Louisville Metro
street guide

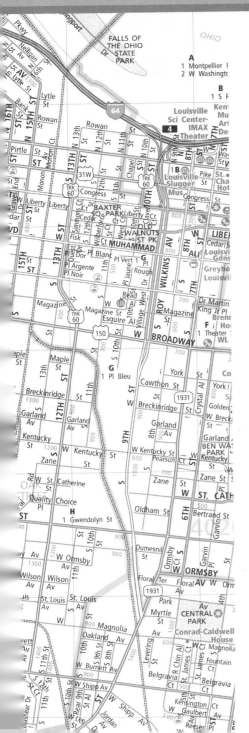

TELL US comment card on last page WHAT YOU THINK

Contents

Introduction

Maps

Lists and Indexes

Rand McNally Consumer Affairs
P.O. Box 7600
Chicago, IL 60680-9915
randmcnally.com

For comments or suggestions, please call
(800) 777-MAPS (-6277)
or email us at:
consumeraffairs@randmcnally.com

Legend

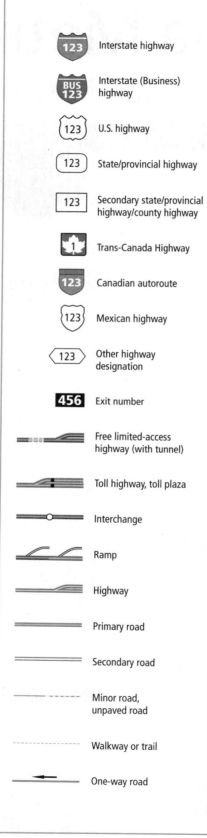

123 Interstate highway

BUS 123 Interstate (Business) highway

123 U.S. highway

123 State/provincial highway

123 Secondary state/provincial highway/county highway

1 Trans-Canada Highway

123 Canadian autoroute

123 Mexican highway

123 Other highway designation

456 Exit number

Free limited-access highway (with tunnel)

Toll highway, toll plaza

Interchange

Ramp

Highway

Primary road

Secondary road

Minor road, unpaved road

Walkway or trail

One-way road

Ferry, waterway

Levee

Trolley

Railroad, station, mass transit line

Bus station

Park and ride

Rest area, service area

Airport

1200 Block number

International boundary, state boundary

County boundary

12345 ZIP code boundary, ZIP code

45°33'30" 90°33'30" Latitude, longitude

Hospital

School

University or college

Information/visitor center/welcome center

Police/sheriff, etc.

City/town/village hall and other government buildings

Courthouse

Lib Library

Museum

Border crossing/Port of entry

Theater/performing arts center

Golf course

Other point of interest

we've got you COVERED

Rand McNally's broad selection of products is perfect for your every need. Whether you're looking for the convenience of write-on wipe-off laminated maps, extra maps for every car, or a Road Atlas to plan your next vacation or to use as a reference, Rand McNally has you covered.

Street Guides

Louisville Metro

Lexington and the Bluegrass Region

Folded Maps

EasyFinder® Laminated Maps

Kentucky

Lexington

Louisville

Paper Maps

Kentucky

Evansville, IN

Lexington

Louisville

Road Atlases

Road Atlas

Road Atlas & Travel Guide

Large Scale Road Atlas

Midsize Road Atlas

Deluxe Midsize Road Atlas

Pocket Road Atlas

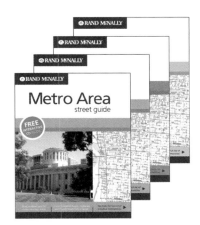

MAP
5180

1:24,000
1 in. = 2000 ft.

0   0.25   0.5
miles

SEE B MAP

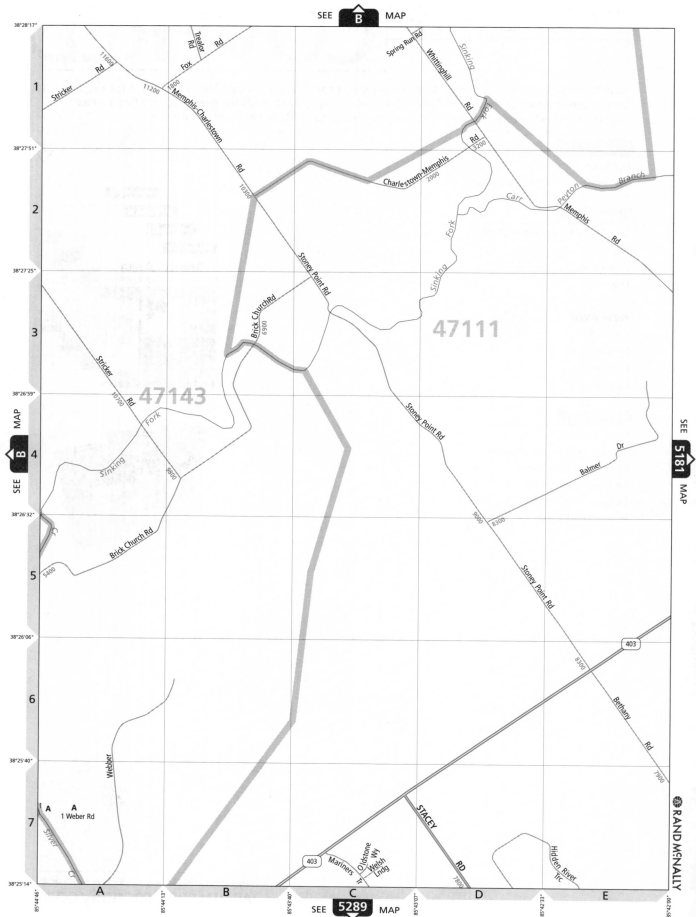

SEE B MAP

SEE 5181 MAP

SEE 5289 MAP

RAND McNALLY

47111

47143

Stricker Rd
11600
11200
1800
Trealor Rd
Fox Rd
Memphis-Charlestown Rd
10300
Spring Run Rd
Whittinghill Rd
Sinking Fork
3200
Charlestown-Memphis 2000
Carr
Peyton
Memphis Rd
Branch
Sinking Fork
Stoney Point Rd
Brick ChurchRd
6900
Stricker Rd
10700
Sinking Fork
9800
9900
Brick Church Rd
5400
Stoney Point Rd
Balmer Dr
9000
8300
Stoney Point Rd
403
8300
Bethany Rd
7900
Webber
1 A   A
1 Weber Rd
Silver Cr
STACEY
RD
403
Mariners Tr
Oldstone Wy
Welsh Lndg
7800
Hidden River Trc

38°28'17"
38°27'51"
38°27'25"
38°26'59"
38°26'32"
38°26'06"
38°25'40"
38°25'14"

85°44'46"
85°44'13"
85°43'40"
85°43'07"
85°42'33"
85°42'00"

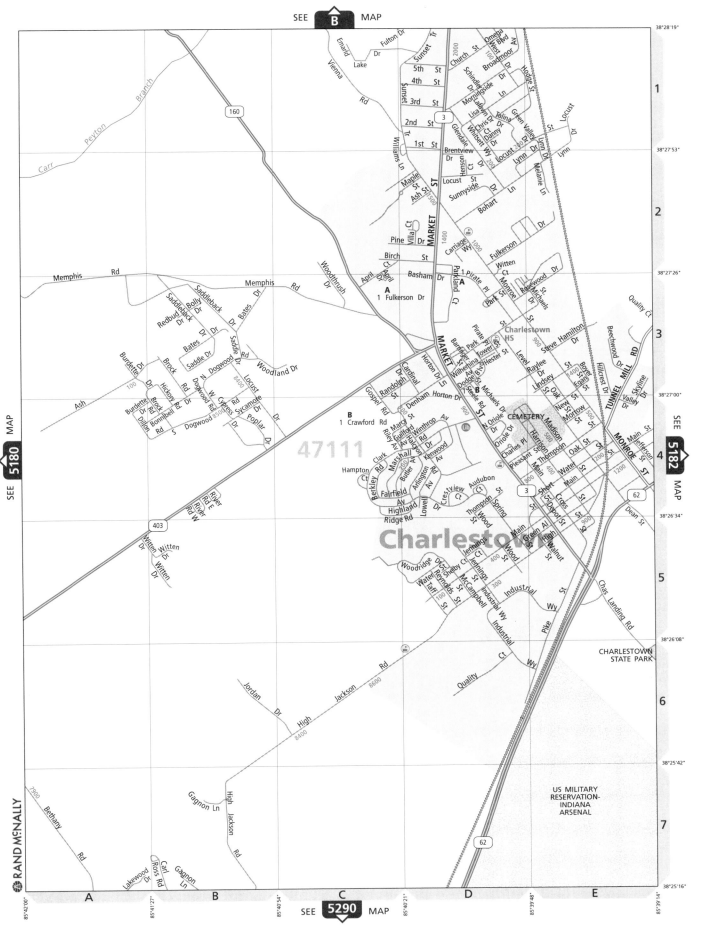

MAP
5182

1:24,000
1 in. = 2000 ft.
0   0.25   0.5
miles

N

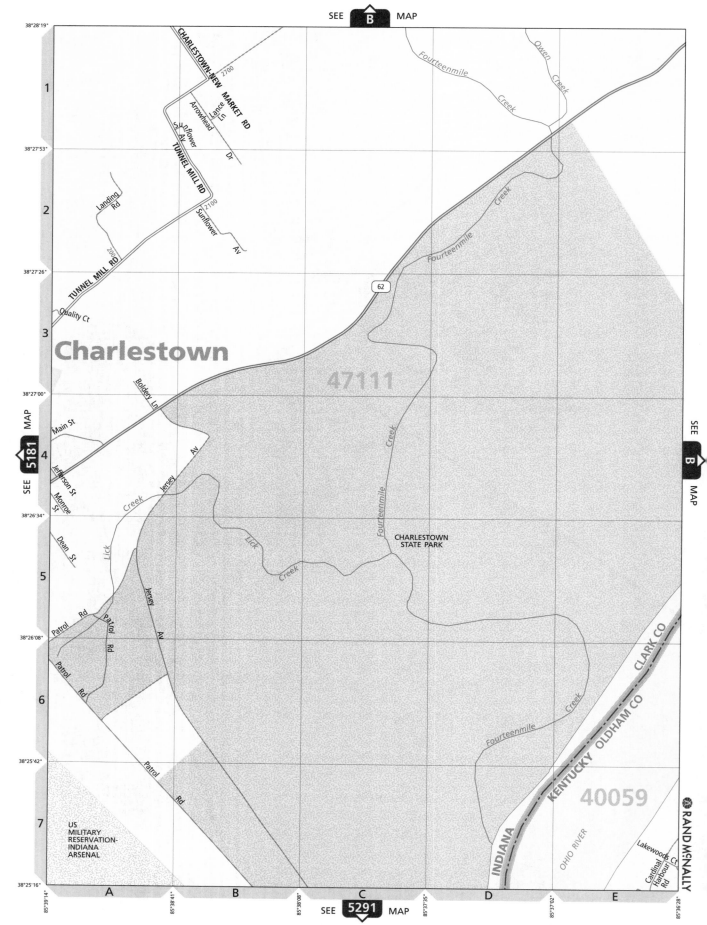

38°28'19"

1

CHARLESTOWN-NEW MARKET RD
2700

Arrowhead
Lance Ln
Sunflower Av
Dr

38°27'53"

TUNNEL MILL RD

Landing Rd

2

2100

Sunflower Av

TUNNEL MILL RD

2000

Quality Ct

38°27'26"

62

Fourteenmile Creek

Owen Creek

Fourteenmile Creek

3

Charlestown

47111

Boldery Ln

38°27'00"

Main St

Av

4

Jefferson St

Jersey

Creek

Monroe St

Fourteenmile Creek

38°26'34"

Dean St

Lick

Lick Creek

CHARLESTOWN STATE PARK

5

Jersey Av

Patrol Rd
Patrol Rd

38°26'08"

Patrol Rd

Patrol Rd

6

CLARK CO

Fourteenmile Creek

KENTUCKY
OLDHAM CO

38°25'42"

Patrol Rd

40059

7

US MILITARY RESERVATION-INDIANA ARSENAL

INDIANA

OHIO RIVER

Lakewoods Ct

Cardinal Harbour Rd

38°25'16"

A   B   C   D   E

85°39'14"   85°38'41"   85°38'08"   85°37'35"   85°37'02"   85°36'58"

MAP
5283

N

1:24,000
1 in. = 2000 ft.
0   0.25   0.5
miles

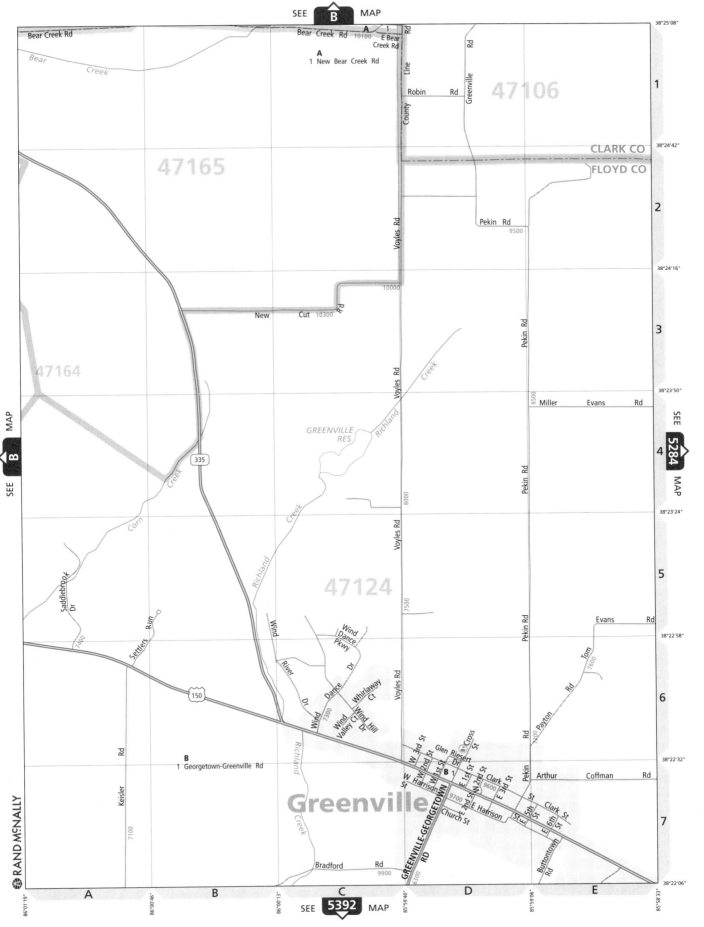

SEE **B** MAP

Bear Creek Rd

Bear Creek Rd   Bear Creek Rd 10100 E Bear Creek Rd   A 1

Bear Creek

38°25'08"

A
1 New Bear Creek Rd

County Line Rd

Greenville Rd

Robin Rd

47106

1

CLARK CO
FLOYD CO

38°24'42"

47165

Voyles Rd

Pekin Rd
9500

2

38°24'16"

New Cut 10300 Rd
10000

Pekin Rd

3

47164

Richland Creek

Voyles Rd

Creek

38°23'50"

Miller   Evans   Rd
8500

GREENVILLE RES

335

Corn Creek

Richland Creek

Voyles Rd

8000

Pekin Rd

SEE **5284** MAP

4

38°23'24"

Saddlebrook Dr

Settlers Run

7400

47124

7500

Richland Creek

Voyles Rd

Pekin Rd

Evans   Rd

5

38°22'58"

Wind

Wind Dance Pkwy

River Dr

Dance Dr

Whirlaway Ct

Tom Payton Rd
7600

150

Wind Dr
7300

Wind Valley Ct

Wind Hill Dr

Voyles Rd

Pekin Rd

6

Keisler Rd

7100

Richland Creek

B
1 Georgetown-Greenville Rd

W 3rd St

W 2nd St
W 1st St

Glen Riesert Dr

Cross St

E 1st St

E 2nd St

N 2nd St

E 3rd St

Clark St
9600

Pekin St

Arthur   Coffman   Rd

38°22'32"

W Harrison St
W St

B 1

9700

E 2nd St

E Harrison

E 5th St

E 6th St

Clark St

Greenville

GREENVILLE-GEORGETOWN RD
6300

Church St

Buttontown Rd

7

Bradford   Rd
9900

38°22'06"

A   B   C   D   E

86°01'19"   86°00'46"   86°00'13"   85°59'40"   85°59'06"   85°58'33"

SEE **5392** MAP

MAP
5284

1:24,000
1 in. = 2000 ft.
0   0.25   0.5
miles

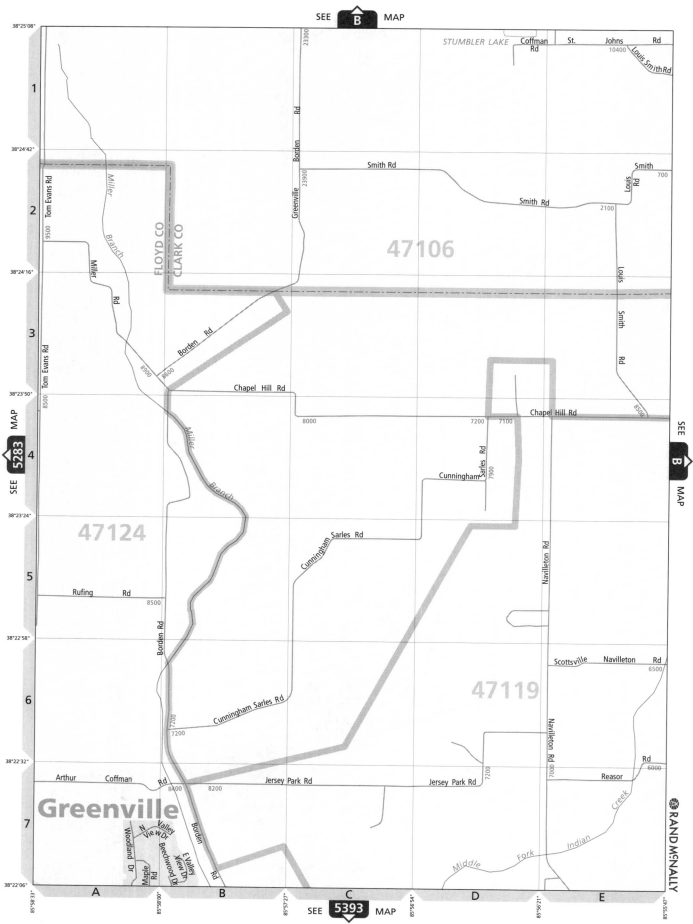

SEE B MAP

N

38°25'08"

STUMBLER LAKE   Coffman   St.   Johns   Rd
Rd   10400
Louis Smith Rd

1

23300

38°24'42"

Smith Rd   Smith
Tom Evans Rd   Louis   Rd   700
Borden   Smith Rd   Rd
Rd   Smith Rd   2100

2

9500   23900

Greenville   47106

FLOYD CO
CLARK CO

Miller

38°24'16"

Louis

Branch

Smith

3

Miller   Borden   Rd   Rd
Rd   8500
8900   8600

Tom Evans Rd

38°23'50"

Chapel Hill Rd
8500   7200 7100   Chapel Hill Rd
SEE 5283 MAP   8000   Chapel Hill Rd

4

Miller   Sarles Rd
Branch   7900
Cunningham

SEE B MAP

38°23'24"

47124   Navilleton Rd

5

Cunningham Sarles Rd
Rufing   Rd
8500   Cunningham Sarles Rd
Borden Rd

38°22'58"

Scottsville   Navilleton   Rd
6500

6

47119
7200   Cunningham Sarles Rd
7200

Navilleton Rd

7000

38°22'32"

Arthur   Coffman   Rd   7200   Reasor   Rd
8400   8200   Jersey Park Rd   Jersey Park Rd   6000

7

Greenville   Creek

N Valley
Woodland   View Dr   Borden   Indian
Dr   E Valley   Rd
Maple   Beechwood Dr View Dr   Fork
Rd   Middle   Fork

RAND McNALLY

38°22'06"

A   B   C   D   E
85°58'33" 85°58'00" 85°57'27" 85°56'54" 85°56'21" 85°55'47"

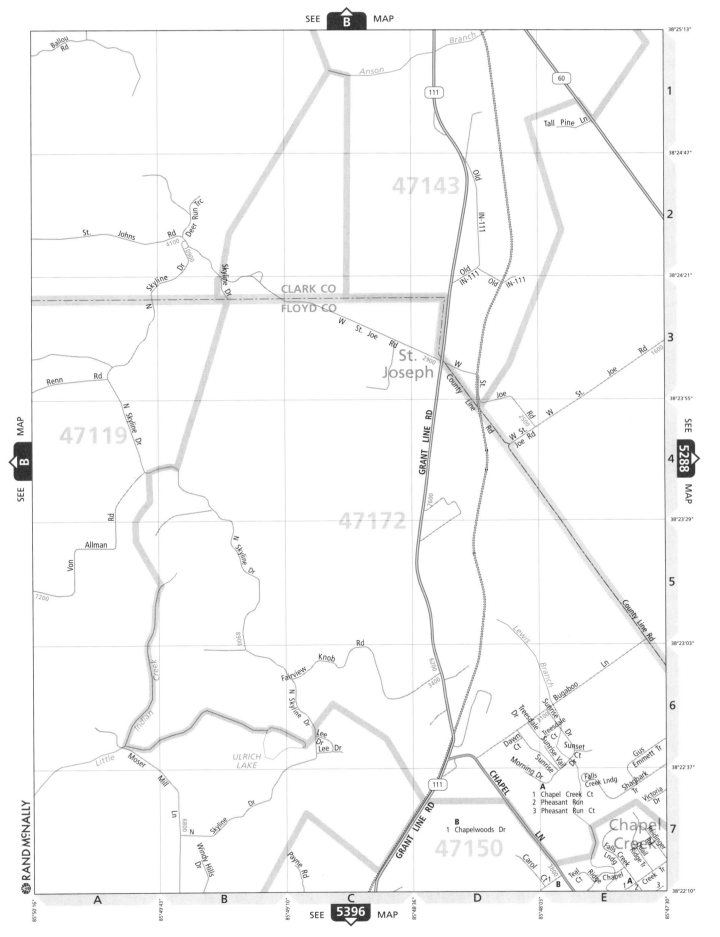

MAP
5287

1:24,000
1 in. = 2000 ft.

0   0.25   0.5
miles

SEE **B** MAP

N

38°25'13"

Ballou Rd

Branch

Anson

60

111

1

Tall Pine Ln

38°24'47"

47143

2

Old IN-111

St. Johns Rd

Deer Run Trc

10900

4100

Skyline Dr

Skyline Dr

N

CLARK CO
FLOYD CO

Old IN-111

Old IN-111

38°24'21"

W St. Joe Rd

St.

3

St. Joseph

2900

W St. Joe Rd

Rd

1600

Renn Rd

W

St. Joe

W St.

Joe Rd

38°23'55"

SEE **5288** MAP

N Skyline Dr

47119

GRANT LINE RD

County Line Rd

2500

4

1600

38°23'29"

47172

38°23'03"

N Skyline Dr

Allman Rd

Von

7200

8900

County Line Rd

5

Lewis

Branch

Little

Indian

Creek

Knob Rd

Fairview

N Skyline Dr

Ln

Bugaboo

6

3100

Treesdale Dr

Sunrise Vall

Treesdale Ct

Sunrise Val Dr

3400

2000

Gus Emmett Tr

Lee Dr

Lee Dr

Dawn Ct

Sunset Ct

Moser Mill

ULRICH
LAKE

Morning Dr

Sunrise

Falls Creek Lndg

Shagbark Tr

38°22'37"

Ln

6800

N Skyline Dr

Windy Hills Dr

111

CHAPEL

Victoria Dr

A
1 Chapel Creek Ct
2 Pheasant Run
3 Pheasant Run Ct

Chapel Creek

Heidinger

Payne Rd

GRANT LINE RD

LN

B
1 Chapelwoods Dr

47150

Falls Creek Lndg

Ridge Tr

7

Carol Ct

3800

Teal Ct

Ridge Chapel

Creek Tr

B

1 2 3

38°22'10"

RAND MCNALLY

A   B   C   D   E

SEE **5396** MAP

85°50'16"

85°49'43"

85°49'10"

85°48'36"

85°48'03"

85°47'30"

MAP
5288

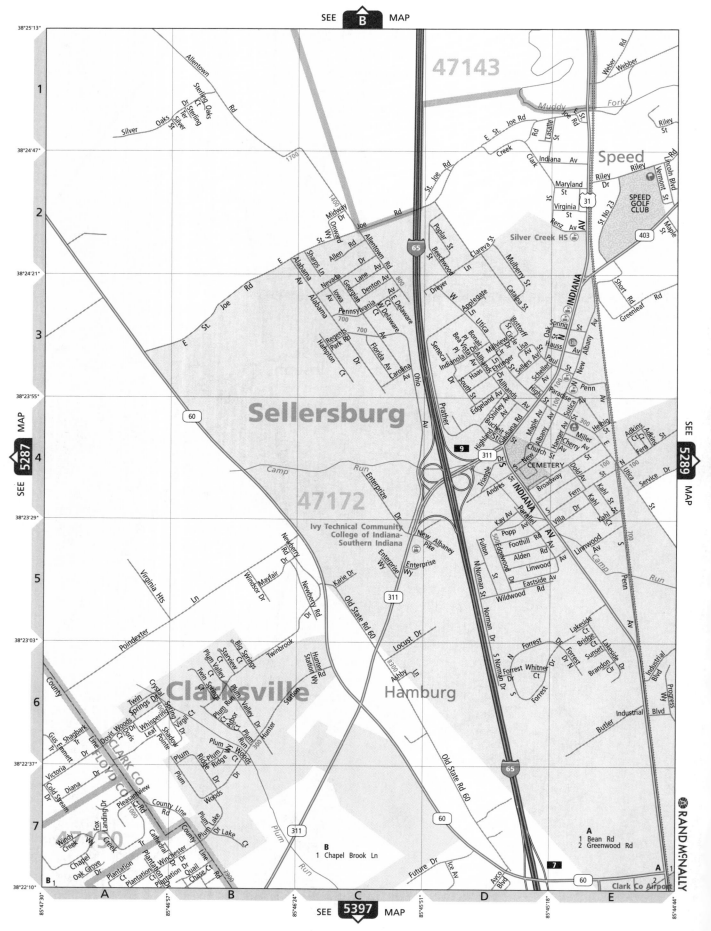

1:24,000
1 in. = 2000 ft.

0   0.25   0.5
miles

MAP
5289

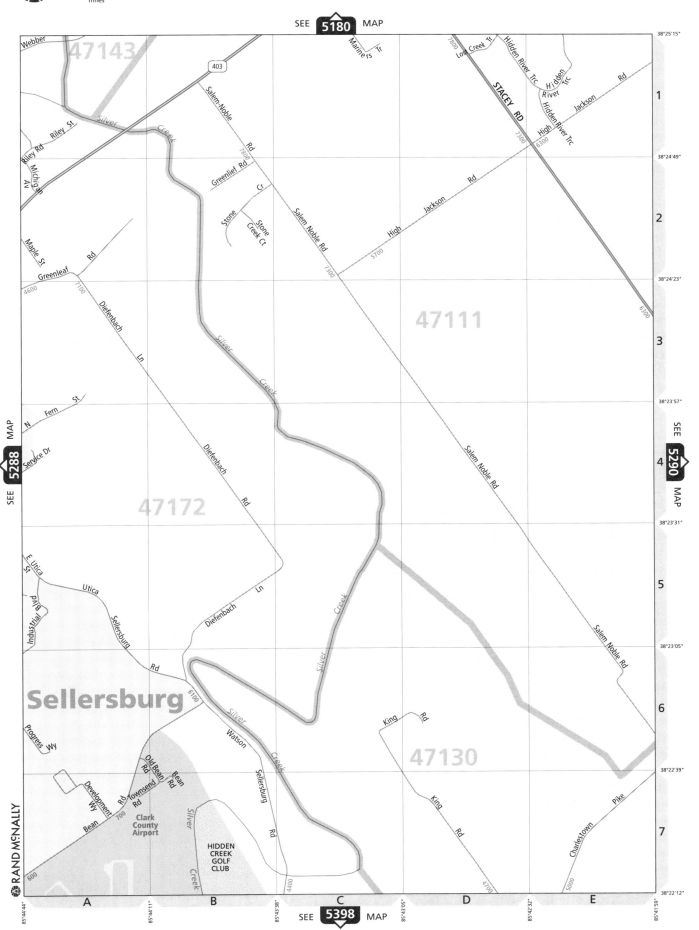

SEE 5180 MAP

Webber

47143

Silver Creek

Riley St

Riley Rd

Michigan Av

Maple St

Greenleaf Rd

4600

7100

Dietenbach Ln

N Fern St

Service Dr

SEE 5288 MAP

47172

E Utica St

Industrial Blvd

Utica

Sellersburg Rd

Sellersburg

6100

Progress Wy

Development Wy

Old Bean Rd

700

Townsend Rd

Bean Rd

Bean

600

Clark County Airport

403

Salem-Noble Rd

7800

Greenlief Rd

Stone Cr

Stone Creek Ct

Salem Noble Rd

7300

Silver

Creek

Dietenbach Rd

Dietenbach Ln

Silver Creek

Watson

Sellersburg Rd

Silver Creek

4400

HIDDEN CREEK GOLF CLUB

Mariners Tr

Lost Creek Tr

STACEY RD

7300

6300

Hidden River Trc

Hidden River Trc

Hidden River Trc

High

Jackson Rd

High Jackson Rd

5700

6300

47111

Salem Noble Rd

47130

King Rd

King Rd

Salem Noble Rd

King Rd

Charlestown Pike

4700

5000

SEE 5290 MAP

SEE 5398 MAP

RAND MCNALLY

38°25'15"
38°24'49"
38°24'23"
38°23'57"
38°23'31"
38°23'05"
38°22'39"
38°22'12"

1
2
3
4
5
6
7

85°44'44"
85°44'11"
85°43'38"
85°43'05"
85°42'32"
85°41'59"

A   B   C   D   E

MAP
5290

1:24,000
1 in. = 2000 ft.
0   0.25   0.5
miles

SEE 5181 MAP

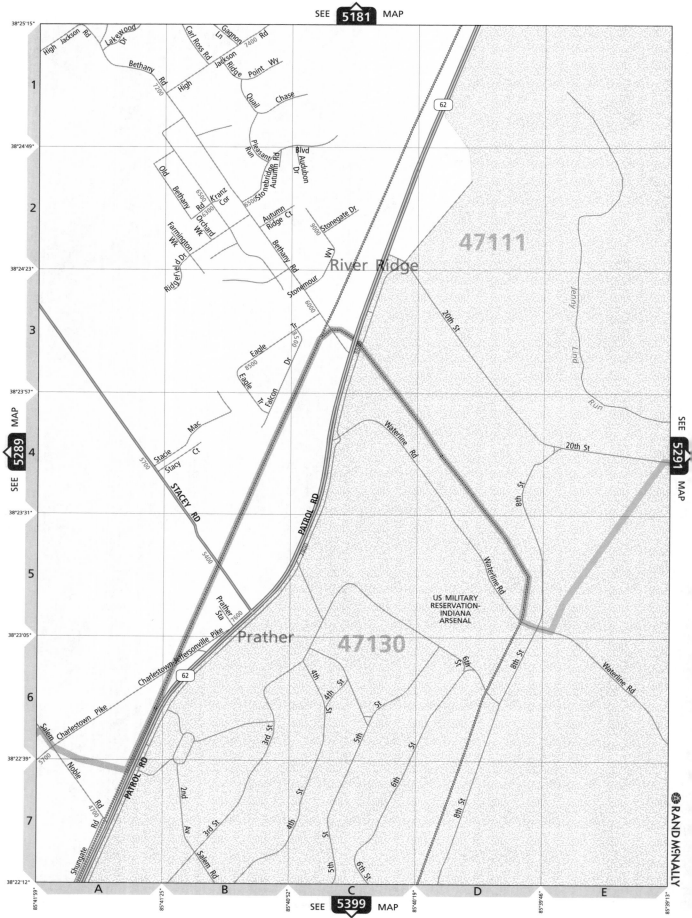

High Jackson Rd
Lakewood Dr
Carl Ross Rd
Gagnon Ln
Jackson Ridge Rd
7400
Bethany Rd
7200
High
Point Wy
Quail
Chase

Pleasant Run
Old Bethany Rd
6500
6300
Kranz Cor
Orchard Wk
Stonebridge
Autumn Rd
Audubon Dr
Blvd
6500
Autumn Ridge Ct
9000
Stonegate Dr

Farmington Wk
Ridgefield Dr
Bethany Rd
6000
River Ridge
Stonemour
Tr
8500

47111

Jenny Lind Run

Eagle Dr
8500
Eagle Tr
Falcon

20th St

Waterline Rd

20th St

SEE 5289 MAP

Mac
Stacie Ct
Stacy
5700
STACEY RD

PATROL RD

8th St

SEE 5291 MAP

5400

7700

Prather Sta
7600

US MILITARY
RESERVATION-
INDIANA
ARSENAL

Waterline Rd

Charlestown-Jeffersonville Pike
Prather
62
47130

8th St

Salem Charlestown Pike
5700

4th St
5th St

6th St

Waterline Rd

Noble Rd
4700
PATROL RD
2nd
3rd St
Av
Salem Rd
Shungate Rd

3rd St

5th St
4th St
5th St

6th St

8th St

5th St
6th St

38°25'15"
38°24'49"
38°24'23"
38°23'57"
38°23'31"
38°23'05"
38°22'39"
38°22'12"

85°41'59"
85°41'25"
85°40'52"
85°40'19"
85°39'46"
*EL6L58

1
2
3
4
5
6
7

A   B   C   D   E

SEE 5399 MAP

MAP
5291

1:24,000
1 in. = 2000 ft.

0   0.25   0.5
miles

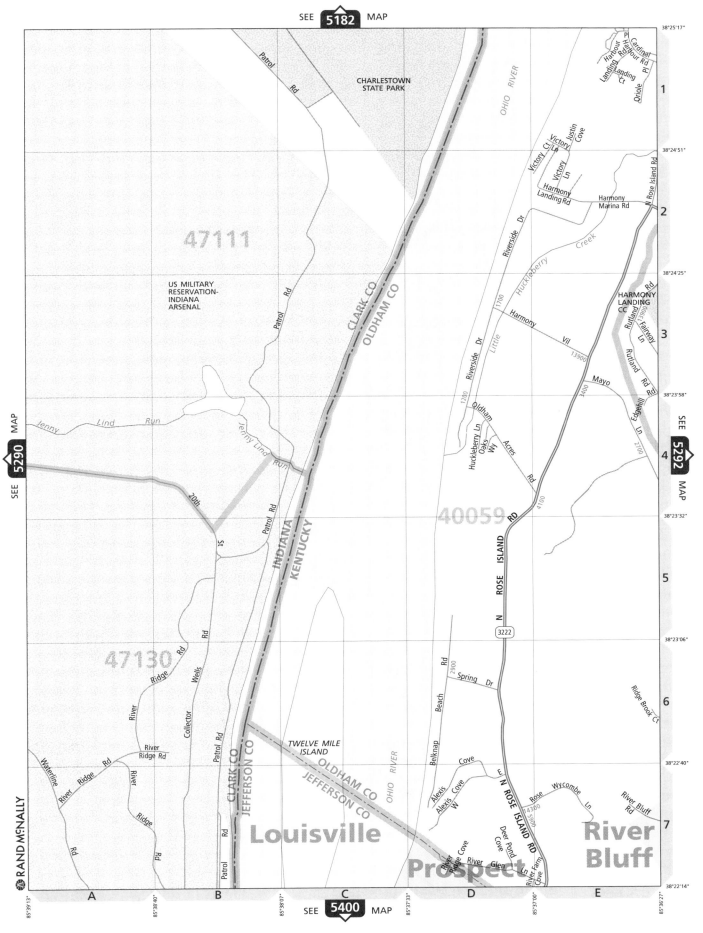

38°25'17"

CHARLESTOWN
STATE PARK

OHIO RIVER

Pl Cardinal
Harbour Rd Harbour Pl
Landing Landing Ct
Oriole

1

47111

Victory Ct Ln Justin
Victory Cove
Ln

Victory
Ln

Harmony
Landing Rd

Harmony
Marina Rd

N Rose Island Rd

38°24'51"

2

US MILITARY
RESERVATION-
INDIANA
ARSENAL

Patrol Rd

CLARK CO
OLDHAM CO

Riverside Dr

Huckleberry Creek

38°24'25"

HARMONY
LANDING
CC

Rd
Rutland Fairway
Rd Ln

3

1700

1300

Harmony
Vil

Little

13900

Rutland Rd Rd

Edgehill Ln

Riverside Dr

1200

Mayo

3400

2700

38°23'58"

SEE 5292 MAP

4

Jenny Lind Run

Jenny Lind Run

Oldham
Ln

Huckleberry Ln

Oaks Wy

Acres Rd

40059

N ROSE ISLAND RD

4100

38°23'32"

20th

St

Patrol Rd

INDIANA
KENTUCKY

5

Patrol Rd

3222

38°23'06"

47130

Ridge Rd

Wells Rd

Beach Rd

2900

Spring Dr

Ridge Brook Ct

38°22'40"

6

River Rd

Collector

River
Ridge Rd

Belknap

Alexis Cove
W
Alexis Cove

E N ROSE ISLAND RD

Rose
4300

Wycombe Ln

River Bluff
Rd

TWELVE MILE
ISLAND

CLARK CO
JEFFERSON CO

OLDHAM CO
JEFFERSON CO

OHIO RIVER

Louisville

Deer Pond
Cove

6005

River
Bluff

38°22'14"

7

Waterline

River Ridge Rd

River
Ridge

Patrol Rd

Patrol Rd

Prospect

River
Ridge Cove

River Glen
Ln

River Farm
Cove

RAND McNALLY

A   B   C   D   E

85°39'13"   85°38'40"   85°38'07"   85°37'33"   85°37'00"   85°36'27"

MAP
5292

1:24,000
1 in. = 2000 ft.
0   0.25   0.5
miles

SEE **B** MAP

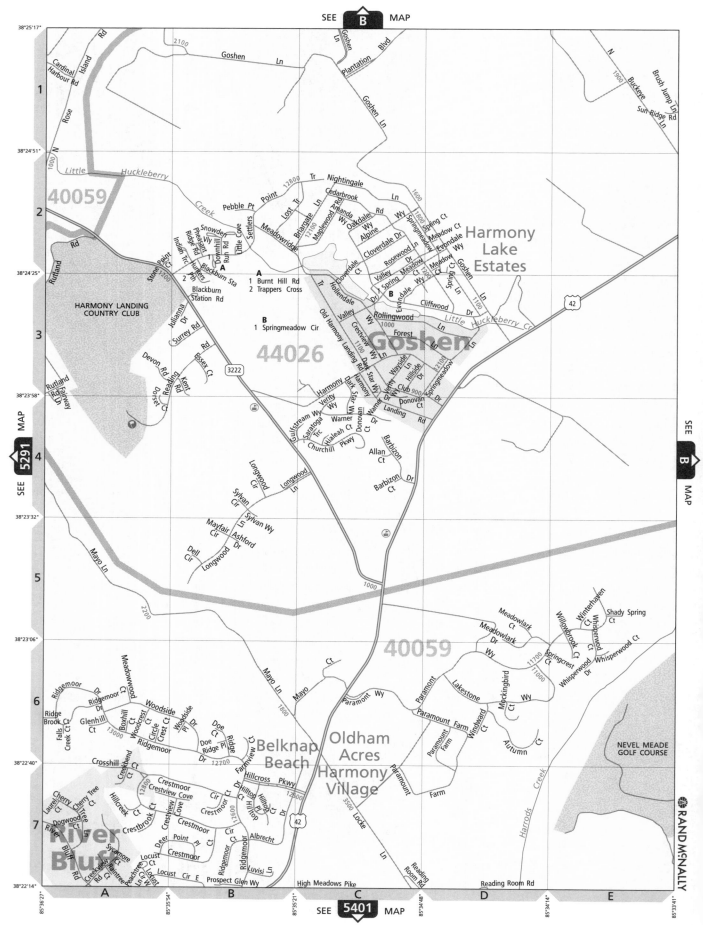

38°25'17"

40059

Goshen Ln

Goshen Ln

Goshen Blvd

Plantation Blvd

Cardinal Ct
Harbour Rd
Island Rd
Rose

N
1000

38°24'51"

Brush Jump Ln
Sun Ridge Ln
Buckeye Rd
1900

Little Huckleberry Creek

1   Nightingale Tr
12800
Pebble Pt Point
Lost Tr
Cedarbrook Rd
Amanda Wy
Oakdale Wy
Alpine Wy
Maplewood Wy
Braidgate Ln
Meadowridge
12100

1600
1800
Spring Ct
Springmeadow Ln
Meadow Wy
Evondale Wy

Harmony
Lake
Estates

Snowden Vly
Pheasant Ct
Ridge Rd
Indian Trc
Hunters Path
Townhill Run Rd
Little Cove
Settlers
Cloverdale Dr
Rosewood Dr
Valley Meadow Dr
Meadow Ct
Goshen Ct
Spring Ct

38°24'25"
Stone Point Ct
1400
Blackburn Sta
A
A
1 Burnt Hill Rd
2 Trappers Cross
2
Cloverdale Dr
Hollendale Tr
Evondale Dr
Spring Wy
1100
Cliffwood Dr

Goshen

Harmony Landing Country Club
Rutland Rd

Blackburn Station Rd
B
1 Springmeadow Cir
44026

Valley Wy
Crestview Wy
Old Harmony Landing Rd
Dark Star Wy
Harmony
Forest Ln
Rollingwood
1000
Ln
B

42
US

Little Huckleberry Cr

Julianna Dr
Surrey Rd
Rd

Verity Ln
Wayside Ln
Hillside Dr
Club Dr
12100
Springmeadow Dr
900

38°23'58"
Devon Rd
Essex Ct
Kent
Reading Rd
Dorset Ct
3222

Harmony Wy
Verity Wy
Saratoga Trc
Hialeah
Churchill
Warner Wy
M M
Donovan Ct
Donovan Dr
Warner Dr
Landing Rd

Rutland Rd
Fairway Ct
Fairway

Gulfstream Wy
Barbizon Ct
Allan Ct
Barbizon Dr
38°23'32"

MAP
5291
SEE

B

SEE **B** MAP

Longwood Cir
Longwood Ln
Sylvan Cir
Sylvan Wy
Mayfair Cir
Ashford Dr
Dell Cir
Longwood

Mayo Ln

38°23'06"
1000

5
2200

Winterhaven Wy
Shady Spring Ct
Whisperwood Ct
Meadowlark Ct
Meadowlark Dr
Willowbrook Ct
Whisperwood Ct
Whisperwood Dr
Springcrest Ct
11700
11000

40059

Ridgemoor Ct
Meadowwood Ct
Ridgemoor Dr
Ridge Brook Ct
Glenhill Ct
Boxhill Ct
Woodcrest Ct
Woodside Ct
Woodside Dr
Doe Ct
Doe Ridge
Circle
Crest Ct
13000

Mayo Ln
1800
Mayo Ct
Paramont Wy
Paramount Ct
Lakestone Wy
Mockingbird Ct
Windyard Ct
Autumn Ct

NEVEL MEADE
GOLF COURSE

Harrods Creek

38°22'40"
Crosshill Ct
Creekband Ct
Ridgemoor Dr
Doe Ridge Pl
12700
Farmview Rd
Hillcross Pkwy
12500
Belknap
Beach
Paramount Farm
Paramount Farm
Paramount Farm

Oldham
Acres
Harmony
Village

3500 Locke Ln

Crestmoor Rd Ct
Crestview Cove
12800
Laurel Ct
Cherry Tree Ct
Hillcreek Ct
Crestbrook Ct
Crestview Cove
Crestmoor Cir
Hilltop Dr
Hilltop Pl
Hilltop Dr
Albrecht
Luvisi Si
12600

42
Reading Room Rd

River
Bluff
Dogwood Ct
River Rd
Sycamore
Cherry Tree Dr
Deer Point
Crestmoor
Locust Cir
Locust Cir E
Prospect Glen Wy
Peachtree
Peachtree Ln Ct
Raintree Dr
Crestview Ct

High Meadows Pike
Reading Room Rd
Reading Room Rd

38°22'14"
85°36'27"
A
85°35'54"
85°35'21"
B
C
85°35'11"
D
85°34'48"
85°34'14"
E
85°33'41"

SEE **5401** MAP

RAND McNALLY

1:24,000
1 in. = 2000 ft.

0   0.25   0.5
miles

MAP
5295

SEE **B** MAP

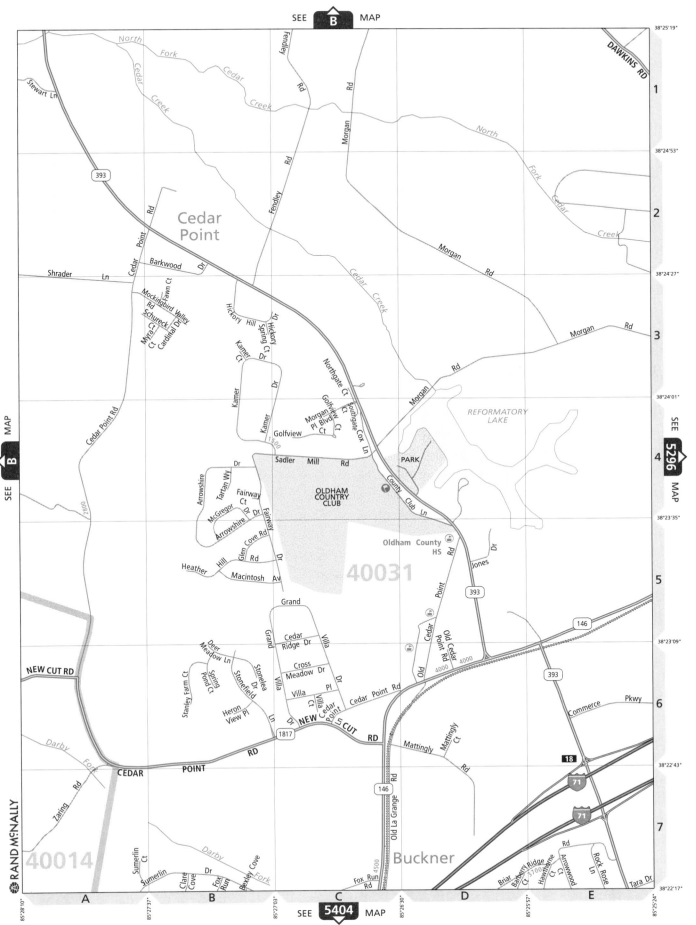

38°25'19"
DAWKINS RD

1

38°24'53"

2

38°24'27"

3

38°24'01"

38°23'35"

4

5

38°23'09"

6

38°22'43"

7

38°22'17"

SEE 5296 MAP

SEE **B** MAP

North Fork Cedar Creek

Stewart Ln

393

Cedar Point

Shrader Ln

Barkwood Dr

Cedar Point Rd

Mockingbird Valley Rd
Fawn Ct
Schureck Ct
Myra Ct
Cardinal Dr

Hickory Hill Rd
Hickory Spring Ct
Kamer Ct
Kamer Dr
Kamer Dr
Kamer

Golfview

Northgate Ct
Golfview Ct
Southgate Ct
Morgan Pl Blvd
Cox Ln

Sadler Mill Rd

Arrowshire
Tartan Wy
Fairway Ct
McGregor Dr
Fairway Dr
Arrowshire Dr

Glen Cove Rd
Heather Hill Rd
Macintosh Av

Grand
Grand
Cedar Ridge Dr
Villa
Cross Meadow Dr
Villa
Villa Pl
Villa Ct

Deer Meadow Ln
Stonelea Dr
Spring Pond Ct
Stonefield Dr
Stanley Farm Ct
Heron View Pl

1817

NEW CUT RD

CEDAR POINT RD

Darby Fork

Zaring Rd

40014

Sumerlin Ct
Sumerlin
Clare Cove
Fox Run
Bexley Cove Dr

Darby Fork

Fendley Rd
Fendley Rd

Rd
Morgan Rd

Morgan Rd

Morgan Rd

Cedar Creek

North Fork Cedar Creek

Morgan Rd

Morgan Rd

REFORMATORY LAKE

PARK

OLDHAM COUNTRY CLUB

40031

County Club Ln

Oldham County HS

Jones Dr
Dr

Cedar Point Rd

393

146

Old Cedar Point Rd
4000 4000

393

Cedar Point Rd

Old Cedar Point Rd

Mattingly Rd
Mattingly Ct

18

71

71

Commerce Pkwy

Old La Grange Rd

146

Buckner

Fox Run Rd

Briar Ridge Ct
Barberry Ct
Hawthorne Ct
Arrowwood Ln
Rock Rose
Rd
Tara Dr

A   B   C   D   E

85°28'10"   85°27'37"   85°27'03"   85°26'30"   85°25'57"   85°25'24"

RAND MCNALLY

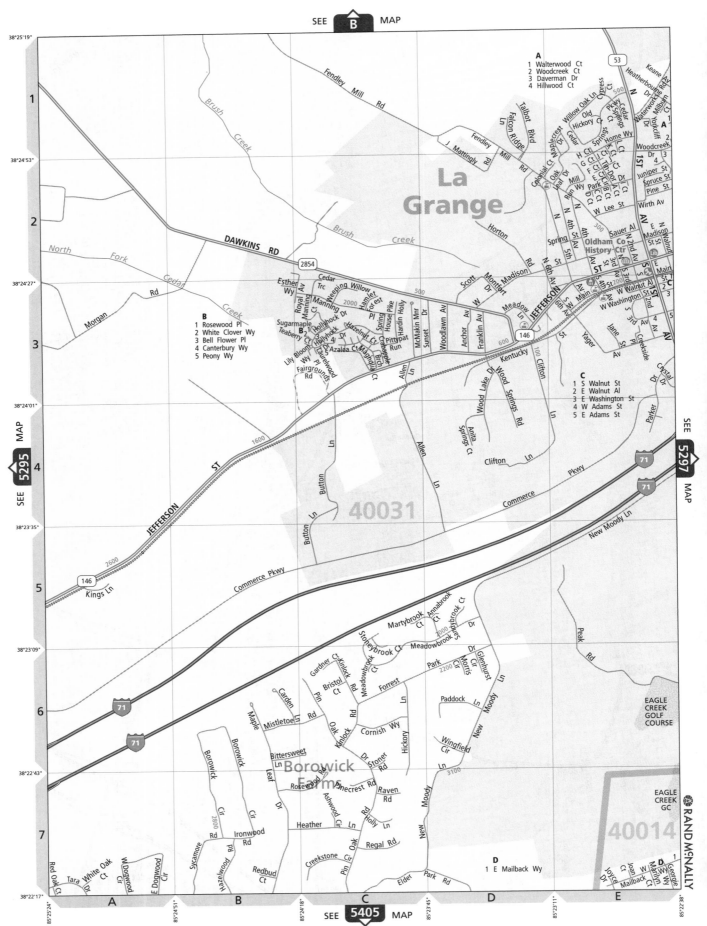

MAP
5296

1:24,000
1 in. = 2000 ft.
0   0.25   0.5
miles

SEE B MAP

38°25'19"

A
1 Walterwood Ct
2 Woodcreek Ct
3 Daverman Dr
4 Hillwood Ct

La
Grange

1

38°24'53"

2

DAWKINS RD

2854

North   Fork   Cedar

Morgan   Rd

Creek

38°24'27"

B
1 Rosewood Pl
2 White Clover Wy
3 Bell Flower Pl
4 Canterbury Wy
5 Peony Wy

Esther
Wy

Cedar
Trc

Weeping Willow

Royal Av

Manning

Hamlet

Forest
Pl

Spring
House Pike

Hardin Holly

Sugarmaple
Teaberry Ct

Hollyhock Dr

Hazelnut Ct

McMakin Mnr

Pittypat
Run

Sunset

Woodlawn Av

Anchor Av

Franklin Av

Meadow
Ln

Scott
Dr

Monfort
Dr

W

Madison

JEFFERSON

146

Oldham Co
History Ctr

Spring   4th Av
St   5th
St   N 6th St

3

Lily Bloom Wy

Fairgrounds
Rd

Azalea

Magnolia Ct

Brch

Crabapple

Allen
Ln

Wood Lake Dr

Wood
Springs Rd

Kentucky

Clifton

C
1 S Walnut St
2 E Walnut Al
3 E Washington St
4 W Adams St
5 E Adams St

38°24'01"

SEE 5295 MAP

1600

Button
Ln

Allen
Ln

Anita
Springs Ct

Clifton   Ln

Pkwy

Commerce

71

71

SEE 5297 MAP

4

JEFFERSON ST

Button
Ln

38°23'35"

2600

146

Kings Ln

Commerce Pkwy

New Moody Ln

5

71

71

Martybrook Ct

Annabrook
Ct

Sandybrook Ct

Dr

Peak
Rd

38°23'09"

Stoneybrook Ct

Meadowbrook

Dr

Park   2200

Glenhurst
Ln

Morris Ln

Paddock
Ln

New Moody Ln

EAGLE
CREEK
GOLF
COURSE

6

Gardner Ct

Kinlock
Ct

Bristol
Ct

Pin

Carden

Mistletoe

Rd

Oak

Kinlock
Rd

Meadowbrook Ln

Forrest

Cornish Wy

Hickory

Wingfield
Cir

Maple

Borowick

Bittersweet
Ln

Leaf
Dr

Rosewood Rd

Pinecrest Rd

Stoner
Rd

Raven
Rd

New Moody

38°22'43"

Borowick
Farms

Borowick

Cir

Sycamore
Rd

Hazelwood Rd

Ironwood
Rd

Redbud
Ct

Heather

Ashwood
Cir

Holly
Ln

Regal Rd

New

3100

EAGLE
CREEK
GC

40014

7

Red Oak Ct

Tara Dr

White Oak
Ct

W Dogwood
Cir

E Dogwood
Cir

Creekstone
Cir

Pin
Oak

Elder

Park
Rd

D
1 E Mailback Wy

Joyce
Dr

Joan
Mailback

W
Martin
Wy

Georgie
Wy

D

38°22'17"

SEE 5405 MAP

A   B   C   D   E

85°25'24"   85°24'51"   85°24'18"   85°23'45"   85°23'11"   85°22'58"

RAND McNALLY

40031

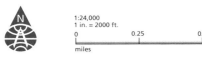
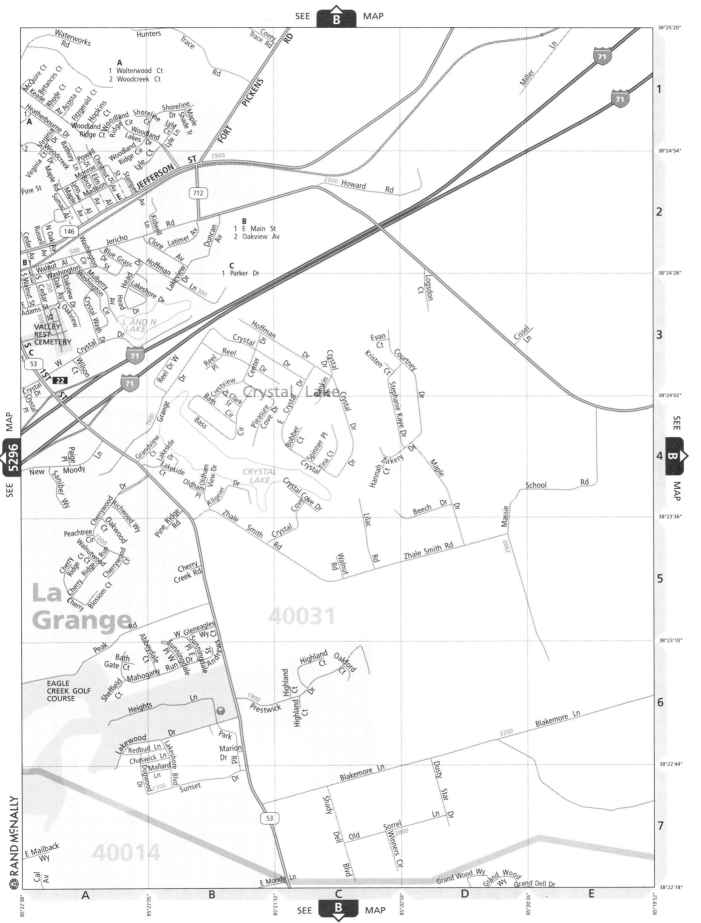

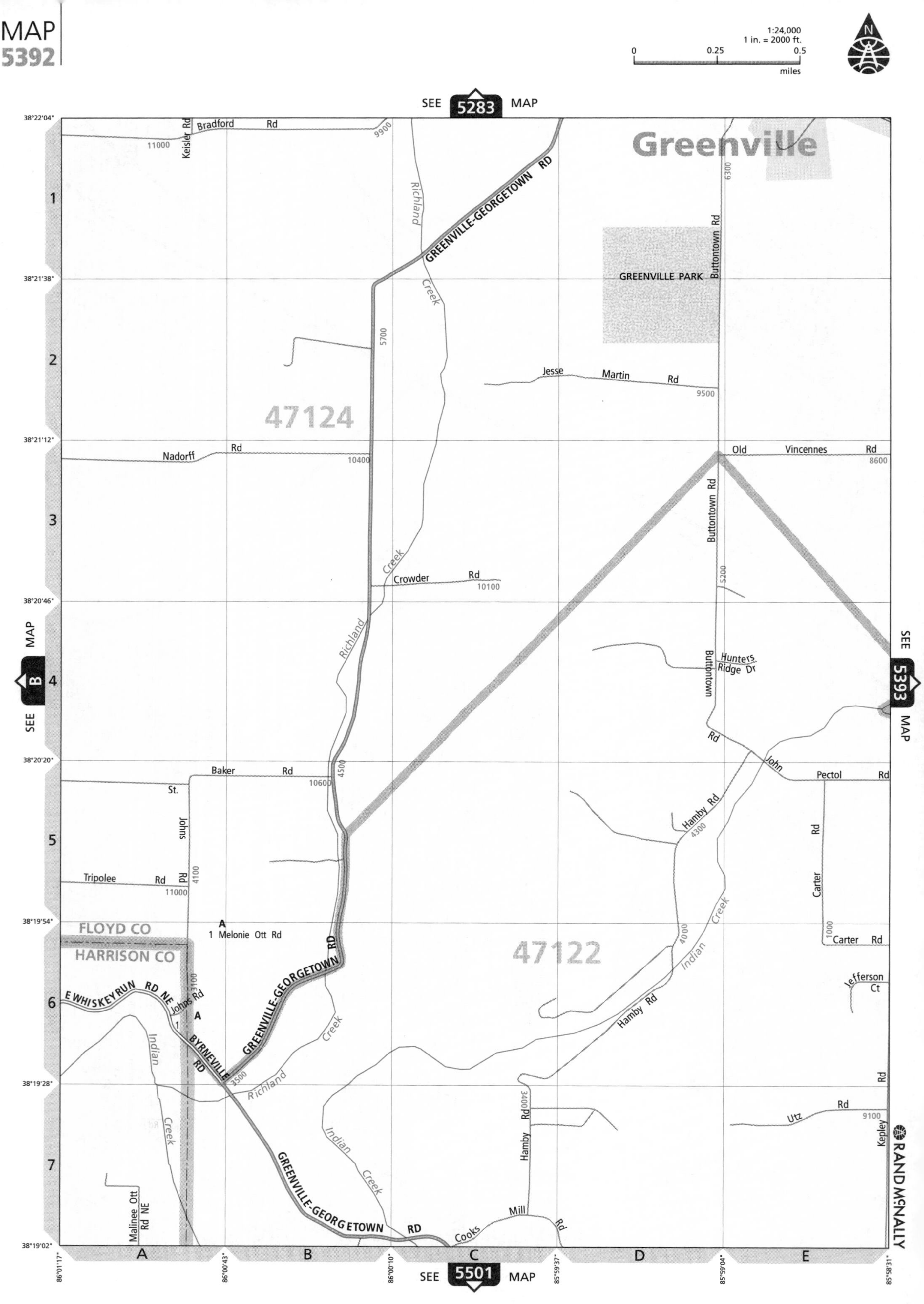

MAP
5392

1:24,000
1 in. = 2000 ft.

0   0.25   0.5
miles

SEE 5283 MAP

Greenville

Keisler Rd   Bradford   Rd
11000
9900

GREENVILLE-GEORGETOWN RD

GREENVILLE PARK

Buttontown Rd

6300

Richland   Creek

1

38°22'04"
38°21'38"

2

5700

Jesse   Martin   Rd
9500

38°21'12"

47124

Nadorff   Rd
10400

Old   Vincennes   Rd
8600

3

Creek

Crowder   Rd
10100

Buttontown Rd
5200

Richland

SEE 5393 MAP

Hunters Ridge Dr

Buttontown Rd

38°20'46"

B MAP

SEE

4

4500

Baker   Rd
1060D

John

Pectol   Rd

St.

Johns

Hamby Rd
4300

Rd

Carter

38°20'20"

5

4100

Tripolee   Rd   Rd
11000

Carter   Rd
1000

A
1 Melonie Ott Rd

Indian Creek
4000

47122

Jefferson Ct

38°19'54"

FLOYD CO
HARRISON CO

6

E WHISKEY RUN   RD NE

Johns Rd
10100

A

BYRNEVILLE RD

GREENVILLE-GEORGETOWN RD

Indian   Creek

Hamby Rd

Rd

38°19'28"

Indian

Richland   Creek
3500

Hamby Rd
34000

Utz   Rd
9100

Kepley   Rd

7

RAND McNALLY

Malinee Ott Rd NE

GREENVILLE-GEORGETOWN   RD

Indian   Creek

Cooks   Mill   Rd

38°19'02"
86°01'17"   86°00'43"   86°00'10"   85°59'37"   85°59'04"   85°58'31"

A   B   C   D   E

SEE 5501 MAP

N

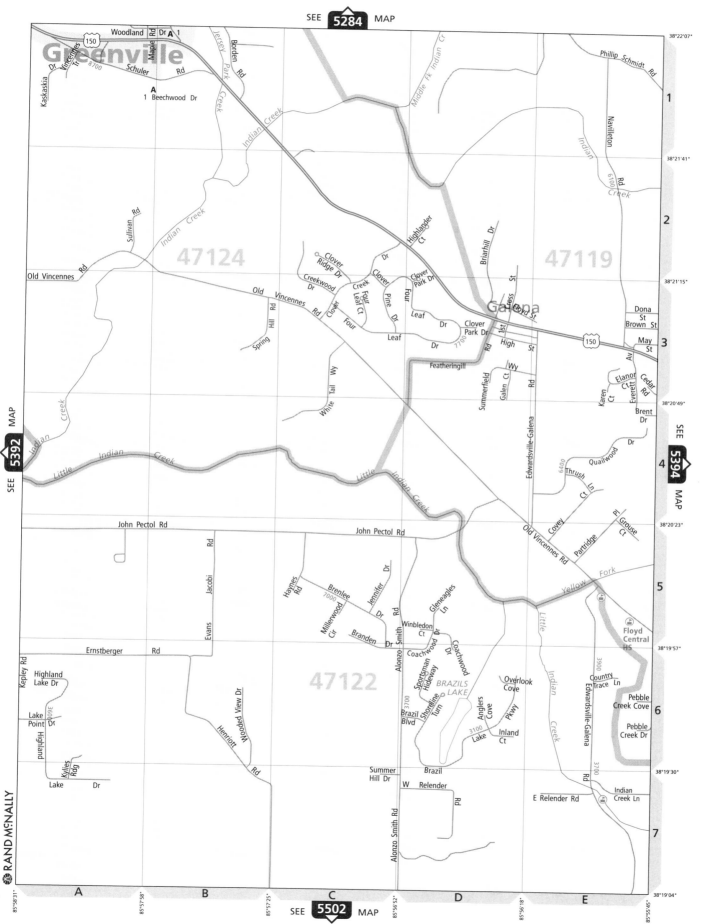

MAP
5393

N

1:24,000
1 in. = 2000 ft.
0   0.25   0.5
miles

SEE 5284 MAP

38°22'07"

1

Greenville

Woodland Rd Dr A 1
150
Vincennes Tr 8700
Maple Rd
Schuler Rd
Borden Rd
Jersey Park Creek

Kaskaskia Dr

A
1 Beechwood Dr

Phillip Schmidt Rd

Navilleton Rd

38°21'41"

2

Sullivan Rd

Indian Creek

47124

Highlander Ct
Dr
Briarhill Dr

Indian Creek

47119

38°21'15"

Old Vincennes Rd

Old Vincennes Rd

Creekwood Dr
Clover Ridge Dr
Creek
Four Leaf Ct
Clover
Four
Clover Park Dr
Tour
Pine Dr
Leaf
Dr

Galena

Lless St
Floyd St

Dona St
Brown St

3

Spring Hill Rd

Clover
Four

Leaf Dr

Leaf Dr
7700
Clover Park Dr

Featheringill

1st
High
St
Rd
Floyd St

150

May St
Av

Elanor Ct
Everett
Cedar Rd
Karen Ct

38°21'15"

White Tail Wy

Summerfield Rd
Galen Ct
Wy
Rd

Brent Dr

38°20'49"

4

SEE 5392 MAP

Little   Indian   Creek

Indian Creek

Little Indian Creek

Edwardsville-Galena

Dr
Quailwood
6400
Thrush Ln
Ct

SEE 5394 MAP

38°20'23"

John Pectol Rd

John Pectol Rd

Old Vincennes Rd

Covey
Partridge
Pl Grouse Ct

Yellow Fork

5

Jacobi Rd

Haynes Rd
Brenlee
7000
Millerwood Cir
Jennifer Dr
Dr
Smith Rd
Branden Dr

Dr
Gleneagles Ln
Winbledon Ct
Coachwood Dr

Little Indian Creek

Floyd Central HS

Evans

Ernstberger Rd

47122

Alonzo Smith

Coachwood Dr
Sportsman Hideway
BRAZILS LAKE
Overlook Cove

Country Trace Ln
3900
Edwardsville-Galena

Pebble Creek Cove

6

Kepley Rd
Highland Lake Dr
3900
Lake Point Dr
Highland

Wooded View Dr

Henriott Rd

Shoreline Turn
3700
Brazil Blvd
Anglers Cove
3100
Lake
Inland Ct
Pkwy

Indian Creek

3700
Rd

Pebble Creek Dr

38°19'57"

38°19'30"

Kylies Rdg
Lake Dr

Summer Hill Dr

W Relender Dr
Rd

Brazil

E Relender Rd

Indian Creek Ln

7

Alonzo Smith Rd

RAND M^CNALLY

85°58'31"
85°57'58"
85°57'25"
85°56'52"
85°56'18"
85°55'45"

38°19'04"

A   B   C   D   E

MAP
5394

1:24,000
1 in. = 2000 ft.

0   0.25   0.5
miles

SEE **B** MAP

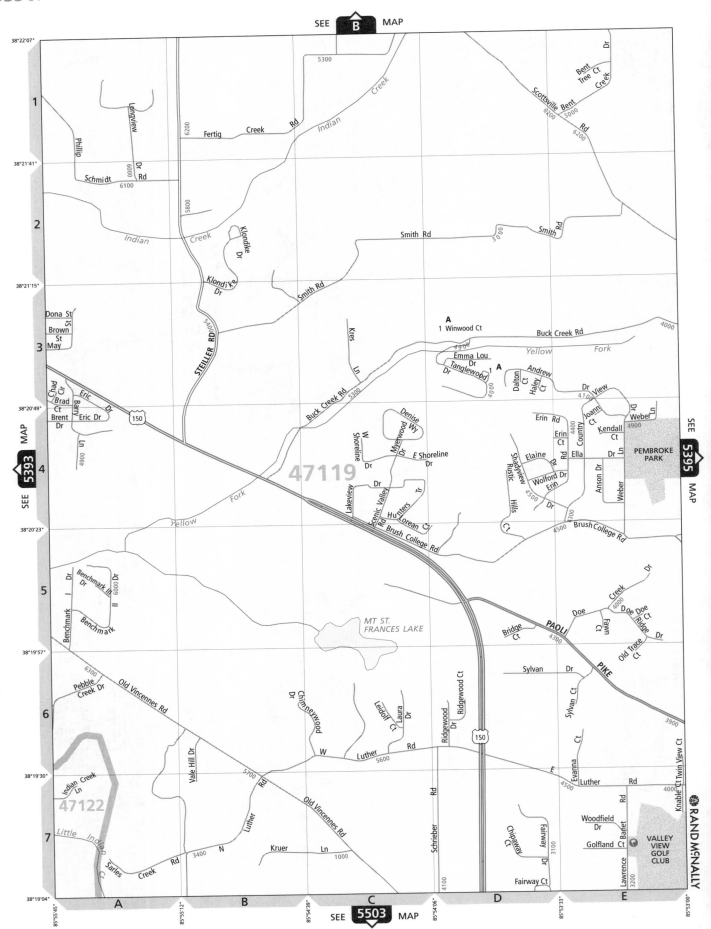

38°22'07"

1

5300

Longview

Phillip

Schmidt   Dr   Rd
6000
6100

Fertig   Creek   Rd   Indian   Creek

6200

Bent Tree Ct
Bent Creek Dr

Scottsville   Bent   Rd
6200   5000   6200

38°21'41"

2

Indian   Creek
5800

Klondike Dr

Klondike Dr
5400

Smith   Rd
5000

Smith   Rd

38°21'15"

Smith Rd

3

Dona St
Brown St
May St

Kres   Ln

STEILLER RD

A
1 Winwood Ct

Buck Creek Rd
4900   4000

Yellow   Fork

Emma Lou Dr
Tanglewood Dr
1   A

Dalton Ct
Haley Ct
Andrew Dr
4100

View

38°20'49"

SEE 5393 MAP

4

Chad Cir
Brad Ct
Brent Dr

Eric Dr
Barry Ln

Eric Dr
4900

150

Buck Creek Rd
5300

47119

Shoreline Dr
W

Myerwood Dr
E Shoreline Dr

Denise Wy

Lakeview Dr

Scenic Valley Rd

Hunters Ct
Lorean Ct

Brush College Rd

Erin Rd
Erin Ct
Erin Rd

Shadyview Rustic
Elaine Dr
Wolford Dr
Erin Dr
4500

Hills Ct
4500

Country
Joann Ct
Ella

Kendall Ct
4900

Weber Ln
Dr
Anson Dr
Weber

Brush College Rd
4500

PEMBROKE PARK

SEE 5395 MAP

38°20'23"

Yellow   Fork

5

Benchmark I Dr
Benchmark III Dr
6000 Dr
Benchmark II

Benchmark   Benchmark

MT ST. FRANCES LAKE

Creek Dr
Doe Ct
Fawn
Doe Ct
Doe Ridge Ct
Dr
4000

Bridge Ct

PAOLI
4300

Old Trace Ct

PIKE

3900

38°19'57"

6

Pebble Creek Dr
6300

Old Vincennes Rd

Chimneywood Dr

Leidolf Ct
Laura Dr

Ridgewood
Ridgewood Ct

150

Sylvan   Dr

Sylvan Ct

Evanna Ct

Knable Ct
Twin View Ct

Vale Hill Dr

Luther   Rd
W   5600

Luther   Rd
E   4500

Luther   Rd
4000

38°19'30"

7

Indian Creek Ln

47122

Little   Indian   Creek

Sarles   Cr

Luther Rd
5700

Old Vincennes Rd

Kruer   Ln
3400   N   1000

Schrieber   Rd
4100

Chipaway Ct

Fairway Dr
3100

Woodfield Dr

Golfland Ct

Banet Rd

Lawrence   Rd
3200

Fairway Ct

VALLEY VIEW GOLF CLUB

RAND M°NALLY

38°19'04"

A   B   C   D   E

SEE 5503 MAP

85°55'45"   85°55'12"   85°54'39"   85°54'06"   85°53'33"   85°53'00"

MAP
5395

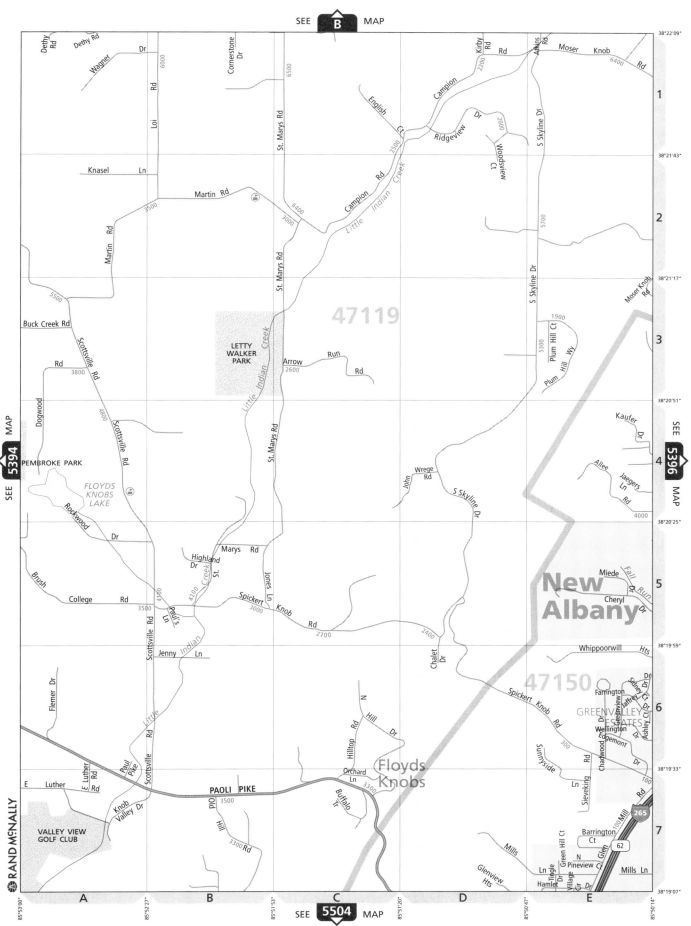

1:24,000
1 in. = 2000 ft.

miles
0   0.25   0.5

SEE B MAP

38°22'09"

Dethy Rd
Dethy Rd
Wagner Dr
Wagner Rd
Loi Rd
6000
Cornerstone Dr
St. Marys Rd
6500
English Ct
Kirby Rd
Rd
Annis Rd
Moser Knob Rd
6400
Campion
Ridgeview Dr
S Skyline Dr
Woodsview Ct
2200
2000

1

Knasel Ln
Martin Rd
3500
Campion Rd
Little Indian Creek
5700

38°21'43"

Martin Rd
Martin Rd
St. Marys Rd
6400
3000
S Skyline Dr

2

5500
Buck Creek Rd
Scottsville Rd
Rd
3800
47119
Little Indian Creek
Plum Hill Ct
5300
1900
Plum Hill Wy

38°21'17"
Moser Knob Rd

SEE
5394
MAP

Dogwood
4800
Scottsville Rd
LETTY WALKER PARK
Arrow Run Rd
2600
Plum Hill

3

38°20'51"
Kaufer Dr

Scottsville Rd
PEMBROKE PARK
St. Marys Rd
Wrege Rd
John
S Skyline Dr
Allee
Jaegers Ln
Rd
4000

SEE
5396
MAP

4

FLOYDS KNOBS LAKE
Rockwood Dr

38°20'25"

Highland Dr
Marys Rd
St.
4200 Creek
Jones Ln
Miede Dr
Fall Run
Cheryl Dr

New Albany

5

Brush
College Rd
3500
Scottsville Rd
4400
Paoli's Ln
Spickert Knob Rd
3000
2700
2400
Chalet Dr
Whippoorwill Hts

38°19'59"

Jenny Ln
Little Indian
47150
Farrington Dr
Greenview Dr
Sidney Ct
Chaffrey Dr
Ashley Ct
GREENVALLEY ESTATES
Wellington
Edgemont
Chadwood Dr
Spickert Knob Rd
Sunnyside Rd
300
Sievekirg Ln
100
Dr

6

Flemer Dr
Scottsville Rd
N Hill Dr
Hilltop Rd
38°19'33"
Mill Rd
100

E Luther Rd
Paul Pike
Orchard Ln
3300
Floyds Knobs
265

E Luther Rd
E Luther
Knob Valley Dr
PAOLI   PIKE
PIO
3500
Buffalo Tr
Barrington Ct
62

7

RAND MƇNALLY
VALLEY VIEW GOLF CLUB
Hill 3300 Rd
Mills
Glenview Hts
Green Hill Ct
Glen
Tingle Ln
Hamlet Dr
N Pineview Ct
Village Cir
Dr
Mills Ln

38°19'07"

85°53'00"   A   85°52'27"   B   85°51'53"   C   85°51'20"   D   85°50'47"   E   85°50'14"

SEE
5504
MAP

MAP
5396

1:24,000
1 in. = 2000 ft.

0   0.25   0.5
miles

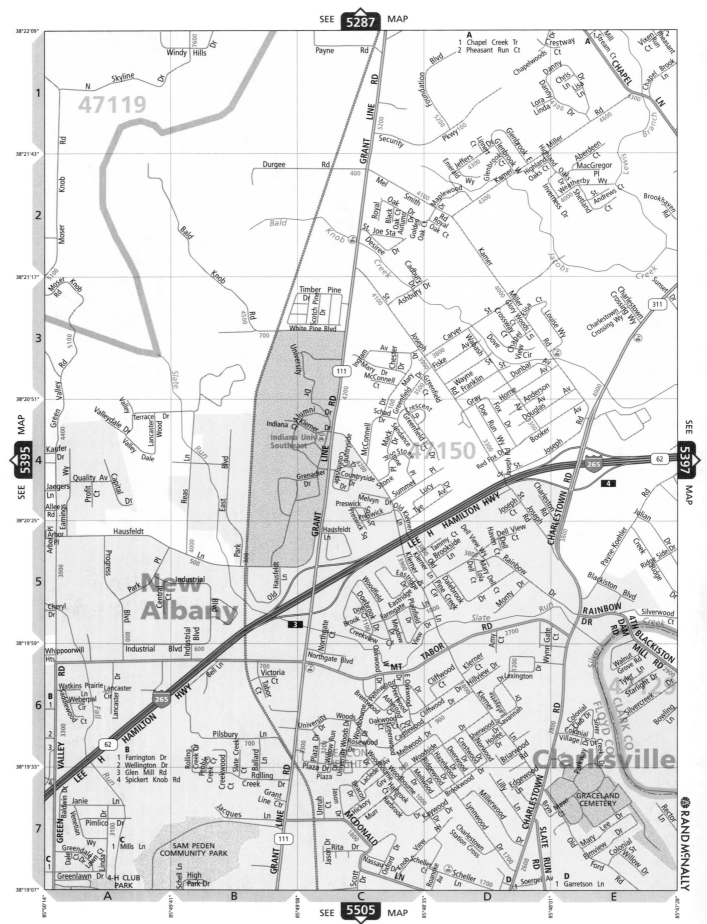

SEE 5287 MAP

SEE 5395 MAP

SEE 5397 MAP

SEE 5505 MAP

47119

47150

New
Albany

Clarksville

A
1 Chapel Creek Tr
2 Pheasant Run Ct

B
1 Farrington Dr
2 Wellington Dr
3 Glen Mill Rd
4 Spickert Knob Rd

C
1 Mills Ln

D
1 Garretson Ln

SAM PEDEN
COMMUNITY PARK

4-H CLUB
PARK

GRACELAND
CEMETERY

RAND McNALLY

38°22'09"
38°21'43"
38°21'17"
38°20'51"
38°20'25"
38°19'59"
38°19'33"
38°19'07"

85°50'14"
85°49'41"
85°49'08"
85°48'35"
85°48'01"
85°47'58"

A   B   C   D   E
1   2   3   4   5   6   7

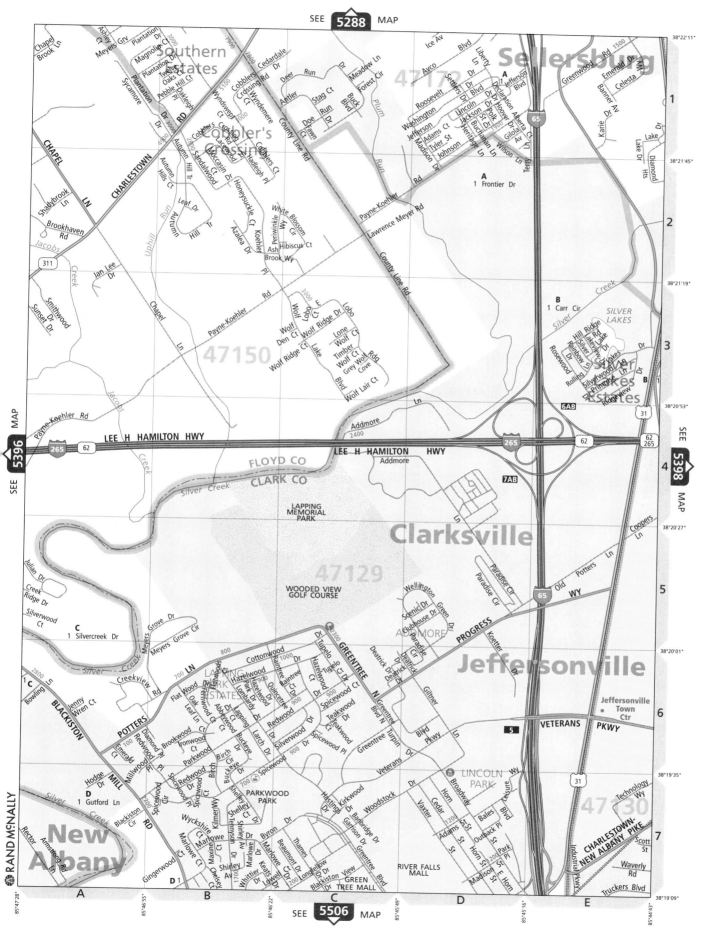

MAP
5397

1:24,000
1 in. = 2000 ft.
0   0.25   0.5
miles

N

SEE 5288 MAP

SEE 5396 MAP

SEE 5398 MAP

SEE 5506 MAP

RAND MCNALLY

Southern States
Cobbler's Crossing
Sellersburg
Silver Lakes
Silver Lakes Estates
Clarksville
Jeffersonville
New Albany

47172
47150
47129
47130

38°22'11"
38°21'45"
38°21'19"
38°20'53"
38°20'27"
38°20'01"
38°19'35"
38°19'09"

85°47'28"
85°46'55"
85°46'22"
85°45'49"
85°45'16"
85°44'43"

1 2 3 4 5 6 7

A B C D E

LEE H HAMILTON HWY
FLOYD CO
CLARK CO
LAPPING MEMORIAL PARK
WOODED VIEW GOLF COURSE
Jeffersonville Town Ctr
Lincoln Park
Parkwood Park
RIVER FALLS MALL
GREEN TREE MALL
CHARLESTOWN-NEW ALBANY PIKE
VETERANS PKWY
PROGRESS

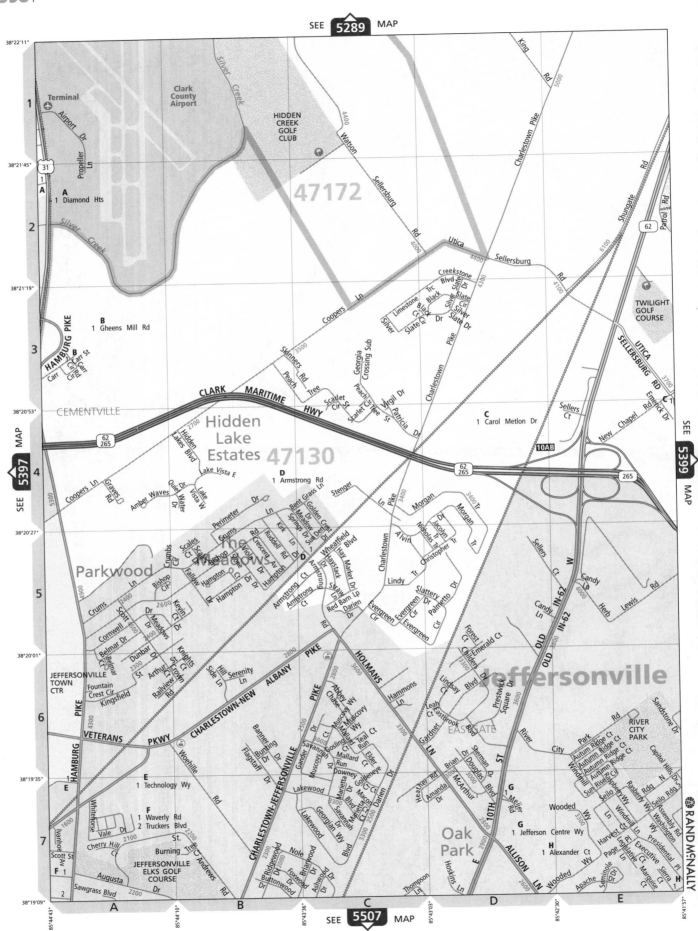

MAP
5398

1:24,000
1 in. = 2000 ft.
0   0.25   0.5
miles

SEE 5289 MAP
SEE 5397 MAP
SEE 5399 MAP
SEE 5507 MAP

RAND MCNALLY

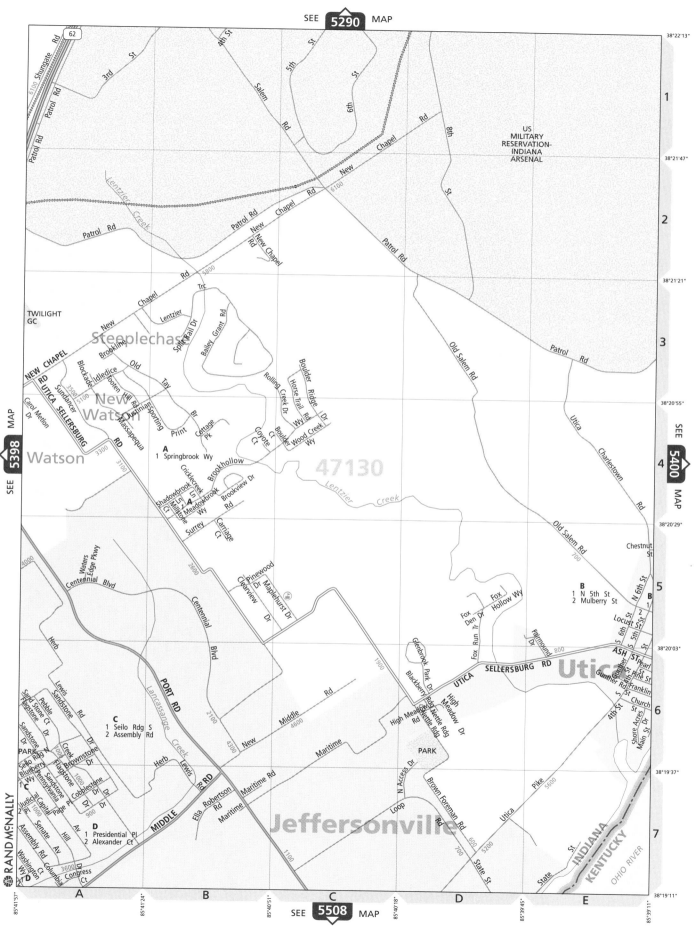

MAP
5399

1:24,000
1 in. = 2000 ft.

0   0.25   0.5
miles

SEE 5290 MAP

62

6100 Shungate Rd

3rd St

Patrol Rd

Patrol Rd

4th St

Salem Rd

5th St

6th St

Chapel Rd

8th St

New Chapel Rd

6100

US
MILITARY
RESERVATION-
INDIANA
ARSENAL

38°22'13"

38°21'47"

1

2

Lentzier Creek

Patrol Rd

Patrol Rd

New Chapel Rd

5800

New Chapel Rd

Patrol Rd

38°21'21"

TWILIGHT
GC

Chapel Trc

New

Steeplechase

Brookline

Lentzier

Bailey Grant Rd

Spur Trail Dr

Old Salem Rd

Patrol Rd

38°20'55"

SEE 5398 MAP

NEW CHAPEL RD

UTICA SELLERSBURG RD

Carol Mellon Dr

Blockade

Idledice

Hooten Hill

Old

3500 5100

Sundancer

Justinian

Sporting

Tay Br

Massapequa

Print

Cottage Pk

Rolling Creek Dr

Horse Trail Rd

Boulder Ridge

Boulder Ct

Wood Creek Wy

Wy Dr

Coyote Ct

Utica Charlestown Rd

New Watson

Watson

3300

3100

A
1 Springbrook Wy

Cricklecreek

Shadowbrook Ln
Millstone Ct

A
Meadowbrook Wy

Brookhollow

Brookview Dr

Meadowbrook Rd

47130

Lentzier Creek

Old Salem Rd
700

Surrey

Carriage Ct

38°20'29"

Chestnut St

2600

Centennial Blvd

Waters Edge Pkwy

Centennial Blvd

Pinewood Dr

Clearview

Maplehurst Dr

Dr

N 6th St

B
1 N 5th St
2 Mulberry St

B

Fox Hollow Wy

Fox Den Dr

Fox Run Tr

Locust St

5th St

S 6th St

38°20'55"

5

Herb

Port Rd

Lancassange Creek

2100

1900

Glenbrook Park Dr

Fairmound

800

High Meadow Dr

ASH ST

UTICA SELLERSBURG RD

Utica

S Gunther Rd

Pearl St

Pine St

Franklin St

Church St

38°20'03"

6

Lewis

Sandstone Rd

Pebble Ct

Flagstone

Sand Stone Ct

Sandstone Dr

C
1 Seilo Rdg S
2 Assembly Rd

4300

New

Middle Rd
4600

Blackberry Dr

Nettle Rdg

High Meadow Rd

High Meadow Dr

4th St

Shore Acres Dr

Main St

PARK

PARK

Brown Foreman Rd

Pike 5600

Utica

38°19'37"

7

Seilo Rdg
Blueberry Wy
Creek
Flagstone
Brownstone Dr
Cobblestone Dr
Dr
Dr
900

Sandstone Dr
Pennsylvania
Page Pl

Judicial
Capital

Senate Av

Hill Av

D
1 Presidential Pl
2 Alexander Ct

MIDDLE RD

Ella Robertson Rd

Maritime Rd

Maritime

N Access Dr

Loop

State St

600

700 5200

State St

Jeffersonville

1100

INDIANA
KENTUCKY

OHIO RIVER

Assembly Rd

Washington

Columbia

Congress Ct

3600

D

A   B   C   D   E

38°19'11"

85°41'57"   85°41'24"   85°40'51"   85°40'18"   85°39'45"   85°39'11"

SEE 5508 MAP

MAP
5400

1:24,000
1 in. = 2000 ft.

0   0.25   0.5
miles

SEE 5291 MAP

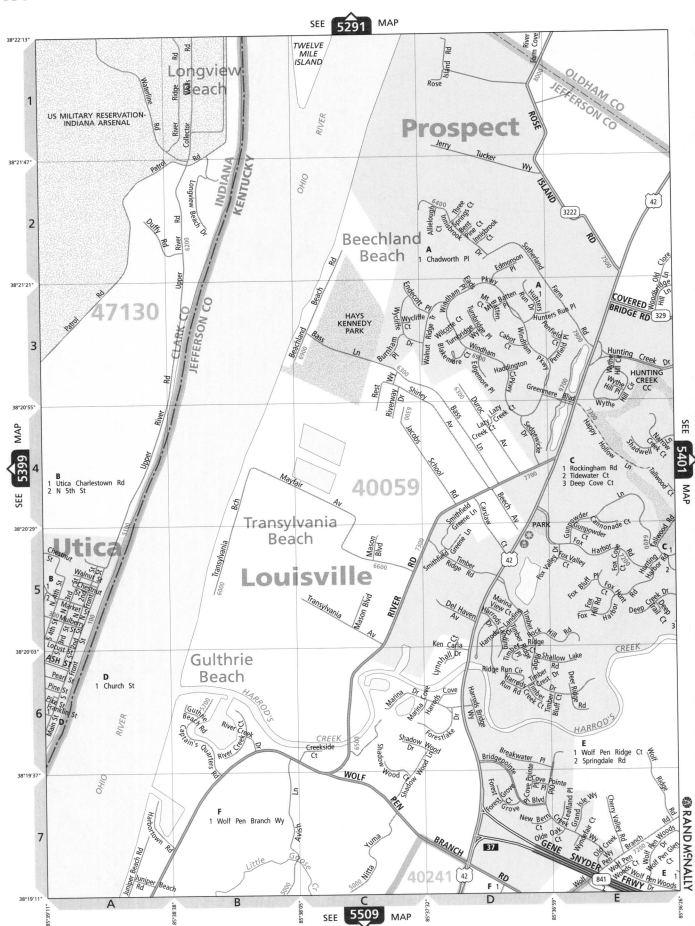

38°22'13"

Longview Beach

TWELVE MILE ISLAND

River Farm Cove

OLDHAM CO
JEFFERSON CO

US MILITARY RESERVATION-
INDIANA ARSENAL

Island Rd
Rose

Prospect

ROSE ISLAND RD

42

3222

Jerry   Tucker   Wy

38°21'47"

Waterline Rd
River Ridge Rd
Wells Rd
Collector Rd

Duffy Rd
River Rd

Patrol Rd

47130

Upper Rd

INDIANA
KENTUCKY

CLARK CO
JEFFERSON CO

38°21'21"

OHIO RIVER

Beechland Beach

Beach Rd

Three Springs Ct
Alielough Ct
Innisbrook Dr
Bent Ct
Pine Ct
Innisbrook Ct

A 1 Chadworth Pl

Edmonson Pl
Easts Pkwy

HUplers Ct
Hunters Run Dr

A

Sutherland
Farm Rd

6400

Woodbridge
Old Clore Rd

Hill Ct

COVERED BRIDGE RD
329

38°20'55"

Burnham Ln

Beechland Bass Ln

HAYS KENNEDY PARK

Endecott Pl
Wycliffe Ct
Walnut Ridge Tr
Wycliffe Dr
Wilcoffe Ct
Blakemore

Mt McP Batten Pl
Mt McP Batten Ct
Turnbridge Wy
Turnbridge Pl

Windham

Cabot Ct

Windham Pkwy

Penfield Pl
Penfield Ct

7900

7500

Wythe Hill Ct
Wythe Hill Pl
Wythe Hill Ct

Hunting Creek Dr

HUNTING CREEK CC

Rest Wy
Riverway Dr
Shirley

6300

Haddington Ct
Edgemore Pl

9700

Greenmere Blvd

Wythe

Happy Hollow Ln

Narrow Creek Rd
Shadwell

SEE 5399 MAP

River Rd

Upper Rd
5100

Jacobs Ln
School Rd

Duroc Ct
Lazy Creek Ct
Lazy Creek Av
Bass Av

Sedgewicke Dr

7700

7200

Tallwood Ln

C
1 Rockingham Rd
2 Tidewater Ct
3 Deep Cove Ct

38°20'29"

Utica

40059

Bch

Transylvania
Beach

Mayfair Av

6300

Smithfield Greene Ln
Smithfield Greene Ct

Carslaw

Beech Av

PARK

Gunpowder Ct
Cannonade Ct
Gunpowder Ct

Tallwood Rd

Fox Harbor Ln

6400

C 1

38°20'03"

Chestnut St
Walnut St
Chestnut St
Front St
2nd St
3rd St

B
1
Market St
Mulberry

Louisville

Transylvania

6000

Mason Blvd

RIVER RD

7300

Smithfield Greene
Timber Ridge Rd

42

Del Haven Av

Marina View Ct
Harrods Landing Dr

Fox Valley Dr

Fox Valley Ct

Fox Bluff Pl

Fox Hill Rd
Fox Harbor

7200

Hunting Harbor Ct

Fox Hill Rd
Fox Hunt Rd

Deep Creek Trail

Deep Creek

38°20'55"

SEE 5401 MAP

ASH ST
4th St
2nd St
Locust St
Pearl St
Pine St
Franklin St
Main St

D
1 Church St

D

Transylvania Av
Mason Blvd

Ken Carla Dr

Lynnhall Dr

Harrods Landing
Timber Ridge
Rock Hill

Harrods Landing Rd
Harrods Landing Ct

Ridge Run Cir
Timber Ridge
Timber Run Rd
Timber Creek Ct
Timber Crest Dr
Bluff Ct

Shallow Lake
Timber Ct

Deer Ridge Rd

CREEK

HARROD'S

38°19'37"

Gulthrie Beach

Guthrie Beach Rd
River Creek Ct
Captain's Quarters Rd
River Creek Dr

5700

HARROD'S

CREEK

Creekside Ct

6500

Marina Dr
Marina Cove

Harrods Cove
Cove Wy

Forestlake

Shadow Wood Dr
Shadow Wood Ct
Shadow Wood Ln

WOLF

Breakwater Pl

Bridgepointe

Cove Pointe Pl
Cove Pointe Pl
Pointe Blvd

E
1 Wolf Pen Ridge Ct
2 Springdale Rd

38°19'11"

Juniper Beach Rd
Juniper Beach

Harbortown Rd

F
1 Wolf Pen Branch Wy

Ln
Avish

Yuma

Little

Goose

Creek

5000 Nitta

WOLF PEN BRANCH RD

40241

37

42

GENE SNYDER FRWY

841

F 1

Forest Grove Ct
Forest Grove
New Bern Ct
Olde Oak Ct

Leafland Pl
Grand Isle Wy
Windfair Wy
Old Creek Rd

Cherry Valley Rd

Wolf Pen Woods Wy
Wolf Pen Woods Ct
Wolf Pen Glen

Wolf Ridge Rd

Wolf Pen Branch Rd

Wolf Pen Woods Dr

E
E 1

B
1 Utica Charlestown Rd
2 N 5th St

A   B   C   D   E

85°39'11"   85°38'38"   85°38'05"   85°37'32"   85°36'59"

MAP
5401

1:24,000
1 in. = 2000 ft.

0   0.25   0.5
miles

SEE 5292 MAP

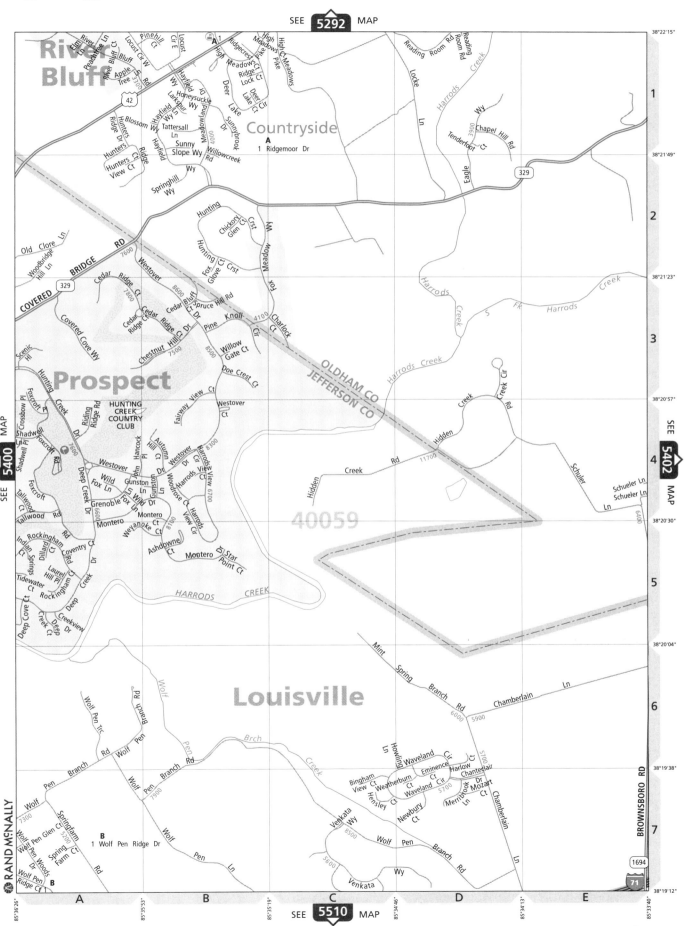

River Bluff

Countryside

A
1 Ridgemoor Dr

Prospect

HUNTING CREEK COUNTRY CLUB

OLDHAM CO
JEFFERSON CO

40059

HARRODS CREEK

Louisville

B
1 Wolf Pen Ridge Dr

SEE 5400 MAP

SEE 5402 MAP

RAND McNALLY

BROWNSBORO RD

SEE 5510 MAP

MAP
5402

1:24,000
1 in. = 2000 ft.

0   0.25   0.5
miles

N

SEE **B** MAP

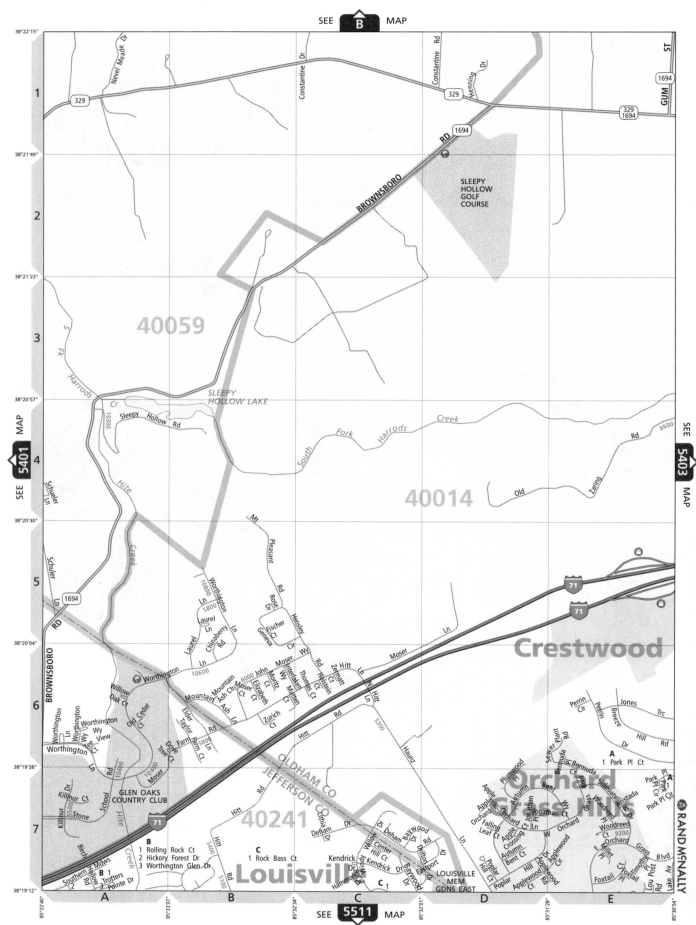

38°22'15"

Nevel Meade Dr

Constantine Dr

Constantine Rd

Henning Dr

GUM ST

1694

329

329

1694

RD

BROWNSBORO

38°21'49"

1694

SLEEPY
HOLLOW
GOLF
COURSE

SEE 5401 MAP

SEE 5403 MAP

1

2

38°21'23"

40059

3

S Fk

Harrods

38°20'57"

Cr

10300

Sleepy Hollow Rd

SLEEPY
HOLLOW LAKE

Creek

South Fork Harrods

Rd

8600

Old

Zaring

4

40014

Rd

Schueler Ln

Hite

38°20'30"

Mt

Creek

Pleasant

Schuler

1694

RD

Rd

71

71

38°20'04"

Worthington Ln

10800

5800

Laurel Ln

Chinaberry Ln

Rd

Laurel Ln

10600

Rose Dr

Fischer Ct

Geneva

Hensley

Cir

Moser Wy

Interlaken

Thomas Rd

Zettmatt

Holstein

Hitt

Ln

Moser

Moser Ln

Ln

Hitt

Crestwood

5

BROWNSBORO

Worthington

Willow
Oak Ct

Old Cedar
Ct

Worthington Ln

Worthington Wy

Worthington
Wy View

Worthington

Elder

Taylor Farm Rd

Dove Ct

Tree Ct

Mountain Mountain

Ash Ct

Moser

Ash Ct

6000 John

Ct

Elizabeth

Moritz

Matten

Wy

Zurich
Ct

Rd

5500

5300

Haunz Ln

Perrin
Cir

Perrin

Jones Trc

Breeze

Hill Rd

Sewer Plant

A

1 Park Pl Ct

6

38°19'38"

Killinur Dr

Killinur Ct

5500

Stone

School

Rd

10400

10400

Moser

GLEN OAKS
COUNTRY CLUB

Hite

OLDHAM CO

JEFFERSON CO

Cithia Dr

Deham Dr

Hitt Rd

Plumwood

Bent

Bermuda Dr

Bermuda
Ct

Autumn

Apple
Crossing Ct

Apple
Orchard

Apple
Falling
Leaf Ct

Orchard

Sideoats

Jonathan

Wy

Woodreed

Orchard

Woodreed
Ct

9200

Park Pl Cir

Tristada

Park Pl Cir

Park Pl
A

Orchard
Grass Hills

7

71

Birch

Southern Mdws

B
1 Rolling Rock Ct
2 Hickory Forest Dr
3 Worthington Glen Dr

Hollow

Trotters
Pointe Dr

Creek

5400

Hitt

Rd

5400

40241

C
1 Rock Bass Ct

Deham Dr

Kendrick Dr

Willow Center Dr

Kendrick Dr

Hammond Indy Dr

Deham Dr

Barwood Dr

Eastport Dr

Barwood Dr

Driftort Ct

LOUISVILLE
MEM
GDNS EAST

Poplar Hill Ct

Poplar

Applewood Rd

Applewood Cir

Applewood
Pl

Hill

E Millet
Pl

Foxtail

Foxtail Pl

Timothy
Ct

Grass
Blvd

Lou Post Rd

Ln

Louisville

C 1

38°19'12"

A   B   C   D   E

85°33'40"   85°33'07"   85°32'34"   101°32.56"   85°31'28"   85°06.58"

SEE 5511 MAP

RAND McNALLY

1:24,000
1 in. = 2000 ft.
0   0.25   0.5
miles

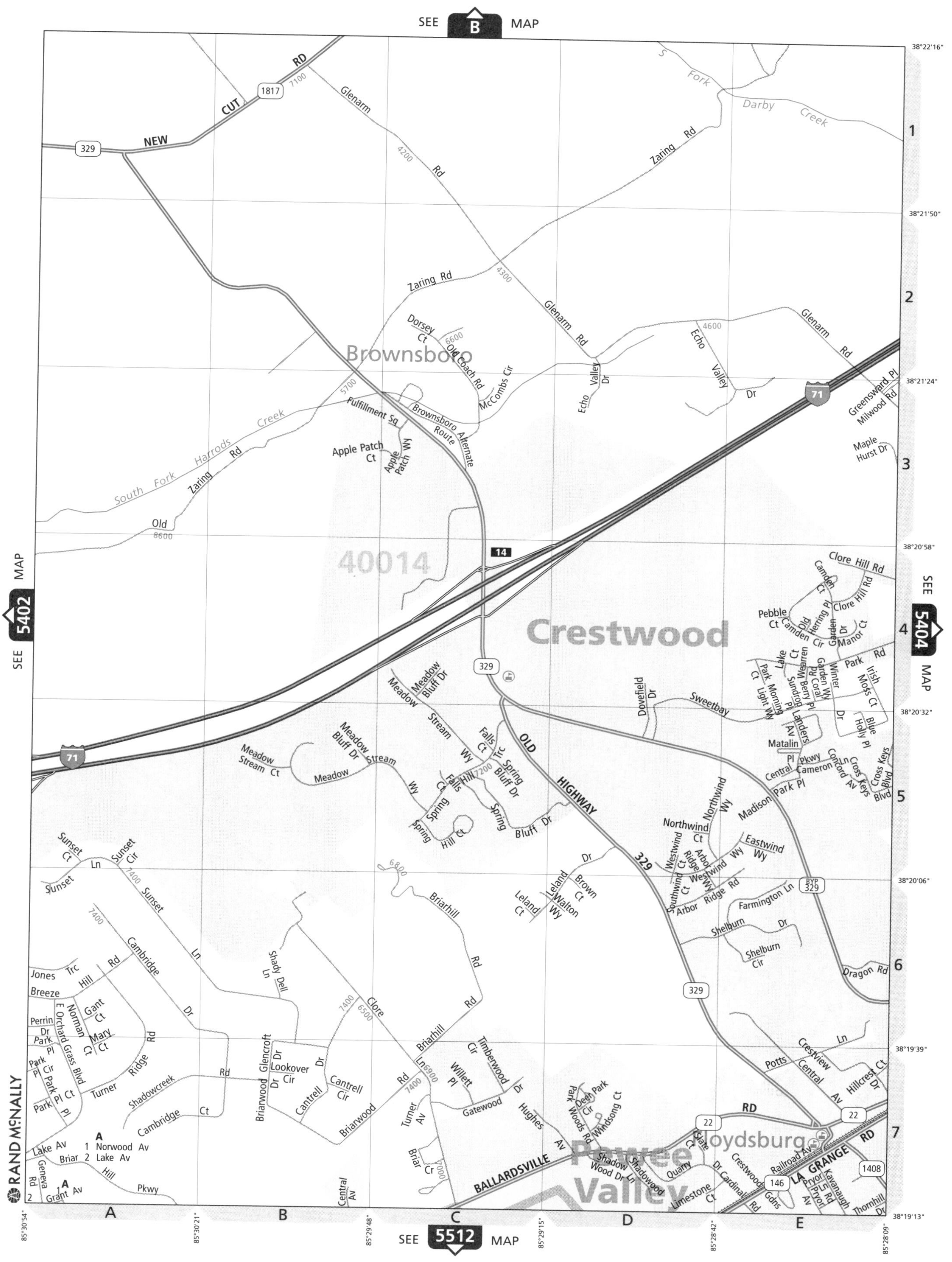

MAP
5403

SEE B MAP

38°22'16"
38°21'50"
38°21'24"
38°20'58"
38°20'32"
38°20'06"
38°19'39"
38°19'13"

1
2
3
4
5
6
7

SEE 5402 MAP
SEE 5404 MAP
SEE 5512 MAP

NEW CUT RD
329
1817
7100
Glenarm
Rd
4200
4300
4600
Zaring Rd
Zaring Rd
Glenarm Rd
Echo Valley Dr
Echo Valley Dr
Glenarm Rd
71
Greensward Pl
Milwood Rd
Maple Hurst Dr

Brownsboro
Dorsey Ct
6600
Old Coach Rd
McCombs Cir
Brownsboro Alternate
Brownsboro Route
5700
Fulfillment Sq
Apple Patch Ct
Apple Patch Wy
South Fork Harrods Creek
Zaring Rd
Old 8600

40014
14
329

Crestwood

Clore Hill Rd
Camden
Clore Hill Pl
Clore Hill
Pebble Ct
Camden Cir
Herring Pl
Manor Rd
Park
Irish
Moss Ct
Winter Dr
Garden Wy
Berry Pl
Coral
Sundrop
Landers
Light Wy
Lake Ct
Park Morning
Ct
Blue Holly Pl
Dovefield Dr
Sweetbay
Matalin Pl
Central Pkwy
Cameron
Cross Keys
Concord Av
Cross Keys Blvd

Meadow Bluff Dr
Meadow Stream
Meadow Bluff Dr
Meadow Stream
Meadow Stream Ct
Meadow
Meadow Stream Wy
Falls Trc
Spring Wy
7200
Falls Hill
Bluff Dr
Spring
Spring Hill Ct
Spring
Bluff Dr
Old HIGHWAY
Madison Park Pl
Northwind Wy
Northwind Ct
Westwind Ct
Eastwind Wy
Southwind Ct
Arbor
Ridge
Westwind Wy
Arbor Ridge Rd
Farmington Ln
BYP 329
Shelburn Dr
Shelburn Cir
Dragon Rd

71
Sunset Ct
Sunset Ln
Sunset Cir
7400
Sunset
Sunset
Shady Dell Ln
6800
Briarhill Rd
Leland Ct
Leland Wy
Walton Wy
Brown Ct
Dr
329

Jones Trc
Breeze
Cambridge Hill Rd
Perrin Dr
E Orchard Grass Blvd
Gant Ct
Mary Ct
Norman
Park Pl
Park Pl Cir
Park Pl Ct
Turner
Ridge Rd
Shadowcreek
Cambridge Ct
Cambridge Dr
Ln
7400
Briarwood
Glencroft Dr
Lookover Cir
Dr
Cantrell Cir
Cantrell Ct
Briarwood
Clore Rd
6500
7400
Briarhill Rd
Timberwood Cir
Willett Pl
6600
Turner Av
Gatewood
Hughes Ln
Dead Park
Park Woods Rd
Windsong Ct
Shadow Wood Dr
Shadowood
Quarry
Slate Dr
Cardinal

RD
22
Floydsburg
146
La Grange
22
1408
Railroad Av
Crestwood Gdns
Pryor Av
Kavanaugh Av
Pryor
Thornhill Dr

CresView
Potts
Central Av
Hillcrest Ct

BALLARDSVILLE
Pewee Valley
Limestone
Central Av

Lake Av
1 Norwood Av
2 Lake Av
A
Briar Hill
Geneva Rd
Grant Av
Pkwy

A   B   C   D   E

85°30'54" 85°30'21" 85°29'48" 85°29'15" 85°28'42" 85°28'09"

MAP
5404

1:24,000
1 in. = 2000 ft.
0   0.25   0.5
miles

SEE 5295 MAP

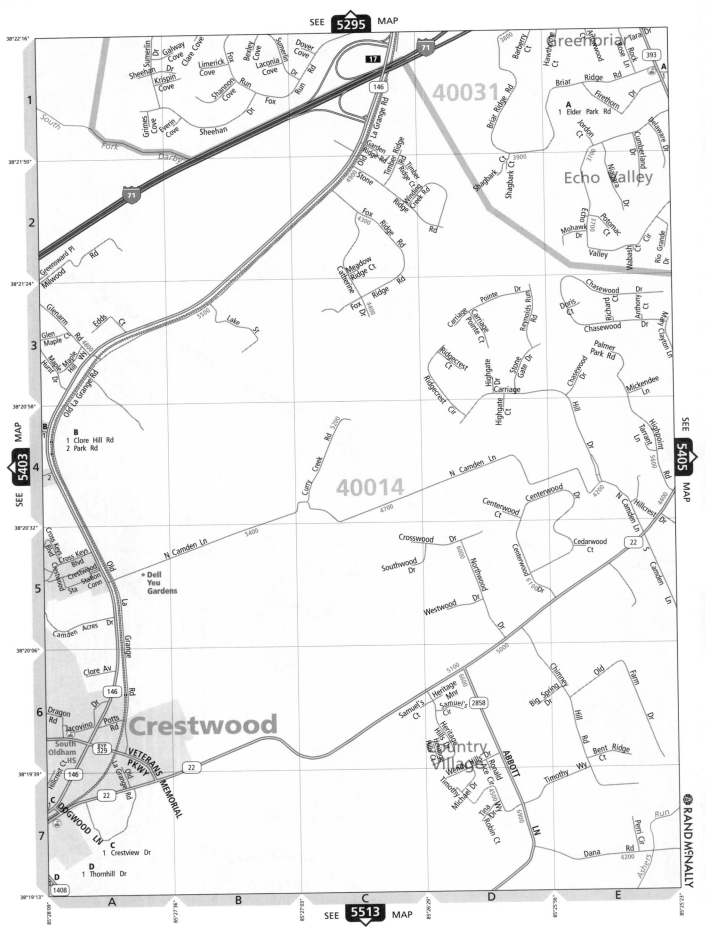

40031

71

17

146

Greenbriar

3800
Barberry Ct
Hawthorne Ct
Arrowwood
Rose Ln
Tara Dr
393
A

Briar Ridge Rd

Firethorn Dr
A
1 Elder Park Rd

Jordan Ct

Delaware Dr
Cumberland Dr
3700
Niagara Dr

Echo Valley

South Fork Darby

Sumerlin Dr
Galway Cove
Clare Cove
Limerick Cove
Fox
Bexley Cove
Laconia Cove
Sumerlin Dr
Dover Cove
Run Rd

Sheehan

Krispin Cove
Shannon Cove
Run
Fox

Grimes Cove
Everin Cove
Sheehan

Old La Grange Rd
Garden Ridge Rd
4900 Stone
Timber Ridge
Timber Ridge Ct
Winding Creek Rd
Ridge Rd

Briar Ridge Rd
3900
Shagbark Ct
Shagbark Ct

Mohawk Dr
3700
Echo Cir
Potomac Ct
Valley
Wabash Ct
Rio Grande Dr

Greensward Pl
Milwood Rd

71

38°22'16"

38°21'50"

38°21'24"

1

2

Fox Ridge Rd
4300

Meadow Ridge Ct
Catherine
Fox Dr
Ridge Rd
4400

5500
Lake St

Chasewood Dr
Doris Ct
Richard Ct
Anthony Dr
Chasewood Dr
Mary Clayton Ln

Glenarm Rd
Edds Ct
4800
Glen Maple Ct
Maple
Maple Hill Wy
Hurst Dr

Old La Grange Rd

Carriage Pointe Dr
Carriage Pointe Ct
Reynolds Run Rd

Palmer Park Rd

Ridgecrest Ct
Highgate Dr
Stone Gate Dr
Carriage
Chasewood Dr

Mickendee Ln

Ridgecrest Cir
Highgate Ct

Hill Dr

Highpoint Rd
Tarrant Ln
5600

38°21'24"

38°20'58"

3

B
B
1 Clore Hill Rd
2 Park Rd

Curry Creek Rd
5200

40014

N Camden Ln

4200
N Camden Ln
Hillcrest Dr
4400

SEE 5405 MAP

SEE 5403 MAP

B
1
2

4700

Centerwood Ct
Centerwood Dr

S Camden Ln

38°20'58"

4

Cross Keys Blvd
Cross Keys Blvd
Crestwood Sta
Station Conn

Old La Grange Rd

Dell Yeu Gardens

N Camden Ln
5400

Crosswood Dr
6000
Northwood Dr
Southwood Dr
Westwood Dr

Centerwood 6100 Dr
Cedarwood Ct
22

38°20'32"

5

Camden Acres Dr

Clore Av

146

Old La Grange Rd

Heritage Mnr
Samuel's Ct
Samuel's Cir
2858
6600

5100
5000

Big Spring Dr
Chimney
Old Farm

38°20'06"

6

Dragon Rd
Jacovino Dr
Potts Rd
Byp 329
South Oldham HS
Hillcrest Ct
146
22

Crestwood

Country Village

VETERANS MEMORIAL PKWY
22

Heritage Hills Dr
Heritage Hills Dr
Heritage Hills Ct
Wendy Dr
Timothy Dr
Michael Dr
Ronald Ace Cir 4500
Tina Dr
Robin Ct
Timothy Wy

Hill Rd
Bent Ridge Ct

ABBOTT LN

6900

Perri Cir
Dana Rd
4200
Ashers Run

38°19'39"

7

C
1 Crestview Dr

D
1 Thornhill Dr

DOGWOOD LN

1408

38°19'13"

A   B   C   D   E

85°28'09"   85°27'36"   85°27'03"   85°26'29"   85°25'56"

SEE 5513 MAP

MAP
5405

1:24,000
1 in. = 2000 ft.

0   0.25   0.5
miles

SEE **5296** MAP

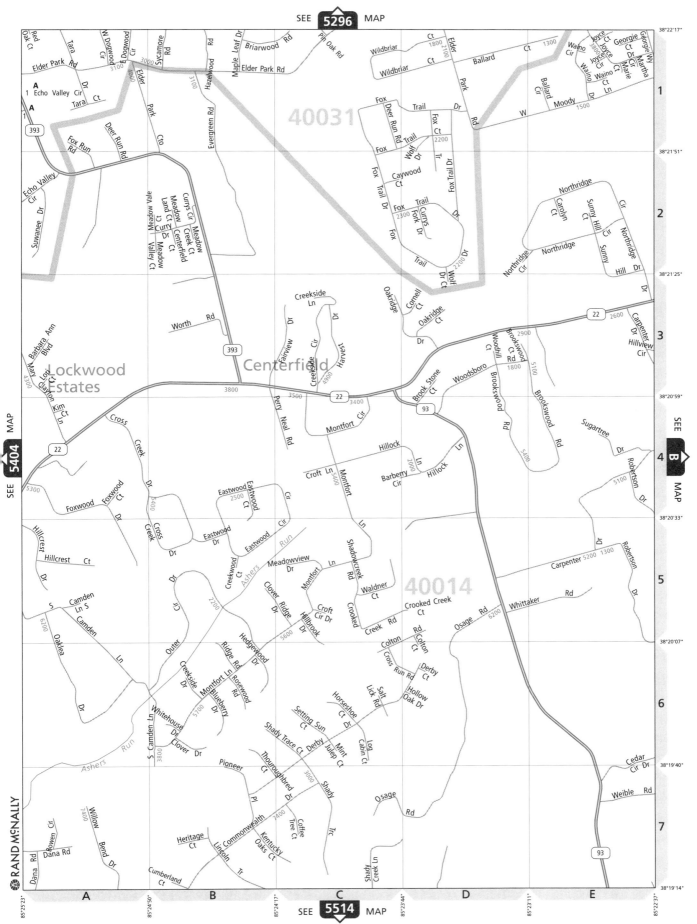

SEE **5404** MAP

SEE **B** MAP

SEE **5514** MAP

RAND McNALLY

38°22'17"
38°21'51"
38°21'25"
38°20'59"
38°20'33"
38°20'07"
38°19'40"
38°19'14"

85°25'23"
85°24'50"
85°24'17"
85°23'44"
85°23'11"
85°22'37"

A   B   C   D   E

40031
40014

Lockwood Estates
Centerfield

MAP
5501

1:24,000
1 in. = 2000 ft.

0   0.25   0.5
miles

N

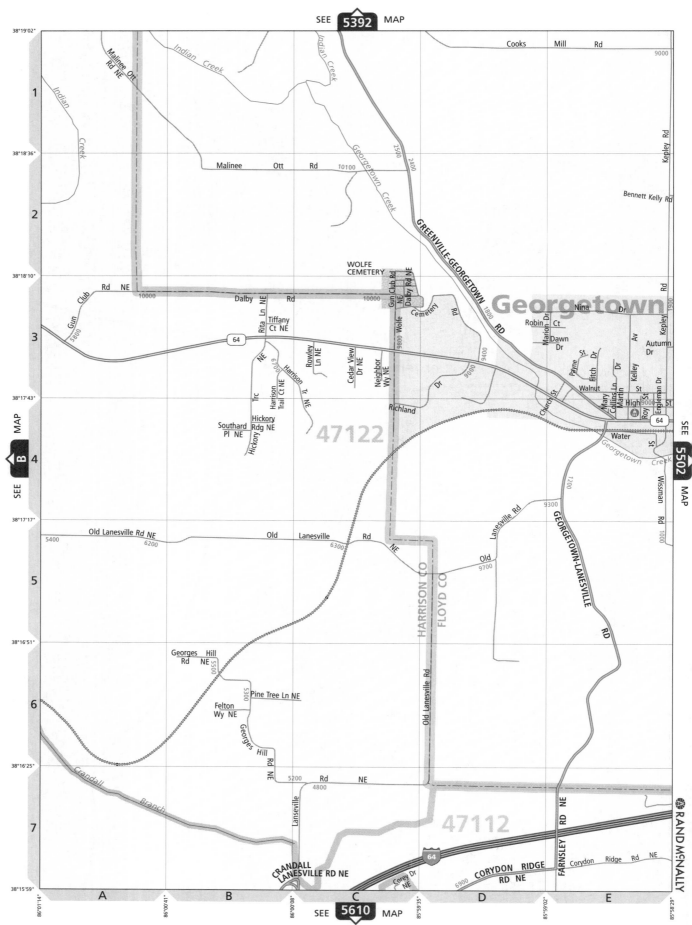

Cooks   Mill   Rd
9000

Indian Creek

Indian Creek

Malinee Ott Rd NE

Malinee   Ott   Rd   10100

Georgetown Creek

2500
2400

GREENVILLE-GEORGETOWN RD

Kepley Rd

Bennett Kelly Rd

1

38°19'02"

38°18'36"

2

38°18'10"

WOLFE CEMETERY

Gun Club Rd NE

Dalby Rd NE

Dalby   Rd   10000

Gun Club Rd

Cemetery

Rd

1800

Georgetown

Nina   Dr

Robin Dr   Ct

Marion Dr

Dawn
Dr

Payne St

Fitch Dr

Autumn
Dr

Av

Kepley Rd

1900

3

38°17'43"

Gun Club Rd NE 10000

5800

64

Rita Ln NE

Tiffany
Ct NE

Trc NE

57?9

Rowley
Ln NE

Harrison Tr NE

Cedar View
Dr NE

Neighbor
Wy NE

9800 Wolfe

9600

9000

Dr

Richland

Kelley
St

Walnut

Collins Ln

Martin

Mary

Church St

Englemn St

Roy

9000

High St

64

38°17'43"

Trc

Harrison
Trail Ct NE

Southard
Pl NE

Hickory
Rdg NE

Hickory

47122

Water

Georgetown Creek

Wissman Rd
1000

SEE [5502] MAP

MAP B

SEE

4

38°17'17"

38°17'17"

Old Lanesville Rd NE

5400   6200

Old   Lanesville   Rd   6300

NE

Lanesville Rd

9300

Old
9700

1200

Lanesville Rd

Georgetown-Lanesville

RD

5

38°16'51"

Georges   Hill
Rd   NE   5500

HARRISON CO

FLOYD CO

Old Lanesville Rd

38°16'51"

6

5300 Pine Tree Ln NE

Felton
Wy NE

Georges Hill Rd NE

38°16'25"

Crandall   Branch

5200   Rd   NE
4800

47112

Farnsley Rd NE

Corey Dr
NE

64

CORYDON RIDGE
RD NE
6900

Corydon Ridge Rd NE

RAND McNALLY

7

38°15'59"

Lanesville

CRANDALL
LANESVILLE RD NE

38°16'25"

86°01'14"   A   86°00'41"   B   86°00'08"   C   85°59'35"   D   85°59'02"   E   ×85°58'58"

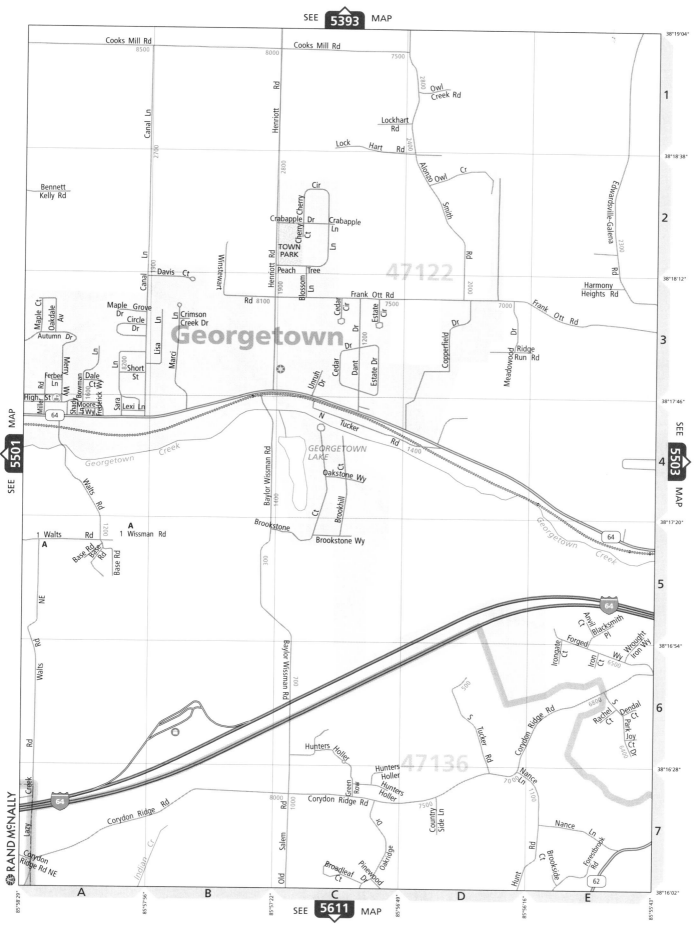

MAP
5502

1:24,000
1 in. = 2000 ft.

0   0.25   0.5
miles

N

SEE 5393 MAP

Cooks Mill Rd
8500   8000   Cooks Mill Rd   7500

Owl
2800   Creek Rd

Lockhart
Rd

Lock   Hart   Rd

2400

Henriott   Rd

Canal Ln

2700

Alonzo Owl   Cr

Smith

Rd

Edwardsville-Galena   Rd

2300

Bennett
Kelly Rd

2800

Cir

Cherry

Crabapple   Cherry   Dr   Crabapple
Ct   Ln

Ln

TOWN
PARK

Ln

Winstewart

1900

Davis   Ct

Canal

Ln

Canal

Peach   Tree

Henriott Rd

Blossom   Ln

1900

Rd   8100

Frank Ott Rd

7500

Cedar   Cir

Estate   Cir

47122

7000

Frank   Ott   Rd

Harmony
Heights Rd

2000

Georgetown

Maple   Grove
Dr   Circle
Dr

Crimson
Creek Dr

Lisa

Marci

Copperfield   Dr

Meadowood   Ridge
Run Rd

Maple Ct   Oakdale
Av

Autumn   Dr

Merry   Wy

Ferber
Rd   Ln

Dale
Ct

8200

Short
St

Ln

1600

Bowman   Frederick Wy

Sara

Lexi   Ln

Cedar

Dr

Dant

Urruh   Dr

1200

Estate Dr

High   St

Miller

Shady   Moore
Ln   Wy

64

MAP
5501
SEE

Walts   Rd

Georgetown   Creek

Baylor Wissman Rd

1400

GEORGETOWN
LAKE

N

Tucker   Rd   1400

Oakstone   Wy

Ct

Brookhill

SEE
5503
MAP

Georgetown   Creek

64

1 Walts   Rd

A

1 Wissman   Rd

A

Base Rd   Base
Rd

Base Rd

1200

Brookstone

Brookstone   Wy

300

NE

Walts

Rd

Baylor Wissman Rd

700

64

Anvil   Blacksmith
Ct   Pl

Forged   Wrought
Wy   Iron Wy

Irongate
Ct

Iron
Ct   6500

500

Corydon Ridge Rd

6800

Rachel   S Dendal   Ct
Ct   Park
Joy   Ct Dr
6400

S Tucker   Rd

Nance   Ln
7000   1100

Creek

Hunters   Holler

47136

Green   Row

Hunters
Holler

Hunters
Holler

Corydon Ridge Rd

8000

1000

Salem   Rd

Corydon Ridge Rd

7500

Country
Side Ln

Nance   Ln

Lazy   Creek   Rd

Corydon
Ridge Rd NE

Indian   Cr

Broadleaf
Ct

Pinewood   Dr

Oakridge

Old

Salem   Rd

Hunt   Rd

Brookside   Ct

Forestbrook
Rd

62

RAND McNALLY

A   B   C   D   E

SEE 5611 MAP

38°19'04"
38°18'38"
38°18'12"
38°17'46"
38°17'20"
38°16'54"
38°16'28"
38°16'02"

85°58'29"   85°57'56"   85°57'22"   85°56'49"   85°56'16"   85°55'43"

1
2
3
4
5
6
7

MAP
5503

1:24,000
1 in. = 2000 ft.

0   0.25   0.5
miles

SEE 5394 MAP

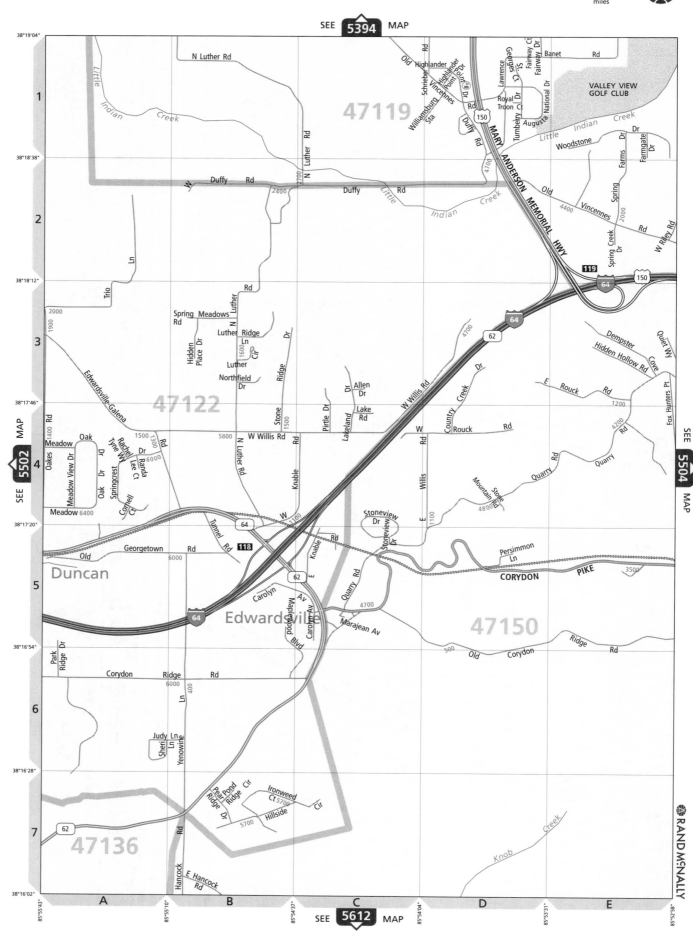

SEE 5502 MAP

SEE 5504 MAP

SEE 5612 MAP

RAND McNALLY

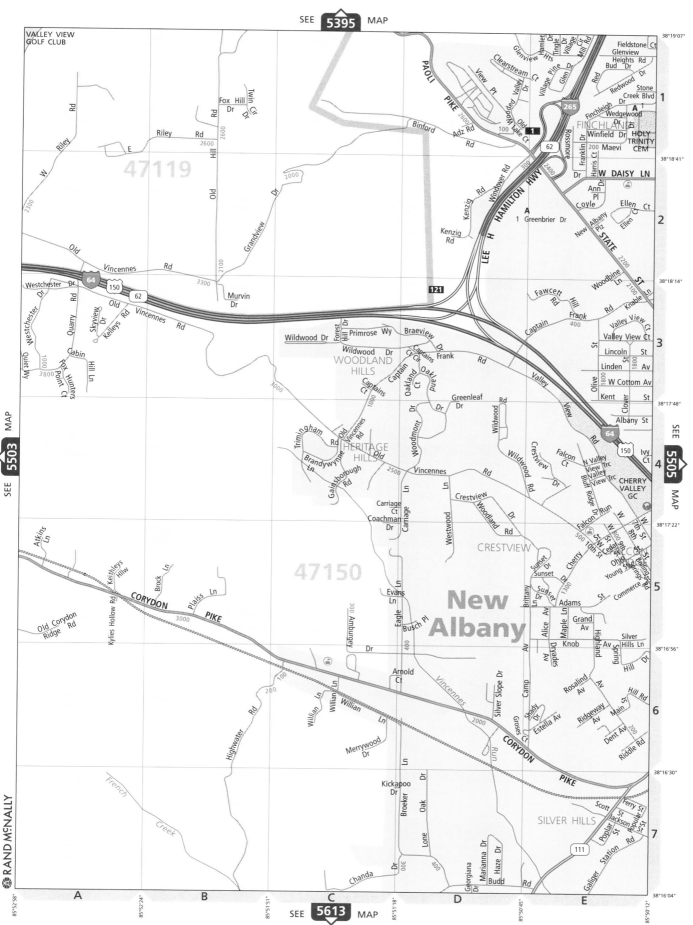

MAP
5504

1:24,000
1 in. = 2000 ft.

0   0.25   0.5
miles

SEE 5395 MAP

SEE 5503 MAP

SEE 5505 MAP

SEE 5613 MAP

VALLEY VIEW
GOLF CLUB

47119

47150

New
Albany

WOODLAND
HILLS

HERITAGE
HILLS

CRESTVIEW

CHERRY
VALLEY
GC

FINCHLANE

HOLY
TRINITY
CEM

SILVER HILLS

RAND McNALLY

PAOLI PIKE

LEE H HAMILTON HWY

CORYDON PIKE

CORYDON PIKE

38°19'07"
38°18'41"
38°18'14"
38°17'48"
38°17'22"
38°16'56"
38°16'30"
38°16'04"

85°52'58"   85°52'24"   85°51'51"   85°51'18"   85°50'45"   85°50'12"

A   B   C   D   E

1   2   3   4   5   6   7

MAP
5505

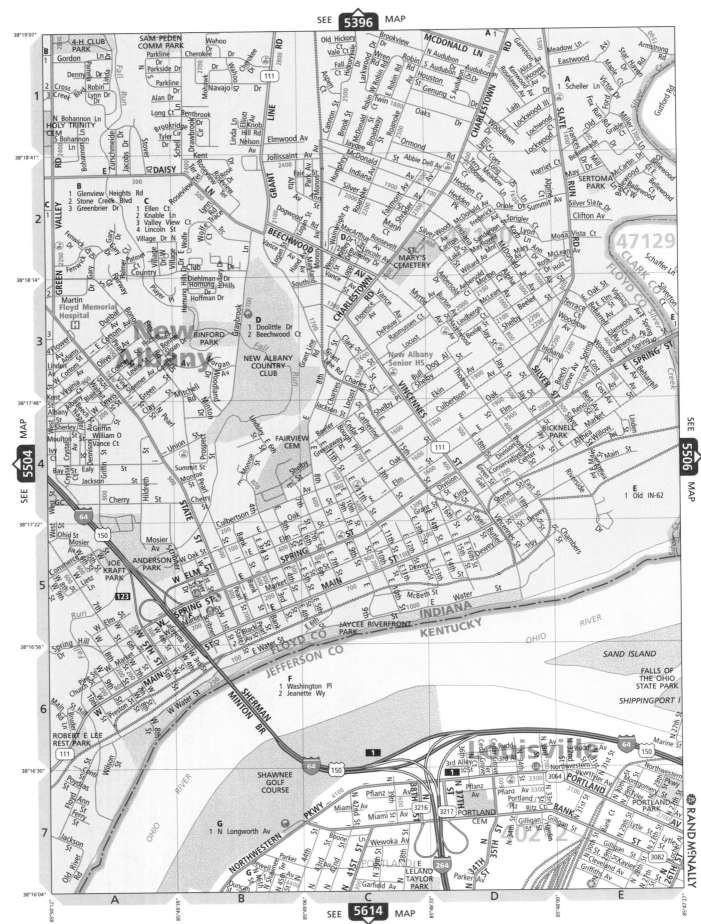

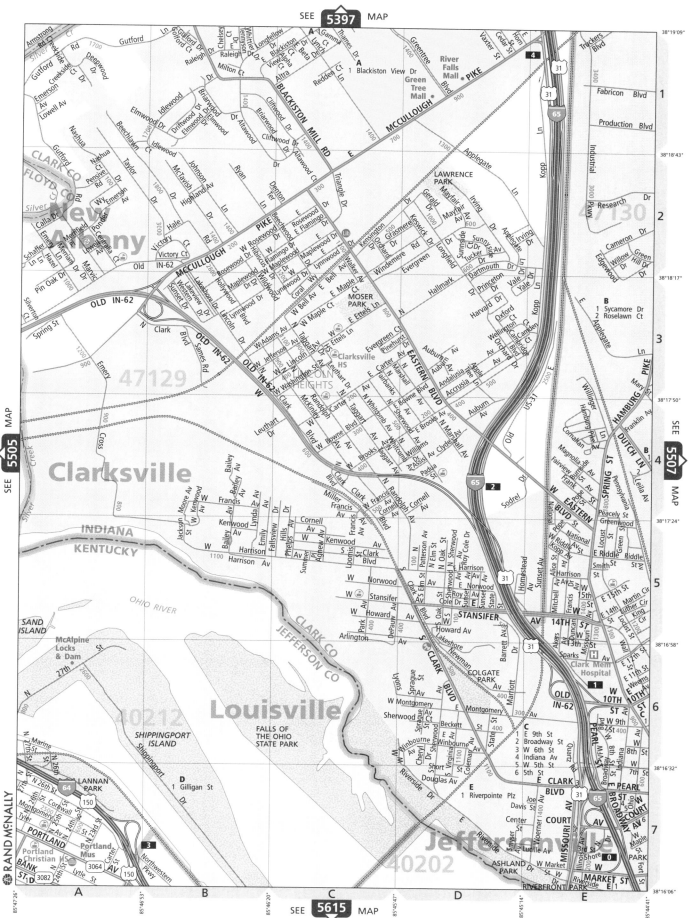

MAP
5506

N
1:24,000
1 in. = 2000 ft.
0   0.25   0.5
miles

SEE 5397 MAP

SEE 5505 MAP

SEE 5507 MAP

SEE 5615 MAP

RAND MCNALLY

38°19'09"
38°18'43"
38°18'17"
38°17'50"
38°17'24"
38°16'58"
38°16'32"
38°16'06"

85°47'26"
85°46'53"
85°46'20"
85°45'47"
85°45'14"
85°44'41"

New Albany
Clarksville
Louisville
Jeffersonville
40202

47130
47129
47219
40212

CLARK CO
FLOYD CO

INDIANA
KENTUCKY

OHIO RIVER

SAND ISLAND
SHIPPINGPORT ISLAND

McAlpine Locks & Dam

FALLS OF THE OHIO STATE PARK

CLARK CO
JEFFERSON CO

A
1 Blackiston View Dr

B
1 Sycamore Dr
2 Roselawn Ct

C
1 E 9th St
2 Broadway St
3 W 6th St
4 Indiana Av
5 W 5th St
6 5th St

D
1 Gilligan St

E
1 Riverpointe Plz

MAP
5507

1:24,000
1 in. = 2000 ft.

0   0.25   0.5
miles

RAND McNALLY

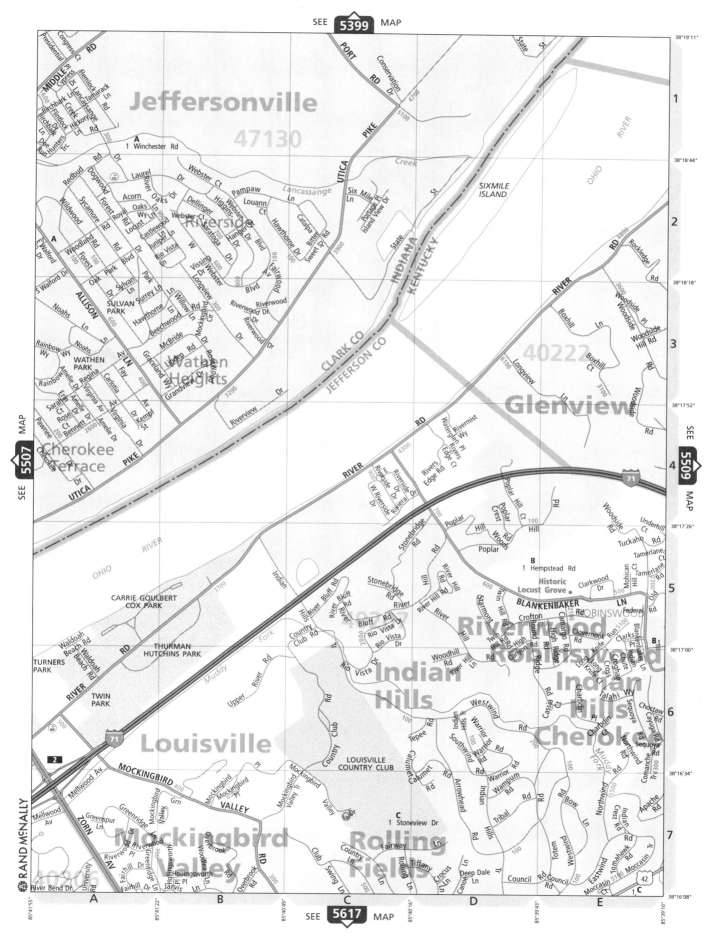

MAP
5508

1:24,000
1 in. = 2000 ft.

0   0.25   0.5
miles

N

SEE 5399 MAP

SEE 5507 MAP

SEE 5509 MAP

SEE 5617 MAP

Jeffersonville
47130

Glenview
40222

Cherokee
Terrace

Wathen
Heights

Riverside

Allison

Sulvan
Park

Wathen
Park

Carrie Goulbert
Cox Park

Thurman
Hutchins Park

Turners
Park

Twin
Park

Louisville

Mockingbird
Valley

Indian
Hills

Louisville
Country Club

Rolling
Fields

Riverwood
Robinswood

Indian
Hills
Cherokee

Historic
Locust Grove

Sixmile
Island

RAND McNALLY

38°19'11"
38°18'44"
38°18'18"
38°17'52"
38°17'26"
38°17'00"
38°16'34"
38°16'08"

85°41'55"
85°41'22"
85°40'49"
85°40'16"
85°39'43"
85°39'10"

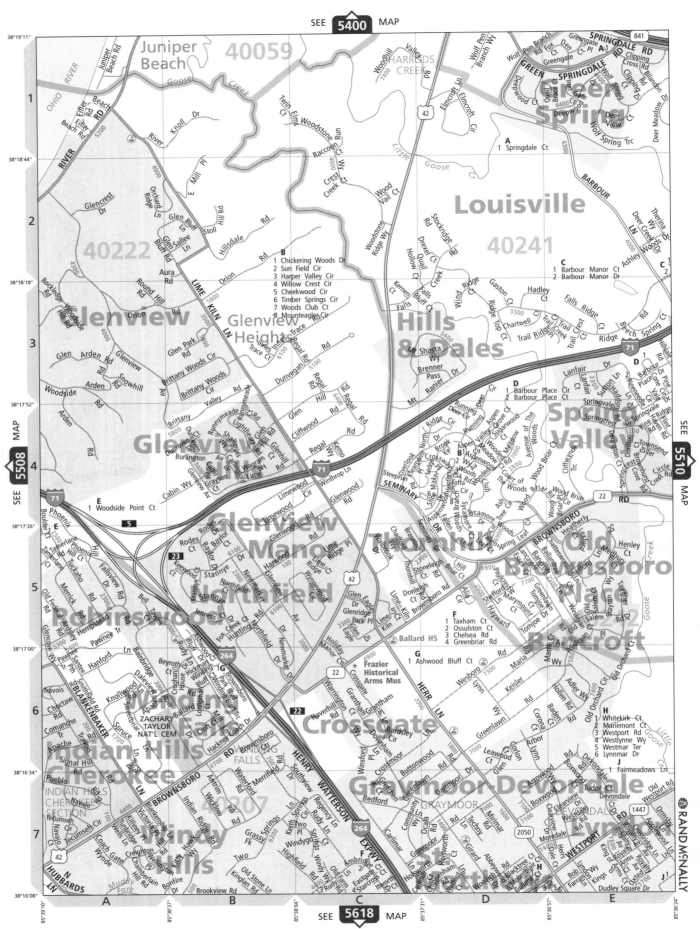

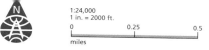
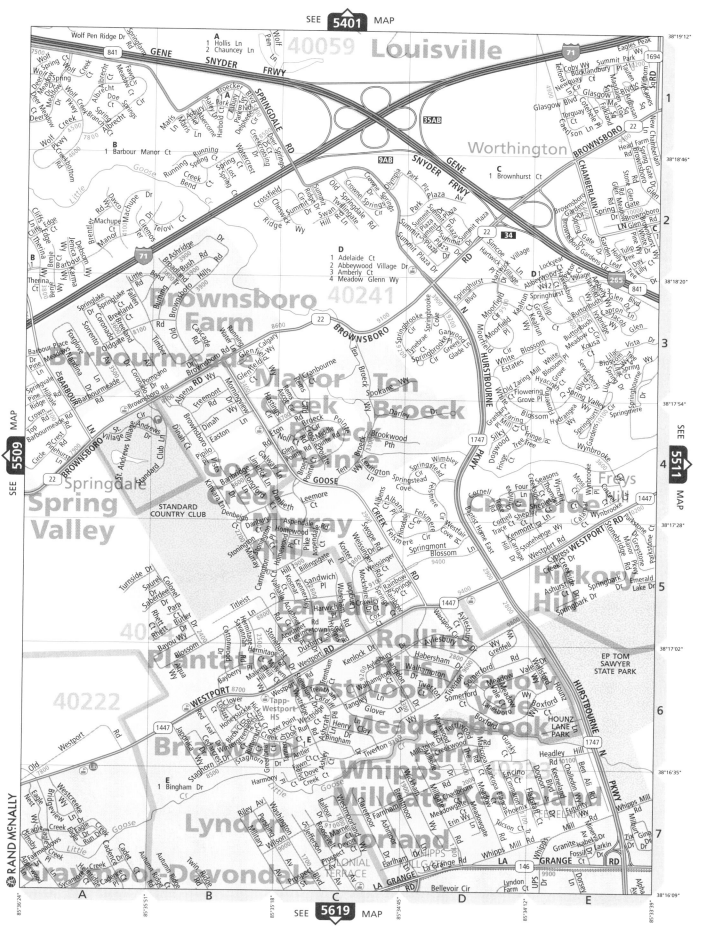

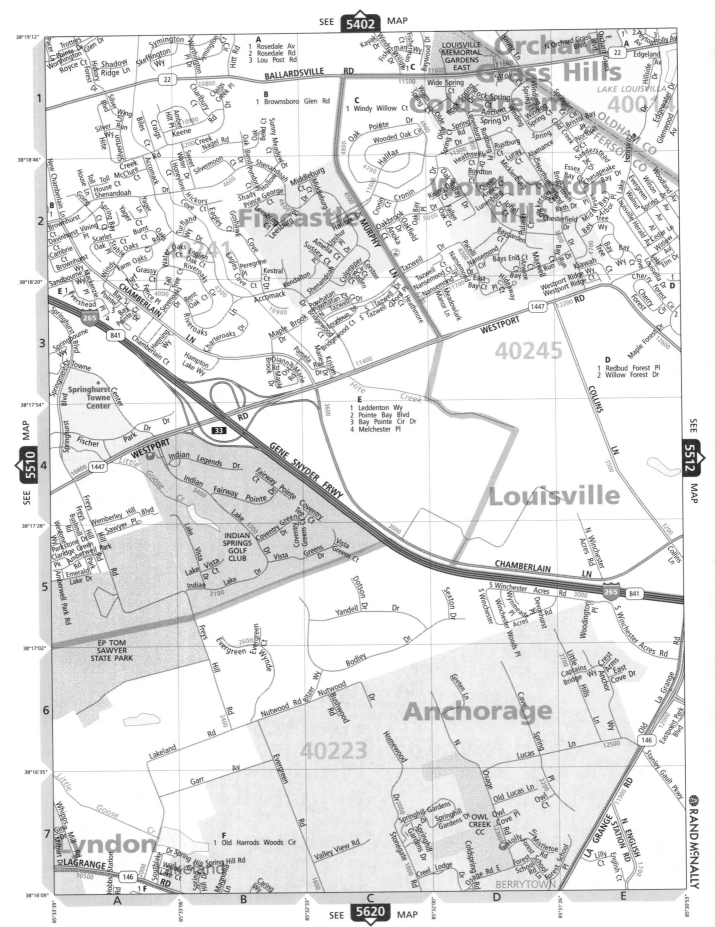

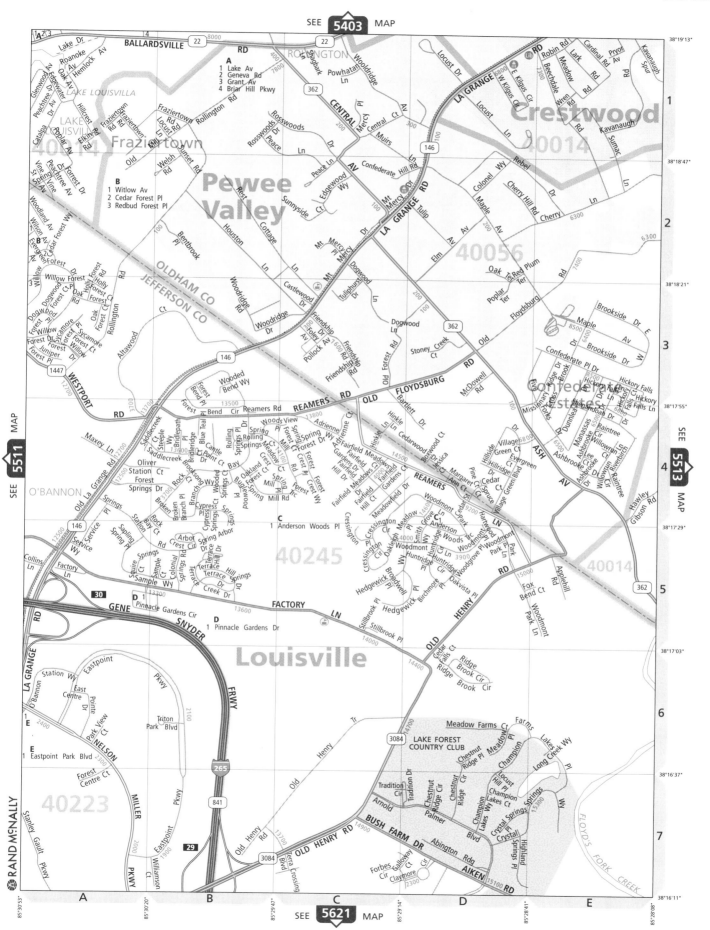

MAP
5512

1:24,000
1 in. = 2000 ft.

0   0.25   0.5
miles

38°19'13"

1

38°18'47"

2

38°18'21"

3

38°17'55"

4

38°17'29"

5

38°17'03"

6

38°16'37"

7

38°16'11"

A   B   C   D   E

85°30'53"   85°30'20"   85°29'47"   85°29'14"   85°28'41"   85°28'08"

RAND M°NALLY

N

Crestwood
40014

Pewee Valley

40056

40141

Frazertown

LAKE LOUISVILLA

LAKE LOUISVILLA

40245

Louisville

Confederate Estates

40014

40223

LAKE FOREST COUNTRY CLUB

FLOYD'S FORK CREEK

A
1 Lake Av
2 Geneva Rd
3 Grant Av
4 Briar Hill Pkwy

B
1 Witlow Av
2 Cedar Forest Pl
3 Redbud Forest Pl

C
1 Anderson Woods Pl

D
1 Pinnacle Gardens Dr

E
1 Eastpoint Park Blvd

MAP
5513

1:24,000
1 in. = 2000 ft.
0   0.25   0.5
miles

SEE 5404 MAP

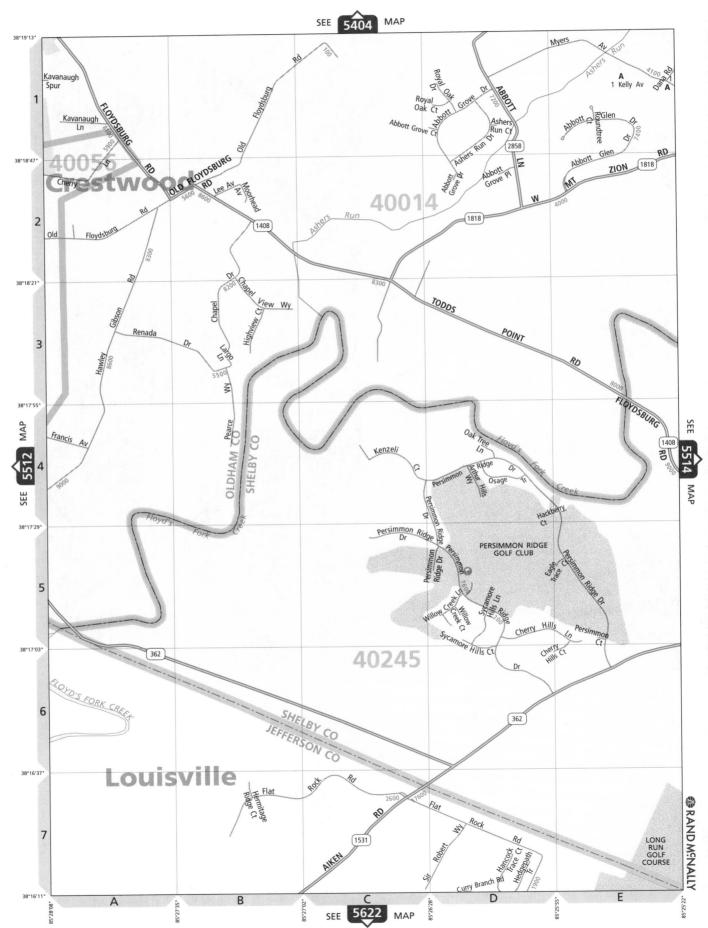

SEE 5512 MAP

SEE 5514 MAP

SEE 5622 MAP

40055
Crestwood

40014

40245

Louisville

PERSIMMON RIDGE
GOLF CLUB

LONG
RUN
GOLF
COURSE

RAND McNALLY

38°19'13"
38°18'47"
38°18'21"
38°17'55"
38°17'29"
38°17'03"
38°16'37"
38°16'11"

85°28'08"
85°27'35"
85°27'02"
85°26'28"
85°25'55"
85°25'22"

A   B   C   D   E
1   2   3   4   5   6   7

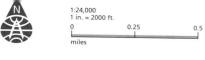

1:24,000
1 in. = 2000 ft.

0   0.25   0.5
miles

MAP
5514

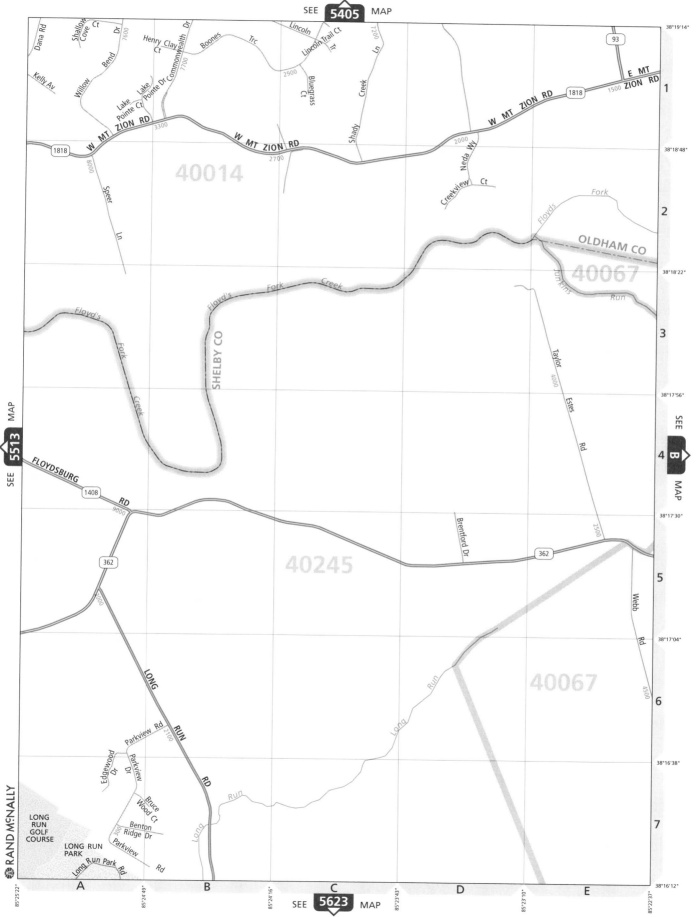

SEE 5513 MAP

SEE B MAP

N

RAND McNALLY

38°19'14"
38°18'48"
38°18'22"
38°17'56"
38°17'30"
38°17'04"
38°16'38"
38°16'12"

85°25'22"   85°24'49"   85°24'16"   85°23'43"   85°23'10"   85°22'37"

A   B   C   D   E

1   2   3   4   5   6   7

Dana Rd
Shallow Cove Ct
Bend Dr
7600
Henry Clay Ct
Commonwealth Dr
Boones Trc
Lincoln
Lincoln Trail Ct
Tr
7200
Ln
93
Willow
Kelly Av
Lake Pointe Ct
Lake Pointe Dr
2900
Bluegrass Ct
Creek
Shady
E MT ZION RD
1818
1500
ZION RD
W MT ZION RD
W MT ZION RD
3300
Neda Wy
2000
1818
W MT ZION RD
W MT ZION RD
2700
40014
8000
Speer Ln
Creekview Ct
Floyds Fork
OLDHAM CO
40067
Junkins Run
Floyd's Fork Creek
SHELBY CO
Floyd's
Fork
Creek
Taylor
4000
Estes Rd
FLOYDSBURG
1408
RD
9000
362
Brentford Dr
2500
362
40245
Webb Rd
4500
2000
40067
LONG
RUN
RD
Parkview Rd
2700
Edgewood Dr
Parkview Dr
Bruce Wood Ct
Benton Ridge Dr
3000
Parkview
Rd
Long Run Park Rd
Run
Long
Run
Long
LONG RUN GOLF COURSE
LONG RUN PARK

MAP
5610

1:24,000
1 in. = 2000 ft.

0   0.25   0.5
miles

SEE 5501 MAP

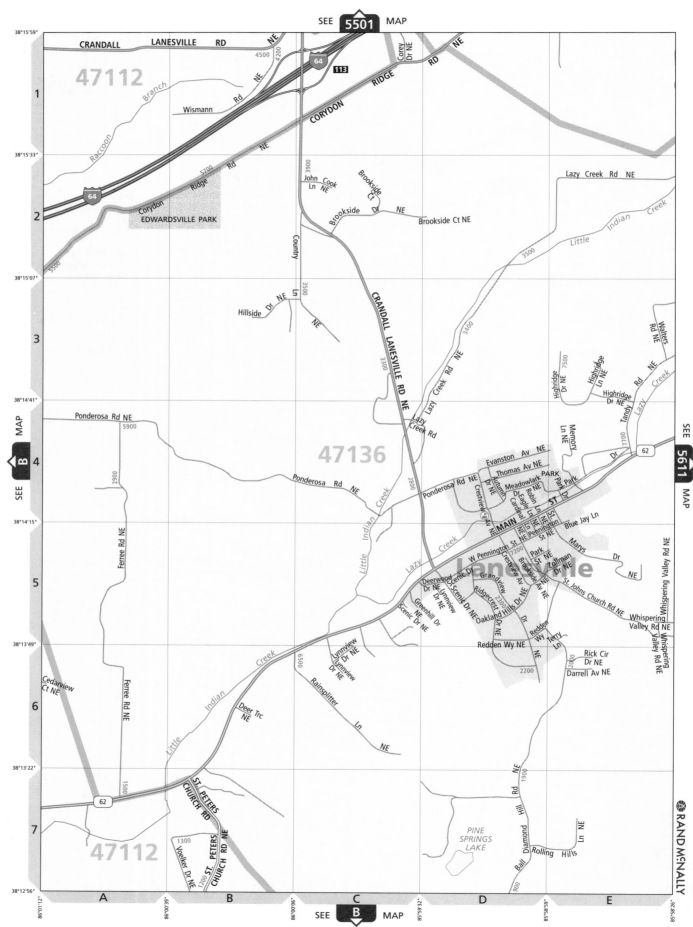

38°15'59"

CRANDALL   LANESVILLE   RD   NE

47112

Corey Dr NE

RD   NE

4500   4200

113

Wismann   Rd   NE

CORYDON   RIDGE

1

Branch

Raccoon

64

38°15'33"

RD   NE

5700

Ridge   Rd   NE

John   Cook   Brookside
Ln   NE   Ct

Lazy   Creek   Rd   NE

5500

Corydon   Ridge

EDWARDSVILLE PARK

2

64

Brookside   Dr   NE

Brookside   Ct   NE

3900

Little   Indian   Creek

3500

Country

38°15'07"

3500

Hillside   Dr   NE   Ln   NE

CRANDALL   LANESVILLE   RD   NE

Lazy   Creek   Rd   NE

3400

Walters
Rd   NE

3300

Highridge
Dr   NE   7500

Highridge
Ln   NE

Tandy   Rd   NE

Highridge
Dr   NE

Creek

3

Lazy

38°14'41"

SEE B MAP

Ponderosa   Rd   NE   5900

47136

Lazy
Creek   Rd

Memory
Ln   NE

7700

62

SEE 5611 MAP

2900

Evanston   Av   NE

Thomas   Av NE

Meadowlark   PARK

Park   Park

Dr   NE

Ponderosa   Rd   NE

Autumn   Dr   NE

Cardinal   St   NE

Robin   Ln   NE

Pennington   St   NE

Blue   Jay   Ln

4

2800

Little   Indian   Creek

Ferree   Rd   NE

2900

MAIN   ST

Crestview   Av   NE

Lanesville

Dr   NE

W Pennington   St   NE   7200

Crestview   Av   NE

Park   St   NE

Man's

Brookside   Av   NE   2300

Zollman   Dr   NE

St Johns   Church   Rd   NE

Whispering   Valley   Rd   Pd   NE

5

38°14'15"

Lazy   Creek

Deerwood
Dr   NE

Scenic   Dr

Lynnview
Dr   NE

Scenic   Dr   NE

Grandview
Av   NE

Ridgecrest

Oakland   Hills   Dr   NE

Dr   NE

Redden
Wy   NE

Terry
Ln   NE

Redden   Wy   NE

Whispering
Valley   Rd   NE

Whispering
Valley   Rd   NE

Greenhill   Dr   NE

Scenic   Dr   NE

2200

Rick   Cir
Dr   NE

Darrell   Av   NE

2000

38°13'49"

Lynnview
Dr   NE

Lynnview
Dr   NE

6500

Cedarview
Ct   NE

Ferree   Rd   NE

Rainsplitter

6

Little   Indian   Creek

Deer   Trc
NE

Ln   NE

38°13'22"

1500

62

ST.   PETERS   CHURCH   RD

Rd   NE   1900

Hill

PINE
SPRINGS
LAKE

Ln   NE

Diamond

7

47112

1300

Voelker   Dr   NE

1200   ST.   PETERS   CHURCH   RD   NE

Ball   900

Rolling   Hills

38°12'56"

A   B   C   D   E

86°01'12"   86°00'39"   86°00'00"   85°59'32"   85°58'59"   85°58'26"

SEE B MAP

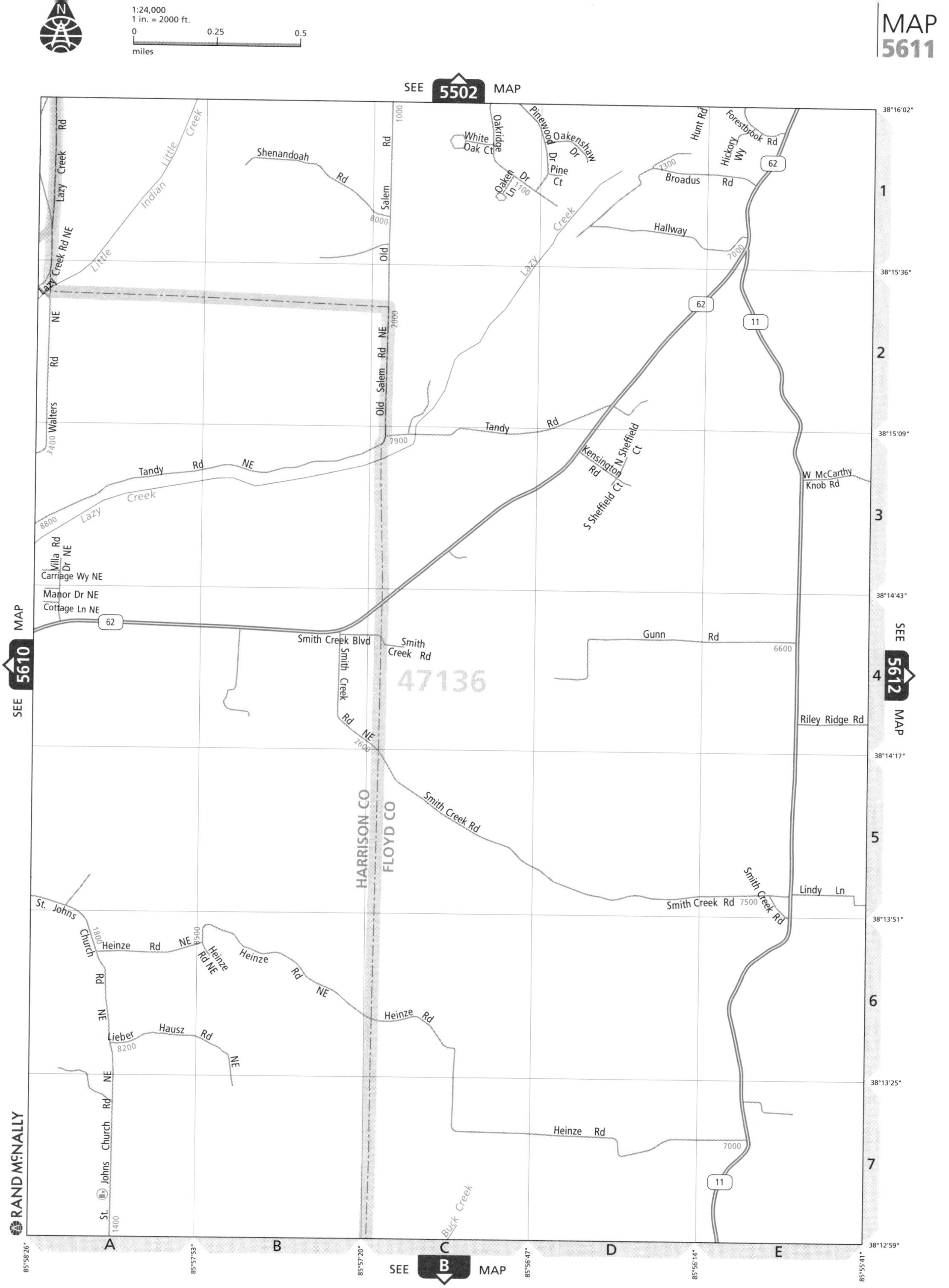

MAP
5611

1:24,000
1 in. = 2000 ft.
0   0.25   0.5
miles

38°16'02"

Lazy Creek Rd

Little Creek

Indian

Little

Shenandoah Rd

Old Salem Rd

1000

8000

White Oak Ct

Oakridge Dr

Pinewood Dr

Oakenshaw Dr

Pine Ct

Oaken Ln

1100

Lazy Creek

Hunt Rd

Forestbrook Rd

Hickory Wy

62

Broadus Rd

Hallway

7000

1

Lazy Creek Rd NE

NE

Rd

38°15'36"

62

11

Old Salem Rd NE

2000

2

Walters

3400

7900

Tandy Rd

38°15'09"

Kensington Rd

N Sheffield Ct

S Sheffield Ct

W McCarthy Knob Rd

3

Tandy Rd NE

Lazy Creek

8800

Villa Rd NE

Dr NE

Carriage Wy NE

Manor Dr NE

Cottage Ln NE

62

38°14'43"

Gunn Rd

6600

Smith Creek Blvd

Smith Creek Rd

Smith Creek

47136

4

Riley Ridge Rd

Smith Creek Rd NE

2600

38°14'17"

HARRISON CO

FLOYD CO

Smith Creek Rd

5

Smith Creek Rd

Lindy Ln

Smith Creek Rd

7500

38°13'51"

St. Johns Church Rd

1800

Heinze Rd NE

NE

600

Heinze Rd NE

Heinze Rd NE

6

NE

Lieber

Hausz Rd

8200

Heinze Rd

NE

38°13'25"

NE

Heinze Rd

7000

7

11

St. Johns Church Rd

1400

Buck Creek

38°12'59"

A   B   C   D   E

85°58'26"   85°57'53"   85°57'20"   85°56'47"   85°56'14"   85°55'41"

MAP
5612

1:24,000
1 in. = 2000 ft.

0   0.25   0.5
miles

SEE 5503 MAP

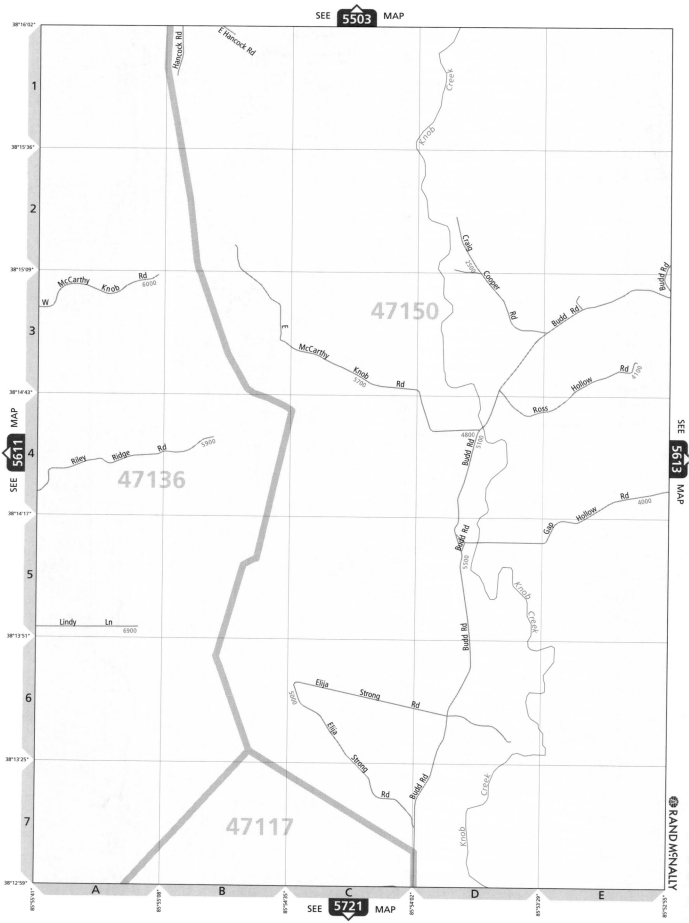

38°16'02"

1

38°15'36"

2

38°15'09"

3

38°14'43"

SEE 5611 MAP

4

38°14'17"

5

38°13'51"

6

38°13'25"

7

38°12'59"

SEE 5613 MAP

Hancock Rd
E Hancock Rd

Knob Creek

Craig
Cooper Rd
2500
Budd Rd
Budd Rd

McCarthy Knob Rd
6000
W

E
McCarthy Knob Rd
5700

Hollow Rd
4100

Ross

4800
Budd Rd
5100

Riley Ridge Rd
5900

47136

47150

Gap Hollow Rd
4000

Budd Rd
5500

Knob Creek

Lindy Ln
6900

Elija Strong Rd
5000

Elija Strong Rd

Budd Rd

Knob Creek

47117

Knob Creek

A   B   C   D   E

85°55'41"   85°55'08"   85°54'35"   85°54'02"   85°53'29"   85°52'56"

SEE 5721 MAP

RAND McNALLY

MAP
5613

1:24,000
1 in. = 2000 ft.

0   0.25   0.5
miles

N

SEE **5504** MAP

38°16'04"

Paradise Highwater
5100
French Rd

Budd Rd

2200

Powder House

Georgiana Dr

Galiger Station Rd

1

38°15'38"

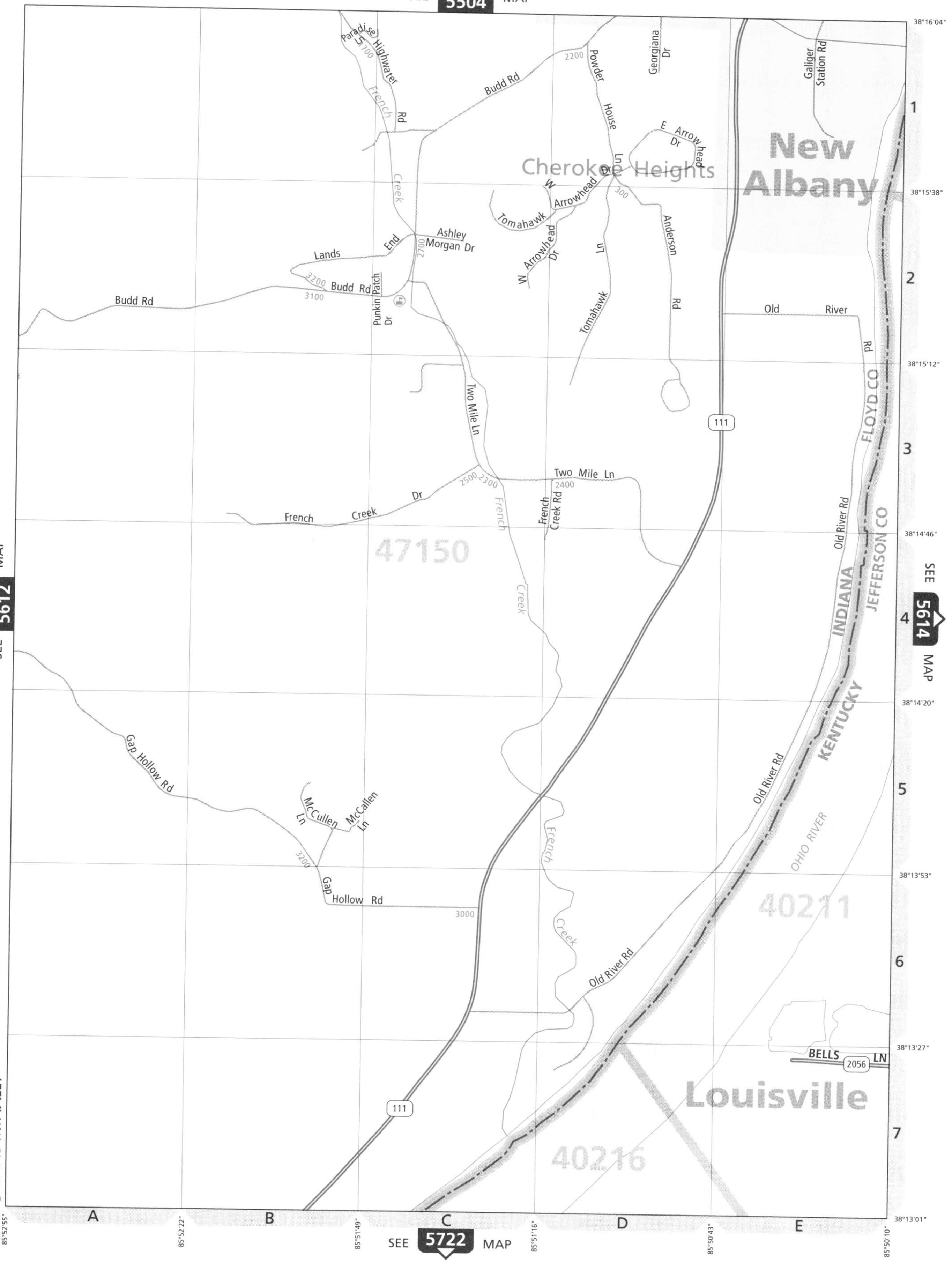

New Albany

Cherokee Heights

E Arrowhead Dr

W Arrowhead

Tomahawk

W Arrowhead Dr

Anderson Rd

300

Ln

Creek

End

Ashley Morgan Dr

2700

Lands

3200

Budd Rd

3100

Punkin Patch Dr

Budd Rd

Tomahawk Ln

Old River

2

38°15'12"

Two Mile Ln

FLOYD CO

Rd

111

3

38°14'46"

French Creek Dr

2500 2300

Two Mile Ln

2400

French Creek Rd

French Creek

47150

Old River Rd

INDIANA

JEFFERSON CO

SEE **5614** MAP

4

38°14'20"

Gap Hollow Rd

KENTUCKY

Old River Rd

5

38°13'53"

McCullen Ln

McCallen Ln

3200

Gap Hollow Rd

3000

French Creek

OHIO RIVER

40211

6

38°13'27"

Old River Rd

BELLS LN

2056

7

111

Louisville

40216

SEE **5722** MAP

A   85°52'55"   85°52'22"   B   85°51'49"   C   85°51'16"   D   85°50'43"   E   85°50'10"

38°13'01"

RAND McNALLY

MAP
5614

1:24,000
1 in. = 2000 ft.

0   0.25   0.5
miles

SEE 5505 MAP

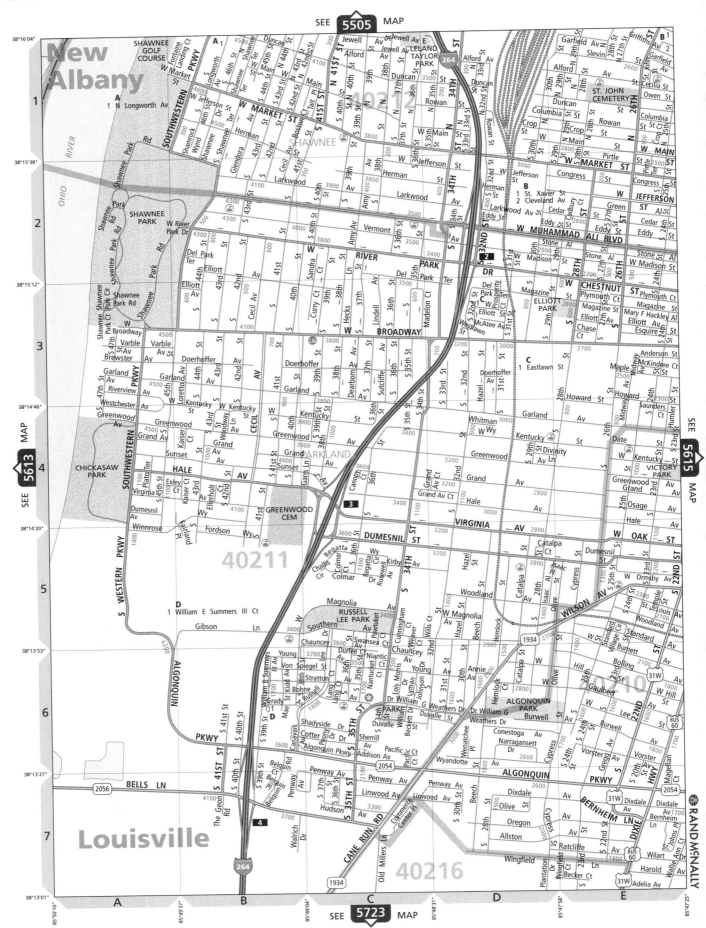

New Albany

Louisville

SEE 5613 MAP

SEE 5615 MAP

SEE 5723 MAP

RAND McNALLY

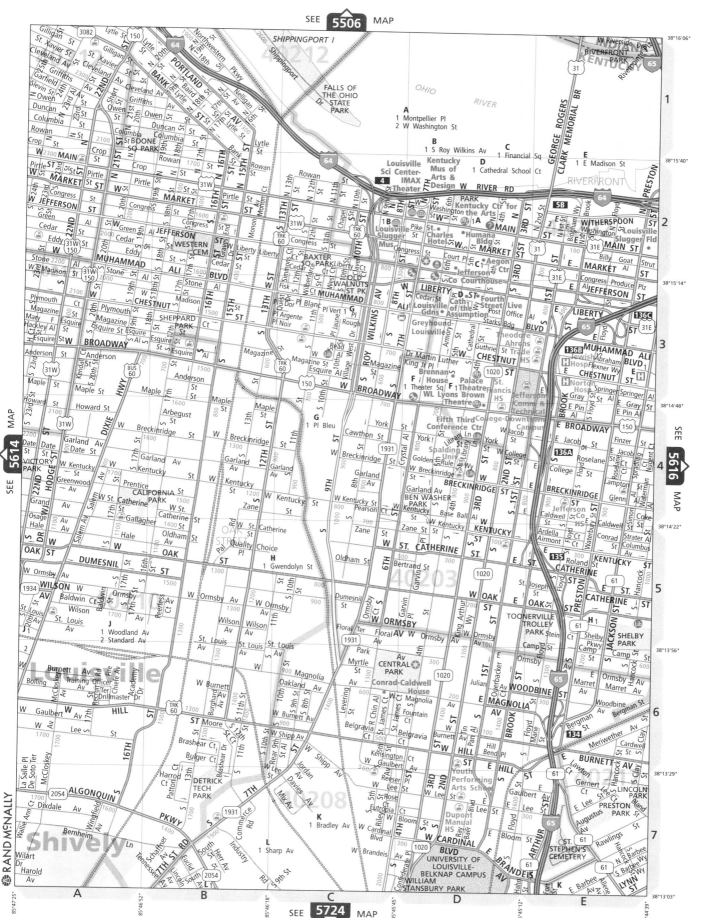

MAP
5615

SEE 5614 MAP

SEE 5616 MAP

1:24,000
1 in. = 2000 ft.
0   0.25   0.5
miles

RAND McNALLY

MAP
5616

1:24,000
1 in. = 2000 ft.

0   0.25   0.5
miles

SEE 5507 MAP

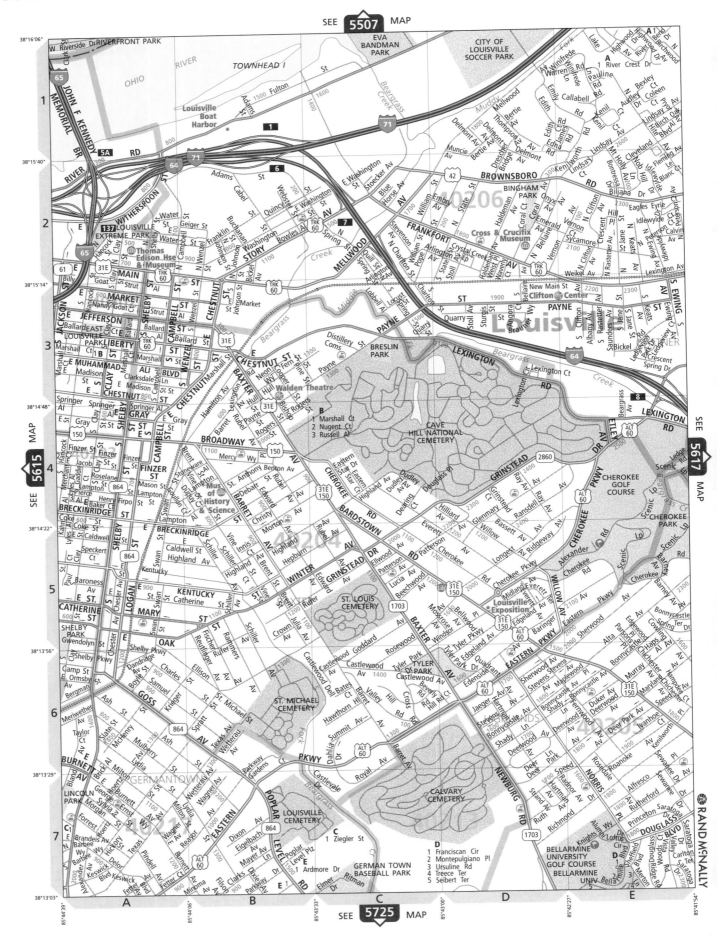

SEE 5615 MAP

SEE 5617 MAP

SEE 5725 MAP

RAND McNALLY

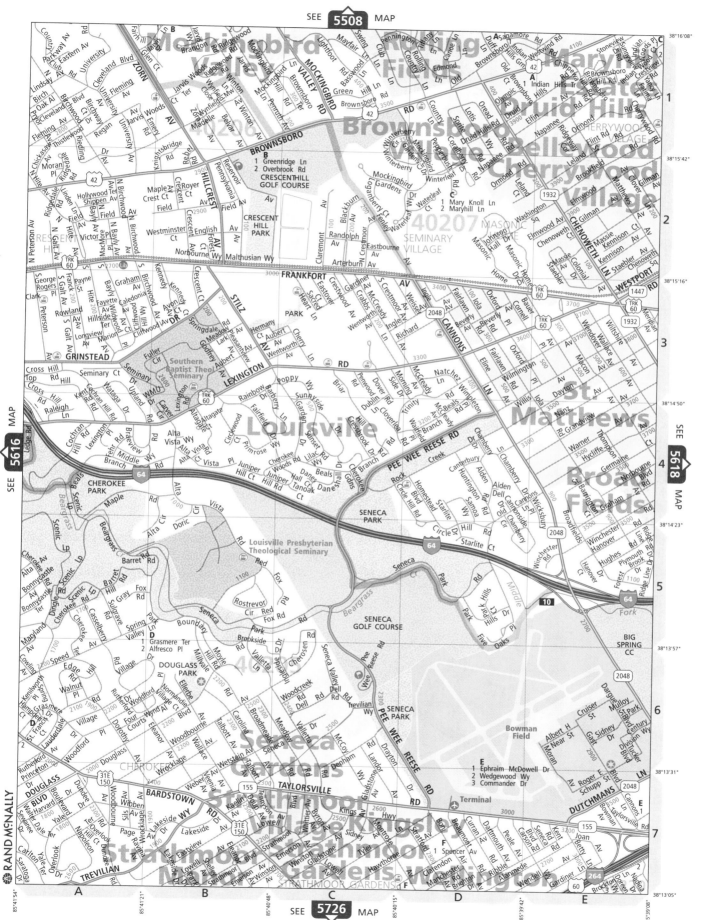

1:24,000
1 in. = 2000 ft.

0   0.25   0.5
miles

SEE 5508 MAP

MAP
5617

SEE 5616 MAP

SEE 5618 MAP

SEE 5726 MAP

RAND MCNALLY

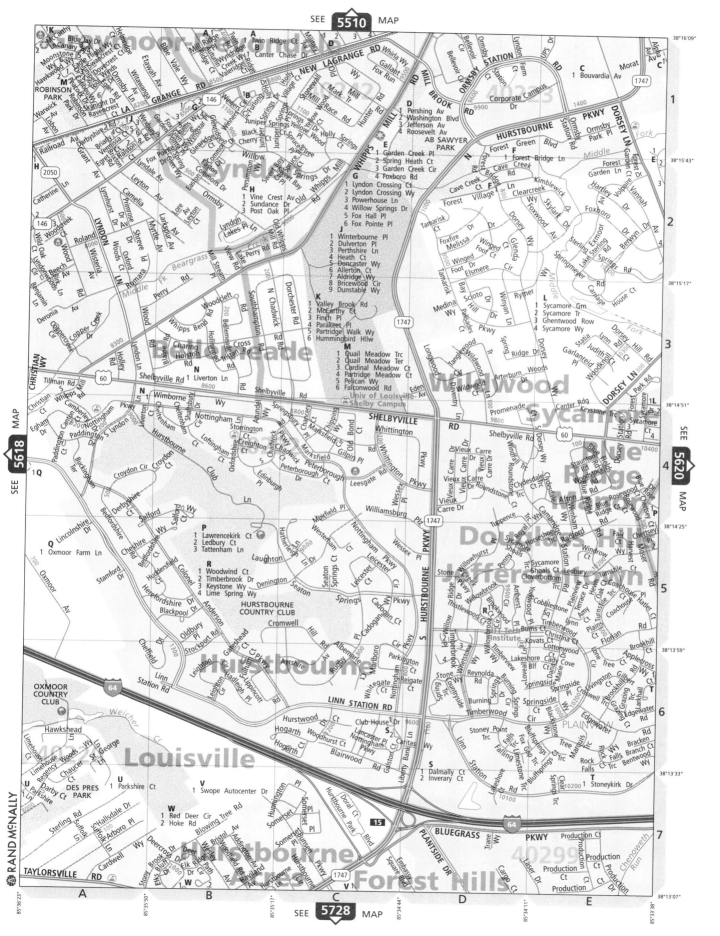

MAP
5619

1:24,000
1 in. = 2000 ft.

0   0.25   0.5

miles

SEE 5618 MAP

SEE 5620 MAP

RAND MCNALLY

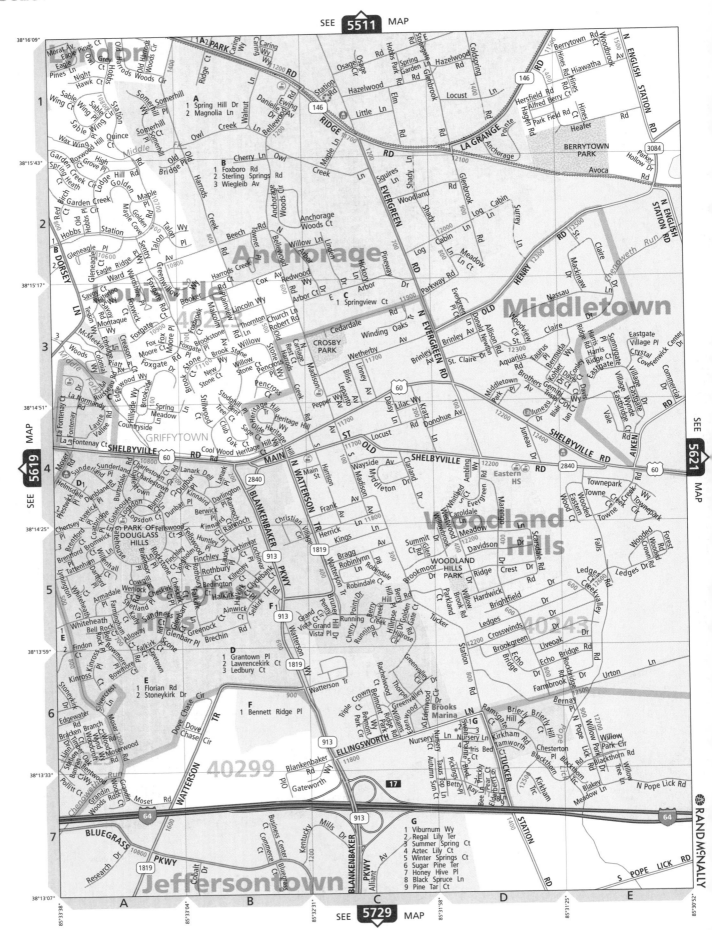

MAP
5620

1:24,000
1 in. = 2000 ft.
0   0.25   0.5
miles

SEE 5511 MAP

SEE 5619 MAP

SEE 5621 MAP

SEE 5729 MAP

A
1 Spring Hill Dr
2 Magnolia Ln

B
1 Foxboro Rd
2 Sterling Springs Rd
3 Wiegleib Av

C
1 Springview Ct

D
1 Grantown Pl
2 Lawrencekirk Ct
3 Ledbury Ct

E
1 Florian Rd
2 Stoneykirk Dr

F
1 Bennett Ridge Pl

G
1 Viburnum Wy
2 Regal Lily Ter
3 Summer Spring Ct
4 Aztec Lily Ct
5 Winter Springs Ct
6 Sugar Pine Ter
7 Honey Hive Pl
8 Black Spruce Ln
9 Pine Tar Ct

Anchorage

Louisville
40223

Middletown

Woodland
Hills

GRIFFYTOWN

Jeffersontown

40299

RAND McNALLY

1:24,000
1 in. = 2000 ft.

0   0.25   0.5
miles

MAP
5621

SEE **5512** MAP

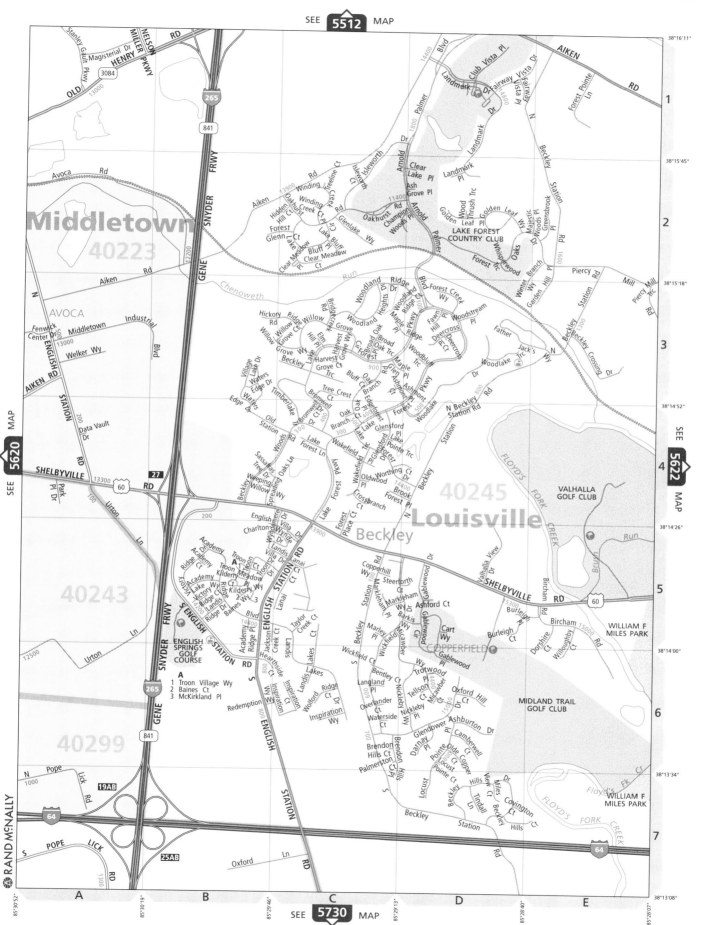

Middletown
40223

Louisville
40245

40243

40299

Beckley

LAKE FOREST
COUNTRY CLUB

VALHALLA
GOLF CLUB

WILLIAM F
MILES PARK

MIDLAND TRAIL
GOLF CLUB

WILLIAM F
MILES PARK

ENGLISH
SPRINGS
GOLF
COURSE

A
1 Troon Village Wy
2 Baines Ct
3 McKirkland Pl

COPPERFIELD

SEE **5620** MAP

SEE **5622** MAP

RAND M^cNALLY

A   B   C   D   E

SEE **5730** MAP

38°16'11"
38°15'45"
38°15'18"
38°14'52"
38°14'26"
38°14'00"
38°13'34"
38°13'08"

1
2
3
4
5
6
7

MAP
5622

1:24,000
1 in. = 2000 ft.

0   0.25   0.5
miles

SEE 5513 MAP

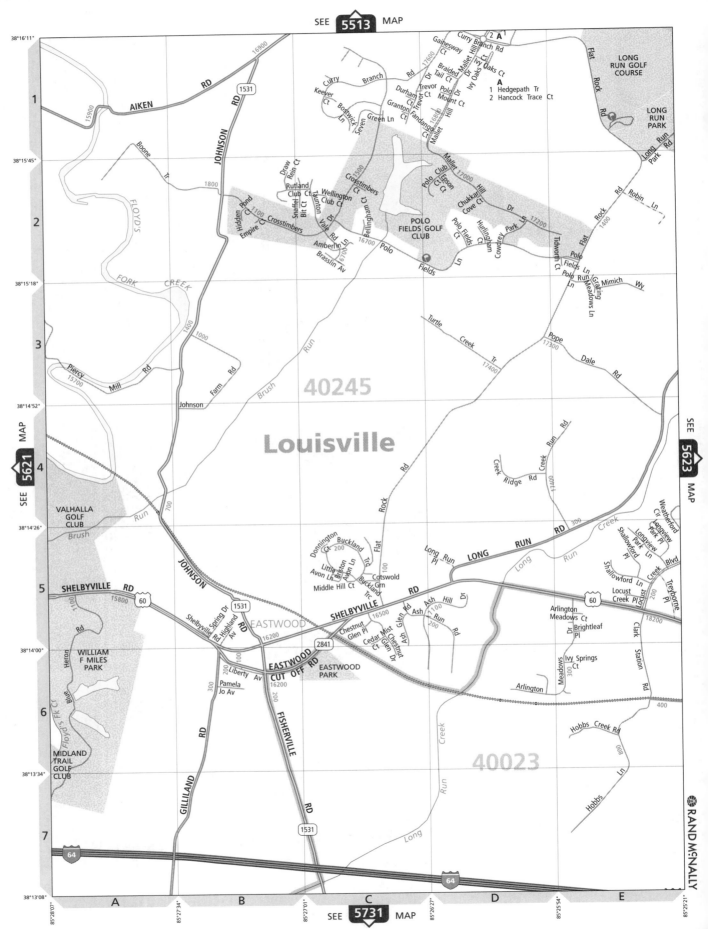

SEE 5621 MAP

SEE 5623 MAP

SEE 5731 MAP

38°16'11"
38°15'45"
38°15'18"
38°14'52"
38°14'26"
38°14'00"
38°13'34"
38°13'08"

85°28'07"   85°27'34"   85°27'01"   85°26'27"   85°25'54"   85°25'58"

A   B   C   D   E

RAND McNALLY

40245
Louisville
40023

A
1 Hedgepath Tr
2 Hancock Trace Ct

LONG RUN GOLF COURSE
LONG RUN PARK
POLO FIELDS GOLF CLUB
VALHALLA GOLF CLUB
WILLIAM F MILES PARK
MIDLAND TRAIL GOLF CLUB
EASTWOOD
EASTWOOD PARK

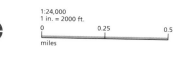

1:24,000
1 in. = 2000 ft.

0   0.25   0.5
miles

MAP
5623

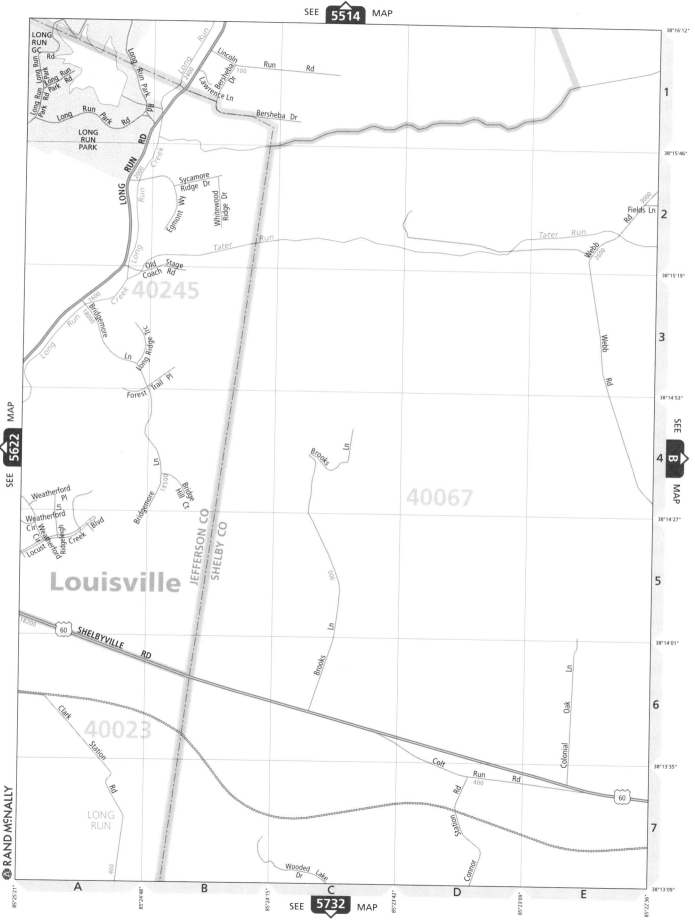

LONG RUN GC

Long Run Park Rd

Long Run Park Rd

Long Run Park Rd

Long Run Park Rd

Long Run Park Rd

LONG RUN PARK

Lincoln   Run   Rd

Bersheba Dr

Lawrence Ln

Bersheba Dr

LONG RUN RD

Long Run Creek

Sycamore Ridge Dr

Egmont Wy

Whitewood Ridge Dr

Tater   Run

Old Stage Coach Rd

40245

Long Creek

Long Run Creek

Bridgemore

Long Ridge Trc

Ln

Forest Trail Pl

Ln

Weatherford Pl

Weatherford Cir

Weatherford Cir

Locust

Ridgeleigh Creek

Bridgemore

Bridge Hill Ct

Blvd

Fields Ln

Tater   Run

Webb

Webb Rd

Brooks   Ln

40067

Louisville

JEFFERSON CO
SHELBY CO

Ln

Brooks   Ln

US 60   SHELBYVILLE   RD

40023

Clark Station Rd

LONG RUN

Colt   Run   Rd

Rd

Station

Connor

Colonial

Oak   Ln

US 60

Wooded Lake Dr

38°16'12"
38°15'46"
38°15'19"
38°14'53"
38°14'27"
38°14'01"
38°13'35"
38°13'09"

1
2
3
4
5
6
7

A   B   C   D   E

85°25'21"   85°24'48"   85°24'15"   85°23'42"   85°23'09"   85°22'36"

RAND McNALLY

MAP
5721

1:24,000
1 in. = 2000 ft.

0   0.25   0.5
miles

SEE 5612 MAP

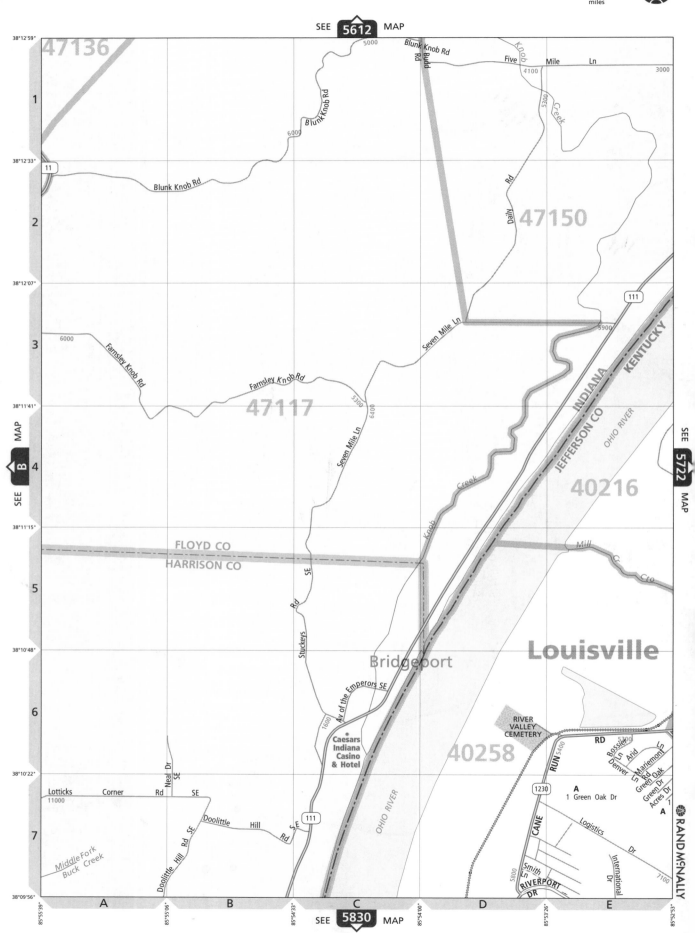

38°12'59"

47136

1

Blunk Knob Rd
5000
Blunk Knob Rd
Budd Rd
Five Mile Ln
Knob
4100
3000

38°12'33"

11

2

Blunk Knob Rd
6000
Blunk Knob Rd

Daily Rd
Creek
5300
47150

38°12'07"

111
5900

3

6000
Farnsley Knob Rd

Seven Mile Ln

Farnsley Knob Rd
5300
6400
47117

INDIANA
KENTUCKY

38°11'41"

JEFFERSON CO
OHIO RIVER

SEE 5722 MAP

MAP
B
4

Seven Mile Ln

Creek
Knob

40216

38°11'15"

SEE

FLOYD CO
HARRISON CO

Mill
Cto

5

SE
Rd
Stuckeys

Louisville

38°10'48"

Bridgeport

Av of the Emperors SE

RIVER
VALLEY
CEMETERY

6

1600

Caesars
Indiana
Casino
& Hotel

40258

RUN 5400
RD
Bossier Ln
Denver Ln
Arid Ln
Mariemont Rd
Green Oak Rd
Green Oak Dr
Acres Dr

38°10'22"

Neal Dr SE

Lotticks Corner Rd SE
11000

Doolittle Hill Rd SE

SE

1230

A
1 Green Oak Dr

A
1

111
SE

Logistics Dr

7

Middle Fork
Buck Creek

Doolittle Hill Rd SE

Doolittle Hill Rd SE

OHIO RIVER

CANE

International Dr

5800
RIVERPORT
DR
Smith Ln

7100

38°09'56"

85°55'39"   A   85°55'06"   B   85°54'33"   C   85°54'00"   D   85°53'26"   E   85°52'58"

SEE 5830 MAP

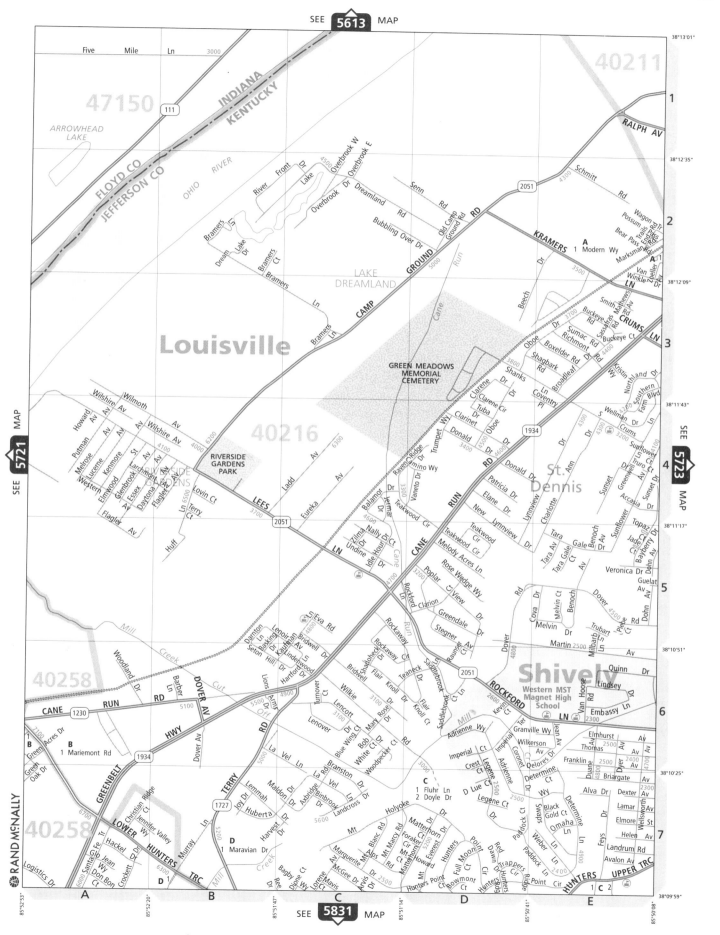

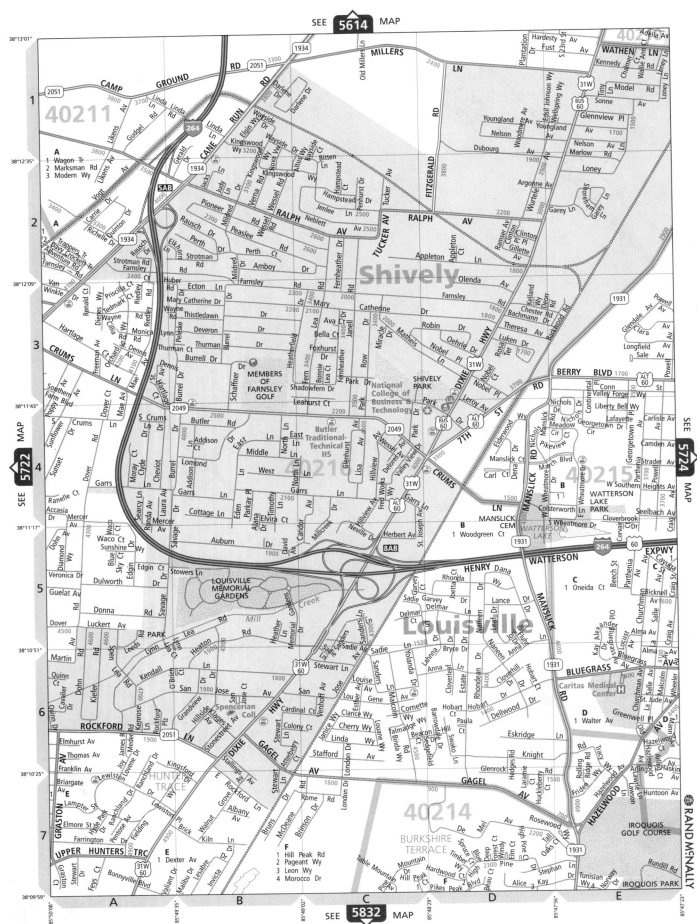

MAP 5724

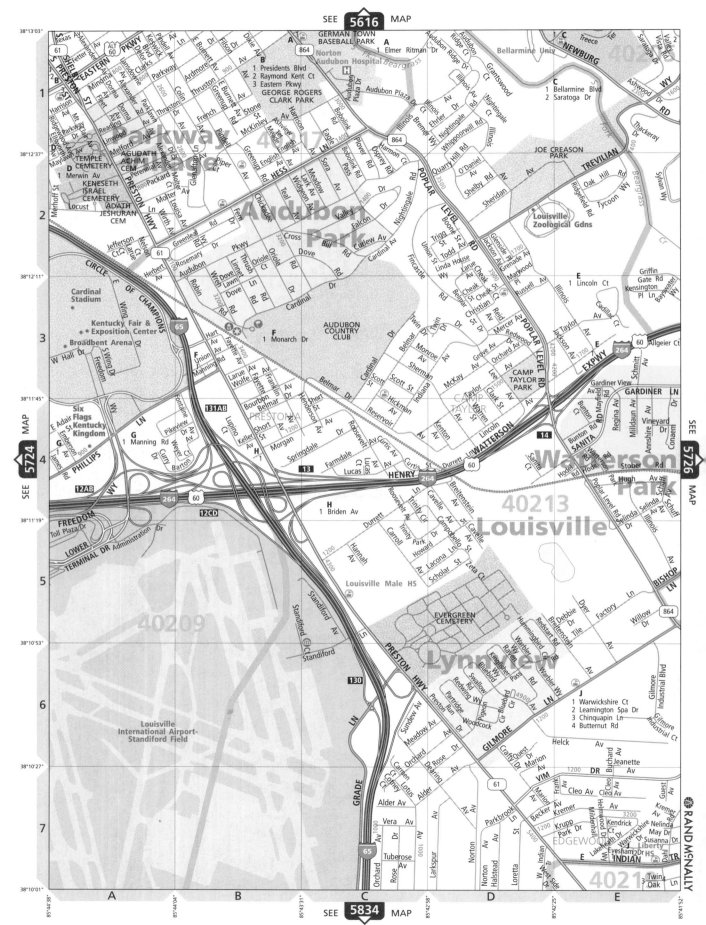

MAP
5725

1:24,000
1 in. = 2000 ft.

0   0.25   0.5
miles

N

SEE 5616 MAP

SEE 5724 MAP

SEE 5726 MAP

SEE 5834 MAP

RAND McNALLY

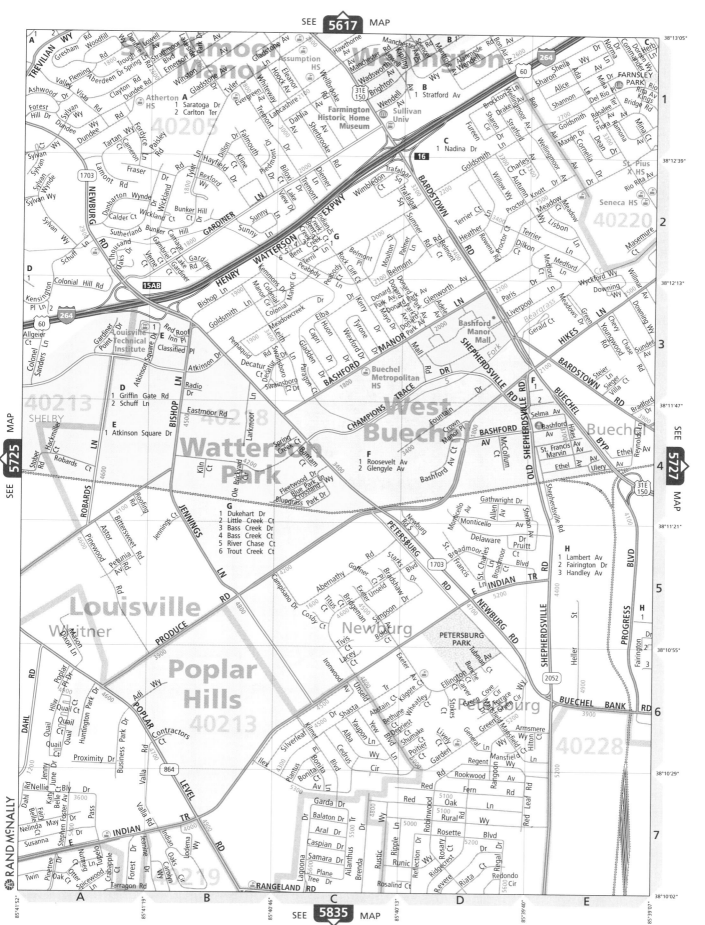

MAP
5726

1:24,000
1 in. = 2000 ft.

0   0.25   0.5
miles

SEE 5617 MAP

SEE 5725 MAP

SEE 5727 MAP

SEE 5835 MAP

RAND MCNALLY

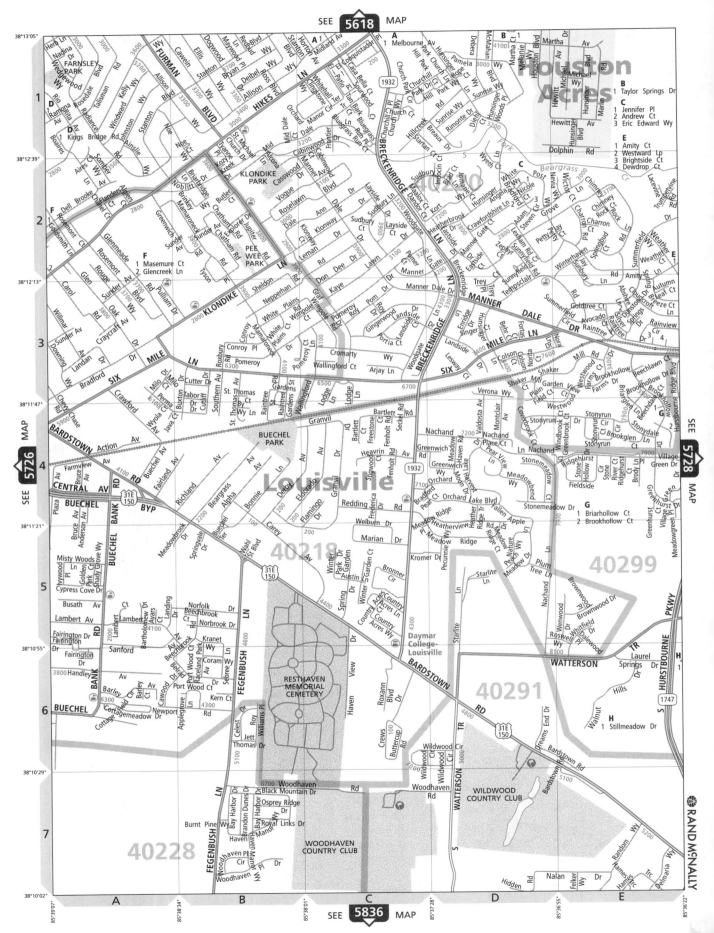

MAP
5728

1:24,000
1 in. = 2000 ft.
0   0.25   0.5
miles

N

SEE 5619 MAP
SEE 5727 MAP
SEE 5729 MAP
SEE 5837 MAP

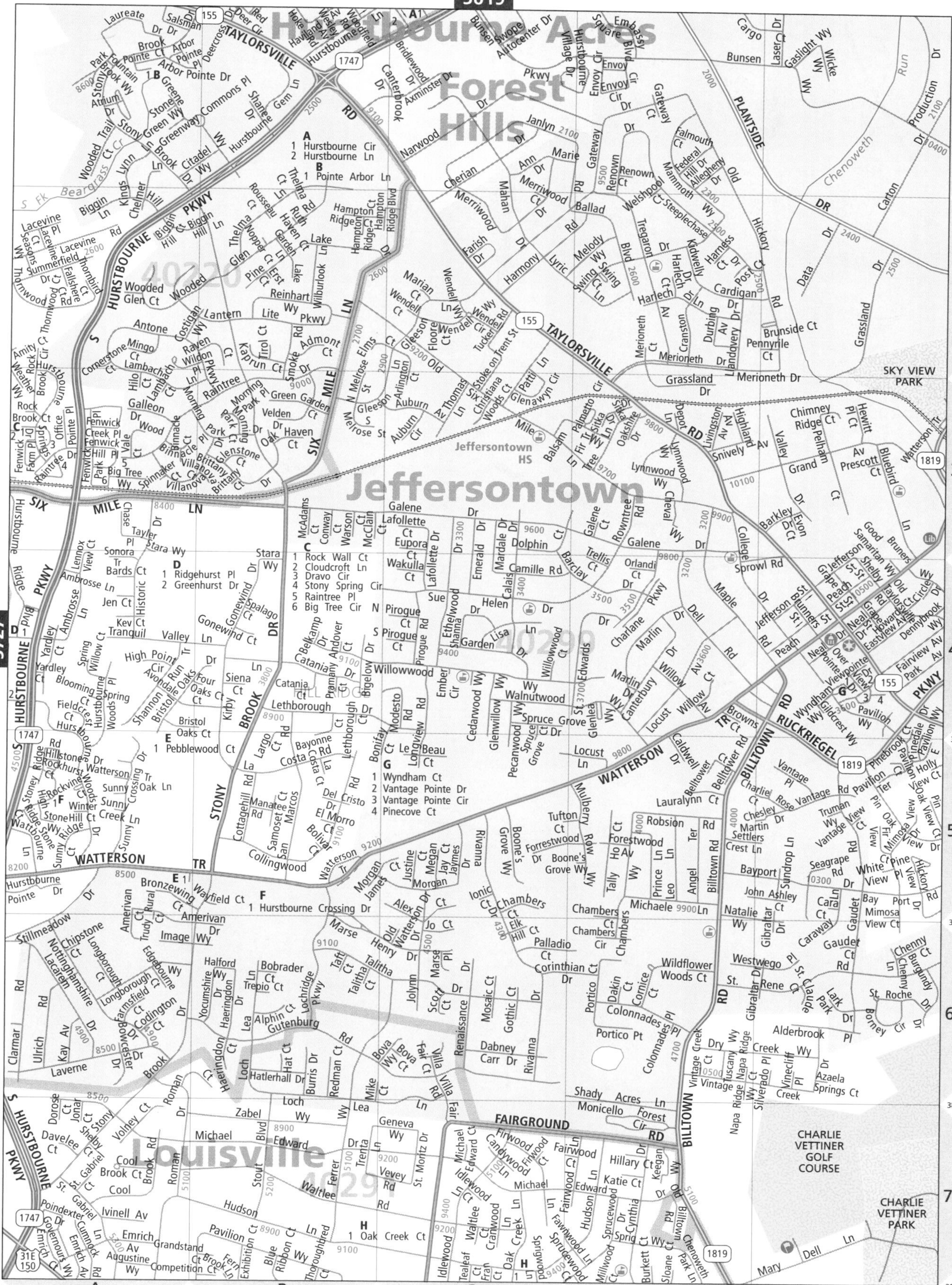

Hurstbourne Acres

Forest Hills

Jeffersontown

Jeffersontown HS

Louisville

40220

40299

40291

TAYLORSVILLE RD

HURSTBOURNE PKWY

SIX MILE LN

WATTERSON TR

STONY BROOK DR

RUCKRIEGEL PKWY

BILLTOWN RD

FAIRGROUND RD

CHARLIE VETTINER GOLF COURSE

CHARLIE VETTINER PARK

SKY VIEW PARK

PLANTSIDE DR

Chenoweth Run

A
1 Hurstbourne Cir
2 Hurstbourne Ln

B
1 Pointe Arbor Ln

C
1 Rock Wall Ln
2 Cloudcroft Ln
3 Dravo Cir
4 Stony Spring Cir
5 Raintree Pl
6 Big Tree Cir

D
1 Ridgehurst Pl
2 Greenhurst Dr

E
1 Pebblewood Ct

F
1 Hurstbourne Crossing Dr

G
1 Wyndham Ct
2 Vantage Pointe Dr
3 Vantage Pointe Cir
4 Pinecove Ct

H
1 Oak Creek Ct

MAP
5729

1:24,000
1 in. = 2000 ft.

0   0.25   0.5
miles

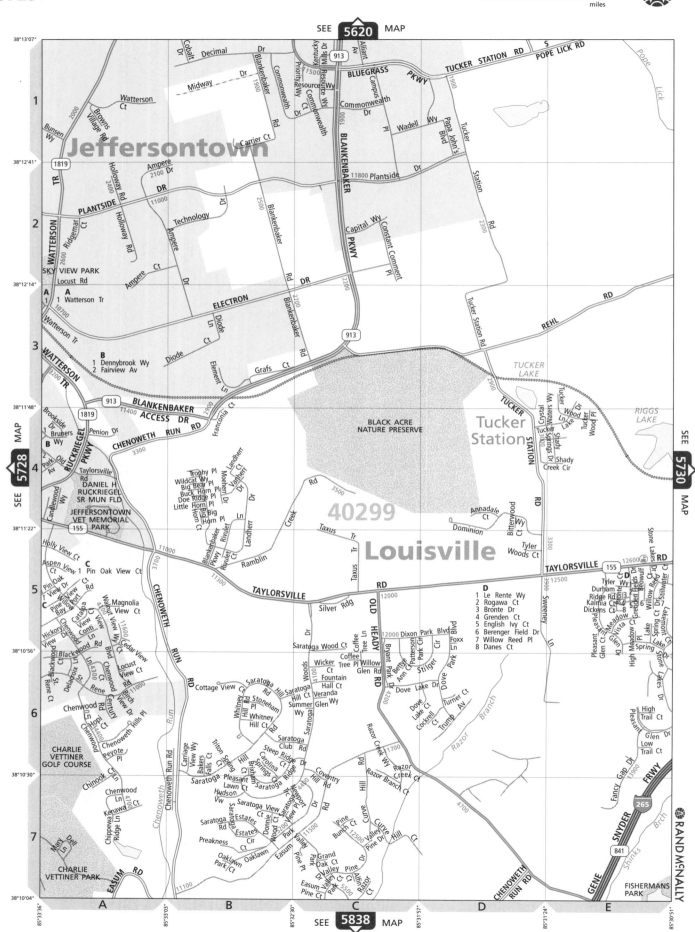

SEE 5620 MAP

SEE 5728 MAP

SEE 5730 MAP

SEE 5838 MAP

Jeffersontown

Louisville

40299

Tucker Station

BLACK ACRE NATURE PRESERVE

TUCKER LAKE

RIGGS LAKE

CHARLIE VETTINER GOLF COURSE

CHARLIE VETTINER PARK

SKY VIEW PARK

DANIEL H RUCKRIEGEL SR MUN FLD

JEFFERSONTOWN VET MEMORIAL PARK

FISHERMANS PARK

RAND McNALLY

A   1 Watterson Tr

B   1 Dennybrook Wy
    2 Fairview Av

C   1 Pin Oak View Ct

D   1 Le Rente Wy
    2 Rogawa Ct
    3 Bronte Dr
    4 Grenden Ct
    5 English Ivy Ct
    6 Berenger Field Dr
    7 Willow Reed Pl
    8 Danes Ct

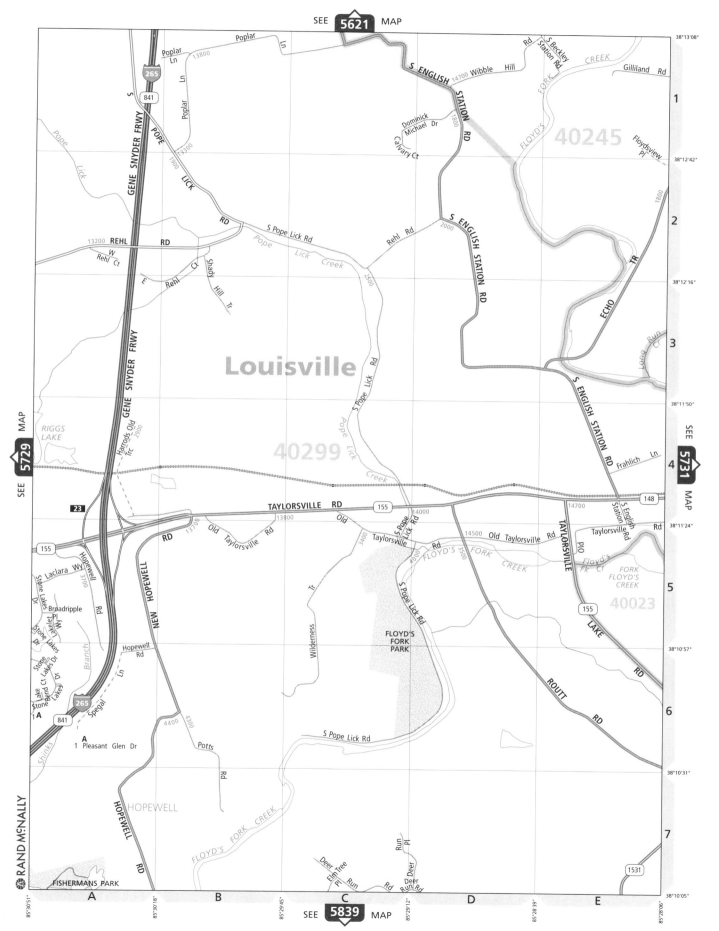

MAP
5730

1:24,000
1 in. = 2000 ft.

0   0.25   0.5
miles

N

SEE 5621 MAP

SEE 5729 MAP

SEE 5731 MAP

SEE 5839 MAP

RAND McNALLY

38°13'08"
38°12'42"
38°12'16"
38°11'50"
38°11'24"
38°10'57"
38°10'31"
38°10'05"

1
2
3
4
5
6
7

A   B   C   D   E

85°30'51"
85°30'18"
85°29'45"
85°29'12"
85°28'39"
85°28'06"

Poplar Ln
13800
Poplar Ln
Poplar Ln

GENE SNYDER FRWY
POPE LICK RD
265
841
S

S ENGLISH STATION RD
14700 Wibble Hill
Rd
S Beckley Station Rd
CREEK
Gilliland Rd
FLOYD'S FORK

Dominick Michael Dr
Calvary Ct
1800
40245
Floydsview Pl
1800

S Pope Lick Rd
Rehl Rd
Pope Lick Creek
S ENGLISH STATION RD
2000

13200 REHL RD
W Rehl Ct
E Rehl Ct
Shady Hill Tr

ECHO TR
Long Run Cr

Louisville

2500

S Pope Lick Rd

40299

S ENGLISH STATION RD
Frahlich Ln

RIGGS LAKE

GENE SNYDER FRWY
Harrods Old Trc 2900

Pope Lick Creek

148

23

TAYLORSVILLE RD 155
13800
Old
14000
14700
S English Station Rd
Taylorsville Rd

155
Old Taylorsville Rd
13700
Old Taylorsville Rd
S Pope Lick Rd
14500 Old Taylorsville Rd
Floyd's Fk Ct
TAYLORSVILLE
FORK FLOYD'S CREEK
40023

HOPEWELL RD
NEW HOPEWELL RD
Laclara Wy
Stone Lakes Dr 3700
Broadripple Rd
Jubilet Wy Pl
Stone Lakes Dr
Stone Ct Lakes Dr
Stone Lakes Dr
Lake Dr
Band Ct Lakes Dr

Branch

Hopewell Rd
Spegal Ln

3600
FLOYD'S FORK CREEK
4000
3500

FLOYD'S FORK PARK

Wilderness Tr

ROUTT RD
LAKE RD
155

265
841
1 A

A
1 Pleasant Glen Dr

4400
4300
Potts Rd

S Pope Lick Rd

Shinks

HOPEWELL RD

HOPEWELL

FLOYD'S FORK CREEK

FISHERMANS PARK

Deer Tree Pl
Elm Tree Pl
Run Pl
Deer Run
Deer Run Rd

1531

MAP
5731

1:24,000
1 in. = 2000 ft.

0   0.25   0.5
miles

N

SEE **5622** MAP

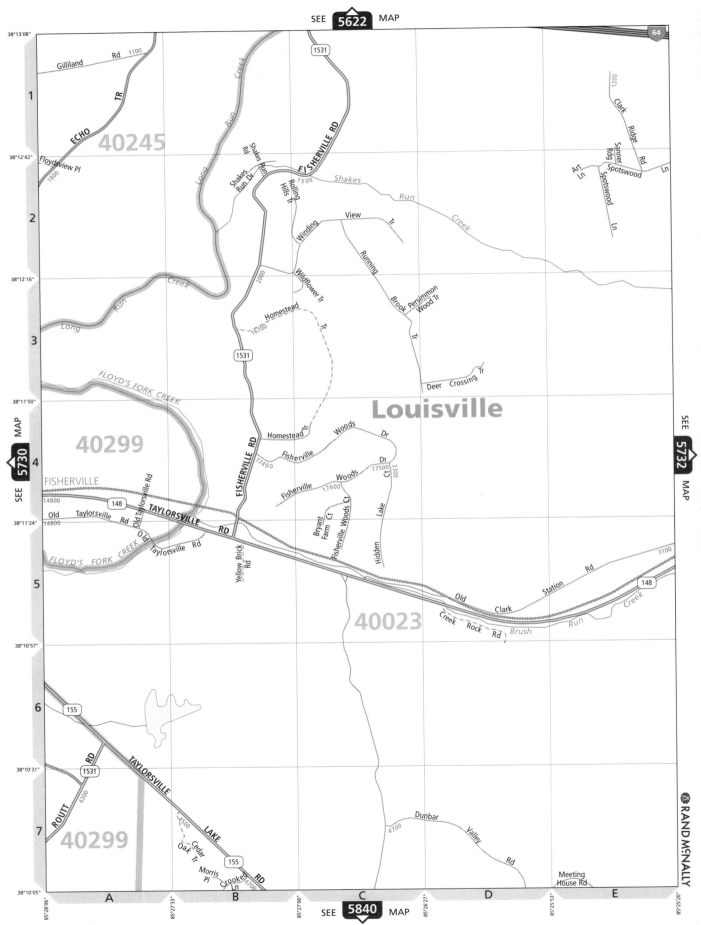

64

38°13'08"

Gilliland   Rd   1100

1 ECHO   TR

40245

38°12'42"   Floydsview Pl
1800

1531

Long   Run   Creek

Shakes
Run Rd

Shakes
Run Dr

Rolling
Hills Tr

FISHERVILLE RD

1500   Shakes   Run   Creek

Clark   Ridge   Rd
1200

Sanner   Rdg
Spotswood
Ln

Art   Spotswood   Ln
Ln

2 Winding   View   Tr

Wildflower Tr

Running   Brook   Persimmon
Wood Tr

2000

38°12'16"   Long   Run   Creek

3 Homestead   Tr

1531   1670

Tr   Tr

Deer   Crossing   Tr

38°11'50"   FLOYD'S FORK CREEK

Louisville

SEE **5730** MAP

40299

4 FISHERVILLE RD

Homestead Tr

Fisherville   17400

Woods   Dr

Woods   Dr   17500   Ct   3300

Lake

SEE **5732** MAP

FISHERVILLE

14800   148

Old   Taylorsville   Rd
14800

TAYLORSVILLE   Fisherville   17600

Fisherville Woods Ct

Bryant
Farm Ct

Hidden

38°11'24"

Old   Taylorsville   Rd

FLOYD'S   FORK   CREEK   Old Taylorsville   Rd

5 Yellow Brick
Rd

40023

Old   Clark   Station   Rd   3100

Creek   Rock   Rd   Brush   Run   Creek

148

38°10'57"

6 155

38°10'31"   1531

RD   TAYLORSVILLE

ROUTT   4300

LAKE

40299   **7**

Dunbar   4700   Valley   Rd

Oak Tr   Cedar   4500

Morris   155
Pl   Crooked   Ln   RD   4700

Meeting
House Rd

A   B   C   D   E

85°28'06"   85°27'33"   85°27'00"   85°26'27"   85°25'53"   85°25'20"

SEE **5840** MAP

RAND MᶜNALLY

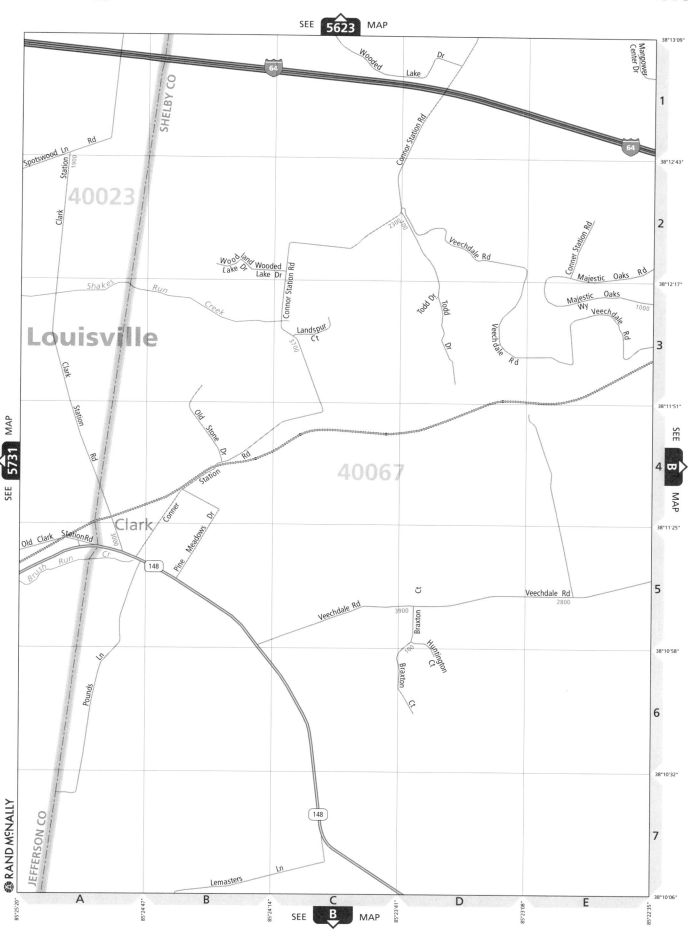

MAP 5732

1:24,000
1 in. = 2000 ft.

0   0.25   0.5
miles

SEE 5623 MAP

SEE 5731 MAP

SEE B MAP

SEE B MAP

RAND McNALLY

Roads and labels:

64 (Interstate 64)

SHELBY CO
JEFFERSON CO

Manpower Center Dr
Wooded Lake Dr
Connor Station Rd
Conner Station Rd
Veechdale Rd
Majestic Oaks Rd
Majestic Oaks Wy
Veechdale Rd
Spotswood Ln
Clark Station Rd
1900
40023
Woodland Lake Dr
Wooded Lake Dr
Connor Station Rd
Shakes Run Creek
Louisville
Landspur Ct
3700
Todd Dr
Todd Dr
2300
1000
Clark Station Rd
Old Stone Dr
Rd
Station
40067
2800
Conner Station
Clark
Pine Meadows Dr
3000
Old Clark Station Rd
Brush Run Cr
148
Veechdale Rd
3900
Braxton Ct
Huntington Ct
Braxton Ct
100
Veechdale Rd
Ln
Pounds
148
Lemasters Ln

38°13'09"
38°12'43"
38°12'17"
38°11'51"
38°11'25"
38°10'58"
38°10'32"
38°10'06"

85°25'20"
85°24'47"
85°24'14"
85°23'41"
85°23'08"
85°22'35"

A   B   C   D   E

1 2 3 4 5 6 7

MAP
5830

1:24,000
1 in. = 2000 ft.

0   0.25   0.5
miles

N

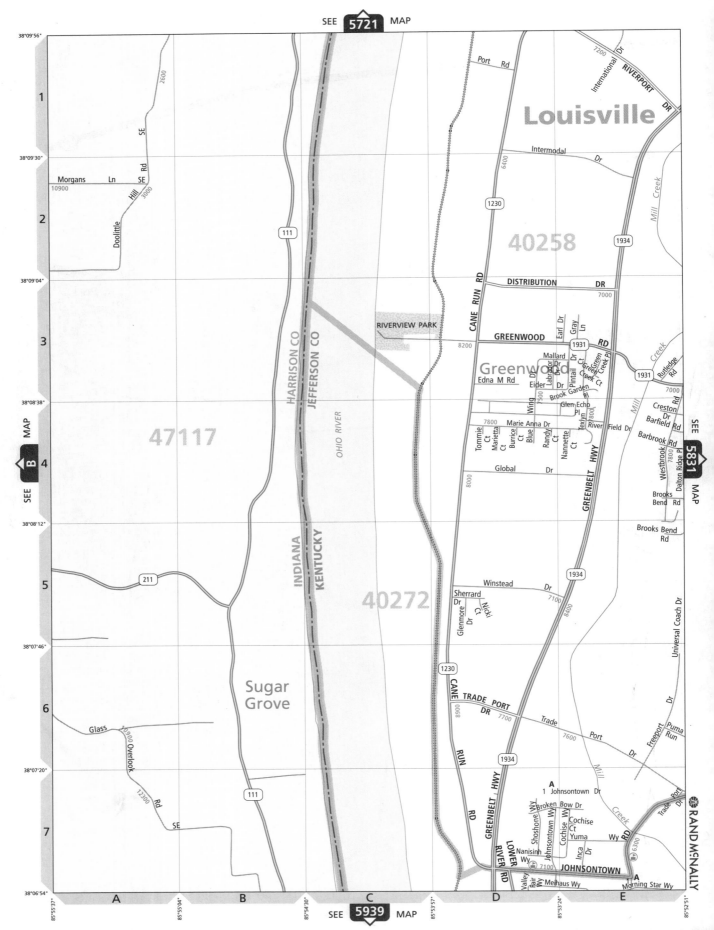

Louisville

Port Rd

International

RIVERPORT DR

7200 Dr

Intermodal Dr

6400

1230

40258

Mill Creek

1934

111

CANE RUN RD

DISTRIBUTION DR
7000

RIVERVIEW PARK

GREENWOOD

8200

1931

Greenwood

RD

Earl Dr Gray Ln

Mallard Dr

Labrador Dr

Pintail Dr

Eider Dr

Green Ct

Green Creek Pl

Creek Ct

1931

Rutledge Rd

7000

Creston Dr

Barfield Rd

Barbrook Rd

Westbrook Rd

Brooks Bend Rd

Dalton Ridge Pl

7800

SEE 5831 MAP

HARRISON CO

JEFFERSON CO

OHIO RIVER

Edna M Rd

Brook Garden

7500

Wirig

Glen Echo Pl

Texlyn

7800

River Field Dr

Marie Anna Dr

7800

Tommie Ct

Marietta Ct

Burrice Ct

Blue

Randy Dr

Nannette Ct

Global Dr

8000

GREENBELT HWY

47117

MAP

B

SEE

40272

Brooks Bend Rd

INDIANA

KENTUCKY

211

Winstead Dr

1934

7100

8400

Sherrard Dr

Glenmore Dr

Nicki Ct

Universal Coach Dr

1230

CANE

TRADE PORT DR

6060

7700

Trade Port

7600

Freeport Dr

Puma Run

Trade Port Dr

RAND McNALLY

Sugar Grove

Glass

10900 Overlook

12300 Rd

SE

111

1934

RUN

GREENBELT HWY

LOWER RIVER RD

A 1 Johnsontown Dr

Shoshone Wy

Johnsontown Wy

Broken Bow Dr

Cochise Ct

Cochise Wy

Yuma Wy

Inca Dr

RD

6300

Mill Creek

7100

Nanisinh Wy

JOHNSONTOWN

Valley Fair Wy

Meihaus Wy

Morning Star Wy

Morgans Ln
10900

SE Rd

3000

Doolittle Hill

SE

38°09'56"

38°09'30"

38°09'04"

38°08'38"

38°08'12"

38°07'46"

38°07'20"

38°06'54"

85°55'37"

85°55'04"

85°54'30"

85°53'57"

85°53'24"

85°52'58"

A   B   C   D   E

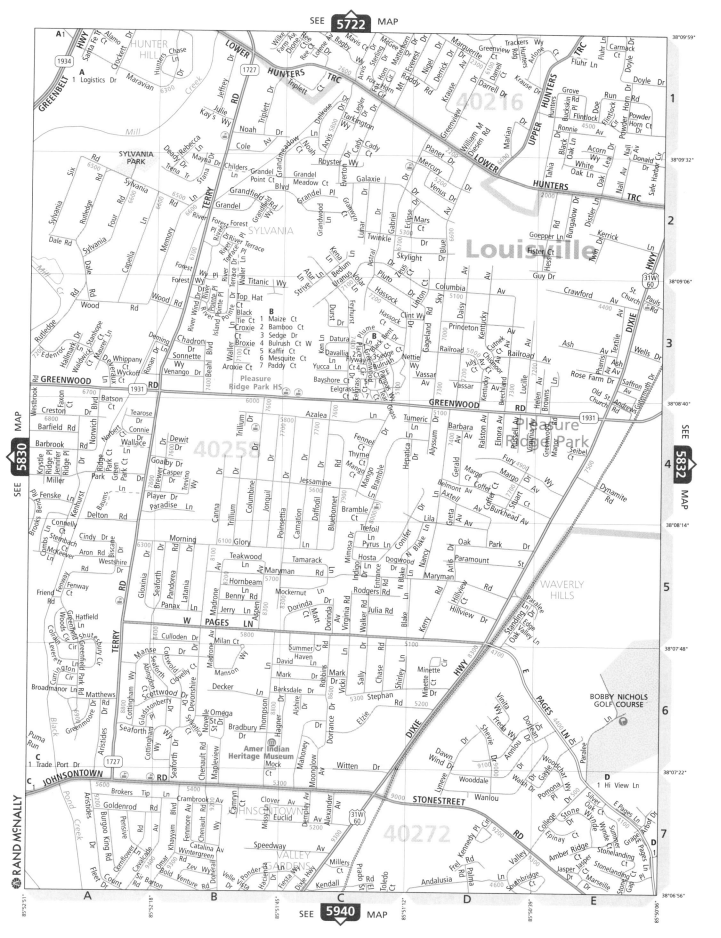

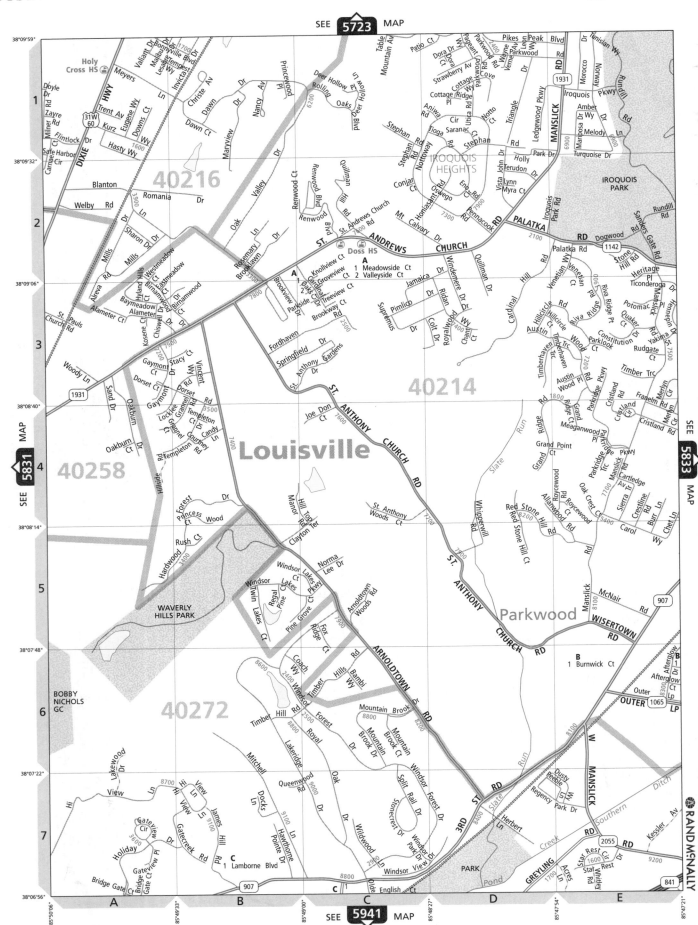

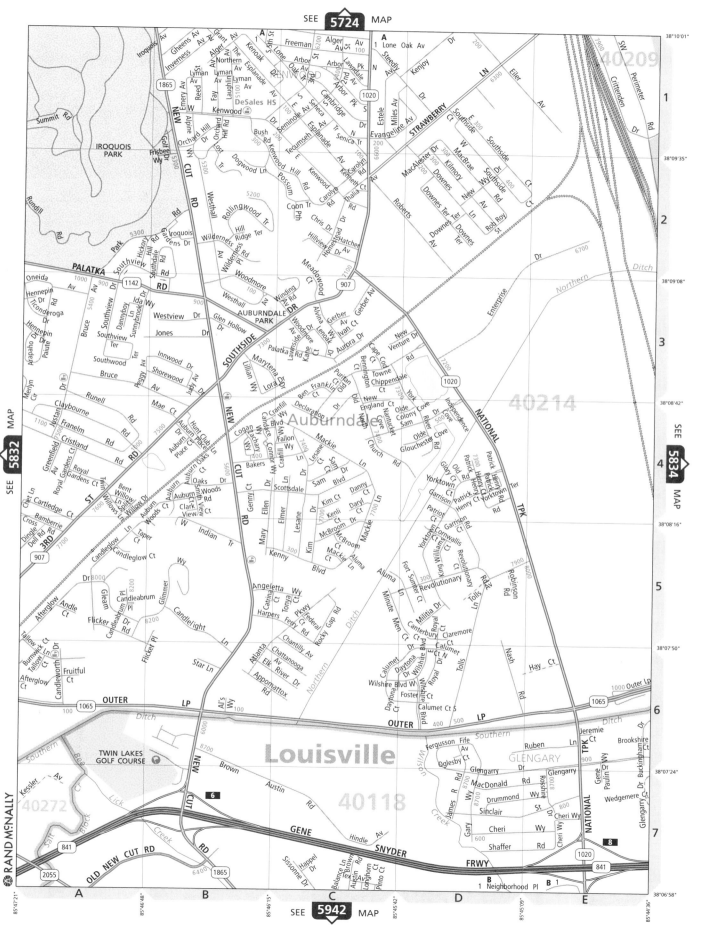

MAP
5833

SEE 5724 MAP

SEE 5832 MAP

SEE 5834 MAP

SEE 5942 MAP

Louisville

40118

40214

40209

40272

Auburndale

IROQUOIS PARK

AUBURNDALE PARK

TWIN LAKES GOLF COURSE

GLENGARY

GENE SNYDER FRWY

1:24,000
1 in. = 2000 ft.

RAND MCNALLY

MAP
5834

1:24,000
1 in. = 2000 ft.
0   0.25   0.5
miles

SEE 5725 MAP

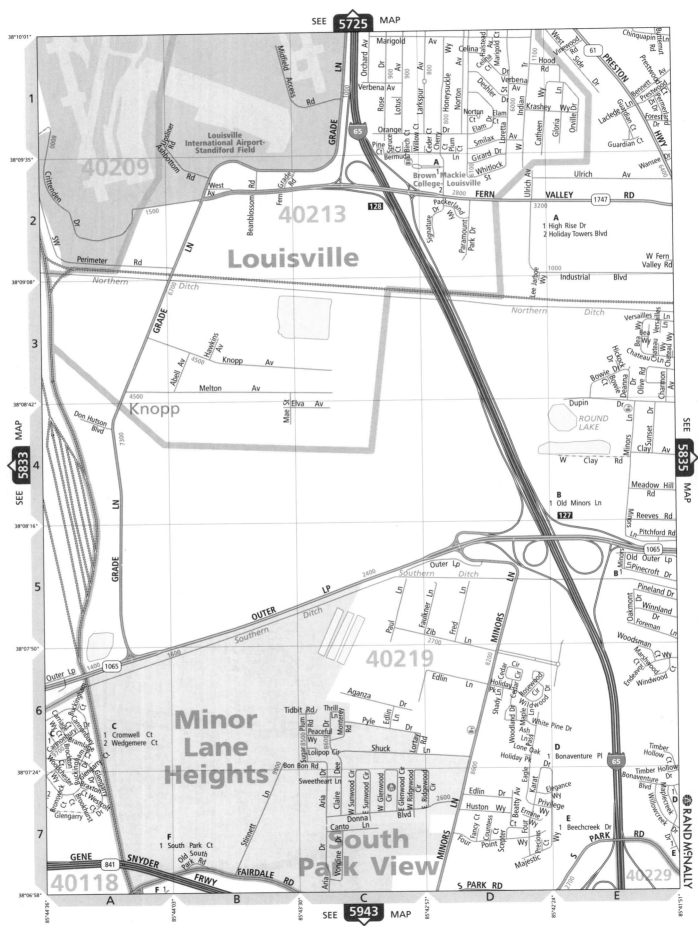

38°10'01"

1

Midfield Access Rd

40209

Louisville International Airport-Standiford Field

38°09'35"

Upsliner Rd
Ashbottom Rd

8000
Crittenden Dr
SW

2

West Av
Beanblossom
Fern Rd
Grade Rd

1500

40213

GRADE LN

Louisville

Marigold Av
Orchard Av
Celina Av
Celina Wy
West Vinewood Side Dr
Chinquapin Rd   Butternut
61   PRESTON HWY
Verbena Av   Halstead Av
Marigold Ct
Hood Rd
1100   Bennett
Prestwood Dr
Fernieland Dr
Rose Dr   Deshler   Verbena Wy
Lotus   Honeysuckle   Norton   Indian Wy   Krashey Wy Dr
Larkspur   800   Ln   Laclede Ln   Guardian Ct   Forest Dr
Orange Av   Norton   Elam   Catheen   Gloria   Orville Dr   Guardian Ct
Pine Ct   Spruce Ct   Elam Ct   Loretta   Smilax   W
Bermuda   Birch Ln   Cedar Ct   Cherry Ct   Plum Ct   Girard Dr   Wansee 6400
Brown Mackie   A   Whitlock St   Ulrich   Av
College-Louisville   2   6100
2800   FERN   VALLEY   1747 RD
Packerland Dr
Signature Dr   Paramount Park Dr   3200   A   W Fern Valley Rd
1   High Rise Dr
2   Holiday Towers Blvd

38°09'08"

128
65

3

Northern   Ditch
6700

GRADE   LN
7300

Hawkins Av
Abell Av   4500   Knopp   Av

Knopp

Melton   Av
4500   Mae St   Elva   Av

Lee Jarboe Dr   1000   Industrial   Blvd
Northern   Ditch
Versailles Ct
Bea   Versailles Wy
Chateau   Wy   Chateau Wy
Hickock Dr
Bowie Dr   Deama
Bowie Ct   Olive Rd   Charmon
Dupin Dr
ROUND   Ln
LAKE   Dr   Sunset Dr
Minors   Clay Av
W   Clay   Rd

38°08'42"

SEE 5833 MAP

4

Don Hutson Blvd

Meadow Hill Rd

B
1   Old Minors Ln

127
Minors   Reeves Rd
Minors   Ln   Pitchford Rd

SEE 5835 MAP

38°08'16"

5

GRADE   LN

Outer Lp
Southern   Ditch
2400   LN
OUTER   LP
Southern   Ditch
1600
Outer Lp   1400   1065

40219

1065   Old Outer Lp
B   Minors
1   Pinecroft Dr
Pineland Dr
Oakmont   Winnland Dr   Dr
Foreman   Ln
Woodsman   Dr
Paul Ln
Faulkner Ln
Fred Ln
Zib Ln
2700   MINORS   LN
8200
Marshwood   Wy
Endeavor   Windwood   Ln

38°07'50"

6

Minor Lane Heights

C
1   Cromwell Ct
2   Wedgemere Ct

Buckingham
Carlisle Wy   Cambridge Dr
Cannonbury   Bramlage Ct
Brockton   Glengary
Glendale Ct   Ct   Braxton   Westolt
Bronston Wy   Ct   Ct   Brookhurst
2   Worchester Wy   Dr
Glengary

Tidbit Rd
Aganza Dr
Thrill
Peaceful Wy   Monterey Rd
Sugar Plum   Pyle
8500 Ln   Lolipop Cir   Shuck
8600
Bon Bon Rd   Dee Ln
Sweetheart Ln

Edlin   Ln
Edlin Ln   Cedar Cir
Holiday   Cir   Rosewood
Pk Ln   Cedar Cir   Wildwood Cir
Shady Ln   Maple   White Pine Dr
Woodland Dr   Ash Ln   Cir
Lone Oak Pass Ln
Holiday Pk   D
1   Bonaventure Pl
8600
Timber Hollow Ct
Timber Hollow Blvd
Bonaventure Blvd
Maplecreek Dr

9900   Ln
Sinnett

F
1   South Park Ct

38°07'24"

7

Aria Dr
Claire Ln   Canto
Donna Ln
Sweetheart Ln   Dee Ln
Aria   Vondale Ln
Dr

W Sunwood Cir
W Sunwood Cir   E Glenwood Cir
W Glenwood   E Ridgewood Cir
Blvd   W Ridgewood Cir
2600

Edlin   Dr
Huston Wy   Beatty Av
Fancy Ct   Karat   Elegance Wy
Countess   Four   Privilege Wy
Point   Scepter Wy   Ermine Wy   Precios Wy
Majestic   Wy

E
1   Beechcreek Dr

S   PARK   RD
2700

40229

South Park View

GENE
841
SNYDER   FRWY   FAIRDALE RD
Old South Park Rd   S PARK RD
F   1

40118

38°06'58"

SEE 5943 MAP

A   B   C   D   E

85°44'36"   85°44'03"   85°43'30"   85°42'57"   85°42'24"

RAND McNALLY

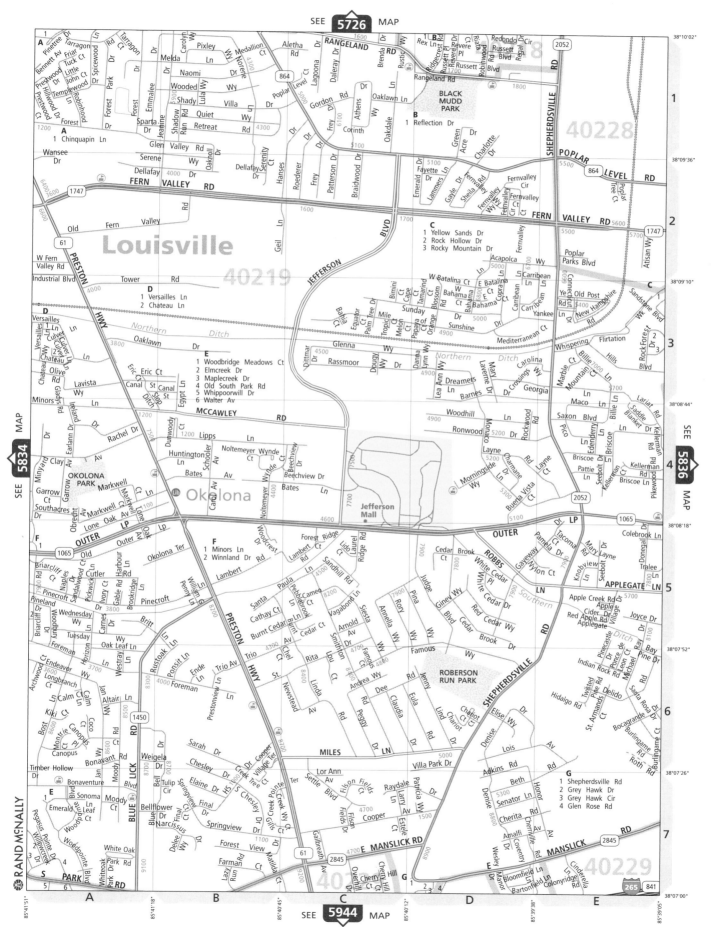

MAP
5835

1:24,000
1 in. = 2000 ft.
0   0.25   0.5
miles

SEE 5726 MAP

SEE 5834 MAP

SEE 5836 MAP

SEE 5944 MAP

Louisville
40219
40228
40229

BLACK MUDD PARK
OKOLONA PARK
Okolona
JEFFERSON MALL
ROBERSON RUN PARK

RAND McNALLY

C
1 Yellow Sands Dr
2 Rock Hollow Dr
3 Rocky Mountain Dr

D
1 Versailles Ln
2 Chateau Ln

E
1 Woodbridge Meadows Ct
2 Elmcreek Dr
3 Maplecreek Dr
4 Old South Park Rd
5 Whippoorwill Dr
6 Walter Av

F
1 Minors Ln
2 Winnland Dr

G
1 Shepherdsville Rd
2 Grey Hawk Dr
3 Grey Hawk Cir
4 Glen Rose Rd

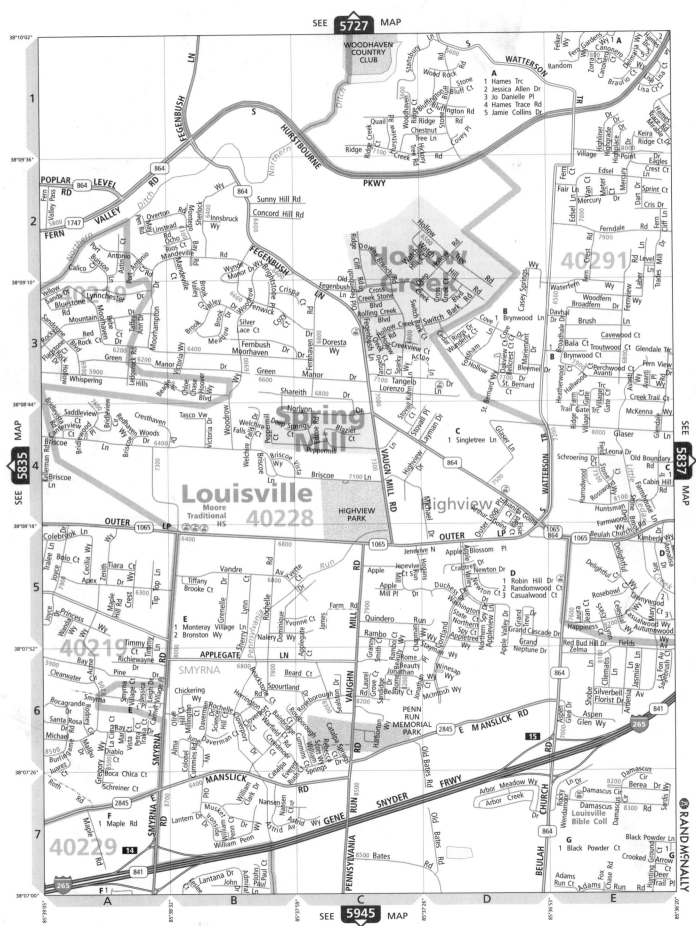

MAP
5837

1:24,000
1 in. = 2000 ft.
0   0.25   0.5
miles

SEE 5728 MAP

SEE 5836 MAP

SEE 5838 MAP

SEE 5946 MAP

40299

40291

40228

Louisville

RAND McNALLY

MAP
5838

1:24,000
1 in. = 2000 ft.

0   0.25   0.5
miles

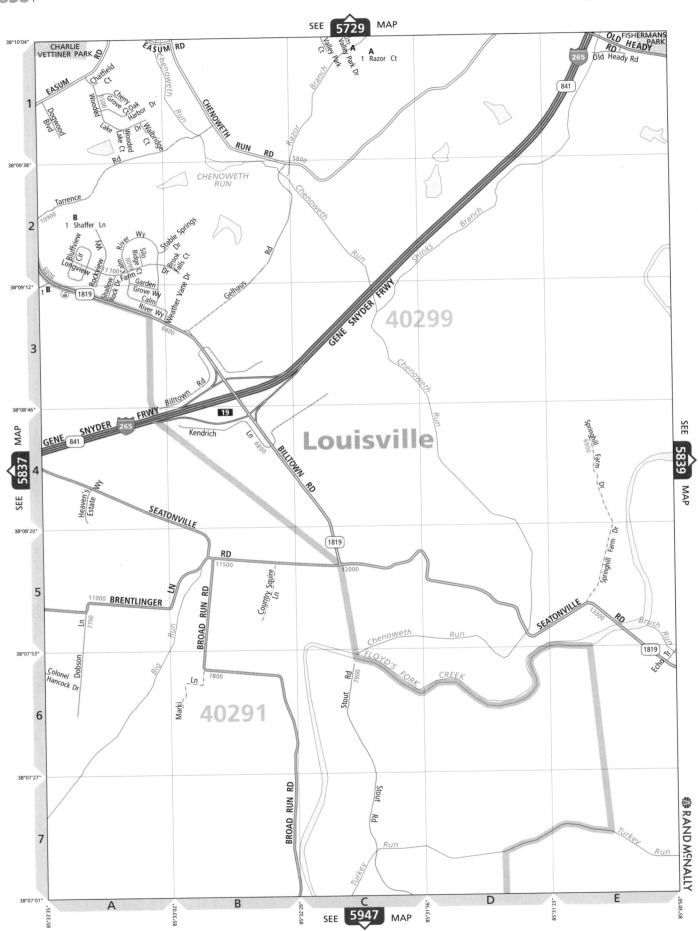

SEE 5729 MAP

38°10'04"

CHARLIE VETTINER PARK

EASUM RD
CHENOWETH RUN RD

265
Old Heady Rd

OLD HEADY RD
FISHERMANS PARK

841

1 Razor Ct
A
A

Valley Park Dr
Valley Park Ct

Branch

1

CHARLIE VETTINER PARK

EASUM

Dogwood Blvd

Chatfield Ct

Cherry Grove Ct
Wooded
Oak Harbor Dr
Wooded Lake Ct
Dr
Walbridge
Wooded Lake Rd

5500

Chenoweth Run

Razor

5800

Chenoweth Branch

38°09'38"

CHENOWETH RUN

Tarrence

Chenoweth Run

Shinks

40299

2

10900

B
1 Shaffer Ln

Bluffview Cir
Longview

Rockview

River Wy
Silo Ridge Ct
Farm

Stable Springs Dr
Brook
Falls Ct

Garden Grove Wy
Calm
Weather Vane Dr

Rd

Gelhaus

1700
10800

6000

38°09'12"
1 B
1819

Shallow Rock Dr
Calm River Wy

6400

GENE SNYDER FRWY

Chenoweth Run

3

Billtown Rd

GENE SNYDER FRWY
265
19

38°08'46"

GENE SNYDER FRWY
841

Kendrich

Ln 6600

BILLTOWN RD

Louisville

Chenoweth Run

Springhill Farm Dr

6900

SEE 5839 MAP

4

Heaven's Estate Wy

SEATONVILLE

1819

Springhill Farm Dr

SEE 5837 MAP

38°08'20"

5

11000 BRENTLINGER

Brentlinger Ln

Ln 7700

BROAD RUN RD

RD
11500

Country Squire Ln

12000

SEATONVILLE RD
13300

Brush Run

1819
Echo Tr

38°07'53"

Colonel Hancock Dr
Dobson Ln

Big Run

Marki Ln
7800

40291

Chenoweth Run

FLOYD'S FORK
CREEK

Stout Rd

7900

6

38°07'27"

Stout Rd

7

BROAD RUN RD

Stout Rd

Run

Turkey Run

Turkey Run

38°07'01"

A   B   C   D   E

85°33'35"   85°33'02"   85°32'29"   85°31'56"   85°31'23"   85°30'50"

SEE 5947 MAP

MAP
5839

SEE **5730** MAP

1:24,000
1 in. = 2000 ft.

0   0.25   0.5

miles

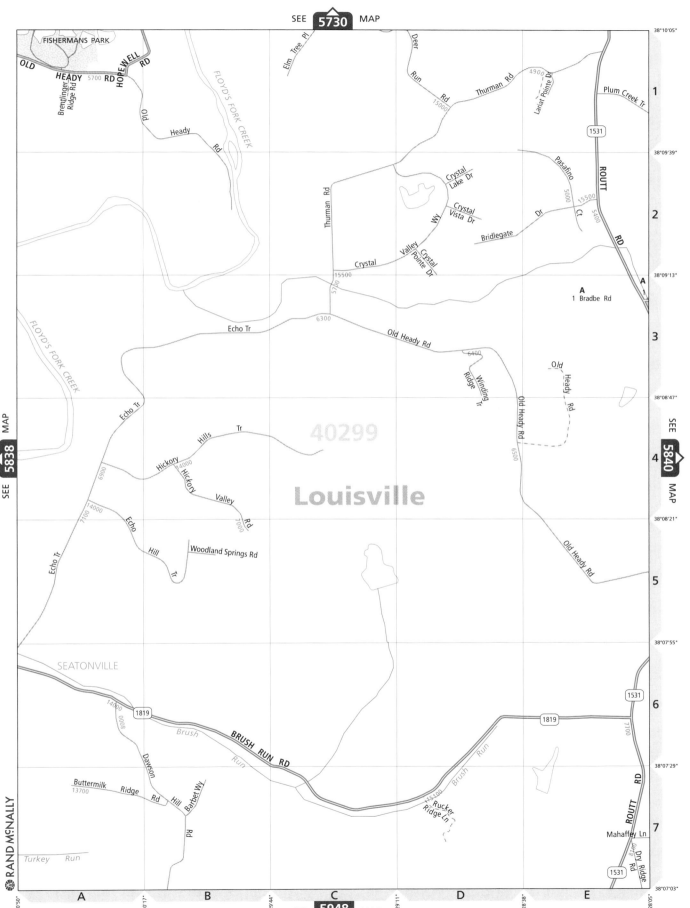

FISHERMANS PARK

OLD HEADY RD

HOPEWELL RD

Brentlinger Ridge Rd

5700

Old Heady Rd

FLOYD'S FORK CREEK

FLOYD'S FORK CREEK

Elm Tree Pl

Deer Run Rd

Thurman Rd

15000

4900

Lariat Pointe Dr

Plum Creek Tr

1531

ROUTT RD

Thurman Rd

Crystal Lake Dr

Crystal Vista Dr

Wy

Pasafino

Dr

5000

5500

15500

5400

Bridlegate

Crystal Valley

Crystal Pointe Dr

15500

5700

A

1 Bradbe Rd

A

Echo Tr

6300

Old Heady Rd

6400

Old Heady Rd

Winding Ridge Tr

Old Heady Rd

6500

Echo Tr

Hills Tr

40299

Louisville

Hickory

14000

Hickory

6900

Valley Rd

7000

14000

Echo

7100

Echo Hill Tr

Woodland Springs Rd

Echo Tr

Old Heady Rd

SEE **5838** MAP

SEE **5840** MAP

SEATONVILLE

14000

8000

1819

1531

1819

7100

Brush Run

BRUSH RUN RD

Brush Run

Dawson

Buttermilk Ridge Rd

13700

Hill

Barber Wy

Rd

+5100

Rucker Ridge Ln

ROUTT RD

8700

Dry Ridge Rd

Mahaffey Ln

1531

Turkey Run

38°10'05"

1

38°09'39"

2

38°09'13"

3

38°08'47"

4

38°08'21"

5

38°07'55"

6

38°07'29"

7

38°07'03"

85°30'50"   85°30'17"   85°29'44"   85°29'11"   85°28'38"   85°28'05"

A   B   C   D   E

MAP
5840

1:24,000
1 in. = 2000 ft.
0   0.25   0.5
miles

SEE 5731 MAP

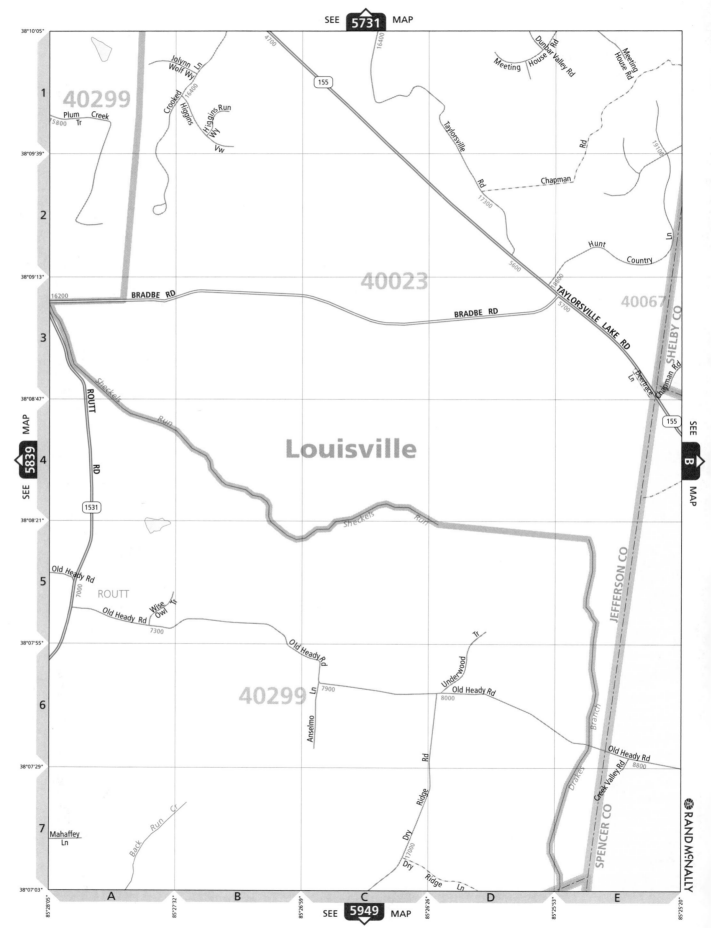

40299

Plum Creek Tr
15800

Jolynn Ln
Wolf Wy
Crooked
Higgins
16400
Higgins Run
Wy
Vw

4700
155
16400
Meeting
Dunbar Valley Rd
Meeting House Rd

Taylorsville Rd
19100
Chapman

17300

Hunt Country
5600

40023

16200
BRADBE RD
BRADBE RD
8600
TAYLORSVILLE LAKE RD
5700

40067

Deerrace Ln
Chapman Rd
SHELBY CO

155

SEE B MAP

ROUTT RD
Sheckels Run

Louisville

Sheckels Run

1531

JEFFERSON CO

Old Heady Rd
7000
ROUTT
Wise Owl Tr
Old Heady Rd
7300

Old Heady Rd

Tr
Underwood
Old Heady Rd
8000

40299

Anselmo Ln
7900

Rd

Branch

Old Heady Rd
8800

Ridge

Dry

Drakes
Creek Valley Rd

SPENCER CO

Mahaffey Ln

Back Run Cr

Dry
17000
Dry Ridge Ln

RAND M^cNALLY

SEE 5949 MAP

38°10'05"
38°09'39"
38°09'13"
38°08'47"
38°08'21"
38°07'55"
38°07'29"
38°07'03"

85°28'05"
85°27'32"
85°26'59"
85°26'26"
85°25'53"
85°25'20"

SEE 5839 MAP

A   B   C   D   E

1
2
3
4
5
6
7

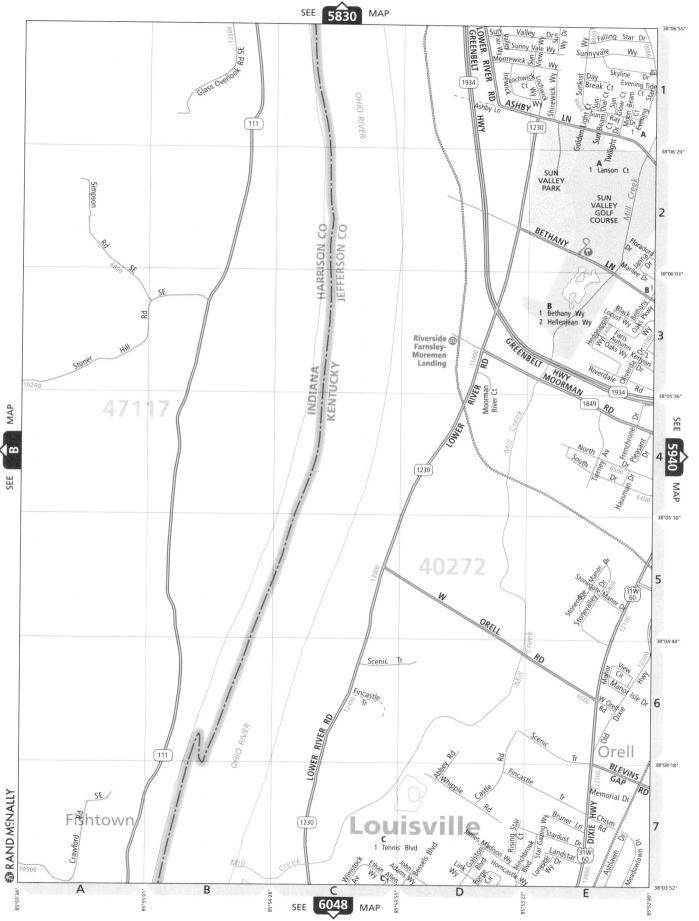

MAP
5939

1:24,000
1 in. = 2000 ft.

0   0.25   0.5
miles

SEE **5830** MAP

SEE **5940** MAP

SEE **B** MAP

SEE **6048** MAP

RAND McNALLY

N

OHIO RIVER

HARRISON CO
JEFFERSON CO

INDIANA
KENTUCKY

47117

40272

Fishtown

Louisville

Orell

Glass Overlook Rd SE

12300

111

Simpson
Rd
SE
6800

Stoner
Hill
Rd
SE
10200

111

Crawford
Rd
SE
10500

OHIO RIVER

Mill   Creek

LOWER RIVER RD

1230

1230

Scenic   Tr

Fincastle
Tr
12400

12000

W   ORELL   RD

LOWER RIVER RD

11000

Mill Creek

Riverside
Farnsley-
Moremen
Landing

Moorman
River Ct

LOWER
GREENBELT
RIVER
RD

1934

ASHBY
HWY

Ashby Ln

BETHANY   LN

GREENBELT   HWY
MOORMAN   RD
1849

1230

Valley
Dr

Sun
Fair
Wy

Sunny
View
Wy

Moorewick
Ln

Irewick
Ct

Irelochwick
Ct

Shirewick
Wy

Valley
Dr
Wy

Sunny
Vale
Wy

9800

Falling Star Dr

Sunnyvale
Wy

Skyline
Dr

Day
Break
Ct

Evening Tide

Golden Light Ct

Sun Beam Ct

Dial Ct

Sun
Glow
Ct

Moon
Beam
Ct

Sun
Ray
Ct

Sunkist

Evening
Star

Twilight

A
1 Lanson Ct

SUN
VALLEY
PARK

SUN
VALLEY
GOLF
COURSE

Mill Creek

Floradora
Dr

Jannat
Dr

Marilee Dr

B
1 Bethany Wy
2 Hellenjean Wy

Black
Locust Wy

Bethany
Oaks Pkwy

Hedgeapple
Wy

Faris
Autumn
Oaks Wy

Kenyon
Dr

Olverda
Dr

Riverdale

Riverdale
Rd

1934

North
Dr

South
Dr

Tierney Av

6500

Frenchrone
Dr

Pleasant
Dr

Hausman Dr
6400

31W
60

Stonedate Manor Dr

Stoneridge
Manor
Dr
6800

Stonevalley
Dr

Manor Dr

12100

Manor
Cir

View
Cir

Manor Isle Dr

W Orell
Rd

Dixie
Hwy

Old
Dixie
Hwy

6500

Scenic
Tr

Orell

BLEVINS
GAP
RD

12700

Memorial Dr

DIXIE   HWY

Chism
Rd

Abbey
Rd

Whipple

Castle
Rd

Rd

Fincastle
Tr

Scenic
Tr

Bruner Ln

James Madison Wy

Rising Star
Ct

Star Gazing Wy

Stardust
Dr

Landstar
Dr

31W
60

13000

Ashlawn
Dr

Meadowlawn Dr

C
1 Tennis Blvd

John Bessels Blvd

Wimstock
Av

Ethan Allen
Wy

Adams
Wy

C

Link
Wy

Galston
Blvd

Hinchbrook
Wy

Horncastle Wy

Longest
Blvd

Forge
Cir

Mill   Creek

38°06'55"
38°06'29"
38°06'03"
38°05'36"
38°05'10"
38°04'44"
38°04'18"
38°03'52"

85°55'34"
85°55'01"
85°54'28"
85°53'55"
85°53'22"
85°52'49"

A   B   C   D   E

1   2   3   4   5   6   7

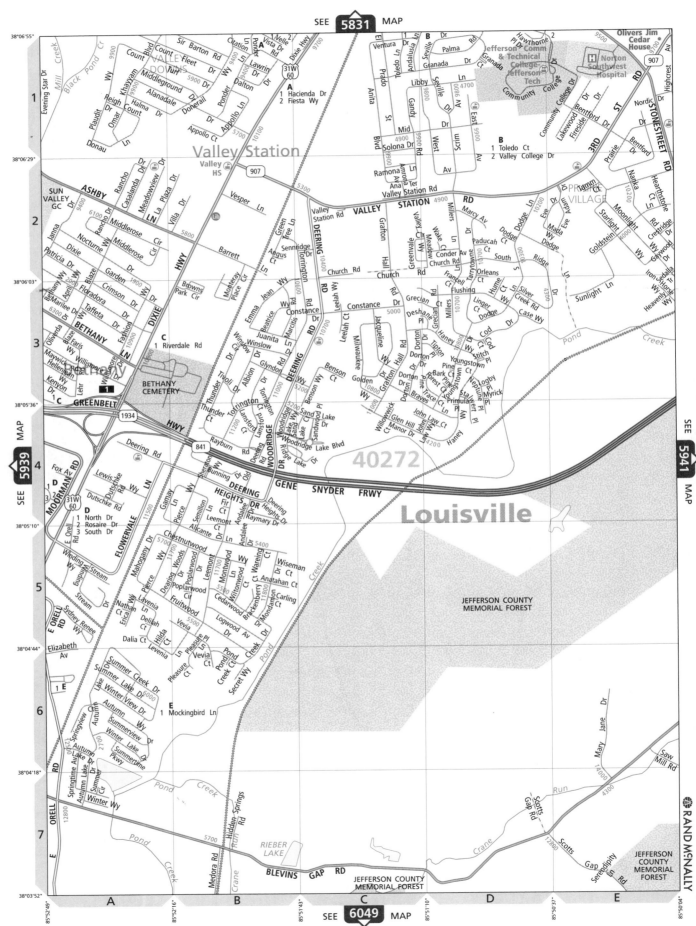

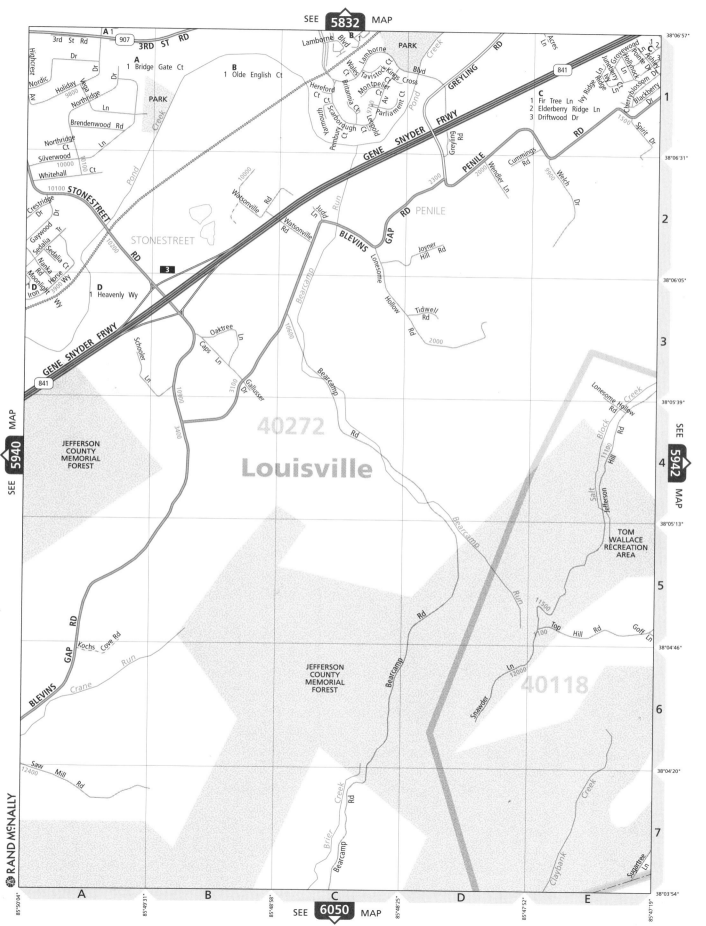

MAP
5942

1:24,000
1 in. = 2000 ft.

0   0.25   0.5
miles

SEE 5833 MAP

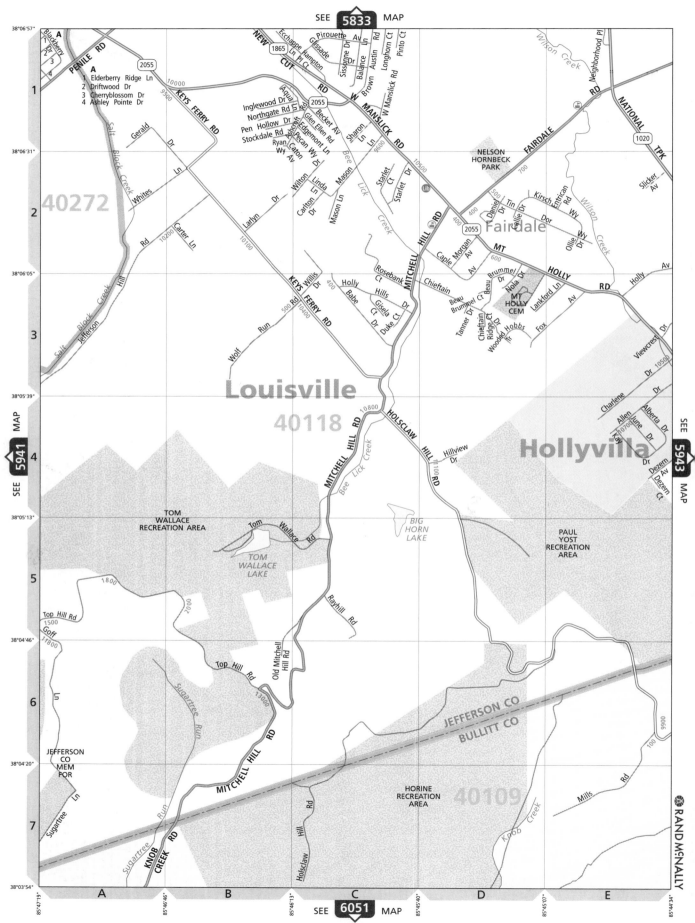

SEE 5941 MAP

SEE 5943 MAP

SEE 6051 MAP

A 1 Elderberry Ridge Ln
2 Driftwood Dr
3 Cherryblossom Dr
4 Ashley Pointe Dr

40272

Louisville
40118

Fairdale

Hollyvilla

NELSON HORNBECK PARK

MT HOLLY CEM

TOM WALLACE RECREATION AREA

TOM WALLACE LAKE

BIG HORN LAKE

PAUL YOST RECREATION AREA

JEFFERSON CO
BULLITT CO

JEFFERSON CO MEM FOR

HORINE RECREATION AREA

40109

RAND McNALLY

MAP
5943

N

1:24,000
1 in. = 2000 ft.
0   0.25   0.5
miles

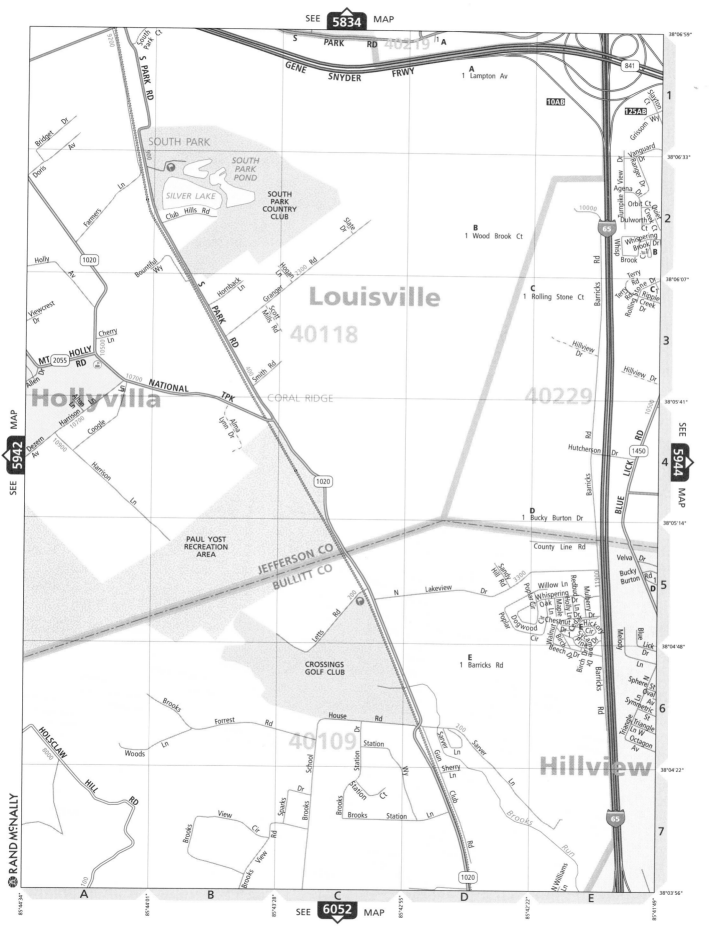

SEE 5834 MAP

38°06'59"

GENE SNYDER FRWY

S PARK RD 40219

1 Lampton Av A

841

10AB

125AB

1

38°06'33"

SOUTH PARK

SILVER LAKE

SOUTH PARK POND

SOUTH PARK COUNTRY CLUB

Club Hills Rd

B
1 Wood Brook Ct

10000

65

Vanguard Dr

Ranger Dr

Agena Dr

Orbit Ct

Dulworth Ct

Whispering Brook Dr B

2

38°06'07"

Louisville
40118

C
1 Rolling Stone Ct

Barricks Rd

Terry Rd

Terry Rd

Rolling Stone Dr

Ripple Creek Dr C

Hillview Dr

3

38°05'41"

Hollyvilla

CORAL RIDGE

S PARK RD

NATIONAL TPK

40229

Hillview Dr

Blue Lick Rd

10500

Hutcherson Dr

1450

Barricks Rd

4

38°05'14"

1020

D
1 Bucky Burton Dr

County Line Rd

Velva Dr

Bucky Burton Rd

D

PAUL YOST RECREATION AREA

JEFFERSON CO
BULLITT CO

N

Lakeview Dr

Sandi Hill Rd

Willow Ln

Poplar Cir

Whispering Oak

Redbud Dr

Holly Ln

Maple Dr

Mulberry Dr

Hickory Cir

5

38°04'48"

CROSSINGS GOLF CLUB

Letts Rd

Dogwood Cir

Poplar Cir

Chestnut Dr

Walnut Dr

Birch Dr

Sycamore Dr

Beech Dr

Pine

E

Barricks Rd

Blue Lick Dr

Ln

Sphere St

Oval Av

Symmetric St

Melody

E
1 Barricks Rd

6

38°04'22"

Brooks Forrest Rd

Woods Ln

House Rd

Station Dr

School Dr

Station Wy

Station Ln

Gun Club Rd

Sarver Ln

Sherry Ln

Sarver Ln

200

Brooks Run

Triangle Ln

Triangle Ln W

Octagon Av

Hillview

40109

HOLSCLAW HILL RD

Brooks View Cir

Sparks Rd

Brooks Dr

Brooks Station Ct

Brooks Station Ln

1020

N Williams Ln

65

7

38°03'56"

SEE 5942 MAP
SEE 5944 MAP
SEE 6052 MAP

A   B   C   D   E

85°44'34"   85°44'01"   85°43'28"   85°42'55"   85°42'22"   85°41'49"

MAP
5944

1:24,000
1 in. = 2000 ft.

0   0.25   0.5
miles

SEE 5835 MAP

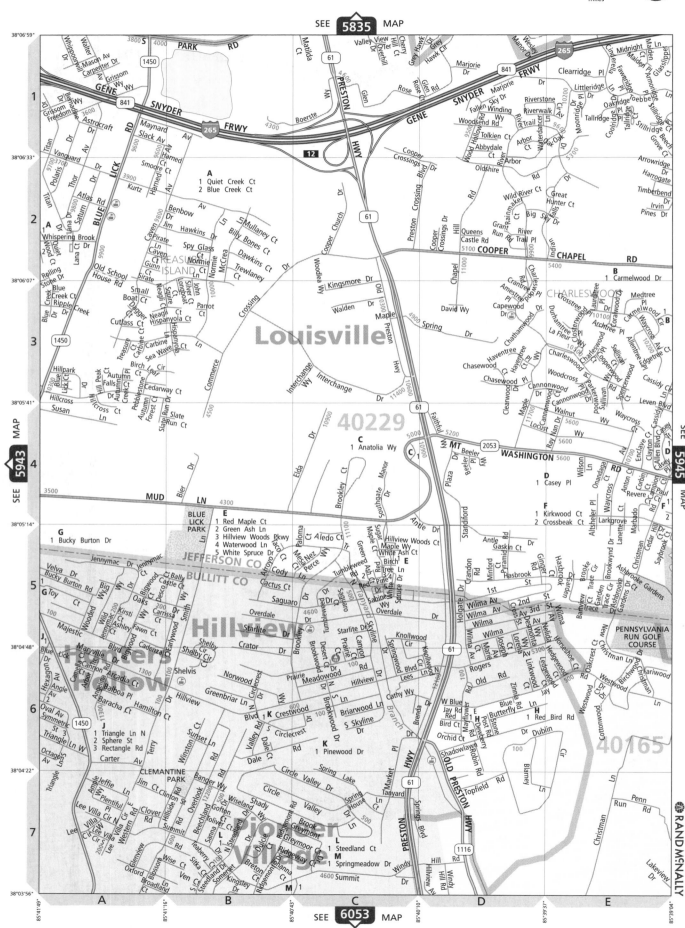

SEE 5943 MAP

SEE 5945 MAP

SEE 6053 MAP

RAND MCNALLY

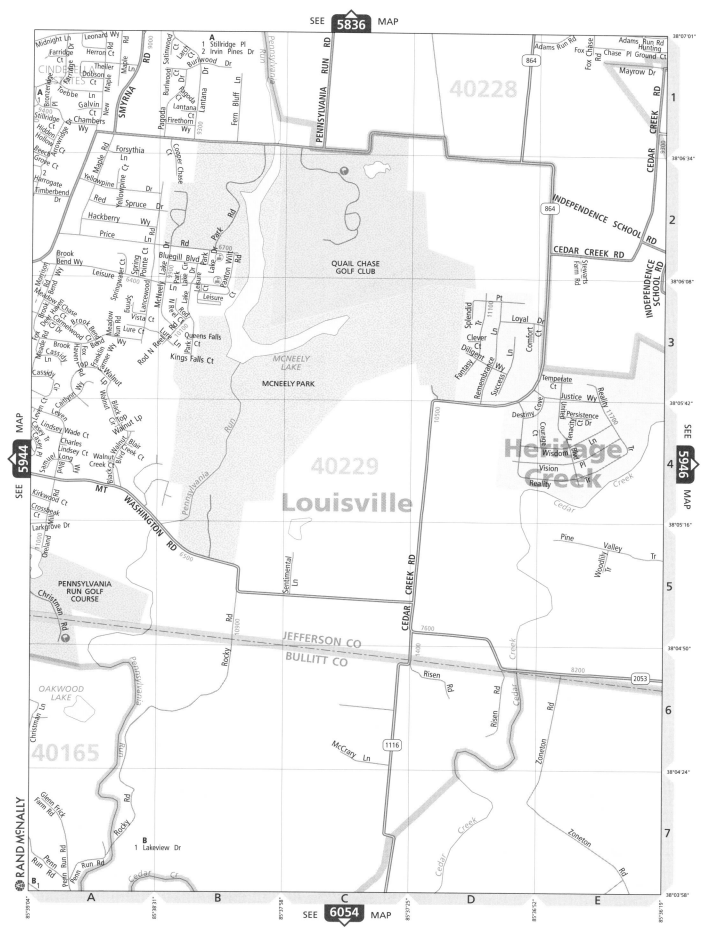

MAP
5945

SEE 5836 MAP

1:24,000
1 in. = 2000 ft.
0   0.25   0.5
miles

N

40228

40229
Louisville

QUAIL CHASE
GOLF CLUB

MCNEELY
LAKE

MCNEELY PARK

Heritage
Creek

PENNSYLVANIA
RUN GOLF
COURSE

JEFFERSON CO
BULLITT CO

OAKWOOD
LAKE

40165

RAND MCNALLY

38°07'01"
38°06'34"
38°06'08"
38°05'42"
38°05'16"
38°04'50"
38°04'24"
38°03'58"

85°39'04"
85°38'31"
85°37'58"
85°37'25"
85°36'52"
85°36'19"

1
2
3
4
5
6
7

A   B   C   D   E

MAP
5946

1:24,000
1 in. = 2000 ft.

0   0.25   0.5
miles

N

SEE 5837 MAP

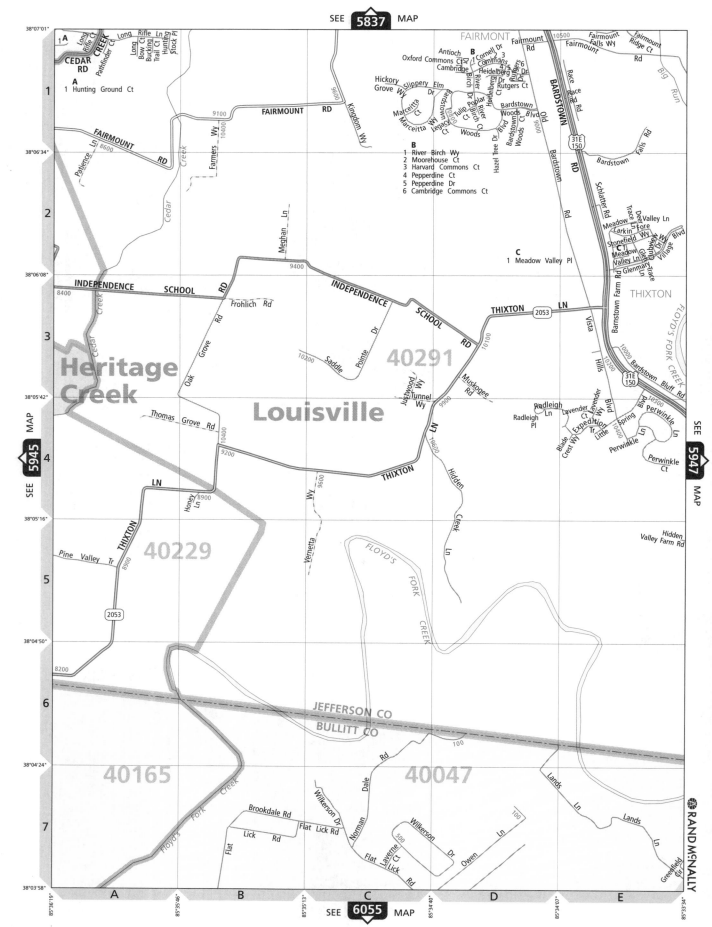

FAIRMONT

CEDAR RD

CREEK

Long Rifle Ct
Long Rifle Ln
Long Bow Ct
Bucking Trail Ct
Hunting Stock Pl
Pathfinder Ct

A
1 Hunting Ground Ct

Antioch
Oxford Commons Ct
Cambridge
B
Cornell Dr
Commons
Rutgers Dr
Heidelberg
Rutgers Ct
Fairmount Rd
Fairmount Falls Wy
Fairmount Ridge Ct
Fairmount Rd
Fairmount

Hickory Grove Wy
Slippery Elm Dr
Marceitta Ct
Marceitta

Tulip Poplar Ct
Legacy Ct
Woods

River Birch Wy
River Birch Ct
Heidelberg

Bardstown

Bardstown Woods Blvd
Bardstown Woods Ct
Old Bardstown

Big Run

Race Rd
Race Rd

31E 150

Bardstown Falls Rd
Bardstown Falls Rd

B
1 River Birch Wy
2 Moorehouse Ct
3 Harvard Commons Ct
4 Pepperdine Ct
5 Pepperdine Dr
6 Cambridge Commons Ct

FAIRMOUNT RD
9100
Kingdom Wy
9600

Farmers Wy
10400

Patience Ln
8600

FAIRMOUNT RD

Creek

Cedar

Meghan Ln

9400

Cedar Creek

INDEPENDENCE SCHOOL RD
8400

Frohlich Rd

INDEPENDENCE SCHOOL RD

Schlatter Rd

Meadow
Stonefield Wy
Larkin Wy
Dee Valley Ln
Fore
Valley Ln
Village Blvd
C
Meadow
Glenman Trace

C
1 Meadow Valley Pl

THIXTON LN
2053

Vista

Barnstown Farm Rd

THIXTON

Grove Rd

Oak

Saddle Pointe Dr
10200

40291

Muskogee Rd

10100

Hills

Floyd's Fork Creek

10200
Bardstown Bluff Rd

31E 150

Heritage Creek

Thomas Grove Rd
10400

Louisville

Juttwood Wy
Tunnel Wy

9900

Radleigh Ln
Radleigh Pl
Blade Crest Wy
Lavender Tr
Expedition
Little
Lavender Blvd
Spring
Perwinkle Ln

Perwinkle Ln
Perwinkle Ct

SEE 5945 MAP

9200

THIXTON LN

THIXTON LN

10600

Hidden Creek Ln

SEE 5947 MAP

Honey Ln
8900

40229

Pine Valley Tr

THIXTON
8900

Vernetta Wy

9600

Hidden Valley Farm Rd

2053

FLOYD'S FORK CREEK

8200

JEFFERSON CO
BULLITT CO

40165

40047

Dale Rd

100

Lands Ln

Brookdale Rd

Wilkerson Dr

Flat Lick Rd

Norman

Wilkerson Dr

Owen Ln

100

Lands Ln

Flat Lick Rd

Floyd's Fork Creek

Flat Laverne Ct
500
Flat Lick Rd

Greenfield Ct

RAND McNALLY

SEE 6055 MAP

MAP
5947

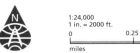

1:24,000
1 in. = 2000 ft.
0   0.25   0.5
miles

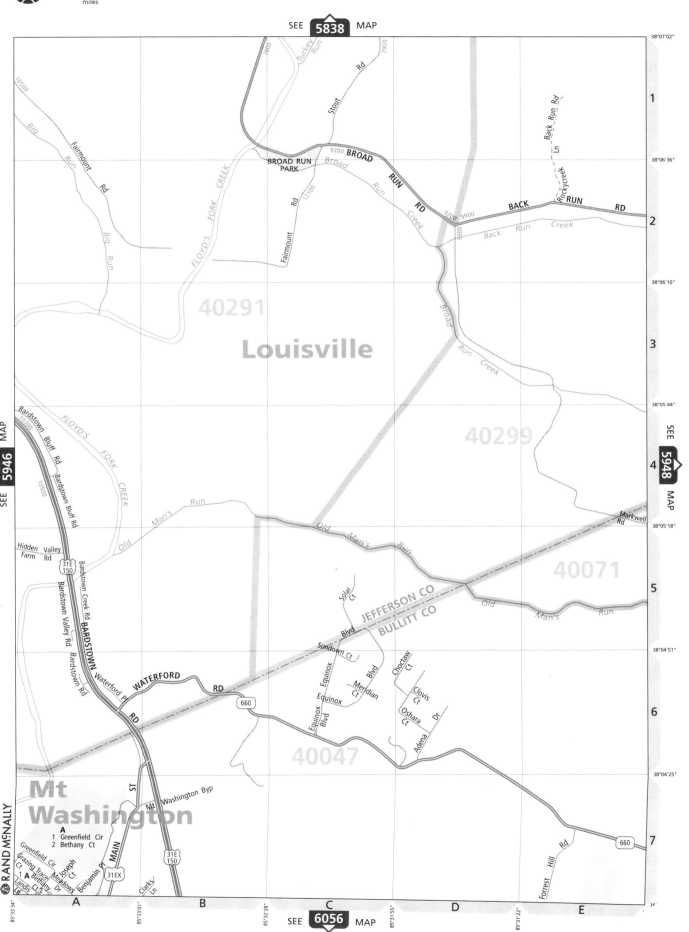

MAP
5948

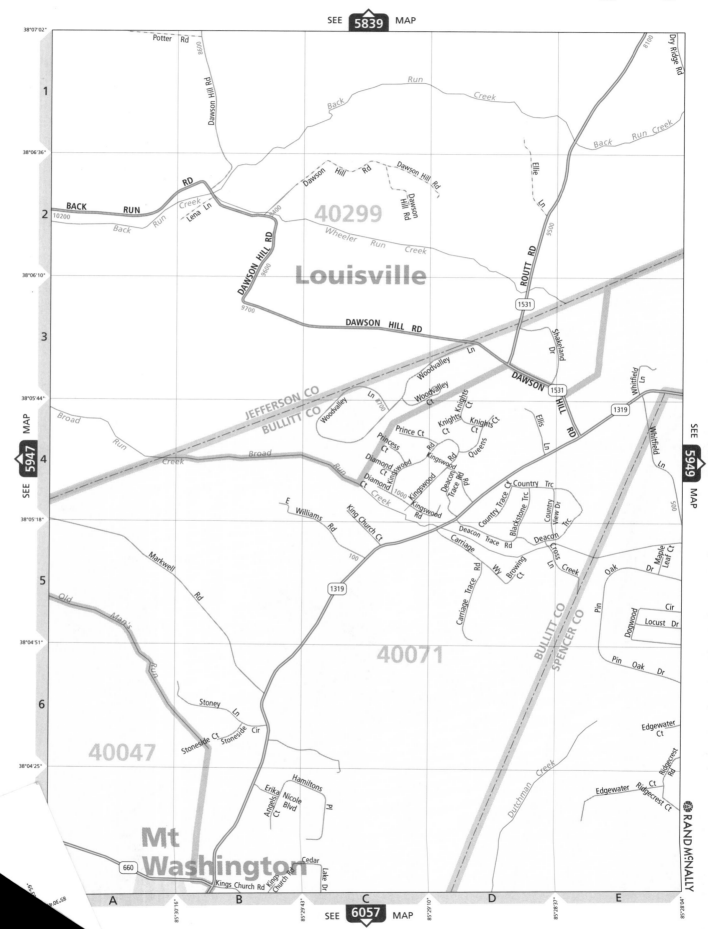

1:24,000
1 in. = 2000 ft.
0   0.25   0.5
miles

N

SEE 5947 MAP

SEE 5949 MAP

SEE 6057 MAP

RAND M^cNALLY

40299

Louisville

40071

40047

Mt
Washington

A   B   C   D   E

38°07'02"
38°06'36"
38°06'10"
38°05'44"
38°05'18"
38°04'51"
38°04'25"

85°30'16"
85°29'43"
85°29'10"
85°28'37"

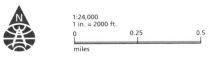

1:24,000
1 in. = 2000 ft.

0   0.25   0.5
miles

MAP
5949

SEE 5840 MAP

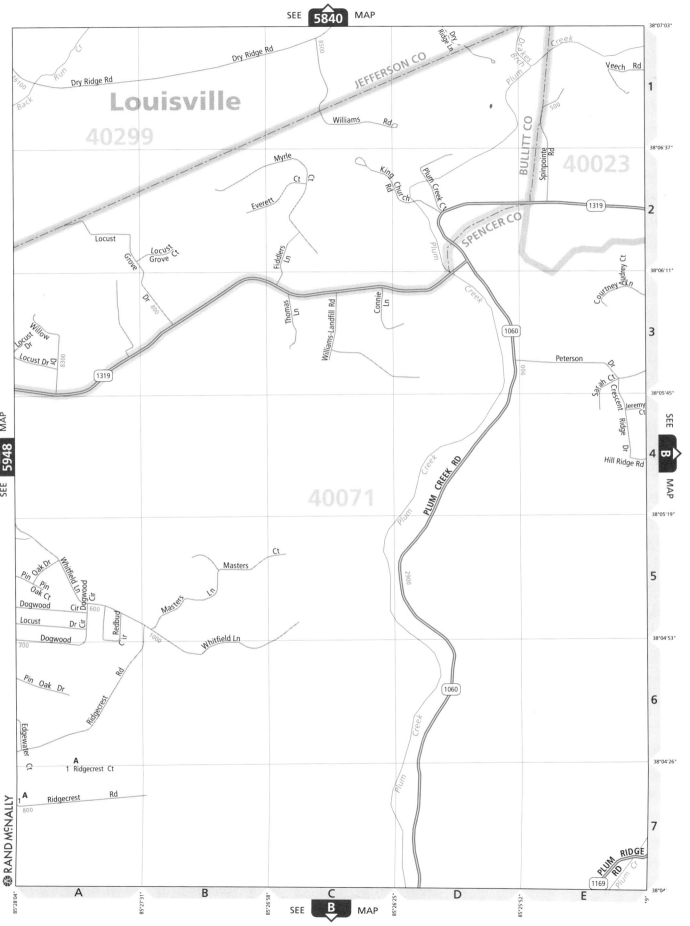

38°07'03"

Dry Ridge Rd

Back Run
Dry Ridge Rd
6100

JEFFERSON CO

8500

Williams Rd

Dry Ridge Ln

Drakes Brch
Plum
Creek

Veech Rd

500

1

Louisville

40299

Myrle Ct
Ct

Everett

Locust
Grove Dr
Locust Ct
Grove
800

Willow Dr
Locust Dr
Locust Dr Q
8300
1319

Fiddlers Ln

Thomas Ln

Williams-Landfill Rd

Connie Ln

King Church Rd

Plum Creek Ct

BULLITT CO

Spinpointe Rd

40023

SPENCER CO

1319

Plum Creek

1060

Courtney Ln
Audrey Ct

Peterson Dr

Sarah Ct
Crescent Ridge Dr
Jeremy Ct

Hill Ridge Rd

38°06'37"

2

38°06'11"

3

38°05'45"

SEE 5948 MAP

SEE B MAP

4

40071

906

Plum Creek RD

Plum Creek

2900

38°05'19"

Masters Ct
Masters Ln

Pin Oak Dr
Whitfield Ln
Dogwood Cir

Pin Oak Ct
Dogwood Cir
600
Locust Dr Cir
Redbud Cir
Dogwood
300
1000

Masters Dr

Whitfield Ln

Pin Oak Dr

Ridgecrest Rd

Edgewater Ct

A
1 Ridgecrest Ct

A
1 Ridgecrest Rd
800

1060

Plum Creek

Plum Creek

5

38°04'53"

6

38°04'26"

7

PLUM RIDGE RD
1169
Plum Cr

38°04'

A   85°28'04"   B   85°27'31"   85°26'58"   C   85°26'25"   D   85°25'52"   E

MAP
6048

1:24,000
1 in. = 2000 ft.
0   0.25   0.5
miles

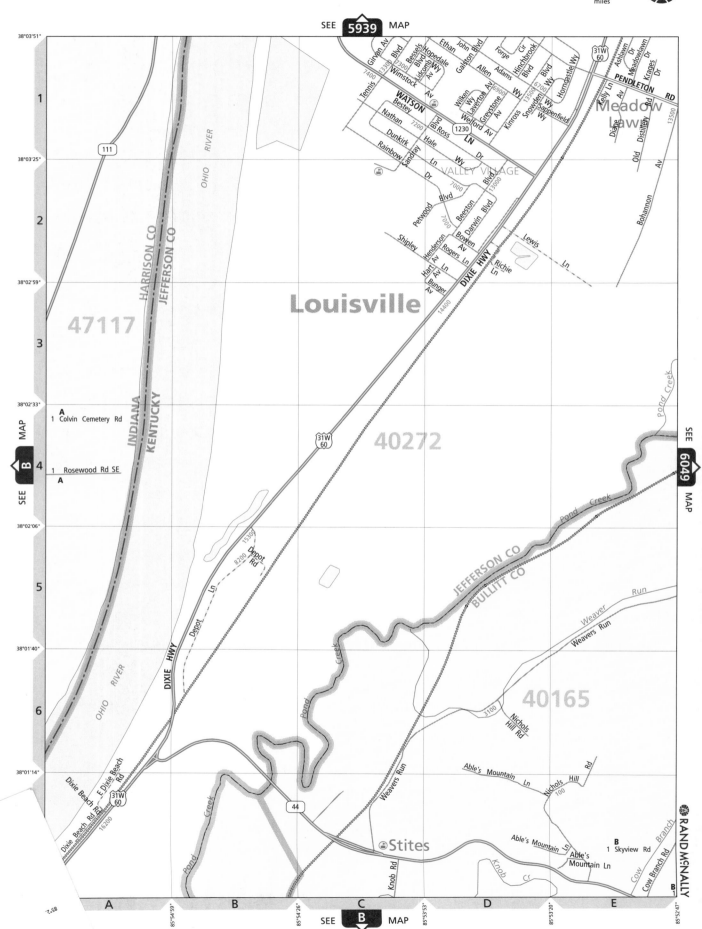

SEE 5939 MAP

38°03'51"

1

111

OHIO RIVER

HARRISON CO
JEFFERSON CO

38°03'25"

2

38°02'59"

47117

INDIANA
KENTUCKY

Louisville

3

38°02'33"

A
1 Colvin Cemetery Rd

SEE B 6049 MAP

SEE B MAP

4

1 Rosewood Rd SE
A

31W
60

40272

38°02'06"

Depot
Rd

13300

8200

Depot
Ln

POND Creek

Pond Creek

JEFFERSON CO
BULLITT CO

Weaver   Run

Weavers Run

5

38°01'40"

DIXIE HWY

DIXIE HWY

Pond Creek

6

40165

3100

Nichols
Hill Rd

OHIO RIVER

38°01'14"

Dixie Beach Rd SE

E Dixie Beach
Rd

31W
60

16200

Pond Creek

44

Weavers Run

Able's Mountain   Ln

Nichols   Hill   Rd

Able's Mountain Ln

Nichols Hill
100

B
1 Skyview Rd

Cow Branch Rd

Cow Branch

⊙Stites

Knob Rd

Knob
Cr

Able's Mountain
Mountain Ln

RAND McNALLY

B
1

WATSON

Girvan Av
Bessels Blvd
Hopedale
Blvd
Lidcomb Wy
Av
Ethan
John Blvd
Galston Blvd
Forge
Cr
Hinchbrook
Blvd
Adams
Allen
Wy
31W
60

Tennis
Blvd 7300
7400
Wimstock
Av

Bestey
Blvd
Wilken
Wy
Lavertou Av 6900
Greystone
Av
13500
Snowden Wy
6100
Kinross
Wy
Sappenfield
Wy
Horngastle Wy

Ashlawn
Kelly Ln
Meadowlawn Dr
Krages
Dr

PENDLETON   RD

Meadow
Lawn

WATSON
LN

Nathan
Bestey
Blvd
7200
Welford
Av
Welford Av
Ross

Diane
Old
Distillery
Rd
Bohannon
Av
13500

Dunkirk
Hale
Ln

Rainbow Candray
Dr
Ln
Wy

VALLEY VILLAGE

Blvd
13000

Petwood
Blvd
7000

Beeston
Darwin Blvd

Shipley
Henderson
Bowen
Av

Rogers
Ln

Hart Av
Ln

Bunger
Av

DIXIE HWY
14400

Lewis
Ln

Richie
Ln

1230

7000

85°2"

A   B   C   D   E

85°54'59"   85°54'26"   85°53'53"   85°53'20"   85°25'58"

SEE B MAP

MAP
6049

1:24,000
1 in. = 2000 ft.

0   0.25   0.5

miles

SEE ⌂ **5940** MAP

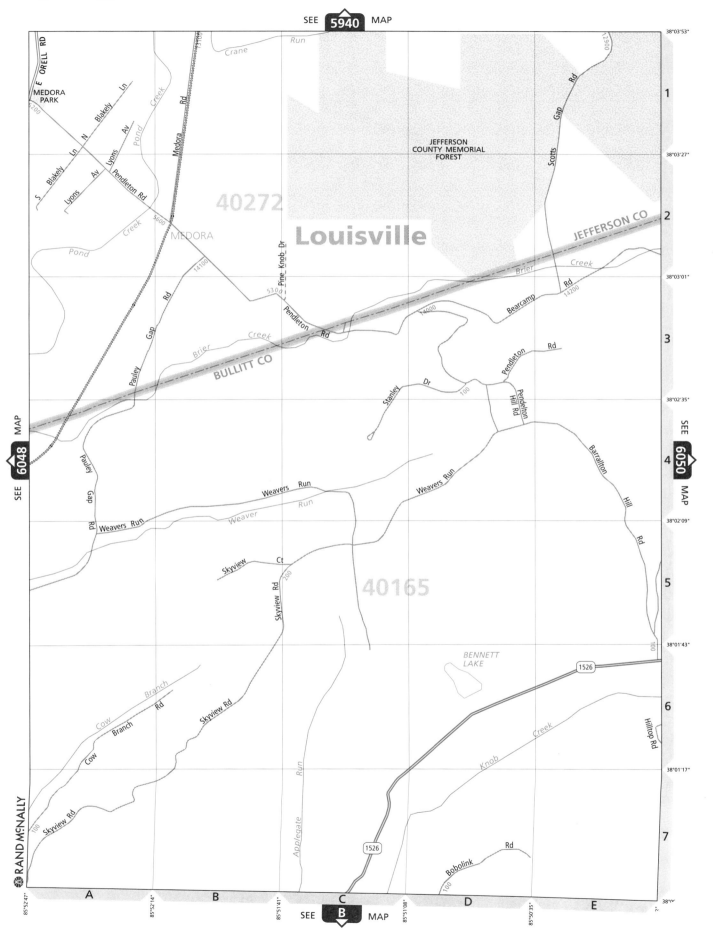

E ORELL RD

MEDORA
PARK

N Blakely Ln

Lyons Av

Medora Rd

Crane Run

Pond Creek

S Blakely Ln

Lyons Av

Pendleton Rd

Creek

Pond

MEDORA

40272

Louisville

JEFFERSON
COUNTY MEMORIAL
FOREST

Scotts Gap Rd

JEFFERSON CO

Pine Knob Dr

Pendleton Rd

Gap Rd

Pauley

Brier Creek

Brier Creek

Bearcamp

Pendleton Rd

BULLITT CO

Stanley Dr

Pendleton Hill Rd

Barrallton Hill Rd

Pauley Gap Rd

Weavers Run

Weavers Run

Weaver Run

Weavers Run

Skyview Ct

Skyview Rd

40165

BENNETT
LAKE

1526

Cow Branch Rd

Skyview Rd

Applegate Run

Knob Creek

Hilltop Rd

Cow

Skyview Rd

1526

Bobolink Rd

A   B   C   D   E

SEE ⌂ **B** MAP

SEE 6048 MAP

SEE 6050 MAP

MAP
6050

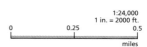

1:24,000
1 in. = 2000 ft.

0   0.25   0.5
miles

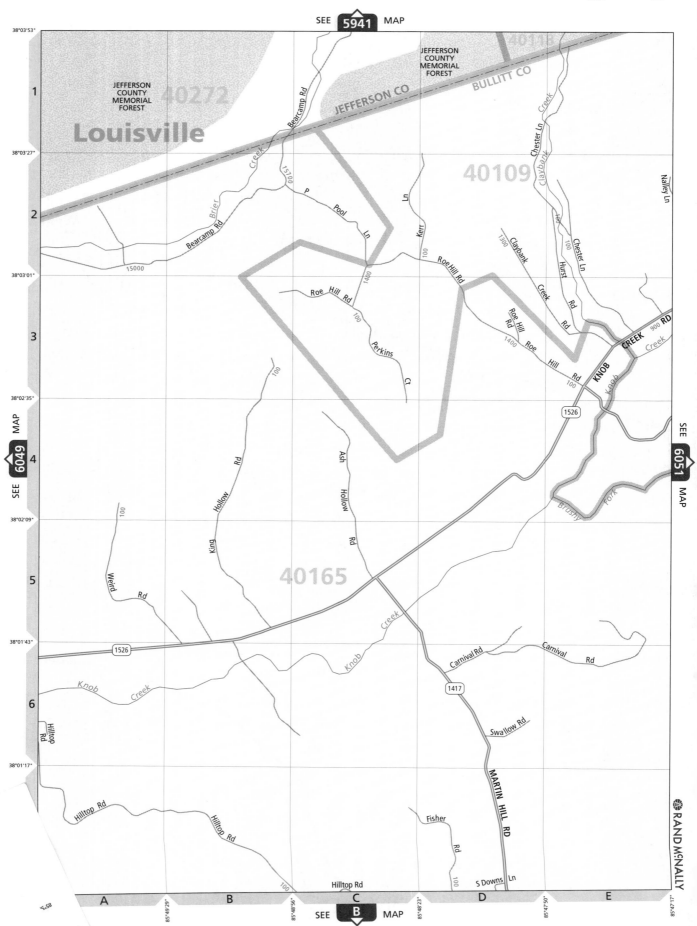

JEFFERSON
COUNTY
MEMORIAL
FOREST

40272

Louisville

JEFFERSON
COUNTY
MEMORIAL
FOREST

4011B

JEFFERSON CO
BULLITT CO

40109

Chester Ln

Claybank

Nalley Ln

Brier   Creek

Bearcamp Rd

15700

Pool Ln

P

Ln

Kerr

100

Roe Hill Rd

1300

Claybank   Creek

Hill

Chester Ln

Hurst   Rd

Bearcamp Rd

15000

1400

Roe   Hill   Rd

100

Roe Hill

Rd

1400

Roe   Hill   Rd

100

KNOB   CREEK   RD

900

Knob   Creek

Perkins

Ct

100

Rd

Hollow

King

Ash

Hollow

Rd

100

40165

Brushy   Fork

100

Weird   Rd

1526

Creek

Knob   Creek

1526

Carnival Rd

Carnival   Rd

1417

Knob   Creek

Hilltop
Rd

Swallow Rd

Hilltop Rd

MARTIN   HILL   RD

Hilltop   Rd

Fisher

Rd

100

S Downs Ln

100

Hilltop Rd

38°03'53"
38°03'27"
38°03'01"
38°02'35"
38°02'09"
38°01'43"
38°01'17"

85°49'29"
85°48'56"
85°48'23"
85°47'50"
85°47'17"

A   B   C   D   E

1   2   3   4   5   6

RAND M^{c}NALLY

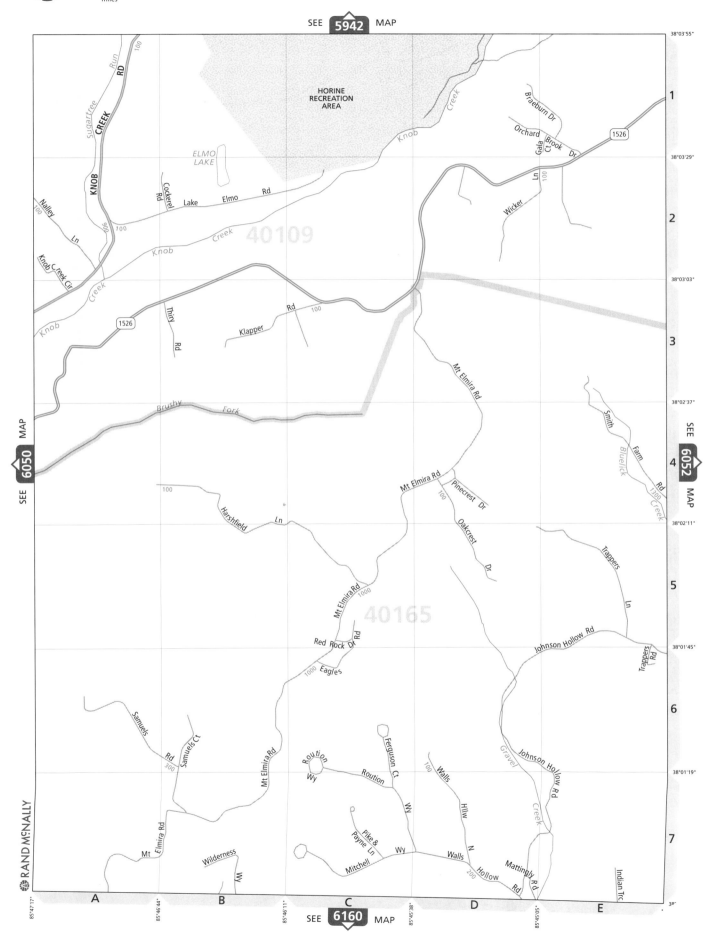

MAP
6051

1:24,000
1 in. = 2000 ft.

0   0.25   0.5
miles

N

SEE 5942 MAP

38°03'55"

HORINE
RECREATION
AREA

Sugartree Run

CREEK RD

KNOB

Knob Creek

Braeburn Dr

Orchard Brook Dr

Gala Ct

1526

Ln

Wicker

100

38°03'29"

ELMO
LAKE

Cockerel Rd

Lake Elmo Rd

Nalley

Ln

100

900

100

Knob   Creek

40109

2

Knob Creek Cir

Creek

38°03'03"

Knob

1526

Thiry Rd

Rd   100

Klapper

Mt Elmira Rd

3

Smith Farm Rd

Bluelick Creek

1300

SEE 6052 MAP

Brushy   Fork

38°02'37"

100

Mt Elmira Rd   Pinecrest Dr

100

4

Harshfield   Ln

OakCrest

Dr

Trappers

38°02'11"

Mt Elmira Rd

1000

40165

Ln

5

Red Rock Dr   Rd

Johnson Hollow Rd

Trappers Rd

38°01'45"

1000   Eagles

Samuels

Rd

Samuels Ct

300

Mt Elmira Rd

Roution

Wy

Roution

Ferguson Ct

Gravel

Johnson Hollow Rd

6

Creek

Wy

Walls

38°01'19"

100

Hllw

N

Mt Elmira Rd

Pike &
Payne Ln

Wy

Walls

Mattingly Rd

7

Wilderness

Wy

Mitchell

Wy

Walls
Hollow
Rd

200

Indian Trc

A   B   C   D   E

85°47'17"   85°46'44"   85°46'11"   85°45'38"   85°45'58"

SEE 6160 MAP

38°

MAP
6052

1:24,000
1 in. = 2000 ft.

0   0.25   0.5
miles

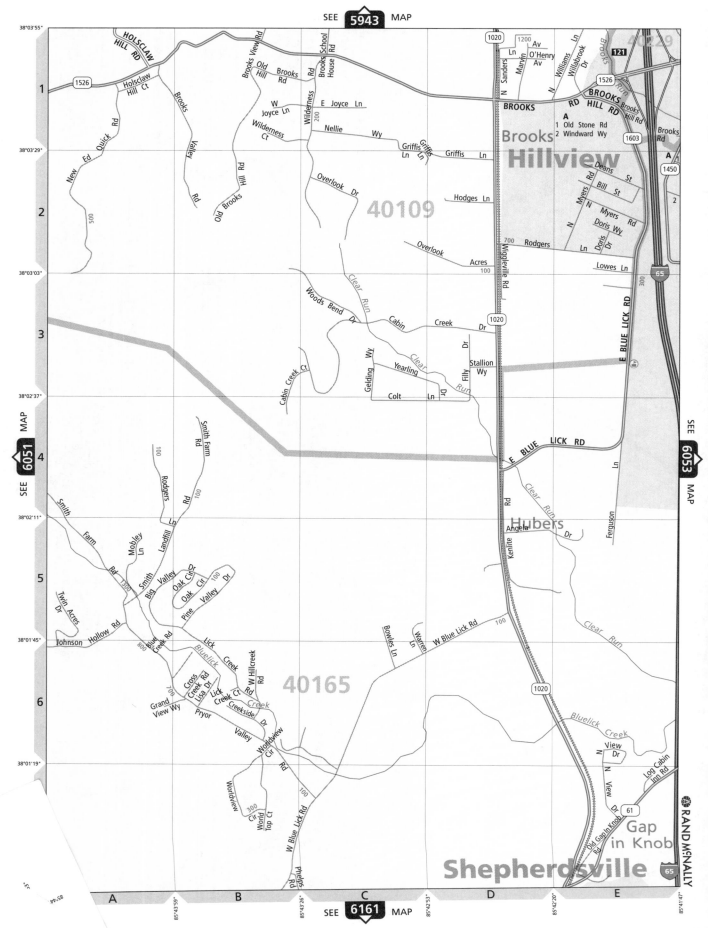

SEE **5943** MAP

SEE **6051** MAP

SEE **6053** MAP

SEE **6161** MAP

HOLSCLAW
HILL RD

Brooks View Rd

Brooks School House Rd

1020

1200
Av
O'Henry Av

N Sanders

N Marvin

N Williams

Willabrook Dr

Brooks Run

121

40229

1526

BROOKS HILL RD

A
1 Old Stone Rd
2 Windward Wy

Brooks Rd

1603

1450

A

2

Brooks
Hillview

40109

1526

Holsclaw Hill Ct

Brooks Valley Rd

Old Hill Brooks Rd

Wilderness

W Joyce Ln

E Joyce Ln

Nellie Wy

Griffis Ln

Griffis Ln

Deans St

Bill St

N Myers Rd

Myers Rd

N Doris Wy

N Doris Dr

Doris Dr

Lowes Ln

Hodges Ln

Overlook Dr

Rodgers

New Ed Quick Rd

Brooks Valley Rd

Old Brooks Hill Rd

Wilderness Ct

Overlook Acres

500

200

700

100

300

I-65

E BLUE LICK RD

Clear Run

Woods Bend Dr

Cabin Creek Dr

1020

Cabin Creek Ct

Gelding Wy

Yearling

Colt Ln

Clear Run

Dr

Filly Dr

Stallion Wy

Smith Farm Rd

Rodgers Ln

100

100

E BLUE LICK RD

Kenlite Rd

Clear Run

Hubers

Angela Dr

Ferguson Ln

Smith Farm Rd

Mobley Ln

Landfill Ln

Smith Big Valley Dr

Oak Cir

Oak Cir

Pine Valley Dr

100

Twin Acres Dr

1300

Johnson Hollow Rd

Blue Creek Rd

800

Lick Creek

Bluelick Creek

Cross Creek Rd

Lisa Dr

Lick Creek Ct

W Hillcreek Rd

Creekside Dr

Grand View Wy

Pryor

Valley

Worldview Cir Rd

700

40165

Bowles Ln

Warren Ln

W Blue Lick Rd

100

1020

Bluelick Creek

Clear Run

View Dr

N View Dr

Log Cabin Inn Rd

61

Old Gap In Knob Rd

Gap in Knob

Worldview Cir

World Top Ct

300

100

W Blue Lick Rd

Phelps Rd

Shepherdsville

RAND McNALLY

65

N

38°03'55"

38°03'29"

38°03'03"

38°02'37"

38°02'11"

38°01'45"

38°01'19"

1

2

3

4

5

6

A   B   C   D   E

85°44'

85°43'58"

85°43'26"

85°42'53"

85°42'20"

85°41'58"

3°

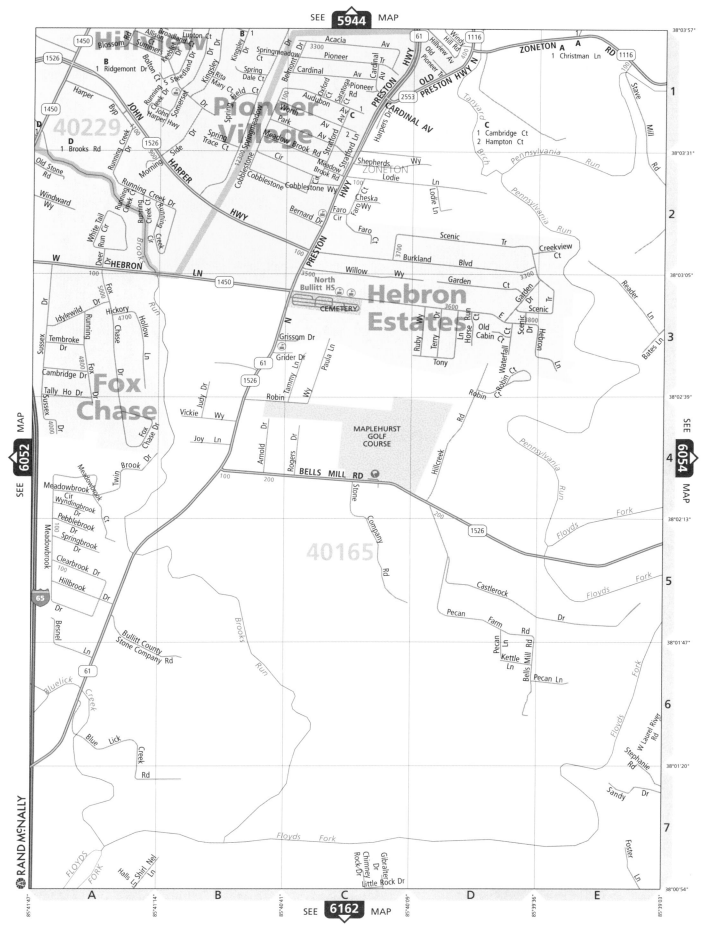

1:24,000
1 in. = 2000 ft.

0   0.25   0.5
miles

MAP
6053

N

SEE 5944 MAP

Hillview

Pioneer Village

40229

Fox Chase

Hebron Estates

ZONETON

Zoneton

North Bullitt HS

CEMETERY

MAPLEHURST GOLF COURSE

40165

BELLS MILL RD

SEE 6052 MAP

SEE 6054 MAP

RAND McNALLY

SEE 6162 MAP

38°03'57"
38°03'31"
38°03'05"
38°02'39"
38°02'13"
38°01'47"
38°01'20"
38°00'54"

1
2
3
4
5
6
7

A   B   C   D   E

MAP
6054

1:24,000
1 in. = 2000 ft.

0   0.25   0.5
miles

SEE ⌄ 5945 ⌄ MAP

40229

40165

40047

Mt
Washington

⟨ 6053 ⟩

SEE 6053 MAP

SEE ⟨ 6055 ⟩ MAP

SEE ⌄ 6163 ⌄ MAP

RAND McNALLY

A   1 Sandy Ln
B   1 Little Kentucky Dr
     2 Meadow Lark Ln

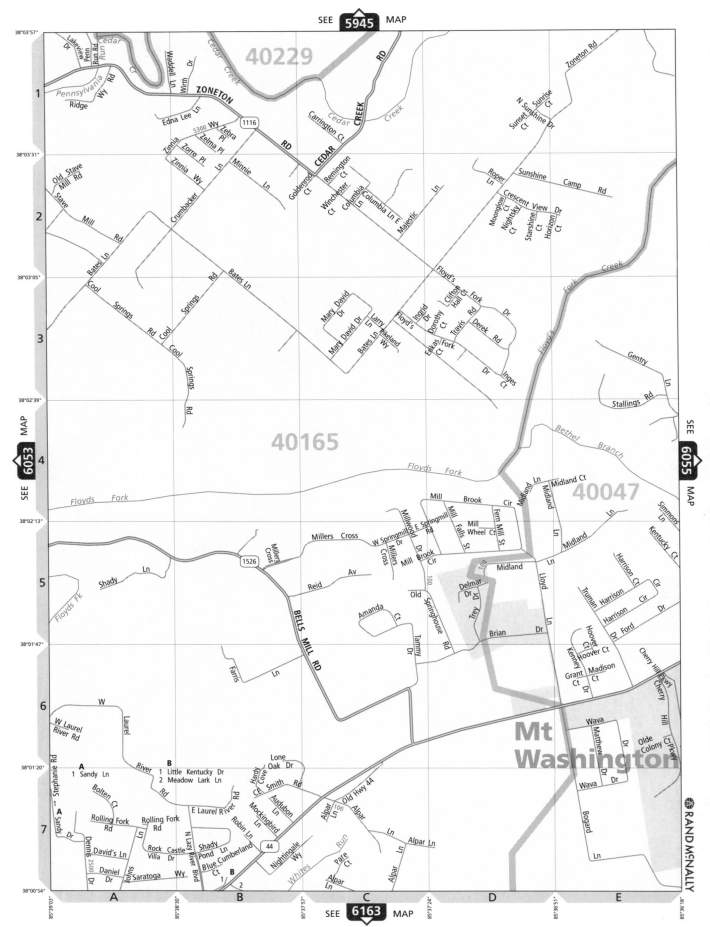

MAP
6055

1:24,000
1 in. = 2000 ft.

0   0.25   0.5
miles

SEE 5946 MAP

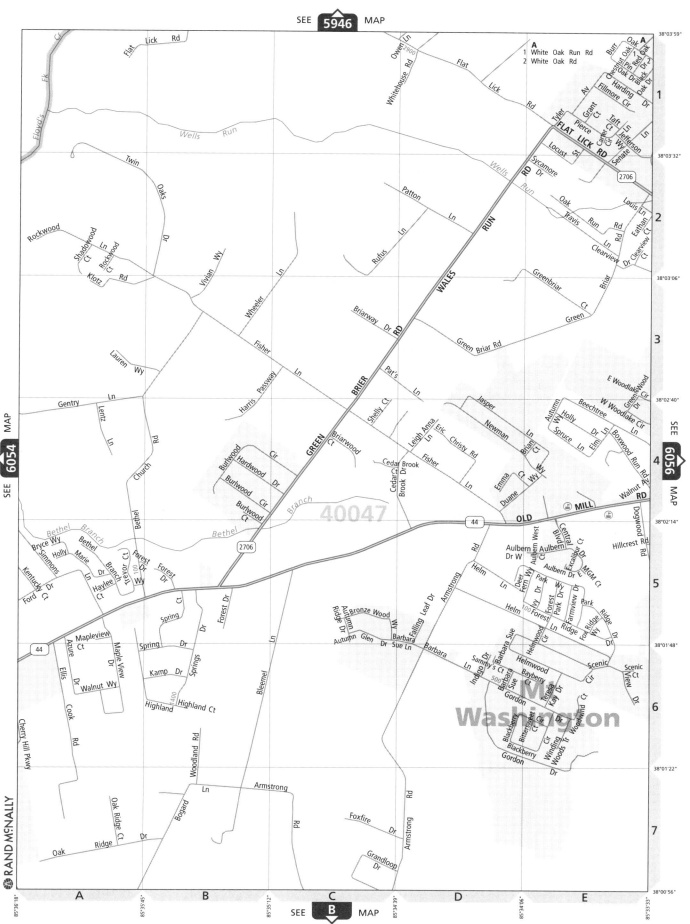

A
1 White Oak Run Rd
2 White Oak Rd

SEE 6054 MAP

SEE 6056 MAP

Mt
Washington

40047

RAND McNALLY

SEE B MAP

38°03'59"
38°03'32"
38°03'06"
38°02'40"
38°02'14"
38°01'48"
38°01'22"
38°00'56"

85°36'18"
85°35'45"
85°35'12"
85°34'39"
85°34'06"
85°33'33"

MAP
6056

1:24,000
1 in. = 2000 ft.

0   0.25   0.5
miles

SEE 5947 MAP

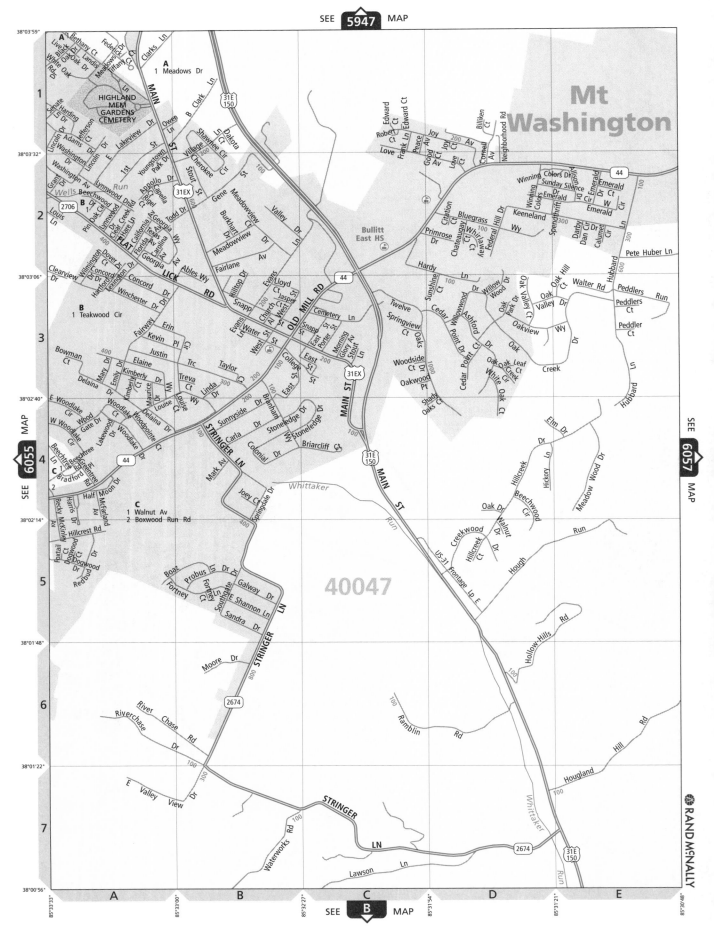

Mt
Washington

40047

SEE 6055 MAP

SEE 6057 MAP

SEE B MAP

A   B   C   D   E

RAND MCNALLY

A
1 Meadows Dr

B
1 Teakwood Cir

C
1 Walnut Av
2 Boxwood Run Rd

38°03'59"
38°03'32"
38°03'06"
38°02'40"
38°02'14"
38°01'48"
38°01'22"
38°00'56"

85°33'33"   85°33'00"   85°32'27"   85°31'54"   85°31'21"

MAP
6057

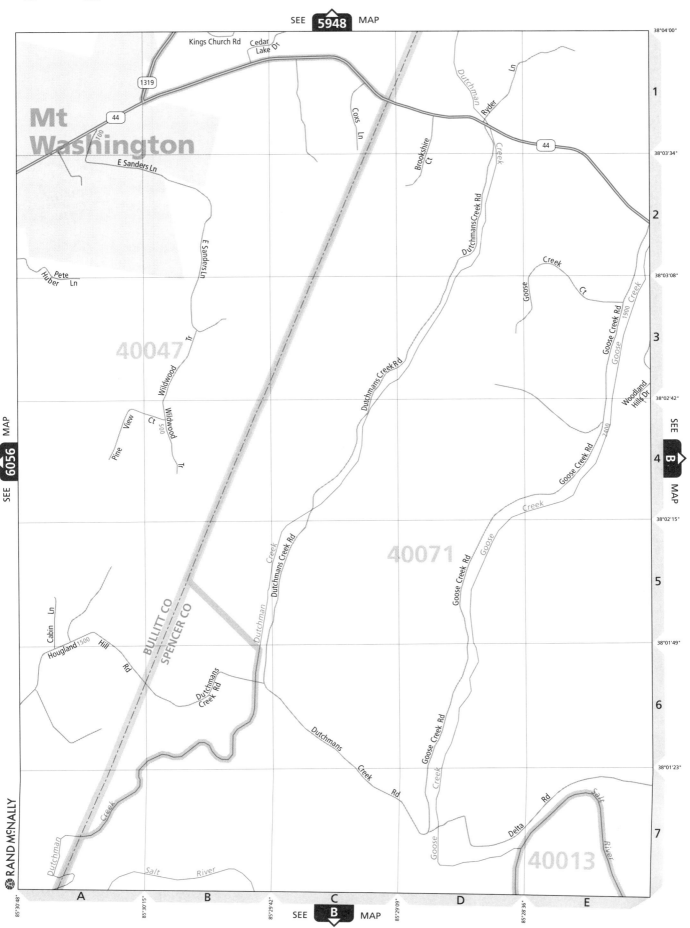

1:24,000
1 in. = 2000 ft.
0   0.25   0.5
miles

N

SEE 5948 MAP

Kings Church Rd
Cedar Lake Dr
1319
44
Mt Washington
100
E Sanders Ln
Coxs Ln
Dutchman
Ryder Ln
Creek
44
Brookshire Ct
Dutchmans Creek Rd
Pete Huber Ln
E Sanders Ln
Goose Creek
Goose
Ct
Goose Creek Rd
1900 Creek
40047
Wildwood Tr
Woodland Hills Dr
Pine View Ct
Wildwood Ct 500
Dutchmans Creek Rd
Goose Creek Rd
2400
Wildwood Tr

SEE 6056 MAP

SEE B MAP

Creek
40071
Goose Creek Rd
Goose
Cabin Ln
Dutchman Creek
Dutchmans Creek Rd
Hougland 1500 Hill Rd
BULLITT CO
SPENCER CO
Dutchmans Creek Rd
Dutchmans Creek Rd
Goose Creek Rd
Dutchmans Creek Rd
Goose
Delta Rd
Salt River
40013
Dutchman Creek
Salt River

RAND McNALLY

SEE B MAP

85°30'48"   85°30'15"   85°29'42"   85°29'09"   85°28'36"

38°04'00"
1
38°03'34"
2
38°03'08"
3
38°02'42"
4
38°02'15"
5
38°01'49"
6
38°01'23"
7

A   B   C   D   E

MAP
6155

1:24,000
1 in. = 2000 ft.

0   0.25   0.5

miles

SEE ▲ B ▲ MAP

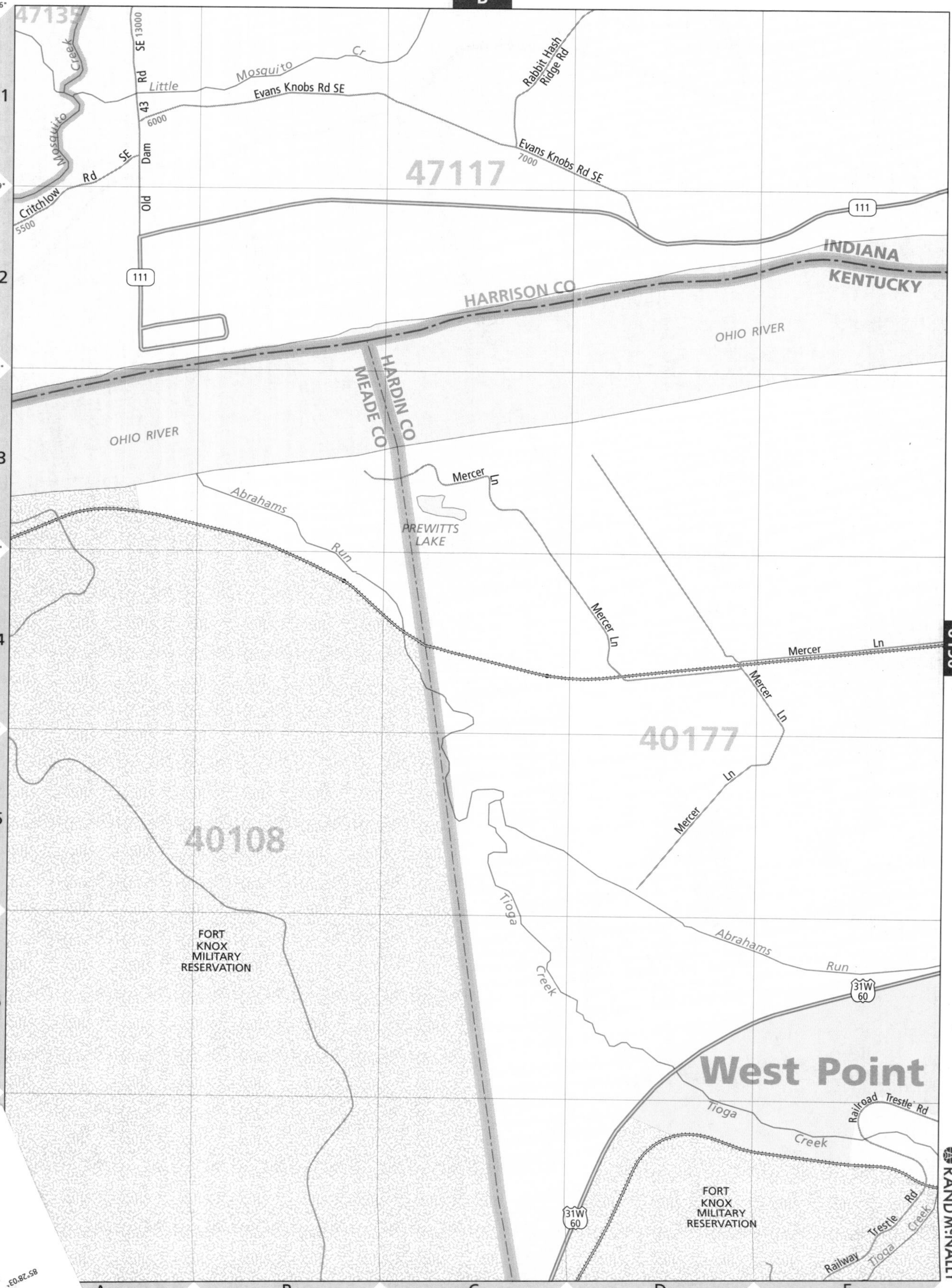

47135

Mosquito Creek

Little Mosquito Cr

SE 13000

Rd 43

6000

Mosquito Cr

Evans Knobs Rd SE

Rabbit Hash Ridge Rd

Evans Knobs Rd SE

7000

47117

38°00'46"

1

Critchlow Rd SE

5500

Old Dam

38°00'19"

111

2

111

INDIANA

KENTUCKY

HARRISON CO

OHIO RIVER

37°59'53"

OHIO RIVER

HARDIN CO

MEADE CO

3

Abrahams Run

Mercer

Mercer

PREWITTS LAKE

37°59'27"

SEE ◄ B MAP

Mercer Ln

Mercer Ln

Mercer Ln

SEE 6156 ► MAP

4

37°59'01"

Mercer Ln

Mercer Ln

40177

5

40108

Tioga Creek

37°58'35"

FORT KNOX MILITARY RESERVATION

Abrahams Run

31W 60

6

West Point

37°58'09"

Tioga Creek

Railroad Trestle Rd

31W 60

FORT KNOX MILITARY RESERVATION

Railway Trestle Rd

Tioga Creek

85°28'03"

86°00'27"

85°59'54"

85°59'21"

85°58'48"

85°58'58"

A   B   C   D   E

SEE 6264 MAP

MAP
6156

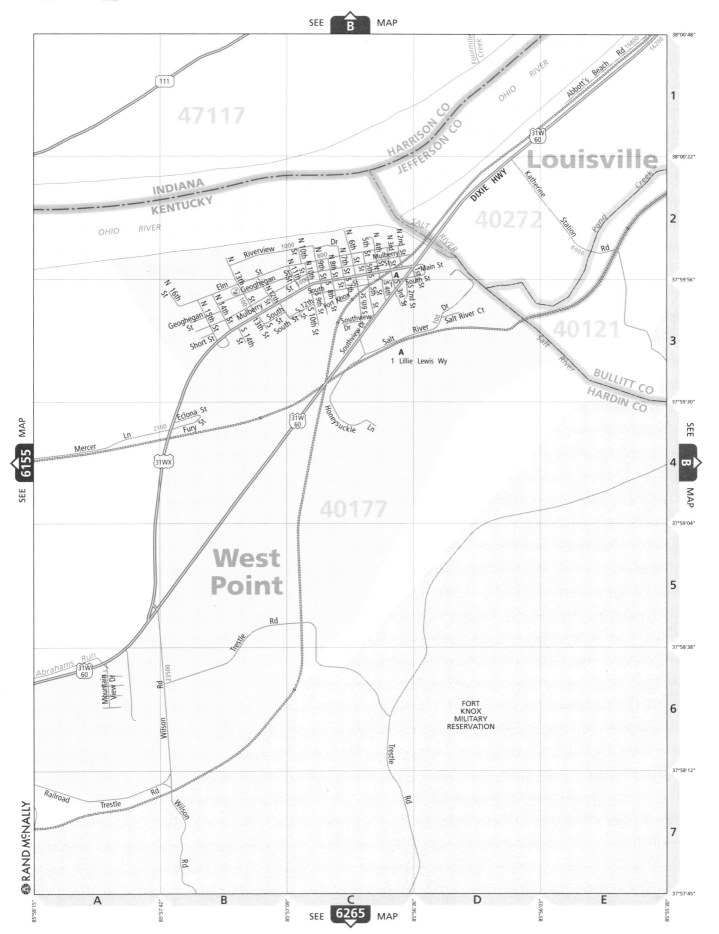

1:24,000
1 in. = 2000 ft.

0   0.25   0.5
miles

SEE B MAP

111

47117

HARRISON CO
JEFFERSON CO

OHIO RIVER

Fourmile Creek

Abbott's Beach Rd 16800   16200

31W 60

DIXIE HWY

Katherine Station Rd

Louisville

40272

Pond Creek

INDIANA
KENTUCKY

OHIO RIVER

SALT RIVER

Riverview 1000   N 10th St
N 13th St   800
N 11th St   N 9th St
N 8th St
N 7th St
N 6th St
N 5th St
N 4th St
N 3rd St
N 2nd St
Dr
Mulberry
1st St
Main St
South St
1000   N 16th St
Elm   Geoghegan   1000
St   S 11th St   S 10th St
Knox
S 9th St   S 8th St
S 7th St
S 6th St
S 5th St
S 4th St
S 3rd St
S 2nd St
A
Geoghegan St   N 14th St
Mulberry   S 13th St   South   S 12th St
South St
South
Southview
Dr
River   100   Salt River Ct
Short St   S 14th St   St   Southview Dr   Salt   River   100
Salt   River

40121

BULLITT CO
HARDIN CO

A
1 Lillie Lewis Wy

Eclona St
2100   Fury St
Ln
31W 60
Honeysuckle Ln

Mercer   Ln
31WX

SEE 6155 MAP

SEE B MAP

40177

West
Point

Trestle Rd

Abrahams Run
31W 60
Mountain View Dr
Wilson Rd   23500

FORT
KNOX
MILITARY
RESERVATION

Trestle Rd

Railroad
Trestle   Rd
Wilson
Rd

SEE 6265 MAP

RAND McNALLY

38°00'48"
38°00'22"
37°59'56"
37°59'30"
37°59'04"
37°58'38"
37°58'12"
37°57'45"

1
2
3
4
5
6
7

A
85°58'15"
85°57'42"
B
85°57'09"
C
85°56'36"
D
85°56'03"
E
85°55'30"

MAP
6160

1:24,000
1 in. = 2000 ft.

0   0.25   0.5
miles

SEE 6051 MAP

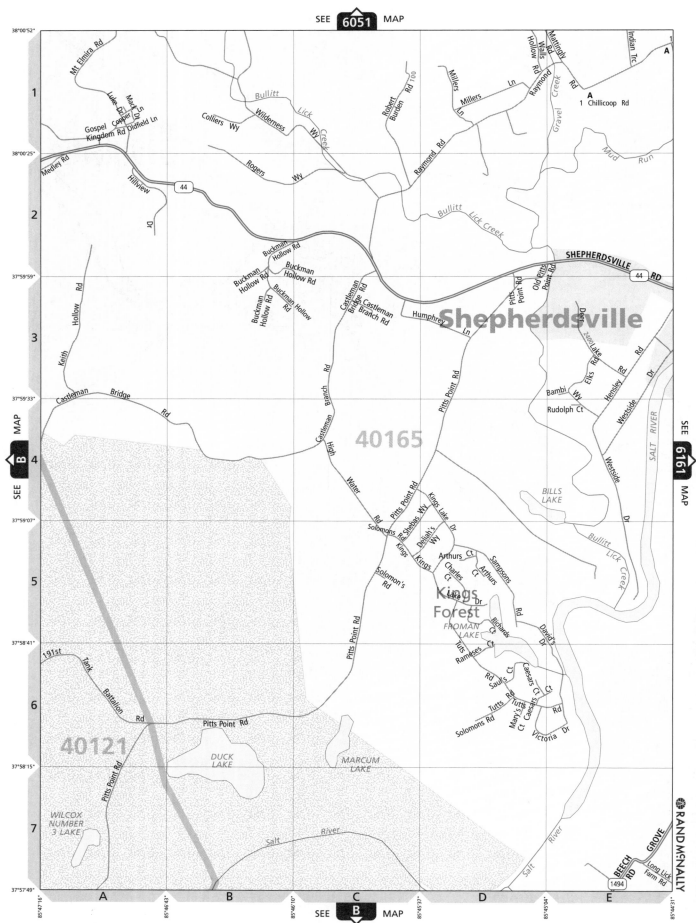

SEE B MAP
SEE 6161 MAP
SEE B MAP

SHEPHERDSVILLE

Shepherdsville

Kings Forest

40165

40121

DUCK LAKE

MARCUM LAKE

WILCOX NUMBER 3 LAKE

FROMAN LAKE

BILLS LAKE

SALT RIVER

Mud Run

Bullitt Lick Creek

Gravel Creek

RAND McNALLY

MAP
6161

SEE 6052 MAP

1:24,000
1 in. = 2000 ft.
0   0.25   0.5
miles

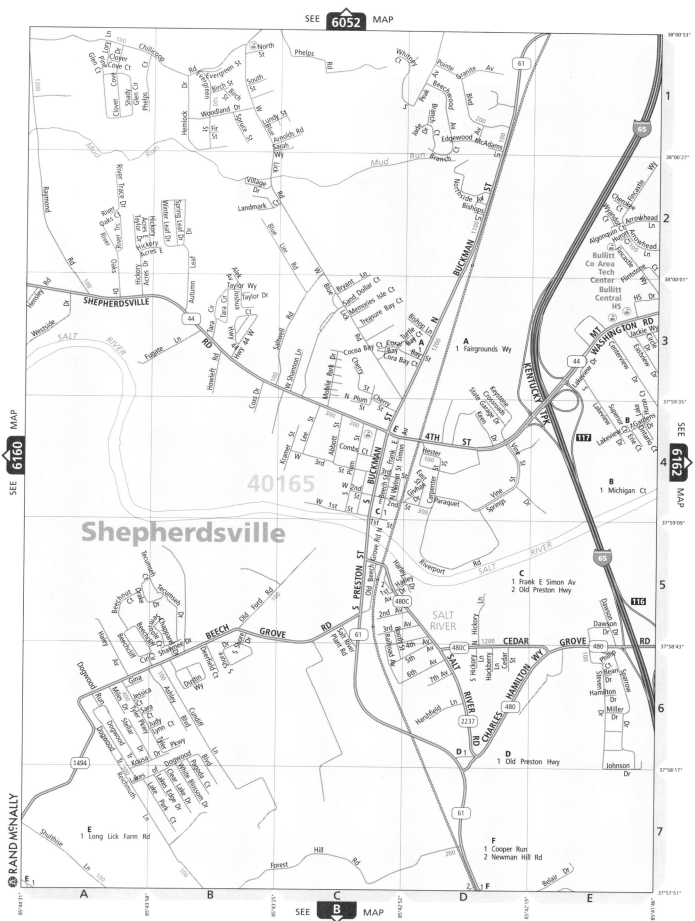

RAND M°NALLY

MAP
6162

1:24,000
1 in. = 2000 ft.

0   0.25   0.5
miles

SEE 6053 MAP

38°00'53"
38°00'27"
38°00'01"
37°59'35"
37°59'09"
37°58'43"
37°58'17"
37°57'51"

SEE 6161 MAP

SEE 6163 MAP

Shepherdsville

40165

RAND MCNALLY

SEE B MAP

A   B   C   D   E

85°41'56"   85°41'13"   85°40'00"   85°40'07"   85°39'34"   85°39'10"

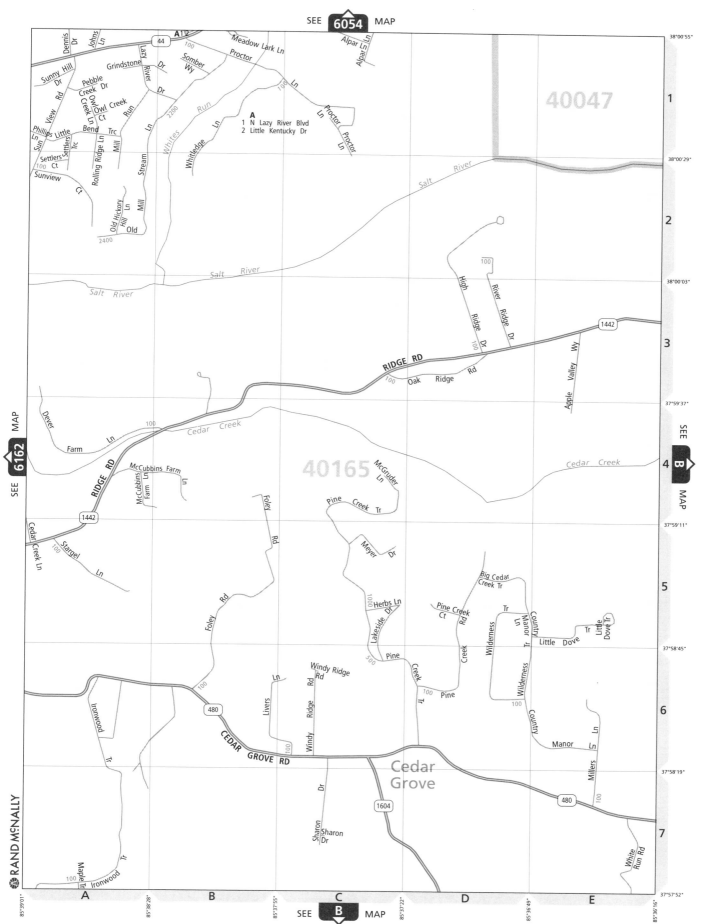

MAP
6163

1:24,000
1 in. = 2000 ft.
0   0.25   0.5
miles

SEE 6054 MAP

A12
44
Dennis Dr
Johns Ln
Meadow Lark Ln
Alpar Ln
Alpar Ln

40047

Sunny Hill Dr
Grindstone
Lazy River Dr
Somber Wy
Proctor
Pebble Creek Dr
Owl Creek Ln
Owl Creek Run
Dr
Proctor Ln

View Rd
2200
Whites
Run
Ln
Proctor Ln

A
1 N Lazy River Blvd
2 Little Kentucky Dr

Phillips Little Ln
Bend
Trc
Mill
Whitledge Dr

1

Settlers Trc
Sun
Settlers Ct
Stream
100
Rolling Ridge Ln
Mill Ln

Salt River

38°00'55"

Sunview Ct
Old Hickory Hill Ln
Old
2400

Salt River

38°00'29"

High Ridge Dr
River Ridge Dr
100

1442

2

Salt River

38°00'03"

Dever Farm Ln
100
Cedar Creek
RIDGE RD
100
Oak Ridge Rd

Apple Valley Wy

3

37°59'37"

McCubbins Farm
McCubbins Farm Ln
McGruder Ln

Cedar Creek

40165

SEE 6162 MAP

SEE B MAP

4

37°59'11"

RIDGE RD
1442
Foley Rd
Pine Creek Tr

Cedar Creek Ln
Stargel Ln
100
Meyer Dr

Big Cedar Creek Tr

5

Foley Rd
Herbs Ln
Lakeside Dr
1000
Pine Creek Ct
Tr
Manor Ln
Country Ln
Little Dove Tr
Tr
Little Dove

Wilderness
Ln

37°58'45"

500
Pine
Creek Tr
100 Pine
Creek
Wilderness

Livers Ln
Windy Ridge Rd
Windy Ridge Rd
Country Ln

6

Ironwood
480
CEDAR GROVE RD
Windy
100

Manor Ln
Millers Ln
100

37°58'19"

Tr
Cedar Grove
Dr
1604
480

7

Maple Tr
100
Ironwood Tr
Sharon Dr
Sharon Dr
White Run Rd

37°57'52"

A   B   C   D   E

85°39'01"   85°38'28"   85°37'55"   85°37'22"   85°36'58"   85°36'16"

SEE B MAP

MAP
6264

1:24,000
1 in. = 2000 ft.
0   0.25   0.5
miles

SEE 6155 MAP

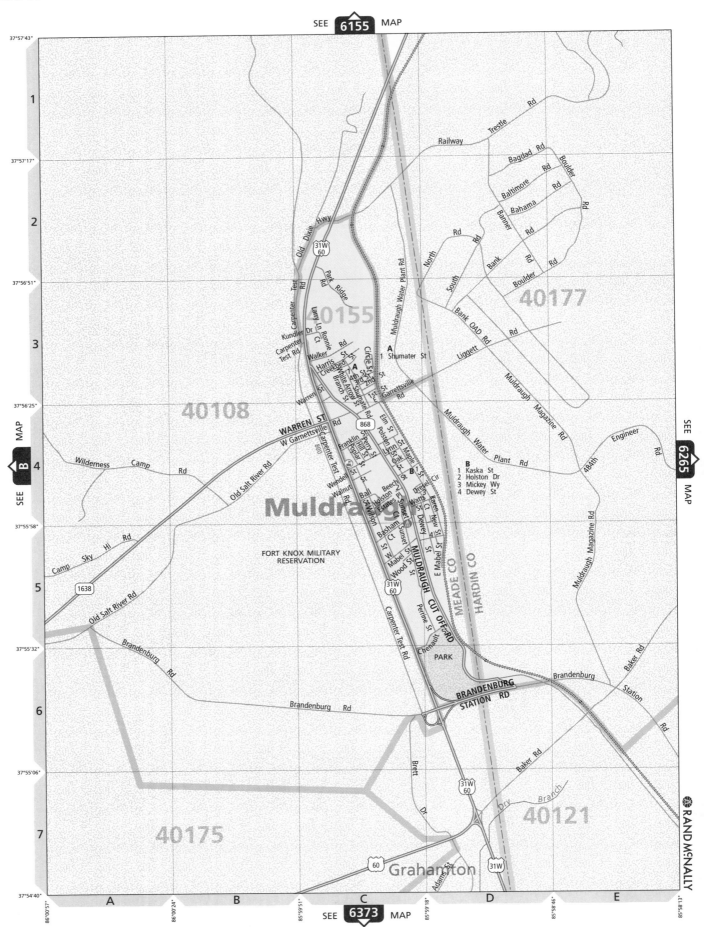

37°57'43"

1

37°57'17"

2

37°56'51"

3

37°56'25"

4

37°55'58"

5

37°55'32"

6

37°55'06"

7

37°54'40"

A   B   C   D   E

86°00'57"   86°00'24"   85°59'51"   85°59'18"   85°58'46"   85°58'13"

SEE 6373 MAP

SEE B MAP

SEE 6265 MAP

40177

40155

40108

Muldraugh

FORT KNOX MILITARY
RESERVATION

40175

40121

Grahamton

BRANDENBURG
STATION RD

PARK

MEADE CO

HARDIN CO

A
1 Shumater St

B
1 Kaska St
2 Holston Dr
3 Mickey Wy
4 Dewey St

RAND MCNALLY

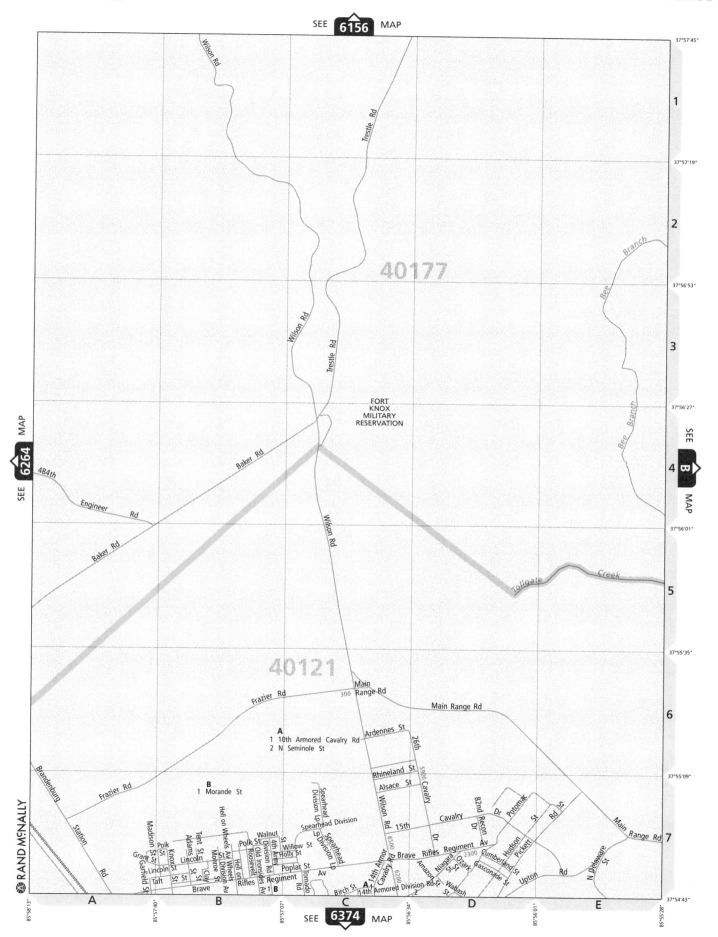

MAP
6265

1:24,000
1 in. = 2000 ft.
0   0.25   0.5
miles

SEE **6156** MAP

SEE **6264** MAP

SEE **B** MAP

37°57'45"
37°57'19"
37°56'53"
37°56'27"
37°56'01"
37°55'35"
37°55'09"
37°54'43"

1
2
3
4
5
6
7

Wilson Rd
Trestle Rd
Bee Branch
Bee Branch

40177

FORT
KNOX
MILITARY
RESERVATION

484th
Engineer Rd
Baker Rd
Baker Rd

Wilson Rd
Trestle Rd
Wilson Rd

Tollgate Creek

40121

Frazier Rd
Main Range Rd
300
Main Range Rd

Brandenburg
Station Rd
Frazier Rd

A
1 10th Armored Cavalry Rd
2 N Seminole St

Ardennes St
26th

Rhineland St
5900 Cavalry

Alsace St

Wilson Rd
15th

Cavalry
82nd Recon
Dr
Potomac
St
Rd

B
1 Morande St

Spearhead Division Lp
Spearhead Division
Spearhead Division Lp
Spearhead Division Lp

Hell on Wheels Av
Madison St
Polk St
Grant St
Garfield St
Taft St
Lincoln St
Knox St
Adams St
Tent St
Clay St
Monroe St
Brave
Walnut St
Polk St
Roosevelt
4th Army
Old Ironsides Av
Division Rd
Willow St
Holly St
Poplar St
Tornado Av
Rifles
Brave
Regiment
B
Birch St
14th Armored Cavalry Rd
14th Armored Division Rd
Amazon St
Niagara St
Ozark St
St
Wabash St
A
2
6500
6200
2300
Recon Dr
Brave
Rifles
Regiment
Cavalry Dr
Hudson St
Pickett
Cumberland St
Gasconade St
Upton St
Rd
N Delaware St
Main Range Rd

SEE **6374** MAP

85°58'13"
85°57'40"
85°57'07"
85°56'34"
85°56'01"
85°55'28"

A   B   C   D   E

MAP
6373

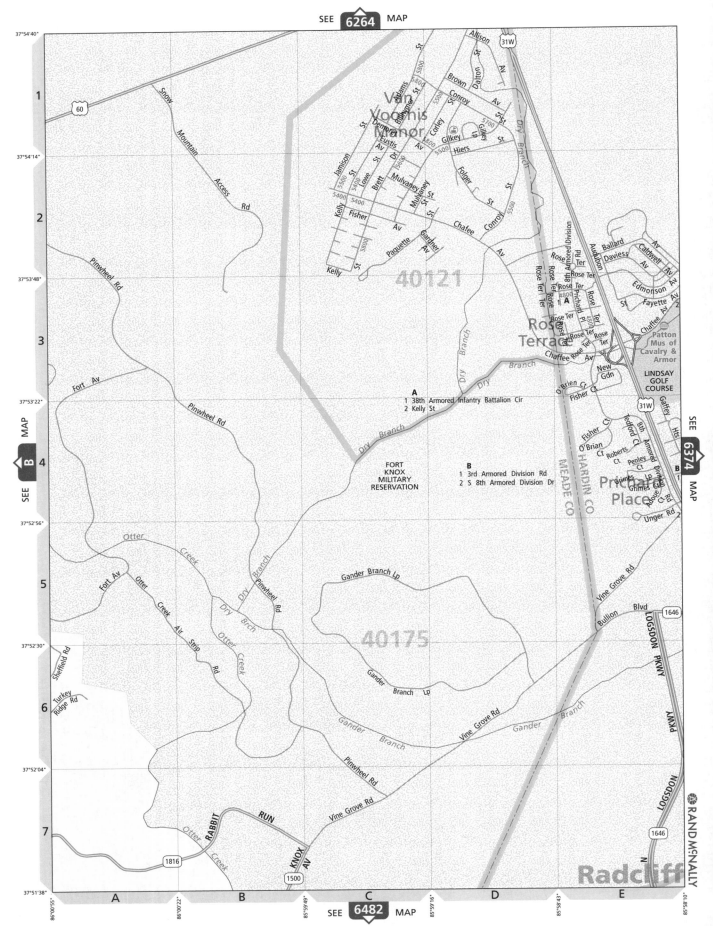

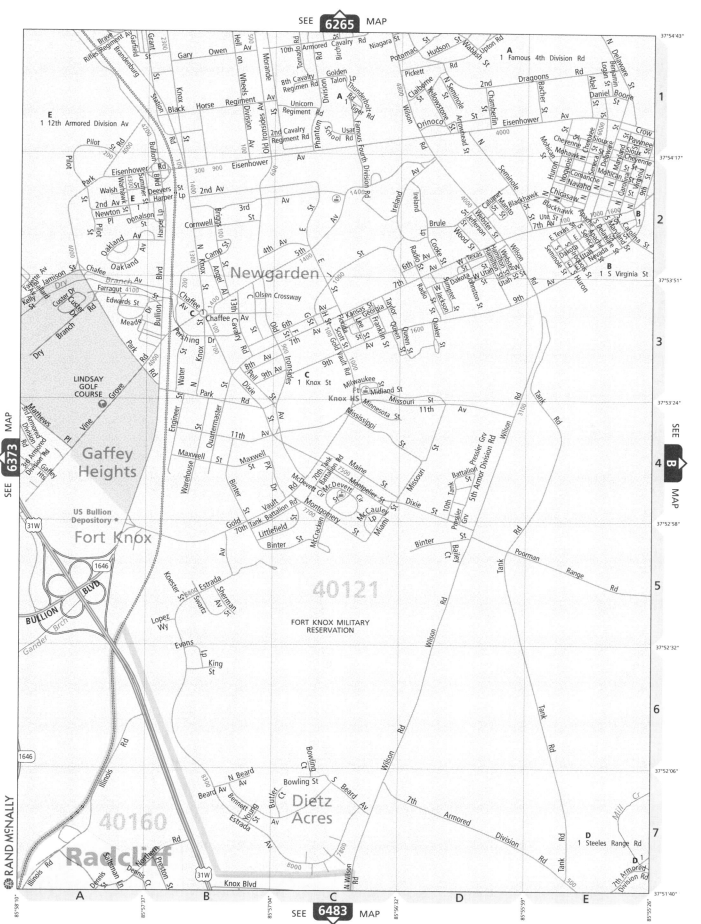

MAP
6482

1:24,000
1 in. = 2000 ft.
0   0.25   0.5
miles

SEE 6373 MAP

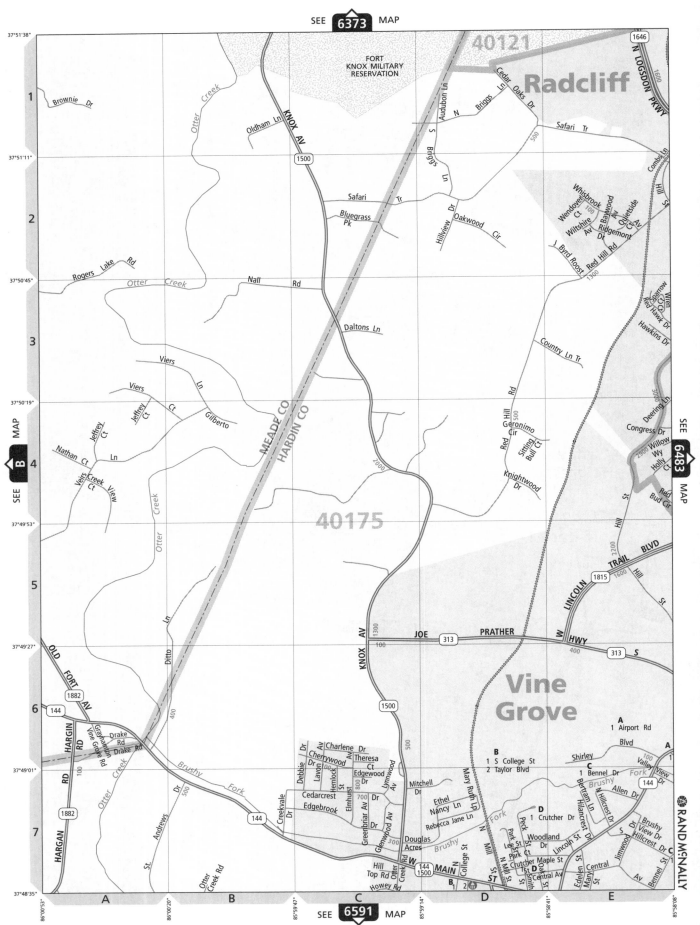

40121

Radcliff

FORT
KNOX MILITARY
RESERVATION

40175

**Vine
Grove**

SEE 6483 MAP

SEE 6591 MAP

RAND McNALLY

MAP
6483

1:24,000
1 in. = 2000 ft.

0   0.25   0.5
miles

SEE 6374 MAP

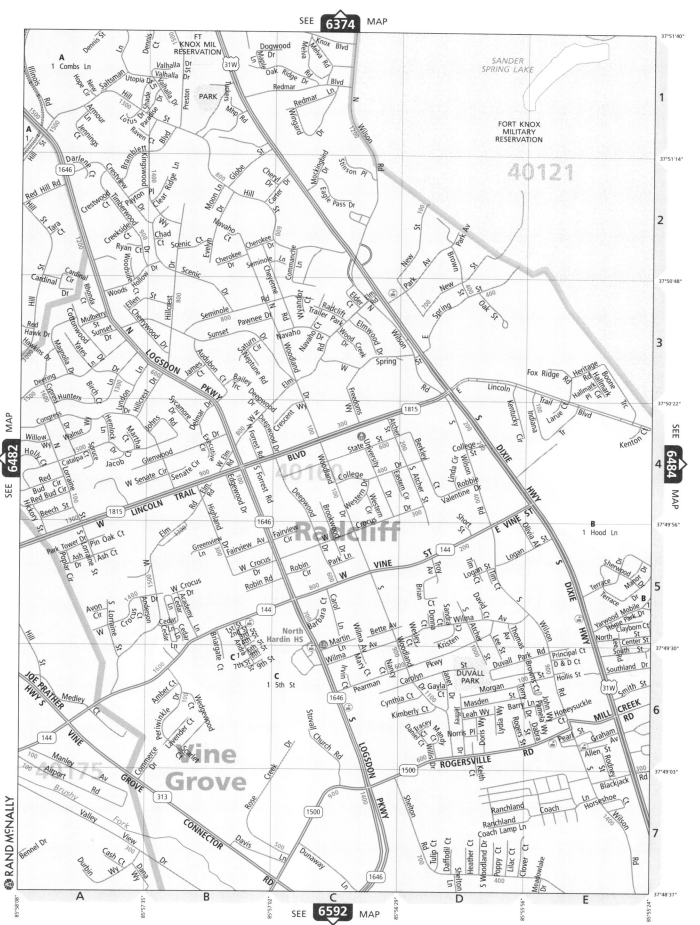

SEE 6482 MAP

SEE 6484 MAP

SEE 6592 MAP

RAND MCNALLY

MAP
6484

1:24,000
1 in. = 2000 ft.

0   0.25   0.5
miles

SEE ▲ B MAP

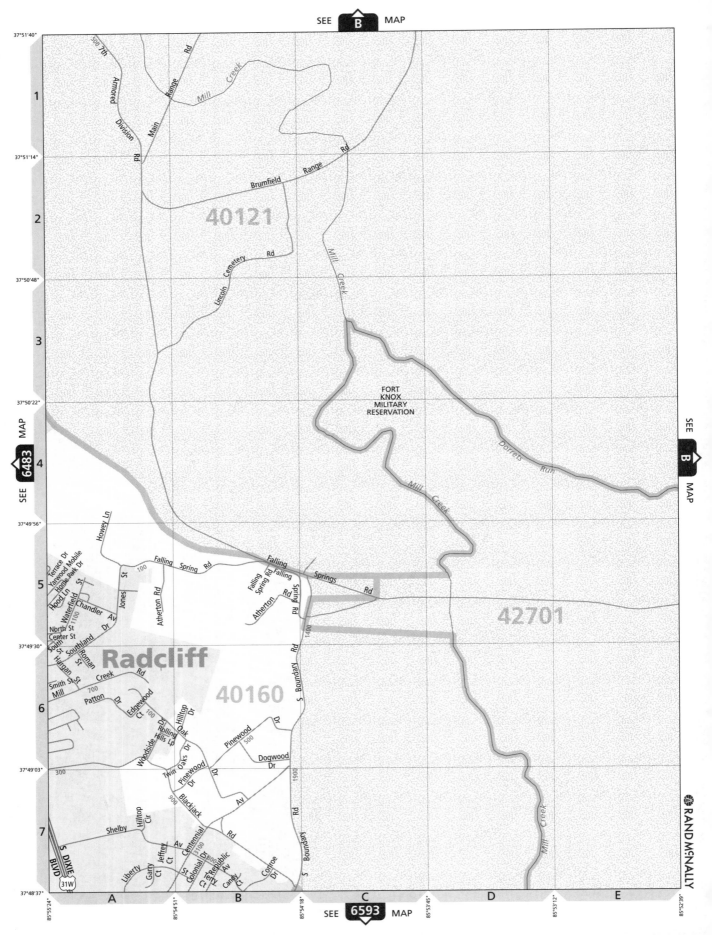

FORT
KNOX
MILITARY
RESERVATION

40121

40160

42701

Radcliff

SEE ◄ 6483 MAP

SEE B ► MAP

SEE 6593 MAP ▼

RAND McNALLY

37°51'40"
37°51'14"
37°50'48"
37°50'22"
37°49'56"
37°49'30"
37°49'03"
37°48'37"

85°55'24"
85°54'51"
85°54'18"
85°53'45"
85°53'12"
85°52'59"

A B C D E

1 2 3 4 5 6 7

Mill Creek
Dorrets Run
Range Rd
Brumfield
Range
Cemetery Rd
Lincoln
Division Rd
Main
Armored
500 7th
Range Rd
Howey Ln
Terrace Dr
Yanwood Mobile
Home Park Dr
Hood Ln
Waterfield
Chandler Av
Jones St
Atherton Rd
Falling Spring Rd
Falling Spring Rd
Falling
Springs Rd
Atherton Rd
North St
Center St
South St
Southland
Roman St
Morgan St
Smith St
Mill Creek Rd
Patton Dr
Edgewood Ct
Hilltop Dr
Rolling Hills Lp
Oak Dr
Woodside Dr
Twin Oaks Dr
Pinewood Dr
Pinewood Dr
Blackjack Rd
Dogwood Dr
Pinewood Dr
Hilltop Cir
Shelby
Liberty Ct
Garry Ct
Jeffrey Ct
Centennial Av
Colonial Dr
Terry Ct
Camp Ct
Republic Av
Conroe Dr
S Boundary Rd
S Boundary Rd
S DIXIE BLVD
31W
100
1100
700
100
500
1900
300
900
1300
800
1400

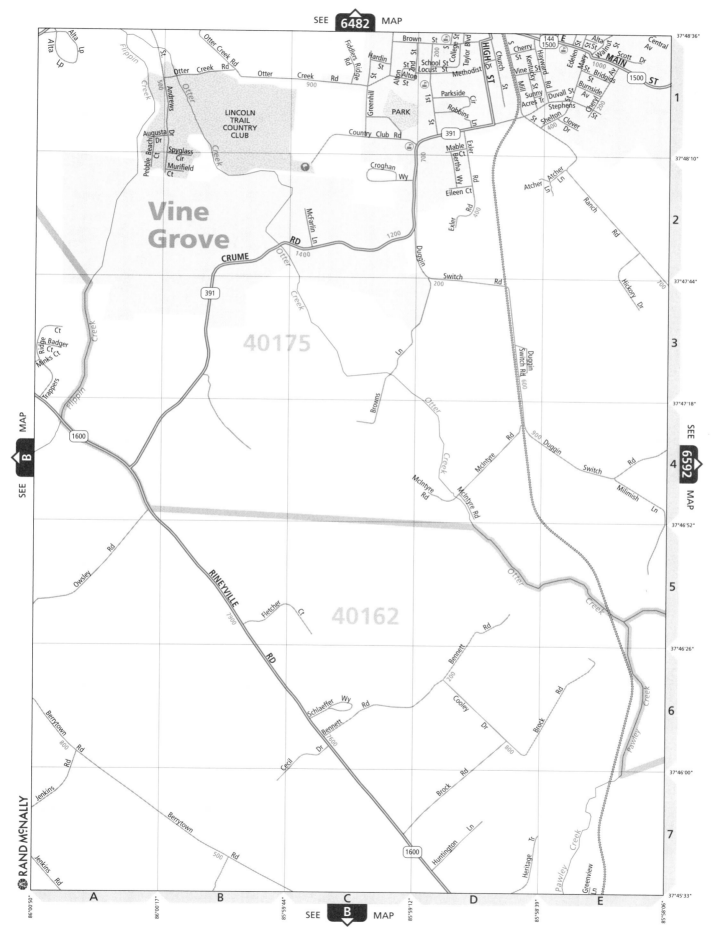

MAP
6592

1:24,000
1 in. = 2000 ft.
0   0.25   0.5
miles

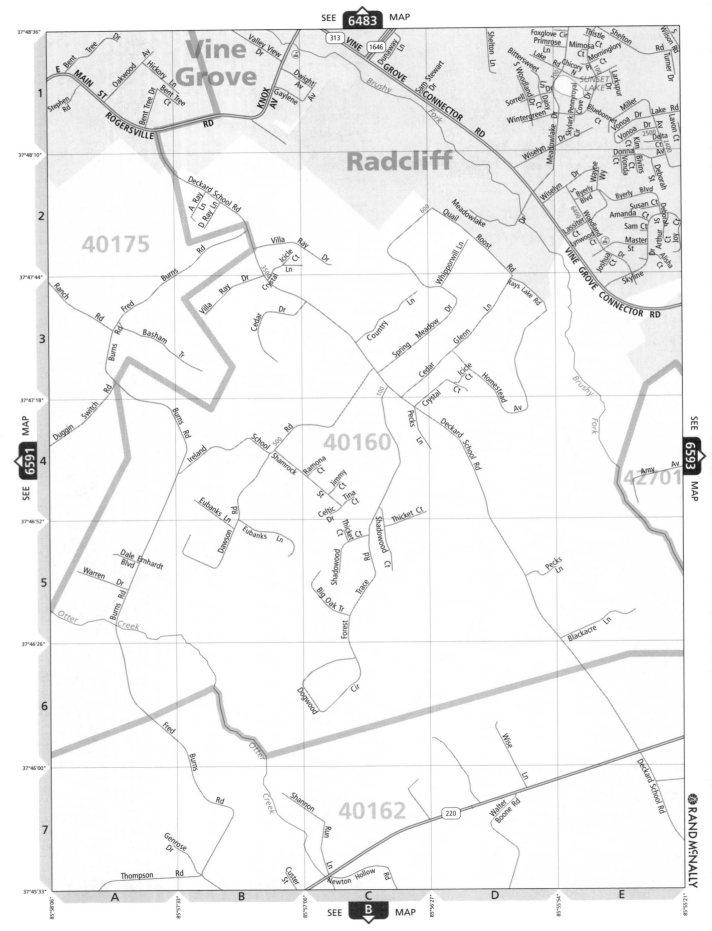

SEE 6483 MAP

37°48'36"

313 VINE
1646

Vine
Grove

Radcliff

40175

40160

40162

40170

42701

SEE 6591 MAP

SEE 6593 MAP

SUNSET
LAKE

37°48'10"

37°47'44"

37°47'18"

37°46'52"

37°46'26"

37°46'00"

37°45'33"

85°58'06"   85°57'33"   85°57'00"   85°56'27"   85°55'54"   85°55'58"

SEE B MAP

RAND McNALLY

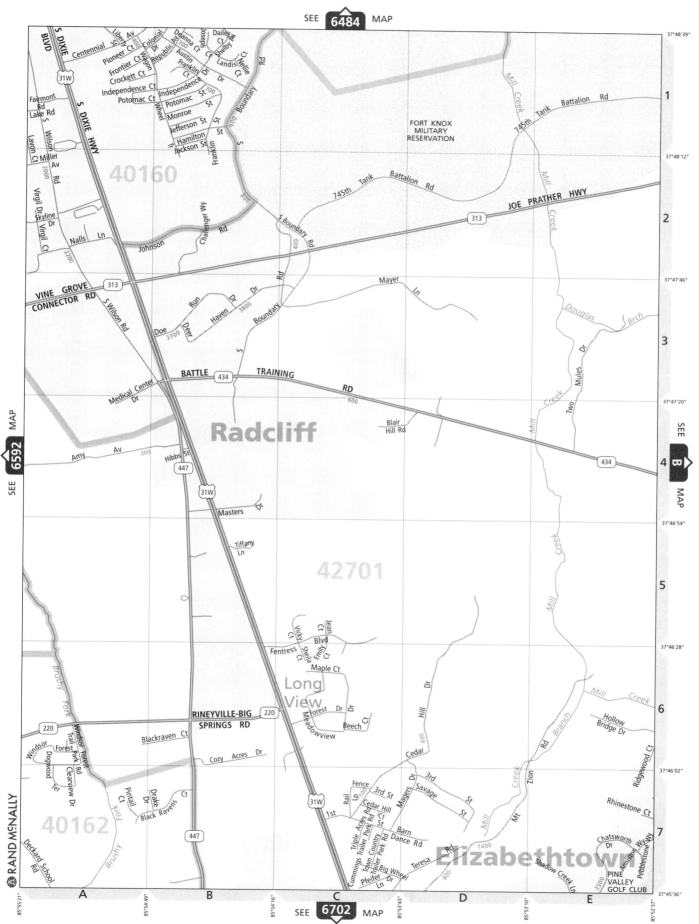

N

1:24,000
1 in. = 2000 ft.
0   0.25   0.5
miles

SEE **6484** MAP

MAP
6593

37°48'39"

1

S DIXIE BLVD
31W
Centennial
Liberty St
Pioneer Ct
Frontier Ct
Crockett Ct
Independence Ct
Potomac Ct
Fairmont Rd
Lake Rd
Wilson Rd
Lavon Ct
Miller Av
Virgil Skyline Dr
Virgil Ct
Nalls Ln

Colonial
Wagon Wheel
Deanna Ct
Republic
Austin Ct
Franklin Ct
Independence St
Potomac St
Monroe St
Jefferson St
Hamilton
Jackson St
Franklin St

Joseph Dr
Dailey
Shelby Ct
Landis Ct
Nellie

Boundary Rd

40160

S DIXIE HWY

Challenger Wy
Rd
Johnson

S Boundary Rd

745th Tank Battalion Rd

FORT KNOX
MILITARY
RESERVATION

Mill Creek

745th Tank Battalion Rd

37°48'12"

2

VINE GROVE
CONNECTOR RD
313
S Wilson Rd

313
Run
Doe
Deer
Haven
Dr
Boundary
Mayer
Ln

JOE PRATHER HWY
313

Douglas Brch

Mill Creek

37°47'46"

SEE **6592** MAP

BATTLE
Medical Center Dr
434
TRAINING RD
600
Blair Hill Rd

Two Miles Dr

Mill Creek

3

Radcliff

Amy Av
Hibbs St
447
31W

434

434

SEE **B** MAP

37°47'20"

4

Masters Dr

Tiffany Ln

42701

37°46'54"

5

Vicky Ct
Jean Ct
Blvd
Emily Ct
Fentress
Sheila Ct
Maple Ct

Mill Creek

37°46'28"

Long View

RINEYVILLE-BIG
220
SPRINGS RD
Blackraven Ct
Cozy Acres Dr
Windsor
Forest
Dogwood Ter
Clearview Dr
Windsor Forest
Trail Park Rd
Pintail Dr
Drake Dr
Black Ravens Ct

220

Forest Dr
Meadowview
Beech Ct

Dr

Hill
400

Cedar
Fence
3rd St
Rail Lp
Cedar Hill
Town Country
Trailer Park Rd
Big Wheel
Pfeifer Ln
1st
Triple Acres Rd
Cummings Trailer Park Rd

Magers Dr
Savage
3rd St
Barn Dance Rd
Teresa

Zion Rd
Branch

Hollow Bridge Dr

Ridgewood Ct

Rhinestone Ct

Mill Creek

6

37°46'02"

Mt Zion Rd
800
1400

Shadow Creek Ln

Chatsworth Dr
Amidon Wy
Pebblestone Wy

PINE VALLEY
GOLF CLUB
2500

7

Elizabethtown

37°45'36"

40162
Brushy Fork
Deckard School Rd
447
Brushy Fork

RAND MCNALLY

A   B   C   D   E

85°55'21"   85°54'49"   85°54'16"   85°53'43"   85°53'10"   85°52'37"

SEE **6702** MAP

MAP
6702

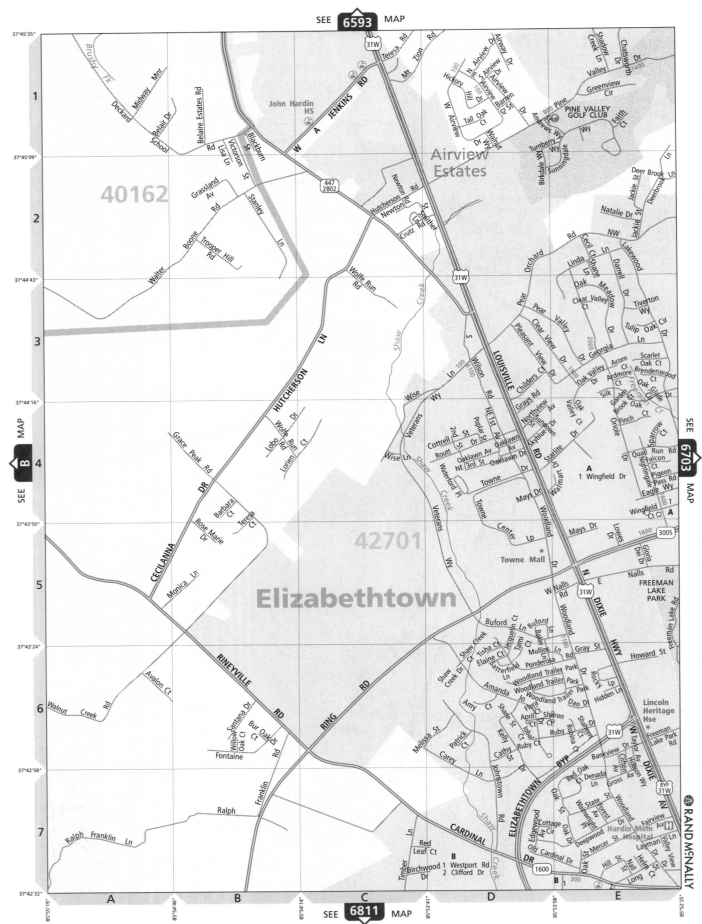

MAP
6703

1:24,000
1 in. = 2000 ft.
0   0.25   0.5
miles

SEE B MAP

37°45'37"
37°45'11"
37°44'45"
37°44'19"
37°43'53"
37°43'27"
37°43'00"
37°42'34"

1
2
3
4
5
6
7

SEE 6702 MAP

SEE B MAP

RAND MCNALLY

42701

Elizabethtown

Tunnel Hill

FREEMAN LAKE PARK

FREEMAN LAKE RESERVOIR

MCCULLUM CEMETERY

A   B   C   D   E

85°52'35"   85°52'02"   85°51'29"   85°50'56"   85°50'24"   85°49'51"

SEE 6812 MAP

MAP
6811

1:24,000
1 in. = 2000 ft.
0   0.25   0.5
miles

SEE 6702 MAP

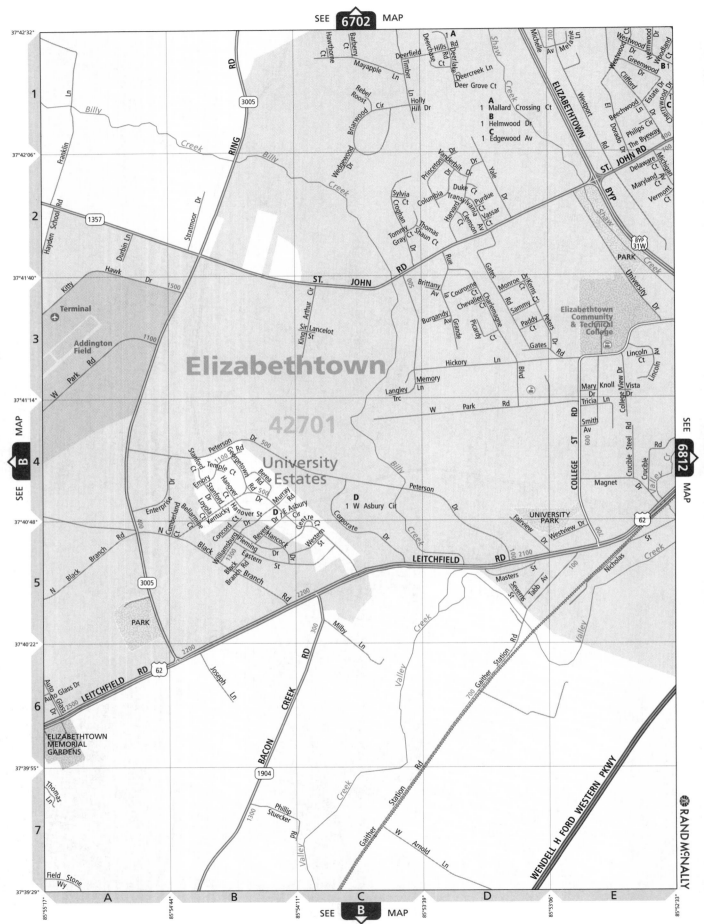

Elizabethtown

42701

University Estates

ELIZABETHTOWN MEMORIAL GARDENS

SEE 6812 MAP

1:24,000
1 in. = 2000 ft.
0   0.25   0.5
miles

MAP
6812

42701

Elizabethtown

RAND MCNALLY

SEE 6811 MAP

SEE B MAP

Cities and Communities

Community Name	Abbr.	County	ZIP Code	Map Page	Community Name	Abbr.	County	ZIP Code	Map Page	Community Name	Abbr.	County	ZIP Code	Map Page
Airview Estates		Hardin	42701	6702	*Goshen	GSHN	Oldham	44026	5292	*Parkway Village	PKWV	Jefferson	40217	5725
*Anchorage	ANCH	Jefferson	40223	5620	Grahamton		Meade	40175	6264	Parkwood		Clark	47130	5398
Auburndale		Jefferson	40214	5833	*Graymoor-Devondale	GYDL	Jefferson	40222	5619	Parkwood		Jefferson	40214	5832
*Audubon Park	ANPK	Jefferson	40213	5725	Greenbriar		Oldham	40031	5404	Petersburg		Jefferson	40218	5726
*Bancroft	BCFT	Jefferson	40222	5509	*Green Spring	GNSP	Jefferson	40241	5509	*Pewee Valley	PWEV	Oldham	40056	5512
*Barbourmeade	BRMD	Jefferson	40241	5510	*Greenville	GNVL	Floyd	47124	5283	*Pioneer Village	PNRV	Bullitt	40229	6053
Beckley		Jefferson	40245	5621	Greenwood		Jefferson	40258	5830	*Plantation	PNTN	Jefferson	40242	5510
Beechland Beach		Jefferson	40059	5400	Gulthrie Beach		Jefferson	40059	5400	Pleasure Ridge Park		Jefferson	40258	5831
*Beechwood Village	BWDV	Jefferson	40207	5618	Hamburg		Clark	47172	5288	*Plymouth Village	PLYV	Jefferson	40207	5618
Belknap Beach		Oldham	40059	5292	--Hardin County	HdnC				*Poplar Hills	PLRH	Jefferson	40213	5726
*Bellemeade	BLMD	Jefferson	40222	5619	Harmony Lake Estates		Oldham	44026	5292	Prather		Clark	47130	5290
*Bellewood	BLWD	Jefferson	40207	5617	Harmony Village		Oldham	40059	5292	Prichard Place		Hardin	40121	6373
Bethany		Jefferson	40272	5940	--Harrison County	HsnC				*Prospect	PROS	Jefferson	40059	5400
*Blue Ridge Manor	BRMR	Jefferson	40223	5619	*Hebron Estates	HBNE	Bullitt	40165	6053	*Radcliff	RDCF	Hardin	40160	6483
Borowick Farms		Oldham	40031	5296	*Heritage Creek	HTCK	Jefferson	40229	5945	*Richlawn	RHLN	Jefferson	40207	5618
*Briarwood	BRWD	Jefferson	40242	5510	*Hickory Hill	HKYH	Jefferson	40241	5510	*River Bluff	RVBF	Oldham	40059	5292
Bridgeport		Harrison	47117	5721	Hidden Lake Estates		Clark	47130	5398	River Ridge		Clark	47111	5290
*Broad Fields	BFLD	Jefferson	40207	5618	Highview		Jefferson	40228	5836	Riverside		Clark	47130	5508
*Broeck Pointe	BKPT	Jefferson	40241	5510	*Hills & Dales	HSDS	Jefferson	40241	5509	*Riverwood	RVWD	Jefferson	40207	5508
Brooks		Bullitt	40109	6052	*Hillview	HLVW	Bullitt	40229	5944	*Robinswood	RBNW	Jefferson	40207	5509
Brownsboro		Oldham	40014	5403	*Hollow Creek	HWCK	Jefferson	40228	5836	*Rolling Fields	RLGF	Jefferson	40207	5508
*Brownsboro Farm	BWNF	Jefferson	40241	5510	*Hollyvilla	HYVA	Jefferson	40118	5942	*Rolling Hills	RLGH	Jefferson	40242	5510
*Brownsboro Village	BWNV	Jefferson	40207	5617	*Houston Acres	HNAC	Jefferson	40220	5727	Rose Terrace		Hardin	40121	6373
Buckner		Oldham	40031	5295	Hubers		Bullitt	40165	6052	St. Dennis		Jefferson	40216	5722
Buechel		Jefferson	40218	5726	*Hunters Hollow	HNTH	Bullitt	40229	5944	St. Joseph		Clark	47143	5287
--Bullitt County	BltC				*Hurstbourne	HTBN	Jefferson	40222	5619	*St. Matthews	STMW	Jefferson	40207	5618
*Cambridge	CMBG	Jefferson	40220	5618	*Hurstbourne Acres	HBNA	Jefferson	40220	5619	*St. Regis Park	SRPK	Jefferson	40220	5618
Cedar Grove		Bullitt	40165	6163	*Indian Hills	INDH	Jefferson	40207	5508	*Sellersburg	SLRB	Clark	47172	5288
Cedar Point		Oldham	40031	5295	*Indian Hills Cherokee	INHC	Jefferson	40207	5509	*Seneca Gardens	SGDN	Jefferson	40205	5617
Centerfield		Oldham	40014	5405	--Jefferson County	JfnC				--Shelby County	SbyC			
Chapel Creek		Floyd	47150	5287	*Jeffersontown	JFTN	Jefferson	40299	5728	*Shepherdsville	SHDV	Bullitt	40165	6161
*Charlestown	CHAN	Clark	47111	5181	*Jeffersonville	JFVL	Clark	47130	5507	*Shively	SVLY	Jefferson	40216	5723
Cherokee Heights		Floyd	47150	5613	Juniper Beach		Jefferson	40059	5509	Silver Lakes Estates		Clark	47129	5397
Cherokee Terrace		Clark	47130	5508	*Keeneland	KNLD	Jefferson	40223	5510	Southern Estates		Floyd	47172	5397
*Cherrywood Village	CYWV	Jefferson	40207	5617	Kings Forest		Bullitt	40165	6160	*South Park View	SPVW	Jefferson	40219	5834
Clark		Shelby	40067	5732	*Kingsley	KGLY	Jefferson	40205	5617	Speed		Clark	47172	5288
--Clark County	ClkC				Knopp		Jefferson	40219	5834	--Spencer County	SpnC			
*Clarksville	CLKV	Clark	47129	5397	*La Grange	LGNG	Oldham	40031	5296	Springdale		Jefferson	40242	5510
Cobbler's Crossing		Floyd	47150	5397	Lakeland		Jefferson	40223	5511	*Springlee	SPLE	Jefferson	40207	5618
*Coldstream	CDSM	Jefferson	40245	5511	*Lanesville	LNVL	Harrison	47136	5610	*Spring Mill	SPML	Jefferson	40228	5836
Confederate Estates		Oldham	40056	5512	*Langdon Place	LDNP	Jefferson	40242	5510	*Spring Valley	SPVL	Jefferson	40241	5509
Countryside		Oldham	40059	5401	*Lincolnshire	LNSH	Jefferson	40220	5618	Steeplechase		Clark	47130	5399
Country Village		Oldham	40014	5404	Lockwood Estates		Oldham	40014	5405	Stites		Bullitt	40165	6048
*Creekside	CKSD	Jefferson	40241	5510	Long View		Hardin	42701	6593	*Strathmoor Gardens	SMRG	Jefferson	40205	5617
*Crestwood	CTWD	Oldham	40014	5512	Longview Beach		Clark	47130	5400	*Strathmoor Manor	SMRM	Jefferson	40205	5617
*Crossgate	CSGT	Jefferson	40222	5509	*Louisville	LSVL	Jefferson	40220	5618	*Strathmoor Village	SMRV	Jefferson	40205	5617
Crystal Lake		Oldham	40031	5297	*Lyndon	LYDN	Jefferson	40222	5619	Sugar Grove		Harrison	47117	5830
Dietz Acres		Hardin	40121	6374	*Lynnview	LYNV	Jefferson	40213	5725	*Sycamore	SCMR	Jefferson	40223	5619
*Douglass Hills	DGSH	Jefferson	40243	5620	*Manor Creek	MRCK	Jefferson	40241	5510	*Ten Broeck	TNBK	Jefferson	40241	5510
*Druid Hills	DRDH	Jefferson	40207	5617	*Maryhill Estates	MYHE	Jefferson	40207	5617	The Meadows		Clark	47130	5398
Duncan		Floyd	47122	5503	--Meade County	MdeC				*Thornhill	TNHL	Jefferson	40222	5509
Echo Valley		Oldham	40031	5404	*Meadowbrook Farm	MBKF	Jefferson	40242	5510	Transylvania Beach		Jefferson	40059	5400
Edwardsville		Floyd	47122	5503	Meadow Lawn		Jefferson	40272	6048	Tucker Station		Jefferson	40299	5729
*Elizabethtown	ELZT	Hardin	42701	6812	*Meadow Vale	MWVL	Jefferson	40242	5510	Tunnel Hill		Hardin	42701	6703
Fairdale		Jefferson	40118	5942	*Meadowview Estates	MVWE	Jefferson	40220	5618	University Estates		Hardin	42701	6811
*Fairmeade	FRMD	Jefferson	40207	5618	*Middletown	MDTN	Jefferson	40243	5620	*Utica	UTCA	Clark	47130	5399
Fern Creek		Jefferson	40291	5837	*Minor Lane Heights	MLHT	Jefferson	40219	5834	Valley Station		Jefferson	40272	5940
*Fincastle	FCSL	Jefferson	40241	5511	*Mockingbird Valley	MKBV	Jefferson	40207	5508	Van Voorhis Manor		Meade	40121	6373
Fishtown		Harrison	47117	5939	*Moorland	MLND	Jefferson	40223	5510	*Vine Grove	VNGV	Hardin	40175	6482
--Floyd County	FydC				*Mt Washington	MTWH	Bullitt	40047	6057	Walford Manor		Clark	47130	5507
Floydsburg		Oldham	40014	5403	*Muldraugh	MRGH	Meade	40155	6264	--Washington County	WasC			
Floyds Knobs		Floyd	47119	5395	*Muldraugh	MRGH	Hardin	40177	6264	Wathen Heights		Clark	47130	5508
*Forest Hills	FTHL	Jefferson	40299	5728	*Murray Hill	MYHL	Jefferson	40241	5510	Watson		Clark	47130	5399
Fort Knox		Hardin	40121	6374	*New Albany	NALB	Floyd	47150	5505	*Watterson Park	WSNP	Jefferson	40218	5726
*Fox Chase	FXCH	Bullitt	40165	6053	Newburg		Jefferson	40218	5726	*Wellington	WLTN	Jefferson	40205	5726
Fraziertown		Oldham	40056	5512	Newgarden		Hardin	40121	6374	*West Buechel	WBHL	Jefferson	40218	5726
Freys Hill		Jefferson	40241	5510	New Watson		Clark	47130	5399	*West Point	WPNT	Hardin	40177	6156
Gaffey Heights		Hardin	40121	6374	*Norbourne Estates	NBNE	Jefferson	40207	5618	*Westwood	WWOD	Jefferson	40242	5510
Galena		Floyd	47119	5393	*Northfield	NHFD	Jefferson	40222	5509	*Whipps Millgate	WPMG	Jefferson	40223	5510
Gap in Knob		Bullitt	40165	6052	*Norwood	NRWD	Jefferson	40222	5618	Whitner		Jefferson	40213	5726
*Georgetown	GEOT	Floyd	47122	5501	Oak Park		Clark	47130	5398	*Wildwood	WDWD	Jefferson	40223	5619
*Glenview	GNVW	Jefferson	40222	5509	Okolona		Jefferson	40219	5835	*Winding Falls	WNDF	Jefferson	40207	5509
Glenview Heights		Jefferson	40222	5509	*Old Brownsboro Place	OBNP	Jefferson	40242	5509	*Windy Hills	WDYH	Jefferson	40207	5509
*Glenview Hills	GNVH	Jefferson	40222	5509	Oldham Acres		Oldham	40059	5292	*Woodland Hills	WDHL	Jefferson	40243	5620
*Glenview Manor	GNVM	Jefferson	40222	5509	--Oldham County	OdmC				*Woodlawn Park	WLNP	Jefferson	40207	5618
Golfview Estates		Clark	47130	5507	*Orchard Grass Hills	ODGH	Oldham	40014	5402	Worthington		Jefferson	40241	5510
*Goose Creek	GSCK	Jefferson	40242	5510	Orell		Jefferson	40272	5939	*Worthington Hills	WTNH	Jefferson	40245	5511

*Indicates incorporated city

List of Abbreviations

Admin	Administration	Cto	Cut Off	Lp	Loop	Ste.	Sainte
Agri	Agricultural	Dept	Department	Mnr	Manor	Sci	Science
Ag	Agriculture	Dev	Development	Mkt	Market	Sci	Sciences
AFB	Air Force Base	Diag	Diagonal	Mdw	Meadow	Sci	Scientific
Arpt	Airport	Div	Division	Mdws	Meadows	Shop Ctr	Shopping Center
Al	Alley	Dr	Drive	Med	Medical	Shr	Shore
Amer	American	Drwy	Driveway	Mem	Memorial	Shrs	Shores
Anx	Annex	E	East	Metro	Metropolitan	Skwy	Skyway
Arc	Arcade	El	Elevation	Mw	Mews	S	South
Arch	Archaeological	Env	Environmental	Mil	Military	Spr	Spring
Aud	Auditorium	Est	Estate	Ml	Mill	Sprs	Springs
Avd	Avenida	Ests	Estates	Mls	Mills	Sq	Square
Av	Avenue	Exh	Exhibition	Mon	Monument	Stad	Stadium
Bfld	Battlefield	Expm	Experimental	Mtwy	Motorway	St For	State Forest
Bch	Beach	Expo	Exposition	Mnd	Mound	St Hist Site	State Historic Site
Bnd	Bend	Expwy	Expressway	Mnds	Mounds	St Nat Area	State Natural Area
Bio	Biological	Ext	Extension	Mt	Mount	St Pk	State Park
Blf	Bluff	Frgds	Fairgrounds	Mtn	Mountain	St Rec Area	State Recreation Area
Blvd	Boulevard	ft	Feet	Mtns	Mountains	Sta	Station
Brch	Branch	Fy	Ferry	Mun	Municipal	St	Street
Br	Bridge	Fld	Field	Mus	Museum	Smt	Summit
Brk	Brook	Flds	Fields	Nat'l	National	Sys	Systems
Bldg	Building	Flt	Flat	Nat'l For	National Forest	Tech	Technical
Bur	Bureau	Flts	Flats	Nat'l Hist Pk	National Historic Park	Tech	Technological
Byp	Bypass	For	Forest	Nat'l Hist Site	National Historic Site	Tech	Technology
Bywy	Byway	Fk	Fork	Nat'l Mon	National Monument	Ter	Terrace
Cl	Calle	Ft	Fort	Nat'l Park	National Park	Terr	Territory
Cljn	Callejon	Found	Foundation	Nat'l Rec Area	National Recreation Area	Theol	Theological
Cmto	Caminito	Frwy	Freeway	Nat'l Wld Ref	National Wildlife Refuge	Thwy	Throughway
Cm	Camino	Gdn	Garden	Nat	Natural	Toll Fy	Toll Ferry
Cap	Capitol	Gdns	Gardens	NAS	Naval Air Station	TIC	Tourist Information Center
Cath	Cathedral	Gen Hosp	General Hospital	Nk	Nook	Trc	Trace
Cswy	Causeway	Gln	Glen	N	North	Trfwy	Trafficway
Cem	Cemetery	GC	Golf Course	Orch	Orchard	Tr	Trail
Ctr	Center	Grn	Green	Ohwy	Outer Highway	Tun	Tunnel
Ctr	Centre	Grds	Grounds	Ovl	Oval	Tpk	Turnpike
Cir	Circle	Grv	Grove	Ovlk	Overlook	Unps	Underpass
Crlo	Circulo	Hbr	Harbor/Harbour	Ovps	Overpass	Univ	University
CH	City Hall	Hvn	Haven	Pk	Park	Vly	Valley
Clf	Cliff	HQs	Headquarters	Pkwy	Parkway	Vet	Veterans
Clfs	Cliffs	Ht	Height	Pas	Paseo	Vw	View
Clb	Club	Hts	Heights	Psg	Passage	Vil	Village
Cltr	Cluster	HS	High School	Pass	Passenger	Wk	Walk
Col	Coliseum	Hwy	Highway	Pth	Path	Wall	Wall
Coll	College	Hl	Hill	Pn	Pine	Wy	Way
Com	Common	Hls	Hills	Pns	Pines	W	West
Coms	Commons	Hist	Historical	Pl	Place	WMA	Wildlife Management Area
Comm	Community	Hllw	Hollow	Pln	Plain		
Co.	Company	Hosp	Hospital	Plns	Plains		
Cons	Conservation	Hse	House	Plgnd	Playground		
Conv & Vis Bur	Convention and Visitors Bureau	Ind Res	Indian Reservation	Plz	Plaza		
Cor	Corner	Info	Information	Pt	Point		
Cors	Corners	Inst	Institute	Pnd	Pond		
Corp	Corporation	Int'l	International	PO	Post Office		
Corr	Corridor	I	Island	Pres	Preserve		
Cte	Corte	Is	Islands	Prov	Provincial		
CC	Country Club	Isl	Isle	Rwy	Railway		
Co	County	Jct	Junction	Rec	Recreation		
Ct	Court	Knl	Knoll	Reg	Regional		
Ct Hse	Court House	Knls	Knolls	Res	Reservoir		
Cts	Courts	Lk	Lake	Rst	Rest		
Cr	Creek	Lndg	Landing	Rdg	Ridge		
Cres	Crescent	Ln	Lane	Rd	Road		
Cross	Crossing	Lib	Library	Rds	Roads		
Curv	Curve	Ldg	Lodge	St.	Saint		

INDEX 3
Louisville Metro Street Index
SR-434 Battle Training

STREET Block City ZIP Map# Grid

HIGHWAYS

ALT - Alternate Route
BUS - Business Route
CO - County Highway/Road
FM - Farm To Market Road
HIST - Historic Highway
I - Interstate Highway
LP - State Loop
P - Provincial Highway
PK - Park & Recreation Road
RTE - Other Route
SPR - State Spur
SR - State Route/Highway
US - United States Highway

I-64
- FydC - 5502 B6
- FydC - 5503 D3
- FydC - 5504 A3
- GEOT - 5502 E5
- HsnC - 5501 D7
- HsnC - 5502 A7
- HsnC - 5610 A2
- HTBN - 5619 A6
- JfnC - 5617 B4
- JFTN - 5619 D7
- JFTN - 5620 A7
- LSVL - 5505 E6
- LSVL - 5506 A7
- LSVL - 5615 B1
- LSVL - 5616 A1
- LSVL - 5617 E5
- LSVL - 5618 A5
- LSVL - 5619 D7
- LSVL - 5620 A7
- LSVL - 5621 A7
- LSVL - 5622 A7
- LSVL - 5731 E1
- LSVL - 5732 B1
- MDTN - 5620 E7
- MDTN - 5621 A7
- NALB - 5504 D3
- NALB - 5505 C7
- SbyC - 5732 B1
- SRPK - 5618 D5
- STMW - 5617 E5
- STMW - 5618 B5
I-64 Sherman Minton Br
- LSVL - 5505 B6
- NALB - 5505 B5
I-65
- BltC - 5943 E6
- BltC - 6052 E6
- BltC - 6053 A5
- BltC - 6161 E5
- BltC - 6162 A1
- ClkC - 5288 D7
- ClkC - 5397 D1
- ClkC - 5506 D4
- CLKV - 5397 E5
- CLKV - 5506 E7
- ELZT - 6812 E1
- HdnC - 6812 E2
- HLVW - 5943 E6
- HLVW - 6052 E7
- HLVW - 6053 A5
- JFVL - 5506 E7
- JFVL - 5615 E1
- LSVL - 5615 E6
- LSVL - 5616 A2
- LSVL - 5724 E2
- LSVL - 5725 C7
- LSVL - 5834 D3
- LSVL - 5943 E1
- SHDV - 6161 E1
- SHDV - 6162 A7
- SLRB - 5288 D7
I-65 John F Kennedy Mem Br
- JFVL - 5506 E7
- JFVL - 5615 E1
- LSVL - 5615 E1
- LSVL - 5616 A1
I-65 Kentucky Tpk
- BltC - 6161 E5
- BltC - 6162 A7
- SHDV - 6161 E5
- SHDV - 6162 A7
I-71
- CTWD - 5402 E5
- CTWD - 5403 A5
- GNVH - 5509 C4
- GNVW - 5508 E4
- GNVW - 5509 A4
- INDH - 5508 E4
- LGNG - 5296 E4
- LGNG - 5297 A3
- LSVL - 5401 E7
- LSVL - 5402 A7
- LSVL - 5507 E7
- LSVL - 5508 E4
- LSVL - 5509 E3
- LSVL - 5510 E1
- LSVL - 5616 A2
- NHFD - 5509 B4
- OdmC - 5295 E7
- OdmC - 5296 E4
- OdmC - 5297 A3
- OdmC - 5402 E5
- OdmC - 5403 E3
- OdmC - 5404 A2
- SPVL - 5509 C4
I-264
- BWDV - 5618 D2
- GYDL - 5509 C7
- LSVL - 5505 D7
- LSVL - 5509 B6
- LSVL - 5614 D1
- LSVL - 5617 E7
- LSVL - 5618 C6
- LSVL - 5723 E5
- LSVL - 5724 D4
I-264
- LSVL - 5725 E3
- LSVL - 5726 A3
- NHFD - 5509 C7
- STMW - 5509 C7
- STMW - 5618 B6
- SVLY - 5723 A2
- WDYH - 5509 C7
- WDYH - 5618 A7
- WLNP - 5618 A7
- WNDF - 5509 B6
- WSNP - 5726 A3
I-264 Henry Watterson Expwy
- BWDV - 5618 D2
- GYDL - 5509 C7
- LSVL - 5509 B6
- LSVL - 5617 E7
- LSVL - 5618 B6
- LSVL - 5723 E5
- LSVL - 5724 C4
- LSVL - 5725 C4
- LSVL - 5726 A3
- NHFD - 5509 B6
- STMW - 5509 C7
- STMW - 5618 D4
- SVLY - 5723 C5
- WDYH - 5509 C7
- WDYH - 5618 A7
- WLNP - 5618 A7
- WSNP - 5726 A3
I-265
- ClkC - 5397 A4
- CLKV - 5397 D4
- FydC - 5395 E7
- FydC - 5396 E4
- FydC - 5397 C4
- JFVL - 5397 D4
- LSVL - 5510 C1
- LSVL - 5511 A3
- LSVL - 5512 B7
- LSVL - 5621 B6
- LSVL - 5729 E7
- LSVL - 5730 A6
- LSVL - 5835 E7
- LSVL - 5836 B7
- LSVL - 5837 A6
- LSVL - 5838 A4
- LSVL - 5944 B1
- MDTN - 5621 B6
- NALB - 5395 E7
- NALB - 5396 D4
- NALB - 5504 E1
I-265 Gene Snyder Frwy
- LSVL - 5510 E3
- LSVL - 5511 E5
- LSVL - 5512 B7
- LSVL - 5621 B1
- LSVL - 5729 E7
- LSVL - 5730 A6
- LSVL - 5835 E7
- LSVL - 5836 A7
- LSVL - 5837 A6
- LSVL - 5838 A4
- LSVL - 5944 B1
- MDTN - 5621 B6
I-265 Lee H Hamilton Hwy
- ClkC - 5397 A4
- CLKV - 5397 D4
- FydC - 5395 E7
- FydC - 5396 A6
- FydC - 5397 C4
- JFVL - 5397 D4
- NALB - 5395 E7
- NALB - 5396 D4
- NALB - 5504 E1
SR-3
- ClkC 47111 5181 E5
100 CHAN 47111 5181 D1
SR-3 Market St
100 CHAN 47111 5181 D1
SR-11
- FydC 47117 5721 A2
- FydC 47136 5611 E7
- FydC 47136 5721 A2
SR-22
- ODGH 40014 5511 E1
2200 OdmC 40014 5405 C4
4400 OdmC 40014 5404 E4
4900 CSGT 40222 5509 C6
4900 LSVL 40222 5509 C6
4900 NHFD 40222 5509 B6
5900 CTWD 40014 5404 E5
6700 CTWD 40014 5403 E7
6700 TNHL 40222 5509 D5
6800 TNHL 40241 5509 D5
6900 LSVL 40241 5509 C6
6900 LSVL 40242 5509 C6
7000 PWEV 40014 5403 D7
7100 OBNP 40242 5509 C6
7100 OdmC 40014 5403 C7
7100 PWEV 40056 5403 C7
7200 OBNP 40241 5509 C6
7200 OdmC 40014 5512 C1
7200 PWEV 40014 5512 B1
7200 PWEV 40056 5512 C1
7300 SPVL 40241 5509 C6
7300 SPVL 40242 5509 C6
7600 LSVL 40241 5510 D2
7600 LSVL 40242 5510 A4
7600 SPVL 40241 5510 A4
7600 SPVL 40242 5510 A4
8000 BRMD 40241 5510 A4
8100 BRMD 40242 5510 B4
8100 BWNF 40241 5510 B3
8400 BWNF 40242 5510 B3
8600 TNBK 40241 5510 C3
10000 LSVL 40241 5511 E1
10900 LSVL 40245 5511 C1
11500 CDSM 40241 5511 C1
11500 CDSM 40245 5511 C1
11600 CDSM 40014 5511 D1
11600 JfnC 40014 5511 D1
SR-22 Ballardsville Rd
- CTWD 40014 5404 A7
- ODGH 40014 5511 E1
6700 CTWD 40014 5403 E7
7000 PWEV 40014 5403 D7
7100 OdmC 40014 5403 C7
7100 PWEV 40056 5403 C7
7200 OdmC 40014 5512 C1
7200 PWEV 40014 5512 B1
7200 PWEV 40056 5512 C1
10000 LSVL 40241 5510 E1
10000 LSVL 40241 5511 E1
10900 LSVL 40245 5511 C1
11500 CDSM 40241 5511 C1
11500 CDSM 40245 5511 C1
11600 CDSM 40014 5511 D1
11600 JfnC 40014 5511 D1
SR-22 Brownsboro Rd
4900 CSGT 40222 5509 C6
4900 LSVL 40222 5509 C6
4900 NHFD 40222 5509 B6
6700 TNHL 40222 5509 D5
6800 TNHL 40241 5509 D5
6900 LSVL 40241 5509 C6
6900 LSVL 40242 5509 C6
7100 OBNP 40242 5509 C6
7200 OBNP 40241 5509 C6
7300 SPVL 40241 5509 C6
7300 SPVL 40242 5509 C6
7600 LSVL 40241 5510 D2
7600 LSVL 40242 5510 A4
7600 SPVL 40241 5510 A4
7600 SPVL 40242 5510 A4
8000 BRMD 40241 5510 A4
8100 BRMD 40242 5510 B4
8100 BWNF 40241 5510 B3
8400 BWNF 40242 5510 B3
8600 TNBK 40241 5510 C3
SR-22 Dogwood Ln
- CTWD 40014 5404 E5
SR-44
- BltC 40047 6054 B7
- BltC 40047 6056 D2
- BltC 40047 6057 E1
- BltC 40071 6057 E1
- BltC 40165 6048 B7
- BltC 40165 6054 C7
- BltC 40165 6160 B2
- BltC 40165 6163 B1
- LSVL 40272 6048 B7
- MTWH 40047 6054 B7
- MTWH 40047 6057 B1
- MTWH 40165 6054 E6
- SHDV 40165 6160 E2
100 MTWH 40047 6056 E2
500 BltC 40047 6055 A6
500 MTWH 40047 6055 D5
2100 SHDV 40165 6161 E3
2100 SHDV 40165 6162 E1
4200 BltC 40165 6162 B2
SR-44 W
10600 BltC 40165 6048 C7
SR-44 E 4th St
1000 SHDV 40165 6161 C4
SR-44 Mt Washington Rd
2100 SHDV 40165 6161 E3
2100 SHDV 40165 6162 E1
4200 BltC 40165 6162 B2
SR-44 Old Mill Rd
- BltC 40047 6056 D2
100 MTWH 40047 6056 B3
500 BltC 40047 6055 D5
500 MTWH 40047 6055 D5
SR-44 Shepherdsville Rd
- SHDV 40165 6160 E2
200 SHDV 40165 6161 B3
SR-53
- LGNG 40014 5297 C7
- OdmC 40014 5297 C7
- OdmC 40031 5297 A4
100 LGNG 40031 5296 E1
100 LGNG 40031 5297 A3
100 OdmC 40031 5296 E1
SR-53 N 1st Av
100 LGNG 40031 5296 E1
100 OdmC 40031 5296 E1
SR-53 S 1st Av
- LGNG 40031 5296 E3
SR-53 S 1st St
100 LGNG 40031 5297 A3
SR-60
- ClkC 47143 5287 E1
- ClkC 47172 5287 E1
- ClkC 47172 5288 B4
- CLKV 47172 5288 C6
- SLRB 47172 5288 B4
SR-61
- BltC 40165 6052 E7
- BltC 40165 6161 C5
- BltC 40229 5944 D6
- LSVL - 5615 E7
- PNRV 40165 5944 C7
- PNRV 40229 5944 C7
- PNRV 40229 6053 D1
- SHDV 40165 6052 E7
100 ELZT 42701 6812 D1
100 LSVL 40202 5615 E5
100 LSVL 40202 5616 A2
100 SHDV 40165 6161 C5
600 LSVL 40203 5615 E4
1600 LSVL 40217 5615 E7
1800 ELZT 42701 6703 E7
2100 LSVL 40217 5724 E1
2200 LSVL 40217 5725 D7
2400 PKWV 40217 5725 A1
3000 LSVL 40213 5725 A2
3100 ANPK 40213 5725 A2
4700 LYNV 40213 5725 C6
5200 BltC 40165 6053 D1
5200 HBNE 40165 6053 C2
5200 PNRV 40165 6053 D1
5300 LSVL 40219 5725 E7
5700 LSVL 40219 5834 E1
6400 LSVL 40219 5835 A2
SR-61
9100 LSVL 40229 5835 C7
9200 LSVL 40229 5944 C2
12100 HLVW 40229 5944 D6
SR-61 Arthur St
1600 LSVL 40208 5615 E7
SR-61 Bardstown Rd
- ELZT 42701 6703 E7
SR-61 E Brandeis Av
400 LSVL 40208 5615 E7
400 LSVL 40217 5615 E7
SR-61 N Buckman St
100 SHDV 40165 6161 D1
SR-61 S Buckman St
100 SHDV 40165 6161 C4
SR-61 S Dixie Av
- ELZT 42701 6812 C3
SR-61 S Jackson St
100 LSVL 40202 5616 A2
400 LSVL 40202 5615 E3
600 LSVL 40203 5615 E4
1200 LSVL 40208 5615 E6
SR-61 Lynn St
700 LSVL 40217 5615 E7
SR-61 N Mulberry St
100 ELZT 42701 6812 D1
1800 ELZT 42701 6703 E7
SR-61 Preston Hwy
- BltC 40165 6053 B3
- BltC 40229 5944 D6
- PNRV 40165 5944 C7
- PNRV 40165 6053 B3
- PNRV 40229 5944 C7
- PNRV 40229 6053 D1
2500 LSVL 40217 5725 A1
2500 PKWV 40217 5725 A1
3000 LSVL 40213 5725 A2
3100 ANPK 40213 5725 A2
4700 LYNV 40213 5725 C6
5300 LSVL 40219 5725 E7
5700 LSVL 40219 5834 E1
6400 LSVL 40219 5835 A2
9100 LSVL 40229 5835 C7
9200 LSVL 40229 5944 C2
12000 HLVW 40229 5944 D5
SR-61 N Preston Hwy
5200 BltC 40165 6053 C2
5200 HBNE 40165 6053 C2
5200 PNRV 40165 6053 C2
SR-61 S Preston St
- BltC 40165 6161 D7
- SHDV 40165 6161 C5
100 LSVL 40202 5615 E5
700 LSVL 40203 5615 E4
1600 LSVL 40208 5615 E7
1600 LSVL 40217 5615 E7
2100 LSVL 40217 5724 E1
2200 LSVL 40217 5725 A1
2400 PKWV 40217 5725 A1
SR-61 S Shelby St
2200 LSVL 40217 5725 D7
2400 PKWV 40217 5725 A1
SR-61 WH Ford Western KY Pkwy
- ELZT 42701 6812 C4
SR-62
- CHAN 47111 5181 D7
- CHAN 47111 5182 A4
- ClkC - 5397 E4
- ClkC 47111 5181 D7
- ClkC 47111 5182 C3
- ClkC 47130 5398 E2
- ClkC 47130 5399 A1
- CLKV - 5397 E4
- FydC - 5395 E7
- FydC - 5396 A6
- FydC - 5397 C4
- FydC - 5503 D3
- FydC - 5504 A3
- FydC 47122 5503 A7
- FydC 47136 5502 E7
- FydC 47136 5503 B7
- FydC 47136 5611 E1
- HsnC 47112 5610 B7
- HsnC 47136 5610 A7
- JFVL - 5397 E4
- JFVL - 5398 A4
- NALB - 5395 E7
- NALB - 5396 D4
- NALB - 5504 E1
6900 LNVL 47136 5610 A7
7900 ClkC 47130 5290 B5
8800 ClkC 47111 5290 D1
SR-62 Clark Maritime Hwy
- ClkC - 5397 E4
- ClkC - 5398 D4
- CLKV - 5397 E4
- JFVL - 5397 E4
- JFVL - 5398 A4
SR-62 Lee H Hamilton Hwy
- ClkC - 5397 A4
- CLKV - 5397 A4
- FydC - 5395 E7
- FydC - 5396 A6
- FydC - 5397 C4
- JFVL - 5397 E4
- NALB - 5395 E7
- NALB - 5396 D4
- NALB - 5504 E1
SR-62 Main St
6900 LNVL 47136 5610 D5
SR-62 Patrol Rd
7900 ClkC 47130 5290 B5
8800 ClkC 47111 5290 C3
SR-64
- FydC 47122 5501 D3
- FydC 47122 5502 C4
- FydC 47122 5503 B5
- GEOT 47122 5501 B3
- GEOT 47122 5502 E5
SR-93
- OdmC 40014 5405 D4
SR-93
- OdmC 40014 5514 E1
SR-111
- FydC 47150 5613 D3
- FydC 47150 5721 C7
- FydC 47150 5722 B1
- HsnC 47117 5721 D5
- HsnC 47117 5830 B7
- HsnC 47117 5939 B1
- HsnC 47117 6048 A1
- HsnC 47117 6155 A2
- HsnC 47117 6156 B1
- NALB 47150 5504 E7
- NALB 47150 5613 D3
10 NALB 47150 5505 A6
2800 NALB 47150 5396 B7
4100 FydC 47150 5396 B7
5400 FydC 47119 5287 D1
5400 FydC 47150 5287 D1
5700 FydC 47172 5287 D1
7600 ClkC 47143 5287 D3
SR-111 Beechwood Av
1300 NALB 47150 5505 C2
SR-111 Charlestown Rd
1700 NALB 47150 5505 C3
SR-111 Grant Line Rd
2100 NALB 47150 5505 A6
2800 NALB 47150 5396 B7
4100 FydC 47150 5396 B7
5400 FydC 47119 5287 D1
5400 FydC 47150 5287 D1
5700 FydC 47172 5287 D1
7600 ClkC 47143 5287 D3
SR-111 E Main St
100 NALB 47150 5505 B5
SR-111 W Main St
100 NALB 47150 5505 B5
SR-111 Vincennes St
10 NALB 47150 5505 D4
SR-144
- MdeC 40175 6482 A6
100 RDCF 40160 6483 A6
100 VNGV 40175 6482 D7
100 VNGV 40175 6591 E1
1500 HdnC 40160 6483 B6
1600 VNGV 40160 6483 B6
1900 VNGV 40175 6483 A6
SR-144 W Main St
100 VNGV 40175 6482 C7
100 VNGV 40175 6591 D1
SR-144 E Vine St
100 RDCF 40160 6483 A6
SR-144 W Vine St
100 RDCF 40160 6483 D5
1500 HdnC 40160 6483 B6
1600 VNGV 40160 6483 B6
1900 VNGV 40175 6483 A6
SR-146
- CTWD 40014 5404 A6
- LSVL 40222 5618 E3
100 LGNG 40031 5296 D3
100 LGNG 40031 5297 A2
100 PWEV 40056 5512 B3
300 OdmC 40056 5512 C3
900 OdmC 40031 5296 C3
2900 OdmC 40031 5297 C1
4000 OdmC 40031 5295 E5
5900 OdmC 40014 5404 A7
5900 OdmC 40031 5404 C1
6500 CTWD 40014 5403 E7
6700 CTWD 40014 5512 D1
6700 PWEV 40014 5512 D1
6800 CTWD 40056 5512 D1
7300 NRWD 40222 5618 E3
7300 STMW 40222 5618 E3
7600 LSVL 40245 5512 A5
7600 LYDN 40222 5618 E3
8000 LYDN 40222 5619 A2
8300 LYDN 40242 5619 A2
9200 LYDN 40223 5619 D1
9400 LYDN 40223 5510 D7
9400 LYDN 40242 5510 D7
9400 MLND 40223 5510 D7
9400 WPMG 40223 5510 D7
10300 LYDN 40223 5511 A7
10600 ANCH 40223 5511 A7
10900 ANCH 40223 5620 D1
10900 LSVL 40223 5620 B1
12000 LSVL 40223 5511 E6
12200 LSVL 40223 5512 A6
SR-146 Bellewood Rd
- ANCH 40223 5620 C1
SR-146 Glenbrook Rd
- ANCH 40223 5620 D1
SR-146 Jefferson St
100 LGNG 40031 5296 E2
900 OdmC 40031 5296 C3
SR-146 E Jefferson St
100 LGNG 40031 5296 D3
100 LGNG 40031 5297 A2
SR-146 La Grange Rd
100 PWEV 40056 5512 B3
300 OdmC 40056 5512 C3
6500 CTWD 40014 5403 E7
6500 CTWD 40014 5404 A7
6700 CTWD 40014 5512 D1
6700 PWEV 40014 5512 D1
6800 CTWD 40056 5512 D1
7600 LSVL 40245 5512 A5
9400 LYDN 40223 5510 D7
9400 LYDN 40242 5510 D7
9400 MLND 40223 5510 D7
9400 WPMG 40223 5510 D7
10300 LSVL 40223 5511 A7
10300 LYDN 40223 5511 A7
10600 ANCH 40223 5511 A7
11500 ANCH 40223 5620 D1
11500 LSVL 40223 5620 D1
12200 LSVL 40223 5512 A6
SR-146 New Lagrange Rd
- LSVL 40222 5618 E3
7300 NRWD 40222 5618 E3
7300 STMW 40222 5618 E3
7600 LYDN 40222 5618 D3
SR-146 New Lagrange Rd
8000 LYDN 40222 5619 A2
8300 LYDN 40242 5619 A2
9200 LYDN 40223 5619 D1
SR-146 Park Rd
10900 ANCH 40223 5620 B1
10900 LSVL 40223 5620 B1
SR-146 Ridge Rd
11400 ANCH 40223 5620 D1
SR-146 Whipps Mill Rd
- LYDN 40223 5510 D7
- LYDN 40242 5510 D7
- MLND 40223 5510 D7
9600 LYDN 40223 5619 D1
9600 LYDN 40242 5619 D1
SR-148
- LSVL 40023 5731 B5
- LSVL 40023 5732 C7
- SbyC 40067 5732 C7
14700 LSVL 40299 5730 E4
14800 LSVL 40299 5731 A4
SR-148 Taylorsville Rd
- LSVL 40023 5731 B5
14700 LSVL 40299 5730 E4
14800 LSVL 40299 5731 A4
SR-155
- LSVL 40205 5618 E7
2200 LSVL 40205 5617 B7
2200 SMRV 40205 5617 B7
2400 SGDN 40205 5617 C7
2500 KGLY 40205 5617 C7
3600 LSVL 40220 5618 A7
3700 MVWE 40220 5618 B7
4000 LSVL 40023 5730 C4
4000 LSVL 40023 5731 B7
4000 LSVL 40299 5731 B7
4100 CMBG 40220 5618 D7
4100 HNAC 40220 5618 D7
4300 HBNA 40220 5619 A7
4300 JFTN 40220 5619 A7
4300 LSVL 40220 5619 A7
4600 HBNA 40220 5728 B1
4600 JFTN 40220 5728 C2
4700 LSVL 40023 5840 E4
6000 SpnC 40023 5840 E3
8900 FTHL 40299 5728 C2
9200 JFTN 40299 5728 C2
10500 JFTN 40299 5729 E5
10600 LSVL 40299 5729 A4
12800 LSVL 40299 5730 A5
SR-155 Taylorsville Rd
- LSVL 40205 5618 E7
2200 LSVL 40205 5617 B7
2200 SMRV 40205 5617 B7
2400 SGDN 40205 5617 C7
2500 KGLY 40205 5617 C7
3700 MVWE 40220 5618 B7
4000 LSVL 40220 5618 D7
4100 CMBG 40220 5618 D7
4100 HNAC 40220 5618 D7
4300 HBNA 40220 5619 A7
4300 JFTN 40220 5619 A7
4300 LSVL 40220 5619 A7
4600 HBNA 40220 5728 B1
4600 JFTN 40220 5728 C2
8900 FTHL 40299 5728 C2
9200 JFTN 40299 5728 C2
10500 JFTN 40299 5729 E5
10600 LSVL 40299 5729 A4
12800 LSVL 40299 5730 A5
SR-155 Taylorsville Lake Rd
4000 LSVL 40023 5730 C4
4000 LSVL 40023 5731 B7
4000 LSVL 40299 5730 C4
4000 LSVL 40299 5731 B7
4700 LSVL 40023 5840 E4
6000 SpnC 40023 5840 E3
SR-160
- CHAN 47111 5181 B1
- ClkC 47111 5181 B1
SR-210
10 ELZT 42701 6812 E7
1000 HdnC 42701 6812 E7
SR-210 Hodgenville Rd
10 ELZT 42701 6812 E7
1000 HdnC 42701 6812 E7
SR-211
- HsnC 47117 5830 A5
SR-220
- HdnC 40162 6592 D7
- HdnC 40162 6593 B6
- HdnC 42701 6593 B6
- RDCF 42701 6593 B6
SR-220 Rineyville-Big Sprs Rd
- HdnC 42701 6593 B6
- RDCF 42701 6593 C6
SR-251
- HdnC 42701 6703 D1
10 ELZT 42701 6703 C7
100 ELZT 42701 6812 C1
SR-251 N Miles St
100 ELZT 42701 6812 C1
900 ELZT 42701 6703 C7
SR-251 Shepherdsville Rd
10 ELZT 42701 6703 C7
SR-265
- ClkC - 5397 E4
- ClkC - 5398 E4
- CLKV - 5397 E4
- JFVL - 5397 E4
- JFVL - 5398 E4
SR-265 Clark Maritime Hwy
- ClkC - 5397 E4
- ClkC - 5398 E4
- CLKV - 5397 E4
- JFVL - 5397 E4
- JFVL - 5398 E4
SR-311
- ClkC 47172 5288 C7
- CLKV 47172 5288 C6
SR-311
- NALB 47150 5396 E4
- SLRB 47172 5288 D4
3900 FydC 47150 5396 E3
4600 FydC 47150 5397 A2
4900 FydC 47172 5397 A2
SR-311 Charlestown Rd
- NALB 47150 5396 E4
3900 FydC 47150 5396 E3
4600 FydC 47150 5397 A2
4900 FydC 47172 5397 A2
SR-313
- HdnC 40160 6592 C1
- HdnC 42701 6593 A3
- RDCF 40160 6592 C1
- RDCF 40160 6593 A3
- RDCF 42701 6593 C2
- VNGV 40160 6483 C7
- VNGV 40160 6592 C1
100 HdnC 40175 6482 C5
100 VNGV 40175 6482 D5
400 VNGV 40175 6483 B7
SR-313 Joe Prather Hwy
- HdnC 42701 6593 A3
- RDCF 40160 6593 A3
- RDCF 42701 6593 C2
SR-313 Joe Prather Hwy S
100 HdnC 40175 6482 C5
100 VNGV 40175 6482 D5
400 VNGV 40175 6483 B7
SR-313 Vine Grove Connector Rd
- HdnC 40160 6592 C1
- RDCF 40160 6592 C1
- RDCF 40160 6593 A3
- RDCF 42701 6593 A3
- VNGV 40160 6483 C7
- VNGV 40160 6592 C1
- VNGV 40175 6483 A6
SR-329
- CTWD 40014 5403 A1
- OdmC 40014 5402 E1
- OdmC 40014 5403 D5
- OdmC 40059 5402 A1
7100 LSVL 40059 5400 E3
7100 PROS 40059 5400 E3
7200 LSVL 40059 5401 A3
7200 PROS 40059 5401 A3
7600 OdmC 40059 5401 A3
SR-329 BYP
- CTWD 40014 5403 E6
- CTWD 40014 5404 A6
- OdmC 40014 5404 A7
SR-329 W
6400 CTWD 40014 5403 E7
SR-329 Covered Bridge Rd
7100 LSVL 40059 5400 E3
7100 PROS 40059 5400 E3
7200 LSVL 40059 5401 A3
7200 PROS 40059 5401 A3
7600 OdmC 40059 5401 A2
SR-329 Old Highway 329
- CTWD 40014 5403 A1
- OdmC 40014 5403 D5
SR-329 BYP Veterans Mem Pkwy
- CTWD 40014 5404 A6
- OdmC 40014 5404 A7
SR-335
- FydC 47124 5283 B4
- FydC 47165 5283 B4
- GNVL 47124 5283 C6
SR-362
- LSVL 40245 5513 A5
- OdmC 40014 5512 E4
- OdmC 40014 5513 A6
- SbyC 40067 5514 E5
- SbyC 40245 5513 A5
- SbyC 40245 5514 E5
100 OdmC 40056 5512 D3
100 PWEV 40056 5512 D3
400 PWEV 40014 5512 B1
SR-362 Ash Av
- OdmC 40014 5512 E4
100 OdmC 40056 5512 D3
100 PWEV 40056 5512 D3
SR-362 Central Av
100 PWEV 40056 5512 C1
400 PWEV 40014 5512 B1
SR-362 La Grange Rd
200 PWEV 40056 5512 C2
SR-391
- HdnC 40162 6591 A4
200 VNGV 40175 6591 D1
700 HdnC 40175 6591 C2
SR-391 Brown St
200 VNGV 40175 6591 D1
SR-391 Crume Rd
300 VNGV 40175 6591 D1
700 HdnC 40175 6591 C2
SR-391 High St
200 VNGV 40175 6591 D1
SR-393
- OdmC 40014 5405 B3
- OdmC 40031 5295 D5
- OdmC 40031 5404 E1
- OdmC 40031 5405 A1
SR-403
- CHAN 47111 5181 B5
- ClkC 47111 5180 C7
- ClkC 47111 5181 D3
- ClkC 47111 5289 B1
- ClkC 47172 5288 E2
- ClkC 47172 5289 A1
- SLRB 47172 5288 E2
SR-434
10 HdnC 42701 6593 B3
10 RDCF 42701 6593 B3
SR-434 Battle Training Rd
10 HdnC 42701 6593 B3
10 RDCF 42701 6593 B3

INDEX 4
SR-447
Louisville Metro Street Index
SR-1819

STREET
Block City ZIP Map# Grid

SR-447
- ELZT 42701 6702 C2
- HdnC 40162 6593 B6
- HdnC 40162 6702 B1
- HdnC 42701 6593 B4
- HdnC 42701 6702 C2
- RDCF 42701 6702 C2
10 RDCF 40160 6593 B7
10 RDCF 42701 6593 B7
SR-447 Battle Training Rd
10 RDCF 40160 6593 B3
10 RDCF 42701 6593 B3
SR-480
- BltC 40165 6163 B6
- SHDV 40165 6161 D6
- SHDV 40165 6162 A5
2200 BltC 40165 6162 C5
SR-480 Cedar Grove Rd
- BltC 40165 6163 B6
- SHDV 40165 6161 D6
- SHDV 40165 6162 A5
2200 BltC 40165 6162 C5
SR-480 Charles Hamilton Wy
- SHDV 40165 6161 D6
SR-480C
900 SHDV 40165 6161 C5
SR-480C Cedar Grove Rd
900 SHDV 40165 6161 E6
SR-567
300 ELZT 42701 6812 D5
800 HdnC 42701 6812 E5
SR-567 Locust Grove Rd
- HdnC 42701 6812 E5
300 ELZT 42701 6812 D5
SR-567 Valley Creek Rd
800 ELZT 42701 6812 E5
800 HdnC 42701 6812 E5
SR-660
- BltC 40047 5948 A7
- BltC 40071 5948 A7
- MTWH 40047 5947 E7
- MTWH 40047 5948 A7
11400 BltC 40047 5947 E7
11400 LSVL 40291 5947 E7
SR-660 Waterford Rd
11400 BltC 40047 5947 E7
11400 LSVL 40291 5947 E7
SR-712
- OdmC 40031 5297 B2
1100 LGNG 40031 5297 B2
SR-712 Fort Pickens Rd
1100 LGNG 40031 5297 B2
SR-841
- LSVL - 5400 E7
- LSVL - 5509 E1
- LSVL - 5510 E3
- LSVL - 5511 A3
- LSVL - 5512 B7
- LSVL - 5621 B1
- LSVL - 5729 E7
- LSVL - 5730 A6
- LSVL - 5832 E7
- LSVL - 5833 A7
- LSVL - 5834 A7
- LSVL - 5835 E7
- LSVL - 5836 B7
- LSVL - 5837 E4
- LSVL - 5838 A4
- LSVL - 5940 B4
- LSVL - 5941 A3
- LSVL - 5943 E1
- LSVL - 5944 D1
- MDTN - 5621 B6
- MLHT - 5834 A7
- PROS - 5400 E7
SR-841 Gene Snyder Frwy
- LSVL - 5400 E7
- LSVL - 5509 E1
- LSVL - 5510 E3
- LSVL - 5511 A3
- LSVL - 5512 B7
- LSVL - 5621 A7
- LSVL - 5729 E7
- LSVL - 5730 A6
- LSVL - 5832 E7
- LSVL - 5833 A7
- LSVL - 5834 A7
- LSVL - 5835 E7
- LSVL - 5836 B7
- LSVL - 5837 E4
- LSVL - 5838 A4
- LSVL - 5940 B4
- LSVL - 5941 A3
- LSVL - 5943 E1
- LSVL - 5944 D1
- MDTN - 5621 B1
- MLHT - 5834 A7
- PROS - 5400 E7
SR-864
600 LSVL 40202 5616 A4
600 LSVL 40203 5616 A4
600 LSVL 40204 5616 A4
900 LSVL 40217 5616 B7
3000 LSVL 40213 5725 E5
3000 LSVL 40217 5725 E5
4300 WSNP 40213 5725 E4
4500 LSVL 40218 5725 E5
4600 LSVL 40213 5726 B7
4600 LSVL 40218 5726 A6
4600 PLRH 40213 5726 A6
4700 LSVL 40219 5726 B7
5000 LSVL 40219 5835 B1
5200 LSVL 40228 5835 E2
6000 LSVL 40228 5945 D1
6000 LSVL 40229 5945 D1
6100 LSVL 40228 5836 D4
6700 HWCK 40228 5836 C3
7000 SPML 40228 5836 C4
7500 LSVL 40291 5836 E6
9900 HTCK 40229 5945 E3
SR-864 Beulah Church Rd
6000 LSVL 40228 5945 D1
6000 LSVL 40229 5945 D1
6500 LSVL 40228 5836 E6
7500 LSVL 40291 5836 E6
SR-864 S Campbell St
600 LSVL 40204 5616 A4
SR-864 Cedar Creek Rd
9900 HTCK 40229 5945 E3
9900 LSVL 40228 5945 E3
9900 LSVL 40229 5945 E3
SR-864 E Chestnut St
- LSVL 40204 5616 B3
SR-864 Cooper Chapel Rd
7900 LSVL 40228 5945 E2
7900 LSVL 40229 5945 E2
SR-864 Fegenbush Ln
6100 LSVL 40228 5836 D4
6700 HWCK 40228 5836 C3
7000 SPML 40228 5836 C4
7900 LSVL 40291 5836 E5
SR-864 Fern Valley Rd
6100 LSVL 40228 5836 A2
SR-864 Finzer St
900 LSVL 40204 5616 A4
SR-864 Goss Av
- LSVL 40203 5616 A6
900 LSVL 40204 5616 A6
900 LSVL 40217 5616 B7
SR-864 E Gray St
800 LSVL 40202 5616 A4
800 LSVL 40204 5616 A4
SR-864 Logan St
700 LSVL 40204 5616 A5
SR-864 Poplar Level Rd
1300 LSVL 40217 5616 B7
3000 LSVL 40213 5725 E5
3000 LSVL 40217 5725 E5
4300 WSNP 40213 5725 E4
4500 LSVL 40218 5725 E5
4600 LSVL 40213 5726 B7
4600 LSVL 40218 5726 A6
4600 PLRH 40213 5726 A6
4700 LSVL 40219 5726 B7
5000 LSVL 40219 5835 B1
5200 LSVL 40228 5835 E2
5800 LSVL 40228 5836 A2
SR-864 S Shelby St
600 LSVL 40202 5616 A4
600 LSVL 40203 5616 A4
600 LSVL 40204 5616 A4
SR-868
- HdnC 40121 6264 D6
- MdeC 40108 6264 C3
- MRGH 40155 6264 C4
- MRGH 40177 6264 D6
SR-868 Brandenburg Station Rd
- HdnC 40121 6264 D6
- MdeC 40108 6264 D6
- MRGH 40155 6264 D6
- MRGH 40177 6264 D6
SR-868 Muldraugh Cut Off Rd
- HdnC 40121 6264 D6
- MRGH 40155 6264 D6
- MRGH 40177 6264 D6
SR-907
4600 LSVL 40272 5940 B2
7100 LSVL 40214 5833 C3
7700 LSVL 40214 5832 E5
8000 LSVL 40272 5832 E6
9300 LSVL 40272 5941 A1
SR-907 3rd St Rd
7400 LSVL 40214 5833 B3
7700 LSVL 40214 5832 E5
8000 LSVL 40272 5832 E6
9300 LSVL 40272 5941 A1
9700 LSVL 40272 5940 E1
SR-907 Southside Dr
7100 LSVL 40214 5833 C3
SR-907 Valley Station Rd
4600 LSVL 40272 5940 B2
SR-913
- JFTN 40299 5620 C7
- LSVL 40299 5620 C7
- MDTN 40299 5620 C6
200 DGSH 40243 5620 C6
200 LSVL 40223 5620 B5
700 MDTN 40243 5620 C7
1800 JFTN 40299 5729 A3
11400 LSVL 40299 5729 A3
SR-913 Blankenbaker Pkwy
- JFTN 40299 5620 C7
- LSVL 40299 5620 C7
- MDTN 40243 5620 C7
200 DGSH 40243 5620 B5
200 LSVL 40223 5620 B5
1800 JFTN 40299 5729 A3
2100 LSVL 40299 5729 C2
SR-913 Blankenbaker Access Dr
11400 JFTN 40299 5729 A3
11400 LSVL 40299 5729 A3
SR-1020
- BltC 40109 6052 D3
- BltC 40165 6052 D6
100 BltC 40109 5943 C5
100 LSVL 40118 5943 A2
200 LSVL 40202 5615 D7
200 LSVL 40214 5724 C7
700 LSVL 40203 5615 D4
1200 LSVL 40208 5615 D5
2000 LSVL 40208 5724 C5
5500 LSVL 40214 5833 D3
8500 LSVL 40118 5833 E6
9100 LSVL 40118 5942 E1
10500 HYVA 40118 5943 A3
SR-1020 S 2nd St
200 LSVL 40202 5615 D5
700 LSVL 40203 5615 D4
1200 LSVL 40208 5615 D5
SR-1020 S 3rd St
200 LSVL 40202 5615 D7
700 LSVL 40203 5615 D4
1200 LSVL 40208 5615 D5
2000 LSVL 40208 5724 C5
3000 LSVL 40214 5724 C2
SR-1020 W Kenwood Wy
200 LSVL 40214 5724 C7
SR-1020 National Tpk
5500 LSVL 40214 5833 C3
8500 LSVL 40118 5833 E6
9100 LSVL 40118 5942 E1
9800 LSVL 40118 5943 A2
10500 HYVA 40118 5943 A3
SR-1020 S Park Rd
100 BltC 40109 5943 C5
100 LSVL 40118 5943 C4
SR-1020 Southern Pkwy
3700 LSVL 40214 5724 C3
SR-1020 Southside Dr
4800 LSVL 40214 5724 C6
5800 LSVL 40214 5833 D3
SR-1060
10 SpnC 40071 5949 D3
SR-1060 Plum Creek Rd
10 SpnC 40071 5949 D3
SR-1065
100 LSVL 40214 5832 E6
600 LSVL 40214 5833 A6
1400 LSVL 40214 5834 A6
1400 LSVL 40219 5834 A6
1400 MLHT 40219 5834 A6
4100 LSVL 40219 5835 A5
5400 LSVL 40299 5837 A4
5600 LSVL 40291 5837 A4
5900 LSVL 40219 5836 C5
6200 LSVL 40228 5836 E5
7800 LSVL 40291 5836 D5
SR-1065 Beulah Church Rd
8000 LSVL 40228 5836 E5
8000 LSVL 40291 5836 E5
8400 LSVL 40291 5837 A5
SR-1065 Fegenbush Ln
7900 LSVL 40228 5836 D5
7900 LSVL 40291 5836 D5
SR-1065 Lovers Ln
5500 LSVL 40299 5837 A4
5600 LSVL 40291 5837 A4
SR-1065 Outer Lp
100 LSVL 40214 5832 E6
600 LSVL 40214 5833 A6
1400 LSVL 40214 5834 A6
1400 LSVL 40219 5834 A6
1400 MLHT 40219 5834 A6
4100 LSVL 40219 5835 A5
5900 LSVL 40219 5836 C5
6200 LSVL 40228 5836 B5
7800 LSVL 40291 5836 D5
SR-1065 Seatonville Rd
9400 LSVL 40291 5837 C3
SR-1116
- BltC 40165 5945 C7
100 BltC 40165 6053 E1
100 BltC 40165 6054 B1
400 BltC 40165 5944 D7
1100 BltC 40229 5944 D7
1100 HLVW 40229 5944 D7
1400 BltC 40229 5945 D6
1400 LSVL 40229 5945 C6
SR-1116 Cedar Creek Rd
- BltC 40165 5945 C7
100 BltC 40165 6054 C2
1400 BltC 40229 5945 D6
1400 LSVL 40229 5945 C6
SR-1116 Old Preston Hwy
- BltC 40165 6053 D1
1100 BltC 40229 5944 D7
1100 HLVW 40229 5944 D7
12300 BltC 40165 5944 D7
SR-1116 Old Preston Hwy N
400 BltC 40165 5944 D7
400 BltC 40165 6053 E1
SR-1116 Zoneton Rd
100 BltC 40165 6053 D1
400 BltC 40165 6054 B1
SR-1136
100 ELZT 42701 6812 C4
1400 HdnC 42701 6812 B6
SR-1136 Bishop Ln
100 ELZT 42701 6812 C4
SR-1136 New Glendale Rd
500 ELZT 42701 6812 C4
1400 HdnC 42701 6812 B6
SR-1142
800 LSVL 40214 5833 A3
1000 LSVL 40214 5832 E2
SR-1142 Palatka Rd
800 LSVL 40214 5833 A3
1000 LSVL 40214 5832 E2
SR-1169
4300 SpnC 40071 5949 E7
SR-1169 Plum Ridge Rd
4300 SpnC 40071 5949 E7
SR-1230
5100 LSVL 40216 5722 A6
5200 LSVL 40216 5721 D7
5200 LSVL 40258 5721 D7
6000 LSVL 40258 5830 D6
6800 LSVL 40272 6048 D1
7000 LSVL 40272 5939 E1
7300 LSVL 40272 5830 D7
SR-1230 Ashby Ln
7000 LSVL 40272 5939 D1
SR-1230 Cane Run Rd
5100 LSVL 40216 5722 A6
5200 LSVL 40216 5721 D7
5200 LSVL 40258 5721 D7
6000 LSVL 40258 5830 D6
SR-1230 Dover Av
- LSVL 40216 5722 B6
SR-1230 Johnsontown Rd
7300 LSVL 40258 5830 D7
7300 LSVL 40272 5830 D7
SR-1230 Lower River Rd
9700 LSVL 40258 5830 D7
9700 LSVL 40272 5830 D7
10100 LSVL 40272 5939 D1
12400 LSVL 40272 6048 C1
SR-1230 Watson Ln
6800 LSVL 40272 6048 D1
SR-1319
- BltC 40047 5948 B7
- BltC 40047 6057 B1
- BltC 40071 5948 E4
- BltC 40071 5949 A3
- BltC 40071 6057 A1
- MTWH 40047 6057 A1
- SpnC 40023 5949 A3
SR-1357
- ELZT 42701 6811 E2
- HdnC 42701 6811 A2
SR-1357 St. John Rd
- ELZT 42701 6811 E2
- HdnC 42701 6811 A2
SR-1408
5500 OdmC 40014 5513 B2
7100 CTWD 40014 5403 E7
7400 CTWD 40014 5404 A7
7400 OdmC 40014 5403 E7
7400 OdmC 40014 5404 A7
7500 CTWD 40014 5513 B2
8000 SbyC 40245 5513 E3
8100 OdmC 40056 5513 A1
9000 SbyC 40245 5514 A4
SR-1408 Floydsburg Rd
7100 CTWD 40014 5403 E7
7400 CTWD 40014 5404 A7
7400 OdmC 40014 5403 E7
7400 OdmC 40014 5404 A7
7500 CTWD 40014 5513 B2
7500 OdmC 40014 5513 B2
8100 OdmC 40056 5513 A1
9000 SbyC 40245 5513 E4
9000 SbyC 40245 5514 A4
SR-1408 Old Floydsburg Rd
5500 OdmC 40014 5513 B2
SR-1408 Todds Point Rd
8000 OdmC 40014 5513 D3
8000 SbyC 40245 5513 E3
SR-1417
- BltC 40165 6050 D6
SR-1417 Martin Hill Rd
- BltC 40165 6050 D6
SR-1442
- BltC 40165 6163 A5
100 BltC 40165 6162 E5
SR-1442 Ridge Rd
- BltC 40165 6163 A5
100 BltC 40165 6162 E5
SR-1447
- WDYH 40222 5618 D1
- WLNP 40222 5618 D1
3900 LSVL 40207 5617 E3
3900 STMW 40207 5617 E3
3900 STMW 40207 5618 A2
4200 WLNP 40207 5618 B1
4300 WDYH 40207 5618 B1
4600 LSVL 40222 5618 D1
4600 STMW 40222 5618 D1
4700 GYDL 40222 5618 D1
4800 GYDL 40222 5509 D7
4800 STMW 40222 5509 D7
7600 LSVL 40222 5509 E7
7600 LYDN 40222 5509 E7
7800 LSVL 40222 5510 A6
7800 LYDN 40222 5510 A6
8300 BRWD 40242 5510 B6
8300 LYDN 40242 5510 A6
8300 PNTN 40242 5510 A6
8700 LSVL 40242 5510 B6
8800 WWOD 40242 5510 C6
8900 LDNP 40242 5510 C6
9100 LSVL 40241 5510 E4
9100 RLGH 40241 5510 C5
9100 RLGH 40242 5510 C6
9700 HKYH 40241 5510 E5
10400 LSVL 40241 5511 A4
11400 LSVL 40245 5511 A4
12200 WTNH 40245 5511 D3
12600 LSVL 40245 5512 A3
SR-1447 Old Lagrange Rd
- LSVL 40245 5512 B4
SR-1447 Old La Grange Rd
13700 LSVL 40245 5512 A4
SR-1447 Westport Rd
- WDYH 40222 5618 D1
- WLNP 40222 5618 D1
3900 LSVL 40207 5617 E3
3900 STMW 40207 5617 E3
3900 STMW 40207 5618 A2
4200 WLNP 40207 5618 B1
4300 WDYH 40207 5618 B1
4600 LSVL 40222 5618 D1
4600 STMW 40222 5618 D1
4700 GYDL 40222 5618 D1
4800 GYDL 40222 5509 D7
4800 STMW 40222 5509 D7
7600 LSVL 40222 5509 E7
7600 LYDN 40222 5509 E7
7800 LSVL 40222 5510 A6
7800 LYDN 40222 5510 A6
8300 BRWD 40242 5510 B6
8300 LYDN 40242 5510 A6
8300 PNTN 40242 5510 A6
8700 LSVL 40242 5510 B6
8800 WWOD 40242 5510 C6
8900 LDNP 40242 5510 C6
9100 LSVL 40241 5510 E4
9100 RLGH 40241 5510 C5
9100 RLGH 40242 5510 C6
9700 HKYH 40241 5510 E5
10400 LSVL 40241 5511 A4
11400 LSVL 40245 5511 A4
12200 WTNH 40245 5511 D3
12600 LSVL 40245 5512 A3
SR-1450
- BltC 40165 6053 A2
- BltC 40229 6053 B3
- HBNE 40165 6053 C3
- HLVW 40165 6052 E2
- HLVW 40165 6053 A1
- HLVW 40229 5944 A6
- HLVW 40229 6053 A1
- PNRV 40229 6053 A2
100 FXCH 40165 6053 B3
100 PNRV 40165 6053 A2
8000 LSVL 40219 5835 A6
9200 LSVL 40219 5944 A1
9200 LSVL 40229 5944 A1
10300 LSVL 40229 5943 E4
10900 HLVW 40229 5943 E5
SR-1450 Blue Lick Rd
8000 LSVL 40219 5835 A6
9200 LSVL 40219 5944 A1
9200 LSVL 40229 5944 A1
10300 LSVL 40229 5943 E4
10900 HLVW 40229 5943 E5
SR-1450 W Hebron Ln
- BltC 40165 6053 A2
- BltC 40229 6053 B3
- HBNE 40165 6053 C3
- PNRV 40229 6053 A2
100 FXCH 40165 6053 B3
100 HLVW 40165 6053 B3
100 PNRV 40165 6053 A2
SR-1494
- BltC 40165 6160 E7
100 SHDV 40165 6161 A7
1400 BltC 40165 6161 A6
SR-1494 Beech Grove Rd
- BltC 40165 6160 E7
100 SHDV 40165 6161 A7
1400 BltC 40165 6161 A6
SR-1500
- MdeC 40175 6373 B7
100 RDCF 40160 6483 E6
100 VNGV 40175 6482 C7
100 VNGV 40175 6591 E1
900 VNGV 40160 6483 C7
1000 VNGV 40160 6592 B1
1500 VNGV 40175 6592 A1
2300 MdeC 40175 6482 C6
SR-1500 Knox Av
- MdeC 40175 6373 B7
- VNGV 40160 6592 B1
300 VNGV 40175 6482 C7
2300 MdeC 40175 6482 C6
SR-1500 E Main St
100 VNGV 40175 6591 E1
1500 VNGV 40175 6592 A1
SR-1500 W Main St
100 VNGV 40175 6482 C7
100 VNGV 40175 6591 D1
SR-1500 Mill Creek Rd
100 RDCF 40160 6483 E6
SR-1500 Rogersville Rd
100 RDCF 40160 6483 E6
900 VNGV 40160 6483 C7
1900 VNGV 40160 6592 B1
1900 VNGV 40175 6592 B1
SR-1500 S Wilson Rd
1000 RDCF 40160 6483 E6
SR-1526
- BltC 40109 6050 A6
- BltC 40109 6051 A3
- BltC 40109 6052 A1
- BltC 40165 6049 C7
- BltC 40165 6050 A6
- BltC 40165 6051 D3
- HLVW 40109 6052 E1
- HLVW 40229 6052 E1
- HLVW 40229 6053 A1
100 BltC 40165 6053 D5
100 HBNE 40165 6053 C2
100 PNRV 40165 6053 B2
200 BltC 40165 6054 B5
500 PNRV 40229 6053 A1
SR-1526 Bells Mill Rd
100 BltC 40165 6053 D5
200 BltC 40165 6054 B5
SR-1526 Brooks Rd
- BltC 40109 6052 E1
- HLVW 40109 6052 E1
SR-1526 John Harper Hwy
100 HBNE 40165 6053 C2
100 PNRV 40165 6053 B2
500 PNRV 40229 6053 A1
900 HLVW 40229 6053 A1
SR-1526 N Preston Hwy
- BltC 40165 6053 B3
- HBNE 40165 6053 B3
- PNRV 40165 6053 C2
SR-1531
100 LSVL 40023 5622 B6
100 LSVL 40245 5622 B7
200 LSVL 40023 5731 B3
4300 LSVL 40299 5730 E7
4300 LSVL 40299 5731 A7
5800 LSVL 40299 5840 A4
7100 LSVL 40299 5839 E7
8100 LSVL 40299 5948 E1
9500 BltC 40299 5948 D3
11000 BltC 40071 5948 D3
11000 LSVL 40245 5513 C7
17600 SbyC 40245 5513 C7
SR-1531 Aiken Rd
16900 LSVL 40245 5513 C7
16900 LSVL 40245 5622 B1
17600 SbyC 40245 5513 C7
SR-1531 Dawson Hill Rd
11000 BltC 40071 5948 D3
11000 BltC 40299 5948 D3
SR-1531 Fisherville Rd
200 LSVL 40023 5622 B7
200 LSVL 40023 5731 B3
200 LSVL 40245 5622 B7
SR-1531 Johnson Rd
100 LSVL 40023 5622 B6
100 LSVL 40245 5622 B7
SR-1531 Routt Rd
4300 LSVL 40023 5731 A7
4300 LSVL 40299 5730 E7
4300 LSVL 40299 5731 A7
5800 LSVL 40299 5840 A4
7100 LSVL 40299 5839 E7
8100 LSVL 40299 5948 E1
9500 BltC 40299 5948 D3
11700 BltC 40071 5948 D3
SR-1600
200 ELZT 42701 6702 E7
300 HdnC 42701 6702 D7
400 ELZT 42701 6812 A1
6800 HdnC 40162 6591 C7
7800 HdnC 40175 6591 C7
SR-1600 Cardinal Dr
200 ELZT 42701 6702 E7
SR-1600 Rineyville Rd
300 ELZT 42701 6702 D7
300 HdnC 42701 6702 D7
6800 HdnC 40162 6591 C7
7800 HdnC 40175 6591 C7
SR-1600 Woodland Dr
400 ELZT 42701 6812 A1
SR-1603
- HLVW 40229 6052 E1
100 BltC 40109 6052 E1
100 BltC 40165 6052 E4
100 HLVW 40165 6052 E3
300 HLVW 40109 6052 E1
SR-1603 E Blue Lick Rd
- HLVW 40229 6052 E1
100 BltC 40109 6052 E3
100 BltC 40165 6052 E4
100 HLVW 40165 6052 E3
300 HLVW 40109 6052 E2
SR-1603 Brooks Hill Rd
- BltC 40109 6052 E1
- HLVW 40109 6052 E1
- HLVW 40229 6052 E1
SR-1604
- BltC 40165 6163 C7
SR-1631
2400 LSVL 40217 5724 E1
2700 LSVL 40209 5724 E2
SR-1631 Crittenden Dr
2400 LSVL 40217 5724 E1
2700 LSVL 40209 5724 E2
SR-1638
- MdeC 40108 6264 A5
- MRGH 40155 6264 A5
SR-1638 Warren St
- MdeC 40108 6264 A5
- MRGH 40155 6264 A5
SR-1646
- HdnC 40121 6373 E7
- HdnC 40121 6374 A6
- RDCF 40160 6373 E7
- RDCF 40175 6373 E7
700 RDCF 40160 6483 B5
1200 RDCF 40175 6483 A2
1400 RDCF 40160 6592 C1
1600 RDCF 40160 6482 E1
1600 RDCF 40175 6482 E1
SR-1646 Bullion Blvd
- HdnC 40121 6373 E5
- HdnC 40121 6374 A5
SR-1646 Hunters Ln
- RDCF 40160 6483 B5
SR-1646 Logsdon Pkwy
- HdnC 40121 6373 E6
SR-1646 N Logsdon Pkwy
- HdnC 40121 6373 E7
- HdnC 40121 6374 A6
- RDCF 40160 6373 E7
- RDCF 40175 6373 E7
100 RDCF 40160 6483 A2
1200 RDCF 40175 6483 A2
1600 RDCF 40160 6482 E1
1600 RDCF 40175 6482 E1
SR-1646 S Logsdon Pkwy
100 RDCF 40160 6483 C7
1400 RDCF 40160 6592 C1
SR-1694
- LSVL 40059 5401 E7
- LSVL 40059 5402 D1
- LSVL 40241 5401 E7
- OdmC 40059 5402 E1
1000 OdmC 40014 5402 E1
10000 LSVL 40241 5510 E1
SR-1694 Brownsboro Rd
- LSVL 40059 5401 E7
- LSVL 40059 5402 D1
- LSVL 40241 5401 E7
- OdmC 40014 5402 D1
- OdmC 40059 5402 D1
10000 LSVL 40241 5510 E1
SR-1694 Gum St
1000 OdmC 40014 5402 E1
SR-1703
- LSVL 40218 5726 A3
1000 LSVL 40204 5616 D7
1400 LSVL 40205 5616 D6
1400 LSVL 40213 5616 D6
2100 LSVL 40205 5725 E1
2400 LSVL 40205 5726 D5
3200 WSNP 40218 5726 B3
3400 WBHL 40218 5726 C4
3500 PLRH 40218 5726 C4
SR-1703 Baxter Av
1000 LSVL 40204 5616 D7
1400 LSVL 40205 5616 D6
1400 LSVL 40213 5616 D6
SR-1703 Newburg Rd
- LSVL 40218 5726 A3
1600 LSVL 40205 5616 D6
1600 LSVL 40213 5616 D6
2100 LSVL 40205 5725 E1
2400 LSVL 40205 5726 D5
3200 WSNP 40218 5726 B3
3400 WBHL 40218 5726 C4
3500 PLRH 40218 5726 C4
SR-1727
4900 LSVL 40216 5722 B7
5200 LSVL 40216 5831 B1
5200 LSVL 40258 5831 B1
8800 LSVL 40272 5831 A7
SR-1727 Terry Rd
4900 LSVL 40216 5722 B7
5200 LSVL 40216 5831 B1
5200 LSVL 40258 5831 B1
8800 LSVL 40272 5831 A7
SR-1747
- LSVL 40220 5619 D7
- LYDN 40223 5510 E7
- MWVL 40242 5510 D5
100 JFTN 40223 5619 D4
100 LSVL 40223 5619 D3
100 LYDN 40223 5619 E1
100 WDWD 40223 5619 D3
900 HTBN 40222 5619 D6
1200 LSVL 40219 5835 E2
1600 FTHL 40299 5619 C7
1600 JFTN 40299 5619 C7
1600 LSVL 40299 5619 C7
1700 HBNA 40220 5619 C7
1700 HBNA 40299 5619 C7
1800 LSVL 40228 5835 E2
1900 FTHL 40299 5728 B1
1900 HBNA 40220 5728 B1
2000 FTHL 40220 5728 B1
2500 JFTN 40220 5728 B1
2700 LSVL 40213 5834 E2
2800 LSVL 40219 5834 D2
2800 LSVL 40220 5728 A2
2800 LSVL 40223 5510 E5
2800 LSVL 40241 5510 D4
2800 MWVL 40223 5510 E5
2800 MWVL 40241 5510 D5
3400 LSVL 40299 5728 A3
4600 LSVL 40299 5727 E6
4700 LSVL 40291 5727 E6
4700 LSVL 40291 5728 A7
6000 LSVL 40228 5836 A2
SR-1747 Fern Valley Rd
1200 LSVL 40219 5835 E2
1800 LSVL 40228 5835 E2
2700 LSVL 40213 5834 E2
2800 LSVL 40219 5834 D2
6000 LSVL 40228 5836 A2
SR-1747 N Hurstbourne Pkwy
- LSVL 40223 5510 E6
- LYDN 40223 5510 E7
- MWVL 40223 5510 E6
- MWVL 40242 5510 D5
100 HTBN 40222 5619 D4
100 JFTN 40223 5619 D4
100 LSVL 40223 5619 D3
100 LYDN 40223 5619 E1
100 WDWD 40223 5619 D3
2800 LSVL 40241 5510 D4
2800 MWVL 40241 5510 D5
SR-1747 S Hurstbourne Pkwy
100 JFTN 40223 5619 D4
100 LYDN 40223 5619 D4
100 WDWD 40223 5619 D4
900 HTBN 40222 5619 D6
1600 FTHL 40299 5619 C7
1600 JFTN 40299 5619 C7
1600 LSVL 40220 5619 C7
1600 LSVL 40299 5619 C7
1700 HBNA 40220 5619 C7
1700 HBNA 40299 5619 C7
1900 FTHL 40299 5728 B1
1900 HBNA 40220 5728 B1
2000 FTHL 40220 5728 B1
2500 JFTN 40220 5728 B1
2800 LSVL 40220 5728 A2
3400 LSVL 40299 5728 A3
4600 LSVL 40299 5727 E6
4700 LSVL 40291 5727 E6
4700 LSVL 40291 5728 A7
SR-1815
100 RDCF 40160 6483 A4
1400 VNGV 40175 6483 A5
1500 VNGV 40175 6482 E5
SR-1815 W Lincoln Trail Blvd
100 RDCF 40160 6483 D3
1400 VNGV 40175 6483 A5
1500 VNGV 40175 6482 E5
SR-1815 S Logsdon Pkwy
- RDCF 40160 6483 A4
SR-1816
- MdeC 40175 6373 A7
SR-1816 Rabbit Run
- MdeC 40175 6373 A7
SR-1817
1400 OdmC 40014 5295 C6
1400 OdmC 40031 5295 C6
6600 OdmC 40014 5403 B1
SR-1817 Cedar Point Rd
1400 OdmC 40014 5295 C6
1400 OdmC 40031 5295 C6
SR-1817 New Cut Rd
5900 OdmC 40014 5295 A6
5900 OdmC 40031 5295 A6
6600 OdmC 40014 5403 B1
SR-1818
1500 OdmC 40014 5514 E1
3600 OdmC 40014 5513 E2
SR-1818 E Mt Zion Rd
2200 OdmC 40014 5514 E1
SR-1818 W Mt Zion Rd
1500 OdmC 40014 5514 E1
3600 OdmC 40014 5513 E2
SR-1818 Todds Point Rd
- OdmC 40014 5513 D2
SR-1819
100 DGSH 40243 5620 C4
100 MDTN 40243 5620 A7
900 DGSH 40299 5620 [illegible]

STREET Block City ZIP Map# Grid

SR-1819
900 LSVL 40299 5620 B6
900 MDTN 40299 5620 B6
1100 JFTN 40299 5620 A7
1600 JFTN 40299 5729 A2
3100 JFTN 40299 5728 E3
3200 LSVL 40299 5729 A3
4400 LSVL 40299 5728 D6
4900 LSVL 40291 5728 D7
5400 LSVL 40291 5837 D1
5400 LSVL 40299 5837 D1
6000 LSVL 40291 5838 C5
6000 LSVL 40299 5838 C5
13800 LSVL 40299 5839 A6
SR-1819 Billtown Rd
3800 JFTN 40299 5728 D5
4400 LSVL 40299 5728 D6
4900 LSVL 40291 5728 D7
5400 LSVL 40291 5837 D1
5400 LSVL 40299 5837 D1
6000 LSVL 40291 5838 C5
6000 LSVL 40299 5838 C5
SR-1819 Blankenbaker Pkwy
600 DGSH 40243 5620 B5
700 MDTN 40243 5620 B6
SR-1819 Brush Run Rd
13800 LSVL 40299 5839 A6
SR-1819 Ruckriegel Pkwy
3200 JFTN 40299 5729 A3
3200 LSVL 40299 5729 A3
3500 JFTN 40299 5728 D7
SR-1819 Seatonville Rd
12000 LSVL 40291 5838 C5
12000 LSVL 40299 5838 D5
SR-1819 Watterson Tr
900 DGSH 40243 5620 B6
900 DGSH 40299 5620 B6
900 LSVL 40299 5620 B6
900 MDTN 40243 5620 B6
900 MDTN 40299 5620 B6
1100 JFTN 40299 5620 A7
1600 JFTN 40299 5729 A2
3100 JFTN 40299 5728 E3
SR-1819 N Watterson Tr
100 DGSH 40243 5620 C4
100 MDTN 40243 5620 A7
SR-1849
6200 LSVL 40272 5940 A4
6400 LSVL 40272 5939 E4
SR-1849 Moorman Rd
6200 LSVL 40272 5940 A4
6400 LSVL 40272 5939 E4
SR-1865
3500 LSVL 40215 5724 A7
4700 LSVL 40214 5724 A7
5000 LSVL 40214 5833 B1
6000 LSVL 40118 5833 B6
6400 LSVL 40118 5942 B1
SR-1865 New Cut Rd
4800 LSVL 40214 5724 A7
4800 LSVL 40215 5724 A7
5000 LSVL 40214 5833 B1
6000 LSVL 40118 5833 B6
6400 LSVL 40118 5942 B1
SR-1865 Taylor Blvd
3500 LSVL 40215 5724 A7
4700 LSVL 40214 5724 A7
SR-1882
10 HdnC 40175 6482 A7
SR-1882 Hargan Rd
10 HdnC 40175 6482 A6
SR-1882 Hargin Rd
100 HdnC 40175 6482 A7
SR-1882 Old Fort Av
- MdeC 40175 6482 A6
SR-1904
10 ELZT 42701 6811 B7
10 HdnC 42701 6811 B7
SR-1904 Bacon Creek Rd
10 ELZT 42701 6811 B7
10 HdnC 42701 6811 B7
SR-1931
700 LSVL 40202 5615 B7
700 LSVL 40203 5615 B7
1200 LSVL 40208 5615 C5
1800 LSVL 40210 5615 B7
2200 LSVL 40208 5724 A1
2200 LSVL 40210 5724 A1
2300 SVLY 40216 5724 A1
2500 LSVL 40215 5724 A1
2900 LSVL 40215 5723 D5
2900 SVLY 40216 5723 E3
4300 LSVL 40216 5723 D5
4500 LSVL 40258 5831 E4
4700 LSVL 40214 5723 E6
6600 LSVL 40214 5832 E1
7000 LSVL 40258 5830 E3
7700 LSVL 40258 5832 B3
SR-1931 S 7th St
700 LSVL 40202 5615 B7
700 LSVL 40203 5615 B7
1200 LSVL 40208 5615 C5
1800 LSVL 40210 5615 B7
SR-1931 7th St Rd
2000 LSVL 40208 5615 B7
2000 LSVL 40210 5615 B7
2200 LSVL 40208 5724 A1
2200 LSVL 40210 5724 A1
2300 SVLY 40216 5724 A1
2500 LSVL 40215 5724 A1
2900 LSVL 40215 5723 E3
2900 SVLY 40216 5723 E3
SR-1931 Greenwood Rd
4500 LSVL 40258 5831 E4
7000 LSVL 40258 5830 E3
SR-1931 Manslick Rd
3500 LSVL 40215 5723 D5
3500 SVLY 40216 5723 E3
4300 LSVL 40216 5723 D5
[illegible]00 LSVL 40214 5723 E6
[illegible] LSVL 40214 5832 E1

SR-1931 St. Andrews Church Rd
7300 LSVL 40214 5832 D2
7700 LSVL 40258 5832 B3
8100 LSVL 40258 5831 E4
SR-1932
100 LSVL 40207 5617 E3
100 STMW 40207 5617 E3
200 BLWD 40207 5617 E2
200 BWNV 40207 5617 E3
200 DRDH 40207 5617 E3
200 LSVL 40207 5618 A3
300 NBNE 40207 5618 A4
400 INDH 40207 5617 E3
500 BFLD 40207 5618 A4
600 PLYV 40207 5618 A4
700 SPLE 40207 5618 A4
900 STMW 40205 5618 C7
900 STMW 40207 5617 E3
1000 LSVL 40205 5618 B6
2800 LSVL 40220 5618 B7
2800 MVWE 40220 5618 C7
3000 LSVL 40220 5727 C1
3600 LSVL 40218 5727 C4
SR-1932 Breckenridge Ln
200 LSVL 40207 5618 A3
200 STMW 40207 5618 A3
300 NBNE 40207 5618 A4
500 BFLD 40207 5618 A4
600 PLYV 40207 5618 A4
700 SPLE 40207 5618 A4
900 STMW 40205 5618 C7
1000 LSVL 40205 5618 B6
2800 LSVL 40220 5618 C7
2800 MVWE 40220 5618 B7
3000 LSVL 40220 5727 C1
3600 LSVL 40218 5727 C4
SR-1932 Chenoweth Ln
100 LSVL 40207 5617 E3
100 STMW 40207 5617 E3
200 BLWD 40207 5617 E2
200 BWNV 40207 5617 E3
200 DRDH 40207 5617 E3
400 INDH 40207 5617 E3
SR-1934
- LSVL 40258 5831 A1
- LSVL 40272 5830 D7
- LSVL 40272 5939 D1
- LSVL 40272 5940 A4
1800 LSVL 40210 5615 A5
2100 LSVL 40210 5614 C7
2500 LSVL 40211 5614 C7
3600 LSVL 40211 5723 C1
3600 LSVL 40216 5614 C7
3600 LSVL 40216 5723 B2
3600 SVLY 40216 5723 B2
4300 LSVL 40216 5722 A6
5500 LSVL 40258 5722 A7
8400 LSVL 40258 5830 E5
SR-1934 Cane Run Rd
3300 LSVL 40210 5614 C7
3300 LSVL 40211 5614 C7
3600 LSVL 40211 5723 C1
3600 LSVL 40216 5614 C7
3600 LSVL 40216 5723 C1
3600 SVLY 40216 5723 B2
4300 LSVL 40216 5722 D4
SR-1934 Greenbelt Hwy
- LSVL 40258 5831 A1
- LSVL 40272 5830 D7
- LSVL 40272 5939 D1
- LSVL 40272 5940 A4
- NHFD 40272 5940 A4
5500 LSVL 40216 5722 B6
5500 LSVL 40258 5722 A7
8400 LSVL 40258 5830 E5
SR-1934 Wilson Av
1800 LSVL 40210 5615 A5
2100 LSVL 40210 5614 D5
2500 LSVL 40211 5614 E5
SR-2048
100 LSVL 40206 5617 E5
100 LSVL 40207 5617 E5
700 STMW 40207 5617 D4
3400 LSVL 40205 5617 E7
3500 LSVL 40205 5618 A6
SR-2048 Cannons Ln
- LSVL 40205 5618 A6
100 LSVL 40206 5617 E5
100 LSVL 40207 5617 E5
700 STMW 40207 5617 D4
2700 LSVL 40205 5617 E6
SR-2048 Dutchmans Ln
3400 LSVL 40205 5617 E7
3500 LSVL 40205 5618 A6
SR-2049
1800 SVLY 40216 5723 B4
2800 LSVL 40216 5723 B4
SR-2049 Crums Ln
1800 SVLY 40216 5723 B4
2800 LSVL 40216 5723 B4
SR-2050
600 LYDN 40222 5619 A2
800 LYDN 40222 5618 E1
1100 GYDL 40222 5618 E1
1100 STMW 40222 5618 E1
1300 GYDL 40222 5509 D7
1300 STMW 40222 5509 E7
1800 LSVL 40222 5509 D7
2000 NHFD 40222 5509 D7
SR-2050 Herr Ln
1100 GYDL 40222 5618 E1
1100 STMW 40222 5618 E1
1300 GYDL 40222 5509 D7
1300 STMW 40222 5509 E7
1800 LSVL 40222 5509 D7
2000 NHFD 40222 5509 D7
SR-2050 Lyndon Ln
- STMW 40222 5618 E1
600 LYDN 40222 5619 A2
800 LYDN 40222 5618 E1
SR-2051
1800 LSVL 40216 5723 A6
2300 LSVL 40216 5722 B5
2300 SVLY 40216 5722 E6

SR-2051
3300 LSVL 40211 5723 A1
3300 SVLY 40216 5723 A1
3800 LSVL 40211 5722 E1
SR-2051 Camp Ground Rd
3300 LSVL 40211 5723 A1
3300 LSVL 40216 5723 A1
3300 SVLY 40216 5723 A1
3800 LSVL 40211 5722 E1
4200 LSVL 40216 5722 B5
SR-2051 Lees Ln
3300 LSVL 40216 5722 C5
SR-2051 Rockford Ln
1800 LSVL 40216 5723 A6
1800 SVLY 40216 5723 A6
2300 LSVL 40216 5722 E6
2300 SVLY 40216 5722 E6
SR-2052
1900 LSVL 40218 5726 E4
1900 WBHL 40218 5726 E6
5000 LSVL 40228 5726 E6
5300 LSVL 40218 5835 E1
5300 LSVL 40219 5835 E4
5300 LSVL 40228 5835 E4
SR-2052 Hikes Ln
2100 LSVL 40218 5726 E3
2100 WBHL 40218 5726 E3
SR-2052 Old Shepherdsville Rd
1900 LSVL 40218 5726 E4
2100 WBHL 40218 5726 E6
SR-2052 Shepherdsville Rd
2100 WBHL 40218 5726 D4
4200 LSVL 40218 5726 E4
5000 LSVL 40228 5726 E6
5300 LSVL 40218 5835 E1
5300 LSVL 40219 5835 E4
5300 LSVL 40228 5835 E4
SR-2053
5200 LSVL 40229 5944 D4
6000 LSVL 40229 5945 E6
8000 BltC 40229 5945 D6
8200 LSVL 40229 5946 A5
8900 LSVL 40291 5946 A5
SR-2053 Cedar Creek Rd
11300 LSVL 40229 5945 D5
SR-2053 Mt Washington Rd
5200 LSVL 40229 5944 D4
6000 LSVL 40229 5945 E6
SR-2053 Thixton Ln
7600 LSVL 40229 5945 D5
8000 BltC 40229 5945 D6
8200 LSVL 40229 5946 A5
8900 LSVL 40291 5946 A5
SR-2054
700 LSVL 40208 5724 B1
1200 LSVL 40208 5615 B7
1200 LSVL 40210 5615 A7
1700 LSVL 40210 5614 E7
2700 LSVL 40211 5614 E7
SR-2054 Algonquin Pkwy
700 LSVL 40208 5724 B1
1200 LSVL 40208 5615 B7
1200 LSVL 40210 5615 A7
1700 LSVL 40210 5614 E7
2700 LSVL 40211 5614 E7
SR-2055
400 LSVL 40118 5942 D2
1100 HYVA 40118 5942 E3
1200 HYVA 40118 5943 A3
1200 LSVL 40118 5943 A3
8600 LSVL 40214 5832 E7
8600 LSVL 40272 5832 E7
9200 LSVL 40118 5833 A7
9200 LSVL 40272 5833 A7
SR-2055 W Manslick Rd
8600 LSVL 40214 5832 E7
8600 LSVL 40272 5832 E7
9200 LSVL 40118 5833 A7
9200 LSVL 40272 5833 A7
9800 LSVL 40118 5942 C1
SR-2055 Mt Holly Rd
400 LSVL 40118 5942 D2
1100 HYVA 40118 5942 E3
1200 HYVA 40118 5943 A3
1200 LSVL 40118 5943 A3
SR-2056
3300 LSVL 40211 5614 A7
4100 LSVL 40211 5613 E7
SR-2056 Bells Ln
3300 LSVL 40211 5614 A7
4100 LSVL 40211 5613 E7
SR-2237
- SHDV 40165 6161 D6
SR-2237 Salt River Rd
- SHDV 40165 6161 D6
SR-2553
100 BltC 40165 6053 C1
100 PNRV 40165 6053 C1
SR-2553 Cardinal Av
- BltC 40165 6053 C1
- PNRV 40165 6053 C1
SR-2553 Old Preston Hwy N
100 BltC 40165 6053 C1
100 PNRV 40165 6053 C1
SR-2674
100 MTWH 40047 6056 B6
300 BltC 40047 6056 B5
SR-2674 Stringer Ln
100 MTWH 40047 6056 B6
300 BltC 40047 6056 B5
SR-2706
100 BltC 40047 6055 B5
100 MTWH 40047 6055 E2
400 MTWH 40047 6056 A2
SR-2706 Flat Lick Rd
- BltC 40047 6055 E1
- MTWH 40047 6055 E2
400 MTWH 40047 6056 A2
SR-2706 Green Brier Rd
100 BltC 40047 6055 B5

SR-2706 Green Brier Rd
100 MTWH 40047 6055 B5
SR-2706 Wales Run Rd
- BltC 40047 6055 E1
- MTWH 40047 6055 E1
SR-2802
10 ELZT 42701 6702 C1
10 RDCF 42701 6702 C1
100 HdnC 42701 6702 C2
SR-2802 W A Jenkins Rd
10 ELZT 42701 6702 C1
10 RDCF 42701 6702 C1
100 HdnC 42701 6702 C1
SR-2802 Cecilanna Dr
100 HdnC 42701 6702 B4
SR-2802 Hutcherson Ln
200 ELZT 42701 6702 C2
200 HdnC 42701 6702 C2
SR-2840
- DGSH 40243 5620 B4
11400 LSVL 40223 5620 B4
11400 MDTN 40243 5620 E4
SR-2840 Main St
- DGSH 40243 5620 B4
11400 LSVL 40223 5620 B4
11400 MDTN 40243 5620 E4
SR-2840 Old Shelbyville Rd
11700 MDTN 40243 5620 C4
SR-2841
16100 LSVL 40023 5622 B6
16100 LSVL 40245 5622 C5
SR-2841 Eastwood Cut Off Rd
16100 LSVL 40023 5622 B6
16100 LSVL 40245 5622 C5
SR-2845
4600 LSVL 40219 5835 C7
4600 LSVL 40229 5835 E7
5500 LSVL 40219 5836 A7
5500 LSVL 40229 5836 A7
6400 LSVL 40228 5836 A7
SR-2845 E Manslick Rd
4600 LSVL 40219 5835 C7
4900 LSVL 40229 5835 E7
5500 LSVL 40219 5836 A7
5500 LSVL 40229 5836 A7
7100 LSVL 40228 5836 D6
SR-2845 Pennsylvania Run Rd
8500 LSVL 40228 5836 C6
SR-2845 Shepherdsville Rd
8900 LSVL 40219 5835 D7
SR-2854
100 LGNG 40031 5296 D3
500 OdmC 40031 5296 C2
1700 OdmC 40031 5295 E1
SR-2854 Dawkins Rd
100 LGNG 40031 5296 D3
500 OdmC 40031 5296 C2
1700 OdmC 40031 5295 E1
SR-2855
1300 LGNG 40031 5297 B2
1300 OdmC 40031 5297 B2
SR-2855 Fort Pickens Rd
1300 LGNG 40031 5297 B2
1300 OdmC 40031 5297 B2
SR-2858
6600 OdmC 40014 5404 D6
7000 OdmC 40014 5513 D1
SR-2858 Abbott Ln
6600 OdmC 40014 5404 D6
7000 OdmC 40014 5513 D1
SR-2860
2000 LSVL 40204 5616 D4
2400 JfnC 40204 5616 D4
SR-2860 Grinstead Dr
2000 LSVL 40204 5616 D4
2400 JfnC 40204 5616 D4
SR-3005
- ELZT 42701 6812 E1
100 ELZT 42701 6811 B1
700 HdnC 42701 6811 B1
1000 HdnC 42701 6702 B7
1700 ELZT 42701 6702 E5
1900 ELZT 42701 6703 A4
2100 HdnC 42701 6703 A4
SR-3005 Louisville Rd
- ELZT 42701 6702 E5
SR-3005 Ring Rd
- ELZT 42701 6812 E1
100 ELZT 42701 6811 B1
700 HdnC 42701 6811 B1
1000 HdnC 42701 6702 B7
1200 ELZT 42701 6702 E5
1900 ELZT 42701 6703 A4
2100 HdnC 42701 6703 A4
SR-3064
2100 LSVL 40203 5506 A7
2100 LSVL 40212 5506 A7
2600 LSVL 40212 5505 D7
SR-3064 Northwestern Pkwy
3200 LSVL 40212 5505 D7
SR-3064 Portland Av
2100 LSVL 40203 5506 A7
2100 LSVL 40212 5506 A7
2600 LSVL 40212 5505 E7
SR-3082
2100 LSVL 40203 5615 A1
2100 LSVL 40212 5615 A1
2400 LSVL 40212 5506 A7
2600 LSVL 40212 5505 E7
SR-3082 Bank St
2100 LSVL 40203 5615 A1
2100 LSVL 40212 5615 A1
2400 LSVL 40212 5506 A7
2600 LSVL 40212 5505 E7
SR-3084
- LSVL 40223 5512 B7
1000 LSVL 40223 5620 E1
1000 MDTN 40223 5620 E2
13300 LSVL 40223 5621 A1

SR-3084
14700 LSVL 40245 5512 B7
SR-3084 N English Station Rd
1000 LSVL 40223 5620 E2
1000 MDTN 40223 5620 E2
SR-3084 Old Henry Rd
- LSVL 40223 5512 B7
12800 LSVL 40223 5620 E1
13300 LSVL 40223 5621 A1
14700 LSVL 40245 5512 B7
SR-3216
500 LSVL 40212 5505 C7
SR-3216 N 38th St
500 LSVL 40212 5505 C7
SR-3217
500 LSVL 40212 5505 D7
SR-3217 N 37th St
500 LSVL 40212 5505 D7
SR-3222
1000 OdmC 44026 5292 B3
1200 OdmC 40059 5291 D5
1200 OdmC 40059 5292 B3
7500 LSVL 40059 5400 E2
7500 PROS 40059 5400 E2
8000 OdmC 40059 5400 E2
SR-3222 Rose Island Rd
7500 LSVL 40059 5400 E2
7500 PROS 40059 5400 E2
8000 OdmC 40059 5400 E2
SR-3222 N Rose Island Rd
2400 OdmC 40059 5291 E2
US-31
- ClkC 47129 5397 E4
- ClkC 47129 5506 E7
- ClkC 47130 5397 E4
- ClkC 47130 5398 A2
- ClkC 47172 5288 E7
- ClkC 47172 5397 E7
- ClkC 47172 5398 A2
- CLKV 47129 5397 E4
- CLKV 47129 5506 D4
- CLKV 47129 5615 E1
- CLKV 47130 5506 E6
- CLKV 47172 5397 E7
- CLKV 47172 5398 A2
- JFVL 47129 5397 E4
- JFVL 47130 5397 E4
- JFVL 47130 5506 E6
- JFVL 47130 5615 E1
- SLRB 47172 5397 E1
100 LSVL 40202 5615 E1
100 SLRB 47172 5288 E2
10900 ClkC 47143 5288 E1
US-31 S 2nd St
100 LSVL 40202 5615 E2
US-31 George R Clark Mem Br
- CLKV 47129 5506 E7
- CLKV 47129 5615 E1
- JFVL 47130 5506 E7
- JFVL 47130 5615 E1
- LSVL 40202 5615 E1
US-31 N Indiana Av
- ClkC 47172 5288 E2
100 SLRB 47172 5288 E2
10900 ClkC 47143 5288 E1
US-31 S Indiana Av
100 SLRB 47172 5288 D4
US-31 Pearl St
- CLKV 47130 5506 E6
- JFVL 47130 5506 E6
US-31E
- BltC 40047 5947 B7
- BltC 40047 6056 C4
- LSVL 40218 5726 E4
- LSVL 40291 5946 E1
- MTWH 40047 6056 C4
- WBHL 40218 5726 E4
100 LSVL 40202 5615 E3
100 LSVL 40206 5616 B3
400 LSVL 40202 5616 B4
400 LSVL 40204 5616 D5
1400 LSVL 40205 5616 D6
1900 LSVL 40205 5617 B7
2700 SMRG 40205 5617 C7
2700 SMRM 40205 5617 B7
2700 SMRV 40205 5617 B7
2800 LSVL 40205 5726 C1
2800 SMRG 40205 5726 C1
2900 WLTN 40205 5726 C1
4100 LSVL 40218 5727 D6
4600 LSVL 40291 5727 D6
5200 LSVL 40291 5728 A7
5300 LSVL 40291 5837 C5
10800 LSVL 40291 5947 A5
US-31E S 1st St
200 LSVL 40202 5615 E2
US-31E Bardstown Rd
- BltC 40047 5947 A6
- LSVL 40291 5946 E1
1000 LSVL 40204 5616 C5
1400 LSVL 40205 5616 D6
1900 LSVL 40205 5617 B7
2700 SMRG 40205 5617 C7
2700 SMRM 40205 5617 B7
2700 SMRV 40205 5617 B7
2800 LSVL 40205 5726 C1
2800 SMRG 40205 5726 C1
2900 WLTN 40205 5726 C1
3300 LSVL 40218 5726 D2
3700 WBHL 40218 5726 D3
4100 LSVL 40218 5727 A4
4600 LSVL 40291 5727 D6
5200 LSVL 40291 5728 A7
5300 LSVL 40291 5837 C5
10800 LSVL 40291 5947 A5
US-31E Baxter Av
100 LSVL 40206 5616 B3
200 LSVL 40204 5616 D5
US-31E Buechel Byp
- LSVL 40218 5726 E4
- WBHL 40218 5726 E4

US-31E Buechel Byp
4100 LSVL 40218 5727 D6
US-31E E Chestnut St
- LSVL 40204 5616 B3
US-31E E Liberty St
100 LSVL 40202 5615 E3
500 LSVL 40202 5616 B4
700 LSVL 40204 5616 A3
US-31E Main St
- BltC 40047 5947 B7
US-31E E Main St
100 LSVL 40202 5615 E2
400 LSVL 40202 5616 B3
700 LSVL 40206 5616 A2
US-31E W Main St
100 LSVL 40202 5615 E2
US-31E W Market St
100 LSVL 40202 5615 E3
US-31EX
- BltC 40047 5947 A7
- MTWH 40047 5947 A7
100 BltC 40047 6056 C4
100 MTWH 40047 6056 C3
US-31EX Main St
- BltC 40047 5947 A7
- MTWH 40047 5947 A7
100 BltC 40047 6056 C4
100 MTWH 40047 6056 C3
US-31W
- ELZT 42701 6593 C7
- ELZT 42701 6703 A7
- ELZT 42701 6812 D6
- HdnC 40121 6373 E4
- HdnC 40121 6374 A5
- HdnC 40160 6374 A6
- HdnC 40160 6483 E4
- HdnC 40177 6155 D7
- HdnC 40177 6156 D2
- HdnC 40177 6264 D7
- HdnC 42701 6593 C6
- HdnC 42701 6702 D3
- LSVL 40272 6156 E1
- MdeC 40108 6264 D7
- MdeC 40121 6264 D7
- MRGH 40155 6264 C4
- RDCF 40160 6374 B7
- RDCF 40160 6483 B1
- RDCF 42701 6593 A2
- RDCF 42701 6702 C1
- WPT 40177 6155 D7
- WPT 40177 6156 D1
100 LSVL 40212 5615 A3
200 LSVL 40202 5615 E2
200 LSVL 40203 5615 A4
400 LSVL 40211 5615 A4
600 LSVL 40210 5615 A4
1000 ELZT 42701 6702 E5
1300 LSVL 40210 5614 E7
2100 LSVL 40216 5614 E7
2100 RDCF 40160 6484 A7
2200 RDCF 40160 6593 A1
2300 LSVL 40210 5723 E1
2300 LSVL 40216 5723 E1
2300 SVLY 40216 5723 E1
5100 LSVL 40216 5832 A1
5300 LSVL 40258 5832 A2
6400 LSVL 40258 5831 C7
9100 LSVL 40272 5831 C7
9700 LSVL 40272 5940 B1
11700 LSVL 40272 5939 E5
13000 LSVL 40272 6048 C4
US-31W BYP
- ELZT 42701 6702 E6
- ELZT 42701 6811 E2
- ELZT 42701 6812 A3
US-31W S 22nd St
100 LSVL 40212 5615 A2
400 LSVL 40211 5615 A3
800 LSVL 40210 5615 A4
1300 LSVL 40210 5614 E7
US-31W Bernheim Ln
- LSVL 40210 5614 E7
US-31W S Dixie Av
- ELZT 42701 6812 C3
US-31W W Dixie Av
- ELZT 42701 6702 E6
- ELZT 42701 6703 A7
600 ELZT 42701 6812 A1
US-31W S Dixie Blvd
2100 RDCF 40160 6484 A7
2200 RDCF 40160 6593 A1
US-31W Dixie Hwy
- HdnC 40177 6156 D2
- LSVL 40272 6156 E1
1900 LSVL 40210 5614 E7
2100 LSVL 40216 5614 E7
2300 LSVL 40210 5723 E1
2300 LSVL 40216 5723 E1
2300 SVLY 40216 5723 E1
5100 LSVL 40216 5832 A1
5300 LSVL 40258 5832 A2
6400 LSVL 40258 5831 C7
9100 LSVL 40272 5831 C7
9700 LSVL 40272 5940 B1
11700 LSVL 40272 5939 E5
13000 LSVL 40272 6048 C4
US-31W N Dixie Hwy
1000 ELZT 42701 6702 E5
US-31W S Dixie Hwy
- HdnC 40160 6483 E4
- RDCF 40160 6483 E5
- RDCF 40160 6484 A7
- RDCF 40160 6593 C7
- RDCF 42701 6593 A2
US-31W Dr WJ Hodge St
200 LSVL 40203 5615 A4
200 LSVL 40212 5615 A3
400 LSVL 40211 5615 A4
600 LSVL 40210 5615 A4
US-31W Dumesnil St
2100 LSVL 40210 5615 A5
US-31W BYP Elizabethtown Byp
- ELZT 42701 6702 E6

US-31W BYP Elizabethtown Byp
- ELZT 42701 6811 E2
- ELZT 42701 6812 A3
US-31W Louisville Rd
- ELZT 42701 6702 D3
US-31W W Main St
200 LSVL 40202 5615 E2
1000 LSVL 40203 5615 B2
2000 LSVL 40212 5615 B2
US-31W W Market St
200 LSVL 40202 5615 E2
1000 LSVL 40203 5615 C2
2000 LSVL 40212 5615 C2
US-31WX
- HdnC 40177 6156 A4
- WPT 40177 6156 A4
US-42
- GSHN 44026 5292 D3
- HSDS 40222 5509 C3
- HSDS 40241 5509 C3
- LSVL 40059 5400 D7
- LSVL 40059 5401 A1
- LSVL 40059 5509 D1
- LSVL 40222 5509 C5
- LSVL 40241 5400 D7
- LSVL 40241 5509 D1
- NHFD 40222 5509 A7
- OdmC 40059 5292 C5
- OdmC 40059 5401 A1
- OdmC 44026 5292 E3
- PROS 40059 5400 E2
- RVBF 40059 5401 B1
- WDYH 40207 5508 E7
1000 LSVL 40206 5616 D2
2700 LSVL 40206 5617 A2
3200 LSVL 40207 5617 A2
3600 BWNV 40207 5617 D1
3700 DRDH 40207 5617 D1
3700 INDH 40207 5617 A2
4200 INDH 40207 5508 E7
4200 INHC 40207 5508 E7
4200 LSVL 40207 5508 E7
4400 INHC 40207 5509 A7
4500 LSVL 40207 5509 A7
4700 WNDF 40207 5509 B6
4800 WDYH 40207 5509 B6
US-42 Brownsboro Rd
- LSVL 40222 5509 B6
- NHFD 40222 5509 A7
- WDYH 40207 5508 E7
1700 LSVL 40206 5616 D2
2700 LSVL 40206 5617 A2
3200 LSVL 40207 5617 A2
3600 BWNV 40207 5617 D1
3700 DRDH 40207 5617 D1
3700 INDH 40207 5617 A2
4200 INDH 40207 5508 E7
4200 INHC 40207 5508 E7
4200 LSVL 40207 5508 E7
4400 INHC 40207 5509 A7
4500 LSVL 40207 5509 A7
4700 WNDF 40207 5509 B6
4800 WDYH 40207 5509 B6
US-42 E Main St
1000 LSVL 40206 5616 B2
US-42 Mellwood Av
1400 LSVL 40206 5616 C2
US-42 Story Av
1000 LSVL 40206 5616 B2
US-60
- HdnC 40177 6155 D7
- HdnC 40177 6156 D2
- HdnC 40177 6264 D7
- LSVL - 5617 E7
- LSVL - 5618 A7
- LSVL - 5723 E5
- LSVL - 5724 B4
- LSVL - 5725 E3
- LSVL - 5726 A3
- LSVL 40272 6156 E1
- MdeC 40108 6264 D7
- MdeC 40121 6264 C7
- MdeC 40175 6264 D7
- MdeC 40175 6373 A1
- MRGH 40155 6264 C4
- STMW - 5618 B6
- WPT 40177 6155 D7
- WPT 40177 6156 D1
- WSNP - 5726 A3
4400 SVLY 40216 5723 A7
5100 LSVL 40216 5832 A1
5300 LSVL 40258 5832 A2
6400 LSVL 40258 5831 C7
7500 LSVL 40222 5618 E3
7500 STMW 40222 5618 E3
7600 NRWD 40222 5618 E3
7800 LYDN 40222 5618 E3
7900 HTBN 40222 5619 A3
7900 LSVL 40222 5619 A3
7900 LYDN 40222 5619 A3
8400 BLMD 40222 5619 B3
8800 BLMD 40223 5619 B4
8900 LYDN 40223 5619 C4
9100 LSVL 40272 5831 C7
9300 JFTN 40223 5619 D4
9400 WDWD 40223 5619 D4
9700 LSVL 40272 5940 B1
9800 LSVL 40223 5619 D4
10000 BRMR 40223 5619 E4
10300 SCMR 40223 5619 E4
10400 BRMR 40223 5620 A4
10400 DGSH 40243 5620 A4
10400 SCMR 40223 5620 A4
10600 LSVL 40243 5620 A4
10700 LSVL 40223 5620 A4
11300 MDTN 40243 5620 A4
11700 LSVL 40272 5939 E7
12700 MDTN 40223 5620 E4
12800 MDTN 40223 5621 A4
12800 MDTN 40243 5621 A4
13000 LSVL 40272 6048 C4
13500 LSVL 40245 5621 B4
13500 MDTN 40245 5621 B4

INDEX 6

US-60 — Louisville Metro Street Index — Alma June Wy

STREET
Block City ZIP Map# Grid

US-60
15700 LSVL 40245 5622 A5
16800 LSVL 40023 5622 E5
18200 LSVL 40023 5623 E7
18200 LSVL 40245 5623 E7
18200 SbyC 40067 5623 E7
US-60 ALT
- JfnC 40206 5617 A4
- LSVL 40204 5617 A4
300 LSVL 40208 5724 A3
400 LSVL 40217 5724 E1
700 LSVL 40217 5725 A1
900 LSVL 40217 5616 A7
1300 LSVL 40204 5616 C6
1300 LSVL 40213 5616 C6
1300 LSVL 40215 5724 A3
1400 LSVL 40205 5616 C6
1500 LSVL 40215 5723 C4
1800 SVLY 40216 5723 C4
2300 JfnC 40204 5616 E5
2400 JfnC 40206 5616 E4
2400 LSVL 40206 5616 E4
2500 LSVL 40206 5617 A4
3300 LSVL 40207 5617 D3
3700 LSVL 40216 5723 D3
US-60 BUS
700 LSVL 40203 5615 A3
700 LSVL 40210 5615 A3
1500 LSVL 40210 5614 E6
2100 LSVL 40216 5614 E7
2300 LSVL 40210 5723 E1
2300 LSVL 40216 5723 E1
2300 SVLY 40216 5723 E1
US-60 TRK
- LSVL 40222 5618 D3
- NRWD 40222 5618 E3
- STMW 40222 5618 D3
100 LSVL 40202 5615 E2
100 LSVL 40203 5615 C2
200 LSVL 40204 5616 B3
400 LSVL 40202 5616 A2
700 LSVL 40206 5616 D2
700 LSVL 40210 5615 C4
2500 LSVL 40206 5617 E3
3300 LSVL 40207 5617 B4
3400 STMW 40207 5617 D3
3900 LSVL 40207 5618 A3
3900 STMW 40207 5618 A3
4100 RHLN 40207 5618 A3
4200 FRMD 40207 5618 B3
4300 BWDV 40207 5618 B3
US-60 TRK S 1st St
200 LSVL 40202 5615 E2
US-60 ALT S 3rd St
2500 LSVL 40208 5724 A3
US-60 ALT 7th St Rd
3700 LSVL 40215 5723 D3
3700 LSVL 40216 5723 D3
3700 SVLY 40216 5723 D3
US-60 TRK S 12th St
700 LSVL 40203 5615 C3
700 LSVL 40210 5615 C4
US-60 TRK S 13th St
100 LSVL 40203 5615 B2
US-60 ALT Bardstown Rd
1300 LSVL 40204 5616 D5
1400 LSVL 40205 5616 D6
US-60 TRK Baxter Av
100 LSVL 40206 5616 B3
200 LSVL 40204 5616 B3
US-60 ALT Berry Blvd
1300 LSVL 40215 5724 A3
1500 LSVL 40215 5723 C4
1800 SVLY 40216 5723 C4
US-60 BUS W Broadway
1200 LSVL 40203 5615 A3
1300 LSVL 40210 5615 A3
US-60 ALT Cherokee Pkwy
2000 LSVL 40204 5616 D6
2300 JfnC 40204 5616 E5
US-60 TRK E Chestnut St
- LSVL 40204 5616 B3
US-60 Dixie Hwy
- HdnC 40177 6156 D2
- LSVL 40272 6156 E1
4400 SVLY 40216 5723 A7
4700 LSVL 40216 5723 B6
5100 LSVL 40216 5832 A1
5300 LSVL 40258 5832 A2
6400 LSVL 40258 5831 C7
9100 LSVL 40272 5831 C7
9700 LSVL 40272 5940 B1
11700 LSVL 40272 5939 E7
13000 LSVL 40272 6048 C4
US-60 ALT Dixie Hwy
4000 LSVL 40216 5723 D4
4000 SVLY 40216 5723 C4
US-60 BUS Dixie Hwy
700 LSVL 40203 5615 A3
700 LSVL 40210 5615 A3
1500 LSVL 40210 5614 E6
2100 LSVL 40216 5614 E7
2300 LSVL 40210 5723 E1
2300 LSVL 40216 5723 E1
2300 SVLY 40216 5723 E1
US-60 ALT Eastern Pkwy
300 LSVL 40208 5724 D1
400 LSVL 40217 5724 E1
700 LSVL 40217 5725 A1
900 LSVL 40217 5616 A7
1300 LSVL 40204 5616 C6
1300 LSVL 40213 5616 C6
1400 LSVL 40205 5616 C6
US-60 TRK Frankfort Av
1600 LSVL 40206 5616 D2
2500 LSVL 40206 5617 E3
3300 LSVL 40207 5617 B4
3400 STMW 40207 5617 D3
US-60 ALT Grinstead Dr
2500 JfnC 40204 5616 E4
2500 JfnC 40206 5616 E4
2500 LSVL 40204 5616 E4
2500 LSVL 40206 5616 E4

US-60 Henry Watterson Expwy
- LSVL - 5617 E7
- LSVL - 5618 C5
- LSVL - 5723 E5
- LSVL - 5724 C4
- LSVL - 5725 D4
- LSVL - 5726 A3
- STMW - 5618 A7
- WSNP - 5726 A3
US-60 TRK W Hill St
1200 LSVL 40210 5615 B6
US-60 ALT Lexington Rd
- JfnC 40206 5617 A4
- LSVL 40204 5617 A4
2400 JfnC 40206 5616 E4
2400 LSVL 40206 5616 E4
2500 LSVL 40206 5617 A4
3300 LSVL 40207 5617 D3
US-60 TRK E Liberty St
100 LSVL 40202 5615 E3
500 LSVL 40202 5616 A3
700 LSVL 40204 5616 A3
US-60 TRK E Main St
100 LSVL 40202 5615 E2
400 LSVL 40202 5616 A2
700 LSVL 40206 5616 A2
US-60 TRK W Main St
100 LSVL 40202 5615 E2
1000 LSVL 40203 5615 C2
US-60 TRK W Market St
100 LSVL 40202 5615 E2
1000 LSVL 40203 5615 C2
US-60 TRK Mellwood Av
1400 LSVL 40206 5616 C2
US-60 Shelbyville Rd
7500 STMW 40222 5618 E3
7600 LSVL 40222 5618 E3
7600 NRWD 40222 5618 E3
7800 LYDN 40222 5618 E3
7900 HTBN 40222 5619 A3
7900 LSVL 40222 5619 A3
7900 LYDN 40222 5619 A3
8400 BLMD 40222 5619 B3
8800 BLMD 40223 5619 B4
8900 LYDN 40223 5619 C4
9300 JFTN 40223 5619 D4
9400 WDWD 40223 5619 D4
9800 LSVL 40223 5619 D4
10000 BRMR 40223 5619 E4
10300 SCMR 40223 5619 E4
10400 BRMR 40223 5620 A4
10400 DGSH 40243 5620 A4
10400 SCMR 40223 5620 A4
10600 LSVL 40243 5620 A4
10700 LSVL 40223 5620 A4
11300 MDTN 40243 5620 A4
12700 MDTN 40223 5620 E4
12800 MDTN 40223 5621 A4
12800 MDTN 40243 5621 A4
13500 LSVL 40245 5621 B4
13500 MDTN 40245 5621 B4
15700 LSVL 40245 5622 A5
16800 LSVL 40023 5622 E5
18200 LSVL 40023 5623 E7
18200 LSVL 40245 5623 E7
18200 SbyC 40067 5623 E7
US-60 TRK Shelbyville Rd
- LSVL 40222 5618 D3
- NRWD 40222 5618 E3
- STMW 40222 5618 D3
3800 LSVL 40207 5617 E3
3800 STMW 40207 5617 E3
3900 LSVL 40207 5618 A3
3900 STMW 40207 5618 A3
4100 RHLN 40207 5618 A3
4200 FRMD 40207 5618 B3
4300 BWDV 40207 5618 B3
US-60 TRK Story Av
1000 LSVL 40206 5616 C2
US-60 ALT Taylor Blvd
2700 LSVL 40208 5724 C1
3000 LSVL 40215 5724 B2
US-60 ALT Winkler Av
300 LSVL 40208 5724 C1
US-62
100 ELZT 42701 6812 D1
1700 ELZT 42701 6811 A6
1800 ELZT 42701 6703 E7
2100 HdnC 42701 6811 A6
US-62 Bardstown Rd
- ELZT 42701 6703 E7
US-62 Leitchfield Rd
1600 ELZT 42701 6812 A4
1700 ELZT 42701 6811 A6
2100 HdnC 42701 6811 A6
US-62 N Mulberry St
100 ELZT 42701 6812 D1
1800 ELZT 42701 6703 E7
US-150
- BltC 40047 5947 B7
- BltC 40047 6056 C4
- FydC - 5503 E2
- FydC - 5504 E4
- FydC 47119 5393 E3
- FydC 47119 5394 A4
- FydC 47119 5503 D1
- FydC 47122 5503 D2
- FydC 47124 5283 A6
- FydC 47124 5393 B1
- GNVL 47124 5283 B6
- GNVL 47124 5393 A1
- LSVL - 5505 E6
- LSVL 40203 5506 A7
- LSVL 40212 5506 A7
- LSVL 40218 5726 E4
- LSVL 40291 5946 E1
- MTWH 40047 6056 C4
- NALB - 5504 D3
- NALB - 5505 A5
- WBHL 40218 5726 E4
100 LSVL 40202 5615 D4
100 LSVL 40203 5615 C3

US-150
100 LSVL 40212 5615 A1
400 LSVL 40211 5615 C3
500 LSVL 40202 5616 B4
500 LSVL 40203 5616 B4
600 LSVL 40210 5615 C3
700 LSVL 40204 5616 D5
1400 LSVL 40205 5616 D6
1900 LSVL 40205 5617 B7
2700 SMRG 40205 5617 C7
2700 SMRM 40205 5617 B7
2700 SMRV 40205 5617 B7
2800 LSVL 40205 5726 C1
2800 SMRG 40205 5726 C1
2900 WLTN 40205 5726 C1
4100 LSVL 40218 5727 B5
4600 LSVL 40291 5727 D6
5200 LSVL 40291 5728 A7
5300 LSVL 40291 5837 C5
10800 LSVL 40291 5947 A5
US-150 N 21st St
100 LSVL 40203 5615 A2
100 LSVL 40212 5615 A2
US-150 N 22nd St
- LSVL 40203 5506 A7
- LSVL 40212 5506 A7
100 LSVL 40212 5615 A1
400 LSVL 40203 5615 A1
US-150 S 22nd St
100 LSVL 40212 5615 A2
400 LSVL 40211 5615 A2
US-150 Bardstown Rd
- BltC 40047 5947 A6
- LSVL 40291 5946 E1
1000 LSVL 40204 5616 C5
1400 LSVL 40205 5616 D6
1900 LSVL 40205 5617 B7
2700 SMRG 40205 5617 C7
2700 SMRM 40205 5617 B7
2700 SMRV 40205 5617 B7
2800 LSVL 40205 5726 C1
2800 SMRG 40205 5726 C1
2900 WLTN 40205 5726 C1
3200 LSVL 40218 5726 D2
3500 WBHL 40218 5726 D3
4100 LSVL 40218 5727 A4
4600 LSVL 40291 5727 D6
5200 LSVL 40291 5728 A7
5300 LSVL 40291 5837 C5
10800 LSVL 40291 5947 A5
US-150 Baxter Av
700 LSVL 40204 5616 D5
US-150 E Broadway
100 LSVL 40202 5615 E4
100 LSVL 40203 5615 E4
500 LSVL 40202 5616 B4
500 LSVL 40203 5616 B4
700 LSVL 40204 5616 A4
US-150 W Broadway
100 LSVL 40202 5615 D4
100 LSVL 40203 5615 C3
1300 LSVL 40210 5615 C3
2000 LSVL 40211 5615 C3
US-150 Buechel Byp
- LSVL 40218 5726 E4
- WBHL 40218 5726 E4
4100 LSVL 40218 5727 B5
US-150 Dr WJ Hodge St
100 LSVL 40203 5615 A3
100 LSVL 40212 5615 A3
400 LSVL 40211 5615 A2
600 LSVL 40210 5615 A3
US-150 Main St
- BltC 40047 5947 B7
US-150 Mary Anderson Mem Hwy
- FydC 47119 5503 D2
- FydC 47122 5503 D2
US-150 Sherman Minton Br
- LSVL - 5505 E6
- NALB - 5505 B6

A

A Ct
10 LGNG 40031 5296 E2
A St
900 JFVL 47130 5507 B4
Abbey Rd
12600 LSVL 40272 5939 D7
Abbey Chase
10 JFVL 47130 5398 C6
Abbeydale Ct
2600 LGNG 40031 5297 A5
Abbeywood Ct
2400 CLKV 47129 5397 B6
Abbeywood Rd
1100 GYDL 40222 5618 D1
1100 STMW 40222 5618 D1
1300 GYDL 40222 5509 D7
Abbeywood Village Dr
4000 LSVL 40241 5510 C2
Abbeywood Village Wy
9700 LSVL 40241 5510 D3
Abbie Dell Av
1700 NALB 47150 5505 C2
Abbott Ln
6600 OdmC 40014 5404 D6
7000 OdmC 40014 5513 D1
Abbott Ln SR-2858
6600 OdmC 40014 5404 D6
7000 OdmC 40014 5513 D1
Abbott St
100 SHDV 40165 6161 C4
Abbott Glen Dr
3900 OdmC 40014 5513 E1
Abbott Grove Ct
7400 OdmC 40014 5513 C1
Abbott Grove Dr
4400 OdmC 40014 5513 D1
Abbott Grove Pl
4500 OdmC 40014 5513 D2

Abbott's Beach Rd
16800 LSVL 40272 6156 E1
Abby Ct
10 ELZT 42701 6812 B4
Abby St
200 ELZT 42701 6812 B4
Abbydale Ct
5000 LSVL 40229 5944 D1
Abel St
10 HdnC 40121 6374 E1
Abell Av
500 LSVL 40213 5834 B3
Abercorne Ter
4600 LSVL 40241 5510 B1
Aberdeen Ct
4200 FydC 47150 5396 E2
Aberdeen Dr
1800 LSVL 40205 5726 A1
Abernathy Rd
1600 LSVL 40218 5726 C5
1600 PLRH 40218 5726 C5
Abigail Dr
2900 LSVL 40205 5618 A7
Abingdon Ct
8800 LSVL 40258 5831 A6
Abington Rdg
15100 LSVL 40245 5512 D7
Ables Wy
100 MTWH 40047 6056 B2
Able's Mountain Ln
- BltC 40165 6048 D7
Abraham Flexner Wy
200 LSVL 40202 5615 E3
Abshire Ln
3200 LSVL 40220 5727 E3
Abstain Ct
4900 LSVL 40213 5726 C6
4900 LSVL 40218 5726 C6
Acacia Av
100 PNRV 40165 6053 C1
Academy Ct
200 LSVL 40245 5621 B5
Academy Dr
- LSVL 40210 5615 A6
Academy Ln
100 RDCF 40160 6483 B5
Academy Lake Wy
300 LSVL 40245 5621 B5
Academy Ridge Blvd
14200 LSVL 40245 5621 B5
14200 MDTN 40245 5621 B5
Academy Ridge Pl
500 LSVL 40245 5621 B6
Acapolca Wy
5000 LSVL 40219 5835 D2
5100 LSVL 40228 5835 E2
Accasia Dr
2500 LSVL 40216 5723 A4
2600 LSVL 40216 5722 E4
N Access Dr
1200 JFVL 47130 5399 D7
Access Rd
- ELZT 42701 6703 E7
- JFVL 47130 5507 C5
Accomack Dr
3900 LSVL 40241 5511 B3
4100 FCSL 40241 5511 B3
Accrusia Av
400 CLKV 47129 5506 D3
Acme Wy
7900 LSVL 40219 5836 A6
8200 LSVL 40228 5836 A6
Acorn Ct
400 ELZT 42701 6702 E3
Acorn Ln
700 JFVL 47130 5508 A2
Acorn Wy
1900 LSVL 40216 5831 E1
Acosta Ct
1600 LGNG 40031 5297 A1
1600 OdmC 40031 5297 A1
Acres Ln
9300 LSVL 40272 5832 E7
9300 LSVL 40272 5941 E1
Action Av
3900 LSVL 40218 5727 A4
Acton Ln
6900 LSVL 40228 5836 C3
Acushnet Ct
2600 LDNP 40242 5510 C5
Acushnet Rd
8900 LDNP 40242 5510 C5
Ada Ln
3500 LSVL 40220 5726 E1
E Adair St
- LSVL 40214 5724 D4
500 LSVL 40209 5724 E4
500 LSVL 40209 5725 A4
W Adair St
100 LSVL 40214 5724 C4
Adair Creek Dr
9900 LSVL 40291 5837 B5
W Adams Av
200 CLKV 47129 5506 B3
Adams Cir
400 ELZT 42701 6703 C7
Adams Ct
2100 ClkC 47172 5397 D1
Adams Dr
100 MTWH 40047 6056 A1
Adams Ln
10 HdnC 42701 6703 E1
Adams Rd
200 ELZT 42701 6812 C4
Adams St
100 LSVL 40206 5616 B2
100 NALB 47150 5505 A3
200 HdnC 40121 6265 B7
1000 CLKV 47129 5397 D7
1200 NALB 47150 5504 E5
5800 MdeC 40121 6264 D7
5800 MdeC 40121 6373 C1
E Adams St
100 LGNG 40031 5296 E4

E Adams St
100 LGNG 40031 5297 A3
W Adams St
100 LGNG 40031 5296 E4
Adams Run Ct
8900 LSVL 40228 5836 E7
Adams Run Rd
8000 LSVL 40228 5945 D1
8100 LSVL 40228 5836 E7
8300 LSVL 40228 5837 A7
Adam Steven Cir
7700 LSVL 40220 5727 D2
Addington Av
1800 HBNA 40220 5619 B7
Addison Av
3400 LSVL 40211 5614 C6
Addison Ct
10 SVLY 40216 5723 B4
Addison Ln
4000 SVLY 40216 5723 B4
Addmore Ln
10 CLKV 47129 5397 C4
Adelaide Ct
4000 LSVL 40241 5510 C2
Adele Av
- LSVL 40218 5726 D3
- WBHL 40218 5726 D3
Adelia Av
1600 LSVL 40210 5723 E1
1700 LSVL 40210 5614 E7
Adena Dr
100 BltC 40047 5947 D6
Adi Wy
- LSVL 40213 5726 A6
- PLRH 40213 5726 A6
Adkins Ct
100 SLRB 47172 5288 E4
Adkins Rd
5300 LSVL 40219 5835 D7
Adler Wy
7500 BCFT 40222 5509 E6
Administration Dr
9100 LSVL 40209 5725 A5
Admiral Dr
8800 LSVL 40229 5836 B7
Admont Ct
9000 JFTN 40220 5728 B2
Adoue Ct
300 HdnC 40121 6373 E4
Adrienne Ct
8900 LSVL 40245 5512 C4
Adrienne Wy
2600 LSVL 40216 5722 D6
2600 SVLY 40216 5722 D6
8900 LSVL 40245 5512 C4
Adventure Rd
10 LSVL 40216 5723 A2
Adz Rd
800 FydC 47150 5504 D1
800 NALB 47150 5504 D1
Aebersold Ct
2000 NALB 47150 5505 D3
Aebersold Dr
1100 NALB 47150 5505 D3
Afterglow Ct
1200 LSVL 40214 5832 E6
1200 LSVL 40214 5833 A6
Afterglow Dr
8000 LSVL 40214 5833 A5
8200 LSVL 40214 5832 E6
Afton Rd
10000 BRMR 40223 5619 E4
10000 JFTN 40223 5619 E4
Aganza Dr
2300 LSVL 40219 5834 C6
Agena Dr
9800 LSVL 40229 5943 E2
Agnew Av
100 CLKV 47129 5506 C5
Ahland Rd
700 WLNP 40207 5618 B1
900 STMW 40207 5618 B1
Aiken Rd
12000 MDTN 40223 5620 E4
12000 MDTN 40243 5620 E4
12300 MDTN 40223 5621 A3
13400 LSVL 40245 5621 A3
15000 LSVL 40245 5512 D7
15500 LSVL 40245 5622 A1
16900 LSVL 40245 5513 C7
17600 SbyC 40245 5513 C7
Aiken Rd SR-1531
16900 LSVL 40245 5513 C7
16900 LSVL 40245 5622 B1
17600 SbyC 40245 5513 C7
Ailanthus Tr
5400 LSVL 40219 5726 C7
Ainslie Wy
3200 LSVL 40220 5727 A1
Aintree Ct
4500 SRPK 40220 5618 D5
Aintree Wy
2400 LSVL 40220 5618 D5
2400 SRPK 40220 5618 D6
Ainwick Ct
11100 DGSH 40243 5620 B5
Aires Ct
3100 LSVL 40220 5727 A2
Airfreight Dr
4600 LSVL 40209 5724 E5
Airline Al
- ELZT 42701 6812 C2
Airmont Ct
300 LSVL 40203 5615 E5
Airport Dr
7000 ClkC 47172 5398 A1
Airport Rd
100 VNGV 40175 6482 E6
100 VNGV 40175 6483 A7
Airview Dr
100 ELZT 42701 6702 D1
100 HdnC 42701 6702 D1
E Airview Dr
10 HdnC 42701 6702 D1

N Airview Dr
- HdnC 42701 6702 D1
S Airview Dr
200 HdnC 42701 6702 D1
W Airview Dr
10 HdnC 42701 6702 D1
Airway Dr
200 HdnC 42701 6702 D1
W A Jenkins Rd
10 ELZT 42701 6702 C1
10 RDCF 42701 6702 C1
100 HdnC 42701 6702 C1
W A Jenkins Rd SR-2802
10 ELZT 42701 6702 C1
10 RDCF 42701 6702 C1
100 HdnC 42701 6702 C1
Akers Av
1200 JFVL 47130 5506 E6
1300 CLKV 47130 5506 E6
Akimbo Rd
800 LSVL 40206 5507 E7
Alabama Av
500 ClkC 47172 5288 B2
500 LYDN 40222 5618 E2
500 SLRB 47172 5288 B2
Alabama Dr
600 SLRB 47172 5288 C3
Alamance Dr
12100 WTNH 40245 5511 D2
Alameter Ct
7200 LSVL 40258 5832 A3
Alameter Dr
3600 LSVL 40214 5832 B3
3600 LSVL 40258 5832 A3
Alamo Ct
6500 LSVL 40258 5831 A1
Alan Dr
400 NALB 47150 5505 A1
Alana Dr
4100 SVLY 40216 5723 B5
Alanadale Dr
5700 LSVL 40272 5940 A1
Alanmede Rd
2500 LSVL 40205 5726 D1
2600 LSVL 40205 5617 D7
Alba Wy
5100 LSVL 40213 5726 C6
Albans Pl
3100 LSVL 40241 5510 C4
Albany Av
200 LSVL 40206 5616 E3
1600 LSVL 40216 5723 B7
Albany St
100 NALB 47150 5505 A4
600 NALB 47150 5504 E4
Albemarle Ct
900 HTBN 40222 5619 C6
Albens Ct
9200 LSVL 40241 5510 C4
Alberta Ct
1900 ClkC 47172 5397 D1
Alberta Dr
10700 HYVA 40118 5942 E4
Albert H Near St
3400 LSVL 40205 5617 E6
Albion Dr
10900 LSVL 40272 5940 B3
Albrecht Cir
7800 LSVL 40241 5510 A1
Albrecht Ct
4800 LSVL 40241 5510 A1
Albrecht Dr
3000 OdmC 40059 5292 B7
Alcona Ln
3700 LSVL 40220 5727 B2
Alcott Rd
200 FRMD 40207 5618 C3
200 STMW 40207 5618 C3
Alden Rd
500 SLRB 47172 5288 D5
800 LSVL 40207 5617 D4
Alden Dell
3200 LSVL 40207 5617 D4
Alder Av
- LYNV 40213 5725 C7
4500 LSVL 40213 5725 C7
Alderbrook Pl
10600 LSVL 40299 5728 E6
10700 JFTN 40299 5728 E6
Aldridge Dr
1100 JFVL 47130 5507 C2
Aldridge Wy
8200 LYDN 40222 5619 C3
Aledo Ct
4700 LSVL 40229 5944 C5
Alek Av
100 BltC 40165 6161 B2
Aletha Rd
1400 LSVL 40219 5835 B1
Alex Ct
9300 JFTN 40299 5728 C5
Alex Dr
1100 ELZT 42701 6703 E5
Alexander Av
2000 LSVL 40217 5616 A7
2200 LSVL 40217 5725 A1
2300 PKWV 40217 5725 A1
9200 LSVL 40258 5831 C7
9200 LSVL 40272 5831 C7
Alexander Ct
3300 JFVL 47130 5398 D7
3300 JFVL 47130 5399 A7
3300 JFVL 47130 5507 E1
Alexander Rd
2500 JfnC 40204 5616 E5
2500 LSVL 40204 5616 D5
Alexis Cove E
10 OdmC 40059 5291 D7
Alexis Cove W
14500 OdmC 40059 5291 D7
Alfin Ct
5400 LSVL 40299 5729 C7
Alford Av
3800 LSVL 40212 5614 C1

Alfred Berry Ct
12400 LSVL 40223 5620 D1
Alfresco Pl
1800 LSVL 40205 5616 E7
1900 LSVL 40205 5617 B6
Alger Av
100 LSVL 40214 5833 C1
300 LSVL 40214 5724 B7
Algiers Ct
100 LSVL 40218 5727 A2
100 LSVL 40220 5727 A2
Algonquin Ct
10 SHDV 40165 6161 E2
Algonquin Pkwy
700 LSVL 40208 5724 B1
1200 LSVL 40208 5615 B7
1200 LSVL 40210 5615 A7
1700 LSVL 40210 5614 E7
2700 LSVL 40211 5614 D7
Algonquin Pkwy SR-2054
700 LSVL 40208 5724 B1
1200 LSVL 40208 5615 B7
1200 LSVL 40210 5615 A7
1700 LSVL 40210 5614 E7
2700 LSVL 40211 5614 D7
Alia Cir
2600 LSVL 40222 5509 D5
2700 TNHL 40222 5509 D5
2700 TNHL 40241 5509 D5
Alicante Ln
5300 LSVL 40272 5940 B5
Alice Av
600 NALB 47150 5504 E5
2600 NALB 47150 5505 D1
2700 LSVL 40220 5726 E1
Alice St
- JFVL 47130 5506 E5
Alice Kay Dr
2200 LSVL 40214 5723 D7
Alicent Ct
4400 WLNP 40207 5618 C1
Alicent Rd
4300 WLNP 40207 5618 C2
Alisha Ct
100 RDCF 40160 6592 E2
Allan Ct
- OdmC 44026 5292 C4
Allanwood Rd
1800 LSVL 40214 5832 D4
Allee Rd
4000 FydC 47150 5395 E4
4000 FydC 47150 5396 A4
4000 NALB 47150 5396 A4
Allegheny Dr
2300 JFTN 40299 5728 D1
Allen Av
2900 LSVL 40208 5724 C2
4200 LSVL 40218 5726 D4
Allen Dr
400 VNGV 40175 6482 E7
1500 FydC 47122 5503 C3
10500 HYVA 40118 5942 E3
10500 HYVA 40118 5943 A3
10500 LSVL 40118 5943 A3
Allen Ln
1700 LGNG 40031 5296 C3
1700 OdmC 40031 5296 C3
Allen Rd
600 SLRB 47172 5288 C2
Allen St
300 RDCF 40160 6483 E6
Allene Av
2000 LSVL 40217 5615 E7
2000 LSVL 40217 5724 E1
Allentown Rd
600 SLRB 47172 5288 C3
1100 ClkC 47143 5288 C2
1100 ClkC 47172 5288 B1
Allentree Pl
10200 LSVL 40229 5944 E3
Allerton Ct
8300 LYDN 40222 5619 C2
Allgeier Ct
1800 LSVL 40213 5725 E3
1800 LSVL 40213 5726 A3
Allgeier Dr
1400 OdmC 40031 5297 B4
Allhands Av
400 SLRB 47172 5288 D3
Alliant Av
1500 JFTN 40299 5620 C7
1500 JFTN 40299 5729 C1
Allielough Ct
8000 PROS 40059 5400 D2
Allison Av
5700 MdeC 40121 6373 D1
Allison Ct
100 HLVW 40229 6053 A1
Allison Dr
- MTWH 40047 6056 E2
Allison Ln
200 JFVL 47130 5508 A3
1300 JFVL 47130 5507 E1
2600 JFVL 47130 5398 D7
Allison Rd
400 MDTN 40243 5620 D3
Allison St
900 ELZT 42701 6812 D1
Allison Wy
3200 LSVL 40220 5727 B1
Allmond Av
4200 LSVL 40214 5724 D4
Alloway Ct
10900 DGSH 40243 5620 A5
Allspice Ct
7000 LSVL 40291 [illegible]
Allston Av
1800 [illegible]
Alma Av
1500 [illegible]
1600 [illegible]
Alma Jun[illegible]
7000 [illegible]

INDEX 7

Alma Lynn Dr — Louisville Metro Street Index — Aster Dr

STREET Block City ZIP Map# Grid

Alma Lynn Dr
12000 LSVL 40118 5943 B4
Almara Cir
1600 LSVL 40205 5618 A6
Almondwood Cir
100 ELZT 42701 6812 A2
Alonzo Smith Rd
2000 FydC 47122 5502 D2
2000 GEOT 47122 5502 D3
3000 FydC 47122 5393 D6
Alpar Ln
- BltC 40165 6163 C1
100 BltC 40165 6054 C7
Alpena Wy
8300 BRMD 40242 5510 B4
Alpha Av
100 LSVL 40218 5727 B4
1500 LYDN 40223 5510 E7
1500 LYDN 40223 5619 E1
Alpha Ct
100 NALB 47150 5505 D2
1400 CLKV 47129 5506 C1
Alphin Ct
8900 JFTN 40299 5728 B6
Alpine Ct
1300 NALB 47150 5505 D2
Alpine Wy
5200 LSVL 40214 5833 B1
12000 OdmC 44026 5292 C2
Alps Rd
2600 LSVL 40216 5722 C7
Alreva Rd
200 LSVL 40216 5832 A3
Al's Wy
8500 LSVL 40214 5833 B6
Alsace St
5900 HdnC 40121 6265 C7
Alshire Dr
8700 LSVL 40258 5831 C6
Alta Av
2000 LSVL 40205 5616 E6
2200 NALB 47150 5505 B2
2300 LSVL 40205 5617 A5
Alta Cir
1000 LSVL 40205 5617 B5
Alta Lp
10 HdnC 40175 6591 A1
Alta St
500 VNGV 40175 6591 E1
Altagate Ct
2800 LSVL 40206 5617 B4
Altagate Rd
500 LSVL 40206 5617 B4
Altair Ln
3900 LSVL 40219 5835 A6
Alta Vista Ct
2800 LSVL 40206 5617 B4
Alta Vista Pl
2800 LSVL 40206 5617 B4
Alta Vista Rd
700 LSVL 40206 5617 B4
900 LSVL 40205 5617 B4
Alta Vista Wy
2800 LSVL 40206 5617 B4
Altawood Ct
- CLKV 47129 5506 C2
3700 LSVL 40245 5512 A3
Altawood Dr
1400 CLKV 47129 5506 B1
Althea
2000 NALB 47150 5505 E4
Althea Av
2000 NALB 47150 5505 E4
Alton Ln
10600 HYVA 40118 5943 A4
10600 LSVL 40118 5943 A4
Alton Rd
3900 SPLE 40207 5618 A5
3900 STMW 40207 5618 B4
Alton St
600 VNGV 40175 6591 C1
Altra Dr
100 CLKV 47129 5506 C1
Altsheler Pl
10900 LSVL 40229 5944 E5
Altus Wy
3100 SVLY 40216 5723 C2
Aluma Ln
- LSVL 40214 5833 C5
Alumni Dr
- LSVL 40205 5616 E7
- NALB 47150 5396 C4
100 ELZT 42701 6703 A2
100 HdnC 42701 6703 A2
Alva Dr
2600 LSVL 40216 5722 E7
Alvarado Wy
6000 LSVL 40205 5618 B6
Alvin Dr
3400 ClkC 47130 5398 C5
Alvina Wy
100 LSVL 40214 5833 C3
[illegible]um Dr
LSVL 40258 5831 D4
[illegible]0219 5835 D7
[illegible]054 C5
[illegible] E2
[illegible] C2
[illegible]02 D6
[illegible] 6265 D7
[illegible]0 6483 B6
[illegible]0 6483 B6
[illegible] 5832 E1
[illegible] 5618 E7

Amber Hill Pl
5100 LSVL 40241 5511 B1
Amberlin Ln
1300 LSVL 40245 5622 C2
Amberly Ct
4200 LSVL 40241 5510 C2
Amberly Wy
4100 LSVL 40241 5510 E2
Amber Ridge Ct
9400 LSVL 40272 5831 E7
Amber Waves Dr
2700 ClkC 47130 5398 A4
Amberwell Park Rd
10300 LSVL 40241 5511 A5
Amberwood Dr
10 HdnC 42701 6703 D3
Ambling Wy
100 MDTN 40243 5620 D4
Amboy Dr
2200 SVLY 40216 5723 B2
Ambridge Cir
6900 WDYH 40207 5618 C1
6900 WLNP 40207 5618 C1
Ambridge Dr
900 WDYH 40207 5618 C1
900 WLNP 40207 5618 C1
1200 WDYH 40207 5509 C7
Ambrosse Ln
8300 LSVL 40299 5728 A4
Amburgey Dr
300 FydC 47150 5504 C5
300 NALB 47150 5504 C5
Amelia Ct
4400 FCSL 40241 5511 C2
Amelie Dr
600 JFVL 47130 5508 A3
Amelle Dr
500 JFVL 47130 5508 A3
America Pl
200 JFVL 47130 5507 A5
Amerivan Ct
4500 JFTN 40299 5728 A6
Amerivan Dr
8500 JFTN 40299 5728 A6
Amestree Pl
5200 LSVL 40229 5944 D3
E Amherst Av
100 LSVL 40214 5724 D6
W Amherst Av
100 LSVL 40214 5724 C6
Amherst Pl
600 JFTN 40223 5619 D5
Amigo Ct
6600 LSVL 40291 5837 D3
Amity Ct
8100 LSVL 40220 5727 E2
8100 LSVL 40220 5728 A2
Amity Ln
8000 LSVL 40220 5727 E3
Ampere Ct
11100 JFTN 40299 5729 A3
Ampere Dr
2100 JFTN 40299 5729 B2
Ample Wy
100 HLVW 40229 5944 A7
Amrona Av
10000 LSVL 40272 5940 C2
Amy Av
10 HdnC 42701 6593 A4
10 RDCF 42701 6593 A4
100 HdnC 42701 6592 E4
200 LSVL 40212 5614 C2
400 LSVL 40211 5614 C2
Amy Ct
10 NALB 47150 5396 D5
100 ELZT 42701 6702 D6
Amy Lynn Ct
10300 JFTN 40223 5619 E5
Ana Ter
4900 LSVL 40272 5940 C2
Anatahan Ct
5300 LSVL 40272 5940 B5
Anatolia Wy
11800 LSVL 40229 5944 C4
Anchor Av
100 LGNG 40031 5296 D3
Anchor Wy
2400 ANCH 40223 5511 E6
Anchorage Pointe
10 ANCH 40223 5620 D1
Anchorage Woods Cir
1000 ANCH 40223 5620 B2
Anchorage Woods Ct
11500 ANCH 40223 5620 C2
Ancient Spring Dr
12000 CDSM 40245 5511 D1
Andalee Dr
11500 LSVL 40272 5940 B4
Andalusia Av
400 CLKV 47129 5506 D3
Andalusia Ln
4600 LSVL 40272 5831 D7
4700 LSVL 40272 5940 C1
Anderson Av
300 LSVL 40218 5727 A5
3800 FydC 47150 5396 D4
Anderson Ct
100 RDCF 40160 6483 A5
Anderson Rd
300 FydC 47150 5613 D2
Anderson St
- LSVL 40211 5614 E3
2100 LSVL 40210 5615 A3
2100 LSVL 40211 5615 A3
Anderson Woods Pl
3900 LSVL 40245 5512 C5
Anderson Woods Trc
14600 LSVL 40245 5512 D5
Andle Ct
1000 LSVL 40214 5833 A5
Andover Ct
3700 LSVL 40299 5728 B4
Andra St
700 RDCF 40160 6483 B5

Andrea Ct
3300 JFVL 47130 5507 A1
Andrea Wy
4700 LSVL 40219 5835 C6
Andres St
300 SLRB 47172 5288 D4
Andrew Ct
7400 LSVL 40220 5727 E1
Andrew Dr
4100 FydC 47119 5394 D3
Angel Al
- HdnC 40121 6374 B2
Angel Ter
4100 JFTN 40299 5728 D5
Angela Dr
100 BltC 40165 6052 D5
Angela Wy
7400 LSVL 40220 5727 D2
Angeletta Wy
200 LSVL 40214 5833 B5
Angelina Rd
11300 HLVW 40229 5944 A6
11300 HNTH 40229 5944 A6
Angels Ct
- BltC 40071 5948 B7
Angle Av
100 HLVW 40229 5944 A6
Anglers Cove
7100 FydC 47122 5393 D6
Angora Ct
10 LSVL 40206 5616 D3
Angus Ct
5400 LSVL 40272 5940 B2
Anita Blvd
9600 LSVL 40272 5940 C1
Anita Springs Ct
500 LGNG 40031 5296 D4
Aniwa Rd
6100 LSVL 40214 5832 D1
Ann Pl
300 NALB 47150 5504 E2
Ann St
2200 NALB 47150 5505 C2
Anna Ln
1400 LSVL 40215 5723 D6
1400 LSVL 40216 5723 D6
Annabrook Ct
2200 OdmC 40031 5296 D5
Annadale Ct
3100 LSVL 40299 5729 D4
Annalisa Dr
7700 LSVL 40291 5836 E5
7700 LSVL 40291 5837 A5
Annella Wy
7900 LSVL 40219 5835 C5
Annie Av
2900 LSVL 40211 5614 D6
Anniston Wy
10 ELZT 42701 6593 E7
Annlou Dr
8800 LSVL 40272 5831 D6
Ann Marie Dr
2100 JFTN 40299 5728 C1
Annshire Av
4300 WSNP 40213 5725 E4
Anoka Ct
11900 LSVL 40245 5511 C2
Anselmo Ln
16900 LSVL 40299 5840 C6
Anson Dr
4100 FydC 47119 5394 E4
Anthony Ct
5200 OdmC 40014 5404 E3
Antioch Dr
9500 LSVL 40291 5946 D1
Antle Dr
5100 LSVL 40229 5944 C4
Antler Ct
9000 BRWD 40242 5510 C6
Antler Dr
100 ClkC 47172 5397 B1
100 CLKV 47172 5397 B1
100 FydC 47150 5397 B1
Anton Ct
10800 LSVL 40229 5944 E4
Antone Pkwy
2600 JFTN 40220 5728 A2
Antrim Rd
700 WDYH 40207 5509 B7
700 WNDF 40207 5509 B7
Anvil Ct
6600 FydC 47122 5502 E5
Apache
- HdnC 40121 6374 E2
Apache Dr
3000 JFVL 47130 5398 E7
3000 JFVL 47130 5507 E1
Apache Rd
5400 INHC 40207 5508 E7
5500 INHC 40207 5509 A6
5500 LSVL 40207 5509 A6
5700 WNDF 40207 5509 A6
Apex Dr
6000 LSVL 40219 5836 A5
6300 LSVL 40228 5836 B5
Apple Ln
1300 JFVL 47130 5507 B5
Apple Blossom Pl
7500 LSVL 40228 5836 D5
Apple Cider Dr
6200 LSVL 40219 5835 E5
Apple Creek Rd
6100 LSVL 40219 5835 E5
Applecross Wy
10500 DGSH 40223 5619 E6
10500 JFTN 40223 5619 E6
Apple Crossing Ct
9500 ODGH 40014 5402 D7
Applegate Ct
8100 LSVL 40228 5836 C6
Applegate Ln
100 SLRB 47172 5288 D3
1100 ClkC 47129 5506 D2
1100 CLKV 47129 5506 D2

Applegate Ln
5500 LSVL 40219 5835 E5
6400 LSVL 40219 5836 B6
6400 LSVL 40228 5836 B6
E Applegate Ln
10 JFVL 47130 5506 E3
10 JFVL 47130 5507 A3
Applegate Village Dr
8700 LSVL 40219 5835 E5
Applegrove Ln
4900 LSVL 40218 5727 B6
Applehill Rd
3100 LSVL 40245 5512 E5
Apple Mill Dr
7200 LSVL 40228 5836 C5
Apple Mill Pl
7700 LSVL 40228 5836 C5
Apple Orchard Ln
7000 ODGH 40014 5402 D7
7000 OdmC 40014 5402 D7
Apple Orchard Pl
9300 ODGH 40014 5402 D7
9300 OdmC 40014 5402 D7
Apple Patch Ct
- CTWD 40014 5403 B3
Apple Patch Wy
- CTWD 40014 5403 C3
Appleton Ct
3200 SVLY 40216 5723 D2
Appleton Ln
1800 SVLY 40216 5723 C2
Apple Tree Ln
500 CLKV 47129 5506 D3
13400 RVBF 40059 5401 A1
Appletree Wy
7500 LSVL 40228 5836 D5
Apple Valley Dr
7700 LSVL 40228 5836 D5
Apple Valley Wy
100 BltC 40165 6163 E4
Appleview Ln
7800 LSVL 40228 5836 D5
Applewood Cir
9500 ODGH 40014 5402 E7
Applewood Ct
9600 ODGH 40014 5402 D7
Applewood Ln
1500 GYDL 40222 5510 A7
1500 GYDL 40222 5618 D4
1600 GYDL 40222 5509 E7
1700 LSVL 40222 5509 E7
Applewood Rd
7100 ODGH 40014 5402 D7
Apollo Ct
9900 LSVL 40272 5940 B1
Apollo Dr
10 MTWH 40047 6056 A2
Appollo Ln
5800 LSVL 40272 5940 B1
Appomattox Rd
200 LSVL 40214 5833 B6
April Ct
10 ELZT 42701 6702 D6
100 CHAN 47111 5181 C3
100 ClkC 47111 5181 C3
April Dr
- CHAN 47111 5181 C2
April Wy
9600 LSVL 40272 5940 A3
Aqua Ln
10200 LSVL 40118 5942 B1
Aqua Wy
2300 PNTN 40242 5510 B6
Aquarius Rd
12400 MDTN 40243 5620 D3
Aral Dr
4500 LSVL 40219 5726 C7
Arapaho Dr
7400 LSVL 40214 5833 A3
A Ray Ln
10 HdnC 40160 6592 B2
Arbegust St
- LSVL 40210 5615 B4
Arbor Av
300 LSVL 40214 5833 C1
Arbor Ct
100 CLKV 47172 5288 B6
11500 ANCH 40223 5620 B3
E Arbor Dr
11500 ANCH 40223 5620 C3
N Arbor Dr
600 ANCH 40223 5620 B2
Arbor Pk N
100 LSVL 40214 5833 C1
Arbor Pk S
100 LSVL 40214 5833 C1
Arbor Pl
10 NALB 47150 5396 A5
Arbor Trc
100 HLVW 40229 5944 A6
Arbor Creek Dr
6600 LSVL 40228 5836 D7
Arbor Crest Cir
13500 LSVL 40245 5512 B5
Arbor Meadow Wy
8300 LSVL 40228 5836 D7
Arboro Pl
1800 HBNA 40220 5619 A7
1900 JFTN 40220 5619 A7
Arbor Oak Ct
5100 LSVL 40229 5944 D1
Arbor Oak Dr
10200 LSVL 40229 5944 D2
Arbor Pointe Dr
2400 JFTN 40220 5728 A1
Arbor Pointe Pl
2300 JFTN 40220 5728 A1
Arbor Ridge Rd
6500 CTWD 40014 5403 D6
6600 OdmC 40014 5403 D6
Arbor Ridge Wy
- CTWD 40014 5403 D5
Arbutus Tr
7500 LSVL 40291 5837 B5

Arcade Av
1200 LSVL 40215 5724 A2
1600 SVLY 40216 5724 A2
Arcadia Ct
3700 HNTH 40229 5944 A6
Archtree Pl
5600 LSVL 40229 5944 E3
Archwood Ct
8400 LSVL 40219 5835 A6
Arctic Springs Rd
10 JFVL 47130 5507 D6
Ardella Ct
200 LSVL 40203 5615 E5
Arden Rd
10 GNVW 40222 5509 A3
2800 LSVL 40220 5618 A7
Ardenia Ln
8100 LSVL 40228 5836 E6
Ardennes St
- HdnC 40121 6265 C6
Ardmore Ct
400 ELZT 42701 6702 E3
Ardmore Dr
900 LSVL 40217 5725 B1
1000 LSVL 40217 5616 B7
Ardossan Sq
5000 LSVL 40241 5510 E1
Ardsley Rd
2200 RBNW 40207 5509 A5
Argonne Av
1800 SVLY 40216 5723 D2
Argyle Ln
3600 LSVL 40220 5618 A7
Aria Dr
8900 MLHT 40219 5834 C7
8900 SPVW 40219 5834 C7
Arid Ln
5500 LSVL 40258 5721 E6
Aristada Pl
9200 ODGH 40014 5402 E7
Aristides Dr
8800 LSVL 40272 5831 A6
9200 LSVL 40258 5831 A7
Arjay Ln
3000 LSVL 40220 5727 C3
Arling Av
1300 LSVL 40215 5724 A6
1600 LSVL 40214 5723 E7
1600 LSVL 40215 5723 E7
Arling Ct
4800 LSVL 40215 5723 E6
Arlington
200 CHAN 47111 5181 D4
Arlington Av
300 CLKV 47129 5506 C5
1600 LSVL 40206 5616 C2
Arlington Ct
2900 JFTN 40299 5728 C3
Arlington Rd
2800 LSVL 40220 5618 B7
Arlington Meadows Ct
18000 LSVL 40023 5622 D5
Arlington Meadows Dr
100 LSVL 40023 5622 D6
100 LSVL 40245 5622 D6
Arlis Dr
7900 LSVL 40258 5831 D5
Arlone Ct
6100 LSVL 40216 5831 D1
Armadale Pl
600 DGSH 40243 5620 A5
Armoridge Pl
9400 LSVL 40229 5944 E1
Armory Pl
300 LSVL 40202 5615 D3
Armour Ln
100 RDCF 40160 6483 A1
Armsmere Wy
5300 LSVL 40218 5726 D6
5400 LSVL 40228 5726 D6
Armstrong Ct
3900 ClkC 47130 5398 B5
3900 JFVL 47130 5398 B5
Armstrong Rd
- BltC 40047 6055 D5
- JFVL 47130 5398 B4
- MTWH 40047 6055 D5
1500 NALB 47150 5505 E1
1600 NALB 47150 5397 A7
1600 NALB 47150 5506 A1
3900 ClkC 47130 5398 C5
Arnold Av
4700 LSVL 40219 5835 C5
Arnold Ct
100 NALB 47150 5504 C6
Arnold Dr
100 BltC 40165 6053 B4
W Arnold Ln
10 HdnC 42701 6811 C7
Arnold Palmer Blvd
1100 LSVL 40245 5621 D2
2100 LSVL 40245 5512 C7
Arnolds Rd
- BltC 40165 6161 B1
- SHDV 40165 6161 B1
Arnoldtown Rd
7200 LSVL 40214 5832 C6
7200 LSVL 40258 5832 C6
7600 LSVL 40272 5832 B4
Arnoldtown Woods Rd
2400 LSVL 40214 5832 C5
2400 LSVL 40272 5832 C5
Aron Rd
6700 LSVL 40258 5831 A5
Aroxie Ct
6200 LSVL 40258 5831 B3
Arrow Creek Rd
100 BltC 40165 6162 A6
100 SHDV 40165 6162 A6
Arrow Creek Farm Rd
- BltC 40165 6162 A7
Arrowhead Dr
2300 ClkC 47111 5182 B1

E Arrowhead Dr
2100 FydC 47150 5613 D1
W Arrowhead Dr
400 FydC 47150 5613 D2
Arrowhead Ln
10 SHDV 40165 6161 E2
10 SHDV 40165 6162 A2
Arrowhead Rd
10 INDH 40207 5508 D7
Arrowhead St
10 HdnC 40121 6374 D1
Arrowood Rd
7100 GYDL 40222 5509 D7
Arrowridge Dr
9500 LSVL 40229 5945 A2
9600 LSVL 40229 5944 E2
Arrow Run Rd
2600 FydC 47119 5395 C3
Arrowshire Dr
5100 OdmC 40031 5295 B4
Arrowwood Ct
3500 OdmC 40031 5295 E7
3500 OdmC 40031 5404 E1
Arroyo Tr
100 HLVW 40229 5944 B5
100 LSVL 40229 5944 B5
Art Ln
17600 LSVL 40023 5731 E2
Arterburn Av
3100 LSVL 40206 5617 C2
Arterburn Dr
- LSVL 40222 5618 E3
100 NRWD 40222 5618 E3
300 LYDN 40222 5618 E3
Arterburn Woods Dr
9900 LSVL 40223 5619 D3
Arthur Ct
100 RDCF 40160 6592 E2
Arthur St
1600 LSVL 40208 5615 E7
1900 LSVL 40208 5724 E1
2300 JFVL 47130 5398 A6
Arthur St SR-61
1600 LSVL 40208 5615 E7
Arthur Coffman Rd
8400 FydC 47106 5284 A7
8400 FydC 47119 5284 A7
8400 FydC 47124 5283 E7
8400 FydC 47124 5284 A7
9300 GNVL 47124 5283 E7
Arthur Ford Ct
2200 LSVL 40217 5724 E1
Arthur Goins Blvd
8100 LSVL 40228 5836 D4
Arthur Hills Wy
- SbyC 40245 5513 D4
Arthurs Ct
- BltC 40165 6160 D5
Artis Pl
7600 LSVL 40291 5837 B4
Artis Wy
8800 LSVL 40291 5837 B4
Arundel Wy
- HTBN 40222 5619 B4
Arvis Dr
5500 LSVL 40216 5722 C7
5500 LSVL 40216 5831 C1
5600 LSVL 40258 5831 C1
Arwine Ct
4300 WTNH 40245 5511 D2
E Asbury Cir
1100 HdnC 42701 6811 B4
W Asbury Cir
- HdnC 42701 6811 C4
Asbury Park Blvd
- LSVL 40241 5510 B1
Asbury Park Ter
4600 LSVL 40241 5510 B1
Ascot Cir
3400 MRCK 40241 5510 C3
Ash Av
- OdmC 40014 5512 E4
100 OdmC 40056 5512 D3
100 PWEV 40056 5512 E4
4500 LSVL 40258 5831 E3
Ash Av SR-362
- OdmC 40014 5512 E4
100 OdmC 40056 5512 D3
100 PWEV 40056 5512 E4
Ash Ct
100 RDCF 40160 6483 A5
1200 JFVL 47130 5507 B2
Ash Dr
- RDCF 40160 6483 A5
100 ClkC 47111 5181 A4
Ash Ln
- LSVL 40219 5834 D6
Ash St
100 CHAN 47111 5181 D2
200 UTCA 47130 5400 A6
300 UTCA 47130 5399 E6
800 LSVL 40203 5616 A6
800 LSVL 40204 5616 A6
800 LSVL 40217 5616 A6
Ashbottom Rd
8000 LSVL 40213 5834 A1
Ashbrook Av
2500 LSVL 40220 5618 C6
Ash Brook Wy
- FydC 47150 5397 B2
Ashbrooke Dr
6500 OdmC 40056 5512 E4
Ashbrooke Gardens Ct
5800 LSVL 40229 5944 E5
Ashbrooke Gardens Dr
11200 LSVL 40229 5944 E5
11300 BltC 40165 5944 E5
Ashburton Dr
17000 LSVL 40245 5621 D6
Ashbury Dr
4800 FydC 47150 5396 C3
Ashbury Rd
200 LSVL 40214 5724 C7

Ashby Ln
10 ClkC 47172 5288 C6
10 SLRB 47172 5288 C6
5800 LSVL 40272 5940 A2
6500 LSVL 40272 5939 D1
Ashby Ln SR-1230
7000 LSVL 40272 5939 D1
Ashcraft Ln
2100 WWOD 40242 5510 C6
Ashcroft Rd
- LSVL 40118 5942 B1
Ashdowne Ct
8000 PROS 40059 5401 B5
Ashers Run Ct
7500 OdmC 40014 5513 D1
Ashers Run Dr
7500 OdmC 40014 5513 D2
Ashfield Ln
1700 LSVL 40220 5618 E7
1700 SRPK 40220 5618 E7
Ashford Ct
14400 LSVL 40245 5621 D5
Ashford Dr
- OdmC 44026 5292 B5
100 MTWH 40047 6056 D3
Ash Glen Rd
16800 LSVL 40245 5622 C5
Ash Grove Pl
14500 LSVL 40245 5621 D2
Ash Hill Dr
16900 LSVL 40245 5622 D5
Ash Hollow Rd
100 BltC 40165 6050 C4
E Ashland Av
100 LSVL 40214 5724 D5
W Ashland Av
100 LSVL 40214 5724 C5
1500 LSVL 40215 5724 A5
Ashlawn Dr
13000 LSVL 40272 5939 E7
13000 LSVL 40272 6048 E1
Ashley Blvd
100 SHDV 40165 6161 B6
Ashley Ct
100 HLVW 40229 5944 A5
2000 WWOD 40242 5510 C6
3000 FydC 47172 5397 A1
3300 NALB 47150 5395 E6
Ashley Dr
2300 JFVL 47130 5507 C1
Ashley Morgan Dr
2700 FydC 47150 5613 C2
Ashley Pointe Dr
- LSVL 40272 5942 A1
10600 LSVL 40272 5941 E1
Ashley Woods Dr
7700 LSVL 40241 5509 E2
Ashmont Ct
14500 LSVL 40245 5621 C3
Ashmont Pl
14500 LSVL 40245 5621 D3
Ashmoor Ln
1600 LYDN 40223 5510 D7
1600 LYDN 40242 5510 D7
1600 MLND 40223 5510 C7
Ashridge Dr
3800 BWNF 40241 5510 B2
Ash Run Rd
100 LSVL 40245 5622 C5
Ash Spring Rd
9200 LSVL 40291 5837 B3
Ashton Av
4400 LSVL 40209 5724 E4
Ash Tree Cir
6900 LSVL 40241 5509 D4
Ashurst Ct
9800 HKYH 40241 5510 E5
Ashview Ter
3000 LSVL 40217 5725 B1
Ashwood Cir
3400 OdmC 40031 5296 C7
Ashwood Ct
3400 NALB 47150 5396 C6
Ashwood Dr
2300 LSVL 40205 5725 E1
2400 JFVL 47130 5398 C7
2400 JFVL 47130 5507 C1
2400 LSVL 40205 5726 A1
Ashwood Bluff Ct
2000 LSVL 40207 5509 C6
Ashwood Bluff Dr
5900 LSVL 40207 5509 B5
5900 WNDF 40207 5509 B6
Aspen Av
8100 LSVL 40258 5831 B5
Aspen Ct
1800 NALB 47150 5505 C1
Aspendale Ct
2900 MYHL 40241 5510 C5
Aspendale Rd
2900 MYHL 40241 5510 C5
Aspen Glen Dr
8000 LSVL 40228 5836 E6
Aspen Glen Wy
8400 LSVL 40228 5836 E6
Aspen Green Ln
8000 LSVL 40291 5837 A4
Aspen Grove Ct
7000 LSVL 40241 5509 D4
Aspen Valley Cir
3200 LSVL 40241 5509 D4
Aspen View Ct
10900 LSVL 40299 5729 A5
Aspenwood Av
- LSVL 40241 5509 D4
Aspenwood Wy
3000 LSVL 40241 5509 D4
Assembly Rd
900 JFVL 47130 5398 E7
900 JFVL 47130 5399 A7
Assisi Av
100 CLKV 47129 5506 D4
Aster Dr
1900 JFVL 47130 5507 C3

INDEX 8
Astin Ct
Louisville Metro Street Index
Bay Cove Ct

STREET Block City ZIP Map# Grid

Astin Ct
7100 LSVL 40219 5836 A2
Astor Rd
4600 LSVL 40218 5726 A5
Astral Dr
6500 LSVL 40258 5831 C2
Astrid Av
8600 LSVL 40228 5836 B7
Astrid Wy
7500 LSVL 40228 5836 B7
Astrocraft Dr
3700 LSVL 40229 5944 A1
Atcher Ln
400 HdnC 40175 6591 D2
Atcher St
- RDCF 40160 6483 C4
S Atcher St
700 RDCF 40160 6483 D5
Athens Dr
6000 LSVL 40219 5835 C1
Atherton Rd
- HdnC 40160 6484 B5
Atisan Wy
6500 LSVL 40228 5835 E2
Atkins Ln
- FydC 47150 5504 A5
Atkins Rd
6500 FydC 47119 5395 E1
Atkinson Dr
4000 LSVL 40218 5726 B3
4000 WSNP 40218 5726 B3
Atkinson Square Dr
3900 WSNP 40218 5726 A4
Atlanta Pkwy
8000 LSVL 40214 5833 B6
Atlas Rd
3800 LSVL 40229 5944 A2
Atlas Cedar Ct
6900 LSVL 40291 5837 A2
Atrium Dr
8500 JFTN 40220 5728 A1
Atterberry Ct
1700 SVLY 40216 5723 B6
Attu Ln
8600 LSVL 40291 5837 A3
Atur Ln
7100 LSVL 40258 5831 C2
Atwood St
- LSVL 40208 5724 D1
400 LSVL 40217 5724 E1
Aubert Av
3000 LSVL 40206 5617 B3
Auburn Av
- CLKV 47129 5506 D3
9200 JFTN 40299 5728 C3
Auburn Cir
3100 JFTN 40299 5728 C3
Auburn Dr
1800 SVLY 40216 5723 B5
Auburndale Av
500 LSVL 40214 5724 B7
Auburn Oaks Ct
7600 LSVL 40214 5833 B4
Auburn Oaks Dr
500 LSVL 40214 5833 B4
Auburn Place Ct
600 LSVL 40214 5833 B4
Auburn Place Dr
7500 LSVL 40214 5833 B4
Auburn Woods Ct
9100 LSVL 40214 5833 A4
Auburn Woods Rd
9000 LSVL 40214 5833 B4
Auction Wy
1000 JFVL 47130 5507 B4
Audley Dr
2700 LSVL 40206 5616 E1
Audrey Ct
- SpnC 40071 5949 E3
Audubon Av
10 PNRV 40165 6053 C1
Audubon Ct
10 ELZT 42701 6812 B3
100 CHAN 47111 5181 D4
300 RDCF 40160 6483 B3
Audubon Dr
- ClkC 47111 5290 C2
N Audubon Dr
1700 NALB 47150 5505 D1
S Audubon Dr
1700 NALB 47150 5505 D1
Audubon Ln
- HdnC 40175 6482 D1
100 BltC 40165 6054 B7
Audubon Pkwy
900 ANPK 40213 5725 B3
900 LSVL 40213 5725 B2
Audubon Pl
1700 NALB 47150 5505 D1
Audubon St
- HdnC 40121 6373 E2
Audubon Plaza Dr
10 LSVL 40213 5725 C1
10 LSVL 40217 5725 C1
Audubon Ridge Ct
3400 LSVL 40213 5725 D1
Audubon Ridge Dr
3300 LSVL 40213 5725 D1
Augusta Dr
700 HdnC 40175 6591 A1
1700 JFVL 47130 5398 A7
2200 JFVL 47130 5507 B1
Augusta National Dr
4500 FydC 47119 5503 D1
Augustine Wy
8600 LSVL 40291 5728 A7
Augustus Av
500 LSVL 40208 5615 E7
500 LSVL 40217 5615 E7
Aulbern Dr
- MTWH 40047 6055 E5
Aulbern Dr E
100 MTWH 40047 6055 E5
Aulbern Dr W
100 MTWH 40047 6055 D5
Aulbern West Ct
100 MTWH 40047 6055 E5
Aura Rd
5800 GNVW 40222 5509 A2
5800 LSVL 40222 5509 A2
Aurora Dr
7200 LSVL 40214 5833 C3
Austin Dr
700 RDCF 40160 6593 B1
900 HdnC 42701 6593 B1
Austin Ln
4400 LSVL 40218 5727 C5
Austin Wood Pl
1800 LSVL 40214 5832 E3
Austin Wood Rd
7000 LSVL 40214 5832 D3
Auto Glass Dr
10 ELZT 42701 6811 A6
10 HdnC 42701 6811 A6
Autumn Ct
2900 OdmC 40059 5292 D6
Autumn Dr
4100 FydC 47150 5396 C2
8100 GEOT 47122 5501 E3
8100 GEOT 47122 5502 A3
Autumn Dr NE
2700 LNVL 47136 5610 D4
Autumn Rd
6600 ClkC 47111 5290 B2
Autumn Wy
10 HdnC 42701 6812 B7
100 BltC 40047 6055 E4
3300 LSVL 40218 5726 D2
4100 LSVL 40272 5940 A6
Autumn Bent Ct
9500 ODGH 40014 5402 D7
9500 OdmC 40014 5402 D7
Autumn Bent Wy
7000 ODGH 40014 5402 D7
7000 OdmC 40014 5402 D7
Autumn Creek Pl
10500 LSVL 40229 5944 A3
Autumn Falls Ct
3900 LSVL 40229 5944 A3
Autumn Forest Ct
11700 LSVL 40229 5944 A4
Autumn Glen Dr
100 MTWH 40047 6055 C5
Autumn Green Wy
3100 JFVL 47130 5507 A1
Autumn Hill Ct
10 PROS 40059 5401 B4
Autumn Hill Tr
3000 FydC 47150 5397 B2
Autumn Hills Ct
3000 FydC 47150 5397 B2
Autumn Lake Dr
2400 LSVL 40272 5940 A6
Autumn Leaf Ct
8000 LSVL 40220 5727 E3
Autumn Leaf Dr
- BltC 40165 6161 B3
- SHDV 40165 6161 B3
Autumn Oaks Wy
6400 LSVL 40272 5939 E3
Autumn Ridge Ct
- JFVL 47130 5398 E6
3200 ClkC 47111 5290 B2
8500 LYDN 40242 5510 B7
8500 LYDN 40242 5619 B1
Autumn Ridge Dr
10 BltC 40047 6055 C5
10 MTWH 40047 6055 C5
Autumn Ridge Rd
1300 LYDN 40222 5619 B1
1300 LYDN 40242 5619 B1
1400 LYDN 40242 5510 A7
Autumn Sun Ct
1200 MDTN 40243 5620 C6
Autumnwood Wy
8200 LSVL 40291 5836 E5
Autum Ridge Ct
- JFVL 47130 5398 E6
Ava Ct
10 SVLY 40216 5723 C3
Avalon Av
2400 LSVL 40216 5722 E7
Avalon Ct
10 HdnC 42701 6702 A6
Avanti Pl
6900 LSVL 40291 5836 E3
Avanti Wy
7900 LSVL 40291 5836 E3
Avco Blvd
1500 ClkC 47172 5288 D7
1500 ClkC 47172 5397 D1
Avenel Ct
10600 LSVL 40291 5837 D6
Avenue of the Emperors SE
11900 HsnC 47117 5721 C6
Avenue of The Woods
2700 LSVL 40241 5509 D4
2700 LSVL 40242 5509 D5
2700 OBNP 40242 5509 E5
Avish Ln
5000 LSVL 40059 5400 C7
Avoca Rd
12200 LSVL 40223 5620 E2
12200 LSVL 40223 5621 A2
12200 MDTN 40223 5620 E2
12200 MDTN 40223 5621 A2
Avocado Ct
3200 LSVL 40220 5727 E3
Avon Cir
1600 RDCF 40160 6483 A5
Avon Ct
- LSVL 40206 5617 B3
3700 LSVL 40220 5618 B7
Avon Rd
2800 LSVL 40220 5618 B7
Avondale Ct
1000 JFVL 47130 5507 C3
8700 LSVL 40299 5728 A4
Axbridge Rd
5600 LSVL 40216 5722 C7
Axminster Dr
9200 FTHL 40299 5728 C1
9200 JFTN 40220 5728 C1
Axtell Av
4900 LSVL 40258 5831 D4
Ayars Ct
2000 LSVL 40218 5727 A5
Ayer St
400 NALB 47150 5505 B5
Aylesbury Ct
2600 RLGH 40242 5510 D5
Aylesbury Dr
9300 RLGH 40242 5510 D5
9500 MWVL 40242 5510 D5
Ayrshire Av
8900 HTBN 40222 5619 C6
Azaela Springs Ct
4700 LSVL 40299 5728 E6
Azalea Ct
100 LGNG 40031 5296 C3
Azalea Dr
3100 FydC 47150 5397 B2
Azalea Ln
5400 LSVL 40258 5831 C4
Aztec Lily Ct
12600 MDTN 40243 5620 C7
Azure Dr
100 BltC 40047 6055 A5
100 MTWH 40047 6055 A5

B

B Ct
10 LGNG 40031 5296 E2
B St
- JFVL 47130 5507 B4
Babe Dr
400 LSVL 40118 5942 C3
Bacher St
10 HdnC 40121 6374 E1
Bachmann Dr
1700 SVLY 40216 5723 D3
Back Run Rd
9900 LSVL 40291 5947 D2
9900 LSVL 40299 5947 D2
10200 LSVL 40299 5948 A2
Bacon Creek Rd
10 ELZT 42701 6811 B6
10 HdnC 42701 6811 B6
Bacon Creek Rd SR-1904
10 ELZT 42701 6811 B6
10 HdnC 42701 6811 B6
Baden Ct
1800 GYDL 40222 5509 E6
Badger Av
100 LSVL 40214 5724 C6
Badger Ct
- HdnC 40162 6591 A3
Bagby Wy
2500 LSVL 40216 5831 C1
2700 LSVL 40216 5722 C7
Bagdad Rd
- HdnC 40177 6264 D2
E Bahama Ct
5000 LSVL 40219 5835 D3
W Bahama Ct
4900 LSVL 40219 5835 D3
Bahama Ln
6700 LSVL 40219 5835 D3
Bahama Rd
- HdnC 40177 6264 D2
Bahia Ct
6800 LSVL 40219 5835 C3
Bailey Av
- CLKV 47129 5506 B4
Bailey Ct
7900 HdnC 40121 6374 D5
Bailey Trc
100 RDCF 40160 6483 B3
Bailey Grant Rd
5600 ClkC 47130 5399 B3
Bainbridge Ct
6800 LSVL 40228 5836 B6
Bainbridge Row Dr
1800 LSVL 40207 5509 B6
1800 WNDF 40207 5509 A6
Baines Ct
- LSVL 40245 5621 B6
Baines Wy
400 LSVL 40245 5621 B5
Baird St
1700 LSVL 40203 5615 B1
Baker Ct
- LSVL 40203 5616 A4
- LSVL 40204 5616 A4
Baker Ln
200 ELZT 42701 6702 D5
Baker Rd
- HdnC 40121 6264 E6
- HdnC 40177 6264 E6
- HdnC 40177 6265 B4
10600 FydC 47124 5392 A5
Bakers Ln
300 LSVL 40214 5833 B4
Bakers Falls Ct
11200 LSVL 40299 5729 B6
Bala Ct
7900 LSVL 40291 5836 E3
Balamor Dr
4500 LSVL 40216 5722 C4
Balance Ln
9300 LSVL 40118 5833 C7
9300 LSVL 40118 5942 C1
Balaton Dr
4500 LSVL 40219 5726 C7
Balboa Pl
3700 HNTH 40229 5944 A6
Bald Knob Rd
100 FydC 47150 5396 B2
100 NALB 47150 5396 C3
Baldwin Ct
- LSVL 40210 5615 A5
Baldwin Dr
100 NALB 47150 5396 A7
Baldwin St
1300 LSVL 40210 5615 A5
Bales Blvd
1000 CLKV 47129 5397 D7
Balfour Dr
1900 LYDN 40242 5510 C7
Ball St
300 MRGH 40155 6264 C4
Ballad Blvd
2400 JFTN 40299 5728 D2
Ballantrae Cir
2500 LSVL 40242 5509 D5
2600 LSVL 40241 5509 D5
Ballard Al
- LSVL 40204 5616 A3
Ballard Av
- HdnC 40121 6373 E2
300 HdnC 40121 6374 A3
Ballard Cir
3900 OdmC 40014 5405 E1
Ballard Ct
700 LSVL 40202 5616 A3
700 LSVL 40204 5616 A3
1300 OdmC 40031 5405 D1
Ballard Ln
3200 NALB 47150 5396 B7
Ballard St
900 LSVL 40204 5616 A3
Ballard Mill Ln
1800 WNDF 40207 5509 B6
Ballardsville Rd
- CTWD 40014 5404 A7
- ODGH 40014 5511 E1
6700 CTWD 40014 5403 C7
7000 PWEV 40014 5403 D7
7100 OdmC 40014 5403 C7
7100 PWEV 40056 5403 C7
7200 OdmC 40014 5512 A1
7200 PWEV 40014 5512 B1
7200 PWEV 40056 5512 A1
10000 LSVL 40241 5511 B1
10900 LSVL 40245 5511 C1
11500 CDSM 40241 5511 C1
11500 CDSM 40245 5511 C1
11600 CDSM 40014 5511 D1
11600 JfnC 40014 5511 D1
Ballardsville Rd SR-22
- CTWD 40014 5404 A7
- ODGH 40014 5511 E1
6700 CTWD 40014 5403 C7
7000 PWEV 40014 5403 D7
7100 OdmC 40014 5403 C7
7100 PWEV 40056 5403 C7
7200 OdmC 40014 5512 A1
7200 PWEV 40014 5512 B1
7200 PWEV 40056 5512 A1
10000 LSVL 40241 5511 B1
10900 LSVL 40245 5511 C1
11500 CDSM 40241 5511 C1
11500 CDSM 40245 5511 C1
11600 CDSM 40014 5511 D1
11600 JfnC 40014 5511 D1
Ball Diamond Hill Rd NE
900 HsnC 47136 5610 D7
2100 LNVL 47136 5610 D7
Ballou Rd
1400 ClkC 47119 5287 A1
Bally Castle Ct
100 HLVW 40229 5944 B5
Balmer Dr
8300 ClkC 47111 5180 E4
Balmoral Dr
1000 STMW 40205 5618 A5
Balmoral Rd
500 ELZT 42701 6812 B1
Balsam Wy
9600 JFTN 40299 5728 C3
Baltimore Rd
- HdnC 40177 6264 D2
Bamberrie Cross Rd
5500 LSVL 40214 5833 A5
Bambi Wy
100 BltC 40165 6160 E3
8500 LSVL 40214 5832 C6
Bamboo Ct
7400 LSVL 40258 5831 B3
Banbridge Dr
1800 CLKV 47129 5397 C7
Banbridge Rd
8600 GSCK 40242 5510 B4
8700 BKPT 40241 5510 B4
8700 BKPT 40242 5510 B4
Bancroft Ln
2600 BCFT 40242 5509 D5
2600 LSVL 40241 5509 D5
2600 LSVL 40242 5509 D5
Banger Wy
100 HLVW 40229 5944 B7
Bank Ct
500 LSVL 40212 5505 E7
Bank Rd
- HdnC 40177 6264 D2
Bank St
10 NALB 47150 5505 B5
1500 LSVL 40203 5615 A1
2000 LSVL 40212 5615 A1
2400 LSVL 40212 5506 A7
2500 LSVL 40212 5505 E7
Bank St SR-3082
2100 LSVL 40203 5615 A1
2100 LSVL 40212 5615 A1
2400 LSVL 40212 5506 A7
2500 LSVL 40212 5505 E7
Bank OAD Rd
- HdnC 40177 6264 D3
Bankview Dr
200 ELZT 42701 6702 E6
Banner Av
7000 ClkC 47172 5397 E1
Banner Dr
3500 JFVL 47130 5398 B6
Banner Rd
- HdnC 40177 6264 D2
Bantam Ct
100 ELZT 42701 6812 D4
3900 WSNP 40218 5726 C4
Banyan Ct
10700 JFTN 40223 5620 A7
Baptist Home East
3000 LSVL 40241 5510 D4
Baracha Ct
3700 HNTH 40229 5944 A6
Barb Ct
9600 LSVL 40291 5837 B5
Barbara Av
5000 LSVL 40258 5831 D4
Barbara Ct
100 HdnC 42701 6702 B4
100 RDCF 40160 6483 C5
1900 JFVL 47130 5507 C3
Barbara Ln
- BltC 40047 6055 D6
- MTWH 40047 6055 D6
Barbara Ann Blvd
3400 OdmC 40014 5405 A3
Barbara Sue
- MTWH 40047 6055 D6
Barbara Sue Ln
100 MTWH 40047 6055 C5
600 BltC 40047 6055 D6
E Barbee Av
100 LSVL 40217 5724 E1
300 LSVL 40208 5724 D1
500 LSVL 40217 5615 E7
N Barbee Wy
600 LSVL 40217 5615 E7
700 LSVL 40217 5616 A7
S Barbee Wy
600 LSVL 40217 5615 E7
700 LSVL 40217 5616 A7
Barber Ln
- LSVL 40216 5722 B6
Barberry Cir
5400 OdmC 40014 5405 C4
Barberry Ct
100 ELZT 42701 6811 C1
3500 OdmC 40031 5295 D7
3500 OdmC 40031 5404 D1
Barberry Ln
500 LSVL 40206 5617 B3
Barbet Wy
15100 LSVL 40299 5839 B7
Barbizon Ct
- OdmC 44026 5292 C4
Barbizon Dr
- OdmC 44026 5292 C4
Barbour Ln
3300 BRMD 40241 5510 A3
3300 LSVL 40241 5510 A3
3300 LSVL 40242 5510 A4
3600 LSVL 40241 5509 E2
4000 GNSP 40241 5509 E2
4300 LSVL 40059 5509 D1
Barbour Manor Ct
3900 LSVL 40241 5509 E2
3900 LSVL 40241 5510 A2
Barbour Manor Dr
7800 LSVL 40241 5509 E3
7800 LSVL 40241 5510 A2
Barbourmeade Rd
7900 BRMD 40241 5510 A4
7900 LSVL 40241 5510 A4
Barbour Place Cir
3500 LSVL 40241 5509 D3
Barbour Place Ct
7600 LSVL 40241 5509 D3
Barbour Place Dr
7700 BRMD 40241 5510 A3
7700 LSVL 40241 5509 E3
7700 LSVL 40241 5510 A3
Barbrook Rd
6600 LSVL 40258 5831 A4
6600 LSVL 40258 5830 E4
Barclay Dr
3400 JFTN 40299 5728 C4
Bardmoor Ct
7900 LSVL 40291 5837 C5
Bards Ct
8700 LSVL 40299 5728 A4
Bardsley Cir
1800 CSGT 40222 5509 C6
Bardstown Rd
- BltC 40047 5947 A6
- LSVL 40291 5946 D1
1000 LSVL 40204 5616 C4
1400 LSVL 40205 5616 D6
1900 LSVL 40205 5617 B7
2700 SMRG 40205 5617 C7
2700 SMRM 40205 5617 B7
2700 SMRV 40205 5617 B7
2800 LSVL 40205 5726 C1
2800 SMRG 40205 5726 C1
2900 WLTN 40205 5726 C1
3200 LSVL 40218 5726 E3
3500 WBHL 40218 5726 E3
3900 LSVL 40218 5727 C6
4600 LSVL 40291 5727 D7
5200 LSVL 40291 5728 A7
5300 LSVL 40291 5837 B3
10300 LSVL 40291 5947 A5
Bardstown Rd US-31E
- BltC 40047 5947 A6
1000 LSVL 40204 5616 C4
1400 LSVL 40205 5616 D6
1900 LSVL 40205 5617 B7
2700 SMRG 40205 5617 C7
2700 SMRM 40205 5617 B7
2700 SMRV 40205 5617 B7
2800 LSVL 40205 5726 C1
2800 SMRG 40205 5726 C1
2900 WLTN 40205 5726 C1
Bardstown Rd US-31E
3200 LSVL 40218 5726 D2
3500 WBHL 40218 5726 D3
4100 LSVL 40218 5727 C6
4600 LSVL 40291 5727 D6
5200 LSVL 40291 5728 A7
5300 LSVL 40291 5837 B3
10200 LSVL 40291 5946 D1
10800 LSVL 40291 5947 A5
Bardstown Rd US-60 ALT
1300 LSVL 40204 5616 D5
1400 LSVL 40205 5616 D6
Bardstown Rd US-150
- BltC 40047 5947 A6
1000 LSVL 40204 5616 C4
1400 LSVL 40205 5616 D6
1900 LSVL 40205 5617 B7
2700 SMRG 40205 5617 C7
2700 SMRM 40205 5617 B7
2700 SMRV 40205 5617 B7
2800 LSVL 40205 5726 C1
2800 SMRG 40205 5726 C1
2900 WLTN 40205 5726 C1
3200 LSVL 40218 5726 D2
3500 WBHL 40218 5726 D3
4100 LSVL 40218 5727 C6
4600 LSVL 40291 5727 D6
5200 LSVL 40291 5728 A7
5300 LSVL 40291 5837 B3
10200 LSVL 40291 5946 D1
10800 LSVL 40291 5947 A5
Bardstown Bluff Rd
10000 LSVL 40291 5946 E3
10000 LSVL 40291 5947 A4
Bardstown Creek Rd
11200 LSVL 40291 5947 A5
Bardstown Falls Rd
11400 LSVL 40291 5946 E2
Bardstown Valley Rd
12200 LSVL 40291 5947 A5
Bardstown Woods Blvd
10700 LSVL 40291 5946 D1
Bardstown Woods Ct
10900 LSVL 40291 5946 D1
Barfield Rd
6700 LSVL 40258 5830 E4
6700 LSVL 40258 5831 A4
Baringer Av
2000 LSVL 40204 5616 D5
Barkis Wy
14200 LSVL 40245 5621 D5
Barkley Dr
10200 JFTN 40299 5728 E3
Barksdale Dr
5500 LSVL 40258 5831 B6
Barkwood Dr
5300 OdmC 40031 5295 B2
Barkwood Rd
3400 SVLY 40216 5723 E3
Barley Av
6000 LSVL 40218 5727 A6
Barley Ct
6200 LSVL 40218 5727 A6
Barn Rd
9500 LSVL 40291 5837 B5
Barn Dance Rd
- HdnC 42701 6593 D7
Barnes Dr
5000 LSVL 40219 5835 D3
Barney Av
- LSVL 40205 5616 E5
Barnlake Dr
9800 LSVL 40291 5837 D3
Barnoak Dr
9000 LSVL 40228 5837 A5
Barnstown Farm Rd
11600 LSVL 40291 5946 E3
Barnwood Rd
7700 LSVL 40291 5837 A5
Baroness Av
700 LSVL 40203 5616 A5
700 LSVL 40204 5616 A5
Barrallton Hill Rd
100 BltC 40165 6049 E4
Barren St
100 HdnC 42701 6702 D1
Barret Av
- LSVL 40213 5616 C6
500 LSVL 40204 5616 B4
Barret Rd
- LSVL 40205 5617 A5
Barret Hill Rd
2400 LSVL 40205 5617 A5
Barrett Av
10 CLKV 47129 5506 D6
Barrett Ln
5600 LSVL 40272 5940 B2
Barricks Rd
- BltC 40109 5943 D6
100 LSVL 40229 5943 E4
Barringer St
10 CHAN 47111 5181 D3
Barrington Ct
900 LSVL 40207 5617 E4
3000 FydC 47150 5395 E7
3000 NALB 47150 5395 E7
Barrowdale Dr
4500 LSVL 40216 5723 D6
Barry Ln
300 RDCF 40160 6483 D6
4900 FydC 47119 5394 A3
Bartholomew Blvd
100 JFVL 47130 5507 E4
Bartholomew Dr
2000 LSVL 40218 5727 A5
Bartlett Ct
3700 LSVL 40218 5727 C4
Bartlett Dr
8900 OdmC 40056 5512 C3
8900 PWEV 40056 5512 C3
Bartlett Rd
6900 LSVL 40218 5727 C4
Bartley Dr
9300 LSVL 40291 5837 C5
Barton Av
- LSVL 40209 5725 B4
Bartonfield Ln
5300 LSVL 40219 5835 D7
Bartview Ct
5700 LSVL 40229 5944 E5
Base Rd
- FydC 47122 5502 A5
Base Ball Al
- LSVL 40203 5615 D4
Basham Ct
100 MdeC 40108 6264 C5
100 MRGH 40155 6264 C5
Basham Dr
800 CHAN 47111 5181 D3
Basham Tr
10 HdnC 40175 6592 A3
Bashford Av
3700 WBHL 40218 5726 E4
Bashford Av Ct
3400 WBHL 40218 5726 D4
Bashford Manor Ln
1800 LSVL 40218 5726 C3
1800 WBHL 40218 5726 C3
1800 WSNP 40218 5726 C4
Basking Dr
4900 LSVL 40216 5722 B6
Bass Cir
1600 OdmC 40031 5297 B4
Bass Ln
6300 LSVL 40059 5400 D4
6300 PROS 40059 5400 D4
Bass Creek Ct
3300 LSVL 40218 5726 B5
Bass Creek Dr
2100 LSVL 40218 5726 B5
Bassett Av
1200 LSVL 40204 5616 D5
Basswood Ct
1300 JFVL 47130 5507 B2
Basswood Ln
3500 LSVL 40207 5617 C1
3600 RLGF 40207 5617 C1
E Batalina Ct
5000 LSVL 40219 5835 D3
W Batalina Ct
4900 LSVL 40219 5835 D3
Bates Av
1200 LSVL 40219 5835 B4
Bates Ct
1200 LSVL 40204 5616 C6
Bates Dr
100 ClkC 47111 5181 B3
Bates Ln
100 BltC 40165 6053 E3
100 BltC 40165 6054 A2
1300 LSVL 40219 5835 C4
Bates Rd
10 HdnC 42701 6703 C3
8500 LSVL 40228 5836 C7
8900 LSVL 40228 5945 D1
8900 LSVL 40229 5945 D1
Bath Dr
4400 WTNH 40245 5511 E2
Bath Gate Ct
1400 LGNG 40031 5297 A6
Bathory Ln
10 LGNG 40031 5297 A1
Batson Ct
6600 LSVL 40258 5831 A4
Battle Training Rd
10 HdnC 42701 6593 B3
10 RDCF 40160 6593 B3
10 RDCF 42701 6593 B3
Battle Training Rd SR-434
10 HdnC 42701 6593 B3
10 RDCF 42701 6593 B3
Battle Training Rd SR-447
10 RDCF 40160 6593 B3
10 RDCF 42701 6593 B3
Bauer Av
100 LSVL 40207 5617 D3
100 STMW 40207 5617 D3
Baumler Ct
8100 LSVL 40291 5837 E5
Baumler Pl
11200 LSVL 40291 5837 E6
Baums Ln
6300 LSVL 40258 5831 A4
Baxter Av
100 LSVL 40206 5616 C5
200 LSVL 40204 5616 B3
1400 LSVL 40205 5616 D6
1400 LSVL 40213 5616 D6
Baxter Av SR-1703
1000 LSVL 40204 5616 C4
1400 LSVL 40205 5616 D6
1400 LSVL 40213 5616 D6
Baxter Av US-31E
100 LSVL 40206 5616 B3
200 LSVL 40204 5616 B3
Baxter Av US-60 TRK
100 LSVL 40206 5616 C5
200 LSVL 40204 5616 B3
Baxter Av US-150
700 LSVL 40204 5616 B4
Bay St
100 SHDV 40165 6161 D3
200 NALB 47150 5505 A4
Bay Arbor Pl
12600 LSVL 40245 5511 E2
Bayberry Ct
100 MTWH 40047 6055 E6
Bayberry Dr
4200 LSVL 40216 5722 E5
Bayberry Pl
8600 BRWD 40242 5510 B6
8600 PNTN 40242 5510 B6
Bayberry Green Ln
9400 LSVL 40291 5837 B4
Bay Cove Ct
4700 LSVL 40245 5511 E2

INDEX 9

Baygarden Ct

Louisville Metro Street Index

Birk Ln

STREET
Block City ZIP Map# Grid

Baygarden Ct
4400 WTNH 40245 5511 D2
Bay Harbor Dr
5700 LSVL 40228 5727 B7
Bay Hill Dr
9600 LSVL 40223 5619 D3
Bayleaf Dr
1100 LYDN 40222 5618 E1
1100 STMW 40222 5618 E1
Baylor Ct
6100 NHFD 40222 5509 B5
Baylor Dr
2400 NHFD 40222 5509 B5
Baylor Wissman Rd
10 GEOT 47122 5502 B4
300 FydC 47122 5502 B5
700 FydC 47136 5502 C6
N Bayly Av
- LSVL 40206 5617 A2
S Bayly Av
100 LSVL 40206 5617 A3
Baymeadow Dr
3600 LSVL 40258 5832 A3
Bayonne Ct
3900 LSVL 40299 5728 B5
Bayou Wy
8400 PNTN 40242 5510 B6
Bay Pine Dr
5900 LSVL 40219 5835 E6
5900 LSVL 40219 5836 A6
6100 LSVL 40228 5836 A6
Bay Pointe Ct
10500 LSVL 40241 5511 A3
Bay Pointe Dr
4100 LSVL 40241 5511 A3
Bay Pointe Cir Dr
10400 LSVL 40241 5511 C4
Bayport Dr
10100 JFTN 40299 5728 D5
Bay Port Rd
10400 JFTN 40299 5728 E5
10400 LSVL 40299 5728 E5
10500 LSVL 40299 5729 A5
Bay Run Ct
4300 WTNH 40245 5511 E2
Bay Run Dr
11000 WTNH 40245 5511 D3
Bays End Ct
4400 WTNH 40245 5511 D2
Bayshore Ct
5500 LSVL 40258 5831 C3
Bayside Ct
10 SVLY 40216 5723 C2
Bayswater Wy
1700 LSVL 40205 5725 E3
Bay Tree Wy
12600 LSVL 40245 5511 E2
12600 WTNH 40245 5511 E2
Baywood Av
100 HdnC 40175 6482 E2
100 RDCF 40175 6482 E2
Baywood Dr
5100 LSVL 40241 5511 D1
5300 LSVL 40241 5402 C7
5300 OdmC 40241 5402 C7
B Clark Ln
- BltC 40047 6056 B1
- MTWH 40047 6056 B1
Bea Wy
- LSVL 40219 5834 E3
Beachland Beach Rd
6900 LSVL 40059 5400 C3
Beackstone Ct
6800 LSVL 40228 5836 B6
Beacon Dr
3100 NALB 47150 5396 C7
Beacon Hill Dr
1500 LSVL 40216 5723 C6
Beagle Pl
7700 LSVL 40219 5836 A3
Beahl Blvd
7300 LSVL 40258 5831 B3
Beals Branch Rd
2600 LSVL 40205 5617 A4
3200 LSVL 40206 5617 D4
3200 LSVL 40207 5617 D4
Bean Dr
100 SHDV 40165 6161 E6
Bean Rd
- ClkC 47172 5289 B7
300 ClkC 47172 5288 E7
300 SLRB 47172 5288 E7
600 SLRB 47172 5289 A7
Beanblossom Rd
700 LSVL 40213 5834 B2
Bearcamp Rd
10600 BltC 40165 6050 B2
10600 BltC 40272 6050 B2
10600 LSVL 40272 5941 C7
10600 LSVL 40272 6050 B2
14000 BltC 40165 6049 D3
Bearcreek Dr
7000 STMW 40207 5618 C4
Bear Creek Rd
10100 FydC 47165 5283 A1
E Bear Creek Rd
10000 ClkC 47106 5283 C1
10000 WasC 47165 5283 C1
Beard Av
- HdnC 40121 6374 B7
N Beard Av
9100 HdnC 40121 6374 B7
S Beard Av
9100 HdnC 40121 6374 C7
Beard Ct
6800 LSVL 40228 5836 B6
Beargrass Av
- LSVL 40206 5616 E4
2200 LSVL 40218 5727 B4
Beargrass Rd
- LSVL 40205 5617 A5
Bear Pass Rd
10 LSVL 40216 5722 E2
Beatrice Wy
10800 LSVL 40272 5940 B3
Beatty Av
- LSVL 40219 5834 D7
Beau Ct
6800 LSVL 40214 5723 D7
Beau Brummel Ct
400 LSVL 40118 5942 D3
Beau Brummel Dr
10200 LSVL 40118 5942 D3
Beaufort Ln
3700 STMW 40207 5618 A5
Beaumont Dr
1700 CLKV 47129 5397 C7
Beaumont Rd
2900 LSVL 40205 5617 D7
Beauty Ct
7400 LSVL 40228 5836 C6
Beaver Rd
4600 BWDV 40207 5618 C2
Beaver St
4000 LSVL 40215 5724 A5
Bea Vista Pl
600 SLRB 47172 5288 D3
Bebe Ct
6800 LSVL 40219 5836 A3
Becker Av
1200 LSVL 40213 5725 D7
Becker Ct
2100 LSVL 40216 5614 E7
Becket Av
10 LSVL 40118 5942 C1
Beckett St
100 CLKV 47129 5506 D6
Beckley Trc
14000 LSVL 40245 5621 C3
Beckley Crossing Dr
15100 LSVL 40245 5621 E3
Beckley Hills Ct
1200 LSVL 40245 5621 D7
Beckley Hills Dr
15400 LSVL 40245 5621 D7
N Beckley Station Rd
700 LSVL 40245 5621 E3
S Beckley Station Rd
100 LSVL 40245 5621 D7
1100 LSVL 40245 5730 E1
Beckley Woods Dr
100 LSVL 40245 5621 B4
Becky McKinley Av
100 MTWH 40047 6056 A4
Bedford Ln
6600 GYDL 40222 5509 C7
Bedfordshire Ct
700 HTBN 40222 5619 A5
Bedfordshire Rd
500 HTBN 40222 5619 A4
Bedington Ct
11100 DGSH 40243 5620 B5
Bedum Ln
7000 LSVL 40258 5831 C2
Bee Ln
1300 MDTN 40243 5620 D7
Beech Av
6800 LSVL 40059 5400 D4
6800 PROS 40059 5400 D4
7900 LYDN 40222 5619 A3
Beech Ct
10 HdnC 42701 6593 C6
Beech Dr
- BltC 40109 5943 E6
2300 OdmC 40031 5297 D4
4700 LSVL 40216 5722 D3
Beech Rd
11000 ANCH 40223 5620 B2
11000 LSVL 40223 5620 B2
Beech St
- SHDV 40165 6161 C4
100 MRGH 40155 6264 C4
300 ELZT 42701 6812 B1
1200 LSVL 40211 5614 D5
1300 NALB 47150 5505 A4
1500 RDCF 40160 6483 A4
1700 LSVL 40210 5614 D6
2000 LSVL 40216 5614 D7
4000 LSVL 40215 5723 E5
Beechbrook Ct
6600 LSVL 40218 5727 B5
Beechbrook Rd
4500 LSVL 40218 5727 A6
Beechcliff Cir
100 SHDV 40165 6161 A5
Beechcreek Dr
8900 LSVL 40219 5834 E7
Beechcrest Av
4200 LSVL 40220 5618 C6
Beechdale Ct
8000 LSVL 40220 5727 E4
Beechdale Rd
7200 CTWD 40014 5512 E1
7600 CTWD 40056 5512 E1
7600 OdmC 40056 5512 E1
7800 PWEV 40056 5512 E1
Beecher St
500 LSVL 40214 5724 C4
500 LSVL 40215 5724 B4
Beech Grove Av
2100 NALB 47150 5505 E3
Beech Grove Ct
3000 JFVL 47130 5507 E1
6500 LSVL 40229 5944 E1
6500 LSVL 40229 5945 A2
Beech Grove Rd
- BltC 40165 6160 E7
100 SHDV 40165 6161 B5
1400 BltC 40165 6161 A6
Beech Grove Rd SR-1494
- BltC 40165 6160 E7
100 SHDV 40165 6161 B5
1400 BltC 40165 6161 A6
Beechland Av
6900 LSVL 40258 5831 D4
Beechland Rd
100 HLVW 40229 5944 B7
Beechlawn Ct
8000 LSVL 40220 5727 E3
Beechlawn Dr
500 CLKV 47129 5506 A1
Beechnut Ct
100 SHDV 40165 6161 A5
Beech Spring Ct
7600 LSVL 40241 5509 E3
Beechtree Ln
100 BltC 40047 6055 E4
100 BltC 40047 6056 A4
Beechtree Rd
- BltC 40047 6056 A4
- MTWH 40047 6056 A4
Beechview Dr
7400 LSVL 40219 5835 C4
Beechwood Av
100 SHDV 40165 6161 D1
1300 NALB 47150 5505 B2
1600 LSVL 40204 5616 C5
Beechwood Av SR-111
1300 NALB 47150 5505 B2
Beechwood Cir
100 BltC 40047 6056 D4
Beechwood Ct
300 NALB 47150 5505 B3
Beechwood Dr
500 CHAN 47111 5181 E3
1200 CLKV 47129 5506 B2
5900 GNVL 47124 5393 A1
6000 GNVL 47124 5284 B7
8000 MTWH 40047 6056 A2
Beechwood Ln
100 ELZT 42701 6811 E1
Beechwood Rd
10 JFVL 47130 5508 A3
700 WLNP 40207 5618 C1
900 WDYH 40207 5618 C1
Beechwood St
800 ClkC 47172 5288 D2
800 SLRB 47172 5288 D2
Beeler Pl
- LSVL 40229 5944 D4
Beeler St
1800 NALB 47150 5505 D3
Beeler Wy
- LSVL 40229 5944 D4
Beeston Blvd
13000 LSVL 40272 6048 D2
Beharrell Av
300 NALB 47150 5505 E3
Behr Ct
3300 LSVL 40220 5727 D3
Belair Dr
100 HdnC 40162 6702 A1
100 SHDV 40165 6161 E7
Belaire Estates Rd
100 HdnC 40162 6702 B1
Belgravia Ct
500 LSVL 40208 5615 C6
Belinda Wy
7500 LSVL 40291 5837 A4
Belkamp Dr
3700 LSVL 40299 5728 B4
Belknap Beach Rd
2400 OdmC 40059 5291 D6
E Bell Av
100 CLKV 47129 5506 C3
W Bell Av
100 CLKV 47129 5506 C3
Bell Ln
1000 NALB 47150 5396 B6
Bella Ct
10 SVLY 40216 5723 C3
N Bellaire Av
100 LSVL 40206 5616 D2
S Bellaire Av
100 LSVL 40206 5616 D3
Bellarmine Blvd
- LSVL 40205 5616 E7
- LSVL 40205 5725 E1
Bellarmine Ct
500 ELZT 42701 6811 B4
500 HdnC 42701 6811 B4
Bellcrest Ct
6900 LSVL 40291 5836 D3
Bellemeade Dr
1400 NALB 47150 5505 E2
Bellemeade Rd
100 BLMD 40222 5619 B3
100 HTBN 40222 5619 B3
200 LYDN 40222 5619 B3
Bellevoir Cir
- LYDN 40223 5510 D7
- LYDN 40223 5619 D1
- LYDN 40242 5619 D1
Bellevue Av
- LSVL 40215 5724 B4
Bellevue Ct
800 LSVL 40215 5724 B5
Bellewood Ct
10 NALB 47150 5505 E2
Bellewood Ct E
10 NALB 47150 5505 E2
Bellewood Ct W
10 NALB 47150 5505 E2
Bellewood Dr
- NALB 47150 5505 E2
Bellewood Rd
500 ANCH 40223 5620 B2
500 LSVL 40223 5620 B3
500 MDTN 40223 5620 B3
500 MDTN 40243 5620 B3
Bellewood Rd SR-146
- ANCH 40223 5620 C1
Bellflower Dr
4000 LSVL 40219 5835 A7
Bell Flower Pl
- LGNG 40031 5296 B3
Bellingham Ct
1500 LSVL 40245 5622 C2
Bellis Wy
8300 LYDN 40242 5619 B1
Bell Rock Ct
10800 DGSH 40243 5620 A5
Bell Rock Pl
700 DGSH 40243 5620 A5
Bells Ln
3300 LSVL 40211 5614 A7
4100 LSVL 40211 5613 E7
Bells Ln SR-2056
3300 LSVL 40211 5614 A7
4100 LSVL 40211 5613 E7
Bells Mill Rd
100 BltC 40165 6053 C4
200 BltC 40165 6054 B5
Bells Mill Rd SR-1526
100 BltC 40165 6053 C4
200 BltC 40165 6054 B5
Bell Tavern Ct
2200 WNDF 40207 5509 A5
Belltower Ct
10000 JFTN 40299 5728 D5
Belltower Rd
3900 JFTN 40299 5728 D5
Bellwood Av
1300 LSVL 40204 5616 D5
Bellwood Dr
500 ELZT 42701 6812 A1
600 ELZT 42701 6703 A7
Belmar Ct
4500 JFVL 47130 5398 A6
Belmar Dr
1200 LSVL 40213 5725 C3
2200 JFVL 47130 5398 A6
Belmont Av
100 ELZT 42701 6812 C3
4900 LSVL 40258 5831 D4
Belmont Ct
3400 LSVL 40218 5726 D2
Belmont Dr
10 PNRV 40165 6053 C1
Belmont Pl
2000 LSVL 40218 5726 C2
Belmont Rd
2100 LSVL 40218 5726 C2
Belmont Park Cir
12100 MDTN 40243 5620 C6
Belmont Park Wy
1100 MDTN 40243 5620 C6
Belquin Ct
3800 LSVL 40211 5614 B6
Belquin Pl
3800 LSVL 40211 5614 B7
Belquin Rd
2100 LSVL 40211 5614 B7
Belrad Dr
4200 LSVL 40218 5727 A6
Belvar Av
300 LSVL 40206 5617 B1
Belvedere Av
2600 LSVL 40220 5618 D6
Ben Ali Rd
2000 KNLD 40223 5510 E6
Benbow Dr
4100 LSVL 40229 5944 B2
Benchmark I Dr
6000 FydC 47119 5394 A5
Benchmark II Dr
6000 FydC 47119 5394 A5
Benchmark III Dr
6000 FydC 47119 5394 A5
Ben Franklin Ct
7200 LSVL 40214 5833 C3
Benjamin Ln
300 LYDN 40222 5618 E3
300 LYDN 40222 5619 A3
Benjamin Pl
100 BltC 40047 5947 A7
100 MTWH 40047 5947 A7
Benjamin Logan St
- HdnC 40121 6374 E1
Benje Ct
3900 LSVL 40241 5510 A2
Benje Wy
3800 LSVL 40241 5510 A3
Bennel Dr
100 VNGV 40175 6482 E7
100 VNGV 40175 6483 A7
Bennel St
100 VNGV 40175 6482 E7
Bennett Av
- JFVL 47130 5507 E4
10 JFVL 47130 5508 A4
3400 LSVL 40219 5834 E1
3400 LSVL 40219 5835 A1
9100 HdnC 40121 6374 B7
Bennett Rd
10 HdnC 40162 6591 C6
Bennett Kelly Rd
8000 FydC 47122 5501 E2
8000 FydC 47122 5502 A2
Bennett Ridge Pl
600 DGSH 40243 5620 B6
Bennington Ct
7100 LSVL 40214 5833 C3
Benny Rd
5800 LSVL 40258 5831 B5
Benoch Av
4300 LSVL 40216 5722 E5
Benson Ct
5200 LSVL 40272 5940 C3
Benson Wy
11000 LSVL 40272 5940 C3
Bentbrook Dr
500 NALB 47150 5505 B1
Bentbrook Pl
8100 OdmC 40056 5512 B2
8100 PWEV 40056 5512 B2
Bent Creek Ct
3300 LSVL 40218 5726 C2
Bent Creek Dr
2100 LSVL 40218 5726 C2
5000 FydC 47119 5394 E1
Bentford Dr
9800 LSVL 40272 5940 E1
Bent Grass Ln
3200 JFVL 47130 5398 B4
Bentley Ct
14100 LSVL 40245 5621 C6
Bent Oak Ct
3800 LSVL 40241 5511 B3
Benton Av
1200 LSVL 40204 5616 B4
Benton Ridge Dr
1000 SbyC 40245 5514 A7
Bent Pine Ct
7900 PROS 40059 5400 D2
Bent Ridge Ct
4100 OdmC 40014 5404 E6
Bent Tree Ct
200 VNGV 40175 6592 A1
300 LSVL 40223 5620 B4
6000 FydC 47119 5394 E1
Bent Tree Dr
- VNGV 40175 6592 A1
Bent Willow Ln
1300 LSVL 40214 5833 A4
Bentwood Wy
1200 JFTN 40223 5619 E6
1200 JFTN 40223 5620 A6
Bentwood Place Ct
1100 WDYH 40207 5618 C1
Beowulf Ct
13700 LSVL 40299 5729 E5
Berea Dr
8300 LSVL 40228 5836 E7
Berea Rd
300 HdnC 42701 6811 B4
Berenger Field Dr
4100 LSVL 40299 5729 D5
Bergman St
500 LSVL 40203 5615 E6
500 LSVL 40203 5616 A6
500 LSVL 40204 5616 A6
1400 LSVL 40208 5615 E6
Berkley Ct
200 RDCF 40160 6483 D4
Berkley Rd
300 CHAN 47111 5181 C4
300 ClkC 47111 5181 C4
Berkshire Av
3900 LSVL 40220 5618 C7
3900 MVWE 40220 5618 C7
Bermuda Ct
9200 ODGH 40014 5402 E6
Bermuda Ln
100 LSVL 40213 5834 C2
Bermuda Pl
7300 ODGH 40014 5402 E7
Bermuda Wy
400 MDTN 40243 5620 D3
Bernadine Dr
9400 LSVL 40229 5944 A1
Bernard Dr
- HBNE 40165 6053 C2
- PNRV 40165 6053 C2
Bernay Pl
12600 DGSH 40299 5620 D6
12600 MDTN 40299 5620 D6
Bernheim Ln
1300 LSVL 40208 5615 B7
1300 LSVL 40210 5615 A7
1400 SVLY 40210 5615 B7
1700 LSVL 40210 5614 E7
Bernheim Ln US-31W
- LSVL 40210 5614 E7
Berry Blvd
1000 LSVL 40215 5724 A3
1500 LSVL 40215 5723 E3
1800 SVLY 40216 5723 E3
Berry Blvd US-60 ALT
1300 LSVL 40215 5724 A3
1500 LSVL 40215 5723 E3
1800 SVLY 40216 5723 E3
Berry Hill Pl
400 DGSH 40243 5620 C5
Berry Hill Rd
11900 DGSH 40243 5620 C5
11900 MDTN 40243 5620 C5
Berrytown Rd
10 HdnC 40162 6591 A6
12400 ANCH 40223 5620 D1
12400 LSVL 40223 5620 E1
Bersheba Dr
- LSVL 40245 5623 B1
10 SbyC 40245 5623 B1
Bertha Wy
400 VNGV 40175 6591 D2
Bertie Av
1800 LSVL 40206 5616 D2
Bertram Ln
800 VNGV 40175 6482 E7
Bertrand St
500 LSVL 40203 5615 C5
Berwick Pl
11100 DGSH 40243 5620 B4
Berwyn Dr
600 LSVL 40223 5619 E2
Besnel Ln
3000 BltC 40165 6053 A5
Bess Ct
600 JFVL 47130 5507 D4
Bessels Blvd
13200 LSVL 40272 5939 D7
13200 LSVL 40272 6048 C1
Best Av SE
300 NALB 47150 5505 E3
Best Ct
8700 BRWD 40242 5510 B6
Bestey Ross Dr
6900 LSVL 40272 6048 C1
E Beta Ct
1400 CLKV 47129 5506 C1
Betances Ct
1600 LGNG 40031 5297 A1
1600 OdmC 40031 5297 A1
Beth Rd
5300 LSVL 40219 5835 D7
Bethaney Rd
- ClkC 47130 5290 C3
Bethany Ct
- BltC 40047 5947 A7
100 BltC 40047 6056 A1
Bethany Ln
6200 LSVL 40272 5940 A3
6300 LSVL 40272 5939 E2
Bethany Rd
5700 ClkC 47111 5290 A1
5700 ClkC 47130 5290 C3
7900 ClkC 47111 5180 E6
7900 ClkC 47111 5181 A7
Bethany Wy
6200 LSVL 40272 5939 E3
6200 LSVL 40272 5940 A3
Bethany Oaks Pkwy
12400 LSVL 40272 5939 E3
Bethel Dr
200 ELZT 42701 6812 D4
Bethel Branch Wy
- BltC 40047 6055 A5
Bethel Church Rd
100 BltC 40047 6055 A5
100 MTWH 40047 6055 B5
Bethune Ct
4900 LSVL 40213 5726 C6
4900 LSVL 40218 5726 C6
Bette Av
500 RDCF 40160 6483 C5
Betty Ln
3000 LSVL 40205 5617 E7
Bettye Ann Ct
12000 LSVL 40299 5729 C6
Betty Ray Ln
- MDTN 40243 5620 D7
- MDTN 40299 5620 D7
Beulah Church Ct
8500 LSVL 40291 5837 C5
Beulah Church Rd
6000 LSVL 40228 5945 D1
6000 LSVL 40229 5945 D2
6500 LSVL 40228 5836 D7
7500 LSVL 40291 5836 D7
8400 LSVL 40291 5837 A4
Beulah Church Rd SR-864
6000 LSVL 40228 5945 D1
6000 LSVL 40229 5945 D2
6500 LSVL 40228 5836 D7
7500 LSVL 40291 5836 E5
Beulah Church Rd SR-1065
8000 LSVL 40228 5836 E5
8000 LSVL 40291 5836 D7
8400 LSVL 40291 5837 A4
Beverly Av
- LSVL 40207 5617 D3
- STMW 40207 5617 D3
Beverly Rd
10 LSVL 40204 5616 C6
Bewley Blvd
500 ELZT 42701 6703 C5
Bewley Hollow Rd
10 ELZT 42701 6703 A1
10 HdnC 42701 6703 A1
Bexley Ct
2800 LSVL 40206 5616 E1
Bexley Cove
5300 OdmC 40031 5295 B7
5300 OdmC 40031 5404 B1
Beyroth Ct
5800 WNDF 40207 5509 A6
Bickel Av
100 LSVL 40206 5616 B2
Bickel Rd
2300 LSVL 40206 5616 E3
Bicknell Av
1000 LSVL 40215 5724 A5
1600 LSVL 40215 5723 E5
Bier Dr
10800 LSVL 40229 5944 B4
Big Bear Pl
12200 LSVL 40299 5729 B4
Big Ben Dr
6200 LSVL 40291 5837 A2
Big Cedar Creek Tr
100 BltC 40165 6163 D5
Big Clifty
10 BltC 40165 6162 C1
Bigelow Dr
3700 LSVL 40299 5728 B4
Biggin Hill Ct
2800 JFTN 40220 5728 A2
Biggin Hill Ln
8400 JFTN 40220 5728 A2
Big Horn Ct
4100 LSVL 40299 5729 B4
Big Horn Pl
11800 LSVL 40299 5729 B4
Big Oak Tr
300 HdnC 40160 6592 C5
Big Oaks Dr
100 HLVW 40229 5944 A5
Big Sky Dr
5300 LSVL 40229 5944 D2
Big Spring Dr
4200 OdmC 40014 5404 D6
Big Springs Ct
100 BltC 40165 6162 E7
8500 CLKV 47172 5288 B6
Big Springs Dr
1100 BltC 40165 6162 D7
Big Tree Cir
8700 LSVL 40220 5728 B4
Big Tree Wy
8800 JFTN 40220 5728 A3
8800 LSVL 40220 5728 A3
Big Valley Dr
10 BltC 40165 6052 A5
Big Wheel Dr
10 HdnC 42701 6593 C7
Bigwood Ct
100 HLVW 40229 5944 A5
Bigwood Wy
100 HLVW 40229 5944 A6
Bilandon Rd
4800 GNSP 40241 5509 E1
4800 LSVL 40241 5509 E1
Biles Ct
4500 LSVL 40241 5511 A1
Biljana Dr
2100 LSVL 40206 5616 E2
Bill St
100 HLVW 40109 6052 E2
Billhymer St
5800 MdeC 40121 6373 C1
Billie Ln
7000 LSVL 40219 5835 E4
Billiken Ct
- BltC 40047 6056 D1
Billingsgate Pl
9000 LDNP 40242 5510 C5
Billtown Rd
3700 JFTN 40299 5728 D7
4400 LSVL 40299 5728 D6
4900 LSVL 40291 5728 D7
5400 LSVL 40291 5837 D1
5400 LSVL 40299 5837 D1
6000 LSVL 40291 5838 B4
6500 LSVL 40299 5838 B3
Billtown Rd SR-1819
3800 JFTN 40299 5728 D7
4400 LSVL 40299 5728 D6
4900 LSVL 40291 5728 D7
5400 LSVL 40291 5837 D1
5400 LSVL 40299 5837 D1
6000 LSVL 40291 5838 B4
6000 LSVL 40299 5838 B4
Billy Bones Ct
4400 LSVL 40229 5944 B2
Billy Goat Strut Al
- LSVL 40202 5615 E2
600 LSVL 40202 5616 A2
700 LSVL 40206 5616 A2
Biloxi Ct
3000 LSVL 40205 5726 C2
Bilsim Ct
8900 LSVL 40291 5837 B3
Bilsim Ln
6400 LSVL 40291 5837 B3
Biltmore Rd
200 BWDV 40207 5618 C3
Bimini Ct
6700 LSVL 40219 5835 C3
Binbrook Dr
5500 LSVL 40216 5722 C7
Binda Wy
4500 LSVL 40216 5723 C6
Binford Rd
600 FydC 47150 5504 D1
600 NALB 47150 5504 D1
Bingham Dr
8900 BRWD 40242 5510 B7
8900 WWOD 40242 5510 B7
Bingham Wy
- LSVL 40202 5615 E2
Bingham View Ct
9100 LSVL 40059 5401 C7
Binnacle Ct
8600 JFTN 40220 5728 A3
Binnacle Pl
3100 JFTN 40220 5728 A3
Binter St
7700 HdnC 40121 6374 B4
Birch Av
200 LGNG 40031 5297 A2
Birch Cir
2200 CLKV 47129 5397 B6
Birch Ct
- LSVL 40213 5834 C1
1600 RDCF 40160 6483 A3
8600 BRWD 40242 5510 B6
Birch Dr
- BltC 40109 5943 E5
600 ELZT 42701 6703 A2
2200 CLKV 47129 5397 B7
Birch St
- HdnC 40121 6265 C7
- HdnC 40121 6374 C1
100 BltC 40165 6161 B1
100 CHAN 47111 5181 C2
Bircham Rd
14800 LSVL 40245 5621 E5
Birchbark Ln
1700 JFVL 47130 5507 E2
1700 JFVL 47130 5508 A1
Birch Hollow Rd
- LSVL 40241 5402 A7
Birch Leaf Ct
3900 LSVL 40229 5944 A3
Birchline Blvd
6300 LSVL 40291 5837 A3
Birchline Ct
8700 LSVL 40291 5837 A3
Birchmore Pl
3400 LSVL 40245 5512 D5
Birch Oak Al
2700 LSVL 40206 5616 E1
2700 LSVL 40206 5617 A1
Birch Tree Ln
4800 LSVL 40229 5944 C5
Birch View Dr
4400 JFTN 40299 5729 A6
Birchway Ct
400 LSVL 40206 5617 A1
N Birchwood Av
300 LSVL 40206 5617 A1
600 LSVL 40206 5616 E1
S Birchwood Av
100 LSVL 40206 5617 A3
Birchwood Dr
10 ELZT 42701 6702 C7
100 BltC 40165 5944 E6
1100 JFVL 47130 5507 B3
Birk Ln
400 LYDN 40222 5619 A3

INDEX 10

Birkdale Wy

Louisville Metro Street Index

Brandenburg Station Rd

STREET Block City ZIP Map# Grid

Birkdale Wy
2300 ELZT 42701 6702 D2
Birnamwood Ct
3600 LSVL 40258 5832 B3
Birnamwood Dr
6900 LSVL 40258 5832 A3
7100 LSVL 40214 5832 B3
Biscane Dr
8100 LSVL 40258 5831 A5
Bishop Cir
2500 JFVL 47130 5398 A5
Bishop Ln
100 ELZT 42701 6812 C4
100 SHDV 40165 6161 D3
1900 LSVL 40218 5726 B4
1900 WSNP 40218 5726 B4
3700 LSVL 40213 5725 E5
3700 LSVL 40213 5726 A5
3700 LSVL 40218 5725 E5
Bishop Ln SR-1136
100 ELZT 42701 6812 C4
Bishop Rd
2300 JFVL 47130 5398 B5
Bishop St
500 LSVL 40204 5616 B4
Bishops Ln
- SHDV 40165 6161 D2
Bitten Ln
3000 SVLY 40216 5723 C2
Bittersweet Ct
100 MTWH 40047 6055 E6
Bittersweet Ln
100 RDCF 40160 6592 D1
2800 OdmC 40031 5296 B6
Bitter Sweet Rd
100 JFVL 47130 5508 C2
Bittersweet Rd
4600 LSVL 40218 5726 A4
Bitterwood Ct
3200 LSVL 40299 5729 D5
Bitzer Wy
11300 ANCH 40223 5511 C6
11300 LSVL 40223 5511 C6
Bivins Ct
100 RDCF 40160 6592 E2
Black Av
10 NALB 47150 5505 B5
Blackacre Ln
600 HdnC 40160 6592 E5
Black Bent Ct
5200 LSVL 40258 5831 C3
Blackberry Cir
100 MTWH 40047 6055 D6
Blackberry Dr
900 LSVL 40272 5942 A1
1300 LSVL 40272 5941 E1
Blackberry Rdg
1300 ClkC 47130 5399 D6
1300 UTCA 47130 5399 D6
Black Branch Rd
- ELZT 42701 6811 B5
N Black Branch Rd
10 ELZT 42701 6811 A5
10 HdnC 42701 6811 B5
Blackburn Av
100 LSVL 40206 5617 C2
200 LSVL 40207 5617 C2
Blackburn St
- HdnC 40162 6702 B1
- HdnC 42701 6702 B1
Blackburn Sta
13300 OdmC 44026 5292 B2
Blackburn Station Rd
13300 OdmC 44026 5292 B3
Black Cherry Ct
8700 LYDN 40242 5619 B1
Black Ct Cir
- ClkC 47130 5398 D3
Black Gold Ct
4900 LSVL 40216 5722 E7
Blackhawk
- HdnC 40121 6374 E2
Blackhawk St
10 HdnC 40121 6374 D2
Blackhorse Dr
6700 LSVL 40291 5837 D4
Black Horse Regiment Av
100 HdnC 40121 6374 B1
Black Iron Rd
10100 LSVL 40291 5837 D6
Blackiston Blvd
3100 FydC 47150 5396 E5
3100 NALB 47150 5396 E5
Blackiston Cir
2200 ClkC 47129 5397 A7
2200 CLKV 47129 5397 A7
Blackiston Mill Rd
- FydC 47150 5396 E5
- NALB 47150 5396 E5
1400 CLKV 47129 5506 A1
1900 ClkC 47129 5397 A6
1900 CLKV 47129 5397 A6
2900 ClkC 47129 5396 E5
2900 CLKV 47129 5396 E5
3200 NALB 47129 5396 E5
Blackiston View Dr
1500 CLKV 47129 5397 C7
1500 CLKV 47129 5506 C1
E Blackiston View Dr
1400 CLKV 47129 5506 B1
Blackjack Rd
10 RDCF 40160 6483 E7
300 HdnC 40160 6484 B7
300 RDCF 40160 6484 B7
1500 HdnC 42701 6484 B7
Black Locust Wy
6700 LSVL 40272 5939 E3
Black Mountain Dr
7000 LSVL 40228 5727 B7
Black Oak Ct
4200 FydC 47150 5396 C2
Black Oak Dr
- BltC 40047 6056 A1
- MTWH 40047 6055 E1

Black Oak Dr
- MTWH 40047 6056 A1
Black Oak Ln
6400 LSVL 40216 5831 E1
Blackpool Dr
8600 HTBN 40222 5619 B5
Black Powder Ct
9400 LSVL 40228 5836 E7
Black Powder Ln
9000 LSVL 40228 5836 E7
9000 LSVL 40228 5837 A7
9000 LSVL 40291 5837 A7
Blackraven Ct
100 HdnC 42701 6593 A6
100 RDCF 42701 6593 A6
Black Ravens Ct
- HdnC 40162 6593 A7
- RDCF 42701 6593 A7
Black Slate Cir
- ClkC 47130 5398 D3
Blacksmith Ct
8000 LSVL 40291 5837 E6
Blacksmith Pl
6700 FydC 47122 5502 E5
Blacksmith Rd
10800 LSVL 40291 5837 E6
Black Spruce Ln
1300 MDTN 40243 5620 C7
Blackstone Trc
13800 BltC 40071 5948 D5
Blackstone Wy
- JFTN 40223 5619 E6
Blackthorn Rd
1200 MDTN 40299 5620 E6
Blackthorn Trc
12600 MDTN 40299 5620 D6
Black Tie Ct
6100 LSVL 40258 5831 B3
Blacktree Ct
4800 GYDL 40222 5509 D7
Black Walnut Blvd
10700 LSVL 40229 5945 A4
Black Walnut Cir
7000 LSVL 40229 5945 A4
Black Willow Ct
7000 LSVL 40291 5837 D3
Blackwood Ct
1300 JFVL 47130 5507 B2
4200 JFTN 40299 5729 A6
Blackwood Rd
10700 JFTN 40299 5729 A6
Blade Crest Wy
11100 LSVL 40291 5946 E4
Blaine Rd
100 BLMD 40222 5619 B3
Blair Ct
300 MDTN 40243 5620 D4
Blair St
100 NALB 47150 5505 A3
Blair Creek Ct
7100 LSVL 40229 5945 A4
Blair Hill Rd
- HdnC 42701 6593 C4
- RDCF 42701 6593 C4
Blairwood Rd
- JFTN 40223 5619 D7
9300 HTBN 40222 5619 C6
Blake Ln
8100 LSVL 40258 5831 C5
N Blake Ln
8000 LSVL 40258 5831 D5
N Blakely Ln
13400 LSVL 40272 6049 A1
S Blakely Ln
13700 LSVL 40272 6049 A2
Blakemore Ct
7300 PROS 40059 5400 D3
Blakemore Ln
2000 LGNG 40031 5297 B7
2000 OdmC 40031 5297 E6
Blakey Meadow Ln
13200 MDTN 40299 5620 E7
Blanca Ct
1800 LSVL 40223 5510 D7
Blanchel Ter
10 JFVL 47130 5507 D5
E Blanchel Ter
10 JFVL 47130 5507 D5
Bland Av
1400 LSVL 40217 5616 A7
Bland St
1600 LSVL 40217 5615 E7
Blankenbaker Ln
100 INHC 40207 5509 A6
100 LSVL 40207 5509 A6
100 WDYH 40207 5509 A7
300 INHC 40207 5508 E6
300 LSVL 40207 5508 D5
300 RBNW 40207 5508 E6
300 RBNW 40207 5509 A6
500 RVWD 40207 5508 E5
600 INDH 40207 5508 D5
Blankenbaker Pkwy
- JFTN 40299 5620 C7
- LSVL 40299 5620 C7
- LSVL 40299 5729 B5
- MDTN 40243 5620 C7
200 DGSH 40243 5620 B4
200 LSVL 40223 5620 B4
800 MDTN 40299 5620 C6
1800 JFTN 40299 5729 C1
Blankenbaker Pkwy SR-913
- JFTN 40299 5620 C7
- LSVL 40299 5620 C7
- MDTN 40243 5620 C7
200 DGSH 40243 5620 B4
200 LSVL 40223 5620 B4
1800 JFTN 40299 5729 C1
2100 LSVL 40299 5729 C2
Blankenbaker Pkwy SR-1819
600 DGSH 40243 5620 B5
700 MDTN 40243 5620 B6

Blankenbaker Rd
1800 JFTN 40299 5729 B3
1800 LSVL 40299 5729 B3
Blankenbaker Access Dr
11400 JFTN 40299 5729 A3
11400 LSVL 40299 5729 A3
Blankenbaker Access Dr SR-913
11400 JFTN 40299 5729 A3
11400 LSVL 40299 5729 A3
Blankenship Ln
4600 INHC 40207 5509 A7
4600 LSVL 40207 5509 A7
4600 WDYH 40207 5509 A7
Blanton Ln
3300 LSVL 40214 5832 B2
3300 LSVL 40258 5832 B2
3400 LSVL 40216 5832 A2
Blarney Ln
100 BltC 40229 5944 D6
Blaze Wy
6200 LSVL 40272 5940 A3
Blazier Ct
7100 SPML 40228 5836 C4
Bleemel Dr
7700 LSVL 40291 5836 D3
Bleemel Ln
100 BltC 40047 6055 B6
100 MTWH 40047 6055 B6
Blenheim Ct
400 BWDV 40207 5618 C2
Blenheim Rd
4100 RHLN 40207 5618 B2
4200 STMW 40207 5618 B2
4300 BWDV 40207 5618 C2
Blevins Gap Rd
2300 LSVL 40272 5941 A6
4000 LSVL 40272 5940 B7
6500 LSVL 40272 5939 E7
Bliss Av
200 MDTN 40243 5620 C3
Blockade
3500 ClkC 47130 5399 A3
E Bloom St
300 LSVL 40208 5615 D7
W Bloom St
400 LSVL 40208 5615 D7
Bloomfield Ln
5300 LSVL 40219 5835 D7
Blooming Spring Ct
3900 LSVL 40299 5728 A4
Blossom Ln
2000 GEOT 47122 5502 C3
8400 PNTN 40242 5510 B6
8800 LDNP 40242 5510 B5
9000 LDNP 40241 5510 B6
9000 LSVL 40242 5510 C5
9200 LSVL 40241 5510 D5
Blossom Rd
100 HLVW 40229 5944 A7
800 HLVW 40229 6053 A1
Blossom Wy
13100 OdmC 40059 5401 A1
Blossom Ridge Dr
200 BltC 40165 6162 E4
Blossom Tree Wy
10100 LSVL 40241 5510 E3
Blossomwood Dr
4000 LSVL 40220 5618 C6
Blowing Tree Rd
9000 HBNA 40220 5619 B7
9000 LSVL 40220 5619 B7
Blue Ash Dr
100 SHDV 40165 6162 A2
Blue Bell Ct
1000 JFVL 47130 5507 D3
Blue Bell Dr
8600 LSVL 40219 5835 B7
Blueberry Dr
5700 OdmC 40014 5405 B6
Blueberry Wy
3700 JFVL 47130 5399 A7
Bluebird Av
4800 LYNV 40213 5725 D6
4900 LSVL 40213 5725 D6
Bluebird Cir
4900 LYNV 40213 5725 D6
Bluebird Ct
100 ELZT 42701 6812 E6
Bluebird Dr
2000 JFVL 47130 5507 E4
Bluebird Ln
3000 JFTN 40299 5728 E3
Bluebonnet Ct
100 RDCF 40160 6592 E1
Bluebonnet Rd
7700 LSVL 40258 5831 C5
Blue Boy Pl
7600 LSVL 40291 5837 A5
Blue Creek Ct
100 LSVL 40229 5944 B2
Blue Creek Dr
10000 LSVL 40229 5944 A3
Blue Creek Rd
10 BltC 40165 6052 A6
Blue Cumberland Ct
100 BltC 40165 6054 B7
Blue Fields Rd
100 BRMR 40223 5619 E4
Bluegill Blvd
6500 LSVL 40229 5945 B2
Bluegrass Av
600 LSVL 40214 5724 B6
900 LSVL 40215 5724 A6
1500 LSVL 40215 5723 E6
1900 LSVL 40216 5723 E6
Bluegrass Ct
3000 JFVL 47130 5507 A1
7700 OdmC 40014 5514 C1
11300 JFTN 40299 5620 B7
Blue Grass Dr
100 LGNG 40031 5297 A2
Bluegrass Dr
100 LGNG 40031 5297 A2

Bluegrass Pk
- HdnC 40175 6482 C2
Bluegrass Pkwy
9500 FTHL 40299 5619 C7
9500 LSVL 40299 5619 C7
9600 JFTN 40299 5619 D7
10300 JFTN 40299 5620 A7
11500 JFTN 40299 5729 C1
12200 LSVL 40299 5729 D1
Blue Grass Rd
10 HdnC 42701 6703 D4
Bluegrass Tr
1100 JFVL 47130 5507 A2
Bluegrass Wy
100 MTWH 40047 6056 D2
Bluegrass Park Dr
- WBHL 40218 5726 C4
3500 WSNP 40218 5726 C4
Bluegrass Run Ct
3100 LSVL 40220 5727 C1
Bluegrass Run Pl
7100 LSVL 40220 5727 C1
Blue Heron Rd
1100 LSVL 40245 5622 A6
Blue Holly Pl
- OdmC 40014 5403 E5
Blue Horse Av
1600 LSVL 40206 5616 C2
Blue Jay Dr
1600 LYDN 40222 5619 A1
Blue Jay Ln
- LNVL 47136 5610 E5
E Blue Jay Rd
100 BltC 40229 5944 D6
100 HLVW 40229 5944 D6
400 BltC 40165 5944 D6
W Blue Jay Rd
100 BltC 40229 5944 D6
100 HLVW 40229 5944 D6
Blue Lick Ct
4100 LSVL 40229 5944 A3
Blue Lick Dr
- HLVW 40229 5943 E5
- HLVW 40229 5944 A6
Blue Lick Rd
8000 LSVL 40219 5835 A7
9200 LSVL 40219 5944 A1
9200 LSVL 40229 5944 A2
10300 LSVL 40229 5943 E4
10900 HLVW 40229 5943 E5
Blue Lick Rd SR-1450
8000 LSVL 40219 5835 A7
9200 LSVL 40219 5944 A1
9200 LSVL 40229 5944 A2
10300 LSVL 40229 5943 E4
10900 HLVW 40229 5943 E5
E Blue Lick Rd
- HLVW 40229 6052 D4
100 BltC 40109 6052 E3
100 BltC 40165 6052 E4
100 HLVW 40165 6052 D4
300 HLVW 40109 6052 D4
E Blue Lick Rd SR-1603
- HLVW 40229 6052 D4
100 BltC 40109 6052 E3
100 BltC 40165 6052 E4
100 HLVW 40165 6052 D4
300 HLVW 40109 6052 D4
W Blue Lick Rd
100 BltC 40165 6052 B7
500 BltC 40165 6161 B1
1500 SHDV 40165 6161 C3
Blue Lick Creek Rd
- BltC 40165 6053 A6
Blue Lier Rd
- BltC 40165 6161 B2
- SHDV 40165 6161 B2
Blue Park Ln
3500 WSNP 40218 5726 C4
Blue Ribbon Ct
9500 LSVL 40291 5728 B7
Blue Ridge Ct
10 HdnC 42701 6703 D4
10200 BRMR 40223 5619 E4
Blue Ridge Rd
10 HdnC 42701 6703 D4
100 BRMR 40223 5619 E4
300 JFTN 40223 5619 E5
Blue Rose Ct
400 BRMR 40223 5619 E4
Blue Sky Ct
4300 LSVL 40216 5723 A5
Blue Spruce Ct
5700 LSVL 40214 5723 D7
Bluestone Rd
5900 LSVL 40219 5836 A3
Blue Teal Ln
1900 JFVL 47130 5507 D1
Blue Teal Pl
4200 LSVL 40245 5512 B4
Blue Vale Wy
1200 LYDN 40222 5619 A1
1200 LYDN 40242 5619 A1
Blue Wing Ct
3000 LSVL 40216 5722 C6
Blue Wing Dr
7400 LSVL 40258 5830 D4
Bluffington Ct
5900 LSVL 40291 5836 D1
Bluffington Rd
7300 LSVL 40291 5836 D1
Bluff Ridge Dr
1000 NALB 47150 5504 E4
Bluffsprings Ct
1300 JFTN 40223 5619 E7
Bluffsprings Trc
10200 JFTN 40223 5619 D6
Bluffview Cir
6600 LSVL 40299 5838 A2
Blunk Knob Rd
5000 FydC 47117 5612 C7
5000 FydC 47117 5721 C1
5000 FydC 47150 5721 C1
6000 FydC 47136 5721 A2

Boaires Ln
3000 LSVL 40220 5727 A1
Boardwalk Av
100 BltC 40165 6162 B2
100 SHDV 40165 6162 B2
Boaz Ln
100 MTWH 40047 6056 A5
Bobber Ct
1600 OdmC 40031 5297 C4
Bobby Ln
1200 RDCF 40160 6483 C2
Bob Farran Wy
- GYDL 40222 5509 E7
- STMW 40222 5509 E7
Bobolink Rd
100 BltC 40165 6049 D7
3000 LSVL 40217 5725 C1
3100 LSVL 40213 5725 C1
Bobrader Ct
8900 JFTN 40299 5728 B6
Bob White Ct
3000 LSVL 40216 5722 C6
Boca Chica Ct
6100 LSVL 40219 5836 A7
Bocagrande Dr
5800 LSVL 40219 5835 E6
5900 LSVL 40219 5836 A6
Bodley Dr
11200 LSVL 40223 5511 C6
Boerste Wy
4300 LSVL 40229 5944 C1
Bogard Ln
100 BltC 40047 6054 E7
100 BltC 40165 6054 E7
100 MTWH 40047 6054 E7
100 MTWH 40165 6054 E7
40000 BltC 40047 6055 B7
Bohannon Av
3100 LSVL 40215 5724 B3
13500 LSVL 40272 6048 E2
Bohannon Ln
2400 NALB 47150 5505 A2
N Bohannon Ln
100 NALB 47150 5505 A1
S Bohannon Ln
100 NALB 47150 5505 A1
Bohannon Station Rd
8100 LSVL 40291 5837 D7
Bohart Ln
200 CHAN 47111 5181 D2
300 ClkC 47111 5181 D2
Bohne Av
3400 LSVL 40211 5614 B6
Boiling Springs Rd
700 NALB 47150 5504 E5
Bold Ct
4800 LSVL 40218 5726 C5
Boldery Ln
12400 ClkC 47111 5182 A3
Bold Venture Rd
5400 LSVL 40272 5831 B7
Bolivar Ct
8900 LSVL 40299 5728 B5
Bolling Av
1700 LSVL 40210 5615 A6
1800 LSVL 40210 5614 E6
2600 LSVL 40211 5614 E6
Bolly Dr
200 ClkC 47111 5181 B3
Bolo Ct
6000 LSVL 40219 5836 A5
Bolten Ct
200 BltC 40165 6054 A7
Bolton Ct
4400 HLVW 40229 6053 A1
Bon Air Av
2900 KGLY 40205 5617 D7
2900 LSVL 40205 5617 D7
3000 LSVL 40205 5726 D1
3000 WLTN 40205 5617 D7
3200 LSVL 40218 5726 D1
3200 LSVL 40220 5726 D1
Bonair Pl
600 SLRB 47172 5288 D3
Bon Aire Dr
700 ELZT 42701 6703 C7
700 ELZT 42701 6812 C1
Bonavant Rd
3900 LSVL 40219 5835 A6
Bonaventure Blvd
3400 LSVL 40219 5834 E7
3700 LSVL 40219 5835 A7
Bonaventure Pl
9800 LSVL 40219 5834 E6
Bon Bon Rd
2100 MLHT 40219 5834 B6
Bond St
- ELZT 42701 6812 B3
Bonfire Dr
5800 WDYH 40207 5509 A7
5800 WDYH 40207 5618 B1
Bonifay Ct
3900 JFTN 40299 5728 B5
Bonita Ct
4500 LSVL 40213 5726 C7
Bonita Ln
5200 LSVL 40213 5726 C6
N Bonner Av
300 STMW 40207 5618 B1
Bonnibell Dr
10 ClkC 47111 5181 B4
Bonnie Ln
100 LSVL 40218 5727 B4
Bonnie Lea Ct
3400 SVLY 40216 5723 C3
Bonnie Sloan Dr
100 NALB 47150 5505 A3
Bonnycastle Av
1600 LSVL 40205 5616 D6
1600 LSVL 40213 5616 D6
2300 LSVL 40205 5617 A5
Bonnycastle Ter
1600 LSVL 40205 5616 E5
1600 LSVL 40205 5617 A5

Bonnyville Blvd
1700 LSVL 40216 5723 A7
1700 LSVL 40216 5832 A1
Bono Rd
1200 NALB 47150 5505 A3
Bontressa Dr
200 LSVL 40206 5616 E2
Booker Av
3800 FydC 47150 5396 D4
Booker Rd
11000 ANCH 40223 5620 B3
11000 LSVL 40223 5620 B3
Boone Ln
- LSVL 40212 5505 C7
Boone St
3700 LSVL 40213 5725 D2
Boone Tr
1800 LSVL 40245 5622 A1
Boone Trc
100 RDCF 40160 6483 E3
Boones Trc
2900 OdmC 40014 5514 B1
Boone's Grove Wy
4200 JFTN 40299 5728 C5
Booth St
100 SHDV 40165 6161 C5
Borden Rd
6300 FydC 47124 5393 B1
6400 FydC 47119 5284 B7
6400 FydC 47124 5284 B3
8600 ClkC 47106 5284 B3
Borney Cir
4500 JFTN 40299 5728 E6
Borowick Cir
2800 OdmC 40031 5296 B6
Bossier Ln
5500 LSVL 40258 5721 E6
Bost Ln
8100 LSVL 40219 5835 A6
Boston Ct
100 LSVL 40212 5614 C1
Bostwick Ln
1500 LSVL 40245 5622 C1
Bottorff St
200 SLRB 47172 5288 D3
Boulder Ct
2700 ClkC 47130 5399 C4
5200 LSVL 40207 5509 A4
Boulder Rd
- HdnC 40177 6264 D3
Boulder Ridge Dr
2700 ClkC 47130 5399 C3
Boulevard Napoleon
2000 LSVL 40205 5617 A7
S Boundary Rd
10 RDCF 42701 6593 B3
500 HdnC 42701 6593 C2
500 RDCF 40160 6593 B1
1000 HdnC 40121 6484 C5
1000 HdnC 40160 6484 C7
1000 HdnC 42701 6484 C7
1900 RDCF 40160 6484 C7
Bountiful Wy
700 LSVL 40118 5943 A3
Bourbon Av
1200 LSVL 40213 5725 B4
Bouvardia Av
1500 LYDN 40223 5619 E1
Bova Ct
9300 JFTN 40291 5728 C6
Bova Wy
4900 JFTN 40291 5728 C6
Bow Ln
100 INDH 40207 5508 E7
Bowcester Dr
4900 JFTN 40299 5728 A6
Bowen Av
6900 LSVL 40272 6048 D2
Bowen Cir
4000 OdmC 40014 5405 A7
Bowie Ct
7100 LSVL 40219 5834 E3
Bowie Dr
3200 LSVL 40219 5834 E3
Bowles Al
- LSVL 40206 5616 B2
Bowles Ln
100 BltC 40165 6052 C5
Bowling
- STMW 40222 5618 D1
Bowling Blvd
4100 STMW 40207 5618 C4
6900 BWDV 40207 5618 C3
Bowling Ct
9100 HdnC 40121 6374 C6
Bowling Ln
100 ClkC 47129 5397 A6
100 CLKV 47129 5396 E6
100 CLKV 47129 5397 A6
Bowling St
9100 HdnC 40121 6374 C7
Bowman Av
2400 LSVL 40217 5724 E2
2900 LSVL 40205 5617 E7
Bowman Ct
100 MTWH 40047 6056 A3
Bowman Ln
1600 GEOT 47122 5502 A3
Bowmont Ct
6000 LSVL 40216 5722 D7
Bowmore Ct
10700 DGSH 40243 5620 A6
Bowmore Pl
800 DGSH 40243 5620 A5
E Bowne Blvd
100 CLKV 47129 5506 D4
W Bowne Blvd
100 CLKV 47129 5506 C4
Boxelder Rd
3400 LSVL 40216 5722 E3
Boxford Ct
9800 MWVL 40242 5510 E6
Boxford Wy
9700 MWVL 40242 5510 D6

Boxhill Ct
2900 OdmC 40059 5292 A6
3100 GNVW 40222 5508 E3
Boxhill Ln
3100 GNVW 40222 5508 E3
Boxley Av
300 LSVL 40209 5724 D2
Boxwood Ct
6800 LSVL 40056 5512 D4
6800 LSVL 40245 5512 D4
6800 OdmC 40056 5512 D4
7400 GYDL 40222 5509 E6
Boxwood Rd
7100 GYDL 40222 5509 D7
Boxwood Hill Ct
10700 LSVL 40223 5620 A1
Boxwood Run Rd
10 BltC 40047 6055 E4
10 BltC 40047 6056 A5
10 MTWH 40047 6056 A5
Boydton Ct
11900 WTNH 40245 5511 D2
Boyer St
700 CHAN 47111 5181 E3
Boyle St
1200 LSVL 40204 5616 A6
1200 LSVL 40217 5616 A6
Brackenberry Ct
11700 LSVL 40272 5940 B5
Bracken Branch Ct
10600 JFTN 40223 5619 E6
10600 JFTN 40223 5620 A6
Brad Ct
3600 LSVL 40220 5727 D2
6500 FydC 47119 5394 A3
Bradbe Rd
16200 LSVL 40023 5840 A3
16200 LSVL 40299 5839 E3
16200 LSVL 40299 5840 A3
Bradbury Dr
5500 LSVL 40258 5831 B6
Braddock Dr
700 STMW 40207 5618 C4
Bradford Dr
2200 LSVL 40218 5726 E4
2200 LSVL 40218 5727 A3
Bradford Pl
100 BltC 40047 6056 A4
100 MTWH 40047 6056 A4
Bradford Rd
9800 FydC 47124 5283 C7
9800 GNVL 47124 5283 C7
9900 FydC 47124 5392 A1
Bradford Grove Ln
2700 LSVL 40220 5727 D2
Bradford Pear Ct
4000 LSVL 40218 5727 C4
Bradley Av
- LSVL 40208 5615 C7
- LSVL 40217 5615 C7
2000 LSVL 40208 5724 E1
2000 LSVL 40217 5724 E1
Bradshaw Pl
4400 LSVL 40218 5726 C5
Braeburn Dr
100 BltC 40109 6051 D1
Braemoor Pl
400 DGSH 40243 5620 A5
Braeview Dr
700 NALB 47150 5504 D3
Braeview Rd
700 LSVL 40206 5617 A4
Bragg Av
11500 DGSH 40243 5620 C5
11500 MDTN 40243 5620 C5
Braided Tail Ct
2300 LSVL 40245 5622 D1
Braidwood Dr
5100 LSVL 40219 5835 C2
Bramble Ct
5400 LSVL 40258 5831 C4
Bramble Ln
7600 LSVL 40258 5831 C4
Bramblett Blvd
1200 RDCF 40160 6483 A2
Bramers Ct
5400 LSVL 40216 5722 B2
Bramers Ln
4100 LSVL 40216 5722 B2
Bramlage Ct
1300 LSVL 40118 5834 A6
Bramton Rd
100 BWDV 40207 5618 C3
100 STMW 40207 5618 C3
Branch Ct
100 SHDV 40165 6161 D1
Branch St
100 MRGH 40155 6264 C3
Branchtree Pl
8400 LSVL 40228 5837 A6
E Brandeis Av
100 LSVL 40208 5615 D7
500 LSVL 40217 5615 E7
600 LSVL 40217 5616 A7
E Brandeis Av SR-61
400 LSVL 40208 5615 E7
400 LSVL 40217 5615 E7
W Brandeis Av
100 LSVL 40208 5615 C7
Branden Dr
7000 FydC 47122 5393 C5
Brandenburg Rd
- MdeC 40108 6264 A5
- MdeC 40121 6264 A5
- MdeC 40175 6264 A5
Brandenburg Station Rd
- HdnC 40121 6264 D6
- HdnC 40121 6265 A7
- HdnC 40177 6264 E6
- MdeC 40108 6264 D6
- MRGH 40155 6264 D6
- MRGH 40177 6264 D6
100 HdnC 40121 6374 A1

STREET Block City ZIP Map# Grid

Brandenburg Station Rd SR-868
- HdnC 40121 6264 D6
- MdeC 40108 6264 D6
- MRGH 40155 6264 D6
- MRGH 40177 6264 D6
Brandon Cir
4500 SLRB 47172 5288 E6
Brandon Rd
500 LSVL 40207 5617 B1
Brandon Dunes Dr
5900 LSVL 40228 5727 B7
Brandywyne Ct
5800 LSVL 40291 5837 C1
Brandywyne Dr
8900 LSVL 40291 5837 B1
Brandywynne Ln
100 FydC 47150 5504 C4
100 NALB 47150 5504 C4
Branham Wy
100 MTWH 40047 6056 B4
Branning Rd
2300 TNHL 40222 5509 C5
Branston Dr
5500 LSVL 40216 5722 C6
Brashear Ct
1200 LSVL 40210 5615 B6
Brashear Dr
1600 LSVL 40210 5615 B7
Brasslin Av
1300 LSVL 40245 5622 C2
Braulio Ct
5600 LSVL 40291 5836 E1
Brauner Wy
200 LSVL 40206 5616 D3
Brave Rifles Regiment Av
- HdnC 40121 6374 A1
2300 HdnC 40121 6265 C7
Braves Ln
4600 LSVL 40272 5940 C3
Braxton Ct
10 SbyC 40067 5732 D6
1400 LSVL 40118 5834 A7
Brazil Blvd
7000 FydC 47122 5393 D6
Brazil Lake Pkwy
3100 FydC 47122 5393 D7
Breakwater Pl
7000 PROS 40059 5400 D6
Breaux Dr
3300 LSVL 40220 5727 D1
Brechin Rd
11000 DGSH 40243 5620 B5
Breckenridge Ln
200 LSVL 40207 5618 A4
200 STMW 40207 5618 A4
300 NBNE 40207 5618 A4
500 BFLD 40207 5618 A4
600 PLYV 40207 5618 A4
700 SPLE 40207 5618 A4
900 STMW 40205 5618 B6
1000 LSVL 40205 5618 B6
2800 LSVL 40220 5618 B6
2800 MVWE 40220 5618 B6
3000 LSVL 40220 5727 C3
3600 LSVL 40218 5727 C4
Breckenridge Ln SR-1932
200 LSVL 40207 5618 A4
200 STMW 40207 5618 A4
300 NBNE 40207 5618 A4
500 BFLD 40207 5618 A4
600 PLYV 40207 5618 A4
700 SPLE 40207 5618 A4
900 STMW 40205 5618 B6
1000 LSVL 40205 5618 B6
2800 LSVL 40220 5618 B6
2800 MVWE 40220 5618 B6
3000 LSVL 40220 5727 C3
3600 LSVL 40218 5727 C4
Breckinridge Sq
10 LSVL 40220 5618 B6
10 MVWE 40220 5618 B6
E Breckinridge St
100 LSVL 40203 5615 E4
500 LSVL 40203 5616 A4
700 LSVL 40204 5616 A5
W Breckinridge St
600 LSVL 40203 5615 C4
1500 LSVL 40210 5615 A4
Breeland Av
3500 BRMD 40241 5510 A3
3500 LSVL 40241 5510 B3
Breeland Ct
8100 BRMD 40241 5510 A3
Breeze Hill Rd
- OdmC 40014 5402 E6
6100 OdmC 40014 5403 A6
Breitenstein Av
- LSVL 40213 5725 D4
4400 LYNV 40213 5725 D5
Bremer Wy
3200 LSVL 40213 5725 C1
Brenda Dr
200 HLVW 40229 5944 D6
4800 LSVL 40213 5726 C7
4800 LSVL 40218 5726 C7
4800 LSVL 40219 5726 C7
4800 LSVL 40219 5835 C1
Brendenwood Ct
10 ELZT 42701 6702 E3
Brendenwood Rd
3600 LSVL 40272 5941 A1
Brendon Hills Ct
14100 LSVL 40245 5621 C6
Brendon Hills Pl
700 LSVL 40245 5621 C6
Brenlee Dr
7000 FydC 47122 5393 C5
Brenner Pass
3300 HSDS 40241 5509 D3
Brent Dr
5100 FydC 47119 5393 E4
5100 FydC 47119 5394 A4

Brent St
700 LSVL 40204 5616 B4
Brentford Ct
300 DGSH 40243 5620 A5
Brentford Dr
10 SbyC 40245 5514 D5
Brentford Pl
10700 DGSH 40243 5620 A5
Brentler Rd
4000 LSVL 40241 5510 A2
Brentlinger Ln
9900 LSVL 40291 5837 D5
10600 LSVL 40291 5838 A5
Brentlinger Ridge Rd
14200 LSVL 40299 5839 A1
Brentmoor Ln
1700 MLND 40223 5510 C7
1900 WPMG 40223 5510 C7
Brentview Dr
100 CHAN 47111 5181 D2
Brentwood Av
500 LSVL 40214 5724 B4
500 LSVL 40215 5724 B4
Brentwood Ct
900 NALB 47150 5396 C6
Breton Ct
4500 PNRV 40229 5944 B7
Brett Dr
- MdeC 40108 6264 C6
5300 MdeC 40121 6264 C6
5300 MdeC 40175 6264 D7
5400 MdeC 40121 6373 C2
5700 ELZT 42701 6703 A3
Brewer Dr
7600 LSVL 40258 5831 B4
Brewster Av
4400 LSVL 40211 5614 A3
Brian Ct
100 MTWH 40047 6055 E4
700 RDCF 40160 6483 D5
Brian Dr
- BltC 40047 6054 D5
- MTWH 40047 6054 D5
- MTWH 40165 6054 D5
100 BltC 40165 6054 D6
3000 JFVL 47130 5398 D6
Briar Cr
- CTWD 40014 5403 C7
- OdmC 40014 5403 C7
Briarbridge Ln
3700 LSVL 40218 5727 B2
3700 LSVL 40220 5727 B2
Briarcliff Ct
10 MTWH 40047 6056 C4
3600 LSVL 40219 5835 A5
Briarcliff Rd
7900 LSVL 40219 5835 A5
Briargate Av
2200 LSVL 40216 5723 A7
2300 LSVL 40216 5722 E7
Briargate Ct
700 RDCF 40160 6483 B5
Briargate Ln
12100 OdmC 44026 5292 C2
Briarglen Ln
3500 LSVL 40220 5727 E3
Briarhill Dr
5500 FydC 47119 5393 D2
Briar Hill Pkwy
7400 OdmC 40014 5403 A7
7400 OdmC 40014 5512 B1
Briar Hill Rd
500 LSVL 40206 5617 C3
Briarhill Rd
6600 OdmC 40014 5403 C6
6800 CTWD 40014 5403 C6
Briarhollow Ct
7900 LSVL 40220 5727 E4
Briarly Ct
1200 LYDN 40222 5619 A1
Briar Ridge Rd
3700 OdmC 40031 5295 D7
3800 OdmC 40031 5404 E1
Briar Turn Dr
10700 LSVL 40291 5837 E6
Briarway Dr
100 BltC 40047 6055 C3
Briarwood Cir
10 ELZT 42701 6811 C1
Briarwood Ct
100 BltC 40047 6055 C4
Briarwood Dr
- JFVL 47130 5398 C7
- JFVL 47130 5507 B1
1600 CLKV 47129 5506 B1
7800 OdmC 40014 5403 B7
Briarwood Ln
4700 HLVW 40229 5944 C6
Briarwood Rd
2700 NALB 47150 5396 D6
2800 OdmC 40031 5405 B1
4200 NBNE 40207 5618 B4
4200 STMW 40207 5618 B4
7400 CTWD 40014 5403 C7
7400 OdmC 40014 5403 B7
Bricewood Cir
- LYDN 40222 5619 C3
Brick Al
1400 LSVL 40217 5616 A7
Brick Church Rd
5400 ClkC 47143 5180 A5
6900 ClkC 47111 5180 B3
Brick Kiln Ln
1600 LSVL 40216 5723 B7
Briden Av
1100 LSVL 40213 5725 C4
Bridge Ct
4200 FydC 47119 5394 D5
4300 SLRB 47172 5288 E6
Bridgecreek Rd
900 LSVL 40245 5621 C3
Bridge Gate Ct
3500 LSVL 40272 5832 A7
3500 LSVL 40272 5941 A1

Bridge Hill Ct
1000 LSVL 40245 5623 B4
Bridgeman Ct
4400 LSVL 40218 5726 C5
Bridgemore Ln
18000 LSVL 40245 5623 A5
Bridgepointe Blvd
6900 LSVL 40059 5400 D6
6900 PROS 40059 5400 D6
Bridget Dr
1200 LSVL 40118 5943 A1
Bridgetown Pl
12500 LSVL 40245 5511 E2
12500 WTNH 40245 5511 E2
Bridgeview Ln
1700 LYDN 40222 5510 A7
Bridgewater Cove
4200 STMW 40207 5618 B4
Bridgewood Ct
- LSVL 40241 5511 C3
Bridlegate Dr
15500 LSVL 40299 5839 D2
Bridlepath Pl
4200 LSVL 40245 5512 B4
Bridleridge Ct
4300 LSVL 40245 5512 B4
Bridleview Cir
6500 LSVL 40228 5836 A4
Bridlevista Rd
7900 LSVL 40228 5836 A3
Bridlewood Dr
2100 FTHL 40299 5728 C1
Bridlewood Pl
7600 LSVL 40228 5836 A4
Bridwell Dr
3000 LSVL 40216 5722 C6
Brierly Hill Ct
900 DGSH 40299 5620 D6
Brierly Hill Pl
12400 DGSH 40299 5620 D6
N Briggs Ln
- RDCF 40175 6482 D1
200 HdnC 40175 6482 D1
S Briggs Ln
10 HdnC 40175 6482 D1
Briggs St
100 HdnC 40121 6374 B2
Brightfield Dr
12200 MDTN 40243 5620 D5
Brightleaf Pl
18000 LSVL 40023 5622 E5
Brighton Av
700 JFVL 47130 5507 C5
Brighton Dr
2200 LSVL 40205 5726 C1
2200 WLTN 40205 5726 C1
2500 LSVL 40205 5617 D7
2500 WLTN 40205 5617 D7
Brighton Hill Ct
9800 LSVL 40291 5837 B2
Brighton Hill Ln
6600 LSVL 40291 5837 B2
Brighton Springs Ct
10000 LSVL 40291 5837 D3
Brighton Springs Ln
6700 LSVL 40291 5837 D4
Brightside Ct
3200 LSVL 40220 5727 E2
Brightstone Pl
6500 LSVL 40228 5836 B2
Brightwood Pl
500 STMW 40207 5618 C4
Brigman Av
1500 JFVL 47130 5507 C5
Brim Dr
700 JFVL 47130 5507 C5
Brinkey Wy
2900 LSVL 40218 5727 B2
Brinley Av
11800 MDTN 40243 5620 D3
Brinson Dr
5500 LSVL 40216 5723 B7
Briscoe Dr
600 JFVL 47130 5507 C5
Briscoe Ln
5500 LSVL 40219 5835 E4
5900 LSVL 40219 5836 A4
5900 LSVL 40228 5836 B4
Briscoe Vista Wy
7200 LSVL 40228 5836 B4
Briscoe Woods Dr
7900 LSVL 40228 5836 A4
Bristol Av
9100 HBNA 40220 5619 B7
Bristol Ct
- ELZT 42701 6703 D6
2600 OdmC 40031 5296 C6
Bristol Bay Pl
12400 CDSM 40245 5511 E1
12400 LSVL 40245 5511 E1
Bristol Oaks Ct
8700 LSVL 40299 5728 A4
Bristol Oaks Dr
3700 LSVL 40299 5728 A4
Briston Avon Ln
16500 LSVL 40245 5622 C5
Britannia Ct
9600 LSVL 40272 5941 C1
Britt Ln
3800 LSVL 40219 5835 A5
Brittany Av
800 ELZT 42701 6811 C3
Brittany Ct
3300 JFTN 40220 5728 B3
Brittany Dr
8700 JFTN 40220 5728 B3
Brittany Ln
700 NALB 47150 5504 E5
Brittany Valley Rd
5800 GNVW 40222 5509 B4
5800 LSVL 40222 5509 B4
Brittany Woods Cir
- LSVL 40222 5509 B3
5800 GNVW 40222 5509 B3

Brixham Ct
4700 LSVL 40299 5729 B6
Brixton Rd
900 LYDN 40222 5619 A2
Broadfern Dr
7900 LSVL 40291 5836 E3
Broadfields Dr
900 LSVL 40207 5617 E4
Broadhale Dr
6600 LSVL 40291 5836 E3
Broadland Ct
100 HLVW 40229 5944 A7
100 HLVW 40229 6053 A1
Broadland Tr
3800 BWNF 40241 5510 B2
Broadleaf Ct
1000 FydC 47136 5502 C7
Broadleaf Dr
4400 LSVL 40216 5722 E3
Broadmanor Ln
6800 LSVL 40258 5831 A6
Broadmeade Rd
2300 LSVL 40205 5617 B6
2300 SGDN 40205 5617 B6
2600 SMRV 40205 5617 C7
Broadmoor Av
100 CHAN 47111 5181 D1
Broadmoor Blvd
4900 LSVL 40218 5726 D5
Broadmoor Ct
4200 LSVL 40218 5726 D5
Broad Oak Pl
14400 LSVL 40245 5621 C3
Broad Oak Trc
14400 LSVL 40245 5621 C3
Broadripple Pl
14000 LSVL 40299 5730 A5
Broad Run Rd
7400 LSVL 40291 5838 B5
7800 LSVL 40291 5947 C1
9200 LSVL 40299 5947 D2
9900 BltC 40071 5947 E4
Broadus Rd
7000 FydC 47136 5611 D1
Broadway
500 ELZT 42701 6812 B1
E Broadway
100 LSVL 40202 5615 E4
100 LSVL 40203 5615 E4
500 JFVL 47130 5506 E7
500 LSVL 40202 5616 B4
500 LSVL 40203 5616 B4
700 LSVL 40204 5616 A4
E Broadway US-150
100 LSVL 40202 5615 E4
100 LSVL 40203 5615 E4
500 LSVL 40202 5616 B4
500 LSVL 40203 5616 B4
700 LSVL 40204 5616 A4
W Broadway
100 LSVL 40202 5615 D4
100 LSVL 40203 5615 C3
1300 LSVL 40210 5615 C3
2000 LSVL 40211 5615 C3
2300 LSVL 40211 5614 A3
W Broadway US-60 BUS
1200 LSVL 40203 5615 B3
1300 LSVL 40210 5615 B3
W Broadway US-150
100 LSVL 40202 5615 D4
100 LSVL 40203 5615 C3
1300 LSVL 40210 5615 C3
2000 LSVL 40211 5615 C3
Broadway St
100 SLRB 47172 5288 D4
700 JFVL 47130 5506 E6
1400 CLKV 47129 5397 D7
2500 NALB 47150 5505 C1
Broadwell Pl
3500 LSVL 40245 5512 C5
Broadwood Ct
8700 LSVL 40291 5837 C6
Broadwood Dr
10500 LSVL 40291 5837 C6
Brock Ln
- FydC 47150 5504 B5
Brock Rd
- ClkC 47111 5181 B4
10 HdnC 40162 6591 D7
Brockton Ct
1300 LSVL 40118 5834 A6
Brockton Ln
- LSVL 40218 5726 D1
- LSVL 40220 5726 D1
3500 LSVL 40220 5617 E7
3500 LSVL 40220 5618 A7
Brody Ln
3800 LSVL 40299 5727 E4
Broecker Blvd
8400 LSVL 40241 5510 B1
Broeck Pointe Cir
3200 BKPT 40241 5510 C4
3200 LSVL 40241 5510 C4
Broeck Pointe Ct
3300 BKPT 40241 5510 C4
Broeker Ln
200 NALB 47150 5504 D7
Broken Bow Dr
7000 LSVL 40258 5830 D7
Broken Branch Pl
3800 LSVL 40245 5512 B4
Broken Branch Wy
13500 LSVL 40245 5512 B4
Brokers Tip Ln
5500 LSVL 40272 5831 A7
Bromwell Ct
300 LSVL 40245 5621 C4
Bromwell Dr
400 LSVL 40245 5621 C3
Bromwick Ct
300 DGSH 40243 5620 A5
Bronner Cir
7000 LSVL 40218 5727 C5

Bronston Wy
8200 LSVL 40228 5836 B5
Bronswick Ct
1200 LSVL 40118 5834 A7
Bronte Ct
4100 LSVL 40299 5729 E5
Bronte Dr
13600 LSVL 40299 5729 D5
Bronzeridge Pl
9400 LSVL 40229 5945 A1
Bronzewing Ct
8500 JFTN 40299 5728 A5
Bronze Wood Wy
- BltC 40047 6055 C5
- MTWH 40047 6055 C5
Brook St
2500 NALB 47150 5505 C1
N Brook St
- LSVL 40202 5615 E2
S Brook St
100 LSVL 40202 5615 D6
600 LSVL 40203 5615 D6
1200 LSVL 40208 5615 D6
2000 LSVL 40208 5724 D1
3900 LSVL 40214 5724 D4
Brook Bend Ct
11100 LSVL 40229 5945 A3
Brook Bend Wy
6500 LSVL 40229 5945 A3
Brookdale Av
2800 LSVL 40220 5618 C6
Brookdale Rd
100 BltC 40047 5946 B7
Brooke Trace Cir
11200 LSVL 40229 5944 E5
Brook Falls Ct
6600 LSVL 40299 5838 B2
Brookfield Rd
3900 BLWD 40207 5617 E2
3900 CYWV 40207 5617 E2
3900 STMW 40207 5617 E2
Brook Forest Pl
14400 LSVL 40245 5621 C4
Brook Garden Pl
7100 LSVL 40258 5830 D4
Brookglen Ct
8000 LSVL 40220 5727 E4
Brookgreen Dr
12200 MDTN 40243 5620 D6
Brookhaven Av
4200 LSVL 40220 5618 C6
Brookhaven Rd
2900 FydC 47150 5397 A2
3000 FydC 47150 5396 E2
Brookhill Ct
- GEOT 47122 5502 C5
10500 JFTN 40223 5619 E5
Brookhill Rd
800 JFTN 40223 5619 E6
Brookhollow Ct
8200 LSVL 40220 5727 E5
Brookhollow Dr
3400 LSVL 40220 5727 E3
3600 LSVL 40299 5727 E4
Brookhollow Wy
- JFVL 47130 5399 B5
2200 ClkC 47130 5399 B4
Brookhurst Ct
1300 LSVL 40118 5834 A7
Brooklawn Dr
6700 LSVL 40214 5832 B2
6700 LSVL 40258 5832 B2
Brookley Ct
4800 LSVL 40229 5944 C4
Brookley Dr
100 HLVW 40229 5944 C5
100 LSVL 40229 5944 C6
Brookline
3500 ClkC 47130 5399 A3
Brookline Av
600 LSVL 40214 5724 A6
700 LSVL 40215 5724 A6
Brook Meadow Dr
7300 LSVL 40228 5836 B3
Brookmoor Dr
12000 DGSH 40243 5620 C5
12000 MDTN 40243 5620 C5
12000 WDHL 40243 5620 C5
Brook Park Dr
700 LSVL 40214 5724 B6
700 LSVL 40215 5724 B6
Brookridge Cir
400 NALB 47150 5505 A1
Brookridge Ln
7900 LSVL 40219 5835 A5
Brookridge Village Blvd
10100 LSVL 40291 5837 C4
Brook Run Dr
11000 LSVL 40291 5837 D4
E Brooks Av
100 CLKV 47129 5506 D4
W Brooks Av
100 CLKV 47129 5506 C4
Brooks Ln
10 SbyC 40067 5623 C4
Brooks Rd
- BltC 40109 6052 D1
- HLVW 40109 6052 D1
- HLVW 40165 6053 A2
- HLVW 40229 6052 E1
- HLVW 40229 6053 A2
Brooks Rd SR-1526
- BltC 40109 6052 D1
- HLVW 40109 6052 D1
Brooks St
100 ELZT 42701 6812 D1
Brooks Bend Rd
9600 LSVL 40258 5831 A5
9700 LSVL 40258 5830 E5
Brooks Forrest Rd
10 BltC 40109 5943 B6
Brooks Hill Rd
- BltC 40109 6052 E1
- HLVW 40109 6052 E1

Brooks Hill Rd
- HLVW 40229 6052 E1
Brooks Hill Rd SR-1603
- BltC 40109 6052 E1
- HLVW 40109 6052 E1
- HLVW 40229 6052 E1
Brookshire Ct
10 SpnC 40071 6057 D2
1000 ELZT 42701 6703 A7
1200 LSVL 40118 5833 E6
Brookshire Dr
2000 JFVL 47130 5507 D1
Brookside Av NE
2400 LNVL 47136 5610 D5
Brookside Ct
3900 HsnC 47136 5610 C2
6200 FydC 47136 5502 E7
Brookside Ct NE
3900 HsnC 47136 5610 C2
Brookside Dr
- DGSH 40243 5620 A4
- LSVL 40243 5620 A4
100 LSVL 40223 5620 A3
2300 LSVL 40205 5617 B5
10800 JFTN 40299 5729 A4
Brookside Dr E
8500 OdmC 40056 5512 E3
Brookside Dr NE
6700 HsnC 47136 5610 C2
Brookside Dr W
8500 OdmC 40056 5512 E3
Brookside Ln
3900 NALB 47150 5396 D5
Brooksong Ct
13600 LSVL 40245 5512 B4
Brooks School House Rd
- BltC 40109 6052 C1
100 BltC 40109 5943 C7
Brooks Station Dr
100 BltC 40109 5943 C7
Brooks Station Ln
100 BltC 40109 5943 C7
Brook Stone Ct
1900 OdmC 40014 5405 D4
11100 LSVL 40223 5620 B3
Brookstone Ct
1000 FydC 47122 5502 B5
1000 GEOT 47122 5502 B5
Brookstone Pl
11200 LSVL 40223 5620 B3
Brook Stone Wy
500 LSVL 40223 5620 B3
Brookstone Wy
1000 GEOT 47122 5502 C5
Brooks Valley Rd
10 BltC 40109 6052 B1
Brooks View Cir
10 BltC 40109 5943 B7
Brooks View Rd
100 BltC 40109 5943 B7
400 BltC 40109 6052 B1
Brookswood Ct
5400 OdmC 40014 5405 D3
Brookswood Rd
5100 OdmC 40014 5405 E3
Brook Valley Ct
6900 LSVL 40228 5836 B3
Brook Valley Dr
6500 LSVL 40228 5836 B3
Brookview Dr
10 NALB 47150 5505 C1
2300 ClkC 47130 5399 B4
7700 LSVL 40214 5832 B3
Brookview Rd
400 WDYH 40207 5618 B1
500 WDYH 40207 5509 B7
Brookway Ct
3000 LSVL 40214 5832 C3
Brookwood Ct
2300 CLKV 47129 5397 B6
10000 JFTN 40223 5619 D5
Brookwood Dr
300 RDCF 40160 6483 C4
900 NALB 47150 5396 D7
N Brookwood Dr
11900 HLVW 40229 5944 C5
S Brookwood Dr
12000 HLVW 40229 5944 C6
Brookwood Pth
9100 TNBK 40241 5510 C4
Brookwynd Dr
11200 LSVL 40229 5944 E5
Brothers Av
12400 MDTN 40243 5620 D3
Browing Ct
100 BltC 40071 5948 D5
Brown Av
100 STMW 40207 5618 A3
5700 MdeC 40121 6373 D1
Brown Ct
- ELZT 42701 6812 C3
- OdmC 40014 5403 D6
Brown St
100 ELZT 42701 6812 D3
200 VNGV 40175 6591 C1
400 RDCF 40160 6483 D2
6000 FydC 47119 5393 E3
6000 FydC 47119 5394 A3
Brown St SR-391
200 VNGV 40175 6591 D1
E Brown St
100 ELZT 42701 6812 C2
W Brown St
100 ELZT 42701 6812 D3
Brown Austin Rd
9100 LSVL 40118 5833 C7
9200 LSVL 40118 5942 C1
Brown Foreman Rd
600 ClkC 47130 5399 D7
600 JFVL 47130 5399 D7
700 UTCA 47130 5399 D7
Brownhurst Ct
10200 LSVL 40241 5510 E2
10200 LSVL 40241 5511 A2

Brownhurst Wy
4300 LSVL 40241 5511 A2
4400 LSVL 40241 5510 E2
Brownhurst Cove Rd
3100 LSVL 40242 5509 E4
3100 SPVL 40241 5509 E4
Brownie Dr
- MdeC 40175 6482 A1
Browning Pl
2900 JFVL 47130 5507 E2
Brownlee Rd
3900 SPLE 40207 5618 B5
3900 STMW 40207 5618 A5
Browns Ct
10 RDCF 40160 6483 E6
100 ELZT 42701 6812 C3
10100 JFTN 40299 5728 D4
Browns Ln
10 HdnC 40175 6591 C4
10 VNGV 40175 6591 C4
100 STMW 40207 5618 B4
200 NBNE 40207 5618 A3
600 ELZT 42701 6812 A1
700 SPLE 40207 5618 B4
1400 LSVL 40207 5618 C5
1400 LSVL 40220 5618 D6
2500 SRPK 40220 5618 D7
2700 LNSH 40220 5618 D7
2800 CMBG 40220 5618 D7
7100 LSVL 40258 5831 E4
Brownsboro Ctr
4800 WDYH 40207 5509 B6
Brownsboro Rd
- LSVL 40059 5401 E7
- LSVL 40059 5402 C2
- LSVL 40241 5401 E7
- OdmC 40014 5402 D1
- OdmC 40059 5402 D1
- WDYH 40207 5508 E7
1700 LSVL 40206 5616 D2
2700 LSVL 40206 5617 A2
3200 LSVL 40207 5617 B2
3600 BWNV 40207 5617 D1
3700 DRDH 40207 5617 D1
3700 INDH 40207 5617 B2
4200 INDH 40207 5508 E7
4200 INHC 40207 5508 E7
4200 LSVL 40207 5508 E7
4400 INHC 40207 5509 A7
4400 WDYH 40207 5509 A7
4500 LSVL 40207 5509 A7
4700 WNDF 40207 5509 A7
4900 CSGT 40222 5509 C6
4900 NHFD 40222 5509 B6
6700 LSVL 40222 5509 C5
6700 TNHL 40222 5509 C5
6800 TNHL 40241 5509 D5
6900 LSVL 40241 5509 D5
6900 LSVL 40242 5509 D5
7100 OBNP 40242 5509 D5
7200 OBNP 40241 5509 D5
7300 SPVL 40241 5509 D5
7300 SPVL 40242 5509 D5
7600 SPVL 40241 5510 A4
7600 STMW 40242 5510 A4
7800 LSVL 40242 5510 A4
8200 BRMD 40241 5510 A4
8200 BRMD 40242 5510 A4
8400 BWNF 40241 5510 B3
8400 BWNF 40242 5510 B3
8400 LSVL 40241 5510 A4
8600 TNBK 40241 5510 C3
Brownsboro Rd SR-22
4900 CSGT 40222 5509 C6
4900 LSVL 40222 5509 C6
4900 NHFD 40222 5509 B6
6700 TNHL 40222 5509 D5
6800 TNHL 40241 5509 D5
6900 LSVL 40241 5509 D5
6900 LSVL 40242 5509 D5
7100 OBNP 40242 5509 D5
7200 OBNP 40241 5509 D5
7300 SPVL 40241 5509 D5
7300 SPVL 40242 5509 D5
7600 LSVL 40241 5510 A4
7600 LSVL 40242 5510 A4
7600 SPVL 40241 5510 A4
7600 SPVL 40242 5510 A4
8000 BRMD 40241 5510 A4
8100 BRMD 40242 5510 A4
8100 BWNF 40241 5510 B3
8100 BWNF 40242 5510 B3
8400 BWNF 40242 5510 B3
8600 TNBK 40241 5510 C3
Brownsboro Rd SR-1694
- LSVL 40059 5401 E7
- LSVL 40059 5402 C2
- LSVL 40241 5401 E7
- OdmC 40014 5402 D1
- OdmC 40059 5402 D1
10000 LSVL 40241 5510 E2
Brownsboro Rd US-42
- LSVL 40222 5509 B6
- NHFD 40222 5509 B6
- WDYH 40207 5508 E7
1700 LSVL 40206 5616 D2
2700 LSVL 40206 5617 A2
3200 LSVL 40207 5617 B2
3600 BWNV 40207 5617 D1
3700 DRDH 40207 5617 D1
3700 INDH 40207 5617 B2
4200 INDH 40207 5508 E7
4200 INHC 40207 5508 E7
4200 LSVL 40207 5508 E7
4400 INHC 40207 5509 A7
4400 WDYH 40207 5509 A7
4500 LSVL 40207 5509 A7
4700 WNDF 40207 5509 A7
Brownsboro Ter
300 LSVL 40207 5617 C1
Brownsboro Alternate Route
7300 CTWD 40014 5403 C3
7300 OdmC 40014 5403 C3

INDEX 12
Brownsboro Gardens Cir — Louisville Metro Street Index — Captains Ct Cir

STREET
Block City ZIP Map# Grid

Brownsboro Gardens Cir
10000 LSVL 40241 5510 E2
Brownsboro Gardens Dr
4700 LSVL 40241 5510 E2
Brownsboro Glen Rd
- LSVL 40241 5511 B1
4300 LSVL 40241 5510 E1
Brownsboro Hill Rd
- DRDH 40207 5617 E1
10 LSVL 40207 5617 E1
Brownsboro Park Blvd
6000 LSVL 40207 5509 B6
6000 WNDF 40207 5509 B6
Brownsboro Vista Dr
2900 GSCK 40242 5510 B4
2900 MYHL 40242 5510 B4
3000 LSVL 40242 5510 B4
3100 BRMD 40242 5510 B4
3300 BRMD 40241 5510 B3
3300 LSVL 40241 5510 B3
Browns Park Cir
6000 LSVL 40272 5940 B3
Brownstone Dr
3800 JFVL 47130 5399 A7
Browns Village Rd
2000 JFTN 40299 5729 A1
Brownwood Dr
7700 LSVL 40218 5727 E5
Brownwood Pl
7700 LSVL 40218 5727 E5
Broxie Ct
6100 LSVL 40258 5831 B3
Bruce Av
600 LSVL 40208 5724 C1
2000 LSVL 40218 5727 A5
5400 LSVL 40214 5833 A3
Bruce Wood Ct
1100 SbyC 40245 5514 B7
Bruder Ln
1200 NALB 47150 5505 A6
Brule St
- HdnC 40121 6374 D2
Brumfield Range Rd
- HdnC 40121 6484 B2
Bruner Ln
6600 LSVL 40272 5939 E7
Bruner Hill Dr
500 DGSH 40243 5620 C5
Bruners Wy
10500 JFTN 40299 5728 E3
10600 JFTN 40299 5729 A4
Brunners St
- JFTN 40299 5728 E4
Bruns Dr
5500 LSVL 40216 5723 B7
Brunside Ct
10100 JFTN 40299 5728 E2
Brunswick Dr
1000 JFVL 47130 5507 A4
Brunswick Rd
200 BWDV 40207 5618 C3
Brush Ln
7900 LSVL 40291 5836 E3
Brush College Rd
3500 FydC 47119 5395 A5
4100 FydC 47119 5394 E5
Brush Jump Ln
1400 OdmC 44026 5292 E1
Brush Run Rd
13800 LSVL 40299 5839 B6
Brush Run Rd SR-1819
13800 LSVL 40299 5839 B6
Brushy View Dr
300 VNGV 40175 6482 E7
E Bryan Rd
10 HdnC 42701 6703 D2
W Bryan Rd
10 HdnC 42701 6703 B2
1300 ELZT 42701 6703 B2
Bryan Wy
3400 LSVL 40220 5727 B1
Bryant Ln
100 SHDV 40165 6161 C3
Bryant Farm Ct
17600 LSVL 40023 5731 C5
Bryant Park Dr
4200 LSVL 40299 5729 C5
Bryce Dr
1400 LSVL 40216 5723 D6
Bryce Wy
- BltC 40047 6055 A5
Bryn Mawr Ct
1600 NALB 47150 5396 D7
Brynwood Ct
7900 LSVL 40291 5836 E3
Brynwood Ln
7800 LSVL 40291 5836 D3
Bubbling Over Dr
4100 LSVL 40216 5722 C2
Buchanan Ln
7200 ClkC 47172 5397 D1
Buchanan St
100 LSVL 40206 5616 B2
Buchard Av
- LSVL 40213 5725 E7
Bucheit St
100 SLRB 47172 5288 D4
Buck Blvd
500 CLKV 47172 5397 C1
Buck Creek Rd
4000 FydC 47119 5394 C4
4000 FydC 47119 5395 A3
Buckeye Ct
3300 LSVL 40216 5722 E3
Buckeye Dr
2200 CLKV 47129 5397 B6
N Buckeye Ln
1500 OdmC 44026 5292 E1
Buckeye Rd
3400 LSVL 40216 5722 E3
Buck Horn Pl
12100 LSVL 40299 5729 B4
Buckingham Ct
1300 LSVL 40118 5834 A6
Buckingham Dr
9600 LSVL 40118 5833 E7
9700 LSVL 40118 5834 A7
Buckingham Ter
300 HTBN 40222 5619 A4
Bucking Trail Ct
8500 LSVL 40291 5946 A1
Buckland Trc
200 LSVL 40245 5622 C5
Bucklandbury Ct
5100 LSVL 40241 5510 E1
N Buckman St
100 SHDV 40165 6161 D2
N Buckman St SR-61
100 SHDV 40165 6161 D2
S Buckman St
100 SHDV 40165 6161 C4
S Buckman St SR-61
100 SHDV 40165 6161 C4
Buckman Hollow Rd
100 BltC 40165 6160 B2
Buckner Av
5300 LSVL 40214 5724 B7
Bucks Ln
5700 LSVL 40291 5837 B1
Buckskin Pl
6300 LSVL 40216 5831 E1
Bucky Burton Dr
- HLVW 40229 5943 E4
- HLVW 40229 5944 A5
Bucky Burton Rd
300 HLVW 40229 5943 E5
300 HLVW 40229 5944 A5
Budd Rd
1900 NALB 47150 5504 D7
2200 FydC 47150 5613 B2
2200 NALB 47150 5613 B2
3300 FydC 47150 5612 D4
6600 FydC 47117 5612 D7
6600 FydC 47117 5721 D1
6600 FydC 47150 5721 D1
Buechel Av
2200 LSVL 40218 5727 A4
Buechel Byp
- LSVL 40218 5726 E3
- WBHL 40218 5726 E3
4100 LSVL 40218 5727 A4
Buechel Byp US-31E
- LSVL 40218 5726 E3
- WBHL 40218 5726 E3
4100 LSVL 40218 5727 A4
Buechel Byp US-150
- LSVL 40218 5726 E3
- WBHL 40218 5726 E3
4100 LSVL 40218 5727 A4
Buechel Ter
100 LSVL 40218 5727 B5
Buechel Bank Rd
1900 LSVL 40218 5727 A5
3900 LSVL 40218 5726 E6
3900 LSVL 40228 5726 E6
Buena Vista Ct
7600 LSVL 40219 5835 D4
Buffalo Tr
3300 FydC 47119 5395 C7
Buffalo Creek Dr
100 ELZT 42701 6703 E7
Buffalo Run Rd
100 SHDV 40165 6162 A6
200 BltC 40165 6162 B7
Buford Ln
200 ELZT 42701 6702 D5
Bugaboo Ln
2800 ClkC 47172 5287 E6
Buglewood Pl
3800 LSVL 40245 5512 B4
Buisson Ln
6500 LSVL 40219 5836 A2
Bulger Ct
- LSVL 40210 5615 B6
Bulkeley Dr
200 NALB 47150 5505 C2
Bull Dog Al
1800 NALB 47150 5505 C3
Bullion Blvd
- HdnC 40121 6373 E5
- MdeC 40175 6373 E5
4200 HdnC 40121 6374 A5
Bullion Blvd SR-1646
- HdnC 40121 6373 E5
- HdnC 40121 6374 A5
Bullitt Ln
100 LSVL 40222 5618 D4
Bullitt Co Stone
Company Rd
- BltC 40165 6053 A5
Bulrush Ct E
5200 LSVL 40258 5831 C3
Bulrush Ct W
5300 LSVL 40258 5831 B3
Bunche Ct
4900 LSVL 40218 5726 D6
Bungalow Dr
5400 LSVL 40216 5831 E2
5400 LSVL 40258 5831 E2
Bunger Av
7100 LSVL 40272 6048 D3
Bunker Hill Ct
1800 LSVL 40205 5726 B2
Bunker Hill Dr
3000 LSVL 40205 5726 A2
Bunning Dr
5500 LSVL 40272 5940 B4
Bunsen Pkwy
- FTHL 40299 5619 C7
- LSVL 40222 5618 D4
9200 HBNA 40220 5619 C7
9200 LSVL 40220 5619 C7
9700 FTHL 40299 5728 C1
9700 JFTN 40299 5728 C1
Bunsen Wy
- FTHL 40299 5728 D1
9800 JFTN 40299 5728 D1
10400 JFTN 40299 5729 A1
Bunting Dr
2400 JFVL 47130 5398 B6
Bunton Ct
4200 WSNP 40213 5725 E4
Bunton Rd
1400 LSVL 40213 5725 E4
1400 WSNP 40213 5725 E4
Burdette Dr
- ClkC 47111 5181 A3
Burgandy Av
800 ELZT 42701 6811 D3
Burghard Av
1400 LSVL 40210 5615 B6
Burgoo King Rd
9200 LSVL 40272 5831 A7
Burgundy Dr
4400 JFTN 40299 5728 E6
4400 LSVL 40299 5728 E6
Burkett Ct
5300 LSVL 40291 5728 D7
Burkhart Dr
- MTWH 40047 6056 B2
Burkhead Av
4800 LSVL 40258 5831 D4
Burkland Blvd
3300 HBNE 40165 6053 C2
3600 PNRV 40165 6053 C2
9100 HdnC 40121 6374 C7
Burkley Av
4700 LSVL 40214 5724 C6
Burleigh Ct
200 LSVL 40245 5621 D5
Burleigh Pl
14800 LSVL 40245 5621 D5
Burlingame Ct
8600 LSVL 40219 5835 E6
Burlingame Rd
8400 LSVL 40219 5836 A6
8500 LSVL 40219 5835 E6
Burlington Av
5900 GNVH 40222 5509 B4
Burlwood Cir
100 BltC 40047 6055 B4
100 MTWH 40047 6055 B4
Burlwood Ct
100 BltC 40047 6055 B4
100 MTWH 40047 6055 B4
9200 LSVL 40229 5945 B1
Burlwood Dr
6400 LSVL 40229 5945 B1
E Burnett Av
400 LSVL 40208 5615 E6
400 LSVL 40217 5615 E6
700 LSVL 40217 5616 A7
1400 LSVL 40217 5725 B1
W Burnett Av
800 LSVL 40208 5615 C6
1200 LSVL 40210 5615 B6
1800 LSVL 40210 5614 E6
2600 LSVL 40211 5614 E6
Burnham Pl
6200 PROS 40059 5400 C3
Burning Bush Rd
3800 BWNF 40241 5510 B3
Burning Springs Cir
900 JFTN 40223 5619 D6
Burning Springs Dr
1000 JFTN 40223 5619 D6
Burning Tree Ct
2400 JFVL 47130 5398 A7
8200 LSVL 40291 5837 C7
Burnley Rd
100 DGSH 40243 5620 A4
100 LSVL 40223 5620 A4
Burns Ct
10500 JFTN 40223 5619 D5
Burns Rd
400 HdnC 40160 6592 A3
400 HdnC 40175 6592 A4
1800 HdnC 40162 6592 A6
Burnsdale Rd
- LSVL 40223 5620 A4
- LSVL 40243 5620 A4
100 DGSH 40243 5620 A4
Burnside Av
500 VNGV 40175 6591 E1
Burnside St
- JFVL 47130 5506 E4
Burnt Cedar Ct
8100 LSVL 40219 5835 C5
Burnt Cedar Ln
4300 LSVL 40219 5835 B5
Burnt Hill Rd
1200 OdmC 44026 5292 B3
Burnt Oaks Ct
10700 LSVL 40241 5511 A2
Burnt Pine Wy
- LSVL 40228 5727 B7
Burnwick Ct
1200 LSVL 40214 5832 E6
1200 LSVL 40214 5833 A6
Bur Oak Ct
10 HdnC 42701 6702 B6
Bur Oak Pl
7100 LSVL 40291 5837 C4
Burr Ln
7700 LSVL 40214 5832 E5
Burrel Dr
2300 SVLY 40216 5723 B3
Burrell Dr
2300 SVLY 40216 5723 B3
Burrice Ct
7600 LSVL 40258 5830 D4
Burris Dr
4800 JFTN 40291 5728 B6
Burr Oak
- BltC 40047 6055 E1
- MTWH 40047 6055 E1
Burton Av
700 LSVL 40208 5724 B2
1100 NALB 47150 5505 D3
Burwell Av
2500 LSVL 40210 5614 D6
Busath Av
4000 LSVL 40218 5727 A5
Busch Pl
200 NALB 47150 5504 D5
Bush Ln
10 ELZT 42701 6812 B5
Bush Rd
200 LSVL 40214 5833 B1
Bush Farm Dr
14900 LSVL 40245 5512 C7
Bushmill Park Rd
3000 LSVL 40241 5511 A4
Bushwood Rd
2600 ANCH 40223 5511 C6
2600 LSVL 40223 5511 C6
Business Center Ct
1600 JFTN 40299 5620 B7
Business Park Dr
3800 LSVL 40213 5726 A7
3800 PLRH 40213 5726 A7
Butler
- SLRB 47172 5288 E6
Butler Av
200 CHAN 47111 5181 D4
Butler Ct
2900 LSVL 40218 5727 B2
2900 LSVL 40220 5727 B2
9100 HdnC 40121 6374 C7
Butler Rd
2600 SVLY 40216 5723 B4
Butler St
100 NALB 47150 5505 D5
Butler National Ct
8000 LSVL 40291 5837 C6
Buttercup Rd
100 LSVL 40218 5727 C6
Butterfly Ln
100 BltC 40229 5944 D6
Buttermilk Ridge Rd
13700 LSVL 40299 5839 A7
Butternut Ct
8500 BRWD 40242 5510 B6
Butternut Rd
5500 LSVL 40213 5725 E7
5500 LSVL 40219 5725 E6
5600 LSVL 40219 5834 E1
Button Ln
1700 LGNG 40031 5296 C4
1700 OdmC 40031 5296 C4
Buttonbush Glen Dr
4200 LSVL 40241 5510 E3
Buttonbush Meadow Ct
4100 LSVL 40241 5510 E3
Buttontown Rd
4600 FydC 47122 5392 D4
5400 FydC 47124 5392 D4
6300 FydC 47124 5283 E7
6300 GNVL 47124 5283 E7
Buttonwood Ct
1600 SHDV 40165 6162 A2
Buttonwood Dr
- JFVL 47130 5398 B7
- JFVL 47130 5507 C1
Buttonwood Rd
1800 GYDL 40222 5509 C7
Buxton Dr
4200 LSVL 40218 5727 B4
Buzzman Dr
10400 LSVL 40291 5837 E4
Byerly Blvd
- RDCF 40160 6592 E2
Byrne Av
300 LSVL 40209 5724 D2
Byrneville Rd
10900 FydC 47122 5392 A6
10900 FydC 47124 5392 A6
Byron Av
2600 SMRV 40205 5617 C7
Byron Dr
1500 CLKV 47129 5397 B7
By Wy Ln
6400 LSVL 40218 5727 B4

C

C Ct
10 LGNG 40031 5296 E2
C St
- HdnC 40121 6374 B3
- JFVL 47130 5507 B4
Cabel St
100 LSVL 40206 5616 B2
Cabin Cir
- GNVH 40222 5509 B4
Cabin Ln
100 BltC 40047 6057 A5
Cabin Wy
5800 GNVH 40222 5509 B4
5800 LSVL 40222 5509 B4
Cabin Creek Ct
- BltC 40109 6052 B4
Cabin Creek Dr
100 BltC 40109 6052 C3
Cabin Hill Ln
3700 FydC 47150 5504 A3
Cabin Hill Rd
8300 LSVL 40291 5836 E4
8300 LSVL 40291 5837 A4
Cabinwood Ct
3800 LSVL 40220 5727 C1
Cabinwood Dr
3000 LSVL 40220 5727 C1
Cabot Ct
6900 PROS 40059 5400 D3
Cactus Ct
100 HLVW 40229 5944 B5
Cadbury Ct
400 LSVL 40212 5614 E2
Cadbury Dr
4200 FydC 47150 5396 C2
Cadence Ct
1400 LYDN 40222 5510 A7
Cadence Pl
8200 LYDN 40222 5510 A7
Cadenza Ct
100 HLVW 40229 5944 A5
Cadet Ct
1400 LYDN 40222 5510 A7
Cadillac Ct
4100 LSVL 40213 5725 E3
Cadogan Ct
700 HTBN 40222 5619 C5
Cadogan Wy
700 HTBN 40222 5619 C5
Cady Ct
- LSVL 40258 5831 C1
Cady Dr
6500 LSVL 40216 5831 C1
6500 LSVL 40258 5831 C1
Cady Cove Ct
10400 JFTN 40223 5619 E6
Caerlson Ln
5000 LSVL 40241 5510 E1
Caesars Ct
900 BltC 40165 6160 D6
Caitlynn Wy
6800 LSVL 40229 5945 A4
Cal Av
3800 OdmC 40014 5297 A7
Calais Dr
3200 JFTN 40299 5728 C4
Calamar Ct
9800 LSVL 40241 5510 E4
Calder Ct
1700 LSVL 40205 5726 A2
Caldwell Av
- HdnC 40121 6373 E2
Caldwell Dr
10100 JFTN 40299 5728 D5
E Caldwell St
100 LSVL 40203 5615 E4
600 LSVL 40203 5616 A5
1000 LSVL 40204 5616 A5
Caledonia Av
10 LSVL 40206 5617 A3
Calgary Wy
3900 LSVL 40241 5510 B3
Calhoun Av
- LSVL 40215 5724 B3
Calico Ct
7200 LSVL 40219 5836 A2
California Av
100 MTWH 40047 6056 A2
Calla Dr
1300 ClkC 47129 5506 A2
1300 CLKV 47129 5506 A2
Callabell Rd
10 LSVL 40206 5616 E1
Callie Dr
9800 LSVL 40118 5942 D2
Callway Dr
3000 JFVL 47130 5507 A2
Calm Ct
3700 LSVL 40219 5835 A6
Calm Ln
8400 LSVL 40219 5835 A6
Calm River Wy
6500 LSVL 40299 5838 A2
Calumet Cir
100 MTWH 40047 6056 E2
Calumet Ct N
10 LSVL 40214 5833 D6
Calumet Ct S
10 LSVL 40214 5833 D6
Calumet Dr
10 LSVL 40214 5833 C6
Calumet Rd
10 INDH 40207 5508 C6
10 LSVL 40207 5508 D6
Calumet St
- HdnC 40121 6374 D2
Calvary Ct
1800 LSVL 40299 5730 C1
Calvin Av
2400 LSVL 40206 5616 E2
Camargo Rd
1900 RVWD 40207 5508 E5
2100 LSVL 40207 5508 E5
Camberley Dr
8200 HTBN 40222 5619 A4
Camberwell Ct
17000 LSVL 40245 5621 D6
Cambridge Blvd
500 CLKV 47129 5506 D3
Cambridge Ct
1700 PNRV 40165 6053 D1
7700 OdmC 40014 5403 A7
Cambridge Dr
100 LSVL 40214 5833 C1
2500 FXCH 40165 6053 A3
2500 HLVW 40165 6053 A3
7400 OdmC 40014 5403 A6
Cambridge Rd
2900 CMBG 40220 5618 E7
2900 SRPK 40220 5618 E7
Cambridge Wy
- ELZT 42701 6703 D6
Cambridge Commons Ct
9600 LSVL 40291 5946 C2
Cambridge Commons Dr
10900 LSVL 40291 5946 D1
Cambridge Station Rd
- LSVL 40223 5619 D4
300 JFTN 40223 5619 E4
Cambrie Ct
10200 LSVL 40241 5511 A2
Camden Av
- LSVL 40215 5723 E4
500 LSVL 40214 5724 C4
1000 LSVL 40215 5724 A4
Camden Cir
6200 CTWD 40014 5403 E4
6200 OdmC 40014 5403 E4
Camden Ct
700 CLKV 47129 5506 D3
5300 CTWD 40014 5403 E4
5300 OdmC 40014 5403 E4
Camden Ln S
- OdmC 40014 5405 A5
N Camden Ln
3800 OdmC 40014 5404 E4
5800 CTWD 40014 5404 A5
S Camden Ln
2800 OdmC 40014 5404 E5
2800 OdmC 40014 5405 A5
Camden Acres Dr
5900 OdmC 40014 5404 A5
6000 CTWD 40014 5404 A5
Camelia Av
- LYDN 40222 5619 A2
Camella Ct
100 HLVW 40229 5944 A6
Camelot Ct
800 JFVL 47130 5507 C4
7600 STMW 40222 5618 E1
Cameo Ct
4400 LSVL 40219 5835 C5
Cameron Ct
2700 LSVL 40205 5726 A1
Cameron Dr
1500 JFVL 47130 5506 E2
1600 JFVL 47130 5507 A2
Cameron Ln
6400 CTWD 40014 5403 E5
Camille Rd
9500 JFTN 40299 5728 C4
Camino Wy
5400 LSVL 40216 5722 D4
Camp Av
10 NALB 47150 5504 E6
Camp St
- HdnC 40121 6374 B2
300 LSVL 40203 5615 E5
600 LSVL 40203 5616 A6
700 LSVL 40204 5616 A6
N Campbell St
- LSVL 40202 5616 B2
100 LSVL 40206 5616 B2
S Campbell St
100 LSVL 40206 5616 A3
200 LSVL 40204 5616 A3
S Campbell St SR-864
600 LSVL 40204 5616 A4
Camp Ground Rd
3300 LSVL 40211 5723 A1
3300 LSVL 40216 5723 A1
3300 SVLY 40216 5723 A1
3800 LSVL 40211 5722 E1
4200 LSVL 40216 5722 C3
Camp Ground Rd SR-2051
3300 LSVL 40211 5723 A1
3300 LSVL 40216 5723 A1
3300 SVLY 40216 5723 A1
3800 LSVL 40211 5722 E1
4200 LSVL 40216 5722 C3
Campion Ct
10800 LSVL 40229 5944 E4
Campion Rd
2100 FydC 47119 5395 D1
Campisano Dr
4300 LSVL 40218 5726 B5
4300 PLRH 40218 5726 B5
Campobello St
4400 LSVL 40213 5725 D5
Camp Sky Hi Rd
- MdeC 40108 6264 A5
Campus Pl
1800 JFTN 40299 5729 C1
Camryn Ct
9200 LSVL 40258 5831 B7
9200 LSVL 40272 5831 B7
Canada Rush Ct
7000 LSVL 40291 5837 D3
Canal Ln
1500 GEOT 47122 5502 A3
1900 FydC 47122 5502 A3
Canal St
- LSVL 40219 5835 B3
Canary Pl
1500 LYDN 40222 5619 A1
Canary Wy
- LYDN 40222 5619 A1
Canavan Av
1900 LSVL 40211 5614 B6
Candace Wy
7300 LSVL 40214 5833 B4
Candleabrum Pl
8200 LSVL 40214 5833 A5
Candleglow Ct
800 LSVL 40214 5833 A5
Candleglow Ln
7900 LSVL 40214 5833 A5
Candlelight Ln
500 LSVL 40214 5833 B5
Candlewood Wy
3700 JFTN 40299 5729 A4
Candleworth Dr
8200 LSVL 40214 5833 A6
Candor Av
4100 SVLY 40216 5723 C5
Candy Ct
100 RDCF 40160 6484 B7
Candy Ln
3900 JFVL 47130 5398 E5
7300 LSVL 40214 5832 B4
Candywood Ln
9400 LSVL 40291 5728 C7
Cane Run Rd
3300 LSVL 40210 5614 C7
3300 LSVL 40211 5614 C7
3600 LSVL 40211 5723 C1
3600 LSVL 40216 5614 C7
3600 LSVL 40216 5723 B1
3600 SVLY 40216 5723 B2
4300 LSVL 40216 5722 D5
5200 LSVL 40216 5721 D7
5200 LSVL 40258 5721 D7
6000 LSVL 40258 5830 D3
Cane Run Rd SR-1230
5100 LSVL 40216 5722 A6
5200 LSVL 40216 5721 D7
5200 LSVL 40258 5721 D7
6000 LSVL 40258 5830 D3
Cane Run Rd SR-1934
3300 LSVL 40210 5614 C7
3300 LSVL 40211 5614 C7
3600 LSVL 40211 5723 C1
3600 LSVL 40216 5614 C7
3600 LSVL 40216 5723 B2
3600 SVLY 40216 5723 B2
4300 LSVL 40216 5722 D5
Canna Dr
7800 LSVL 40258 5831 B4
Cannon Ct
100 HLVW 40229 5944 A6
Cannon St
2500 NALB 47150 5505 C1
Cannonade Ct
7100 PROS 40059 5400 E5
Cannonbury Ct
1200 LSVL 40118 5834 A6
Cannonbury Dr
9600 LSVL 40118 5834 A6
Cannons Ln
- LSVL 40205 5618 A6
100 LSVL 40206 5617 D3
100 LSVL 40207 5617 D3
700 STMW 40207 5617 D4
2900 LSVL 40205 5617 E7
Cannons Ln SR-2048
- LSVL 40205 5618 A6
100 LSVL 40206 5617 D3
100 LSVL 40207 5617 D3
700 STMW 40207 5617 D4
2700 LSVL 40205 5617 E6
Cannonside Dr
800 LSVL 40207 5617 D4
Cannonwood Ct
5400 LSVL 40229 5944 D4
Cannonwood Dr
5400 LSVL 40229 5944 D3
Canoe Ln
3700 INDH 40207 5508 D7
3700 RLGF 40207 5508 D7
3700 RLGF 40207 5617 D1
Canonade Ct
10 HdnC 42701 6703 E4
Canonero Ct
10 HdnC 42701 6703 E4
5600 LSVL 40291 5836 E1
Canonero Wy
7800 LSVL 40291 5836 E1
Canopus Ct
3600 LSVL 40219 5835 A6
Canopus Pl
8600 LSVL 40219 5835 A6
Canopy Ct
1100 LSVL 40211 5614 C4
Canter Rdg
10100 LSVL 40223 5619 E4
Canterbrook Dr
2100 FTHL 40299 5728 B1
Canterbury Ct
- ELZT 42701 6703 D6
10 LSVL 40214 5833 D5
Canterbury Dr
10 CMBG 40220 5618 D7
10 LNSH 40220 5618 D7
3500 JFTN 40299 5728 D4
Canterbury Ln
3200 LSVL 40207 5617 D4
Canterbury Wy
- LGNG 40031 5296 B3
Canter Chase Dr
1200 LYDN 40242 5619 B1
Canterview Ct
6400 LSVL 40228 5836 A4
Cantle Point Ct
4000 LSVL 40245 5512 B4
Canto Ln
2300 SPVW 40219 5834 C7
Canton Ct
300 HTBN 40222 5619 A4
Cantrell Cir
6800 OdmC 40014 5403 B7
Cantrell Dr
7400 OdmC 40014 5403 B7
Canyon Ct
100 HLVW 40229 5944 C5
Cape Ct
6700 LSVL 40219 5835 C3
Cape Cod Ct
7100 LSVL 40214 5833 C3
Capella Ct
10 MTWH 40047 6056 A2
Capella Ln
6600 LSVL 40258 5831 A2
Capewood Dr
5100 LSVL 40229 5944 D3
Capital Dr
4100 FydC 47150 5396 A4
4100 NALB 47150 5396 A4
Capital Wy
11800 JFTN 40299 5729 C2
Capital Hill Dr
800 JFVL 47130 5399 A7
Capitol Hills Dr
1100 JFVL 47130 5398 E6
Caple Av
300 LSVL 40118 5942 D2
Capri Dr
3400 LSVL 40218 5726 C3
Capron Ln
9900 LSVL 40241 5510 E3
Caps Ln
10700 LSVL 40272 5941 B3
Captain Pl
- LSVL 40291 5837 D6
Captain Frank Rd
100 NALB 47150 5504 E3
Captains Ct
10 NALB 47150 5504 C3
Captains Bridge Wy
12400 ANCH 40223 5511 E6
Captains Ct Cir
10 NALB 47150 5504 D3

INDEX 13
Captain's Quarters Rd
Louisville Metro Street Index
Chapel Brook Ln

STREET
Block City ZIP Map# Grid

Captain's Quarters Rd
5300 LSVL 40059 5400 B6
Cara Ct
10300 JFTN 40299 5728 E5
Caraway Ln
4300 JFTN 40299 5728 E6
Carbine Ct
10300 LSVL 40229 5944 A3
Carbine Ln
3800 LSVL 40229 5944 A3
Carden Ln
2900 OdmC 40031 5296 B6
Cardiff Rd
8900 WWOD 40242 5510 C6
Cardigan Dr
10000 JFTN 40299 5728 D2
Cardin St
300 ELZT 42701 6812 B3
Cardinal Av
- ANPK 40213 5725 C2
- BltC 40165 6053 C1
- LSVL 40213 5725 C2
3200 PNRV 40165 6053 C1
Cardinal Av SR-2553
- BltC 40165 6053 C1
- PNRV 40165 6053 C1
W Cardinal Blvd
100 LSVL 40208 5615 C7
Cardinal Cir
10 RDCF 40175 6483 A2
Cardinal Ct
1700 SVLY 40216 5723 B6
Cardinal Dr
10 RDCF 40175 6483 A3
100 NALB 47150 5505 A3
200 ELZT 42701 6702 D7
300 CHAN 47111 5181 D3
300 ClkC 47111 5181 D3
900 ANPK 40213 5725 B3
900 LSVL 40213 5725 B3
1100 OdmC 40031 5295 B3
Cardinal Dr SR-1600
200 ELZT 42701 6702 D7
Cardinal Ln
1900 JFVL 47130 5507 D1
Cardinal Ln NE
2600 LNVL 47136 5610 D4
Cardinal Rd
7200 CTWD 40014 5403 E7
7200 CTWD 40014 5512 E1
Cardinal Harbour Rd
1900 OdmC 40059 5291 E1
1900 OdmC 40059 5292 A1
2100 OdmC 40059 5182 E7
Cardinal Hill Rd
7300 LSVL 40214 5832 D3
Cardinal Meadow Ct
8000 LYDN 40222 5619 C3
Cardinal Oaks Dr
3000 LSVL 40214 5832 C3
Cardwell St
600 LSVL 40217 5615 E6
Cardwell Wy
10 HBNA 40220 5619 A7
10 JFTN 40220 5619 A7
Carey Av
100 LSVL 40218 5727 B5
Carey Ln
100 ELZT 42701 6702 D6
200 HdnC 42701 6702 C6
Cargo Ct
1700 JFTN 40299 5619 D7
1700 JFTN 40299 5728 D1
Caribou Wy
1100 LYDN 40222 5619 A1
Caring Wy
1600 ANCH 40223 5511 B7
1600 ANCH 40223 5620 B1
Caritas Wy
- HTBN 40222 5619 C6
- JFTN 40223 5619 C6
Carl Ct
1800 LSVL 40215 5723 D4
Carla Dr
100 MTWH 40047 6056 B4
Carlimar Ct
6900 STMW 40222 5509 C7
Carlimar Ln
1100 STMW 40222 5509 D7
1100 STMW 40222 5618 D1
1300 GYDL 40222 5509 C7
Carling Ct
5400 LSVL 40272 5940 B5
Carlingford Dr
2900 GNVH 40222 5509 B4
Carlisle Av
- LSVL 40215 5723 E4
1000 LSVL 40215 5724 A4
Carlotia Dr
10 JFVL 47130 5508 A3
Carl Ross Rd
7000 ClkC 47111 5181 B7
7000 ClkC 47111 5290 B1
Carlton Dr
2100 NALB 47150 5505 D2
9800 LSVL 40118 5942 C2
Carlton Ter
2300 LSVL 40205 5616 E7
2300 LSVL 40205 5617 A7
2300 LSVL 40205 5726 B1
Carmack Ct
2200 LSVL 40216 5831 E1
Carmel Village Pl
8200 LSVL 40228 5836 A6
Carmelwood Cir
5800 LSVL 40229 5944 E3
Carmelwood Dr
5900 LSVL 40229 5944 E2
5900 LSVL 40229 5945 A3
Carmen Av
1800 JFVL 47130 5507 D5
Carmen Ct
4500 LSVL 40213 5725 C7
Carmil Ct
7600 LSVL 40291 5837 A5
Carmil Dr
8400 LSVL 40291 5837 A5
Carnae Ct
5400 LSVL 40216 5832 A2
Carnation Dr
7700 LSVL 40258 5831 C5
Carnes Dr
8100 LSVL 40219 5835 A5
Carnival Rd
500 BltC 40165 6050 E6
Carol Av
7700 LSVL 40219 5835 B4
Carol Ct
10 FydC 47150 5287 D7
Carol Ln
700 RDCF 40160 6483 C5
Carol Rd
3700 LSVL 40218 5727 A3
Carol Wy
5400 LSVL 40214 5832 E5
Caroldale Ln
300 WDHL 40243 5620 D4
Carolina Av
600 SLRB 47172 5288 C3
2200 LSVL 40205 5617 B6
2500 SMRV 40205 5617 C7
9600 MTWH 40047 6056 A2
N Carolina St
- HdnC 40121 6374 E2
S Carolina St
- HdnC 40121 6374 E2
Carolina Crossings Wy
5300 LSVL 40219 5835 D3
Carolina Springs Ct
4700 LSVL 40299 5729 B6
Carol Jean Ct
1300 LSVL 40215 5724 A7
Carol Metlon Dr
3500 ClkC 47130 5398 D4
3500 ClkC 47130 5399 A4
Carolyn Av
- FydC 47150 5503 C5
100 FydC 47122 5503 B5
Carolyn Ct
4400 OdmC 40014 5405 E2
Carolyn Rd
6800 LSVL 40214 5833 C2
Carolyn St
500 RDCF 40160 6483 D6
Carolyn Wy
5600 LSVL 40219 5726 B7
5600 LSVL 40219 5835 B1
Carolyns Cove
100 BltC 40165 6162 C1
Carpenter Dr
1200 OdmC 40014 5405 E3
3700 LSVL 40229 5944 A1
Carpenter St
100 SHDV 40165 6161 D4
Carpenter Test Rd
100 MdeC 40108 6264 C3
100 MRGH 40155 6264 C3
Carr Cir
- ClkC 47130 5397 E3
6000 ClkC 47130 5398 A3
Carr St
- ClkC 47130 5398 A3
Carraige Wy
100 ELZT 42701 6812 D4
Carr Cir Rd
6000 ClkC 47130 5398 A3
Carriage Ct
1900 NALB 47150 5504 C4
2300 ClkC 47130 5399 B5
3100 LSVL 40205 5726 B2
Carriage Ln
1100 NALB 47150 5504 D5
Carriage Wy
100 BltC 40071 5948 D5
1300 CHAN 47111 5181 D2
Carriage Wy NE
8000 HsnC 47136 5611 A3
Carriage Hill Dr
3100 LSVL 40241 5510 D5
3800 OdmC 40014 5404 D3
Carriage House Ct
10300 LSVL 40223 5619 E3
Carriage Pointe Ct
5100 OdmC 40014 5404 D3
Carriage Pointe Dr
3800 OdmC 40014 5404 D3
Carriage Rest Ct
11500 MDTN 40243 5620 B3
Carriage Trace Rd
100 BltC 40071 5948 D5
Carriage View Wy
11200 LSVL 40299 5729 B6
Carriage Wy Ct
1200 LSVL 40118 5834 A6
Carribean Ln
6700 LSVL 40219 5835 D2
Carrico Av
- LSVL 40215 5724 A5
Carrie Dr
3200 LSVL 40216 5723 A2
Carrier Ct
11900 JFTN 40299 5729 B1
11900 LSVL 40299 5729 B1
Carrington Ct
100 BltC 40165 6054 C1
2800 MYHL 40242 5510 B5
Carrissa Ct
100 HLVW 40229 5944 A5
Carroll Av
4300 LSVL 40213 5725 C5
Carslaw Ct
6800 LSVL 40059 5400 D4
6800 PROS 40059 5400 D4
Carson Wy
3000 LSVL 40205 5617 D7
Cart Wy
14500 LSVL 40245 5621 D5
Carter Av
100 HLVW 40229 5944 A6
E Carter Av
100 CLKV 47129 5506 C3
W Carter Av
100 CLKV 47129 5506 C4
Carter Cir
100 MTWH 40047 6055 E1
Carter Dr
100 RDCF 40160 6483 B2
Carter Ln
10200 LSVL 40118 5942 B2
Carter Rd
1000 FydC 47122 5392 E6
Carter St
600 LSVL 40212 5506 A7
Cartledge Av
- LSVL 40214 5832 E4
Cartledge Ct
5500 LSVL 40214 5833 A4
Carton Dr
2100 JFTN 40299 5728 E2
Carver Cir
- LSVL 40206 5617 B4
Carver Ct
4900 LSVL 40218 5726 D6
Carver St
3800 FydC 47150 5396 D3
Casa Bella Ct
100 LSVL 40220 5727 C1
Casalanda Dr
10200 LSVL 40272 5940 A2
Cascade Rd
3600 BWNF 40241 5510 B3
Case Wy
4400 LSVL 40272 5940 D3
Casey Cir
- HdnC 42701 6703 E4
Casey Pl
6800 LSVL 40229 5944 E4
6800 LSVL 40229 5945 A4
Casey Tr
- LSVL 40229 5944 E4
10600 LSVL 40229 5945 A4
Casey Springs Wy
6500 LSVL 40291 5836 D3
Cash Ct
100 VNGV 40175 6483 A7
Casper Dr
6200 LSVL 40258 5831 B4
Caspian Dr
4500 LSVL 40219 5726 C7
Casselberry Rd
1700 LSVL 40205 5617 A5
Cassia Ct
4800 RVWD 40207 5508 E6
Cassidy Cir
6700 LSVL 40229 5944 E3
6700 LSVL 40229 5945 A3
Cassidy Ln
11300 LSVL 40229 5945 A3
11400 LSVL 40229 5944 E4
Casswood Dr
3000 LSVL 40220 5727 B2
Casteel Ct
9900 LSVL 40241 5510 E4
Castle Rd
12600 LSVL 40272 5939 D7
Castleman Branch Rd
- BltC 40165 6160 C3
Castleman Bridge Rd
- BltC 40165 6160 C3
Castle Pines Ct
7900 LSVL 40291 5837 D6
Castlerock Dr
10 BltC 40165 6053 D5
Castlevale Dr
1100 LSVL 40204 5616 C7
Castleview Dr
300 STMW 40207 5618 B1
Castlewood Av
1300 LSVL 40204 5616 C6
Castlewood Dr
100 PWEV 40056 5512 C3
800 NALB 47150 5396 C6
Castlewood Ln
3300 JFVL 47130 5508 A2
Castlewood Dell
1200 LSVL 40204 5616 B6
Casualwood Ct
8000 LSVL 40291 5836 D5
Casualwood Wy
8200 LSVL 40291 5836 E5
8300 LSVL 40291 5837 A5
Catalina Av
5400 LSVL 40272 5831 B7
Catalpa Ct
1200 LSVL 40211 5614 D5
Catalpa Dr
200 JFVL 47130 5508 C2
1400 RDCF 40160 6483 A4
7600 OdmC 40014 5512 A1
Catalpa St
500 ClkC 47172 5288 D3
500 SLRB 47172 5288 D3
1200 LSVL 40211 5614 D6
Catalpa Springs Ct
8400 LSVL 40228 5836 C6
Catalpa Springs Dr
6900 LSVL 40228 5836 B7
Catalpa View Ct
11400 LSVL 40299 5729 A5
Catania Ct
3800 LSVL 40299 5728 B4
Catania Dr
9000 LSVL 40299 5728 B4
Catawba Ln
2500 LSVL 40217 5724 E2
Cathay Ct
4300 LSVL 40219 5835 B5
Cathcart Ct
900 WDYH 40207 5618 C1
Cathedral Dr
8300 FydC 47172 5288 A7
Cathedral Wy
- LSVL 40202 5615 D3
Cathedral School Ct
10 LSVL 40202 5615 D2
Catheen Wy
5900 LSVL 40213 5834 D1
Catherine Dr
4300 OdmC 40014 5404 C2
Catherine Ln
8000 LYDN 40222 5619 A2
Catherine Pl
800 NALB 47150 5505 C4
Cathy St
10 ELZT 42701 6702 D6
Cathy Wy
100 HLVW 40229 5944 C6
Caton Av
10 LSVL 40118 5942 B1
Catrina Ct
8100 LSVL 40214 5833 B5
Cattail Ct
7000 LSVL 40291 5837 D4
Cattleya Ct
800 WLNP 40207 5618 C1
Cavalcade Av
9200 LSVL 40272 5831 A7
Cavalier Dr
2200 SVLY 40216 5723 A6
Cave Creek Ct
10000 LYDN 40223 5619 D2
Cave Creek Rd
10100 LYDN 40223 5619 D2
Cavel St
200 NALB 47150 5505 D4
Cavelle Av
4300 LSVL 40213 5725 D4
Caven Av
9600 LSVL 40229 5944 A2
Caven Ct
4100 LSVL 40229 5944 A2
Cave Run Ct
- ELZT 42701 6703 B5
Cave Run Ln
1100 ELZT 42701 6703 A5
Cave Spring Pl
2100 ANCH 40223 5511 D6
Cavewood Ct
8000 LSVL 40291 5836 E3
Cawein Wy
3100 LSVL 40220 5618 A7
3200 LSVL 40220 5727 B1
Cawood Dr
4900 LSVL 40218 5727 A6
Cawthon St
700 LSVL 40203 5615 C4
Cayuga Rd
200 INHC 40207 5508 E6
Cayuga St
1500 LSVL 40215 5724 A5
1600 LSVL 40215 5723 E5
Caywood Ct
1900 OdmC 40031 5405 C2
Cecil Av
200 LSVL 40212 5614 B2
600 LSVL 40211 5614 B3
Cecil Ct
100 ELZT 42701 6702 E2
100 HdnC 42701 6702 E2
Cecil Dr
10 HdnC 40162 6591 C7
Cecilanna Dr
100 HdnC 42701 6702 A5
Cecilanna Dr SR-2802
100 HdnC 42701 6702 A5
Cecilia Wy
7700 LSVL 40219 5836 A5
Cedar Av
- LGNG 40031 5297 A2
Cedar Cir
- LSVL 40219 5834 D6
1100 FydC 47122 5502 C3
1100 GEOT 47122 5502 C3
Cedar Ct
900 LSVL 40203 5615 C2
6900 LSVL 40245 5512 D4
6900 OdmC 40056 5512 D4
Cedar Dr
- BltC 40109 5943 E5
500 HdnC 40160 6592 B3
600 ELZT 42701 6703 B6
1100 GEOT 47122 5502 C3
Cedar Ln
- HdnC 40160 6483 B5
- LSVL 40245 5511 E2
- RDCF 40160 6483 B5
- VNGV 40160 6483 B5
Cedar Rd
7300 FydC 47119 5393 E3
Cedar St
- CLKV 47129 5506 D1
- LSVL 40245 5512 D4
- OdmC 40056 5512 D4
100 SHDV 40165 6161 D6
600 LSVL 40202 5615 D3
600 LSVL 40203 5615 D3
900 NALB 47150 5504 E5
1200 CLKV 47129 5397 D7
2000 LSVL 40212 5615 A2
2400 LSVL 40212 5614 E2
S Cedar St
100 LGNG 40031 5297 A3
Cedar Trc
1100 LGNG 40031 5296 C2
Cedar Bluff Ct
7400 OdmC 40059 5401 B3
7400 PROS 40059 5401 B3
Cedar Bough Pl
800 NALB 47150 5505 C4
Cedar Branch Ct
6400 LSVL 40291 5837 C3
Cedar Brook Ct
100 BltC 40047 6055 C4
4900 LSVL 40219 5835 D5
Cedar Brook Dr
100 BltC 40047 6055 C4
100 MTWH 40047 6055 D5
7700 LSVL 40219 5835 D5
Cedarbrook Rd
1200 OdmC 44026 5292 C2
Cedar Cir Dr
1400 OdmC 40014 5405 E6
Cedar Creek Ln
100 BltC 40165 6162 E4
100 BltC 40165 6163 A5
Cedar Creek Rd
- BltC 40165 5945 C7
100 BltC 40165 6054 C2
1400 BltC 40229 5945 D6
1400 LSVL 40229 5945 D6
7500 LSVL 40291 5837 A7
8700 LSVL 40228 5837 A7
8800 LSVL 40228 5946 A1
8800 LSVL 40291 5946 A1
9100 LSVL 40228 5945 E2
9100 LSVL 40291 5945 E2
9900 HTCK 40229 5945 C5
Cedar Creek Rd SR-864
9900 HTCK 40229 5945 C5
9900 LSVL 40228 5945 E3
9900 LSVL 40229 5945 E3
Cedar Creek Rd SR-1116
- BltC 40165 5945 C7
100 BltC 40165 6054 C2
1400 BltC 40229 5945 D6
1400 LSVL 40229 5945 D6
Cedar Creek Rd SR-2053
11300 LSVL 40229 5945 D5
Cedarcrest Dr
500 VNGV 40175 6482 C7
900 HdnC 40175 6482 B7
2000 BRWD 40242 5510 B6
Cedar Dale Ct
100 BltC 40165 6162 D6
Cedardale Dr
6700 ClkC 47172 5397 B1
6700 FydC 47150 5397 B1
Cedardale Rd
11500 ANCH 40223 5620 C3
11500 LSVL 40223 5620 C3
11500 MDTN 40223 5620 C3
11500 MDTN 40243 5620 C3
Cedar Falls Ct
- LSVL 40245 5512 D6
Cedar Forest Pl
4800 LSVL 40245 5512 A2
Cedar Forest Wy
13000 LSVL 40245 5512 A2
Cedar Glen Ct
10400 LSVL 40291 5837 E6
Cedar Glen Ln
8000 LSVL 40291 5837 D6
Cedar Glenn Ln
10 HdnC 40160 6592 C3
500 RDCF 40160 6592 C3
Cedar Grove Ct
700 LSVL 40212 5505 D6
Cedar Grove Rd
- BltC 40165 6162 A6
- BltC 40165 6163 B6
- SHDV 40165 6161 D5
- SHDV 40165 6162 A6
Cedar Grove Rd SR-480
- BltC 40165 6163 B6
- SHDV 40165 6161 D5
- SHDV 40165 6162 A5
2200 BltC 40165 6162 A5
Cedar Grove Rd SR-480C
900 SHDV 40165 6161 E6
Cedar Grove Ter
700 LSVL 40212 5505 D6
Cedar Haven Dr
9200 LSVL 40291 5837 B4
Cedar Heights Ct
9600 LSVL 40291 5837 B5
Cedar Hill Ct
10 HdnC 42701 6593 C7
11000 LSVL 40229 5944 E5
Cedar Hill Dr
10 HdnC 42701 6593 D6
Cedar Hollow Dr
7500 HWCK 40228 5836 D3
7500 LSVL 40291 5836 D3
Cedar Knoll Dr
7000 LSVL 40291 5837 B4
Cedar Knoll Pl
7000 LSVL 40291 5837 A3
Cedar Lake Ct
6900 LSVL 40291 5837 C3
Cedar Lake Dr
10 BltC 40047 6057 B1
10 BltC 40071 5948 C7
10 BltC 40071 6057 B1
9500 LSVL 40291 5837 C3
Cedar Look Dr
9400 LSVL 40291 5837 C3
Cedar Mist Ct
16600 LSVL 40245 5622 C5
Cedar Oak Tr
17000 LSVL 40023 5731 B7
Cedar Oaks Dr
100 HdnC 40175 6482 D1
100 RDCF 40175 6482 D1
200 HdnC 40121 6482 D1
Cedar Place Dr
100 BltC 40165 6162 D6
Cedar Point Ct
100 MTWH 40047 6056 D3
Cedar Point Dr
100 MTWH 40047 6056 D3
Cedar Point Ln
- OdmC 40031 5295 C6
Cedar Point Rd
1400 OdmC 40014 5295 A4
1400 OdmC 40031 5295 A4
Cedar Point Rd SR-1817
1400 OdmC 40014 5295 A7
1400 OdmC 40031 5295 A7
Cedar Post Ct
6300 LSVL 40291 5837 C2
Cedar Ridge Ct
100 BltC 40165 6162 E6
7700 PROS 40059 5401 A3
Cedar Ridge Dr
5100 OdmC 40031 5295 C5
Cedar Run Rd
7000 LSVL 40291 5837 B3
Cedar Springs Blvd
7100 LSVL 40291 5837 C3
Cedar Springs Ct
1600 LGNG 40031 5296 E1
9200 LSVL 40291 5837 B3
Cedar Springs Pkwy
- LSVL 40291 5837 B4
500 LGNG 40031 5296 E1
500 OdmC 40031 5296 E1
Cedar Springs Pl
9200 LSVL 40291 5837 B3
Cedar View Ct
4200 JFTN 40299 5729 A5
4200 LSVL 40299 5729 A5
Cedarview Ct NE
5600 HsnC 47112 5610 A6
Cedarview Dr
1100 JFVL 47130 5507 B3
2300 SHDV 40165 6162 A3
Cedar View Dr NE
6600 HsnC 47122 5501 C3
Cedarway Ct
4000 LSVL 40229 5944 A3
Cedarwood Ct
3900 OdmC 40014 5404 E5
Cedarwood Dr
5400 LSVL 40272 5940 B5
6800 LSVL 40245 5512 D4
6800 OdmC 40056 5512 C4
Cedarwood Wy
3600 JFTN 40299 5728 C5
Ceder Ct
- LSVL 40213 5834 D1
Cedrus Cir
5200 LSVL 40213 5726 C6
5300 LSVL 40218 5726 D6
Celest Dr
4900 LSVL 40228 5727 B6
Celesta Wy
1300 SLRB 47172 5397 E1
1400 ClkC 47172 5397 E1
Celestial Wy
7900 LSVL 40291 5836 E5
Celina Ct
5800 LSVL 40213 5834 D1
Celina Dr
2800 LSVL 40213 5834 D1
Celtic Dr
1000 HdnC 40160 6592 C4
Cemetery Ln
- MTWH 40047 6056 C3
Centennial Av
2800 RDCF 40160 6593 A1
2900 RDCF 40160 6484 A7
3100 HdnC 40160 6484 B7
Centennial Blvd
2100 JFVL 47130 5399 A5
Center Dr
1800 OdmC 40031 5297 B3
Center St
10 JFVL 47130 5507 C4
10 RDCF 40160 6483 E5
10 RDCF 40160 6484 A5
200 CLKV 47129 5506 D7
1800 NALB 47150 5505 D4
3700 LSVL 40215 5724 B4
Centerfield Ct
4900 OdmC 40014 5405 B2
Center Hill Ct
11400 LSVL 40241 5402 C7
Center Park Ln
- LSVL 40214 5724 D7
Centerview Dr
100 SHDV 40165 6161 E3
100 SHDV 40165 6162 A4
Centerwood Ct
5900 OdmC 40014 5404 D4
Centerwood Dr
4000 OdmC 40014 5404 D4
Central Av
- PWEV 40014 5403 B7
- VNGV 40175 6591 E1
100 ELZT 42701 6812 C2
100 PWEV 40056 5512 C1
100 VNGV 40175 6482 D7
200 LSVL 40208 5724 C2
200 LSVL 40209 5724 C2
200 LSVL 40214 5724 C2
300 LSVL 40215 5724 C2
400 PWEV 40014 5512 B1
1500 SVLY 40216 5724 A1
3900 LSVL 40218 5727 A4
6800 CTWD 40014 5403 E7
6800 OdmC 40014 5403 E7
Central Av SR-362
100 PWEV 40056 5512 C1
400 PWEV 40014 5512 B1
N Central Av
7300 LSVL 40222 5618 D1
7300 STMW 40222 5618 D1
S Central Av
7300 LSVL 40222 5618 D1
7300 STMW 40222 5618 D1
Central Blvd
100 BltC 40047 6055 E5
100 MTWH 40047 6055 E5
Central Ct
100 PWEV 40056 5512 C1
500 NALB 47150 5396 A5
Central Pkwy
6500 CTWD 40014 5403 E5
Centralia Ct
1000 CLKV 47129 5506 A2
Centre Ct
- ELZT 42701 6703 E6
300 HdnC 42701 6811 C5
Century Rd
4400 JFTN 40299 5729 A6
Century Division Wy
3500 LSVL 40205 5617 E6
3500 LSVL 40205 5618 A6
CE Smith Rd
100 BltC 40165 6054 B7
Chad Cir
5200 FydC 47119 5394 A3
Chad Ct
900 RDCF 40160 6483 B2
Chadbourn Ct
9500 WPMG 40223 5510 D7
Chadford Wy
2400 TNHL 40222 5509 C5
Chadron Dr
6300 LSVL 40258 5831 B3
Chadwick Ct
8800 HTBN 40222 5619 B4
N Chadwick Rd
- HTBN 40222 5619 C4
100 BLMD 40223 5619 B3
200 BLMD 40222 5619 B2
200 LYDN 40222 5619 B2
200 LYDN 40242 5619 B2
S Chadwick Rd
100 BLMD 40223 5619 B4
100 HTBN 40222 5619 B4
Chadwood Dr
- FydC 47150 5395 E6
3300 NALB 47150 5395 E6
Chadworth Pl
6800 PROS 40059 5400 D2
Chafee Av
- HdnC 40121 6374 A2
5400 MdeC 40121 6373 D2
Chaffee Av
1300 HdnC 40121 6374 B3
5500 MdeC 40121 6373 D3
Chain Ivy Ct
10700 LSVL 40291 5837 E6
Chalet Dr
3000 FydC 47119 5395 D6
Challedon Wy
2000 KNLD 40223 5510 E6
Challenger Wy
- RDCF 40160 6593 B2
- RDCF 42701 6593 B2
Challis Cir
1300 LSVL 40211 5614 C5
Chalmer Ct
2300 LSVL 40210 5723 E1
2300 LSVL 40216 5723 E1
2300 SVLY 40216 5723 E1
Chamberlain Ct
3700 LSVL 40241 5511 A3
Chamberlain Ln
- LSVL 40245 5512 A5
3000 LSVL 40241 5511 D5
4600 LSVL 40241 5510 E2
4900 LSVL 40059 5510 E1
5100 LSVL 40059 5401 D6
12500 LSVL 40245 5511 E5
Chamberlain Hill Rd
1100 WDYH 40207 5509 A7
Chamberlin St
10 HdnC 40121 6374 D1
Chamberry Cir
10 LSVL 40207 5617 D4
Chamberry Dr
700 LSVL 40207 5617 D4
Chambers Cir
9800 JFTN 40299 5728 D6
Chambers Ct
9500 JFTN 40299 5728 C5
Chambers St
10 NALB 47150 5505 E5
Chambers Wy
4000 JFTN 40299 5728 D6
6100 LSVL 40229 5945 A1
Champion Rd
10 JFVL 47130 5507 A5
Champion Lakes Ct
2500 LSVL 40245 5512 D7
Champion Lakes Pl
15300 LSVL 40245 5512 D6
Champion Lakes Wy
15200 LSVL 40245 5512 D7
Champions Trace Dr
4000 WSNP 40218 5726 B4
4400 WBHL 40218 5726 C4
Champion Woods Pl
14400 LSVL 40245 5621 C2
Chancery Ct
100 HTBN 40222 5619 C4
Chanda Dr
300 FydC 47150 5504 C7
300 NALB 47150 5504 C7
Chandler Av
600 RDCF 40160 6484 A5
Chandler St
200 ELZT 42701 6812 C1
Chanel Ct
300 LSVL 40218 5727 A2
300 LSVL 40220 5727 A2
Chant Ct
7400 LSVL 40214 5832 D3
Chanteclair Dr
9400 LSVL 40059 5401 D7
Chantilly Av
100 LSVL 40214 5833 C5
Chapel Dr
8000 OdmC 40014 5513 B3
Chapel Ln
2600 FydC 47150 5397 A1
3200 FydC 47150 5396 E1
3700 FydC 47150 5287 D7
3800 FydC 47172 5287 D7
Chapel St
100 LSVL 40202 5615 C2
Chapel Brook Ln
4800 FydC 47150 5288 C7

Louisville Metro Street Index

STREET
Block City ZIP Map# Grid

Clay Ct W
10 ELZT 42701 6812 B3
W Clay Rd
900 LSVL 40219 5834 E4
Clay St
- HdnC 40121 6265 B7
100 NALB 47150 5505 A4
N Clay St
100 LSVL 40202 5616 A2
S Clay St
100 LSVL 40202 5616 A3
600 LSVL 40203 5616 A6
1200 LSVL 40208 5616 A6
1400 LSVL 40217 5615 E7
Claybank Creek Rd
1300 BltC 40109 6050 D2
1300 BltC 40165 6050 D2
Clayborn Ct
- RDCF 40160 6483 E5
Claybourne Rd
1000 LSVL 40214 5833 A4
Claymore Cir
2200 LSVL 40245 5512 C7
Clayton Rd
1700 LSVL 40205 5726 A1
Clayton Ter
4600 LSVL 40214 5832 B5
4600 LSVL 40272 5832 B5
Clayton Allen Blvd
10500 LSVL 40229 5944 E4
Clearbrook Dr
100 BltC 40165 6053 A5
2500 LSVL 40220 5618 C6
Clear Creek Rd
100 MTWH 40047 6056 A2
Clearcreek Wy
10000 LSVL 40223 5619 D2
Clear Lake Dr
- SHDV 40165 6161 B7
Clear Lake Pl
14500 LSVL 40245 5621 D2
Clear Meadow Ct
14500 LSVL 40245 5621 C2
Clear Meadow Pl
1200 LSVL 40245 5621 C2
Clearpoint Pl
2900 LSVL 40241 5509 C4
Clear Ridge Ln
1200 RDCF 40160 6483 B2
Clearridge Pl
5600 LSVL 40229 5944 E1
Clear Springs Trc
1300 JFTN 40223 5619 E7
Clear Stream Ct
11000 LSVL 40291 5837 D4
Clearstream Ct
2600 NALB 47150 5504 D1
Clearstream Wy
3000 JFVL 47130 5507 A1
Clear Valley Ct
400 ELZT 42701 6702 E3
Clearview Ct
100 BltC 40047 6055 E2
Clear View Dr
1900 ELZT 42701 6702 D3
Clearview Dr
100 BltC 40047 6055 E2
100 ClkC 47130 5399 B5
300 BltC 40047 6056 A2
300 HdnC 40162 6593 A7
1600 GYDL 40222 5509 E7
Clearwater Cir
6000 LSVL 40219 5836 A6
Clearwood Dr
- LSVL 40229 5944 D4
Cleaver St
300 ELZT 42701 6812 B1
Clemson Ct
600 ELZT 42701 6811 D2
Cleo Av
1300 LSVL 40213 5725 E7
Clerkenwell Ct
900 WDYH 40207 5618 B1
Clerkenwell Rd
1000 WDYH 40207 5618 C1
Cleveland Av
- LSVL 40203 5615 A1
- LSVL 40212 5615 A1
2500 LSVL 40212 5614 D2
2800 LSVL 40212 5505 E7
Cleveland Blvd
2600 LSVL 40206 5616 E2
3000 LSVL 40206 5617 A1
3000 LSVL 40207 5617 A1
Cleveland St
500 ELZT 42701 6703 C7
Clever Ct
- HTCK 40229 5945 D3
Cliff Av
3800 LSVL 40215 5724 B5
Clifford Dr
600 ELZT 42701 6811 E1
800 ELZT 42701 6702 D7
Cliff Ridge Ct
1400 ELZT 42701 6703 D6
Cliffs Edge Ct
7800 LSVL 40241 5510 A2
Cliffs Edge Ln
4100 LSVL 40241 5510 A2
Cliffside Dr
100 SHDV 40165 6162 A2
Cliffview Ct
10 SHDV 40165 6162 A2
Cliffwood Av
2700 LSVL 40206 5617 A3
Cliffwood Ct
1800 NALB 47150 5396 D6
Cliffwood Dr
1000 NALB 47150 5396 D6
1000 OdmC 44026 5292 C3
Cliffwood Rd
5000 GNVH 40222 5509 C4
5000 LSVL 40222 5509 C4
Cliffwood Hill Wy
300 LSVL 40206 5617 A3
Cliffwynde Trc
2900 LSVL 40241 5509 E4
2900 LSVL 40242 5509 E4
2900 OBNP 40241 5509 E4
2900 OBNP 40242 5509 E4
Clifton Av
100 ELZT 42701 6702 E6
1500 NALB 47150 5505 E2
N Clifton Av
100 LSVL 40206 5616 E2
S Clifton Av
100 LSVL 40206 5616 E3
Clifton Ln
100 LGNG 40031 5296 D3
Clifton Hall Ct
100 BltC 40165 6054 D3
Cliftwood Dr
1500 CLKV 47129 5506 B1
Clingstone Wy
3400 LSVL 40220 5727 C1
Clint Wy
5200 LSVL 40258 5831 C3
Clinton Pl
1800 SVLY 40216 5723 D2
Clinton St
- HLVW 40229 5944 A7
Clipping Ct
4800 GNSP 40241 5509 E1
Clipping Cross Rd
7500 GNSP 40241 5509 E1
7500 LSVL 40241 5509 E1
Cllematis Ln
8100 LSVL 40228 5836 E6
Clore Av
100 LGNG 40031 5297 B2
6000 OdmC 40014 5404 A6
Clore Ln
6400 OdmC 40014 5403 B6
6800 CTWD 40014 5403 C7
7200 PWEV 40014 5403 C7
7200 PWEV 40056 5403 C7
Clore Hill Rd
- CTWD 40014 5404 A4
- OdmC 40014 5404 A4
5200 CTWD 40014 5403 E4
5200 OdmC 40014 5403 E4
Closterwood Dr
10100 LSVL 40229 5944 E3
Cloudcroft Ln
8000 LSVL 40220 5727 E3
8000 LSVL 40220 5728 B4
Clovelly Ct
6100 LSVL 40258 5831 B6
Clover Av
5300 LSVL 40272 5831 B7
Clover Ct
100 RDCF 40160 6483 E7
8700 BRWD 40242 5510 B6
Clover Dr
100 VNGV 40175 6591 E1
5700 OdmC 40014 5405 B6
Clover Ln
200 STMW 40207 5617 E2
200 STMW 40207 5618 A2
400 CYWV 40207 5617 E2
500 ELZT 42701 6812 A1
Clover Rd
100 HLVW 40229 5944 A7
Clover St
1200 NALB 47150 5504 E4
Cloverbottom Trc
10100 JFTN 40223 5619 D5
Cloverbrook Dr
1700 LSVL 40215 5723 E5
Clover Cove Ct
- BltC 40165 6161 A1
Clover Cove Dr
- BltC 40165 6161 A1
Clover Creek Dr
5000 FydC 47124 5393 C3
Cloverdale Ct
12000 OdmC 44026 5292 C3
Cloverdale Dr
12100 OdmC 44026 5292 C2
Cloverhill Dr
1400 LSVL 40216 5723 D6
Cloverlea Rd
500 LSVL 40206 5617 C4
Cloverleaf Dr
4300 LSVL 40216 5723 D6
Clovernook Rd
4900 LSVL 40207 5508 E5
4900 RVWD 40207 5508 E5
Clover Park Dr
4800 FydC 47124 5393 D3
Clover Pine Dr
4900 FydC 47124 5393 C2
Cloverport Ct
8000 LSVL 40228 5836 B6
Cloverport Dr
8300 LSVL 40228 5836 B6
Clover Ridge Dr
5100 FydC 47124 5393 C2
5500 OdmC 40014 5405 B5
Cloverwood Ln
9300 LSVL 40291 5837 C1
Clovis Ct
100 BltC 40047 5947 D6
Club Dr
900 GSHN 44026 5292 C3
900 OdmC 44026 5292 D4
Club Ln
400 RLGF 40207 5617 C1
500 MKBV 40207 5508 C7
500 RLGF 40207 5508 C7
Club Hills Rd
1900 LSVL 40118 5943 B2
Club House Dr
1200 HTBN 40222 5619 C6
Clubhouse Dr
1300 CLKV 47129 5397 D5
Club Oak Ct
200 LSVL 40223 5620 B4
Clubview Dr
9600 LSVL 40291 5946 E2
Club Vista Pl
2100 LSVL 40245 5621 D1
Clyde Av
300 CLKV 47129 5506 D4
Clyde Dr
4000 SVLY 40216 5723 A4
Clydebank Ct
400 DGSH 40243 5620 B5
Clydesdale Ct
10000 JFTN 40223 5619 D4
Clydesdale Trc
200 JFTN 40223 5619 E4
Coach Wy
8400 LSVL 40272 5832 B6
Coach Gate Wynde
- INHC 40207 5509 A7
5600 WDYH 40207 5509 A7
5600 WDYH 40207 5618 B2
Coachman Dr
1900 NALB 47150 5504 C4
Coachouse Ct
500 JFTN 40223 5619 E5
Coachouse Pl
10400 JFTN 40223 5619 E5
Coachwood Dr
7100 FydC 47122 5393 D6
Coatbridge Pl
300 DGSH 40243 5620 A5
Coats Ln
- HdnC 42701 6812 E2
Cobalt Dr
1700 JFTN 40299 5620 B7
1700 JFTN 40299 5729 B1
Cobblers Ct
3300 FydC 47150 5397 B1
Cobblers Crossing Rd
3000 ClkC 47172 5397 B1
3000 FydC 47150 5397 B1
Cobblestone Cir
1000 PNRV 40165 6053 B2
Cobblestone Ct
1100 ELZT 42701 6703 C7
Cobblestone Dr
3800 JFVL 47130 5399 A7
Cobblestone Sq
600 JFTN 40223 5619 E5
Cobblestone Wy
1000 BltC 40165 6053 C2
1000 PNRV 40165 6053 B2
Coby Wy
9900 LSVL 40241 5510 E1
Cochise Ct
7000 LSVL 40258 5830 E7
Cochise Wy
9500 LSVL 40258 5830 E7
Cochran Hill Rd
- LSVL 40205 5617 A4
- LSVL 40206 5617 A4
Cockerel Rd
100 BltC 40109 6051 B2
Cockrell Ct
12900 LSVL 40299 5729 D6
Coco Ct
8500 LSVL 40219 5835 A6
Cocoa Bay Ct
100 SHDV 40165 6161 C3
Cod Ct
10800 LSVL 40272 5940 D3
Cod Dr
4500 LSVL 40272 5940 D3
Codington Ct
8600 JFTN 40299 5728 A6
Cody Ln
4400 LSVL 40229 5944 B5
4500 HLVW 40229 5944 B5
Coes Ln
1600 NALB 47150 5505 D2
Coffee Tree Ct
3000 OdmC 40014 5405 C7
Coffee Tree Ln
4500 LSVL 40299 5729 C5
Coffee Tree Pl
12600 LSVL 40299 5729 C6
Coffer Ct
4800 LSVL 40258 5831 D4
Coffman Rd
10600 ClkC 47106 5284 D1
Cogan Blvd
7300 LSVL 40214 5833 B4
Coin Rd
9600 LSVL 40291 5837 B5
Coke St
- LSVL 40203 5615 E4
700 LSVL 40203 5616 A4
Cold Creek Dr
- CDSM 40245 5511 E1
- LSVL 40245 5511 D1
Coldspring Rd
- ANCH 40223 5511 D7
1400 ANCH 40223 5620 D1
Cold Stream Dr
8800 FydC 47172 5288 A7
Cole Av
5800 LSVL 40258 5831 B1
Colebrook Ln
5900 LSVL 40219 5835 E5
6000 LSVL 40219 5836 A5
Coleen Ct
2800 LSVL 40206 5616 E1
Coleman Av
1100 CLKV 47129 5506 D7
Colin Av
2600 LSVL 40217 5725 B1
Collector Wells Rd
- ClkC 47130 5291 B6
- ClkC 47130 5400 B1
College Av
200 ELZT 42701 6812 B3
College Dr
200 RDCF 40160 6483 C4
3200 JFTN 40299 5728 D3
College St
100 ELZT 42701 6812 B3
100 MTWH 40047 6056 B3
100 RDCF 40160 6483 D4
E College St
100 LSVL 40202 5615 D4
100 LSVL 40203 5615 E4
N College St
100 VNGV 40175 6482 D7
S College St
100 VNGV 40175 6482 D6
100 VNGV 40175 6591 D1
W College St
100 LSVL 40202 5615 D4
100 LSVL 40203 5615 D4
College St Rd
100 ELZT 42701 6811 E4
100 ELZT 42701 6812 A3
College View Dr
400 ELZT 42701 6811 E4
Colliers Wy
100 BltC 40165 6160 B1
Collingwood Rd
8900 LSVL 40299 5728 B5
E Collins Ct
100 LSVL 40214 5724 D3
W Collins Ct
100 LSVL 40214 5724 C3
Collins Ln
3100 LSVL 40245 5511 E5
3100 LSVL 40245 5512 A5
Colmar Ct
1300 LSVL 40211 5614 C5
Colmar Dr
3500 LSVL 40211 5614 C5
Colonel Dr
2400 PNTN 40242 5510 B5
2800 LSVL 40242 5510 B5
Colonel Wy
400 PWEV 40056 5512 D2
Colonel Anderson Pkwy
400 HTBN 40222 5619 B5
Colonel Cummins Rd
9200 LSVL 40228 5836 B6
Colonel Hancock Dr
10100 LSVL 40291 5837 D5
10800 LSVL 40291 5838 A6
Colonel Sanders Ln
1900 LSVL 40213 5726 A3
1900 WSNP 40213 5726 A3
Colonial Ct
500 LGNG 40031 5296 D2
Colonial Dr
10 MTWH 40047 6056 B4
100 STMW 40207 5617 E2
900 ELZT 42701 6703 C7
2800 RDCF 40160 6484 B7
2800 RDCF 40160 6593 A1
Colonial St
2700 NALB 47150 5396 E7
Colonial Club Dr
100 NALB 47150 5396 E6
Colonial Hill Rd
3000 LSVL 40205 5726 A3
Colonial Manor Cir
3300 LSVL 40218 5726 B3
Colonial Oak Ln
10 SbyC 40067 5623 E7
Colonial Park Dr
800 JFVL 47130 5507 C3
Colonial Springs Rd
3500 LSVL 40245 5512 B5
Colonial Village Dr
1600 NALB 47150 5396 E6
Colonial Woods Wy
10600 LSVL 40223 5620 A3
10700 DGSH 40223 5620 A3
10700 DGSH 40243 5620 A3
Colonnades Pl
9800 JFTN 40299 5728 D6
9900 LSVL 40299 5728 D6
Colony Ct
1700 SVLY 40216 5723 B6
Colony Dr
1100 ELZT 42701 6703 D6
Colonyridge Rd
5400 LSVL 40229 5835 E7
Colorado Av
- LSVL 40215 5724 A2
2400 LSVL 40208 5724 B1
Colrain Cir
6900 LSVL 40258 5831 A5
Colson Ct
3400 LSVL 40220 5727 D3
Colson Dr
7400 LSVL 40220 5727 D3
Colsterworth Ln
1700 LSVL 40215 5723 D4
Colt Dr
7400 LSVL 40214 5832 D3
Colt Ln
10 BltC 40109 6052 C4
Colton Ct
3100 OdmC 40014 5405 D5
Colton Rd
6900 OdmC 40014 5405 C6
Colt Run Rd
10 SbyC 40067 5623 D7
Columbia Av
4900 LSVL 40258 5831 D3
7000 STMW 40222 5618 D2
7200 LYDN 40222 5618 D2
Columbia Ct
800 JFVL 47130 5399 A7
Columbia Dr
600 ELZT 42701 6811 D2
Columbia Ln
100 BltC 40165 6054 C2
Columbia Ln E
10 BltC 40165 6054 C2
Columbia St
1600 LSVL 40203 5615 B1
2000 LSVL 40212 5615 A1
2800 LSVL 40212 5614 D1
Columbine Dr
7600 LSVL 40258 5831 B4
Columbus Av
500 LSVL 40203 5615 E5
Columbus Dr
10 ELZT 42701 6703 B3
10 HdnC 42701 6703 B3
Colvin Cemetery Rd
- HsnC 47117 6048 A4
Comanche St
- HdnC 40121 6374 E2
Comanche Tr
4300 INHC 40207 5508 E7
4400 INHC 40207 5509 A6
Combs Ct
100 SHDV 40165 6161 C4
Combs Ln
10 RDCF 40175 6482 E2
10 RDCF 40175 6483 A1
9600 LSVL 40258 5831 A5
Comfort Ct
- HTCK 40229 5945 D3
Commanche Dr
100 ELZT 42701 6703 D7
100 ELZT 42701 6812 D1
Commanche Ln
300 RDCF 40160 6483 C2
Commander Dr
3000 LSVL 40220 5726 E1
3100 LSVL 40220 5617 D7
Commerce Ct
1700 JFTN 40299 5620 B7
Commerce Dr
- ELZT 42701 6812 D3
10 ELZT 42701 6703 E7
100 VNGV 40160 6483 A7
Commerce Pkwy
- OdmC 40031 5295 E6
- OdmC 40031 5296 D4
1000 LGNG 40031 5296 D4
Commerce Rd
1800 LSVL 40208 5615 B7
Commerce St
600 NALB 47150 5505 A5
800 NALB 47150 5504 E5
Commerce Center Pl
- LSVL 40210 5614 C7
- LSVL 40211 5614 C7
- LSVL 40216 5614 C7
Commerce Crossing Dr
4500 LSVL 40229 5944 B3
Commercial Dr
400 MDTN 40223 5620 E3
Commonwealth Ct
1900 JFTN 40299 5729 C1
Commonwealth Dr
7400 OdmC 40014 5405 B7
7600 OdmC 40014 5514 B1
11500 JFTN 40299 5729 C1
Community Wy
1400 GYDL 40222 5509 C7
Community College Dr
1000 LSVL 40272 5940 D1
Competition Ct
9300 LSVL 40291 5728 A7
Compton St
500 LSVL 40208 5724 C1
Conaem Dr
4300 WSNP 40213 5725 E4
Concord Av
5900 CTWD 40014 5403 E5
Concord Ct
100 ELZT 42701 6811 B5
Concord Dr
100 MTWH 40047 6056 A3
2400 LSVL 40217 5724 E2
Concord Hill Rd
6600 LSVL 40228 5836 B2
Conder Av
4700 LSVL 40272 5940 D2
Conestoga Av
2600 LSVL 40210 5614 D6
Confederate Pl
- LSVL 40208 5724 C1
2000 LSVL 40208 5615 D7
Confederate Hill Rd
- PWEV 40056 5512 C2
Confederate Pl Dr
8500 OdmC 40056 5512 E3
8600 PWEV 40056 5512 E3
Congress Al
400 LSVL 40202 5615 E2
Congress Ct
800 JFVL 47130 5399 A7
800 JFVL 47130 5508 A1
Congress Dr
200 RDCF 40160 6483 A4
500 RDCF 40160 6482 E4
500 RDCF 40175 6482 E4
Congress St
100 LSVL 40202 5615 C2
1000 LSVL 40203 5615 C2
2000 LSVL 40212 5615 A2
2600 LSVL 40212 5614 E2
Conifer Dr
7700 LSVL 40258 5831 C5
Conjar Ct
7400 LSVL 40214 5832 C2
Conley Ct
400 MDTN 40243 5620 E3
Conn St
- LSVL 40215 5724 A4
1600 LSVL 40215 5723 E3
Connecticut Ct
100 ELZT 42701 6812 A2
Connecticut Dr
6900 LSVL 40219 5835 E2
Connelly Ct
6700 LSVL 40258 5831 A5
Conner St
100 NALB 47150 5505 A3
Conner Station Rd
900 SbyC 40067 5732 E2
Connie Dr
6500 LSVL 40258 5831 A4
Connie Ln
10 BltC 40071 5949 C3
Connor Wy
7500 LSVL 40214 5833 B4
Connor Station Rd
10 SbyC 40067 5623 D7
200 SbyC 40067 5732 D2
Conrad St
400 LSVL 40203 5615 E5
Conroe Dr
- HdnC 40160 6484 B7
100 RDCF 40160 6484 B7
Conroy Ct
4000 LSVL 40218 5727 B3
Conroy Pl
2800 LSVL 40218 5727 B3
Conroy St
5500 MdeC 40121 6373 D1
Conservation Dr
6200 JFVL 47130 5508 C1
Conservative St
1800 NALB 47150 5505 D4
Constance Dr
5000 LSVL 40272 5940 B3
Constant Comment Pl
2400 JFTN 40299 5729 C2
2400 LSVL 40299 5729 C2
Constantine Dr
3500 OdmC 40059 5402 C1
Constantine Rd
- OdmC 40059 5402 D1
Constitution Dr
1200 LSVL 40214 5832 E3
Conti Ln
10900 JFTN 40299 5729 A5
Conti St
10 NALB 47150 5505 A7
Continental Pl
- LSVL 40215 5723 E4
Contractors Ct
4000 LSVL 40213 5726 B6
4000 PLRH 40213 5726 B6
Conway Ct
3300 JFTN 40299 5728 B3
Coogle Ln
10700 LSVL 40118 5943 A4
Cooke St
800 HdnC 40121 6374 D2
Cooks Mill Rd
7500 FydC 47122 5502 C1
8500 FydC 47122 5501 D1
9000 FydC 47122 5392 C7
Cool Brook Ct
8600 LSVL 40291 5728 A7
Cool Brook Rd
5000 LSVL 40291 5728 A7
Cooley Dr
10 HdnC 40162 6591 D6
Coolridge Dr
9300 LSVL 40229 5944 E1
Cool Springs Rd
100 BltC 40165 6054 A3
Cool Wood Rd
11200 LSVL 40223 5620 B4
11200 MDTN 40243 5620 B4
Coon Tr
6900 LSVL 40214 5833 C2
Cooper Av
1200 LSVL 40219 5835 C7
Cooper Run
- BltC 40165 6161 D7
- SHDV 40165 6161 D7
Cooper St
400 LSVL 40204 5616 B3
Cooper Chapel Rd
4700 LSVL 40229 5944 D2
5900 LSVL 40229 5945 A2
7000 LSVL 40228 5945 C1
Cooper Chapel Rd SR-864
7900 LSVL 40228 5945 E2
7900 LSVL 40229 5945 E2
Cooper Chase Ct
9500 LSVL 40229 5945 B1
Cooper Church Dr
9700 LSVL 40229 5944 C2
Cooper Crossings Dr
- LSVL 40229 5944 D2
Coopers Ln
2000 ClkC 47130 5398 A4
2000 CLKV 47129 5397 E5
2000 JFVL 47129 5397 E5
2000 JFVL 47130 5397 E5
2000 JFVL 47130 5398 A4
3500 ClkC 47130 5398 C3
Cooper Village Ter
4800 LSVL 40219 5835 B6
Cooperwood Ct
10300 LSVL 40229 5944 E3
Coots Av
1000 JFVL 47130 5507 C3
Copper Ln
100 BltC 40165 6160 A1
Coppercreek Cir
200 LYDN 40222 5619 A3
Copper Creek Dr
8100 LYDN 40222 5619 A3
Copperfield Ct
1000 WDYH 40207 5618 C1
Copperfield Dr
- FydC 47122 5502 D3
- GEOT 47122 5502 D3
Copperfield Rd
6700 WDYH 40207 5618 C1
Copperhill Wy
15000 LSVL 40245 5621 C5
Copra Ln
6700 LSVL 40219 5835 D3
Cora Bay Ct
100 SHDV 40165 6161 C3
Coral Av
100 LSVL 40206 5616 D2
Coral Ct
100 LSVL 40206 5616 D2
Coral Wy
100 CLKV 47129 5506 C3
Coral Bay
100 SHDV 40165 6161 C3
Coral Berry Pl
- OdmC 40014 5403 E4
Coralberry Rd
200 LSVL 40207 5617 D1
Coralwood Dr
10100 LSVL 40229 5944 E3
Coram Wy
4400 LSVL 40218 5727 B6
Corbin Ct
10800 LSVL 40229 5944 E4
Cordova Rd
- STMW 40207 5618 C3
4400 BWDV 40207 5618 C3
Corey Dr NE
4400 HsnC 47136 5501 C7
4400 HsnC 47136 5610 C1
Corinth Wy
6000 LSVL 40219 5835 C1
Corinthian Dr
9500 JFTN 40299 5728 C6
Corley St
5600 MdeC 40121 6373 D1
Corlon Ct
1700 GYDL 40222 5509 D6
Cornahan Av
- JFVL 47130 5506 E4
Cornelia Dr
3300 LSVL 40220 5726 E1
Cornell Av
- BltC 40047 6056 D2
- MTWH 40047 6056 D2
200 CLKV 47129 5506 D4
Cornell Ct
1000 OdmC 40014 5405 D3
6300 FydC 47122 5503 A4
Cornell Dr
9600 LSVL 40291 5946 D1
Cornell Pl
100 LSVL 40207 5617 D3
100 STMW 40207 5617 D3
Cornell Trace Ct
3300 LSVL 40241 5510 D5
Cornell Trace Rd
9700 LSVL 40241 5510 D4
Cornerstone Ct
3000 JFTN 40220 5728 A3
Cornerstone Dr
6400 FydC 47119 5395 B1
Cornette Wy
1500 LSVL 40216 5723 C6
Cornflower Rd
9200 LSVL 40272 5831 A7
Cornice Ct
4500 JFTN 40299 5728 D6
Cornish Wy
2400 OdmC 40031 5296 C6
Corn Island Ct
1000 STMW 40207 5618 A5
Cornwall Av
1400 ELZT 42701 6703 D6
Cornwall St
2400 LSVL 40212 5506 A7
Cornwallis Ct
300 LSVL 40214 5833 D5
Cornwell Dr
2200 JFVL 47130 5398 A5
Cornwell St
1300 HdnC 40121 6374 B2
Corona Ct
1800 GYDL 40222 5509 D6
Coronado Dr
- LSVL 40241 5510 A4
3500 BRMD 40241 5510 A3
Coronet Dr
2500 LSVL 40216 5722 D6
Corporate Dr
200 ELZT 42701 6811 C4
200 HdnC 42701 6811 C4
Corporate Campus Dr
9900 LYDN 40223 5619 D1
Corston Ct
11300 FCSL 40241 5511 C2
Cortland Dr
7900 LSVL 40228 5836 D5
Corvair Ct
3800 LSVL 40215 5723 E5
Corydon Pike
1100 NALB 47150 5504 E7
2700 FydC 47150 5504 A5
3400 FydC 47150 5503 D5
4900 FydC 47122 5503 C5
Corydon Ridge Rd
5600 FydC 47122 5503 A6
5600 FydC 47150 5503 A6
6400 FydC 47122 5502 A7
6400 FydC 47136 5502 E6
6600 GEOT 47136 5502 E6
8000 HsnC 47112 5502 A7
Corydon Ridge Rd NE
5500 HsnC 47112 5610 C1
5500 HsnC 47136 5610 A2
6900 HsnC 47112 5501 D7
7800 FydC 47136 5502 A7
7800 HsnC 47112 5502 A7
Cosby Ct
4400 LSVL 40218 5726 C5
Cost Av
300 NALB 47150 5505 E3
Costigan Wy
2700 JFTN 40220 5728 A2
Cotehele Pl
5000 LSVL 40241 5510 E1
Cotney Ct
4500 LSVL 40213 5725 C7
Cotswold Dr
8500 LSVL 40258 5831 B6

INDEX 16
Cotswold Grn
Cypress Dr

Louisville Metro Street Index

STREET
Block City ZIP Map# Grid

Cotswold Grn
16400 LSVL 40245 5622 C5
Cottage Cir
100 ELZT 42701 6702 D7
Cottage Ln
2200 SVLY 40216 5723 B4
Cottage Ln NE
8000 HsnC 47136 5611 A4
Cottage Pk
3100 ClkC 47130 5399 B4
Cottage Cove Wy
7600 LSVL 40214 5832 D1
Cottage Field Cir
6300 LSVL 40218 5727 A6
Cottagehill Rd
4100 LSVL 40299 5728 B5
Cottagemeadow Dr
6300 LSVL 40218 5727 A6
Cottage Ridge Pl
6200 LSVL 40214 5832 D1
Cottage View Ct
11300 LSVL 40299 5729 B6
Cotter Dr
3500 LSVL 40211 5614 B6
Cottingham Wy
8900 LSVL 40258 5831 A6
E Cottom Av
100 NALB 47150 5505 A3
W Cottom Av
10 NALB 47150 5505 A3
600 NALB 47150 5504 E3
Cottonwood Ct
10400 JFTN 40223 5619 E5
Cottonwood Dr
100 BltC 40165 5944 E6
600 RDCF 40160 6483 A3
900 CLKV 47129 5397 B6
2500 PNTN 40242 5510 B5
Cottrell St
10 ELZT 42701 6702 D4
Council Rd
- INDH 40207 5508 E7
Countess Ct
- LSVL 40219 5834 D7
Count Fleet Dr
5400 LSVL 40272 5940 A1
5600 LSVL 40272 5831 A7
Country Ln
300 HdnC 40160 6592 C3
400 LSVL 40207 5617 D1
400 RLGF 40207 5617 C1
500 LSVL 40207 5508 C7
500 RLGF 40207 5508 C7
Country Ln NE
3300 HsnC 47136 5610 B2
Country Trc
13500 BltC 40071 5948 D4
Country Acres Ct
- LSVL 40218 5727 C5
Country Acres Ln
100 LSVL 40218 5727 C5
Country Acres Wy
- LSVL 40218 5727 C5
Country Acres In
500 LSVL 40218 5727 C5
S Country Club Dr
300 NALB 47150 5505 A2
Country Club Ln
- ELZT 42701 6812 E6
3000 JFVL 47130 5507 A1
Country Club Rd
- INDH 40207 5508 C5
- LSVL 40207 5508 C5
100 VNGV 40175 6591 C1
600 LSVL 40206 5617 A1
Country Creek Dr
1500 FydC 47150 5503 D4
Country Ln Tr
10 HdnC 40175 6482 D3
Country Manor Ln
100 BltC 40165 6163 D5
Countryside Dr
100 NALB 47150 5396 C4
Country Side Ln
1000 FydC 47136 5502 D7
Countryside Ln
100 LSVL 40223 5620 A4
Countryside Trc
1000 JFTN 40223 5619 D6
Country Squire Ln
7500 LSVL 40291 5838 B5
Country Trace Ct
100 BltC 40071 5948 D5
Country Trace Ln
6700 FydC 47122 5393 E6
Country View Dr
4300 FydC 47119 5394 E4
13500 BltC 40071 5948 D4
Count Turf Dr
5900 LSVL 40272 5940 A1
County Club Ln
1800 OdmC 40031 5295 C4
County Line Rd
- ClkC 47143 5287 E5
10 BltC 40109 5943 E5
10 LSVL 40229 5943 E5
6300 ClkC 47129 5397 D3
6300 FydC 47150 5397 B1
7500 CLKV 47172 5397 B1
7600 ClkC 47172 5397 B1
7900 CLKV 47172 5288 B7
8400 ClkC 47172 5288 A6
8400 FydC 47150 5288 A7
9100 ClkC 47172 5287 E5
22600 ClkC 47106 5283 D1
22600 FydC 47124 5283 D2
23500 WasC 47165 5283 D1
Courage Ct
11400 HTCK 40229 5945 E4
Couronne Ct
10 ELZT 42701 6811 D3
Court Av
- JFVL 47130 5506 E7
E Court Av
1300 JFVL 47130 5507 C5
W Court Av
100 JFVL 47130 5507 A7
200 JFVL 47130 5506 E7
Court Pl
500 LSVL 40202 5615 D2
E Court St
1200 JFVL 47130 5507 B6
Courtney Dr
2000 OdmC 40031 5297 C3
Courtney Ln
- SpnC 40071 5949 E3
Courtney Rd
3500 LSVL 40214 5832 B4
Court of The Woods
7000 LSVL 40241 5509 D4
Court Yard
100 JFVL 47130 5507 E2
Cova Dr
4800 LSVL 40216 5722 E5
Cove Ct
6800 LSVL 40291 5836 D3
Cove Dr
7500 LSVL 40291 5836 D3
Coventry Ct
6400 PROS 40059 5401 A5
Coventry Ln
9100 LSVL 40219 5835 D7
Coventry Pl
100 LSVL 40216 5722 E3
Coventry Greens Ct
3400 LSVL 40241 5511 B5
Coventry Greens Dr
11100 LSVL 40241 5511 B5
Coventry Hill Rd
11700 LSVL 40299 5729 C6
Coventry Tee Ct
3500 LSVL 40241 5511 B4
Cove Pointe Pl
7000 PROS 40059 5400 D7
Coverbrook Ct
4100 LSVL 40220 5727 D4
Covered Bridge Rd
7100 LSVL 40059 5400 E3
7100 PROS 40059 5400 E3
7200 LSVL 40059 5401 A3
7200 PROS 40059 5401 A3
7600 OdmC 40059 5401 A3
Covered Bridge Rd SR-329
7100 LSVL 40059 5400 E3
7100 PROS 40059 5400 E3
7200 LSVL 40059 5401 A3
7200 PROS 40059 5401 A3
7600 OdmC 40059 5401 A3
Covered Cove Wy
7100 LSVL 40059 5401 A3
7100 PROS 40059 5401 A3
Covey Ct
6200 FydC 47119 5393 E5
Covey Pl
7400 LSVL 40291 5836 D1
Covey Trace Rd
1800 OdmC 40031 5297 B1
Covington Ct
1100 LSVL 40245 5621 D7
Cow Branch Rd
100 BltC 40165 6048 E7
100 BltC 40165 6049 A6
Cowdrey Park Ln
1500 LSVL 40245 5622 D2
Cowgill Pl
10900 DGSH 40243 5620 A5
Cowling Av
1500 LSVL 40205 5616 E5
1700 LSVL 40205 5617 A6
Cox Av
11300 ANCH 40223 5620 B3
11300 LSVL 40223 5620 B3
Cox Ct
9100 LSVL 40241 5510 C5
Cox Ln
500 ELZT 42701 6812 D2
2000 OdmC 40031 5295 C4
Coxs Dr
100 SHDV 40165 6161 B4
Coxs Ln
100 BltC 40047 6057 C1
100 BltC 40071 6057 C1
Coyle Dr
2300 NALB 47150 5504 E2
Coyote Ct
2800 ClkC 47130 5399 B4
Cozy Ct
6800 LSVL 40228 5836 B3
Cozy Acres Dr
10 HdnC 40162 6593 B6
10 HdnC 42701 6593 B6
10 RDCF 42701 6593 B6
Crabapple Brch
100 LGNG 40031 5296 C3
Crabapple Ct
5600 LSVL 40219 5726 A7
Crabapple Dr
300 ELZT 42701 6703 A3
7000 FydC 47122 5502 B2
7000 GEOT 47122 5502 B2
Crabapple Ln
7000 GEOT 47122 5502 C2
Crabbs Ln
100 LSVL 40206 5617 C3
Crabtree Dr
100 ELZT 42701 6812 C4
7300 LSVL 40228 5836 D5
Crafty Dr
5000 LSVL 40213 5725 D6
5000 LYNV 40213 5725 D6
Craig Av
3500 LSVL 40215 5724 A4
3700 LSVL 40215 5723 E5
Craig St
3900 LSVL 40215 5723 E5
Craig Cooper Rd
2300 FydC 47150 5612 D2
Craigs Creek Dr
5100 LSVL 40241 5511 A1
Craigs Creek Pl
11000 LSVL 40241 5511 B1
Crambrook Av
5400 LSVL 40272 5831 B7
Cranbourne Ct
8800 LSVL 40241 5510 C3
Crandall Lanesville Rd NE
- HsnC 47112 5501 B7
- HsnC 47122 5501 B7
2600 HsnC 47136 5610 C3
2600 LNVL 47136 5610 D5
4400 HsnC 47112 5610 A1
Crandon Rd
11200 LSVL 40229 5944 D5
Cranfill Wy
7300 LSVL 40214 5833 B4
Cranston Dr
2600 JFTN 40299 5728 D2
Crantree Pl
5300 LSVL 40229 5944 D3
Cranwood Ln
5300 LSVL 40291 5728 C7
Crator Dr
100 HLVW 40229 5944 B5
Crawford Av
4000 LSVL 40218 5727 A3
4400 LSVL 40258 5831 E3
Crawford Rd
10 CHAN 47111 5181 C4
Crawford Rd SE
10500 HsnC 47117 5939 A7
Crawfordshire Ln
7400 LSVL 40220 5727 D2
Crawley Ct
9100 LSVL 40241 5510 C5
Craycraft Av
2600 LSVL 40218 5727 A3
Creason Ct
300 DGSH 40223 5620 A3
300 LSVL 40223 5620 A3
Creedmoor Ct
6800 LSVL 40228 5836 B6
Creek Cir
5000 OdmC 40059 5401 D3
Creek Rd
100 ClkC 47172 5288 D2
200 JFVL 47130 5508 A1
Creekbed St
100 MRGH 40155 6264 C3
Creek Bend Ct
4300 LSVL 40241 5510 B2
Creekbend Ct
12800 RVBF 40059 5292 A7
Creekbottom Rd
7800 LSVL 40241 5510 A2
Creekcrossing Dr
4400 LSVL 40241 5510 B1
Creek Pointe Ter
4900 LSVL 40219 5835 B7
Creek Ridge Dr
3000 FydC 47150 5396 E5
3000 FydC 47150 5397 A5
Creek Ridge Rd
17200 LSVL 40245 5622 D4
Creek Rock Rd
17000 LSVL 40023 5731 D5
Creek Run Rd
17400 LSVL 40245 5622 D4
Creekside Cir
4800 OdmC 40014 5405 C3
Creekside Ct
10 LSVL 40059 5400 C6
100 RDCF 40160 6483 A2
400 ELZT 42701 6812 A2
1800 CLKV 47129 5506 A1
Creekside Dr
10 BltC 40165 6052 B6
200 JFVL 47130 5507 E1
1700 CLKV 47129 5506 A1
1800 ClkC 47129 5506 A1
2800 HKYH 40241 5510 E5
3000 LSVL 40241 5510 E5
3100 CKSD 40241 5510 D4
5600 OdmC 40014 5405 B6
Creekside Ln
2300 OdmC 40014 5405 C3
Creekside Pl
100 LGNG 40031 5296 E3
Creek Stone Blvd
7100 HWCK 40228 5836 C3
7100 LSVL 40228 5836 C3
Creekstone Blvd
4400 ClkC 47130 5398 D2
Creekstone Cir
2700 OdmC 40031 5296 C7
Creek Trail Ct
8300 LSVL 40291 5836 E3
Creek Tree Ct
4700 LSVL 40219 5835 B7
Creekvale Dr
100 HdnC 40175 6482 B7
Creek Valley Rd
100 SpnC 40023 5840 E7
Creekvalley Rd
600 MDTN 40243 5620 E5
Creekview Cir
1100 NALB 47150 5396 C5
Creek View Ct
10 MdeC 40175 6482 A4
Creekview Ct
10 HBNE 40165 6053 E2
1900 OdmC 40014 5514 D2
7300 HWCK 40228 5836 C3
Creekview Dr
13200 PROS 40059 5401 A5
Creekview Rd
- ClkC 47129 5397 A6
13200 RVBF 40059 5292 A7
Creekwood Ct
3200 NALB 47150 5396 B7
5600 OdmC 40014 5405 B5
Creekwood Dr
100 BltC 40047 6056 D5
5100 FydC 47124 5393 C3
Creekwood Rd
9600 MBKF 40223 5510 D6
Creek Wy Ct
8900 LSVL 40219 5835 B7
Creel Av
500 LSVL 40208 5724 C1
Creel Lodge Dr
11900 ANCH 40223 5511 C7
Creetown Ct
800 DGSH 40243 5620 A6
Creighton Ct
8700 HTBN 40222 5619 B4
Creighton Hill Rd
1200 WDYH 40207 5509 A7
Cresap Ct
100 ELZT 42701 6812 B3
Crescent Av
100 LSVL 40206 5617 B2
4500 JFVL 47130 5398 B5
Crescent Ct
100 LSVL 40206 5617 B2
Crescent Lp
200 FydC 47150 5396 C4
Crescent Wy
600 RDCF 40160 6483 C4
Crescent Hill Pl
200 LSVL 40206 5616 E2
Crescent Ridge Dr
10 SpnC 40071 5949 E3
Crescent Spring Dr
300 LSVL 40206 5616 E3
Crescent View Dr
100 BltC 40165 6054 D2
Cressbrook Dr
600 LSVL 40206 5617 C4
Cressington Cir
14600 LSVL 40245 5512 C5
Cressington Pl
3800 LSVL 40245 5512 C4
Crest Ct
4900 SVLY 40216 5722 D6
Crest Wy
7700 LSVL 40219 5836 A5
Crest Arms
12600 ANCH 40223 5511 E6
Crestbrook Ct
3200 OdmC 40059 5292 A7
Crest Creek Ct
6300 LSVL 40241 5509 C2
Cresthaven Dr
7900 LSVL 40228 5836 A4
Crestline Rd
7700 LSVL 40214 5832 E4
N Crestmoor Av
100 LSVL 40206 5617 C2
100 LSVL 40207 5617 C2
S Crestmoor Av
100 LSVL 40206 5617 C3
Crestmoor Cir
12700 OdmC 40059 5292 A7
12700 RVBF 40059 5292 A7
Crestmoor Ct
3100 OdmC 40059 5292 B7
Creston Dr
6600 LSVL 40258 5831 A4
6900 LSVL 40258 5830 E4
Crestridge Dr
3800 LSVL 40272 5940 E2
3800 LSVL 40272 5941 A2
Crestview Av NE
2400 LNVL 47136 5610 D5
2900 HsnC 47136 5610 D4
Crestview Ct
100 CHAN 47111 5181 D4
400 JFVL 47130 5507 C5
Crestview Dr
- NALB 47150 5504 E4
1400 RDCF 40160 6483 A2
1400 RDCF 40175 6483 A2
1600 OdmC 40031 5297 B3
6000 CTWD 40014 5403 E6
6000 OdmC 40014 5403 E6
6700 CTWD 40014 5404 A7
Crestview Rd
4100 MYHE 40207 5617 E1
Crestview Wy
1100 GSHN 44026 5292 C3
Crestview Cove
- OdmC 40059 5292 A7
12800 RVBF 40059 5292 A7
Crestway Ct
10 FydC 47150 5396 D1
Crestwood Av
100 LSVL 40206 5617 C3
Crestwood Ct
100 RDCF 40160 6483 A2
Crestwood Dr
3300 NALB 47150 5396 D6
Crestwood Gdns
7200 CTWD 40014 5403 E7
Crestwood Ln
100 HLVW 40229 5944 B6
N Crestwood St
100 ELZT 42701 6812 C3
Crestwood Sta
6000 CTWD 40014 5404 A5
Crestwood Station Conn
- CTWD 40014 5404 A5
- OdmC 40014 5404 A5
Crews Dr
100 LSVL 40218 5727 C6
Cricklecreek Ln
2300 ClkC 47130 5399 B4
Crimson Dr
1900 LSVL 40272 5940 A3
Crimson Creek Ct
100 ELZT 42701 6703 E6
Crimson Creek Dr
- GEOT 47122 5502 B3
10 ELZT 42701 6703 E6
Cris Dr
8100 LSVL 40291 5836 E2
Crispa Ct
6700 LSVL 40228 5836 B3
Cristland Cir
1600 LSVL 40214 5832 E4
Cristland Rd
1000 LSVL 40214 5833 A4
1600 LSVL 40214 5832 E4
Critchlow Rd SE
5500 HsnC 47117 6155 A2
Crittenden Dr
2100 LSVL 40208 5724 E2
2100 LSVL 40217 5724 E2
2700 LSVL 40209 5724 E3
7900 LSVL 40209 5833 E1
7900 LSVL 40209 5834 A2
7900 LSVL 40214 5724 E7
Crittenden Dr SR-1631
- LSVL 40217 5724 E4
2700 LSVL 40209 5724 E4
Crockett Ct
2900 RDCF 40160 6593 A1
Crockett Dr
5800 LSVL 40258 5722 A7
5800 LSVL 40258 5831 A1
W Crocus Dr
- VNGV 40160 6483 A5
300 RDCF 40160 6483 B5
Crocus Ln
3700 RLGF 40207 5508 D7
Croft Ct
5900 WNDF 40207 5509 B6
Croft Ln
2100 OdmC 40014 5405 C4
Croft Cir Dr
2000 OdmC 40014 5405 C5
Crofton Rd
4700 RVWD 40207 5508 D5
Croghan Cross
2100 LSVL 40207 5508 E6
Croghan Dr
100 ELZT 42701 6811 C2
Croghan Wy
10 HdnC 40175 6591 C2
10 VNGV 40175 6591 C2
Croghan House Dr
2000 LSVL 40207 5509 B6
2000 WNDF 40207 5509 B6
Cromarty Wy
2900 LSVL 40218 5727 C3
2900 LSVL 40220 5727 C3
Cromwell Ct
1200 LSVL 40118 5834 A6
Cromwell Hill Rd
8900 HTBN 40222 5619 B5
Cronin Ct
11700 LSVL 40245 5511 C2
Cronin Dr
4900 LSVL 40245 5511 C2
Crooked Ln
- LSVL 40023 5731 B7
16300 LSVL 40023 5840 A1
Crooked Arrow Ct
9500 LSVL 40228 5836 E7
Crooked Creek Ct
2000 OdmC 40014 5405 D5
Crooked Creek Rd
2000 OdmC 40014 5405 C5
Crooked Stick Ct
10000 LSVL 40291 5837 C6
Crop Ct
100 LSVL 40212 5614 E1
Crop St
1600 LSVL 40203 5615 A2
2300 LSVL 40212 5615 A1
2400 LSVL 40212 5614 D1
Cross Rd
10 LSVL 40204 5616 C6
10 LSVL 40213 5616 C6
Cross St
200 HLVW 40229 5944 D5
200 LSVL 40229 5944 D5
7000 FydC 47124 5283 D6
7000 GNVL 47124 5283 D6
Crossbeak Ct
6000 LSVL 40229 5944 E4
2800 LSVL 40229 5945 A4
Cross Bill Rd
- LSVL 40213 5725 C2
3200 ANPK 40213 5725 B2
Crossbow Pl
6900 PROS 40059 5401 A4
Crossbranch Ct
14000 LSVL 40245 5621 C4
Cross Brook Dr
6400 OdmC 40056 5512 E4
Cross Country Ct
6800 LSVL 40291 5837 A3
Cross Creek Blvd
10 NALB 47150 5505 A1
7100 HWCK 40228 5836 C3
7100 LSVL 40228 5836 C3
Cross Creek Ct
7400 HWCK 40228 5836 D3
Cross Creek Dr
5300 OdmC 40014 5405 B5
Cross Creek Ln
100 BltC 40071 5948 D5
Cross Creek Rd
100 BltC 40165 6052 B6
Crossfield Cir
4600 LSVL 40241 5510 B2
Crossgate Ln
1800 CSGT 40222 5509 C6
1900 NHFD 40222 5509 C6
Crossgate Rd
100 ELZT 42701 6812 D5
Cross Hill Ct
2500 LSVL 40206 5507 D7
Crosshill Ct
3200 OdmC 40059 5292 A7
3200 RVBF 40059 5292 A6
Cross Hill Rd
2200 LSVL 40206 5617 A3
Cross Keys Blvd
- CTWD 40014 5403 E5
100 CTWD 40014 5404 A5
100 OdmC 40014 5404 A5
Crossland Wy
3500 WSNP 40218 5726 C4
Cross Meadow Dr
5100 OdmC 40031 5295 C6
Crossmoor Ln
6700 GYDL 40222 5509 C7
6800 LSVL 40222 5509 C7
Cross Pointe Rd
3300 BKPT 40241 5510 C4
3300 TNBK 40241 5510 C4
Crossridge Ln
1600 GYDL 40222 5509 E7
Cross Run Rd
3100 OdmC 40014 5405 C6
Crosstimbers Ct
16800 LSVL 40245 5622 C2
Crosstimbers Dr
1100 LSVL 40245 5622 B2
Crosstree Pl
5400 LSVL 40229 5944 E3
Crossway Ct
3700 FydC 47150 5396 D3
Crossways Pl
6700 LSVL 40241 5509 D4
Crosswinds Dr
12200 MDTN 40243 5620 D5
Crosswood Ct
5500 LSVL 40291 5837 C1
Crosswood Dr
4300 OdmC 40014 5404 C5
Croswell Trc
10400 JFTN 40223 5619 E6
Crow
- HdnC 40121 6374 E1
Crowder Rd
10100 FydC 47124 5392 C3
Crown Av
1200 LSVL 40204 5616 B5
Crown Ct
4200 JFVL 47130 5398 A6
Crowne Springs Cir
- LSVL 40241 5510 C2
Crowne Springs Dr
4300 LSVL 40241 5510 C2
Crown Manor Pl
5000 WBHL 40218 5726 D4
Crown Pointe Dr
1100 ELZT 42701 6703 E7
Crown Top Rd
7800 LSVL 40241 5510 A4
Croxie Ct
6000 LSVL 40258 5831 B3
Croydon Cir
8300 HTBN 40222 5619 A4
Croydon Ct
500 HTBN 40222 5619 B4
Crucible Rd
10 ELZT 42701 6811 E4
10 ELZT 42701 6812 A4
Crucible Steel Rd
10 ELZT 42701 6811 E4
Cruiser St
3500 LSVL 40205 5617 E6
Crumbacker Ln
5300 BltC 40165 6054 B2
Crumbs Cir
- JFVL 47130 5398 A5
Crume Rd
100 VNGV 40175 6591 B2
700 HdnC 40175 6591 C2
Crume Rd SR-391
300 VNGV 40175 6591 B2
700 HdnC 40175 6591 C2
Crums Ln
1500 LSVL 40215 5723 D4
1500 LSVL 40216 5723 A3
1500 SVLY 40216 5723 D4
2300 JFVL 47130 5398 A5
3100 LSVL 40216 5722 E3
Crums Ln SR-2049
1800 SVLY 40216 5723 C4
2800 LSVL 40216 5723 A3
S Crums Ln
2900 SVLY 40216 5723 A4
3000 LSVL 40216 5723 A4
3100 LSVL 40216 5722 E4
Crutcher Dr
100 VNGV 40175 6482 D7
Crutcher Ln
500 ELZT 42701 6812 B1
Crutcher St
- ELZT 42701 6812 D3
100 VNGV 40175 6482 D7
E Crutcher St
100 ELZT 42701 6812 C2
W Crutcher St
100 ELZT 42701 6812 C2
Crutz Rd
10 ELZT 42701 6702 C2
10 HdnC 42701 6702 C2
Crystal Al
- LSVL 40203 5615 D4
Crystal Av
1100 NALB 47150 5505 A4
Crystal Ct
10 HdnC 40160 6592 C4
200 NALB 47150 5505 A4
Crystal Dr
- LGNG 40031 5296 E3
- LGNG 40031 5297 A3
600 OdmC 40031 5297 B3
E Crystal Dr
1400 OdmC 40031 5297 C4
W Crystal Dr
100 LGNG 40031 5297 A3
W Crystal Dr
100 OdmC 40031 5297 A3
Crystal Ln
- HdnC 40160 6592 B3
Crystal Pl
600 LGNG 40031 5297 A4
Crystal Cove
1800 OdmC 40031 5297 C5
13300 MDTN 40223 5620 E3
Crystal Cove Dr
- OdmC 40031 5297 C4
Crystal Creek Lp
2000 LSVL 40206 5616 D2
Crystal Lake Dr
5800 LSVL 40299 5839 D2
Crystal Pointe Dr
6200 LSVL 40299 5839 D2
Crystal Spring Dr
7000 ClkC 47172 5288 A6
7100 CLKV 47172 5288 A6
Crystal Springs Pl
2400 LSVL 40245 5512 D7
Crystal Springs Wy
15200 LSVL 40245 5512 D7
Crystal Valley Wy
15500 LSVL 40299 5839 C2
Crystal Vista Dr
6000 LSVL 40299 5839 D2
Crystal Wash Dr
300 LGNG 40031 5297 A3
Crystal Waters Wy
3000 LSVL 40299 5729 D4
Cub Ct
6700 LSVL 40291 5837 A3
Culbertson Av
100 NALB 47150 5505 D4
Culloden Dr
6100 LSVL 40258 5831 B5
Culpepper Cir
4300 FCSL 40241 5511 C3
Culver Ln
7000 LSVL 40219 5835 A3
Cumberland Av
200 LSVL 40214 5724 C7
Cumberland Ct
500 ELZT 42701 6811 B5
3100 OdmC 40014 5405 B7
Cumberland Dr
4000 OdmC 40031 5404 E1
Cumberland St
- HdnC 40121 6265 D7
Cummings Rd
1800 LSVL 40272 5941 D2
Cummings Trailer Park Rd
- HdnC 42701 6593 C7
Cumnock Rd
5400 LSVL 40291 5728 A7
5500 LSVL 40291 5837 A1
Cundiff Ln
100 SHDV 40165 6161 B6
Cunningham Ct
1400 LSVL 40211 5614 C5
Cunningham Sarles Rd
7200 FydC 47106 5284 B6
7200 FydC 47124 5284 B6
7900 FydC 47119 5284 B6
Curlew Av
1200 ANPK 40213 5725 C2
1200 LSVL 40213 5725 C2
Curran Rd
2900 LSVL 40205 5617 D7
Currington Cir
6700 LSVL 40258 5831 A6
Curry Ct
600 LSVL 40211 5614 C3
Curry Dr
- LSVL 40209 5725 A4
2600 OdmC 40014 5405 B2
Curry Branch Rd
17300 LSVL 40245 5622 C1
17600 LSVL 40245 5513 D7
Curry Creek Rd
5200 OdmC 40014 5404 C4
Currys Cir
- OdmC 40014 5405 B2
Currys Fork Dr
2000 OdmC 40031 5405 D2
Curtis Av
4200 LSVL 40213 5725 C4
Curtis St
4200 LSVL 40213 5725 C4
Curve Hill Ct
11300 LSVL 40299 5729 C7
Curve Hill Rd
4600 LSVL 40299 5729 C7
Custer Dr
4000 HdnC 40121 6374 A3
Custer St
10 HdnC 40162 6592 B7
Cutlass Ct
4000 LSVL 40229 5944 A3
Cutler Rd
3600 LSVL 40219 5835 A5
Cutliff Dr
4200 LSVL 40218 5727 B4
Cutnek Ct
4900 LSVL 40258 5831 D3
Cutter Dr
6200 LSVL 40218 5727 B3
Cynthia Ct
600 RDCF 40160 6483 C6
Cynthia Dr
5100 JFTN 40299 5728 D7
5100 LSVL 40291 5728 D7
5300 LSVL 40291 5837 D1
Cypress Av
800 JFVL 47130 5507 B6
Cypress Ct
1700 LGNG 40031 5296 E1
Cypress Dr
10 JFVL 47130 5508 A1
1500 RDCF 40160 6483 A3
8300 ClkC 47111 5181 B4

INDEX 17

Cypress St

Louisville Metro Street Index

Diefenbach Rd

STREET
Block City ZIP Map# Grid

Cypress St
1200 LSVL 40211 5614 E5
1300 LSVL 40210 5614 D6
2000 LSVL 40216 5614 D7
Cypress Cove Dr
4000 LSVL 40218 5727 A5
Cypress Creek Dr
9800 HKYH 40241 5510 E5
9900 LSVL 40241 5510 E5
Cypress Green Wy
7900 LSVL 40291 5837 A4
Cypress Point Rd
2200 JFVL 47130 5507 B1
Cypress Springs Ct
13500 LSVL 40245 5512 B5
Cypress Springs Pl
3700 LSVL 40245 5512 B4
Cypress Station Dr
700 STMW 40207 5618 C4

D

D Ct
10 LGNG 40031 5296 E2
D St
- JFVL 47130 5507 B4
D & D Ct
10 RDCF 40160 6483 E6
Dabney Carr Dr
9500 JFTN 40299 5728 C6
Dabra St
1400 RDCF 40160 6483 E6
Daffodil Ct
100 RDCF 40160 6483 D7
Daffodil Dr
7600 LSVL 40258 5831 C4
Dagger Ct
3900 LSVL 40229 5944 A3
Dahl Rd
- LSVL 40219 5725 E7
1200 LSVL 40213 5726 A6
5300 LSVL 40213 5725 E7
Dahlia Av
2000 LSVL 40205 5726 C1
Dahlia Dr
1200 LSVL 40204 5616 C6
Dailey Ct
100 RDCF 40160 6593 B1
Daily Rd
5000 FydC 47150 5721 D2
5300 FydC 47117 5721 D3
Daisy Av
6800 LSVL 40258 5831 D3
Daisy Ct
100 RDCF 40160 6592 D1
Daisy Ln
200 MDTN 40243 5620 C3
E Daisy Ln
10 NALB 47150 5505 A2
W Daisy Ln
100 NALB 47150 5504 E2
Dakin Ct
4500 JFTN 40299 5728 D6
Dakota Av
500 LSVL 40209 5724 E4
Dakota Ct
100 BltC 40047 6056 B1
E Dakota St
10 HdnC 40121 6374 E2
W Dakota St
- HdnC 40121 6374 D3
Dalby Rd
10000 FydC 47122 5501 B3
Dalby Rd NE
6500 FydC 47122 5501 C3
6500 GEOT 47122 5501 C3
Dale Av
500 LSVL 40214 5724 B7
Dale Ct
100 HLVW 40229 5944 B6
100 NALB 47150 5396 A7
8000 GEOT 47122 5502 A3
Dale Rd
- INHC 40207 5509 A6
- LSVL 40207 5509 A6
4200 HLVW 40229 5944 B6
7000 LSVL 40258 5831 A2
Dale Ann Dr
2900 LSVL 40220 5727 B2
Dalebrook Dr
3800 NALB 47150 5396 D5
Dale Ernhardt Blvd
- HdnC 40160 6592 A5
Daleray Dr
4900 LSVL 40219 5835 C1
Daleview Ln
200 LSVL 40207 5509 A6
Dalewood Pl
4300 LSVL 40218 5727 E5
Dalia Ct
6100 LSVL 40272 5940 A5
Dalmally Ct
1200 HTBN 40222 5619 D7
Dalton Ct
4300 FydC 47119 5394 D3
Dalton Dr
9400 LSVL 40272 5940 B1
Dalton St
5700 MdeC 40121 6373 D1
Dalton Ridge Pl
8300 LSVL 40258 5830 E4
Daltons Ln
2200 HdnC 40175 6482 C3
Damascus Cir
8200 LSVL 40228 5836 E7
Damascus Rd
8000 LSVL 40228 5836 E7
Dana Dr
4000 LSVL 40216 5723 D5
Dana Rd
4000 OdmC 40014 5405 A7
4000 OdmC 40014 5513 E1
4000 OdmC 40014 5514 A1
4100 OdmC 40014 5404 E7
Dana Wy
100 VNGV 40175 6483 A7
Dana Marie Dr
800 JFTN 40223 5619 E6
Danbury Ct
3100 MYHL 40242 5510 B5
Danby Ct
9100 LSVL 40291 5837 B1
Dandor Ct
2800 LSVL 40220 5727 C2
Dandridge Av
900 LSVL 40204 5616 A6
Dane Cir
2500 JFVL 47130 5507 C1
Danes Ct
13600 LSVL 40299 5729 D5
Danes Hall Ct
3000 LSVL 40206 5617 C4
Daneshall Dr
700 LSVL 40206 5617 C4
Daniel Ct
100 RDCF 40160 6483 D6
Daniel Dr
100 BltC 40165 6054 A7
9900 LSVL 40118 5942 D2
Daniel Boone St
10 HdnC 40121 6374 E1
Danielle Dr
- ANCH 40223 5620 B1
Danna Lynn Wy
7000 LSVL 40219 5835 D3
Danny Ct
100 LSVL 40214 5833 C4
Danny Dr
100 CHAN 47111 5181 D1
4200 FydC 47150 5396 D1
Dannyboy Ln
5400 LSVL 40214 5833 A3
Dannywood Rd
4300 LSVL 40220 5618 D6
4300 SRPK 40220 5618 D6
Dant Dr
1100 GEOT 47122 5502 C3
1200 FydC 47122 5502 C3
Dao Dr
- ELZT 42701 6702 E6
Darbrook Rd
4100 STMW 40207 5618 B2
4100 WLNP 40207 5618 B2
Darby Ct
8200 LSVL 40220 5619 A7
Darby Dan Cir
100 MTWH 40047 6056 E2
Darbyshire Rd
900 LYDN 40222 5619 A1
Dargue Blvd
- LSVL 40205 5617 E6
Darien Dr
- ClkC 47130 5398 C5
- JFVL 47130 5398 C5
Dark Star Wy
1000 GSHN 44026 5292 C3
1000 OdmC 44026 5292 C3
Darlene Ct
1300 RDCF 40160 6483 A2
Darlene Dr
- LSVL 40211 5723 B1
3800 SVLY 40216 5723 B1
Darley Dr
9100 TNBK 40241 5510 C4
Darlington Pl
11200 DGSH 40243 5620 B4
Darnay Pl
600 LSVL 40245 5621 D6
Darnton Ln
4900 LSVL 40216 5722 B5
Darrell Av NE
7500 HsnC 47136 5610 E6
Darrell Ct
6200 LSVL 40216 5831 D1
Darrell Dr
200 ELZT 42701 6702 E2
2200 LSVL 40216 5831 D1
Dart Dr
6200 LSVL 40291 5836 E2
Dartford Pl
10800 DGSH 40243 5620 A5
Dartmoor Dr
6800 GYDL 40222 5509 D7
Dartmouth Av
2900 LSVL 40205 5617 D7
Dartmouth Dr
600 CLKV 47129 5506 D3
Darwin Blvd
13900 LSVL 40272 6048 D2
Daryl Ct
100 LSVL 40214 5833 C4
Data Dr
2400 JFTN 40299 5728 E2
Data Vault Dr
13200 MDTN 40223 5621 A4
Date St
1800 LSVL 40210 5615 A4
2200 LSVL 40210 5614 E4
2500 LSVL 40211 5614 E4
Datura Ln
5100 LSVL 40258 5831 C3
Davallia Ln
5500 LSVL 40258 5831 C3
Davco Wy
4100 LSVL 40241 5510 A2
Davelee Ct
8500 LSVL 40291 5728 A7
Daventry Ln
100 JFTN 40223 5619 D3
100 WDWD 40223 5619 D3
Daverman Ct
6500 LSVL 40228 5836 B6
Daverman Dr
1500 LGNG 40031 5296 D1
8300 LSVL 40228 5836 B6
Davhal Dr
7800 LSVL 40291 5836 E3
David Av
4200 SVLY 40216 5723 B5
David Ct
900 ELZT 42701 6703 D7
1000 RDCF 40160 6483 D5
David Ln
5500 LSVL 40258 5831 B6
David Wy
5100 LSVL 40229 5944 D3
David Fairleigh Ct
700 LSVL 40217 5724 D3
David's Dr
100 BltC 40165 6160 D5
David's Ln
100 BltC 40165 6054 A7
Davidson Dr
12200 WDHL 40243 5620 D5
Davies Av
600 LSVL 40208 5615 C7
Daviess Av
- HdnC 40121 6373 E2
Davinhurst Ct
10200 LSVL 40241 5510 E2
10200 LSVL 40241 5511 A2
Davis Ct
8500 FydC 47122 5502 B3
8500 GEOT 47122 5502 B3
12500 MDTN 40243 5620 E3
Davis Dr
100 ELZT 42701 6812 B3
Davis Ln
10 VNGV 40160 6483 B7
Davy Crockett Tr
- SVLY 40216 5723 A2
10 LSVL 40216 5723 A2
Dawkins Ct
4300 LSVL 40229 5944 B2
Dawkins Rd
100 LGNG 40031 5296 D3
500 OdmC 40031 5296 B2
1700 OdmC 40031 5295 E1
Dawkins Rd SR-2854
100 LGNG 40031 5296 D3
500 OdmC 40031 5296 B2
1700 OdmC 40031 5295 E1
Dawn Ct
- LSVL 40216 5832 B1
3200 FydC 47172 5287 D6
Dawn Dr
1500 LSVL 40214 5832 C1
1500 LSVL 40216 5832 B1
9100 GEOT 47122 5501 E3
9200 FydC 47122 5501 D3
Dawn Wind Dr
- LSVL 40272 5831 D6
Dawson Dr
- SHDV 40165 6161 E5
Dawson Rd
10 HdnC 40160 6592 B5
Dawson Hill Rd
100 BltC 40071 5948 D3
100 BltC 40299 5948 D3
8000 LSVL 40299 5839 B6
8300 LSVL 40299 5948 C3
Dawson Hill Rd SR-1531
11000 BltC 40071 5948 D3
11000 BltC 40299 5948 D3
Day Ct
100 ELZT 42701 6812 B2
Day Break Ct
6900 LSVL 40272 5939 E1
Day Lilly Ct
10100 LSVL 40241 5510 E2
Dayton Av
- LSVL 40207 5618 A3
- STMW 40207 5618 A3
3300 LSVL 40207 5617 E3
3300 STMW 40207 5617 E3
Daytona Av
6500 LSVL 40216 5722 A4
Daytona Ct
10 LSVL 40214 5833 C6
Daytona Dr
10 LSVL 40214 5833 D6
Deacon Trc
13800 BltC 40071 5948 D5
Deacon Trace Rd
- BltC 40071 5948 D4
Dea Dea Ct
9800 LSVL 40291 5837 D1
Dea Dea Dr
5500 LSVL 40291 5837 D1
Deady Dr
6100 LSVL 40258 5831 B1
Dean Dr
3300 LSVL 40220 5726 E1
Dean St
11100 CHAN 47111 5181 E4
11100 ClkC 47111 5181 E4
11100 ClkC 47111 5182 A5
Deanna Ct
800 RDCF 40160 6593 B1
Deanna Dr
7100 LSVL 40219 5834 E3
Deans St
- HLVW 40165 6052 E2
1600 HLVW 40109 6052 E2
Dearborn Av
700 LSVL 40211 5614 C3
Dearcy Av
3300 LSVL 40215 5724 B3
Dearing Av
4500 LSVL 40213 5725 C7
Dearing Ct
2200 LSVL 40204 5616 C4
Dearing Woods Dr
11700 LSVL 40272 5940 A5
Deatrick Dr
- CLKV 47129 5397 D6
Debarr St
1300 LSVL 40204 5616 B4
Debbie Dr
100 HdnC 40175 6482 C7
100 VNGV 40175 6482 C7
Debbie Dr
1200 LSVL 40213 5725 E5
1200 LYNV 40213 5725 E5
Debby Ln
- HdnC 42701 6703 E4
Debera Wy
3000 LSVL 40220 5618 D7
3000 LSVL 40220 5727 D1
Deborah St
- RDCF 40160 6592 E2
Debra Ln
600 ELZT 42701 6703 C7
Debsom Wy
3800 LSVL 40241 5510 A2
Decatur Ct
3500 LSVL 40218 5726 B3
Decatur Dr
1900 LSVL 40218 5726 B3
1900 WSNP 40218 5726 B3
Decimal Dr
11000 JFTN 40299 5729 B1
Deckard School Rd
10 HdnC 40162 6702 A1
10 HdnC 42701 6702 B1
10 RDCF 42701 6702 B1
300 HdnC 40162 6592 E7
300 HdnC 40162 6593 A7
800 HdnC 40160 6592 E7
3600 HdnC 40175 6592 B2
4500 VNGV 40160 6592 B2
4500 VNGV 40175 6592 A2
Decker Ln
5400 LSVL 40258 5831 B6
Declaration Dr
100 LSVL 40214 5833 C4
7200 ClkC 47172 5397 D1
Decoy Rd
6700 LSVL 40291 5837 A3
Dee Rd
4900 LSVL 40219 5835 C6
Deebet Dr
- LSVL 40220 5618 B7
- MVWE 40220 5618 B7
Deep Cove Ct
6200 PROS 40059 5400 E5
6200 PROS 40059 5401 A5
Deep Creek Ct
6200 PROS 40059 5401 A5
Deep Creek Dr
6100 PROS 40059 5400 E5
6700 PROS 40059 5401 A4
Deep Dale Ln
3700 RLGF 40207 5508 D7
Deep Forest Ct
5700 LSVL 40214 5723 D7
Deep Hollow Rd
7400 HWCK 40228 5836 D3
Deep Springs Ct
6900 SPML 40228 5836 B4
Deep Trail Ct
7800 PROS 40059 5400 E5
Deep Well Ct
7300 LSVL 40291 5837 A4
Deepwood Ct
4600 GNSP 40241 5509 D1
Deepwood Dr
- RDCF 40160 6483 B3
200 ELZT 42701 6702 E7
1700 CLKV 47129 5506 A1
4400 GNSP 40241 5509 E1
N Deepwood Dr
100 RDCF 40160 6483 B4
Deer Ln
1600 LSVL 40205 5616 D7
1600 LSVL 40213 5616 D6
Deer Trc NE
6200 HsnC 47136 5610 B6
Deerbourne Ct
1000 ELZT 42701 6703 B7
Deer Brook Ln
- HdnC 42701 6702 E2
- HdnC 42701 6703 A2
Deerbrook Ln
100 ELZT 42701 6702 E2
100 HdnC 42701 6702 E2
Deerchase Ct
100 ELZT 42701 6811 D1
Deer Creek Dr
4000 LSVL 40241 5509 E2
Deercreek Ln
100 ELZT 42701 6811 D1
Deercross Ct
800 LSVL 40245 5621 D3
Deercross Dr
1800 HBNA 40220 5619 B7
2200 HBNA 40220 5728 B1
2200 JFTN 40220 5728 B1
Deercross Pl
14500 LSVL 40245 5621 D3
Deer Crossing Tr
17100 LSVL 40023 5731 D3
Deerfield Ct
100 SHDV 40165 6161 B6
Deerfield Ln
400 STMW 40207 5618 A1
400 WDYH 40207 5618 A1
Deerfield Hills Rd
100 ELZT 42701 6811 C1
Deer Grove Ct
100 ELZT 42701 6811 D1
Deer Haven Ct
11100 LSVL 40229 5945 A3
Deer Haven Dr
3700 RDCF 42701 6593 B3
3800 HdnC 42701 6593 B3
Deer Hollow Ln
7400 LSVL 40214 5832 C1
Deer Hollow Pl
3300 LSVL 40214 5832 C1
Deering Ln
1200 RDCF 40160 6483 A3
1500 RDCF 40160 6482 E4
1500 RDCF 40175 6482 E4
Deering Rd
10300 LSVL 40272 5940 B3
Deering Heights Dr
5400 LSVL 40272 5940 B4
Deer Lake Cir
3800 OdmC 40059 5401 B1
Deer Lake Ct
3900 OdmC 40059 5401 B1
Deer Lake Rd
2400 BltC 40165 6160 E3
2400 SHDV 40165 6160 E3
Deerlake Rd
400 ELZT 42701 6811 D1
Deer Meadow Ct
4600 LSVL 40241 5509 E1
4600 LSVL 40241 5510 A1
Deer Meadow Dr
7600 LSVL 40241 5509 E1
7600 LSVL 40241 5510 A1
Deer Meadow Ln
- OdmC 40031 5295 B6
Deer Park Av
1600 LSVL 40213 5616 D7
1900 LSVL 40205 5616 E6
Deer Park Cir
1000 CTWD 40014 5403 D7
Deer Park Wy
- BltC 40047 6055 D5
Deer Path Cir
8800 HBNA 40220 5619 B7
Deer Point Ct
8700 BRWD 40242 5510 B6
Deer Point Pl
3200 OdmC 40059 5292 A7
Deer Pond Cove
3600 OdmC 40059 5291 D7
Deer Ridge Rd
7200 PROS 40059 5400 E6
Deer Run Dr
- FXCH 40165 6053 A2
- PNRV 40165 6053 A2
200 CLKV 47172 5397 B1
600 ClkC 47172 5397 B1
Deer Run Pl
4500 LSVL 40299 5730 D7
Deer Run Rd
1800 OdmC 40031 5405 C1
1900 OdmC 40014 5405 A1
15000 LSVL 40299 5839 D1
15200 LSVL 40299 5730 D7
Deer Run Trc
100 ClkC 47119 5287 B2
Deer Run Wy
10 HdnC 42701 6703 C3
Deer Springs Ct
4400 LSVL 40241 5510 B1
Deer Trace Ln
11500 LSVL 40291 5946 E2
Deertrace Ln
17800 LSVL 40023 5840 E3
Deer Trail Pl
9500 LSVL 40228 5836 E7
Deer View Ct
7500 GNSP 40241 5509 E1
7500 LSVL 40241 5509 E1
Deerwood Av
1900 LSVL 40205 5616 E6
Deerwood Ct
- JFVL 47130 5507 B1
Deerwood Dr
- JFVL 47130 5507 C1
3400 NALB 47150 5396 C6
Deerwood Dr NE
6900 HsnC 47136 5610 D5
6900 LNVL 47136 5610 D5
Deevers St
4300 HdnC 40121 6374 B2
Deham Dr
9600 LSVL 40241 5402 C7
11200 OdmC 40241 5402 C7
Deham Rd
9600 OdmC 40241 5402 C7
Deibel Ct
3100 LSVL 40220 5618 B7
Deibel Wy
3400 LSVL 40220 5727 B1
3600 LSVL 40220 5618 B7
Delacroix Ln
4300 JFTN 40299 5729 A6
Delaina Dr
9400 MTWH 40047 6056 A3
Delaware Ct
10 ELZT 42701 6811 E2
E Delaware Ct
700 SLRB 47172 5288 C3
W Delaware Ct
700 SLRB 47172 5288 C3
Delaware Dr
4000 OdmC 40031 5404 E1
4900 LSVL 40218 5726 D5
N Delaware St
- HdnC 40121 6265 E7
100 HdnC 40121 6374 E2
S Delaware St
- HdnC 40121 6374 E2
Del Cristo Dr
8900 LSVL 40299 5728 B5
Delee Wy
9000 LSVL 40219 5835 B7
Del Haven Av
6600 PROS 40059 5400 D5
Deliah's Wy
100 BltC 40165 6160 D5
Delido Rd
8200 LSVL 40219 5835 E6
Delightful Ct
8300 LSVL 40291 5836 E5
Delightful Wy
7800 LSVL 40291 5836 E5
Delilah Ct
6000 LSVL 40272 5940 A5
Dell Cir
- OdmC 44026 5292 B5
Dell Rd
- SGDN 40205 5617 C6
3200 JFTN 40299 5728 D4
Dellafay Dr
3900 LSVL 40219 5835 A2
Dell Brooke Av
2800 LSVL 40220 5727 A2
Dell Haven Ct
- NALB 47150 5396 D5
Dellinger Dr
600 JFVL 47130 5508 B2
Dellridge Dr
4100 STMW 40207 5618 A2
Dellrose Dr
5800 LSVL 40258 5831 C1
Dell View Ct
- NALB 47150 5396 D5
Dell View Wy
- NALB 47150 5396 D5
Dellwood Dr
1400 LSVL 40216 5723 D6
Delmar Ct
1500 LSVL 40216 5723 C5
Delmar Dr
100 MTWH 40165 6054 D5
200 BltC 40165 6054 D5
1000 RDCF 40160 6483 B4
Delmar Ln
1300 LSVL 40216 5723 D5
Delmaria Wy
5400 LSVL 40291 5727 E7
5500 LSVL 40291 5836 E1
Delmont Av
200 LSVL 40206 5616 D1
Delor Av
800 LSVL 40217 5616 A7
2300 LSVL 40217 5725 A1
2900 LSVL 40213 5725 B2
Delores Av
4000 SVLY 40216 5723 C4
Delores Dr
2500 LSVL 40216 5722 E6
Del Park Ter
4400 LSVL 40211 5614 B2
Delphene Cir
4600 LSVL 40241 5510 B1
Delray Rd
300 STMW 40207 5618 B3
Del Rio Pl
2800 LSVL 40220 5726 E1
Delta Ct
2600 RDCF 40160 6592 E1
Delta Rd
10 SpnC 40071 6057 D7
Delton Rd
6500 LSVL 40258 5831 A4
De Mel Av
2100 LSVL 40214 5723 D7
2200 LSVL 40216 5723 D7
Deming Ln
6400 LSVL 40258 5831 A3
Demoret Av
5600 MdeC 40121 6373 C1
Dempley Av
9200 LSVL 40258 5831 C7
9200 LSVL 40272 5831 C7
Dempster Cove
1000 FydC 47150 5503 E3
Dena Dr
3600 LSVL 40215 5723 D4
Denada Ln
1200 ELZT 42701 6702 E7
Denbeigh Ct
3100 MYHL 40242 5510 B4
Dendal Ct
6100 FydC 47122 5502 E6
Denham Ln
700 CHAN 47111 5181 D4
700 ClkC 47111 5181 C4
Denham Rd
10 LSVL 40205 5617 C7
2500 SGDN 40205 5617 C6
Denington Dr
8800 HTBN 40222 5619 B5
Denise Dr
8200 LSVL 40219 5835 D7
Denise Wy
5000 FydC 47119 5394 C4
Denmark St
500 LSVL 40214 5724 B3
500 LSVL 40215 5724 B3
Dennis Ct
100 RDCF 40160 6374 A7
1000 RDCF 40160 6483 A1
Dennis Dr
100 BltC 40165 6054 A7
100 BltC 40165 6163 A1
Dennis St
100 RDCF 40160 6374 A7
100 RDCF 40160 6483 A1
Dennison Av
1100 NALB 47150 5505 A4
Denny Dr
100 NALB 47150 5505 A1
Dennybrook Wy
10700 JFTN 40299 5728 E4
10700 JFTN 40299 5729 A3
Dent Av
1300 NALB 47150 5504 E6
Denton Av
600 SLRB 47172 5288 C3
Denton Ter
10 CLKV 47129 5506 B2
Denver Ln
7100 LSVL 40258 5721 E6
Deorr Rd
3400 SVLY 40216 5723 D3
DePauw Av
300 CLKV 47129 5506 C5
1700 NALB 47150 5505 C3
Depot Ln
8200 LSVL 40272 6048 B5
9800 JFTN 40299 5728 D3
Depot Rd
8200 LSVL 40272 6048 B5
Depot St
900 CHAN 47111 5181 E4
Depriest Ct
4900 LSVL 40213 5726 C6
4900 LSVL 40218 5726 C6
Derby Av
200 LSVL 40218 5727 B4
Derby Ct
3000 OdmC 40014 5405 D6
Derby Dr
- BltC 40165 6162 C2
- SHDV 40165 6162 C2
100 ELZT 42701 6812 D4
6900 OdmC 40014 5405 C6
Derbyshire Ct
8200 HTBN 40222 5619 A4
Derek Av
300 ELZT 42701 6703 C5
Derek Rd
100 BltC 40165 6054 D3
Derington Ct
3000 LSVL 40241 5509 E4
3000 SPVL 40241 5509 E4
Deronia Av
7900 LYDN 40222 5619 A3
Derrick Dr
6200 LSVL 40216 5831 D1
Desco Ct
100 HLVW 40229 5944 A5
Desert Ct
100 HLVW 40229 5944 C5
Deshane Pl
10700 LSVL 40272 5940 C3
Deshler Dr
2800 LSVL 40213 5834 D1
Desiree Dr
4200 FydC 47150 5396 C2
Desmonta Wy
100 HLVW 40229 5944 D5
De Soto Ter
1700 LSVL 40210 5615 A7
Destiny Cove
8700 HTCK 40229 5945 D4
Determine Ct
2400 LSVL 40216 5722 E7
Determine Ln
4800 LSVL 40216 5722 E7
Dethy Rd
3700 FydC 47119 5395 A1
Development Wy
3000 ClkC 47172 5289 A7
3000 SLRB 47172 5289 A7
Deveraux Ln
7400 LSVL 40258 5831 A3
Dever Farm Ln
100 BltC 40165 6163 A4
Deveron Dr
2200 SVLY 40216 5723 B3
Devers Av
5300 LSVL 40214 5724 B7
Devon Ct
1600 LYDN 40242 5510 C7
Devon Rd
10 OdmC 44026 5292 A3
Devondale Ct
7600 GYDL 40222 5509 E7
Devondale Dr
1700 GYDL 40222 5509 E6
Devonhurst Pl
12500 LSVL 40223 5511 D5
Devonshire Dr
8100 LSVL 40258 5831 B6
Dewberry Rd
5300 BltC 40229 5944 D6
Dewdrop Ct
3200 LSVL 40220 5727 E2
Dewey St
100 MRGH 40155 6264 C4
1800 NALB 47150 5505 D5
Dewit Dr
6200 LSVL 40258 5831 B4
Dexter Av
2300 LSVL 40216 5722 E7
2300 LSVL 40216 5723 A7
Dezern Av
10800 HYVA 40118 5942 E4
10800 HYVA 40118 5943 A4
10800 LSVL 40118 5942 E4
10800 LSVL 40118 5943 A4
Dezern Ct
1000 HYVA 40118 5942 E4
1000 LSVL 40118 5942 E4
Diablo Ct
6100 LSVL 40219 5836 A6
Diamond Ct
- BltC 40071 5948 C4
Diamond Hts
6800 ClkC 47172 5397 E1
6800 ClkC 47172 5398 A2
Diamond Pl
2400 ClkC 47129 5397 A6
2400 CLKV 47129 5397 A6
Diamond Wy
4300 LSVL 40216 5723 A5
Diana Dr
2700 ClkC 47172 5288 A7
Diane Av
13400 LSVL 40272 6048 E1
Diann Marie Rd
3700 LSVL 40241 5511 B3
Dickens Ct
13600 LSVL 40299 5729 E5
Dickerson Ct
4500 WTNH 40245 5511 D2
Diecks Dr
100 ELZT 42701 6703 A7
100 ELZT 42701 6812 A1
Diefenbach Ln
- SLRB 47172 5289 B5
- ClkC 47172 5289 A3
Diefenbach Rd
7100 ClkC 47172 5289 B4

Louisville Metro Street Index

STREET
Block City ZIP Map# Grid

Eagle Tr
8500 ClkC 47111 5290 B3
Eagle Wy
200 ELZT 42701 6702 E4
300 ELZT 42701 6703 A4
3900 OdmC 40059 5401 D2
Eagle Creek Dr
- GYDL 40222 5510 A7
8000 LYDN 40222 5510 A7
Eagle Creek Pl
1700 LYDN 40222 5510 A7
Eagle Flight Wy
8300 LYDN 40222 5619 A1
Eagle Nest Wy
1500 LYDN 40222 5510 A7
1600 LSVL 40222 5510 A7
Eagle Pass
- LSVL 40219 5834 D7
3000 ANPK 40213 5725 C1
3000 LSVL 40217 5725 C1
3200 LSVL 40213 5725 C2
Eagle Pass Dr
200 RDCF 40160 6483 C2
Eagle Pines Ct
1600 LYDN 40223 5620 A1
Eagle Pines Ln
10500 LYDN 40223 5620 A1
Eagle Ridge Pl
10700 LSVL 40223 5620 A2
Eagle Run Dr
1400 LYDN 40222 5510 A7
Eagles Rd
100 BltC 40165 6051 C6
Eagles Cove Ct
4400 LSVL 40241 5511 B2
Eagles Cove Dr
10900 LSVL 40241 5511 B2
Eagles Crest Ct
8100 LSVL 40291 5836 E2
Eagles Eyrie Ct
2400 LSVL 40206 5616 E2
Eagles Peak Wy
5200 LSVL 40241 5510 E1
Eagle Trace Ct
- SbyC 40245 5513 D5
Eagle Trace Dr
7900 LSVL 40291 5837 C5
Ealy St
100 NALB 47150 5505 A4
Earl Av
1500 LSVL 40215 5724 A2
Earl Dr
7200 LSVL 40258 5830 E3
Earlann Dr
5400 LSVL 40219 5835 A4
Earlham Dr
9200 LYDN 40242 5510 C7
9200 MLND 40223 5510 C7
9400 WPMG 40223 5510 C7
Earlywood Wy
100 HLVW 40229 5944 B6
100 HNTH 40229 5944 A6
Earnings Wy
4000 NALB 47150 5396 A5
East Av
9800 LSVL 40272 5940 D1
East Ln
2100 SVLY 40216 5723 B4
East St
100 SHDV 40165 6161 D4
200 MTWH 40047 6056 C3
200 NALB 47150 5505 D4
East Bay Ct
12100 WTNH 40245 5511 D3
Eastbourne Av
3300 LSVL 40206 5617 C2
Eastbridge Ct
100 MDTN 40223 5620 E3
100 MDTN 40243 5620 E3
Eastbrook Blvd
3000 JFVL 47130 5398 D6
East Cove Dr
12700 ANCH 40223 5511 E6
Eastern Av
3000 LSVL 40206 5617 A1
Eastern Blvd
100 ClkC 47129 5506 E4
100 CLKV 47129 5506 D3
100 CLKV 47130 5506 E4
100 JFVL 47130 5506 E4
W Eastern Blvd
100 JFVL 47130 5506 E4
300 CLKV 47129 5506 E4
300 CLKV 47130 5506 E4
Eastern Cir
300 RDCF 40160 6483 C4
Eastern Pkwy
300 LSVL 40208 5724 E1
400 LSVL 40217 5724 E1
700 LSVL 40217 5725 A1
900 LSVL 40217 5616 A7
1200 LSVL 40213 5616 B7
1300 LSVL 40204 5616 D6
1500 LSVL 40205 5616 D6
Eastern Pkwy US-60 ALT
300 LSVL 40208 5724 E1
400 LSVL 40217 5724 E1
700 LSVL 40217 5725 A1
900 LSVL 40217 5616 A7
1100 LSVL 40204 5616 B7
1200 LSVL 40213 5616 B7
1500 LSVL 40205 5616 D6
Eastern St
1200 ELZT 42701 6811 B5
1200 HdnC 42701 6811 C5
Eastern Star Ct
900 LSVL 40204 5616 C4
Eastern Star Dr
- LSVL 40204 5616 C4
Eastern Wood Ct
200 MDTN 40243 5620 E4
Eastgate Ct
6800 WDYH 40207 5509 C7
Eastgate Village Dr
13200 MDTN 40223 5620 E3
Eastgate Village Pl
700 MDTN 40223 5620 E3
Eastgate Village Wynde
400 MDTN 40223 5620 E3
Eastlawn St
600 LSVL 40211 5614 D3
Eastlawn Arms Dr
10 JFVL 47130 5507 C5
Eastmeadow Ct
3600 LSVL 40258 5832 A3
Eastmoor Rd
4000 WSNP 40218 5726 B4
Easton Ln
8300 BRMD 40242 5510 B4
8300 LSVL 40241 5510 B4
Easton Commons Dr
8500 LYDN 40242 5619 B2
Eastover Ct
10 LSVL 40206 5617 C3
Eastpoint Ctr
- LSVL 40223 5512 A6
Eastpoint Pkwy
2000 LSVL 40223 5512 A6
East Pointe Centre Dr
13400 LSVL 40223 5512 A6
Eastpoint Park Blvd
13100 LSVL 40223 5512 A6
13200 LSVL 40223 5511 E6
Eastport Dr
6900 OdmC 40241 5402 C7
Eastridge Dr
1100 NALB 47150 5396 C5
Eastside Av
500 SLRB 47172 5288 D5
Eastside Ct
4300 LSVL 40220 5727 D2
Eastside Dr
3200 LSVL 40220 5727 D2
Eastview Av
1900 LSVL 40205 5617 B7
10300 JFTN 40299 5728 E4
Eastview Dr
100 SHDV 40165 6161 E3
300 SHDV 40165 6162 A3
Eastwind Rd
10 INDH 40207 5508 E7
Eastwind Wy
- CTWD 40014 5403 E5
Eastwood Av
1500 NALB 47150 5505 E1
Eastwood Cir
2400 OdmC 40014 5405 B5
Eastwood Ct
5500 OdmC 40014 5405 B4
Eastwood Dr
3000 OdmC 40014 5405 B5
Eastwood Cut Off Rd
16100 LSVL 40023 5622 B6
16100 LSVL 40245 5622 B6
Eastwood Cut Off Rd SR-2841
16100 LSVL 40023 5622 B6
16100 LSVL 40245 5622 B6
Easum Rd
10200 LSVL 40299 5837 E1
10600 LSVL 40299 5838 A1
11100 LSVL 40299 5729 B7
Easum Pine Ct
5500 LSVL 40299 5729 C7
Eathan Ct
100 BltC 40047 6055 E2
100 BltC 40047 6056 A2
100 MTWH 40047 6055 E2
100 MTWH 40047 6056 A2
Ecchappe Ln
400 LSVL 40118 5942 B1
Echo Tr
1400 LSVL 40245 5731 A1
1800 LSVL 40245 5730 E3
1800 LSVL 40299 5730 E3
6300 LSVL 40299 5839 A5
7100 LSVL 40299 5838 E6
Echo Bridge Dr
800 MDTN 40243 5620 D6
Echo Bridge Rd
12500 MDTN 40243 5620 D6
Echo Hill Tr
14000 LSVL 40299 5839 A5
Echo Valley Cir
3500 OdmC 40031 5404 E2
3500 OdmC 40031 5405 A1
Echo Valley Dr
4600 OdmC 40014 5403 D2
Eclipse Dr
6600 LSVL 40258 5831 C2
Eclona St
- HdnC 40177 6156 B4
- WPT 40177 6156 B4
Ecton Ln
2300 SVLY 40216 5723 B3
Edcoe Rd
7200 LSVL 40228 5836 C4
7200 SPML 40228 5836 C4
Edds Ct
4700 OdmC 40014 5404 A3
Eddy St
- LSVL 40212 5614 D2
1500 LSVL 40203 5615 A2
2100 LSVL 40212 5615 A2
Edelen St
100 VNGV 40175 6482 E7
100 VNGV 40175 6591 E1
Eden Av
- HTBN 40222 5619 C4
- LYDN 40223 5619 D3
- WDWD 40223 5619 D3
Eden Ln
4000 SVLY 40216 5723 B4
Edenderry Ln
7300 LSVL 40219 5835 E4
Edenroc Ln
7300 LSVL 40258 5831 A3
Edenside Av
1600 LSVL 40204 5616 D6
Edenwood Cir
800 DGSH 40243 5620 C6
Edenwood Dr
12000 DGSH 40243 5620 C6
12000 MDTN 40243 5620 C6
Edgebourne Ct
4600 JFTN 40299 5728 A6
Edgebrook Dr
300 VNGV 40175 6482 C7
700 HdnC 40175 6482 C7
Edgeforest Pl
500 LSVL 40245 5621 C3
Edge Hill Rd
2100 LSVL 40205 5617 A6
Edgehill Rd
13900 OdmC 44026 5291 E4
Edgeland Av
200 SLRB 47172 5288 D4
2000 LSVL 40204 5616 D5
8700 OdmC 40014 5511 E1
Edgemont Dr
100 NALB 47150 5395 E6
Edgemont Ln
10 LSVL 40118 5942 C1
Edgemore Pl
7300 PROS 40059 5400 D3
Edgetree Ct
5900 LSVL 40229 5944 E3
Edge Valley Ln
4800 LSVL 40272 5831 D5
Edgeware Ln
8100 LSVL 40220 5618 E6
Edgewater Ct
10 SpnC 40071 5948 E6
10 SpnC 40071 5949 A6
Edgewater Dr
600 ELZT 42701 6703 B6
7400 OdmC 40014 5512 A1
7500 OdmC 40014 5511 E1
Edgewater Rd
10300 JFTN 40223 5619 E6
10400 DGSH 40223 5620 A6
10500 DGSH 40223 5619 E6
Edgewood Av
100 ELZT 42701 6702 D7
100 SHDV 40165 6161 D1
200 ELZT 42701 6812 A1
300 ELZT 42701 6811 D1
Edgewood Ct
1700 RDCF 40160 6484 A6
Edgewood Dr
- JFVL 47130 5507 D1
100 RDCF 40160 6483 B4
100 VNGV 40175 6482 C7
500 SLRB 47172 5288 D5
1500 JFVL 47130 5506 E2
2200 SbyC 40245 5514 A7
Edgewood Ln
100 JFVL 47130 5507 E2
2700 NALB 47150 5396 D7
Edgewood Pl
1500 LSVL 40205 5616 E5
Edgewood Wy
100 LSVL 40223 5620 A3
100 PWEV 40056 5512 C2
Edgin Ct
2300 LSVL 40216 5723 A5
2300 SVLY 40216 5723 A5
Edgin Dr
4200 LSVL 40216 5723 A5
Edinburgh Pl
400 HTBN 40222 5619 B4
Edith Ct
1900 LSVL 40206 5616 D1
Edith Rd
- LSVL 40206 5507 D7
600 LSVL 40206 5616 D1
Edlin Dr
2800 LSVL 40219 5834 D7
2800 MLHT 40219 5834 D7
Edlin Ln
- MLHT 40219 5834 C6
2600 LSVL 40219 5834 D6
Edmond Ln
3700 RLGF 40207 5617 D1
Edmonia Av
2900 LNSH 40220 5618 D7
2900 LSVL 40220 5618 D7
Edmonson Av
- HdnC 40121 6373 E3
Edmonson Pl
7200 PROS 40059 5400 D2
Edna Rd
600 LSVL 40206 5616 D1
Edna Lee Ln
100 BltC 40165 6054 A1
Edna M Rd
7700 LSVL 40258 5830 D3
Edsel Ln
7800 LSVL 40291 5836 E2
Edsil Johnson Wy
2600 SVLY 40216 5723 E1
Edward Av
800 LSVL 40204 5616 B4
Edward Ct
100 MTWH 40047 6056 C1
Edwards St
400 HdnC 40121 6374 A3
Edwardsville-Galena Rd
1200 FydC 47122 5503 A3
2000 FydC 47122 5502 E2
2800 FydC 47122 5393 E6
4600 FydC 47119 5393 E4
Eelgrass Ct
5300 LSVL 40258 5831 C3
Egan St
1400 CHAN 47111 5181 E3
Egham Dr
- HTBN 40222 5619 A4
- LSVL 40222 5619 A4
Egmont Wy
1900 LSVL 40245 5623 B2
Egret Ct
8200 LYDN 40222 5619 A2
Egret Rd
- LYDN 40222 5619 A1
Egypt Ln
7200 LSVL 40219 5835 B4
Ehret Av
600 ELZT 42701 6812 A1
Ehringer Dr
100 SLRB 47172 5288 D3
Ehrler Dr
1600 LSVL 40213 5725 D1
Eider Dr
7500 LSVL 40258 5830 D3
Eifler Beach Rd
5100 GNVW 40222 5509 A1
5100 LSVL 40222 5509 A1
Eigelbach Av
1000 LSVL 40217 5616 B7
Eileen Ct
500 HdnC 40175 6591 D2
500 VNGV 40175 6591 D2
Eiler Av
200 LSVL 40214 5724 D7
200 LSVL 40214 5833 D1
Eisenhower Av
100 HdnC 40121 6374 B2
Eisenhower Rd
- HdnC 40121 6374 A2
Ekin Av
1100 NALB 47150 5505 D3
Elaine Ct
700 ELZT 42701 6702 D6
Elaine Dr
1000 LSVL 40219 5835 B7
4800 FydC 47119 5394 D4
Elaine Wy
100 MTWH 40047 6056 A3
Elam Ct
2800 LSVL 40213 5834 D1
Elam Dr
2800 LSVL 40213 5834 D1
Elane Dr
3200 LSVL 40216 5722 D4
Elanor Ct
6200 FydC 47119 5393 E3
Elba Dr
1900 LSVL 40218 5726 C3
El Coco Ct
10200 LSVL 40291 5837 D3
El Conquistador Pl
200 LSVL 40220 5727 C1
Elda Dr
10900 LSVL 40229 5944 C4
Elder Ct
500 RDCF 40160 6483 C3
2600 JFVL 47130 5398 C6
Elder Ln
10500 LSVL 40059 5402 B6
10500 OdmC 40014 5402 B6
Elderberry Ln
1200 MDTN 40243 5620 D7
Elderberry Ridge Ln
1200 LSVL 40272 5941 E1
1200 LSVL 40272 5942 A1
Elder Park Cto
4000 OdmC 40014 5405 A1
4000 OdmC 40031 5405 A1
Elder Park Rd
2000 OdmC 40031 5405 D1
2200 OdmC 40031 5296 C7
2800 OdmC 40014 5405 B1
3200 OdmC 40031 5404 E1
Elderwood Wy
3600 LSVL 40215 5723 D4
Eldorado Av
200 LSVL 40218 5727 C4
5800 LSVL 40291 5837 B1
El Dorado Dr
600 ELZT 42701 6811 E1
Eleanor Av
- SMRM 40205 5617 B7
2200 LSVL 40205 5617 B6
2800 LSVL 40205 5726 C1
Electron Dr
10700 JFTN 40299 5729 B3
11400 LSVL 40299 5729 B3
Elegance Wy
- LSVL 40219 5834 D7
Element Ln
3000 JFTN 40299 5729 B3
3000 LSVL 40299 5729 B3
Elfin Av
3900 BWNV 40207 5617 D1
3900 DRDH 40207 5617 D1
3900 LSVL 40207 5617 D1
Elgin Wy
3900 SVLY 40216 5723 B1
Elija Strong Rd
5000 FydC 47150 5612 C6
Eline Av
200 LSVL 40207 5617 D3
200 STMW 40207 5617 D3
Elisa Ct
3000 FydC 47150 5396 D3
Elise Wy
5300 LSVL 40219 5835 D6
Elizabeth Av
6100 LSVL 40272 5940 A6
Elizabeth Ct
6200 OdmC 40014 5402 B6
Elizabeth St
200 ELZT 42701 6812 B2
Elizabethtown Byp
- ELZT 42701 6702 D7
- ELZT 42701 6811 E1
- ELZT 42701 6812 B4
Elizabethtown Byp US-31W BYP
- ELZT 42701 6702 D7
- ELZT 42701 6811 E1
- ELZT 42701 6812 B4
Elk Hill Ct
9400 JFTN 40299 5728 C6
Elkhorn Ln
2400 SVLY 40216 5723 B2
Elkin Rd
- OdmC 40014 5512 A1
Elk Pointe
1000 JFVL 47130 5507 A1
Elk Pointe Blvd
1700 JFVL 47130 5507 A1
Elk Pointe Ct
2300 JFVL 47130 5507 A1
Elk Ridge Dr
1800 HBNA 40220 5619 B7
Elk River Dr
100 LSVL 40214 5833 B6
Elks Rd
1400 BltC 40165 6160 E3
Elks Bluff Dr
8900 HBNA 40220 5619 B7
Ella Dr
4200 FydC 47119 5394 E4
Ella Robertson Rd
- JFVL 47130 5399 B7
Ellen Ct
100 NALB 47150 5504 E2
100 NALB 47150 5505 A2
Ellen St
1000 RDCF 40160 6483 A3
Ellerbe Av
2100 LSVL 40205 5617 B6
Ellerholt Ct
1100 LSVL 40211 5614 B4
Ellie Ln
15500 LSVL 40299 5948 D2
Ellingsworth Ln
1200 DGSH 40243 5620 C6
1200 MDTN 40243 5620 C6
11800 LSVL 40299 5620 C6
12100 DGSH 40299 5620 C6
Ellington Av
5000 LSVL 40218 5726 D6
Elliott Av
1500 JFVL 47130 5507 C5
2500 NALB 47150 5505 B1
4400 LSVL 40211 5614 B3
W Elliott St
3100 LSVL 40211 5614 D3
Ellis Ln
7800 BltC 40071 5948 D4
Ellis Wy
3200 LSVL 40220 5618 A7
3200 LSVL 40220 5727 B1
Ellis Cook Rd
100 BltC 40047 6055 A6
100 MTWH 40047 6055 A6
Ellison Av
900 LSVL 40204 5616 B6
Ellsworth Av
2500 LSVL 40217 5724 E1
2500 LSVL 40217 5725 A1
Ellwanger Dr
1500 JFVL 47130 5507 C5
Ellwood Av
1600 LSVL 40204 5616 C5
Elm Al
- LGNG 40031 5297 A2
Elm Av
200 PWEV 40056 5512 D2
Elm Dr
- LSVL 40245 5511 E2
100 BltC 40047 6056 D4
Elm Ln
100 BltC 40047 6055 E4
13400 OdmC 40059 5401 A1
13400 RVBF 40059 5401 A1
Elm Rd
- RDCF 40160 6483 C3
200 ELZT 42701 6703 A3
1200 ANCH 40223 5620 C1
W Elm Rd
1200 RDCF 40160 6483 B5
1400 VNGV 40160 6483 B5
Elm St
100 MRGH 40155 6264 C4
100 WPT 40177 6156 B3
E Elm St
1000 NALB 47150 5505 C4
N Elm St
100 CLKV 47129 5506 D5
S Elm St
100 CLKV 47129 5506 D5
W Elm St
100 NALB 47150 5505 B5
Elmcreek Dr
8900 LSVL 40219 5835 B3
Elmcroft Cir
6700 LSVL 40241 5509 D1
Elmcroft Ln
4800 LSVL 40059 5509 D1
4800 LSVL 40241 5509 D1
Elmer Ln
5600 LSVL 40214 5833 C5
Elmer Ritman Dr
- LSVL 40217 5616 C7
- LSVL 40217 5725 C1
Elm Hill Pl
900 LSVL 40245 5621 C3
Elmhurst Av
300 VNGV 40175 6482 C7
2100 LSVL 40216 5723 A6
2400 LSVL 40216 5722 E6
Elm Lake Dr
9500 LSVL 40291 5837 C3
Elmore St
1900 LSVL 40216 5723 A7
2300 LSVL 40216 5722 E7
El Morro Ct
8900 LSVL 40299 5728 B5
Elms Ct
9100 JFTN 40299 5728 B2
Elm Tree Pl
4800 LSVL 40299 5730 C7
4800 LSVL 40299 5839 C1
Elmview Dr
1700 NALB 47150 5396 E7
Elmwood Av
800 NALB 47150 5505 B1
3800 BLWD 40207 5617 D2
3800 LSVL 40207 5617 D2
3800 STMW 40207 5617 D2
3900 CYWV 40207 5617 E2
4000 CYWV 40207 5618 A1
4000 STMW 40207 5618 A1
4000 WDYH 40207 5618 A1
Elmwood Ct
400 STMW 40207 5618 A1
Elmwood Dr
200 RDCF 40160 6483 C3
1700 CLKV 47129 5506 B1
Elmwood St
6500 LSVL 40216 5722 A4
Elnora Av
7400 LSVL 40258 5831 D4
El Patio Pl
2600 LSVL 40220 5727 C1
El Prado St
9600 LSVL 40272 5831 C7
9600 LSVL 40272 5940 C1
El Rancho Rd
6500 LSVL 40291 5837 D3
Elsie Ct
8400 LSVL 40228 5836 D5
Elsmere Cir
600 LSVL 40223 5619 D2
El Toro Ct
6600 LSVL 40291 5837 D3
Elva Av
- LSVL 40213 5834 B4
El Ventoso Ct
10200 LSVL 40291 5837 D3
Elvira Ct
2100 SVLY 40216 5723 B4
Elysean Ct
7000 LSVL 40291 5837 A4
Elzie Rd
5200 LSVL 40258 5831 C6
Emarld Lake Dr
- CHAN 47111 5181 C1
- ClkC 47111 5181 C1
Embassy Ln
2300 SVLY 40216 5722 E6
Embassy Square Blvd
1800 FTHL 40299 5619 C7
1800 JFTN 40299 5619 C7
1900 FTHL 40299 5728 D1
1900 JFTN 40299 5728 D1
Ember Cir
3600 JFTN 40299 5728 C4
Emberson Av
4300 LSVL 40209 5725 A4
Embry Av
1800 LSVL 40206 5616 D2
Emerald Av
2000 LSVL 40206 5616 D2
Emerald Cir
- MTWH 40047 6056 D2
W Emerald Cir
10 MTWH 40047 6056 E2
Emerald Ct
100 MTWH 40047 6056 E2
1800 CLKV 47129 5397 A6
3100 JFVL 47130 5398 D6
Emerald Dr
100 MTWH 40047 6056 E2
1400 ClkC 47172 5397 E1
1400 SLRB 47172 5397 E1
3300 JFTN 40299 5728 C4
5100 LSVL 40219 5835 D2
Emerald Wy
10 HdnC 42701 6703 D4
4300 FydC 47150 5396 D2
Emerald Green Wy
8000 LSVL 40291 5837 B5
Emerald Lake Dr
- LSVL 40241 5511 A5
3000 LSVL 40241 5510 E5
Emerald Leaf Ct
3900 LSVL 40219 5835 A7
Emerick Dr
4900 ClkC 47130 5398 E3
Emerson Av
- ClkC 47129 5506 A1
200 CLKV 47129 5506 A2
1900 LSVL 40205 5726 B1
1900 SMRM 40205 5726 B1
2000 LSVL 40205 5617 B7
2000 SMRM 40205 5617 B7
2100 SMRV 40205 5617 B7
2300 KGLY 40205 5617 C7
Emery Av
5000 LSVL 40214 5833 B1
Emery Cross
200 CLKV 47129 5506 B5
1100 ClkC 47129 5506 A3
Emery Ln
1000 CLKV 47129 5506 A2
1200 ClkC 47129 5506 A2
Emery Rd
500 LSVL 40206 5617 A1
Emil Av
2400 LSVL 40217 5724 E2
Emily Av
100 CLKV 47129 5506 B5
Emily Ct
10 HdnC 42701 6593 C6
Emily Dr
4500 MTWH 40047 6056 A3
Emily Rd
600 LSVL 40206 5616 D1
Eminence Ct
9200 LSVL 40059 5401 D7
Emma Ct
4500 MTWH 40047 6055 D4
Emma Jean Wy
10600 LSVL 40272 5940 B3
Emmalee Dr
5700 LSVL 40219 5835 A1
Emma Lou Dr
4100 FydC 47119 5394 D3
Emmet Av
2000 LSVL 40217 5724 E1
Emory Rd
300 HdnC 42701 6811 B4
1400 ELZT 42701 6811 B4
Empire Ct
16900 LSVL 40245 5622 B2
Emrich Av
5400 LSVL 40291 5728 A7
Emrich Ct
8300 LSVL 40291 5728 A7
Encino Ct
9800 LSVL 40223 5510 D7
Enclave Ct
10700 LSVL 40229 5944 E4
Ende Ln
8300 LSVL 40219 5835 B6
Endeavor Wy
3300 LSVL 40219 5834 E6
3500 LSVL 40219 5835 A6
Endecott Pl
7600 PROS 40059 5400 C3
Engineer St
10 HdnC 40121 6374 B4
Engleman Dr
- GEOT 47122 5501 E4
Englewood Av
2600 LSVL 40220 5618 C6
English Av
1100 LSVL 40217 5725 B1
2900 LSVL 40206 5617 B2
English Ct
1600 LSVL 40223 5511 E7
6000 FydC 47119 5395 C1
English Ivy Ct
13700 LSVL 40299 5729 D5
English Oak Ct
10700 LSVL 40241 5511 B2
English Station Rd
- LSVL 40245 5621 B5
N English Station Rd
200 MDTN 40223 5621 A3
200 MDTN 40243 5621 A4
500 MDTN 40223 5620 E2
1000 LSVL 40223 5620 E1
1700 ANCH 40223 5511 E7
1700 LSVL 40223 5511 E7
N English Station Rd SR-3084
1000 LSVL 40223 5620 E2
1000 MDTN 40223 5620 E2
S English Station Rd
200 LSVL 40245 5621 B6
200 MDTN 40245 5621 B5
800 LSVL 40299 5621 C7
1100 LSVL 40245 5730 E3
1100 LSVL 40299 5730 E4
English Villa Dr
- LSVL 40245 5621 B4
Ennis Trc
7100 LSVL 40291 5837 B4
Eno Rd
2500 LSVL 40214 5832 D2
Enridge Dr
3300 LSVL 40220 5727 D3
Enterprise Dr
- ELZT 42701 6811 A4
6700 LSVL 40214 5833 D3
Enterprise Wy
100 SLRB 47172 5288 C5
Enterprize Dr
- SLRB 47172 5288 C4
Entrance Rd
8100 LSVL 40258 5831 C5
Entrican Rd
- LSVL 40118 5942 E2
Envoy Cir
100 JFTN 40299 5728 D1
Ephraim McDowell Dr
3500 LSVL 40205 5617 D7
3500 LSVL 40205 5618 A7
Epinay Ct
4500 LSVL 40272 5831 E7
Epson Ct
17000 LSVL 40245 5622 D2
Equator Ct
6800 LSVL 40219 5835 C3
Equinox Blvd
- BltC 40047 5947 C6
- LSVL 40047 5947 C6
Eric Ct
100 LSVL 40219 5835 A3
Eric Dr
6200 FydC 47119 5394 A4
Erica Wy
6100 LSVL 40272 5940 A5
Eric Christy Rd
100 BltC 40047 6055 D4
Eric Edward Wy
7400 LSVL 40220 5727 E1
Erie Ct
100 SHDV 40165 6161 E4
Erika Nicole Blvd
- BltC 40071 5948 B7
Erikas Ct
100 BltC 40165 6054 D3
Erin Cir
100 MTWH 40047 6056 A3
Erin Ct
4400 FydC 47119 5394 E4
Erin Dr
400 JFVL 47130 5508 A3
Erin Rd
4300 FydC 47119 5394 D4
Erin Wy
9500 WPMG 40223 5510 D7
Ermine Wy
- LSVL 40219 5834 D7
Erni Av
100 NALB 47150 5505 A3
Ernstberger Rd
8400 FydC 47122 5393 A6
Erst Ct
2600 JFTN 40220 5728 B2

INDEX 20
Ervay Av
Louisville Metro Street Index
Filly Dr

STREET Block City ZIP Map# Grid

Ervay Av
600 LSVL 40217 5724 E2
Eskridge Ln
1500 LSVL 40214 5723 D6
1500 LSVL 40216 5723 D6
E Esplanade Av
100 LSVL 40214 5833 C1
Esquire Al
- LSVL 40210 5615 B3
900 LSVL 40203 5615 C3
Esquire St
- LSVL 40203 5615 A3
- LSVL 40211 5615 A3
1700 LSVL 40210 5615 A3
2500 LSVL 40211 5614 E3
Essex Av
6500 LSVL 40216 5722 A4
Essex Ct
1000 OdmC 44026 5292 B3
1400 ELZT 42701 6703 C6
Essex Rd
3700 LSVL 40220 5618 A7
Essex Bay Ct
12500 LSVL 40245 5511 E2
Estate Cir
1000 FydC 47122 5502 C3
1000 GEOT 47122 5502 C3
Estate Dr
300 ELZT 42701 6811 E1
1100 GEOT 47122 5502 C3
4100 LSVL 40216 5723 D6
4600 LSVL 40214 5723 D7
Estele Av
6500 LSVL 40214 5833 C1
Estele Ct
6100 LSVL 40219 5835 C7
Estella Av
200 NALB 47150 5504 E6
Esther Av
4400 LSVL 40216 5723 C6
Esther Blvd
2800 LSVL 40220 5618 C6
Esther Wy
- LGNG 40031 5296 B3
Estrada Av
7800 HdnC 40121 6374 B5
Etawah Av
1200 LYDN 40222 5619 A1
1200 LYDN 40242 5619 A1
Ethan Allen Wy
6900 LSVL 40272 6048 D1
7200 LSVL 40272 5939 C7
Ethel Av
3700 WBHL 40218 5726 E4
3800 LSVL 40218 5726 E4
Ethel Nancy Ln
- VNGV 40175 6482 D7
Ethelwood Dr
3300 JFTN 40299 5728 C4
Ethridge Av
300 LSVL 40223 5620 A3
400 DGSH 40223 5620 A3
Etley Av
- JfnC 40204 5616 E4
- JfnC 40206 5616 E4
- LSVL 40204 5616 E4
- LSVL 40206 5616 E4
Eton Rd
- LSVL 40242 5510 B4
8700 LSVL 40241 5510 B4
8700 MRCK 40241 5510 B4
E Ettels Ln
10 CLKV 47129 5506 C3
W Ettels Ln
100 CLKV 47129 5506 C3
Eubanks Ln
- HdnC 40160 6592 B4
Euclid Av
900 LSVL 40208 5724 B1
1200 LSVL 40208 5615 B7
1200 LSVL 40210 5615 B7
5100 LSVL 40272 5831 B7
Euclid St
- ELZT 42701 6812 A3
Eugene Wy
5200 LSVL 40216 5832 A1
Eula Rd
8500 LSVL 40219 5835 D6
Eupora Ct
9200 JFTN 40299 5728 C3
Eureka Av
6200 LSVL 40216 5722 C4
Eustis Av
5400 MdeC 40121 6373 C1
Eutropia Ct
10 LSVL 40208 5615 C7
Eva Rd
3400 LSVL 40216 5722 C5
Evan Ct
1700 OdmC 40031 5297 C3
Evangeline Av
200 LSVL 40214 5833 C1
Evanna Ct
3000 FydC 47119 5394 E7
Evans Ln
- BltC 40047 6056 B3
200 MTWH 40047 6056 B3
2300 FydC 47150 5504 C5
2300 NALB 47150 5504 C5
Evans Lp
7800 HdnC 40121 6374 B6
Evans Rd
10 HdnC 42701 6812 E7
Evans Jacobi Rd
4000 FydC 47122 5393 B5
Evans Knobs Rd SE
6000 HsnC 47117 6155 C1
Evanston Av NE
7300 HsnC 47136 5610 D4
7300 LNVL 47136 5610 D4
Eve Dr
10200 LSVL 40272 5940 D2
Eve Adam Dr
10200 LSVL 40272 5940 E2

STREET Block City ZIP Map# Grid

E Evelyn Av
100 LSVL 40214 5724 D3
W Evelyn Av
100 LSVL 40214 5724 C3
400 LSVL 40215 5724 C3
Evelyn Dr
1000 RDCF 40160 6483 B2
Evening Star Dr
9800 LSVL 40272 5939 E1
9900 LSVL 40272 5940 A1
Evening Tide Ct
6600 LSVL 40272 5939 E1
Everett Av
1400 LSVL 40204 5616 D5
5100 FydC 47119 5393 E3
Everett Ct
100 BltC 40071 5949 B2
Everett Ter
- LSVL 40204 5616 D5
Everett Rush Ct
8600 LSVL 40228 5836 B7
Evergreen Av
- LSVL 40245 5511 E2
- LSVL 40245 5512 A2
2000 LSVL 40205 5726 B1
Evergreen Cir
3100 ClkC 47130 5398 C5
Evergreen Ct
100 CLKV 47129 5506 C3
2600 LSVL 40223 5511 B6
9200 OdmC 40056 5512 D4
Evergreen Dr
400 CLKV 47129 5506 D2
Evergreen Ln
- ELZT 42701 6703 C3
Evergreen Rd
400 ANCH 40223 5620 C2
400 MDTN 40223 5620 C3
400 MDTN 40243 5620 C2
1600 ANCH 40223 5511 B6
2300 LSVL 40223 5511 B6
3100 OdmC 40014 5405 B1
3100 OdmC 40031 5405 B1
N Evergreen Rd
100 MDTN 40243 5620 C3
300 MDTN 40223 5620 C3
400 ANCH 40223 5620 C3
S Evergreen Rd
- MDTN 40243 5620 D4
200 WDHL 40243 5620 D4
Evergreen St
10 BltC 40165 6161 B1
Evergreen Tr
- ELZT 42701 6703 C4
Evergreen Garden Dr
- ELZT 42701 6703 C3
- HdnC 42701 6703 C3
Evergreen Pl Ct
500 MDTN 40223 5620 D3
500 MDTN 40243 5620 D3
Evergreen Wynde
2600 ANCH 40223 5511 B6
2600 LSVL 40223 5511 B5
Everin Cove
4100 OdmC 40031 5404 B1
Evershead Pl
4200 LSVL 40241 5511 A3
Everton Dr
6600 LSVL 40258 5831 C2
Evesham Dr
3400 LSVL 40213 5725 E7
Evon Ct
3100 JFTN 40299 5728 E3
Evondale Wy
- OdmC 44026 5292 D2
Ewing Av
- ANCH 40223 5620 B1
N Ewing Av
100 LSVL 40206 5616 E2
S Ewing Av
100 LSVL 40206 5616 E3
Ewing Ln
200 JFVL 47130 5507 D4
Excalibur Cor
1000 STMW 40222 5618 D1
Excalibur Ct
100 MTWH 40047 6055 E5
Exchange Av
200 STMW 40207 5618 A2
Executive Cir
100 RDCF 40160 6483 B4
Executive Ct
1000 JFVL 47130 5398 E7
Executive Dr
1000 ELZT 42701 6703 E7
1000 ELZT 42701 6812 E1
Executive Pk
100 STMW 40207 5618 D4
Exeter Av
4400 LSVL 40218 5726 C6
Exhibition Ct
9400 LSVL 40291 5728 B7
Exler Rd
300 HdnC 40175 6591 D2
300 VNGV 40175 6591 D2
Exley Ct
4400 LSVL 40211 5614 A4
Exmoor Av
700 LSVL 40223 5619 E2
Expedition Tr
11400 LSVL 40291 5946 E4
Explorer Dr
2900 LSVL 40218 5727 B2
2900 LSVL 40220 5727 B2
Expressway Av
- LSVL 40214 5724 B4
- LSVL 40215 5724 B4

F

F Ct
10 LGNG 40031 5296 E2
F St
- HdnC 40121 6374 C3

STREET Block City ZIP Map# Grid

Fabricon Blvd
1300 JFVL 47130 5506 E1
1400 JFVL 47130 5507 A2
Factory Ln
12900 LSVL 40245 5512 A5
Fair Av
400 ELZT 42701 6812 A2
Fair Ln
7800 LSVL 40291 5836 E2
Fair St
2200 NALB 47150 5505 B2
N Fairbanks Av
500 CLKV 47129 5506 C3
Fairdale Rd
- LSVL 40118 5834 B7
- MLHT 40219 5834 B7
400 LSVL 40118 5942 D1
1100 LSVL 40118 5943 A1
Fairfax Av
100 LSVL 40207 5618 A3
100 STMW 40207 5618 A3
200 NBNE 40207 5618 A3
Fairfield Av
300 CHAN 47111 5181 C4
Fairfield Dr
500 LSVL 40206 5617 B4
Fairfield Gardens Ct
4000 LSVL 40245 5512 C4
Fairfield Gardens Dr
14400 LSVL 40245 5512 C4
Fairfield Hill Ct
3900 LSVL 40245 5512 C4
Fairfield Hill Dr
14300 LSVL 40245 5512 C4
Fairfield Meadows Ct
14200 LSVL 40245 5512 C4
Fairfield Meadows Dr
3900 LSVL 40245 5512 C4
Fairground Rd
8800 LSVL 40291 5837 B1
9300 LSVL 40291 5728 C7
9400 JFTN 40291 5728 C7
9400 JFTN 40299 5728 C7
9900 LSVL 40299 5728 D7
Fairgrounds Rd
- LSVL 40209 5725 A3
- OdmC 40031 5296 C3
Fairgrounds Wy
- SHDV 40165 6161 D3
Fairhill Dr
700 LSVL 40207 5508 A7
700 LSVL 40207 5617 A1
Fairington Dr
- LSVL 40218 5726 E6
- LSVL 40218 5727 A5
Fairland Av
2200 LSVL 40218 5727 A4
Fairland Pl
1200 LSVL 40211 5614 B4
Fairlane Av
100 MTWH 40047 6056 B2
Fairlawn Rd
100 LSVL 40207 5617 D3
100 STMW 40207 5617 D3
Fairmeade Ct
400 STMW 40207 5618 C4
Fairmeade Rd
100 FRMD 40207 5618 B3
200 STMW 40207 5618 B3
Fairmeadows Ln
7700 GYDL 40222 5618 D4
7800 GYDL 40222 5509 E7
7800 GYDL 40222 5510 A7
7800 LYDN 40222 5510 A7
Fairmont Av
2200 NALB 47150 5505 C2
E Fairmont Av
100 LSVL 40214 5724 D4
W Fairmont Av
100 LSVL 40214 5724 C4
400 LSVL 40215 5724 C4
Fairmont Rd
10 RDCF 40160 6593 A1
Fairmound Dr
100 ClkC 47130 5399 E5
100 UTCA 47130 5399 E5
Fairmount Rd
9600 LSVL 40291 5837 C7
10500 LSVL 40291 5946 E1
12100 LSVL 40291 5947 C2
Fairmount Falls Wy
10500 LSVL 40291 5946 E1
10600 LSVL 40291 5837 E7
Fairmount Ridge Ct
8700 LSVL 40291 5837 E7
8700 LSVL 40291 5946 E1
Fairview Av
100 ELZT 42701 6702 E7
100 JFVL 47130 5506 E4
900 RDCF 40160 6483 B5
2800 LSVL 40208 5724 B2
10500 JFTN 40299 5728 E4
10500 JFTN 40299 5729 A3
Fairview Cir
800 RDCF 40160 6483 C5
Fairview Dr
200 ELZT 42701 6811 D5
4900 OdmC 40014 5405 C3
Fairview Ln
100 BltC 40165 6053 A7
100 BltC 40165 6162 A1
Fairview Knob Rd
3400 FydC 47172 5287 B6
Fairway Ct
2100 NALB 47150 5505 A2
3100 FydC 47119 5394 D7
3100 FydC 47119 5503 D1
5100 OdmC 40031 5295 B4
Fairway Dr
100 MTWH 40047 6056 A3
1700 OdmC 40031 5295 B4
3000 FydC 47119 5394 D7
3000 FydC 47119 5503 D1

STREET Block City ZIP Map# Grid

Fairway Ln
3700 RLGF 40207 5508 C7
13000 OdmC 44026 5292 A4
13100 OdmC 44026 5291 E3
Fairway Pointe Ct
4600 LSVL 40241 5511 B4
Fairway Pointe Dr
10900 LSVL 40241 5511 B4
Fairway View Ct
6800 PROS 40059 5401 B4
Fairway Vista Dr
2000 LSVL 40245 5621 D1
Fairway Vista Pl
15300 LSVL 40245 5621 D1
Fairwood Av
200 JFVL 47130 5508 B2
Fairwood Ct
5700 LSVL 40291 5728 C7
Fairwood Ln
5000 JFTN 40299 5728 D7
5000 LSVL 40291 5728 D7
Fairwood Oaks Pl
5500 LSVL 40291 5837 B1
Fairy Belle Ct
5300 LSVL 40213 5726 A7
Faith Ct
10 ELZT 42701 6702 E1
Faithful Wy
10800 LSVL 40229 5944 D4
Falcon Ct
300 ELZT 42701 6702 E4
1000 NALB 47150 5504 E4
Falcon Dr
1200 ANPK 40213 5725 C2
1200 LSVL 40213 5725 C2
8500 ClkC 47111 5290 B4
Falcon Run
900 NALB 47150 5504 E5
Falcon Ridge Ln
- LGNG 40031 5296 D1
Falconwood Rd
1000 LYDN 40222 5619 C3
Falkirk Ct
500 DGSH 40243 5620 B5
Falkirk Rd
10800 DGSH 40243 5620 A6
Falkland Ln
5000 LSVL 40241 5510 E1
Fall Ct
- NALB 47150 5505 C1
Fallen Apple Ln
4400 LSVL 40218 5727 D4
Fallen Leaf Cir
6700 LSVL 40241 5509 D4
Fallen Leaf Ct
2600 LSVL 40241 5509 D5
Fallen Oak Ct
12000 LSVL 40245 5511 D2
12000 WTNH 40245 5511 D2
Fallen Sky Dr
10100 LSVL 40229 5944 D1
Fallen Timber Dr
3600 BWNF 40241 5510 A3
Fallgate Ct
900 WDYH 40207 5618 C1
Fall Harvest Ct
300 JFTN 40223 5619 E5
Falling Leaf Ct
9600 ODGH 40014 5402 D7
9600 OdmC 40014 5402 D7
Falling Leaf Dr
100 BltC 40047 6055 D5
100 MTWH 40047 6055 D5
Falling Spring Rd
10 RDCF 40160 6484 A5
300 HdnC 40121 6484 B5
600 HdnC 40160 6484 B5
800 HdnC 42701 6484 C5
Falling Springs Rd
- HdnC 40121 6484 B5
- HdnC 40160 6484 B5
- HdnC 42701 6484 C5
Falling Star Dr
6500 LSVL 40272 5939 E1
Falling Tree Wy
10000 JFTN 40223 5619 D6
Fallon Wy
400 LSVL 40214 5833 C4
Fallow Dr
4500 JFVL 47130 5398 B5
Falls Ct
5600 CTWD 40014 5403 C5
Falls Trc
1200 JFTN 40223 5619 D6
Falls Bluff Ct
3600 LSVL 40241 5509 D3
Falls Creek Ct
3200 OdmC 40059 5292 A6
Falls Creek Lndg
- FydC 47172 5287 E7
1200 FydC 47150 5287 E7
Falls Creek Rd
6600 LSVL 40241 5509 C3
Fallshere Ct
3200 LSVL 40220 5728 A2
Falls Ridge Ct
7400 LSVL 40241 5509 E3
Fallsview Dr
100 CLKV 47129 5506 C5
Fallsview Rd
2300 LSVL 40207 5509 A5
2300 WNDF 40207 5509 A5
Falmouth Ct
9900 JFTN 40299 5728 D1
Falmouth Dr
2900 LSVL 40205 5726 B1
Famous Ct
8400 LSVL 40219 5835 C6
Famous Wy
4700 LSVL 40219 5835 D6
Famous 4th Division Rd
10 HdnC 40121 6374 D1

STREET Block City ZIP Map# Grid

Famous Fourth Division Rd
- HdnC 40121 6374 C1
Fancy Ct
- LSVL 40219 5834 D7
Fancy Gap Dr
13800 LSVL 40299 5729 E7
Fandango Ct
2000 LSVL 40245 5622 C1
Fantasy Tr
11100 HTCK 40229 5945 D3
Faris Wy
6200 LSVL 40272 5940 A3
6300 LSVL 40272 5939 E3
Farish Dr
9300 JFTN 40299 5728 C2
Fariwood
- BltC 40165 5944 E6
Farman Ct
1100 LSVL 40219 5835 B7
1100 LSVL 40229 5835 B7
Farmbrook Dr
12500 MDTN 40243 5620 D6
Farmdale Av
1200 LSVL 40213 5725 C4
Farmers Ln
9200 LSVL 40118 5943 A2
Farmers Rd
10 HdnC 42701 6703 B2
Farmers Wy
10400 LSVL 40291 5946 B2
Farmgate Ct
6400 LSVL 40291 5837 C2
Farmgate Dr
2000 FydC 47119 5503 E1
Farmgate Ln
1000 NALB 47150 5396 C5
Farmhill Ct
6300 LSVL 40291 5837 C2
Farmhouse Ln
7500 LSVL 40291 5836 E4
Farmingdale Dr
1300 ELZT 42701 6703 D5
Farmingham Rd
700 DGSH 40243 5620 A5
Farmington Av
300 LSVL 40209 5724 D3
Farmington Ln
6600 CTWD 40014 5403 E6
Farmington Wk
8900 ClkC 47111 5290 B2
Farm Oaks Ct
10600 LSVL 40241 5511 A2
Farmsfield Ct
8600 JFTN 40299 5728 A6
Farmstead Ct
6400 LSVL 40291 5837 C3
Farmstead Ln
9400 LSVL 40291 5837 C2
Farmview Av
3900 LSVL 40218 5727 A4
Farmview Ct
2900 OdmC 40059 5292 B7
Farmview Dr
- BltC 40047 6055 E5
Farmwood Wy
8200 LSVL 40291 5836 E5
Farnham Rd
9100 LYDN 40242 5510 C7
9100 MLND 40223 5510 C7
9400 WPMG 40223 5510 D7
9500 LSVL 40223 5510 C7
9800 KNLD 40223 5510 D6
Farnsley Rd
2400 LSVL 40216 5723 A2
3300 SVLY 40216 5723 A2
Farnsley Rd NE
4700 HsnC 47112 5501 E7
4800 FydC 47122 5501 E7
Farnsley Knob Rd
5300 FydC 47117 5721 B3
Faro Cir
5300 BltC 40165 6053 C2
5300 PNRV 40165 6053 C2
Faro Ct
3900 BltC 40165 6053 C2
3900 HBNE 40165 6053 C2
Farragut St
4000 HdnC 40121 6374 A3
Farridge Ct
6000 LSVL 40229 5945 A1
Farridge Dr
9100 LSVL 40229 5945 A1
Farrington Dr
100 NALB 47150 5395 E6
100 NALB 47150 5396 A6
1900 LSVL 40216 5723 A7
Farris Ln
100 BltC 40165 6054 B6
Fashion Wy
10900 LSVL 40272 5940 A3
Father Jack's Wy
- LSVL 40245 5621 D3
Fatima Ln
600 MYHE 40207 5617 E1
Faulkner Ln
8000 LSVL 40219 5834 D5
Fawcett Hill Rd
2100 NALB 47150 5504 E3
Fawn Ct
100 CLKV 47172 5397 C1
100 HLVW 40229 5944 A5
1100 OdmC 40031 5295 B3
4200 FydC 47119 5394 E5
9000 BRWD 40242 5510 C7
Fawn Hill Pl
14500 LSVL 40245 5621 D3
Fawn Meadow Ct
4800 LSVL 40241 5510 A1
Fawnridge Pl
9200 LSVL 40229 5944 E1
Fawnwood Ln
5200 LSVL 40291 5728 C7

STREET Block City ZIP Map# Grid

Faxon Ct
7500 LSVL 40258 5831 A4
Fay Av
10 JFVL 47130 5508 A3
5000 LSVL 40214 5833 B1
Fayette Av
- HdnC 40121 6374 A3
200 HdnC 40121 6373 E3
2700 LSVL 40206 5617 A3
3400 LSVL 40213 5725 B3
Fayette Dr
1400 LSVL 40219 5835 D2
Faywood Wy
2900 LSVL 40215 5724 A2
Featheringill Rd
5000 FydC 47119 5393 D3
5000 FydC 47124 5393 D3
E Federal Av
10 JFVL 47130 5507 A6
Federal Ct
200 LSVL 40214 5833 C5
Federal Hill Dr
100 MTWH 40047 6056 D2
2200 JFTN 40299 5728 D1
Federick Ct
100 BltC 40047 6056 A1
Fegenbush Ln
4300 LSVL 40218 5727 B6
4900 LSVL 40228 5727 B6
5900 LSVL 40228 5836 B2
6800 HWCK 40228 5836 C3
7000 SPML 40228 5836 C4
7900 LSVL 40291 5836 D4
Fegenbush Ln SR-864
6100 LSVL 40228 5836 B2
6700 HWCK 40228 5836 C3
7000 SPML 40228 5836 C4
7900 LSVL 40291 5836 D4
Fegenbush Ln SR-1065
7900 LSVL 40228 5836 E5
7900 LSVL 40291 5836 E5
Fehr Rd
700 LSVL 40206 5617 A4
Felker Wy
5500 LSVL 40291 5727 E7
5500 LSVL 40291 5836 E1
Fellswood Ct
11000 DGSH 40243 5620 A5
Fellswood Pl
400 DGSH 40243 5620 B5
Felsmere Cir
9100 LSVL 40241 5510 D4
Felton Wy NE
6200 HsnC 47122 5501 B6
Fence Pl
4300 LSVL 40241 5511 A3
Fendley Rd
1000 OdmC 40031 5295 C2
Fendley Mill Rd
300 LGNG 40031 5296 C1
600 OdmC 40031 5296 D1
Fenholt Rd
3700 LSVL 40218 5727 C4
Fenley Av
100 LSVL 40206 5617 C2
100 LSVL 40207 5617 C2
500 LYDN 40222 5618 E2
700 STMW 40222 5618 D1
Fenmore Av
9200 LSVL 40272 5831 B7
Fennel Ct
5400 LSVL 40258 5831 C4
Fenske Ln
6700 LSVL 40258 5831 A4
Fentress Blvd
10 HdnC 42701 6593 B6
10 RDCF 42701 6593 B6
Fenway Ct
8400 LSVL 40258 5831 A5
Fenway Rd
6700 LSVL 40258 5831 A5
Fenwick Dr
500 NALB 47150 5505 A2
6500 LSVL 40228 5836 B3
Fenwick Center Dr
12800 MDTN 40223 5620 E3
12800 MDTN 40223 5621 A3
Fenwick Creek Pl
8600 JFTN 40220 5728 A3
8600 LSVL 40220 5728 A3
Fenwick Farm Pl
8200 LSVL 40220 5728 A3
Fenwick Hill Pl
8700 JFTN 40220 5728 A3
8700 LSVL 40220 5728 A3
Fenwick Park Pl
3400 LSVL 40220 5728 A3
Ferber Ln
1700 GEOT 47122 5502 A3
Ferguson Ct
- BltC 40165 6051 C6
Ferguson Ln
100 BltC 40165 6052 E5
100 HLVW 40165 6052 E5
Fergusson Fife Av
500 LSVL 40118 5833 D6
Fern Ct
6100 LSVL 40291 5836 E2
Fern Dr
- LSVL 40213 5725 B2
- LSVL 40217 5725 B2
Fern St
1200 LSVL 40204 5616 B3
N Fern St
100 SLRB 47172 5288 E4
200 ClkC 47172 5289 A4
200 SLRB 47172 5289 A4
S Fern St
100 SLRB 47172 5288 E4
Fern Wy
- BltC 40047 6055 E5
Fern Bluff Ln
9200 LSVL 40229 5945 B1

STREET Block City ZIP Map# Grid

Fern Brook Ln
5400 LSVL 40291 5728 B7
5400 LSVL 40291 5837 B1
Fernbush Dr
6600 LSVL 40228 5836 B3
Fern Cliff Ln
6300 LSVL 40291 5836 E2
Fern Creek Rd
9200 LSVL 40291 5837 C2
Fern Crest Rd
6400 LSVL 40291 5836 E3
Ferndale Rd
7800 LSVL 40291 5836 E2
8200 LSVL 40291 5837 A2
Fern Gardens Wy
7800 LSVL 40291 5836 E1
Fern Grade Rd
- LSVL 40213 5834 B2
Fernhaven Rd
6700 LSVL 40228 5836 C3
Fernheather Dr
3300 SVLY 40216 5723 C3
Fern Hill Dr
9300 LSVL 40291 5837 B2
Fern Lea Rd
3300 SVLY 40216 5723 C3
Fern Mill St
100 BltC 40165 6054 D4
Fernvalley Cir
6400 LSVL 40219 5835 D2
Fernvalley Ct
6300 LSVL 40219 5835 D2
Fern Valley Rd
1200 LSVL 40219 5835 D2
1500 LSVL 40209 5834 A2
1800 LSVL 40228 5835 E2
2800 LSVL 40213 5834 D2
2800 LSVL 40219 5834 D2
6000 LSVL 40228 5836 A2
Fern Valley Rd SR-864
6100 LSVL 40228 5836 A2
Fern Valley Rd SR-1747
1200 LSVL 40219 5835 D2
1800 LSVL 40228 5835 E2
2800 LSVL 40213 5834 D2
2800 LSVL 40219 5834 D2
6000 LSVL 40228 5836 A2
W Fern Valley Rd
1100 LSVL 40219 5834 E2
1100 LSVL 40219 5835 A2
Fernvalley Wy
6200 LSVL 40219 5835 D2
Fern Valley Pass
6200 LSVL 40228 5836 A2
Fern View Dr
8400 LSVL 40291 5836 E3
8400 LSVL 40291 5837 A3
Fernview Rd
6300 LSVL 40291 5836 E3
Fernwood Av
1500 LSVL 40204 5616 E6
1500 LSVL 40205 5616 E6
Fernwood Ct
700 CLKV 47129 5397 B6
Ferree Rd NE
1500 HsnC 47112 5610 A7
1500 HsnC 47136 5610 A5
Ferrer Wy
4700 JFTN 40291 5728 B7
4700 JFTN 40299 5728 B7
4900 LSVL 40291 5728 B7
Ferry St
10 NALB 47150 5504 E7
10 NALB 47150 5505 A7
Fertig Creek Rd
5000 FydC 47119 5394 B1
Fetter Av
700 LSVL 40217 5725 A1
900 LSVL 40217 5616 A7
Fetter Ct
- LSVL 40217 5616 A7
Feyhurst Dr
7000 LSVL 40258 5831 C3
Feys Ct
5100 LSVL 40216 5723 A7
Feys Dr
4900 LSVL 40216 5722 E7
Fiddlers Ln
100 BltC 40071 5949 C2
Fiddlers Ridge Rd
10 HdnC 40175 6591 C1
10 VNGV 40175 6591 C1
Fiddlestick Ct
8200 LSVL 40291 5837 C6
Field Av
2700 LSVL 40206 5617 A2
Field Dr
1700 JFVL 47130 5507 C3
Fieldcrest Ct
8400 LSVL 40299 5728 A4
Fielding Wy
4800 LSVL 40216 5723 A7
Field Ridge Ct
7100 LSVL 40291 5837 A4
Fields Ln
10 SbyC 40067 5623 E2
Fieldside Cir
3800 LSVL 40299 5727 E4
Fieldstone Ct
10 NALB 47150 5504 E1
Field Stone Wy
- HdnC 42701 6811 A7
7300 LSVL 40291 5836 E4
Field Trails Ct
8500 LSVL 40291 5837 A3
Field View Ct
7000 LSVL 40291 5837 A4
Fiesta Wy
9300 LSVL 40272 5831 C7
9300 LSVL 40272 5940 B1
Fillmore Ct
10 MTWH 40047 6055 E1
Filly Dr
10 BltC 40109 6052 D3

INDEX 21
Filson Av
Louisville Metro Street Index
Frisbee Wy

STREET Block City ZIP Map# Grid
Filson Av
- LSVL 40217 5616 B7
2500 LSVL 40217 5725 B1
Filson Fields Ct
8700 LSVL 40219 5835 C7
Filson Fields Dr
8900 LSVL 40219 5835 C7
Final Ct
100 LSVL 40219 5835 B7
Final Dr
4200 LSVL 40219 5835 B7
Financial Dr
100 ELZT 42701 6703 C4
Financial Sq
10 LSVL 40202 5615 D2
Fincastle Ct
100 SHDV 40165 6162 A2
Fincastle Rd
3500 LSVL 40213 5725 C2
Fincastle Tr
6600 LSVL 40272 5939 D7
Fincastle Wy
10 SHDV 40165 6161 E2
400 SHDV 40165 6162 A2
Finch Ct
300 ELZT 42701 6702 E4
Finch Pl
1600 LYDN 40222 5619 C3
Finchleigh Dr
200 NALB 47150 5504 E1
Finchley Ct
500 DGSH 40243 5620 A5
Finchley Rd
11000 DGSH 40243 5620 B5
Findon Ct
10600 DGSH 40223 5620 A5
10600 DGSH 40243 5620 A5
Finn Av
2800 LSVL 40208 5724 C2
Finzer St
400 LSVL 40203 5615 E4
700 LSVL 40203 5616 A4
800 LSVL 40204 5616 A4
Finzer St SR-864
900 LSVL 40204 5616 A4
Fir Ct
5600 LSVL 40272 5940 B4
Fir St
100 BltC 40165 6161 B1
Fir Tr
3000 JFTN 40299 5728 D3
Fire Chiefe Av
- LSVL 40210 5615 A6
Fireside Dr
9800 LSVL 40272 5940 E1
Firestone Ct
10100 LSVL 40291 5837 D6
Firethorn Dr
3700 OdmC 40031 5404 E1
Firethorn Wy
6500 LSVL 40229 5945 B1
Fir Green Wy
7900 LSVL 40291 5837 B4
Fir Tree Ln
10700 LSVL 40272 5941 E1
Fir View Ct
10500 LSVL 40299 5728 E5
Firwood Ct
1200 JFVL 47130 5507 B2
9600 LSVL 40291 5728 C7
Firwood Ln
5000 LSVL 40291 5728 C7
Fischer Av
1100 LSVL 40204 5616 B5
Fischer Ct
- OdmC 40014 5402 B5
Fischer Dr
100 NALB 47150 5505 A3
Fischer Park Dr
10500 LSVL 40241 5511 A4
Fisher Av
5300 MdeC 40121 6373 C2
Fisher Ct
100 HdnC 40121 6373 E4
Fisher Ln
10 ELZT 42701 6703 D5
100 BltC 40047 6055 D4
100 MTWH 40047 6055 D4
Fisher Rd
100 BltC 40165 6050 D7
Fisherman Ct
5200 LSVL 40241 5511 C1
Fisherman Wy
11500 LSVL 40241 5511 C1
Fisherville Rd
200 LSVL 40023 5622 B6
200 LSVL 40023 5731 B4
200 LSVL 40245 5622 B6
Fisherville Rd SR-1531
200 LSVL 40023 5622 B6
200 LSVL 40023 5731 B4
200 LSVL 40245 5622 B6
Fisherville Woods Ct
3400 LSVL 40023 5731 C5
Fisherville Woods Dr
17400 LSVL 40023 5731 B4
Fisk Ct
1000 LSVL 40203 5615 C3
Fiske Av
3300 FydC 47150 5396 D3
Fister Ct
4700 LSVL 40258 5831 D2
Fitch Dr
1700 GEOT 47122 5501 E3
Fitzgerald Ct
1600 LGNG 40031 5297 A1
Fitzgerald Rd
3800 LSVL 40216 5723 D2
3800 SVLY 40216 5723 D2
Five Forks Dr
6500 OdmC 40056 5512 D3
Five Mile Ln
3000 FydC 47150 5721 D1
3000 FydC 47150 5722 A1

STREET Block City ZIP Map# Grid
Five Oaks Dr
10 HdnC 42701 6703 C1
Five Oaks Pl
3200 LSVL 40207 5617 D5
Flagler Av
6500 LSVL 40216 5722 B4
Flagstaff Ct
1700 LSVL 40223 5510 E7
Flagstaff Dr
3500 JFVL 47130 5398 B6
Flagstone Ct
5800 LSVL 40219 5836 A3
Flagstone Dr
1000 JFVL 47130 5399 A6
Flair Knoll Ct
2900 LSVL 40216 5722 D6
Flair Knoll Dr
3000 LSVL 40216 5722 C6
Flamingo Dr
100 BltC 40165 6162 D1
200 LSVL 40218 5727 C4
E Flamingo Dr
100 CLKV 47129 5506 C2
W Flamingo Dr
100 CLKV 47129 5506 B2
Flanders Ct
200 LSVL 40218 5727 A2
200 LSVL 40220 5727 A2
Flat Lick Rd
- BltC 40047 5946 B7
- BltC 40047 6055 A1
- MTWH 40047 6055 E1
400 MTWH 40047 6056 A2
Flat Lick Rd SR-2706
- BltC 40047 6055 E1
- MTWH 40047 6055 E1
400 MTWH 40047 6056 A2
Flat Rock Rd
100 LSVL 40245 5622 E1
1500 JfnC 40245 5622 E1
2600 LSVL 40245 5513 B7
Flat Wood Dr
700 CLKV 47129 5397 B6
Flatwoods Ct
- CLKV 47129 5397 B6
Fleet Av
2300 LSVL 40217 5725 A1
2300 PKWV 40217 5725 A1
Fleetwood Dr
3500 WSNP 40218 5726 C4
Flemer Dr
3700 FydC 47119 5395 A6
Fleming Av
2700 LSVL 40206 5616 E2
3000 LSVL 40206 5617 A1
Fleming Dr
1200 ELZT 42701 6811 B5
1200 HdnC 42701 6811 B5
Fleming Rd
1700 LSVL 40205 5726 A1
Fletcher Ct
10 HdnC 40162 6591 B5
Flicker Pl
8200 LSVL 40214 5833 B6
Flicker Rd
700 LSVL 40214 5833 A5
Flint Rd
4000 BLWD 40207 5617 E1
4000 CYWV 40207 5617 E1
Flint Haven Rd
3400 LSVL 40241 5509 E4
Flintlock Cir
6300 LSVL 40216 5831 E1
Flintlock Dr
1600 JFVL 47130 5508 A1
4100 LSVL 40216 5832 A1
4200 LSVL 40216 5831 E1
Flintstone Ct
100 SHDV 40165 6161 E3
100 SHDV 40165 6162 A2
Flirtation Wk
100 LSVL 40219 5835 E3
Floore Ct
2800 JFTN 40299 5728 C2
Flora Av
2800 LSVL 40220 5726 E1
Flora Ct
100 ELZT 42701 6702 D6
Floradora Dr
1900 LSVL 40272 5940 A3
2000 LSVL 40272 5939 E2
Floral Av
600 LSVL 40208 5615 C5
Floral Ter
600 LSVL 40203 5615 C5
600 LSVL 40208 5615 C5
Florence Av
1700 NALB 47150 5505 C3
E Florence Av
100 LSVL 40214 5724 D4
200 LSVL 40209 5724 D4
W Florence Av
100 LSVL 40214 5724 C4
400 LSVL 40215 5724 C4
Florian Rd
10300 JFTN 40223 5619 E5
10400 DGSH 40243 5620 A6
10400 JFTN 40223 5620 A6
Florida Av
- LYDN 40222 5618 E2
- STMW 40222 5618 E2
100 MTWH 40047 6056 A2
600 SLRB 47172 5288 C3
Florida St
- HdnC 40121 6374 C3
Florist Dr
8100 LSVL 40228 5836 E6
Flower Av
100 NALB 47150 5505 A3
Flowering Grove Ct
3800 LSVL 40241 5510 E4
Flowering Grove Pl
9800 LSVL 40241 5510 D3

STREET Block City ZIP Map# Grid
Flowervale Ln
11400 LSVL 40272 5940 A5
Floyd St
700 NALB 47150 5505 A7
7000 FydC 47119 5393 D3
N Floyd St
100 LSVL 40202 5615 E2
S Floyd St
100 LSVL 40202 5615 E4
600 LSVL 40203 5615 E6
1200 LSVL 40208 5615 E6
2100 LSVL 40208 5724 D3
2400 LSVL 40209 5724 D2
Floydsburg Rd
7100 CTWD 40014 5403 E7
7400 OdmC 40014 5403 E7
7500 CTWD 40014 5404 A7
7500 CTWD 40014 5513 A1
7500 OdmC 40014 5404 A7
8100 OdmC 40056 5513 A1
9000 OdmC 40014 5513 E4
9000 SbyC 40245 5513 E4
9000 SbyC 40245 5514 A4
Floydsburg Rd SR-1408
7100 CTWD 40014 5403 E7
7400 OdmC 40014 5403 E7
7500 CTWD 40014 5404 A7
7500 CTWD 40014 5513 A1
7500 OdmC 40014 5404 A7
7500 OdmC 40014 5513 A1
8100 OdmC 40056 5513 A1
9000 SbyC 40245 5513 E4
9000 SbyC 40245 5514 A4
Floyd's Fork Dr
100 BltC 40165 6054 D2
Floydsview Pl
15500 LSVL 40245 5730 E1
15500 LSVL 40245 5731 A2
Fluhr Dr
4300 LSVL 40216 5723 D5
Fluhr Ln
2400 LSVL 40216 5722 D7
2400 LSVL 40216 5831 E1
Flushing Wy
4500 LSVL 40272 5940 D3
Flyway Ct
5300 LSVL 40258 5831 C3
Foeburn Ln
- WLNP 40207 5618 C1
300 WDYH 40207 5618 B1
Foeburn Wy
300 WDYH 40207 5618 B1
Foley Av
8600 OdmC 40056 5512 C3
8600 PWEV 40056 5512 C3
Foley Rd
100 BltC 40165 6163 B4
Folger St
5500 MdeC 40121 6373 D2
Fontaine Av
- LSVL 40209 5725 B4
Fontaine Dr
10 ELZT 42701 6702 B6
10 HdnC 42701 6702 B6
Fontaine Landing Ct
100 LSVL 40212 5614 B1
Fontendleau Wy
7000 LSVL 40291 5837 A4
Foothill Rd
500 SLRB 47172 5288 D5
Foraker Cir
5200 LSVL 40216 5722 D7
Forbes Cir
14700 LSVL 40245 5512 C7
Ford Dr
7000 BltC 40047 6054 E5
7000 BltC 40047 6055 A5
Ford Pl
11500 LSVL 40241 5511 C3
Fordham Ln
6700 LSVL 40291 5836 D3
Fordhaven Rd
2500 LSVL 40214 5832 B3
Fordson Wy
4100 LSVL 40211 5614 B5
Fordyce Ln
2600 LSVL 40205 5726 A1
Foreman Ln
3400 LSVL 40219 5834 E5
3400 LSVL 40219 5835 B6
Forest Av
1100 ELZT 42701 6702 E7
Forest Cir
700 CLKV 47172 5397 C1
Forest Ct
10 LSVL 40206 5617 B2
3300 JFVL 47130 5398 D5
Forest Dr
- BltC 40047 6055 B5
- LSVL 40219 5834 E1
- MTWH 40047 6055 B5
10 HdnC 42701 6593 C6
10 JFVL 47130 5508 A2
1200 LSVL 40219 5835 A1
1400 LSVL 40213 5726 A7
1400 LSVL 40219 5726 A7
Forest Ln
300 NRWD 40222 5618 E3
300 STMW 40222 5618 E3
1000 GSHN 44026 5292 C3
1000 OdmC 44026 5292 C3
Forest Trc
3900 LSVL 40245 5512 C4
Forest Bend Cir
13500 LSVL 40245 5512 B4
Forest Bend Pl
4300 LSVL 40245 5512 B3
Forest Bridge Ln
- LSVL 40223 5619 D2
- LYDN 40223 5619 D2
Forest Bridge Rd
- LYDN 40223 5619 D1
Forest Brook Dr
3500 LSVL 40207 5617 E5

STREET Block City ZIP Map# Grid
Forestbrook Rd
6000 FydC 47136 5502 E7
6000 FydC 47136 5611 E1
Forest Centre Ct
13000 LSVL 40223 5512 A7
Forest Creek Wy
14700 LSVL 40245 5621 D3
Forest Crest Pl
4000 LSVL 40245 5512 C4
Forest Crest Wy
3900 LSVL 40245 5512 C4
Forest Garden Ct
1300 LYDN 40223 5619 E1
Forest Garden Ln
10400 LYDN 40223 5619 E2
10500 LSVL 40223 5619 E2
Forest Glenn Ct
14400 LSVL 40245 5621 B2
Forest Green Blvd
9900 LYDN 40223 5619 D1
Forest Grove Ct
5100 PROS 40059 5400 D7
Forest Grove Pl
5100 PROS 40059 5400 D7
Forest Hill Dr
800 FydC 47150 5504 C3
800 NALB 47150 5504 C3
1600 LSVL 40205 5726 A1
Forest Hill Rd
100 SHDV 40165 6161 C7
Forestlake Dr
5000 LSVL 40059 5400 D6
Forest Oaks Dr
14600 LSVL 40245 5621 D2
Forest Park Dr
100 BltC 40047 6055 E5
100 MTWH 40047 6055 E5
4800 LSVL 40219 5835 A1
Forest Park Rd
800 BRMR 40223 5619 E4
800 LSVL 40223 5619 E4
Forest Place Ct
100 LSVL 40245 5621 C5
Forest Pointe Ln
2000 LSVL 40245 5621 E1
Forest Ridge Ct
4500 LSVL 40219 5835 C5
Forest Ridge Dr
100 BltC 40047 6055 E5
Forest School Ln
- ANCH 40223 5511 D7
Forest School Pl
- ANCH 40223 5511 D7
Forest School Rd
12300 ANCH 40223 5511 D7
Forest Springs Dr
13400 LSVL 40245 5512 A4
Forest Trace Rd
100 HdnC 40160 6592 C5
Forest Trail Pl
1100 LSVL 40245 5623 A4
Forest View Dr
1000 LSVL 40219 5835 B7
Forest Village Ln
9800 LSVL 40223 5619 D2
9800 LYDN 40223 5619 D2
Forestwood Av
- JFTN 40299 5728 D5
Forest Wy Dr
8500 LSVL 40258 5831 B3
Forest Wy Pl
6300 LSVL 40258 5831 B2
Forge Cir
13200 LSVL 40272 5939 D7
13200 LSVL 40272 6048 D1
Forged Wy
6500 FydC 47122 5502 E5
Forrest Dr
- SLRB 47172 5288 D6
8000 OdmC 40014 5512 A2
Forrest Dr N
- SLRB 47172 5288 E6
N Forrest Dr
600 SLRB 47172 5288 D6
S Forrest Dr
700 SLRB 47172 5288 D6
N Forrest Rd
100 RDCF 40160 6483 B4
S Forrest Rd
100 RDCF 40160 6483 B4
Forrest St
800 LSVL 40217 5616 A7
Forrest Hill Rd
6400 BltC 40047 5947 E7
Forrest Park Dr
2000 OdmC 40031 5296 C6
Forrest Spring Dr
10 HdnC 42701 6703 C3
Forrestwood Dr
9700 JFTN 40299 5728 C5
Forsythia Ln
6200 LSVL 40229 5945 A1
Fort Av
- MdeC 40175 6373 A5
Fort St
100 JFVL 47130 5506 E7
2000 LSVL 40208 5615 E7
2000 LSVL 40208 5724 E1
2000 LSVL 40217 5615 E7
2100 LSVL 40217 5724 E1
Fortas Ct
3300 LSVL 40220 5727 D3
Fort Knox
- WPT 40177 6156 C3
Fortney Ct
100 MTWH 40047 6056 B5
Fortney Ln
100 MTWH 40047 6056 A5
Fort Pickens Rd
1300 LGNG 40031 5297 B2
1300 OdmC 40031 5297 B1
Fort Pickens Rd SR-712
1100 LGNG 40031 5297 B2

STREET Block City ZIP Map# Grid
Fort Pickens Rd SR-2855
1300 LGNG 40031 5297 B2
1300 OdmC 40031 5297 B1
Fort Sumter Ct
7500 LSVL 40214 5833 D5
Forum Av
500 LSVL 40214 5724 B6
Fossil Ct
10100 LYDN 40223 5510 E7
Foster Ct
10 LSVL 40214 5833 D6
Foster Ln
100 BltC 40165 6053 E7
100 BltC 40165 6162 E1
100 BltC 40165 6163 A1
Foster Holly Wy
6700 LSVL 40291 5837 B4
Foundation Blvd
5200 FydC 47150 5396 D1
Fountain Av
500 LYDN 40222 5618 E2
700 LSVL 40222 5618 D1
900 STMW 40222 5618 D1
Fountain Ct
400 LSVL 40208 5615 D6
Fountain Dr
3400 WBHL 40218 5726 D4
Fountain Brook Wy
- JFTN 40220 5728 A1
Fountain Crest Cir
2100 JFVL 47130 5398 A6
Fountain Hall Ct
11700 LSVL 40299 5729 C6
Four Courts Al
2100 LSVL 40205 5617 A6
Four Karat Dr
- LSVL 40219 5834 D7
Four Leaf Ct
5000 FydC 47124 5393 C3
Four Leaf Dr
7200 FydC 47124 5393 C3
Four Oaks Ct
8700 LSVL 40299 5728 B4
Four Point Wy
- LSVL 40219 5834 D7
- SPVW 40219 5834 D7
Four Seasons Ln
9800 CKSD 40241 5510 D4
9800 LSVL 40241 5510 D4
Four Winds Dr
8100 LYDN 40222 5619 A1
Fox Av
6200 LSVL 40272 5940 A4
10300 LSVL 40118 5942 D3
Fox Rd
1800 ClkC 47143 5180 B1
Fox Run
- OdmC 40031 5295 B7
- OdmC 40031 5404 B1
Fox Tr
2200 OdmC 40031 5405 D1
Fox Bend Ct
14800 LSVL 40245 5512 D5
Fox Bluff Pl
7300 PROS 40059 5400 E5
Foxboro Dr
10000 LSVL 40223 5619 E2
Foxboro Rd
10500 LSVL 40223 5619 C2
10500 LSVL 40223 5620 B2
Foxbrook Ct
11100 LSVL 40223 5620 B3
Fox Chase Dr
4300 FXCH 40165 6053 A3
4900 PNRV 40165 6053 A3
Fox Chase Pl
8800 LSVL 40228 5945 E1
Fox Chase Rd
- LSVL 40228 5836 E7
9000 LSVL 40228 5945 E1
Fox Cove Ct
6100 PROS 40059 5400 E5
Fox Creek Ct
6000 NHFD 40222 5509 B5
Foxcroft Pl
6900 PROS 40059 5401 A3
Foxcroft Rd
6800 PROS 40059 5401 A4
Fox Den Ct
4700 GNSP 40241 5509 E1
Fox Den Dr
1500 ClkC 47130 5399 D5
Foxfire Dr
100 BltC 40047 6055 C7
800 LSVL 40223 5619 D2
Foxfire Rd
600 ELZT 42701 6703 A5
Fox Gap Trc
1200 JFTN 40223 5619 D6
Foxgate Ct
10800 LSVL 40223 5620 A3
Foxgate Pl
11100 LSVL 40223 5620 B3
Foxgate Rd
800 LSVL 40223 5620 A2
Fox Glen Wy
1100 LYDN 40242 5619 B1
Foxglove Cir
100 RDCF 40160 6592 D1
Fox Glove Ct
4300 OdmC 40059 5401 B2
Foxglove Dr
800 JFVL 47130 5507 D3
Foxglove Ln
3500 BRMD 40241 5510 A3
Fox Hall Pl
8200 LYDN 40242 5619 C2
Fox Harbor Rd
6900 PROS 40059 5400 E5
Fox Haven Rd
11200 LSVL 40229 5945 A3
Fox Hill Dr
3000 FydC 47119 5504 B1

STREET Block City ZIP Map# Grid
Fox Hill Rd
6000 PROS 40059 5400 E5
Fox Hollow Wy
1700 ClkC 47130 5399 D5
Fox Horn Cir
5600 LSVL 40216 5831 C1
5600 LSVL 40258 5831 C1
Fox Hound Rd
6700 LSVL 40291 5837 A3
Fox Hunt Ct
6100 PROS 40059 5400 E5
Fox Hunters Pt
1000 FydC 47150 5503 E4
Fox Hunters Point Ct
1000 FydC 47150 5504 A3
Foxhurst Dr
2000 SVLY 40216 5723 C3
Fox Landing Dr
2000 FydC 47150 5288 A7
Fox Ledge Ct
7600 LSVL 40291 5837 A4
Fox Meade Rd
11200 LSVL 40229 5945 A3
Fox Meadow Wy
4000 OdmC 40059 5401 C3
4000 PROS 40059 5401 C3
Fox Moore Ct
11000 LSVL 40223 5620 A3
Fox Moore Pl
11000 LSVL 40223 5620 A3
Fox Pointe Dr
1200 LYDN 40242 5619 A2
Fox Pointe Pl
8400 LYDN 40242 5619 C2
Fox Ridge Ct
8400 LSVL 40272 5832 C5
Fox Ridge Rd
100 RDCF 40160 6483 E3
4200 OdmC 40014 5404 C2
Fox Ridge Wy
100 BltC 40047 6055 E5
Fox Run Rd
300 BWDV 40207 5618 C2
1400 NALB 47150 5505 E1
4100 OdmC 40014 5405 A1
4800 OdmC 40031 5295 C7
4800 OdmC 40031 5404 B1
Fox Run Tr
1500 ClkC 47130 5399 D6
1500 UTCA 47130 5399 D6
Foxtail Ct
100 MTWH 40047 6056 A5
9200 ODGH 40014 5402 E7
Foxtail Pl
7500 ODGH 40014 5402 E7
Fox Trail Ct
2200 OdmC 40031 5405 C2
Fox Trail Dr
1800 OdmC 40031 5405 C2
Fox Valley Ct
7000 PROS 40059 5400 E5
Fox Valley Dr
6100 PROS 40059 5400 D5
Foxwick Ct
500 LSVL 40223 5620 A3
Foxwood Av
800 LSVL 40223 5619 D2
Foxwood Ct
3300 OdmC 40014 5405 A4
Foxwood Dr
- JFVL 47130 5398 B7
5300 OdmC 40014 5405 A4
Foxx Ln
- LSVL 40299 5729 D5
Foxy Poise Rd
2400 SRPK 40220 5618 D5
Frahlich Ln
16200 LSVL 40299 5730 E4
Fran Ct
5500 LSVL 40291 5728 C7
Francell Ct
4700 LSVL 40272 5940 D2
Frances Dr
1300 NALB 47150 5505 E1
Francis Av
- CLKV 47129 5506 C4
6000 OdmC 40014 5513 A4
E Francis Av
100 LSVL 40214 5724 D5
W Francis Av
400 CLKV 47129 5506 C4
Francis Ct
400 JFVL 47130 5507 A6
Francis Dr
1400 JFVL 47130 5506 E5
Franciscan Cir
- LSVL 40205 5616 C7
Franck Av
100 LSVL 40206 5617 A3
Franconia Ct
12100 LSVL 40299 5729 B4
Franelm Rd
1000 LSVL 40214 5833 A4
1100 LSVL 40214 5832 E3
Frank Av
4700 LSVL 40213 5725 E7
11600 DGSH 40243 5620 C4
11600 MDTN 40243 5620 C4
Frank Ln
100 MTWH 40047 6056 C2
Frank St
100 ELZT 42701 6812 C2
100 JFVL 47130 5506 E4
Frank E Simon Av
100 SHDV 40165 6161 C4
Frankfort Av
1400 LSVL 40206 5616 C2
2500 LSVL 40206 5617 C3
3300 LSVL 40207 5617 D3
3400 STMW 40207 5617 D3
Frankfort Av US-60 TRK
1600 LSVL 40206 5616 C2
2500 LSVL 40206 5617 C3
3300 LSVL 40207 5617 D3

STREET Block City ZIP Map# Grid
Frankfort Av US-60 TRK
3400 STMW 40207 5617 D3
Franklin Av
10 JFVL 47130 5506 E4
10 JFVL 47130 5507 A4
100 LGNG 40031 5296 D3
400 ELZT 42701 6812 A4
2200 LSVL 40216 5723 A6
2400 LSVL 40216 5722 E6
3500 LSVL 40213 5725 B3
Franklin Ct
600 RDCF 40160 6593 B1
Franklin Dr
100 NALB 47150 5504 E2
Franklin Ln
10 HdnC 42701 6811 A2
Franklin Sq
600 JFVL 47130 5507 A6
Franklin St
- HdnC 40121 6374 C3
100 MdeC 40108 6264 C4
100 MRGH 40155 6264 C4
200 UTCA 47130 5399 E6
200 UTCA 47130 5400 A6
500 LSVL 40202 5616 A2
500 LSVL 40206 5616 B2
700 RDCF 40160 6593 B2
3800 FydC 47150 5396 D3
Franklin Farmer Wy
6900 LSVL 40229 5945 A3
Frank Ott Rd
6500 FydC 47122 5502 C3
7000 GEOT 47122 5502 C3
Fraser Dr
1700 LSVL 40205 5726 A2
Frazier Rd
300 HdnC 40121 6265 A7
Fraziertown Rd
7500 OdmC 40056 5512 A1
7500 PWEV 40056 5512 B1
Fred Ln
8000 LSVL 40219 5834 D5
Freda Wy
4500 LSVL 40272 5831 D6
Fred Burns Rd
10 HdnC 40160 6592 A3
10 HdnC 40175 6592 A3
2100 HdnC 40162 6592 A6
Frederica Dr
- LSVL 40218 5727 C4
Frederick Av
1400 JFVL 47130 5507 B5
2300 NALB 47150 5505 D2
Frederick Wy
- GEOT 47122 5502 A4
Frederick Stamm Ct
700 LSVL 40217 5724 D3
Fred Works Wy
4100 SVLY 40216 5723 C4
Freedom Wy
- LSVL 40209 5725 A3
3600 LSVL 40229 5944 A1
Freedoms Wy
200 RDCF 40160 6483 C3
Freeman Av
100 LSVL 40214 5833 C1
4200 LSVL 40216 5723 A3
Freeman Green Dr
100 ELZT 42701 6812 A2
Freeman Lake Ln
- ELZT 42701 6703 A5
Freeman Lake Rd
- ELZT 42701 6702 E6
700 ELZT 42701 6703 B7
Freeman Lake Park Rd
10 ELZT 42701 6702 E6
10 ELZT 42701 6703 A6
Fremont Rd
8300 BRMD 40242 5510 B4
Freeport Dr
7300 LSVL 40258 5830 E6
Freestone Ct
3700 LSVL 40218 5727 C4
Frel Rd
4600 LSVL 40272 5831 D7
French Av
800 LSVL 40217 5725 B1
French St
200 ELZT 42701 6812 D1
800 JFVL 47130 5507 A5
E French St
100 ELZT 42701 6812 D1
W French St
100 ELZT 42701 6812 D1
200 ELZT 42701 6703 C7
French Creek Dr
2500 FydC 47150 5613 B3
French Creek Rd
2600 FydC 47150 5613 D3
Frenchrone Dr
11300 LSVL 40272 5939 E4
Frey Dr
5100 LSVL 40219 5835 C2
Freys Hill Rd
2400 LSVL 40223 5511 B6
2500 LSVL 40241 5511 A4
Friar Tuck Ct
3600 LSVL 40219 5835 A1
Friden Wy
4900 LSVL 40214 5723 E7
4900 LSVL 40216 5723 E7
Friend Rd
10100 LSVL 40258 5831 A5
Friendship Dr
7400 PWEV 40056 5512 C3
Friendship Rd
7600 PWEV 40056 5512 C3
Fringe Tree Ct
9900 LSVL 40241 5510 D4
Fringe Tree Pl
3700 LSVL 40241 5510 D4
Frisbee Wy
- LSVL 40214 5833 B2

INDEX 22
Frohlich Rd
Louisville Metro Street Index
Glensford Pl

STREET Block City ZIP Map# Grid

Frohlich Rd
9400 LSVL 40291 5946 B3
N Front St
100 UTCA 47130 5400 A5
S Front St
100 UTCA 47130 5400 A6
Frontier Ct
2800 RDCF 40160 6593 A1
Frontier Dr
7300 ClkC 47172 5397 D2
Frontier Tr
3300 LSVL 40220 5727 C1
Front Nine Dr
100 ELZT 42701 6812 E6
Fruitful Ct
1100 LSVL 40214 5833 A6
Fruitwood Dr
5400 LSVL 40272 5940 B5
Fugate Ln
100 SHDV 40165 6161 A3
Fulfillment Sq
- CTWD 40014 5403 B3
Fulham Ct
1000 HTBN 40222 5619 B6
Fulkerson Dr
- CHAN 47111 5181 C3
Fuller Cir
- LSVL 40206 5617 A3
Full Moon Ct
5900 LSVL 40216 5722 D7
Fulton Dr
2000 ClkC 47111 5181 C1
Fulton St
200 JFVL 47130 5507 A6
500 SLRB 47172 5288 D5
1500 LSVL 40206 5616 B1
Fureen Dr
2500 LSVL 40218 5726 D1
Furlong Dr
8800 LYDN 40242 5619 B1
Furman Blvd
3000 LSVL 40220 5618 A7
3200 LSVL 40220 5727 A1
Fury St
- HdnC 40177 6156 B4
- WPT 40177 6156 B4
Fury Wy
4700 LSVL 40258 5831 D4
Fust Av
1800 LSVL 40216 5723 E1
1800 SVLY 40216 5723 D1
Future Dr
2100 ClkC 47172 5288 C7
Futurity Wy
10100 KNLD 40223 5510 E7

G

G Ct
10 LGNG 40031 5296 E2
G St
- HdnC 40121 6374 C3
Gable Rd
7900 LSVL 40219 5835 A5
Gablewood Cir
300 LSVL 40245 5621 D5
Gablewood Dr
200 LSVL 40245 5621 D5
Gablewood Pl
14500 LSVL 40245 5621 D6
Gabriel Dr
6400 LSVL 40216 5831 C2
6400 LSVL 40258 5831 C2
Gaddie Ct
700 LSVL 40203 5616 A4
Gaffey Hts
100 HdnC 40121 6374 A4
4500 HdnC 40121 6373 E4
Gagel Av
700 LSVL 40214 5723 D7
700 LSVL 40216 5723 D7
1600 SVLY 40216 5723 B6
Gageland Rd
7000 LSVL 40258 5831 D3
Gagnon Ln
- ClkC 47111 5290 B1
7400 ClkC 47111 5181 B7
Gail Ct
1100 JFVL 47130 5507 C2
Gail Dr
1100 JFVL 47130 5507 B2
Gailbreath Av
6100 LSVL 40219 5835 C7
6100 LSVL 40229 5835 C7
Gainesway Ct
2500 LSVL 40245 5622 D1
Gainsborough Ct
7900 LSVL 40291 5837 A5
Gainsborough Dr
8400 LSVL 40291 5837 A5
Gainsborough Rd
- FydC 47150 5504 C4
10 NALB 47150 5504 C4
Gaither Station Rd
100 ELZT 42701 6811 D6
100 HdnC 42701 6811 D6
Gala Ct
100 BltC 40109 6051 E1
Galaxie Dr
5100 LSVL 40258 5831 C2
Galen Ct
5100 FydC 47119 5393 D3
Galene Ct
3200 JFTN 40299 5728 D3
Galene Dr
9000 JFTN 40299 5728 C3
9000 LSVL 40299 5728 C3
Galiger Station Rd
1700 NALB 47150 5504 E7
1700 NALB 47150 5613 E1
Gallagher St
1400 LSVL 40210 5615 A5
Gallant Fox Run
1200 LYDN 40223 5619 C1
Gallant Fox Run
1200 LYDN 40242 5619 C1
Galleon Dr
3000 JFTN 40220 5728 A3
Gallery Pl
600 ELZT 42701 6812 C4
Galloway Ct
2400 LSVL 40245 5512 C7
Gallusser Dr
- LSVL 40272 5941 B3
Galston Blvd
14800 LSVL 40272 5939 D7
15000 LSVL 40272 6048 D1
Galston Ct
1300 HTBN 40222 5619 C7
N Galt Av
100 LSVL 40206 5617 A2
S Galt Av
100 LSVL 40206 5617 A3
Galt St
10 NALB 47150 5505 D4
Galvin Ct
6100 LSVL 40229 5945 A1
Galway Dr
100 BltC 40047 6056 B5
100 MTWH 40047 6056 B5
Galway Ln
3100 GSCK 40242 5510 B4
Galway Cove
- OdmC 40031 5404 B1
Gamay Ln
11600 LSVL 40272 5940 A4
Gambriel Ct
3100 LSVL 40205 5726 B2
Gamekeeper Ct
8600 LSVL 40291 5837 A3
Gamma Ct
1400 CLKV 47129 5506 C1
Gander Dr
3400 JFVL 47130 5398 B6
Gander Branch Lp
- MdeC 40175 6373 C6
Gandy Rd
9700 LSVL 40272 5940 C1
Gant Ct
8400 OdmC 40014 5403 A6
Gap Hollow Rd
3000 FydC 47150 5613 B6
3200 FydC 47150 5612 E5
Garda Dr
4500 LSVL 40219 5726 C7
Garden Ct
1000 JFVL 47130 5507 D3
3600 HBNE 40165 6053 D3
Garden Dr
500 LSVL 40206 5617 C4
5000 HBNE 40165 6053 D3
5300 CTWD 40014 5403 E4
5300 OdmC 40014 5403 E4
9400 JFTN 40299 5728 C4
Garden Wy
- LSVL 40205 5618 A6
Garden Brook Ct
100 ELZT 42701 6702 E4
Garden Creek Cir
1000 LSVL 40223 5619 C2
1100 LSVL 40223 5620 A1
Garden Creek Pl
10600 LSVL 40223 5619 C2
Garden Gate Cir
8600 LSVL 40291 5837 D7
Garden Green Wy
4900 LSVL 40218 5726 D6
Garden Grove Wy
- LSVL 40299 5838 A2
Garden Hill Pl
1300 LSVL 40245 5621 E3
Gardenia Ct
3900 LSVL 40220 5618 C7
Garden Lake Ln
2500 JFTN 40220 5728 B2
Garden Leaf Dr
- LSVL 40241 5510 E2
Garden Pointe Pl
1000 LYDN 40242 5619 A1
Garden Ridge Rd
4200 OdmC 40014 5404 C1
Garden Trace Cir
5700 LSVL 40229 5944 E5
Garden Trace Dr
11200 LSVL 40229 5944 E5
Garden View Ct
7600 LSVL 40220 5727 D3
Gardiner Av
10 LSVL 40206 5617 C3
Gardiner Ct
10 LSVL 40205 5726 B2
Gardiner Ln
1200 WSNP 40213 5725 E3
1400 WSNP 40213 5726 A3
1500 LSVL 40205 5726 B2
1500 WSNP 40218 5726 A3
2700 LSVL 40205 5617 E7
Gardiner Lake Rd
100 LSVL 40205 5726 B2
Gardiner Point Dr
4000 WSNP 40213 5726 A3
Gardiner View Av
4200 LSVL 40213 5725 E3
4200 WSNP 40213 5725 E3
Gardner Av
5300 MdeC 40121 6373 C2
Gardner Blvd
3000 JFVL 47130 5398 C6
Gardner Ct
2600 OdmC 40031 5296 C6
Gardner St
- ELZT 42701 6812 B3
Garey Ln
2900 SVLY 40216 5723 E2
Garfield Av
2200 LSVL 40212 5615 A1
2800 LSVL 40212 5614 E1
3800 LSVL 40212 5505 C7
Garfield St
- HdnC 40121 6265 A7
- HdnC 40121 6374 A1
Garland Av
- LSVL 40203 5615 C4
1800 LSVL 40210 5615 A4
1800 LSVL 40211 5615 A4
2200 LSVL 40210 5614 E4
2200 LSVL 40211 5614 D4
Garlanreid Pl
10200 LSVL 40223 5619 E3
W Garnettsville Rd
100 MdeC 40108 6264 B4
100 MRGH 40155 6264 B4
Garr Av
11800 ANCH 40223 5511 B7
11800 LSVL 40223 5511 B7
Garretson Ln
1600 NALB 47150 5396 E7
1600 NALB 47150 5505 D1
E Garrett St
100 LSVL 40214 5724 D3
W Garrett St
100 LSVL 40214 5724 C3
E Garrettsville Rd
200 MdeC 40155 6264 C3
200 MdeC 40177 6264 C3
200 MRGH 40155 6264 C3
Garrison Ct
400 LSVL 40214 5833 D5
Garrison Dr
1800 CLKV 47129 5397 C7
Garrison Rd
7300 LSVL 40214 5833 D4
Garrow Av
5500 LSVL 40219 5835 A4
Garrow Ct
1000 LSVL 40219 5835 A4
Garrs Ln
- LSVL 40211 5614 C4
2300 SVLY 40216 5723 A4
2400 LSVL 40216 5723 A4
Garry Ct
3000 RDCF 40160 6484 A7
Garvey Ct
4200 LSVL 40216 5723 C5
Garvey Dr
1400 LSVL 40216 5723 D5
Garvin Pl
1000 LSVL 40203 5615 D5
1200 LSVL 40208 5615 D5
Garwood Pl
3800 LSVL 40241 5510 D3
Gary Dr
2100 NALB 47150 5505 A2
Gary Wy
600 LSVL 40118 5833 D7
Garydon Dr
8600 LSVL 40291 5837 A5
Gary Owen Av
2300 HdnC 40121 6374 B1
Gasconade St
- HdnC 40121 6265 D7
Gaskin Ct
5400 LSVL 40229 5944 D5
Gaslight Wy
10300 JFTN 40299 5728 E1
Gast Blvd
2700 LSVL 40205 5617 E6
Gaston Ct
3700 LSVL 40241 5509 D3
Gatecreek Rd
3300 LSVL 40272 5832 B7
Gatehouse Ln
200 DGSH 40243 5620 A4
Gate Run Ct
9700 LSVL 40291 5837 D4
Gate Run Rd
7000 LSVL 40291 5837 D4
Gates Rd
10 ELZT 42701 6811 D3
Gateshead Ct
1000 HTBN 40222 5619 B6
Gateview Cir
3600 LSVL 40272 5832 A7
Gateview Pl
3500 LSVL 40272 5832 A7
Gateway Ct
2100 JFTN 40299 5728 D1
Gateway Dr
300 ELZT 42701 6812 D4
9500 JFTN 40299 5728 D1
Gateway Plz
1400 JFVL 47130 5507 B5
Gatewood Dr
7300 CTWD 40014 5403 C7
7300 OdmC 40014 5403 C7
Gatewood St
4400 LSVL 40215 5724 C4
Gateworth Wy
11700 LSVL 40299 5620 B7
Gathwright Dr
5100 LSVL 40218 5726 D4
Gaudet Ct
10400 JFTN 40299 5728 E6
Gaudet Rd
3900 JFTN 40299 5728 E6
E Gaulbert Av
300 LSVL 40208 5615 D7
W Gaulbert Av
200 LSVL 40208 5615 C6
1700 LSVL 40210 5615 A6
1800 LSVL 40210 5614 E6
2600 LSVL 40211 5614 E6
Gayeway Dr
7700 LSVL 40219 5835 D5
Gayla Ct
600 RDCF 40160 6483 D6
Gayle Dr
6200 LSVL 40219 5835 D2
9000 LSVL 40272 5831 E7
Gaylene Av
100 VNGV 40160 6592 B1
Gaymont Ct
3600 LSVL 40214 5832 A3
Gaymont Dr
7200 LSVL 40214 5832 A4
7200 LSVL 40258 5832 A4
Gaywood Dr
3800 LSVL 40272 5940 E2
3800 LSVL 40272 5941 A2
Geiger St
900 LSVL 40206 5616 B2
Geil Ln
6300 LSVL 40219 5835 B2
Gelding Wy
10 BltC 40109 6052 C3
Gelhaus Rd
6000 LSVL 40299 5838 B3
Gemini Wy
12100 MDTN 40243 5620 D3
Gemma Cir
10 ELZT 42701 6703 C5
Gemma Dr
500 ELZT 42701 6703 C5
Gene St
100 BltC 40047 6056 B2
100 MTWH 40047 6056 B2
Gene Paulin Wy
- LSVL 40118 5833 E7
General Ln
5100 LSVL 40218 5726 D6
Gene Snyder Frwy
- LSVL - 5400 E7
- LSVL - 5509 E1
- LSVL - 5510 D2
- LSVL - 5511 B4
- LSVL - 5512 A5
- LSVL - 5621 B3
- LSVL - 5729 E7
- LSVL - 5730 A2
- LSVL - 5832 E7
- LSVL - 5833 C7
- LSVL - 5834 A7
- LSVL - 5835 E7
- LSVL - 5836 B7
- LSVL - 5837 B5
- LSVL - 5838 C3
- LSVL - 5940 B4
- LSVL - 5941 A3
- LSVL - 5943 C1
- LSVL - 5944 A1
- MDTN - 5621 B6
- MLHT - 5834 A7
- PROS - 5400 D7
Gene Snyder Frwy I-265
- LSVL - 5510 A1
- LSVL - 5511 B4
- LSVL - 5512 A5
- LSVL - 5621 B3
- LSVL - 5729 E7
- LSVL - 5730 A2
- LSVL - 5835 E7
- LSVL - 5836 B7
- LSVL - 5837 A6
- LSVL - 5838 C3
- LSVL - 5944 A1
- MDTN - 5621 B6
Gene Snyder Frwy SR-841
- LSVL - 5400 D7
- LSVL - 5509 E1
- LSVL - 5510 D2
- LSVL - 5511 E5
- LSVL - 5512 A5
- LSVL - 5621 B3
- LSVL - 5729 E7
- LSVL - 5730 A2
- LSVL - 5832 E7
- LSVL - 5833 C7
- LSVL - 5834 A7
- LSVL - 5835 E7
- LSVL - 5836 B7
- LSVL - 5837 A6
- LSVL - 5838 C3
- LSVL - 5940 B4
- LSVL - 5941 A3
- LSVL - 5943 E1
- LSVL - 5944 A1
- MDTN - 5621 B3
- MLHT - 5834 A7
- PROS - 5400 D7
Geneva Cir
- OdmC 40014 5402 B5
Geneva Rd
7300 OdmC 40014 5403 A7
7300 OdmC 40014 5512 B1
Geneva Wy
9300 LSVL 40291 5728 C7
Genny Ct
5600 LSVL 40214 5833 B4
Genrose Dr
10 HdnC 40162 6592 A7
Gentry Ln
- BltC 40047 6055 A4
100 BltC 40047 6054 E3
8500 LSVL 40291 5837 C7
Genung Dr
1300 NALB 47150 5505 D1
Geoghegan St
1100 WPT 40177 6156 B3
George Ernst Wy
- LSVL 40217 5616 A7
George Rogers Clark Pl
2500 LSVL 40206 5617 A3
George Rogers Clark Mem Br
- CLKV 47129 5506 E7
- CLKV 47129 5615 E2
- JFVL 47130 5506 E7
- JFVL 47130 5615 E2
- LSVL 40202 5615 E2
George R Clark Mem Br US-31
- CLKV 47129 5506 E7
- CLKV 47129 5615 E2
- JFVL 47130 5506 E7
- JFVL 47130 5615 E2
George R Clark Mem Br US-31
- LSVL 40202 5615 E2
Georges Hill Rd NE
5200 HsnC 47122 5501 B6
Georgetown Cir
3400 LSVL 40215 5723 E4
Georgetown Pl
3500 LSVL 40215 5723 E4
Georgetown Rd
400 HdnC 42701 6811 B4
Georgetown-Greenville Rd
- GNVL 47124 5283 B7
Georgetown-Lanesville Rd
10 FydC 47122 5501 E6
10 HsnC 47112 5501 E7
1200 GEOT 47122 5501 E4
Georgia
- HdnC 40121 6374 C3
Georgia Av
9600 MTWH 40047 6056 A2
Georgia Ln
200 ELZT 42701 6702 E3
5300 LSVL 40219 5835 D3
Georgia Wy
500 MTWH 40047 6056 A2
Georgia Crossing Sub
- ClkC 47130 5398 C3
Georgian Av
600 SLRB 47172 5288 C3
Georgian Wy
3100 JFVL 47130 5398 C7
Georgiana Dr
500 FydC 47150 5613 D1
500 NALB 47150 5504 D7
500 NALB 47150 5613 D1
Georgie Ct
1000 OdmC 40014 5405 E1
Georgie Wy
3600 OdmC 40014 5296 E7
3700 OdmC 40014 5405 E1
Gerald Av
7500 LSVL 40258 5831 D4
Gerald Ct
2200 LSVL 40218 5726 E3
Gerald Dr
600 CLKV 47129 5506 D2
3000 LSVL 40216 5723 B2
9600 LSVL 40118 5942 A1
Gerber Av
7100 LSVL 40214 5833 C3
Gernert Ct
400 LSVL 40208 5615 E7
400 LSVL 40217 5615 E7
Geronimo Cir
10 HdnC 40175 6482 D4
Gerrard Ct
10 ELZT 42701 6812 B4
Gheens Av
200 LSVL 40214 5724 C7
700 LSVL 40214 5833 B1
Gheens Mill Rd
6200 ClkC 47130 5398 A3
Ghentwood Row
10400 BRMR 40223 5619 E3
Gibraltar Dr
4200 JFTN 40299 5728 E6
Gibralter Dr
10 BltC 40165 6053 C7
10 BltC 40165 6162 C1
Gibson Ln
3800 LSVL 40211 5614 B5
Gibson Rd
100 RHLN 40207 5618 B3
Gilberto
10 MdeC 40175 6482 B4
Gildcrest Wy
3800 JFTN 40299 5728 E4
Gilkey Lp
5600 MdeC 40121 6373 D1
Gilkey St
5400 MdeC 40121 6373 D1
Gillette Av
100 LSVL 40214 5724 D5
1800 SVLY 40216 5723 D2
Gilligan St
2100 LSVL 40203 5615 A1
2400 LSVL 40212 5615 A1
2500 LSVL 40212 5506 B7
3300 LSVL 40212 5505 D7
Gilliland Rd
100 LSVL 40245 5622 B7
300 LSVL 40245 5731 A1
1100 LSVL 40245 5730 E1
Gills Ct
4400 LSVL 40219 5835 B7
Gilman Av
3900 STMW 40207 5617 E2
4000 CYWV 40207 5617 E2
4000 CYWV 40207 5618 A2
4000 STMW 40207 5618 A2
Gilmore Av
400 JFVL 47130 5507 C5
Gilmore Ln
1200 LSVL 40213 5725 D6
1200 LYNV 40213 5725 D6
1300 LSVL 40218 5725 D6
Gilmore Industrial Blvd
3300 LSVL 40213 5725 E6
Gilmore Industrial Ct
5000 LSVL 40213 5725 E6
Gilola Av
1900 ClkC 47129 5397 D1
1900 ClkC 47172 5397 D1
1900 CLKV 47129 5397 D1
Gilpin Pl
9700 HTBN 40222 5619 C4
Giltner Ln
1900 CLKV 47129 5397 D6
Gina
- SHDV 40165 6161 A6
Gina Dr
10300 LSVL 40223 5511 A7
10300 LYDN 40223 5510 E7
10300 LYDN 40223 5511 A7
Ginev Wy
4900 LSVL 40219 5835 D5
Ginger Rd
11200 LSVL 40229 5944 D5
Gingerwood Ct
1400 ClkC 47129 5397 B7
1400 CLKV 47129 5397 B7
Gingerwood Dr
4000 LSVL 40220 5727 C3
Girard Ct
1000 STMW 40222 5618 D1
Girard Dr
800 STMW 40222 5618 D1
1100 GYDL 40222 5618 D1
1300 GYDL 40222 5509 D7
2800 LSVL 40213 5834 D2
Girvan Av
13300 LSVL 40272 6048 C1
Gisela Ct
10400 LSVL 40118 5942 C3
Givhan Dr
1100 SHDV 40165 6161 D4
Gladden Dr
3400 LSVL 40218 5726 C3
3500 WBHL 40218 5726 C3
Gladstonberry Pl
8800 LSVL 40258 5831 A6
Gladstone Av
2100 LSVL 40205 5726 B1
2300 KGLY 40205 5617 C7
2300 LSVL 40205 5617 C7
2300 SMRG 40205 5617 C7
Gladys Rd
6900 LSVL 40219 5835 A3
Glaser Ln
7500 LSVL 40228 5836 D4
7500 LSVL 40291 5836 D4
8300 LSVL 40291 5837 A4
Glasgow Blvd
10000 LSVL 40241 5510 E1
Glasslipper Ct
9100 LSVL 40229 5944 E1
Glass Overlook Rd SE
10900 HsnC 47117 5830 A6
12300 HsnC 47117 5939 B1
Glastonburg Ln
6600 LSVL 40291 5837 C2
Gleam Dr
800 LSVL 40214 5833 A5
Gleeson Ln
2600 JFTN 40299 5728 C2
3000 JFTN 40220 5728 B3
Glen Ct
600 LSVL 40207 5617 A1
Glen Rd
300 MDTN 40243 5620 C5
Glenabbey
2200 JFVL 47130 5507 A1
Glen Abbey Dr
10100 LSVL 40291 5837 D6
Glenafton Ln
2900 LSVL 40217 5725 B2
Glen Arbor Rd
7100 GYDL 40222 5509 D6
7300 BCFT 40222 5509 D7
Glen Arden Rd
10 GNVW 40222 5509 A3
Glenarm Rd
3900 OdmC 40014 5403 B1
4800 OdmC 40014 5404 A3
Glenawyn Cir
9600 JFTN 40299 5728 C3
Glenbarr Ct
10900 DGSH 40243 5620 A5
Glenbarr Pl
800 DGSH 40243 5620 A5
Glen Bluff Ln
3900 GNVW 40222 5509 B2
Glen Bluff Rd
- LSVL 40222 5509 B2
3700 GNVW 40222 5509 B2
Glenbrook E
4200 FydC 47150 5396 D1
Glenbrook W
4200 FydC 47150 5396 D1
Glenbrook Av
6500 LSVL 40216 5722 A4
Glenbrook Ct
4200 FydC 47150 5396 D2
Glenbrook Rd
800 ANCH 40223 5620 D2
800 MDTN 40223 5620 D2
Glenbrook Rd SR-146
- ANCH 40223 5620 D1
Glenbrook Park Dr
1500 ClkC 47130 5399 D5
1500 UTCA 47130 5399 D5
Glen Cir Dr
500 ELZT 42701 6812 C4
Glencony Ct
10500 LSVL 40291 5837 E7
Glen Cove Rd
5100 OdmC 40031 5295 B5
Glencove Wy
- INHC 40207 5509 A6
2000 LSVL 40207 5509 A6
2000 RBNW 40207 5509 A5
2100 RBNW 40207 5508 E5
Glencreek Ln
3600 LSVL 40218 5726 E2
3600 LSVL 40218 5727 A2
Glencrest Av
500 ELZT 42701 6812 C4
Glencrest Dr
5300 GNVW 40222 5509 A2
Glencroft Dr
6600 OdmC 40014 5403 B7
Glenda Ct
9900 LSVL 40223 5619 D2
Glendale Av
3400 LSVL 40215 5723 E3
Glendale Dr
100 CHAN 47111 5181 D1
Glendale Rd
6400 LSVL 40291 5837 A3
6800 LSVL 40291 5836 E4
Glendale Trc
8400 LSVL 40291 5836 E3
8400 LSVL 40291 5837 A3
Glendora Av
200 LSVL 40212 5614 B2
Glendower Dr
14100 LSVL 40245 5621 D6
Gleneagle Ct
800 LSVL 40223 5620 A2
Glen Eagle Dr
2300 NHFD 40222 5509 C5
Gleneagle Pl
10600 LSVL 40223 5620 A2
Gleneagles Ln
7300 FydC 47122 5393 D5
W Gleneagles Wy
1800 LGNG 40031 5297 B5
1800 OdmC 40031 5297 B5
Glen Echo Pl
7100 LSVL 40258 5830 E4
Glen Ellen Rd
10 LSVL 40118 5942 C1
Glen Falls Ct
8100 LSVL 40291 5837 E6
Glenfield Ct
3600 LSVL 40241 5510 B3
Glenfield Wy
8600 BRMD 40242 5510 B3
8600 LSVL 40241 5510 B3
Glengarry Ct
9900 LSVL 40118 5834 A7
Glengarry Dr
800 LSVL 40118 5833 E7
1200 LSVL 40118 5834 A7
Glengyle Av
3600 WBHL 40218 5726 C4
Glenhill Ct
2900 GNVH 40222 5509 B4
3000 OdmC 40059 5292 A6
Glen Hill Rd
6000 GNVH 40222 5509 B4
6200 LSVL 40222 5509 B4
Glen Hill Manor Dr
4100 LSVL 40272 5940 C4
Glen Hollow Dr
800 LSVL 40214 5833 B3
Glenhope Dr
8600 LSVL 40291 5837 E7
Glenhurst Av
4000 SVLY 40216 5723 C4
Glenhurst Cir
2900 OdmC 40031 5296 D6
Glenlake Wy
1100 LSVL 40245 5621 C2
Glenlea Wy
3700 JFTN 40299 5728 D4
Glen Maple Ct
6000 OdmC 40014 5404 A3
Glenmary Av
2200 LSVL 40204 5616 D5
Glenmary St
200 ELZT 42701 6812 B2
Glenmary Farm Ct
7900 LSVL 40291 5837 D6
Glenmary Farm Dr
10100 LSVL 40291 5837 D6
Glenmary Village Blvd
- LSVL 40291 5946 E2
Glenmeade Rd
3700 LSVL 40218 5727 A2
Glen Meadow Rd
10000 LSVL 40241 5510 E2
Glen Mill Rd
10 FydC 47150 5395 E7
10 NALB 47150 5395 E7
10 NALB 47150 5396 A7
10 NALB 47150 5504 E1
Glenmore Dr
8400 LSVL 40258 5830 D5
Glenn Al
- LSVL 40203 5615 E4
Glenna Wy
4500 LSVL 40219 5835 C3
Glenn Frick Farm Rd
100 BltC 40165 5945 A7
Glennview Pl
1700 SVLY 40216 5723 E1
Glen Oak Dr
3700 LSVL 40218 5727 A2
Glen Park Rd
5800 GNVW 40222 5509 B3
5800 LSVL 40222 5509 B3
Glen Pointe Rd
8700 BKPT 40241 5510 C4
8700 BKPT 40242 5510 C4
8700 GSCK 40242 5510 C4
Glenridge Ct
8500 LYDN 40242 5619 B2
Glenridge Dr
1000 LYDN 40242 5619 B1
Glenridge Park Pl
6500 NHFD 40222 5509 C5
Glen Riesert Dr
- GNVL 47124 5283 D6
Glenrock Rd
1500 LSVL 40214 5723 E7
1500 LSVL 40216 5723 D7
Glen Rose Ct
10100 LSVL 40229 5944 D1
Glen Rose Rd
4600 LSVL 40229 5944 C1
4900 LSVL 40219 5835 E7
4900 LSVL 40229 5835 E7
Glensford Dr
400 LSVL 40245 5621 C4
Glensford Pl
14300 LSVL 40245 5621 C4

INDEX 23
Glenside Pl
Louisville Metro Street Index
Gum St

STREET
Block City ZIP Map# Grid

Glenside Pl
3800 LSVL 40213 5725 D2
Glenstone Ct
3200 JFTN 40220 5728 B3
Glen Trace Ln
9500 LSVL 40291 5946 E2
Glen Valley Rd
3900 LSVL 40219 5835 A1
Glenview Av
2000 NHFD 40222 5509 B5
2200 GNVM 40222 5509 B5
2300 LSVL 40222 5509 B5
3400 GNVH 40222 5509 B4
3400 GNVW 40222 5509 A3
Glenview Dr
2000 ELZT 42701 6703 D6
Glenview Hts
400 FydC 47150 5504 D1
400 NALB 47150 5504 D1
600 FydC 47150 5395 D7
Glenview Rd
100 HLVW 40229 5944 A7
Glenview Heights Rd
100 NALB 47150 5504 E1
100 NALB 47150 5505 A2
Glenway Ct
8200 LSVL 40291 5837 D5
Glenway Pl
10800 LSVL 40291 5837 D5
Glenwillow Wy
3700 JFTN 40299 5728 C5
Glenwood Av
300 VNGV 40175 6482 C7
7400 OdmC 40014 5511 E1
7400 OdmC 40014 5512 A1
E Glenwood Cir
8600 MLHT 40219 5834 C7
W Glenwood Cir
8500 MLHT 40219 5834 C7
Glenwood Ct
2500 NALB 47150 5505 E3
Glenwood Dr
900 RDCF 40160 6483 B4
Glenwood Pk
2500 NALB 47150 5505 E3
Glenwood Rd
6400 GNVM 40222 5509 C4
6400 LSVL 40222 5509 C4
Glenworth Av
2000 LSVL 40218 5726 D3
Glimmer Wy
8100 LSVL 40214 5833 B5
Glissade Dr
100 LSVL 40118 5942 C1
Global Dr
7000 LSVL 40258 5830 D4
Globe St
200 RDCF 40160 6483 B2
Glo Jean Wy
6500 LSVL 40258 5722 A7
Gloria Ln
5900 LSVL 40213 5834 E1
Gloria Dei Dr
- ELZT 42701 6702 E5
Glory Woods Ct
3700 FydC 47150 5396 D3
Gloucester Rd
4000 STMW 40207 5618 A4
Glover Ln
9000 WWOD 40242 5510 C6
9100 RLGH 40242 5510 C6
Gloxinia Dr
8100 LSVL 40258 5831 A5
Glyndon Wy
5300 LSVL 40272 5940 B3
Goalby Dr
6200 LSVL 40258 5831 A4
Goddard Av
1300 LSVL 40204 5616 C6
Godfrey Av
300 LSVL 40206 5617 B3
Goepper Ln
4700 LSVL 40258 5831 D2
Goff Ln
11800 LSVL 40118 5941 E5
11800 LSVL 40118 5942 A5
Goffner Ct
4400 LSVL 40218 5726 C5
Gofton Ct
100 HLVW 40229 5944 B7
Going Ct
10300 LSVL 40241 5511 A2
Golden Dr
10700 LSVL 40272 5940 C3
Golden Crest Dr
4500 JFVL 47130 5398 C4
Goldeneye Ct
2500 JFVL 47130 5398 C7
Golden Gate Ct
400 DGSH 40243 5620 C5
Golden Leaf Pl
14600 LSVL 40245 5621 D2
Golden Leaf Wy
1600 LSVL 40245 5621 D2
Golden Light Ct
11700 LSVL 40272 5939 E1
Golden Maple Pl
10800 LSVL 40223 5620 A2
Golden Maple Cove
1000 LSVL 40223 5620 A2
Golden Oak Ct
4100 FydC 47150 5396 C2
Golden Park Ct
2000 LSVL 40218 5727 A5
Goldenrod Ct
5400 BltC 40165 6054 B2
Goldenrod Rd
5500 LSVL 40272 5831 A7
Golden Rule Wy
- LSVL 40203 5615 D4
Golden Springs Ct
1300 STMW 40205 5618 A6
Golden Talon Lp
- HdnC 40121 6374 C1
Goldsmith Ln
1900 LSVL 40218 5726 B3
1900 WSNP 40218 5726 B3
2600 LSVL 40220 5726 E1
3500 LSVL 40220 5727 A2
3600 LSVL 40218 5727 A2
Goldstein Ln
3800 LSVL 40272 5940 E2
Goldtree Ct
3200 LSVL 40220 5727 E3
Gold Vault Rd
100 HdnC 40121 6374 C3
Golf Dr
- LSVL 40214 5833 B1
Golf Hill Dr
1500 JFVL 47130 5507 A1
Golfland Ct
4300 FydC 47119 5394 E7
Golford Ct
- ClkC 47129 5506 B1
- CLKV 47129 5506 B1
Golfview Ct
- OdmC 40031 5295 C4
Gonewind Ct
8900 LSVL 40299 5728 B4
Gonewind Dr
3400 LSVL 40299 5728 B4
Good Ct
100 MTWH 40047 6056 D2
Good Samaritan Wy
3500 JFTN 40299 5728 E3
Goose Creek Ct
10 SpnC 40071 6057 E3
Goose Creek Rd
10 SpnC 40071 6057 D5
2700 MWVL 40242 5510 D6
2700 RLGH 40242 5510 D6
2800 LSVL 40241 5510 C4
2800 LSVL 40242 5510 D5
2800 RLGH 40241 5510 D5
2900 LDNP 40241 5510 C5
2900 MYHL 40241 5510 C4
2900 TNBK 40241 5510 C4
3100 BKPT 40241 5510 C4
3100 BKPT 40242 5510 C4
3100 GSCK 40241 5510 C4
3100 GSCK 40242 5510 C4
3300 BRMD 40242 5510 C4
3400 BWNF 40241 5510 C4
Gordon Dr
100 BltC 40047 6055 E6
500 MTWH 40047 6055 D6
Gordon Ln
100 NALB 47150 5505 A1
Gordon Rd
4500 LSVL 40219 5835 C1
Gorham Ct
8700 LSVL 40291 5837 A4
Gorham Wy
6900 LSVL 40291 5837 A4
Goshawk Ct
4500 LSVL 40241 5511 B2
Goshen Ln
- OdmC 44026 5292 C1
Gosling Ct
3500 JFVL 47130 5398 C6
Gospel Rd
200 CHAN 47111 5181 C3
200 ClkC 47111 5181 C3
Gospel Kingdom Rd
- BltC 40165 6160 A1
Goss Av
- LSVL 40203 5616 A6
900 LSVL 40204 5616 A6
900 LSVL 40217 5616 A6
Goss Av SR-864
- LSVL 40203 5616 A6
900 LSVL 40204 5616 A6
1200 LSVL 40217 5616 B7
Gothic Ct
4400 JFTN 40299 5728 C6
Goullon Ct
700 LSVL 40204 5616 A4
Governors Ct
100 ELZT 42701 6812 A1
Governours Wy
5300 LSVL 40291 5728 A7
Goyne Av
500 JFVL 47130 5507 D4
Grable Ct
1300 NALB 47150 5505 E1
Grace
- ELZT 42701 6812 B4
Graceland Wy
10 JFVL 47130 5508 A3
Grace Peak Rd
10 HdnC 42701 6702 B4
Grade Ln
- MLHT 40219 5834 A6
700 LSVL 40219 5834 A3
1000 LSVL 40213 5725 C7
7200 LSVL 40219 5834 A4
Grady Av
3800 LSVL 40211 5614 B6
Graf Dr
3900 LSVL 40218 5727 C3
3900 LSVL 40220 5727 C3
Grafton Hall Rd
10300 LSVL 40272 5940 C3
Grafs Ct
11500 JFTN 40299 5729 B3
11500 LSVL 40299 5729 B3
Graham Av
100 RDCF 40160 6483 E6
2700 LSVL 40206 5617 A3
Graham Rd
3500 BFLD 40207 5617 E4
3500 LSVL 40207 5617 E4
3600 BFLD 40207 5618 A4
3600 STMW 40207 5618 A4
Graham St
200 JFVL 47130 5507 B6
Granada Ct
9600 LSVL 40272 5940 D1
Granada Dr
4700 LSVL 40272 5940 D1
Granbury Pl
9800 LSVL 40241 5510 D4
Grand Av
1300 NALB 47150 5504 E5
1800 LSVL 40210 5615 A4
2200 LSVL 40210 5614 E4
2600 LSVL 40211 5614 D4
10100 JFTN 40299 5728 E3
Grand Av Ct
- LSVL 40211 5614 D4
Grand Cascade Dr
7800 LSVL 40228 5836 D5
Grand Cypress Ct
10100 LSVL 40291 5837 C7
Grand Dell Dr
- OdmC 40014 5297 D7
Grandel Blvd
5400 LSVL 40258 5831 B2
Grandel Pl
8200 LSVL 40258 5831 C2
Grandel Meadow Ct
5900 LSVL 40258 5831 C2
Grandel Point Ct
6000 LSVL 40258 5831 B2
Grandfield Rd
6700 LSVL 40258 5831 B2
Grandfield Wy
8200 LSVL 40258 5831 B2
Grandin Woods Ct
1500 JFTN 40299 5620 A7
Grandin Woods Rd
- LSVL 40299 5620 A7
9700 JFTN 40299 5620 A7
Grand Isle Wy
7300 PROS 40059 5400 E7
Grandloop Dr
100 BltC 40047 6055 C7
Grandmeadow Ln
7900 LSVL 40258 5831 B2
Grand Neptune Dr
8500 LSVL 40228 5836 D5
Grand Oak Ct
12500 LSVL 40299 5729 C7
Grand Point Ct
9000 LSVL 40214 5832 D4
Grand Ridge Ct
8800 LSVL 40214 5832 E4
Grand Ridge Rd
1800 LSVL 40214 5832 D4
Grandstand Ct
9300 LSVL 40291 5728 A7
Grand Trevi Dr
8300 LSVL 40228 5836 D5
Grandview Av
3300 LSVL 40207 5617 E4
3300 STMW 40207 5617 E4
3900 LSVL 40207 5618 A3
3900 STMW 40207 5618 A3
Grandview Ct
1400 LGNG 40031 5297 A4
1400 OdmC 40031 5297 A4
Grandview Dr
- FydC 47150 5504 B2
10 JFVL 47130 5508 B3
100 SHDV 40165 6162 A2
2000 FydC 47119 5504 B2
4500 SVLY 40216 5723 B6
4600 LSVL 40216 5723 A6
Grandview Dr NE
2100 LNVL 47136 5610 D5
Grand View Wy
- BltC 40165 6052 A6
Grand Villa Dr
1700 OdmC 40031 5295 B5
Grand Vista Ct
11600 DGSH 40243 5620 B5
Grand Vista Pl
500 DGSH 40243 5620 C5
Grandwood Ln
8200 LSVL 40258 5831 C2
Grand Wood Wy
4300 OdmC 40014 5297 D7
Grange Dr
900 OdmC 40031 5297 B4
1300 LGNG 40031 5297 B4
Granger Rd
2000 LSVL 40118 5943 B3
Granite Av
100 BltC 40165 6161 D1
Granite Dr
800 LYDN 40223 5510 E7
Grannel Ct
3500 LSVL 40214 5832 A4
Grannel Rd
7300 LSVL 40214 5832 B4
Granny Smith Ct
8700 LSVL 40228 5836 C6
Grant Av
- LSVL 40214 5833 B1
- OdmC 40014 5403 A7
- OdmC 40014 5512 A1
600 LYDN 40222 5619 A2
3100 LSVL 40214 5724 D3
Grant Cir
700 ELZT 42701 6703 C6
Grant Ct
- BltC 40047 6054 E6
100 MTWH 40047 6055 E1
Grant Dr
100 MTWH 40047 6056 A2
Grant St
- HdnC 40121 6265 A7
600 HdnC 40121 6374 A1
1400 NALB 47150 5505 C4
Grantham Ct
1800 CSGT 40222 5509 C6
Grantham Pl
4800 CSGT 40222 5509 C6
Grant Line Ctr
100 NALB 47150 5396 B7
Grant Line Rd
1400 NALB 47150 5505 B2
2800 NALB 47150 5396 B7
4100 FydC 47150 5396 C2
5400 FydC 47119 5287 D4
5400 FydC 47150 5287 D4
5700 FydC 47172 5287 D4
7600 ClkC 47143 5287 D3
Grant Line Rd SR-111
2100 NALB 47150 5505 B2
2800 NALB 47150 5396 B7
4100 FydC 47150 5396 C2
5400 FydC 47119 5287 D4
5400 FydC 47150 5287 D4
5700 FydC 47172 5287 D4
7600 ClkC 47143 5287 D3
Granton Ct
- LSVL 40245 5622 C1
Grantown Pl
200 DGSH 40243 5620 B6
Grant Run Rd
9900 LSVL 40229 5944 D2
Grantswood Ct
3500 LSVL 40213 5725 D1
Granvil Dr
100 LSVL 40218 5727 C4
Granville Wy
2500 LSVL 40216 5722 D6
Granwyn Ct
8200 LSVL 40258 5831 C2
Grape St
10400 JFTN 40299 5728 E4
Grape Arbor Dr
10700 LSVL 40272 5831 E7
Grasmere Dr
400 CLKV 47129 5506 C2
2000 LSVL 40205 5617 A6
Grasmere Ter
- LSVL 40205 5617 B6
Grassland Av
10 HdnC 40162 6702 B2
Grassland Dr
2500 JFTN 40299 5728 E2
Grassy Ct
10600 LSVL 40241 5511 A2
Grassy Fk
1300 WDYH 40207 5509 B7
Graston Av
4700 LSVL 40216 5723 A7
4700 SVLY 40216 5723 A7
Graston Ct
5100 LSVL 40216 5723 A7
Graves Rd
5200 ClkC 47130 5398 A4
Graves End Dr
300 LSVL 40203 5615 B2
Gray Ln
7200 LSVL 40258 5830 E3
Gray St
100 ELZT 42701 6702 E6
E Gray St
100 LSVL 40202 5615 E3
500 LSVL 40202 5616 A4
800 LSVL 40204 5616 A4
E Gray St SR-864
800 LSVL 40202 5616 A4
800 LSVL 40204 5616 A4
Graybrook Ln
200 NALB 47150 5505 B3
Gray Fox Dr
3600 FydC 47150 5396 D4
Gray Fox Rd
2300 LSVL 40205 5617 A5
Grayhamton Vine Grove Rd
- MdeC 40175 6482 A6
Graymoor Rd
6800 GYDL 40222 5509 C7
Grays Rd
100 ELZT 42701 6702 D4
Grayson Ct
5900 GNVH 40222 5509 B4
5900 LSVL 40222 5509 B4
Grazing Ct
10400 JFTN 40223 5619 E6
Grazing Trc
10400 JFTN 40223 5619 E6
Grazing Meadows Ln
1000 LSVL 40245 5622 E3
Grazing Trace Ct
100 BltC 40047 5947 A7
Great Hunter Ct
5300 LSVL 40229 5944 E2
Grecian Ct
4800 LSVL 40272 5940 C3
Grecian Rd
10500 LSVL 40272 5940 D3
Green Al
700 CHAN 47111 5181 D5
1800 LSVL 40203 5615 A2
2000 LSVL 40212 5615 A2
2400 LSVL 40212 5614 E2
Green Row
800 FydC 47136 5502 C7
Green St
300 NALB 47150 5505 D4
1700 JFVL 47130 5506 E5
Green Acre Dr
- LSVL 40219 5835 D1
Green Acres Dr
5500 LSVL 40216 5722 A6
5500 LSVL 40258 5722 A6
5500 LSVL 40258 5721 E7
Green Ash Ct
11200 LSVL 40229 5944 C5
Green Ash Ln
4800 LSVL 40229 5944 B5
Greenaway Pl
1100 NALB 47150 5505 C4
Greenbelt Hwy
- LSVL 40258 5831 A1
- LSVL 40272 5830 D7
- LSVL 40272 5939 D3
- LSVL 40272 5940 A4
5500 LSVL 40216 5722 A7
5500 LSVL 40258 5722 A7
8400 LSVL 40258 5830 D7
Greenbelt Hwy SR-1934
- LSVL 40258 5831 A1
- LSVL 40272 5830 D7
- LSVL 40272 5939 D3
- LSVL 40272 5940 A4
5500 LSVL 40216 5722 A7
5500 LSVL 40258 5722 A7
8400 LSVL 40258 5830 D7
Greenbriar Av
300 VNGV 40175 6482 C7
Greenbriar Ct
100 BltC 40047 6055 E2
1600 JFVL 47130 5507 A1
8600 BRWD 40242 5510 B7
Greenbriar Ln
100 HLVW 40229 5944 B6
Green Briar Rd
1400 BltC 40047 6055 D3
1400 MTWH 40047 6055 D3
Greenbriar Rd
4400 WDYH 40207 5509 D5
4400 WDYH 40207 5618 B1
Greenbrier Dr
100 NALB 47150 5504 D2
100 NALB 47150 5505 A2
Green Brier Rd
100 BltC 40047 6055 C4
100 MTWH 40047 6055 B5
Green Brier Rd SR-2706
100 BltC 40047 6055 C4
100 MTWH 40047 6055 B5
Greenbrook Ct
4000 LSVL 40220 5727 E4
Green Cove Cir
5100 LSVL 40218 5726 D6
Green Creek Ct
7700 LSVL 40258 5830 E3
Green Creek Pl
7000 LSVL 40258 5830 E3
Greendale Dr
100 NALB 47150 5396 A7
3100 LSVL 40216 5722 D5
Greene Wy
2300 JFTN 40220 5728 A1
Greenfield Av
7600 LSVL 40214 5833 A4
Greenfield Cir
10 BltC 40047 5946 E7
10 BltC 40047 5947 A7
Greenfield Ct
3800 FydC 47150 5396 D3
Greenfield Dr
3500 FydC 47150 5396 C4
Greenfield Park Rd
8800 LSVL 40258 5831 A6
Greenfield Woods Cir
10100 LSVL 40258 5831 A5
Green Garden Ct
9000 JFTN 40220 5728 B3
9000 JFTN 40299 5728 B3
Greengate Ct
7100 GNSP 40241 5509 E1
Greengate Pl
7100 GNSP 40241 5509 E1
Green Glade Ln
9300 LSVL 40241 5510 D3
Green Hill Ct
10 NALB 47150 5395 E7
Green Hill Dr
2700 JFVL 47130 5506 E2
Greenhill Dr NE
2000 HsnC 47136 5610 C5
2000 LNVL 47136 5610 C5
Green Hill Ln
3300 LSVL 40207 5617 C1
Greenhill St
200 VNGV 40175 6591 C1
Greenhurst Ct
8000 LSVL 40299 5727 E5
Greenhurst Dr
- LSVL 40299 5728 A4
3800 LSVL 40299 5727 E4
Greenlawn Dr
100 NALB 47150 5396 A7
Greenlawn Rd
6700 GYDL 40222 5509 C7
6900 LSVL 40222 5509 C7
7300 BCFT 40222 5509 E6
7500 BCFT 40242 5509 E5
7500 LSVL 40242 5509 D6
7700 LSVL 40241 5509 D6
Greenleaf Dr
800 NALB 47150 5504 D3
Greenleaf Rd
900 LSVL 40213 5725 B2
4100 ClkC 47172 5288 E3
4100 SLRB 47172 5288 E3
4600 ClkC 47172 5289 A2
Greenleaves Dr
1600 JFVL 47130 5507 A1
Greenlief Rd
5200 ClkC 47111 5289 B2
Green Manor Dr
6000 LSVL 40219 5836 A3
6000 LSVL 40228 5836 A3
Green Meadow Cir
6800 WLNP 40207 5618 C2
Green Meadow Ct
6700 WLNP 40207 5618 C2
Green Meadows Dr
3600 LSVL 40218 5726 E3
Greenmere Blvd
6900 PROS 40059 5400 D3
Greenmoore Dr
8900 LSVL 40258 5831 A6
Green Oak Dr
7100 LSVL 40258 5721 E7
7100 LSVL 40258 5722 A7
Greenock Ct
11000 DGSH 40243 5620 B5
Green Park Ct
8000 LSVL 40258 5831 A4
Green Pine Ct
4300 LSVL 40220 5618 E7
Green Pine Dr
4400 LSVL 40220 5618 E7
Greenridge Ln
700 LSVL 40207 5508 A7
700 LSVL 40207 5617 B2
Greensbrook Pl
1600 LSVL 40245 5621 E2
Green Springdale Rd
7000 GNSP 40241 5509 D1
7000 LSVL 40059 5509 D1
7000 LSVL 40241 5509 D1
Greenspur Ln
800 LSVL 40207 5508 A7
Greensward Pl
5900 OdmC 40014 5403 E3
5900 OdmC 40014 5404 A2
Greentree N
2100 CLKV 47129 5397 C6
Greentree Blvd
1400 CLKV 47129 5506 D1
1500 CLKV 47129 5397 C6
Greentree Blvd N
2000 CLKV 47129 5397 C6
Green Tree Ln
10300 LSVL 40272 5940 B2
Greentree Rd
- BltC 40047 6056 A4
- MTWH 40047 6056 A4
Greenup Rd
3000 ANPK 40213 5725 B2
3000 LSVL 40217 5725 B1
Greenvale Cir
4800 LSVL 40272 5940 C2
Greenvalley Cir
- DGSH 40243 5620 C6
Green Valley Dr
400 CHAN 47111 5181 D1
12000 DGSH 40243 5620 C6
12000 MDTN 40243 5620 C6
Greenvalley Dr
12000 DGSH 40243 5620 C6
12000 MDTN 40243 5620 C6
Green Valley Rd
2000 NALB 47150 5505 A3
2800 NALB 47150 5396 A7
3400 FydC 47150 5396 A4
Greenview Cir
700 ELZT 42701 6702 E1
Greenview Ct
4900 LSVL 40216 5831 D1
Greenview Dr
3300 NALB 47150 5395 E6
6100 LSVL 40216 5831 D1
6400 LSVL 40258 5831 D1
Greenview Ln
100 HdnC 40162 6591 E7
300 RDCF 40160 6483 B5
Greenville Rd
- ClkC 47106 5283 D1
- FydC 47124 5283 D2
Greenville Borden Rd
23300 ClkC 47106 5284 C2
23900 FydC 47124 5284 B3
Greenville-Georgetown Rd
1200 GEOT 47122 5501 E4
1600 FydC 47122 5501 C2
3000 FydC 47122 5392 B7
3100 FydC 47124 5392 B7
6300 FydC 47124 5283 D7
6300 GNVL 47124 5283 D7
Greenway Dr
900 ELZT 42701 6812 E5
7800 LYDN 40222 5618 E2
7800 STMW 40222 5618 E2
Greenway Commons Pl
8900 JFTN 40220 5728 A1
Greenwell Ln
4200 LSVL 40216 5722 E4
Greenwell Pl
- LSVL 40215 5723 E6
Greenwich Rd
3700 LSVL 40218 5727 A2
Greenwich Wy
3800 LSVL 40218 5727 D4
Greenwillow Wy
800 LSVL 40223 5620 A2
Greenwood
100 JFVL 47130 5506 E5
Greenwood Av
1800 LSVL 40210 5615 A4
2200 LSVL 40210 5614 E4
2500 LSVL 40211 5614 E4
Greenwood Ct
900 NALB 47150 5396 C6
Green Wood Dr
- MTWH 40047 6055 E4
Greenwood Dr
700 ELZT 42701 6811 E1
Greenwood Rd
1300 ClkC 47172 5288 E7
1300 SLRB 47172 5288 E7
1300 SLRB 47172 5397 E1
1400 ClkC 47172 5397 E1
4500 LSVL 40258 5831 D4
7000 LSVL 40258 5830 D3
Greenwood Rd SR-1931
4500 LSVL 40258 5831 D4
7000 LSVL 40258 5830 D3
Greenwood Manor Rd
7400 LSVL 40258 5831 E4
Greenwood Place Cir
7500 LSVL 40258 5831 C3
Gregg Av
1700 LSVL 40210 5614 E7
Gregory Wy
8500 LSVL 40219 5836 A7
Grenade Av
1700 LSVL 40213 5725 D2
Grenadier Dr
- NALB 47150 5396 C4
Grenden Ct
13600 LSVL 40299 5729 D5
Grenden Fields Dr
4100 LSVL 40299 5729 E5
Grenelle Dr
7900 LSVL 40228 5836 B5
Grenfell Wy
9800 MWVL 40242 5510 D6
Grenoble Ln
7800 PROS 40059 5401 A4
Gresham Rd
1700 LSVL 40205 5726 A1
Greta Av
7700 LSVL 40258 5831 D4
Gretchen K Ct
1800 GYDL 40222 5509 C7
Greten Ln
2400 ANCH 40223 5511 D6
Grey Hawk Cir
5500 LSVL 40219 5835 E7
5500 LSVL 40219 5944 D1
Grey Hawk Dr
10000 LSVL 40219 5835 E7
10000 LSVL 40219 5944 C1
Greyling Rd
1600 LSVL 40272 5832 D7
2100 LSVL 40272 5941 D1
Greymont Dr
4500 PNRV 40229 5944 C7
Greymoor Ct
4800 PNRV 40229 5944 B7
Grey Owl Ct
1600 LSVL 40223 5620 A1
Greystone Av
13500 LSVL 40272 6048 D1
Greystone Manor Pkwy
2900 LSVL 40241 5510 E5
Grey Wolf Cove
3000 FydC 47150 5397 C3
Grider Dr
- BltC 40165 6053 B3
Griffin St
900 NALB 47150 5505 A4
Griffin Gate Rd
1700 LSVL 40205 5725 E2
1700 LSVL 40205 5726 A3
Griffis Ln
10 BltC 40109 6052 D2
Griffiths Av
1800 LSVL 40203 5615 A1
2000 LSVL 40212 5615 A1
2500 LSVL 40212 5614 E1
2800 LSVL 40212 5505 E7
Grimes Ct
200 HdnC 40121 6373 E4
Grimes Lp
- HdnC 40121 6373 E4
Grimes Cove
4100 OdmC 40031 5404 A1
Grindstone Dr
2300 BltC 40165 6163 A1
Grinstead Ct
1000 LSVL 40204 5616 D4
Grinstead Dr
1500 ELZT 42701 6703 D6
1600 LSVL 40204 5616 C5
2400 JfnC 40204 5616 D4
2500 JfnC 40206 5616 D4
2500 LSVL 40206 5616 D4
2500 LSVL 40206 5617 A3
Grinstead Dr SR-2860
2000 LSVL 40204 5616 C5
2400 JfnC 40204 5616 E4
Grinstead Dr US-60 ALT
2500 JfnC 40204 5616 D4
2500 JfnC 40206 5616 D4
2500 LSVL 40204 5616 D4
2500 LSVL 40206 5616 D4
Grissom Dr
- BltC 40165 6053 B3
- HBNE 40165 6053 B3
Grissom Ln
500 ELZT 42701 6812 C4
Grissom Wy
3500 LSVL 40229 5943 E1
3700 LSVL 40229 5944 A1
Groses Ct
10 NALB 47150 5504 D6
Gross Av
100 ELZT 42701 6702 E7
Grouse Ct
6000 FydC 47119 5393 E4
Grove Av
1600 LSVL 40213 5725 D3
Groveview Ct
3000 LSVL 40214 5832 C3
Grovewood Ln
1300 LSVL 40272 5941 E1
Grubbs Av
1400 JFVL 47130 5507 B5
Guardian Ct
6100 LSVL 40219 5834 E1
Gudgel Rd
2900 LSVL 40211 5723 A1
Guelat Av
2500 LSVL 40216 5722 E5
2500 LSVL 40216 5723 A5
Guenevere Ct
1000 STMW 40222 5618 D1
Guest Av
5300 LSVL 40213 5725 E7
Guilford Av
200 CHAN 47111 5181 C4
200 ClkC 47111 5181 C4
Gulford Dr
- CLKV 47129 5506 B1
Gulfstream Wy
1600 OdmC 44026 5292 B4
Gullane Ct
4800 GYDL 40222 5509 D7
Gum St
1000 OdmC 40014 5402 E1

INDEX 24
Gum St SR-1694
Louisville Metro Street Index
Hemlock St

STREET Block City ZIP Map# Grid

Gum St SR-1694
1000 OdmC 40014 5402 E1
Gun Club Rd
100 BltC 40109 5943 D6
Gun Club Rd NE
- FydC 47122 5501 C3
- GEOT 47122 5501 C3
Gunn Ct
4000 LSVL 40229 5944 A2
Gunn Rd
6600 FydC 47136 5611 D4
Gunpowder Ct
7100 PROS 40059 5400 E5
Gunpowder Ln
6400 PROS 40059 5400 E5
Gunston Ln
700 PROS 40059 5401 A4
Gunther Rd
- UTCA 47130 5399 E6
Gunther St
400 UTCA 47130 5399 E6
Gursky Ct
2200 LSVL 40223 5510 D6
Gus Emmett Tr
10 FydC 47172 5287 E6
2200 FydC 47172 5288 A6
Gutenburg Rd
8800 JFTN 40299 5728 B6
8900 JFTN 40291 5728 B6
Gutermuth Dr
4300 LSVL 40258 5831 E4
Gutford Ln
- ClkC 47129 5397 A7
- CLKV 47129 5397 A7
1700 ClkC 47129 5506 A1
1700 CLKV 47129 5506 A1
Gutford Rd
1600 ClkC 47129 5506 A2
2100 ClkC 47129 5505 E1
2200 CLKV 47129 5506 A1
Guthrie Pl
200 ELZT 42701 6812 C3
Guthrie St
200 LSVL 40202 5615 D3
300 ELZT 42701 6812 C2
Guthrie Beach Rd
6200 LSVL 40059 5400 B6
Guy Dr
4700 LSVL 40258 5831 D2
Gwendolyn St
400 LSVL 40203 5615 C5
700 LSVL 40203 5616 A5
700 LSVL 40204 5616 A5

H

H Ct
- LSVL 40211 5615 A3
10 LGNG 40031 5296 E2
H St
- HdnC 40121 6374 C3
Haas Ln
100 SLRB 47172 5288 D3
Habersham Dr
9300 RLGH 40242 5510 D6
Hacienda Dr
9300 LSVL 40272 5831 B7
9300 LSVL 40272 5940 B1
Hackberry Ct
- SbyC 40245 5513 D4
Hackberry Ln
2300 SHDV 40165 6161 D6
Hackberry Wy
6200 LSVL 40229 5945 A2
Hackel Dr
6400 LSVL 40258 5722 A7
Hackmiller Ct
- WSNP 40218 5726 A4
Hackney Coach Dr
6000 WNDF 40207 5509 B6
Haddington Ct
7400 PROS 40059 5400 D3
Haddon Rd
3100 SPVL 40241 5509 E3
Hadleigh Pl
1400 HTBN 40222 5619 B6
3200 FydC 47150 5397 B2
Hadley Ct
7000 LSVL 40241 5509 D3
Haeringdon Ct
4700 JFTN 40299 5728 B6
Haeringdon Dr
4600 JFTN 40299 5728 B6
Hagan Av
- ELZT 42701 6812 B1
Hagen Rd
1300 LSVL 40223 5620 D1
Hagner Dr
8700 LSVL 40258 5831 C6
Hahn St
2000 LSVL 40208 5615 D7
2000 LSVL 40208 5724 D1
Hail Dr
- BltC 40165 6162 D2
Hail Ln
- BltC 40165 6162 C2
Halcyon Rd
100 CHAN 47111 5181 D4
100 ClkC 47111 5181 D4
Haldeman Av
200 LSVL 40206 5616 D2
Hale Av
1800 LSVL 40210 5615 A5
2200 LSVL 40210 5614 E5
2600 LSVL 40211 5614 D4
Hale Rd
400 CLKV 47129 5506 B2
Haley Av
100 SHDV 40165 6161 A5
Haley Ct
4300 FydC 47119 5394 D3
Haley Ln
4700 LSVL 40241 5510 B1
Half Moon Dr
100 MTWH 40047 6056 A4
Halford Wy
8800 JFTN 40299 5728 B6
Halifax Dr
11300 FCSL 40241 5511 C2
11400 LSVL 40245 5511 C2
11800 WTNH 40245 5511 C2
Halkirk Ct
500 DGSH 40243 5620 B5
Halkirk Pl
11100 DGSH 40243 5620 B5
Hall Ct
7900 LSVL 40291 5837 E6
W Hall Dr
- LSVL 40209 5724 E3
- LSVL 40209 5725 A3
Hall Ln
2000 JFVL 47130 5507 C2
Hall Farm Ct
11700 LSVL 40291 5837 E6
Hall Farm Dr
7700 LSVL 40291 5837 E6
Hallmark Cir
100 RDCF 40160 6483 E3
Hallmark Dr
7400 LSVL 40258 5831 A3
N Hallmark Dr
400 CLKV 47129 5506 D3
Hallmark Pl
100 RDCF 40160 6483 E3
Halls Ln
- BltC 40165 6162 C1
- SHDV 40165 6162 C2
100 BltC 40165 6053 A7
Hallsdale Dr
10 HBNA 40220 5619 A7
10 JFTN 40220 5619 A7
10 LSVL 40220 5619 A7
Hallway
7000 FydC 47136 5611 D1
Hallwood Ct
6900 LSVL 40291 5836 E3
Halma Dr
5900 LSVL 40272 5940 A1
Halsey Ct
5300 LSVL 40214 5724 B7
Halstead Av
5500 LSVL 40213 5725 D7
5500 LSVL 40213 5834 D1
Halston Ct
8200 LYDN 40222 5619 A2
Hamburg Pike
- CLKV 47172 5398 A3
2100 JFVL 47130 5506 E4
2200 JFVL 47130 5507 A1
3600 JFVL 47130 5398 A7
4800 ClkC 47130 5398 A6
5700 ClkC 47130 5397 E3
6000 ClkC 47172 5398 A3
Hamby Rd
3200 FydC 47122 5392 D6
Hames Trc
4800 LSVL 40291 5727 E7
4800 LSVL 40291 5836 D1
Hames Trace Rd
5300 LSVL 40291 5836 E1
5300 LSVL 40291 5837 A1
Hamilton Av
1000 LSVL 40204 5616 B4
Hamilton Ct
100 HLVW 40229 5944 A6
Hamilton Dr
100 SHDV 40165 6161 E6
Hamilton St
- HdnC 40121 6374 D2
100 HdnC 42701 6593 B1
100 RDCF 40160 6593 B1
Hamiltons Pl
- BltC 40071 5948 B7
Hamlet Dr
400 NALB 47150 5395 E7
500 NALB 47150 5504 E1
Hamlet Forest
1100 LGNG 40031 5296 C3
Hammond Dr
11400 LSVL 40241 5402 C7
Hammons Ln
100 JFVL 47130 5398 C6
Hampden Ct
1800 LSVL 40205 5616 E6
1800 LSVL 40205 5617 A6
Hampshire Dr
900 STMW 40207 5618 A5
Hampstead Ct
3200 SVLY 40216 5723 C2
Hampstead Dr
2500 SVLY 40216 5723 C2
Hampton Ct
300 CHAN 47111 5181 C4
300 ClkC 47111 5181 C4
600 SLRB 47172 5288 C3
1800 PNRV 40165 6053 D1
3300 JFVL 47130 5398 B5
Hampton Dr
2700 JFVL 47130 5398 B5
Hampton Lake Wy
4100 LSVL 40241 5511 B3
Hampton Pl Ct
200 LSVL 40118 5942 C1
Hampton Ridge Blvd
- JFTN 40299 5728 B2
2500 JFTN 40220 5728 B2
Hampton Ridge Ct
9100 JFTN 40220 5728 B2
Hancock Dr
1200 ELZT 42701 6811 B5
Hancock Rd
1000 FydC 47122 5503 B7
1000 FydC 47136 5503 B7
1000 FydC 47150 5503 B7
1400 FydC 47150 5612 B1
E Hancock Rd
5800 FydC 47150 5503 B7
5800 FydC 47150 5612 B1
N Hancock St
100 LSVL 40202 5616 A2
S Hancock St
100 LSVL 40202 5616 A4
600 LSVL 40203 5616 A4
900 LSVL 40203 5615 E5
1200 LSVL 40208 5615 E6
1400 LSVL 40217 5615 E7
Hancock Trace Ct
- LSVL 40245 5622 D1
11700 LSVL 40245 5513 D7
Hand Av
1900 NALB 47150 5505 B2
Handley Av
3800 LSVL 40218 5726 E5
3800 LSVL 40218 5727 A6
Haney Wy
4200 LSVL 40272 5940 D4
Hanford Ln
4600 LSVL 40207 5509 A6
Hanger Av
100 SLRB 47172 5288 E4
Hanger St
- JFVL 47130 5508 B2
Hannah Av
4300 LSVL 40213 5725 C5
Hannah Ct
1900 OdmC 40031 5297 C4
Hanover Ct
400 HdnC 42701 6811 B4
3400 LSVL 40207 5617 E5
Hanover Rd
3500 BFLD 40207 5617 E5
3500 LSVL 40207 5617 E5
3600 BFLD 40207 5618 A4
Hanover St
400 ELZT 42701 6811 B4
400 HdnC 42701 6811 B4
Hanses Dr
6200 LSVL 40219 5835 B2
Happel Dr
100 LSVL 40118 5833 C7
Happiness Wy
8100 LSVL 40228 5836 E5
8100 LSVL 40291 5836 E5
Happy Hollow Ln
7300 PROS 40059 5400 E4
Happy Hollow Rd
200 ELZT 42701 6812 D7
200 HdnC 42701 6812 D7
Haps Al
- LSVL 40205 5616 E6
Harbold Ct
4600 LSVL 40241 5510 B1
Harborton Wy
7200 LSVL 40228 5836 C6
Harbortown Rd
5400 LSVL 40059 5400 A7
Harbour Ln
7800 LSVL 40219 5835 A5
Harbour Pl
13900 OdmC 40059 5291 E1
Harbrook Ct
3100 NALB 47150 5396 C7
Harbrook Dr
1000 NALB 47150 5396 C7
Hardesty Av
1800 LSVL 40210 5723 E1
1800 LSVL 40216 5723 D1
Hardin St
200 ELZT 42701 6812 C2
400 LSVL 40212 5505 D7
700 VNGV 40175 6591 C1
Harding Dr
100 MTWH 40047 6056 A1
300 MTWH 40047 6055 E1
Hardin Holly
1000 LGNG 40031 5296 C3
Hardwick Rd
12200 WDHL 40243 5620 D5
Hardwood Ct
2600 LSVL 40214 5723 D7
Hardwood Dr
10 BltC 40047 6055 B4
10 MTWH 40047 6055 B4
Hardwood Forest Dr
3100 LSVL 40214 5832 A5
3400 LSVL 40272 5832 A5
Hardy Av
700 LSVL 40208 5724 C2
Hardy Ln
100 MTWH 40047 6056 C2
Hardy Cove
2100 BltC 40165 6054 B7
Hare Ln
100 MTWH 40047 6056 A2
Hargan Rd
10 HdnC 40175 6482 A7
Hargan Rd SR-1882
10 HdnC 40175 6482 A7
Hargan St
1400 RDCF 40160 6484 A6
Hargin Rd
100 HdnC 40175 6482 A6
Hargin Rd SR-1882
100 HdnC 40175 6482 A6
Harlan Av
100 LSVL 40214 5724 C3
Harlech Ct
2600 JFTN 40299 5728 D2
Harlech Ln
9900 JFTN 40299 5728 D2
Harley Dr
100 SHDV 40165 6161 C5
Harlow Ct
9400 LSVL 40059 5401 D7
Harmon Ct
3100 LSVL 40213 5725 C1
Harmony Ln
1000 GSHN 44026 5292 C3
1000 OdmC 44026 5292 D3
1100 JFVL 47130 5507 B3
Harmony Rd
2400 JFTN 40299 5728 C2
Harmony Vil
13900 OdmC 40059 5291 D3
Harmony Heights Rd
6700 FydC 47122 5502 E3
Harmony Landing Rd
- OdmC 40059 5291 E2
900 GSHN 44026 5292 C3
900 OdmC 44026 5292 C3
Harmony Marina Rd
- OdmC 40059 5291 E2
Harmony Pl Ct
8900 BRWD 40242 5510 B7
Harned Av
9600 LSVL 40229 5944 A2
Harned Ct
10 LSVL 40229 5944 A2
Harness Ct
2500 JFTN 40299 5728 D2
Harold Av
1600 LSVL 40210 5615 A7
1700 LSVL 40210 5614 E7
1700 LSVL 40216 5614 E7
Harper Byp
- HLVW 40229 6053 A1
Harper Lp
4300 HdnC 40121 6374 B2
Harpers Dr
- BltC 40165 6053 C1
- PNRV 40165 6053 C1
Harpers Ferry Rd
100 LSVL 40214 5833 B5
Harper Valley Cir
6800 LSVL 40241 5509 B2
Harriet Ct
1600 NALB 47150 5505 D2
Harris Ct
2400 NALB 47150 5504 E2
Harris Dr
100 MTWH 40047 6056 A4
Harris Pl
400 STMW 40222 5618 D2
Harris St
100 MRGH 40155 6264 C3
Harrison Av
- CLKV 47129 5506 B5
100 JFVL 47130 5506 E5
600 LSVL 40217 5724 E1
2900 LSVL 40217 5725 B1
3000 ANPK 40213 5725 C2
5800 LSVL 40291 5837 C1
E Harrison Av
100 CLKV 47129 5506 D5
S Harrison Av
100 MDTN 40243 5620 C4
W Harrison Av
100 CLKV 47129 5506 B5
Harrison Cir
100 BltC 40047 6054 E5
Harrison Ct
100 BltC 40047 6054 E5
Harrison Ln
10600 HYVA 40118 5943 A4
10600 LSVL 40118 5943 A4
Harrison St
100 CHAN 47111 5181 E4
E Harrison St
9400 GNVL 47124 5283 D7
W Harrison St
9700 GNVL 47124 5283 D7
Harrison Tr NE
6600 HsnC 47122 5501 B3
Harrison Trail Ct NE
6700 HsnC 47122 5501 B4
Harris Passway
100 BltC 40047 6055 B4
Harris Ridge Ct
13300 MDTN 40223 5620 E3
Harris Ridge Rd
600 MDTN 40223 5620 E3
Harrod Ct
1700 LSVL 40210 5615 B7
Harrods Bridge Wy
- PROS 40059 5400 D6
Harrods Cove
5000 LSVL 40059 5400 D6
Harrods Creek Ct
11100 ANCH 40223 5620 B2
11100 LSVL 40223 5620 B2
Harrods Landing Dr
10 PROS 40059 5400 D5
Harrods Old Trc
2900 LSVL 40299 5730 A4
Harrods Run Rd
5600 PROS 40059 5400 D6
Harrods View Cir
6500 PROS 40059 5401 B4
Harrods View Ct
8200 PROS 40059 5401 B4
Harrodwood Ct
8000 LSVL 40291 5836 E4
Harrogate
6500 LSVL 40229 5944 E2
6500 LSVL 40229 5945 A2
Harrow Ct
8100 LSVL 40220 5618 E7
Harshfield Ln
- SHDV 40165 6161 D6
100 BltC 40165 6051 B4
Hart Av
- LSVL 40272 6048 D2
1200 LSVL 40213 5725 B3
Hartford Dr
100 MTWH 40047 6056 A3
Hartford Ln
4900 LSVL 40216 5722 C6
Hartlage Ct
2900 SVLY 40216 5723 A3
3000 LSVL 40216 5723 A3
Hartley Dr
10200 LSVL 40223 5619 E2
Hartman Av
- LSVL 40205 5616 D6
Hartwell Ct
100 LSVL 40214 5724 C7
Hartwick Village Dr
10000 LSVL 40241 5510 D3
Hartwick Village Pl
4100 LSVL 40241 5510 D2
Hartwood Pl
14700 LSVL 40245 5512 D4
Harvard Dr
600 CLKV 47129 5506 D3
600 ELZT 42701 6811 D2
1700 LSVL 40205 5617 A7
Harvard Commons Ct
9600 LSVL 40291 5946 C2
Harvest Ct
1200 JFVL 47130 5398 E7
Harvest Dr
4700 OdmC 40014 5405 C3
5100 LSVL 40216 5722 B7
Harvest Gold Ct
9000 LSVL 40291 5837 B3
Harvest Gold Wy
7000 LSVL 40291 5837 A2
Harvest Grove Ct
800 LSVL 40245 5621 C3
Harvest Grove Wy
800 LSVL 40245 5621 C3
Harvest Moon Dr
4300 LSVL 40218 5727 D4
Harvey Ln
- LSVL 40220 5618 B7
Harwell Av
2700 LSVL 40209 5724 E2
Harwich Pl
9000 LDNP 40242 5510 C5
Harwood Rd
10 GNVM 40222 5509 B5
10 NHFD 40222 5509 B5
Hasbrook Ct
11200 LSVL 40229 5944 E5
Hasbrook Dr
5200 LSVL 40229 5944 D5
Haskin Av
1300 LSVL 40215 5724 A7
1600 LSVL 40215 5723 E7
Hassock Ct
5200 LSVL 40258 5831 C3
Hassock Dr
7200 LSVL 40258 5831 C3
Hastings Cir
3400 MRCK 40241 5510 B3
Hastings Dr
1800 CLKV 47129 5397 C7
Hasty Wy
1700 LSVL 40216 5832 A1
Hat Ct
4800 JFTN 40291 5728 B6
Hatcher Av
300 LSVL 40214 5833 C2
Hatfield Ln
6800 LSVL 40258 5831 A5
Hathaway Av
1000 LSVL 40215 5724 A4
Hatherleigh Ln
600 HTBN 40222 5619 C5
Hatler Ct
600 JFTN 40223 5619 E5
Hatlerhall Dr
8900 JFTN 40291 5728 B6
Haunz Ln
5300 ODGH 40014 5402 D7
5300 OdmC 40014 5402 C6
5400 ODGH 40014 5511 D1
5400 OdmC 40014 5511 D1
Hausfeldt Ln
100 FydC 47150 5396 A5
100 NALB 47150 5396 A5
Hausman Dr
- LSVL 40272 5939 E4
Hauss Av
400 SLRB 47172 5288 D3
Haven Manor Wy
5800 LSVL 40228 5727 B7
Haventree Ct
5300 LSVL 40229 5944 D3
Haventree Pl
5300 LSVL 40229 5944 D3
Haven View Dr
2100 LSVL 40218 5727 C6
Haverhill Rd
6400 CSGT 40222 5509 C6
Haviland Av
9000 HBNA 40220 5619 B7
9000 HBNA 40220 5728 B1
Hawick Pl
300 DGSH 40243 5620 A4
Hawkesbury Ct
4000 LSVL 40241 5510 E2
Hawkins Av
600 LSVL 40213 5834 B3
Hawkins Dr
600 ELZT 42701 6812 D6
1400 RDCF 40175 6482 E3
1400 RDCF 40175 6483 A3
Hawkins Rill Ct
9700 LSVL 40291 5837 D4
Hawkins Rill Dr
7000 LSVL 40291 5837 C4
Hawkshead Ln
1400 LSVL 40220 5619 A6
Hawkwood Wy
8000 LYDN 40222 5619 A1
Hawley Gibson Rd
8100 OdmC 40014 5513 A3
8900 OdmC 40014 5512 E4
8900 OdmC 40056 5512 E4
Hawthorn Hl
10 LSVL 40204 5616 C6
Hawthorne Av
2200 LSVL 40205 5617 C7
2200 LSVL 40205 5726 C1
Hawthorne Ct
200 ELZT 42701 6811 C1
3500 OdmC 40031 5295 E7
3500 OdmC 40031 5404 E1
Hawthorne Dr
300 JFVL 47130 5508 B2
Hawthorne Ln
10 JFVL 47130 5508 A3
Hawthorne Pl Dr
4700 LSVL 40272 5940 D1
Hawthorne Pointe Dr
9100 LSVL 40272 5832 B7
Hay Ct
700 LSVL 40214 5833 E6
Haycraft St
100 ELZT 42701 6812 C3
Hayden School Rd
10 ELZT 42701 6811 A2
10 HdnC 42701 6811 A2
Hayes Av
9300 LSVL 40291 5837 C1
Hayfield Dr
3000 LSVL 40205 5726 B2
Hayfield Wy
4200 OdmC 40059 5401 B1
Haylee Ct
- BltC 40047 6055 A5
Hay Market Dr
3900 ClkC 47130 5398 C5
Haynes Rd
7000 FydC 47122 5393 C5
Hays Ct
100 ELZT 42701 6812 A4
Haystack Dr
300 ClkC 47130 5398 C5
Hayward Rd
100 VNGV 40175 6591 D1
2200 BCFT 40222 5509 D6
2200 LSVL 40242 5509 D5
2500 LSVL 40241 5509 D5
Haze Dr
300 NALB 47150 5504 D7
Hazel Ln
1100 ClkC 47129 5506 A2
1100 CLKV 47129 5506 A2
Hazel St
700 LSVL 40211 5614 D3
Hazelnut Ct
100 LGNG 40031 5296 C3
Hazel Tree Dr
9900 LSVL 40291 5946 D2
Hazelwood Av
- LSVL 40214 5723 E7
- LSVL 40216 5723 E7
10 NALB 47150 5505 D3
4100 LSVL 40215 5724 A6
4300 LSVL 40215 5723 E7
Hazelwood Ct
1000 CLKV 47129 5397 C6
1900 LSVL 40214 5723 E6
Hazelwood Dr
900 CLKV 47129 5397 B6
3300 NALB 47150 5396 D6
Hazelwood Rd
3400 OdmC 40014 5405 B1
3400 OdmC 40031 5296 B7
3400 OdmC 40031 5405 B1
12000 ANCH 40223 5620 D1
Hazelwood Park Dr
900 CLKV 47129 5397 B6
Head Dr
200 LGNG 40031 5297 A3
Head Farm Rd
9900 LSVL 40241 5510 E1
Headley Hill Rd
10100 KNLD 40223 5510 E6
10100 LSVL 40223 5510 E6
Heady Av
100 RHLN 40207 5618 B3
100 STMW 40207 5618 B3
Heafer Rd
1100 LSVL 40223 5620 E1
1400 ANCH 40223 5620 D1
Hearthside Ct
14500 LSVL 40245 5621 B6
Hearthstone Ct
10200 LSVL 40272 5940 E2
Heartland Dr
100 ELZT 42701 6703 A7
Heath Ct
8100 LYDN 40222 5619 C2
Heather Ct
100 RDCF 40160 6483 D7
Heather Ln
2200 LSVL 40218 5726 D2
2700 OdmC 40031 5296 B7
4400 SVLY 40216 5723 B5
Heather Rd
2900 JFVL 47130 5398 C7
Heatherbourne Dr
1100 LGNG 40031 5296 E1
1100 LGNG 40031 5297 A1
1100 OdmC 40031 5296 E1
Heatherbrook Dr
4400 LSVL 40220 5727 D2
Heatherfield Dr
3400 SVLY 40216 5723 B3
Heather Hill Rd
5100 OdmC 40031 5295 B5
Heatherly Sq
7200 OBNP 40242 5509 E5
Heather Ridge Tr
7300 LSVL 40218 5727 D5
Heatherview Rd
4000 LSVL 40218 5727 D5
Heatherwood Ct
6900 LSVL 40291 5836 E3
Heathmore Ct
4900 LSVL 40241 5511 C3
Heathsville Ct
11900 WTNH 40245 5511 D2
Heaton Rd
1800 SVLY 40216 5723 B6
Heavenly Wy
3900 LSVL 40272 5940 E3
3900 LSVL 40272 5941 A3
Heaven's Estate Wy
7600 LSVL 40291 5838 A4
Heavrin Av
6900 LSVL 40218 5727 C4
E Hebron Ln
3000 BltC 40165 6053 E3
3000 HBNE 40165 6053 E3
3000 PNRV 40165 6053 E3
W Hebron Ln
- BltC 40165 6053 A2
- BltC 40229 6053 B3
- HBNE 40165 6053 C3
- PNRV 40229 6053 A2
100 FXCH 40165 6053 A2
100 HLVW 40165 6053 A2
100 PNRV 40165 6053 A2
W Hebron Ln SR-1450
- BltC 40165 6053 A2
- BltC 40229 6053 B3
- HBNE 40165 6053 C3
- PNRV 40229 6053 A2
100 FXCH 40165 6053 A2
100 HLVW 40165 6053 A2
100 PNRV 40165 6053 A2
Hecks Ln
600 LSVL 40211 5614 C3
Hedden Ct
1600 NALB 47150 5505 D2
Hedden Pk
1600 NALB 47150 5505 D2
Hedgeapple Wy
12400 LSVL 40272 5939 E3
Hedgepath Tr
2600 LSVL 40245 5513 D7
2600 LSVL 40245 5622 D1
Hedgerow Ct
4600 SRPK 40220 5618 E6
Hedges Rd
4600 LSVL 40216 5723 D7
Hedgewick Pl
3500 LSVL 40245 5512 C5
Hedgewick Wy
14700 LSVL 40245 5512 C5
Hedgewood Ct
100 BltC 40165 5944 E6
100 BltC 40229 5944 E5
100 HLVW 40229 5944 E5
Hedgewood Dr
5700 OdmC 40014 5405 B5
Heidelberg Ct
9700 LSVL 40291 5946 D1
Heidelberg Dr
11000 LSVL 40291 5946 D1
Heights Dr
7600 LSVL 40291 5837 B6
Heights Ln
2700 LGNG 40031 5297 A6
2800 OdmC 40031 5297 A6
Heights Wy
8000 LSVL 40291 5837 B6
Heinze Rd
- HsnC 47136 5611 D7
Heinze Rd NE
8200 HsnC 47136 5611 B6
Helbig St
100 SLRB 47172 5288 E4
200 ClkC 47172 5288 E4
Helck Av
1200 LSVL 40213 5725 E6
1200 LYNV 40213 5725 D6
Helen Av
2300 LSVL 40216 5722 E7
7200 LSVL 40258 5831 E4
Hellenjean Wy
6200 LSVL 40272 5939 E3
6200 LSVL 40272 5940 A3
Heller St
4900 LSVL 40218 5726 E6
4900 LSVL 40228 5726 E6
Hell on Wheels Av
2300 HdnC 40121 6265 B7
Hell on Wheels Division Av
- HdnC 40121 6265 B7
100 HdnC 40121 6374 B1
Helm Av
100 ELZT 42701 6812 B3
Helm Ct
100 ELZT 42701 6702 E7
Helm Ln
100 BltC 40047 6055 D5
300 MTWH 40047 6055 E5
Helm St
100 ELZT 42701 6812 B3
2600 LSVL 40209 5724 D2
Helmridge Ct
1400 LYDN 40222 5510 A7
1400 LYDN 40222 5619 A1
Helmsdale Ln
10600 BRMR 40223 5620 A4
10600 DGSH 40243 5620 A4
Helmwood Cir
10 BltC 40047 6055 E6
10 MTWH 40047 6055 D6
Helmwood Dr
100 ELZT 42701 6812 A1
200 ELZT 42701 6811 D1
5300 LSVL 40213 5725 E7
Hemingway Rd
100 FRMD 40207 5618 B3
200 STMW 40207 5618 C4
Hemlock Av
7300 OdmC 40014 5512 A1
Hemlock Ct
1600 LSVL 40211 5614 D6
Hemlock Dr
100 BltC 40165 6161 B1
Hemlock Ln
1600 RDCF 40160 6483 A4
Hemlock Rd
400 JFVL 47130 5508 A1
Hemlock St
100 VNGV 40175 6482 C7
1300 LSVL 40211 5614 D5

INDEX 25

Hempstead Rd
Louisville Metro Street Index
Holly Ct

STREET
Block City ZIP Map# Grid

Hempstead Rd
5200 LSVL 40207 5508 D5
5200 RBNW 40207 5508 D5
5300 RBNW 40207 5509 A5
5500 WNDF 40207 5509 A5
Henderson Av
4000 LSVL 40213 5725 B3
14100 LSVL 40272 6048 D2
Hendon Rd
3000 LSVL 40220 5618 A7
Henley Ct
2400 OBNP 40242 5509 E5
Hennepin Dr
1100 LSVL 40214 5832 E3
1100 LSVL 40214 5833 A3
Henning Dr
- OdmC 40059 5402 D1
Henning Wy
10600 LSVL 40241 5511 A3
Henon Ln
500 ELZT 42701 6812 C2
Henrietta Av
2900 LSVL 40220 5618 A7
Henriott Rd
1500 GEOT 47122 5502 B3
1900 FydC 47122 5502 B3
2900 FydC 47122 5393 B6
Henry
1700 JFVL 47130 5507 A4
Henry Av
3500 LSVL 40215 5724 A4
Henry St
200 ELZT 42701 6812 B2
Henry Clay Ct
3100 OdmC 40014 5514 A1
Henry Clay Dr
- LSVL 40242 5510 C6
9000 WWOD 40242 5510 C6
Henry Firpo St
700 LSVL 40203 5616 A4
700 LSVL 40204 5616 A4
Henry Watterson Expwy
- BWDV - 5618 D2
- GYDL - 5509 C7
- LSVL - 5509 C6
- LSVL - 5617 E7
- LSVL - 5618 C5
- LSVL - 5723 D5
- LSVL - 5724 B4
- LSVL - 5725 B4
- LSVL - 5726 D1
- NHFD - 5509 B6
- STMW - 5509 C7
- STMW - 5618 B6
- SVLY - 5723 C5
- WDYH - 5509 B6
- WDYH - 5618 C1
- WLNP - 5618 C1
- WSNP - 5726 A3
Henry Watterson Expwy I-264
- BWDV - 5618 D2
- GYDL - 5509 C7
- LSVL - 5509 B6
- LSVL - 5617 E7
- LSVL - 5618 A7
- LSVL - 5723 D5
- LSVL - 5724 B4
- LSVL - 5725 C4
- LSVL - 5726 B3
- NHFD - 5509 B6
- STMW - 5509 C7
- STMW - 5618 B6
- SVLY - 5723 C5
- WDYH - 5509 B6
- WDYH - 5618 C1
- WLNP - 5618 C1
- WSNP - 5726 A3
Henry Watterson Expwy US-60
- LSVL - 5617 E7
- LSVL - 5618 A7
- LSVL - 5723 D5
- LSVL - 5724 B4
- LSVL - 5725 B4
- LSVL - 5726 B3
- STMW - 5618 C5
- WSNP - 5726 A3
Hensley Ct
9100 LSVL 40059 5401 C7
Hensley Rd
- OdmC 40014 5402 B5
100 BltC 40165 6160 E3
100 BltC 40165 6161 A3
12300 LSVL 40223 5620 E1
100 SHDV 40165 6161 A3
Henson Ct
1500 CHAN 47111 5181 D2
Hepatica Dr
7700 LSVL 40258 5831 C4
Hepburn Av
1300 LSVL 40204 5616 B5
Herb Ln
3500 LSVL 40220 5618 A7
3500 LSVL 40220 5726 E1
3500 LSVL 40220 5727 A1
Herbert Av
- LSVL 40213 5725 A3
1600 SVLY 40216 5723 C5
Herbert Ln
1900 LSVL 40272 5832 D7
Herb Lewis Rd
4000 JFVL 47130 5398 E5
4000 JFVL 47130 5399 A6
Herbs Ln
100 BltC 40165 6163 C5
Herby Dr
1700 JFVL 47130 5507 C5
Hereford Ct
2400 LSVL 40272 5941 C1
Herefordshire Dr
8600 HTBN 40222 5619 A5
Heritage Ct
1300 ELZT 42701 6703 C7
3100 OdmC 40014 5405 B7
Heritage Ln
7200 ClkC 47172 5397 D1
Heritage Mnr
- OdmC 40014 5404 D6
Heritage Pl
1200 LSVL 40214 5832 E2
Heritage Rd
500 RDCF 40160 6483 E3
Heritage Tr
10 HdnC 40162 6591 D7
Heritage Hill Ct
11300 MDTN 40243 5620 B4
Heritage Hill Tr
200 MDTN 40243 5620 B4
Heritage Hill Wy
11400 MDTN 40243 5620 B4
Heritage Hills Ct
- OdmC 40014 5404 D6
Heritage Hills Dr
- OdmC 40014 5404 D6
Herman St
4000 LSVL 40212 5614 B1
Hermany Ct
3000 LSVL 40206 5617 B3
Hermitage Ct
8800 PNTN 40242 5510 B6
Hermitage Wy
2400 LSVL 40242 5510 B6
2400 PNTN 40242 5510 B5
Hermitage Ridge Ct
16200 LSVL 40245 5513 B7
Hermits Run Rd
7700 LSVL 40291 5837 D5
Heron View Pl
- OdmC 40031 5295 B6
Herr Av
1200 LSVL 40208 5615 B7
Herr Ln
1100 GYDL 40222 5618 E1
1100 STMW 40222 5618 E1
1300 GYDL 40222 5509 C6
1300 STMW 40222 5509 E7
1800 LSVL 40222 5509 C6
2000 NHFD 40222 5509 C6
Herr Ln SR-2050
1100 GYDL 40222 5618 E1
1100 STMW 40222 5618 E1
1300 GYDL 40222 5509 C6
1300 STMW 40222 5509 E7
1800 LSVL 40222 5509 C6
2000 NHFD 40222 5509 C6
Herrick Ln
11500 DGSH 40243 5620 C5
11500 MDTN 40243 5620 C5
Herring Ct
11100 LSVL 40291 5837 E5
Herrington Ct
8300 LSVL 40228 5836 B6
Herron Ct
6100 LSVL 40229 5945 A1
Herrs Dale Ct
1500 GYDL 40222 5509 E7
Hersfield Rd
12400 LSVL 40223 5620 D1
Hertsch Rd
100 JFVL 47130 5507 E5
Hess Ln
900 LSVL 40213 5725 B2
900 LSVL 40217 5725 B2
1000 ANPK 40213 5725 B2
Hess Rd
5400 LSVL 40216 5831 E2
5400 LSVL 40258 5831 E2
Hester St
10 CHAN 47111 5181 D3
100 SHDV 40165 6161 D4
Hetzil Ct
7000 LSVL 40291 5837 B4
Hewitt Av
3100 HNAC 40220 5727 E1
Hewitt Pl Ct
2900 JFTN 40299 5728 E3
Hewn Oak Ct
10300 JFTN 40223 5619 E5
Hexagon Av
3500 HLVW 40229 5944 A6
Heywood Av
700 LSVL 40208 5724 B2
Hialeah Ct
1600 OdmC 44026 5292 C4
Hiawatha Av
200 LSVL 40214 5724 D5
300 LSVL 40209 5724 D5
12300 LSVL 40223 5620 E1
Hibbs St
- RDCF 42701 6593 B4
Hibiscus Ct
3100 FydC 47150 5397 B2
Hibiscus Dr
1100 CLKV 47129 5506 B2
Hickman Av
4100 LSVL 40213 5725 C4
Hickman Ct
5900 LSVL 40207 5509 B6
5900 WNDF 40207 5509 B6
Hickock Dr
7000 LSVL 40219 5834 E3
Hickory Cir
- BltC 40109 5943 E5
Hickory Ct
8700 BRWD 40242 5510 B6
Hickory Dr
900 HdnC 40175 6591 E3
Hickory Grv
3100 NALB 47150 5396 C7
Hickory Ln
100 BltC 40047 6056 D4
100 ELZT 42701 6811 D3
100 VNGV 40175 6592 A1
700 ANCH 40223 5620 C2
1700 JFVL 47130 5508 A1
2900 OdmC 40031 5296 C6
N Hickory Ln
100 SHDV 40165 6161 D5
S Hickory Ln
2300 SHDV 40165 6161 D6
Hickory Rd
10 ClkC 47111 5181 B3
Hickory Rdg NE
6400 HsnC 47122 5501 B4
Hickory St
100 RDCF 40160 6483 A4
1300 LSVL 40204 5616 A7
1300 LSVL 40217 5616 A7
Hickory Trc NE
6300 HsnC 47122 5501 B4
Hickory Wy
6000 FydC 47136 5611 E1
Hickory Acres E
- BltC 40165 6161 A2
Hickory Acres Dr
- BltC 40165 6161 A3
- SHDV 40165 6161 A3
Hickory Cove Ct
10700 LSVL 40241 5511 B2
Hickory Falls Ct
8600 OdmC 40056 5512 E3
Hickory Falls Ln
8600 OdmC 40056 5512 E3
Hickory Forest Dr
- LSVL 40241 5402 A7
- LSVL 40241 5511 A1
Hickory Grove Wy
10600 LSVL 40291 5946 C1
Hickory Hill Dr
10 HdnC 42701 6702 D1
5000 OdmC 40031 5295 B3
Hickory Hill Rd
5400 LSVL 40214 5833 A2
Hickory Hills Tr
14000 LSVL 40299 5839 B4
Hickory Hollow Ln
4700 FXCH 40165 6053 A3
Hickory Ridge Rd
14000 LSVL 40245 5621 B3
Hickory Spring Ct
2900 OdmC 40031 5295 B3
Hickory Tree Rd
6000 LSVL 40291 5836 D1
Hickoryvale Dr
2500 NALB 47150 5505 C1
Hickory Valley Rd
7000 LSVL 40299 5839 B4
Hickory View Dr
4100 LSVL 40299 5728 E5
4200 LSVL 40299 5729 A5
Hidalgo Rd
8400 LSVL 40219 5835 E6
Hidden Ln
100 ELZT 42701 6702 E6
Hidden Rd
5500 LSVL 40291 5727 D7
Hidden Creek Ln
10600 LSVL 40291 5946 D4
Hidden Creek Rd
11600 OdmC 40059 5401 D4
11700 LSVL 40059 5401 C4
Hidden Grove Pl
8700 LSVL 40291 5837 D7
Hidden Hill Ct
1100 LSVL 40245 5621 B2
Hidden Hollow Ct
6600 LSVL 40229 5945 A1
Hidden Hollow Rd
1000 FydC 47150 5503 E3
Hidden Lake Ct
3300 LSVL 40023 5731 C5
Hidden Lakes Blvd
5300 ClkC 47130 5398 B4
Hidden Oak Ct
7800 NRWD 40222 5618 E3
Hidden Oak Pl
200 NRWD 40222 5618 E3
Hidden Oak Wy
300 NRWD 40222 5618 E3
400 LYDN 40222 5618 E3
Hidden Place Dr
1700 FydC 47122 5503 B3
Hidden Pond Ct
16900 LSVL 40245 5622 B2
Hidden River Trc
- ClkC 47111 5289 E1
7600 ClkC 47111 5180 E7
Hidden Springs Rd
13000 LSVL 40272 5940 B7
Hidden Valley Farm Rd
11000 LSVL 40291 5946 E5
11000 LSVL 40291 5947 A5
Hideaway Ct
12200 WTNH 40245 5511 D3
Hiers St
5500 MdeC 40121 6373 D2
Higgins Dr
600 JFVL 47130 5508 B2
Higgins Vw
4900 LSVL 40023 5840 B1
Higgins Run Wy
16500 LSVL 40023 5840 B1
High Al
200 JFVL 47130 5507 C6
High St
- SLRB 47172 5288 D3
10 CHAN 47111 5181 E5
100 JFVL 47130 5507 C6
200 VNGV 40175 6591 D1
300 ELZT 42701 6812 C2
7000 FydC 47119 5393 D3
7100 FydC 47124 5393 D3
8800 GEOT 47122 5502 A4
8900 GEOT 47122 5501 E4
High St SR-391
200 VNGV 40175 6591 D1
E High St
100 JFVL 47130 5507 C6
W High St
100 JFVL 47130 5507 C6
High Canyon Rd
2000 RVWD 40207 5508 D5
Highcrest Av
9700 LSVL 40272 5940 E1
9700 LSVL 40272 5941 A1
High Fern Rd
7500 LSVL 40291 5837 A4
Highfield Rd
400 WDYH 40207 5509 B7
Highgate Ct
3800 OdmC 40014 5404 D4
Highgate Dr
- OdmC 40014 5404 D3
Highgrade Dr
6000 LSVL 40291 5836 E1
High Grove Pl
10700 LSVL 40223 5620 A1
High Jackson Rd
5400 ClkC 47111 5289 C2
7200 ClkC 47111 5290 B1
7400 ClkC 47111 5181 C6
8400 CHAN 47111 5181 C6
Highland Av
10 CLKV 47129 5506 B2
100 LSVL 40245 5622 B5
200 NALB 47150 5504 E5
200 SLRB 47172 5288 D4
1300 LSVL 40204 5616 B5
2900 JFTN 40299 5728 D3
Highland Ct
- BltC 40047 6055 B6
200 SHDV 40165 6162 A2
2000 LGNG 40031 5297 C6
Highland Dr
100 RDCF 40160 6483 B4
200 CHAN 47111 5181 C4
300 ClkC 47111 5181 C4
1100 JFVL 47130 5507 B3
3300 FydC 47119 5395 B5
Highlander Ct
5500 FydC 47124 5393 D2
Highlander Point Dr
700 FydC 47119 5503 D1
Highland Lake Dr
3300 FydC 47122 5393 A6
Highland Oaks Ct
4100 FydC 47150 5396 D2
Highland Oaks Dr
4100 FydC 47150 5396 D1
Highland Springs Dr
100 BltC 40047 6055 B6
3900 MTWH 40047 6055 B6
Highland Springs Pl
2100 LSVL 40245 5512 D7
Highliner Dr
6000 LSVL 40291 5836 E1
High Meadow Dr
1100 UTCA 47130 5399 D6
High Meadow Pl
4300 LSVL 40299 5729 E6
High Meadow Rd
1400 UTCA 47130 5399 C6
High Meadows Ct
3700 OdmC 40059 5401 B1
High Meadows Pike
12000 OdmC 40059 5292 C7
12000 OdmC 40059 5401 C1
High Park Dr
100 NALB 47150 5396 B7
High Pine Ct
5700 LSVL 40214 5723 D7
High Pine Dr
100 BltC 40165 6162 E6
2200 LSVL 40214 5723 D7
Highplace Dr
6000 LSVL 40291 5836 E2
High Point Cir
8800 LSVL 40299 5728 A4
Highpoint Rd
5300 OdmC 40014 5404 E4
High Ridge Dr
100 BltC 40165 6163 D3
Highridge Dr NE
7500 HsnC 47136 5610 E3
Highridge Ln NE
3200 HsnC 47136 5610 E3
High Ridge Rd
2000 RVWD 40207 5508 E5
High Rise Dr
- LSVL 40213 5834 E2
High School Dr
- SHDV 40165 6161 E3
800 CLKV 47129 5506 C3
800 LSVL 40219 5835 B7
High Stone Wy
4200 LSVL 40299 5728 A5
High Trail Ct
13800 LSVL 40299 5729 E6
Highview Ct
8200 OdmC 40014 5513 B3
Highview Dr
7300 LSVL 40228 5836 C4
High Water Rd
100 BltC 40165 6160 C4
Highwater Rd
100 FydC 47150 5504 C6
100 NALB 47150 5504 B6
200 FydC 47150 5613 B1
Highwood Dr
- LSVL 40206 5507 D7
100 LSVL 40206 5616 E1
Highwood Pl
10 LSVL 40206 5507 E7
Hikes Av
3700 WBHL 40218 5726 E4
Hikes Ln
- PLRH 40218 5726 C4
- WSNP 40218 5726 C4
1800 LSVL 40218 5726 E3
1800 WBHL 40218 5726 D4
2600 LSVL 40218 5727 A2
2800 LSVL 40220 5727 B1
3300 LSVL 40220 5618 C7
Hikes Ln SR-2052
2100 LSVL 40218 5726 E3
2100 WBHL 40218 5726 E3
Hilancrest Dr
2000 VNGV 40175 6482 E7
Hi-Land Dr
100 BltC 40165 6162 D2
Hilda Ct
12000 LSVL 40272 5940 A5
Hildreth St
700 NALB 47150 5505 A4
N Hill Dr
10 FydC 47119 5395 C6
Hill Rd
- LSVL 40213 5616 D6
10 LSVL 40204 5616 C6
Hill Sq
- RDCF 40160 6483 C2
Hill St
100 ELZT 42701 6702 E7
100 MRGH 40155 6264 C4
300 RDCF 40160 6483 A2
1600 RDCF 40175 6482 E2
1600 RDCF 40175 6483 A2
2000 VNGV 40175 6482 E5
2000 VNGV 40175 6483 A5
2200 HdnC 40175 6482 E4
2200 RDCF 40160 6482 E5
E Hill St
- LSVL 40217 5615 E6
- LSVL 40217 5616 A7
100 LSVL 40208 5615 D7
W Hill St
100 LSVL 40208 5615 D6
900 LSVL 40210 5615 A6
1800 LSVL 40210 5614 E6
2600 LSVL 40211 5614 E6
W Hill St US-60 TRK
1200 LSVL 40210 5615 A6
Hillary Ct
9800 LSVL 40291 5728 D7
Hill Bend Pl
100 LSVL 40208 5615 D6
Hill Briar Ct
2600 LSVL 40241 5509 D5
Hillbrook Ct
2500 LSVL 40220 5618 C6
Hillbrook Dr
100 BltC 40165 6053 A5
3900 LSVL 40220 5618 C6
3900 MVWE 40220 5618 C7
5700 OdmC 40014 5405 C5
Hillcircle Ct
7100 LSVL 40214 5832 D3
Hillcircle Rd
1900 LSVL 40214 5832 D3
Hillcreek Ct
- OdmC 40059 5292 A7
100 BltC 40047 6056 D5
Hillcreek Dr
100 BltC 40047 6056 D4
Hillcreek Rd
- HBNE 40165 6053 D4
100 BltC 40165 6053 D4
3500 LSVL 40220 5727 C1
W Hillcreek Rd
10 BltC 40165 6052 B6
Hillcrest
200 ELZT 42701 6812 B2
Hillcrest Av
100 LSVL 40206 5617 B2
Hillcrest Ct
- OdmC 40014 5405 A5
6200 CTWD 40014 5403 E7
6200 CTWD 40014 5404 A7
Hillcrest Dr
- OdmC 40014 5404 E4
- OdmC 40014 5405 A5
500 RDCF 40160 6483 B3
1400 CHAN 47111 5181 E3
N Hillcrest Dr
400 VNGV 40175 6482 E7
S Hillcrest Dr
100 VNGV 40175 6482 E7
Hillcrest Rd
7600 OdmC 40014 5512 A1
8800 BltC 40047 6055 E5
8800 MTWH 40047 6056 A5
Hillcross Ct
10600 LSVL 40229 5944 A3
Hillcross Dr
3500 LSVL 40229 5944 A3
Hillcross Pkwy
12500 OdmC 40059 5292 B7
Hilliard Av
1100 LSVL 40204 5616 D4
Hillock Dr
9700 LSVL 40291 5837 C6
Hillock Ln
2000 OdmC 40014 5405 D4
Hill Park Ct
3100 LSVL 40220 5727 C1
Hillpark Dr
10500 LSVL 40229 5944 A3
Hill Park Wy
7200 LSVL 40220 5727 D1
Hill Peak Ct
6800 LSVL 40214 5723 C7
10500 LSVL 40229 5944 A3
Hill Peak Rd
6800 LSVL 40214 5723 B7
Hill Rd Ct
1500 LSVL 40204 5616 C6
Hillridge Dr
9200 OdmC 40056 5512 D4
Hill Ridge Rd
10 CLKV 47129 5397 E3
10 SpnC 40071 5949 E4
Hill Ridge Ter
500 LSVL 40214 5833 B2
Hillrose Cir
12000 DGSH 40243 5620 C5
Hillrose Dr
500 DGSH 40243 5620 C5
Hills Dr
100 CLKV 47129 5506 C5
Hillsboro Ct
3500 STMW 40207 5618 A5
Hillsboro Rd
3900 SPLE 40207 5618 B4
3900 STMW 40207 5618 B4
Hillsdale Rd
3700 GNVW 40222 5509 B2
3700 LSVL 40222 5509 B2
Hillside Cir
5700 FydC 47122 5503 B7
Hillside Dr
4300 SVLY 40216 5723 B6
4600 LSVL 40216 5723 B6
6700 OdmC 40056 5512 D4
7500 OdmC 40014 5511 E1
12100 GSHN 44026 5292 C3
Hillside Dr NE
3300 HsnC 47136 5610 B3
Hill Side Ln
4300 JFVL 47130 5398 B6
Hillside Ln
500 WDYH 40207 5618 A1
Hillside Rd
100 HLVW 40229 5944 B7
7200 LSVL 40214 5832 A4
Hillside Ter
2700 LSVL 40206 5617 A3
Hillside Wy
100 LSVL 40223 5620 A4
Hillstone Dr
9200 LSVL 40299 5728 A5
Hilltop Cir
2500 RDCF 40160 6484 A7
Hilltop Ct
- OdmC 40059 5292 B7
10 LSVL 40214 5724 C5
10 LSVL 40215 5724 C5
Hilltop Dr
10 HdnC 40160 6484 B6
10 RDCF 40160 6484 B6
100 MTWH 40047 6056 B3
Hilltop Pl
3000 OdmC 40059 5292 B7
Hill Top Rd
100 VNGV 40175 6482 C7
4200 WDYH 40207 5618 A1
Hilltop Rd
10 FydC 47119 5395 C6
100 BltC 40165 6049 E6
100 BltC 40165 6050 B7
Hill Top Manor Rd
7600 LSVL 40214 5832 B4
Hillvale Rd
3300 LSVL 40241 5510 A3
3500 LSVL 40241 5509 E3
Hillview Av
100 BltC 40165 5944 D7
100 PNRV 40165 5944 D7
200 BltC 40165 6053 D1
200 PNRV 40165 6053 D1
4000 SVLY 40216 5723 C4
Hillview Blvd
100 HLVW 40229 5944 C6
1200 HNTH 40229 5944 A6
Hillview Cir
1200 OdmC 40014 5405 E3
Hillview Ct
8200 LSVL 40258 5831 D5
Hillview Dr
100 BltC 40165 6160 A2
100 HdnC 40175 6482 D2
300 LSVL 40214 5833 C2
500 LSVL 40118 5942 D4
2700 NALB 47150 5396 D6
3200 LSVL 40229 5943 E3
4800 LSVL 40258 5831 D5
Hillview Woods Ct
4900 LSVL 40229 5944 C5
Hillview Woods Pkwy
11000 LSVL 40229 5944 B5
11300 HLVW 40229 5944 C5
Hillwood Ct
1200 LGNG 40031 5296 D1
Hillwood Dr
5800 LSVL 40219 5835 A1
Hilo Ct
3000 JFTN 40220 5728 A3
Hilton Ct
5100 LSVL 40218 5726 E6
Hinchbrook Blvd
13200 LSVL 40272 5939 D7
13300 LSVL 40272 6048 D1
Hindle Av
200 LSVL 40118 5833 C7
Hines Ct
1200 LSVL 40223 5620 E1
Hines Rd
1400 LSVL 40223 5620 E1
Hines Mill Wy
6200 LSVL 40291 5837 C1
Hinkle Ln
- LSVL 40245 5512 C4
- OdmC 40056 5512 C4
Hinsdale Ct
3000 LSVL 40241 5510 C5
Hisham Ct
600 ELZT 42701 6812 A1
Hish Pine Dr
- BltC 40165 6162 E7
Hispanyola Ct
4000 LSVL 40229 5944 A3
Hispanyola Ln
10200 LSVL 40229 5944 B3
Historic Dr
3300 JFTN 40220 5728 A4
3300 LSVL 40299 5728 A4
N Hite Av
100 LSVL 40206 5617 A2
300 LSVL 40206 5616 E1
S Hite Av
100 LSVL 40206 5617 A3
Hite Creek Rd
10400 LSVL 40241 5511 A1
Hitt Ln
- OdmC 40014 5402 C6
N Hitt Ln
- OdmC 40014 5402 C6
Hitt Rd
5100 LSVL 40241 5402 B7
5100 LSVL 40241 5511 B1
5400 OdmC 40014 5402 B7
Hi View Ln
8600 LSVL 40272 5832 B7
9100 LSVL 40272 5831 E7
Hobart Ct
4400 LSVL 40216 5723 D6
Hobart Dr
1400 LSVL 40215 5723 D6
1400 LSVL 40216 5723 D6
Hobbs Ln
600 LSVL 40023 5622 E7
Hobbs Creek Rd
18200 LSVL 40023 5622 E6
Hobbs Park Rd
1500 ANCH 40223 5620 C1
Hobbs Station Rd
10700 LSVL 40223 5620 A1
10900 LSVL 40223 5511 A7
Hobson Wy
100 ELZT 42701 6702 E6
Hodel Rd
1200 LSVL 40213 5725 E4
1200 WSNP 40213 5725 E4
Hodge Dr
100 CLKV 47129 5397 A7
Hodge St
100 CHAN 47111 5181 D1
Hodgenville Rd
10 ELZT 42701 6812 E6
1000 HdnC 42701 6812 E7
Hodgenville Rd SR-210
10 ELZT 42701 6812 E6
1000 HdnC 42701 6812 E7
Hodges Ln
100 BltC 40109 6052 D2
Hoertz Av
1300 LSVL 40204 5616 A7
1300 LSVL 40217 5616 A7
Hofelich Ct
5600 LSVL 40291 5837 C1
Hofelich Ln
9600 LSVL 40291 5837 C1
Hoffman Dr
500 NALB 47150 5505 B3
1700 OdmC 40031 5297 B3
Hoffman Ln
100 LGNG 40031 5297 B2
300 OdmC 40031 5297 B3
Hogan Ln
2200 LSVL 40118 5943 C2
Hogans Run
7700 LSVL 40228 5836 C5
Hogarth Ct
9100 HTBN 40222 5619 C6
Hogarth Dr
1200 HTBN 40222 5619 C6
Hoke Rd
1900 HBNA 40220 5619 B7
1900 HBNA 40220 5728 B1
Holgate Dr
- HLVW 40229 5944 D5
- LSVL 40229 5944 D5
Holiday Dr
9300 LSVL 40272 5832 A7
9500 LSVL 40272 5941 A1
Holiday Pk
10 LSVL 40219 5834 D6
Holiday Manor Ctr
2200 CSGT 40222 5509 C5
2200 NHFD 40222 5509 C5
Holiday Towers Blvd
- LSVL 40213 5834 E2
Hollary Dr
400 NALB 47150 5505 B3
Hollee Dr
1000 NALB 47150 5396 D6
Hollen Rd
1900 BCFT 40222 5509 E6
1900 GYDL 40222 5509 E6
Hollendale Wy
1100 GSHN 44026 5292 C3
Holley Rd
100 HTBN 40222 5619 A3
100 LYDN 40222 5619 A3
Hollingsworth Pl
700 LSVL 40207 5508 B7
Hollins Rd
4900 LSVL 40214 5724 D6
Hollis Ln
4700 LSVL 40241 5510 B1
Hollis St
100 RDCF 40160 6483 E6
Holliswood Rd
100 BLMD 40222 5619 B3
Holloway Rd
2400 JFTN 40299 5729 A2
Hollow Bridge Dr
200 HdnC 42701 6593 E6
Hollow Creek Ct
6800 HWCK 40228 5836 C3
Hollow Creek Rd
7100 HWCK 40228 5836 C3
7100 LSVL 40228 5836 C3
Hollow-Hills Rd
100 BltC 40047 6056 D6
Hollow Oak Dr
3000 OdmC 40014 5405 D6
Hollow Tree Rd
6400 HWCK 40228 5836 D2
Holly Av
- OdmC 40014 5511 E1
- OdmC 40014 5512 A1
1100 LSVL 40118 5942 E3
1100 LSVL 40118 5943 A2
Holly Ct
1700 RDCF 40160 6482 E4
1700 RDCF 40160 6483 A4

INDEX 26
Holly Dr
Louisville Metro Street Index
Indian Oaks Cir

STREET Block City ZIP Map# Grid

Holly Dr
100 BltC 40047 6055 E4
800 JFVL 47130 5507 D3
Holly Ln
- BltC 40109 5943 E5
2500 OdmC 40031 5296 C7
12200 ANCH 40223 5511 D7
Holly St
- HdnC 40121 6265 B7
Holly Forest Ct
4700 LSVL 40245 5512 A3
Holly Forest Rd
13200 LSVL 40245 5512 A3
Holly Hill Dr
10 ELZT 42701 6811 C1
Holly Hills Dr
10 LSVL 40118 5942 C3
Hollyhock Dr
- LGNG 40031 5296 C3
Hollyhock Ln
10800 LSVL 40272 5941 E1
Holly Lake Ct
6600 LSVL 40291 5837 C3
Holly Lake Dr
6600 LSVL 40291 5837 C3
Holly Marie Dr
- BltC 40047 6055 A5
Holly Oak Ct
5800 LSVL 40291 5837 B1
Holly Park Dr
2700 LSVL 40214 5832 D2
Holly Springs Ct
9100 LYDN 40242 5619 C1
Holly Springs Dr
1000 LYDN 40242 5619 B1
Holly Tree Dr
4200 LSVL 40241 5510 E2
Holly View Ct
10800 LSVL 40299 5728 E5
10800 LSVL 40299 5729 A5
Holly Village Ct
9000 LYDN 40242 5619 B1
Hollywood Blvd
2500 CLKV 47129 5506 B3
Hollywood Ter
2700 LSVL 40206 5617 A2
Holmans Ln
2800 JFVL 47130 5398 C6
Holsclaw Hill Ct
100 BltC 40109 6052 A1
Holsclaw Hill Rd
- BltC 40109 5942 C7
100 BltC 40109 5943 A6
100 BltC 40109 6052 A1
9900 LSVL 40118 5942 C4
Holstein Ct
- OdmC 40014 5402 C6
Holston Dr
200 MRGH 40155 6264 D4
Holston Rd
8500 BLMD 40222 5619 B3
8500 LYDN 40222 5619 A3
Holston Estates Pl
- MRGH 40155 6264 C4
Holsworth Ct
7000 STMW 40222 5509 D7
Holsworth Ln
1200 STMW 40222 5509 C7
1200 STMW 40222 5618 B2
Holz Ct
800 NALB 47150 5505 E2
Home Wy
10 LGNG 40031 5296 E1
Homestead Av
10 HdnC 40160 6592 D3
100 CLKV 47129 5506 D5
600 RDCF 40160 6592 D3
Homestead Blvd
700 LSVL 40207 5617 D4
Homestead Dr
6800 LSVL 40214 5833 C2
Homestead Tr
16700 LSVL 40023 5731 B4
Homeview Dr
1300 LSVL 40215 5724 A1
1500 SVLY 40216 5724 A1
Homewood Ct
8800 MYHL 40241 5510 C5
Homewood Dr
2000 ANCH 40223 5511 C6
Homewood Pl
2900 MYHL 40241 5510 C5
Honey Ln
10000 LSVL 40229 5946 B4
Honey Hive Pl
1200 MDTN 40243 5620 C7
Honeylore Ct
4900 LSVL 40241 5511 B2
Honeysuckle Ct
100 RDCF 40160 6483 E6
1000 JFVL 47130 5507 D3
3100 FydC 47150 5397 B2
8700 BRWD 40242 5510 B6
Honeysuckle Ln
- WPT 40177 6156 C4
Honeysuckle Wy
800 LSVL 40213 5834 D1
13000 OdmC 40059 5401 B1
Honiasant Rd
7000 LSVL 40214 5832 C2
Honor Av
8600 LSVL 40219 5835 E7
Hoock Av
2800 LSVL 40205 5726 B1
Hood Ln
- RDCF 40160 6483 E5
- RDCF 40160 6484 A5
Hood Rd
4800 LSVL 40213 5834 D1
Hooper Ct
1700 JFVL 47130 5507 A1
Hoosier Ct
1600 NALB 47150 5505 D2

Hoot Owl Camp Rd
2300 SHDV 40165 6162 B2
Hoover Av
2600 NALB 47150 5505 D1
Hoover Ct
100 BltC 40047 6054 E5
Hoover Dr
7200 ClkC 47172 5397 D1
Hoover Wy
7700 LSVL 40219 5836 B3
Hope Ct
4000 LSVL 40220 5727 D1
Hopedale Wy
13400 LSVL 40272 6048 D1
Hopewell Rd
3600 LSVL 40299 5730 A5
4400 LSVL 40299 5839 A1
Hopi Ct
11500 LSVL 40299 5729 A6
Hopkins Ct
1600 LGNG 40031 5297 A1
1600 OdmC 40031 5297 A1
Hopkins Ln
200 JFVL 47130 5507 D4
Horizon Ct
100 BltC 40165 6054 D2
Horizon Ln
8100 LSVL 40219 5835 A6
Horn St
1200 CLKV 47129 5397 D7
E Horn St
- CLKV 47129 5397 D7
- CLKV 47129 5506 D1
Hornback Ln
2100 LSVL 40118 5943 B3
Hornbeam Ln
5800 LSVL 40258 5831 B5
Horncastle Wy
13300 LSVL 40272 5939 D7
13300 LSVL 40272 6048 E1
Horne Av
3800 FydC 47150 5396 D3
Hornung Hills Dr
500 NALB 47150 5505 B3
Horse Run Ct
3500 HBNE 40165 6053 D3
Horseshoe Ct
100 BltC 40165 5944 E5
100 HLVW 40229 5944 E5
100 RDCF 40160 6483 E7
3100 OdmC 40014 5405 C6
Horseshoe Trc
10100 JFTN 40223 5619 D5
Horse Trail Rd
2800 ClkC 47130 5399 C3
Horton Av
3100 LSVL 40220 5618 B7
3100 LSVL 40220 5727 C1
Horton Ct
- ELZT 42701 6812 D5
Horton Dr
- CHAN 47111 5181 D3
Horton Rd
300 LGNG 40031 5296 D2
Hoskins Ln
- JFVL 47130 5507 D1
2800 JFVL 47130 5398 D7
Hosta Ln
5300 LSVL 40258 5831 C5
Hough Run
10 BltC 40047 6056 D5
Hougland Hill Rd
100 BltC 40047 6056 E7
100 BltC 40047 6057 A6
Houle
- SHDV 40165 6161 B3
Hounz Ln
2000 KNLD 40223 5510 E6
2000 LSVL 40223 5510 E7
2500 LSVL 40242 5510 E6
2500 MWVL 40223 5510 E6
2500 MWVL 40242 5510 E6
Houston Blvd
3000 CMBG 40220 5618 E7
3000 HNAC 40220 5618 E7
3000 HNAC 40220 5727 D1
Houston Ln
8000 PWEV 40056 5512 B2
8200 OdmC 40056 5512 B2
Houston St
1700 NALB 47150 5505 C1
Howard Av
800 JFVL 47130 5507 B5
6500 LSVL 40216 5722 A4
W Howard Av
200 CLKV 47129 5506 D5
Howard Ct
10600 JFTN 40299 5728 E4
Howard Rd
2000 OdmC 40031 5297 C2
Howard St
100 ELZT 42701 6702 E6
1200 LSVL 40213 5725 C5
1900 LSVL 40210 5615 A4
2100 LSVL 40211 5615 A4
2300 LSVL 40211 5614 E3
Howell St
400 JFVL 47130 5507 C5
Howell Wy
6200 LSVL 40291 5837 D2
Howey Ln
10 HdnC 40160 6484 A5
10 RDCF 40160 6484 A5
Howey Rd
700 VNGV 40175 6482 C7
700 VNGV 40175 6591 C1
Howleft Rd
100 SHDV 40165 6161 B3
Howling Ln
- LSVL 40059 5401 C6
Hubbard Ln
100 BltC 40047 6056 E3
100 MTWH 40047 6056 E3

Hubbards Ct
5400 WDYH 40207 5618 A1
N Hubbards Ln
100 RHLN 40207 5618 B3
100 STMW 40207 5618 B3
400 WDYH 40207 5618 A1
500 INHC 40207 5509 A7
500 LSVL 40207 5509 A7
500 MYHE 40207 5509 A7
500 WDYH 40207 5509 A7
S Hubbards Ln
100 RHLN 40207 5618 B3
100 STMW 40207 5618 B3
Huber Rd
2300 SVLY 40216 5723 A3
Huber Station Rd
100 BltC 40165 6052 D5
Huberta Dr
3000 LSVL 40216 5722 B7
Huckleberry Ct
4700 LSVL 40216 5723 D7
Huckleberry Ln
1800 OdmC 40059 5291 D4
Huddersfield Ct
800 HTBN 40222 5619 B5
Hudson Av
3300 LSVL 40211 5614 C7
Hudson Ln
8100 LSVL 40291 5837 A1
8400 LSVL 40291 5728 B7
9700 JFTN 40299 5728 D7
Hudson St
- HdnC 40121 6265 D7
- HdnC 40121 6374 D1
Hudson Vw
12000 LSVL 40299 5729 B7
Hudson Lake Dr
5800 LSVL 40291 5837 A1
Huff Ln
6500 LSVL 40216 5722 B5
Hugh Av
1400 LSVL 40213 5725 E4
Hughes Av
6900 CTWD 40014 5403 C7
6900 PWEV 40014 5403 C7
Hughes Rd
3500 LSVL 40207 5617 E5
3500 PLYV 40207 5617 E5
3600 PLYV 40207 5618 A4
Hull St
1100 LSVL 40204 5616 B3
Hume Ct
10600 LSVL 40272 5940 D3
Humler St
800 LSVL 40210 5614 E4
800 LSVL 40211 5614 E4
Hummingbird Cir
4800 LYNV 40213 5725 D5
Hummingbird Hllw
8000 LYDN 40222 5619 C3
Humphrey Ln
100 BltC 40165 6160 C3
Humphry
2400 NALB 47150 5505 C2
Hunnington Pl
1600 HBNA 40220 5619 C7
Hunsinger Blvd
- HNAC 40220 5727 E1
Hunsinger Ln
3000 LSVL 40220 5618 C7
3000 LSVL 40220 5727 D1
Hunsinger Woods Pl
4100 LSVL 40220 5727 D1
Hunt Rd
1100 FydC 47136 5502 D7
1200 FydC 47136 5611 D1
Hunt Club Ln
5500 LSVL 40214 5833 B4
Hunt Country Ln
18800 LSVL 40023 5840 E2
Hunter Av
- LSVL 40214 5724 B6
- LSVL 40215 5724 B6
Hunter Ln
100 ELZT 42701 6812 A1
Hunter Rd
9200 LYDN 40242 5619 C1
Hunter Green Wy
6000 LSVL 40291 5837 B5
Hunter Pointe
1700 JFVL 47130 5507 A1
Hunters Ln
1200 RDCF 40160 6483 A4
Hunters Ln SR-1646
- RDCF 40160 6483 A3
Hunters Pth
1200 OdmC 44026 5292 B2
Hunters Rdg
6000 LSVL 40216 5722 D7
6000 LSVL 40216 5831 D1
Hunters Tr
10 FydC 47119 5394 C4
Hunters Trc
1800 JFVL 47130 5508 A1
Hunters Branch Dr
2800 LSVL 40241 5509 D4
Hunters Chase Ln
6500 LSVL 40258 5831 A1
Hunters Grove Rd
6300 LSVL 40216 5831 E1
Hunters Holler
- FydC 47136 5502 C6
Hunters Point Cir
4600 LSVL 40216 5722 D7
4900 LSVL 40216 5831 D1
Hunters Point Ct
6100 LSVL 40216 5722 D7
Hunters Ridge Ct
13500 OdmC 40059 5401 A2
Hunters Ridge Dr
3700 OdmC 40059 5401 A1
9400 FydC 47122 5392 E4
Hunters Run Dr
7200 PROS 40059 5400 D3

Hunters Run Pl
6800 PROS 40059 5400 D3
Hunter Station Rd
100 ClkC 47172 5288 B6
100 CLKV 47172 5288 B6
Hunter Station Wy
100 CLKV 47172 5288 C6
Hunters Trace Rd
10 OdmC 40031 5297 A1
Hunters Trail Ct
8500 LSVL 40228 5837 A7
Hunters View Ct
13500 OdmC 40059 5401 A2
Hunting Cr
3600 JFVL 47130 5507 A1
Hunting Rd
6000 NHFD 40222 5509 B5
Hunting Creek Dr
6500 PROS 40059 5400 E3
7000 PROS 40059 5401 A3
Hunting Crst
12000 OdmC 40059 5401 B2
12000 PROS 40059 5401 B2
Hunting Ground Ct
9500 LSVL 40228 5836 E7
9700 LSVL 40228 5945 E1
9700 LSVL 40228 5946 A1
Hunting Harbor Rd
6300 PROS 40059 5400 E5
Hunting Stock Pl
800 LSVL 40291 5946 A1
Huntington Ct
10 SbyC 40067 5732 D5
Huntington Ln
10 HdnC 40162 6591 D7
1200 LSVL 40219 5835 B4
Huntington Rd
800 LSVL 40207 5617 D4
Huntington Park Dr
100 PLRH 40213 5726 A6
Huntley Pl
11100 DGSH 40243 5620 B5
Huntoon Av
1300 LSVL 40215 5724 A7
1600 LSVL 40214 5723 E7
1600 LSVL 40215 5723 E7
Huntridge Cir
14800 LSVL 40245 5512 D5
Huntridge Pl
3600 LSVL 40245 5512 D5
Huntsman Tr
7900 LSVL 40291 5836 E4
Huon Dr
3500 LSVL 40218 5726 C3
3500 WBHL 40218 5726 C3
Hurdle Wy
2600 SRPK 40220 5618 E6
Hurlingham Ct
1500 LSVL 40245 5622 D2
S Huron
- HdnC 40121 6374 E3
Huron Av
300 LSVL 40209 5724 E4
Huron Ct
100 SHDV 40165 6161 E2
N Huron St
100 HdnC 40121 6374 E2
Hurst Rd
100 BltC 40109 6050 E2
100 BltC 40165 6050 E2
Hurstbourne Cir
1900 FTHL 40299 5619 C7
1900 FTHL 40299 5728 B1
1900 HBNA 40220 5619 C7
1900 HBNA 40220 5728 B1
Hurstbourne Ln
9000 FTHL 40299 5728 C1
9000 HBNA 40220 5619 B7
9000 HBNA 40220 5728 B1
9000 JFTN 40220 5728 B1
N Hurstbourne Pkwy
- LYDN 40223 5510 E7
- MWVL 40223 5510 E6
- MWVL 40242 5510 D5
100 HTBN 40222 5619 D4
100 JFTN 40223 5619 D4
100 LSVL 40223 5619 D3
100 LYDN 40223 5619 D1
100 WDWD 40223 5619 D3
2800 LSVL 40223 5510 E5
2800 LSVL 40241 5510 E6
2800 MWVL 40241 5510 D5
N Hurstbourne Pkwy SR-1747
- LYDN 40223 5510 E7
- MWVL 40223 5510 E6
- MWVL 40242 5510 D5
100 HTBN 40222 5619 D4
100 JFTN 40223 5619 D4
100 LSVL 40223 5619 D3
100 LYDN 40223 5619 D1
100 WDWD 40223 5619 D3
2800 LSVL 40223 5510 E5
2800 LSVL 40241 5510 E6
2800 MWVL 40241 5510 D5
S Hurstbourne Pkwy
- JFTN 40299 5619 D7
- LSVL 40220 5619 D7
- LSVL 40228 5836 C2
- LSVL 40291 5836 B1
100 HTBN 40222 5619 D5
100 JFTN 40223 5619 D5
100 LYDN 40223 5619 D5
100 WDWD 40223 5619 D4
1600 FTHL 40299 5619 C7
1600 LSVL 40299 5619 C7
1700 HBNA 40220 5619 C7
1700 HBNA 40299 5619 C7
1900 FTHL 40299 5728 A4
1900 HBNA 40220 5728 A4
2000 FTHL 40220 5728 B1
2500 JFTN 40220 5728 A2
2800 LSVL 40220 5728 A2
3400 LSVL 40299 5728 A3

S Hurstbourne Pkwy
4600 LSVL 40299 5727 E6
4700 LSVL 40291 5727 E6
4700 LSVL 40291 5728 A7
S Hurstbourne Pkwy SR-1747
- JFTN 40299 5619 D7
100 HTBN 40222 5619 D5
100 JFTN 40223 5619 D5
100 LYDN 40223 5619 D5
100 WDWD 40223 5619 D4
1600 FTHL 40299 5619 C7
1600 LSVL 40220 5619 C7
1600 LSVL 40299 5619 C7
1700 HBNA 40220 5619 C7
1700 HBNA 40299 5619 C7
1900 FTHL 40299 5728 A4
1900 HBNA 40220 5728 A4
2000 FTHL 40220 5728 B1
2500 JFTN 40220 5728 A2
2800 LSVL 40220 5728 A2
3400 LSVL 40299 5728 A3
4600 LSVL 40299 5727 E6
4700 LSVL 40291 5727 E6
4700 LSVL 40291 5728 A7
Hurstbourne Club Ln
9000 HTBN 40222 5619 B4
Hurstbourne Crossing Dr
9300 LSVL 40299 5728 B5
Hurstbourne Gem Ln
2500 HBNA 40220 5728 B1
2500 JFTN 40220 5728 B1
Hurstbourne Park Blvd
9300 LSVL 40220 5619 C7
9300 LSVL 40299 5619 C7
Hurstbourne Pointe Dr
- LSVL 40299 5728 A5
Hurstbourne Ridge Blvd
- LSVL 40220 5728 A3
3400 LSVL 40299 5727 E3
3500 LSVL 40299 5728 A3
Hurstbourne Springs Dr
3200 JFTN 40220 5728 A3
3200 LSVL 40220 5728 A3
Hurstbourne Village Dr
2300 FTHL 40299 5728 C1
Hurstbourne Woods Dr
3900 LSVL 40299 5728 A4
Hurstbourne Woods Pl
8400 LSVL 40299 5728 A4
Hurstview Rd
6000 LSVL 40291 5836 C1
Hurstwood Ct
9000 HTBN 40222 5619 C6
Huston Dr
300 JFVL 47130 5507 E4
Huston Wy
2800 LSVL 40219 5834 D7
2800 MLHT 40219 5834 D7
Hutcherson Dr
- LSVL 40229 5943 E4
Hutcherson Ln
200 ELZT 42701 6702 B4
200 HdnC 42701 6702 B4
Hutcherson Ln SR-2802
200 ELZT 42701 6702 B4
200 HdnC 42701 6702 B4
Hutcherson Rd
10 ELZT 42701 6702 C2
10 HdnC 42701 6702 C2
Hwy 44
- BltC 40165 6161 B3
- SHDV 40165 6161 B3
Hwy 44 W
- BltC 40165 6161 B3
- SHDV 40165 6161 B3
Hyacinth Ct
9900 LSVL 40241 5510 E3
Hyannis Pl
2600 LDNP 40242 5510 C5
Hycliffe Av
- STMW 40207 5618 A3
3400 LSVL 40207 5617 E4
3400 STMW 40207 5617 E4
3800 NBNE 40207 5618 A4
Hyde Park Dr
4900 LSVL 40216 5723 A7
Hydrangea Wy
10000 LSVL 40241 5510 E4
Hyland Hills Ct
6900 LSVL 40258 5832 A3

I

I Ct
10 LGNG 40031 5296 E2
I-64
- FydC - 5502 B6
- FydC - 5503 B5
- FydC - 5504 E4
- GEOT - 5502 D6
- HsnC - 5501 D7
- HsnC - 5502 A7
- HsnC - 5610 A2
- HTBN - 5619 C7
- JfnC - 5617 B4
- JFTN - 5619 D7
- JFTN - 5620 A7
- LSVL - 5505 E6
- LSVL - 5506 A7
- LSVL - 5615 C2
- LSVL - 5616 A2
- LSVL - 5617 C5
- LSVL - 5618 A5
- LSVL - 5619 D7
- LSVL - 5620 A7
- LSVL - 5621 C7
- LSVL - 5622 D7
- LSVL - 5731 E1
- LSVL - 5732 B1
- MDTN - 5620 C7
- MDTN - 5621 E7
- NALB - 5504 D3
- NALB - 5505 C7

I-64
- SbyC - 5732 B1
- SRPK - 5618 D5
- STMW - 5617 E5
- STMW - 5618 B5
I-64 Sherman Minton Br
- LSVL - 5505 B6
- NALB - 5505 B5
I-65
- BltC - 5943 E6
- BltC - 6052 E6
- BltC - 6053 A5
- BltC - 6161 E1
- BltC - 6162 A1
- ClkC - 5288 D7
- ClkC - 5397 D1
- ClkC - 5506 D4
- CLKV - 5397 D1
- CLKV - 5506 E1
- ELZT - 6812 E1
- HdnC - 6812 E2
- HLVW - 5943 E6
- HLVW - 6052 E7
- HLVW - 6053 A5
- JFVL - 5506 E7
- LSVL - 5615 E6
- LSVL - 5616 A2
- LSVL - 5724 E1
- LSVL - 5725 C7
- LSVL - 5834 E7
- LSVL - 5943 E2
- SHDV - 6161 E1
- SLRB - 5288 C2
I-65 John F Kennedy Mem Br
- JFVL - 5506 E7
- JFVL - 5615 E1
- LSVL - 5615 E1
- LSVL - 5616 A1
I-65 Kentucky Tpk
- BltC - 6161 E5
- BltC - 6162 A7
- SHDV - 6161 E5
- SHDV - 6162 A7
I-71
- CTWD - 5402 E5
- CTWD - 5403 A5
- GNVH - 5509 C4
- GNVW - 5508 E4
- GNVW - 5509 A4
- INDH - 5508 A6
- LGNG - 5296 E4
- LGNG - 5297 A3
- LSVL - 5401 E7
- LSVL - 5402 A7
- LSVL - 5507 E7
- LSVL - 5508 A7
- LSVL - 5509 E3
- LSVL - 5510 E1
- LSVL - 5616 A2
- NHFD - 5509 B4
- OdmC - 5295 E7
- OdmC - 5296 E4
- OdmC - 5297 E1
- OdmC - 5402 E5
- OdmC - 5403 A5
- OdmC - 5404 A2
- SPVL - 5509 C4
I-264
- LSVL - 5505 D7
- LSVL - 5509 B6
- LSVL - 5614 B7
- LSVL - 5723 B1
- NHFD - 5509 C7
- SVLY - 5723 A2
- WNDF - 5509 B6
I-264 Henry Watterson Expwy
- BWDV - 5618 D2
- GYDL - 5509 C7
- LSVL - 5509 C7
- LSVL - 5617 E7
- LSVL - 5618 C5
- LSVL - 5723 E5
- LSVL - 5724 D4
- LSVL - 5725 B4
- LSVL - 5726 A3
- NHFD - 5509 B6
- STMW - 5509 C7
- STMW - 5618 D4
- SVLY - 5723 C5
- WDYH - 5509 C7
- WDYH - 5618 A7
- WLNP - 5618 A7
- WSNP - 5726 A3
I-265 Gene Snyder Frwy
- LSVL - 5510 E3
- LSVL - 5511 E5
- LSVL - 5512 B7
- LSVL - 5621 B1
- LSVL - 5729 E7
- LSVL - 5730 A6
- LSVL - 5835 E7
- LSVL - 5836 B7
- LSVL - 5837 A6
- LSVL - 5838 A4
- LSVL - 5944 B1
- MDTN - 5621 B6
I-265 Lee H Hamilton Hwy
- ClkC - 5397 A4
- CLKV - 5397 D4
- FydC - 5395 E7
- FydC - 5396 A6
- FydC - 5397 C4
- JFVL - 5397 A4
- NALB - 5395 E7
- NALB - 5396 D4
- NALB - 5504 E1
Ian Ct
300 MDTN 40243 5620 E4
Ice Av
- ClkC 47172 5288 D7
- ClkC 47172 5397 D1

Ichabod Dr
10500 LSVL 40291 5837 C6
Icicle Ct
- HdnC 40160 6592 B2
Ida Wy
900 LSVL 40214 5833 A3
Idledice
5100 ClkC 47130 5399 A3
Idle Hour Dr
4600 LSVL 40216 5722 C5
Idlewood Ct
1700 CLKV 47129 5506 B1
9500 LSVL 40291 5728 C7
Idlewood Dr
1500 CLKV 47129 5506 B1
Idlewood Ln
5100 JFTN 40299 5728 C7
5100 LSVL 40291 5728 C7
5500 LSVL 40291 5837 C1
Idlewylde Ct
2400 LSVL 40206 5616 E2
Idlewylde Dr
200 LSVL 40206 5616 E2
Idylewild Dr
2500 FXCH 40165 6053 A3
Ilex Av
- PLRH 40213 5726 B6
5200 LSVL 40213 5726 B6
Illinois Av
100 JFVL 47130 5506 E7
1500 LSVL 40217 5725 C1
3400 LSVL 40213 5725 D1
4600 LSVL 40218 5725 E5
Illinois Ct
3100 LSVL 40213 5725 C1
Illinois Rd
1500 RDCF 40160 6374 A7
1500 RDCF 40160 6483 A1
1700 HdnC 40160 6374 A7
Image Wy
8500 JFTN 40299 5728 A6
Imperial Ct
4900 LSVL 40216 5722 D6
4900 SVLY 40216 5722 D6
Imperial Ter
4800 LSVL 40216 5722 D6
4800 SVLY 40216 5722 D6
Inca Dr
9600 LSVL 40258 5830 E7
9600 LSVL 40272 5830 E7
Independence Ct
500 RDCF 40160 6593 A1
Independence Dr
300 RDCF 40160 6593 B1
Independence Cove
7400 LSVL 40214 5833 D4
Independence School Rd
8400 LSVL 40228 5945 E2
8400 LSVL 40228 5946 A3
8400 LSVL 40291 5946 C3
E Indian Tr
3200 LSVL 40213 5725 E7
3200 LSVL 40219 5725 E7
3700 LSVL 40213 5726 A7
3700 LSVL 40219 5726 A7
4000 PLRH 40213 5726 A7
4300 PLRH 40218 5726 C6
4600 LSVL 40218 5726 D5
W Indian Tr
900 LSVL 40213 5834 D1
1100 LSVL 40213 5725 D7
5600 LSVL 40214 5833 B5
Indian Trc
100 BltC 40165 6051 E7
100 BltC 40165 6160 E1
1200 OdmC 44026 5292 B2
Indiana Av
100 ClkC 47172 5288 D2
700 JFVL 47130 5506 E6
1400 LSVL 40213 5725 C4
1700 NALB 47150 5505 C2
N Indiana Av
- ClkC 47172 5288 E1
100 SLRB 47172 5288 E3
10900 ClkC 47143 5288 E1
N Indiana Av US-31
- ClkC 47172 5288 E1
100 SLRB 47172 5288 E3
10900 ClkC 47143 5288 E1
S Indiana Av
100 SLRB 47172 5288 D4
S Indiana Av US-31
100 SLRB 47172 5288 D4
Indiana Ct
100 NALB 47150 5396 B4
Indiana Tr
100 RDCF 40160 6483 E4
Indian Chute
2000 LSVL 40207 5508 E6
Indian Creek Ct
3300 LSVL 40218 5726 C2
Indian Creek Ln
3400 FydC 47122 5393 E7
3400 FydC 47122 5394 A7
Indian Crest Rd
5300 INDH 40207 5508 E7
Indian Falls Dr
9800 LSVL 40229 5944 E2
Indian Hills Dr
900 ELZT 42701 6812 D1
Indian Hills Grn
4700 INDH 40207 5617 D1
Indian Hills Tr
10 INDH 40207 5508 D6
10 INDH 40207 5617 D1
10 LSVL 40207 5508 B5
Indian Lake Dr
3000 LSVL 40241 5511 B5
Indian Legends Dr
11000 LSVL 40241 5511 A4
Indian Oaks Cir
5500 LSVL 40213 5726 B7
5500 LSVL 40219 5726 B7

INDEX 27
Indianola Dr — Louisville Metro Street Index — Julian Av

STREET Block City ZIP Map# Grid

Indianola Dr
200 SLRB 47172 5288 D3
Indian Ridge Rd
500 WDYH 40207 5509 B7
500 WDYH 40207 5618 A1
600 LSVL 40207 5509 B7
Indian Rock Rd
5600 LSVL 40219 5835 E6
Indian Springs Ct
6100 PROS 40059 5401 A5
Indian Stone Rd
10 BltC 40165 6162 E7
E Indian Stone Rd
100 BltC 40165 6162 E7
Indian Wells Ct
8100 LSVL 40291 5837 C6
Indian Wood Ct
5200 LSVL 40207 5617 E1
Indian Woods Pl
5400 LSVL 40207 5617 E1
Indigo Dr
100 MTWH 40047 6055 D6
8100 LSVL 40258 5831 C5
Indocin Ct
3500 LSVL 40220 5727 D2
Industrial Blvd
- ClkC 47172 5289 A5
- SLRB 47172 5288 E6
- SLRB 47172 5289 A5
400 NALB 47150 5396 A6
1000 LSVL 40219 5834 E3
1000 LSVL 40219 5835 A3
Industrial Pkwy
- JFVL 47130 5397 E7
2900 JFVL 47130 5506 E1
Industrial Wy
10 CHAN 47111 5181 D5
Industry Rd
400 LSVL 40208 5724 C1
500 LSVL 40208 5615 B7
Inges Ct
100 BltC 40165 6054 D3
Ingle Av
3200 LSVL 40206 5617 C3
3400 LSVL 40207 5617 D3
3400 STMW 40207 5617 D3
Ingleside Dr
2300 LSVL 40205 5617 C6
Inglewood Dr
100 LSVL 40118 5942 B1
Ingram Av
200 FydC 47150 5396 C3
Ingrid Dr
100 BltC 40165 6054 C3
Inkberry Ct
7000 LSVL 40291 5837 A2
Inland Ct
7200 FydC 47122 5393 D6
Innes Trace Ct
3300 LSVL 40222 5509 B3
Innes Trace Rd
6000 GNVW 40222 5509 B3
6000 LSVL 40222 5509 B3
Innis Ct
1100 LSVL 40204 5616 B5
Innisbrook Ct
7900 PROS 40059 5400 D2
Innisbrook Dr
6300 PROS 40059 5400 D2
Innsbruck Wy
6500 LSVL 40228 5836 B2
Innwood Dr
5500 LSVL 40214 5833 B3
Inspiration Ct
14600 LSVL 40245 5621 C6
Inspiration Wy
700 LSVL 40245 5621 C6
Interchange Dr
11400 LSVL 40229 5944 C3
Interchange Wy
5100 LSVL 40229 5944 B3
Interlaken Wy
6200 OdmC 40014 5402 B6
Intermodal Dr
7000 LSVL 40258 5830 D1
International Dr
7000 LSVL 40258 5721 E7
7000 LSVL 40258 5830 E1
Intramural Pl
- LSVL 40208 5724 D1
Inverary Ct
1200 HTBN 40222 5619 D7
Inverness Av
200 LSVL 40214 5724 C7
400 LSVL 40214 5833 B1
Inverness Dr
4100 FydC 47150 5396 D2
Invicta Dr
4900 LSVL 40216 5723 B7
4900 LSVL 40216 5832 B1
Iobal Ct
- ELZT 42701 6702 D6
Iola Rd
100 LSVL 40207 5617 E3
100 STMW 40207 5617 D3
Iona Ct
9000 LSVL 40291 5837 B3
Ionic Ct
9400 JFTN 40299 5728 C5
Iowa Av
200 LSVL 40208 5724 C2
800 SLRB 47172 5288 C3
Iowa Ct
10 ELZT 42701 6812 A2
Ireland Av
200 HdnC 40121 6374 C2
Ireland Dr
1100 LSVL 40219 5835 A4
Ireland Lp
10 HdnC 40121 6374 D2
Ireland School Rd
10 HdnC 40160 6592 B4
Irewick Wy
7000 LSVL 40272 5939 D1
Iris Ct
800 JFVL 47130 5507 D3
Iris Wy
2900 LSVL 40220 5618 C7
Iris Bed Ct
12600 MDTN 40243 5620 D6
Irish Moss Ct
- OdmC 40014 5403 E4
Iron Ct
6600 FydC 47122 5502 E6
Iron Gate Ct
7200 GNSP 40241 5509 E1
Irongate Ct
6800 FydC 47122 5502 E6
Iron Horse Wy
3700 LSVL 40272 5941 A3
4000 LSVL 40272 5940 E3
Ironweed Ct
5700 FydC 47122 5503 B7
Ironwood Av
- LSVL 40213 5726 C6
- PLRH 40218 5726 C6
Ironwood Cir
200 ELZT 42701 6812 E6
Ironwood Ct
1200 JFVL 47130 5507 B2
2300 CLKV 47129 5397 B6
Ironwood Rd
1800 OdmC 40031 5296 B7
Ironwood Tr
100 BltC 40165 6163 A7
Iroquois Av
200 LSVL 40214 5724 C7
800 LSVL 40214 5833 A1
Iroquois Ct
5300 LSVL 40214 5724 B7
Iroquois Pkwy
1400 LSVL 40214 5832 E1
N Iroquois St
10 HdnC 40121 6374 E2
S Iroquois St
- HdnC 40121 6374 E2
Iroquois Gardens Dr
100 LSVL 40214 5833 B2
Iroquois Park Rd
6600 LSVL 40214 5832 D2
Irvin Ct
100 RDCF 40160 6483 C6
Irving Dr
- ClkC 47129 5506 D2
700 CLKV 47129 5506 D2
Irvin Pines Dr
10500 LSVL 40229 5945 B1
10600 LSVL 40229 5944 E2
Irwin Av
100 ELZT 42701 6812 D1
Isaac Al
100 LSVL 40211 5614 D5
Isaac Pl
2700 LSVL 40211 5614 D5
Isabel Dr
10200 LYDN 40223 5510 E7
Island Pointe Pl
6700 LSVL 40258 5831 B3
Island View Dr
10 JFVL 47130 5508 C2
Isleworth Ct
14700 LSVL 40245 5621 C2
Isleworth Dr
1200 LSVL 40245 5621 C2
Itworth Ct
6800 WDYH 40207 5509 C7
Ivan Ct
7200 LSVL 40214 5833 C3
Ivanhoe Av
3800 JFVL 47130 5398 A7
Ivanhoe Ct
1800 LSVL 40205 5616 E6
Ivinell Av
8500 LSVL 40291 5728 A7
Ivory Ct
7900 LSVL 40219 5835 A5
Ivy Ct
10 NALB 47150 5504 E4
10 NALB 47150 5505 A4
Ivy Dr
- BltC 40047 6055 E5
Ivy Rd
- LSVL 40213 5725 B2
- LSVL 40217 5725 B2
Ivybridge Cir
10000 LSVL 40241 5510 E3
Ivy Oaks Ct
2500 LSVL 40245 5622 D1
Ivy Ridge Ln
1900 LSVL 40272 5941 E1
Ivy Springs Ct
18000 LSVL 40023 5622 E6
Ivywood Pl
2000 LSVL 40218 5727 A5

J

J Ct
100 LGNG 40031 5296 E2
J Dr
100 SHDV 40165 6161 D1
J St
1000 HdnC 40121 6374 C2
Jackie St
100 ELZT 42701 6702 E2
100 HdnC 42701 6702 E2
Jackie Wy
2100 SHDV 40165 6161 E3
2100 SHDV 40165 6162 A3
Jacks Ln
3200 SVLY 40216 5723 B2
Jackson Av
- LSVL 40213 5725 D2
Jackson Dr
1800 ClkC 47172 5397 D1
Jackson St
- HdnC 40121 6374 D3
10 NALB 47150 5504 E7
100 CLKV 47129 5506 B5
100 RDCF 40160 6593 B2
500 JFVL 47130 5507 C5
600 ELZT 42701 6703 C7
1100 NALB 47150 5505 C4
S Jackson St
100 LSVL 40202 5616 A3
300 LSVL 40202 5615 E5
600 LSVL 40203 5615 E4
1200 LSVL 40208 5615 E6
S Jackson St SR-61
100 LSVL 40202 5616 A3
300 LSVL 40202 5615 E6
600 LSVL 40203 5615 E4
1200 LSVL 40208 5615 E6
Jackson Creek Ct
500 LSVL 40245 5621 B6
Jacob Ct
1300 RDCF 40160 6483 A4
E Jacob St
100 LSVL 40202 5615 E4
100 LSVL 40203 5615 E4
500 LSVL 40203 5616 A4
700 LSVL 40204 5616 A4
W Jacob St
100 LSVL 40202 5615 D4
100 LSVL 40203 5615 D4
Jacob Glen Wy
4300 LSVL 40241 5510 E3
Jacobs Dr
2400 NALB 47150 5505 A2
Jacobs School Rd
6300 LSVL 40059 5400 C4
6300 PROS 40059 5400 C4
Jacolyn Tr
3600 ClkC 47130 5398 D4
Jacovino Dr
- CTWD 40014 5404 A6
Jacquelin Ct
600 ELZT 42701 6702 D6
Jacqueline Wy
10700 LSVL 40272 5940 C3
Jacques Ln
500 NALB 47150 5396 B7
Jade Ct
4300 LSVL 40216 5722 E5
Jade Dr
100 SHDV 40165 6161 D1
Jade Green Wy
7900 LSVL 40291 5837 B4
Jaeger Av
1600 LSVL 40205 5616 D6
1900 LSVL 40213 5616 D6
Jaegers Ln
4000 FydC 47150 5395 E4
4000 FydC 47150 5396 A4
4000 NALB 47150 5396 A4
Jaffa Cir
6800 LSVL 40241 5509 D4
Jaffrey Dr
3400 NALB 47150 5395 E6
Jamaica Dr
7400 LSVL 40214 5832 C3
James Ct
500 RDCF 40160 6483 B3
James Dr
600 JFVL 47130 5507 D4
James Rd
400 LSVL 40206 5616 E1
4500 LSVL 40209 5724 E4
4500 LSVL 40209 5725 A4
James St
100 ELZT 42701 6812 C2
James Farm Rd
6900 LSVL 40228 5836 C5
James Guthrie Ct
2200 LSVL 40217 5724 E1
James Hill Rd
9100 LSVL 40272 5832 B7
James Madison Wy
6800 LSVL 40272 5939 D7
James Pirtle Ct
2200 LSVL 40217 5724 E1
James R Rd
8600 LSVL 40118 5833 D7
James R Meder Rd
- LSVL 40216 5723 A6
- SVLY 40216 5723 A6
Jamestown Ct
1000 STMW 40207 5618 A5
Jamie Collins Dr
6100 LSVL 40291 5836 D1
Jamison St
5400 MdeC 40121 6373 C2
5500 HdnC 40121 6374 A3
Jan Wy
8400 LSVL 40219 5835 A7
Jane Av
400 JFVL 47130 5507 C5
Jane St
200 LGNG 40031 5296 E3
300 JFVL 47130 5507 C5
N Jane St
100 LSVL 40206 5616 E2
S Jane St
100 LSVL 40206 5616 E3
Janell Rd
3300 SVLY 40216 5723 C3
Janet Dr
1000 RDCF 40160 6483 D6
Janet Lee Ct
9900 LSVL 40291 5837 D1
Janet Lee Dr
5700 LSVL 40291 5837 D1
Janice Wy
4500 LSVL 40216 5723 C6
Janie Ln
100 NALB 47150 5396 A7
Jan Lee Dr
4700 FydC 47150 5397 A3
Janlyn Rd
1800 JFTN 40299 5728 C1
2000 FTHL 40299 5728 C1
Janna Dr
9400 LSVL 40272 5940 A2
9600 LSVL 40272 5939 E2
Japonica Wy
2000 BRWD 40242 5510 B6
2100 PNTN 40242 5510 B6
Jarvis Ln
300 LSVL 40206 5617 C1
400 MKBV 40207 5617 B1
500 MKBV 40207 5508 B7
600 LSVL 40207 5508 B7
600 LSVL 40207 5617 A1
Jarvis Wy
500 LSVL 40207 5617 B1
500 MKBV 40207 5617 B1
Jarvis Woods Ct
3000 LSVL 40206 5617 A1
Jarvis Woods Ter
700 LSVL 40206 5617 B1
Jasmine Ln
8100 LSVL 40228 5836 E6
Jason Dr
- NALB 47150 5396 C7
Jasper Ct
100 MTWH 40047 6056 B3
4300 LSVL 40272 5831 E7
Jasper Dr
9300 LSVL 40272 5831 E7
Jasper Ln
100 MTWH 40047 6055 D4
Java Ct
4300 LSVL 40218 5727 A4
Jay St
800 NALB 47150 5505 D3
Jaycee St
2000 NALB 47150 5505 C1
J Byrd Roost
- HdnC 40175 6482 E2
Jean Av
4800 LSVL 40216 5722 E6
4800 SVLY 40216 5722 E6
Jean Ct
10 HdnC 42701 6593 C5
Jean Dr
1000 JFVL 47130 5507 C3
Jeanette Av
1300 LSVL 40213 5725 E6
Jeanette Wy
- NALB 47150 5505 B6
Jeanine Dr
5500 LSVL 40213 5726 A7
5500 LSVL 40219 5726 A7
5700 LSVL 40219 5835 B1
Jeffers Dr
4200 FydC 47150 5396 D2
Jefferson Av
1600 LYDN 40242 5510 C7
1600 LYDN 40242 5619 C1
9100 LSVL 40291 5837 B2
W Jefferson Av
200 CLKV 47129 5506 B3
Jefferson Blvd
- ClkC 47172 5397 D1
- LSVL 40219 5835 C3
Jefferson Ct
100 JFVL 47130 5507 A4
100 MTWH 40047 6056 A1
700 LSVL 40217 5725 A2
9000 FydC 47122 5392 E6
Jefferson Pl
800 ELZT 42701 6703 C6
Jefferson St
- HdnC 40121 6374 D2
- JFTN 40299 5728 E4
100 CHAN 47111 5181 E4
100 CHAN 47111 5182 A4
100 ClkC 47111 5181 E4
100 ClkC 47111 5182 A4
100 LGNG 40031 5296 A5
100 RDCF 40160 6593 B1
300 ELZT 42701 6812 B2
500 JFVL 47130 5507 B6
900 OdmC 40031 5296 C3
Jefferson St SR-146
100 LGNG 40031 5296 A5
900 OdmC 40031 5296 C3
E Jefferson St
100 LGNG 40031 5296 E2
100 LGNG 40031 5297 A2
100 LSVL 40202 5615 E3
500 LSVL 40202 5616 A3
700 LSVL 40204 5616 A3
700 LSVL 40206 5616 A3
E Jefferson St SR-146
100 LGNG 40031 5296 E2
100 LGNG 40031 5297 A2
W Jefferson St
100 LSVL 40202 5615 E3
600 LSVL 40203 5615 B2
2000 LSVL 40212 5615 B2
3200 LSVL 40212 5614 C2
Jefferson Wy
10 MTWH 40047 6055 E1
Jefferson Centre Wy
2700 JFVL 47130 5398 D7
Jefferson Hill Rd
10000 LSVL 40118 5942 A3
10200 LSVL 40118 5941 E4
Jefferson Trace Blvd
11200 LSVL 40291 5837 E3
Jefferson Trace Ct
6600 LSVL 40291 5837 E2
Jeffie Ln
2200 HLVW 40229 5944 A7
Jeffrey Ct
10 MdeC 40175 6482 A4
2600 RDCF 40160 6484 A7
Jeffrey Dr
10 RDCF 40160 6483 D6
6000 LSVL 40216 5831 B1
6000 LSVL 40258 5831 B1
Jen Ct
8700 LSVL 40299 5728 A4
Jenevive N
7400 LSVL 40228 5836 C5
Jenevive Ct S
7300 LSVL 40228 5836 C5
Jenica Wy
3900 LSVL 40241 5510 A2
Jenkins Rd
10 HdnC 40162 6591 A7
Jenlee Ln
2500 SVLY 40216 5723 C2
Jenness Ct
5900 NHFD 40222 5509 B5
Jennifer Dr
7000 FydC 47122 5393 C5
Jennifer Pl
7500 LSVL 40220 5727 E1
Jennifer Ridge Pl
7900 LSVL 40258 5831 A4
Jennifer Valley Wy
6500 LSVL 40258 5722 A7
Jennings Ct
10 CHAN 47111 5181 D5
100 RDCF 40160 6483 A1
4000 LSVL 40218 5726 B5
4000 PLRH 40218 5726 B5
Jennings Ln
4500 LSVL 40218 5726 B4
4500 PLRH 40218 5726 B4
4500 WSNP 40218 5726 B4
4800 LSVL 40213 5726 C6
Jennings St
200 CHAN 47111 5181 D5
Jenny Av
10 ELZT 42701 6812 B4
Jenny Ln
3200 FydC 47119 5395 B6
Jenny June Dr
5200 LSVL 40213 5726 A7
Jenny Lind Dr
8200 LSVL 40219 5835 D6
Jennymac Ct
- HLVW 40229 5944 A5
Jennymac Dr
100 HLVW 40229 5944 A5
Jenny Wren Ct
10 ClkC 47129 5397 A6
10 CLKV 47129 5397 A6
Jeremie Ct
900 LSVL 40118 5833 E6
Jeremy Ct
10 SpnC 40071 5949 E4
Jericho Rd
500 LGNG 40031 5297 A2
Jermar Dr
4600 LSVL 40216 5722 C4
Jerry Ln
5800 LSVL 40258 5831 B5
Jerry Tucker Wy
- LSVL 40059 5400 D1
- PROS 40059 5400 D1
Jersey Av
- ClkC 47111 5182 A5
Jersey Ct
10 ELZT 42701 6812 A2
Jersey Park Rd
7000 FydC 47119 5284 B7
8200 FydC 47106 5284 B7
8200 FydC 47124 5284 B7
Jessamine Ln
5300 LSVL 40258 5831 C4
Jesse Wy
4400 BltC 40165 6162 D1
Jesse Martin Rd
9500 FydC 47124 5392 C2
Jessica Ct
100 SHDV 40165 6161 A6
6900 LSVL 40245 5512 D4
6900 OdmC 40056 5512 D4
Jessica Allen Dr
8600 LSVL 40291 5836 D1
Jessica Leigh Dr
9000 LSVL 40228 5836 A6
Jester Cir
1100 STMW 40222 5618 E1
Jett Thomas Dr
4500 LSVL 40228 5727 B6
Jewell Av
- LSVL 40212 5614 C1
4400 LSVL 40212 5505 B7
Jim Ct
100 HLVW 40229 5944 A7
Jim Hawkins Dr
4100 LSVL 40229 5944 B2
Jim Julius Al
- LSVL 40215 5724 A5
Jimmy Ct
900 HdnC 40160 6592 C4
Jimwood Dr
500 VNGV 40175 6482 E7
J Mattingly Rd
- LGNG 40031 5296 D1
- OdmC 40031 5296 D1
Jo Ct
9400 JFTN 40299 5728 C6
Joan Av
300 ELZT 42701 6812 C1
500 ELZT 42701 6703 B7
2800 LSVL 40205 5617 E7
Joan Ct
3600 OdmC 40014 5296 E7
Joann Ct
4300 FydC 47119 5394 E4
Jo Danielle Pl
6000 LSVL 40291 5836 D1
Joe Davis St
300 CLKV 47129 5506 E7
Joe Don Ct
2600 LSVL 40214 5832 C4
Joe Prather Hwy
- HdnC 42701 6593 D2
- RDCF 40160 6593 A3
- RDCF 42701 6593 C2
Joe Prather Hwy SR-313
- HdnC 42701 6593 D2
- RDCF 40160 6593 A3
- RDCF 42701 6593 C2
Joe Prather Hwy S
100 HdnC 40175 6482 C5
100 VNGV 40175 6482 D5
400 VNGV 40175 6483 A6
Joe Prather Hwy S SR-313
100 HdnC 40175 6482 C5
100 VNGV 40175 6482 C5
400 VNGV 40175 6483 A6
Joetta Ct
4100 LSVL 40216 5723 D5
Joey Ct
100 BltC 40047 6056 B4
100 MTWH 40047 6056 B4
Johanna Ct
4600 PNRV 40229 5944 B7
John St
500 JFVL 47130 5507 A6
John Wy
300 RDCF 40160 6483 E6
John Adams Wy
6700 LSVL 40272 6048 D1
7000 LSVL 40272 5939 D7
John Ashley Ct
10100 JFTN 40299 5728 D5
John Cook Ln NE
6600 HsnC 47136 5610 C2
John F Kennedy Memorial Br
- JFVL - 5506 E7
- JFVL - 5615 E1
- LSVL - 5615 E1
- LSVL - 5616 A1
John F Kennedy Mem Br I-65
- JFVL - 5506 E7
- JFVL - 5615 E1
- LSVL - 5615 E1
- LSVL - 5616 A1
John Hancock Pl
6700 PROS 40059 5401 A4
John Harper Hwy
- HLVW 40229 6053 A1
- PNRV 40229 6053 A1
100 HBNE 40165 6053 C2
100 PNRV 40165 6053 B2
John Harper Hwy SR-1526
100 HBNE 40165 6053 C2
100 PNRV 40165 6053 B2
500 PNRV 40229 6053 A1
900 HLVW 40229 6053 A1
John Law Ct
4700 LSVL 40272 5940 C4
John Law Wy
11200 LSVL 40272 5940 C4
John Moser Wy
6000 OdmC 40014 5402 B6
Johnny Dr
700 JFVL 47130 5507 D5
John Paul Ct
9000 LSVL 40229 5836 B7
John Paul Ln
6800 LSVL 40229 5836 B7
John Pectol Rd
7100 FydC 47119 5393 C5
7100 FydC 47122 5393 C5
8900 FydC 47122 5392 E5
Johns Ln
100 BltC 40165 6163 A1
300 BltC 40165 6054 A7
Johns Rd
- FydC 47122 5392 A6
- FydC 47124 5392 A6
100 RDCF 40160 6483 B4
John Silver Ct
10000 LSVL 40229 5944 B3
Johnson Dr
100 SHDV 40165 6161 E6
1900 ClkC 47172 5397 D2
Johnson Ln
100 CLKV 47129 5506 B2
Johnson Rd
10 HdnC 42701 6593 A2
10 RDCF 40160 6593 A2
10 RDCF 42701 6593 A2
100 LSVL 40023 5622 B6
100 LSVL 40245 5622 B2
Johnson Rd SR-1531
100 LSVL 40023 5622 B6
100 LSVL 40245 5622 B2
N Johnson St
- LSVL 40206 5616 B2
S Johnson St
100 LSVL 40206 5616 B3
Johnson Farm Rd
1000 LSVL 40245 5622 B4
Johnson Green Blvd
9400 LSVL 40291 5837 A4
Johnson Hall Dr
- LSVL 40207 5617 D2
Johnson Hollow Rd
- BltC 40165 6051 D6
100 BltC 40165 6052 A6
Johnson School Rd
7400 LSVL 40291 5837 A6
Johnsontown Dr
- LSVL 40258 5830 D7
- LSVL 40272 5830 D7
Johnsontown Rd
5100 LSVL 40258 5831 A7
5100 LSVL 40272 5831 A7
5800 LSVL 40258 5830 E7
5800 LSVL 40272 5830 E7
Johnsontown Rd SR-1230
7300 LSVL 40258 5830 D7
7300 LSVL 40272 5830 D7
Johnsontown Wy
- LSVL 40272 5830 D7
9500 LSVL 40258 5830 D7
Johnston St
- HdnC 40121 6374 D3
Johnston Wy
3500 LSVL 40220 5727 A1
Johnstown Rd
1100 ELZT 42701 6702 D7
John Wrege Rd
2400 FydC 47119 5395 D4
Jollissaint Av
2200 NALB 47150 5505 B2
Jolynn Dr
4500 JFTN 40299 5728 C6
Jolynn Wolf Wy
4800 LSVL 40023 5840 A1
Jomarie Ct
2800 LSVL 40220 5727 D2
Jonar Ct
5100 LSVL 40291 5728 A7
Jonathan Ct
7100 ODGH 40014 5402 D7
8200 LSVL 40228 5836 C6
Jonathan Pl
9400 ODGH 40014 5402 D7
Jonathan Wy
7300 LSVL 40228 5836 C6
Jonel Ct
12200 WTNH 40245 5511 D2
Jones Dr
800 LSVL 40214 5833 B3
3700 OdmC 40031 5295 D5
Jones Ln
3200 FydC 47119 5395 B5
Jones St
1100 HdnC 40160 6484 A5
1100 RDCF 40160 6484 A5
Jones Trc
- OdmC 40014 5402 E6
- OdmC 40014 5403 A6
Joni Dr
1300 LSVL 40216 5723 D5
Jonlyn Ct
4400 WDYH 40207 5618 C1
Jonquil Dr
1000 JFVL 47130 5507 C3
7700 LSVL 40258 5831 B4
Jordan Av
600 LSVL 40208 5615 C6
Jordan Dr
8100 ClkC 47111 5181 B6
Jordon Ct
3900 OdmC 40031 5404 E1
Joseph Av
100 HLVW 40229 5944 D5
Joseph Ct
100 BltC 40047 5947 A7
100 MTWH 40047 5947 A7
100 RDCF 40160 6593 B1
3500 NALB 47150 5396 D4
Joseph Ln
- ELZT 42701 6811 B6
10 HdnC 42701 6811 B6
Joshua Ct
100 BltC 40165 6161 B3
100 RDCF 40160 6592 E2
Joy Av
100 MTWH 40047 6056 D1
Joy Ct
100 MTWH 40047 6056 D1
100 RDCF 40160 6592 E2
1900 JFVL 47130 5507 E4
6200 FydC 47122 5502 E6
Joy Dr
5100 LSVL 40216 5722 B7
Joy Ln
2400 BltC 40165 6053 B4
Joy St
1900 JFVL 47130 5507 E5
Joyce Cir
1100 OdmC 40014 5405 E1
Joyce Ct
1100 OdmC 40014 5405 E1
Joyce Dr
3600 OdmC 40014 5296 E7
3600 OdmC 40014 5405 E1
7700 LSVL 40219 5836 A5
8100 LSVL 40219 5835 E5
E Joyce Ln
100 BltC 40109 6052 C1
W Joyce Ln
300 BltC 40109 6052 B1
Joy Lovene Dr
4800 LSVL 40216 5723 A6
Joyner Hill Rd
2200 LSVL 40272 5941 D2
Juanita Ln
5300 LSVL 40272 5940 B3
Juanita Goins Ct
8300 LSVL 40228 5836 D4
Juarez Ct
8600 LSVL 40219 5836 A7
Judd Ln
2700 LSVL 40272 5941 C2
Jude Ct
100 ELZT 42701 6703 C7
Judge Blvd
7900 LSVL 40219 5835 D5
Judicial Pl
- JFVL 47130 5399 A7
Judith Ct
10200 LSVL 40223 5619 E3
Judy Av
7400 LSVL 40214 5833 B3
Judy Dr
4400 BltC 40165 6053 B4
Judy Ln
3200 SVLY 40216 5723 B2
6000 FydC 47122 5503 A6
Judy Lynn Ct
100 SHDV 40165 6161 B6
Julia Av
1100 LSVL 40204 5616 B5
Julia Rd
5200 LSVL 40258 5831 C5
Julian Av
- LSVL 40208 5615 D6

INDEX 28
Julian Dr
Louisville Metro Street Index
Krupp Park Dr

STREET Block City ZIP Map# Grid
Julian Dr
3000 FydC 47150 5396 E5
3000 FydC 47150 5397 A5
Julianna Ct
1100 ELZT 42701 6703 E5
Julianna Dr
1100 OdmC 44026 5292 B3
Julie Kay's Wy
6100 LSVL 40258 5831 B1
July Ct
5000 LSVL 40258 5831 D3
Jumper Ct
6800 LSVL 40291 5837 A3
Jumper Pl
8700 LSVL 40291 5837 A3
June Dr
10700 HYVA 40118 5942 E4
Juneau Dr
100 MDTN 40243 5620 D4
Juneberry Ct
10800 LSVL 40272 5941 E1
Junell St
100 ELZT 42701 6812 D1
Juniper Dr
1300 LYDN 40222 5619 A1
Juniper Ln
1300 JFVL 47130 5508 A2
Juniper St
10 LGNG 40031 5296 E2
Juniper Beach Rd
5300 LSVL 40059 5509 A1
5600 LSVL 40059 5400 A7
Juniper Forest Pl
4300 LSVL 40245 5512 A3
Juniper Hill Ct
2800 LSVL 40206 5617 B4
Juniper Hill Rd
2900 LSVL 40206 5617 B4
Juniper Springs Ct
8300 LYDN 40242 5619 B1
Juniper Springs Dr
1000 LYDN 40242 5619 B1
Juniper Springs Pl
8800 LYDN 40242 5619 B1
Jupiter Rd
3800 LSVL 40218 5727 B2
Justan Dr
7400 LSVL 40214 5833 A4
Justice Wy
8700 HTCK 40229 5945 E3
Justin Trc
100 MTWH 40047 6056 A3
Justin Cove
1800 OdmC 40059 5291 E1
Justine Ct
9300 JFTN 40299 5728 C5
Justinian
3300 ClkC 47130 5399 A4
Justwood Wy
10900 LSVL 40291 5946 C4

K

K Ct
100 LGNG 40031 5296 E1
Kaelin Av
2200 LSVL 40205 5617 B7
Kaelin Dr
400 STMW 40207 5618 A1
400 WDYH 40207 5618 A1
Kaffir Ct
5200 LSVL 40258 5831 B3
Kahl Ct
200 SLRB 47172 5288 E4
Kahl St
200 SLRB 47172 5288 E4
Kahlert Av
3500 LSVL 40215 5724 A4
Kahn Al
- LSVL 40203 5616 A5
Kaiser Ct
1100 LSVL 40211 5614 B4
Kalmia Ct
13600 LSVL 40299 5729 E5
Kamer Ct
5300 OdmC 40031 5295 B3
Kamer Dr
- OdmC 40031 5295 B4
Kamer Miller Rd
3300 FydC 47150 5396 D2
Kames Sq
5000 LSVL 40241 5510 E1
Kamp Dr
100 BltC 40047 6055 B6
Kane Ct
7200 LSVL 40214 5833 C3
Kansas St
- HdnC 40121 6374 C3
Kanzig Rd
- FydC 47150 5504 D2
- NALB 47150 5504 D2
Kaprun Ct
8900 JFTN 40220 5728 B2
Karen Ct
600 MRGH 40155 6264 D4
5200 FydC 47119 5393 E4
Karie Dr
- SLRB 47172 5288 C5
100 ClkC 47172 5397 E1
100 CLKV 47172 5397 E1
Karly Ct
700 DGSH 40243 5620 A5
Karma Wy
3800 LSVL 40241 5510 A2
Kasey Wy
5500 LSVL 40291 5837 D1
Kaska St
300 MdeC 40155 6264 D4
300 MRGH 40155 6264 D4
Kaskaskia Dr
6000 FydC 47124 5393 A1
Katherine Av
1800 JFVL 47130 5507 D5
Katherine Station Rd
600 BltC 40121 6156 D2
600 BltC 40272 6156 D2
6900 LSVL 40272 6156 E2
Kathleen Av
600 LSVL 40214 5724 B5
600 LSVL 40215 5724 B5
Katie Ct
9800 LSVL 40291 5728 D7
Katy Belle Ct
5300 LSVL 40213 5726 A7
Kaufer Dr
100 FydC 47150 5395 E4
100 FydC 47150 5396 A4
100 NALB 47150 5396 A4
Kaufman Ln
4800 LSVL 40216 5722 C6
Kavanaugh Ln
5900 OdmC 40014 5513 A1
Kavanaugh Rd
- CTWD 40014 5403 E7
7200 CTWD 40014 5512 E1
7200 OdmC 40014 5512 E1
Kavanaugh Spur
- CTWD 40014 5512 E1
- OdmC 40014 5512 E1
- OdmC 40014 5513 A1
Kay Av
500 SLRB 47172 5288 D5
4900 JFTN 40299 5728 A6
Kay Dr
10700 HYVA 40118 5942 E4
Kayak Dr
- LSVL 40241 5511 C1
Kay Alexander Dr
- LSVL 40215 5723 E6
Kaye Lawn Dr
3000 LSVL 40218 5727 C3
3000 LSVL 40220 5727 C3
Kaywood Dr
2700 NALB 47150 5396 D7
Kealrun Ct
9700 LSVL 40241 5510 D3
Kealrun Wy
3900 LSVL 40241 5510 D3
Keane Av
1100 LGNG 40031 5296 E1
1100 LGNG 40031 5297 A1
1100 OdmC 40031 5296 E1
N Keats Av
100 LSVL 40206 5616 E2
S Keats Av
100 LSVL 40206 5616 E3
Keats Dr
1700 CLKV 47129 5397 B7
Keebler Dr
100 HLVW 40229 6053 B1
Keegan Wy
5100 JFTN 40299 5728 D7
5100 LSVL 40291 5728 D7
Keeling Pl Ct
9700 LSVL 40291 5837 C2
Keeling Pl Rd
6500 LSVL 40291 5837 C2
Keen Dr
- SHDV 40165 6161 D4
Keene Rd
10900 LSVL 40241 5511 B1
Keeneland Blvd
2000 KNLD 40223 5510 E7
2000 LYDN 40223 5510 E7
Keeneland Dr
- BltC 40047 6056 E2
100 MTWH 40047 6056 D2
Keever Ct
1600 LSVL 40245 5622 C1
Keewood Ct
5800 NHFD 40222 5509 B5
Kehoe Ln
1000 JFVL 47130 5507 C3
Keira Ridge Ct
8100 LSVL 40291 5836 E1
Keisler Rd
6600 FydC 47124 5283 A7
6600 FydC 47124 5392 A1
Keisler Wy
7300 BCFT 40222 5509 D6
7300 LSVL 40222 5509 D6
Keith Ct
100 RDCF 40160 6483 D6
Keith Hollow Rd
100 BltC 40165 6160 A3
Keithleys Hllw
- FydC 47150 5504 A5
Keith Springs Cir
6400 WDYH 40207 5509 B7
Kelland Wy
3400 SVLY 40216 5723 D3
Keller Av
1100 LSVL 40213 5725 B4
Kellerman Ct
5700 LSVL 40219 5835 E4
Kellerman Rd
8000 LSVL 40219 5835 E4
8000 LSVL 40219 5836 A4
Kelley Av
1700 GEOT 47122 5501 E3
Kelley Dr
200 NALB 47150 5505 C2
Kelleys Rd
1000 FydC 47150 5504 A3
Kelly Av
4000 OdmC 40014 5513 E1
4000 OdmC 40014 5514 A1
Kelly Dr
1200 ELZT 42701 6702 D6
Kelly Ln
13500 LSVL 40272 6048 E1
Kelly St
5300 HdnC 40121 6374 A3
5300 MdeC 40121 6373 C2
Kelly Wy
3600 LSVL 40220 5727 A1
Kelly Green Wy
8000 LSVL 40291 5837 B5
Kemmons Dr
3200 LSVL 40218 5726 B2
Kemo Wy
3000 LSVL 40222 5509 C4
Kempf St
- JFVL 47130 5508 A4
Ken Ln
5500 LSVL 40258 5831 C3
Kena Ln
7100 LSVL 40258 5831 C2
Kenawa Ct
11700 LSVL 40299 5729 A7
Ken Carla Dr
6600 LSVL 40059 5400 D5
6600 PROS 40059 5400 D6
Kendall Ct
700 LSVL 40210 5615 A3
4000 FydC 47119 5394 E4
Kendall Ln
1800 SVLY 40216 5723 A6
Kendall Rd
4900 LSVL 40272 5831 C7
Kendalton Pl
11200 FCSL 40241 5511 B3
Kendrich Ln
6800 LSVL 40299 5838 B4
Kendrick Ct
3000 LSVL 40213 5725 E7
Kendrick Dr
11400 LSVL 40241 5402 C7
Kendrick Crossing Ln
7500 LSVL 40291 5837 E6
Kenhurst Dr
7600 LSVL 40258 5831 A4
Kenil Ct
10 LSVL 40206 5616 E1
Kenilworth Pl
2000 LSVL 40205 5616 E6
2100 LSVL 40205 5617 A6
Kenilworth Rd
300 LSVL 40206 5616 E2
Kenjoy Dr
6300 LSVL 40214 5724 D7
6300 LSVL 40214 5833 D1
Kenli Ct
200 LSVL 40214 5833 C4
Kenlite Rd
- BltC 40165 6052 D5
Kenlock Dr
9100 LDNP 40242 5510 C6
9100 RLGH 40242 5510 C6
Kenmont Ln
9700 CKSD 40241 5510 D5
9700 LSVL 40241 5510 D5
Kenmore Av
6400 LSVL 40216 5722 A4
Kennedy Av
100 LSVL 40206 5617 B2
Kennedy Ct
200 LSVL 40206 5617 B3
Kennedy Rd
1700 LSVL 40216 5723 E1
1700 SVLY 40216 5723 E1
Kennedy St
100 ELZT 42701 6812 C4
Kennedy Pl Cir
4500 LSVL 40272 5831 D7
Kennersley Dr
2600 LDNP 40242 5510 C5
2800 MYHL 40242 5510 C5
Kenneth Ct
- LSVL 40214 5833 C2
Kenney Dr
- BltC 40047 6054 E6
- MTWH 40047 6054 E6
Kennison Av
3900 STMW 40207 5617 E2
Kennison Ct
3900 STMW 40207 5617 E2
Kenny Blvd
300 LSVL 40214 5833 C5
Kenoak Dr
200 LSVL 40214 5833 B1
Kenrose Ln
4700 LSVL 40216 5723 A6
4700 SVLY 40216 5723 A6
Kensington Ct
400 LSVL 40208 5615 C6
Kensington Dr
400 CLKV 47129 5506 C2
Kensington Rd
7400 FydC 47136 5611 D3
Kensington Pl Ln
1700 LSVL 40205 5725 E3
1700 LSVL 40205 5726 A3
Kent Dr
500 NALB 47150 5505 B2
Kent Rd
- LSVL 40206 5617 A4
1000 OdmC 44026 5292 B3
3000 LSVL 40205 5617 E7
Kent St
600 NALB 47150 5504 E3
600 NALB 47150 5505 A3
Kenton Av
4200 LSVL 40213 5725 D4
Kenton Ct
100 RDCF 40160 6483 E4
E Kenton St
100 LSVL 40214 5724 D3
W Kenton St
100 LSVL 40214 5724 C3
400 LSVL 40215 5724 C3
Kentucky Av
400 NRWD 40222 5618 E3
500 JFVL 47130 5507 A5
700 STMW 40222 5618 D2
6800 LSVL 40258 5831 D3
9100 LSVL 40291 5837 B2
Kentucky Cir
10 RDCF 40160 6483 D4
Kentucky Ct
100 BltC 40047 6054 E5
100 BltC 40047 6055 A5
Kentucky Dr
200 ELZT 42701 6811 C5
200 HdnC 42701 6811 B5
Kentucky St
100 VNGV 40175 6591 D1
400 LGNG 40031 5296 D3
E Kentucky St
- LSVL 40204 5616 A5
100 LSVL 40203 5615 E5
600 LSVL 40203 5616 A5
W Kentucky St
100 LSVL 40203 5615 D5
1800 LSVL 40210 5615 A4
2200 LSVL 40210 5614 E4
2500 LSVL 40211 5614 E4
Kentucky Tpk
- BltC - 6161 D3
- BltC - 6162 A7
- SHDV - 6161 D3
- SHDV - 6162 A6
Kentucky Tpk I-65
- BltC - 6161 D3
- BltC - 6162 A7
- SHDV - 6161 D3
- SHDV - 6162 A6
Kentucky Mills Dr
1200 JFTN 40299 5620 B7
1200 JFTN 40299 5729 C1
Kentucky Oaks Ct
3000 OdmC 40014 5405 B7
Kenwood Av
100 CHAN 47111 5181 D4
1000 CLKV 47129 5506 B5
1600 NALB 47150 5505 D1
W Kenwood Av
1000 CLKV 47129 5506 B4
Kenwood Ct
100 LSVL 40214 5724 D6
W Kenwood Dr
200 LSVL 40214 5833 B1
E Kenwood Rd
300 LSVL 40214 5833 C2
E Kenwood Wy
100 LSVL 40214 5724 C6
W Kenwood Wy
100 LSVL 40214 5724 D6
W Kenwood Wy SR-1020
200 LSVL 40214 5724 C6
Kenwood Hill Rd
200 LSVL 40214 5833 B1
Kenyon Dr
6200 LSVL 40272 5939 E3
6200 LSVL 40272 5940 A3
Kenzeli Ct
- SbyC 40245 5513 C4
Kenzig Rd
100 FydC 47150 5504 D2
100 NALB 47150 5504 D2
Kepley Rd
1700 GEOT 47122 5501 E2
1900 FydC 47122 5501 E3
3000 FydC 47122 5392 E7
3900 FydC 47122 5393 A6
Kern Ct
4400 LSVL 40218 5727 B6
Kernen Ct
3700 LSVL 40241 5509 C3
Kerns Ct
500 ELZT 42701 6811 D3
Kerr Ln
100 BltC 40109 6050 D2
Kerrick Ln
4500 LSVL 40258 5831 E2
Kerry Dr
3400 LSVL 40218 5726 C3
3500 WBHL 40218 5726 C3
Kerry Rd
8100 LSVL 40258 5831 D5
Kessler Av
8900 LSVL 40272 5832 E7
8900 LSVL 40272 5833 A7
Kestral Ct
11000 LSVL 40241 5511 B2
Keswick Blvd
800 LSVL 40217 5616 A7
2300 LSVL 40217 5725 A1
Keswick Dr
300 CLKV 47129 5506 D2
Kettle Ln
- BltC 40165 6053 D6
Kev Ct
8700 LSVL 40299 5728 A4
Kevin Ct
4600 JFVL 47130 5398 B5
4800 LSVL 40216 5722 D6
4800 SVLY 40216 5722 D6
Kevin Pl
100 MTWH 40047 6056 A3
Kewanna Dr
200 JFVL 47130 5507 D5
Keys Ferry Rd
9500 LSVL 40118 5942 B3
Keystone Trc
10300 BRMR 40223 5619 E4
Keystone Wy
800 JFTN 40223 5619 B5
Keystone Crossroads
- SHDV 40165 6161 D3
Kiawah Ct
12000 LSVL 40245 5511 E2
12000 WTNH 40245 5511 E2
Kickapoo Dr
- NALB 47150 5504 C7
Kidwell Ln
600 LGNG 40031 5297 B2
Kidwelly Dr
9900 JFTN 40299 5728 D2
Kiefer Rd
4600 LSVL 40216 5723 A6
4600 SVLY 40216 5723 A6
Kiki Ct
3600 LSVL 40219 5835 A6
Kilderry Ct
- LSVL 40245 5621 B5
Kilderry Wy
300 LSVL 40245 5621 B5
Kilgore Ct
4900 LSVL 40218 5726 D6
E Kilgus Cir
7400 CTWD 40014 5512 D1
7400 PWEV 40014 5512 D1
W Kilgus Cir
7400 CTWD 40014 5512 D1
7400 PWEV 40014 5512 D1
Killiney Pl
1300 INHC 40207 5509 A7
1300 WDYH 40207 5509 A7
Killinur Ct
10200 LSVL 40059 5402 A7
Killinur Dr
5400 LSVL 40059 5402 A7
Kilmer Blvd
- PLRH 40213 5726 C6
- PLRH 40218 5726 C6
5100 LSVL 40213 5726 C6
5400 LSVL 40219 5726 C7
Kilmer Wy
1300 CLKV 47129 5397 B7
Kilmory Av
300 LSVL 40214 5833 D2
Kiln Ct
4400 WSNP 40218 5726 B4
Kilrenny Ct
11100 DGSH 40243 5620 B5
Kim Ct
100 RDCF 40160 6592 E1
100 SHDV 40165 6162 A3
200 LSVL 40214 5833 C4
3500 OdmC 40014 5405 A4
Kim Dr
7700 LSVL 40214 5833 C5
Kimball Dr
100 ELZT 42701 6812 D1
Kimberly Ct
10 MTWH 40047 6056 A3
600 RDCF 40160 6483 C6
Kimberly Dr
100 MTWH 40047 6056 A3
Kimberly Wy
8100 LSVL 40291 5836 E5
8400 LSVL 40291 5837 A5
Kimblewick Dr
10100 LSVL 40223 5619 D2
King Cir
200 JFVL 47130 5506 E5
King Rd
4700 ClkC 47130 5289 C6
4700 ClkC 47130 5398 D1
King St
1600 NALB 47150 5505 D4
7800 HdnC 40121 6374 B6
King Arthur Cir
100 ELZT 42701 6811 C3
King Arthur Ct
7500 STMW 40222 5618 E1
King Arthur Ln
1000 STMW 40222 5618 E1
King Arthur Wy
- LSVL 40203 5615 D5
- LSVL 40208 5615 D5
King Church Ct
100 BltC 40071 5948 C4
King Church Rd
- BltC 40071 5949 C2
Kingdom Wy
9100 LSVL 40291 5946 C1
Kingfisher Wy
4800 LYNV 40213 5725 D6
King Hollow Rd
100 BltC 40165 6050 B5
Kinglan Rd
400 WDYH 40207 5509 B7
400 WDYH 40207 5618 B1
King of Arms Ct
1600 GYDL 40222 5509 E7
Kings
- BltC 40165 6160 C5
Kings Ct
7100 STMW 40207 5618 C4
Kings Hwy
2500 KGLY 40205 5617 C7
2500 SGDN 40205 5617 C7
2600 LSVL 40205 5617 D7
3500 LSVL 40220 5618 A7
Kings Ln
3300 OdmC 40031 5296 A5
11600 DGSH 40243 5620 C5
11600 MDTN 40243 5620 C5
Kings Bridge Rd
2900 LSVL 40220 5726 E1
2900 LSVL 40220 5727 A1
Kingsbury Dr
3700 STMW 40207 5618 A5
Kings Church Rd
- BltC 40047 5948 B7
- BltC 40071 5948 B7
- BltC 40071 6057 B1
Kings Cross Ct
2400 LSVL 40272 5941 C1
Kings Falls Ct
6700 LSVL 40229 5945 B3
Kingsfield St
2100 JFVL 47130 5398 A6
Kingsford Dr
1800 LSVL 40216 5723 A6
Kings Lake Dr
100 BltC 40165 6160 D4
Kingsley Dr
12300 PNRV 40229 5944 B7
12300 PNRV 40229 6053 B1
Kingslook Ct
6700 WDYH 40207 5618 C1
Kings Lynn Ln
8700 JFTN 40220 5728 A2
Kingsmill Ct
7900 LSVL 40291 5837 C6
Kingsmill Dr
- LSVL 40291 5837 D6
Kingsmore Dr
4600 LSVL 40229 5944 C3
Kings of Arms Ct
1600 GYDL 40222 5509 E7
E Kingston Av
100 LSVL 40214 5724 D7
N Kingston Av
- LSVL 40214 5724 C7
W Kingston Av
200 LSVL 40214 5724 C7
Kingswood Rd
200 BltC 40071 5948 C4
Kingswood Wy
1300 RDCF 40160 6483 A2
3100 SVLY 40216 5723 B1
3200 LSVL 40216 5723 B1
King Williams Ct
7400 LSVL 40214 5833 D5
Kinloch Rd
700 WLNP 40207 5618 C2
Kinlock Rd
2600 OdmC 40031 5296 C6
Kinnaird Ct
11100 DGSH 40243 5620 B5
Kinnaird Ln
200 DGSH 40243 5620 B4
Kinross Blvd
13400 LSVL 40272 6048 D1
Kinross Ct
10600 DGSH 40223 5620 A6
10600 DGSH 40243 5620 A6
Kinross Pl
800 DGSH 40243 5620 A6
Kinvara Ln
3100 GSCK 40242 5510 B4
Kipling Wy
3000 WLTN 40205 5726 C1
3100 LSVL 40205 5726 C1
Kirby Av
3200 LSVL 40211 5614 C5
Kirby Ln
3500 LSVL 40299 5728 B4
Kirby Rd
6500 FydC 47119 5395 D1
Kirk Ln
4500 JFVL 47130 5398 B4
Kirkham Rd
12400 DGSH 40299 5620 D6
12400 MDTN 40243 5620 D6
12400 MDTN 40299 5620 D6
Kirkham Trc
1100 MDTN 40299 5620 D7
Kirkwood Ct
6100 LSVL 40229 5944 E4
6100 LSVL 40229 5945 A4
Kirkwood Dr
900 CLKV 47129 5397 C7
Kirsch Wy
600 LSVL 40118 5942 D2
Kirsti Ct
100 HLVW 40229 5944 A5
Kitty Hawk Dr
1500 ELZT 42701 6811 A3
Kitty Hawk Wy
4700 WDYH 40207 5509 B7
Klages Av
1800 SVLY 40216 5723 B6
Klapper Rd
100 BltC 40109 6051 B3
Kleier Av
- LSVL 40208 5724 C2
Klerner Ct
2700 NALB 47150 5396 D6
Klerner Dr
10 FydC 47150 5396 C4
10 NALB 47150 5396 C4
Klerner Ln
1700 NALB 47150 5396 D6
3900 FydC 47150 5396 C5
Kline Ct
1800 LSVL 40205 5726 B2
Klondike Dr
5000 FydC 47119 5394 B2
Klondike Ln
2700 LSVL 40218 5727 B3
2900 LSVL 40220 5727 B3
Klonway Ct
3800 LSVL 40220 5727 C2
Klonway Dr
3000 LSVL 40218 5727 B2
3000 LSVL 40220 5727 C2
Klotz Rd
- BltC 40047 6055 A3
Knable Ct
3900 FydC 47119 5394 E7
Knable Ln
- NALB 47150 5504 E3
- NALB 47150 5505 A2
E Knable Rd
900 FydC 47122 5503 C5
W Knable Rd
1000 FydC 47122 5503 C4
Knasel Ln
3600 FydC 47119 5395 A2
Knight Rd
1400 LSVL 40214 5723 E6
1400 LSVL 40216 5723 D6
Knights Ct
- BltC 40071 5948 D4
4200 JFVL 47130 5398 B5
Knights Wy
- LSVL 40205 5616 E7
Knightsbridge Rd
400 LSVL 40206 5617 B2
Knightwood Dr
10 HdnC 40175 6482 D4
Knob Av
1200 NALB 47150 5504 E5
Knob Rd
100 BltC 40165 6048 C7
Knob Creek Cir
100 BltC 40109 6051 A2
Knob Creek Rd
100 BltC 40109 5942 A7
100 BltC 40109 6051 A2
100 LSVL 40118 5942 A7
900 BltC 40109 6050 E3
1000 BltC 40165 6050 E3
Knob Hill Rd
600 NALB 47150 5505 B1
1500 ELZT 42701 6703 C5
Knobloch Av
200 JFVL 47130 5507 C5
Knob Valley Dr
3400 FydC 47119 5395 A7
Knob View Av
2600 NALB 47150 5396 C7
Knobview Ln
5500 LSVL 40219 5835 E5
Knollview Ct
3000 LSVL 40214 5832 C2
Knollwood Cir
100 HLVW 40229 5944 C5
Knollwood Rd
1800 LSVL 40207 5509 A6
Knopp Av
4500 LSVL 40213 5834 B3
Knox Av
- MdeC 40175 6373 B7
- VNGV 40160 6592 B1
300 VNGV 40175 6482 C7
2300 MdeC 40175 6482 B1
Knox Av SR-1500
- MdeC 40175 6373 B7
- VNGV 40160 6592 B1
300 VNGV 40175 6482 C7
2300 MdeC 40175 6482 B1
Knox Blvd
100 RDCF 40160 6374 B7
200 RDCF 40160 6483 C1
500 HdnC 40121 6483 C1
Knox St
- HdnC 40121 6265 B7
1300 HdnC 40121 6374 B1
N Knox St
1200 HdnC 40121 6374 B2
Kochs Cove Rd
13500 LSVL 40272 5941 A6
Koehler Pl
3100 FydC 47150 5397 B2
Koester St
7800 HdnC 40121 6374 B5
Koetter Dr
2200 CLKV 47129 5397 D5
Kohler Dr
400 MDTN 40243 5620 D3
Kopp Av
200 JFVL 47130 5506 E5
Kopp Ln
400 CLKV 47129 5506 E3
600 ClkC 47129 5506 E3
Korb Av
900 NALB 47150 5505 D2
Kort Wy
7200 LSVL 40220 5727 D2
Kosene Ct
7200 LSVL 40258 5832 A3
Kosman Ct
2800 LDNP 40242 5510 C5
Koster Pl
2900 LDNP 40241 5510 C5
Kousa Ct
4100 LSVL 40241 5510 E3
Kousa Dr
100 SHDV 40165 6161 A6
Kovats Ct
10500 JFTN 40223 5619 D5
Kozy Kreek Dr
2900 LSVL 40218 5727 B2
2900 LSVL 40220 5727 B2
Krages Dr
13300 LSVL 40272 6048 E1
Kramer St
500 SHDV 40165 6161 C4
Kramers Ln
3300 LSVL 40216 5722 E2
3300 LSVL 40216 5723 A3
Kranet Wy
4300 LSVL 40218 5727 B5
Kranz Cor
6500 ClkC 47111 5290 B2
Krashey Wy
3000 LSVL 40213 5834 D1
Kratz Ln
100 MDTN 40243 5620 C4
Krause Av
5000 LSVL 40216 5831 D1
Krause Dr
5000 LSVL 40216 5831 D1
Kremer Av
3300 LSVL 40213 5725 E7
Kres Ln
5000 FydC 47119 5394 C3
Kresge Wy
4000 STMW 40207 5618 B5
Krieger St
- LSVL 40217 5616 A6
1100 LSVL 40204 5616 A6
Krispin Cove
- OdmC 40031 5404 A1
Kristen Ct
100 RDCF 40160 6483 D6
1800 OdmC 40031 5297 C3
Kristen Marie Dr
3700 LSVL 40241 5511 C3
Kristin Wy
3200 LSVL 40216 5722 E3
Kromer Dr
7100 LSVL 40218 5727 C5
Kruer Ln
1000 FydC 47119 5394 B7
Krupp Park Dr
1200 LSVL 40213 5725 E7

INDEX 29
Krystle Ridge Pl
Louisville Metro Street Index
Leesgate Rd

STREET Block City ZIP Map# Grid

Krystle Ridge Pl
8100 LSVL 40258 5831 A4
Kuhn Ln
7000 LSVL 40228 5836 C3
Kundler Dr
- MRGH 40155 6264 B3
Kurtz Av
3900 LSVL 40229 5944 A2
Kurz Wy
1600 LSVL 40216 5832 A1
Kylies Rdg
8800 FydC 47122 5393 A7
Kylies Hollow Rd
- FydC 47150 5504 A5

L

L Ct
100 LGNG 40031 5296 E1
Laber Ln
6300 LSVL 40291 5836 E3
Labrador Dr
7600 LSVL 40258 5830 D3
Lacarem Dr
4700 JFTN 40299 5728 A6
4700 LSVL 40299 5728 A6
Lacevine Ct
2700 LSVL 40220 5728 A2
Lacevine Pl
8400 LSVL 40220 5728 A2
Lacevine Rd
8100 LSVL 40220 5727 E2
8200 LSVL 40220 5728 A2
Lacewood Ln
3100 FydC 47150 5397 B1
Lacey Ct
4700 LSVL 40218 5726 C6
4700 PLRH 40218 5726 C6
La Cima Ct
8400 LSVL 40219 5836 A6
Laclara Wy
13900 LSVL 40299 5730 A5
Laclede Av
3200 NALB 47150 5396 C7
Laclede Ln
- LSVL 40219 5834 E1
Lacona Ln
1300 LSVL 40213 5725 D5
Laconia Cove
5200 OdmC 40031 5404 B1
La Costa Ct
4000 LSVL 40299 5728 B5
La Costa Rd
8900 LSVL 40299 5728 B5
Ladd Av
6300 LSVL 40216 5722 C4
Lafawn Dr
100 CHAN 47111 5181 D1
Lafayette Dr
1100 NALB 47150 5396 D6
1700 LSVL 40215 5723 E4
Lafayette St
200 NALB 47150 5505 A5
La Fleur Wy
5500 LSVL 40229 5944 E3
Lafollette Ct
3200 JFTN 40299 5728 C3
Lafollette Dr
3300 JFTN 40299 5728 C4
La Fon Av
8000 LSVL 40228 5836 E6
La Fontenay Ct
100 DGSH 40243 5620 A4
100 SCMR 40223 5620 A4
La Fontenay Dr
100 DGSH 40243 5620 A4
Lagoona Dr
4900 LSVL 40219 5835 C1
5400 LSVL 40219 5726 C7
La Grange Rd
100 PWEV 40056 5512 C2
300 OdmC 40056 5512 C3
6500 CTWD 40014 5403 E7
6500 CTWD 40014 5404 A7
6600 CTWD 40014 5512 D1
6700 PWEV 40014 5512 D1
6800 CTWD 40056 5512 D1
7600 LSVL 40245 5512 A6
8100 LYDN 40222 5619 A1
8200 LYDN 40242 5619 A1
9300 LYDN 40242 5510 C7
9300 MLND 40223 5510 C7
9300 MLND 40242 5510 C7
9400 LYDN 40223 5510 D7
9400 WPMG 40223 5510 D7
10300 LYDN 40223 5511 A7
11500 ANCH 40223 5511 E7
11500 ANCH 40223 5620 D1
11500 LSVL 40223 5511 E7
11500 LSVL 40223 5620 D1
12200 LSVL 40223 5512 A6
La Grange Rd SR-146
100 PWEV 40056 5512 C2
300 OdmC 40056 5512 C3
6500 CTWD 40014 5403 E7
6500 CTWD 40014 5404 A7
6600 CTWD 40014 5512 D1
6700 PWEV 40014 5512 D1
6800 CTWD 40056 5512 D1
7600 LSVL 40245 5512 A6
9400 LYDN 40223 5510 D7
9400 LYDN 40242 5510 D7
9400 MLND 40223 5510 D7
9400 WPMG 40223 5510 D7
10300 LYDN 40223 5511 A7
11500 ANCH 40223 5511 E7
11500 ANCH 40223 5620 D1
11500 LSVL 40223 5511 E7
11500 LSVL 40223 5620 D1
12200 LSVL 40223 5512 A6
La Grange Rd SR-362
200 PWEV 40056 5512 C2
Lahnna Dr
4300 LSVL 40216 5723 D6

Laib Dr
1400 NALB 47150 5505 D1
Lake Av
10 LSVL 40206 5616 E1
7300 OdmC 40014 5402 E7
7300 OdmC 40014 5403 A7
7300 OdmC 40014 5512 B1
8100 LYDN 40222 5618 E1
8100 STMW 40222 5618 E1
Lake Ct
5500 CTWD 40014 5403 E4
5500 OdmC 40014 5403 E4
Lake Dr
100 CLKV 47129 5397 E3
7000 ClkC 47172 5397 E1
7400 OdmC 40014 5512 A1
Lake Pl
1000 STMW 40222 5618 E1
Lake Rd
1100 RDCF 40160 6592 E1
1100 RDCF 40160 6593 A1
1500 FydC 47122 5503 C4
Lake Rd N
2600 RDCF 40160 6592 D1
Lake St
- OdmC 40014 5404 B3
2100 NALB 47150 5505 D2
Lake Ter
- LYDN 40222 5618 E1
8100 STMW 40222 5618 E1
Lake Wy
1000 STMW 40222 5618 E1
Lake Bend Ct
13900 LSVL 40299 5730 A6
Lake Bluff Cir
1100 LSVL 40245 5621 C2
Lake Bluff Pl
14600 LSVL 40245 5621 C2
Lake Buckhorn Ct
6800 LSVL 40291 5837 C3
Lakecrest Ct
100 BltC 40165 6162 E5
Lake Dreamland Rd
4100 LSVL 40216 5722 C2
Lake Elkhorn Ct
6800 LSVL 40291 5837 D3
Lake Elkhorn Dr
9700 LSVL 40291 5837 C3
Lake Elmo Rd
100 BltC 40109 6051 B2
Lake Erie Dr
5800 LSVL 40291 5837 A1
Lake Forest Dr
14200 LSVL 40245 5621 C4
Lake Forest Ln
14100 LSVL 40245 5621 C4
Lake Forest Pkwy
400 LSVL 40245 5621 C3
Lakegreen Ct
6900 LSVL 40291 5837 C4
Lakeheath Dr
2900 LSVL 40213 5725 E7
Lake Huron Ct
100 SHDV 40165 6161 E4
5900 LSVL 40291 5837 A1
Lakeland Dr
1500 FydC 47122 5503 C4
Lakeland Rd
2000 LSVL 40223 5511 A6
Lakelet Wy
4300 LSVL 40299 5730 A5
Lake Louisvilla Dr
3900 LSVL 40245 5511 E2
4500 OdmC 40014 5511 E2
Lakemont Ct
13800 LSVL 40299 5729 E5
13800 LSVL 40299 5730 A5
Lake Park Ct
100 SHDV 40165 6161 B7
Lake Point Dr
8800 FydC 47122 5393 A6
Lake Pointe Ct
3200 OdmC 40014 5514 A1
Lake Pointe Dr
7600 OdmC 40014 5514 A1
Lake Pointe Trc
400 LSVL 40245 5621 C4
Lakeridge Dr
8600 LSVL 40272 5832 B6
Lakes Edge Dr
100 SHDV 40165 6161 B7
Lakeshore
10 CLKV 47129 5506 D5
Lakeshore Blf
10400 JFTN 40223 5619 D6
Lakeshore Blvd
3100 LGNG 40031 5297 B6
3100 OdmC 40031 5297 B6
Lakeshore Ct
1500 JFTN 40223 5619 D7
Lakeshore Dr
10 CLKV 47129 5506 B3
200 LGNG 40031 5297 A3
Lakeside Ct
1300 LGNG 40031 5297 B4
1300 OdmC 40031 5297 B4
4200 SLRB 47172 5288 E5
Lakeside Dr
100 BltC 40165 6163 C5
800 ELZT 42701 6703 B7
1400 OdmC 40031 5297 B4
2000 LSVL 40205 5617 B7
2600 LSVL 40205 5726 B1
2600 SMRM 40205 5726 B1
4100 SLRB 47172 5288 E6
Lakes of Dogwood Blvd
100 SHDV 40165 6161 A7
400 BltC 40165 6161 A7
Lake Spring Ct
4200 LSVL 40299 5729 E5
Lake Spring Dr
13700 LSVL 40299 5729 E5
Lake Sterling Rd
600 LSVL 40223 5619 E2

Lakestone Wy
11000 OdmC 40059 5292 D6
Lake Storm Ct
6900 LSVL 40291 5837 C3
Lake Superior Ct
5700 LSVL 40291 5837 A1
Lake Superior Dr
8300 LSVL 40291 5837 A1
Lake View Dr
100 ELZT 42701 6703 B6
3100 LSVL 40205 5726 C2
Lakeview Dr
- BltC 40165 5944 E7
- BltC 40165 5945 A7
- BltC 40165 6054 A1
- CLKV 47129 5397 E3
10 CLKV 47129 5506 B3
100 LGNG 40031 5297 B3
3200 SHDV 40165 6161 E3
4600 FydC 47119 5394 C4
E Lakeview Dr
10 MTWH 40047 6056 A1
N Lakeview Dr
10 BltC 40109 5943 D5
S Lakeview Dr
100 SHDV 40165 6161 E4
Lake View Rd
800 BLMD 40222 5619 B2
800 BLMD 40223 5619 B2
800 LYDN 40222 5619 B2
Lakeview Gardens Dr
- SHDV 40165 6161 E4
Lake Vista E
2900 ClkC 47130 5398 B4
Lake Vista W
2800 ClkC 47130 5398 B4
Lake Vista Ct
10900 LSVL 40241 5511 B5
Lake Vista Dr
2900 LSVL 40241 5511 B5
Lakewood Blvd
2400 JFVL 47130 5398 C7
Lakewood Dr
- MTWH 40047 6056 A4
100 ELZT 42701 6702 E2
200 LGNG 40031 5297 A6
200 OdmC 40031 5297 A6
1600 ELZT 42701 6703 A4
8500 ClkC 47111 5181 A7
8500 ClkC 47111 5290 A1
9000 LSVL 40272 5832 A7
9800 LSVL 40272 5940 E1
Lakewoods Ct
13800 OdmC 40059 5182 E7
Lamar Av
2300 LSVL 40216 5722 E7
La Marr Cir
100 ELZT 42701 6703 A2
Lambach Ct
3000 JFTN 40220 5728 A3
Lambach Ln
8600 JFTN 40220 5728 A2
Lambert Av
4000 LSVL 40218 5726 E5
4000 LSVL 40218 5727 A5
Lambert Ct
2000 LSVL 40218 5727 A5
Lambert Rd
4300 LSVL 40219 5835 C5
Lamborne Blvd
9600 LSVL 40272 5941 C1
9700 LSVL 40272 5832 B7
Lammers Ln
5100 LSVL 40219 5835 D2
Lamont Rd
2700 LSVL 40205 5726 A2
Lampter St
1900 LSVL 40216 5723 A7
Lampton Al
1000 LSVL 40204 5616 A4
Lampton Av
9300 LSVL 40219 5943 D1
Lampton St
400 LSVL 40203 5615 E4
500 LSVL 40203 5616 A4
1000 LSVL 40204 5616 B4
Lana Ct
100 LSVL 40229 5944 A2
Lana Dr
9900 LSVL 40229 5944 A2
Lanai Ct
- LSVL 40245 5621 C5
Lanark Pl
200 DGSH 40243 5620 B4
Lanark Dell
200 DGSH 40243 5620 B4
Lancashire Av
2000 LSVL 40205 5726 B1
Lancassange Dr
300 JFVL 47130 5508 A1
Lancaster Av
- LSVL 40215 5724 A7
Lancaster Cir
200 NALB 47150 5396 A6
Lancaster Dr
3400 NALB 47150 5396 A6
Lancaster Pl
1300 HTBN 40222 5619 C6
Lancaster Essex Ct
1400 LSVL 40242 5509 D5
Lancaster Wood
200 FydC 47150 5396 A4
Lance Dr
1200 LSVL 40216 5723 D5
Lance Ln
- ClkC 47111 5182 B1
Lancelot Ct
800 JFVL 47130 5507 C4
7600 STMW 40222 5618 E1
Lancewood Rd
9600 LSVL 40229 5945 A3
Landan Dr
2200 LSVL 40218 5727 A3

Landcross Dr
5500 LSVL 40216 5722 C7
Landers Av
- CTWD 40014 5403 E5
Landherr Ct
12100 LSVL 40299 5729 B4
Landherr Dr
3800 LSVL 40299 5729 B5
Landing Ct
- OdmC 40059 5291 E1
Landing Dr
2000 LSVL 40218 5727 A5
Landing Rd
200 ClkC 47111 5182 A2
1700 OdmC 40059 5291 E1
Landis Ct
100 RDCF 40160 6593 B1
Landis Ln
100 BltC 40047 6056 A1
100 MTWH 40047 6056 A1
800 BltC 40047 5947 A7
800 MTWH 40047 5947 A7
900 BltC 40047 5946 E7
900 MTWH 40047 5946 E7
Landis Lakes Ct
400 LSVL 40245 5621 C6
Landis Lakes Dr
14500 LSVL 40245 5621 C5
Landis Ridge Dr
400 LSVL 40245 5621 B5
Landis Villa Dr
14500 LSVL 40245 5621 B5
Landmark Ct
1200 SHDV 40165 6161 B2
Landmark Dr
14800 LSVL 40245 5621 D1
Landmark Pl
1700 LSVL 40245 5621 D2
Landor Av
2600 KGLY 40205 5617 C6
2600 LSVL 40205 5617 C6
Landrew Ct
7000 LSVL 40291 5837 A3
Landrum Rd
2300 LSVL 40216 5722 E7
Lands Ln
- BltC 40047 5946 E7
- LSVL 40291 5946 E7
Landsdowne Ct
700 ELZT 42701 6703 B7
Lands End
3200 FydC 47150 5613 B2
Landside Ct
4400 LSVL 40220 5727 C3
Landside Dr
4000 LSVL 40220 5727 D3
Landspur Ct
100 SbyC 40067 5732 C3
Landstar Dr
6800 LSVL 40272 5939 E7
Landwood Dr
10100 LSVL 40291 5837 C7
Landwood Wy
8600 LSVL 40291 5837 D7
Lane Av
600 SLRB 47172 5288 C3
Lanesboro Wy
9700 MWVL 40242 5510 D6
Lanette Ct
10900 LSVL 40229 5944 E5
Lanfair Ct
3300 SPVL 40241 5509 E3
Lanfair Dr
7400 SPVL 40241 5509 E3
7500 LSVL 40241 5509 E3
Lang Ct
1700 LSVL 40211 5614 C6
Langdon Dr
2300 RLGH 40242 5510 C6
2500 LDNP 40242 5510 C6
2500 LSVL 40241 5510 C6
2500 LSVL 40242 5510 C6
2500 RLGH 40241 5510 C6
2600 LDNP 40241 5510 C5
Langholm Pl
500 DGSH 40243 5620 A5
Langland Pl
14100 LSVL 40245 5621 C6
Langley Trc
500 ELZT 42701 6811 C3
Lankford Ln
10300 LSVL 40118 5942 D3
La Normandy Rd
200 DGSH 40243 5620 A3
Lansdowne Av
2300 LSVL 40217 5725 A1
2300 PKWV 40217 5725 A1
Lanseville Rd NE
4700 HsnC 47112 5501 C7
4700 HsnC 47122 5501 C7
Lansford Ct
5300 LSVL 40272 5940 B4
Lansford Dr
11000 LSVL 40272 5940 B4
E Lansing Av
- LSVL 40214 5724 D4
W Lansing Av
100 LSVL 40214 5724 C4
400 LSVL 40215 5724 C4
Lanson Ct
10100 LSVL 40272 5939 E2
Lantana Ct
6500 LSVL 40229 5945 B1
Lantana Dr
8800 LSVL 40229 5836 B7
9000 LSVL 40229 5945 B1
Lantern Ct
1300 ELZT 42701 6703 D7
Lantern Dr
6500 LSVL 40228 5836 B7
Lantern Lite Pkwy
8700 JFTN 40220 5728 B2
9100 JFTN 40299 5728 B2

La Plaza Dr
10300 LSVL 40272 5940 A2
Lapping Ct
2400 CLKV 47129 5397 B6
Laramie Ct
4700 LSVL 40216 5723 D7
Larch Ct
6500 LSVL 40229 5945 B1
Larch Dr
2200 CLKV 47129 5397 B6
Larchmont Av
1100 LSVL 40215 5724 A1
1500 SVLY 40216 5724 A1
4000 LSVL 40216 5722 A4
Largo Ct
8900 LSVL 40299 5728 B5
Largo Ln
5600 OdmC 40014 5513 B3
Lariat Rd
7800 LSVL 40219 5835 E3
Lariat Pointe Dr
15400 LSVL 40299 5839 E1
Larimda Ct
7000 LSVL 40291 5837 C4
Lark Rd
7300 CTWD 40014 5512 E1
Larkgrove Dr
5600 LSVL 40229 5944 E4
6000 LSVL 40229 5945 A5
Larkhall Ct
10500 DGSH 40223 5619 E6
Larkin Dr
10300 LYDN 40223 5510 E7
Larkin Fore Wy
11500 LSVL 40291 5946 E2
Larkmoor Ln
1700 LSVL 40218 5726 B4
1700 WSNP 40218 5726 B4
Lark Park Dr
10300 JFTN 40299 5728 E6
Larkspur Av
- LYDN 40222 5619 B2
800 LSVL 40213 5834 D1
1000 LSVL 40213 5725 D7
Larkspur Dr
100 RDCF 40160 6592 E1
E Larkspur Dr
800 JFVL 47130 5507 D3
N Larkspur Dr
1700 JFVL 47130 5507 D3
W Larkspur Dr
800 JFVL 47130 5507 C4
Larkspur Ln
13000 OdmC 40059 5401 B1
Larkwood Av
3200 LSVL 40212 5614 C2
Larkwood Dr
2500 NALB 47150 5505 C1
Larlyn Dr
9900 LSVL 40118 5942 B2
Larry Ln
100 BltC 40165 6054 C3
300 MRGH 40155 6264 C3
6500 LSVL 40219 5835 C7
Larue Av
1600 LSVL 40213 5725 D2
Larue Ct
100 RDCF 40160 6483 E4
3000 LSVL 40217 5725 A2
La Ruisseau Rd
200 DGSH 40243 5620 A3
La Salle Av
4000 LSVL 40215 5723 E6
La Salle Pl
1700 LSVL 40210 5615 A7
Lasalle St
10 ClkC 47172 5288 D1
Laser Dr
1800 JFTN 40299 5619 D7
1800 JFTN 40299 5728 E1
Lassiter Ct
200 HdnC 40160 6592 E2
200 RDCF 40160 6592 E2
Latania Dr
8100 LSVL 40258 5831 B5
Latimer Av
700 LGNG 40031 5297 B2
Lauder Pl
500 DGSH 40243 5620 B5
Lauderdale Rd
1800 LSVL 40205 5617 A6
Laughlin Av
5000 LSVL 40214 5833 B1
Laughton Ln
8000 HTBN 40222 5619 B5
Laura Av
4200 SVLY 40216 5723 A4
Laura Ct
- HdnC 42701 6703 E3
Laura Dr
3000 FydC 47119 5394 C6
Laura Jean Ct
7900 LSVL 40291 5836 E5
Lauralynn Ct
10000 JFTN 40299 5728 D5
Laurel Ct
13300 RVBF 40059 5292 A7
Laurel Dr
10 JFVL 47130 5508 A2
Laurel Ln
5800 OdmC 40014 5402 B5
Laurel Grove Ct
8200 LSVL 40228 5836 C6
Laurel Hill Pl
7600 PROS 40059 5401 A5
Laurel Ridge Rd
7700 LSVL 40219 5835 C5
E Laurel River Rd
- BltC 40165 6054 B7
W Laurel River Rd
- BltC 40165 6053 E6
- BltC 40165 6054 A6
Laurel Springs Dr
8100 LSVL 40299 5727 E6

Laureltree Pl
5400 LSVL 40229 5944 E3
Laurelwood Av
4000 LSVL 40220 5618 C6
Laurelwood Pl
- LGNG 40031 5296 C3
Lauren Wy
100 BltC 40047 6055 A3
Laurie Vallee Rd
100 DGSH 40243 5620 A4
La Vel Ln
3200 LSVL 40216 5722 B6
Lavender Ct
100 VNGV 40160 6483 B6
11400 LSVL 40291 5946 E4
Lavender Wy
11000 LSVL 40291 5946 E4
Lavenia Ln
13200 LSVL 40272 5940 A5
Laverne Ct
100 BltC 40047 5946 C7
Laverne Dr
8300 JFTN 40299 5728 A6
Laverton Av
13500 LSVL 40272 6048 D1
Lavista Wy
1000 LSVL 40219 5835 A3
Lavon Av
100 VNGV 40175 6482 C7
200 HdnC 40175 6482 C7
Lavon Ct
2600 RDCF 40160 6592 E1
2600 RDCF 40160 6593 A1
Lawn Ct
200 NALB 47150 5396 A7
Lawndale Av
100 LSVL 40214 5833 C1
Lawnside Dr
7200 LSVL 40214 5833 C3
Lawrence Dr
3300 LSVL 40215 5724 A3
Lawrence Ln
- SbyC 40245 5623 B1
Lawrence Banet Rd
3000 FydC 47119 5503 D1
3200 FydC 47119 5394 E7
Lawrencekirk Ct
10500 BRMR 40223 5619 B5
10500 DGSH 40243 5619 B5
10500 DGSH 40243 5620 B6
Lawrence Meyer Rd
- ClkC 47129 5397 C2
- FydC 47150 5397 C2
Lawrie Ln
4800 LSVL 40214 5723 E7
4800 LSVL 40215 5723 E7
Lawrin Dr
5300 LSVL 40272 5940 B1
Lawson Blvd
100 ELZT 42701 6812 C7
Lawson Ln
- BltC 40047 6056 C7
100 LSVL 40214 5723 E7
Lawton Ct
400 LSVL 40208 5615 E6
400 LSVL 40217 5615 E6
Layman Dr
7200 LSVL 40228 5836 D4
Layman Ln
100 ELZT 42701 6702 E7
Layne Ct
7400 LSVL 40219 5835 E4
Layne Rd
5200 LSVL 40219 5835 D4
Layside Ct
3200 LSVL 40220 5727 C2
Layside Dr
3800 LSVL 40220 5727 C2
Lazy Creek Ct
6500 LSVL 40059 5400 D4
7700 PROS 40059 5400 D4
Lazy Creek Rd
1100 FydC 47122 5502 A7
1100 HsnC 47112 5502 A7
1200 FydC 47136 5502 A7
1300 HsnC 47112 5611 A1
1300 HsnC 47136 5610 C4
1300 HsnC 47136 5611 A1
Lazy Creek Rd NE
2900 HsnC 47136 5610 D4
4600 HsnC 47136 5611 A2
N Lazy River Blvd
- BltC 40165 6054 B7
- BltC 40165 6163 B1
Lazy River Dr
100 BltC 40165 6163 A1
Lazy Run Rd
6100 LSVL 40219 5835 B7
6100 LSVL 40229 5835 B7
Lea Ann Wy
4900 LSVL 40219 5835 D3
Leaf Dr
3000 FydC 47150 5397 B2
4300 LSVL 40216 5723 D5
Leafland Pl
7200 PROS 40059 5400 E7
Leah Ct
3000 JFVL 47130 5398 D6
Leah Wy
200 RDCF 40160 6483 D6
Leahurst Ct
2000 SVLY 40216 5723 C4
Leamington Spa Dr
5500 LSVL 40213 5725 E6
5500 LSVL 40219 5725 E6
Leaning Trace Ct
10100 LSVL 40291 5837 C5
Leawood Ct
1800 GYDL 40222 5509 D6
Le Beau Ct
9200 JFTN 40299 5728 C5
Le Blanc Ct
2600 LSVL 40206 5616 E2

Ledbury Ct
10600 DGSH 40243 5619 B5
10600 DGSH 40243 5620 B6
10600 JFTN 40223 5619 B5
Ledbury Wy
10100 JFTN 40223 5619 E5
10300 DGSH 40243 5619 E5
Leddenton Wy
10400 LSVL 40241 5511 C4
Ledge Rd
- JfnC 40206 5616 E4
- JfnC 40206 5617 A4
- LSVL 40204 5616 E4
- LSVL 40204 5617 A4
- LSVL 40206 5617 A4
Ledge Brook Ct
3000 LSVL 40241 5509 D4
Ledge Pointe Ct
7600 LSVL 40291 5837 B4
Ledgerock Rd
6900 LSVL 40219 5836 A3
6900 LSVL 40228 5836 A3
Ledges Ct
500 MDTN 40243 5620 E5
Ledges Dr
12200 MDTN 40243 5620 E5
Ledgeview Ct
500 LSVL 40206 5616 E3
Ledgeview Park Dr
400 LSVL 40206 5616 E3
Ledgewood Ct
100 BltC 40229 5944 D6
100 HLVW 40229 5944 D6
Ledgewood Pkwy
6100 LSVL 40214 5832 D1
Ledyard Rd
4100 RHLN 40207 5618 B2
Lee Av
4100 LSVL 40213 5725 D3
5300 OdmC 40014 5513 B2
Lee Ct
1600 LSVL 40217 5615 E7
8600 OdmC 40056 5512 E4
Lee Dr
100 FydC 47119 5287 C6
100 FydC 47172 5287 C6
Lee Rd
400 ELZT 42701 6812 B1
400 RDCF 40160 6483 E5
500 ELZT 42701 6703 B7
Lee St
- HdnC 40121 6374 C3
100 SHDV 40165 6161 C4
100 VNGV 40175 6482 D7
400 RDCF 40160 6483 D5
1600 JFVL 47130 5507 B3
E Lee St
100 LSVL 40208 5615 E7
400 LSVL 40217 5615 E7
W Lee St
100 LGNG 40031 5296 E2
900 LSVL 40208 5615 C7
1500 LSVL 40210 5615 A6
1800 LSVL 40210 5614 E6
Leeds Rd
4400 LSVL 40216 5723 A6
4400 SVLY 40216 5723 A6
Lee H Hamilton Hwy
- ClkC - 5397 A4
- CLKV - 5397 C4
- FydC - 5395 E7
- FydC - 5396 C5
- FydC - 5397 C4
- JFVL - 5397 A4
- NALB - 5395 E7
- NALB - 5396 D4
- NALB - 5504 D2
Lee H Hamilton Hwy I-265
- ClkC - 5397 A4
- CLKV - 5397 C4
- FydC - 5395 E7
- FydC - 5396 C5
- FydC - 5397 C4
- JFVL - 5397 C4
- NALB - 5395 E7
- NALB - 5396 D4
- NALB - 5504 D2
Lee H Hamilton Hwy SR-62
- ClkC - 5397 A4
- CLKV - 5397 C4
- FydC - 5395 E7
- FydC - 5396 C5
- FydC - 5397 C4
- JFVL - 5397 C4
- NALB - 5395 E7
- NALB - 5396 D4
- NALB - 5504 D2
Lee Jarboe Wy
- LSVL 40219 5834 D3
Leelah Ct
10700 LSVL 40272 5940 C3
Leelah Wy
- LSVL 40272 5940 C3
Leemont Ct
5600 LSVL 40272 5940 B4
Leemont Dr
11500 LSVL 40272 5940 B5
Leemore Ct
8900 MYHL 40241 5510 C4
Lees Ln
1600 SHDV 40165 6162 A2
3300 LSVL 40216 5722 B4
Lees Ln SR-2051
3300 LSVL 40216 5722 B4
Lees Ln N
100 HLVW 40229 5944 C6
Leesburg Ct
4600 FCSL 40241 5511 B2
Leesburg Pl
11300 FCSL 40241 5511 B2
Leesgate Rd
9100 HTBN 40222 5619 C4

INDEX 30

Lee Villa Cir E

Louisville Metro Street Index

Long Lick Farm Rd

STREET
Block City ZIP Map# Grid

Lee Villa Cir E
10 HLVW 40229 5944 A7
Lee Villa Cir N
100 HLVW 40229 5944 A7
Lee Villa Cir S
100 HLVW 40229 5944 A7
Lee Villa Cir W
- HLVW 40229 5944 A7
Leeward Ct
5500 LSVL 40291 5837 C1
Legacy Ct
9900 LSVL 40291 5946 D1
Legend Wy
- STMW 40222 5618 D1
Legene Ct
2500 LSVL 40216 5722 D7
Legene Dr
2500 LSVL 40216 5722 D7
2500 SVLY 40216 5722 D6
Legion Wy
- STMW 40207 5618 C3
Legislative Ln
1000 JFVL 47130 5398 E7
Legler Dr
7700 LSVL 40258 5831 C1
Lehigh Av
1100 LSVL 40215 5724 A6
Lehr Rd
11000 LSVL 40272 5940 A3
Leicester Cir
500 HTBN 40222 5619 C5
Leicester Ct
9100 HTBN 40222 5619 C5
Leidolf Ct
3000 FydC 47119 5394 C6
Leigh Anna Ln
100 BltC 40047 6055 D4
Leighton Cir
1300 HTBN 40222 5619 B6
Leila Av
10 JFVL 47130 5506 E4
Leisure Ct
- LSVL 40229 5945 B3
Leisure Ln
6200 LSVL 40229 5945 A2
Leisure Wy
1400 CLKV 47129 5397 D7
Leitchfield Rd
1600 ELZT 42701 6812 B3
1700 ELZT 42701 6811 C5
2100 HdnC 42701 6811 D5
Leitchfield Rd US-62
1600 ELZT 42701 6812 B3
1700 ELZT 42701 6811 C5
2100 HdnC 42701 6811 D5
Leith Ln
3200 LSVL 40218 5726 B3
3500 WBHL 40218 5726 C3
Leland Ct
- OdmC 40014 5403 C6
200 STMW 40207 5617 D2
Leland Dr
- CTWD 40014 5403 D6
- OdmC 40014 5403 D6
Leland Rd
3800 BLWD 40207 5617 E2
3800 LSVL 40207 5617 D2
3800 STMW 40207 5617 E2
3900 CYWV 40207 5617 E2
Leman Dr
3000 LSVL 40218 5727 C2
3000 LSVL 40220 5727 C2
Lemasters Ln
10 SbyC 40067 5732 B7
Lemmah Dr
3100 LSVL 40216 5722 B7
Lena Ln
9200 LSVL 40299 5948 B2
Lencott Dr
2800 LSVL 40216 5722 C6
Lennox Av
300 LSVL 40209 5724 D3
Lennox View Ct
3500 LSVL 40299 5728 A4
Lenoak Dr
100 LSVL 40214 5833 C3
Lenoir Av
3400 LSVL 40216 5722 B5
Lenover Dr
3000 LSVL 40216 5722 C6
Lentz Av
3500 LSVL 40215 5724 A4
Lentz Ln
100 BltC 40047 6055 A4
Lentzier Trc
5600 ClkC 47130 5399 B3
Leo Ln
4100 JFTN 40299 5728 D5
Leon Wy
5900 LSVL 40214 5723 B7
5900 LSVL 40214 5832 D1
Leona Dr
8100 LSVL 40291 5836 E4
Leonard Wy
6100 LSVL 40229 5945 A1
Leopold Ct
9700 LSVL 40272 5941 C1
Lepanto Av
200 MDTN 40243 5620 C3
Le Rente Wy
4100 LSVL 40299 5729 D5
Leroy Av
1700 LSVL 40216 5723 D4
1700 SVLY 40216 5723 D3
Lesabre Dr
4900 LSVL 40216 5723 B7
4900 LSVL 40216 5832 A1
Lesane Ct
200 LSVL 40214 5833 C4
Lesane Dr
7400 LSVL 40214 5833 C5
Leslee Ct
9000 LSVL 40229 5836 B7
Lester Av
3300 LSVL 40215 5724 A3
Lesway Ct
3400 LSVL 40220 5727 D3
Lethborough Ct
3900 LSVL 40299 5728 B5
Lethborough Dr
8900 LSVL 40299 5728 B4
9000 JFTN 40299 5728 B4
Letts Rd
100 BltC 40109 5943 C5
Leuthart Dr
- CLKV 47129 5506 C3
Level Ln
8200 LSVL 40291 5836 E2
Level St
100 CHAN 47111 5181 D3
100 ClkC 47111 5181 E4
Leven Blvd
- LSVL 40229 5944 E4
10500 LSVL 40229 5945 A4
Leven Ct
6600 LSVL 40229 5945 A4
Levenia Ln
12000 LSVL 40272 5940 A6
Leverett Ln
6700 LSVL 40258 5831 A6
Levering St
1400 LSVL 40208 5615 C6
Lewis Dr
1100 ELZT 42701 6703 C7
Lewis Ln
6500 LSVL 40272 6048 D2
E Lewis St
200 NALB 47150 5505 A3
W Lewis St
100 NALB 47150 5505 A4
Lewis Wy
6000 LSVL 40272 5940 A4
Lewis & Clark Pkwy
1300 ClkC 47129 5506 E1
1300 CLKV 47129 5506 E1
Lewiston Dr
1800 LSVL 40216 5723 A7
Lewiston Pl
1800 LSVL 40216 5723 A7
Lexford Ct
2400 OBNP 40242 5509 E5
Lexham Rd
2800 LSVL 40220 5727 D2
Lexi Ln
8300 GEOT 47122 5502 A4
Lexington Av
- LSVL 40206 5616 E3
- LSVL 40206 5617 A2
400 ELZT 42701 6812 A3
Lexington Cir
- LSVL 40204 5616 D4
Lexington Ct
- LSVL 40204 5616 D3
Lexington Dr
100 MTWH 40047 6056 A3
1200 NALB 47150 5396 D6
Lexington Ln
9100 LSVL 40241 5510 C4
9100 TNBK 40241 5510 C4
Lexington Pl
700 LSVL 40206 5617 A4
Lexington Rd
- JfnC 40206 5617 A4
- LSVL 40204 5617 A4
1000 LSVL 40204 5616 E4
1400 LSVL 40206 5616 E4
2300 JfnC 40206 5616 E4
2800 LSVL 40206 5617 B4
3300 LSVL 40207 5617 B3
Lexington Rd US-60 ALT
- JfnC 40206 5617 A4
- LSVL 40204 5617 A4
2400 JfnC 40206 5616 E4
2400 LSVL 40206 5616 E4
2500 LSVL 40206 5617 A4
3300 LSVL 40207 5617 B3
Leyton Av
300 LYDN 40222 5619 A2
Leyton Ct
8500 LYDN 40222 5619 B2
Libby Ln
4700 LSVL 40272 5940 C1
Liberty Av
16000 LSVL 40245 5622 B6
16100 LSVL 40023 5622 B6
Liberty Ct
1200 LSVL 40203 5615 B2
Liberty Ln
7300 ClkC 47172 5397 D1
Liberty St
400 ELZT 42701 6812 A2
2800 RDCF 40160 6484 A7
3000 RDCF 40160 6593 A1
E Liberty St
100 LSVL 40202 5615 E3
500 LSVL 40202 5616 A3
700 LSVL 40204 5616 A3
E Liberty St US-31E
100 LSVL 40202 5615 E3
500 LSVL 40202 5616 A3
700 LSVL 40204 5616 A3
E Liberty St US-60 TRK
100 LSVL 40202 5615 E3
500 LSVL 40202 5616 A3
700 LSVL 40204 5616 A3
W Liberty St
100 LSVL 40202 5615 D3
1300 LSVL 40203 5615 B2
Liberty Bank Ln
1200 HTBN 40222 5619 D7
Liberty Bell Wy
1700 LSVL 40215 5723 E4
Library Ln
- LSVL 40202 5615 D4
- LSVL 40203 5615 D4
Lick Creek Ct
10 BltC 40165 6052 B6
Lick Creek Rd
10 BltC 40165 6052 B6
Lickskillet Dr
100 BltC 40165 6162 E7
Lidcomb Av
13400 LSVL 40272 6048 C1
Lido Ct
4500 LSVL 40219 5835 C5
Lieber Hausz Rd NE
8200 HsnC 47136 5611 A6
Lietz Ln
- NALB 47150 5505 A5
Liggett Rd
- HdnC 40177 6264 D3
- MdeC 40155 6264 D3
Lightfoot Rd
400 LSVL 40207 5617 C1
400 MKBV 40207 5617 C1
Lightheart Rd
2900 GNVH 40222 5509 B4
Likens Av
3000 LSVL 40211 5723 A1
Lila Av
4900 LSVL 40258 5831 D4
Lilac Ct
200 RDCF 40160 6483 D7
Lilac Rd
2100 OdmC 40031 5297 C4
Lilac Wy
2900 LSVL 40206 5617 C4
11900 MDTN 40243 5620 C4
Lilac Spring Ct
10300 LSVL 40241 5510 E3
Lilac Spring Dr
4000 LSVL 40241 5510 E3
Lilac Vista Dr
4100 LSVL 40241 5510 E3
Lillian Av
1300 LSVL 40208 5724 B1
1400 LSVL 40210 5724 A1
1400 SVLY 40216 5724 A1
Lillian Wy
200 LSVL 40214 5833 B3
Lillie Lewis Wy
200 WPT 40177 6156 C3
Lilly Av
500 LSVL 40208 5724 E1
500 LSVL 40217 5724 E1
Lilly Ct
12500 ANCH 40223 5511 E7
12500 LSVL 40223 5511 E7
Lilly Ln
800 JFVL 47130 5507 D3
1700 NALB 47150 5396 D7
Lily Run
10 JFVL 47130 5507 B1
Lily Bloom Wy
- LGNG 40031 5296 B3
Lime Rd
6300 GNVH 40222 5509 B4
6300 LSVL 40222 5509 B4
Limehouse Ct
1700 LSVL 40220 5619 A6
Limehouse Ln
8100 LSVL 40220 5618 E7
8100 LSVL 40220 5619 A7
Lime Kiln Ct
2300 LSVL 40222 5509 C5
2300 NHFD 40222 5509 C5
Lime Kiln Ln
2300 NHFD 40222 5509 C5
2400 LSVL 40222 5509 B3
2700 GNVM 40222 5509 C4
2800 GNVH 40222 5509 C4
3100 GNVW 40222 5509 B3
Limerick Ln
3100 GSCK 40242 5510 B4
Limerick Cove
- OdmC 40031 5404 B1
Lime Ridge Ct
6400 NHFD 40222 5509 C5
Lime Ridge Pl
6400 LSVL 40222 5509 C5
6400 NHFD 40222 5509 C5
Lime Spring Wy
900 JFTN 40223 5619 B5
Limestone Ct
7200 CTWD 40014 5403 D7
Limestone Trc
- ClkC 47130 5398 C3
1300 JFTN 40223 5619 D6
Limewood Cir
6300 LSVL 40222 5509 B4
Lincoln Av
- ELZT 42701 6811 E3
900 LSVL 40208 5724 B1
1300 LSVL 40208 5615 B7
1300 LSVL 40210 5615 B7
1300 NALB 47150 5505 C2
1400 LSVL 40213 5725 D4
W Lincoln Av
200 CLKV 47129 5506 C3
Lincoln Blvd
600 ClkC 47172 5288 E2
Lincoln Ct
100 ELZT 42701 6811 E3
4300 LSVL 40213 5725 E3
Lincoln Dr
1900 ClkC 47172 5397 D1
2500 CLKV 47129 5506 B3
8500 MTWH 40047 6055 E1
8500 MTWH 40047 6056 A1
Lincoln Pkwy
- ELZT 42701 6812 D7
Lincoln Rd
4300 LNSH 40220 5618 D6
4300 LSVL 40220 5618 D6
4300 SRPK 40220 5618 D6
Lincoln St
- HdnC 40121 6265 B7
200 VNGV 40175 6482 E7
600 NALB 47150 5504 E3
600 NALB 47150 5505 A2
Lincoln Tr
3000 OdmC 40014 5514 C1
3100 OdmC 40014 5405 B7
Lincoln Wy
11100 LSVL 40223 5620 B3
Lincoln Cemetery Rd
- HdnC 40121 6484 B3
Lincoln Run Rd
10 SbyC 40245 5623 B1
Lincolnshire Dr
- HTBN 40222 5619 A5
E Lincoln Trail Blvd
100 RDCF 40160 6483 D3
W Lincoln Trail Blvd
100 RDCF 40160 6483 A4
1400 VNGV 40175 6483 A5
1500 VNGV 40175 6482 E5
W Lincoln Trail Blvd SR-1815
800 RDCF 40160 6483 A4
1400 VNGV 40175 6483 A5
1500 VNGV 40175 6482 E5
Lincoln Trail Ct
3000 OdmC 40014 5514 C1
Linda Cir
400 RDCF 40160 6483 D4
Linda Dr
100 MTWH 40047 6056 B3
2600 NALB 47150 5505 A1
2800 NALB 47150 5396 A7
Linda Ln
- LSVL 40211 5723 A1
200 LSVL 40118 5942 C2
300 ELZT 42701 6702 E2
2600 NALB 47150 5505 B1
3300 LSVL 40216 5723 B1
3300 SVLY 40216 5723 B1
Linda Rd
3300 LSVL 40211 5723 B1
3300 LSVL 40216 5723 B1
8000 LSVL 40219 5835 C6
Linda Wy
1600 LSVL 40216 5723 C6
Linda House Wy
1700 LSVL 40213 5725 D2
Lindbergh Ct
2000 NALB 47150 5505 D3
Lindbergh Dr
- LSVL 40215 5724 A1
2400 LSVL 40208 5724 A1
Lindell Av
600 LSVL 40211 5614 C3
Linden Av
600 NALB 47150 5504 E3
600 NALB 47150 5505 A3
Linden Dr
600 ANCH 40223 5620 C2
Linden Ln
100 LSVL 40206 5617 A2
Linden Rd
10 JFVL 47130 5508 B3
Linden St
600 NALB 47150 5505 E4
Lindenwood Dr
3300 LSVL 40216 5722 C6
Lindsay Av
2400 LSVL 40206 5616 E2
2900 LSVL 40206 5617 A1
Lindsay Ct
400 LSVL 40206 5616 E2
3100 JFVL 47130 5398 D6
Lindsey Dr
2300 SVLY 40216 5722 E6
Lindsey St
1100 CHAN 47111 5181 E3
Lindsey Wade Ct
6800 LSVL 40229 5945 A4
Lindsley St
400 NALB 47150 5505 B4
Lindy Ln
6900 FydC 47136 5611 E5
6900 FydC 47136 5612 A5
Lindy Tr
3400 ClkC 47130 5398 C5
Linger Ct
4600 LSVL 40272 5940 D3
Link Wy
6900 LSVL 40272 5939 D7
Linkwood Ct
100 BltC 40229 5944 D6
100 HLVW 40229 5944 D6
Linnert Ct
4200 FydC 47150 5396 D1
Linnet Rd
3200 ANPK 40213 5725 B2
3300 LSVL 40213 5725 B3
Linney Av
200 MDTN 40243 5620 C3
Linn Station Rd
8700 HTBN 40222 5619 C6
9600 JFTN 40223 5619 D6
11600 JFTN 40223 5620 A6
11800 DGSH 40243 5620 A6
Linnwood Av
200 SLRB 47172 5288 E5
Linstead Rd
6300 LSVL 40228 5836 A2
Linton Ct
7000 LSVL 40258 5831 D3
Linwood Av
400 SLRB 47172 5288 D5
800 LSVL 40217 5725 A1
800 PKWV 40217 5725 A1
3000 LSVL 40210 5614 C7
3000 LSVL 40211 5614 C7
Lions Arms Dr
5800 LSVL 40216 5722 B6
Lippincott Rd
8900 HTBN 40222 5619 B6
Lipps Ln
1200 LSVL 40219 5835 B4
Lisa Av
300 SLRB 47172 5288 D3
4000 SVLY 40216 5723 C4
Lisa Ct
5800 LSVL 40291 5836 E1
Lisa Dr
10 BltC 40165 6052 B6
Lisa Ln
10 HdnC 40162 6702 B1
100 CHAN 47111 5181 D1
3500 JFTN 40299 5728 C4
4500 FydC 47150 5396 E1
8100 GEOT 47122 5502 B3
Lisbon Av
800 LYDN 40222 5619 A1
Lisbon Ln
3500 LSVL 40218 5726 E2
Lithia Dr
5400 LSVL 40241 5402 C7
Little Ln
11600 ANCH 40223 5620 C1
Little Avon Ln
- LSVL 40245 5622 C5
Little Bend Rd
3800 BWNF 40241 5510 A3
Little Bend Trc
100 BltC 40165 6163 A1
Little Bridge Dr
11100 LSVL 40291 5837 E4
Little Cove
1200 OdmC 44026 5292 B2
Little Creek Ct
2100 LSVL 40218 5726 B5
Little Dove Tr
100 BltC 40165 6163 E5
Littlefield St
7700 HdnC 40121 6374 B5
Little Hills Ln
2300 ANCH 40223 5511 E6
Little Horn Pl
11900 LSVL 40299 5729 B4
Little John Ct
3600 LSVL 40219 5835 A1
Little Kentucky Dr
100 BltC 40165 6054 A7
100 BltC 40165 6163 B1
Littleleaf Ct
7000 LSVL 40291 5837 A3
Littleridge Dr
5500 LSVL 40229 5944 E1
Little Rock Dr
- BltC 40165 6053 C7
Little Spring Blvd
11000 LSVL 40291 5946 E4
Lively Ct
5000 LSVL 40218 5726 D6
Live Oak Dr
- MTWH 40047 6056 A1
Liveoak Dr
12500 MDTN 40243 5620 D6
Liverpool Ln
2200 LSVL 40218 5726 D3
2200 WBHL 40218 5726 D3
Livers Ln
100 BltC 40165 6163 B6
Liverton Ct
200 HTBN 40222 5619 A4
Liverton Ln
100 HTBN 40222 5619 B3
Livingston Av
900 LSVL 40215 5724 B5
2900 JFTN 40299 5728 D3
Livingston Gilbert Ct
10400 JFTN 40223 5619 E6
Llandovery Dr
2600 JFTN 40299 5728 D2
Lloyd Ct
100 MTWH 40047 6056 B3
Lloyd Ln
100 BltC 40047 6054 D5
100 BltC 40165 6054 E6
100 MTWH 40047 6054 D5
100 MTWH 40165 6054 E6
Lobbell Al
- LSVL 40206 5616 C3
Lobo Ct
3000 FydC 47150 5397 C3
Lobo Dr
1000 HdnC 42701 6702 B4
E Lobo Rdg
3000 FydC 47150 5397 C3
Locher Al
500 LSVL 40212 5505 E7
Lochinvar Ct
11200 DGSH 40243 5620 B5
Lochinvar Pl
400 DGSH 40243 5620 B5
Loch Lea Ln
8700 JFTN 40299 5728 B6
8800 JFTN 40291 5728 B6
Lochmoor Ct
8300 LSVL 40291 5837 C7
Lochridge Pkwy
4300 JFTN 40291 5728 B6
4300 JFTN 40299 5728 B6
4300 LSVL 40299 5728 B6
Lochwick Ct
7000 LSVL 40272 5939 D1
Lochwick Wy
9900 LSVL 40272 5939 E1
Lochwood Ct
10 NALB 47150 5505 D1
Locke Ln
3000 OdmC 40059 5401 D1
3300 OdmC 40059 5292 C7
Lock Hart Rd
- FydC 47122 5502 C1
Lockhart Rd
7500 FydC 47122 5502 C1
Locklee Rd
3500 LSVL 40214 5832 A4
Lockwood II
- NALB 47150 5505 D2
Lockwood III
- NALB 47150 5505 D1
Lockyear Ct
9800 LSVL 40241 5510 E2
Locust
- ClkC 47111 5181 E1
Locust Av
3500 JFTN 40299 5728 D4
4100 LSVL 40215 5723 E6
Locust Cir E
3600 OdmC 40059 5292 A7
3600 OdmC 40059 5401 B1
Locust Cir W
3600 OdmC 40059 5292 A7
3600 OdmC 40059 5401 A1
Locust Ct
3500 OdmC 40059 5292 A7
8600 BRWD 40242 5510 B6
Locust Dr
- CTWD 40014 5512 D1
- CTWD 40056 5512 D1
- PWEV 40056 5512 D1
10 SpnC 40071 5948 E5
7700 ClkC 47172 5288 C6
7700 SLRB 47172 5288 C6
8300 ClkC 47171 5181 B3
14600 BltC 40071 5949 A3
Locust Ln
100 CTWD 40014 5512 D1
600 LSVL 40217 5724 E2
600 LSVL 40217 5725 A2
3300 JFVL 47130 5508 A2
7500 PWEV 40014 5512 D1
7500 PWEV 40056 5512 D1
7700 OdmC 40056 5512 B1
9600 JFTN 40299 5728 D5
12000 ANCH 40223 5620 D1
Locust Rd
10700 JFTN 40299 5729 A2
11800 MDTN 40243 5620 C4
Locust St
- UTCA 47130 5399 E5
- UTCA 47130 5400 A5
100 BltC 40047 6055 E1
100 CHAN 47111 5181 D2
100 MTWH 40047 6055 E1
300 ClkC 47111 5181 D2
300 VNGV 40175 6591 D1
900 JFVL 47130 5507 A6
1000 JFVL 47130 5506 E5
1300 NALB 47150 5505 C4
1400 LSVL 40206 5616 C3
Locust Wy
5500 LSVL 40229 5944 D4
Locust Creek Blvd
100 LSVL 40023 5622 E5
100 LSVL 40245 5622 E5
300 LSVL 40245 5623 A5
Locust Creek Pl
18500 LSVL 40245 5622 E5
Locust Grove Ct
10 BltC 40071 5949 B2
Locust Grove Dr
- LSVL 40299 5949 A2
10 BltC 40071 5949 A2
Locust Grove Rd
300 ELZT 42701 6812 D6
600 HdnC 42701 6812 D6
Locust Grove Rd SR-567
- HdnC 42701 6812 D6
300 ELZT 42701 6812 D6
Locust Hill Pl
2600 LSVL 40245 5512 D7
Locust Pointe Ct
800 LSVL 40245 5621 D6
Locust Pointe Pl
700 LSVL 40245 5621 D7
Locust View Ct
1600 JFTN 40299 5729 A6
Lodema Wy
5400 LSVL 40213 5726 B7
5400 LSVL 40219 5726 B7
Lodge Ln
3500 LSVL 40220 5727 C4
Lodge Hill Rd
900 LSVL 40223 5620 A2
Lodie Ln
100 BltC 40165 6053 C2
100 PNRV 40165 6053 C2
Loft Ct
7900 LSVL 40291 5837 B5
Loft Ln
9500 LSVL 40291 5837 B5
Loftingham Ct
8600 HTBN 40222 5619 B4
Loftus Cir
- LSVL 40205 5616 E7
Logan Av
100 ELZT 42701 6812 D2
Logan Ct
100 ELZT 42701 6812 B4
Logan Ln
2400 JFVL 47130 5507 D2
Logan St
200 RDCF 40160 6483 D5
700 LSVL 40204 5616 A5
1800 NALB 47150 5505 B2
Logan St SR-864
700 LSVL 40204 5616 A5
Loganberry Ct
200 LSVL 40207 5617 C2
Logby Pl
4600 LSVL 40272 5940 D3
Log Cabin Ct
3000 OdmC 40014 5405 C6
Log Cabin Ln
11900 ANCH 40223 5620 C2
Log Cabin Inn Rd
- BltC 40165 6052 E7
Logistics Dr
7100 LSVL 40258 5721 E7
7100 LSVL 40258 5722 A7
7100 LSVL 40258 5831 A1
Logsdon Ct
100 DGSH 40243 5620 A4
1000 OdmC 40031 5297 D3
Logsdon Pkwy
- HdnC 40121 6373 E5
Logsdon Pkwy SR-1646
- HdnC 40121 6373 E5
N Logsdon Pkwy
- HdnC 40121 6373 E7
- HdnC 40121 6374 A6
- RDCF 40160 6373 E7
- RDCF 40175 6373 E7
100 RDCF 40160 6483 B3
1200 RDCF 40175 6483 A3
1600 RDCF 40160 6482 E1
1600 RDCF 40175 6482 E1
N Logsdon Pkwy SR-1646
- HdnC 40121 6373 E7
- HdnC 40121 6374 A6
- RDCF 40160 6373 E7
- RDCF 40175 6373 E7
100 RDCF 40160 6483 A3
1200 RDCF 40175 6483 A3
1600 RDCF 40160 6482 E1
1600 RDCF 40175 6482 E1
S Logsdon Pkwy
100 RDCF 40160 6483 C6
1600 RDCF 40160 6592 C1
S Logsdon Pkwy SR-1646
100 RDCF 40160 6483 C6
1600 RDCF 40160 6592 C1
S Logsdon Pkwy SR-1815
- RDCF 40160 6483 B4
Logwood Av
5300 LSVL 40272 5940 B5
Loi Rd
6000 FydC 47119 5395 B1
Lois Av
5300 LSVL 40219 5835 D6
Lois Morris Dr
1600 LSVL 40211 5614 C6
Lola Dell Ct
3800 NALB 47150 5396 D5
Lolipop Cir
2200 MLHT 40219 5834 C6
E Loma Vista Ct
100 JFVL 47130 5507 D3
W Loma Vista Dr
100 JFVL 47130 5507 D3
Lombardy Dr
2100 CLKV 47129 5397 B6
Lomond Dr
2600 SVLY 40216 5723 B4
London Dr
5500 LSVL 40216 5723 C7
Lone Oak
- LSVL 40219 5834 D6
Lone Oak Av
1100 LSVL 40219 5835 A4
6200 LSVL 40214 5833 C1
Lone Oak Dr
100 BltC 40165 6054 B6
200 NALB 47150 5504 D7
Lone Oak Tr
500 LSVL 40214 5724 B7
6300 LSVL 40214 5833 B1
Lonesome Hollow Rd
1900 LSVL 40272 5941 C2
3000 LSVL 40118 5941 E3
Lonestar Wy
13100 LSVL 40272 5939 E7
Lone Tree Ct
900 JFTN 40223 5619 E6
Lone Wolf Ct
3000 FydC 47150 5397 C3
Loney Ln
2300 LSVL 40210 5723 E1
2300 SVLY 40210 5723 E1
2300 SVLY 40216 5723 E1
Long Ct
400 NALB 47150 5505 A1
Long St
200 ELZT 42701 6702 E7
1700 JFVL 47130 5507 C4
Long Barn Ct
10300 LSVL 40291 5837 D6
Longboat Ct
10000 LSVL 40229 5944 B3
Longborough Ct
4700 JFTN 40299 5728 A6
Longborough Wy
8600 JFTN 40299 5728 A6
Long Bow Ct
8500 LSVL 40291 5946 A1
Longbranch Ct
3600 LSVL 40219 5835 A6
Long Creek Wy
2900 LSVL 40245 5512 E6
Longest Av
2000 LSVL 40204 5616 D5
2500 JfnC 40204 5616 D5
Longfellow Av
1100 CLKV 47129 5397 C7
1300 CLKV 47129 5506 B1
Longfield Av
500 LSVL 40214 5724 B3
500 LSVL 40215 5724 B3
1600 LSVL 40215 5723 E3
Longfield Dr
500 CLKV 47129 5506 D2
Longford Ln
3100 GSCK 40242 5510 B4
Long Home Rd
10300 LSVL 40291 5837 D7
Longhorn Ct
9300 LSVL 40118 5833 C7
9300 LSVL 40118 5942 C1
Long Knife Ct
2000 LSVL 40207 5508 E6
Long Knife Run
5000 LSVL 40207 5508 E6
Longlake Ct
6700 LSVL 40291 5837 C3
Longlake Dr
6700 LSVL 40291 5837 C3
Long Lick Farm Rd
100 BltC 40165 6160 E7
100 BltC 40165 6161 A7

INDEX 31

Long Meadow Dr — W Manslick Rd

Louisville Metro Street Index

STREET
Block City ZIP Map# Grid

Long Meadow Dr
1600 NALB 47150 5505 D2
Long Ridge Trc
1200 LSVL 40245 5623 A3
Long Rifle Ct
8500 LSVL 40228 5946 A1
Long Rifle Ln
9600 LSVL 40228 5837 A7
9600 LSVL 40228 5946 A1
9600 LSVL 40291 5946 A1
Long Run Pl
17700 LSVL 40245 5622 C5
Long Run Rd
100 LSVL 40245 5622 D5
1000 LSVL 40245 5623 A3
2000 SbyC 40245 5514 B6
2000 SbyC 40245 5623 A2
Long Run Park Rd
- LSVL 40245 5622 E2
- LSVL 40245 5623 A1
- SbyC 40245 5514 A7
- SbyC 40245 5623 A1
Longview Av
2600 LSVL 40206 5617 A3
Longview Dr
10 JFVL 47130 5508 B3
6000 FydC 47119 5394 A1
Longview Ln
6100 GNVW 40222 5508 D3
Longview Rd
3700 JFTN 40299 5728 C5
Longview Beach Dr
6400 ClkC 47130 5400 B2
Longview Farm Dr
11600 LSVL 40299 5838 A2
Longview Park Ln
18500 LSVL 40245 5622 E5
Longview Park Pl
300 LSVL 40245 5622 E5
Longwood Cir
- OdmC 44026 5292 B4
9800 WDWD 40223 5619 D3
Longwood Ln
- OdmC 44026 5292 B5
N Longworth Av
100 LSVL 40212 5614 A1
100 LSVL 40212 5505 B7
S Longworth Av
100 LSVL 40212 5614 B1
Lonlipman Ct
1900 WNDF 40207 5509 B6
Lonsdale Av
4300 LSVL 40215 5724 A6
Lookover Cir
6600 OdmC 40014 5403 B7
Loomis St
100 CLKV 47129 5506 C5
Loop Rd
700 JFVL 47130 5399 C7
Lopez Wy
7800 HdnC 40121 6374 B5
Lopp Av
200 NALB 47150 5505 C2
Lora Dr
7200 LSVL 40214 5833 B3
Lora Linda
4200 FydC 47150 5396 D1
Lor Ann Av
4600 LSVL 40219 5835 C7
Lore Av
8500 LYDN 40222 5619 B2
Lorean Ct
5000 FydC 47119 5394 C4
Lorena Ct
11900 HLVW 40229 5944 D5
Lorene Av
2400 LSVL 40216 5722 C7
2500 LSVL 40216 5831 C1
Lorenzo Ln
7100 LSVL 40228 5836 C3
Loretta St
1100 LSVL 40213 5725 D7
5700 LSVL 40213 5834 D1
Loretto Av
700 LSVL 40211 5614 B3
Lori Ct
3500 OdmC 40014 5405 A3
Lorien Ct
1000 HdnC 42701 6702 B4
N Lorraine St
100 RDCF 40160 6483 A4
S Lorraine St
100 RDCF 40160 6483 A5
200 VNGV 40160 6483 A6
Lortay Rd
8500 LSVL 40219 5834 C6
8500 MLHT 40219 5834 C6
Lory Ln
100 BltC 40165 6161 A1
Lost Tr
5300 LSVL 40214 5833 B1
13000 OdmC 44026 5292 B2
Lost Creek Tr
7800 ClkC 47111 5289 D1
Lost Spring Ct
4300 LSVL 40241 5510 B2
Lost Tree Ct
10200 LSVL 40291 5837 D6
Lotis Wy
300 BWNV 40207 5617 D1
400 INDH 40207 5617 D1
Lotticks Corner Rd SE
11000 HsnC 47117 5721 A7
Lotus Av
800 LSVL 40213 5834 C1
1000 LSVL 40213 5725 C7
Lotus Dr
1400 RDCF 40160 6483 A1
Lou Ct
8400 LSVL 40219 5835 C6
Louane Wy
4500 LSVL 40216 5723 C6
Louann Ct
400 JFVL 47130 5508 B2
Loudoun Trc
11300 LSVL 40241 5511 C3
Lou Gene Av
1500 LSVL 40216 5723 C6
1600 SVLY 40216 5723 C6
Lough Dr
8700 LSVL 40291 5837 C6
Louis Ln
100 BltC 40047 6055 E2
100 BltC 40047 6056 A2
100 MTWH 40047 6055 E2
100 MTWH 40047 6056 A2
Louisa Av
3000 LSVL 40213 5725 B2
3000 LSVL 40217 5725 A2
Louise Av
1600 LSVL 40216 5723 C6
1600 SVLY 40216 5723 C6
Louise Ct
100 MTWH 40047 6056 B3
Louise St
10 JFVL 47130 5507 C4
Louise Wy
100 MTWH 40047 6056 A4
3000 FydC 47150 5396 D3
Louisiana Dock Rd
2000 LSVL 40206 5507 D7
Louis Smith Rd
100 ClkC 47106 5284 E1
8500 FydC 47119 5284 E4
Louisville Av
4100 LSVL 40209 5724 D5
4100 LSVL 40214 5724 D5
Louisville Rd
- ELZT 42701 6702 D3
Louisville Rd SR-3005
- ELZT 42701 6702 E5
Louisville Rd US-31W
- ELZT 42701 6702 D3
Louisville Herald Av
- LSVL 40245 5511 E2
Lou Post Rd
7300 OdmC 40014 5402 E7
7300 OdmC 40014 5511 B1
Love Av
- MTWH 40047 6056 C2
Love Ct
100 MTWH 40047 6056 D2
Loveall Ln
900 JFTN 40223 5619 D6
Lovers Ln
5500 LSVL 40299 5837 D2
5600 LSVL 40291 5837 D2
Lovers Ln SR-1065
5500 LSVL 40299 5837 D2
5600 LSVL 40291 5837 D2
Lovin Ct
3900 LSVL 40216 5722 B4
Lowe Rd
4300 CMBG 40220 5618 D7
4300 LNSH 40220 5618 D7
4300 SRPK 40220 5618 D7
4400 LSVL 40220 5618 D7
Lowe St
5400 MdeC 40121 6373 C2
Lowell Av
- ClkC 47129 5506 A1
- CLKV 47129 5506 A2
- LSVL 40205 5617 C7
- SMRG 40205 5617 C7
200 CHAN 47111 5181 D4
1900 LSVL 40205 5726 A1
1900 SMRM 40205 5617 B7
2600 SMRV 40205 5617 B7
3000 WLTN 40205 5726 C1
Lowell Ct
1300 CLKV 47129 5397 B7
Lower Hunters Trc
1800 LSVL 40216 5831 D2
1800 LSVL 40258 5831 D2
6200 LSVL 40216 5722 A7
6200 LSVL 40258 5722 A7
Lower Rill Dr
9800 LSVL 40291 5837 D4
Lower River Rd
9700 LSVL 40258 5830 D7
9700 LSVL 40272 5830 D7
10100 LSVL 40272 5939 C7
12400 LSVL 40272 6048 C1
Lower River Rd SR-1230
9700 LSVL 40258 5830 D7
9700 LSVL 40272 5830 D7
9700 LSVL 40272 5939 D1
12400 LSVL 40272 6048 C1
Lower Terminal Dr
- LSVL 40209 5724 E5
- LSVL 40209 5725 A5
Lowes Dr
100 ELZT 42701 6702 E5
Lowes Ln
100 BltC 40109 6052 E2
100 HLVW 40165 6052 E2
Low Trail Ct
4300 LSVL 40299 5729 E6
Loyal Dr
- HTCK 40229 5945 D3
- LSVL 40228 5945 D3
Loyola Ct
500 HdnC 42701 6811 B4
Lucas Av
1200 LSVL 40213 5725 C4
Lucas Ct
4200 LSVL 40213 5725 C4
Lucas Ln
12100 ANCH 40223 5511 D6
12600 LSVL 40223 5511 E6
Lucerne Av
6500 LSVL 40216 5722 A4
Lucia Av
1600 LSVL 40204 5616 C5
Lucille Av
10 CLKV 47129 5506 E7
7000 LSVL 40258 5831 D3
Luckert Av
- LSVL 40216 5723 A5
- SVLY 40216 5723 A5
Lucy Dr
4000 FydC 47150 5396 D4
Luke Dr
- BltC 40165 6160 A1
Luken Dr
1700 SVLY 40216 5723 D3
Lula Wy
4000 LSVL 40219 5835 B1
Lunar Dr
6600 LSVL 40258 5831 C2
Lundy St
10 BltC 40165 6161 B1
Lunenburg Ct
11000 WTNH 40245 5511 D2
Lunenburg Dr
4500 WTNH 40245 5511 D2
4800 CDSM 40245 5511 D1
4900 LSVL 40241 5511 D1
Lupino Ct
4000 LSVL 40213 5725 B4
Lupton Ct
100 HLVW 40229 6053 B1
Luray Ct
12000 WTNH 40245 5511 D2
Lure Ct
6300 LSVL 40229 5945 A3
Lure Ln
6500 LSVL 40229 5945 B3
Luther Cir
200 JFVL 47130 5506 E5
5700 FydC 47122 5503 B3
E Luther Rd
3100 FydC 47119 5395 A7
4000 FydC 47119 5394 E7
N Luther Rd
1000 FydC 47122 5503 B4
2300 FydC 47119 5503 B2
2700 FydC 47119 5394 B7
W Luther Rd
4900 FydC 47119 5394 C6
Luther Ridge Ln
5700 FydC 47122 5503 B3
Lutz Ln
- JFVL 47130 5507 E1
Luvisi Ln
- OdmC 40059 5292 B7
Lydgate Dr
7100 STMW 40222 5618 D2
Lydgate Cove
700 STMW 40222 5618 D2
Lydia St
800 LSVL 40217 5616 A6
Lydia Wy
100 RDCF 40160 6483 D6
Lyle Ct
- LGNG 40031 5297 B1
Lyle Ln
- LGNG 40031 5297 B1
Lyles Al
- LSVL 40203 5616 A4
Lyman Av
400 LSVL 40214 5833 B1
Lyman Johnson Dr
1600 LSVL 40211 5614 C6
Lymington Ct
500 DGSH 40243 5620 A5
Lynch Ln
1400 CLKV 47129 5506 C1
Lynda Av
100 CLKV 47129 5506 B5
Lyndale Av
400 LYDN 40222 5619 A2
Lyndon Ln
100 HTBN 40222 5619 A3
100 LYDN 40222 5619 A3
800 LYDN 40222 5618 E1
1000 STMW 40222 5618 E1
1100 GYDL 40222 5618 E1
1100 RDCF 40160 6483 A4
1200 GYDL 40222 5509 E7
Lyndon Ln SR-2050
- STMW 40222 5618 E1
600 LYDN 40222 5619 A2
800 LYDN 40222 5618 E1
S Lyndon Ln
100 HTBN 40222 5619 A4
100 LYDN 40222 5619 A4
Lyndon Wy
4100 RHLN 40207 5618 A2
4100 STMW 40207 5618 A2
Lyndon Crossing Ct
8600 LYDN 40242 5619 C2
Lyndon Crossing Wy
1200 LYDN 40242 5619 C2
Lyndon Farm Ct
1600 LYDN 40223 5510 D7
1600 LYDN 40223 5619 D1
Lyndon Lakes Pl
8900 LYDN 40242 5619 B2
Lyndonwoods Cir
300 LYDN 40222 5619 A2
400 LYDN 40222 5618 E2
Lyneve Dr
9000 LSVL 40272 5831 D7
Lynn Al
- LGNG 40031 5297 A2
Lynn Ct
2500 NALB 47150 5505 D1
Lynn Dr
- CHAN 47111 5181 E1
- ClkC 47111 5181 E2
Lynn Rd
600 NALB 47150 5505 B2
Lynn St
100 MRGH 40155 6264 C4
600 LSVL 40217 5724 E1
700 LSVL 40217 5615 E7
Lynn St SR-61
700 LSVL 40217 5615 E7
Lynn Wy
1500 GYDL 40222 5509 D6
2000 LSVL 40222 5509 D6
Lynnbrook Ct
2600 LSVL 40220 5618 C6
Lynnbrook Dr
4200 LSVL 40220 5618 C6
4400 SRPK 40220 5618 D6
Lynnchester Dr
6100 LSVL 40219 5836 A3
6200 LSVL 40228 5836 A3
Lynndale Dr
1500 JFVL 47130 5507 B5
Lynnhall Ct
8700 LSVL 40059 5400 D6
8800 PROS 40059 5400 D6
Lynnhurst Av
1400 LSVL 40215 5724 A6
Lynnhurst Dr
500 LYDN 40222 5619 A2
Lynn Lea Ct
10 SVLY 40216 5723 B5
Lynn Lea Rd
1800 SVLY 40216 5723 A6
4700 LSVL 40216 5723 A6
Lynnmar Dr
1300 STMW 40222 5509 E7
1300 STMW 40222 5618 E1
Lynn Myra Ct
1200 LSVL 40214 5832 D2
Lynnview Dr
4300 LSVL 40216 5722 D4
Lynnview Dr NE
- HsnC 47136 5610 C6
2000 LNVL 47136 5610 D5
Lynnwood Av
400 VNGV 40175 6482 C7
Lynnwood Dr
100 CLKV 47129 5506 B3
1700 NALB 47150 5396 D7
8000 MTWH 40047 6056 A2
E Lynnwood Dr
100 CLKV 47129 5506 C2
W Lynnwood Dr
100 CLKV 47129 5506 C3
Lynnwood Wy
3000 JFTN 40299 5728 D3
Lynwood Ct
200 RDCF 40160 6592 E2
Lyon Ln
2400 NALB 47150 5505 D2
Lyons Av
100 CLKV 47129 5506 C6
13600 LSVL 40272 6049 A2
Lyric Ln
9600 JFTN 40299 5728 C2
Lytle St
2000 LSVL 40203 5615 A1
2000 LSVL 40212 5615 A1
2100 LSVL 40212 5506 A7
2700 LSVL 40212 5505 E7

M

M St
700 LSVL 40208 5724 C2
Maalox Ct
3500 LSVL 40220 5727 C2
E Mabel St
200 MdeC 40155 6264 D5
200 MRGH 40155 6264 D5
W Mabel St
100 MdeC 40108 6264 C5
100 MRGH 40155 6264 C5
Mable Ct
200 HdnC 40175 6591 D1
200 VNGV 40175 6591 D1
MacAlester Dr
6600 LSVL 40214 5833 D2
MacArthur Dr
100 FRMD 40207 5618 B3
100 STMW 40207 5618 B3
300 NALB 47150 5505 C2
MacBrae Rd
300 LSVL 40214 5833 D1
MacDonald Rd
600 LSVL 40118 5833 D7
MacGregor Pl
4200 FydC 47150 5396 E2
Machupe Ct
7900 LSVL 40241 5510 A2
Machupe Dr
4000 LSVL 40241 5510 A2
Macintosh Av
5100 OdmC 40031 5295 B5
Mack Dr
- BltC 40165 6160 A1
100 FydC 47150 5396 C4
Mackenzie Pl
4400 LSVL 40241 5511 A2
Mackie Ct
100 LSVL 40214 5833 C5
Mackie Ln
100 LSVL 40214 5833 C4
Mackinaw Dr
12700 MDTN 40243 5620 E2
MacLean Av
400 LSVL 40209 5724 E6
400 LSVL 40214 5724 E6
MacMore Pl
2700 LSVL 40206 5617 A2
Maco Ln
5500 LSVL 40219 5835 E4
Macon Av
300 LSVL 40207 5617 E3
300 STMW 40207 5617 E3
600 BFLD 40207 5618 A4
600 STMW 40207 5618 A4
700 PLYV 40207 5618 A5
Macon Ct
3500 JFVL 47130 5398 C7
Mada Wy
4200 LSVL 40272 5940 E2
Madelle Av
3000 LSVL 40206 5617 B1
Madelon Ct
600 LSVL 40211 5614 D3
N Madison Av
100 MDTN 40243 5620 C3
300 ANCH 40223 5620 C3
300 LSVL 40223 5620 C3
300 MDTN 40223 5620 C3
S Madison Av
100 MDTN 40243 5620 C4
Madison Ct
100 BltC 40047 6054 E6
Madison Dr
- ELZT 42701 6703 C6
7200 ClkC 47172 5397 D1
7300 CLKV 47129 5397 D2
Madison St
- HdnC 40121 6265 A7
200 CHAN 47111 5181 E4
500 ELZT 42701 6812 C4
1000 CLKV 47129 5397 D7
E Madison St
- LSVL 40202 5615 E2
100 LGNG 40031 5296 E2
500 LGNG 40031 5297 A2
500 LSVL 40202 5616 A3
800 LSVL 40204 5616 A3
W Madison St
100 LGNG 40031 5296 D3
1300 LSVL 40203 5615 B3
2000 LSVL 40211 5615 B3
2300 LSVL 40211 5614 E2
Madison Park Pl
- CTWD 40014 5403 E5
Madrone Av
8100 LSVL 40258 5831 B6
Mae Av
4100 LSVL 40216 5723 A4
Mae Ct
5500 LSVL 40214 5833 B4
Mae St
- LSVL 40213 5834 B4
Mae St Kidd Av
1600 LSVL 40211 5614 B6
Maevi Dr
100 NALB 47150 5504 E1
Magazine St
700 LSVL 40202 5615 C3
1300 LSVL 40203 5615 B3
1300 LSVL 40210 5615 B3
2000 LSVL 40211 5615 A3
2300 LSVL 40211 5614 E3
W Magazine St
1000 LSVL 40203 5615 C3
Magdalen Sq
5100 LSVL 40241 5510 E1
Magellan Ct
1900 LSVL 40210 5614 E7
Magers Dr
10 HdnC 42701 6593 D7
Magisterial Dr
13000 LSVL 40223 5621 A1
Magnet Dr
10 ELZT 42701 6811 E4
Magnolia Av
100 JFVL 47130 5506 E4
E Magnolia Av
100 LSVL 40208 5615 D6
W Magnolia Av
100 LSVL 40208 5615 C6
900 LSVL 40210 5615 C6
3100 LSVL 40211 5614 D5
Magnolia Ct
100 LGNG 40031 5296 C3
100 OdmC 40031 5296 C3
3200 FydC 47172 5397 A1
Magnolia Dr
700 RDCF 40160 6483 A3
Magnolia Ln
1700 ANCH 40223 5511 B7
1700 ANCH 40223 5620 B1
Magnolia Ridge Ct
8000 LSVL 40291 5837 A5
Magnolia Ridge Dr
9400 LSVL 40291 5837 A5
Magnolia View Ct
11500 LSVL 40299 5729 A5
Mahaffey Ln
16100 LSVL 40299 5839 E7
16100 LSVL 40299 5840 A7
Mahan Dr
2100 JFTN 40299 5728 C2
2200 FTHL 40299 5728 C1
Mahogany Dr
11700 LSVL 40272 5940 A5
Mahogany Run Dr
1500 LGNG 40031 5297 A6
Mahoney Dr
8900 LSVL 40258 5831 C6
9000 LSVL 40272 5831 C7
Maiden Ct
9100 LSVL 40229 5944 E1
Maiden Ln
200 JFVL 47130 5507 A7
Maiden Pl
9100 LSVL 40229 5944 E1
E Mailback Wy
1000 LGNG 40014 5297 A7
1000 OdmC 40014 5296 D7
1000 OdmC 40014 5297 A7
W Mailback Wy
1000 OdmC 40014 5296 E7
Main St
- BltC 40047 5947 A7
- MTWH 40047 5947 A7
- UTCA 47130 5399 E6
- UTCA 47130 5400 A6
10 CHAN 47111 5181 D5
10 WPT 40177 6156 D2
100 BltC 40047 6056 C4
100 MTWH 40047 6056 A1
200 JFVL 47130 5507 C6
1400 ClkC 47111 5181 E4
1500 ClkC 47111 5182 A4
6900 LNVL 47136 5610 D5
11400 DGSH 40243 5620 B4
11400 LSVL 40223 5620 B4
11500 MDTN 40243 5620 C4
Main St SR-62
6900 LNVL 47136 5610 D5
Main St SR-2840
11400 DGSH 40243 5620 B4
11400 LSVL 40223 5620 B4
11400 MDTN 40243 5620 B4
Main St US-31E
- BltC 40047 5947 B6
Main St US-31EX
- BltC 40047 5947 A7
- MTWH 40047 5947 A7
100 BltC 40047 6056 C4
100 MTWH 40047 6056 A1
Main St US-150
- BltC 40047 5947 B6
E Main St
- NALB 47150 5505 E4
100 LGNG 40031 5296 E2
100 LSVL 40202 5615 E2
100 VNGV 40175 6591 E1
300 LGNG 40031 5297 B2
400 LSVL 40202 5616 A2
700 LSVL 40206 5616 A2
1500 VNGV 40175 6592 A1
E Main St SR-111
100 NALB 47150 5505 C5
E Main St SR-1500
100 VNGV 40175 6591 E1
1500 VNGV 40175 6592 A1
E Main St US-31E
100 LSVL 40202 5615 E2
400 LSVL 40202 5616 A2
700 LSVL 40206 5616 A2
E Main St US-42
1000 LSVL 40206 5616 B2
E Main St US-60 TRK
100 LSVL 40202 5615 E2
400 LSVL 40202 5616 A2
700 LSVL 40206 5616 A2
N Main St
100 ELZT 42701 6812 D1
S Main St
100 ELZT 42701 6812 B3
W Main St
100 LGNG 40031 5296 E3
100 LSVL 40202 5615 E2
100 NALB 47150 5505 A6
100 VNGV 40175 6482 D7
100 VNGV 40175 6591 E1
1000 LSVL 40203 5615 D2
2000 LSVL 40212 5615 D2
3200 LSVL 40212 5614 D1
W Main St SR-111
100 NALB 47150 5505 A6
W Main St SR-144
100 VNGV 40175 6482 D7
100 VNGV 40175 6591 E1
W Main St SR-1500
100 VNGV 40175 6482 D7
100 VNGV 40175 6591 E1
W Main St US-31E
100 LSVL 40202 5615 E2
W Main St US-31W
200 LSVL 40202 5615 E2
1000 LSVL 40203 5615 D2
2000 LSVL 40212 5615 D2
W Main St US-60 TRK
100 LSVL 40202 5615 E2
1000 LSVL 40203 5615 C2
Main Cross St
100 CHAN 47111 5181 E4
Maine St
100 HdnC 40121 6374 C4
Main Range Rd
- HdnC 40121 6265 E7
- HdnC 40121 6484 A1
Main St Hill Rd
1100 NALB 47150 5505 A6
1200 NALB 47150 5504 E6
Maize Ct
5200 LSVL 40258 5831 B3
Majestic Blvd
100 HLVW 40229 5944 A5
Majestic Ln
100 BltC 40165 6054 C2
Majestic Wy
- LSVL 40219 5834 D7
Majestic Oaks Rd
- SbyC 40067 5732 E2
Majestic Oaks Wy
1000 SbyC 40067 5732 E3
Majestic Woods Pl
1600 LSVL 40245 5621 D2
Major Ln
- LSVL 40291 5837 D5
Malcolm Av
400 LSVL 40223 5620 B3
4300 LSVL 40215 5723 E6
Malcolm Rd
4400 LSVL 40216 5723 C6
4500 LSVL 40214 5723 C7
Maldon Dr
5700 LSVL 40216 5722 B7
Malibu Dr
5100 LSVL 40216 5723 B7
5100 LSVL 40216 5832 A1
8500 LSVL 40219 5836 A6
Malinee Ott Rd
10000 FydC 47122 5501 B2
Malinee Ott Rd NE
7700 FydC 47122 5501 A1
7700 HsnC 47122 5392 A7
Mall Rd
- LSVL 40218 5726 D3
- WBHL 40218 5726 D3
Mallard Dr
7500 LSVL 40258 5830 D3
Mallard Ln
1300 OdmC 40031 5297 B7
Mallard Run
2400 JFVL 47130 5398 C6
Mallard Creek Rd
900 STMW 40207 5618 C5
Mallard Crossing Ct
100 ELZT 42701 6811 D1
Mallet Hill Dr
16700 LSVL 40245 5622 D1
Mallgate Pl
7000 STMW 40207 5618 C4
Mallory St
300 ELZT 42701 6812 B1
Malthusian Wy
2900 LSVL 40206 5617 B2
Malvern Hill Ct
2400 PNTN 40242 5510 B6
Malvern Hill Rd
8800 PNTN 40242 5510 B6
Mamaroneck Rd
3700 LSVL 40218 5727 B3
Mammoth Wy
2100 JFTN 40299 5728 D1
Manassas Dr
6500 OdmC 40056 5512 E4
Manatee Rd
8900 LSVL 40299 5728 B5
Manchester Dr
- ELZT 42701 6703 D6
Manchester Rd
2200 LSVL 40205 5726 C1
2300 WLTN 40205 5726 C1
2400 WLTN 40205 5617 D7
2500 LSVL 40205 5617 D7
Mandeville Ct
6500 LSVL 40228 5836 B2
Mandeville Rd
6300 LSVL 40228 5836 A2
Mandy Ct
100 RDCF 40160 6483 D6
Mango Ct
10 LSVL 40258 5831 C4
Mango Dr
7600 LSVL 40258 5831 C4
Manitau Av
1200 LSVL 40215 5724 A5
Manito St
- HdnC 40121 6374 D2
Manley Av
100 VNGV 40175 6483 A6
Mann Av
4400 LSVL 40215 5723 E6
Mann Ct
10 NALB 47150 5505 C2
Manner Dale Dr
3800 LSVL 40220 5727 C3
Manner Gate Ct
4300 LSVL 40220 5727 D2
Manner Gate Dr
4100 LSVL 40220 5727 C2
Manning Ct
- LGNG 40031 5296 C3
Manning Pl
1100 LGNG 40031 5296 C3
Manning Rd
700 LSVL 40209 5724 E4
700 LSVL 40209 5725 A4
1100 LSVL 40213 5725 B3
Manor Ct
5200 CTWD 40014 5403 E4
5200 OdmC 40014 5403 E4
Manor Dr
200 RDCF 40160 6483 E5
Manor Dr NE
8000 HsnC 47136 5611 A4
Manor House Dr
1800 LSVL 40220 5618 B7
1800 MVWE 40220 5618 B7
Manor Isle Dr
6400 LSVL 40272 5939 E6
Manor View Cir
6400 LSVL 40272 5939 E6
Man O War Dr
- SHDV 40165 6162 C2
Manpower Center Dr
- SbyC 40067 5732 E1
Manse Dr
6000 LSVL 40258 5831 A6
Mansfield Ct
5300 LSVL 40218 5726 D6
Mansfield Dr
5000 LSVL 40218 5726 D6
Mansfield Ln
5000 LSVL 40218 5726 D6
5200 LSVL 40228 5726 D6
Manslick Ct
3700 LSVL 40215 5723 D4
Manslick Rd
3500 LSVL 40215 5723 D4
3500 SVLY 40216 5723 E3
4300 LSVL 40216 5723 D5
4700 LSVL 40214 5723 E6
7300 LSVL 40214 5832 E3
Manslick Rd SR-1931
3500 LSVL 40215 5723 D4
3500 SVLY 40216 5723 E3
4300 LSVL 40216 5723 D5
4700 LSVL 40214 5723 E6
6600 LSVL 40214 5832 E1
E Manslick Rd
4600 LSVL 40229 5835 C7
4900 LSVL 40219 5835 E7
5500 LSVL 40219 5836 A7
5500 LSVL 40229 5836 A7
7100 LSVL 40228 5836 D6
E Manslick Rd SR-2845
4600 LSVL 40229 5835 C7
4900 LSVL 40219 5835 E7
5500 LSVL 40219 5836 A7
5500 LSVL 40229 5836 A7
7100 LSVL 40228 5836 D6
W Manslick Rd
8600 LSVL 40214 5832 E7
8600 LSVL 40272 5832 E6
9200 LSVL 40118 5833 A7

INDEX 32
W Manslick Rd
Louisville Metro Street Index
Meadowbrook Dr

STREET Block City ZIP Map# Grid

W Manslick Rd
9200 LSVL 40272 5833 A7
10400 LSVL 40118 5942 C1
W Manslick Rd SR-2055
8600 LSVL 40214 5832 E6
8600 LSVL 40272 5832 E6
9200 LSVL 40118 5833 A7
9200 LSVL 40272 5833 A7
9700 LSVL 40118 5942 C1
Manson Wy
5900 LSVL 40258 5831 B6
N Mantle Av
100 ELZT 42701 6812 B1
600 ELZT 42701 6703 C7
S Mantle Av
100 ELZT 42701 6812 A2
Maple Av
100 PWEV 40056 5512 D2
100 SLRB 47172 5288 D4
200 LGNG 40031 5297 A2
400 OdmC 40056 5512 E3
Maple Ct
10 HdnC 42701 6593 C6
10 LSVL 40214 5724 C5
10 LSVL 40215 5724 C5
1500 NALB 47150 5505 E1
1800 GEOT 47122 5502 A3
E Maple Ct
100 CLKV 47129 5506 C3
W Maple Ct
100 CLKV 47129 5506 C3
Maple Dr
1900 OdmC 40031 5297 D4
Maple Ln
- BltC 40109 5943 E5
- LSVL 40219 5834 D6
600 NALB 47150 5504 E5
1200 ANCH 40223 5620 C2
1600 RDCF 40160 6483 B1
Maple Rd
10 LGNG 40031 5297 A2
2700 LSVL 40205 5617 A4
3200 JFTN 40299 5728 D4
6200 GNVL 47124 5284 A7
6200 GNVL 47124 5393 A1
8800 LSVL 40219 5836 A7
8800 LSVL 40229 5836 A7
9000 LSVL 40229 5945 A1
Maple St
10 ClkC 47172 5288 E2
10 ClkC 47172 5289 A2
100 CHAN 47111 5181 D2
100 MRGH 40155 6264 C4
200 VNGV 40175 6482 D7
2000 LSVL 40210 5615 A3
2000 LSVL 40211 5615 A3
2300 LSVL 40211 5614 E3
E Maple St
100 JFVL 47130 5507 B6
N Maple St
10 SHDV 40165 6162 A2
100 ELZT 42701 6812 B2
S Maple St
200 ELZT 42701 6812 A3
W Maple St
100 JFVL 47130 5507 A7
400 JFVL 47130 5506 E7
Maple Tr
100 BltC 40165 6163 A7
Maple Wy
11500 LSVL 40229 5944 D4
Maple Brook Dr
- LSVL 40241 5511 B3
Maplecreek Dr
8800 LSVL 40219 5834 E7
9000 LSVL 40219 5835 B3
Maple Crest Ct
10 LSVL 40206 5617 A2
Maplecrest Dr
500 LGNG 40031 5296 E2
Maple Crest Wy
500 ELZT 42701 6703 A2
Maple Forest Dr
4400 LSVL 40245 5511 E3
Maple Glen Pl
14500 LSVL 40245 5621 C3
Maple Grove Dr
8000 GEOT 47122 5502 A3
Maple Hill Rd
7900 LSVL 40219 5836 A5
Maple Hill Wy
6000 OdmC 40014 5404 A3
Maple Hurst Dr
4000 OdmC 40014 5403 E3
4000 OdmC 40014 5404 A3
Maplehurst Dr
100 ClkC 47130 5399 B5
Maple Leaf Ct
- SpnC 40071 5948 E5
Maple Leaf Dr
2900 OdmC 40031 5296 B6
3400 OdmC 40031 5405 B1
Maple Ridge Pl
14400 LSVL 40245 5621 C3
Maple Shade Tr
- LGNG 40031 5297 B1
Maple Spring Dr
4900 LSVL 40229 5944 C3
Mapleton Av
4000 LSVL 40215 5724 B5
Mapleview Ct
100 BltC 40047 6055 A5
Maple View Dr
- MTWH 40047 6055 A5
100 BltC 40047 6055 A6
Mapleview Dr
8800 LSVL 40258 5831 B7
9000 LSVL 40272 5831 B7
Maplewood Blvd
500 FydC 47122 5503 B5
Maplewood Dr
100 CLKV 47129 5506 B3
4100 FydC 47150 5396 D2
E Maplewood Dr
100 CLKV 47129 5506 C2
W Maplewood Dr
100 CLKV 47129 5506 B2
Maplewood Pl
1900 LSVL 40205 5616 D6
Maplewood Rd
12100 OdmC 44026 5292 C2
Marajean Av
100 FydC 47150 5503 C5
Maravian Dr
6100 LSVL 40216 5722 B7
6100 LSVL 40258 5722 B7
6100 LSVL 40258 5831 A1
Marbado Ct
10900 LSVL 40229 5944 E5
Marble Ct
5400 LSVL 40219 5835 E3
Marceitta Ct
10700 LSVL 40291 5946 C1
Marceitta Wy
9500 LSVL 40291 5946 C1
March Blvd
1700 LSVL 40215 5723 D4
Marci Ln
1000 GEOT 47122 5502 B3
Marcitis Rd
10700 LSVL 40272 5940 B3
Marcy Av
4600 LSVL 40272 5940 D2
Marcy St
200 CHAN 47111 5181 C4
200 ClkC 47111 5181 C4
Mardale Dr
3300 JFTN 40299 5728 C4
Marengo Dr
200 WDHL 40243 5620 D4
500 MDTN 40243 5620 D5
800 DGSH 40299 5620 D6
Margaret Ann Ct
9200 OdmC 40056 5512 D4
Margo Av
4800 LSVL 40258 5831 D4
Margo Ct
5100 LSVL 40258 5831 D4
Margot Av
600 ELZT 42701 6812 B1
Marguerite Dr
2300 LSVL 40216 5831 D1
2500 LSVL 40216 5722 C7
Maria Av
7300 BCFT 40222 5509 D6
7300 LSVL 40222 5509 D6
Maria Ct
2300 BCFT 40222 5509 E6
Marian Ct
9100 JFTN 40299 5728 C2
Marian Dr
100 LSVL 40218 5727 C5
6700 LSVL 40216 5831 D1
Marianna Dr
300 NALB 47150 5504 D7
Maricopa Ct
1900 LSVL 40223 5510 D6
Maricopa Rd
2000 LSVL 40223 5510 D6
2000 MBKF 40223 5510 D6
Marie Ct
3800 OdmC 40014 5405 E1
11900 HLVW 40229 5944 D5
Marie St
1400 LSVL 40208 5615 E6
Marie Anna Dr
7400 LSVL 40258 5830 D4
Mariemont Ct
1300 STMW 40222 5509 E6
Mariemont Dr
6800 LSVL 40291 5836 D3
Mariemont Rd
5500 LSVL 40216 5722 A6
5500 LSVL 40258 5721 E6
5500 LSVL 40258 5722 A6
Marietta Ct
2500 JFVL 47130 5398 C7
7600 LSVL 40258 5830 D4
Marietta Dr
2500 JFVL 47130 5398 C7
Marigold Av
2800 LSVL 40213 5834 C1
Marigold Ct
5700 LSVL 40213 5834 D1
Marigold Dr
800 JFVL 47130 5507 C3
Marilee Dr
2000 LSVL 40272 5939 E2
2000 LSVL 40272 5940 A3
Marilyn Ct
3600 OdmC 40014 5296 E7
Marina Dr
6000 LSVL 40059 5400 C6
6600 PROS 40059 5400 D6
Marina Cove
5000 LSVL 40059 5400 C6
Marina View Ct
5900 PROS 40059 5400 D5
Marine St
- LSVL 40212 5505 E6
2700 LSVL 40212 5506 A6
Mariners Tr
5900 ClkC 47111 5180 C7
6100 ClkC 47111 5289 C1
Marion Av
4600 LSVL 40213 5725 D7
Marion Ct
3200 LSVL 40206 5617 A3
Marion Dr
- LGNG 40031 5297 B6
- OdmC 40031 5297 B6
1800 GEOT 47122 5501 E3
Mariposa Dr
6800 LSVL 40214 5832 E1
Maris Ln
4600 LSVL 40241 5510 B1
Maritime
5100 ClkC 47130 5399 C6
5100 JFVL 47130 5399 B7
Maritime Rd
- JFVL 47130 5399 B7
Marjorie Dr
5000 LSVL 40229 5944 D1
Mark Av
100 MTWH 40047 6056 B4
Mark Ct
900 ELZT 42701 6703 D7
Mark Dr
5500 LSVL 40258 5831 C6
Mark Tr
1300 LYDN 40242 5619 C1
Market St
100 CHAN 47111 5181 D3
100 UTCA 47130 5400 A5
Market St SR-3
100 CHAN 47111 5181 D3
E Market St
100 JFVL 47130 5507 A7
100 LSVL 40202 5615 E2
500 LSVL 40202 5616 A3
700 LSVL 40206 5616 B3
1700 NALB 47150 5505 E4
W Market St
100 JFVL 47130 5507 A7
100 LSVL 40202 5615 E2
100 NALB 47150 5505 A6
500 JFVL 47130 5506 E7
900 CLKV 47129 5506 E7
1000 LSVL 40203 5615 D2
2000 LSVL 40212 5615 D2
2500 LSVL 40212 5614 B1
W Market St US-31E
100 LSVL 40202 5615 E2
W Market St US-31W
200 LSVL 40202 5615 E2
1000 LSVL 40203 5615 D2
2000 LSVL 40212 5615 D2
W Market St US-60 TRK
100 LSVL 40202 5615 E2
1000 LSVL 40203 5615 C2
Market Cart Wy
7600 LSVL 40291 5837 A5
Market Pl Dr
100 HLVW 40229 5944 C7
Markham Ln
800 STMW 40207 5618 A5
Marki Ln
12300 LSVL 40291 5838 B6
Markleham Pl
100 LSVL 40245 5621 C5
Markleham Wy
14200 LSVL 40245 5621 C5
Marksfield Cir
200 HTBN 40222 5619 C4
Marksfield Rd
8800 HTBN 40222 5619 C4
Marksman Rd
10 LSVL 40216 5722 E2
10 LSVL 40216 5723 A2
Markwell Ct
300 LSVL 40219 5835 A4
Markwell Ln
1100 LSVL 40219 5835 A4
Markwell Rd
- BltC 40071 5947 E4
- BltC 40071 5948 A5
- LSVL 40299 5947 E4
Markwood Rd
2100 MBKF 40223 5510 D6
Marlboro Cir
9200 HTBN 40222 5619 C6
Marley Pl
14100 LSVL 40245 5621 C5
Marlin Dr
3500 JFTN 40299 5728 D4
Marlin Rd
3100 HNAC 40220 5727 E1
Marlow Rd
1700 SVLY 40216 5723 E2
Marlowe Ct
1900 CLKV 47129 5397 B7
Marlowe Dr
1000 ClkC 47129 5397 B7
1000 CLKV 47129 5397 B7
Marne Ct
1600 LYDN 40242 5510 C7
Marquette Dr
400 STMW 40222 5618 D2
Marquis Trc
1100 JFTN 40223 5619 E6
Marquise Ct
900 JFVL 47130 5398 E7
900 JFVL 47130 5507 D1
Marret Av
400 LSVL 40208 5615 E6
Marret Pl
1300 LSVL 40214 5724 A7
1300 LSVL 40215 5724 A7
Marriott Dr
500 CLKV 47129 5506 D6
Mars Ct
5200 LSVL 40258 5831 D2
Marse Pl
4500 JFTN 40299 5728 C6
Marse Henry Dr
9200 JFTN 40299 5728 B6
Marseille Dr
4200 LSVL 40272 5831 E7
N Marshall Av
500 CLKV 47129 5506 C3
Marshall Ct
500 LSVL 40202 5616 A3
700 LSVL 40204 5616 A3
Marshall Dr
100 BWDV 40207 5618 B3
100 CHAN 47111 5181 C4
100 FRMD 40207 5618 B3
Marshall St
800 LSVL 40202 5616 A3
800 LSVL 40204 5616 A3
Marshall Wk
400 LSVL 40214 5724 B7
Marshwood Ct
8300 LSVL 40219 5834 E6
Martha Av
600 JFVL 47130 5507 D4
4100 HNAC 40220 5727 D1
4100 LSVL 40220 5727 D1
Martha Cir
3900 OdmC 40014 5405 E1
Martha Ct
500 RDCF 40160 6483 A4
3100 LSVL 40220 5727 D1
Martha Moloney Dr
500 LSVL 40209 5724 E5
Martha's Ct
- MTWH 40047 6054 E7
Marthas Ct
1800 JFVL 47130 5507 A1
Martin Av
2500 LSVL 40216 5722 E5
2500 LSVL 40216 5723 A6
2500 SVLY 40216 5722 E5
2500 SVLY 40216 5723 A6
Martin Cir
100 JFVL 47130 5506 E5
Martin Dr
10 NALB 47150 5505 A3
1700 GEOT 47122 5501 E4
Martin Ln
10 RDCF 40160 6483 C5
Martin Rd
3000 FydC 47119 5395 B2
Martin Hill Rd
- BltC 40165 6050 D7
Martin Hill Rd SR-1417
- BltC 40165 6050 D7
Martinside Dr
10400 LSVL 40291 5837 E7
Martybrook Ct
2100 OdmC 40031 5296 C5
Marvic Dr
10 CLKV 47129 5506 A2
Marvin Av
100 BltC 40109 6052 D1
100 HLVW 40109 6052 D1
3700 WBHL 40218 5726 E4
Mar Vista Ct
8500 LSVL 40219 5836 A6
Marwood Pl
1700 LSVL 40213 5725 D3
Mary Ct
800 RDCF 40160 6483 C6
8400 OdmC 40014 5403 A7
Mary Dr
300 FydC 47150 5396 C3
4500 MTWH 40047 6056 A3
Mary St
100 JFVL 47130 5506 E3
100 JFVL 47130 5507 A4
100 VNGV 40175 6482 E7
100 VNGV 40175 6591 E1
800 LSVL 40203 5616 A5
800 LSVL 40204 5616 A5
Mary Anderson Memorial Hwy
- FydC 47119 5503 D1
- FydC 47122 5503 D2
Mary Anderson Mem Hwy US-150
- FydC 47119 5503 D1
- FydC 47122 5503 D2
Mary Ann Dr
2400 NALB 47150 5505 D2
Mary Catherine Dr
2300 SVLY 40216 5723 B3
Mary Clayton Ln
3500 OdmC 40014 5405 A3
4600 OdmC 40014 5404 E3
Mary Collins Ln
- GEOT 47122 5501 E4
Mary David Dr
100 BltC 40165 6054 C3
Mary Dell Ct
3800 NALB 47150 5396 D5
Mary Dell Ln
9600 LSVL 40291 5837 D1
9900 LSVL 40299 5837 D1
10100 LSVL 40299 5728 E7
10300 LSVL 40299 5729 A7
Mary Ellen Dr
5600 LSVL 40214 5833 B5
Mary F Hackley Al
- LSVL 40211 5614 E3
- LSVL 40211 5615 A3
Maryhill Ln
600 MYHE 40207 5617 D2
600 MYHE 40207 5618 A1
Mary Jane Dr
14000 LSVL 40272 5940 E6
Mary Knoll Dr
600 ELZT 42701 6811 E3
Mary Knoll Ln
4200 MYHE 40207 5617 D2
4200 MYHE 40207 5618 A1
4200 WDYH 40207 5618 A1
Maryland Av
- LSVL 40205 5617 A6
2000 LSVL 40205 5616 E6
2000 NALB 47150 5505 C2
Maryland Ct
500 ELZT 42701 6811 E2
Maryland St
100 ClkC 47172 5288 E2
N Maryland St
10 HdnC 40121 6374 E2
S Maryland St
- HdnC 40121 6374 E2
Mary Laverne Dr
7000 LSVL 40219 5835 D3
Mary Layne Rd
5500 LSVL 40219 5835 E5
Mary Lee Dr
1900 NALB 47150 5396 E7
Marylee Ln
7600 LSVL 40291 5837 C4
Maryman Rd
4800 LSVL 40258 5831 B5
Marymount Ct
2400 LSVL 40242 5509 D5
Mary Rose Dr
2900 LSVL 40216 5722 C6
Mary Ruth Lp
- VNGV 40175 6482 D7
Mary's Ct
100 BltC 40165 6160 D6
Mary Sue Dr
7600 LSVL 40291 5836 E5
8000 LSVL 40228 5836 E5
Marytena Dr
200 LSVL 40214 5833 B3
Mary T Meagher Dr
1100 ELZT 42701 6703 D6
Maryview Dr
5100 LSVL 40216 5832 B1
Maryville Dr
1400 HLVW 40229 5944 A6
1400 HNTH 40229 5944 A6
Masden St
10 RDCF 40160 6483 D6
Masemure Ct
2500 LSVL 40220 5726 E2
2500 LSVL 40220 5727 A2
Mason Av
3600 LSVL 40229 5944 A1
Mason Blvd
6100 LSVL 40059 5400 C5
Mason Ln
9600 LSVL 40118 5942 C2
Mason St
800 LSVL 40203 5616 A4
800 LSVL 40204 5616 A4
Mason Dixon Ln
4500 LSVL 40213 5726 A5
Masonic Home Dr
- LSVL 40207 5617 D2
- STMW 40207 5617 D2
Massapequa
- ClkC 47130 5399 A4
Massie Av
3800 STMW 40207 5617 E2
4000 STMW 40207 5618 A2
Massie School Rd
1700 OdmC 40031 5297 D5
Master St
100 RDCF 40160 6592 E2
Masters Ct
10 SpnC 40071 5949 B5
8500 LSVL 40291 5837 A3
Masters Dr
10 RDCF 42701 6593 B4
Masters Ln
10 SpnC 40071 5949 B5
Masters St
10 ELZT 42701 6811 D5
Matalin Pl
- CTWD 40014 5403 E5
Matha Av
1200 LSVL 40215 5724 A5
Matheis Ln
1900 SVLY 40216 5723 C3
Mathews Av
- LSVL 40216 5722 E3
Mathews Pl
4000 HdnC 40121 6374 A4
Matilda Ct
9200 LSVL 40219 5835 B7
9200 LSVL 40229 5835 B7
9200 LSVL 40229 5944 C1
Matt Ct
8300 LSVL 40258 5831 C5
Matten Ct
- OdmC 40014 5402 B6
Matterhorn Ct
5200 LSVL 40216 5722 D7
Matterhorn Dr
5200 LSVL 40216 5722 D7
5400 LSVL 40216 5831 C1
Matthew Dr
- BltC 40047 6054 E6
- MTWH 40047 6054 E6
Matthews Rd
6600 LSVL 40258 5831 A6
Mattingly Ct
4500 OdmC 40031 5295 D6
Mattingly Rd
100 BltC 40165 6051 D7
100 BltC 40165 6160 E1
3500 OdmC 40031 5295 D6
Maurer Ln
7300 LSVL 40258 5831 A3
Maurice Dr
4500 MTWH 40047 6056 A4
Mavis Ct
2500 LSVL 40216 5722 C7
2500 LSVL 40216 5831 C1
Maxey Ln
2700 LSVL 40245 5512 A4
Maxine Ct
1800 CLKV 47129 5397 B7
Maxon Dr
2700 LSVL 40218 5726 E1
2700 LSVL 40220 5726 E1
Maxwell Ct
4400 WTNH 40245 5511 D2
Maxwell St
- HdnC 40121 6374 B4
May Av
2000 LSVL 40217 5724 E1
May Dr
1400 NALB 47150 5505 E2
May St
6000 FydC 47119 5393 E3
6000 FydC 47119 5394 A3
Mayan Ct
- ELZT 42701 6812 A3
Mayapple Ln
10 ELZT 42701 6811 C1
Mayer Av
1000 LSVL 40217 5616 B7
Mayer Ln
10 HdnC 42701 6593 C3
10 RDCF 42701 6593 C3
Mayfair Av
1000 CLKV 47129 5506 D2
6100 LSVL 40059 5400 B4
6600 PROS 40059 5400 C5
Mayfair Cir
- OdmC 44026 5292 B5
Mayfair Dr
1600 ClkC 47172 5288 B5
Mayfair Ln
400 LSVL 40207 5617 C1
400 MKBV 40207 5617 C1
Mayfield Rd
4300 WSNP 40213 5725 E4
Mayflower Mnr
2200 NALB 47150 5505 D2
Mayflower Rd
100 HLVW 40229 5944 D6
200 BltC 40229 5944 D6
Mayford Wy
2800 SRPK 40220 5618 D7
Maylawn Av
500 LSVL 40217 5724 E2
600 LSVL 40217 5725 A2
Mayna Dr
6100 LSVL 40258 5831 B2
Maynard Av
4000 LSVL 40229 5944 A1
Mayo Ct
12500 OdmC 40059 5292 C6
Mayo Dr
3500 LSVL 40218 5726 C3
3500 WBHL 40218 5726 C3
Mayo Ln
1800 OdmC 40059 5292 B6
2200 OdmC 40059 5291 E3
May Pen Rd
6300 LSVL 40228 5836 A2
Mayrow Dr
7300 LSVL 40228 5945 E1
7300 LSVL 40291 5945 E1
Mays Dr
- ELZT 42701 6702 D4
Maywick Rd
6200 LSVL 40272 5940 A3
Maywood Pl
3000 LSVL 40220 5618 B7
3100 LSVL 40220 5727 B1
McAdams Ct
3300 JFTN 40299 5728 B3
McAdams Ln
300 SHDV 40165 6161 D1
McArthur
2900 JFVL 47130 5398 D7
McAtee Av
3100 LSVL 40211 5614 D3
McBeth St
1000 NALB 47150 5505 C5
McBride Dr
10 JFVL 47130 5508 B3
McBroom Ct
200 LSVL 40214 5833 C5
McBroom Dr
100 LSVL 40214 5833 C5
McCallen Ln
3000 FydC 47150 5613 B5
McCamish Dr
10 ELZT 42701 6812 B5
McCampbell St
100 CHAN 47111 5181 D5
McCarthy Ct
1500 GYDL 40222 5619 C3
McCarthy Ln
7800 GYDL 40222 5618 D4
7800 GYDL 40222 5619 A1
7800 STMW 40222 5618 C4
E McCarthy Knob Rd
4800 FydC 47150 5612 C3
W McCarthy Knob Rd
6000 FydC 47136 5611 E3
6000 FydC 47136 5612 A3
McCartin Dr
1400 NALB 47150 5505 E2
McCauley Lp
7500 HdnC 40121 6374 C4
McCawley Rd
1200 LSVL 40219 5835 B4
McClain Ct
3300 JFTN 40299 5728 B3
McCloskey Av
1600 LSVL 40210 5615 A7
McClure Ct
10500 LSVL 40241 5511 A2
McCollum Ct
4000 WBHL 40218 5726 D4
McCombs Cir
4300 OdmC 40014 5403 C3
McConnell Ct
- FydC 47150 5396 C3
McConnell Dr
10 FydC 47150 5396 C4
10 NALB 47150 5396 C4
McCoy Av
1400 LSVL 40215 5724 A3
McCoy Wy
2600 LSVL 40205 5617 C6
2600 SGDN 40205 5617 C6
McCracken St
7500 HdnC 40121 6374 C5
McCrary Ln
10 BltC 40229 5945 C6
McCrea Ln
9800 LSVL 40229 5944 B2
McCready Av
100 LSVL 40206 5617 D3
McCubbins Farm Ln
100 BltC 40165 6163 A4
McCullen Ln
- FydC 47150 5613 B5
McCullough Pike
10 CLKV 47129 5506 B3
500 ClkC 47129 5506 A3
E McCullough Pike
100 CLKV 47129 5506 C1
McCullum Av
600 ELZT 42701 6703 B7
600 ELZT 42701 6812 B1
McDeane Rd
5400 LSVL 40216 5723 B7
McDevett Cir
7500 HdnC 40121 6374 C4
McDonald Av
1700 NALB 47150 5505 C2
McDonald Ln
1700 NALB 47150 5396 C7
1700 NALB 47150 5505 D1
McDonald St
2500 NALB 47150 5505 C1
McDowell Rd
- OdmC 40056 5512 D3
- PWEV 40056 5512 D3
McFarland Av
100 MTWH 40047 6056 A4
McFarlin Ln
10 VNGV 40175 6591 C2
McGee Dr
2400 LSVL 40216 5722 C7
2400 LSVL 40216 5831 C1
McGill Dr
4400 LSVL 40215 5724 A6
McGregor Dr
5100 OdmC 40031 5295 B5
McGruder Ln
100 BltC 40165 6163 C4
McHenry St
1300 LSVL 40204 5616 A6
1300 LSVL 40217 5616 A6
McIntosh Wy
7500 LSVL 40228 5836 D6
McIntyre Rd
10 HdnC 40175 6591 D4
McKay Av
1500 LSVL 40213 5725 D3
McKeever Ln
6800 LSVL 40258 5831 A5
McKenna Ct
7100 LSVL 40291 5837 A4
McKenna Wy
8300 LSVL 40291 5836 E4
8500 LSVL 40291 5837 A4
McKindree Ct
2400 LSVL 40211 5614 E3
McKinley Av
- CLKV 47129 5506 C4
800 LSVL 40217 5725 B1
N McKinley Av
500 CLKV 47129 5506 C4
McKirkland Pl
400 LSVL 40245 5621 B6
McLean Av
2400 NALB 47150 5505 E2
McLeod Pl
- ELZT 42701 6812 C2
McLeod St
300 ELZT 42701 6812 C3
McMahan Blvd
- LNSH 40220 5618 D7
- SRPK 40220 5618 D7
2900 CMBG 40220 5618 D7
2900 LSVL 40220 5618 E7
3000 LSVL 40220 5727 D1
McMakin Mnr
100 LGNG 40031 5296 C3
McMeekin Ln
10500 DGSH 40223 5620 A3
10500 LSVL 40223 5620 A3
McNair Rd
8300 LSVL 40214 5832 E5
McNeely Lake Dr
9600 LSVL 40229 5945 B3
McQuire Ct
1600 LGNG 40031 5297 A1
McTavish Dr
1400 CLKV 47129 5506 B2
Meade Av
2900 LSVL 40217 5725 B1
3000 ANPK 40213 5725 B2
Meade Dr
4000 HdnC 40121 6374 A3
Meadow Av
1100 LSVL 40213 5725 C6
1100 LYNV 40213 5725 C6
Meadow Ct
- OdmC 44026 5292 D2
3500 LSVL 40218 5726 E2
Meadow Dr
2200 LSVL 40218 5726 D2
2500 LSVL 40220 5726 E2
Meadow Ln
- ELZT 42701 6812 B1
10 LGNG 40031 5296 D3
100 CLKV 47172 5397 C1
100 HdnC 42701 6812 B7
1500 NALB 47150 5505 E1
12000 MDTN 40243 5620 C5
12100 WDHL 40243 5620 D5
Meadow Rd
2300 LSVL 40205 5617 C6
2300 SGDN 40205 5617 C6
2600 SMRV 40205 5617 C7
7300 CTWD 40014 5512 E1
Meadowbend Wy
4200 LSVL 40218 5727 D4
Meadow Bluff Dr
5500 CTWD 40014 5403 B5
Meadowbrook Cir
100 BltC 40165 6053 A4
Meadowbrook Ct
100 BltC 40165 6053 A4
500 LSVL 40214 5724 B6
2300 OdmC 40031 5296 C6
Meadowbrook Dr
100 BltC 40165 6053 A5

INDEX 33
Meadowbrook Dr
Monroe St

Louisville Metro Street Index

STREET Block City ZIP Map# Grid

Meadowbrook Dr
2000 LGNG 40031 5296 C6
2000 OdmC 40031 5296 C6
4200 LSVL 40218 5727 A5
Meadow Brook Rd
- BltC 40165 6053 C2
- PNRV 40165 6053 B1
Meadowbrook Wy
2200 ClkC 47130 5399 B4
Meadow Chase Ct
11100 LSVL 40229 5945 A3
Meadow Creek Ct
4900 OdmC 40014 5405 B2
Meadowcreek Dr
1900 LSVL 40218 5726 B3
1900 WSNP 40218 5726 B3
Meadow Crest Ct
4000 LSVL 40245 5512 B4
Meadow Farms Ct
15100 LSVL 40245 5512 D6
Meadow Farms Pl
2900 LSVL 40245 5512 D6
Meadowfield Dr
3900 LSVL 40245 5512 C4
Meadowgate Ct
9500 WPMG 40223 5510 D7
Meadowgate Ln
1700 WPMG 40223 5510 D7
2000 LSVL 40223 5510 D7
Meadow Glenn Wy
10200 LSVL 40241 5510 C3
Meadowgreen Pl
8000 LSVL 40299 5727 E5
Meadow Haven Rd
3800 LSVL 40218 5727 D4
Meadow Hill Rd
900 LSVL 40219 5834 E4
Meadowkark Ct
- OdmC 40059 5292 D5
Meadowlake Dr
10 RDCF 40160 6483 E7
10 RDCF 40160 6592 D2
Meadow Land Ct
4900 OdmC 40014 5405 B2
Meadowland Dr
3900 OdmC 40059 5401 B1
Meadow Lark Av
2900 LSVL 40206 5617 B3
3100 ANPK 40213 5725 C2
3100 LSVL 40217 5725 C2
Meadowlark Dr
2500 OdmC 40059 5292 D5
Meadowlark Dr NE
7300 LNVL 47136 5610 D4
Meadow Lark Ln
- BltC 40165 6163 B1
100 BltC 40165 6054 A7
Meadowlark Rd
2900 JFVL 47130 5507 D1
Meadowlark Manor Ln
4500 LSVL 40245 5511 D3
Meadowlawn Dr
13000 LSVL 40272 5939 E7
13000 LSVL 40272 6048 E1
Meadow Ln Ct
2100 ANCH 40223 5620 D2
Meadow Oak Dr
6300 FydC 47122 5503 A4
Meadowood Ct
300 LSVL 40214 5833 C2
Meadowood Dr
1900 FydC 47122 5502 D3
Meadowood Rd
100 HLVW 40229 5944 C6
Meadow Ridge Ct
4100 LSVL 40218 5727 D5
5300 OdmC 40014 5404 C2
Meadow Ridge Dr
7100 LSVL 40218 5727 D5
Meadow Ridge Pl
3900 LSVL 40218 5727 C5
Meadowridge Tr
1100 GSHN 44026 5292 B2
1200 OdmC 44026 5292 B2
Meadow Run Rd
11100 LSVL 40229 5945 A3
Meadows Dr
100 BltC 40047 5947 A7
100 MTWH 40047 6056 A1
800 BltC 40047 6056 A1
4600 JFVL 47130 5398 A5
Meadowside Ct
3100 LSVL 40214 5832 C2
Meadow Springs Dr
4500 JFVL 47130 5398 C4
Meadow Springs Wy
8700 LSVL 40291 5837 D6
Meadow Stream Ct
- CTWD 40014 5403 B5
Meadow Stream Wy
5500 CTWD 40014 5403 C4
Meadow Vale Ct
2500 MWVL 40242 5510 D6
4900 OdmC 40014 5405 B2
Meadow Vale Dr
9700 MWVL 40242 5510 D6
9800 MWVL 40223 5510 D6
Meadow Valley Ct
4900 OdmC 40014 5405 B2
Meadow Valley Ln
9300 LSVL 40291 5946 E2
Meadow Valley Pl
9500 LSVL 40291 5946 D2
Meadowview Cir
2900 LSVL 40220 5618 B7
2900 MVWE 40220 5618 B7
Meadowview Ct
100 MTWH 40047 6056 B2
Meadow View Dr
1000 NALB 47150 5396 C5
6300 FydC 47122 5503 A4
Meadowview Dr
10 HdnC 42701 6593 C6
100 MTWH 40047 6056 B2
2000 OdmC 40014 5405 B5
10300 LSVL 40272 5940 A2
Meadow Vista Ct
13600 LSVL 40299 5729 E5
Meadowwood Ct
2700 OdmC 40059 5292 A6
Meadow Wood Dr
- BltC 40047 6056 E4
Meaganwood Pl
7500 LSVL 40214 5832 E4
Mechanic St
200 JFVL 47130 5507 A6
Medallion Ct
4200 LSVL 40219 5835 B1
Medbury Ct
2400 OBNP 40242 5509 E5
Medford Ct
3500 LSVL 40218 5726 E2
Medford Ln
2200 LSVL 40218 5726 E2
Medical Center Dr
100 RDCF 40160 6593 A4
Medina Wy
9600 LSVL 40223 5619 D3
Mediterranean Ct
5100 LSVL 40219 5835 D3
Medley Ct
3900 VNGV 40175 6483 A6
Medley Rd
- BltC 40165 6160 A2
Medora Rd
13100 LSVL 40272 5940 B7
13100 LSVL 40272 6049 B1
Medtree Pl
5800 LSVL 40229 5944 E3
Meeting House Rd
16900 LSVL 40023 5840 E1
17000 LSVL 40023 5731 E7
Megan Jay Ct
9400 JFTN 40299 5728 C5
Meghan Ln
9600 LSVL 40291 5946 B2
Meigs Av
100 JFVL 47130 5507 A6
Meihaus Wy
7000 LSVL 40272 5830 D7
Meijer Rd
2700 JFVL 47130 5398 D7
Melanie Ln
100 CHAN 47111 5181 E2
100 ELZT 42701 6811 E1
Melanie Wy
3100 LSVL 40220 5727 D1
Melbourne Av
3000 LSVL 40220 5618 C7
3000 LSVL 40220 5727 C1
Melchester Pl
10600 LSVL 40241 5511 C4
Melda Ln
3800 LSVL 40219 5835 B1
Melford Av
800 LSVL 40217 5725 A2
800 PKWV 40217 5725 A2
Melissa Dr
9800 LSVL 40223 5619 D2
Melissa St
100 ELZT 42701 6702 C6
Mellwood Av
- LSVL 40206 5508 A7
1400 LSVL 40206 5616 C2
2300 LSVL 40206 5507 E7
3000 LSVL 40207 5508 A7
Mellwood Av US-42
1400 LSVL 40206 5616 C2
Mellwood Av US-60 TRK
1400 LSVL 40206 5616 C2
Mellwood Dr
900 NALB 47150 5396 C6
Melody Ln
100 HLVW 40229 5943 E5
1200 JFVL 47130 5507 B3
1400 LSVL 40214 5832 E1
Melody Wy
2400 JFTN 40299 5728 D2
Melody Acres Ln
3100 LSVL 40216 5722 D5
Melon Ct
6800 LSVL 40219 5835 C3
Melonie Ott Rd
- FydC 47124 5392 A6
- HsnC 47122 5392 A6
Melrose Av
6500 LSVL 40216 5722 A4
N Melrose St
2900 JFTN 40299 5728 B3
S Melrose St
3000 JFTN 40299 5728 B3
Mel Smith Rd
4100 FydC 47150 5396 C2
Melton Av
4500 LSVL 40213 5834 B3
Melva Rd
- RDCF 40160 6483 C1
Melvin Ct
2700 LSVL 40216 5722 E5
Melvin Dr
4500 LSVL 40216 5722 E5
Melvyn Dr
4000 FydC 47150 5396 C4
4000 NALB 47150 5396 C4
Melwood Dr
100 SHDV 40165 6162 A3
Memorial Ct
900 ELZT 42701 6703 A7
Memorial Dr
- LSVL 40272 5939 E7
E Memorial Dr
100 ELZT 42701 6703 A7
Memorial Gardens Dr
- SVLY 40216 5723 B5
Memories Isle Ct
100 SHDV 40165 6161 C3
Memory Ln
600 ELZT 42701 6811 C3
6500 LSVL 40258 5831 B2
Memory Ln NE
2800 HsnC 47136 5610 E4
2800 LNVL 47136 5610 E4
Memphis Rd
- CHAN 47111 5181 C3
2700 ClkC 47111 5180 E2
2700 ClkC 47111 5181 A3
Memphis-Charlestown Rd
10300 ClkC 47111 5180 B2
10300 ClkC 47143 5180 B1
Mercer Av
1600 LSVL 40213 5725 D3
2300 SVLY 40216 5723 A4
2400 LSVL 40216 5723 A4
Mercer Ln
- MdeC 40108 6155 C3
2100 HdnC 40177 6155 E4
2100 HdnC 40177 6156 A4
2100 WPT 40177 6156 A4
Mercer St
200 ELZT 42701 6702 E7
Merchant Ct
700 LSVL 40203 5616 A4
Mercury Dr
5100 LSVL 40258 5831 D2
5900 LSVL 40291 5836 E2
Mercy Pl
- PWEV 40056 5512 C1
Mercy Wy
- LSVL 40204 5616 B4
Merhoff St
2600 LSVL 40217 5724 E2
2600 LSVL 40217 5725 A2
Meridale Av
4500 LSVL 40214 5724 C5
Meridian Av
- SPLE 40207 5618 A4
- STMW 40207 5618 A4
100 LSVL 40207 5617 E3
100 LSVL 40207 5618 A3
100 STMW 40207 5617 E3
300 NBNE 40207 5618 A3
Meridian Ct
- BltC 40047 5947 C6
Merioneth Ct
9800 JFTN 40299 5728 D2
Merioneth Dr
9800 JFTN 40299 5728 D2
Meriwether Av
500 LSVL 40217 5615 E6
600 LSVL 40217 5616 A6
Merlyn Cir
7500 LSVL 40214 5832 E4
7500 LSVL 40214 5833 A4
Merriam Dr
900 CLKV 47129 5506 A2
Merribrook Ln
5600 LSVL 40059 5401 D7
Merrick Rd
2200 RBNW 40207 5509 A5
Merrifield Pl
10 CLKV 47129 5506 A2
Merrifield Rd
700 WDYH 40207 5509 B7
Merriman Rd
200 STMW 40207 5618 B3
Merriwood Ct
2100 JFTN 40299 5728 C1
Merriwood Dr
2400 FTHL 40299 5728 C2
2400 JFTN 40299 5728 C2
Merry Wy
- GEOT 47122 5502 A3
Merryman Dr
400 JFVL 47130 5507 D5
Merrywood Dr
200 FydC 47150 5504 C6
200 NALB 47150 5504 C6
Merton Ln
- LSVL 40205 5616 E7
Merton Sq
4900 LSVL 40241 5510 E1
Merwin Av
600 LSVL 40217 5724 E2
600 LSVL 40217 5725 A2
Mesa Ct
4500 LSVL 40229 5944 C5
Mesquite Ct
7500 LSVL 40258 5831 B3
Metal Ln
- LSVL 40206 5507 D7
Meter Ct
6200 LSVL 40291 5836 E2
Methodist Dr
- VNGV 40175 6591 D1
Metts Ct
200 ELZT 42701 6703 C7
Meyer Dr
100 BltC 40165 6163 C5
Meyers Grv
3400 FydC 47172 5397 A1
Meyers Ln
1700 LSVL 40216 5832 A1
Meyers Grove Cir
600 ClkC 47129 5397 B6
700 CLKV 47129 5397 B6
Meyers Grove Dr
600 ClkC 47129 5397 A6
MGM Ct
100 MTWH 40047 6055 E5
Miami Av
4100 LSVL 40212 5505 C7
Miami St
7500 HdnC 40121 6374 C5
Micawber Ct
500 LSVL 40245 5621 D6
Micawber Wy
14300 LSVL 40245 5621 C5
Michael Dr
3000 HNAC 40220 5727 E1
6700 OdmC 40014 5404 D7
7400 LSVL 40228 5836 D4
Michael Wy
4300 HNAC 40220 5727 E1
Michaele Ln
9900 JFTN 40299 5728 D5
Michael Edward Ct
5200 LSVL 40291 5728 C7
Michael Edward Dr
8400 LSVL 40291 5728 C7
9900 LSVL 40299 5728 D7
Michael Ray Dr
8100 LSVL 40219 5835 E6
8400 LSVL 40219 5836 A6
8700 LSVL 40228 5836 A6
Michelle Av
200 ELZT 42701 6811 D1
Michigan Av
400 ELZT 42701 6812 A2
500 ELZT 42701 6811 E2
500 JFVL 47130 5507 A7
800 ClkC 47172 5289 A2
Michigan Ct
100 ELZT 42701 6812 A2
100 SHDV 40165 6161 E4
Mickendee Ln
3700 OdmC 40014 5404 E3
Mickey Wy
500 MRGH 40155 6264 D4
Micklenburg Ct
4500 WTNH 40245 5511 D2
Mid Dr
4700 LSVL 40272 5940 C1
Mid Dale Ct
3700 LSVL 40220 5727 B1
Mid Dale Ln
3000 LSVL 40218 5727 B2
3000 LSVL 40220 5727 B1
Middle Ln
2100 SVLY 40216 5723 B4
Middle Rd
2100 JFVL 47130 5507 E3
3400 JFVL 47130 5508 A1
3600 JFVL 47130 5399 B7
4500 ClkC 47130 5399 C6
Middle Wy
700 LSVL 40206 5617 A4
Middlebrook Rd
4200 WLNP 40207 5618 B2
Middleburg Ct
4600 FCSL 40241 5511 B2
Middleground Dr
5900 LSVL 40272 5940 A1
Middle Hill Ct
16600 LSVL 40245 5622 C5
Middle Pointe Rd
8900 BKPT 40241 5510 C4
Middlerose Cir
5900 LSVL 40272 5940 A2
Middlesex Dr
4700 WTNH 40245 5511 E2
4800 LSVL 40245 5511 E2
5100 CDSM 40245 5511 E2
Middletown Industrial Blvd
13000 MDTN 40223 5621 A3
Middletown Park Pl
300 MDTN 40243 5620 D3
Midfield Access Rd
- LSVL 40213 5834 B1
Midland Av
2000 LSVL 40204 5616 D5
4000 LSVL 40220 5618 C7
4000 LSVL 40220 5727 C1
Midland Ct
500 BltC 40047 6054 E4
Midland Ln
100 MTWH 40047 6054 D5
200 BltC 40047 6054 E5
Midland St
- HdnC 40121 6374 C3
Midnight Ln
5700 LSVL 40229 5944 E1
5900 LSVL 40229 5945 A1
Midway Av
700 LSVL 40211 5614 E3
800 LSVL 40210 5614 E4
Midway Dr
700 ClkC 47172 5288 C2
11200 JFTN 40299 5729 B1
11200 LSVL 40299 5729 B1
Midway Mnr
10 HdnC 40162 6702 A1
Miede Dr
100 NALB 47150 5395 E5
Mike Ct
4800 JFTN 40291 5728 B6
Mike St
300 ELZT 42701 6703 D5
Milan Ct
5800 LSVL 40258 5831 B5
Milbarb Ln
4500 LSVL 40216 5722 E6
4500 SVLY 40216 5722 E6
Milburn Av
2800 SRPK 40220 5618 E6
Milburn Ct
1500 LGNG 40031 5296 E1
Milburt Dr
1800 LYDN 40223 5510 E7
1800 LYDN 40223 5511 A7
Milby Ln
10 HdnC 42701 6811 C5
Milby St
200 ELZT 42701 6812 C1
Mildenhall Wy
- LSVL 40219 5725 E7
5300 LSVL 40213 5725 E7
Mildred Dr
3100 SVLY 40216 5723 B2
Mile of Sunshine Dr
4500 LSVL 40219 5835 C3
Miles Av
6500 LSVL 40214 5833 C1
Miles Dr
100 SHDV 40165 6161 A6
Miles Ln
4500 LSVL 40219 5835 C6
Miles Rd
2900 CMBG 40220 5618 D7
2900 SRPK 40220 5618 D7
N Miles St
100 ELZT 42701 6812 C1
900 ELZT 42701 6703 C7
N Miles St SR-251
100 ELZT 42701 6812 C1
900 ELZT 42701 6703 C7
S Miles St
100 ELZT 42701 6812 B3
Miles View Ct
1100 LSVL 40245 5621 D7
Milford Ct
800 STMW 40207 5618 A4
Milford Ln
900 STMW 40207 5618 A5
Milimish Ln
10 HdnC 40175 6591 E4
Military Av
1600 LYDN 40242 5510 C7
1600 LYDN 40242 5619 C1
Militia Dr
200 LSVL 40214 5833 D5
Mill Ln
1300 NALB 47150 5505 E2
E Mill Pl
10 GNVW 40222 5509 B2
10 LSVL 40222 5509 B2
Mill Run
100 BltC 40165 6163 A1
N Mill St
100 VNGV 40175 6482 D7
S Mill St
100 VNGV 40175 6591 D1
400 HdnC 40175 6591 D1
Mill Brook Cir
100 BltC 40165 6054 C5
Mill Brook Rd
9400 LYDN 40223 5619 D1
9400 LYDN 40242 5619 D1
Millcreek Dr
4100 SVLY 40216 5723 C5
Mill Creek Rd
100 RDCF 40160 6483 E6
500 RDCF 40160 6484 A6
Mill Creek Rd SR-1500
100 RDCF 40160 6483 E6
Milldaun Av
4300 WSNP 40213 5725 E4
Miller Av
100 RDCF 40160 6593 A2
200 RDCF 40160 6592 E1
300 CLKV 47129 5506 C4
400 SLRB 47172 5288 E4
Miller Dr
100 SHDV 40165 6161 E6
9700 LSVL 40291 5837 C2
Miller Ln
1300 NALB 47150 5505 E1
1900 OdmC 40031 5297 D1
Miller Rd
1600 GEOT 47122 5502 A4
8900 FydC 47124 5284 A2
Miller St
200 ELZT 42701 6812 C3
Miller Evans Rd
- FydC 47124 5283 E4
Miller Park Dr
6500 LSVL 40258 5831 A4
Millers Cross
- BltC 40165 6054 B5
Millers Ct
5000 LSVL 40272 5831 C7
Millers Ln
- BltC 40165 6160 D1
100 BltC 40165 6163 E7
1800 LSVL 40216 5723 C1
1800 SVLY 40216 5723 C1
2800 LSVL 40211 5723 C1
10400 LSVL 40272 5940 D3
Millerwood Cir
7000 FydC 47122 5393 C5
Millerwood Dr
1700 NALB 47150 5396 D7
Millet Pl
7500 ODGH 40014 5402 E7
Mill Falls St
100 BltC 40165 6054 D4
Millgate Rd
- LYDN 40223 5510 D7
1700 WPMG 40223 5510 D7
Millington Ct
8300 LSVL 40228 5836 B6
Mill Race Rd
1300 LYDN 40242 5619 C1
Mill Ridge Pl
8400 LYDN 40242 5619 B1
Mill Run Wy
10 LGNG 40031 5296 E2
Mills Ct
- BltC 40165 6162 C2
- SHDV 40165 6162 C2
100 ELZT 42701 6812 B4
Mills Dr
100 LSVL 40216 5832 A2
Mills Ln
100 NALB 47150 5395 E7
100 NALB 47150 5396 A7
500 FydC 47150 5395 D7
Mills Rd
100 BltC 40109 5942 E7
Millside Dr
2100 WPMG 40223 5510 D6
Millstone Ct
2800 ClkC 47130 5399 B4
Millstone Dr
9500 MBKF 40223 5510 D6
9500 WPMG 40223 5510 D6
Mill Stream Ct
1000 FydC 47150 5287 E7
1000 FydC 47150 5396 E1
Mill Stream Pl
300 BLMD 40222 5619 B2
300 LYDN 40222 5619 B2
Millvale Rd
2000 LSVL 40205 5617 B6
Millview Cir
100 SLRB 47172 5288 D3
Mill Wheel Ct
100 BltC 40165 6054 D5
Millwood Ct
5300 LSVL 40291 5728 D7
5300 LSVL 40291 5837 D1
Millwood Dr
100 BltC 40165 6054 C4
Millwood Pl
500 CLKV 47129 5397 A7
Milner Rd
5100 LSVL 40216 5832 A1
Milo Ct
6300 LSVL 40218 5727 A3
Milo Dr
4200 LSVL 40218 5727 A3
Milton Ct
1500 CLKV 47129 5506 B1
Milton St
800 LSVL 40217 5616 A6
Milwaukee St
- HdnC 40121 6374 C3
Milwaukee Wy
10700 LSVL 40272 5940 C3
Milwood Rd
- OdmC 40014 5403 E3
- OdmC 40014 5404 A3
Mimich Wy
17500 LSVL 40245 5622 E3
Mimosa Ct
100 RDCF 40160 6592 E1
Mimosa Dr
8000 LSVL 40258 5831 C5
Mimosa View Ct
10400 LSVL 40299 5728 E5
Mimosa View Dr
3900 LSVL 40299 5728 E5
Mina Ct
3400 LSVL 40220 5726 E1
Mina Ter
3500 LSVL 40220 5726 E1
Minerva Av
900 LYDN 40223 5510 E7
Minette Cir
100 LSVL 40258 5831 D6
Minette Ct
100 LSVL 40258 5831 D6
Minford Ct
11200 LSVL 40229 5944 D5
Mingo Ct
8500 JFTN 40220 5728 A2
Minks Ct
- HdnC 40162 6591 A3
Minnesota St
- HdnC 40121 6374 C4
Minnie Ln
5800 BltC 40165 6054 B2
Minoma Av
800 LSVL 40217 5725 A1
900 LSVL 40217 5616 A7
Minors Ln
- LSVL 40219 5835 B5
1000 LSVL 40219 5834 E4
8300 MLHT 40219 5834 D6
8900 SPVW 40219 5834 D7
Mint Julep Ct
3000 OdmC 40014 5405 C6
Minton Dr
1200 NALB 47150 5505 B4
Mint Spring Branch Rd
6000 LSVL 40059 5401 C6
Minute Men Ct
9300 LSVL 40214 5833 C5
Minyard Dr
5400 LSVL 40219 5835 A4
Mirable Dr
- LSVL 40291 5836 E1
- LSVL 40291 5837 A1
Miracle Dr
3400 SVLY 40216 5723 C3
Mirimar Rd
1400 GYDL 40222 5509 D7
Missionary Ct
8500 LSVL 40291 5837 C6
Missionary Ridge Dr
200 OdmC 40056 5512 D4
Mississippi St
7400 HdnC 40121 6374 C4
Missoure Av
- ELZT 42701 6812 A2
Missouri Av
100 CLKV 47129 5506 E7
1200 JFVL 47130 5506 E6
Missouri St
7500 HdnC 40121 6374 C4
Missy Ln
- LSVL 40272 5831 B7
Mistletoe Rd
2700 OdmC 40031 5296 B6
12300 ANCH 40223 5511 D7
Misty Green Wy
7900 LSVL 40291 5837 B4
Misty Woods Ln
4000 LSVL 40218 5727 A5
Mitchell Av
1400 CLKV 47130 5506 E5
1400 JFVL 47130 5506 E5
Mitchell Dr
10 VNGV 40175 6482 C7
Mitchell Ln
8800 LSVL 40272 5832 B6
Mitchell Rd
200 NALB 47150 5505 B3
Mitchell Wy
100 BltC 40165 6051 C7
Mitchell Hill Rd
10000 LSVL 40118 5942 B7
13000 BltC 40109 5942 B7
Mitscher Av
5300 LSVL 40214 5724 C7
Mix Av
600 LSVL 40208 5615 C7
Mobile Park Dr
- SHDV 40165 6161 C3
Mobley Ln
100 BltC 40165 6052 A5
Moccasin Ct
2900 FydC 47150 5397 B2
5100 INDH 40207 5508 E7
Moccasin Tr
5100 INDH 40207 5508 E7
Mock Al
300 ELZT 42701 6812 B2
Mock Ct
5500 LSVL 40258 5831 B6
Mockernut Ln
5600 LSVL 40258 5831 B5
Mockingbird Cir
10 JFVL 47130 5508 B3
Mockingbird Ct
2800 OdmC 40059 5292 D6
Mockingbird Dr
100 RDCF 40160 6483 C2
200 JFVL 47130 5507 D4
Mockingbird Ln
100 BltC 40165 6054 B7
3200 LSVL 40207 5617 B1
6200 LSVL 40272 5940 A6
Mockingbird Pl
- MKBV 40207 5508 B7
10 LSVL 40207 5508 B7
Mockingbird Gardens Dr
300 LSVL 40207 5617 D1
Mockingbird Hill Rd
300 LSVL 40207 5617 B1
400 MKBV 40207 5617 B1
Mockingbird Valley Dr
10 LSVL 40207 5508 C6
Mockingbird Valley Grn
1400 LSVL 40207 5508 A7
Mockingbird Valley Rd
300 LSVL 40207 5617 C1
300 MKBV 40207 5508 B7
300 MKBV 40207 5617 C1
400 LSVL 40207 5508 A7
5200 OdmC 40031 5295 A3
Mockingbird Valley Tr
10 LSVL 40207 5508 B7
10 MKBV 40207 5508 B7
Mockshire Dr
2600 LDNP 40241 5510 C5
2600 LSVL 40241 5510 C5
Model Rd
1700 SVLY 40216 5723 E1
Modern Wy
10 LSVL 40216 5722 E2
10 LSVL 40216 5723 A2
Modesto Rd
3700 JFTN 40299 5728 C4
Moeherr Dr
3900 LSVL 40299 5729 B4
Mohave Ct
800 ELZT 42701 6812 C1
Mohawk Av
300 LSVL 40209 5724 D5
300 LSVL 40214 5724 D5
Mohawk Dr
400 JFVL 47130 5507 D5
2700 NALB 47150 5505 B1
3700 OdmC 40031 5404 E2
Mohawk St
- HdnC 40121 6374 E1
Mohican St
- HdnC 40121 6374 E1
Mohican Hill Ct
2300 LSVL 40207 5508 E5
2300 RVWD 40207 5508 E5
Molter Av
800 LSVL 40217 5725 A2
Molter Ct
2900 LSVL 40217 5725 A2
Monaco Ln
4900 LSVL 40219 5835 D4
Monarch Dr
3400 LSVL 40213 5725 B3
Mona Vista Ct
1500 NALB 47150 5505 E2
Mondamon Dr
11700 LSVL 40272 5940 B5
Monica Ln
10 HdnC 42701 6702 B5
Monica Lynn Rd
3000 LSVL 40216 5723 A3
Monicello Forest Cir
- LSVL 40299 5728 D7
10400 JFTN 40299 5728 D7
Monin Rd
500 ELZT 42701 6703 B7
Moninda Ln
400 ELZT 42701 6812 B1
Monohan Dr
200 STMW 40207 5618 B3
Monon Av
- LSVL 40203 5615 B2
1700 NALB 47150 5505 C2
Monon Ct
100 LSVL 40203 5615 B2
Monroe Av
4100 LSVL 40213 5725 C3
Monroe Dr
800 ELZT 42701 6811 D3
Monroe St
- HdnC 40121 6265 B7
100 ClkC 47111 5182 A4
100 RDCF 40160 6593 B1
200 CHAN 47111 5181 D3
200 ClkC 47111 5181 E4
500 LGNG 40031 5297 A2
900 NALB 47150 5505 B4

INDEX 34
Montana Av — Louisville Metro Street Index — New Lagrange Rd SR-146

STREET
Block City ZIP Map# Grid

Montana Av
400 LSVL 40208 5724 C1
3100 LSVL 40215 5724 A2
Montaque Wy
10600 LSVL 40223 5620 A3
Montclair Av
3600 LSVL 40218 5727 D4
Montecito Ln
6800 LSVL 40291 5837 D4
Montego Bay Rd
6300 LSVL 40228 5836 B2
Montepulgiano Pl
- LSVL 40205 5616 C7
Monteray Place Cir
10500 LSVL 40272 5940 B3
Monteray Village Ln
8200 LSVL 40228 5836 B5
Monterey Rd
8500 MLHT 40219 5834 C6
Montero Ct
8000 PROS 40059 5401 A4
Montero Dr
6500 PROS 40059 5401 A5
Montfort Cir
2000 OdmC 40014 5405 C4
Montfort Ln
5300 OdmC 40014 5405 B6
Montgomery Av
100 CLKV 47129 5506 E6
100 CLKV 47130 5506 E6
100 JFVL 47130 5506 E6
600 ELZT 42701 6812 C2
E Montgomery Av
100 CLKV 47129 5506 D6
W Montgomery Av
100 CLKV 47129 5506 D6
Montgomery St
2300 LSVL 40212 5506 A7
2700 LSVL 40212 5505 E7
7500 HdnC 40121 6374 C4
Monticello Av
4200 LSVL 40218 5726 D4
Monticello Pl
10 HdnC 42701 6703 B2
Montpelier Ct
2500 LSVL 40272 5941 C1
Montpelier St
7500 HdnC 40121 6374 C4
Montpellier Pl
- LSVL 40202 5615 C1
Montrie Ct
8600 LSVL 40219 5835 A6
Montrose Av
- LSVL 40205 5726 D1
- WLTN 40205 5726 D1
2600 KGLY 40205 5617 C7
2800 LSVL 40205 5617 D7
2900 WLTN 40205 5617 D7
Montwood Ln
11700 LSVL 40272 5940 B5
Monty Dr
3800 NALB 47150 5396 D5
Monty Ln
6600 LSVL 40291 5837 D4
Moody Ct
3900 LSVL 40219 5835 A7
E Moody Ln
1000 LGNG 40014 5297 B7
1000 LGNG 40031 5297 B7
1000 OdmC 40014 5297 B7
1000 OdmC 40031 5297 B7
W Moody Ln
1200 OdmC 40014 5405 E1
1700 OdmC 40031 5405 D1
Moody Rd
8500 LSVL 40219 5835 A7
Moon Ln
1200 RDCF 40160 6483 B2
Moon St
100 ELZT 42701 6812 C3
Moon Beam Ct
10000 LSVL 40272 5939 E1
Mooney Ln
100 BltC 40165 6162 C4
Moonglow Av
9000 LSVL 40258 5831 C7
9000 LSVL 40272 5831 C7
Moonglow Ct
100 BltC 40165 6054 D2
Moonlight Wy
10200 LSVL 40272 5940 E2
10500 LSVL 40272 5941 A3
Moonridge Pl
9300 LSVL 40229 5944 E1
Moonstone Wy
1300 LYDN 40222 5619 A1
Moore Av
- CLKV 47129 5506 B4
Moore Ct
1200 LSVL 40210 5615 B6
Moore Dr
- BltC 40047 6056 B6
- MTWH 40047 6056 B6
Moore St
100 ELZT 42701 6812 B4
Moore Wy
- GEOT 47122 5502 A4
Moorehouse Ct
9600 LSVL 40291 5946 C2
Moorewick Wy
6900 LSVL 40272 5939 D1
Moorfield Cir
9500 LSVL 40241 5510 D3
Moorfield Pl
3900 LSVL 40241 5510 D3
Moorhampton Dr
6600 LSVL 40219 5836 A3
6600 LSVL 40228 5836 A3
Moorhaven Dr
6000 LSVL 40219 5836 B3
6200 LSVL 40228 5836 A3
Moorhead Av
8100 OdmC 40014 5513 B2
Moorman Rd
6200 LSVL 40272 5939 E4
6200 LSVL 40272 5940 A4
Moorman Rd SR-1849
6200 LSVL 40272 5939 E4
6200 LSVL 40272 5940 A4
Moorman River Ct
7300 LSVL 40272 5939 D4
Moran Av
2700 LSVL 40205 5617 E6
Moran Pl
2900 LSVL 40206 5617 A2
Morande St
- HdnC 40121 6265 B7
10 HdnC 40121 6374 B1
Morat Av
10400 LYDN 40223 5619 E1
10400 LYDN 40223 5620 A1
Moray Ct
4000 SVLY 40216 5723 A4
Moredale Rd
7400 GYDL 40222 5509 D7
Morgan Av
100 NALB 47150 5505 B3
1200 LSVL 40213 5725 B4
10000 LSVL 40118 5942 D2
Morgan Rd
- OdmC 40031 5295 C1
3000 OdmC 40031 5296 A3
Morgan St
10 RDCF 40160 6483 D6
700 LSVL 40217 5616 A7
Morgan Tr
3400 ClkC 47130 5398 C4
Morgan James Ct
9200 JFTN 40299 5728 B5
Morgan Jaymes Dr
4100 JFTN 40299 5728 C5
Morgan Pl Blvd
- OdmC 40031 5295 C4
Morgans Ln SE
10900 HsnC 47117 5830 A2
Moritz Ct
6200 OdmC 40014 5402 B6
Morning Dr
4100 FydC 47172 5287 D6
Morning Glory Av
100 MTWH 40047 6056 C3
Morning Glory Ln
5500 LSVL 40258 5831 B5
Morning Light Wy
- OdmC 40014 5403 E4
Morninglory Ct
100 RDCF 40160 6592 E1
Morning Park Ct
3100 JFTN 40220 5728 B3
Morning Park Dr
8800 JFTN 40220 5728 A3
Morning Park Pl
3000 JFTN 40220 5728 B3
Morning Side Dr
500 LSVL 40206 5617 C3
12000 PNRV 40229 6053 A2
Morningside Dr
100 CHAN 47111 5181 D1
200 ELZT 42701 6812 B1
800 JFVL 47130 5507 B5
Morningside Wy
5200 LSVL 40219 5835 D4
Morning Star Wy
6600 LSVL 40272 5830 E7
6600 LSVL 40272 5939 E1
Morningview Dr
3200 BRMD 40242 5510 B3
Morocco Dr
6600 LSVL 40214 5723 B7
6600 LSVL 40214 5832 E1
Morris Av
800 JFVL 47130 5507 C4
Morris Cir
2900 OdmC 40031 5296 D6
Morris Pl
4800 LSVL 40023 5731 B7
Morrison Av
5600 LSVL 40214 5724 B7
Morrison Rd
10200 LSVL 40229 5945 A3
Morrow St
1200 CHAN 47111 5181 E4
Morton Av
1300 LSVL 40204 5616 B5
2100 NALB 47150 5505 D3
Mosaic Ct
4400 JFTN 40299 5728 C6
Moser Ct
6100 OdmC 40014 5402 B6
Moser Ln
- OdmC 40014 5402 C6
Moser Rd
200 BRMR 40223 5619 E5
200 BRMR 40223 5620 A4
200 DGSH 40243 5619 E5
200 DGSH 40243 5620 A4
200 JFTN 40223 5619 E4
500 JFTN 40223 5620 A7
700 DGSH 40223 5620 A5
1200 JFTN 40299 5620 A6
1200 LSVL 40299 5620 A6
1300 LSVL 40223 5620 A7
Moser Farm Rd
5700 LSVL 40059 5402 A7
5900 OdmC 40014 5402 A7
Moser Knob Rd
5100 FydC 47119 5396 A3
5100 FydC 47150 5396 A3
6300 FydC 47119 5395 E1
Moser Mill Ln
6800 FydC 47119 5287 A6
Moserwood Rd
11100 DGSH 40243 5620 A6
11100 JFTN 40223 5620 A6
Mosier Av
200 NALB 47150 5505 A5
Moss Ct
9900 LSVL 40241 5510 E4
Moss Green Wy
7900 LSVL 40291 5837 B5
Mossrose Av
1300 LSVL 40204 5616 C5
Mosswood Ct
1200 JFVL 47130 5507 B2
Mosswood Ln
5500 LSVL 40291 5837 C1
Mossy Oaks Dr
6400 LSVL 40291 5837 C2
Moulton Ln
3300 LSVL 40218 5726 C2
Moulton St
400 NALB 47150 5505 A4
Mountain Ct
7000 LSVL 40219 5835 E3
Mountain Ash Ct
6100 OdmC 40014 5402 B6
Mountain Ash Ln
10500 LSVL 40059 5402 B6
10500 OdmC 40014 5402 B6
Mountain Brook Ct
8900 LSVL 40272 5832 C6
Mountain Brook Dr
8700 LSVL 40214 5832 C6
8700 LSVL 40272 5832 C6
Mountain View Dr
- HdnC 40177 6156 A6
10 WPT 40177 6156 A6
Mt Batten Ct
6500 PROS 40059 5400 D3
Mt Batten Pl
7000 PROS 40059 5400 D3
Mountblair Ct
4800 GYDL 40222 5509 D7
Mt Blanc Rd
5100 LSVL 40216 5722 C7
Mt Calvary Dr
6700 LSVL 40214 5832 C2
Mt Clair Av
2300 LSVL 40217 5725 A1
Mounteagle Cir
6800 LSVL 40241 5509 B3
Mt Eastes Ln
8700 LSVL 40291 5837 A3
Mt Elmira Rd
100 BltC 40109 6051 B7
100 BltC 40165 6051 B7
1100 BltC 40165 6160 A1
Mt Everest Dr
5800 LSVL 40216 5722 D7
6100 LSVL 40216 5831 C1
6300 LSVL 40258 5831 C1
Mt Gerald Ct
8800 LSVL 40291 5837 B3
Mt Holly Av
200 LSVL 40206 5616 E2
Mt Holly Rd
400 LSVL 40118 5942 D2
1100 HYVA 40118 5942 E3
1200 HYVA 40118 5943 A3
1200 LSVL 40118 5943 A3
Mt Holly Rd SR-2055
400 LSVL 40118 5942 D2
1100 HYVA 40118 5942 E3
1200 HYVA 40118 5943 A3
1200 LSVL 40118 5943 A3
Mt Holyoke Dr
4900 LSVL 40216 5722 C7
Mt Howard Ct
5200 LSVL 40216 5722 D7
Mt Marcy Rd
5100 LSVL 40216 5722 C7
Mt Mercy Dr
300 PWEV 40056 5512 C2
Mt Mercy Pl
100 PWEV 40056 5512 C2
Mt Pleasant Rd
- OdmC 40014 5402 B4
Mt Ranier Dr
3200 HSDS 40241 5509 C4
3200 LSVL 40222 5509 C4
3200 LSVL 40241 5509 C4
Mt Shasta Wy
3300 HSDS 40241 5509 C3
Mt Tabor Rd
200 FydC 47150 5396 A6
200 NALB 47150 5396 C6
Mt Vernon Ct
2600 SRPK 40220 5618 E6
Mt Vernon Ln
100 ELZT 42701 6812 A2
Mt Vernon Rd
4300 LSVL 40220 5618 D6
4300 SRPK 40220 5618 D6
Mt Washington Byp
- BltC 40047 5947 B7
Mt Washington Rd
2100 SHDV 40165 6161 E3
2100 SHDV 40165 6162 A2
4200 BltC 40165 6162 B2
5200 LSVL 40229 5944 D4
6000 LSVL 40229 5945 A4
Mt Washington Rd SR-44
2100 SHDV 40165 6161 E3
2100 SHDV 40165 6162 A3
4200 BltC 40165 6162 B2
Mt Washington Rd SR-2053
5200 LSVL 40229 5944 D4
6000 LSVL 40229 5945 A4
Mt Zion Rd
- RDCF 42701 6702 C1
10 ELZT 42701 6702 C1
10 HdnC 42701 6702 C1
200 HdnC 42701 6593 D7
E Mt Zion Rd
2200 OdmC 40014 5514 E1
E Mt Zion Rd SR-1818
2200 OdmC 40014 5514 E1
W Mt Zion Rd
1500 OdmC 40014 5514 B2
3600 OdmC 40014 5513 E2
W Mt Zion Rd SR-1818
1500 OdmC 40014 5514 B2
3600 OdmC 40014 5513 E2
Moyle Hill Rd
2100 LSVL 40205 5617 B6
Mozart Ct
9500 LSVL 40059 5401 D7
Mud Ln
3500 LSVL 40229 5943 E4
3500 LSVL 40229 5944 A4
Mugho Pine Ct
9000 LSVL 40291 5837 A2
E Muhammad Ali Blvd
100 LSVL 40202 5615 E3
500 LSVL 40202 5616 A3
700 LSVL 40204 5616 A3
W Muhammad Ali Blvd
100 LSVL 40202 5615 E3
500 LSVL 40203 5615 C3
2000 LSVL 40211 5615 A2
2000 LSVL 40212 5615 A2
2400 LSVL 40211 5614 D2
2400 LSVL 40212 5614 D2
Muirfield Pl
10 HTBN 40222 5619 C5
Muirs Ln
100 PWEV 40056 5512 C1
Mulberry
- BltC 40109 5943 E5
Mulberry Av
400 LGNG 40031 5297 A3
Mulberry St
- JFVL 47130 5507 A7
100 UTCA 47130 5400 A5
200 WPT 40177 6156 B3
500 ClkC 47172 5288 D2
500 SLRB 47172 5288 D2
500 UTCA 47130 5399 E5
800 LSVL 40217 5616 A6
1200 RDCF 40160 6483 A3
N Mulberry St
100 ELZT 42701 6812 C2
1800 ELZT 42701 6703 E7
N Mulberry St SR-61
100 ELZT 42701 6812 C2
1800 ELZT 42701 6703 E7
N Mulberry St US-62
100 ELZT 42701 6812 C2
1800 ELZT 42701 6703 E7
Mulberry Row Wy
3900 JFTN 40299 5728 D5
Muldraugh Cut Off Rd
- HdnC 40121 6264 D6
- MRGH 40155 6264 C5
- MRGH 40177 6264 D6
Muldraugh Cut Off Rd SR-868
- HdnC 40121 6264 D6
- MRGH 40155 6264 C5
- MRGH 40177 6264 D6
Muldraugh Magazine Rd
- HdnC 40177 6264 E5
Muldraugh Water Plant Rd
- HdnC 40177 6264 C3
- MdeC 40155 6264 C3
Mullaney Ct
4400 LSVL 40229 5944 B2
Mullins Ln
300 ELZT 42701 6702 D6
Mulloy St
- LSVL 40205 5617 E6
Mulvaney St
5400 MdeC 40121 6373 C2
Muncie Av
1900 LSVL 40206 5616 D1
Murifield Ct
500 HdnC 40175 6591 B2
Murphy Dr
100 ELZT 42701 6812 D4
Murphy Ln
4100 LSVL 40241 5511 C2
4100 LSVL 40245 5511 C2
4300 FCSL 40241 5511 C2
Murr Ln
3100 NALB 47150 5396 C7
Murray Av
2000 LSVL 40205 5616 E6
Murray Ln
5100 LSVL 40216 5722 B7
5100 LSVL 40258 5722 B7
Murray Rd
1100 HdnC 42701 6811 B4
Murray Hill Pike
- BKPT 40241 5510 C4
- GSCK 40241 5510 C4
- TNBK 40241 5510 C4
2700 MYHL 40242 5510 B5
2900 MYHL 40241 5510 B5
Murvin Dr
2000 FydC 47119 5504 B3
Muscovy Ct
2500 JFVL 47130 5398 C7
Muscovy Wy
2500 JFVL 47130 5398 C6
Musket Dr
6600 LSVL 40228 5836 B7
Muskogee Rd
10300 LSVL 40291 5946 D3
Myddleton Dr
1800 MDTN 40243 5620 C4
Myers Av
4100 OdmC 40014 5513 E1
N Myers Rd
- HLVW 40165 6052 E2
100 HLVW 40109 6052 E2
1100 BltC 40109 6052 E2
Myerwood Dr
4700 FydC 47119 5394 C4
Mylanta Pl
3100 LSVL 40220 5618 B7
Myra Ct
1300 OdmC 40031 5295 B3
Myrick Pl
4600 LSVL 40272 5940 D3
Myrle Ct
100 BltC 40071 5949 C2
Myrtle Av
- LYDN 40222 5619 A2
1100 NALB 47150 5505 C3
Myrtle St
100 JFVL 47130 5507 A3
600 LSVL 40203 5615 C6
600 LSVL 40208 5615 C6

N

Nachand Ln
800 JFVL 47130 5507 B4
3800 LSVL 40218 5727 D5
4300 LSVL 40291 5727 D6
7500 LSVL 40299 5727 D4
Nachand Place Ct
7300 LSVL 40218 5727 D4
Nadina Dr
3000 LSVL 40220 5617 E7
3000 LSVL 40220 5726 D1
3000 LSVL 40220 5727 A1
Nadorff Rd
10400 FydC 47124 5392 A3
Nagel Rd
10900 LSVL 40241 5511 B1
Naghel St
100 NALB 47150 5505 A4
Nalan Dr
7700 LSVL 40291 5727 D7
Nalery Wy
6800 LSVL 40228 5836 B5
Nall Av
5200 LSVL 40216 5831 E1
5300 LSVL 40258 5831 E2
Nall Rd
10 MdeC 40175 6482 B3
Nall St
10 ELZT 42701 6702 E7
Nalley Ln
100 BltC 40109 6050 E2
100 BltC 40109 6051 A2
Nalls Ln
10 RDCF 40160 6593 A2
E Nalls Rd
10 ELZT 42701 6702 E5
200 ELZT 42701 6703 A5
W Nalls Rd
100 ELZT 42701 6702 E5
Nally Ct
5500 LSVL 40216 5722 C5
Nance Ln
900 FydC 47136 5502 D7
Nancy Av
5100 LSVL 40216 5832 B1
Nancy Ct
100 RDCF 40160 6483 C6
Nancy Ln
7400 LSVL 40258 5831 D5
Nandina Dr
3400 BRMD 40241 5510 A3
Naneen Dr
4100 LSVL 40216 5723 D6
Nanisinh Wy
7100 LSVL 40258 5830 D7
Nanka Rd
9900 LSVL 40272 5940 E2
10400 LSVL 40272 5941 A2
Nannette Ct
7600 LSVL 40258 5830 E4
Nanny Goat Strut Al
- LSVL 40202 5616 A3
- LSVL 40206 5616 A3
Nansemond Cir
11800 WTNH 40245 5511 D2
Nansemond Ct
11600 LSVL 40245 5511 C3
Nansemond Dr
11600 LSVL 40241 5511 C3
11600 LSVL 40245 5511 D3
11800 WTNH 40245 5511 D3
Nansemond Pl
11700 LSVL 40245 5511 D2
Nansen Ct
8700 LSVL 40228 5836 B7
Nansen Tr
6900 LSVL 40228 5836 B7
Nantucket Ct
1500 LSVL 40211 5614 C6
Nantucket Cove
7300 LSVL 40214 5833 C4
Nanz Av
3300 LSVL 40207 5617 E4
3500 STMW 40207 5617 E4
3900 LSVL 40207 5618 A3
3900 STMW 40207 5618 A3
Naomi Dr
4000 LSVL 40219 5835 B1
Napanee Rd
3700 BWNV 40207 5617 D2
3800 DRDH 40207 5617 D2
3900 BLWD 40207 5617 E1
3900 LSVL 40207 5617 E1
Napa Ridge Ct
4700 LSVL 40299 5728 D6
Napa Ridge Wy
4700 LSVL 40299 5728 D7
Naples Dr
7900 LSVL 40219 5835 A5
Narcissus Dr
4100 LSVL 40219 5835 B7
Narragansett Dr
2600 LSVL 40210 5614 D6
Narrow Creek Ct
6900 PROS 40059 5400 E4
Narwood Dr
10 FTHL 40299 5728 C1
10 JFTN 40220 5728 C1
10 JFTN 40299 5728 C1
Nash Rd
8200 LSVL 40214 5833 D6
Nashua Ct
300 CLKV 47129 5506 A2
Nashua Dr
10 CLKV 47129 5506 A1
Nassau Dr
10 NALB 47150 5396 C7
Nassau Ln
12400 MDTN 40243 5620 D3
Natalie Dr
100 ELZT 42701 6702 E2
Natalie Wy
10100 JFTN 40299 5728 D5
Natchez Ln
3300 LSVL 40206 5617 D3
Nathan Ct
10 MdeC 40175 6482 A4
13100 LSVL 40272 5940 A5
Nathan Hale Wy
7000 LSVL 40272 6048 C1
National Av
200 JFVL 47130 5506 E5
National Tpk
5500 LSVL 40214 5833 D4
8500 LSVL 40118 5833 E6
9000 LSVL 40118 5942 E1
9800 LSVL 40118 5943 B3
10500 HYVA 40118 5943 A3
National Tpk SR-1020
5500 LSVL 40214 5833 D4
8500 LSVL 40118 5833 E6
9000 LSVL 40118 5942 E1
9800 LSVL 40118 5943 A3
10500 HYVA 40118 5943 A3
Nature Wy
7900 LSVL 40218 5727 D5
Navaho
- HdnC 40121 6374 E2
Navaho Ct
- RDCF 40160 6483 C3
Navaho Dr
100 RDCF 40160 6483 C3
1000 ELZT 42701 6812 D1
Navaho Pl
1000 LSVL 40215 5724 B5
Navajo Ct
1200 INHC 40207 5509 A7
Navajo Dr
500 NALB 47150 5505 B1
Navajo Rd
5400 INHC 40207 5509 A7
Naval Ordinance Dr
- LSVL 40214 5724 D7
Navilleton Rd
5300 FydC 47119 5393 E1
6500 FydC 47119 5284 E5
8000 FydC 47106 5284 E5
Navy Dr
100 LSVL 40214 5724 C7
Neagli Ct
4000 LSVL 40229 5944 A3
Neal Dr
3400 JFTN 40299 5728 E4
Neal Dr SE
1700 HsnC 47117 5721 B7
Neblett Av
2500 SVLY 40216 5723 C2
Neda Wy
7800 OdmC 40014 5514 D2
Neighbor Wy NE
6600 HsnC 47122 5501 C3
Neighborhood Pl
1000 LSVL 40118 5833 D7
1000 LSVL 40118 5942 E1
Neighborhood Rd
- BltC 40047 6056 D2
- MTWH 40047 6056 D2
Nelida Wy
100 HLVW 40229 5944 D5
Nelinda May Dr
3300 LSVL 40213 5725 E7
3400 LSVL 40213 5726 A7
Nellie Ct
100 RDCF 40160 6593 B1
Nellie Wy
10 BltC 40109 6052 C1
Nellie Bly Dr
3400 LSVL 40213 5726 A7
Nelligan Av
1600 LSVL 40203 5615 B1
Nelson Av
600 NALB 47150 5505 B1
1800 SVLY 40216 5723 D1
Nelson Ct
3000 LSVL 40217 5725 A2
Nelson Miller Pkwy
- LSVL 40223 5511 E6
1800 LSVL 40223 5512 A6
1800 LSVL 40223 5621 A1
Neon Wy
1100 LSVL 40204 5616 B3
Nepperhan Rd
2800 LSVL 40218 5727 B3
2900 LSVL 40220 5727 B3
Neptune Pl
11000 LSVL 40272 5940 D3
Neptune Rd
100 RDCF 40160 6483 B3
Netsedge Ct
9700 LSVL 40291 5837 D4
Nettie Wy
5200 LSVL 40258 5831 C3
Nettle Rdg
- UTCA 47130 5399 D6
Neubert Dr
10 ELZT 42701 6812 B3
Nevada Av
300 LSVL 40209 5724 D5
300 LSVL 40214 5724 D5
Nevada Dr
600 SLRB 47172 5288 C3
Nevada St
400 LSVL 40209 5724 E5
E Nevada St
10 HdnC 40121 6374 E2
Nevel Meade Dr
3100 OdmC 40059 5402 A1
Nevia Wy
7700 LSVL 40220 5727 D2
Neville Dr
1800 SVLY 40216 5723 C5
Nevis Dr
400 ELZT 42701 6703 C6
New Gdn
- HdnC 40121 6373 E3
New St
100 HdnC 40121 6483 D3
100 RDCF 40160 6483 D3
600 MdeC 40155 6264 D4
600 MRGH 40155 6264 D4
1200 CHAN 47111 5181 E4
New Albaney Pike
- SLRB 47172 5288 C5
N New Albany Av
100 SLRB 47172 5288 E3
400 ClkC 47172 5288 E3
S New Albany Av
100 SLRB 47172 5288 D4
New Albany Plz
200 NALB 47150 5504 E2
New Bear Creek Rd
- ClkC 47106 5283 C1
- FydC 47165 5283 C1
New Bern Ct
7000 PROS 40059 5400 D7
Newberry Rd
8900 ClkC 47172 5288 B5
Newbridge Pl
6600 LSVL 40291 5837 B2
Newbridge Rd
9700 LSVL 40291 5837 B2
Newburg Rd
1600 LSVL 40205 5616 D7
1600 LSVL 40213 5616 D7
2100 LSVL 40205 5725 E1
2400 LSVL 40205 5726 A2
3200 LSVL 40218 5726 D5
3200 WSNP 40218 5726 D5
3400 WBHL 40218 5726 C4
3500 PLRH 40218 5726 C4
Newburg Rd SR-1703
1600 LSVL 40205 5616 D7
1600 LSVL 40213 5616 D7
2100 LSVL 40205 5725 E1
2400 LSVL 40205 5726 A2
3200 LSVL 40218 5726 D5
3200 WSNP 40218 5726 D5
3400 WBHL 40218 5726 C4
3500 PLRH 40218 5726 C4
Newburg Rd S
- LSVL 40218 5726 D4
Newbury Ct
9200 LSVL 40059 5401 D7
New Chamberlain Ln
- LSVL 40241 5510 E1
- LSVL 40241 5511 A2
New Chapel Rd
- ClkC 47130 5399 B2
3000 ClkC 47130 5398 E4
New Christman Ln
- BltC 40165 5944 E5
- LSVL 40229 5944 E5
New Cut Rd
- OdmC 40031 5295 C6
4800 LSVL 40214 5724 A7
4800 LSVL 40215 5724 A7
5000 LSVL 40214 5833 B6
5900 OdmC 40014 5295 A6
6000 LSVL 40118 5833 B6
6400 LSVL 40118 5942 B1
6600 OdmC 40014 5403 A1
10000 FydC 47124 5283 B3
10000 FydC 47165 5283 B3
New Cut Rd SR-1817
- OdmC 40031 5295 C6
5900 OdmC 40014 5295 A6
6600 OdmC 40014 5403 A1
New Cut Rd SR-1865
4800 LSVL 40214 5724 A7
4800 LSVL 40215 5724 A7
5000 LSVL 40214 5833 B6
6000 LSVL 40118 5833 B6
6400 LSVL 40118 5942 B1
New Ed Quick Rd
10 BltC 40109 6052 A2
New England Ct
300 LSVL 40214 5833 C4
New Glendale Dr
- ELZT 42701 6812 C4
New Glendale Rd
100 ELZT 42701 6812 C4
1400 HdnC 42701 6812 B6
New Glendale Rd SR-1136
500 ELZT 42701 6812 C4
1400 HdnC 42701 6812 B6
New Hampshire Rd
5500 LSVL 40219 5835 E3
New High St
2700 LSVL 40209 5724 E2
New Hope Cir
- RDCF 40160 6483 A1
New Hopewell Rd
13700 LSVL 40299 5730 B5
New Lagrange Rd
- LSVL 40222 5618 E3
7300 NRWD 40222 5618 E3
7300 STMW 40222 5618 E3
7600 LYDN 40222 5618 E3
8000 LYDN 40222 5619 A2
8300 LYDN 40242 5619 C1
9200 LYDN 40223 5619 D1
New Lagrange Rd SR-146
- LSVL 40222 5618 E3
7300 NRWD 40222 5618 E3
7300 STMW 40222 5618 E3
7600 LYDN 40222 5618 E3
8000 LYDN 40222 5619 A2

Louisville Metro Street Index

STREET
Block City ZIP Map# Grid

New Lagrange Rd SR-146
8300 LYDN 40242 5619 C1
9200 LYDN 40223 5619 D1
New Lynnview Dr
3100 LSVL 40216 5722 D4
New Main St
1900 LSVL 40206 5616 D3
Newman Av
100 CLKV 47129 5506 D6
Newman Wy
100 MTWH 40047 6055 D4
Newman Hill Rd
- SHDV 40165 6161 D7
New Maple Rd
9100 LSVL 40229 5945 A1
Newmarket Dr
2000 NHFD 40222 5509 B5
New Middle Rd
4600 ClkC 47130 5399 B6
4600 JFVL 47130 5399 B6
New Millennium Dr
2300 SVLY 40210 5724 A1
2300 SVLY 40216 5724 A1
New Moody Ln
1000 LGNG 40031 5297 A4
1500 LGNG 40031 5296 C7
2200 OdmC 40031 5296 D5
Newport Rd
4200 LSVL 40218 5727 A6
Newport Trc
12300 LSVL 40299 5729 B7
Newquay Cir
9800 LSVL 40241 5510 E1
Newstead Av
8400 LSVL 40219 5835 C6
New Stone Ct
11200 LSVL 40223 5620 B3
Newton Ct
7600 LSVL 40228 5836 D5
Newton Dr
7500 LSVL 40228 5836 D5
Newton Pl
100 HdnC 40121 6374 A2
Newton Rd
10 ELZT 42701 6702 C2
10 HdnC 42701 6702 C2
Newton St
10 HdnC 42701 6702 C2
Newton Hollow Rd
10 HdnC 40162 6592 C7
New Venture Dr
300 LSVL 40214 5833 C3
New Wy Dr
6600 LSVL 40214 5833 D2
Nez Perce Wy
11300 LSVL 40229 5944 C5
11400 HLVW 40229 5944 C5
Niagara Dr
4000 OdmC 40031 5404 E2
Niagara St
- HdnC 40121 6265 D7
- HdnC 40121 6374 C1
Niantic Ct
3400 LSVL 40211 5614 C6
Niblick Ct
100 ELZT 42701 6812 E6
Nicholas St
100 ELZT 42701 6812 A4
600 ELZT 42701 6811 E5
N Nicholas St
100 ELZT 42701 6812 C3
Nicholas Tr
3600 ClkC 47130 5398 C5
Nichols Dr
10 LSVL 40215 5723 E4
Nichols Hill Rd
- BltC 40165 6048 D6
Nichols Meadow Cir
3600 LSVL 40215 5723 D4
Nicki Ct
8400 LSVL 40258 5830 D5
Nickleby Pl
500 LSVL 40245 5621 D6
Nickleby Wy
400 LSVL 40245 5621 C6
Nicole Ct
7500 LSVL 40220 5727 D2
Niemann Dr
7800 LSVL 40291 5837 E5
Nigel Dr
6200 LSVL 40216 5831 D1
Night Hawk Ct
1600 LSVL 40223 5620 A1
Nightingale Ct
1600 ELZT 42701 6702 E4
1700 LSVL 40213 5725 D1
Nightingale Ln
1200 OdmC 44026 5292 C2
Nightingale Rd
1400 ANPK 40213 5725 C2
1600 LSVL 40213 5725 D1
Nightingale Wy
100 BltC 40165 6054 B7
Nightsky Ct
100 BltC 40165 6054 D2
Nimitz Ct
5400 LSVL 40214 5724 C7
Nina Dr
9000 GEOT 47122 5501 E3
9200 FydC 47122 5501 E3
Nina Rd
1400 JFVL 47130 5507 C2
Nitta Yuma
5000 LSVL 40059 5400 C7
Noah Ct
5900 LSVL 40258 5831 C1
Noah Dr
5800 LSVL 40258 5831 B1
Noahs Ln
- JFVL 47130 5507 E2
- JFVL 47130 5508 A3
Nobel Ct
3700 SVLY 40216 5723 D3
Nobel Pl
1700 LSVL 40216 5723 D3
1800 SVLY 40216 5723 D3
Nob Hill Ln
100 LSVL 40206 5616 E2
Noblitt Dr
3700 LSVL 40218 5727 B2
3700 LSVL 40220 5727 A2
Nocturne Dr
1900 LSVL 40272 5940 A2
Noe Ct
2900 LSVL 40220 5727 B1
Noe Wy
3300 LSVL 40218 5727 B2
3300 LSVL 40220 5727 A1
Nola Dr
10100 LSVL 40118 5942 D3
Nole Dr
1400 JFVL 47130 5398 B7
1400 JFVL 47130 5507 C1
Nolin Pl
100 LSVL 40214 5724 D7
Noll Ct
8700 BKPT 40241 5510 C4
Noltemeyer Wynde Ct
- LSVL 40219 5835 B4
Nopper Ct
2400 JFTN 40220 5728 B2
Nora Ln
3300 LSVL 40220 5727 E3
Norbert Ct
6500 LSVL 40258 5831 A4
Norbourne Av
7500 NRWD 40222 5618 E3
Norbourne Blvd
3500 LSVL 40207 5617 E4
3500 STMW 40207 5617 E4
3700 STMW 40207 5618 A4
3800 NBNE 40207 5618 A4
Norbourne Wy
2900 LSVL 40206 5617 B2
Norbrook Dr
4100 LSVL 40218 5727 B5
Nordic Dr
9700 LSVL 40272 5940 E1
9700 LSVL 40272 5941 A1
Norene Ln
3900 LSVL 40219 5835 B1
Norfolk Dr
4300 LSVL 40218 5727 B5
Norita Ct
3400 LSVL 40220 5727 D3
Norlynn Dr
6900 LSVL 40228 5836 B4
6900 SPML 40228 5836 B4
Norma Ct
3300 JFVL 47130 5507 A2
Norma Dr
3300 JFVL 47130 5507 A1
Norma Ln
3200 LSVL 40220 5726 E1
Norma Lee Dr
3000 LSVL 40214 5832 C5
Norman Ct
6500 OdmC 40014 5403 A6
Norman Dr
500 SLRB 47172 5288 D5
S Norman Dr
600 SLRB 47172 5288 D6
N Norman St
500 SLRB 47172 5288 D5
Norman Dale Rd
100 BltC 40047 5946 C7
100 LSVL 40291 5946 C7
Normandie Village Ct
10 LSVL 40205 5617 B6
Normie Ct
4100 LSVL 40229 5944 B2
Normie Ln
9800 LSVL 40229 5944 B2
Norris Pl
200 RDCF 40160 6483 D6
1400 LSVL 40204 5616 E7
1400 LSVL 40205 5616 E7
Norseman Dr
500 JFVL 47130 5507 D4
North Dr
6400 LSVL 40272 5939 E4
6400 LSVL 40272 5940 A4
North Ln
4000 SVLY 40216 5723 B4
North Rd
- HdnC 40177 6264 D2
North St
10 RDCF 40160 6483 E5
100 BltC 40165 6161 B1
400 RDCF 40160 6484 A5
Northern Av
400 LSVL 40214 5833 B1
Northern Rd
1900 HdnC 40160 6374 A7
1900 RDCF 40160 6374 B7
Northern Spy Ct
7600 LSVL 40228 5836 D5
Northern Spy Dr
7900 LSVL 40228 5836 D6
Northfield Ct
2400 NHFD 40222 5509 B5
Northfield Dr
1500 FydC 47122 5503 B3
2000 NHFD 40222 5509 B5
Northgate Blvd
800 NALB 47150 5396 C6
Northgate Ct
- OdmC 40031 5295 C3
3600 NALB 47150 5396 C6
Northgate Rd
10 LSVL 40118 5942 B1
Northhaven Ct
1700 JFVL 47130 5507 C2
Northhaven Dr
1400 JFVL 47130 5507 B1
Northland Dr
3100 LSVL 40216 5722 E3
Northolt Ct
12500 LSVL 40245 5511 E1
North Ridge Cir
6600 LSVL 40241 5509 D4
Northridge Cir
4500 OdmC 40014 5405 E2
Northridge Ct
10000 LSVL 40272 5941 A1
Northridge Dr
1000 ELZT 42701 6703 E6
4600 OdmC 40014 5405 E2
9700 LSVL 40272 5941 A1
Northside Av
200 SHDV 40165 6161 D2
Northumberland Dr
3800 LSVL 40245 5511 E2
3800 WTNH 40245 5511 D2
Northview Av
100 ELZT 42701 6702 D4
Northwestern Pkwy
100 LSVL 40212 5505 B7
100 LSVL 40212 5614 B1
1500 LSVL 40203 5615 B1
1900 LSVL 40203 5506 B7
2100 LSVL 40212 5506 B7
Northwestern Pkwy SR-3064
3200 LSVL 40212 5505 D7
Northwind Ct
- CTWD 40014 5403 D5
Northwind Rd
1400 INDH 40207 5508 E7
1500 LSVL 40207 5508 E6
Northwind Wy
- CTWD 40014 5403 D5
Northwood Dr
4300 LSVL 40220 5618 C5
6000 OdmC 40014 5404 D5
Norton Av
800 LSVL 40213 5834 D1
1100 LSVL 40213 5725 D7
Norton Ct
2800 LSVL 40213 5834 D1
Norway Dr
6500 LSVL 40214 5723 E7
6500 LSVL 40214 5832 E1
Norwich Blvd
7500 LSVL 40258 5831 A4
Norwood Av
- OdmC 40014 5403 A7
E Norwood Av
100 CLKV 47129 5506 D5
W Norwood Av
300 CLKV 47129 5506 C5
Norwood Dr
- LSVL 40222 5618 E3
100 ELZT 42701 6812 D5
100 NRWD 40222 5618 E3
100 STMW 40222 5618 E3
3300 NALB 47150 5396 D6
Norwood Wy
100 HLVW 40229 5944 B6
Nottingham Pkwy
- HTBN 40222 5619 C6
Nottinghamshire Dr
4700 JFTN 40299 5728 A6
4700 LSVL 40299 5728 A6
Notto Ct
6300 LSVL 40214 5832 D1
Nottoway Cir
7300 LSVL 40214 5832 D2
Nova Vw
3100 SVLY 40216 5723 B2
Novelle St
8900 LSVL 40258 5831 B6
Nugent Ct
700 LSVL 40203 5615 E4
700 LSVL 40203 5616 A4
Nursery Ct
1100 MDTN 40243 5620 C6
Nursery Ln
12500 MDTN 40243 5620 C6
Nutmeg Ct
3600 LSVL 40219 5726 A7
Nutwood Dr
2500 ANCH 40223 5511 C6
2500 LSVL 40223 5511 C6
Nutwood Rd
11100 ANCH 40223 5511 B6
11100 LSVL 40223 5511 B6
Nylon Ct
5400 LSVL 40219 5835 D5

O

Oak Av
7400 OdmC 40014 5512 A1
N Oak Av
100 LGNG 40031 5297 A2
S Oak Av
100 LGNG 40031 5297 A3
Oak Cir
10 BltC 40165 6052 B5
Oak Ct
1400 JFVL 47130 5507 B2
Oak Dr
- JFVL 47130 5507 C2
10 RDCF 40160 6484 B6
100 BltC 40047 6056 D4
100 HdnC 40160 6484 A6
1100 ELZT 42701 6702 E7
Oak St
100 MRGH 40155 6264 C4
100 VNGV 40175 6482 D7
300 RDCF 40160 6483 D3
300 SLRB 47172 5288 D3
500 CHAN 47111 5181 E3
1100 ELZT 42701 6702 E7
E Oak St
100 LSVL 40203 5615 E5
600 LSVL 40203 5616 A5
700 LSVL 40204 5616 A5
2500 NALB 47150 5505 E3
N Oak St
100 CLKV 47129 5506 D5
1500 SHDV 40165 6162 A3
S Oak St
100 CLKV 47129 5506 D5
W Oak St
100 LSVL 40203 5615 D5
100 NALB 47150 5505 B5
800 LSVL 40210 5615 A5
2200 LSVL 40210 5614 E5
2500 LSVL 40211 5614 E5
Oak Ter
7100 PWEV 40056 5512 D2
Oak Bay Dr
11700 WTNH 40245 5511 D2
11800 LSVL 40245 5511 D2
Oak Bay Pl
11900 LSVL 40245 5511 C2
Oak Bend Ct
11100 LSVL 40241 5511 B1
Oak Bend Dr
4700 LSVL 40241 5511 B1
Oak Bluff Ct
14300 LSVL 40245 5621 C3
Oak Branch Ct
14200 LSVL 40245 5621 C4
Oak Branch Rd
500 LSVL 40245 5621 C4
Oakbrook Dr
4900 FCSL 40241 5511 C2
4900 LSVL 40245 5511 C2
5000 WTNH 40245 5511 C2
Oakburn Ct
3600 LSVL 40258 5832 A4
Oakburn Dr
7200 LSVL 40258 5832 A3
Oak Creek Cir
100 MTWH 40047 6056 D3
Oak Creek Ct
5500 LSVL 40291 5728 B7
5500 LSVL 40291 5837 C1
Oak Creek Dr
100 MTWH 40047 6056 D3
200 BltC 40047 6056 D3
Oak Creek Ln
5300 LSVL 40291 5728 C7
Oak Crest Ct
1800 LSVL 40214 5832 E4
Oakcrest Ct
100 BltC 40165 5944 E6
100 HLVW 40229 5944 E6
Oakcrest Dr
100 BltC 40165 6051 D5
Oakdale Av
1800 GEOT 47122 5502 A3
3100 LSVL 40214 5724 C2
3100 LSVL 40215 5724 C2
Oakdale Ln
5900 LSVL 40219 5835 C1
Oakdale Wy
12100 OdmC 44026 5292 C2
Oaken Ln
- FydC 47136 5611 C1
Oakenshaw Dr
1100 FydC 47136 5611 D1
Oakes Rd
1000 FydC 47122 5503 A4
Oakfield Dr
11700 LSVL 40245 5511 C2
Oakford Ct
- LGNG 40031 5297 C6
Oak Forest Ct
13300 LSVL 40245 5512 A3
Oak Forest Rd
4600 LSVL 40245 5512 A3
Oak Glade Cir
100 ELZT 42701 6702 E3
Oak Grove Dr
1700 FydC 47150 5288 A7
Oak Grove Rd
10000 LSVL 40291 5946 B3
Oak Harbor Dr
10800 LSVL 40299 5838 A1
Oak Haven Ct
3200 JFTN 40220 5728 B3
Oak Hill Ct
10 BltC 40047 6056 E3
Oak Hill Rd
1300 LSVL 40213 5725 E2
Oakhurst Rd
11100 LSVL 40245 5621 C2
Oakland Av
700 LSVL 40208 5615 C6
800 LSVL 40210 5615 C6
4200 HdnC 40121 6374 A2
Oakland Ct
900 NALB 47150 5504 D3
Oakland Dr
900 NALB 47150 5504 D3
Oakland Forest Ct
4000 LSVL 40245 5512 B4
Oakland Hills Dr NE
7200 LNVL 47136 5610 D5
Oaklawn Av
200 ELZT 42701 6702 D4
Oaklawn Dr
300 ELZT 42701 6702 D4
1100 JFVL 47130 5507 B3
3800 LSVL 40219 5835 A3
Oaklawn Ln
4700 LSVL 40219 5835 C1
Oaklawn Park Ct
12100 LSVL 40299 5729 B7
Oaklawn Park Dr
5100 LSVL 40299 5729 B7
Oak Lea Dr
5300 LSVL 40216 5831 E2
5300 LSVL 40258 5831 E2
Oaklea Dr
6200 OdmC 40014 5405 A5
Oak Leaf Ct
100 MTWH 40047 6056 D3
Oak Leaf Dr
500 LGNG 40031 5296 E2
Oak Leaf Ln
2400 ClkC 47129 5397 B6
2400 CLKV 47129 5397 B6
3800 LSVL 40219 5835 A6
Oakleigh Pl
3000 FydC 47172 5397 B1
Oakleigh Meadow Pl
3900 LSVL 40245 5512 C5
Oak Meadow Dr
2000 ELZT 42701 6702 E3
Oakmont Dr
1500 JFVL 47130 5507 A2
8000 LSVL 40219 5834 E5
Oaknoll Dr
6100 LSVL 40219 5835 B2
Oak Park Blvd
10 JFVL 47130 5508 A3
Oak Park Dr
10 MTWH 40047 6056 D3
4700 LSVL 40258 5831 D5
Oak Pointe Dr
4500 LSVL 40245 5511 C1
Oak Ridge Ct
100 BltC 40047 6055 A7
Oakridge Ct
1000 OdmC 40014 5405 D3
Oak Ridge Dr
100 RDCF 40160 6483 B1
200 BltC 40047 6055 A7
200 MTWH 40047 6055 A7
Oakridge Dr
1000 FydC 47136 5502 C7
1100 FydC 47136 5611 C1
1900 JFVL 47130 5507 C2
4000 OdmC 40014 5405 C3
Oakridge Pl
5600 LSVL 40229 5944 E1
Oak Ridge Rd
100 BltC 40165 6163 D3
Oak Run Rd
100 BltC 40047 6055 E2
Oaks Wy
1800 OdmC 40059 5291 D4
Oakshire Dr
9800 JFTN 40299 5728 D3
Oak Side Ct
7000 LSVL 40291 5837 B3
Oakstone Wy
1000 GEOT 47122 5502 C4
Oak Tree Ln
- SbyC 40245 5513 D4
Oaktree Ln
10600 LSVL 40272 5941 B3
Oak Valley Ct
100 BltC 40047 6056 D3
100 MTWH 40047 6056 D3
200 ELZT 42701 6702 E4
Oak Valley Dr
10 BltC 40047 6056 D3
300 ELZT 42701 6702 E3
6200 LSVL 40214 5832 B2
6200 LSVL 40216 5832 B2
6200 LSVL 40258 5832 B2
Oakview
- LGNG 40031 5297 A3
Oakview Av
- LGNG 40031 5297 B2
Oakview Ct
6800 LSVL 40291 5836 D3
Oakview Dr
100 LGNG 40031 5297 A3
Oakview Wy
- BltC 40047 6056 D3
100 MTWH 40047 6056 D3
Oakvista Pl
3600 LSVL 40245 5512 D5
Oakwood Av
10 VNGV 40175 6592 A1
1000 LSVL 40215 5724 A6
Oakwood Cir
300 HdnC 40175 6482 D2
Oakwood Ct
900 NALB 47150 5396 C6
1000 LGNG 40031 5297 A5
Oakwood Dr
10 JFVL 47130 5507 D1
200 ELZT 42701 6703 D7
200 ELZT 42701 6812 C1
E Oakwood Dr
3500 NALB 47150 5396 C6
W Oakwood Dr
3500 NALB 47150 5396 C6
Oakwood Pt
100 MTWH 40047 6056 C3
O'Bannon Station Wy
13200 LSVL 40223 5512 A6
Oboe Dr
3700 LSVL 40216 5722 D3
Obrecht Av
5600 LSVL 40219 5835 A5
O'Brian Ct
- HdnC 40121 6373 E4
O'Brien Ct
200 HdnC 40121 6373 E3
200 MdeC 40175 6373 E3
2000 SVLY 40216 5723 B6
Ocala Rd
1500 GYDL 40222 5509 D7
Ocho Rios Ct
6300 LSVL 40228 5836 B2
Octagon Av
2200 HLVW 40229 5943 E6
2200 HLVW 40229 5944 A6
O'Daniel Av
1700 LSVL 40213 5725 D2
Oechsli Av
4100 STMW 40207 5618 A2
Oehrle Dr
1800 SVLY 40216 5723 D3
Office Pointe Pl
3200 LSVL 40220 5728 A3
Oglesby Ct
8600 LSVL 40118 5833 D6
O'Henry Av
100 BltC 40109 6052 D1
Ohio Av
100 SLRB 47172 5288 C3
200 JFVL 47130 5506 E7
Ohio St
600 NALB 47150 5505 A5
700 NALB 47150 5504 E5
OHM Dr
- BltC 40165 6162 B7
Okolona Ter
1100 LSVL 40219 5835 A5
Old Rd
100 HLVW 40229 5944 D6
Old Altar Ct
10300 LSVL 40291 5837 D7
Old Bardstown Rd
8000 LSVL 40291 5837 D6
8800 LSVL 40291 5946 D1
Old Bates Rd
8600 LSVL 40228 5836 C6
Old Bean Rd
- ClkC 47172 5289 A6
- SLRB 47172 5289 A6
Old Beech Grove Rd N
100 SHDV 40165 6161 C5
Old Bethany Rd
6300 ClkC 47111 5290 A2
Old Billtown Rd
5100 LSVL 40291 5728 D7
5100 LSVL 40299 5728 D7
Old Blankenbaker Rd
1200 LSVL 40299 5620 B7
1200 MDTN 40243 5620 B7
Old Bluegrass Av
- LSVL 40215 5723 E5
Old Bond Ct
100 HTBN 40222 5619 C4
Old Boundary Rd
8200 LSVL 40291 5836 E4
8400 LSVL 40291 5837 A4
Old Bridge Pl
10900 ANCH 40223 5620 A2
Old Brooks Hill Rd
100 BltC 40109 6052 B1
Old Brownsboro Ct
4700 INDH 40207 5617 D1
4700 RLGF 40207 5617 D1
Old Brownsboro Rd
3700 BWNV 40207 5617 D1
3700 INDH 40207 5617 D1
3700 LSVL 40207 5617 D1
3700 RLGF 40207 5617 D1
3900 DRDH 40207 5617 E1
Old Brownsboro Hills Rd
3600 BRMD 40242 5510 B3
3600 BWNF 40241 5510 B3
3600 BWNF 40242 5510 B3
Oldbury Pl
8700 HTBN 40222 5619 B5
Old Cabin Ct
3600 HBNE 40165 6053 D3
Old Camp Ground Rd
4800 LSVL 40216 5722 D2
Old Cannons Ln
- STMW 40207 5617 D4
1000 LSVL 40207 5617 D4
Old Cardinal Dr
100 ELZT 42701 6702 D7
Old Cedar Ct
5900 LSVL 40059 5402 A6
Old Cedar Point Rd
2700 OdmC 40031 5295 D6
Old Clark Station Rd
- SbyC 40067 5732 A5
3000 LSVL 40023 5732 A5
3100 LSVL 40023 5731 D5
Old Clore Ln
- PROS 40059 5400 E3
7200 LSVL 40059 5400 E3
7200 LSVL 40059 5401 A2
Old Coach Rd
4300 OdmC 40014 5403 C2
Old Corydon Ridge Rd
- FydC 47150 5504 A5
200 FydC 47150 5503 D6
Old Creek Wy
- LSVL 40059 5400 E7
4900 PROS 40059 5400 D7
Old Dam 43 Rd SE
13000 HsnC 47117 6155 A2
Old Deering Rd
11300 LSVL 40272 5940 B4
Old Distillery Rd
13500 LSVL 40272 6048 E1
Old Dixie Hwy
- MdeC 40108 6264 C2
- MRGH 40155 6264 C2
12300 LSVL 40272 5939 E6
Olde Colony Ct
- MTWH 40047 6054 E6
Olde Colony Cove
400 LSVL 40214 5833 C4
Olde Copper Ct
17000 LSVL 40245 5621 D6
Olde English Ct
- LSVL 40272 5941 B1
100 LSVL 40272 5832 C7
Olde Glouchester Cove
400 LSVL 40214 5833 D4
Olde Oak Ct
7100 PROS 40059 5400 D7
Olde Sage Ct
11300 MDTN 40243 5620 B4
Olde Spring Ct
11900 CDSM 40245 5511 D1
Olde Spring Rd
11800 CDSM 40245 5511 D1
Old Farm Dr
4000 OdmC 40014 5404 E6
Old Farm Rd
300 WDYH 40207 5509 C7
300 WDYH 40207 5618 C1
Old Federal Rd
5000 LSVL 40207 5508 E5
5000 LSVL 40207 5509 A5
Old Fegenbush Ln
- LSVL 40228 5836 C3
6800 HWCK 40228 5836 C3
Old Fern Valley Rd
1200 LSVL 40219 5835 A2
Oldfield Ln
- BltC 40165 6160 A1
Old Floydsburg Rd
100 OdmC 40014 5513 A2
6300 OdmC 40056 5512 D3
6300 OdmC 40056 5513 A2
6300 PWEV 40056 5512 D3
Old Floydsburg Rd SR-1408
5500 OdmC 40014 5513 B2
Old Ford Rd
100 SHDV 40165 6161 B5
1400 NALB 47150 5505 E1
1500 NALB 47150 5396 E7
Old Forest Rd
100 OdmC 40056 5512 C3
100 PWEV 40056 5512 C3
Old Fort Av
- MdeC 40175 6482 A6
Old Fort Av SR-1882
- MdeC 40175 6482 A6
Old Gap In Knob Rd
2800 SHDV 40165 6052 E7
2900 BltC 40165 6052 E7
Oldgate Rd
8100 BRMD 40241 5510 A3
8100 BWNF 40241 5510 A3
Old Georgetown Rd
4900 FydC 47122 5503 A5
Old Glendale Rd
100 ELZT 42701 6812 C4
Old Glory Ct
7300 LSVL 40214 5833 D4
Oldham Ct
5600 LSVL 40291 5837 A1
Oldham Ln
- MdeC 40175 6482 B1
Oldham Pl
400 OdmC 40031 5297 B4
Oldham St
700 LSVL 40203 5615 C5
1400 LSVL 40210 5615 B5
Oldham Acres Rd
14300 OdmC 40059 5291 D4
Oldham View Dr
1400 OdmC 40031 5297 B4
Old Harmony Landing Rd
12400 GSHN 44026 5292 C3
12400 OdmC 44026 5292 C3
Old Harrods Creek Rd
200 LSVL 40223 5620 B3
200 MDTN 40243 5620 B4
300 MDTN 40223 5620 B3
600 ANCH 40223 5620 B1
Old Harrods Woods Cir
10900 ANCH 40223 5620 A1
10900 LSVL 40223 5511 B7
10900 LSVL 40223 5620 A1
Old Harrods Woods Ct
1600 LSVL 40223 5620 A1
Old Hausfeldt Ln
700 FydC 47150 5396 B5
700 NALB 47150 5396 B5
Old Hazlewood Av
4500 LSVL 40214 5723 E6
4500 LSVL 40215 5723 E6
Old Heady Rd
4000 LSVL 40299 5729 C5
5000 LSVL 40299 5838 E1
6300 LSVL 40299 5839 E3
6500 LSVL 40299 5840 A5
8000 LSVL 40023 5840 E6
8000 SpnC 40023 5840 E6
Old Henry Rd
- LSVL 40223 5512 B7
- LSVL 40245 5512 C7
9200 OdmC 40056 5512 E5
12000 MDTN 40223 5620 D3
12000 MDTN 40243 5620 D3
12800 LSVL 40223 5620 E1
12800 LSVL 40223 5621 A1
Old Henry Rd SR-3084
- LSVL 40223 5512 B7
- LSVL 40245 5512 C7
12800 LSVL 40223 5620 E1
12800 LSVL 40223 5621 A1
Old Henry Tr
13700 LSVL 40245 5512 C7
Old Herring Pl
5300 CTWD 40014 5403 E4
5300 OdmC 40014 5403 E4
Old Hickory Ct
1100 LGNG 40031 5296 E1
1800 NALB 47150 5505 C1
Old Hickory Ln
10 ELZT 42701 6812 A1
Old Hickory Rd
2000 JFTN 40299 5728 D1
Old Hickory Hill Ln
2200 BltC 40165 6163 A2
Old Highway 44
4100 BltC 40165 6054 C7
Old Highway 329
- CTWD 40014 5403 C5
- OdmC 40014 5403 D5
Old Highway 329 SR-329
- CTWD 40014 5403 C5
- OdmC 40014 5403 D5
Old Hill Rd
2000 FydC 47119 5504 B2
2900 FydC 47119 5395 B7
Old Hobbs Pl
900 LSVL 40223 5620 A2
Old IN-62
- ClkC 47129 5506 A3
- ClkC 47130 5398 E4

INDEX 36

Old IN-62

Louisville Metro Street Index

W Park Rd

STREET
Block City ZIP Map# Grid

Old IN-62
- CLKV 47130 5506 E6
- JFVL 47130 5506 E6
- JFVL 47130 5507 C4
400 CLKV 47129 5506 A2
1300 ClkC 47129 5505 E4
1300 NALB 47150 5505 E4
3400 JFVL 47130 5398 D6
Old IN-62 W
- JFVL 47130 5507 C3
1000 ClkC 47129 5506 B3
1000 CLKV 47129 5506 B3
3400 JFVL 47130 5398 D5
Old IN-64
- FydC 47122 5503 A5
Old IN-111
7600 ClkC 47143 5287 D3
Old Ironside Dr
8700 LSVL 40228 5836 B7
Old Ironsides Av
200 HdnC 40121 6265 B7
500 HdnC 40121 6374 B3
Old Klerner Ln
3800 FydC 47150 5396 D5
3800 NALB 47150 5396 D5
Old Lagrange Rd
- LSVL 40245 5512 B4
Old La Grange Rd
4300 OdmC 40031 5295 C7
6300 CTWD 40014 5404 A6
6300 OdmC 40014 5404 A7
11900 ANCH 40223 5511 E6
11900 LSVL 40223 5511 E6
12300 LSVL 40223 5512 A5
12300 LSVL 40245 5512 A4
Old Lagrange Rd SR-1447
- LSVL 40245 5512 B4
Old La Grange Rd SR-1447
13700 LSVL 40245 5512 A4
Old Lake Ct
2600 NALB 47150 5504 D1
Old Lanesville Rd
100 FydC 47122 5501 D6
Old Lanesville Rd NE
5400 HsnC 47122 5501 B5
Old Lucas Ln
12200 ANCH 40223 5511 D7
Old Mill Rd
- BltC 40047 6056 B3
100 MTWH 40047 6056 B3
500 BltC 40047 6055 E5
500 MTWH 40047 6055 D5
1200 LYDN 40223 5619 C1
1200 LYDN 40242 5619 C1
8100 OdmC 40056 5512 A2
8100 PWEV 40056 5512 A2
Old Mill Rd SR-44
- BltC 40047 6056 B3
100 MTWH 40047 6056 B3
500 BltC 40047 6055 D5
500 MTWH 40047 6055 D5
Old Millers Ln
3200 LSVL 40211 5614 C7
3200 LSVL 40216 5614 C7
3200 LSVL 40216 5723 C1
Old Mill Stream Ln
100 BltC 40165 6163 A2
Old Minors Ln
7900 LSVL 40219 5834 E4
Old Mitchell Hill Rd
11700 LSVL 40118 5942 B6
Old New Cut Rd
6400 LSVL 40118 5833 A7
Old North Church Rd
7200 LSVL 40214 5833 C4
Old Orchard Cir
7600 BCFT 40222 5509 E6
Old Orchard Ct
7600 BCFT 40222 5509 E6
Old Outer Lp
3300 LSVL 40219 5834 E5
3700 LSVL 40219 5835 A5
Old Park Blvd
4200 LSVL 40209 5724 D4
Old Pioneer Tr
- BltC 40165 6053 D1
- PNRV 40165 6053 D1
Old Pitts Point Rd
100 BltC 40165 6160 D3
Old Potters Ln
- CLKV 47129 5397 E5
- JFVL 47129 5397 E5
- JFVL 47130 5397 E5
Old Preston Hwy
- BltC 40165 6053 D1
- SHDV 40165 6161 D5
1100 BltC 40229 5944 D6
1100 HLVW 40229 5944 D6
10100 LSVL 40229 5944 C3
12300 BltC 40165 5944 D7
Old Preston Hwy SR-1116
- BltC 40165 6053 D1
1100 BltC 40229 5944 D6
1100 HLVW 40229 5944 D6
12300 BltC 40165 5944 D7
Old Preston Hwy N
100 BltC 40165 6053 D1
100 PNRV 40165 6053 D1
400 BltC 40165 5944 D7
Old Preston Hwy N SR-1116
400 BltC 40165 5944 D7
400 BltC 40165 6053 D1
Old Preston Hwy N SR-2553
100 BltC 40165 6053 D1
100 PNRV 40165 6053 D1
Old River Rd
- FydC 47150 5613 D6
1700 NALB 47150 5505 A7
Old St. Andrews Church Rd
8400 LSVL 40258 5831 E3
Old Salem Ct
7600 BCFT 40242 5509 E5
Old Salem Rd
600 ClkC 47130 5399 E5
600 UTCA 47130 5399 E5
1000 FydC 47136 5502 C7
1000 FydC 47136 5611 C1
7600 BCFT 40222 5509 E5
7600 BCFT 40242 5509 E5
Old Salem Rd NE
2000 FydC 47136 5611 C2
Old Salt River Rd
- MdeC 40108 6264 B4
- MdeC 40175 6264 A5
- MRGH 40155 6264 B4
Old School House Rd
3800 LSVL 40229 5944 A2
Old Shelbyville Rd
11700 MDTN 40243 5620 C4
Old Shelbyville Rd SR-2840
11700 MDTN 40243 5620 C4
Old Shepherdsville Rd
1900 LSVL 40218 5726 E4
1900 WBHL 40218 5726 E4
Old Shepherdsville Rd SR-2052
1900 LSVL 40218 5726 E4
1900 WBHL 40218 5726 E4
Oldshire Rd
4900 LSVL 40229 5944 D2
Old Six Mile Ln
9100 JFTN 40220 5728 C2
9100 JFTN 40299 5728 C2
Old Sorrel Ln
2000 OdmC 40031 5297 C7
Old South Park Rd
- LSVL 40118 5834 B7
- MLHT 40118 5834 B7
- MLHT 40219 5834 B7
8900 LSVL 40219 5835 B3
8900 LSVL 40229 5835 A7
Old Springdale Rd
4300 LSVL 40241 5510 C2
Old Springhouse Rd
100 BltC 40165 6054 C5
Old Stage Coach Rd
- LSVL 40245 5623 B3
Old State Rd 60
7600 ClkC 47172 5288 D6
8600 SLRB 47172 5288 D6
Old Station Rd
14000 LSVL 40245 5621 B4
Old Stave Mill Rd
- BltC 40165 6054 A2
Old Stone Dr
10 SbyC 40067 5732 B4
Old Stone Ln
400 WDYH 40207 5509 B7
400 WDYH 40207 5618 B1
Old Stone Rd
100 HLVW 40165 6052 E1
100 HLVW 40165 6053 A2
Oldstone Wy
6000 ClkC 47111 5180 C7
Old Tay Br
3000 ClkC 47130 5399 A3
Old Taylorsville Rd
10500 JFTN 40299 5728 E4
10700 LSVL 40299 5729 A4
10800 LSVL 40299 5729 A4
13200 LSVL 40299 5730 B5
15100 LSVL 40299 5731 A5
15200 LSVL 40023 5731 B5
Old Toll Rd
8200 LSVL 40291 5837 E5
Old Towne Rd
100 LSVL 40214 5833 C3
Old Trace Ct
4400 FydC 47119 5394 E6
Old Tree Run
7800 LYDN 40222 5618 E2
Old Tunnel Hill Rd
10 ELZT 42701 6703 D5
Old US-31 E
2000 ClkC 47129 5506 D4
Old Vincennes Rd
- FydC 47122 5503 D2
2700 FydC 47150 5504 A3
2700 NALB 47150 5504 C4
3300 FydC 47119 5504 A2
4700 FydC 47119 5503 C1
5000 FydC 47119 5394 A6
6400 FydC 47119 5393 D5
6400 FydC 47122 5393 E5
7200 FydC 47124 5393 D5
8600 FydC 47122 5392 E3
8600 FydC 47124 5392 E3
Old Watterson Dr
4500 JFTN 40299 5728 C6
Old Westport Rd
7700 LSVL 40222 5509 E7
7700 LSVL 40222 5510 A7
7700 LYDN 40222 5509 E7
7800 LYDN 40222 5510 A7
Old Whipps Mill Rd
9000 BLMD 40223 5619 B2
9000 LYDN 40242 5619 C2
Oldwood Pl
14000 LSVL 40245 5621 C4
Old Zaring Rd
5700 OdmC 40014 5403 A3
8600 OdmC 40014 5402 D4
Old Zaring Mill Ct
3900 LSVL 40241 5510 D3
Oleanda Av
1400 LSVL 40215 5724 A2
1500 SVLY 40216 5724 A2
Ole Brickyard Cir
4400 WSNP 40218 5726 B4
Olenda Av
1800 SVLY 40216 5723 D3
Olenda Ct
1500 LSVL 40215 5724 A2
Olive Av
100 NALB 47150 5505 A3
Olive Rd
3400 LSVL 40219 5834 E3
3500 LSVL 40219 5835 A3
Olive St
1300 LSVL 40210 5614 D6
1300 LSVL 40211 5614 D6
1600 NALB 47150 5504 E3
Olive Hill Ct
8300 LSVL 40228 5836 B6
Oliverda Dr
11000 LSVL 40272 5939 E3
11000 LSVL 40272 5940 A3
Oliver Station Ct
13500 LSVL 40245 5512 A4
Olivia Al
600 RDCF 40160 6483 D5
Ollie Dr
- LSVL 40118 5942 E2
Olsen Crossway
- HdnC 40121 6374 B3
Olympia Park Plz
- LSVL 40241 5510 C2
Olympic Av
3900 BWNV 40207 5617 D1
3900 DRDH 40207 5617 D1
Omaha Ln
2400 LSVL 40216 5722 E7
Omaha St
- SHDV 40165 6162 C2
Omaho Ct
10 HdnC 42701 6703 E4
Omar Khayyam Blvd
9200 LSVL 40258 5831 B7
9200 LSVL 40272 5831 B7
9900 LSVL 40272 5940 A1
Omega Blvd
200 CHAN 47111 5181 D1
Omega Pkwy
10 BltC 40165 6162 B6
Omega St
5700 LSVL 40258 5831 B6
Omicron Ct
100 BltC 40165 6162 C7
Onandaga Ct
10800 LSVL 40229 5944 E4
Oneida Av
1000 LSVL 40214 5833 A3
Oneida Ct
1500 LSVL 40215 5723 E5
1500 LSVL 40215 5724 A5
Ontario Ct
100 SHDV 40165 6161 E4
Onward Wy
1300 ClkC 47172 5288 C2
1300 SLRB 47172 5288 C2
Onyx Av
- LSVL 40206 5616 D2
Optimist Av
1700 JFVL 47130 5507 C4
Orange Dr
4500 LSVL 40213 5834 C1
Orange Blossom Rd
6700 LSVL 40219 5835 D3
Orbit Ct
3500 LSVL 40229 5943 E2
Orchard Av
900 LSVL 40213 5834 C1
1100 LYNV 40213 5725 C7
1600 LSVL 40213 5725 D3
Orchard Dr
300 CLKV 47129 5506 C2
500 ELZT 42701 6812 B1
Orchard Ln
10 FydC 47119 5395 C7
Orchard Wk
6100 ClkC 47111 5290 B2
Orchard Wy
4100 LSVL 40216 5723 A3
4100 SVLY 40216 5723 A3
Orchard Brook Dr
200 BltC 40109 6051 D1
E Orchard Grass Blvd
7200 ODGH 40014 5402 E7
7200 OdmC 40014 5402 E7
7200 OdmC 40014 5403 A6
7500 ODGH 40014 5511 E1
7600 OdmC 40014 5511 E1
N Orchard Grass Blvd
- ODGH 40014 5511 E1
W Orchard Grass Blvd
7100 ODGH 40014 5402 E7
Orchard Hill Dr
600 LSVL 40214 5833 B1
Orchard Hill Rd
- LSVL 40214 5833 B1
Orchard Lake Blvd
7100 LSVL 40218 5727 D4
Orchard Lake Dr
3900 LSVL 40218 5727 D4
Orchard Manor Cir
3100 LSVL 40220 5727 B1
Orchard Ridge Ln
5400 GNVW 40222 5509 A2
5400 LSVL 40222 5509 A2
Orchid Ct
100 BltC 40229 5944 D6
Orchid Hill Pl
6400 WLNP 40207 5618 C1
Ordinance Station Dr
100 LSVL 40214 5724 D7
Ordnance Dr
100 LSVL 40214 5724 C7
Oread Rd
300 BWNV 40207 5617 D1
Oregon Av
1800 LSVL 40210 5614 D7
Oreland Mill Rd
10800 LSVL 40229 5945 A5
E Orell Rd
11800 LSVL 40272 5940 A5
11900 LSVL 40272 5939 E5
12800 LSVL 40272 6049 A1
W Orell Rd
6400 LSVL 40272 5939 E6
Orinoco St
- HdnC 40121 6374 D1
Oriole Ct
1000 ANPK 40213 5725 B2
Oriole Dr
100 CHAN 47111 5181 D4
1600 NALB 47150 5505 D2
1700 ELZT 42701 6702 E4
3100 ANPK 40213 5725 B2
3100 LSVL 40217 5725 B2
3300 LSVL 40213 5725 B3
N Oriole Dr
200 CHAN 47111 5181 D4
Oriole Pl
1900 OdmC 40059 5291 E1
Orion Rd
5800 GNVW 40222 5509 A3
5800 LSVL 40222 5509 B3
Orlandi Ct
9800 JFTN 40299 5728 D4
Orleans Ct
4600 LSVL 40272 5940 D2
Ormond Rd
1700 NALB 47150 5505 C1
3800 BLWD 40207 5617 D2
3800 STMW 40207 5617 D2
3900 LSVL 40207 5617 E1
4100 MYHE 40207 5617 E1
4100 MYHE 40207 5618 A1
E Ormsby Av
100 LSVL 40203 5615 D6
400 LSVL 40208 5615 E6
500 LSVL 40203 5616 A6
500 LSVL 40208 5616 A6
600 LSVL 40204 5616 A6
W Ormsby Av
100 LSVL 40203 5615 D5
100 LSVL 40208 5615 D5
1800 LSVL 40210 5615 A5
2100 LSVL 40210 5614 E5
Ormsby Ct
1200 LSVL 40203 5615 C5
1200 LSVL 40208 5615 C5
Ormsby Ln
800 LYDN 40242 5619 B2
1200 LYDN 40222 5619 A1
1500 GYDL 40222 5510 A7
1500 LYDN 40222 5510 A7
1700 GYDL 40222 5509 E7
1700 LSVL 40222 5509 E7
1700 LYDN 40222 5509 E7
Ormsby Park Pl
10300 LYDN 40223 5619 E1
Ormsby Station Ct
1500 LYDN 40223 5619 D1
Ormsby Station Rd
9500 LYDN 40223 5619 D1
Orville Dr
5900 LSVL 40213 5834 E1
Osage Av
1800 LSVL 40210 5615 A5
2200 LSVL 40210 5614 E4
2500 LSVL 40211 5614 E4
Osage Cir
1600 ANCH 40223 5620 C1
Osage Ct
10 ELZT 42701 6812 A1
Osage Rd
6200 OdmC 40014 5405 D5
Osage Rd E
11600 ANCH 40223 5620 C1
12100 ANCH 40223 5511 D7
N Osage Rd
12200 ANCH 40223 5511 D7
Osage Tr
- SbyC 40245 5513 D4
Osborn Dr
7800 LYDN 40222 5618 E1
7800 STMW 40222 5618 E1
Oscar Rd
11200 LSVL 40241 5511 B3
Oshara Ct
100 BltC 40047 5947 D6
Osprey Rd
3100 LSVL 40213 5725 C1
Osprey Ridge Dr
7000 LSVL 40228 5727 B7
Ossulston Ct
6800 WDYH 40207 5509 D5
Oswego Cir
7300 LSVL 40214 5832 D2
Ottawa Av
100 LSVL 40214 5724 D5
300 LSVL 40209 5724 D5
Otter Ct
3600 LSVL 40219 5726 A7
Otter Creek Rd
- HdnC 40175 6591 B1
100 VNGV 40175 6482 C7
100 VNGV 40175 6591 B1
1100 HdnC 40175 6482 B7
Otter Creek Air Strip Rd
- MdeC 40175 6373 A5
Ouerbacker Ct
1300 LSVL 40208 5615 D6
Outback Pl
- CLKV 47129 5397 D7
Outer Lp
100 LSVL 40214 5832 E6
1000 LSVL 40214 5833 E6
1200 LSVL 40214 5834 A6
1400 LSVL 40219 5834 B5
1400 MLHT 40219 5834 B5
4100 LSVL 40219 5835 D5
5900 LSVL 40219 5836 A4
6200 LSVL 40228 5836 B5
7800 LSVL 40291 5836 D5
Outer Lp SR-1065
100 LSVL 40214 5832 E6
100 LSVL 40214 5833 A6
1400 LSVL 40214 5834 A6
1400 LSVL 40219 5834 B5
1400 MLHT 40219 5834 B5
4100 LSVL 40219 5835 D5
5900 LSVL 40219 5836 A4
6200 LSVL 40228 5836 B5
7800 LSVL 40291 5836 D5
Outer Cir Dr
2100 OdmC 40014 5405 B6
Outer Loop Plz
- LSVL 40228 5836 D5
Oval Av
- HLVW 40229 5943 E6
2200 HLVW 40229 5944 A6
Overbrook E
4600 LSVL 40216 5722 C2
Overbrook W
4800 LSVL 40216 5722 C2
Overbrook Dr
4700 LSVL 40216 5722 C2
Overbrook Rd
10 MKBV 40207 5508 B7
10 MKBV 40207 5617 B1
Overdale Dr
10 HLVW 40229 5944 B5
Overhill Dr
6100 LSVL 40219 5835 C7
6100 LSVL 40229 5835 C7
6100 LSVL 40229 5944 C1
Overlander Ct
14100 LSVL 40245 5621 C6
Overlook Dr
10 BltC 40109 6052 C2
6800 LSVL 40241 5509 C4
Overlook Rd
11900 HLVW 40229 5944 B7
Overlook Ter
1800 LSVL 40205 5617 A7
Overlook Acres
100 BltC 40109 6052 C2
Overlook Cove
7200 FydC 47122 5393 D6
Overlook Hill Ct
2400 LSVL 40205 5617 A7
Overoaks Ct
10200 LSVL 40291 5837 D5
Overton Rd
6300 LSVL 40228 5836 A2
Over View Pointe Dr
10300 JFTN 40299 5728 E4
Owen Ln
100 BltC 40047 5946 D7
100 BltC 40047 6055 C1
100 BltC 40047 6056 A1
100 MTWH 40047 6056 A1
Owen St
1700 LSVL 40203 5615 A1
2100 LSVL 40212 5615 A1
2500 LSVL 40212 5614 E1
Owl Cr
- FydC 47122 5502 D2
- GEOT 47122 5502 D2
Owl Ct
12300 ANCH 40223 5511 D7
Owl Cove Pl
12200 ANCH 40223 5511 D7
Owl Creek Ct
4700 BltC 40165 6163 A1
Owl Creek Ln
100 BltC 40165 6163 A1
11000 ANCH 40223 5620 B1
Owl Creek Rd
7200 FydC 47122 5502 D1
Owsley Rd
10 HdnC 40162 6591 A5
10 HdnC 40175 6591 A5
Oxford Ct
900 CLKV 47129 5506 D3
1500 ELZT 42701 6703 D6
1500 PNRV 40165 6053 C1
5600 LSVL 40291 5837 A2
Oxford Dr
10 NALB 47150 5396 C7
Oxford Ln
200 HLVW 40229 5944 A7
14300 LSVL 40245 5621 B7
14300 LSVL 40299 5621 B7
Oxford Pl
100 LSVL 40207 5617 D3
100 STMW 40207 5617 D3
5600 LSVL 40291 5837 A1
Oxford Commons Ct
10900 LSVL 40291 5946 C1
Oxford Hill Ct
14700 LSVL 40245 5621 D6
Oxfordshire Ln
200 HTBN 40222 5619 B4
Oxford Woods Ct
8400 LYDN 40222 5619 A2
Oxmoor Av
700 LSVL 40222 5618 E4
700 LSVL 40222 5619 A5
Oxmoor Ct
100 LSVL 40222 5618 D3
Oxmoor Ln
100 LSVL 40222 5618 E3
100 NRWD 40222 5618 E3
Oxmoor Farm Ln
8200 LSVL 40222 5618 E4
8200 LSVL 40222 5619 A5
Oxmoor Glen Pl
2900 LSVL 40220 5618 E7
2900 SRPK 40220 5618 E6
Oxmoor Woods Pkwy
- LSVL 40222 5618 E4
- LSVL 40222 5619 A4
700 HTBN 40222 5619 A4
Oxted Ln
7700 GYDL 40222 5509 E7
Ozark St
- HdnC 40121 6265 D7

P

Pacelli Pl
4000 WTNH 40245 5511 D2
4300 LSVL 40245 5511 D2
Pacer Ln
5300 LSVL 40241 5511 A1
Pacific Ct
3300 LSVL 40211 5614 C6
Packard Av
800 LSVL 40217 5725 A2
800 PKWV 40217 5725 A2
Packerland Wy
2800 LSVL 40213 5834 D2
Paddington Ct
300 HTBN 40222 5619 A4
Paddington Dr
8200 HTBN 40222 5619 A4
Paddock Ct
2500 LSVL 40216 5722 D7
Paddock Ln
2000 LGNG 40031 5296 D6
2000 OdmC 40031 5296 D6
2400 LSVL 40216 5722 D7
Paddy Ct
800 ELZT 42701 6811 D3
7600 LSVL 40258 5831 B3
Padua St
100 CLKV 47129 5506 D4
Paducah Ct
4500 LSVL 40272 5940 D2
Page Av
2300 LSVL 40205 5617 A7
Page Pl
- JFVL 47130 5399 A7
1000 JFVL 47130 5398 E7
Pageant Wy
5900 LSVL 40214 5723 D7
5900 LSVL 40214 5832 D1
E Pages Ln
3900 LSVL 40272 5831 E7
4700 LSVL 40258 5831 E6
W Pages Ln
4900 LSVL 40258 5831 B5
Pagoda Ct
- SHDV 40165 6161 B6
6500 LSVL 40229 5945 B1
Pagoda Dr
9200 LSVL 40229 5945 B1
Paige Pl
1000 LGNG 40031 5297 A4
Paisley Rd
1700 LSVL 40205 5726 B1
Paiute Rd
7300 LSVL 40214 5833 A3
Pal Rd
1100 LSVL 40210 5615 B5
Palatka Rd
700 LSVL 40214 5833 B3
1000 LSVL 40214 5832 D2
Palatka Rd SR-1142
800 LSVL 40214 5833 A2
1000 LSVL 40214 5832 D2
Palisades Ct
500 LSVL 40223 5619 D3
Palladio Ct
9500 JFTN 40299 5728 C6
Palma Rd
4600 LSVL 40272 5831 D7
4600 LSVL 40272 5940 D1
Palmer Ct
2200 NALB 47150 5505 A2
Palmer Ln
3300 LSVL 40218 5726 D2
Palmer Park Rd
3700 OdmC 40014 5404 E3
Palmerston Ct
14100 LSVL 40245 5621 C7
Palmetto Cir
- JFTN 40299 5728 D3
Palmetto Dr
3400 ClkC 47130 5398 D5
Palmetto Dunes
3600 JFVL 47130 5507 A1
Palm Tree Dr
6800 LSVL 40219 5835 C3
Paloma Ct
11200 LSVL 40229 5944 C5
Pamela Dr
800 NALB 47150 5505 A1
5300 LSVL 40219 5835 E5
Pamela Wy
300 RDCF 40160 6483 E6
3000 LSVL 40220 5727 D1
Pamela Jo Av
16200 LSVL 40245 5622 B6
Pamela Rae Dr
3700 LSVL 40241 5511 B3
Pampas Wy
7200 LSVL 40258 5831 C3
Pampaw Ln
300 JFVL 47130 5508 B2
Panax Ln
6100 LSVL 40258 5831 B5
Pandorea Rd
8100 LSVL 40258 5831 B5
Panther Ln
100 ELZT 42701 6812 C1
Paoli Pike
2600 FydC 47150 5504 D1
2600 NALB 47150 5504 D1
2900 FydC 47119 5395 B7
2900 FydC 47150 5395 C7
3900 FydC 47119 5394 D5
Papa John's Blvd
2000 JFTN 40299 5729 D1
Papaya Ct
6800 LSVL 40219 5835 D3
Paquette St
5300 MdeC 40121 6373 C2
Par Ln
100 ELZT 42701 6812 E6
Para Ct
8500 PNTN 40242 5510 B5
Paradise Av
200 SLRB 47172 5288 E3
Paradise Cir
2200 CLKV 47129 5397 D5
Paradise Dr
- RDCF 40160 6483 A1
Paradise Ln
100 LSVL 40258 5831 A4
2000 FydC 47150 5613 B1
Paragon Ct
3500 LSVL 40218 5726 C3
3500 WBHL 40218 5726 C3
Parakeet Pl
1500 LYDN 40222 5619 C3
Paralee Ln
- LSVL 40258 5831 D5
- LSVL 40272 5831 D5
Parallel Av
600 SLRB 47172 5288 D4
Paramont Wy
11000 OdmC 40059 5292 C6
Paramount St
4800 LSVL 40258 5831 D5
Paramount Farm
- OdmC 40059 5292 D6
Paramount Park Dr
2800 LSVL 40213 5834 D2
Paraquet Springs Dr
10 SHDV 40165 6161 D4
Pare Ct
100 BltC 40165 6054 C7
Paris Dr
2200 LSVL 40218 5726 D3
2200 WBHL 40218 5726 D3
Parish Pl
300 JFVL 47130 5507 A7
Park Av
10 PNRV 40165 6053 B1
100 CLKV 47129 5506 C5
300 ELZT 42701 6812 A3
300 LSVL 40208 5615 C6
300 RDCF 40160 6483 D2
600 LSVL 40203 5615 C6
2200 NALB 47150 5505 C2
10500 JFTN 40299 5728 E4
10500 JFTN 40299 5729 A4
Park Blvd
4100 LSVL 40209 5724 D4
S Park Cir
10 ELZT 42701 6812 E5
Park Ct
100 VNGV 40175 6482 D7
5500 CTWD 40014 5403 E4
5500 OdmC 40014 5403 E4
Park Dr
- HsnC 47136 5610 E4
- LNVL 47136 5610 E4
- LSVL 40216 5723 D4
- SVLY 40216 5723 C3
10 LGNG 40031 5296 E2
2600 SMRM 40205 5617 B7
2600 SMRM 40205 5726 B1
S Park Dr
6100 FydC 47122 5502 E6
6100 FydC 47136 5502 E6
Park Ln
10 JFVL 47130 5508 A2
300 ELZT 42701 6812 A2
600 RDCF 40160 6483 C5
Park Pl
- OdmC 40014 5403 A7
800 NALB 47150 5396 A5
900 FydC 47150 5396 A5
1400 CLKV 47129 5397 D7
6500 OdmC 40014 5402 E7
E Park Pl
100 JFVL 47130 5507 C5
N Park Pl
7500 NRWD 40222 5618 E3
7500 STMW 40222 5618 E3
S Park Pl
- LYDN 40222 5618 E3
7400 NRWD 40222 5618 E3
7400 STMW 40222 5618 E3
W Park Pl
- JFVL 47130 5507 C6
Park Rd
- LSVL 40229 5945 B2
10 HdnC 40121 6374 B3
3100 LGNG 40031 5297 B6
3100 OdmC 40031 5297 B6
5300 LSVL 40214 5833 A2
6100 CTWD 40014 5403 E4
6100 CTWD 40014 5404 A4
6100 OdmC 40014 5403 E4
6100 OdmC 40014 5404 A4
10900 ANCH 40223 5620 B1
10900 LSVL 40223 5620 B1
Park Rd SR-146
10900 ANCH 40223 5620 B1
10900 LSVL 40223 5620 B1
S Park Rd
100 BltC 40109 5943 C5
100 LSVL 40118 5943 B3
800 ELZT 42701 6812 D5
1600 LSVL 40118 5834 A7
1600 MLHT 40219 5834 A7
1800 MLHT 40118 5834 B7
2000 MLHT 40219 5943 C1
2000 SPVW 40219 5943 C1
2300 LSVL 40219 5943 C1
2700 LSVL 40219 5834 E7
2700 LSVL 40229 5834 E7
3600 LSVL 40219 5835 A7
3600 LSVL 40229 5835 A7
3800 LSVL 40219 5944 B1
3800 LSVL 40229 5944 B1
S Park Rd SR-1020
100 BltC 40109 5943 C5
100 LSVL 40118 5943 C4
W Park Rd
1100 ELZT 42701 6811 A3

STREET
Block City ZIP Map# Grid

Park St
100 VNGV 40175 6482 D7
700 CHAN 47111 5181 D3
Park St NE
7400 LNVL 47136 5610 D5
Parkay Pl
4300 SVLY 40216 5723 B4
Park Boundary Rd
1700 LSVL 40205 5617 B5
Parkbrook Ln
2800 LSVL 40213 5725 D7
Park Church Ln
3100 LSVL 40220 5727 C1
Parkdale Av
2400 LSVL 40220 5618 D5
Park East Blvd
300 FydC 47150 5396 B5
300 NALB 47150 5396 B5
Parker Av
3600 LSVL 40212 5505 B7
Parker Dr
200 LGNG 40031 5296 E4
200 LGNG 40031 5297 B3
Parker Hollow Dr
1500 LSVL 40223 5620 E2
Parkerwood Pl
10500 LSVL 40229 5944 E3
Park Field Rd
12300 LSVL 40223 5620 D1
Park Hills Ct
1200 LSVL 40207 5617 D5
Park Hills Dr
1200 LSVL 40207 5617 D5
Parkhurst Ct
10500 LSVL 40291 5837 C6
Parkington Ct
9200 HTBN 40222 5619 C6
Park Lake Cir
9900 LSVL 40229 5945 B3
Park Lake Dr
- LSVL 40229 5945 B2
Parkland Ct
100 CHAN 47111 5181 D2
12000 DGSH 40243 5620 D5
12000 MDTN 40243 5620 D5
Park Laureate Dr
8600 JFTN 40220 5728 A1
Parklawn Dr
2600 LSVL 40217 5725 A1
N Parkline Dr
400 NALB 47150 5505 A1
S Parkline Dr
400 NALB 47150 5505 A1
Parklook Ct
7100 LSVL 40214 5832 E3
Park Pl Cir
- OdmC 40014 5402 E7
- OdmC 40014 5403 A7
Park Pl Ct
- OdmC 40014 5402 E6
- OdmC 40014 5403 A7
Park Pl Dr
100 MDTN 40223 5621 A4
100 MDTN 40243 5621 A4
Park Plaza Av
- LSVL 40241 5510 D2
Park Ridge Dr
- MTWH 40047 6055 E6
100 BltC 40047 6055 E5
500 FydC 47122 5503 A6
Parkridge Pkwy
1600 LSVL 40214 5832 E4
Park Ridge Rd
400 MRGH 40155 6264 C2
Parkridge Trc
7600 LSVL 40214 5832 E4
Park Row Dr
3400 SVLY 40216 5723 C4
Parkshire Ct
8100 LSVL 40220 5618 E7
8100 LSVL 40220 5619 A7
Parkshire Ln
1600 LSVL 40220 5618 E6
1700 LSVL 40220 5619 A7
Parkside Cir
100 VNGV 40175 6591 D1
Parkside Ct
3100 LSVL 40214 5832 B3
Parkside Dr
400 NALB 47150 5505 A1
Parkstone Ct
2900 LSVL 40241 5510 E5
2900 LSVL 40241 5511 A5
Parkstone Dr
10200 LSVL 40241 5510 E5
10300 LSVL 40241 5511 A5
Park Tower Dr
- RDCF 40160 6483 A5
Park View Ct
13400 LSVL 40223 5512 A6
Parkview Dr
200 SbyC 40245 5514 A7
Parkview Rd
300 SbyC 40245 5514 A7
Parkway Av
3000 LSVL 40206 5617 A1
Parkway Dr
700 LSVL 40217 5725 A1
800 PKWV 40217 5725 A1
1000 LSVL 40217 5616 B7
2800 NALB 47150 5396 E7
Parkway Rd
12100 ANCH 40223 5620 C3
12100 MDTN 40243 5620 C3
Parkway Gardens Ct
1200 LSVL 40204 5616 B6
1200 LSVL 40217 5616 B7
Parkwood Dr
400 ClkC 47129 5397 A7
400 CLKV 47129 5397 B6
Parkwood Rd
2200 LSVL 40214 5832 D1
Park Woods Rd
6000 CTWD 40014 5403 D7
8000 PWEV 40014 5403 D7
Parliament Ct
2400 LSVL 40272 5941 C1
Parret Ln
- ELZT 42701 6812 B5
Parrot Ct
4100 LSVL 40229 5944 B3
Parsons Pl
1500 LSVL 40205 5616 E5
Parthenia Av
3500 LSVL 40215 5723 E4
Partridge Pl
6100 FydC 47119 5393 E5
Partridge Run
10 BltC 40165 6162 D4
4800 LYNV 40213 5725 D6
Partridge Meadow Ct
8000 LYDN 40222 5619 C3
Partridge Walk Wy
- LYDN 40222 5619 C3
Pasafino Ct
4900 LSVL 40299 5839 E2
Pathfinder Ct
8500 LSVL 40291 5946 A1
Patience Ln
10100 LSVL 40291 5946 A2
Patio Ct
2600 LSVL 40214 5832 C1
Patricia Dr
2000 LSVL 40272 5940 A2
3200 LSVL 40216 5722 D4
4000 ClkC 47130 5398 C4
Patricia Wy
- HdnC 42701 6703 E3
6500 LSVL 40219 5835 D7
Patrick Ct
100 ELZT 42701 6702 D6
Patrick Henry Ct
7400 LSVL 40214 5833 D4
Patrick Henry Rd
7300 LSVL 40214 5833 D4
Patriot Ct
300 LSVL 40214 5833 D4
Patrol Rd
- ClkC 47111 5182 A5
- ClkC 47111 5291 B6
- ClkC 47130 5291 B6
- ClkC 47130 5398 E2
- ClkC 47130 5399 A2
- ClkC 47130 5400 A2
7900 ClkC 47130 5290 A7
8800 ClkC 47111 5290 C3
Patrol Rd SR-62
7900 ClkC 47130 5290 A7
8800 ClkC 47111 5290 C3
Pat's Ln
100 BltC 40047 6055 C3
Patterson Av
2000 LSVL 40204 5616 C5
N Patterson Av
100 CLKV 47129 5506 D5
Patterson Dr
5100 LSVL 40219 5835 C2
Patterson St
100 ELZT 42701 6812 C2
Patterson Park Cir
4200 LSVL 40299 5729 C6
Patti Ln
2800 JFTN 40299 5728 C3
Pattie Ln
5500 LSVL 40219 5835 E4
Patton Ct
1600 LSVL 40210 5615 B7
Patton Dr
500 RDCF 40160 6484 A6
Patton Ln
100 BltC 40047 6055 D2
Paul Av
1400 LSVL 40215 5724 A3
Paul Ln
8000 LSVL 40219 5834 C5
Paula Ct
1500 LSVL 40216 5723 D6
Paula Ln
4500 BltC 40165 6053 C3
4500 HBNE 40165 6053 C3
Paul Alan Wy
6700 LSVL 40291 5837 A3
Paula Marie Pl
6000 LSVL 40291 5837 B2
Paulcrest Ct
2500 LSVL 40242 5509 D5
Pauley Gap Rd
300 BltC 40165 6049 A3
300 LSVL 40165 6049 A3
300 LSVL 40272 6049 A3
Pauline Rd
10 LSVL 40206 5616 E1
Paul Pike
- FydC 47119 5395 A7
Paul Revere Ct
5900 LSVL 40229 5944 E4
Paul's Ln
4100 FydC 47119 5395 B5
Pavilion Ct
10500 JFTN 40299 5728 E5
Pavilion Ter
4000 JFTN 40299 5728 E5
Pavilion Wy
5200 LSVL 40291 5728 B7
5500 LSVL 40291 5837 B1
10400 JFTN 40299 5728 E4
Pavilion Wy E
10600 JFTN 40299 5728 E5
Pavillion Dr
- LSVL 40209 5724 E3
Pawnee
- HdnC 40121 6374 E1
Pawnee Dr
100 JFVL 47130 5508 A4
200 JFVL 47130 5507 E3
600 RDCF 40160 6483 B3
900 ELZT 42701 6703 D7
1100 ELZT 42701 6812 D1
Pawnee Tr
10 INHC 40207 5509 A6
10 LSVL 40207 5509 A5
Pawtuket Ct
1500 LSVL 40211 5614 C5
Paxton Wilt Rd
- LSVL 40229 5945 B3
Payne Rd
500 FydC 47150 5287 C7
500 FydC 47150 5396 C1
Payne St
1100 LSVL 40204 5616 C3
1400 LSVL 40206 5616 C3
1700 GEOT 47122 5501 E3
2600 LSVL 40206 5617 A3
Payne-Koehler Rd
- NALB 47150 5396 E5
1800 ClkC 47172 5397 C2
1900 CLKV 47129 5397 C2
1900 CLKV 47172 5397 C2
3800 FydC 47150 5396 E5
4000 FydC 47150 5397 A4
4500 ClkC 47129 5397 A4
Paynter Pt
1700 JFVL 47130 5507 A1
Payton Pl
1200 RDCF 40160 6483 A2
Payton Rd
9000 FydC 47124 5283 E6
9000 GNVL 47124 5283 E6
Peabody Ct
2000 LSVL 40218 5726 C3
Peabody Ln
1900 LSVL 40218 5726 C2
Peace Av
100 MTWH 40047 6056 C1
Peace Ln
100 PWEV 40056 5512 C2
Peaceful Wy
100 BltC 40165 6162 C7
2200 MLHT 40219 5834 C6
Peacely St
100 JFVL 47130 5506 E4
Peach Rd
1300 JFVL 47130 5507 B5
Peach St
10400 JFTN 40299 5728 E4
Peach Meadow Dr
4700 LSVL 40218 5727 D5
Peachtree Av
3300 LSVL 40215 5724 B3
4900 LSVL 40214 5724 B6
7600 OdmC 40014 5512 A2
Peachtree Cir
1000 LGNG 40031 5297 A5
Peach Tree Ln
7100 FydC 47122 5502 C2
7100 GEOT 47122 5502 B2
Peachtree Ln
13300 RVBF 40059 5292 A7
13300 RVBF 40059 5401 A1
Peach Tree St
- ClkC 47130 5398 B3
Peachtree St
100 ELZT 42701 6812 A2
Peacock Dr
1100 LYDN 40222 5619 A1
S Peak Av
100 BltC 40165 6161 D1
100 SHDV 40165 6161 D1
Peak Rd
- LGNG 40031 5296 E5
- LGNG 40031 5297 A5
- OdmC 40031 5297 A6
Peale Av
2900 LSVL 40205 5617 D7
Pearce Wy
5400 OdmC 40014 5513 B4
Pearl St
- CLKV 47130 5506 E7
- JFVL 47130 5506 E7
- JFVL 47130 5507 A7
- UTCA 47130 5399 E6
- UTCA 47130 5400 A6
100 RDCF 40160 6483 E6
1700 NALB 47150 5505 A3
Pearl St US-31
- CLKV 47130 5506 E6
- JFVL 47130 5506 E6
N Pearl St
1200 NALB 47150 5505 A4
Pearman Pkwy
400 RDCF 40160 6483 C6
Pear Orchard Rd
100 ELZT 42701 6703 B4
1200 HdnC 42701 6703 B4
Pear Orchard Rd NW
10 ELZT 42701 6702 D3
200 HdnC 42701 6702 D3
500 ELZT 42701 6703 A2
600 HdnC 42701 6703 A2
Pear Orchard Cove
600 ELZT 42701 6703 B6
Pear Orchard Estates Dr
100 ELZT 42701 6703 B6
Pear Ridge Dr
1100 FydC 47122 5503 B7
Pearson Ct
600 LSVL 40203 5615 C4
Pear Valley Dr
2000 ELZT 42701 6702 D3
Pear View Ln
7700 LSVL 40218 5727 D4
Peaslee Rd
2100 SVLY 40216 5723 B2
Pebble Brch
3000 JFVL 47130 5507 A1
Pebble Ct
6200 CTWD 40014 5403 E4
6200 OdmC 40014 5403 E4
Pebble Pt
1200 OdmC 44026 5292 B2
Pebble Beach Ct
800 HdnC 40175 6591 A2
10100 LSVL 40291 5837 D6
Pebblebrook Dr
2300 BltC 40165 6053 A5
Pebblebrook Ln
8000 LSVL 40219 5835 C5
Pebble Creek Ct
3200 NALB 47150 5396 B7
Pebble Creek Dr
100 BltC 40165 6163 A1
800 JFVL 47130 5399 A6
6000 FydC 47119 5393 E6
6000 FydC 47119 5394 A6
Pebble Creek Cove
6100 FydC 47119 5393 E6
Pebble Hill Ct
3100 FydC 47172 5397 B1
Pebblestone Cir
10400 LSVL 40229 5944 A4
Pebblestone Wy
100 ELZT 42701 6593 E7
Pebblewood Ct
4400 JFTN 40299 5728 A5
4400 LSVL 40299 5728 A5
Pecan Ln
- BltC 40165 6053 E6
Pecan Wy
10 LSVL 40118 5942 C1
Pecan Farm Rd
- BltC 40165 6053 D5
Pecanwood Wy
3800 JFTN 40299 5728 C5
Peck St
200 VNGV 40175 6482 D7
Pecks Ln
10 HdnC 40160 6592 D5
Pecunnie Wy
4100 LSVL 40218 5727 D5
Peddler Ct
100 BltC 40047 6056 E3
Peddlers Ct
100 BltC 40047 6056 E3
Peddlers Run
- BltC 40047 6056 E3
Peeble Ln
8700 LSVL 40272 5832 D7
Peerless Ct
1300 LSVL 40210 5615 B5
Pee Wee Reese Rd
- JfnC 40207 5617 C5
- KGLY 40205 5617 D7
- LSVL 40206 5617 C6
- LSVL 40207 5617 C6
2300 JfnC 40205 5617 C6
2300 LSVL 40205 5617 C6
Pegasus Pointe Dr
9000 LSVL 40219 5835 A7
Peggy Av
7400 LSVL 40214 5833 A3
Peggy Dr
8400 LSVL 40219 5835 C6
Pekin Rd
6900 GNVL 47124 5283 D4
7200 FydC 47124 5283 E5
9700 ClkC 47106 5283 D2
Peleske Dr
3400 SVLY 40216 5723 B3
Pelham Ct
2900 JFTN 40299 5728 E3
Pelican Wy
8000 LYDN 40222 5619 C3
Pell St
400 HdnC 40121 6374 B3
Pemaquid Rd
3400 LSVL 40218 5726 B3
Pembroke Rd
10 LNSH 40220 5618 C7
10 LSVL 40220 5618 D7
10 SRPK 40220 5618 C7
Pembury Ct
9600 LSVL 40272 5941 C1
Pencross Ct
11300 LSVL 40223 5620 B3
Pencross Pl
300 LSVL 40223 5620 B3
Pendelton Hill Rd
- BltC 40165 6049 D3
Pendleton Rd
100 BltC 40165 6049 D3
4000 LSVL 40272 6049 C3
6300 LSVL 40272 6048 E1
Penfield Ct
6800 PROS 40059 5400 D3
Penfield Pl
7000 PROS 40059 5400 E3
Penguin St
600 LSVL 40217 5724 E2
Pen Hollow Dr
10 LSVL 40118 5942 B1
Penhurst Dr
3200 SVLY 40216 5723 C2
Penile Rd
1100 LSVL 40118 5942 A1
1100 LSVL 40272 5942 A1
1500 LSVL 40272 5941 D2
Penion Dr
10800 JFTN 40299 5729 A4
10800 LSVL 40299 5729 A4
Penley Ct
100 HdnC 40121 6373 E4
Penn Av
300 ClkC 47172 5288 E3
300 SLRB 47172 5288 E3
S Penn Av
500 SLRB 47172 5288 E5
Penn St
200 JFVL 47130 5507 B6
Pennacook Rd
2500 LSVL 40214 5832 D2
Pennington Ln
400 BWNV 40207 5617 D1
400 LSVL 40207 5617 D1
400 RLGF 40207 5617 C1
Pennington St NE
- LNVL 47136 5610 D5
W Pennington St NE
2300 LNVL 47136 5610 D5
Penn Run Rd
- BltC 40165 5944 E7
- BltC 40165 6054 A1
100 BltC 40165 5945 A7
Pennsylvania Av
100 LSVL 40206 5617 B2
400 ELZT 42701 6812 A2
600 SLRB 47172 5288 C3
900 JFVL 47130 5399 A7
1300 JFVL 47130 5507 A5
1500 JFVL 47130 5506 E5
Pennsylvania Run Rd
8200 LSVL 40228 5836 C7
8700 LSVL 40228 5945 C1
8700 LSVL 40229 5945 C1
Pennsylvania Run Rd SR-2845
8500 LSVL 40228 5836 C6
Pennwood Dr
900 NALB 47150 5396 C6
Penny Cir
500 DGSH 40243 5620 C5
Pennyrile Ct
10100 JFTN 40299 5728 D2
Penny Royal Wy
400 JFTN 40223 5619 D5
Pennyroyal Cove
300 RDCF 40160 6592 E1
Penruth Av
300 LSVL 40206 5617 B1
300 LSVL 40207 5617 B1
Pensive Ln
9200 LSVL 40272 5831 A7
Pensive Rd
100 CLKV 47129 5506 A2
Pentel Ln
9900 LSVL 40291 5837 D1
Pentose Av
4900 LSVL 40216 5723 A7
Penway Av
3000 LSVL 40210 5614 D7
3000 LSVL 40211 5614 C7
Penwern Ct
6800 WDYH 40207 5618 C1
Penwood Rd
500 LSVL 40206 5617 C3
Peony Dr
1900 LSVL 40211 5614 C6
Peony Wy
- LGNG 40031 5296 B3
Pepper Wy
- MDTN 40243 5620 C4
Pepperbush Rd
200 LSVL 40207 5617 D1
Pepperdine Ct
11000 LSVL 40291 5946 C2
Pepperdine Dr
9700 LSVL 40291 5946 C2
Peppermill Ct
7200 SPML 40228 5836 B4
Peppermill Ln
6900 SPML 40228 5836 C4
7000 LSVL 40228 5836 C4
Perchwood Ct
8000 LSVL 40291 5836 E3
Peregrine Pl
4400 LSVL 40241 5511 B2
Perennial Dr
800 LSVL 40217 5725 A2
800 PKWV 40217 5725 A2
Perimeter Dr
2900 JFVL 47130 5398 B4
SW Perimeter Rd
- LSVL 40209 5724 E7
- LSVL 40209 5833 E1
- LSVL 40209 5834 A2
- LSVL 40213 5834 A2
Periwinkle Dr
100 HdnC 40160 6483 B6
100 VNGV 40160 6483 B6
Periwinkle Wy
3100 FydC 47150 5397 B2
Perkins Ct
100 BltC 40109 6050 C3
Perma Dr
6100 LSVL 40218 5727 A3
Permerland Dr
5900 LSVL 40219 5834 E1
Perri Cir
6900 OdmC 40014 5404 E7
Perrin Cir
- OdmC 40014 5402 E6
Perrin Dr
- OdmC 40014 5402 E6
6100 OdmC 40014 5403 A6
Perrin Ln
200 JFVL 47130 5507 E4
Perrine St
- MRGH 40155 6264 C5
Perry Av
600 ELZT 42701 6812 B1
Perry Rd
8500 LYDN 40222 5619 B3
Perry St
200 MRGH 40155 6264 C4
Perryman Rd
800 WLNP 40207 5618 B1
900 STMW 40207 5618 B1
Perry Neal Rd
5300 OdmC 40014 5405 B4
Pershing Av
1600 LYDN 40242 5619 C1
1700 LYDN 40242 5510 B7
Pershing Dr
200 HdnC 40121 6374 B3
Persimmon Ct
- SbyC 40245 5513 E5
Persimmon Ln
4000 FydC 47150 5503 D5
Persimmon Wy
900 LYDN 40242 5619 B2
Persimmon Ridge Dr
10 SbyC 40245 5513 D5
Persimmon Wood Tr
17000 LSVL 40023 5731 C3
Persistence Dr
8800 HTCK 40229 5945 E4
Perth Ct
2200 SVLY 40216 5723 B2
Perth Dr
2300 SVLY 40216 5723 B2
Perthshire Ln
900 LYDN 40222 5619 C2
Perwinkle Ct
10300 LSVL 40291 5946 E4
Perwinkle Ln
10000 LSVL 40291 5946 E4
Pete Huber Ln
100 BltC 40047 6056 E2
100 BltC 40047 6057 A2
100 MTWH 40047 6056 E2
Peterborough Ct
9000 HTBN 40222 5619 C4
Peterborough Dr
8800 HTBN 40222 5619 C4
Peters Dr
500 ELZT 42701 6811 D3
Petersburg Rd
- WSNP 40218 5726 C5
3600 LSVL 40218 5726 C5
3600 PLRH 40218 5726 C5
N Peterson Av
100 LSVL 40206 5616 E2
100 LSVL 40206 5617 A2
S Peterson Av
100 LSVL 40206 5617 A3
N Peterson Ct
2400 LSVL 40206 5616 E2
Peterson Dr
10 SpnC 40071 5949 E3
100 ELZT 42701 6811 B4
500 HdnC 42701 6811 B4
Petra Ct
8300 LSVL 40219 5836 A6
Petty Jay Ct
7600 LSVL 40220 5727 D2
Petty Jay Rd
2800 LSVL 40220 5727 D2
Petunia Av
1500 LSVL 40218 5726 A5
Petwood Blvd
13900 LSVL 40272 6048 C2
Peyote Pl
11700 LSVL 40299 5729 A6
Peyton Av
7300 ODGH 40014 5511 E1
7300 OdmC 40014 5511 E1
Pfeifer Ln
10 HdnC 42701 6593 C7
Pflanz Av
3800 LSVL 40212 5505 C7
Phantom Division Rd
10 HdnC 40121 6374 C1
Pharris Av
7100 LSVL 40258 5831 E3
Pheasant Run
1400 FydC 47150 5287 E7
1400 FydC 47150 5396 E1
Pheasant Ridge Rd
1200 OdmC 44026 5292 B2
Pheasant Run Ct
1500 FydC 47150 5287 E7
1500 FydC 47150 5396 D1
Phelps Av
200 CLKV 47129 5506 C5
Phelps Ct
- BltC 40165 6161 A1
Phelps Rd
- BltC 40165 6052 B7
100 BltC 40165 6161 C1
Philips Cir
400 ELZT 42701 6811 E1
Phillip Ct
100 SHDV 40165 6161 E6
Phillips Ln
10 BltC 40165 6162 E1
10 BltC 40165 6163 A1
500 LSVL 40209 5724 E4
500 LSVL 40209 5725 A4
1100 LSVL 40213 5725 A4
Phillip Schmidt Rd
6000 FydC 47119 5394 A1
6100 FydC 47119 5393 E1
Phillip Stuecker Rd
10 HdnC 42701 6811 B7
Phoenix Tr
9800 LSVL 40223 5510 D7
9800 WPMG 40223 5510 D7
9900 KNLD 40223 5510 D7
Phoenix Hill Ct
5500 LSVL 40207 5509 A5
5500 WNDF 40207 5509 A5
Phoenix Hill Dr
2300 LSVL 40207 5509 A4
2300 WNDF 40207 5509 A5
Phyllis Av
1500 LSVL 40215 5724 A2
1600 SVLY 40216 5724 A1
Piatt Pl
300 DGSH 40223 5620 A3
300 LSVL 40223 5620 A3
Picadilly Av
4500 LSVL 40215 5724 B5
Picardy Ct
600 ELZT 42701 6811 D3
Pickett Rd
10 HdnC 40121 6265 D7
10 HdnC 40121 6374 D1
Pickings Pl
1200 MDTN 40243 5620 D6
Pickwick Ln
7900 LSVL 40219 5835 A5
Pico Ln
5500 LSVL 40219 5835 E4
Pictor Ct
- LSVL 40241 5510 E2
Piedmont Dr
3000 LSVL 40205 5726 B2
Pierce Al
- LSVL 40203 5616 A4
Pierce Ln
100 MTWH 40047 6055 E1
Pierce St
400 ELZT 42701 6812 C3
Pierce Wy
11500 LSVL 40272 5940 B4
Piercy Mill Rd
14100 LSVL 40245 5621 E2
15400 LSVL 40245 5622 A3
Piercy Mill Trc
1400 LSVL 40245 5621 E3
Pigeon Pass Rd
- LSVL 40213 5725 D6
300 ELZT 42701 6702 E4
300 ELZT 42701 6703 A4
1200 LYNV 40213 5725 D6
Pike St
- LSVL 40202 5615 D2
10 CHAN 47111 5181 E5
200 UTCA 47130 5400 A6
600 ELZT 42701 6703 C7
Pike & Payne Ln
100 BltC 40165 6051 C7
Pikeland Wy
100 BltC 40165 6054 C3
Pikes Peak Blvd
2200 LSVL 40214 5832 D1
2500 LSVL 40214 5723 D7
Pikeview Ct
1700 LSVL 40215 5723 D4
Pikeview Dr
- LSVL 40209 5725 A4
Pikewood Rd
5800 LSVL 40219 5835 E4
Pilot St
200 HdnC 40121 6374 A2
Pilsbury Ln
700 NALB 47150 5396 B6
Pimlico Dr
200 NALB 47150 5396 A7
7500 LSVL 40214 5832 C3
E Pin Al
- LSVL 40202 5615 E4
Pina Wy
8000 LSVL 40219 5835 D5
Pindell Av
1200 LSVL 40217 5616 A7
2500 LSVL 40217 5725 B1
2900 ANPK 40213 5725 B2
Pine Ct
- LSVL 40213 5834 C1
1100 FydC 47136 5611 D1
9200 OdmC 40056 5512 D4
Pine Dr
- BltC 40109 5943 E5
100 CHAN 47111 5181 C2
Pine Pt
12400 LSVL 40299 5729 C7
Pine St
10 LGNG 40031 5296 E2
10 LGNG 40031 5297 A2
400 LSVL 40204 5616 B3
900 NALB 47150 5505 A6
5800 UTCA 47130 5399 E6
5800 UTCA 47130 5400 A6
Pine Bark Ct
3100 LSVL 40272 5940 D3
Pinebrook Ct
10600 JFTN 40299 5728 E5
Pine Bunch Ct
5200 LSVL 40299 5729 C7
Pinecastle Dr
8100 LSVL 40219 5835 E6
Pine Cone Cir
3500 LSVL 40241 5509 E3
Pinecove Ct
3600 JFTN 40299 5728 C5
Pine Creek Cir
3800 NALB 47150 5396 D5
Pine Creek Ct
100 BltC 40165 6163 D5
Pine Creek Rd
100 BltC 40165 6163 D6
Pine Creek Tr
100 BltC 40165 6163 C6
Pinecrest Dr
100 BltC 40165 6051 D4
300 ELZT 42701 6812 D2
Pinecrest Rd
300 ELZT 42701 6812 D2
2700 OdmC 40031 5296 C7
Pinecroft Dr
3400 LSVL 40219 5834 E5
3400 LSVL 40219 5835 A5
Pinecroft Ln
3900 LSVL 40219 5835 A5
Pinedale Dr
10700 JFTN 40299 5728 E5
Pine Forest Ct
3200 LSVL 40272 5940 D3
Pine Glen Cir
10400 LSVL 40291 5837 C6
Pine Glen Ct
- BltC 40165 6161 A1
Pine Grove Ct
8300 LSVL 40214 5832 B5
Pine Hill Ct
2200 JFVL 47130 5507 B1
Pinehill Ct
13000 OdmC 40059 5401 B1
Pinehurst Dr
10 CLKV 47129 5506 C3
1500 JFVL 47130 5507 B3
Pinehurst Ln
3300 LSVL 40241 5510 A4
3300 LSVL 40242 5510 A4

STREET Block City ZIP Map# Grid

Pine Knob Dr
15800 LSVL 40272 6049 C3
Pine Knoll Cir
7400 PROS 40059 5401 B3
Pine Lake Dr
8800 JFTN 40220 5728 B2
9100 JFTN 40299 5728 B2
Pineland Dr
3400 LSVL 40219 5834 E5
3400 LSVL 40219 5835 A5
Pine Meadows Dr
10 SbyC 40067 5732 B5
Pine Meadows Ln
7800 BRMD 40241 5510 A3
7800 LSVL 40241 5510 A3
Pine Mountain Dr
5800 LSVL 40214 5723 C7
Pineneedle Ln
3300 LSVL 40241 5509 E3
Pine Ridge Rd
- LGNG 40031 5297 B5
- OdmC 40031 5297 B5
7700 LSVL 40241 5509 E4
7700 SPVL 40241 5509 E4
7800 LSVL 40241 5510 A4
Pine Spring Dr
9100 LSVL 40291 5837 B4
Pine Springs Ct
7000 LSVL 40291 5837 B4
Pine Springs Dr
8700 LSVL 40291 5837 B4
Pine Tar Ct
1300 MDTN 40243 5620 C7
Pine Trace Ct
3100 LSVL 40272 5940 C3
Pinetree Dr
5500 LSVL 40213 5726 A7
5500 LSVL 40219 5726 A7
5600 LSVL 40219 5835 A1
Pine Tree Ln NE
6500 HsnC 47122 5501 B6
Pine Valley Dr
10 ELZT 42701 6702 E1
10 HdnC 42701 6702 D2
100 BltC 40165 6052 B5
1400 ELZT 42701 6703 A1
Pine Valley Tr
8300 LSVL 40229 5945 E5
8400 LSVL 40229 5946 A5
Pine View Ct
100 BltC 40047 6057 A4
10800 LSVL 40299 5729 A5
N Pineview Ct
400 NALB 47150 5395 E7
Pineway
700 ANCH 40223 5620 C2
Pinewood Dr
100 HdnC 40160 6484 B6
1100 FydC 47136 5502 C7
1100 FydC 47136 5611 C1
2100 ClkC 47130 5399 B5
2100 JFVL 47130 5399 B5
12000 HLVW 40229 5944 C6
Pinewood Rd
4600 LSVL 40213 5726 A5
4600 LSVL 40218 5726 A5
4600 PLRH 40213 5726 B6
4600 PLRH 40218 5726 B6
Pinnacle Gardens Cir
13500 LSVL 40245 5512 A5
Pinnacle Gardens Dr
3400 LSVL 40245 5512 B5
Pin Oak Cir
8000 MTWH 40047 6056 A2
Pin Oak Ct
- SpnC 40071 5949 A5
100 ELZT 42701 6812 D1
1500 RDCF 40160 6483 A5
Pin Oak Dr
- BltC 40047 6055 E1
- MTWH 40047 6055 E1
- SpnC 40071 5948 E6
- SpnC 40071 5949 A5
10 ClkC 47129 5506 A3
1000 CLKV 47129 5506 A3
2900 OdmC 40031 5296 C6
Pin Oak Ln
10 WDYH 40207 5618 A1
Pin Oak Rd
3300 OdmC 40031 5296 C7
3500 OdmC 40031 5405 C1
Pin Oak View Ct
3900 LSVL 40299 5728 E5
3900 LSVL 40299 5729 A5
Pin Oak View Dr
10400 JFTN 40299 5728 E5
10400 LSVL 40299 5728 E5
10600 LSVL 40299 5729 A5
Pintail Ct
- HdnC 40162 6593 A7
Pintail Dr
7500 LSVL 40258 5830 E3
Pinto Ct
9300 LSVL 40118 5833 C7
9300 LSVL 40118 5942 C1
Pinwheel Rd
- MdeC 40175 6373 B4
Pioneer Ct
2700 RDCF 40160 6593 A1
Pioneer Pl
3000 OdmC 40014 5405 B6
Pioneer Rd
- PNRV 40165 6053 C1
2600 SVLY 40216 5723 B2
Pioneer Tr
3300 PNRV 40165 6053 C1
Piper Ct
2900 LSVL 40217 5725 B2
Pipilo Pl
8200 LSVL 40242 5510 B4
Pirate Ln
4100 LSVL 40229 5944 A2
Pirate Pl
- CHAN 47111 5181 D3

N Pirogue Ct
9200 JFTN 40299 5728 C4
S Pirogue Ct
9200 JFTN 40299 5728 C4
Pirogue Rd
3500 JFTN 40299 5728 C4
Pirouette Av
9300 LSVL 40118 5942 C1
Pirtle Dr
1500 FydC 47122 5503 C4
Pirtle St
1400 LSVL 40203 5615 B2
2000 LSVL 40212 5615 A2
2500 LSVL 40212 5614 E2
Pirtle Ter
- LSVL 40212 5614 E2
Pitchford Rd
1000 LSVL 40219 5834 E5
Pitts Point Rd
- BltC 40121 6160 A7
- BltC 40165 6160 D3
Pittypat Run
1900 LGNG 40031 5296 C3
Pixley Wy
4000 LSVL 40219 5835 B1
Plain Field Ct
7500 LSVL 40220 5727 D3
Plainfield Dr
1000 NALB 47150 5396 C5
Plains Ct
10300 JFTN 40223 5619 E5
Plainview Rd
500 LSVL 40223 5620 B3
Plainview Terrace Dr
600 JFTN 40223 5619 E5
Plaiss Ln
100 FydC 47150 5504 B5
Planet Dr
5200 LSVL 40258 5831 D1
Plane Tree Ct
1600 SHDV 40165 6162 A2
Plane Tree Dr
4500 LSVL 40219 5726 C7
Plank Rd
1400 JFVL 47130 5507 B4
Plantation Blvd
12100 OdmC 44026 5292 C1
Plantation Ct
2800 FydC 47172 5288 A7
2800 FydC 47172 5397 A1
Plantation Dr
2200 LSVL 40210 5614 D7
2200 LSVL 40216 5614 D7
2200 LSVL 40216 5723 D1
2200 SVLY 40216 5723 D1
3000 FydC 47150 5397 A1
3000 FydC 47172 5288 A7
3000 FydC 47172 5397 A1
Plantside Dr
1700 JFTN 40299 5619 D7
1700 JFTN 40299 5728 D1
11000 LSVL 40299 5729 B2
11800 JFTN 40299 5729 C2
Plantus Pl
4300 LSVL 40213 5726 C7
Pl Argente
10 LSVL 40203 5615 B3
Plato Ter
1100 LSVL 40211 5614 A4
Plaudit Wy
9900 LSVL 40272 5940 A1
Player Dr
6100 LSVL 40258 5831 A4
Player Pl
2000 NALB 47150 5505 A3
Plaza Av
200 LSVL 40218 5727 A4
Plaza Dr
10 NALB 47150 5396 C7
700 JFVL 47130 5507 C4
Pl Blanc
1100 LSVL 40203 5615 C3
Pl Bleu
900 LSVL 40203 5615 C4
Pl Dor
10 LSVL 40203 5615 B3
Pleasant Dr
11400 LSVL 40272 5939 E4
Pleasant Run
6600 ClkC 47111 5290 B1
Pleasant St
800 CHAN 47111 5181 D4
Pleasant Glen Ct
13500 LSVL 40299 5729 E6
Pleasant Glen Dr
4000 LSVL 40299 5729 E5
4300 LSVL 40299 5730 A6
Pleasant Lawn Ct
12000 LSVL 40299 5729 B7
Pleasant Valley Ct
7900 LSVL 40291 5837 C6
Pleasantview Av
200 LSVL 40206 5617 B3
Pleasantview Ct
2100 FydC 47150 5288 A7
2100 FydC 47172 5288 A7
Pleasant View Dr
2000 ELZT 42701 6702 D3
Pleasure Ct
5600 LSVL 40272 5940 B6
Pleasure Ln
12100 LSVL 40272 5940 B6
Pleasure Cove Dr
1600 OdmC 40031 5297 B4
Plebe Ct
4900 LSVL 40216 5722 E5
Plentiful Pl
100 HLVW 40229 5944 A7
Pl Jaune
1000 LSVL 40203 5615 C3
Pl Noir
10 LSVL 40203 5615 B3
Plover Rd
3100 LSVL 40213 5725 C1

Plover Rd
3100 LSVL 40217 5725 C1
Pl Rough
900 LSVL 40203 5615 C3
Plum Al
200 ELZT 42701 6812 B2
Plum Av
- ELZT 42701 6812 C3
Plum Ct
- LSVL 40213 5834 D1
Plum Run
8400 CLKV 47172 5288 B6
N Plum St
100 SHDV 40165 6161 C4
S Plum St
100 SHDV 40165 6161 C4
Plum Creek Ct
100 BltC 40071 5949 D2
Plum Creek Rd
10 SpnC 40071 5949 D4
Plum Creek Rd SR-1060
10 SpnC 40071 5949 D5
Plum Creek Tr
15800 LSVL 40299 5839 E1
15800 LSVL 40299 5840 A1
Plume Dr
5200 LSVL 40258 5831 C3
Plum Hill Ct
1900 FydC 47119 5395 E3
Plum Hill Wy
1900 FydC 47119 5395 E3
Plum Hollow Ct
10000 LSVL 40291 5837 C6
Plum Lake Ct
100 CLKV 47172 5288 B7
Plum Lake Dr
100 CLKV 47172 5288 B7
100 FydC 47172 5288 B7
Plum Ridge Dr
1000 CLKV 47172 5288 B6
Plum Ridge Rd
4300 SpnC 40071 5949 E7
Plum Ridge Rd SR-1169
4300 SpnC 40071 5949 E7
Plum Ridge Wy
100 CLKV 47172 5288 B6
Plum Run Ct
100 CLKV 47172 5288 B6
Plum Tree Ln
4700 LSVL 40218 5727 D5
4700 LSVL 40299 5727 D5
Plum Valley Ct
8500 CLKV 47172 5288 B6
Plum Valley Dr
8300 CLKV 47172 5288 B6
Plumwood Pl
9300 ODGH 40014 5402 D7
9300 OdmC 40014 5402 D7
Plumwood Rd
9400 LSVL 40291 5837 C1
Plum Woods Ct
1000 CLKV 47172 5288 B6
Plum Woods Dr
2200 CLKV 47172 5288 B7
2500 ClkC 47172 5288 B6
Pluto Dr
5200 LSVL 40258 5831 C2
Pl Vert
1000 LSVL 40203 5615 C3
Plymouth Ct
1500 LSVL 40203 5615 A3
2300 LSVL 40211 5615 A3
2600 LSVL 40211 5614 E3
Plymouth Rd
- LSVL 40207 5617 E5
3500 LSVL 40207 5618 A5
3500 PLYV 40207 5618 A5
3800 STMW 40207 5618 A5
Poco Pl
10200 LSVL 40291 5837 D3
Poindexter Dr
5300 LSVL 40291 5728 A7
Poindexter Ln
1600 ClkC 47172 5288 A6
1600 SLRB 47172 5288 A6
Poinsettia Dr
7700 LSVL 40258 5831 C5
Pointe Blvd
100 SHDV 40165 6161 D1
200 BltC 40165 6161 D1
Pointe Ct
2400 JFTN 40220 5728 A1
N Pointe Ct
100 ELZT 42701 6703 A3
N Pointe Dr
100 ELZT 42701 6703 B3
100 HdnC 42701 6703 B3
Pointe Arbor Ln
8700 JFTN 40220 5728 B1
Pointe Bay Blvd
10500 LSVL 40241 5511 C4
Poitier Ct
4900 LSVL 40213 5726 D6
4900 LSVL 40218 5726 D6
Polaris Dr
9500 LSVL 40229 5944 A2
Polk St
400 HdnC 40121 6265 B7
7200 ClkC 47172 5397 D1
Pollitt Ct
1300 JFTN 40223 5620 A7
Pollock Av
7500 OdmC 40056 5512 C3
7500 PWEV 40056 5512 C3
Polo Club Ct
1600 LSVL 40245 5622 D2
Polo Fields Ct
1500 LSVL 40245 5622 D2
Polo Fields Ln
16700 LSVL 40245 5622 E2
Polo Mount Ct
2200 LSVL 40245 5622 D1
Polo Run Ln
17400 LSVL 40245 5622 E3

Polston St
- MRGH 40155 6264 C4
Pomer Ct
3200 LSVL 40220 5727 C2
Pomeroy Ct
4100 LSVL 40218 5727 B3
Pomeroy Dr
2800 LSVL 40218 5727 B3
3000 LSVL 40220 5727 C3
Pomona Pl
9100 LSVL 40272 5831 E7
Pompano Dr
8100 BRMD 40241 5510 A3
8100 LSVL 40241 5510 A3
Ponce de Leon Ct
8100 LSVL 40219 5835 E6
Pond Creek Ct
5500 LSVL 40272 5940 B6
Pond Creek Dr
11700 LSVL 40272 5940 B6
Ponder Ln
9200 LSVL 40272 5831 B7
9300 LSVL 40272 5940 B1
Ponder Wy
200 CLKV 47129 5506 A2
Ponderosa Rd
200 ELZT 42701 6702 D6
Ponderosa Rd NE
- LNVL 47136 5610 D4
5300 HsnC 47136 5610 A4
Pondoray Ct
4500 LSVL 40241 5511 B2
Pond Ridge Cir
5700 FydC 47122 5503 B7
Pond View Ct
9200 LSVL 40291 5837 B3
Ponsit Ln
8300 LSVL 40219 5835 B6
Poorman Range Rd
- HdnC 40121 6374 D5
Pope St
- JFVL 47130 5506 E5
100 LSVL 40206 5616 C2
Pope Dale Rd
17300 LSVL 40245 5622 E3
Pope Farm Rd
- BltC 40165 6162 A4
- SHDV 40165 6162 A4
N Pope Lick Rd
800 DGSH 40243 5620 D6
800 DGSH 40299 5620 E6
800 MDTN 40243 5620 E6
800 MDTN 40299 5620 E6
1000 MDTN 40299 5621 A7
S Pope Lick Rd
1300 LSVL 40299 5620 E7
1300 LSVL 40299 5621 A7
1300 LSVL 40299 5730 C4
12600 LSVL 40299 5729 D1
Poplar Av
7900 OdmC 40014 5512 A1
Poplar Cir
- BltC 40109 5943 D5
100 RDCF 40160 6483 A5
Poplar Dr
200 ELZT 42701 6812 B2
700 JFVL 47130 5507 A4
8300 ClkC 47111 5181 B4
Poplar Ln
13700 LSVL 40299 5730 B1
13800 LSVL 40245 5730 B1
Poplar St
- ELZT 42701 6702 D4
- HdnC 40121 6265 C7
200 MRGH 40155 6264 C4
700 SLRB 47172 5288 D2
700 NALB 47150 5504 E7
E Poplar St
100 ELZT 42701 6812 D3
W Poplar St
100 ELZT 42701 6812 B2
Poplar Ter
7100 PWEV 40056 5512 D3
Poplar Crest Rd
2500 INDH 40207 5508 D4
Poplar Forest Ln
6600 LSVL 40291 5837 E2
Poplar Hill Ct
2700 INDH 40207 5508 D4
7000 ODGH 40014 5402 D7
7000 OdmC 40014 5402 D7
Poplar Hill Dr
- OdmC 40014 5402 D7
9500 ODGH 40014 5402 D7
Poplar Hill Rd
10 INDH 40207 5508 D5
Poplar Hill Woods
4300 INDH 40207 5508 D5
Poplar Level Ct
100 LSVL 40219 5835 B1
Poplar Level Plz
1100 LSVL 40217 5616 B7
Poplar Level Rd
1300 LSVL 40217 5616 B7
1600 LSVL 40217 5725 D3
3200 LSVL 40213 5725 C2
4300 WSNP 40213 5725 E4
4500 LSVL 40218 5725 E5
4600 LSVL 40213 5726 A6
4600 LSVL 40218 5726 A6
4600 PLRH 40213 5726 A6
4700 LSVL 40219 5726 B7
5000 LSVL 40219 5835 E1
5200 LSVL 40228 5835 E2
5900 LSVL 40228 5836 A2
Poplar Level Rd SR-864
1300 LSVL 40217 5616 B7
3000 LSVL 40213 5725 C2
3000 LSVL 40217 5725 C2
4300 WSNP 40213 5725 E4
4500 LSVL 40218 5725 E5
4600 LSVL 40213 5726 A6
4600 LSVL 40218 5726 A6
4600 PLRH 40213 5726 A6

Poplar Level Rd SR-864
4700 LSVL 40219 5726 B7
5000 LSVL 40219 5835 E1
5200 LSVL 40228 5835 E2
5900 LSVL 40228 5836 A2
Poplar Parks Blvd
5500 LSVL 40219 5835 E2
5500 LSVL 40228 5835 E2
Poplar Pl Dr
4800 LSVL 40213 5726 A6
Poplar Tree Ct
6200 LSVL 40228 5835 E2
Poplar View Dr
3200 LSVL 40216 5722 D5
Poplarwood Cir
5600 LSVL 40272 5940 B5
Poplarwood Dr
11800 LSVL 40272 5940 B5
Popp Av
100 SLRB 47172 5288 D5
Poppy Av
4200 LSVL 40216 5723 A4
Poppy Ct
100 RDCF 40160 6483 D7
Poppy Pl
900 JFVL 47130 5507 D3
Poppy Wy
500 LSVL 40206 5617 C3
Popular St
1700 NALB 47150 5504 E7
Port Rd
- ClkC 47130 5399 B6
700 JFVL 47130 5399 B6
700 JFVL 47130 5508 C1
7600 LSVL 40258 5830 D1
Portage Pl
10 JFVL 47130 5508 C2
Portage Tr
200 JFVL 47130 5507 E2
Port Antonio Ct
6600 LSVL 40228 5836 A2
Port Antonio Rd
6100 LSVL 40219 5836 A2
6200 LSVL 40228 5836 A2
Porter St
100 MTWH 40047 6056 C3
Portia Ct
4000 LSVL 40220 5727 C3
Portico Ct
4500 JFTN 40299 5728 D6
Portico Pt
4600 JFTN 40299 5728 D6
Portland Av
1300 LSVL 40203 5615 B1
2100 LSVL 40203 5506 A7
2100 LSVL 40212 5506 A7
2600 LSVL 40212 5505 E7
Portland Av SR-3064
2100 LSVL 40203 5506 A7
2100 LSVL 40212 5506 A7
2600 LSVL 40212 5505 E7
Portland Plz
3400 LSVL 40212 5505 D7
Port Royal Ct
8000 LSVL 40291 5837 C6
Port Wood Ct
- LSVL 40218 5727 A6
Possum Pth
100 LSVL 40214 5833 C2
Possum Pass
10 LSVL 40216 5722 E2
Post Ct
2500 JFTN 40299 5728 D2
Post Oak Pl
8000 LYDN 40222 5619 B2
Post Office Al
300 LSVL 40202 5615 D3
Potomac Ct
100 RDCF 40160 6593 A1
3500 OdmC 40031 5404 E2
Potomac Pl
1200 LSVL 40214 5832 E3
Potomac St
- HdnC 40121 6265 D7
- HdnC 40121 6374 C1
100 RDCF 40160 6593 B1
Potter Rd
14700 LSVL 40299 5948 A1
Potters Ln
300 ClkC 47129 5397 B6
300 CLKV 47129 5397 A6
Potts Ln
6000 CTWD 40014 5403 E7
6000 OdmC 40014 5403 E7
Potts Rd
4300 LSVL 40299 5730 B6
6900 CTWD 40014 5404 A6
6900 OdmC 40014 5404 A6
Pounds Ln
10 LSVL 40023 5732 A6
10 SbyC 40067 5732 A6
Powder Horn Ct
10 LSVL 40216 5831 E1
Powder Horn Dr
5200 LSVL 40216 5831 E1
Powder House Ln
100 FydC 47150 5613 D1
Powell Av
3300 LSVL 40215 5723 E3
Powell St
600 LGNG 40031 5297 A2
Powerhouse Ln
1100 LYDN 40242 5619 C2
Powhatan Ct
11300 LSVL 40241 5511 C3
Powhatan Ln
7400 PWEV 40056 5512 C1
Poydras St
10 NALB 47150 5505 A7
P Pool Ln
- BltC 40109 6050 C2
- BltC 40165 6050 C2
Prairie Ct
100 HLVW 40229 5944 C5

Prairie Dr
100 HLVW 40229 5944 B6
9900 LSVL 40272 5940 E2
Pramany Ct
3800 LSVL 40299 5728 B4
Prather St
100 SLRB 47172 5288 D4
Prather Sta
7600 ClkC 47130 5290 B5
Pratt St
800 JFVL 47130 5507 B5
Preakness Ct
12100 LSVL 40299 5729 B7
Preakness Dr
200 ELZT 42701 6812 C3
Precious Ct
- LSVL 40219 5834 D7
Prentice St
1500 LSVL 40210 5615 A4
Prescott Ct
10400 JFTN 40299 5728 E3
Presidential Pl
800 JFVL 47130 5508 A1
1000 JFVL 47130 5398 E7
1000 JFVL 47130 5399 A7
Presidents Blvd
700 LSVL 40217 5724 E1
700 LSVL 40217 5725 B1
Pressler Grv
- HdnC 40121 6374 D4
Preston Dr
4800 LSVL 40213 5725 D6
4800 LYNV 40213 5725 D6
Preston Hwy
- BltC 40165 6053 C1
- BltC 40229 5944 D6
- PNRV 40165 5944 C7
- PNRV 40165 6053 C1
- PNRV 40229 5944 C7
- PNRV 40229 6053 D1
2500 LSVL 40217 5725 A2
2500 PKWV 40217 5725 A2
3000 LSVL 40213 5725 A2
3100 ANPK 40213 5725 A2
4700 LYNV 40213 5725 C6
5300 LSVL 40219 5725 E7
5700 LSVL 40219 5834 E1
6400 LSVL 40219 5835 A2
9100 LSVL 40229 5835 C7
9200 LSVL 40229 5944 C1
12000 HLVW 40229 5944 D5
Preston Hwy SR-61
- BltC 40165 6053 C1
- BltC 40229 5944 D6
- PNRV 40165 5944 C7
- PNRV 40165 6053 C1
- PNRV 40229 5944 C7
- PNRV 40229 6053 D1
2500 LSVL 40217 5725 A2
2500 PKWV 40217 5725 A2
3000 LSVL 40213 5725 A2
3100 ANPK 40213 5725 A2
4700 LYNV 40213 5725 C6
5300 LSVL 40219 5725 E7
5700 LSVL 40219 5834 E1
6400 LSVL 40219 5835 A2
9100 LSVL 40229 5835 C7
10600 LSVL 40229 5944 C7
12000 HLVW 40229 5944 D5
N Preston Hwy
5200 BltC 40165 6053 C2
5200 HBNE 40165 6053 C2
5200 PNRV 40165 6053 C2
N Preston Hwy SR-61
5200 BltC 40165 6053 C2
5200 HBNE 40165 6053 C2
5200 PNRV 40165 6053 C2
N Preston Hwy SR-1526
- BltC 40165 6053 B3
- HBNE 40165 6053 B3
- PNRV 40165 6053 C2
Preston St
800 NALB 47150 5505 A6
1500 RDCF 40160 6374 B7
1500 RDCF 40160 6483 B1
N Preston St
100 LSVL 40202 5615 E2
S Preston St
- BltC 40165 6161 D7
- SHDV 40165 6161 C5
100 LSVL 40202 5615 E5
700 LSVL 40203 5615 E6
1200 LSVL 40208 5615 E6
1400 LSVL 40217 5615 E6
2100 LSVL 40217 5724 E1
2200 LSVL 40217 5725 A1
2400 PKWV 40217 5725 A1
S Preston St SR-61
- BltC 40165 6161 D7
- SHDV 40165 6161 C5
100 LSVL 40202 5615 E5
700 LSVL 40203 5615 E4
1200 LSVL 40208 5615 E6
1600 LSVL 40217 5615 E7
2100 LSVL 40217 5724 E1
2200 LSVL 40217 5725 A1
2400 PKWV 40217 5725 A1
Preston Crossing Blvd
9700 LSVL 40229 5944 C2
Prestonview Ln
8200 LSVL 40219 5835 B6
Prestwick Dr
1900 LGNG 40031 5297 B6
Prestwick Pl
200 DGSH 40243 5620 A4
Prestwick Square Dr
3400 JFVL 47130 5398 D6
Prestwood Ct
5900 LSVL 40219 5834 E1
5900 LSVL 40219 5835 A1
Prestwood Dr
3400 LSVL 40219 5834 E1
3400 LSVL 40219 5835 A1

Preswick Sq
4000 FydC 47150 5396 C4
4000 NALB 47150 5396 C4
Price Ln Rd
6100 LSVL 40229 5945 A2
Prichard Pl
4600 HdnC 40121 6373 E3
Prickly Pear Ct
1200 MDTN 40243 5620 D7
Primrose Ct
300 STMW 40207 5618 A2
Primrose Dr
- LYDN 40222 5619 A2
100 MTWH 40047 6056 D2
300 STMW 40207 5618 A2
1000 JFVL 47130 5507 C3
Primrose Ln
100 RDCF 40160 6592 D1
200 CLKV 47129 5397 E3
Primrose Wy
- NALB 47150 5504 C3
500 LSVL 40206 5617 B4
Primula Pl
4600 LSVL 40272 5940 D4
Prince Ct
- BltC 40071 5948 C4
Prince Ln
4000 JFTN 40299 5728 D5
Prince George Ct
11300 FCSL 40241 5511 B2
Princess Ct
- BltC 40071 5948 C4
Princess Wy
6000 LSVL 40219 5836 A5
Princess Wood Ct
7900 LSVL 40214 5832 B4
Princeton Av
4800 LSVL 40258 5831 D3
Princeton Dr
600 CLKV 47129 5506 D3
600 ELZT 42701 6813 D2
1800 LSVL 40205 5616 E7
1800 LSVL 40205 5617 A7
Prince William St
5700 STMW 40207 5618 A5
Princewood Pl
5100 LSVL 40216 5832 B1
Principal Ct
100 RDCF 40160 6483 E6
Priority Wy
1800 JFTN 40299 5729 C1
Priscilla Ct
10 LSVL 40216 5723 A3
Privilege Wy
- LSVL 40219 5834 D7
Probus Dr
100 MTWH 40047 6056 B5
Proctor Ct
2400 LSVL 40218 5726 D2
Proctor Dr
200 ELZT 42701 6703 C7
Proctor Ln
100 BltC 40165 6163 C1
Proctor Knott Dr
2400 LSVL 40218 5726 D2
2600 LSVL 40220 5726 D2
Produce Plz
200 LSVL 40202 5615 E3
Produce Rd
3800 LSVL 40213 5726 A6
3800 LSVL 40218 5726 B5
3800 PLRH 40213 5726 A6
3800 PLRH 40218 5726 B6
4200 WSNP 40218 5726 C4
Production Blvd
1400 JFVL 47130 5506 E1
1400 JFVL 47130 5507 A2
Production Ct
200 ELZT 42701 6812 E7
1800 JFTN 40299 5619 E7
Production Dr
1900 JFTN 40299 5619 E7
1900 JFTN 40299 5728 E1
Profit Ct
4100 NALB 47150 5396 A4
Progress Blvd
800 NALB 47150 5396 A5
900 FydC 47150 5396 A5
4100 LSVL 40218 5726 E5
Progress Wy
1000 SLRB 47172 5288 E6
1700 CLKV 47129 5397 D5
1800 JFVL 47129 5397 D5
1800 JFVL 47130 5397 D5
5000 SLRB 47172 5289 A6
Promenade Ct
- JFTN 40223 5619 D4
100 LSVL 40223 5619 D4
Propeller Ln
6000 ClkC 47172 5398 A2
Prospect Av
9200 LYDN 40242 5510 C7
Prospect St
1000 NALB 47150 5505 B4
8900 LYDN 40242 5510 C7
Prospect Glen Wy
13100 OdmC 40059 5292 B7
Prosperity Ct
100 LSVL 40211 5614 D3
Providence
10500 LSVL 40291 5837 C7
Provincetown Pl
8900 LDNP 40242 5510 C5
Proximity Dr
4600 LSVL 40213 5726 A6
Pruitt Ct
4300 LSVL 40218 5726 D5
Pryor Av
- LSVL 40206 5616 E1
- LSVL 40206 5617 A1
7100 CTWD 40014 5403 E7
7200 CTWD 40014 5512 E1
Pryor Ln
- CTWD 40014 5403 E7

STREET Block City ZIP Map# Grid

Pryor Valley Rd
100 BltC 40165 6052 B6
Pueblo Rd
5300 INHC 40207 5509 A7
Pulaski Ct
4500 WTNH 40245 5511 D2
Pulliam Dr
3700 LSVL 40218 5727 A3
Puma Run
10 LSVL 40258 5830 E6
10 LSVL 40258 5831 A6
Punkin Patch Dr
- FydC 47150 5613 C2
Purdue Ct
10 ELZT 42701 6811 D2
Puritan Ct
7100 LSVL 40214 5833 C3
Putman Av
6300 LSVL 40216 5722 A4
PX Dr
- HdnC 40121 6374 B4
Pyle Dr
2400 LSVL 40219 5834 C6
2400 MLHT 40219 5834 C6
Pyramid Rd
11200 LSVL 40229 5944 D5
Pyrus Ln
5200 LSVL 40258 5831 C5

Q

Quad Rd
1000 JFVL 47130 5507 B5
Quadrant Av
1400 LSVL 40204 5616 D6
1400 LSVL 40205 5616 D6
Quail Ct
4900 LSVL 40213 5726 A6
4900 PLRH 40213 5726 A6
Quail Hllw
4900 LSVL 40213 5726 A6
Quail Brace Ct
7000 GNSP 40241 5509 E1
Quail Chase
6800 ClkC 47111 5290 B1
Quail Chase Ct
2500 CLKV 47172 5288 B7
2500 FydC 47172 5288 B7
Quail Hollow Ct
3700 LSVL 40241 5509 D2
Quail Hollow Rd
100 BltC 40165 6162 D5
Quail Meadow Ter
8000 LYDN 40222 5619 C3
Quail Meadow Trc
8000 LYDN 40222 5619 C3
Quail Ridge Rd
7100 LSVL 40291 5836 C1
Quail Ridge Tr
1500 FydC 47150 5287 E7
Quail Roost Rd
- HdnC 40160 6592 D2
- RDCF 40160 6592 D2
Quail Run Rd
100 ELZT 42701 6702 E4
300 ELZT 42701 6703 A4
Quails Run
500 STMW 40207 5618 C4
Quailwood Dr
6400 FydC 47119 5393 E4
Quaker Ct
1200 LSVL 40214 5832 E3
Quaker St
- HdnC 40121 6374 D3
Quality Av
100 NALB 47150 5396 A4
Quality Ct
- CHAN 47111 5181 D6
100 ClkC 47111 5181 E3
100 ClkC 47111 5182 A3
Quality Choice Pl
1100 LSVL 40210 5615 B5
Quarry Dr
7000 CTWD 40014 5403 D7
Quarry Rd
1400 JFVL 47130 5507 A3
3400 FydC 47119 5504 A3
3400 FydC 47150 5504 A3
3900 FydC 47150 5503 C5
Quarry St
1800 LSVL 40206 5616 D3
Quarry Hill Rd
1600 LSVL 40213 5725 D2
Quartermaster St
10 HdnC 40121 6374 B4
Quartz Rd
1100 CLKV 47129 5506 E6
Queen Av
1000 LSVL 40215 5724 B3
Queen St
10 HdnC 40121 6374 C3
Queen Annes Ct
11900 WTNH 40245 5511 D2
Queens Ct
- BltC 40071 5948 D4
Queens Castle Rd
5100 LSVL 40229 5944 D2
Queens Falls Ct
6600 LSVL 40229 5945 B3
Queenwood Rd
3200 LSVL 40272 5832 B7
Quest Dr
500 LSVL 40203 5615 C3
1200 LSVL 40213 5725 D6
Quiet Wy
1100 FydC 47150 5503 E3
1100 FydC 47150 5504 A3
4000 LSVL 40219 5835 B1
Quiet Creek Ct
100 LSVL 40229 5943 E2
100 LSVL 40229 5944 B2
Quietside Ct
100 RDCF 40175 6482 E2
Quiet Water Dr
5200 ClkC 47130 5398 B4
Quiet Wood Ct
100 LSVL 40229 5944 A2
Quill St
100 LSVL 40206 5616 C2
Quillman Dr
2100 LSVL 40214 5832 D2
Quillman Hill Rd
2200 LSVL 40214 5832 C2
Quince Al
200 ELZT 42701 6812 C3
Quince Ct
10800 LSVL 40223 5620 A1
Quincetree Dr
2300 CLKV 47129 5397 B6
Quincy St
1300 LSVL 40206 5616 B2
Quindero Run
7200 LSVL 40228 5836 C5
Quinn Ct
2200 SVLY 40216 5723 A6
Quinn Dr
2300 SVLY 40216 5722 E6
4700 LSVL 40216 5723 A6
4700 SVLY 40216 5723 A6
Quinton Dr
3200 LSVL 40216 5723 A2

R

Rabbit Run
- MdeC 40175 6373 B7
Rabbit Run SR-1816
- MdeC 40175 6373 B7
Rabbit Hash Ridge Rd
11500 HsnC 47117 6155 C1
Raccoon Run Ct
6200 LSVL 40241 5509 C2
Race Rd
11300 LSVL 40291 5946 E1
Raceland Park Av
- LSVL 40218 5727 B6
Rachel Ct
6000 FydC 47122 5502 E6
Rachel Dr
1100 LSVL 40219 5835 A4
Rachel Tyne Wy
6200 FydC 47122 5503 A4
Rachelwood Ct
11000 DGSH 40243 5620 C6
11000 MDTN 40243 5620 C6
Racine Av
900 LSVL 40215 5724 B2
Radclift Trailer Park
- RDCF 40160 6483 C3
Radford Rd
10100 BRMR 40223 5619 E5
10100 JFTN 40223 5619 E5
Radiance Rd
3000 LSVL 40220 5618 A7
3000 LSVL 40220 5727 A1
Radio Dr
4000 WSNP 40218 5726 B3
Radio St
100 HdnC 40121 6374 D2
Radleigh Ln
11000 LSVL 40291 5946 D4
Radleigh Pl
- LSVL 40291 5946 D4
Radnor Av
1800 LSVL 40205 5616 D7
Rail Fence Lp
10 HdnC 42701 6593 C7
Railroad Av
1100 SHDV 40165 6161 C5
5000 LSVL 40258 5831 D3
6400 CTWD 40014 5403 E7
8100 LYDN 40222 5619 A2
Railroad Av W
300 ELZT 42701 6812 C3
E Railroad Av
200 ELZT 42701 6812 C3
Railroad Trestle Rd
10 HdnC 40177 6155 E7
10 HdnC 40177 6156 A7
10 WPT 40177 6155 E7
10 WPT 40177 6156 A7
Railview Rd
2300 JFVL 47130 5398 A6
Railway Trestle Rd
- HdnC 40177 6155 E7
- HdnC 40177 6264 D1
- MdeC 40108 6264 C2
- MRGH 40155 6264 C2
Rainbow Dr
10 CLKV 47129 5397 E3
2800 LSVL 40206 5617 B4
3800 NALB 47150 5396 E5
7000 LSVL 40272 6048 C1
Rainbow Wy
- JFVL 47130 5507 E3
200 JFVL 47130 5508 A3
Rainbow Springs Ct
- LDNP 40241 5510 C5
9100 LSVL 40241 5510 C5
Rainfield Ct
3000 JFVL 47130 5507 A2
Rainmaker Ct
5200 LSVL 40229 5944 D2
Rainsplitter Ln NE
6500 HsnC 47136 5610 C6
Raintree Cir
- OdmC 40056 5512 E4
Raintree Ct
2300 CLKV 47129 5397 C6
3400 RVBF 40059 5292 A7
Raintree Dr
2300 CLKV 47129 5397 B6
7800 LSVL 40220 5727 E3
8500 LSVL 40220 5728 A3
8600 JFTN 40220 5728 B3
9000 JFTN 40299 5728 B3
Raintree Pl
3600 LSVL 40220 5727 E3
8600 JFTN 40220 5728 B4
8600 LSVL 40220 5728 B4
Raintree Gardens St
100 LSVL 40218 5727 B4
Rainview Cir
3200 LSVL 40220 5727 E3
Raleigh Dr
1600 CLKV 47129 5506 B1
E Raleigh Dr
1500 CLKV 47129 5506 B1
Raleigh Ln
2300 LSVL 40206 5617 A4
Raleigh Wy
100 ELZT 42701 6703 E7
Ralph Av
- LSVL 40216 5722 E1
2500 SVLY 40216 5723 B2
3100 LSVL 40216 5723 B2
3500 LSVL 40211 5723 A2
3800 LSVL 40211 5722 E1
Ralph Franklin Ln
- HdnC 42701 6702 A7
Ralph Franklin Rd
10 ELZT 42701 6702 B7
10 HdnC 42701 6702 B7
Ralston Av
7400 LSVL 40258 5831 D4
Ramblin Rd
100 BltC 40047 6056 C6
Ramblin Creek Rd
3500 LSVL 40299 5729 B5
Rambo Ct
8700 LSVL 40228 5836 C6
Rambo Wy
7200 LSVL 40228 5836 C5
Rameses Ct
100 BltC 40165 6160 D6
Rammers Av
1100 LSVL 40204 5616 B5
Ramona Av
3500 LSVL 40220 5726 E1
3500 LSVL 40220 5727 A1
Ramona Ct
800 HdnC 40160 6592 C4
Ramona Ln
4900 LSVL 40272 5940 C2
Ramser Av
3100 SVLY 40216 5723 D2
Ramsgate Ct
900 DGSH 40299 5620 D6
Ramsgate Gdns
200 BWDV 40207 5618 C3
200 STMW 40207 5618 C3
Ranch Rd
600 HdnC 40175 6592 A3
700 HdnC 40175 6591 E2
Ranchland Dr
4800 LSVL 40216 5723 A7
Ranchland Coach Ln
- RDCF 40160 6483 D7
Ranchland Coach Lamp Ln
- RDCF 40160 6483 D7
Rancho Dr
10200 LSVL 40272 5940 A2
Randa Lee Ct
6100 FydC 47122 5503 A4
Randolph Av
- CLKV 47129 5506 C4
3100 LSVL 40206 5617 C2
N Randolph Av
500 CLKV 47129 5506 C4
Randolph St
300 CHAN 47111 5181 C4
300 ClkC 47111 5181 C3
Random Wy
5300 LSVL 40291 5727 E7
5500 LSVL 40291 5836 E1
Randomwood Ct
8300 LSVL 40291 5836 D5
Randy Ct
7600 LSVL 40258 5830 D4
Ranelle Ct
2500 LSVL 40216 5723 A4
Rangeland Rd
1500 LSVL 40213 5726 B7
1500 LSVL 40219 5726 B7
1500 LSVL 40219 5835 C1
1700 LSVL 40218 5835 D1
1800 LSVL 40228 5835 E1
Ranger Dr
9700 LSVL 40229 5943 E2
Rangoon Wy
5100 LSVL 40218 5726 D7
Rankin Dr
1700 OdmC 40031 5297 C3
Rankin St
3900 LSVL 40214 5724 D3
Rannoch Ct
300 DGSH 40243 5620 B4
Rannoch Ln
11200 DGSH 40243 5620 B5
Ransdell Av
2400 LSVL 40204 5616 D4
Rasberry Wy
- JFVL 47130 5398 E7
Rasmussen Ct
1700 NALB 47150 5505 C3
Raspberry Wy
- JFVL 47130 5398 E7
Rassmoor Dr
4500 LSVL 40219 5835 C3
N Rastetter Av
100 LSVL 40206 5616 E2
S Rastetter Av
100 LSVL 40206 5616 E3
Ratcliffe Av
1800 LSVL 40210 5614 E7
Raunser Ct
10 LSVL 40216 5722 D6
Rausch Dr
2300 SVLY 40216 5723 B2
Raven Ct
1500 RDCF 40160 6483 A1
2900 JFTN 40220 5728 A2
Raven Rd
2500 OdmC 40031 5296 C7
4800 LYNV 40213 5725 D6
Ravencrest Ct
8100 LYDN 40222 5619 A1
Raven Ridge Dr
4300 LSVL 40216 5722 C4
Ravenwood Dr
4300 LSVL 40220 5618 C5
Ravina Av
2000 LSVL 40205 5617 A7
Rawlings St
500 LSVL 40208 5615 E7
500 LSVL 40217 5615 E7
Ray Av
1100 LSVL 40204 5616 D4
Ray Baer Blvd
- LSVL 40208 5615 D7
Rayburn Rd
5300 LSVL 40272 5940 B4
Raydale Dr
1500 LSVL 40219 5835 C7
Rayhill Rd
100 LSVL 40118 5942 C5
Raylee Dr
1200 CHAN 47111 5181 E3
Raymary Dr
5400 LSVL 40272 5940 B4
Raymond Rd
100 BltC 40165 6161 A2
100 SHDV 40165 6161 A2
1200 BltC 40165 6160 D2
Raymond Kent Ct
700 LSVL 40217 5724 E1
700 LSVL 40217 5725 B1
Ray Nan Dr
5600 LSVL 40229 5944 E4
Rays Lake Rd
- HdnC 40160 6592 D3
- RDCF 40160 6592 D3
Razor Ct
12600 LSVL 40299 5729 C7
12600 LSVL 40299 5838 C1
Razor Branch Ct
12700 LSVL 40299 5729 C6
Razor Creek Ct
12800 LSVL 40299 5729 C6
Razor Creek Wy
4500 LSVL 40299 5729 C6
R Chin Al
- LSVL 40208 5615 C6
Read Al
900 LSVL 40203 5615 C3
Reader Ln
100 BltC 40165 6053 E3
Reading Rd
800 LSVL 40217 5725 A1
800 PKWV 40217 5725 A1
1800 OdmC 44026 5292 A3
Reading Room Rd
11900 OdmC 40059 5292 D7
11900 OdmC 40059 5401 D1
Reality Tr
11400 HTCK 40229 5945 E3
Reamers Ln
- PWEV 40056 5512 D4
8900 LSVL 40245 5512 D4
9300 OdmC 40056 5512 D4
Reamers Rd
8600 LSVL 40245 5512 C4
8600 OdmC 40056 5512 C4
8600 PWEV 40056 5512 C4
Rear 9th St Al
1500 LSVL 40208 5615 C6
Rear South Pkwy
- LSVL 40214 5724 C4
Reas Ln
4000 FydC 47150 5396 B4
4000 NALB 47150 5396 B4
Reasor Av
900 LSVL 40217 5616 A7
Reasor Rd
6000 FydC 47119 5284 E7
Rebecca Ln
6600 LSVL 40258 5831 B2
Rebecca Jane Ln
- VNGV 40175 6482 D7
Rebecca Scott Wy
8500 LSVL 40228 5836 C6
Rebel Dr
100 PWEV 40056 5512 D2
Rebel Rd
10 LSVL 40206 5617 B2
Rebel Roost
300 ELZT 42701 6811 C1
Recruit Rd
- LSVL 40210 5615 A6
Rectangle Rd
100 HLVW 40229 5944 A6
Rector Ln
1500 NALB 47150 5396 E7
1500 NALB 47150 5397 A7
Red Apple Rd
6300 LSVL 40219 5835 E5
Red Barn Lp
- ClkC 47130 5398 C5
- JFVL 47130 5398 C5
Redberry Ct
7000 LSVL 40291 5837 A3
Red Birch Ct
10600 LSVL 40223 5620 A2
Red Bird Ct
100 BltC 40229 5944 D6
Red Bird Rd
5200 BltC 40229 5944 D6
Red Bud Cir
1600 RDCF 40160 6482 E4
1600 RDCF 40160 6483 A4
Redbud Cir
10 SpnC 40071 5949 A5
Redbud Ct
2900 OdmC 40031 5296 B7
Red Bud Dr
300 ELZT 42701 6703 A2
300 NALB 47150 5504 E1
Redbud Dr
100 MTWH 40047 6056 A5
8000 ClkC 47111 5181 B3
Redbud Ln
- BltC 40109 5943 E5
- LGNG 40031 5297 A6
- OdmC 40031 5297 A6
3000 LSVL 40220 5618 B7
3100 LSVL 40220 5727 B1
Redbud Rd
10 JFVL 47130 5508 A2
Redbud Forest Pl
4700 LSVL 40245 5511 E3
4700 LSVL 40245 5512 A2
Red Bud Hill Dr
8000 LSVL 40228 5836 E5
Red Cedar Wy
7900 LSVL 40219 5835 D5
Redcoat Ct
8700 LSVL 40291 5837 A3
Red Dawn Dr
4800 LSVL 40216 5722 D7
Red Deer Cir
8700 HBNA 40220 5619 B7
8700 HBNA 40220 5728 B1
Redden Ct
100 CLKV 47129 5506 C1
Redden Wy
- HsnC 47136 5610 D5
- LNVL 47136 5610 D5
Redden Wy NE
7200 LNVL 47136 5610 D6
Redding Rd
200 LSVL 40218 5727 C4
Redemption Wy
- LSVL 40245 5621 B6
Red Fern Rd
4900 LSVL 40218 5726 D7
Red Fox Dr
3600 FydC 47150 5396 D4
Red Fox Rd
1100 LSVL 40205 5617 B5
Redhaven Wy
- LSVL 40228 5836 A4
Red Hawk Dr
10 RDCF 40175 6482 E3
10 RDCF 40175 6483 A3
Red Hill Rd
10 RDCF 40160 6483 A2
10 RDCF 40175 6483 A2
100 HdnC 40175 6482 D4
1000 RDCF 40175 6482 E2
Red Leaf Ct
100 ELZT 42701 6702 C7
Red Leaf Dr
1900 BRWD 40242 5510 B6
2000 PNTN 40242 5510 B6
Redleaf Dr
- BRWD 40242 5510 B6
- PNTN 40242 5510 B6
Red Leaf Rd
5200 LSVL 40218 5726 E7
Redman Ct
4800 JFTN 40291 5728 B6
Red Maple Ct
11100 LSVL 40229 5944 B4
Red Maple Wy
4700 LSVL 40229 5944 C5
Redmar Blvd
100 RDCF 40160 6483 C1
300 HdnC 40121 6483 C1
Redmar Ln
100 RDCF 40160 6483 C1
Red Oak Ct
100 ELZT 42701 6702 E7
3900 OdmC 40031 5296 A7
3900 OdmC 40031 5405 A1
Red Oak Dr
- MTWH 40047 6055 E1
Red Oak Ln
4800 LSVL 40218 5726 D7
4800 LSVL 40219 5726 D7
Redondo Cir
5500 LSVL 40218 5726 D7
5500 LSVL 40218 5835 D1
Red Pine Dr
4700 HLVW 40229 5944 C5
4700 LSVL 40229 5944 C5
Red Plum Ter
7000 PWEV 40056 5512 D2
Red Rock Ct
6000 LSVL 40219 5836 A3
Red Rock Dr
- BltC 40165 6051 C5
Red Roof Inn Pl
3300 WSNP 40218 5726 B3
Red Run Ct
9900 LSVL 40291 5837 C6
Red Spruce Dr
6100 LSVL 40229 5945 A2
Redstart Rd
4800 LYNV 40213 5725 D5
Red Stone Hill Ct
8100 LSVL 40214 5832 D4
Red Stone Hill Rd
8200 LSVL 40214 5832 D4
Redwing Wy
4800 LYNV 40213 5725 D6
Redwood Ct
1200 JFVL 47130 5507 B2
Redwood Dr
200 NALB 47150 5504 E1
600 CLKV 47129 5397 C6
1600 LSVL 40213 5725 D3
Redwood Pl
2300 CLKV 47129 5397 A6
Redwood Wy
11500 ANCH 40223 5620 B3
Ree Ct
6200 LSVL 40216 5831 C1
Ree Dr
5600 LSVL 40216 5831 C1
5700 LSVL 40216 5722 C7
Reed St
300 LSVL 40217 5724 E2
5000 LSVL 40214 5833 B1
Reeds Ln
1100 JFVL 47130 5507 B3
Reel Dr
1600 OdmC 40031 5297 B3
Reel Dr W
1600 OdmC 40031 5297 B3
Reel Pl
1600 OdmC 40031 5297 B3
Reelfoot Lake Ct
6800 LSVL 40291 5837 C3
Reeser Pl
10 LSVL 40208 5615 C7
Reeves Rd
1000 LSVL 40219 5834 E4
Reflection Dr
5400 LSVL 40218 5726 D7
5600 LSVL 40218 5835 D1
Regal Dr
5400 LSVL 40218 5726 D7
5600 LSVL 40218 5835 D1
Regal Rd
- LSVL 40222 5509 C3
2500 OdmC 40031 5296 C7
6300 GNVH 40222 5509 C4
Regal Lily Ter
12600 MDTN 40243 5620 C7
Regal Pine Ct
8200 LSVL 40214 5832 B5
Regal Springs Ct
1400 STMW 40205 5618 A6
Regal Springs Dr
- LSVL 40205 5618 A6
6000 STMW 40205 5618 A5
Regan Av
2800 LSVL 40206 5617 A1
Regatta Cir
1300 LSVL 40211 5614 C5
Regatta Wy
3500 LSVL 40211 5614 C5
Regency Ct
400 STMW 40207 5618 B4
Regency Ln
6400 WDYH 40207 5509 C7
Regency Wy
1100 ELZT 42701 6703 E6
Regency Park Dr
1700 LSVL 40272 5832 D7
Regency Woods Wy
8000 LSVL 40220 5618 E7
8000 LSVL 40220 5619 A7
Regent Wy
5100 LSVL 40218 5726 D6
5400 LSVL 40228 5726 E7
Regents Park Rd
800 SLRB 47172 5288 C3
Regina Av
10 JFVL 47130 5508 A3
4200 WSNP 40213 5725 E4
E Rehl Ct
13600 LSVL 40299 5730 B3
W Rehl Ct
13500 LSVL 40299 5730 A2
Rehl Rd
10900 LSVL 40299 5729 E3
12400 LSVL 40299 5730 A2
Reichmuth Ln
100 BltC 40165 6161 A7
100 SHDV 40165 6161 A7
Reid Av
100 BltC 40165 6054 C5
100 LSVL 40213 5725 D3
Reidinger Rd
1600 FydC 47150 5287 E7
1600 FydC 47150 5288 A7
Reigate Ct
9200 HTBN 40222 5619 D6
Reigh Count Dr
6000 LSVL 40272 5940 A1
Reinhart Wy
8900 JFTN 40220 5728 B2
E Relender Rd
6700 FydC 47122 5393 E7
W Relender Rd
7000 FydC 47122 5393 D7
Remembrance Ln
11100 HTCK 40229 5945 D3
11200 LSVL 40229 5945 D3
Remington Ct
100 BltC 40165 6054 C2
Rems Ct
3500 LSVL 40241 5510 C3
3500 MRCK 40241 5510 C3
Rems Rd
- BKPT 40241 5510 C4
3400 LSVL 40241 5510 C3
3400 MRCK 40241 5510 C3
Renada Dr
5500 OdmC 40014 5513 A3
Renaissance Dr
4400 JFTN 40299 5728 C6
Renate Rd
6200 LSVL 40291 5837 A2
Rene Cir
2500 JFVL 47130 5507 C1
Renn Rd
1200 FydC 47119 5287 A3
Reno Av
2100 NALB 47150 5505 E4
Renown Ct
9800 JFTN 40299 5728 D1
Renown Dr
2200 JFTN 40299 5728 D1
Renwood Blvd
3200 LSVL 40214 5832 C2
Renwood Ct
7400 LSVL 40214 5832 C2
Renz Av
500 ClkC 47172 5288 E2
500 SLRB 47172 5288 D2
Republic Av
2800 RDCF 40160 6593 B1
2900 RDCF 40160 6484 B7
Research Dr
1500 JFVL 47130 5506 E2
1500 JFVL 47130 5507 A2
1700 JFTN 40299 5620 A7
Reservoir Av
200 LSVL 40206 5617 B2
4100 LSVL 40213 5725 C4
Resource Wy
1800 JFTN 40299 5729 C1
Rest Wy
6700 LSVL 40059 5400 C3
Rest Cottage Ln
10 PWEV 40056 5512 B2
Retreat Rd
4000 LSVL 40219 5835 B1
Reutlinger Av
1100 LSVL 40204 5616 B5
Reva Ridge Rd
10 HdnC 42701 6703 D4
Revere Dr
1200 ELZT 42701 6811 B5
1200 HdnC 42701 6811 B5
5400 LSVL 40218 5726 D7
5600 LSVL 40218 5835 D1
Revere Pl
5700 LSVL 40218 5835 D1
Revolutionary Ct
7500 LSVL 40214 5833 D5
Revolutionary Rd
200 LSVL 40214 5833 D5
Rex Ln
5000 LSVL 40218 5835 D1
Rexford Wy
3000 LSVL 40205 5726 B2
Reynolda Rd
9800 JFTN 40223 5619 D6
Reynolds Ln
2100 LSVL 40218 5726 E4
Reynolds St
200 CHAN 47111 5181 D5
Reynolds Run Rd
5100 OdmC 40014 5404 D3
Rhett Ct
2500 PNTN 40242 5510 B5
Rhett Butler Dr
8400 LSVL 40242 5510 B5
8400 PNTN 40242 5510 B5
Rhineland St
5900 HdnC 40121 6265 C7
Rhinestone Ct
100 ELZT 42701 6593 E7
Rhode Ct
1600 LGNG 40031 5297 A1
1600 OdmC 40031 5297 A1
Rhodes Dr
800 ELZT 42701 6812 D4
Rhonda Ct
800 RDCF 40160 6483 A3
Rhonda Dr
1000 JFVL 47130 5507 C3
Rhonda Wy
1300 LSVL 40216 5723 D5
Rhondean Dr
4300 LSVL 40216 5723 D6
Riata Ct
5300 LSVL 40218 5726 D7
5600 LSVL 40218 5835 D1
Ribble Rd
- LSVL 40205 5617 D7
- WLTN 40205 5617 D7
Rice Av
4400 LSVL 40209 5724 E4
Richard Av
3200 LSVL 40206 5617 D3
3200 LSVL 40207 5617 C3
3400 STMW 40207 5617 C3
Richard Ct
5200 OdmC 40014 5404 E3
Richards Ct
100 BltC 40165 6160 D5
Richardson Ct
100 ELZT 42701 6812 B4
Richelle Dr
3300 LSVL 40216 5723 A2
3300 SVLY 40216 5723 A2
Richie Ln
- LSVL 40272 6048 C2
Richiewayne Dr
6100 LSVL 40219 5836 A6
6200 LSVL 40228 5836 A6
Richland Av
2200 LSVL 40218 5727 B4
2800 LSVL 40220 5618 C6
4000 STMW 40207 5618 A2
Richland Dr
9000 GEOT 47122 5501 C4
9000 HsnC 47122 5501 C4
Richmond Dr
1600 LSVL 40205 5616 D7
Richmont Rd
3400 LSVL 40216 5722 E3
Richwood Wy
1000 LGNG 40031 5297 A4
Rick Cir Dr NE
7500 HsnC 47136 5610 E6
Ridan Wy
7300 LSVL 40214 5832 D3
Riddle Rd
1200 NALB 47150 5504 E6
Riddle St
- JFVL 47130 5506 E5
E Riddle St
100 JFVL 47130 5506 E5
W Riddle St
100 JFVL 47130 5506 E5
Riders Row Ct
4600 SRPK 40220 5618 E5

INDEX 40
Ridge Ct
Rose Ter

Louisville Metro Street Index

STREET Block City ZIP Map# Grid

Ridge Ct
1400 ANCH 40223 5620 B1
Ridge Rd
- BltC 40165 6163 C3
10 LSVL 40205 5616 E7
100 BltC 40165 6162 E5
300 CHAN 47111 5181 C5
300 ClkC 47111 5181 C4
5600 OdmC 40014 5405 B6
11000 ANCH 40223 5620 C1
12100 LSVL 40223 5620 D2
12400 MDTN 40223 5620 E2
Ridge Rd SR-146
11400 ANCH 40223 5620 C1
Ridge Rd SR-1442
- BltC 40165 6163 C3
100 BltC 40165 6162 E5
Ridgeback Rd
- LSVL 40291 5837 D7
Ridge Brook Cir
- LSVL 40245 5512 D6
Ridge Brook Ct
3200 OdmC 40059 5291 E6
3200 OdmC 40059 5292 A6
Ridge Cliff Rd
6400 HWCK 40228 5836 C2
6400 LSVL 40228 5836 C2
Ridge Creek Ct
6000 LSVL 40291 5836 C1
Ridge Creek Rd
7100 LSVL 40291 5836 C1
Ridgecrest Cir
3900 OdmC 40014 5404 D3
Ridgecrest Ct
100 BltC 40165 6162 E5
700 SpnC 40071 5948 E7
700 SpnC 40071 5949 A7
3700 OdmC 40059 5401 B1
5100 OdmC 40014 5404 D3
Ridge Crest Dr
12200 WDHL 40243 5620 D5
Ridgecrest Dr
300 ELZT 42701 6703 C5
Ridgecrest Dr NE
2200 LNVL 47136 5610 D5
Ridgecrest Rd
10 SpnC 40071 5949 A6
600 SpnC 40071 5948 E7
5300 LSVL 40218 5726 D7
5500 LSVL 40218 5835 D1
5700 LSVL 40219 5835 D1
Ridgedale Rd
300 LSVL 40206 5617 A2
Ridge Farm Ct
7000 LSVL 40291 5836 E4
Ridgefield Dr
5600 ClkC 47111 5290 B3
Ridgefield Rd
- LSVL 40213 5725 E2
Ridgehurst Ct
3800 LSVL 40299 5727 E4
Ridgehurst Pl
- LSVL 40218 5727 E4
- LSVL 40299 5728 A4
7700 LSVL 40299 5727 E4
Ridge Lake Dr
11300 LSVL 40272 5940 B4
Ridgeleigh Ln
18900 LSVL 40245 5623 A5
Ridge Line Dr
1100 LSVL 40207 5617 E5
1100 LSVL 40207 5618 A5
Ridge Lock Ct
12800 OdmC 40059 5401 B1
Ridgemar Ct
2500 JFTN 40299 5729 A2
Ridgemont Dr
10 RDCF 40175 6482 E2
12200 PNRV 40229 5944 B7
12300 PNRV 40229 6053 A1
Ridgemont Rd
12300 PNRV 40229 5944 B7
Ridgemoor Ct
3100 OdmC 40059 5292 B7
Ridgemoor Dr
12500 OdmC 40059 5292 A6
12500 OdmC 40059 5401 C1
Ridge Park Ct
7900 LSVL 40258 5831 A4
Ridge Point Wy
6800 ClkC 47111 5290 B1
Ridge Run Cir
6900 PROS 40059 5400 D6
Ridge Run Rd
6900 FydC 47122 5502 D3
7000 GEOT 47122 5502 D3
Ridgeside Ct
7000 LSVL 40291 5837 D4
Ridge Side Dr
- FydC 47150 5396 E5
Ridgeside Dr
9500 LSVL 40291 5837 C4
Ridge Stone Ct
9500 LSVL 40299 5728 A5
Ridgestone Dr
2400 ELZT 42701 6703 A1
2400 HdnC 42701 6703 A1
Ridge Top Ct
3500 LSVL 40241 5509 D3
Ridgeview Av
2400 LSVL 40220 5618 D5
Ridge View Ct
- SHDV 40165 6162 A7
100 BltC 40165 6162 E6
Ridgeview Dr
100 CLKV 47129 5397 E3
2000 FydC 47119 5395 D1
Ridgeway Av
200 STMW 40207 5618 A2
1300 NALB 47150 5504 E6
2300 LSVL 40204 5616 D5
Ridgeway Cor
200 BLWD 40207 5617 E1

Ridgeway Ct
1300 JFVL 47130 5507 B2
4700 PNRV 40229 5944 B7
Ridgeway Dr
1200 JFVL 47130 5507 B2
E Ridgeway Dr
1400 JFVL 47130 5507 C2
Ridgewood Av
2500 LSVL 40217 5725 A1
E Ridgewood Cir
8600 MLHT 40219 5834 D7
W Ridgewood Cir
8500 MLHT 40219 5834 C7
Ridgewood Ct
10 HdnC 42701 6593 E7
3100 FydC 47119 5394 D6
Ridgewood Dr
1900 JFVL 47130 5398 B7
1900 JFVL 47130 5507 B1
3000 FydC 47119 5394 D6
3300 NALB 47150 5396 C6
Ridgewood Rd
500 LSVL 40207 5617 B1
500 MKBV 40207 5617 B1
Ridge Wy Rd
100 BltC 40165 6054 A1
Riding Ridge Rd
10 PROS 40059 5401 A4
Riedley Ct
4100 LSVL 40216 5723 A3
4100 SVLY 40216 5723 A3
Riedley Rd
3500 LSVL 40216 5723 A2
3500 SVLY 40216 5723 A3
Riedling Dr
2700 LSVL 40206 5617 A1
Rigel Ct
10 MTWH 40047 6056 A2
Riggs Dr
6800 LSVL 40291 5836 D3
Rihn Ct
10 ELZT 42701 6812 B1
Riley Av
100 CHAN 47111 5181 C4
100 ClkC 47111 5181 C4
1700 LSVL 40208 5615 C7
8900 LYDN 40242 5510 B7
Riley Dr
- ClkC 47172 5288 E2
Riley Rd
- ClkC 47172 5288 E2
700 ClkC 47172 5289 A2
E Riley Rd
2600 FydC 47119 5504 B1
W Riley Rd
2300 FydC 47119 5503 E2
2300 FydC 47119 5504 A1
Riley St
100 ClkC 47172 5288 E1
100 ClkC 47172 5289 A1
Riley Ridge Rd
5900 FydC 47136 5611 E4
5900 FydC 47136 5612 A4
Rimfire Rd
10000 LSVL 40291 5837 C1
Rimonte Dr
- LSVL 40220 5727 D1
Rineyville Rd
300 ELZT 42701 6702 D7
300 HdnC 42701 6702 B6
6800 HdnC 40162 6591 B5
7800 HdnC 40175 6591 B5
Rineyville Rd SR-1600
300 ELZT 42701 6702 D7
300 HdnC 42701 6702 B6
6800 HdnC 40162 6591 B5
7800 HdnC 40175 6591 B5
Rineyville-Big Springs Rd
- HdnC 42701 6593 B6
- RDCF 42701 6593 B6
Rineyville-Big Sprs Rd SR-220
- HdnC 42701 6593 B6
- RDCF 42701 6593 B6
Ring Rd
- ELZT 42701 6812 E1
100 ELZT 42701 6811 B2
200 BWDV 40207 5618 C3
700 HdnC 42701 6811 B1
1000 HdnC 42701 6702 B7
1200 ELZT 42701 6702 C6
1900 ELZT 42701 6703 B4
2100 HdnC 42701 6703 D7
Ring Rd SR-3005
- ELZT 42701 6812 E1
100 ELZT 42701 6811 B2
700 HdnC 42701 6811 B2
1000 HdnC 42701 6702 B7
1200 ELZT 42701 6702 C6
1900 ELZT 42701 6703 B4
2100 HdnC 42701 6703 B4
Ringold Al
- ELZT 42701 6812 C3
Rio Grande Dr
4000 OdmC 40031 5404 E2
Rio Rita Av
2800 LSVL 40220 5726 E2
2800 LSVL 40220 5727 A1
Rio Vista Dr
- LSVL 40207 5508 C6
10 INDH 40207 5508 C5
Rio Vista Ln
- JFVL 47130 5508 A2
Ripple Ln
500 LSVL 40218 5726 C7
Ripple Creek Dr
3500 LSVL 40229 5943 E3
3600 LSVL 40229 5944 A3
Risen Rd
- BltC 40229 5945 D6
100 LSVL 40229 5945 D6
Rising Oak Ct
5100 LSVL 40245 5511 D2

Rising Oak Ct
5100 WTNH 40245 5511 D2
Rising Star Ct
14700 LSVL 40272 5939 D7
Rita Dr
1800 NALB 47150 5396 C7
Rita Ln NE
6900 FydC 47122 5501 B3
Rita Mary Ct
4500 PNRV 40229 6053 B1
Ritz Ct
- LSVL 40212 5505 D7
Rivanna Dr
4100 JFTN 40299 5728 C5
Riva Ridge Pt
7800 LSVL 40214 5832 E3
Riva Ridge Rd
1900 LSVL 40214 5832 E3
River Rd
100 LSVL 40202 5616 A2
300 LSVL 40206 5616 A2
2000 LSVL 40206 5507 D7
2900 LSVL 40207 5507 D7
3000 LSVL 40207 5508 A6
3700 INDH 40207 5508 B5
4400 GNVW 40207 5508 D3
4400 GNVW 40222 5508 C4
4800 GNVW 40222 5509 A2
4900 LSVL 40222 5509 A1
5300 LSVL 40059 5509 A1
5600 LSVL 40059 5400 A7
6500 PROS 40059 5400 C5
River Rd E
100 ClkC 47111 5181 B4
River Rd W
200 ClkC 47111 5181 B4
W River Rd
- LSVL 40202 5615 D2
River Trc
100 BltC 40165 6161 A2
River Bend Dr
2500 LSVL 40206 5507 D7
2500 LSVL 40206 5508 A7
2500 LSVL 40206 5616 E1
River Birch Ct
9800 LSVL 40291 5946 D1
River Birch Dr
9600 LSVL 40291 5946 D1
Riverbirch Dr
6600 OdmC 40056 5512 E4
River Birch Wy
11000 LSVL 40291 5946 C2
River Bluff Ct
13300 RVBF 40059 5401 A1
River Bluff Rd
10 INDH 40207 5508 C5
10 LSVL 40207 5508 C5
3300 OdmC 40059 5401 B1
3300 RVBF 40059 5401 A1
3500 RVBF 40059 5292 A7
3600 RVBF 40059 5291 E7
3700 OdmC 40059 5291 E7
River Chase Ct
3300 LSVL 40218 5726 B5
Riverchase Dr
100 BltC 40047 6056 A6
River Chase Rd
- BltC 40047 6056 A6
River City Park Rd
2700 JFVL 47130 5398 D6
River Creek Ct
5300 LSVL 40059 5400 B6
River Creek Dr
5800 LSVL 40059 5400 B6
River Crest Ct
800 LSVL 40206 5507 D7
River Crest Dr
800 LSVL 40206 5507 D7
800 LSVL 40206 5616 E1
Riverdale Rd
6200 LSVL 40272 5939 E3
6200 LSVL 40272 5940 A3
River Dell Ct
800 LSVL 40206 5507 E7
River Dell Dr
800 LSVL 40206 5507 E7
River Edge Dr
- BltC 40165 6162 C2
- SHDV 40165 6162 C2
River Farm Cove
3700 OdmC 40059 5291 D7
3700 OdmC 40059 5400 D1
River Field Dr
7100 LSVL 40258 5830 E4
River Forest Cir
200 JFVL 47130 5507 E4
River Forest Dr
6200 LSVL 40258 5831 B2
River Forest Pkwy
- JFVL 47130 5507 E3
River Forest Pl
8300 LSVL 40258 5831 B2
River Front Dr
4500 LSVL 40216 5722 B2
River Glen Ln
13900 OdmC 40059 5291 D7
River Green Cir
2600 LSVL 40206 5507 E7
River Hill Ln
4300 INDH 40207 5508 D6
River Hill Rd
10 INDH 40207 5508 D5
10 RVWD 40207 5508 D6
River Knoll Dr
5000 GNVW 40222 5509 A1
5000 LSVL 40222 5509 A1
Rivermist Wy
4400 LSVL 40207 5508 D4
Rivermont Ct
2500 LSVL 40206 5507 D7
Riveroaks Cir
3800 LSVL 40241 5511 B2
River Oaks Cir
- BltC 40165 6161 A2

River Oaks Dr
100 BltC 40165 6161 A2
100 SHDV 40165 6161 A3
800 JFVL 47130 5508 A2
2500 LSVL 40206 5507 E7
Riveroaks Ln
3800 LSVL 40241 5511 B3
W River Park Dr
3000 LSVL 40211 5614 C2
River Pointe Dr
6200 LSVL 40258 5831 B3
River Pointe Pl
6800 LSVL 40258 5831 B3
Riverpointe Plz
10 JFVL 47130 5506 D7
10 JFVL 47130 5615 E1
Riverport Dr
6900 LSVL 40258 5830 E1
7300 LSVL 40258 5721 D7
Riverport Rd
- SHDV 40165 6161 D5
River Ridge Dr
100 BltC 40165 6163 D3
River Ridge Rd
- ClkC 47130 5400 B1
10 ClkC 47130 5291 A6
River Ridge Cove
3600 OdmC 40059 5291 D7
3600 PROS 40059 5291 D7
River Rock Dr
100 BltC 40165 6162 C1
Rivers Edge Ct
4200 LSVL 40207 5508 D4
Rivers Edge Rd
2800 LSVL 40207 5508 D4
Riverside Dr
10 NALB 47150 5505 E4
900 LSVL 40207 5508 C4
1000 OdmC 40059 5291 D3
E Riverside Dr
100 JFVL 47130 5507 A7
400 CLKV 47129 5506 D7
900 LSVL 40207 5508 C4
W Riverside Dr
100 CLKV 47129 5506 D7
100 JFVL 47130 5507 A7
200 JFVL 47130 5616 A1
400 JFVL 47130 5615 E1
600 JFVL 47130 5506 E7
900 LSVL 40207 5508 C4
Riverstone Cir
10200 LSVL 40229 5944 D1
River Terrace Dr
8500 LSVL 40258 5831 B3
River Terrace Pl
6200 LSVL 40258 5831 B2
River Trace Dr
- BltC 40165 6161 A2
River Trail Dr
9400 LSVL 40229 5944 D2
River Trail Pl
5200 LSVL 40229 5944 D2
Riverview Av
4500 LSVL 40211 5614 A3
Riverview Dr
700 WPT 40177 6156 B2
3100 JFVL 47130 5508 B4
Riverview Ln
100 SHDV 40165 6162 A3
Riverwalk Av
9600 LSVL 40229 5944 D1
Riverway Dr
6700 LSVL 40059 5400 C4
River Wind Dr
6900 LSVL 40258 5831 B3
Riverwood Dr
200 JFVL 47130 5508 B3
600 LSVL 40207 5508 A7
Riverwood Pl
600 LSVL 40207 5508 A7
River Woods Ct
2300 JFVL 47130 5507 E3
Riviera Dr
4200 INDH 40207 5508 C5
4200 LSVL 40207 5508 C4
Rivulet Ct
4100 LSVL 40299 5729 B5
Rivulet Ln
4000 LSVL 40299 5729 B5
Roadway Av
900 LSVL 40208 5724 B1
Roanoke Av
- OdmC 40014 5512 A1
1800 LSVL 40205 5616 E7
2500 NALB 47150 5505 C1
2600 NALB 47150 5396 D7
Robards Ct
3400 WSNP 40213 5726 A4
3400 WSNP 40218 5726 A4
Robards Ln
4300 WSNP 40213 5726 A4
4300 WSNP 40218 5726 A4
4600 LSVL 40218 5726 A4
Robbie Valentine Dr
400 RDCF 40160 6483 D4
Robbins Ln
10 VNGV 40175 6591 D1
Robbins Rd
8400 LSVL 40258 5831 C6
Robbs Ln
5100 LSVL 40219 5835 D5
Robert Ct
100 MTWH 40047 6056 C1
Robert Rd
11500 ANCH 40223 5620 B3
11500 LSVL 40223 5620 B3
Roberta Ct
8600 LSVL 40291 5837 C6
Robert Burden Rd
100 BltC 40165 6160 C1
Roberts Av
400 LSVL 40214 5833 C2
Roberts Ct
100 HdnC 40121 6373 E4

Robertson Dr
1400 OdmC 40014 5405 E4
Robin Cir
800 RDCF 40160 6483 C5
Robin Ct
- BltC 40165 6053 D3
- HBNE 40165 6053 D3
10 NALB 47150 5505 C1
6800 OdmC 40014 5404 D7
9100 GEOT 47122 5501 D3
9200 FydC 47122 5501 D3
Robin Dr
1000 JFVL 47130 5507 A4
3500 SVLY 40216 5723 D3
Robin Ln
100 BltC 40165 6054 B7
2000 JFVL 47130 5507 D1
17400 LSVL 40245 5622 E2
Robin Ln NE
2600 LNVL 47136 5610 D4
Robin Rd
100 BltC 40229 5944 D6
300 ELZT 42701 6812 B2
900 RDCF 40160 6483 B5
2600 NALB 47150 5505 C1
3200 ANPK 40213 5725 B3
3200 LSVL 40213 5725 B3
6600 CTWD 40014 5512 E1
29600 ClkC 47106 5283 D1
29600 FydC 47165 5283 D1
E Robin Rd
2500 NALB 47150 5505 C1
W Robin Rd
2500 NALB 47150 5505 C1
Robin Wy
100 BltC 40165 6053 B4
Robina Ct
200 ELZT 42701 6702 E6
Robindale Ct
11800 MDTN 40243 5620 C5
Robindale Rd
11700 DGSH 40243 5620 C5
11700 MDTN 40243 5620 C5
Robin Hill Ct
8400 LSVL 40291 5837 A5
Robin Hill Dr
8400 LSVL 40291 5836 D5
8400 LSVL 40291 5837 A5
Robinhood Ln
5800 LSVL 40219 5835 A1
Robin Lynn Dr
200 NALB 47150 5505 A1
Robinlynn Ln
11700 MDTN 40243 5620 C5
Robinson Ct
10 ELZT 42701 6812 B3
Robinson Rd
10 LSVL 40214 5833 D5
Robinson Park Dr
- LYDN 40222 5619 A1
Robinwood Rd
5200 LSVL 40218 5726 D7
5700 LSVL 40218 5835 D1
5800 LSVL 40219 5835 D1
Rob Roy St
6600 LSVL 40214 5833 D2
Robsion Rd
9900 JFTN 40299 5728 D5
Rochelle Rd
7600 LSVL 40228 5836 B6
Rochester Dr
100 LSVL 40214 5724 D7
Rochester Rd
200 LSVL 40214 5724 C7
Rockaway Cir
4800 LSVL 40216 5722 C5
Rockaway Dr
2900 LSVL 40216 5722 C5
Rock Bass Ct
11500 LSVL 40241 5402 B7
Rock Bay Ct
13500 LSVL 40245 5512 B4
Rock Bay Dr
3600 LSVL 40245 5512 B4
Rockbridge Rd
800 MDTN 40243 5620 E6
800 MDTN 40299 5620 D6
Rock Brook Cir
8400 LSVL 40220 5728 A3
Rock Brook Ct
3200 LSVL 40220 5728 A3
Rock Castle Villa Dr
100 BltC 40165 6054 A7
Rock Cliff Ct
100 LSVL 40218 5726 C2
Rock Creek Dr
- LSVL 40206 5617 C4
3000 LSVL 40207 5617 C4
Rock Falls Ct
10300 JFTN 40223 5619 E6
Rock Falls Trc
1200 JFTN 40223 5619 E6
Rockfish Ct
10100 LSVL 40291 5837 D6
Rockford Ln
1500 LSVL 40216 5723 A6
1800 SVLY 40216 5723 A6
2300 SVLY 40216 5722 E6
3100 LSVL 40216 5722 D6
Rockford Ln SR-2051
1800 LSVL 40216 5723 A6
1800 SVLY 40216 5723 A6
2300 LSVL 40216 5722 D6
2300 SVLY 40216 5722 E6
E Rockford Ln
1600 LSVL 40216 5723 B7
1600 SVLY 40216 5723 B7
Rockford Plz
4700 LSVL 40216 5723 A6
4700 SVLY 40216 5723 A6
Rock Forest Dr
6800 LSVL 40219 5835 E3
Rockhaven Dr
2800 LSVL 40220 5618 C6

Rock Hill Rd
7000 PROS 40059 5400 D5
Rock Hollow Dr
6800 LSVL 40219 5835 D2
6800 LSVL 40219 5836 A3
Rockhurst Ct
9200 LSVL 40299 5728 A5
Rockingham Ct
6300 PROS 40059 5401 A5
Rockingham Rd
7500 PROS 40059 5400 E4
7500 PROS 40059 5401 A5
Rockledge Rd
10 GNVW 40222 5508 E2
10 GNVW 40222 5509 A3
Rock Moss Ct
10700 LSVL 40291 5837 E6
Rock Rose Ln
3500 OdmC 40031 5295 E7
3500 OdmC 40031 5404 E1
Rock Spring Ct
12000 CDSM 40245 5511 D1
Rock Spring Dr
11900 CDSM 40245 5511 D1
Rockstone Pl
400 DGSH 40243 5620 A5
Rockview Wy
6600 LSVL 40299 5838 A2
Rockvine Ct
8300 LSVL 40299 5728 A5
Rock Wall Ct
8200 LSVL 40220 5728 B4
Rockwood Ct
100 BltC 40047 6055 A2
Rockwood Dr
3600 FydC 47119 5395 A4
4300 LSVL 40220 5618 D6
Rockwood Ln
100 BltC 40047 6055 A2
Rockwood Rd
7200 LSVL 40219 5835 D4
Rocky Ln
7100 LSVL 40228 5836 E7
Rocky Lp
1300 ELZT 42701 6702 E6
Rocky Rd
10900 BltC 40229 5945 B5
10900 LSVL 40229 5945 A7
11500 BltC 40165 5945 A7
Rocky Tr
9700 LSVL 40299 5837 D1
Rockycreek Ln
9500 LSVL 40299 5947 E2
Rocky Gap Rd
8100 LSVL 40214 5833 C6
Rocky Mountain Dr
5800 LSVL 40219 5835 D2
5900 LSVL 40219 5836 A3
6200 LSVL 40228 5836 A3
Roddy Rd
2400 LSVL 40216 5831 C1
Roden Ct
11300 FCSL 40241 5511 C2
11300 LSVL 40241 5511 C2
Rodes Ct
6000 NHFD 40222 5509 B5
Rodes Dr
6100 LSVL 40222 5509 B5
6100 NHFD 40222 5509 B5
Rodgers Ln
100 BltC 40109 6052 D2
100 BltC 40165 6052 A4
100 HLVW 40109 6052 D2
700 HLVW 40165 6052 E2
Rodgers Rd
5200 LSVL 40258 5831 C5
Rodman St
- LSVL 40215 5724 C2
2300 LSVL 40208 5724 C1
Rodney Cir
8400 LSVL 40219 5836 A6
Rodney St
1700 RDCF 40160 6483 E6
Rod N Reel Ct
6500 LSVL 40229 5945 B3
Rod N Reel Rd
9800 LSVL 40229 5945 A3
Roederer Dr
5500 LSVL 40219 5835 C2
Roe Hill Rd
100 BltC 40165 6050 D3
1400 BltC 40109 6050 C3
Rogawa Ct
13700 LSVL 40299 5729 D5
Roger E Schupp St
3300 LSVL 40205 5617 E7
Rogers Av
5200 BltC 40165 5944 D6
5200 HLVW 40229 5944 D6
Rogers Dr
100 BltC 40165 6053 C4
Rogers Ln
7000 LSVL 40272 6048 D2
Rogers St
1000 LSVL 40204 5616 B4
1400 RDCF 40160 6483 D6
Rogers Wy
- BltC 40165 6160 B2
Rogers Lake Rd
10 MdeC 40175 6482 A2
Rogersville Rd
100 RDCF 40160 6483 E6
900 VNGV 40160 6483 D6
1000 VNGV 40160 6592 B1
1900 VNGV 40175 6592 A1
Rogersville Rd SR-1500
100 RDCF 40160 6483 E6
900 VNGV 40160 6483 D6
1000 VNGV 40160 6592 B1
1900 VNGV 40175 6592 A1
Roland Av
8000 LYDN 40222 5619 A2
Roland St
300 LSVL 40203 5615 E5

Rolling Ln
10 CLKV 47129 5397 E3
400 RLGF 40207 5508 C7
400 RLGF 40207 5617 D1
Rolling Creek Blvd
7100 HWCK 40228 5836 C3
7100 LSVL 40228 5836 C3
Rolling Creek Dr
- NALB 47150 5396 B6
2800 ClkC 47130 5399 B3
Rolling Fork Rd
- BltC 40165 6054 A7
Rolling Hills Ln NE
7500 HsnC 47136 5610 D7
Rolling Hills Lp
- RDCF 40160 6484 A6
Rolling Hills Tr
1900 LSVL 40023 5731 B2
Rolling Oaks Blvd
3200 LSVL 40214 5832 C1
3300 LSVL 40216 5832 C1
Rolling Ridge Ln
2300 BltC 40165 6163 A2
Rolling Ridge Rd
5400 LSVL 40214 5723 E7
Rolling Rock Ct
5300 LSVL 40241 5402 A7
Rolling Springs Ct
14000 LSVL 40245 5512 B4
Rolling Springs Pl
13900 LSVL 40245 5512 B4
Rolling Stone Ct
3600 LSVL 40229 5943 E3
Rolling Stone Dr
10100 LSVL 40229 5943 E3
10100 LSVL 40229 5944 A2
Rollington Rd
100 LSVL 40056 5512 A2
100 LSVL 40245 5512 A2
100 OdmC 40056 5512 B1
100 PWEV 40056 5512 B1
Rollingwood Ln
1000 GSHN 44026 5292 C3
Rollingwood Tr
5200 LSVL 40214 5833 B2
Roma Av
600 JFVL 47130 5507 D4
Roman Ct
8800 LSVL 40291 5728 A7
Roman Dr
4900 JFTN 40291 5728 A7
4900 JFTN 40299 5728 A7
4900 LSVL 40291 5728 A7
Roman St
1400 RDCF 40160 6484 A6
Romania Dr
3600 LSVL 40216 5832 A2
Romara Pl
500 LYDN 40222 5619 A3
Rome Rd
3100 LSVL 40216 5723 C7
Rome Beauty Pl
7400 LSVL 40228 5836 C6
Rome Beauty Wy
8100 LSVL 40228 5836 C6
Ronald Ct
4100 LSVL 40216 5723 A3
4100 SVLY 40216 5723 A3
Ronald Ace Cir
6800 OdmC 40014 5404 D6
Ronan Dr
7300 LSVL 40258 5831 A3
Ronda Av
4300 SVLY 40216 5723 A5
Ronnie Av
2100 LSVL 40216 5831 E1
Ronnie Ct
300 MRGH 40155 6264 C3
Ronwood Dr
4900 LSVL 40219 5835 D4
Roofing Rd
4600 LSVL 40218 5726 A4
Rookwood Av
5100 LSVL 40218 5726 D7
Roosevelt
- HdnC 40121 6265 B7
Roosevelt Av
1300 NALB 47150 5505 C2
1600 LYDN 40242 5510 C7
1600 LYDN 40242 5619 C1
3700 WBHL 40218 5726 C4
4100 LSVL 40213 5725 C4
Roosevelt Dr
1100 JFVL 47130 5507 B3
1900 ClkC 47172 5397 D1
Roper Ln
- BltC 40165 6054 D2
Rory Wy
8000 LSVL 40219 5835 C5
Rosa Ter
3700 SVLY 40216 5723 D3
Rosaire Dr
- LSVL 40272 5940 A5
Rosalee Av
2800 LSVL 40220 5726 E1
Rosalind Av
- NALB 47150 5504 E6
Rosalind Ct
4900 LSVL 40218 5726 C7
Rosary Ct
5500 LSVL 40218 5726 D7
Rose Av
700 JFVL 47130 5507 D4
Rose Ct
10 LSVL 40208 5615 C7
400 JFVL 47130 5508 A4
Rose Dr
- OdmC 40014 5402 B5
600 NALB 47150 5505 B2
800 LSVL 40213 5834
1100 LSVL 40213 572
1100 LYNV 40213 572
Rose Ter
- HdnC 40121

INDEX 41

Rosebank Ct

Louisville Metro Street Index

Santee Pth

STREET
Block City ZIP Map# Grid

Rosebank Ct
100 LSVL 40118 5942 C2
Roseborough Ct
6900 LSVL 40228 5836 B6
Roseborough Rd
8200 LSVL 40228 5836 C6
Rosebowl Ct
8300 LSVL 40291 5836 E5
Rose Creek Dr
500 VNGV 40160 6483 B7
Rosedale Av
- ODGH 40014 5511 B1
- OdmC 40014 5511 B1
1800 LSVL 40205 5616 E6
Rosedale Blvd
3000 LSVL 40220 5618 A7
3000 LSVL 40220 5727 A1
Rosedale Dr
300 ELZT 42701 6812 A3
Rosedale Rd
7300 ODGH 40014 5402 E7
7300 ODGH 40014 5511 B1
7300 OdmC 40014 5402 E7
7300 OdmC 40014 5511 B1
Rose Farm Dr
4500 LSVL 40258 5831 E3
Rose Island Rd
7500 LSVL 40059 5400 D1
7500 PROS 40059 5400 D1
8000 OdmC 40059 5400 D1
Rose Island Rd SR-3222
7500 LSVL 40059 5400 D1
7500 PROS 40059 5400 D1
8000 OdmC 40059 5400 D1
N Rose Island Rd
1000 OdmC 40059 5291 E2
1000 OdmC 40059 5292 A1
N Rose Island Rd SR-3222
2400 OdmC 40059 5291 D7
Roselane Ct
- LSVL 40203 5615 E4
Roselane St
700 LSVL 40203 5616 A4
700 LSVL 40204 5616 A4
Roselawn Av
300 JFVL 47130 5507 A4
1600 NALB 47150 5505 D1
Roselawn Blvd
3000 LSVL 40220 5727 B2
Roselawn Ct
10 JFVL 47130 5506 E3
Rose Marie Dr
10 HdnC 42701 6702 B5
Rosemary Dr
900 LSVL 40213 5725 B2
Rosemary Ln
7500 LSVL 40214 5832 B2
7500 LSVL 40258 5832 B2
Rosemont Av
3800 LSVL 40220 5618 C7
Rosemont Blvd
3700 LSVL 40218 5727 A2
Rosemont Ct
3600 LSVL 40218 5727 A2
3600 LSVL 40220 5727 A2
Rosette Blvd
5000 LSVL 40218 5726 D7
Roseview Ter
500 NALB 47150 5505 B2
Rose Wedge Wy
3200 LSVL 40216 5722 D5
Rosewell Av
1300 LSVL 40211 5614 C5
Rosewood Av
1400 LSVL 40204 5616 C6
Rosewood Cir
- LSVL 40219 5834 D6
Rosewood Ct
400 BRMR 40223 5619 E4
Rosewood Dr
- CLKV 47129 5397 E3
- DGSH 40243 5619 E4
10 CLKV 47129 5506 B3
10 JFVL 47130 5508 B3
100 NALB 47150 5396 C6
200 BRMR 40223 5619 E4
500 CHAN 47111 5181 D3
E Rosewood Dr
100 CLKV 47129 5506 C2
W Rosewood Dr
100 CLKV 47129 5506 B2
Rosewood Ln
12100 OdmC 44026 5292 C2
Rosewood Pl
- LGNG 40031 5296 B3
Rosewood Rd
2800 OdmC 40031 5296 B7
5700 OdmC 40014 5405 B6
Rosewood Rd SE
- HsnC 47117 6048 A4
Rosewood Wy
2200 LSVL 40214 5723 D7
Rose Wycombe Ln
14300 OdmC 40059 5291 E7
Ross Av
1600 JFVL 47130 5507 A4
Ross Blvd
3300 LSVL 40220 5727 B1
Ross Dr
2400 NALB 47150 5505 D2
Rosshire Dr
8700 LSVL 40118 5833 E7
Ross Hollow Rd
4100 FydC 47150 5612 D4
Rossmore Dr
100 NALB 47150 5504 E1
Rosswood Ct
8100 LSVL 40291 5836 E4
Rosswoods Dr
100 PWEV 40056 5512 B1
Rostrevor Cir
1100 LSVL 40205 5617 B5

Roswell Wy
7700 LSVL 40218 5727 D5
Roth Rd
8500 LSVL 40219 5835 E6
8500 LSVL 40219 5836 A7
8500 LSVL 40229 5836 A7
Rothbury Ct
11100 DGSH 40243 5620 B5
Rothbury Ln
500 DGSH 40243 5620 B5
E Rouck Rd
1200 FydC 47150 5503 E3
W Rouck Rd
4700 FydC 47150 5503 D4
Rouge Wy
3700 LSVL 40218 5727 A2
Round Hill Rd
5800 GNVW 40222 5509 A3
Round Ridge Rd
1800 RVWD 40207 5508 D5
Roundstone Ct
200 JFTN 40223 5619 D4
Roundstone Trc
9900 JFTN 40223 5619 D4
Round Table Ct
1000 STMW 40222 5618 D1
Roundtree Ct
3800 OdmC 40014 5513 E1
Rousseau Ct
2400 JFTN 40220 5728 B2
Roution Wy
- BltC 40165 6051 C6
Routt Dr
10 ELZT 42701 6702 D4
Routt Rd
200 LSVL 40299 5730 E6
3500 LSVL 40299 5731 A7
4300 LSVL 40023 5731 A7
5800 LSVL 40299 5840 A3
7100 LSVL 40299 5839 E7
8100 LSVL 40299 5948 D3
9500 BltC 40299 5948 D3
11700 BltC 40071 5948 D3
Routt Rd SR-1531
4300 LSVL 40023 5731 A7
4300 LSVL 40299 5730 E7
4300 LSVL 40299 5731 A7
5800 LSVL 40299 5840 A3
7100 LSVL 40299 5839 E7
8100 LSVL 40299 5948 D3
9500 BltC 40299 5948 D3
11700 BltC 40071 5948 D3
Rowan St
1100 LSVL 40202 5615 C2
1400 LSVL 40203 5615 B2
2000 LSVL 40212 5615 A1
2500 LSVL 40212 5614 E1
Rowena Rd
3400 LSVL 40218 5726 D2
Rowland Av
2600 LSVL 40206 5617 A3
Rowley Ln NE
6600 HsnC 47122 5501 C3
Rowntree Rd
9800 JFTN 40299 5728 D3
Roxann Blvd
4600 LSVL 40218 5727 C6
Roxbury Rd
4100 LSVL 40218 5727 B3
Roy Dr
4100 LSVL 40220 5727 C3
Roy St
- GEOT 47122 5501 E4
Royal Av
- LGNG 40031 5296 C3
1200 LSVL 40204 5616 C7
1200 LSVL 40213 5616 C7
Royal Ct
10 LSVL 40214 5833 D5
Royal Dr
10 LSVL 40214 5833 D6
Royal Gardens Ct
1000 LSVL 40214 5833 A4
Royal Links Dr
7000 LSVL 40228 5727 B7
Royal Oak Ct
4000 FydC 47150 5396 D2
4400 OdmC 40014 5513 C1
Royal Oak Dr
4100 FydC 47150 5396 C2
7400 OdmC 40014 5513 D1
8800 LSVL 40272 5832 C6
Royal Oaks Wy
3300 JFVL 47130 5508 A2
Royal Troon Ct
4800 FydC 47119 5503 D1
Royalty Av
7800 GYDL 40222 5509 E7
Royalwood Dr
7300 LSVL 40214 5832 D3
Royce Ct
10300 LSVL 40241 5511 A1
Roycewood Ct
1900 LSVL 40214 5832 E4
Roycewood Rd
7900 LSVL 40214 5832 E4
Roy Cole Dr
- CLKV 47129 5506 D5
Royer Ct
100 LSVL 40206 5617 B2
Roy Pom Dr
3000 LSVL 40220 5727 C3
Royster Wy
2400 LSVL 40258 5831 C2
S Roy Wilkins Av
300 LSVL 40202 5615 C3
300 LSVL 40203 5615 C2
Roy Williams Pl
5000 LSVL 40218 5727 B6
5000 LSVL 40228 5727 B6
Rubel Av
500 LSVL 40204 5616 B4
Ruben Ln
600 LSVL 40118 5833 E6

Ruby Ct
10 ELZT 42701 6702 D6
Ruby Dr
100 ELZT 42701 6702 E6
Ruby Wy
4900 HBNE 40165 6053 D3
Ruck Ln
1900 JFVL 47130 5507 C2
Rucker Ridge Ln
8700 LSVL 40299 5839 D7
Ruckriegel Pkwy
3200 JFTN 40299 5729 A4
3200 LSVL 40299 5729 A4
3500 JFTN 40299 5728 E4
Ruckriegel Pkwy SR-1819
3200 JFTN 40299 5729 A4
3200 LSVL 40299 5729 A4
3500 JFTN 40299 5728 E4
Rudd Av
3000 LSVL 40212 5505 D6
Ruddell Rd
4500 JFVL 47130 5398 B5
Rudgate Ct
1200 LSVL 40214 5832 E3
Rudie Dr
2000 JFVL 47130 5507 D4
Rudolph Ct
100 BltC 40165 6160 E4
Rudy Ln
600 WDYH 40207 5509 B7
1800 LSVL 40207 5509 C7
1800 WNDF 40207 5509 C7
4200 STMW 40207 5618 B1
4300 WDYH 40207 5618 B1
Rue la Grande
500 ELZT 42701 6811 D2
Rufer Av
1200 LSVL 40204 5616 B5
Rufing Rd
8500 FydC 47124 5284 A5
Rufus Ln
100 BltC 40047 6055 C2
Rugby Ct
1100 HTBN 40222 5619 C6
Rugby Pl
700 HTBN 40222 5619 C6
Rundill Rd
- LSVL 40214 5832 E2
- LSVL 40214 5833 A2
1500 LSVL 40214 5723 E7
1500 LSVL 40214 5724 A7
Runell Rd
1000 LSVL 40214 5833 A4
Runic Wy
4900 LSVL 40218 5726 C7
4900 LSVL 40219 5726 C7
Running Brook Tr
2300 LSVL 40023 5731 C2
Running Creek Cir
100 PNRV 40229 6053 A2
Running Creek Ct
100 PNRV 40229 6053 A2
Running Creek Dr
- HLVW 40229 6053 A1
100 PNRV 40229 6053 A2
Running Creek Pl
500 DGSH 40243 5620 C5
Running Creek Rd
11600 DGSH 40243 5620 C5
Running Deer Cir
3000 LSVL 40241 5509 D4
Running Fox Cir
8600 LSVL 40291 5837 A3
Running Fox Dr
4700 FXCH 40165 6053 A3
Running Spring Ct
4500 LSVL 40241 5510 B2
Running Spring Dr
8300 LSVL 40241 5510 B2
Running Water Ln
4000 BWNF 40241 5510 B3
4000 LSVL 40241 5510 B3
Runnymeade Ct
3100 GNVH 40222 5509 B4
Runnymeade Rd
3100 GNVH 40222 5509 B4
Rural Wy
4900 LSVL 40218 5726 D7
5400 LSVL 40228 5726 E7
Rush Ct
8000 LSVL 40214 5832 B5
Russell Al
- LSVL 40203 5616 C4
Russell Av
100 LGNG 40031 5297 A2
1600 LSVL 40213 5725 D3
7400 LSVL 40258 5831 D4
Russell Lee Dr
1500 LSVL 40211 5614 C6
Russett Blvd
5300 LSVL 40218 5835 D1
Russett Pl
5800 LSVL 40218 5835 D1
Rustburg Ct
12000 WTNH 40245 5511 D1
Rustburg Pl
4700 WTNH 40245 5511 D1
Rustic Wy
5400 LSVL 40218 5726 C7
5400 LSVL 40219 5726 C7
5600 LSVL 40218 5835 C1
5600 LSVL 40219 5835 C1
Rustic Hills Ct
4000 FydC 47119 5394 D4
Rustling Tree Wy
9500 LSVL 40291 5837 B1
Rustoak Ln
8200 LSVL 40219 5835 B6
Rutgers Ct
11100 LSVL 40291 5946 D1
Rutgers Dr
9700 LSVL 40291 5946 D1
Ruth Av
1600 LSVL 40205 5616 D7

Ruth Av
1600 LSVL 40213 5616 D7
Rutherford Av
1800 LSVL 40205 5616 E7
1900 LSVL 40205 5617 A7
Rutherford Wynd
2200 LSVL 40205 5617 A6
Ruth Haven Ct
2400 JFTN 40220 5728 B2
N Rutland Av
4600 LSVL 40215 5724 B5
S Rutland Av
4600 LSVL 40215 5724 B6
Rutland Rd
13600 OdmC 44026 5292 A3
13700 OdmC 44026 5291 E3
13900 OdmC 40059 5292 A3
Rutland Club Ct
1400 LSVL 40245 5622 B2
Rutledge Rd
6600 LSVL 40258 5831 A3
7200 LSVL 40258 5830 E3
Ryan Ct
1000 RDCF 40160 6483 A2
Ryan Ln
1400 CLKV 47129 5506 B2
Ryan Wy
10 LSVL 40118 5942 B1
Ryder Ln
- SpnC 40071 6057 D1
Rymer Wy
600 LSVL 40223 5619 D3

S

Saberdee Dr
8400 PNTN 40242 5510 A5
Sabine Wy
- HLVW 40229 5944 C5
Sable Mill Ln
2800 JFVL 47130 5507 A1
Sable Wing Cir
1400 LSVL 40223 5620 A1
Sable Wing Ct
10500 LSVL 40223 5620 A1
Sable Wing Pl
10900 LSVL 40223 5620 A1
Sacred Heart Ln
100 LSVL 40206 5617 C3
Saddle Ct
2600 SRPK 40220 5618 E6
Saddle Dr
- ClkC 47111 5181 B3
Saddleback Dr
10 ClkC 47111 5181 B3
Saddle Blanket Dr
5900 LSVL 40219 5835 E4
Saddlebrook Ct
4900 LSVL 40216 5722 D6
Saddlebrook Dr
7400 FydC 47124 5283 A5
Saddlebrook Ln
4800 LSVL 40216 5722 D6
Saddlecreek Ct
4000 LSVL 40245 5512 A4
Saddlecreek Dr
13500 LSVL 40245 5512 A4
Saddle Horn Dr
2800 LSVL 40220 5618 E6
2800 SRPK 40220 5618 E6
Saddle Horse Wy
7500 LSVL 40291 5837 A4
Saddle Pointe Dr
10200 LSVL 40291 5946 C3
Saddleview Ct
6400 LSVL 40228 5836 A4
Saddlewood Ct
3300 NALB 47150 5396 A6
Sadie Av
1700 LSVL 40216 5723 C5
1700 SVLY 40216 5723 C6
Sadie Ln
- SVLY 40216 5723 C6
1500 LSVL 40216 5723 C6
Sadler Mill Rd
4600 OdmC 40031 5295 C4
Safari Tr
10 HdnC 40175 6482 E1
10 RDCF 40175 6482 E2
Safe Harbor Cir
1900 LSVL 40216 5831 E2
1900 LSVL 40216 5832 A1
Saffron Av
1700 LSVL 40258 5831 E3
Sagamore Rd
100 INDH 40207 5617 D1
Sage Rd
100 BWDV 40207 5618 C3
100 STMW 40207 5618 C3
Sagebrush Ct
9000 LSVL 40228 5836 E6
Saginaw St
300 LSVL 40209 5724 D5
300 LSVL 40214 5724 D5
Saguaro Ct
100 HLVW 40229 5944 C5
Saguaro Dr
100 HLVW 40229 5944 B5
Sailor Rd
7600 LSVL 40291 5837 B6
St. Andrews Ct
1800 LGNG 40031 5297 B6
4200 FydC 47150 5396 E2
St. Andrews Dr
500 HdnC 40175 6482 A7
500 HdnC 40175 6591 A1
8200 LSVL 40291 5837 D6
St. Andrews Rd
2000 JFVL 47130 5398 B7
2400 JFVL 47130 5507 C1
St. Andrews Wy
- ELZT 42701 6702 D1
St. Andrews Church Rd
7300 LSVL 40214 5832 C2

St. Andrews Church Rd
7700 LSVL 40258 5832 B3
8100 LSVL 40258 5831 E4
St. Andrews Church Rd SR-1931
7300 LSVL 40214 5832 C2
7700 LSVL 40258 5832 B3
8100 LSVL 40258 5831 E4
St. Andrews Village Cir
3500 LSVL 40241 5510 A4
St. Andrews Village Dr
8000 LSVL 40241 5510 A4
St. Anthony Pl
700 LSVL 40204 5616 B4
St. Anthony Church Rd
7100 LSVL 40214 5832 C3
7100 LSVL 40258 5832 C3
St. Anthony Gardens Dr
3000 LSVL 40214 5832 B3
St. Anthony Woods Ct
7800 LSVL 40214 5832 C4
St. Armands Ct
8300 LSVL 40219 5835 E6
St. Bernard Ct
7700 LSVL 40291 5836 D3
St. Bernard Wy
7600 LSVL 40291 5836 D4
St. Bridgids St
500 VNGV 40175 6591 E1
E St. Catherine St
100 LSVL 40203 5615 E5
600 LSVL 40203 5616 A5
800 LSVL 40204 5616 A5
W St. Catherine St
100 LSVL 40203 5615 D5
1100 LSVL 40210 5615 B5
St. Cecilia St
2500 LSVL 40212 5614 E1
St. Charles Ln
4100 LSVL 40218 5726 D5
St. Claire Dr
12300 MDTN 40243 5620 E2
12700 MDTN 40223 5620 E2
St. Claude Ct
4500 JFTN 40299 5728 E6
St. Dennis Av
3000 LSVL 40216 5723 A3
4200 SVLY 40216 5723 A3
St. Edwards Dr
3500 JFTN 40299 5728 D4
St. Francis Av
3700 WBHL 40218 5726 E4
St. Francis Ct
100 LSVL 40205 5617 A6
St. Francis Ln
4000 LSVL 40218 5726 D5
St. Gabriel Ct
5200 LSVL 40291 5728 A7
St. Gabriel Ln
5200 LSVL 40291 5728 A7
5400 LSVL 40291 5837 A1
St. George Ln
8400 LSVL 40220 5619 A6
St. Georges Ct
4600 FydC 47119 5503 D1
St. Germaine Ct
3500 LSVL 40207 5617 E4
3500 STMW 40207 5617 E4
3700 STMW 40207 5618 A4
3900 NBNE 40207 5618 A3
St. Ives Ct
3900 NBNE 40207 5618 A4
St. James Av
300 ELZT 42701 6812 B1
St. James Ct
1400 LSVL 40208 5615 D6
St. Joe Rd
- ClkC 47172 5288 D2
E St. Joe Rd
100 ClkC 47172 5288 B3
400 ClkC 47143 5288 C2
400 SLRB 47172 5288 B3
W St. Joe Rd
1600 ClkC 47172 5287 E3
1600 ClkC 47172 5288 A3
2500 ClkC 47143 5287 D3
St. Joe Sta
4200 FydC 47150 5396 C2
St. John Rd
- HdnC 42701 6811 C3
100 ELZT 42701 6812 A1
600 ELZT 42701 6811 E2
St. John Rd SR-1357
- ELZT 42701 6811 E2
- HdnC 42701 6811 C3
St. John St
- LSVL 40212 5614 E1
St. Johns Pl
2100 LSVL 40210 5614 E7
St. Johns Rd
- ClkC 47143 5287 D3
- FydC 47172 5287 B3
3100 FydC 47122 5392 A6
3100 FydC 47124 5392 A5
4100 ClkC 47119 5287 A2
10100 ClkC 47106 5284 E1
St. Johns Church Rd NE
1400 HsnC 47136 5611 A5
2000 HsnC 47136 5610 E5
2100 LNVL 47136 5610 E5
St. Joseph Av
4100 SVLY 40216 5723 C5
St. Joseph Rd
- NALB 47150 5396 D4
3000 FydC 47150 5396 C3
St. Joseph St
200 LSVL 40203 5615 D5
St. Jude Av
1400 LSVL 40215 5723 E6
St. Leo Pl
4800 LSVL 40214 5724 D6
St. Louis Av
1000 LSVL 40208 5615 B6
2000 LSVL 40210 5615 A5

St. Louis Av
2100 LSVL 40210 5614 E5
St. Marys Dr NE
- HsnC 47136 5610 E5
2500 LNVL 47136 5610 E4
St. Marys Rd
3000 FydC 47119 5395 B5
St. Matthews Av
100 LSVL 40207 5618 A3
100 STMW 40207 5617 E2
100 STMW 40207 5618 A2
200 BLWD 40207 5617 E1
200 CYWV 40207 5617 E2
200 DRDH 40207 5617 E1
200 LSVL 40207 5617 E1
St. Michael St
1100 LSVL 40204 5616 B6
St. Michael Church Dr
3700 LSVL 40220 5727 B1
St. Michaels Dr
100 CHAN 47111 5181 D3
St. Moritz Dr
9200 LSVL 40291 5728 C7
St. Paul Ct
1000 LSVL 40203 5616 A5
St. Paul St
100 SLRB 47172 5288 D3
St. Pauls Church Rd
4200 LSVL 40258 5831 E3
4200 LSVL 40258 5832 A3
St. Peters Church Rd
- HsnC 47112 5610 B7
- HsnC 47136 5610 B7
St. Peters Church Rd NE
1200 HsnC 47112 5610 B7
1300 HsnC 47136 5610 B7
St. Regis Ln
4300 LNSH 40220 5618 D7
4300 SRPK 40220 5618 D7
St. Rene Ct
4300 JFTN 40299 5729 A6
St. Rene Rd
10100 JFTN 40299 5728 D6
10700 JFTN 40299 5729 A6
11000 LSVL 40299 5729 A6
St. Rita Dr
4400 LSVL 40219 5835 B6
St. Roche Dr
10400 JFTN 40299 5728 E6
St. Thomas Av
4200 LSVL 40218 5727 B4
St. Thomas Ct
6400 LSVL 40218 5727 B3
St. Xavier St
2100 LSVL 40203 5615 A1
2100 LSVL 40212 5615 A1
2500 LSVL 40212 5614 D2
2600 LSVL 40212 5505 E7
Sale Av
1000 LSVL 40215 5724 A3
1600 LSVL 40215 5723 E3
Salem Av
1000 LSVL 40210 5615 A4
Salem Rd
- ClkC 47130 5290 B7
- ClkC 47130 5399 B1
Salem Noble Rd
4700 ClkC 47111 5290 A6
4700 ClkC 47130 5290 A6
5000 ClkC 47111 5289 E5
Salem-Noble Rd
7800 ClkC 47111 5289 B1
Salford Ct
700 HTBN 40222 5619 B5
Salford Wy
8200 HTBN 40222 5619 A5
Salisbury Sq
4700 BWDV 40207 5618 C3
4700 STMW 40207 5618 C3
Sallee Ln
3700 GNVW 40222 5509 B2
Sally Dr
8400 LSVL 40258 5831 C6
Salsman Dr
8800 JFTN 40220 5728 A1
Salt Lick Rd
3000 OdmC 40014 5405 C6
Salt River Ct
- WPT 40177 6156 D3
Salt River Dr
10 WPT 40177 6156 C3
2300 SHDV 40165 6162 A3
Salt River Rd
- SHDV 40165 6161 D6
Salt River Rd SR-2237
- SHDV 40165 6161 D6
Salt River Plant Rd
100 SHDV 40165 6161 C5
Saltsman Ln
100 RDCF 40160 6483 A1
500 RDCF 40160 6374 A7
Saltwell Rd
- BltC 40165 6161 C3
100 SHDV 40165 6161 B3
Sam Ct
100 RDCF 40160 6592 E2
7500 LSVL 40214 5833 C4
Sam Dr
400 LSVL 40214 5833 D4
Samara Dr
4500 LSVL 40219 5726 C7
Sames Rd
1000 CLKV 47129 5506 B3
Sammy Ct
700 ELZT 42701 6811 D3
Sammy's Ct
100 MTWH 40047 6055 D6
Samoa Wy
800 LSVL 40207 5617 D4
Samoset Ct
4100 LSVL 40299 5728 B5
Sample Ct
13600 LSVL 40245 5512 B5

Sample Wy
3400 LSVL 40245 5512 A5
Sampsons Rd
100 BltC 40165 6160 D5
Sam Stewart Dr
1800 RDCF 40160 6592 C1
Samuel St
900 LSVL 40204 5616 A6
1100 LSVL 40217 5616 B6
Samuel Long Wy
6800 LSVL 40229 5945 A4
Samuel's Cir
- OdmC 40014 5404 D6
Samuel's Ct
- OdmC 40014 5404 C6
Samuels Ct
100 BltC 40165 6051 B6
Samuels Rd
300 BltC 40165 6051 A6
Sanctuary Ln
8600 LSVL 40291 5837 C7
Sand Dr
1400 LSVL 40258 5832 A3
Sandalwood Ct
7900 LSVL 40219 5835 A5
Sandalwood Dr
2800 FydC 47150 5397 B2
Sandbourne Wy
10400 LSVL 40241 5511 A3
Sand Dollar
3600 JFVL 47130 5507 A1
Sand Dollar Ct
100 SHDV 40165 6161 C3
Sanders Ln
1500 LSVL 40216 5723 C6
1700 SVLY 40216 5723 C5
E Sanders Ln
100 BltC 40047 6057 B2
100 MTWH 40047 6057 B2
N Sanders Ln
1200 BltC 40109 6052 D1
1200 HLVW 40109 6052 D1
Sanders Gate Rd
7000 LSVL 40214 5832 E2
Sanderson St
2300 NALB 47150 5505 D2
Sanderstead Trc
12600 LSVL 40245 5511 E2
Sandhill Rd
4500 LSVL 40219 5835 C5
Sandidge Dr
8200 LSVL 40228 5836 C6
Sand Lake Ct
1100 LSVL 40272 5940 B4
Sand Lake Dr
5200 LSVL 40272 5940 C4
Sandness Ct
800 DGSH 40243 5620 A5
Sandra Ct
600 LSVL 40211 5614 C2
700 RDCF 40160 6483 D5
Sandra Dr
100 BltC 40047 6056 B5
100 MTWH 40047 6056 B5
800 JFVL 47130 5507 C4
Sandray Blvd
13700 LSVL 40272 6048 C2
Sandstone Blvd
6800 LSVL 40219 5835 E3
6800 LSVL 40219 5836 A3
Sand Stone Ct
- JFVL 47130 5399 A6
Sandstone Dr
900 JFVL 47130 5399 A7
1200 JFVL 47130 5398 E6
Sandwich Pl
9000 LDNP 40242 5510 C5
Sandwood Pl
11200 LSVL 40272 5940 C4
Sandy Dr
- BltC 40165 6054 A7
100 BltC 40165 6053 E7
Sandy Ln
- BltC 40165 6054 A7
Sandybrook Ct
2100 OdmC 40031 5296 D5
Sandy Hill Rd
7500 BltC 40109 5943 D5
Sanford Av
4100 LSVL 40218 5727 A6
Sanibel Wy
1000 LGNG 40031 5297 A4
Sanita Ct
4300 LSVL 40213 5725 D4
Sanita Rd
1400 LSVL 40213 5725 E4
1400 WSNP 40213 5725 E4
San Jose Av
1500 SVLY 40216 5723 C6
San Jose Ct
- SVLY 40216 5723 B6
San Marcos Rd
3900 LSVL 40299 5728 B5
4300 JFTN 40299 5728 B5
Sanna Dr
12200 HLVW 40229 5944 B7
Sanner Rdg
18000 LSVL 40023 5731 E1
Santa Fe Tr
5700 LSVL 40216 5722 A7
5700 LSVL 40258 5722 A7
6000 LSVL 40258 5831 A1
Santana Dr
10 ELZT 42701 6702 B6
10 HdnC 42701 6702 B6
Santa Paula Ln
4300 LSVL 40219 5835 B5
Santa Rosa Dr
5900 LSVL 40219 5835 E6
5900 LSVL 40219 5836 A6
Santee Pth
200 LSVL 40207 5509 A6
300 RBNW 40207 5509 A6

STREET Block	City	ZIP	Map#	Grid
Santom Ln				
6700	LSVL	40291	5837	B3
Sapling Spring Pl				
13400	LSVL	40245	5512	A5
Sappenfield Wy				
6700	LSVL	40272	6048	D1
Sara Ct				
100	SHDV	40165	6161	A6
Sara Ln				
8100	GEOT	47122	5502	A4
Sarah Ct				
10	SpnC	40071	5949	E3
500	JFVL	47130	5508	A4
Sarah Dr				
1000	LSVL	40219	5835	B6
Sarah Wy				
100	BltC	40165	6161	B1
100	SHDV	40165	6161	B1
Saranac Ct				
6300	LSVL	40214	5832	D1
Saratoga Ct				
1600	PNRV	40165	6053	C1
Saratoga Dr				
700	JFVL	47130	5508	B2
2300	LSVL	40205	5616	E7
2300	LSVL	40205	5617	A7
2300	LSVL	40205	5725	E1
2300	LSVL	40205	5726	B1
Saratoga Trc				
1600	OdmC	44026	5292	C4
Saratoga Wy				
100	BltC	40165	6054	A7
Saratoga Club Rd				
11500	LSVL	40299	5729	B6
Saratoga Estates Cir				
5300	LSVL	40299	5729	B7
Saratoga Estates Rd				
12100	LSVL	40299	5729	B7
Saratoga Hill Ct				
11500	LSVL	40299	5729	B6
Saratoga Hill Rd				
4300	LSVL	40299	5729	B6
Saratoga Ridge Dr				
11400	LSVL	40299	5729	B7
Saratoga View Ct				
12300	LSVL	40299	5729	B7
Saratoga View Pl				
5200	LSVL	40299	5729	B7
Saratoga Wood Ct				
11700	LSVL	40299	5729	C5
Saratoga Woods Dr				
4000	LSVL	40299	5729	C6
Sardis Wy				
8600	LSVL	40228	5836	E7
Sarles Creek Rd				
6000	FydC	47119	5394	A7
Sarver Ln				
10	HdnC	42701	6812	B7
100	BltC	40109	5943	D6
Sassafras Av				
800	JFVL	47130	5507	B6
Sassafras Rd				
4300	LSVL	40216	5722	E3
Sassafras Tree Dr				
13900	LSVL	40245	5621	B4
Satinwood Ct				
9100	LSVL	40229	5945	B1
Satterfield Ln				
500	ELZT	42701	6702	D6
Saturn Cir				
100	RDCF	40160	6483	B3
Saturn Dr				
9700	LSVL	40229	5944	A2
Sauer Al				
100	LGNG	40031	5296	E2
Saul's Ct				
100	BltC	40165	6160	D6
Saunders Av				
200	LSVL	40206	5616	E3
Saunders Ct				
100	LSVL	40211	5614	E4
Saurel Dr				
8500	PNTN	40242	5510	A5
Savage Dr				
4200	SVLY	40216	5723	B5
Savage St				
-	HdnC	42701	6593	D7
Savannah Dr				
400	ELZT	42701	6812	B1
500	ELZT	42701	6703	B7
1100	NALB	47150	5396	D6
2700	JFVL	47130	5398	C6
Savannah Rd				
2500	PNTN	40242	5510	B5
Savoy Ct				
10600	LSVL	40223	5620	A3
Savoy Rd				
600	LSVL	40223	5620	A3
Sawgrass Blvd				
3500	JFVL	47130	5398	A7
3500	JFVL	47130	5507	A1
Sawgrass Ct				
8100	LSVL	40291	5837	D6
Saw Mill Rd				
12400	LSVL	40272	5940	E6
12400	LSVL	40272	5941	A7
Sawyer Pl				
10500	LSVL	40241	5511	A5
Saxon Blvd				
5500	LSVL	40219	5835	E4
Saybrook Ct				
11000	LSVL	40229	5944	E5
11000	LSVL	40229	5945	A5
Scales Ct				
2700	JFVL	47130	5398	B5
Scales Dr				
4800	JFVL	47130	5398	B5
Scanlon St				
-	LSVL	40214	5724	C3
Scarborough Av				
9600	LSVL	40272	5941	C1
Scarlet Cir				
3500	ClkC	47130	5398	C4
Scarlet Ct				
200	VNGV	40160	6483	B6
Scarlet Oak Ct				
100	ELZT	42701	6702	E3
10400	LSVL	40241	5511	A2
Scarsdale Rd				
400	WDHL	40243	5620	D5
Scenic Ct				
-	MTWH	40047	6055	E6
-	RDCF	40160	6483	B2
Scenic Dr				
-	HsnC	47136	5610	D5
-	LNVL	47136	5610	D5
700	RDCF	40160	6483	B2
1300	CLKV	47129	5397	D5
3900	HBNE	40165	6053	D3
Scenic Dr NE				
-	LNVL	47136	5610	D5
2400	HsnC	47136	5610	C5
Scenic Hl				
10	PROS	40059	5401	A3
Scenic Lp				
-	JfnC	40204	5616	E4
-	JfnC	40206	5616	E5
-	LSVL	40204	5616	E5
-	LSVL	40205	5616	E5
-	LSVL	40205	5617	A5
-	LSVL	40206	5616	E4
-	LSVL	40206	5617	A5
Scenic Tr				
3700	HBNE	40165	6053	D2
7200	LSVL	40272	5939	C6
Scenic Valley Rd				
4000	FydC	47119	5394	C4
Scenic View Dr				
10	MTWH	40047	6055	E6
Scepter Ct				
-	LSVL	40219	5834	D7
Schad Dr				
3500	FydC	47150	5396	C4
Schaffer Ln				
-	ClkC	47129	5505	E2
1100	ClkC	47129	5506	A2
1100	CLKV	47129	5506	A2
Schaffner Av				
2100	LSVL	40210	5615	B7
Schaffner Dr				
2200	SVLY	40216	5723	B3
Schell Ln				
2400	NALB	47150	5505	B1
2700	NALB	47150	5396	B7
Scheller Av				
200	SLRB	47172	5288	D3
Scheller Ct				
1800	NALB	47150	5396	C7
Scheller Ln				
1700	NALB	47150	5396	D7
1700	NALB	47150	5505	E1
Schiller Av				
1000	LSVL	40204	5616	B5
Schiller Ct				
900	LSVL	40204	5616	B5
Schindler Dr				
1700	CHAN	47111	5181	D1
Schlaeffer Wy				
10	HdnC	40162	6591	C6
Schlatter Rd				
10500	LSVL	40291	5946	E2
Schmitt Av				
4100	LSVL	40213	5725	E3
4100	WSNP	40213	5725	E3
Schmitt Rd				
3800	LSVL	40216	5722	E2
Schneiter Av				
3100	LSVL	40215	5724	A2
Scholar St				
1300	LSVL	40213	5725	D5
School St				
200	VNGV	40175	6591	D1
School Wy				
500	LSVL	40214	5724	B6
Schooler Av				
5500	LSVL	40219	5835	B4
Schooler Ln				
3400	LSVL	40272	5941	A3
Schreiner Ct				
6100	LSVL	40219	5836	A7
Schrieber Rd				
3300	FydC	47119	5394	D7
4100	FydC	47119	5503	D1
Schroering Dr				
8000	LSVL	40291	5836	E4
Schueler Ln				
5400	OdmC	40059	5401	E4
5400	OdmC	40059	5402	A4
Schuff Av				
4400	LSVL	40213	5725	E4
Schuff Ln				
1500	LSVL	40205	5726	A2
Schuler Dr				
2000	JFVL	47130	5507	E4
Schuler Ln				
5400	OdmC	40059	5401	E4
6400	LSVL	40059	5402	A5
6400	OdmC	40059	5402	A5
Schuler Rd				
8200	FydC	47124	5393	A1
8200	GNVL	47124	5393	A1
Schureck Ct				
5200	OdmC	40031	5295	B3
Schuwey Ct				
4200	WLNP	40207	5618	B2
Schweirmann Av				
-	LSVL	40209	5724	E4
Science Hill Ct				
8300	LSVL	40228	5836	B6
Scioto Dr				
500	LSVL	40223	5619	D3
Scone Ct				
800	DGSH	40243	5620	A5
Scotch Pine Dr				
4700	FydC	47150	5396	C3
Scott Ct				
4600	JFTN	40299	5728	C6
Scott Dr				
100	VNGV	40175	6591	E1
1800	NALB	47150	5396	C7
4300	JFVL	47130	5398	A5
Scott St				
-	HdnC	40121	6374	C3
-	LSVL	40213	5725	C3
1500	JFVL	47130	5397	E7
1500	JFVL	47130	5398	A7
1700	NALB	47150	5504	E7
Scott Mills Rd				
11500	LSVL	40118	5943	B3
Scott Montfort Dr				
600	LGNG	40031	5296	D3
Scottsdale Blvd				
100	LSVL	40214	5833	C4
Scotts Gap Rd				
100	LSVL	40272	5940	D7
12900	BltC	40165	6049	E2
12900	LSVL	40272	6049	E2
Scottsville Rd				
3500	FydC	47119	5395	B7
5500	FydC	47119	5394	D1
Scottsville Navilleton Rd				
6500	FydC	47119	5284	E6
Scottwood Dr				
6100	LSVL	40258	5831	A6
Scribner Dr				
10	NALB	47150	5505	B5
Scrim Av				
9800	LSVL	40272	5940	D1
Sea Pns				
3600	JFVL	47130	5507	A1
Seaforth Dr				
9000	LSVL	40258	5831	B7
9100	LSVL	40272	5831	B7
Seaforth Wy				
6000	LSVL	40258	5831	A6
Seagrape Rd				
4200	JFTN	40299	5728	E5
Sealston Dr				
8200	LSVL	40228	5836	C6
Sea Pines Ct				
10100	LSVL	40291	5837	D6
Searcy Ln				
4200	SVLY	40216	5723	A4
Sears Av				
100	STMW	40207	5618	A3
Seasons Wy				
2700	LSVL	40220	5728	A2
Seaton Ln				
6300	LSVL	40291	5837	C3
Seaton Brook Ln				
9600	LSVL	40291	5837	C3
Seaton Springs Ct				
500	HTBN	40222	5619	C5
Seaton Springs Pkwy				
-	JFTN	40223	5619	D5
9000	HTBN	40222	5619	C5
Seatonville Rd				
9400	LSVL	40291	5837	D3
10700	LSVL	40291	5838	D5
11500	LSVL	40299	5838	D5
Seatonville Rd SR-1065				
9400	LSVL	40291	5837	C3
Seatonville Rd SR-1819				
12000	LSVL	40291	5838	D5
12000	LSVL	40299	5838	D5
Seaton Woods Ct				
10300	LSVL	40291	5837	D3
Seaton Woods Dr				
6800	LSVL	40291	5837	D4
Sea Wave Ct				
4000	LSVL	40229	5944	A3
Sebree Ln				
4700	LSVL	40218	5727	B6
Seckel Rd				
3600	LSVL	40218	5727	C4
Secret Wy				
5600	LSVL	40272	5940	B6
Secretariat Rd				
10	HdnC	42701	6703	E4
Security Pkwy				
100	FydC	47150	5396	C1
Sedalia Ct				
10500	LSVL	40272	5941	A2
Sedalia Tr				
3800	LSVL	40272	5941	A2
3900	LSVL	40272	5940	E3
Sedge Ct				
5200	LSVL	40258	5831	C3
Sedge Dr				
7400	LSVL	40258	5831	B3
Sedgefield Ct				
4500	LSVL	40216	5723	C6
Sedgewicke Dr				
6500	PROS	40059	5400	D4
Seebolt Dr				
7800	LSVL	40219	5835	E5
Seelbach Av				
-	LSVL	40215	5723	E4
1300	LSVL	40215	5724	A4
Seibel Ct				
4600	LSVL	40258	5831	E4
Seibert Ter				
-	LSVL	40205	5616	C7
-	LSVL	40205	5725	E1
Seilo Rdg N				
3400	JFVL	47130	5398	E7
3700	JFVL	47130	5399	A7
Seilo Rdg S				
3400	JFVL	47130	5398	E7
3600	JFVL	47130	5399	A6
Selbert St				
-	ELZT	42701	6812	D5
Selinda Av				
1400	LSVL	40213	5725	E4
Selinda Dr				
1400	LSVL	40213	5725	E5
Selkirk Ln				
500	DGSH	40243	5620	B5
Sellers Av				
200	SLRB	47172	5288	D3
Sellers Ct				
-	ClkC	47130	5398	E4
2800	JFVL	47130	5398	D5
Selma Av				
3700	WBHL	40218	5726	E4
Semillon Ln				
11400	LSVL	40272	5940	B4
Seminary Ct				
2700	LSVL	40206	5617	A3
Seminary Dr				
-	LSVL	40222	5509	C4
-	LSVL	40242	5509	D5
2600	LSVL	40241	5509	C5
2800	LSVL	40206	5617	A3
Seminole Av				
6700	LSVL	40214	5833	C1
Seminole Ct				
100	SHDV	40165	6161	B5
Seminole Dr				
3000	JFVL	47130	5398	E7
3000	JFVL	47130	5507	E1
Seminole Ln				
-	RDCF	40160	6483	B2
Seminole Rd				
-	ELZT	42701	6703	D7
200	ELZT	42701	6812	D1
300	RDCF	40160	6483	B3
N Seminole St				
-	HdnC	40121	6265	C6
200	HdnC	40121	6374	D2
S Seminole St				
10	HdnC	40121	6374	E2
Senate Av				
900	JFVL	47130	5399	A7
Senate Cir				
100	RDCF	40160	6483	B4
W Senate Cir				
1200	RDCF	40160	6483	A4
Senate Ln				
100	MTWH	40047	6055	E1
300	MTWH	40047	6056	A1
Senator Ln				
5300	LSVL	40219	5835	D7
Seneca Av				
300	LSVL	40209	5724	E4
Seneca Blvd				
3000	LSVL	40205	5617	E7
Seneca Dr				
-	SLRB	47172	5288	D3
2400	LSVL	40205	5617	B6
2400	SGDN	40205	5617	B6
N Seneca St				
10	HdnC	40121	6374	E2
S Seneca St				
-	HdnC	40121	6374	E2
Seneca Tr				
100	LSVL	40214	5833	C1
Seneca Park Rd				
-	JfnC	40207	5617	C5
2900	JfnC	40205	5617	B5
2900	LSVL	40205	5617	B5
3200	LSVL	40207	5617	C5
Seneca Valley Rd				
2300	LSVL	40205	5617	C6
2300	SGDN	40205	5617	C6
N Senica Tr				
100	LSVL	40214	5833	C1
Senn Rd				
4100	LSVL	40216	5722	D2
Sennridge Dr				
5300	LSVL	40272	5940	B2
Sentimental Ln				
11100	LSVL	40229	5945	C5
Sentry Wy				
700	LSVL	40223	5620	A2
Sequoya Rd				
100	INHC	40207	5508	E6
Serendipity Ln				
4000	LSVL	40272	5940	E7
Serene Wy				
3900	LSVL	40219	5835	A2
Serenity Ct				
6200	LSVL	40219	5835	B2
Serenity Ln				
2500	JFVL	47130	5398	B6
Service Dr				
1000	ClkC	47172	5288	E4
1000	ClkC	47172	5289	A4
1000	SLRB	47172	5288	E4
1000	SLRB	47172	5289	A4
Service Pl				
-	LSVL	40245	5512	A5
Service Wy				
-	LSVL	40245	5512	A5
Serviceberry Ct				
4000	LSVL	40241	5510	E3
Seton Hill Dr				
3400	LSVL	40216	5722	B6
Setting Sun Ct				
3100	OdmC	40014	5405	C6
Settle Blvd				
4600	LSVL	40219	5835	C7
Settlers Ct				
100	BltC	40165	6163	A2
Settlers Dr				
-	ClkC	47172	5397	D1
Settlers Run				
7400	FydC	47124	5283	A6
Settlers Trc				
2300	BltC	40165	6163	A2
Settlers Crest Ln				
10100	JFTN	40299	5728	D5
Settlers Point Tr				
12800	OdmC	44026	5292	B2
Settlers Trace Rd				
10	LSVL	40291	5837	A1
Seven Green Ln				
17200	LSVL	40245	5622	C1
Seven Mile Ln				
5900	FydC	47117	5721	D3
5900	FydC	47150	5721	D3
Sevenoaks Dr				
10700	LSVL	40241	5511	A3
Severns St				
10	ELZT	42701	6811	D5
10	HdnC	42701	6811	D5
Seville Dr				
4700	LSVL	40272	5940	D1
Sewanee Dr				
-	LSVL	40205	5616	E7
-	LSVL	40205	5617	A7
Sewell Dr				
11100	LSVL	40291	5837	E5
Sewer Plant Rd				
-	ODGH	40014	5402	E6
-	OdmC	40014	5402	E6
Sexton Dr				
2800	LSVL	40223	5511	D5
Shade Ln				
-	RDCF	40160	6483	A1
Shadoheck Dr				
4900	LSVL	40216	5722	C6
Shadowbrook Ln				
2200	ClkC	47130	5399	B4
2200	JFVL	47130	5399	B4
Shadow Creek Ln				
2500	ELZT	42701	6593	E7
2500	ELZT	42701	6702	E1
Shadowcreek Rd				
-	OdmC	40014	5405	C5
7900	OdmC	40014	5403	A7
Shadow Creek Wy				
8700	LSVL	40291	5837	A4
Shadowfern Dr				
2000	SVLY	40216	5723	B3
Shadowlawn Dr				
5100	BltC	40229	5944	D6
5100	HLVW	40229	5944	D6
Shadowood Ct				
-	HdnC	40160	6592	C5
100	BltC	40047	6055	A2
Shadowood Ln				
7200	CTWD	40014	5403	D7
Shadow Pointe				
7000	ClkC	47172	5288	A6
Shadow Ridge Ln				
10400	LSVL	40241	5511	A1
Shadow Run Rd				
6000	LSVL	40219	5835	B1
Shadow Wood Ct				
6300	LSVL	40059	5400	C6
Shadow Wood Dr				
-	CTWD	40014	5403	D7
-	PWEV	40014	5403	D7
6300	LSVL	40059	5400	C6
Shadow Wood Ln				
5100	LSVL	40059	5400	C7
Shadwell Ln				
7300	PROS	40059	5400	E4
7400	PROS	40059	5401	A4
Shadwell Pl				
6800	PROS	40059	5401	A4
Shady Dr				
200	NALB	47150	5504	E6
Shady Ln				
-	LSVL	40219	5834	D6
100	BltC	40165	6054	A5
1100	ANCH	40223	5620	C2
1600	GEOT	47122	5502	A4
1600	LSVL	40205	5616	D6
1600	LSVL	40213	5616	D6
Shady Trc				
3000	OdmC	40014	5405	C7
Shady Acres Ln				
9500	JFTN	40299	5728	D6
9500	LSVL	40299	5728	D6
Shady Brook Ln				
100	HLVW	40229	5944	B7
100	PNRV	40229	5944	B7
Shadybrook Ln				
3000	FydC	47150	5397	A2
Shady Creek Cir				
13300	LSVL	40299	5729	E4
Shady Creek Ln				
7200	OdmC	40014	5405	C7
7200	OdmC	40014	5514	C1
Shady Dell Blvd				
3400	LGNG	40031	5297	C7
3400	OdmC	40014	5297	C7
3400	OdmC	40031	5297	C7
Shady Dell Ln				
7400	OdmC	40014	5403	B6
Shady Glen Cir				
-	BltC	40165	6161	A1
Shady Grove Wy				
2000	LSVL	40218	5727	A5
Shady Hill Tr				
2400	LSVL	40299	5730	B2
Shady Hollow Dr				
10900	LSVL	40241	5511	B2
Shady Oaks Ct				
100	MTWH	40047	6056	D4
Shady Pond Ln				
100	BltC	40165	6054	B7
Shadyside Dr				
3500	LSVL	40211	5614	B6
Shady Spring Ct				
2200	OdmC	40059	5292	E5
Shady Springs Dr				
3100	LSVL	40299	5729	E4
Shady Trace Ct				
3100	OdmC	40014	5405	B6
Shadyview Dr				
4500	FydC	47119	5394	D4
Shady Villa Dr				
4000	LSVL	40219	5835	B1
Shaffer Ln				
6300	LSVL	40291	5837	E3
6300	LSVL	40291	5838	A2
6300	LSVL	40299	5838	A2
Shaffer Rd				
700	LSVL	40118	5833	D7
Shaftsbury Dr				
-	BLMD	40222	5619	B4
-	HTBN	40222	5619	B4
Shagbark Ct				
3600	OdmC	40031	5404	D2
Shagbark Ln				
7300	OdmC	40014	5512	C1
7300	PWEV	40056	5512	C1
Shagbark Rd				
3400	LSVL	40216	5722	D3
Shagbark Tr				
3000	ClkC	47172	5288	A6
3000	FydC	47172	5287	E7
Shaheen Ct				
-	ELZT	42701	6702	E6
Shakeland Dr				
13900	BltC	40071	5948	D3
13900	BltC	40299	5948	D3
Shaker Mill Ct				
3600	LSVL	40220	5727	D3
Shaker Mill Rd				
7600	LSVL	40220	5727	D3
Shakes Run Dr				
1500	LSVL	40023	5731	B2
Shakes Run Rd				
-	LSVL	40023	5731	B1
Shallcross Wy				
3000	GNVH	40222	5509	B4
Shallow Cove Ct				
3300	OdmC	40014	5514	A1
Shallowford Ln				
18400	LSVL	40245	5622	E5
Shallowford Pl				
300	LSVL	40245	5622	E5
Shallow Lake Rd				
7000	PROS	40059	5400	D6
Shallow Rock Dr				
6700	LSVL	40291	5838	A3
6700	LSVL	40299	5838	A3
Shamrock St				
1000	HdnC	40160	6592	B4
Shamrock Wynd				
300	LSVL	40212	5614	B1
Shane Dr				
-	JFTN	40220	5728	B1
Shane Ln				
200	ELZT	42701	6702	E2
Shane St				
-	ELZT	42701	6702	D6
Shanks Ln				
3400	LSVL	40216	5722	D3
Shanna Dr				
9400	JFTN	40299	5728	C4
Shannon Dr				
2700	LSVL	40220	5726	E1
E Shannon Ln				
100	BltC	40047	6056	B5
100	MTWH	40047	6056	B5
W Shannon Ln				
100	SHDV	40165	6161	C3
Shannon Cove				
-	OdmC	40031	5404	B1
Shannon Run Ln				
10	HdnC	40162	6592	B7
Shannon Run Tr				
3600	LSVL	40299	5728	A4
Shareith Dr				
6700	LSVL	40228	5836	B3
6800	SPML	40228	5836	C4
Sharon Cir				
2500	LSVL	40218	5726	D1
Sharon Ct				
100	ELZT	42701	6702	D6
Sharon Dr				
100	BltC	40165	6163	C7
900	JFVL	47130	5507	C4
1500	LSVL	40216	5832	A2
Sharon Ln				
1700	LSVL	40118	5942	C1
Sharon Wy				
2700	LSVL	40218	5726	D1
2700	LSVL	40220	5726	E1
Sharp Av				
-	LSVL	40208	5615	C7
-	LSVL	40208	5724	B1
Sharps Ln				
1200	ClkC	47172	5288	C2
1200	SLRB	47172	5288	C2
Shasta Tr				
4300	LSVL	40213	5726	C6
4800	LSVL	40218	5726	C6
Shaun Cir				
2500	JFVL	47130	5507	C1
Shaw Ct				
7800	LSVL	40291	5837	A5
Shaw Creek Ct				
100	ELZT	42701	6702	D6
Shaw Creek Dr				
-	ELZT	42701	6702	D6
Shawnee Cir				
100	MTWH	40047	6056	B1
Shawnee Dr				
-	SHDV	40165	6161	B6
200	LSVL	40212	5614	B1
1000	ELZT	42701	6703	D7
1000	ELZT	42701	6812	D1
N Shawnee Ter				
100	LSVL	40212	5614	B1
200	LSVL	40212	5505	B7
S Shawnee Ter				
200	LSVL	40212	5614	B1
Shawnee Park Cir				
-	LSVL	40211	5614	A3
Shawnee Park Ct				
-	LSVL	40211	5614	A3
Shawnee Park Rd				
-	LSVL	40211	5614	A3
-	LSVL	40212	5614	A2
Shean Ct				
6000	LSVL	40291	5837	B2
Shebas Wy				
100	BltC	40165	6160	C5
Sheehan Dr				
-	OdmC	40031	5404	B1
Sheffield Blvd				
2200	LSVL	40205	5616	E7
Sheffield Ct				
2600	LGNG	40031	5297	A6
N Sheffield Ct				
7400	FydC	47136	5611	D3
S Sheffield Ct				
7400	FydC	47136	5611	D3
Sheffield Rd				
10	MdeC	40175	6373	A6
Shefford Ln				
7100	LSVL	40242	5509	E5
7100	OBNP	40242	5509	E5
Shefford Ln W				
7000	LSVL	40242	5509	D5
Sheila Ct				
10	HdnC	42701	6593	C6
Sheila Dr				
2700	LSVL	40220	5726	E1
Sheila Rd				
6100	LSVL	40219	5835	D2
Shelburn Cir				
6500	CTWD	40014	5403	E6
Shelburn Dr				
6500	CTWD	40014	5403	D6
6500	OdmC	40014	5403	D6
Shelby Av				
100	RDCF	40160	6484	A7
800	RDCF	40160	6593	B1
Shelby Cir				
-	HLVW	40229	5944	B6
Shelby Ct				
100	CHAN	47111	5181	D5
8600	LSVL	40291	5728	A7
Shelby Pkwy				
400	LSVL	40203	5615	E5
700	LSVL	40203	5616	A6
700	LSVL	40204	5616	A6
Shelby Pl				
1500	NALB	47150	5505	C4
Shelby Rd				
1700	LSVL	40213	5725	D2
Shelby St				
2100	NALB	47150	5505	D3
5800	LSVL	40291	5837	B1
10400	JFTN	40299	5728	E4
N Shelby St				
100	LSVL	40202	5616	A2
100	LSVL	40206	5616	A2
S Shelby St				
100	LSVL	40202	5616	A3
100	LSVL	40206	5616	A3
500	LSVL	40204	5616	A4
600	LSVL	40203	5616	A5
1300	LSVL	40217	5616	A6
2200	LSVL	40217	5725	A1
2400	PKWV	40217	5725	A1
S Shelby St SR-61				
2200	LSVL	40217	5725	A1
2400	PKWV	40217	5725	A1
S Shelby St SR-864				
600	LSVL	40202	5616	A5
600	LSVL	40203	5616	A5
600	LSVL	40204	5616	A5
Shelbyville Rd				
3800	LSVL	40207	5617	E3
3800	STMW	40207	5617	E3
3900	LSVL	40207	5618	A3
3900	STMW	40207	5618	D3
4100	RHLN	40207	5618	A3
4200	FRMD	40207	5618	B3
4300	BWDV	40207	5618	B3
7500	LSVL	40222	5618	E3
7500	STMW	40222	5618	E3
7600	NRWD	40222	5618	E3
7800	LYDN	40222	5618	E3
7900	LSVL	40222	5619	C4
7900	LYDN	40222	5619	C4
8500	BLMD	40222	5619	A3
8800	BLMD	40223	5619	B3
8800	HTBN	40222	5619	C4
8900	LYDN	40223	5619	C4
9400	WDWD	40223	5619	D4
9800	LSVL	40223	5619	D4
9900	JFTN	40223	5619	D4
10000	BRMR	40223	5619	E4
10300	SCMR	40223	5619	E4
10400	BRMR	40223	5620	A4
10400	DGSH	40243	5620	A4
10400	SCMR	40223	5620	A4
10600	LSVL	40243	5620	A4
10700	LSVL	40223	5620	A4
11300	MDTN	40243	5620	A4
12700	MDTN	40223	5620	E4
12800	MDTN	40223	5621	D5
12800	MDTN	40243	5621	A4
13500	LSVL	40245	5621	B4
13500	MDTN	40245	5621	D5
15700	LSVL	40245	5622	A5
16800	LSVL	40023	5622	C5
18200	LSVL	40023	5623	A5
18200	LSVL	40245	5623	A5
18200	SbyC	40067	5623	A5
Shelbyville Rd US-60				
7500	NRWD	40222	5618	E3
7500	STMW	40222	5618	E3
7600	LSVL	40222	5618	E3
7800	LYDN	40222	5618	E3
7900	HTBN	40222	5619	A3
7900	LSVL	40222	5619	C4
7900	LYDN	40222	5619	C4
8400	BLMD	40222	5619	B3
8800	BLMD	40223	5619	B4
8900	LYDN	40223	5619	C4
9300	JFTN	40223	5619	D4
9400	WDWD	40223	5619	D4
9800	LSVL	40223	5619	D4
10000	BRMR	40223	5619	E4
10300	SCMR	40223	5619	E4
10400	BRMR	40223	5620	A4
10400	DGSH	40243	5620	A4
10400	SCMR	40223	5620	A4
10600	LSVL	40243	5620	A4
10700	LSVL	40223	5620	A4
11300	MDTN	40243	5620	A4
12700	MDTN	40223	5620	E4
12800	MDTN	40223	5621	D5
12800	MDTN	40243	5621	A4

Louisville Metro Street Index

STREET
Block City ZIP Map# Grid

Shelbyville Rd US-60
13500 MDTN 40245 5621 D5
15700 LSVL 40245 5621 E5
15700 LSVL 40245 5622 A5
16800 LSVL 40023 5622 C5
18200 LSVL 40023 5623 A5
18200 LSVL 40245 5623 A5
18200 SbyC 40067 5623 A5
Shelbyville Rd US-60 TRK
- LSVL 40222 5618 D3
- NRWD 40222 5618 E3
- STMW 40222 5618 D3
3800 LSVL 40207 5617 E3
3800 STMW 40207 5617 E3
3900 LSVL 40207 5618 A3
3900 STMW 40207 5618 A3
4100 RHLN 40207 5618 A3
4200 FRMD 40207 5618 B3
4300 BWDV 40207 5618 B3
Sheldon Rd
2800 LSVL 40218 5727 B3
Shelley Av
2700 SMRM 40205 5617 B7
Shelley Ct
1900 CLKV 47129 5397 B7
Shelley Dr
1900 CLKV 47129 5397 B7
Shelly Ct
100 BltC 40047 6055 C4
Shelton Av
4100 LSVL 40218 5726 D4
Shelton Ln
10 RDCF 40160 6483 D7
10 RDCF 40160 6592 D1
Shelton Rd
100 RDCF 40160 6592 E1
300 RDCF 40160 6483 D7
Shelton St
100 VNGV 40175 6591 E1
400 HdnC 40175 6591 D1
Shelvis Ct
- HLVW 40229 5944 B6
Shenandoah Dr
4200 FCSL 40241 5511 C3
4600 LSVL 40241 5511 C3
8500 OdmC 40056 5512 E3
Shenandoah Rd
8000 FydC 47136 5611 B1
Shepherds Ct
8700 LSVL 40291 5837 A5
Shepherds Wy
100 BltC 40165 6053 C2
100 PNRV 40165 6053 C2
Shepherdsville Rd
- SHDV 40165 6160 E2
10 ELZT 42701 6703 C7
200 SHDV 40165 6161 A3
4200 LSVL 40218 5726 E6
4200 WBHL 40218 5726 E6
5000 LSVL 40228 5726 E6
5300 LSVL 40218 5835 E1
5300 LSVL 40219 5835 E1
5300 LSVL 40228 5835 E1
Shepherdsville Rd SR-44
- SHDV 40165 6160 E2
200 SHDV 40165 6161 A3
Shepherdsville Rd SR-251
10 ELZT 42701 6703 C7
Shepherdsville Rd SR-2052
4200 LSVL 40218 5726 E6
4200 WBHL 40218 5726 E6
5000 LSVL 40228 5726 E6
5300 LSVL 40218 5835 E1
5300 LSVL 40219 5835 E1
5300 LSVL 40228 5835 E1
Shepherdsville Rd SR-2845
8900 LSVL 40219 5835 D7
Sheplet Ct
9900 CKSD 40241 5510 E4
Sheraton Wy
- LSVL 40272 5940 B4
Sherbrooke Rd
3000 LSVL 40205 5726 C1
Sherburn Ln
- STMW 40207 5618 C4
Sheri Ln
200 FydC 47122 5503 A6
Sheridan Av
1700 LSVL 40213 5725 D2
Sheridan Rd
3700 LSVL 40220 5618 B7
Sherley St
400 NALB 47150 5505 A4
Sherlock Wy
6300 LSVL 40228 5836 B2
Sherman Av
4100 LSVL 40213 5725 C3
5800 HdnC 40121 6374 B5
Sherman Dr
2900 JFVL 47130 5398 D6
Sherman Minton Br
- LSVL - 5505 B6
- NALB - 5505 B6
Sherman Minton Br I-64
- LSVL - 5505 B6
- NALB - 5505 B6
Sherman Minton Br US-150
- LSVL - 5505 B6
- NALB - 5505 B6
Sherrard Dr
7400 LSVL 40258 5830 D5
Sherrill Av
3400 LSVL 40211 5614 C6
Sherrin Av
- NBNE 40207 5618 B4
- SPLE 40207 5618 B4
- STMW 40207 5618 B4
N Sherrin Av
100 STMW 40207 5618 A3
S Sherrin Av
100 STMW 40207 5618 A3
300 NBNE 40207 5618 A3
Sherry Ln
- BltC 40109 5943 D7
6800 LSVL 40291 5837 B3
Sherry Rd
2400 LSVL 40217 5724 E2
Sherry Lynn Ct
7700 LSVL 40228 5836 B6
Sherwood Av
2000 LSVL 40205 5616 E5
N Sherwood Av
300 CLKV 47129 5506 C4
S Sherwood Av
100 CLKV 47129 5506 D5
Sherwood Ct
100 CLKV 47129 5506 C6
Sherwood Dr
1000 NALB 47150 5396 D6
1000 RDCF 40160 6483 E5
Shetland Ct
4200 FydC 47150 5396 E2
Shetland Pl
10900 DGSH 40243 5620 A5
Shevie Dr
8900 LSVL 40272 5831 D6
Shibley Av
6700 LSVL 40291 5837 D4
Shingo Av
1300 LSVL 40215 5724 A6
Shipley Ln
7000 LSVL 40272 6048 C2
W Shipp Av
600 LSVL 40208 5615 C6
900 LSVL 40210 5615 C6
Shippen Av
2700 LSVL 40206 5617 A2
Shippingport Dr
2600 LSVL 40202 5615 B1
2600 LSVL 40212 5506 A6
2600 LSVL 40212 5615 B1
Shirewick Wy
9900 LSVL 40272 5939 E1
Shirley Av
200 SLRB 47172 5288 D4
1800 CLKV 47129 5397 B7
6400 LSVL 40059 5400 C3
Shirley Blvd
100 VNGV 40175 6482 E6
Shirley Ln
8500 LSVL 40258 5831 C6
Shirl Nel Ln
100 BltC 40165 6053 A7
Shobe Ln
8100 LSVL 40228 5836 E6
Shoel Creek Ct
10200 LSVL 40291 5837 C5
Shoe Maker Dr
2800 LSVL 40241 5509 D4
N Shore Dr
600 JFVL 47130 5506 E7
S Shore Dr
100 SHDV 40165 6161 B6
Shore Acres Dr
400 UTCA 47130 5399 E6
Shoreham Ln
3000 SVLY 40216 5723 E2
Shoreline Ct
- LGNG 40031 5297 A1
Shoreline Dr
- LGNG 40031 5297 B1
E Shoreline Dr
5000 FydC 47119 5394 C4
W Shoreline Dr
5100 FydC 47119 5394 C4
Shoreline Turn
3000 FydC 47122 5393 D6
Shorewood Dr
5500 LSVL 40214 5833 B3
Short Ct
10 JFVL 47130 5507 B4
Short Rd
300 BWDV 40207 5618 D2
4200 ClkC 47172 5288 E3
Short St
- RDCF 40160 6483 D4
200 CLKV 47129 5506 D7
300 LSVL 40212 5615 A1
600 ELZT 42701 6812 B1
800 CHAN 47111 5181 E4
1300 LSVL 40213 5725 C4
1300 SHDV 40165 6162 A3
1500 WPT 40177 6156 B3
8300 GEOT 47122 5502 A3
Short Jackson St
700 JFVL 47130 5507 B5
Shoshone Wy
9500 LSVL 40258 5830 D7
Shrader Av
2200 NALB 47150 5505 C2
Shrader Ln
6100 OdmC 40031 5295 A2
Shreve Dr
400 LYDN 40222 5619 A2
Shuck Ln
2300 LSVL 40219 5834 C6
2300 MLHT 40219 5834 C6
Shulthise Ln
100 BltC 40165 6161 A7
Shumake Ct
4900 LSVL 40213 5726 D6
4900 LSVL 40218 5726 D6
Shumate Rd
100 MRGH 40155 6264 C3
Shumater St
- MRGH 40155 6264 C3
Shungate Rd
5100 ClkC 47130 5398 E2
6100 ClkC 47130 5290 A7
6100 ClkC 47130 5399 A1
Shutesbury Cir
6800 LSVL 40258 5831 A5
Sideoats Dr
7300 ODGH 40014 5402 E7
Sidney Av
2300 KGLY 40205 5617 C7
Sidney Ct
100 NALB 47150 5395 E6
Sidney Park Dr
3500 LSVL 40205 5617 E6
Sieger Villa Ct
2200 LSVL 40218 5726 E3
Siena Ct
8900 LSVL 40299 5728 B4
Sierra Ct
900 JFVL 47130 5398 E7
Sierra Tr
7700 LSVL 40214 5832 E4
Siesta Wy
8200 LSVL 40219 5835 C5
Sieveking Rd
3000 FydC 47150 5395 E7
Signal Hill Rd
4400 INHC 40207 5509 A6
Signature Dr
6500 LSVL 40213 5834 D2
Silk Oak Dr
300 ELZT 42701 6702 E3
500 ELZT 42701 6703 A3
Silky Dogwood Ct
9800 LSVL 40241 5510 D4
Silo Ct
8000 LSVL 40291 5837 B6
Silo Wy
9900 LSVL 40291 5837 B6
Silo Ridge Ct
6600 LSVL 40299 5838 A2
Sils Av
1800 LSVL 40205 5617 A7
Silver Rdg
11600 LSVL 40299 5729 C5
Silver St
- ClkC 47172 5288 B1
200 NALB 47150 5505 E4
Silverado Pl
4700 LSVL 40299 5728 E7
Silverbell Av
8100 LSVL 40228 5836 E6
Silverbrook Av
2400 LSVL 40220 5618 C6
Silver Creek Dr
1600 NALB 47150 5396 E6
Silvercreek Dr
100 ClkC 47129 5397 A5
100 CLKV 47129 5396 E6
100 CLKV 47129 5397 A5
Silver Creek Rd
4200 LSVL 40272 5940 D3
Silvercrest Ln
1000 DGSH 40223 5620 A6
Silver Fox Ct
6700 LSVL 40291 5837 A3
Silver Fox Rd
8300 LSVL 40291 5837 A3
Silver Hills Ln
1100 NALB 47150 5504 E5
Silver Lace Ct
6600 LSVL 40228 5836 B3
Silver Lakes Dr
- ClkC 47129 5397 E3
10 CLKV 47129 5397 E3
Silverleaf Dr
4300 LSVL 40213 5726 C6
Silvermoon Ct
10800 LSVL 40241 5511 B2
Silver Oak Ct
4300 LSVL 40272 5831 E7
Silver Oaks Dr
- ClkC 47172 5288 A1
Silver Run Wy
5000 LSVL 40241 5511 A1
Silver Slate Dr
- ClkC 47130 5398 D3
1400 NALB 47150 5505 E2
Silver Slope Dr
200 NALB 47150 5504 D6
Silver Springs Dr
3200 LSVL 40220 5727 E3
Silverton Ct
1000 ClkC 47129 5505 E3
1000 ClkC 47129 5506 A3
Silverton Ln
5100 LSVL 40241 5511 A1
Silver Wing Blvd
5300 LSVL 40241 5511 A1
Silverwood Ct
1100 FydC 47150 5396 E5
1100 FydC 47150 5397 A5
1100 NALB 47150 5396 E5
Silverwood Dr
900 CLKV 47129 5397 C6
Silverwood Ln
100 CLKV 47129 5397 E3
9800 LSVL 40272 5941 A2
Simcoe Ln
4100 LSVL 40241 5510 D2
Simmons Ct
300 LSVL 40203 5615 C3
Simmons Ln
100 BltC 40047 6054 E4
100 BltC 40047 6055 A5
400 MTWH 40047 6055 A5
Simon Al
- LSVL 40203 5615 E4
Simpson Dr
4800 LSVL 40218 5726 C5
Simpson Rd SE
6700 HsnC 47117 5939 A2
Sinclair St
500 LSVL 40118 5833 D7
Sindiana Rd
- SLRB 47172 5288 D4
Singer Ct
6900 LSVL 40220 5727 D3
Singletree Ln
7400 LSVL 40291 5836 D4
Sioux
- HdnC 40121 6374 E1
Sirate Ln
4000 LSVL 40229 5944 A2
Sir Barton Rd
5400 LSVL 40272 5831 A7
5400 LSVL 40272 5940 B1
Sir Johns Ct
2400 SRPK 40220 5618 D5
Sir Lancelot Ln
1000 STMW 40222 5618 E1
Sir Lancelot St
- ELZT 42701 6811 C3
Sir Robert Wy
2400 LSVL 40245 5513 C7
Sissonne Dr
9200 LSVL 40118 5833 C7
9300 LSVL 40118 5942 C1
Sitka Ct
100 HLVW 40229 5944 B7
Sitka Dr
2900 JFTN 40299 5728 D3
Sitting Bull Ct
- HdnC 40175 6482 D4
Six Mile Ln
- FTHL 40299 5728 B3
10 JFVL 47130 5508 C2
2500 JFTN 40220 5728 B3
2500 JFTN 40299 5728 B3
5900 LSVL 40218 5727 A3
6400 LSVL 40220 5727 D3
8000 LSVL 40299 5727 E3
8100 LSVL 40220 5728 A3
8100 LSVL 40299 5728 A3
Skeffington Wy
5400 LSVL 40241 5511 A1
Skinners Rd
- ClkC 47130 5398 B3
Sky Blue Av
6400 LSVL 40216 5831 D3
6400 LSVL 40258 5831 D3
Skyblue Dr
100 ELZT 42701 6702 D4
Skylark Cir
200 RDCF 40160 6592 E1
Skylark Dr
800 LSVL 40223 5619 E2
Skylight Dr
5200 LSVL 40258 5831 C2
Skyline Dr
- FydC 47119 5287 B2
- FydC 47172 5287 B2
100 HdnC 40160 6592 E3
100 RDCF 40160 6592 E3
100 RDCF 40160 6593 A2
200 ELZT 42701 6812 B3
1300 JFVL 47130 5507 B2
1400 CHAN 47111 5181 E3
6500 LSVL 40272 5939 E1
11300 LSVL 40229 5944 C5
11400 HLVW 40229 5944 C5
N Skyline Dr
100 HLVW 40229 5944 C5
500 LSVL 40229 5944 C5
7000 FydC 47119 5396 A1
7600 FydC 47119 5287 B5
8000 FydC 47172 5287 C6
S Skyline Dr
100 HLVW 40229 5944 C6
4300 FydC 47119 5395 E1
Skynight Dr
8100 LYDN 40222 5619 A1
Skyview Ct
10 BltC 40165 6049 B5
Skyview Dr
10 FydC 47150 5504 A3
Skyview Rd
10 BltC 40165 6049 B5
200 BltC 40165 6048 E7
Slack Av
4000 LSVL 40229 5944 A1
Slate Av
- ELZT 42701 6812 E7
Slate Ct
7100 CTWD 40014 5403 D7
Slate Dr
10200 LSVL 40118 5943 C2
Slate St
1400 LSVL 40217 5616 A6
Slate Creek Ct
3200 NALB 47150 5396 B7
Slate Run Ct
4600 LSVL 40229 5944 B4
Slate Run Dr
11700 LSVL 40229 5944 A4
Slate Run Rd
800 NALB 47150 5505 E1
1500 NALB 47150 5396 D7
Slattery Dr
- ClkC 47130 5398 C5
Slayton Ct
9400 LSVL 40229 5943 E1
Sleepy Hollow Rd
10300 OdmC 40059 5402 A4
Slevin St
2400 LSVL 40212 5615 A1
2500 LSVL 40212 5614 E1
Slicker Av
1100 LSVL 40118 5942 E2
Slippery Elm Dr
10700 LSVL 40291 5946 C1
Sloane Ct
5300 LSVL 40291 5728 D7
5300 LSVL 40291 5837 D1
Sloemer Av
100 NALB 47150 5505 A3
Slone Dr
2900 JFVL 47130 5398 B5
Slop Ditch
- LSVL 40219 5835 A3
Small Boat Ct
3900 LSVL 40229 5944 A3
Smilax Av
2800 LSVL 40213 5834 D1
Smith Av
400 ELZT 42701 6811 E4
Smith Ln
- LSVL 40291 5837 A5
100 HLVW 40229 5944 B5
100 LSVL 40229 5944 B5
7200 LSVL 40258 5721 D7
Smith Rd
2100 ClkC 47106 5284 D2
2100 LSVL 40118 5943 B3
3300 LSVL 40216 5722 E3
4200 FydC 47119 5394 C2
Smith St
100 JFVL 47130 5506 E5
100 VNGV 40175 6482 D7
300 RDCF 40160 6483 E6
300 RDCF 40160 6484 A6
Smith Creek Blvd
- FydC 47136 5611 B4
Smith Creek Rd
6800 FydC 47136 5611 E5
Smith Creek Rd NE
2600 HsnC 47136 5611 B4
Smither Ln
10 HdnC 42701 6702 C2
Smith Farm Rd
- BltC 40165 6052 B4
1300 BltC 40165 6051 E4
Smithfield Rd
200 INHC 40207 5509 A6
200 LSVL 40207 5509 A6
Smithfield Greene Ln
7400 PROS 40059 5400 D4
Smith Grove Wy
3900 LSVL 40245 5512 D5
Smith Landfill Rd
100 BltC 40165 6052 A5
Smithton Rd
8100 LSVL 40219 5835 C5
Smith View Ct
800 LSVL 40214 5833 B4
Smithwood Dr
2900 FydC 47150 5397 A3
Smoke Rd
2800 JFTN 40220 5728 B3
Smoore Ct
10 LSVL 40229 5944 A2
Smyrna Pl
6000 LSVL 40219 5836 A6
6000 LSVL 40228 5836 A6
Smyrna Rd
7300 LSVL 40219 5836 A7
7300 LSVL 40228 5836 A7
8300 LSVL 40229 5836 A7
9000 LSVL 40229 5945 A1
Smyrna Village Ct
8200 LSVL 40228 5836 A6
Smyser Av
1400 CLKV 47129 5506 D7
Snaffel Bit Ct
16400 LSVL 40245 5622 C2
Snapp St
100 MTWH 40047 6056 C3
Snawder Ln
11000 LSVL 40118 5941 D6
Snively Av
10100 JFTN 40299 5728 D3
Snowden Vly
13200 OdmC 44026 5292 B2
Snowden Wy
13400 LSVL 40272 6048 D1
Snow Flake Ln
10 HdnC 42701 6812 A7
Snowhill Rd
5400 GNVW 40222 5509 A3
Snow Mountain Access Rd
- MdeC 40175 6373 A1
Snyder Dr
2000 JFVL 47130 5507 C1
Sodrel Dr
10 ClkC 47129 5506 D4
10 CLKV 47129 5506 D4
Soergel Av
1600 NALB 47150 5396 D7
Solar Ct
- BltC 40047 5947 C5
- LSVL 40047 5947 C5
Solomon's Rd
- BltC 40165 6160 C5
Solomons Rd
100 BltC 40165 6160 C5
Solona Dr
4900 LSVL 40272 5940 C1
Somber Wy
3000 LSVL 40220 5727 A2
4800 BltC 40165 6163 B1
Somerford Ct
9600 MWVL 40242 5510 D6
Somerford Rd
9700 MWVL 40242 5510 D6
Somerhill Ct
10800 ANCH 40223 5620 A1
Somerhill Pl
1300 ANCH 40223 5620 A1
Somerhill Wy
1400 ANCH 40223 5620 A1
Somerset Dr
12100 PNRV 40229 5944 B7
12300 PNRV 40229 6053 B1
Somerset Pl
1700 HBNA 40220 5619 B7
Sonic Dr
10300 LSVL 40291 5837 D4
Sonne Av
1600 SVLY 40216 5723 E1
Sonnette Wy
6300 LSVL 40258 5831 B3
Sonoma Ln
3700 LSVL 40219 5835 A7
Sonora Tr
8700 LSVL 40299 5728 A4
Sonrisa Dr
9800 LSVL 40291 5837 C3
Sora Av
3100 ANPK 40213 5725 C2
3100 LSVL 40217 5725 C2
Sorrell Dr
100 RDCF 40160 6592 D1
Sorrento Av
3500 BRMD 40241 5510 A3
Sourwood Ct
3700 LSVL 40220 5727 C1
South Dr
6400 LSVL 40272 5939 E4
6400 LSVL 40272 5940 A5
South Rd
- HdnC 40177 6264 D3
South St
- LSVL 40208 5615 B7
10 RDCF 40160 6484 A6
10 WPT 40177 6156 C3
100 BltC 40165 6161 B1
100 RDCF 40160 6483 E6
400 SLRB 47172 5288 D3
1300 NALB 47150 5505 B3
Southacres Dr
1000 LSVL 40219 5835 A4
Southard Pl NE
6300 HsnC 47122 5501 B4
Southbridge Ct
4400 LSVL 40272 5831 D7
Southcrest Dr
4500 LSVL 40215 5724 B5
Southdale Rd
5300 LSVL 40214 5833 B3
Southern Av
1000 LSVL 40218 5727 B4
2900 LSVL 40211 5614 C5
Southern Mdws
10300 LSVL 40241 5402 A7
Southern Pkwy
4600 LSVL 40214 5724 C5
5700 LSVL 40215 5724 A7
Southern Pkwy SR-1020
3700 LSVL 40214 5724 C4
Southern Farm Blvd
- LSVL 40216 5723 A3
4200 LSVL 40216 5722 E3
E Southern Heights Av
100 LSVL 40214 5724 D5
500 LSVL 40209 5724 E4
W Southern Heights Av
- LSVL 40215 5723 E4
100 LSVL 40214 5724 C4
1400 LSVL 40215 5724 A4
Southgate Av
1300 LSVL 40215 5724 A3
Southgate Ct
- OdmC 40031 5295 C4
Southgate Dr
100 MTWH 40047 6056 B5
300 BltC 40047 6056 B5
Southgate Manor Dr
10800 LSVL 40229 5944 C4
Southhampton Rd
100 BLMD 40223 5619 B3
Southlake Dr
1700 ANCH 40223 5511 A7
1700 LSVL 40223 5511 A7
E Southland Blvd
100 LSVL 40214 5724 D7
W Southland Blvd
200 LSVL 40214 5724 C7
5700 LSVL 40215 5724 A7
Southland Dr
200 RDCF 40160 6483 E6
700 RDCF 40160 6484 A6
Southland Ter
5700 LSVL 40214 5724 B7
South Park Ct
1700 LSVL 40118 5834 A7
1700 LSVL 40118 5943 A1
South Ridge Dr
4300 LSVL 40272 5940 D2
Southside Ct
200 LSVL 40214 5833 D1
E Southside Ct
300 LSVL 40214 5833 D1
W Southside Ct
300 LSVL 40214 5833 D2
Southside Dr
4800 LSVL 40214 5724 C7
5800 LSVL 40214 5833 B3
Southside Dr SR-907
7100 LSVL 40214 5833 C3
Southside Dr SR-1020
4800 LSVL 40214 5724 C7
5800 LSVL 40214 5833 B3
Southview Dr
- WPT 40177 6156 C3
600 WDYH 40207 5509 B6
5400 LSVL 40214 5833 A3
Southview Rd
900 LSVL 40214 5833 A2
Southview Ter
100 LSVL 40214 5833 A3
Southwestern Pkwy
100 LSVL 40212 5614 B1
700 LSVL 40211 5614 A4
Southwind Ct
- CTWD 40014 5403 D6
Southwind Rd
10 INDH 40207 5508 D6
Southwood Dr
6000 OdmC 40014 5404 C5
Southwood Ter
200 LSVL 40214 5833 A3
Spalago Ct
8900 LSVL 40299 5728 B4
Spanish Ct
500 LSVL 40214 5724 C5
500 LSVL 40215 5724 C5
Sparks Av
100 JFVL 47130 5506 E6
Sparks Dr
100 BltC 40109 5943 C7
Sparky Wy
6900 HWCK 40228 5836 C3
6900 LSVL 40228 5836 C3
Sparrow Ct
- RDCF 40175 6482 E3
1800 ELZT 42701 6702 E4
Sparrow Dr
100 SHDV 40165 6161 E6
Sparta Dr
3900 LSVL 40219 5835 A1
Spearhead Division Lp
- HdnC 40121 6265 C7
Speckert Ct
700 LSVL 40203 5616 A5
Speed Av
1600 LSVL 40213 5616 D7
2000 LSVL 40205 5616 E6
2000 LSVL 40205 5617 A6
Speedway Av
5200 LSVL 40272 5831 B7
Speer Ln
8000 OdmC 40014 5514 A2
Spegal Ln
14100 LSVL 40299 5730 A6
Spencer Av
2900 LSVL 40205 5617 D7
2900 WLTN 40205 5617 D7
2900 WLTN 40205 5726 D1
Spencerwood Ct
6500 LSVL 40229 5944 E3
Spendthrift
- MTWH 40047 6056 E2
Spen Lea Rd
4600 LSVL 40216 5723 A6
4600 SVLY 40216 5723 A5
Sphere St
100 HLVW 40229 5943 E6
100 HLVW 40229 5944 A6
Spicewood Cir
500 CLKV 47129 5397 B7
Spicewood Ct
1000 CLKV 47129 5397 C6
Spicewood Dr
500 CLKV 47129 5397 B7
Spicewood Ln
5600 LSVL 40219 5726 A7
5600 LSVL 40219 5835 A1
Spicewood Pl
- CLKV 47129 5397 C6
Spickert Knob Rd
100 NALB 47150 5395 E7
100 NALB 47150 5396 A7
200 FydC 47150 5395 D6
300 FydC 47119 5395 D6
Spindletop
1000 ELZT 42701 6703 B7
Spinnaker Ct
8600 JFTN 40220 5728 A3
Spinner Pl
1600 OdmC 40031 5297 C4
Spinpointe Rd
10 BltC 40071 5949 E2
10 SpnC 40023 5949 E2
Spirit Dr
1600 LSVL 40272 5941 E1
Splendid Pt
- HTCK 40229 5945 D3
Split Rail Dr
5600 ClkC 47130 5399 B3
9000 LSVL 40272 5832 C7
Split Willow Dr
9000 LSVL 40214 5833 A4
Spokane Wy
9100 LSVL 40241 5510 C3
9100 TNBK 40241 5510 C3
Sporting Print
3200 ClkC 47130 5399 A4
Sportsman Ct
1300 JFVL 47130 5507 B1
Sportsman Dr
1100 JFVL 47130 5507 B2
Sportsman Hideway
7000 FydC 47122 5393 D6
Sportsman Lake Rd
10 ELZT 42701 6812 D7
200 HdnC 42701 6812 D7
Spotswood Ln
1800 LSVL 40023 5731 E2
1800 LSVL 40023 5732 A2
Spourtland Dr
6800 LSVL 40228 5836 B6
Spradling Ct
700 LSVL 40203 5615 E4
Sprague St
700 CLKV 47129 5506 D6
Spratt St
- LSVL 40217 5616 A6
1200 LSVL 40204 5616 B6
Spreading Oaks Ln
200 LSVL 40245 5621 B4
Sprig Wy
9800 LSVL 40291 5728 D7
Sprigler Ct
1500 NALB 47150 5505 D2
Sprigwood Ln
5300 LSVL 40291 5728 C7
5300 LSVL 40291 5837 C1
Spring Av
2100 NALB 47150 5505 E3
Spring Ct
- OdmC 44026 5292 D2
100 BltC 40047 6055 B5
100 MTWH 40047 6055 B5
Spring Dr
10 HdnC 42701 6703 D3
10 LSVL 40245 5622 B5
100 BltC 40047 6055 A6
500 ELZT 42701 6812 B1
1600 LSVL 40205 5616 E5
1600 LSVL 40205 5617 A6
2400 OdmC 40059 5291 D6
7700 LSVL 40245 5511 E2
7700 OdmC 40014 5512 A2
8900 LSVL 40245 5512 A2

STREET Block City ZIP Map# Grid

Spring Dr
8900 OdmC 40245 5512 A2
Spring St
- ClkC 47129 5506 A3
- LGNG 40031 5296 E2
- SLRB 47172 5288 E3
100 CHAN 47111 5181 D4
100 JFVL 47130 5507 A6
900 JFVL 47130 5506 E4
E Spring St
- ClkC 47129 5505 E3
100 NALB 47150 5505 B5
100 RDCF 40160 6483 D3
400 HdnC 40121 6483 D3
N Spring St
100 LSVL 40206 5616 C2
S Spring St
100 LSVL 40206 5616 C3
W Spring St
100 NALB 47150 5505 B5
200 RDCF 40160 6483 C3
Spring Arbor Dr
3800 LSVL 40245 5512 B5
Springbark Dr
9800 HKYH 40241 5510 E5
10100 LSVL 40241 5510 E5
Spring Bay Ct
4400 LSVL 40241 5511 A2
Spring Bluff Dr
- CTWD 40014 5403 C5
Springbourne Wy
4000 LSVL 40241 5510 E4
4100 LSVL 40241 5511 A3
Spring Branch Ct
4600 LSVL 40241 5510 A1
Spring Breeze Ct
3100 LSVL 40220 5727 E2
Springbrook Dr
2300 BltC 40165 6053 A5
Springbrook Wy
2800 ClkC 47130 5399 B4
Springbrooke Cir
9200 LSVL 40241 5510 C3
Springbrooke Cove
3900 LSVL 40241 5510 D3
Springbud Ct
2800 LSVL 40220 5727 E2
Spring Creek Ct
100 WBHL 40218 5726 C4
100 WSNP 40218 5726 C4
Spring Creek Dr
2000 FydC 47119 5503 E2
Springcrest Ct
- BltC 40165 6162 D5
2700 OdmC 40059 5292 D6
Springcrest Dr
3000 LSVL 40241 5509 E4
3000 LSVL 40242 5509 E4
3000 OBNP 40241 5509 E4
3000 OBNP 40242 5509 E4
3000 SPVL 40241 5509 E4
3000 SPVL 40242 5509 E4
6000 FydC 47122 5503 A4
Spring Dale Ct
4600 PNRV 40229 6053 B1
Springdale Ct
4800 GNSP 40241 5509 D1
Springdale Dr
100 BltC 40047 6056 B4
100 MTWH 40047 6056 B5
400 ELZT 42701 6812 B1
800 JFVL 47130 5507 C3
1200 LSVL 40213 5725 B4
Springdale Rd
2900 LSVL 40206 5617 B3
4100 LSVL 40241 5510 B1
7200 GNSP 40241 5400 E6
7200 GNSP 40241 5509 E1
7200 LSVL 40059 5400 E6
7200 LSVL 40241 5400 E6
7200 LSVL 40241 5509 E1
7500 GNSP 40241 5510 A1
Springer Al
- LSVL 40202 5615 E3
- LSVL 40204 5616 A3
500 LSVL 40202 5616 A3
Spring Farm Ct
7800 LSVL 40059 5401 A7
Springfarm Rd
5000 LSVL 40059 5401 A7
5000 LSVL 40059 5510 A1
Spring Farms Dr
2000 FydC 47119 5503 E2
Spring Field Ct
4600 PNRV 40229 6053 B1
Springfield Dr
3000 LSVL 40214 5832 B3
Springfield Rd
10 ELZT 42701 6812 E3
500 HdnC 42701 6812 E3
Spring Forest Ct
14000 LSVL 40245 5512 C4
Spring Forest Dr
4000 LSVL 40245 5512 C4
Spring Garden Dr
100 LSVL 40218 5727 C5
Spring Garden Ln
11800 ANCH 40223 5620 C1
Spring Gate Dr
9800 LSVL 40241 5510 E2
Spring Glen Wy
900 LYDN 40242 5619 B2
Spring Grove Wy
9200 LSVL 40291 5837 B3
Spring Heath Ct
10500 LSVL 40223 5619 C2
10500 LSVL 40223 5620 A2
Spring Hill Ct
1800 ANCH 40223 5511 A7
5700 CTWD 40014 5403 C5
Spring Hill Dr
500 NALB 47150 5504 E6
800 NALB 47150 5505 A6
1700 ANCH 40223 5511 B7

Spring Hill Dr
1700 ANCH 40223 5620 B1
Spring Hill Rd
1700 ANCH 40223 5511 B7
5200 FydC 47124 5393 B3
Springhill Rd
3900 PLYV 40207 5618 A4
3900 SPLE 40207 5618 A4
3900 STMW 40207 5618 A4
Spring Hill Trc
7200 CTWD 40014 5403 C5
Springhill Wy
13100 OdmC 40059 5401 B2
Springhill Farm Dr
6900 LSVL 40299 5838 E4
Springhill Gardens Dr
11800 ANCH 40223 5511 C7
Spring House Ln
100 HLVW 40229 5944 C7
7400 LSVL 40291 5837 A4
Spring House Pike
1000 LGNG 40031 5296 C3
1000 OdmC 40031 5296 C3
Springhurst Blvd
3400 LSVL 40241 5511 A4
3800 LSVL 40241 5510 D3
Springhurst Gardens Cir
10100 LSVL 40241 5510 E4
Spring Lake Ct
100 HLVW 40229 5944 C6
Springlake Ct
8100 BRMD 40241 5510 A3
Springlake Dr
8100 BRMD 40241 5510 A3
Spring Lawn Ct
6800 LSVL 40291 5837 D4
Spring Lawn Dr
10700 LSVL 40291 5837 D3
Spring Leaf Cir
6900 LSVL 40241 5509 D5
Spring Leaf Dr
- BltC 40165 6161 B2
Springlet Ct
4900 CDSM 40245 5511 E1
Springmeadow Cir
- OdmC 44026 5292 B3
Spring Meadow Ct
11800 OdmC 44026 5292 C3
Springmeadow Ct
4600 PNRV 40229 6053 B1
Spring Meadow Dr
100 HdnC 40160 6592 C3
600 RDCF 40160 6592 C3
12300 PNRV 40229 6053 B1
Springmeadow Dr
12300 PNRV 40229 5944 C7
12300 PNRV 40229 6053 B1
Spring Meadow Ln
100 LSVL 40223 5620 A4
Springmeadow Ln
12000 GSHN 44026 5292 D3
12000 OdmC 44026 5292 D3
Spring Meadows Rd
5800 FydC 47122 5503 B3
Springmere Dr
10200 LSVL 40241 5511 A3
10300 LSVL 40241 5510 E4
Springmeyer Rd
3800 LSVL 40223 5619 E2
W Springmill Dr
100 BltC 40165 6054 C5
Spring Mill Pl
4000 LSVL 40245 5512 B4
Spring Mill Rd
14000 LSVL 40245 5512 B4
E Springmill Rd
- BltC 40165 6054 C5
Springmont Pl
9300 LSVL 40241 5510 D5
Spring Pointe Ct
9800 LSVL 40229 5945 A2
Spring Pond Ct
- OdmC 40031 5295 B6
Spring Ridge Dr
9900 LSVL 40223 5619 D3
Spring Run Ct
10900 LSVL 40291 5837 D4
Spring Run Dr
7300 LSVL 40291 5837 D4
Spring Run Rd
3200 ClkC 47143 5180 C1
Springsbury Pl
8800 HTBN 40222 5619 B4
Springside Ct
1100 JFTN 40223 5619 D6
Springside Pl
10200 JFTN 40223 5619 E6
Springside Wy
1000 JFTN 40223 5619 D6
Springs Station Rd
13400 LSVL 40245 5512 A4
Springstead Cir
3100 LSVL 40241 5510 D4
Springstead Cove
9200 LSVL 40241 5510 C4
Springtime Av
3000 LSVL 40272 5940 A7
Spring Trace Ct
12400 PNRV 40229 6053 B1
Springvale Dr
2100 LSVL 40218 5727 B5
7400 SPVL 40241 5509 E4
7500 LSVL 40241 5509 E4
7700 LSVL 40241 5510 A3
Spring Valley Ln
2400 LSVL 40205 5617 A5
Spring Valley Wy
3800 LSVL 40241 5510 E3
Springview Ct
100 LSVL 40223 5620 C3
100 MTWH 40047 6056 C3
1000 LSVL 40219 5835 B7
2700 LSVL 40272 5940 A6

Springview Dr
1000 LSVL 40219 5835 B7
Spring Vista Ct
7000 LSVL 40229 5945 A3
Springwater Ct
9700 LSVL 40229 5945 A3
Spring Willow Ct
3800 LSVL 40299 5728 A4
Springwood Dr
100 HLVW 40229 5944 C5
Springwood Ln
400 STMW 40207 5618 A1
400 WDYH 40207 5618 A1
Sprint Ct
8100 LSVL 40291 5836 E2
Sprite Rd
300 BWNV 40207 5617 D1
Sprowl Rd
3000 JFTN 40299 5728 D4
Spruce Ct
- LSVL 40213 5834 C1
1400 RDCF 40160 6483 A4
9200 OdmC 40056 5512 D4
Spruce Dr
1100 JFVL 47130 5507 B3
Spruce Ln
10 ELZT 42701 6703 A3
100 BltC 40047 6055 E4
100 LSVL 40207 5509 A6
100 WDYH 40207 5509 A7
700 HdnC 42701 6703 A3
Spruce St
10 LGNG 40031 5296 E2
100 BltC 40165 6161 B1
Sprucedale Ct
6900 LSVL 40291 5837 A2
Sprucedale Wy
9000 LSVL 40291 5837 B3
Spruce Grove Ct
4200 JFTN 40299 5728 C5
Spruce Grove Dr
10000 JFTN 40299 5728 C4
Spruce Hill Rd
8400 OdmC 40059 5401 B3
8400 PROS 40059 5401 B3
Spruce Tree Ct
- LYDN 40242 5619 C2
Spruce Tree Pl
9000 LYDN 40242 5619 C1
Sprucewood Ct
5400 LSVL 40291 5728 C7
Sprucewood Dr
5000 LSVL 40291 5728 D7
5300 LSVL 40291 5837 C1
Spyglass Cir
100 HdnC 40175 6591 B1
Spy Glass Ct
4100 LSVL 40229 5944 B2
Squire Neagli Ct
10100 LSVL 40229 5944 A3
Squires Dr
1400 LSVL 40215 5724 A5
Squires Ln
11800 ANCH 40223 5620 C2
Squire Springs Ct
13500 LSVL 40245 5512 A5
SR-3
- CHAN 47111 5181 E5
- ClkC 47111 5181 E5
SR-3 Market St
100 CHAN 47111 5181 D1
SR-11
- FydC 47117 5721 A2
- FydC 47136 5611 E7
- FydC 47136 5721 A2
SR-22 Ballardsville Rd
- CTWD 40014 5404 A7
- ODGH 40014 5511 E1
6700 CTWD 40014 5403 E7
7000 PWEV 40014 5403 D7
7100 OdmC 40014 5403 C7
7100 PWEV 40056 5403 C7
7200 OdmC 40014 5512 C1
7200 PWEV 40014 5512 B1
7200 PWEV 40056 5512 C1
10000 LSVL 40241 5510 E1
10000 LSVL 40241 5511 E1
10900 LSVL 40245 5511 C1
11500 CDSM 40241 5511 C1
11500 CDSM 40245 5511 C1
11600 CDSM 40014 5511 D1
11600 JfnC 40014 5511 D1
SR-22 Brownsboro Rd
4900 CSGT 40222 5509 C6
4900 LSVL 40222 5509 C6
4900 NHFD 40222 5509 B6
6700 TNHL 40222 5509 D5
6800 TNHL 40241 5509 D5
6900 LSVL 40241 5509 C6
6900 LSVL 40242 5509 C6
7100 OBNP 40242 5509 C6
7200 OBNP 40241 5509 C6
7300 SPVL 40241 5509 C6
7300 SPVL 40242 5509 C6
7600 LSVL 40241 5510 D2
7600 LSVL 40242 5510 A4
7600 SPVL 40241 5510 A4
7600 SPVL 40242 5510 A4
8000 BRMD 40241 5510 A4
8100 BRMD 40242 5510 B4
8100 BWNF 40241 5510 B3
8400 BWNF 40242 5510 B3
8600 TNBK 40241 5510 C3
SR-22 Dogwood Ln
- CTWD 40014 5404 E5
SR-44
- BltC 40047 6054 B7
- BltC 40047 6055 A6
- BltC 40047 6057 E1
- BltC 40071 6057 E1
- BltC 40165 6048 B7
- BltC 40165 6054 C7
- BltC 40165 6160 B2
- BltC 40165 6162 E1

SR-44
- BltC 40165 6163 A1
- LSVL 40272 6048 B7
- MTWH 40047 6054 B7
- MTWH 40047 6055 A6
- MTWH 40047 6056 E2
- MTWH 40047 6057 B1
- MTWH 40165 6054 E6
- SHDV 40165 6160 E2
- SHDV 40165 6162 C2
SR-44 E 4th St
1000 SHDV 40165 6161 C4
SR-44 Mt Washington Rd
2100 SHDV 40165 6161 E3
2100 SHDV 40165 6162 E1
4200 BltC 40165 6162 B2
SR-44 Old Mill Rd
- BltC 40047 6056 D2
100 MTWH 40047 6056 B3
500 BltC 40047 6055 D5
500 MTWH 40047 6055 D5
SR-44 Shepherdsville Rd
- SHDV 40165 6160 E2
200 SHDV 40165 6161 B3
SR-53
- LGNG 40014 5297 C7
- LGNG 40031 5296 E1
- LGNG 40031 5297 A3
- OdmC 40014 5297 C7
- OdmC 40031 5296 E1
- OdmC 40031 5297 A4
SR-53 N 1st Av
100 LGNG 40031 5296 E1
100 OdmC 40031 5296 E1
SR-53 S 1st Av
- LGNG 40031 5296 E3
SR-53 S 1st St
100 LGNG 40031 5297 A3
SR-60
- ClkC 47143 5287 E1
- ClkC 47172 5287 E1
- ClkC 47172 5288 B4
- CLKV 47172 5288 C6
- SLRB 47172 5288 B4
SR-61
- BltC 40165 6161 C5
- ELZT 42701 6812 D6
- LSVL - 5615 E7
- LSVL 40217 5615 E7
- SHDV 40165 6052 E7
- SHDV 40165 6161 C5
SR-61 Arthur St
1600 LSVL 40208 5615 E7
SR-61 Bardstown Rd
- ELZT 42701 6703 E7
SR-61 E Brandeis Av
400 LSVL 40208 5615 E7
400 LSVL 40217 5615 E7
SR-61 N Buckman St
100 SHDV 40165 6161 D1
SR-61 S Buckman St
100 SHDV 40165 6161 C4
SR-61 S Dixie Av
- ELZT 42701 6812 C3
SR-61 S Jackson St
100 LSVL 40202 5616 A2
400 LSVL 40202 5615 E3
600 LSVL 40203 5615 E4
1200 LSVL 40208 5615 E6
SR-61 Lynn St
700 LSVL 40217 5615 E7
SR-61 N Mulberry St
100 ELZT 42701 6812 D1
1800 ELZT 42701 6703 E7
SR-61 Preston Hwy
- BltC 40165 6053 B3
- BltC 40229 5944 D6
- PNRV 40165 5944 C7
- PNRV 40165 6053 B3
- PNRV 40229 5944 C7
- PNRV 40229 6053 D1
2500 LSVL 40217 5725 A1
2500 PKWV 40217 5725 A1
3000 LSVL 40213 5725 A2
3100 ANPK 40213 5725 A2
4700 LYNV 40213 5725 C6
5300 LSVL 40219 5725 E7
5700 LSVL 40219 5834 E1
6400 LSVL 40219 5835 A2
9100 LSVL 40229 5835 C7
9200 LSVL 40229 5944 C2
12000 HLVW 40229 5944 D5
SR-61 N Preston Hwy
5200 BltC 40165 6053 C2
5200 HBNE 40165 6053 C2
5200 PNRV 40165 6053 C2
SR-61 S Preston St
- BltC 40165 6161 D7
- SHDV 40165 6161 C5
100 LSVL 40202 5615 E5
700 LSVL 40203 5615 E4
1600 LSVL 40208 5615 E7
1600 LSVL 40217 5615 E7
2100 LSVL 40217 5724 E1
2200 LSVL 40217 5725 A1
2400 PKWV 40217 5725 A1
SR-61 S Shelby St
2200 LSVL 40217 5725 D7
2400 PKWV 40217 5725 A1
SR-61 WH Ford Western KY Pkwy
- ELZT 42701 6812 C4
SR-62
- CHAN 47111 5181 D7
- CHAN 47111 5182 A4
- ClkC - 5397 E4
- ClkC 47111 5181 D7
- ClkC 47111 5182 C3
- ClkC 47111 5290 D1
- ClkC 47130 5290 A7
- ClkC 47130 5399 A1
- CLKV - 5397 E4
- FydC - 5503 D3
- FydC - 5504 A2

SR-62
- FydC 47122 5503 A7
- FydC 47136 5502 E7
- FydC 47136 5503 B7
- FydC 47136 5611 E1
- HsnC 47112 5610 B7
- HsnC 47136 5610 A7
- JFVL - 5397 E4
- JFVL 47130 5398 E4
- LNVL 47136 5610 A7
SR-62 Clark Maritime Hwy
- ClkC - 5397 E4
- ClkC - 5398 D4
- CLKV - 5397 E4
- JFVL - 5397 E4
- JFVL - 5398 A4
SR-62 Lee H Hamilton Hwy
- ClkC - 5397 A4
- CLKV - 5397 A4
- FydC - 5395 E7
- FydC - 5396 A6
- FydC - 5397 C4
- JFVL - 5397 E4
- NALB - 5395 E7
- NALB - 5396 D4
- NALB - 5504 E1
SR-62 Main St
6900 LNVL 47136 5610 D5
SR-62 Patrol Rd
7900 ClkC 47130 5290 B5
8800 ClkC 47111 5290 C3
SR-64
- FydC 47122 5501 D3
- FydC 47122 5502 C4
- FydC 47122 5503 B5
- GEOT 47122 5501 B3
- GEOT 47122 5502 E5
SR-93
- OdmC 40014 5405 D4
- OdmC 40014 5514 E1
SR-111
- ClkC 47143 5287 D1
- FydC 47150 5613 D3
- FydC 47150 5721 C7
- FydC 47150 5722 B1
- FydC 47172 5287 D3
- HsnC 47117 5721 D5
- HsnC 47117 5830 B7
- HsnC 47117 5939 B1
- HsnC 47117 6048 A1
- HsnC 47117 6155 A2
- HsnC 47117 6156 A1
- NALB 47150 5504 E7
- NALB 47150 5505 A6
- NALB 47150 5613 D3
SR-111 Beechwood Av
1300 NALB 47150 5505 C2
SR-111 Charlestown Rd
1700 NALB 47150 5505 C3
SR-111 Grant Line Rd
2100 NALB 47150 5505 A6
2800 NALB 47150 5396 B7
4100 FydC 47150 5396 B7
5400 FydC 47119 5287 D1
5400 FydC 47150 5287 D1
5700 FydC 47172 5287 D1
7600 ClkC 47143 5287 D3
SR-111 E Main St
100 NALB 47150 5505 B5
SR-111 W Main St
100 NALB 47150 5505 B5
SR-111 Vincennes St
10 NALB 47150 5505 D4
SR-144
- MdeC 40175 6482 A6
- VNGV 40175 6482 E7
- VNGV 40175 6483 A6
SR-144 W Main St
100 VNGV 40175 6482 C7
100 VNGV 40175 6591 D1
SR-144 E Vine St
100 RDCF 40160 6483 A6
SR-144 W Vine St
100 RDCF 40160 6483 D5
1500 HdnC 40160 6483 B6
1600 VNGV 40160 6483 B6
1900 VNGV 40175 6483 A6
SR-146
- CTWD 40014 5404 A6
SR-146 Bellewood Rd
- ANCH 40223 5620 C1
SR-146 Glenbrook Rd
- ANCH 40223 5620 D1
SR-146 Jefferson St
100 LGNG 40031 5296 E2
900 OdmC 40031 5296 C3
SR-146 E Jefferson St
100 LGNG 40031 5296 D3
100 LGNG 40031 5297 A2
SR-146 La Grange Rd
100 PWEV 40056 5512 B3
300 OdmC 40056 5512 C3
6500 CTWD 40014 5403 E7
6500 CTWD 40014 5404 A7
6700 CTWD 40014 5512 D1
6700 PWEV 40014 5512 D1
6800 CTWD 40056 5512 D1
7600 LSVL 40245 5512 A5
9400 LYDN 40223 5510 D7
9400 LYDN 40242 5510 D7
9400 MLND 40223 5510 D7
9400 WPMG 40223 5510 D7
10300 LSVL 40223 5511 A7
10300 LYDN 40223 5511 A7
10600 ANCH 40223 5511 A7
11500 ANCH 40223 5620 D1
11500 LSVL 40223 5620 D1
12200 LSVL 40223 5512 A6
SR-146 New Lagrange Rd
- LSVL 40222 5618 E3
7300 NRWD 40222 5618 E3
7300 STMW 40222 5618 E3

SR-146 New Lagrange Rd
7600 LYDN 40222 5618 D3
8000 LYDN 40222 5619 A2
8300 LYDN 40242 5619 A2
9200 LYDN 40223 5619 D1
SR-146 Park Rd
10900 ANCH 40223 5620 B1
10900 LSVL 40223 5620 B1
SR-146 Ridge Rd
11400 ANCH 40223 5620 D1
SR-146 Whipps Mill Rd
- LYDN 40223 5510 D7
- LYDN 40242 5510 D7
- MLND 40223 5510 D7
9600 LYDN 40223 5619 D1
9600 LYDN 40242 5619 D1
SR-148
- LSVL 40023 5731 C5
- LSVL 40023 5732 C7
- SbyC 40067 5732 C7
SR-148 Taylorsville Rd
- LSVL 40023 5731 B5
14700 LSVL 40299 5730 E4
14800 LSVL 40299 5731 A4
SR-155
- LSVL 40023 5840 E3
- SpnC 40023 5840 E3
SR-155 Taylorsville Rd
- LSVL 40205 5618 E7
2200 LSVL 40205 5617 B7
2200 SMRV 40205 5617 B7
2400 SGDN 40205 5617 C7
2500 KGLY 40205 5617 C7
3700 MVWE 40220 5618 B7
4000 LSVL 40220 5618 D7
4100 CMBG 40220 5618 D7
4100 HNAC 40220 5618 D7
4300 HBNA 40220 5619 A7
4300 JFTN 40220 5619 A7
4300 LSVL 40220 5619 A7
4600 HBNA 40220 5728 B1
4600 JFTN 40220 5728 C2
8900 FTHL 40299 5728 C2
9200 JFTN 40299 5728 C2
10500 JFTN 40299 5729 E5
10600 LSVL 40299 5729 A4
12800 LSVL 40299 5730 A5
SR-155 Taylorsville Lake Rd
4000 LSVL 40023 5730 C4
4000 LSVL 40023 5731 B7
4000 LSVL 40299 5730 C4
4000 LSVL 40299 5731 B7
4700 LSVL 40023 5840 A4
6000 SpnC 40023 5840 E3
SR-160
- CHAN 47111 5181 B1
- ClkC 47111 5181 B1
SR-210
- ELZT 42701 6812 E7
- HdnC 42701 6812 E7
SR-210 Hodgenville Rd
10 ELZT 42701 6812 E7
1000 HdnC 42701 6812 E7
SR-211
- HsnC 47117 5830 A5
SR-220
- HdnC 40162 6592 D7
- HdnC 40162 6593 B6
- HdnC 42701 6593 B6
- RDCF 42701 6593 B6
SR-220 Rineyville-Big Sprs Rd
- HdnC 42701 6593 B6
- RDCF 42701 6593 C6
SR-251
- ELZT 42701 6703 D4
- HdnC 42701 6703 D1
SR-251 N Miles St
100 ELZT 42701 6812 C1
900 ELZT 42701 6703 C7
SR-251 Shepherdsville Rd
10 ELZT 42701 6703 C7
SR-265
- ClkC - 5397 E4
- CLKV - 5397 E4
- JFVL - 5397 E4
SR-265 Clark Maritime Hwy
- ClkC - 5397 E4
- ClkC - 5398 E4
- CLKV - 5397 E4
- JFVL - 5397 E4
- JFVL - 5398 E4
SR-311
- ClkC 47172 5288 C7
- ClkC 47172 5397 B1
- CLKV 47172 5288 C6
- FydC 47150 5397 B1
- SLRB 47172 5288 D4
SR-311 Charlestown Rd
- NALB 47150 5396 E4
3900 FydC 47150 5396 E3
4600 FydC 47150 5397 A2
4900 FydC 47172 5397 A2
SR-313 Joe Prather Hwy
- HdnC 42701 6593 A3
- RDCF 40160 6593 A3
- RDCF 42701 6593 C2
SR-313 Joe Prather Hwy S
100 HdnC 40175 6482 C5
100 VNGV 40175 6482 D5
400 VNGV 40175 6483 B7
SR-313 Vine Grove Connector Rd
- HdnC 40160 6592 C1
- RDCF 40160 6592 C1
- RDCF 40160 6593 A3
- RDCF 42701 6593 A3
- VNGV 40160 6483 C7
- VNGV 40160 6592 C1
- VNGV 40175 6483 A6

SR-329
- CTWD 40014 5403 B3
- LSVL 40059 5401 A2
- OdmC 40014 5402 E1
- OdmC 40014 5403 D6
- OdmC 40059 5401 A3
- OdmC 40059 5402 A1
- PROS 40059 5401 A2
SR-329 BYP
- CTWD 40014 5403 E6
- CTWD 40014 5404 A6
SR-329 Covered Bridge Rd
7100 LSVL 40059 5400 E3
7100 PROS 40059 5400 E3
7200 LSVL 40059 5401 A3
7200 PROS 40059 5401 A3
7600 OdmC 40059 5401 A2
SR-329 Old Highway 329
- CTWD 40014 5403 A1
- OdmC 40014 5403 D5
SR-329 BYP Veterans Mem Pkwy
- CTWD 40014 5404 A6
- OdmC 40014 5404 A7
SR-335
- FydC 47124 5283 B4
- FydC 47165 5283 B4
- GNVL 47124 5283 C6
SR-362
- LSVL 40245 5513 A5
- OdmC 40014 5512 E5
- OdmC 40014 5513 A6
- OdmC 40056 5512 E4
- SbyC 40067 5514 E5
- SbyC 40245 5513 A5
- SbyC 40245 5514 E5
SR-362 Ash Av
- OdmC 40014 5512 E4
100 OdmC 40056 5512 D3
100 PWEV 40056 5512 D3
SR-362 Central Av
100 PWEV 40056 5512 C1
400 PWEV 40014 5512 B1
SR-362 La Grange Rd
200 PWEV 40056 5512 C2
SR-391
- HdnC 40162 6591 A4
- HdnC 40175 6591 B3
- VNGV 40175 6591 B3
SR-391 Brown St
200 VNGV 40175 6591 D1
SR-391 Crume Rd
300 VNGV 40175 6591 D1
700 HdnC 40175 6591 C2
SR-391 High St
200 VNGV 40175 6591 D1
SR-393
- OdmC 40014 5405 B3
- OdmC 40031 5295 D5
- OdmC 40014 5404 E1
- OdmC 40031 5405 A1
SR-403
- CHAN 47111 5181 B5
- ClkC 47111 5180 C7
- ClkC 47111 5181 D3
- ClkC 47111 5289 B1
- ClkC 47172 5288 E2
- ClkC 47172 5289 A1
- SLRB 47172 5288 E2
SR-434
- HdnC 42701 6593 E4
- RDCF 42701 6593 C4
SR-434 Battle Training Rd
10 HdnC 42701 6593 B3
10 RDCF 42701 6593 B3
SR-447
- ELZT 42701 6702 C2
- HdnC 40162 6593 B6
- HdnC 40162 6702 B1
- HdnC 42701 6593 B4
- HdnC 42701 6702 C2
- RDCF 40160 6593 B7
- RDCF 42701 6593 B7
- RDCF 42701 6702 C2
SR-447 Battle Training Rd
10 RDCF 40160 6593 B3
10 RDCF 42701 6593 B3
SR-480
- BltC 40165 6163 C6
SR-480 Cedar Grove Rd
- BltC 40165 6163 B6
- SHDV 40165 6161 D6
- SHDV 40165 6162 A5
2200 BltC 40165 6162 C5
SR-480 Charles Hamilton Wy
- SHDV 40165 6161 D6
SR-480C
- SHDV 40165 6161 C5
SR-480C Cedar Grove Rd
900 SHDV 40165 6161 E6
SR-567 Locust Grove Rd
- HdnC 42701 6812 E5
300 ELZT 42701 6812 D5
SR-567 Valley Creek Rd
800 ELZT 42701 6812 E5
800 HdnC 42701 6812 E5
SR-660
- BltC 40047 5947 B6
- BltC 40047 5948 A7
- BltC 40071 5948 A7
- LSVL 40291 5947 B6
- MTWH 40047 5947 E7
- MTWH 40047 5948 A7
SR-660 Waterford Rd
11400 BltC 40047 5947 E7
11400 LSVL 40291 5947 E7
SR-712
- LGNG 40031 5297 B2
- OdmC 40031 5297 B2

INDEX 45
SR-712 Fort Pickens Rd
Louisville Metro Street Index
Stable Pl

STREET
Block City ZIP Map# Grid
SR-712 Fort Pickens Rd
1100 LGNG 40031 5297 B2
SR-841 Gene Snyder Frwy
- LSVL - 5400 E7
- LSVL - 5509 E1
- LSVL - 5510 E3
- LSVL - 5511 E5
- LSVL - 5512 B7
- LSVL - 5621 B1
- LSVL - 5729 E7
- LSVL - 5730 A6
- LSVL - 5832 E7
- LSVL - 5833 A7
- LSVL - 5834 A7
- LSVL - 5835 E7
- LSVL - 5836 B7
- LSVL - 5837 E4
- LSVL - 5838 A4
- LSVL - 5940 B4
- LSVL - 5941 A3
- LSVL - 5943 E1
- LSVL - 5944 D1
- MDTN - 5621 B6
- MLHT - 5834 A7
- PROS - 5400 E7
SR-864
- LSVL 40228 5836 B1
SR-864 Beulah Church Rd
6000 LSVL 40228 5945 D1
6000 LSVL 40229 5945 D1
6500 LSVL 40228 5836 E6
7500 LSVL 40291 5836 E6
SR-864 S Campbell St
600 LSVL 40204 5616 A4
SR-864 Cedar Creek Rd
9900 HTCK 40229 5945 E3
9900 LSVL 40228 5945 E3
9900 LSVL 40229 5945 E3
SR-864 E Chestnut St
- LSVL 40204 5616 B3
SR-864 Cooper Chapel Rd
7900 LSVL 40228 5945 E2
7900 LSVL 40229 5945 E2
SR-864 Fegenbush Ln
6100 LSVL 40228 5836 D4
6700 HWCK 40228 5836 C3
7000 SPML 40228 5836 C4
7900 LSVL 40291 5836 E5
SR-864 Fern Valley Rd
6100 LSVL 40228 5836 A2
SR-864 Finzer St
900 LSVL 40204 5616 A4
SR-864 Goss Av
- LSVL 40203 5616 A6
900 LSVL 40204 5616 A6
900 LSVL 40217 5616 B7
SR-864 E Gray St
800 LSVL 40202 5616 A4
800 LSVL 40204 5616 A4
SR-864 Logan St
700 LSVL 40204 5616 A5
SR-864 Poplar Level Rd
1300 LSVL 40217 5616 B7
3000 LSVL 40213 5725 E5
3000 LSVL 40217 5725 E5
4300 WSNP 40213 5725 E4
4500 LSVL 40218 5725 E5
4600 LSVL 40213 5726 B7
4600 LSVL 40218 5726 A6
4600 PLRH 40213 5726 A6
4700 LSVL 40219 5726 B7
5000 LSVL 40219 5835 B1
5200 LSVL 40228 5835 E2
5800 LSVL 40228 5836 A2
SR-864 S Shelby St
600 LSVL 40202 5616 A4
600 LSVL 40203 5616 A4
600 LSVL 40204 5616 A4
SR-868
- MdeC 40108 6264 C3
- MRGH 40155 6264 C4
SR-868 Brandenburg Station Rd
- HdnC 40121 6264 D6
- MdeC 40108 6264 D6
- MRGH 40155 6264 D6
- MRGH 40177 6264 D6
SR-868 Muldraugh Cut Off Rd
- HdnC 40121 6264 D6
- MRGH 40155 6264 D6
- MRGH 40177 6264 D6
SR-907 3rd St Rd
7400 LSVL 40214 5833 B3
7700 LSVL 40214 5832 E5
8000 LSVL 40272 5832 E6
9300 LSVL 40272 5941 A1
9700 LSVL 40272 5940 E1
SR-907 Southside Dr
7100 LSVL 40214 5833 C3
SR-907 Valley Station Rd
4600 LSVL 40272 5940 B2
SR-913
- DGSH 40243 5620 C6
- LSVL 40299 5620 C6
- MDTN 40243 5620 C6
- MDTN 40299 5620 C6
SR-913 Blankenbaker Pkwy
- JFTN 40299 5620 C7
- LSVL 40299 5620 C7
- MDTN 40243 5620 C7
200 DGSH 40243 5620 B5
200 LSVL 40223 5620 B5
1800 JFTN 40299 5729 A3
2100 LSVL 40299 5729 C2
SR-913 Blankenbaker Access Dr
11400 JFTN 40299 5729 A3
11400 LSVL 40299 5729 A3
SR-1020
- BltC 40109 5943 C6
- BltC 40109 6052 D3
SR-1020
- BltC 40165 6052 D6
- LSVL 40118 5943 C5
SR-1020 S 2nd St
200 LSVL 40202 5615 D5
700 LSVL 40203 5615 D4
1200 LSVL 40208 5615 D5
SR-1020 S 3rd St
200 LSVL 40202 5615 D7
700 LSVL 40203 5615 D4
1200 LSVL 40208 5615 D5
2000 LSVL 40208 5724 C5
3000 LSVL 40214 5724 C2
SR-1020 W Kenwood Wy
200 LSVL 40214 5724 C7
SR-1020 National Tpk
5500 LSVL 40214 5833 C3
8500 LSVL 40118 5833 E6
9100 LSVL 40118 5942 E1
9800 LSVL 40118 5943 A2
10500 HYVA 40118 5943 A3
SR-1020 S Park Rd
100 BltC 40109 5943 C5
100 LSVL 40118 5943 C4
SR-1020 Southern Pkwy
3700 LSVL 40214 5724 C3
SR-1020 Southside Dr
4800 LSVL 40214 5724 C6
5800 LSVL 40214 5833 D3
SR-1060 Plum Creek Rd
10 SpnC 40071 5949 D3
SR-1065 Beulah Church Rd
8000 LSVL 40228 5836 E5
8000 LSVL 40291 5836 E5
8400 LSVL 40291 5837 A5
SR-1065 Fegenbush Ln
7900 LSVL 40228 5836 D5
7900 LSVL 40291 5836 D5
SR-1065 Lovers Ln
5500 LSVL 40299 5837 A4
5600 LSVL 40291 5837 A4
SR-1065 Outer Lp
100 LSVL 40214 5832 E6
600 LSVL 40214 5833 A6
1400 LSVL 40214 5834 A6
1400 LSVL 40219 5834 A6
1400 MLHT 40219 5834 A6
4100 LSVL 40219 5835 A5
5900 LSVL 40219 5836 C5
6200 LSVL 40228 5836 B5
7800 LSVL 40291 5836 D5
SR-1065 Seatonville Rd
9400 LSVL 40291 5837 C3
SR-1116 Cedar Creek Rd
- BltC 40165 5945 C7
100 BltC 40165 6054 C2
1400 BltC 40229 5945 D6
1400 LSVL 40229 5945 C6
SR-1116 Old Preston Hwy
- BltC 40165 6053 D1
1100 BltC 40229 5944 D7
1100 HLVW 40229 5944 D7
12300 BltC 40165 5944 D7
SR-1116 Old Preston Hwy N
400 BltC 40165 5944 D7
400 BltC 40165 6053 E1
SR-1116 Zoneton Rd
100 BltC 40165 6053 D1
400 BltC 40165 6054 B1
SR-1136 Bishop Ln
100 ELZT 42701 6812 C4
SR-1136 New Glendale Rd
500 ELZT 42701 6812 C4
1400 HdnC 42701 6812 B6
SR-1142 Palatka Rd
800 LSVL 40214 5833 A3
1000 LSVL 40214 5832 E2
SR-1169 Plum Ridge Rd
4300 SpnC 40071 5949 E7
SR-1230 Ashby Ln
7000 LSVL 40272 5939 D1
SR-1230 Cane Run Rd
5100 LSVL 40216 5722 A6
5200 LSVL 40216 5721 D7
5200 LSVL 40258 5721 D7
6000 LSVL 40258 5830 D6
SR-1230 Dover Av
- LSVL 40216 5722 B6
SR-1230 Johnsontown Rd
7300 LSVL 40258 5830 D7
7300 LSVL 40272 5830 D7
SR-1230 Lower River Rd
9700 LSVL 40258 5830 D7
9700 LSVL 40272 5830 D7
10100 LSVL 40272 5939 D1
12400 LSVL 40272 6048 C1
SR-1230 Watson Ln
6800 LSVL 40272 6048 D1
SR-1319
- BltC 40047 5948 B7
- BltC 40047 6057 A1
- BltC 40071 5948 E4
- BltC 40071 5949 A3
- BltC 40071 6057 A1
- MTWH 40047 6057 A1
- SpnC 40023 5949 A3
SR-1357 St. John Rd
- ELZT 42701 6811 E2
- HdnC 42701 6811 A2
SR-1408 Floydsburg Rd
7100 CTWD 40014 5403 E7
7400 CTWD 40014 5404 A7
7400 OdmC 40014 5403 E7
7400 OdmC 40014 5404 A7
7500 CTWD 40014 5513 B2
7500 OdmC 40014 5513 B2
8100 OdmC 40056 5513 A1
9000 SbyC 40245 5513 E4
9000 SbyC 40245 5514 A4
SR-1408 Old Floydsburg Rd
5500 OdmC 40014 5513 B2
SR-1408 Todds Point Rd
8000 OdmC 40014 5513 D3
8000 SbyC 40245 5513 E3
SR-1417 Martin Hill Rd
- BltC 40165 6050 D6
SR-1442 Ridge Rd
- BltC 40165 6163 A5
100 BltC 40165 6162 E5
SR-1447 Old Lagrange Rd
- LSVL 40245 5512 B4
SR-1447 Old La Grange Rd
13700 LSVL 40245 5512 A4
SR-1447 Westport Rd
- WDYH 40222 5618 D1
- WLNP 40222 5618 D1
3900 LSVL 40207 5617 E3
3900 STMW 40207 5617 E3
3900 STMW 40207 5618 A2
4200 WLNP 40222 5618 B1
4300 WDYH 40207 5618 B1
4600 LSVL 40222 5618 D1
4600 STMW 40222 5618 D1
4700 GYDL 40222 5618 D1
4800 GYDL 40222 5509 D7
4800 STMW 40222 5509 D7
7600 LSVL 40222 5509 E7
7600 LYDN 40222 5509 E7
7800 LSVL 40222 5510 A6
7800 LYDN 40222 5510 A6
8300 BRWD 40242 5510 B6
8300 LYDN 40242 5510 A6
8300 PNTN 40242 5510 A6
8700 LSVL 40242 5510 B6
8800 WWOD 40242 5510 C6
8900 LDNP 40242 5510 C6
9100 LSVL 40241 5510 E4
9100 RLGH 40241 5510 C5
9100 RLGH 40242 5510 C6
9700 HKYH 40241 5510 E5
10400 LSVL 40241 5511 A4
11400 LSVL 40245 5511 A4
12200 WTNH 40245 5511 D3
12600 LSVL 40245 5512 A3
SR-1450
- HLVW 40165 6052 E2
- HLVW 40165 6053 A1
- HLVW 40229 5943 E5
- HLVW 40229 5944 A6
- HLVW 40229 6053 A1
- LSVL 40229 5943 E5
SR-1450 Blue Lick Rd
8000 LSVL 40219 5835 A6
9200 LSVL 40219 5944 A1
9200 LSVL 40229 5944 A1
10300 LSVL 40229 5943 E4
10900 HLVW 40229 5943 E5
SR-1450 W Hebron Ln
- BltC 40165 6053 A2
- BltC 40229 6053 B3
- HBNE 40165 6053 C3
- PNRV 40229 6053 A2
100 FXCH 40165 6053 B3
100 HLVW 40165 6053 B3
100 PNRV 40165 6053 A2
SR-1494 Beech Grove Rd
- BltC 40165 6160 E7
100 SHDV 40165 6161 A7
1400 BltC 40165 6161 A6
SR-1500 Knox Av
- MdeC 40175 6373 B7
- VNGV 40160 6592 B1
300 VNGV 40175 6482 C7
2300 MdeC 40175 6482 C6
SR-1500 E Main St
100 VNGV 40175 6591 E1
1500 VNGV 40175 6592 A1
SR-1500 W Main St
100 VNGV 40175 6482 C7
100 VNGV 40175 6591 D1
SR-1500 Mill Creek Rd
100 RDCF 40160 6483 E6
SR-1500 Rogersville Rd
100 RDCF 40160 6483 E6
900 VNGV 40160 6483 C7
1900 VNGV 40160 6592 B1
1900 VNGV 40175 6592 B1
SR-1500 S Wilson Rd
1000 RDCF 40160 6483 E6
SR-1526
- BltC 40109 6050 A6
- BltC 40109 6051 A3
- BltC 40109 6052 A1
- BltC 40165 6049 C7
- BltC 40165 6050 A6
- BltC 40165 6051 D3
- HLVW 40109 6052 E1
- HLVW 40229 6052 E1
- HLVW 40229 6053 A1
SR-1526 Bells Mill Rd
100 BltC 40165 6053 D5
200 BltC 40165 6054 B5
SR-1526 Brooks Rd
- BltC 40109 6052 E1
- HLVW 40109 6052 E1
SR-1526 John Harper Hwy
100 HBNE 40165 6053 C2
100 PNRV 40165 6053 B2
500 PNRV 40229 6053 A1
900 HLVW 40229 6053 A1
SR-1526 N Preston Hwy
- BltC 40165 6053 B3
- HBNE 40165 6053 B3
- PNRV 40165 6053 C2
SR-1531
- LSVL 40245 5513 C7
- SbyC 40245 5513 D7
SR-1531 Aiken Rd
16900 LSVL 40245 5513 C7
16900 LSVL 40245 5622 B1
17600 SbyC 40245 5513 C7
SR-1531 Dawson Hill Rd
11000 BltC 40071 5948 D3
11000 BltC 40299 5948 D3
SR-1531 Fisherville Rd
200 LSVL 40023 5622 B7
200 LSVL 40023 5731 B3
200 LSVL 40245 5622 B7
SR-1531 Johnson Rd
100 LSVL 40023 5622 B6
100 LSVL 40245 5622 B7
SR-1531 Routt Rd
4300 LSVL 40023 5731 A7
4300 LSVL 40299 5730 E7
4300 LSVL 40299 5731 A7
5800 LSVL 40299 5840 A4
7100 LSVL 40299 5839 E7
8100 LSVL 40299 5948 E1
9500 BltC 40299 5948 D3
11700 BltC 40071 5948 D3
SR-1600 Cardinal Dr
200 ELZT 42701 6702 E7
SR-1600 Rineyville Rd
300 ELZT 42701 6702 D7
300 HdnC 42701 6702 D7
6800 HdnC 40162 6591 C7
7800 HdnC 40175 6591 C7
SR-1600 Woodland Dr
400 ELZT 42701 6812 A1
SR-1603 E Blue Lick Rd
- HLVW 40229 6052 E1
100 BltC 40109 6052 E3
100 BltC 40165 6052 E4
100 HLVW 40165 6052 E3
300 HLVW 40109 6052 E2
SR-1603 Brooks Hill Rd
- BltC 40109 6052 E1
- HLVW 40109 6052 E1
- HLVW 40229 6052 E1
SR-1604
- BltC 40165 6163 C7
SR-1631 Crittenden Dr
2400 LSVL 40217 5724 E1
2700 LSVL 40209 5724 E2
SR-1638
- MdeC 40108 6264 B4
SR-1638 Warren St
- MdeC 40108 6264 A5
- MRGH 40155 6264 A5
SR-1646 Bullion Blvd
- HdnC 40121 6373 E5
- HdnC 40121 6374 A5
SR-1646 Hunters Ln
- RDCF 40160 6483 B5
SR-1646 Logsdon Pkwy
- HdnC 40121 6373 E6
SR-1646 N Logsdon Pkwy
- HdnC 40121 6373 E7
- HdnC 40121 6374 A6
- RDCF 40160 6373 E7
- RDCF 40175 6373 E7
100 RDCF 40160 6483 A2
1200 RDCF 40175 6483 A2
1600 RDCF 40160 6482 E1
1600 RDCF 40175 6482 E1
SR-1646 S Logsdon Pkwy
100 RDCF 40160 6483 C7
1400 RDCF 40160 6592 C1
SR-1694
- OdmC 40014 5402 E1
- OdmC 40059 5402 E1
SR-1694 Brownsboro Rd
- LSVL 40059 5401 E7
- LSVL 40059 5402 D1
- LSVL 40241 5401 E7
- OdmC 40014 5402 D1
- OdmC 40059 5402 D1
10000 LSVL 40241 5510 E1
SR-1694 Gum St
1000 OdmC 40014 5402 E1
SR-1703
- LSVL 40205 5616 D6
- LSVL 40213 5616 D6
SR-1703 Baxter Av
1000 LSVL 40204 5616 D7
1400 LSVL 40205 5616 D6
1400 LSVL 40213 5616 D6
SR-1703 Newburg Rd
- LSVL 40218 5726 A3
1600 LSVL 40205 5616 D6
1600 LSVL 40213 5616 D6
2100 LSVL 40205 5725 E1
2400 LSVL 40205 5726 D5
3200 WSNP 40218 5726 B3
3400 WBHL 40218 5726 C4
3500 PLRH 40218 5726 C4
SR-1727 Terry Rd
4900 LSVL 40216 5722 B7
5200 LSVL 40216 5831 B1
5200 LSVL 40258 5831 B1
8800 LSVL 40272 5831 A7
SR-1747 Fern Valley Rd
1200 LSVL 40219 5835 E2
1800 LSVL 40228 5835 E2
2700 LSVL 40213 5834 E2
2800 LSVL 40219 5834 D2
6000 LSVL 40228 5836 A2
SR-1747 N Hurstbourne Pkwy
- LSVL 40223 5510 E6
- LYDN 40223 5510 E7
- MWVL 40223 5510 E6
- MWVL 40242 5510 D5
100 HTBN 40222 5619 D4
100 JFTN 40223 5619 D4
100 LSVL 40223 5619 D3
100 LYDN 40223 5619 E1
100 WDWD 40223 5619 D3
2800 LSVL 40241 5510 D4
2800 MWVL 40241 5510 D5
SR-1747 S Hurstbourne Pkwy
100 JFTN 40223 5619 D4
100 LYDN 40223 5619 D3
100 WDWD 40223 5619 D4
900 HTBN 40222 5619 D6
1600 FTHL 40299 5619 C7
1600 JFTN 40299 5619 C7
SR-1747 S Hurstbourne Pkwy
1600 LSVL 40220 5619 C7
1600 LSVL 40299 5619 C7
1700 HBNA 40220 5619 C7
1700 HBNA 40299 5619 C7
1900 FTHL 40299 5728 B1
1900 HBNA 40220 5728 B1
2000 FTHL 40220 5728 B1
2500 JFTN 40220 5728 B1
2800 LSVL 40220 5728 A2
3400 LSVL 40299 5728 A3
4600 LSVL 40299 5727 E6
4700 LSVL 40291 5727 E6
4700 LSVL 40291 5728 A7
SR-1815
- RDCF 40160 6483 D4
SR-1815 W Lincoln Trail Blvd
100 RDCF 40160 6483 D3
1400 VNGV 40175 6483 A5
1500 VNGV 40175 6482 E5
SR-1815 S Logsdon Pkwy
- RDCF 40160 6483 A4
SR-1816 Rabbit Run
- MdeC 40175 6373 A7
SR-1817 Cedar Point Rd
1400 OdmC 40014 5295 C6
1400 OdmC 40031 5295 C6
SR-1817 New Cut Rd
5900 OdmC 40014 5295 A6
5900 OdmC 40031 5295 A6
6600 OdmC 40014 5403 B1
SR-1818 E Mt Zion Rd
2200 OdmC 40014 5514 E1
SR-1818 W Mt Zion Rd
1500 OdmC 40014 5514 E1
3600 OdmC 40014 5513 E2
SR-1818 Todds Point Rd
- OdmC 40014 5513 D2
SR-1819 Billtown Rd
3800 JFTN 40299 5728 D5
4400 LSVL 40299 5728 D6
4900 LSVL 40291 5728 D7
5400 LSVL 40291 5837 D1
5400 LSVL 40299 5837 D1
6000 LSVL 40291 5838 C5
6000 LSVL 40299 5838 C5
SR-1819 Blankenbaker Pkwy
600 DGSH 40243 5620 B5
700 MDTN 40243 5620 B6
SR-1819 Brush Run Rd
13800 LSVL 40299 5839 A6
SR-1819 Ruckriegel Pkwy
3200 JFTN 40299 5729 A3
3200 LSVL 40299 5729 A3
3500 JFTN 40299 5728 D7
SR-1819 Seatonville Rd
12000 LSVL 40291 5838 C5
12000 LSVL 40299 5838 D5
SR-1819 Watterson Tr
900 DGSH 40243 5620 B6
900 DGSH 40299 5620 B6
900 LSVL 40299 5620 B6
900 MDTN 40243 5620 B6
900 MDTN 40299 5620 B6
1100 JFTN 40299 5620 A7
1600 JFTN 40299 5729 A2
3100 JFTN 40299 5728 E3
SR-1819 N Watterson Tr
100 DGSH 40243 5620 C4
100 MDTN 40243 5620 A7
SR-1849 Moorman Rd
6200 LSVL 40272 5940 A4
6400 LSVL 40272 5939 E4
SR-1865 New Cut Rd
4800 LSVL 40214 5724 A7
4800 LSVL 40215 5724 A7
5000 LSVL 40214 5833 B1
6000 LSVL 40118 5833 B6
6400 LSVL 40118 5942 B1
SR-1865 Taylor Blvd
3500 LSVL 40215 5724 A7
4700 LSVL 40214 5724 A7
SR-1882 Hargan Rd
10 HdnC 40175 6482 A6
SR-1882 Hargin Rd
100 HdnC 40175 6482 A7
SR-1882 Old Fort Av
- MdeC 40175 6482 A6
SR-1904 Bacon Creek Rd
10 ELZT 42701 6811 B7
10 HdnC 42701 6811 B7
SR-1931 S 7th St
700 LSVL 40202 5615 B7
700 LSVL 40203 5615 B7
1200 LSVL 40208 5615 C5
1800 LSVL 40210 5615 B7
SR-1931 7th St Rd
2000 LSVL 40208 5615 B7
2000 LSVL 40210 5615 B7
2200 LSVL 40208 5724 A1
2200 LSVL 40210 5724 A1
2300 SVLY 40216 5724 A1
2500 LSVL 40215 5724 A1
2900 LSVL 40215 5723 E3
2900 SVLY 40216 5723 E3
SR-1931 Greenwood Rd
4500 LSVL 40258 5831 E4
7000 LSVL 40258 5830 E3
SR-1931 Manslick Rd
3500 LSVL 40215 5723 D5
3500 SVLY 40216 5723 E3
4300 LSVL 40216 5723 D5
4700 LSVL 40216 5723 E6
6600 LSVL 40214 5832 E1
SR-1931 St. Andrews Church Rd
7300 LSVL 40214 5832 D2
7700 LSVL 40258 5832 B3
8100 LSVL 40258 5831 E4
SR-1932
- LSVL 40207 5617 E3
SR-1932
- STMW 40207 5617 E3
SR-1932 Breckenridge Ln
200 LSVL 40207 5618 A3
200 STMW 40207 5618 A3
300 NBNE 40207 5618 A4
500 BFLD 40207 5618 A4
600 PLYV 40207 5618 A4
700 SPLE 40207 5618 A4
900 STMW 40205 5618 C7
1000 LSVL 40205 5618 B6
2800 LSVL 40220 5618 C7
2800 MVWE 40220 5618 B7
3000 LSVL 40220 5727 C1
3600 LSVL 40218 5727 C4
SR-1932 Chenoweth Ln
100 LSVL 40207 5617 E3
100 STMW 40207 5617 E3
200 BLWD 40207 5617 E2
200 BWNV 40207 5617 E3
200 DRDH 40207 5617 E3
400 INDH 40207 5617 E3
SR-1934 Cane Run Rd
3300 LSVL 40210 5614 C7
3300 LSVL 40211 5614 C7
3600 LSVL 40211 5723 C1
3600 LSVL 40216 5614 C7
3600 LSVL 40216 5723 C1
3600 SVLY 40216 5723 B2
4300 LSVL 40216 5722 D4
SR-1934 Greenbelt Hwy
- LSVL 40258 5831 A1
- LSVL 40272 5830 D7
- LSVL 40272 5939 D1
- LSVL 40272 5940 A4
5500 LSVL 40216 5722 B6
5500 LSVL 40258 5722 A7
8400 LSVL 40258 5830 E5
SR-1934 Wilson Av
1800 LSVL 40210 5615 A5
2100 LSVL 40210 5614 D5
2500 LSVL 40211 5614 E5
SR-2048 Cannons Ln
- LSVL 40205 5618 A6
100 LSVL 40206 5617 E5
100 LSVL 40207 5617 E5
700 STMW 40207 5617 D4
2700 LSVL 40205 5617 E6
SR-2048 Dutchmans Ln
3400 LSVL 40205 5617 E7
3500 LSVL 40205 5618 A6
SR-2049 Crums Ln
1800 SVLY 40216 5723 B4
2800 LSVL 40216 5723 B4
SR-2050 Herr Ln
1100 GYDL 40222 5618 E1
1100 STMW 40222 5618 E1
1300 GYDL 40222 5509 D7
1300 STMW 40222 5509 E7
1800 LSVL 40222 5509 D7
2000 NHFD 40222 5509 D7
SR-2050 Lyndon Ln
- STMW 40222 5618 E1
600 LYDN 40222 5619 A2
800 LYDN 40222 5618 E1
SR-2051
- LSVL 40216 5722 C5
SR-2051 Camp Ground Rd
3300 LSVL 40211 5723 A1
3300 LSVL 40216 5723 A1
3300 SVLY 40216 5723 A1
3800 LSVL 40211 5722 E1
4200 LSVL 40216 5722 B5
SR-2051 Lees Ln
3300 LSVL 40216 5722 C5
SR-2051 Rockford Ln
1800 LSVL 40216 5723 A6
1800 SVLY 40216 5723 A6
2300 LSVL 40216 5722 E6
2300 SVLY 40216 5722 E6
SR-2052
- WBHL 40218 5726 D4
SR-2052 Hikes Ln
2100 LSVL 40218 5726 E3
2100 WBHL 40218 5726 E3
SR-2052 Old Shepherdsville Rd
1900 LSVL 40218 5726 E4
2100 WBHL 40218 5726 E6
SR-2052 Shepherdsville Rd
2100 WBHL 40218 5726 D4
4200 LSVL 40218 5726 E4
5000 LSVL 40228 5726 E6
5300 LSVL 40218 5835 E1
5300 LSVL 40219 5835 E4
5300 LSVL 40228 5835 E4
SR-2053 Cedar Creek Rd
11300 LSVL 40229 5945 D5
SR-2053 Mt Washington Rd
5200 LSVL 40229 5944 D4
6000 LSVL 40229 5945 E6
SR-2053 Thixton Ln
7600 LSVL 40229 5945 D5
8000 BltC 40229 5946 D6
8200 LSVL 40229 5946 A5
8900 LSVL 40291 5946 A5
SR-2054 Algonquin Pkwy
700 LSVL 40208 5724 B1
1200 LSVL 40208 5615 B7
1200 LSVL 40210 5615 A7
1700 LSVL 40210 5614 E7
2700 LSVL 40211 5614 E7
SR-2055 W Manslick Rd
8600 LSVL 40214 5832 E7
8600 LSVL 40272 5832 E7
9200 LSVL 40118 5833 A7
9200 LSVL 40272 5833 A7
9700 LSVL 40118 5942 C1
SR-2055 Mt Holly Rd
400 LSVL 40118 5942 D2
1100 HYVA 40118 5942 E3
1200 HYVA 40118 5943 A3
SR-2055 Mt Holly Rd
1200 LSVL 40118 5943 A3
SR-2056 Bells Ln
3300 LSVL 40211 5614 A7
4100 LSVL 40211 5613 E7
SR-2237 Salt River Rd
- SHDV 40165 6161 D6
SR-2553 Cardinal Av
- BltC 40165 6053 C1
- PNRV 40165 6053 C1
SR-2553 Old Preston Hwy N
100 BltC 40165 6053 C1
100 PNRV 40165 6053 C1
SR-2674 Stringer Ln
100 MTWH 40047 6056 B6
300 BltC 40047 6056 B5
SR-2706 Flat Lick Rd
- BltC 40047 6055 E1
- MTWH 40047 6055 E2
400 MTWH 40047 6056 A2
SR-2706 Green Brier Rd
100 BltC 40047 6055 B5
100 MTWH 40047 6055 B5
SR-2706 Wales Run Rd
- BltC 40047 6055 E1
- MTWH 40047 6055 E1
SR-2802
- ELZT 42701 6702 C2
- HdnC 42701 6702 C2
- RDCF 42701 6702 C1
SR-2802 W A Jenkins Rd
10 ELZT 42701 6702 C1
10 RDCF 42701 6702 C1
100 HdnC 42701 6702 C1
SR-2802 Cecilanna Dr
100 HdnC 42701 6702 B4
SR-2802 Hutcherson Ln
200 ELZT 42701 6702 C2
200 HdnC 42701 6702 C2
SR-2840 Main St
- DGSH 40243 5620 B4
11400 LSVL 40223 5620 B4
11400 MDTN 40243 5620 E4
SR-2840 Old Shelbyville Rd
11700 MDTN 40243 5620 C4
SR-2841 Eastwood Cut Off Rd
16100 LSVL 40023 5622 B6
16100 LSVL 40245 5622 C5
SR-2845
- LSVL 40219 5835 C7
- LSVL 40229 5835 C7
SR-2845 E Manslick Rd
4600 LSVL 40219 5835 C7
4900 LSVL 40229 5835 E7
5500 LSVL 40219 5836 A7
5500 LSVL 40229 5836 A7
7100 LSVL 40228 5836 D6
SR-2845 Pennsylvania Run Rd
8500 LSVL 40228 5836 C6
SR-2845 Shepherdsville Rd
8900 LSVL 40219 5835 D7
SR-2854 Dawkins Rd
100 LGNG 40031 5296 D3
500 OdmC 40031 5296 C2
1700 OdmC 40031 5295 E1
SR-2855 Fort Pickens Rd
1300 LGNG 40031 5297 B2
1300 OdmC 40031 5297 B2
SR-2858 Abbott Ln
6600 OdmC 40014 5404 D6
7000 OdmC 40014 5513 D1
SR-2860 Grinstead Dr
2000 LSVL 40204 5616 D4
2400 JfnC 40204 5616 D4
SR-3005 Louisville Rd
- ELZT 42701 6702 E5
SR-3005 Ring Rd
- ELZT 42701 6812 E1
100 ELZT 42701 6811 B1
700 HdnC 42701 6811 B1
1000 HdnC 42701 6702 B7
1200 ELZT 42701 6702 E5
1900 ELZT 42701 6703 A4
2100 HdnC 42701 6703 A4
SR-3064 Northwestern Pkwy
3200 LSVL 40212 5505 D7
SR-3064 Portland Av
2100 LSVL 40203 5506 A7
2100 LSVL 40212 5506 A6
2600 LSVL 40212 5505 E7
SR-3082 Bank St
2100 LSVL 40203 5615 A1
2100 LSVL 40212 5615 A1
2400 LSVL 40212 5506 A7
2600 LSVL 40212 5505 E7
SR-3084 N English Station Rd
1000 LSVL 40223 5620 E2
1000 MDTN 40223 5620 E2
SR-3084 Old Henry Rd
- LSVL 40223 5512 B7
12800 LSVL 40223 5620 E1
13300 LSVL 40223 5621 A1
14700 LSVL 40245 5512 B7
SR-3216 N 38th St
500 LSVL 40212 5505 C7
SR-3217 N 37th St
500 LSVL 40212 5505 D7
SR-3222 Rose Island Rd
7500 LSVL 40059 5400 E2
7500 PROS 40059 5400 E2
8000 OdmC 40059 5400 E2
SR-3222 N Rose Island Rd
2400 OdmC 40059 5291 E2
Stable Pl
4200 LSVL 40241 5511 A2

INDEX 46
Stable Lake Ct
Louisville Metro Street Index
Sunridge Av

STREET Block City ZIP Map# Grid

Stable Lake Ct
6900 LSVL 40291 5837 C3
Stable Springs Dr
11900 LSVL 40299 5838 B2
Stacey Rd
5100 ClkC 47111 5290 B4
5100 ClkC 47130 5290 B5
6300 ClkC 47111 5289 D1
7800 ClkC 47111 5180 D7
Stacie Mac
- ClkC 47111 5290 A4
Stacy Ct
3600 LSVL 40214 5832 B3
5600 ClkC 47111 5290 B4
Stacy Lynn Ct
7900 LSVL 40291 5836 E5
Staebler Av
100 STMW 40207 5617 E2
Stafford Av
1600 LSVL 40216 5723 C6
Stag Ct
300 CLKV 47172 5397 C1
Staghorn Dr
8400 BRWD 40242 5510 B7
8400 LYDN 40242 5510 B7
Stall Ct
9500 LSVL 40291 5837 B5
Stallings Av
1600 SVLY 40216 5723 B6
Stallings Rd
- BltC 40047 6054 E4
Stallion Wy
100 BltC 40109 6052 D3
Stalwert Pl
11100 LSVL 40272 5940 D3
Stamford Dr
- HTBN 40222 5619 A5
Stamper Av
200 LGNG 40031 5297 A2
Stana Dr
6600 LSVL 40258 5831 B2
Stanalouise Dr
9700 LSVL 40291 5837 D1
Standard Av
1800 LSVL 40210 5614 E5
1800 LSVL 40210 5615 A6
Standard Club Ln
- BRMD 40241 5510 A4
- LSVL 40241 5510 A4
Standard Village Cir
1400 LSVL 40210 5614 E6
Standiford Av
1100 LSVL 40213 5725 C5
Standiford Ct
1100 LSVL 40213 5725 B5
Standiford Ln
1100 LSVL 40213 5725 C6
Standiford Plaza Dr
11800 LSVL 40229 5944 D5
Standing Oak Dr
8500 LSVL 40272 5831 D5
Stanford Ct
600 HdnC 42701 6811 B4
Stanford Dr
500 HdnC 42701 6811 B4
Stanhope Ct
7400 LSVL 40258 5831 A3
Stanley Av
900 LSVL 40215 5724 A4
Stanley Dr
100 BltC 40165 6049 C4
Stanley Ln
10 HdnC 40162 6702 B2
Stanley Farm Ct
- OdmC 40031 5295 B6
Stanley Gault Pkwy
1900 LSVL 40223 5621 A1
2000 ANCH 40223 5511 E6
2000 LSVL 40223 5511 E7
2000 LSVL 40223 5512 A7
Stannye Ct
2400 NHFD 40222 5509 B5
Stannye Dr
2200 NHFD 40222 5509 B5
6100 GNVM 40222 5509 B5
6100 LSVL 40222 5509 B5
Stansbury Ln
5600 LSVL 40291 5836 C1
E Stansifer Av
100 CLKV 47129 5506 D5
600 CLKV 47130 5506 E5
600 JFVL 47130 5506 E5
W Stansifer Av
100 CLKV 47129 5506 C5
Stanton Blvd
3500 LSVL 40218 5727 A2
3500 LSVL 40220 5727 A1
3700 LSVL 40220 5618 C7
Star Ln
7400 LSVL 40214 5833 B6
Stara Wy
8800 LSVL 40299 5728 A3
Starcross Ct
6800 WDYH 40207 5509 C7
Stardust Dr
6800 LSVL 40272 5939 E7
Star Gazing Wy
14800 LSVL 40272 5939 E7
Stargel Ln
100 BltC 40165 6163 A5
Star Haven Dr
1500 NALB 47150 5505 E1
Starks Dr
4400 LSVL 40218 5726 C5
Starks Bdg
500 LSVL 40202 5615 D3
Starlet Ct
200 LSVL 40118 5942 C2
Starlet Dr
9700 LSVL 40118 5942 C2
Starlight Dr
100 ClkC 47129 5396 E6
100 CLKV 47129 5396 E6
Starlight Wy
10200 LSVL 40272 5940 E2
Starlite Ct
800 LSVL 40207 5617 D5
Starlite Dr
100 ELZT 42701 6702 D4
800 LSVL 40207 5617 D4
4800 HLVW 40229 5944 C5
Starlite Ln
4200 LSVL 40291 5727 D5
Starmont Rd
2000 RVWD 40207 5508 D5
Star Point Ct
8300 PROS 40059 5401 B5
Star Rest Cir
9200 LSVL 40272 5832 E7
Star Rest Dr
1600 LSVL 40272 5832 E7
Starshine Ct
100 BltC 40165 6054 D2
Startan Ct
3300 LSVL 40220 5727 C1
Starview Ct
3000 JFVL 47130 5507 A2
8500 CLKV 47172 5288 B6
State St
- ClkC 47130 5399 E7
- JFVL 47130 5399 E7
- JFVL 47130 5508 D1
10 NALB 47150 5505 B5
200 CLKV 47129 5506 D5
200 ELZT 42701 6702 E7
400 RDCF 40160 6483 C4
2100 NALB 47150 5504 E2
2400 FydC 47150 5504 E2
N State St
100 LSVL 40206 5616 D2
S State St
100 LSVL 40206 5616 D2
State Garage Dr
- SHDV 40165 6161 D3
Statia Lynn Ct
10200 LSVL 40223 5619 E3
Station Ct
10 BltC 40109 5943 C7
Station Rd
- ANCH 40223 5620 C1
Station Wy
10 BltC 40109 5943 C6
Statton Rd
4300 CMBG 40220 5618 D7
4300 SRPK 40220 5618 D7
Staunton Rd
10200 BRMR 40223 5619 E4
Stave Mill Rd
100 BltC 40165 6053 E1
100 BltC 40165 6054 A2
Stayman Wy
7500 LSVL 40228 5836 D6
Stayton Wy
2400 BCFT 40242 5509 E5
2400 OBNP 40242 5509 E5
Steedland Ct
100 HLVW 40229 5944 C7
100 PNRV 40229 5944 C7
N Steedland Dr
100 HLVW 40229 5944 B7
100 PNRV 40229 5944 B7
S Steedland Dr
100 HLVW 40229 5944 B7
100 PNRV 40229 5944 B7
300 HLVW 40229 6053 B1
Steedly Dr
100 LSVL 40214 5833 C1
Steel Dr
200 ELZT 42701 6812 D5
Steele Rd
10 CHAN 47111 5181 D3
Steeles Range Rd
- HdnC 40121 6374 E7
Steeple Wy
4100 LSVL 40245 5512 B4
Steeplechase Dr
2200 JFTN 40299 5728 D2
Steeplecrest Cir
7400 LSVL 40222 5618 D4
Steeplecrest Ct
400 LSVL 40222 5618 D4
Steep Ridge Ct
4600 LSVL 40299 5729 B6
Steeprun Rd
6800 LSVL 40241 5509 C4
Steerforth Ct
14100 LSVL 40245 5621 C5
Stegner Av
3200 LSVL 40216 5722 D5
Steier Ln
2200 LSVL 40218 5726 E3
Steiller Rd
5000 FydC 47119 5394 B3
Stein Ct
300 LSVL 40203 5615 E5
Stellar Dr
- SHDV 40165 6161 A6
Stenger Ln
3400 ClkC 47130 5398 C4
Stephan Dr
5000 LSVL 40258 5831 C6
Stephan Ln
2100 LSVL 40214 5723 D7
Stephan Rd
2400 LSVL 40214 5832 C1
Stephanie Rd
10 BltC 40165 6053 E6
10 BltC 40165 6054 A7
Stephanie Kaye Dr
2000 OdmC 40031 5297 C3
Stephen Rd
- VNGV 40175 6592 A1
Stephen Foster Av
5200 LSVL 40213 5726 A7
Stephens St
10 VNGV 40175 6591 E1
Sterling Dr
5500 LSVL 40216 5831 C1
5600 LSVL 40258 5831 C1
Sterling Rd
10 LSVL 40220 5618 E7
10 LSVL 40220 5619 A7
Sterling Ter
- ClkC 47172 5288 B1
Sterling Oaks Ct
- ClkC 47172 5288 B1
Sterling Springs Rd
10200 LSVL 40223 5619 E2
10400 LSVL 40223 5620 B2
Sternbach Ct
6700 LSVL 40258 5831 A5
Steve Hamilton Dr
100 CHAN 47111 5181 E3
100 ClkC 47111 5181 E3
Steven Dr
100 SHDV 40165 6161 E6
Stevens Av
1600 LSVL 40205 5616 D6
1600 LSVL 40213 5616 D6
Stevenson Av
100 LSVL 40206 5616 C2
Stewart Dr
5100 LSVL 40216 5723 A7
Stewart Ln
1700 SVLY 40216 5723 C6
4000 OdmC 40031 5295 A1
Stewart St
600 ELZT 42701 6812 C2
Stewarts Farm Rd
10800 LSVL 40228 5945 E2
Stigwood Ct
3800 LSVL 40218 5727 C4
Stilger Cir
4200 LSVL 40299 5729 D6
Stillbrook Pl
3500 LSVL 40245 5512 C5
Stillmeadow Dr
8200 LSVL 40299 5727 E6
8300 JFTN 40299 5728 A6
8300 LSVL 40299 5728 A6
Stillridge Ct
6000 LSVL 40229 5944 E1
6000 LSVL 40229 5945 A1
Stillridge Pl
9500 LSVL 40229 5944 E1
9500 LSVL 40229 5945 B1
Stillwater Ct
13800 LSVL 40299 5729 E5
Stillwood Ct
200 LSVL 40223 5620 B3
Stilz Av
100 LSVL 40206 5617 B3
Stinnett Ln
8700 LSVL 40118 5834 B7
8700 MLHT 40219 5834 B7
Stinson Pl
1000 RDCF 40160 6483 C2
Stitch Pl
10900 LSVL 40272 5940 D3
Stivers Ct
4200 WLNP 40207 5618 C2
Stivers Rd
600 WLNP 40207 5618 B2
800 STMW 40207 5618 B2
St No 23
- ClkC 47172 5288 E2
Stober Rd
3100 LSVL 40213 5725 E4
3100 WSNP 40213 5725 E4
3100 WSNP 40213 5726 A4
Stockdale Rd
10 LSVL 40118 5942 B1
Stockport Rd
8700 HTBN 40222 5619 B6
Stockridge Rd
3800 LSVL 40241 5509 D2
Stockton Ct
9000 LSVL 40291 5837 B1
Stodghill Pl
300 LSVL 40223 5620 B3
Stoecker Av
100 LSVL 40206 5616 C2
Stoke on Trent St
100 JFTN 40299 5728 C3
Stokes Ct
4900 LSVL 40218 5726 D6
Stoll Av
100 LSVL 40206 5616 D3
Stoll Hill Rd
5700 GNVW 40222 5509 B2
5700 LSVL 40222 5509 B2
Stoltz Ct
4300 LSVL 40215 5724 A6
Stone Al
1800 LSVL 40203 5615 A3
2100 LSVL 40211 5615 A2
2600 LSVL 40211 5614 E2
Stone Cr
5300 ClkC 47111 5289 B2
Stone Pl
- NALB 47150 5396 C4
4100 FydC 47150 5396 C4
Stone St
900 LSVL 40217 5725 B1
1700 NALB 47150 5505 D4
Stone Bluff Ct
7400 LSVL 40291 5836 D1
Stone Bluff Rd
5700 LSVL 40291 5836 D1
Stone Breaker Ct
10500 LSVL 40291 5837 E7
Stone Breaker Rd
10600 LSVL 40291 5837 E7
Stonebridge Blvd
6500 ClkC 47111 5290 B2
Stonebridge Rd
10 INDH 40207 5508 C5
10 LSVL 40207 5508 C5
3000 LSVL 40241 5510 E5
Stone Brook Dr
7500 LSVL 40291 5836 E4
Stone Company Rd
- BltC 40165 6053 C4
Stone Creek Blvd
200 NALB 47150 5504 E1
200 NALB 47150 5505 A2
Stone Creek Ct
7700 ClkC 47111 5289 B2
Stone Creek Pkwy
- HTBN 40222 5619 D5
800 JFTN 40223 5619 D5
Stonecrest Dr
9100 LSVL 40272 5832 C7
Stonefield Ln
- OdmC 40031 5295 B6
Stonefield Wy
11500 LSVL 40291 5946 E2
Stone Gap Ct
4100 LSVL 40272 5831 E7
Stonegate Av
- ELZT 42701 6812 E7
Stone Gate Dr
3800 OdmC 40014 5404 D3
Stonegate Dr
9100 ClkC 47111 5290 C2
Stonegate Rd
1700 ANCH 40223 5511 C7
1700 ANCH 40223 5620 C1
Stonegate Manor Dr
- LSVL 40272 5939 E5
Stone Glen Rd
4300 LSVL 40241 5510 E2
Stone Green Wy
8900 JFTN 40220 5728 A1
Stoneham Pl
4400 LSVL 40299 5729 B6
Stonehaven Ct
- LSVL 40205 5618 A7
Stonehenge Dr
200 BWDV 40207 5618 D3
200 STMW 40207 5618 D3
Stonehenge Wy
9800 LSVL 40241 5510 D5
Stone Hill Rd
6800 LSVL 40214 5832 E2
Stone Hollow Dr
3900 LSVL 40299 5727 E4
Stonehurst Dr
2200 WWOD 40242 5510 C6
2400 PNTN 40242 5510 B5
Stone Lakes Dr
4000 LSVL 40299 5729 E5
4400 LSVL 40299 5730 A6
Stonelanding Ct
4000 LSVL 40272 5831 E7
Stonelanding Pl
9400 LSVL 40272 5831 E7
Stonelea Dr
- OdmC 40031 5295 B6
Stone Ledge Ct
9600 LSVL 40291 5837 B4
Stoneledge Dr
100 MTWH 40047 6056 B4
Stone Ledge Rd
7600 LSVL 40291 5837 B4
Stoneleigh Ct
2300 TNHL 40222 5509 C5
Stonemeadow Ct
4200 LSVL 40218 5727 D4
Stonemeadow Dr
7900 LSVL 40218 5727 D4
8000 LSVL 40299 5727 D4
Stonemill Ct
7300 LSVL 40291 5837 A4
Stonemill Dr
- LSVL 40222 5618 D2
- STMW 40222 5618 D1
2600 ELZT 42701 6703 A1
Stone Mountain Rd
4200 FydC 47150 5503 D4
Stonemour Wy
8800 ClkC 47111 5290 C3
Stone Point Ct
13300 OdmC 44026 5292 A3
Stone Post Rd
- BltC 40229 5944 D6
Stoner Rd
2500 OdmC 40031 5296 C6
Stoner Hill Rd SE
10200 HsnC 47117 5939 A3
Stoneridge Ct
100 BltC 40165 6162 D5
Stone Ridge Dr
1500 FydC 47122 5503 B4
Stone Ridge Rd
1600 OdmC 40014 5404 C2
Stoneridge Manor Dr
13600 LSVL 40272 5939 E5
Stone River Ct
3800 LSVL 40299 5727 E4
Stone School Rd
10100 LSVL 40059 5402 A7
Stoneside Cir
100 BltC 40071 5948 B6
Stoneside Ct
- BltC 40071 5948 B6
Stone Spring Wy
1000 JFTN 40223 5619 D6
Stonestreet Av
4500 LSVL 40216 5723 B6
4500 SVLY 40216 5723 B6
Stonestreet Rd
8900 LSVL 40258 5831 D7
8900 LSVL 40272 5831 D7
9500 LSVL 40272 5940 E1
10000 LSVL 40272 5941 A2
Stonevalley Dr
6700 LSVL 40272 5939 E5
Stoneview Dr
500 FydC 47150 5503 C4
4000 LSVL 40207 5617 E1
4100 LSVL 40207 5508 E7
Stonewall Wy
1200 LYDN 40242 5619 C1
Stoneware Al
- LSVL 40204 5616 A4
Stonewood Ct
7800 LSVL 40220 5618 E7
Stone Wynde Dr
4400 LSVL 40272 5831 E7
Stoney Ln
100 BltC 40071 5948 B6
Stoneybrook Ct
2300 OdmC 40031 5296 C5
Stoney Creek Ct
100 PWEV 40056 5512 D3
Stoneykirk Dr
800 DGSH 40223 5619 E6
800 DGSH 40223 5620 A6
800 DGSH 40243 5620 A6
Stoney Point Rd
8300 ClkC 47111 5180 C4
11400 ClkC 47143 5180 C4
Stoney Point Trc
1200 JFTN 40223 5619 D6
Stoney Ridge Rd
4100 LSVL 40299 5728 A5
Stoneyridge Wynde
100 BltC 40165 6162 D5
Stonington Ct
3100 MYHL 40242 5510 B5
Stonington Pl
3200 MYHL 40242 5510 B5
Stony Brook Dr
- HBNA 40220 5619 A7
- HBNA 40220 5728 A1
- LSVL 40220 5619 A7
2000 JFTN 40220 5728 A1
3300 JFTN 40299 5728 B5
3300 LSVL 40299 5728 B3
4800 JFTN 40291 5728 A6
4800 LSVL 40291 5728 A7
Stonydale Ln
7800 LSVL 40220 5727 E4
Stonyrun Cir
3600 LSVL 40220 5727 E4
Stonyrun Ct
8100 LSVL 40220 5727 E4
Stonyrun Dr
3600 LSVL 40220 5727 D4
Stony Spring Cir
3400 LSVL 40220 5728 B4
Storage Wy
9300 LSVL 40291 5837 B2
Stormon Ct
4600 SRPK 40220 5618 E5
Storrington Ct
8700 HTBN 40222 5619 B4
Story Av
1000 LSVL 40206 5616 B2
Story Av US-42
1000 LSVL 40206 5616 B2
Story Av US-60 TRK
1000 LSVL 40206 5616 B2
Stout Blvd
4900 JFTN 40291 5728 B7
4900 LSVL 40291 5728 B7
Stout Ln
100 MTWH 40047 6056 C3
Stout Rd
7900 LSVL 40291 5838 C6
7900 LSVL 40291 5947 C1
Stout St
100 MTWH 40047 6056 B2
Stovall Ct
100 ELZT 42701 6812 B4
7900 LSVL 40228 5836 C4
Stovall Pl
7600 LSVL 40228 5836 C4
Stovall Church Rd
10 RDCF 40160 6483 C6
10 VNGV 40160 6483 C6
Stover Dr
2400 NALB 47150 5505 A1
Stowers Ln
2200 SVLY 40216 5723 B5
Strader Av
- LSVL 40215 5723 E4
1300 LSVL 40215 5724 A4
Strand Av
1800 LSVL 40205 5616 D7
Strater Al
- LSVL 40203 5615 E5
Stratford Av
- KGLY 40205 5617 D7
- WLTN 40205 5617 D7
- WLTN 40205 5726 D1
10 PNRV 40165 6053 C2
2800 LSVL 40205 5617 D7
3200 LSVL 40218 5726 D1
Stratford Ln
1000 PNRV 40165 6053 C2
3700 STMW 40207 5618 A5
Strathmoor Blvd
1900 LSVL 40205 5726 B1
1900 SMRM 40205 5726 B1
2100 SMRM 40205 5617 B7
2100 SMRV 40205 5617 B7
2300 SGDN 40205 5617 C7
Stratmoor Dr
10 ELZT 42701 6811 B2
10 HdnC 42701 6811 B2
Stratton Av
3500 LSVL 40211 5614 C6
Straw Ln
- ClkC 47130 5398 C5
Strawberry Al
200 ELZT 42701 6812 B3
Strawberry Av
2500 LSVL 40214 5832 D1
Strawberry Ln
700 JFVL 47130 5507 D4
4700 LSVL 40214 5724 D6
6200 LSVL 40214 5833 D1
Stricker Rd
1000 ClkC 47143 5180 A1
Stringer Ln
100 MTWH 40047 6056 C7
300 BltC 40047 6056 B5
Stringer Ln SR-2674
100 MTWH 40047 6056 C7
300 BltC 40047 6056 B5
Strive Ln
7200 LSVL 40258 5831 C3
Stroll Ct
12100 CDSM 40245 5511 D1
Strotman Rd
2300 SVLY 40216 5723 B2
Stuart Dr
7700 LSVL 40258 5831 D4
Stuckeys Rd SE
1400 FydC 47117 5721 C6
Sturgis St
- LSVL 40206 5616 D3
Success Ln
11100 HTCK 40229 5945 D3
Sudbury Ct
3100 LSVL 40220 5727 C2
Sudbury Ln
3100 LSVL 40220 5727 C2
Sue Helen Dr
9200 JFTN 40299 5728 C4
Suffolk Ln
- HBNA 40220 5619 A7
- LSVL 40220 5619 A7
Sugar Maple Ct
11000 LSVL 40229 5944 C5
Sugarmaple Dr
2000 LGNG 40031 5296 B3
Sugar Pine Ter
1200 MDTN 40243 5620 C7
Sugar Plum Rd
8500 MLHT 40219 5834 C6
Sugartree Dr
1200 OdmC 40014 5405 E4
Sugartree Ln
1200 BltC 40109 5941 E7
1200 LSVL 40118 5941 E7
1200 LSVL 40118 5942 A7
Sugarwood Ct
7000 LSVL 40241 5509 D4
Sulgrave Rd
1700 LSVL 40205 5617 A5
Sullivan Ct
11300 LSVL 40229 5944 E3
Sullivan Rd
- FydC 47124 5393 A2
Sullivan Wy
5500 LSVL 40229 5944 E4
Sumac Al
- LGNG 40031 5297 A2
Sumac Ln
6200 CTWD 40014 5512 E1
6500 OdmC 40014 5512 E1
6600 OdmC 40056 5512 E1
Sumac Rd
3400 LSVL 40216 5722 E3
Sumerlin Ct
- OdmC 40031 5295 A7
Sumerlin Dr
- OdmC 40031 5404 A1
3900 OdmC 40031 5295 A7
Summer Cir
3000 LSVL 40272 5940 A7
Summer Pl
100 CLKV 47129 5506 C5
4000 FydC 47150 5396 C4
4000 NALB 47150 5396 C4
Summer St
4300 HdnC 40121 6374 A2
Summer Creek Dr
5900 LSVL 40272 5940 A6
Summerfield Cir
8000 LSVL 40220 5727 D3
Summerfield Dr
2600 LSVL 40220 5728 A2
2700 LSVL 40220 5727 E2
Summerfield Wy
7000 FydC 47119 5393 D4
Summer Glen Wy
11600 LSVL 40299 5729 B6
Summer Haven Ct
8400 LSVL 40258 5831 C6
Summer Hill Dr
7000 FydC 47122 5393 C7
Summer Lake Dr
6200 LSVL 40272 5940 A6
Summerlin Pl
1700 JFVL 47130 5507 A1
Summers Av
- LSVL 40214 5724 B7
Summers Dr
4300 HLVW 40229 6053 A1
4400 PNRV 40229 6053 B1
Summer Spring Ct
12600 MDTN 40243 5620 C7
Summertime Pkwy
4000 LSVL 40272 5940 A6
Summertree Ln
8600 LSVL 40291 5837 C6
Summerview Dr
4100 LSVL 40272 5940 A6
Summer Wynde Ct
9400 LSVL 40272 5831 E7
Summit Av
1200 LSVL 40204 5616 C6
1600 NALB 47150 5505 D2
Summit Ct
300 MDTN 40243 5620 C5
Summit Dr
100 HLVW 40229 5944 B7
4400 PNRV 40229 5944 B7
4800 PNRV 40165 5944 C7
Summit Rd
- LSVL 40214 5833 A1
Summit St
200 NALB 47150 5505 B4
Summit Park Pl
10100 LSVL 40241 5510 E1
Summit Plaza Dr
3900 LSVL 40241 5510 C2
Summit Ridge Dr
8800 LSVL 40241 5510 C2
Sumner Rd
3300 LSVL 40218 5726 D2
Sumpter St
- HdnC 40121 6374 D3
Sun Beam Ct
11700 LSVL 40272 5939 E1
Sunbury Ln
7700 LSVL 40220 5727 E2
Sundance Ct
3500 FydC 47150 5396 C4
Sundance Dr
- LYDN 40222 5619 B2
7700 LYDN 40222 5618 E2
7700 NRWD 40222 5618 E2
Sundancer
3400 ClkC 47130 5399 A3
Sunday Dr
4600 LSVL 40219 5835 C3
Sunday Silence Dr
10 MTWH 40047 6056 D2
Sun Den Dr
3200 JFVL 47130 5398 C5
Sunder Av
- LSVL 40218 5726 E3
- LSVL 40218 5727 B2
Sunderland Pl
10700 DGSH 40243 5620 A4
Sunderland Rd
10600 DGSH 40243 5620 A4
Sundew Av
1100 LSVL 40213 5725 C6
Sun Dial Ct
11600 LSVL 40272 5939 E1
Sundown Ct
- BltC 40047 5947 C5
5000 LYDN 40222 5618 E2
Sundown St
1800 ELZT 42701 6702 D4
Sundrop Ln
4300 JFTN 40299 5728 E5
Sundrop Pl
- OdmC 40014 5403 E4
Sun Field Cir
3100 LSVL 40241 5509 B2
Sunflower Av
2100 ClkC 47111 5182 A1
3900 LSVL 40216 5723 A4
4100 LSVL 40216 5722 E5
Sunflower Ct
10 LSVL 40216 5722 E4
1000 JFVL 47130 5507 C3
Sun Glow Ct
11600 LSVL 40272 5939 E1
Sunkist Wy
9800 LSVL 40272 5939 E1
Sunlight Ln
10300 LSVL 40272 5940 E3
Sunningdale Pl E
2600 LGNG 40031 5297 B5
Sunningdale Pl W
2600 LGNG 40031 5297 B6
Sunningdale Wy
400 ELZT 42701 6702 E2
Sunnside Ct
- CLKV 47129 5506 D2
Sunny Ln
3100 LSVL 40205 5726 B2
Sunny St
100 ELZT 42701 6812 C3
Sunny Acres Tr
10 VNGV 40175 6591 D1
Sunnybrook Dr
5400 LSVL 40214 5833 A3
12900 OdmC 40059 5401 B1
Sunny Creek Ln
8400 LSVL 40299 5728 A5
Sunny Crossing Dr
4100 LSVL 40299 5728 A5
4200 JFTN 40299 5728 A5
Sunnyfield Ct
7500 LSVL 40220 5727 D3
Sunnyfield Rd
2900 LSVL 40220 5727 D2
Sunnygate Pl
600 MDTN 40223 5620 E3
Sunny Hill Ct
4600 OdmC 40014 5405 E2
Sunny Hill Dr
100 BltC 40165 6163 A1
4600 OdmC 40014 5405 E2
Sunny Hill Rd
6600 LSVL 40228 5836 B2
Sunny Meadow Ct
4700 LSVL 40241 5511 B1
Sunny Oak Ln
8400 LSVL 40299 5728 A5
Sunny Ridge Ct
8300 LSVL 40299 5728 A5
Sunnyside Ct
100 PWEV 40056 5512 C2
Sunnyside Dr
100 CHAN 47111 5181 D2
100 MTWH 40047 6056 B4
500 LSVL 40206 5617 C4
900 CLKV 47129 5506 D2
Sunnyside Ln
300 FydC 47150 5395 E6
Sunny Slope Wy
13000 OdmC 40059 5401 B1
Sunny Vale Wy
6900 LSVL 40272 5939 D1
Sunnyvale Wy
6500 LSVL 40272 5939 E1
Sunnyview Rd
- INDH 40207 5617 E1
400 LSVL 40207 5617 E1
Sun Ray Dr
6000 LSVL 40272 5939 E1
Sunridge Av
4400 LSVL 40220 5618 D5

INDEX 47
Sunridge Av
Louisville Metro Street Index
Thomas Av

STREET
Block City ZIP Map# Grid
Sunridge Av
4500 SRPK 40220 5618 D5
Sun Ridge Rd
10900 OdmC 44026 5292 E1
Sun Rise Cir
3300 JFVL 47130 5398 E7
Sunrise Ct
100 BltC 40165 6054 D1
Sunrise Dr
3100 FydC 47172 5287 E6
Sunrise Ln
500 ELZT 42701 6812 B1
600 ELZT 42701 6703 B7
Sunrise Wy
4100 LSVL 40220 5727 D1
Sunrise Vail
4300 FydC 47172 5287 E6
Sunset
4400 SLRB 47172 5288 E6
Sunset Av
100 CLKV 47129 5506 E5
3800 LSVL 40211 5614 B4
Sunset Cir
6500 OdmC 40014 5403 A5
Sunset Ct
100 BltC 40165 6054 D1
500 MRGH 40155 6264 C4
4400 FydC 47172 5287 E6
5000 LYDN 40222 5618 E2
6500 OdmC 40014 5403 A5
Sunset Dr
10 CLKV 47129 5506 B3
100 LGNG 40031 5296 D3
300 RDCF 40160 6483 A3
1300 OdmC 40031 5297 B7
1500 NALB 47150 5504 E5
2900 FydC 47150 5396 E3
2900 FydC 47150 5397 A3
4100 LSVL 40216 5723 A4
4300 LSVL 40216 5722 E4
5400 LSVL 40219 5834 E4
Sunset Ln
4200 HLVW 40229 5944 B6
7200 OdmC 40014 5403 A6
Sunset Rd
100 ELZT 42701 6812 A1
500 LSVL 40206 5617 C4
7700 OdmC 40056 5512 B1
7700 PWEV 40056 5512 B1
Sunset St
100 MRGH 40155 6264 C5
Sunset Tr
1500 CHAN 47111 5181 D1
1500 ClkC 47111 5181 D1
Sunshine Ct
100 MTWH 40047 6056 D3
N Sunshine Dr
100 BltC 40165 6054 D1
Sunshine Ln
1100 JFVL 47130 5507 A2
Sunshine Wy
2400 LSVL 40216 5723 A5
Sunshine Camp Rd
100 BltC 40165 6054 D2
Sun Valley Dr
7000 LSVL 40272 5939 D1
Sunview Ct
100 BltC 40165 6163 A2
Sun View Rd
- BltC 40165 6162 E2
300 BltC 40165 6163 A1
Sun View Wy
- LSVL 40272 5939 E1
Sunway Ct
5000 LYDN 40222 5618 E2
E Sunwood Cir
8600 MLHT 40219 5834 C7
W Sunwood Cir
8500 MLHT 40219 5834 C7
Sun Wy Dr
9800 LSVL 40272 5939 E1
Superior Ct
100 SHDV 40165 6161 E4
Supremus Dr
7100 LSVL 40214 5832 C3
Surrey Ln
- MDTN 40243 5620 D2
10 JFVL 47130 5508 A3
800 ANCH 40223 5620 D2
800 MDTN 40223 5620 D2
Surrey Rd
2100 ClkC 47130 5399 B5
2100 JFVL 47130 5399 B5
13000 OdmC 44026 5292 B3
Susan Ct
100 RDCF 40160 6592 E2
Susan Ln
3600 LSVL 40229 5944 A4
Susanna Dr
3300 LSVL 40213 5725 E7
3400 LSVL 40213 5726 A7
Sussex Ct
4400 FCSL 40241 5511 C2
Sussex Dr
4000 FXCH 40165 6053 A3
4000 HLVW 40165 6053 A3
Sutcliffe Av
700 LSVL 40211 5614 C3
Sutherland Dr
1600 LSVL 40205 5726 A2
Sutherland Farm Rd
7900 PROS 40059 5400 D2
Sutica St
- SLRB 47172 5288 E4
Sutton Ln
900 ELZT 42701 6812 D2
3300 SPVL 40241 5509 E3
Suwanee Dr
4100 OdmC 40031 5405 A2
Swainsboro Ct
3500 LSVL 40218 5726 B3
Swainsboro Dr
1900 LSVL 40218 5726 B3
Swako Ln
4500 LSVL 40216 5723 D6
Swallow Rd
100 BltC 40165 6050 D6
4800 LYNV 40213 5725 D6
Swan St
1000 LSVL 40204 5616 A5
Swancrest Ct
8300 LYDN 40222 5619 A1
Swan Hill Rd
8800 LSVL 40241 5510 C2
Swan Pointe Blvd
- DGSH 40243 5620 D6
1100 MDTN 40243 5620 D6
Swansea Ct
3400 LSVL 40211 5614 C5
Swaps Ln
4900 LSVL 40216 5722 E7
Swartz St
7800 HdnC 40121 6374 B5
Sweeney Ln
3900 LSVL 40299 5729 D5
Sweet Bay Ct
8900 LYDN 40242 5619 B2
Sweetbay Dr
- CTWD 40014 5403 E5
- OdmC 40014 5403 D4
Sweet Bay Pl
8900 LYDN 40242 5619 B2
Sweetbriar Ln
100 LSVL 40207 5509 A6
Sweetheart Ln
2300 MLHT 40219 5834 C7
Sweet Water Dr
10800 LSVL 40241 5511 B1
Swindon Ct
1100 STMW 40222 5618 D1
Swing Ct
2600 JFTN 40299 5728 D2
Swing Dr
2300 JFTN 40299 5728 D2
Swing Ln
400 LSVL 40207 5617 C1
400 MKBV 40207 5508 C7
400 MKBV 40207 5617 C1
400 RLGF 40207 5508 C7
400 RLGF 40207 5617 C1
Switch Bark Ct
6800 HWCK 40228 5836 C3
Switch Bark Rd
7300 HWCK 40228 5836 D3
Swope Rd
2900 LDNP 40241 5510 C5
2900 LSVL 40241 5510 C5
Swope Autocenter Dr
10 FTHL 40299 5619 B7
10 FTHL 40299 5728 C1
Sycamore Ct
3500 RVBF 40059 5292 A7
10600 BRMR 40223 5619 E4
10600 SCMR 40223 5619 E4
Sycamore Dr
- BltC 40109 5943 E5
100 BltC 40047 6055 E2
100 BRMR 40223 5619 E4
100 SCMR 40223 5619 E4
100 SHDV 40165 6162 A2
300 RDCF 40160 6483 B4
900 JFVL 47130 5506 E3
900 JFVL 47130 5507 A4
3000 FydC 47150 5397 A1
7700 ClkC 47111 5181 B4
Sycamore Grn
10600 BRMR 40223 5619 E3
10600 SCMR 40223 5619 E3
Sycamore Rd
10 JFVL 47130 5508 A2
3400 OdmC 40014 5405 B1
3400 OdmC 40031 5296 B7
3400 OdmC 40031 5405 B1
Sycamore St
100 ELZT 42701 6812 B1
2100 LSVL 40206 5616 E2
Sycamore Tr
10600 BRMR 40223 5619 E3
10600 SCMR 40223 5619 E3
Sycamore Wy
10600 BRMR 40223 5619 E3
10600 SCMR 40223 5619 E3
Sycamore Bend Trc
6600 LSVL 40291 5837 E2
Sycamore Creek Dr
8000 LYDN 40222 5510 A7
Sycamore Forest Ct
13200 LSVL 40245 5512 A3
Sycamore Forest Pl
4400 LSVL 40245 5512 A3
Sycamore Hills Ct
200 SbyC 40245 5513 D5
Sycamore Hills Ln
200 SbyC 40245 5513 D5
Sycamore Ridge Dr
19100 LSVL 40245 5623 B2
Sycamore Shoals Ct
10100 JFTN 40223 5619 E5
Sycamore Shoals Trc
500 JFTN 40223 5619 D5
Sycamore Woods Ct
2700 LSVL 40241 5509 D4
Sycamore Woods Dr
6700 LSVL 40241 5509 D4
Sydney Renee Wy
6300 LSVL 40272 5940 A5
Sylvan Cir
- OdmC 44026 5292 B4
Sylvan Ct
1500 LSVL 40205 5726 A2
4000 FydC 47119 5394 E6
Sylvan Dr
4000 FydC 47119 5394 D6
Sylvan Ln
10 JFVL 47130 5508 A3
Sylvan Wy
- OdmC 44026 5292 B5
1400 LSVL 40205 5725 E2
1500 LSVL 40205 5726 A2
Sylvania Rd
6500 LSVL 40258 5831 A2
Sylvania Four Rd
6600 LSVL 40258 5831 A2
Sylvania Six Rd
6500 LSVL 40258 5831 A2
Sylvan Wynde
1500 LSVL 40205 5726 A2
Sylvatica Ct
6000 LSVL 40258 5831 B6
Sylvia Ct
- ELZT 42701 6811 C2
Sylvia St
800 LSVL 40217 5616 A7
Symington Cir
10800 LSVL 40241 5511 A1
Symington Ct
5500 LSVL 40241 5402 B7
5500 LSVL 40241 5511 B1
Symmetric St
2200 HLVW 40229 5943 E6
2200 HLVW 40229 5944 A6

T

Tabb Av
- ELZT 42701 6811 D5
- HdnC 42701 6811 D5
Table Mountain Av
6000 LSVL 40214 5723 C7
6000 LSVL 40214 5832 C1
Tabor Ct
700 NALB 47150 5396 B6
Tabor Dr
6200 LSVL 40218 5727 B3
Taco Ct
11200 LSVL 40229 5944 B5
Tacoma Ct
5400 LSVL 40219 5835 E5
Taff St
200 CHAN 47111 5181 D5
200 ClkC 47111 5181 D5
Taffeta Dr
1900 LSVL 40272 5940 A3
Taffey Ann Dr
6800 LSVL 40219 5836 A3
6800 LSVL 40228 5836 A3
Taft Ct
100 MTWH 40047 6055 E1
4400 JFTN 40299 5728 B6
Taft St
- HdnC 40121 6265 A7
N Taggart Av
500 CLKV 47129 5506 C4
Taggart Dr
- RHLN 40207 5618 B3
4300 BWDV 40207 5618 B3
4300 STMW 40207 5618 B3
Tahia Dr
5300 LSVL 40216 5831 E2
5300 LSVL 40258 5831 E2
Tait Pl
100 LSVL 40212 5614 C1
Talahi Wy
4300 INHC 40207 5508 E6
Talbot Blvd
- LGNG 40031 5296 D1
Talbott Av
2500 LSVL 40205 5617 B6
Talina Dr
200 CHAN 47111 5181 D1
Talisman Rd
3000 LSVL 40220 5618 A7
3000 LSVL 40220 5727 A1
Talitha Ct
4400 JFTN 40299 5728 B6
Talitha Dr
9100 JFTN 40299 5728 B6
Tall Oak Ct
10 HdnC 42701 6702 D1
Tall Oaks Ct
5600 LSVL 40214 5723 D7
Tall Oaks Dr
1600 JFVL 47130 5507 B1
Tallow Ct
8300 LSVL 40214 5833 A6
Tallow Ln
1100 LSVL 40214 5833 A5
Tall Pine Ln
11100 ClkC 47143 5287 E1
11100 ClkC 47172 5287 E1
Tallridge Ct
9400 LSVL 40229 5944 E1
Tallridge Pl
5700 LSVL 40229 5944 E1
Tall Tree Ct
10700 LSVL 40241 5511 A3
Tallulah Av
300 LSVL 40209 5724 D5
300 LSVL 40214 5724 D5
Tallwood Ct
6600 PROS 40059 5400 E4
6600 PROS 40059 5401 A4
Tallwood Rd
7400 PROS 40059 5400 E5
7600 PROS 40059 5401 A4
Tally Ho Ct
3900 JFTN 40299 5728 D5
Tally Ho Dr
2500 FXCH 40165 6053 A3
2500 HLVW 40165 6053 A3
Talmadge Wy
1500 LSVL 40216 5723 C6
Talon Pl
700 LSVL 40223 5620 A2
Talon Wy
10900 ANCH 40223 5620 B2
10900 LSVL 40223 5620 A2
Tamarack Ln
10 JFVL 47130 5508 A1
5500 LSVL 40258 5831 C5
Tamarind Ct
6700 LSVL 40219 5835 D3
Tamarisk Ct
900 LSVL 40223 5619 D2
Tamarisk Pkwy
9400 LSVL 40223 5619 D2
9400 LYDN 40223 5619 D2
Tamerlane Ct
- LSVL 40207 5509 A5
2500 LSVL 40207 5508 E5
Tamerlane Rd
5200 LSVL 40207 5508 E5
5200 LSVL 40207 5509 A5
Tami Ct
500 ELZT 42701 6702 D6
Tamm Ct
4200 LSVL 40272 5940 E2
Tammy Ct
3900 NALB 47150 5396 D5
Tammy Dr
100 BltC 40165 6054 C5
Tammy Ln
100 BltC 40165 6053 C3
Tamworth Ct
12400 DGSH 40299 5620 D6
12400 MDTN 40243 5620 D6
Tan Bark Ct
3700 LSVL 40220 5727 C1
Tandy Rd
7300 FydC 47136 5611 C3
Tandy Rd NE
7700 HsnC 47136 5610 E4
8800 FydC 47136 5611 A3
Tangelo Ct
6900 LSVL 40228 5836 C3
Tangelo Dr
7100 LSVL 40228 5836 C3
Tanglewood Dr
4000 FydC 47119 5394 D3
Tanglewood Tr
100 WDWD 40223 5619 D3
Tangley Ln
9100 RLGH 40242 5510 C6
9100 WWOD 40242 5510 C6
Tank Rd
- HdnC 40121 6374 E3
Tannen Dr
8600 BRWD 40242 5510 C6
Tanner Ct
100 ELZT 42701 6812 B4
Tanner Dr
10400 LSVL 40118 5942 D3
Tanoak Ct
3100 LSVL 40206 5617 C4
Tanyard Springs Blvd
10 HLVW 40229 5944 C7
Taper Ct
800 LSVL 40214 5833 A5
Taproot Ln
100 JFVL 47130 5507 E2
Tara Av
4400 LSVL 40216 5722 E5
Tara Cir
100 SHDV 40165 6161 B3
200 BltC 40165 6161 B3
Tara Ct
1300 RDCF 40175 6483 A2
3200 OdmC 40031 5405 A1
Tara Dr
3800 OdmC 40031 5295 E7
3800 OdmC 40031 5296 A7
3800 OdmC 40031 5404 E1
3900 OdmC 40031 5405 A1
Tara Gale Ct
4400 LSVL 40216 5722 E5
Tara Gale Dr
3100 LSVL 40216 5722 E5
Tarkington Wy
2500 LSVL 40258 5831 C1
Tarragon Ct
5700 LSVL 40219 5835 A1
Tarragon Rd
3500 LSVL 40219 5835 A1
3700 LSVL 40213 5726 A7
3700 LSVL 40219 5726 A7
Tarrant Ln
5400 OdmC 40014 5404 E4
Tarrence Rd
10900 LSVL 40291 5837 E2
10900 LSVL 40299 5837 E2
10900 LSVL 40299 5838 A2
Tarrytowne Dr
10400 LSVL 40272 5940 D3
Tartan Wy
1600 LSVL 40205 5726 A1
1800 OdmC 40031 5295 B4
Tasco Vw
6400 LSVL 40228 5836 B4
Tattenham Ln
10700 DGSH 40243 5619 B5
10700 DGSH 40243 5620 A5
10700 JFTN 40223 5619 B5
Tattersall Ln
13000 OdmC 40059 5401 B1
Taunton Vale Rd
16500 LSVL 40245 5622 C2
Taurus Pl
400 MDTN 40243 5620 D3
Tauten Sq
5100 LSVL 40241 5510 E1
Tavener Dr
2300 BCFT 40242 5509 E5
Tavistock Ct
2500 LSVL 40272 5941 C1
Tawnywood Ct
8200 LSVL 40291 5836 E5
Taxham Ct
6800 WDYH 40207 5509 D5
Taxus Tr
3600 LSVL 40299 5729 C5
Taxus Top Ln
1200 MDTN 40243 5620 C6
Taylor
- HdnC 40121 6374 C3
Taylor Av
200 ELZT 42701 6702 E6
1400 LSVL 40213 5725 D3
Taylor Blvd
100 VNGV 40175 6482 D7
100 VNGV 40175 6591 D1
2700 LSVL 40208 5724 B2
3000 LSVL 40215 5724 B2
4700 LSVL 40214 5724 A7
Taylor Blvd SR-1865
3500 LSVL 40215 5724 A3
4700 LSVL 40214 5724 A7
Taylor Blvd US-60 ALT
2700 LSVL 40208 5724 B2
3000 LSVL 40215 5724 B2
Taylor Ct
100 MTWH 40047 6056 B3
700 LSVL 40217 5616 A6
Taylor Dr
- BltC 40165 6161 A2
2900 CLKV 47129 5506 A2
Taylor Ln
100 ELZT 42701 6812 B4
Taylor Wy
100 BltC 40165 6161 B3
Taylor Creek Ct
400 LSVL 40245 5621 C5
Taylor Estes Rd
2500 SbyC 40245 5514 E3
Taylor Farm Ct
10600 LSVL 40059 5402 B6
Taylor Springs Dr
3000 LSVL 40220 5618 A7
3000 LSVL 40220 5727 E1
Taylorsville Rd
- LSVL 40205 5618 A7
2200 LSVL 40205 5617 C7
2200 SMRV 40205 5617 C7
2400 SGDN 40205 5617 C7
2500 KGLY 40205 5617 C7
3700 MVWE 40220 5618 B7
4000 LSVL 40220 5618 D7
4100 CMBG 40220 5618 D7
4100 HNAC 40220 5618 D7
4300 HBNA 40220 5619 A7
4300 JFTN 40220 5619 A7
4300 LSVL 40220 5619 A7
4600 HBNA 40220 5728 B1
4600 JFTN 40220 5728 B1
8900 FTHL 40299 5728 B1
9200 JFTN 40299 5728 C2
10500 JFTN 40299 5729 B5
10600 LSVL 40299 5729 E5
12800 LSVL 40299 5730 B4
14800 LSVL 40299 5731 A4
15500 LSVL 40299 5731 C6
16400 LSVL 40023 5840 D1
Taylorsville Rd SR-148
- LSVL 40023 5731 B5
14700 LSVL 40299 5730 B4
14800 LSVL 40299 5731 A4
Taylorsville Rd SR-155
- LSVL 40205 5618 A7
2200 LSVL 40205 5617 C7
2200 SMRV 40205 5617 C7
2400 SGDN 40205 5617 C7
2500 KGLY 40205 5617 C7
3700 MVWE 40220 5618 B7
4000 LSVL 40220 5618 C7
4100 CMBG 40220 5618 D7
4100 HNAC 40220 5618 D7
4300 HBNA 40220 5619 A7
4300 JFTN 40220 5619 A7
4300 LSVL 40220 5619 A7
4600 HBNA 40220 5728 B1
4600 JFTN 40220 5728 B1
8900 FTHL 40299 5728 B1
9200 JFTN 40299 5728 C2
10500 JFTN 40299 5729 B5
10600 LSVL 40299 5729 D5
12800 LSVL 40299 5730 A5
Taylorsville Lake Rd
4000 LSVL 40023 5730 E5
4000 LSVL 40023 5731 A6
4000 LSVL 40299 5730 E4
4000 LSVL 40299 5731 A6
4700 LSVL 40023 5840 E3
6000 SpnC 40023 5840 E3
Taylorsville Lake Rd SR-155
4000 LSVL 40023 5730 E4
4000 LSVL 40023 5731 A6
4000 LSVL 40299 5730 E4
4000 LSVL 40299 5731 A6
4700 LSVL 40023 5840 E3
6000 SpnC 40023 5840 E3
Tazwell Ct
11700 LSVL 40245 5511 C3
Tazwell Dr
11600 LSVL 40241 5511 C2
11600 LSVL 40245 5511 C2
11700 WTNH 40245 5511 C2
N Tazwell Dr
11300 LSVL 40241 5511 C3
S Tazwell Dr
11300 LSVL 40241 5511 C3
Teaberry Ct
- LGNG 40031 5296 B3
100 HLVW 40229 5944 B7
Teakwood Cir
3000 LSVL 40216 5722 D5
8000 MTWH 40047 6056 A3
Teakwood Ct
- CLKV 47129 5397 C6
Teakwood Dr
1000 CLKV 47129 5397 C6
Teakwood Ln
5800 LSVL 40258 5831 B5
Teal Av
3100 ANPK 40213 5725 B2
3100 LSVL 40217 5725 B2
Teal Ct
3500 JFVL 47130 5398 C6
Tealeaf Ct
5500 LSVL 40291 5728 C7
Teal Ridge Ct
1100 FydC 47150 5287 E7
Teaneck Ln
4800 LSVL 40216 5722 D6
Tear Grass Ct
7600 LSVL 40258 5831 C3
Tearose Dr
6500 LSVL 40258 5831 A4
Technology Dr
2500 LSVL 40299 5729 B2
2600 JFTN 40299 5729 B2
Technology Dr S
- LSVL 40214 5724 D7
Technology Wy
100 JFVL 47130 5397 E7
100 JFVL 47130 5398 A7
Technology Park Dr
- LSVL 40214 5724 D7
Techny Ln
1300 GYDL 40222 5509 D7
Tecumseh Av
- LSVL 40214 5833 C2
Tecumseh Cir
5500 INHC 40207 5509 A7
Tecumseh Ct
- SHDV 40165 6161 A5
Tecumseh Dr
100 SHDV 40165 6161 B5
Tedford Ct
200 HdnC 40121 6373 E4
Tedmark Ct
10 LSVL 40216 5723 A3
Tee View Ct
5800 LSVL 40059 5402 A6
Telford Ln
5100 LSVL 40241 5510 E1
Tellson Ct
500 LSVL 40245 5621 D6
Telovi Ct
4200 LSVL 40241 5510 B2
Tembroke Dr
2400 FXCH 40165 6053 A3
Temperate Ct
8800 HTCK 40229 5945 E3
Tempest Wy
1700 LSVL 40216 5832 B1
Temple Ct
500 HdnC 42701 6811 B4
Temple St
1300 LSVL 40210 5614 E5
Templeton Ct
3500 LSVL 40214 5832 B4
Templeton Dr
7300 LSVL 40214 5832 A4
Templewood Dr
3500 LSVL 40219 5835 A1
Tempsclair Rd
7500 LSVL 40220 5727 D3
Tenacity Ct
11300 HTCK 40229 5945 E4
Ten Broeck Wy
3200 MYHL 40241 5510 C4
3200 TNBK 40241 5510 C4
3600 LSVL 40241 5510 C4
Tenderfoot Ct
11600 OdmC 40059 5401 D1
Tennessee Av
1000 LSVL 40208 5724 B1
1300 LSVL 40208 5615 A7
1300 LSVL 40210 5615 A7
Tennis Blvd
13300 LSVL 40272 5939 C7
13300 LSVL 40272 6048 C1
E Tenny Av
100 LSVL 40214 5724 D6
W Tenny Av
100 LSVL 40214 5724 C6
Tennyson Av
2500 LSVL 40205 5617 B7
2500 SMRV 40205 5617 B7
Tennyson Dr
1600 CLKV 47129 5506 B1
1700 CLKV 47129 5397 B7
Ten Pin Ln
100 STMW 40207 5618 D3
Tent St
- HdnC 40121 6265 B7
Tepee Rd
10 INDH 40207 5508 D6
Teresa Ct
100 HdnC 42701 6702 B5
Teresa Pl
- LSVL 40214 5724 C7
Teresa Rd
10 ELZT 42701 6702 C1
10 HdnC 42701 6593 D7
10 HdnC 42701 6702 C1
Teresa Kay Dr
100 MTWH 40047 6055 E6
Terminal Dr
600 LSVL 40209 5724 E5
600 LSVL 40209 5725 A4
Terrace Ct
600 NALB 47150 5505 E3
1900 JFVL 47130 5507 D3
Terrace Dr
200 RDCF 40160 6483 E5
300 RDCF 40160 6484 A5
Terrace Hts
10 JFVL 47130 5507 D5
E Terrace Hts
400 JFVL 47130 5507 D5
Terrace Creek Dr
13500 LSVL 40245 5512 B5
Terrace Green Cir
5100 LSVL 40218 5726 D6
Terrace Hill Dr
3700 LSVL 40245 5512 B5
Terrace Springs Dr
3500 LSVL 40245 5512 B5
Terra Crossing Blvd
- LSVL 40245 5512 C7
Terrier Ct
2300 LSVL 40218 5726 D2
Terrier Ln
3300 LSVL 40218 5726 D2
Terril Ln
2000 LSVL 40218 5726 C2
Terriwood Ct
2100 MBKF 40223 5510 D6
Terry Av
200 ELZT 42701 6812 B3
Terry Ct
2900 RDCF 40160 6484 B7
3900 LSVL 40216 5722 B4
Terry Dr
100 HLVW 40229 5944 A6
300 RDCF 40160 6483 D6
4900 HBNE 40165 6053 D3
Terry Ln
- HsnC 47136 5610 E5
- LNVL 47136 5610 E5
1600 NALB 47150 5505 D2
7000 ClkC 47129 5397 D2
7000 ClkC 47172 5397 D2
Terry Pl
- LSVL 40214 5724 D7
Terry Rd
3500 LSVL 40229 5943 E2
4900 LSVL 40216 5722 B7
5200 LSVL 40216 5831 A6
5200 LSVL 40258 5831 A6
8800 LSVL 40272 5831 A7
Terry Rd SR-1727
4900 LSVL 40216 5722 B7
5200 LSVL 40216 5831 A6
5200 LSVL 40258 5831 A6
8800 LSVL 40272 5831 A7
Terudon Dr
1200 LSVL 40214 5832 D2
Tessin Wy
600 DGSH 40223 5620 A3
600 LSVL 40223 5620 A3
Tex Av
100 LSVL 40118 5833 C7
Texas Av
800 LSVL 40217 5616 A7
800 LSVL 40217 5725 A1
1200 LSVL 40204 5616 A7
5900 MTWH 40047 6056 A2
E Texas St
10 HdnC 40121 6374 E2
W Texas St
- HdnC 40121 6374 D2
Texlyn Ct
7600 LSVL 40258 5830 E4
Textile Av
6900 LSVL 40258 5831 E3
Thackeray Dr
1500 LSVL 40205 5725 E1
Thalia Av
6700 LSVL 40214 5833 C2
Thames Av
2800 LSVL 40220 5618 A7
Thames Dr
1400 CLKV 47129 5506 C1
1600 CLKV 47129 5397 C7
Theater Sq
10 LSVL 40202 5615 D3
The Byeway
400 ELZT 42701 6811 E1
The Esplanade Av
100 LSVL 40214 5833 B1
The Geon Rd
- LSVL 40211 5614 B7
Theiler Ln
6100 LSVL 40229 5945 A1
Thelma Ct
2400 JFTN 40220 5728 B1
Thelma Ln
8900 JFTN 40220 5728 B2
The Meadow Rd
1700 LSVL 40223 5510 D6
1700 LYDN 40223 5510 D7
1700 WPMG 40223 5510 D6
2000 MBKF 40223 5510 D6
Theodore Burnett Ct
700 LSVL 40217 5724 D3
Theresa Av
1700 SVLY 40216 5723 D3
Theresa Ct
700 VNGV 40175 6482 C6
Therina Ct
7800 LSVL 40241 5510 A3
Therina Wy
3800 LSVL 40241 5510 A2
4000 LSVL 40241 5509 E2
Thicket Ct
10 HdnC 40160 6592 C5
Thierman Ln
100 STMW 40207 5618 A2
Thiry Rd
300 BltC 40109 6051 B3
Thistle Ct
100 RDCF 40160 6592 E1
Thistledawn Dr
2200 SVLY 40216 5723 B3
Thistlewood Ct
9900 JFTN 40223 5619 D5
Thistlewood Dr
2800 LSVL 40206 5617 A2
Thixton Ln
7600 LSVL 40229 5945 D5
8000 BltC 40229 5945 D6
8200 LSVL 40229 5946 A5
8900 LSVL 40291 5946 D3
Thixton Ln SR-2053
7600 LSVL 40229 5945 D5
8000 BltC 40229 5945 D6
8200 LSVL 40229 5946 A5
8900 LSVL 40291 5946 D3
Thomas Av
1100 RDCF 40160 6483 D5
2200 LSVL 40216 5723 A6
2400 LSVL 40216 5722 E6

Louisville Metro Street Index

STREET: Block City ZIP Map# Grid

Thomas Av NE
- 7300 LNVL 47136 5610 D4

Thomas Ct
- - OdmC 40014 5402 C6

Thomas Ln
- - HdnC 42701 6811 A7
- 10 BltC 40071 5949 C3
- 2900 JFTN 40299 5728 C3

Thomas St
- 100 ELZT 42701 6812 B2
- 300 NALB 47150 5505 D3

Thomas Grove Rd
- 8900 LSVL 40291 5946 A4

Thomas Shaun Ct
- - ELZT 42701 6811 D2

Thompson Av
- - BFLD 40207 5617 E4
- - LSVL 40207 5618 A5
- - PLYV 40207 5618 A4
- - STMW 40207 5618 A5
- 100 LSVL 40206 5616 D1
- 400 STMW 40207 5617 E4
- 600 BFLD 40207 5618 A4

Thompson Ln
- 100 JFVL 47130 5398 C7
- 100 JFVL 47130 5507 C1
- 8500 LSVL 40258 5831 B6
- 9100 LSVL 40272 5831 B7

Thompson Rd
- 10 HdnC 40162 6592 A7

Thompson St
- 800 CHAN 47111 5181 E4

Thor Av
- 9400 LSVL 40229 5944 A2

Thornberry Av
- 1600 LSVL 40215 5724 A1

Thornbird Ct
- 2800 LSVL 40220 5728 A2

Thorndell Ct
- 3200 CKSD 40241 5510 E4

Thornhill Dr
- - CTWD 40014 5403 E7
- - CTWD 40014 5404 A7
- - OdmC 40014 5404 A7

Thornhill Rd
- - LSVL 40222 5509 D5
- 2300 TNHL 40222 5509 C5

Thornton Ln
- 11200 LSVL 40223 5620 B3

Thornwood Ct
- 2700 LSVL 40220 5728 A2

Thornwood Rd
- 8100 LSVL 40220 5728 A2

Thoroughbred Ct
- 9000 LSVL 40291 5728 B7
- 9000 LSVL 40291 5837 B1

Thorpe Dr
- 700 DGSH 40243 5620 C6
- 900 MDTN 40243 5620 C6

Thouroughbred Ct
- 3100 OdmC 40014 5405 B6

Thousand Oaks Dr
- 3100 LSVL 40205 5726 A2

Three Springs Ct
- 8000 PROS 40059 5400 D2

Thrill Ln
- 2300 MLHT 40219 5834 C6

Thrush Ln
- 6300 FydC 47119 5393 E4

Thrush Rd
- 3200 ANPK 40213 5725 B2
- 3300 LSVL 40213 5725 B3

Thruston Av
- 900 LSVL 40217 5725 B1

Thruston Dr
- 800 LSVL 40217 5725 A1

Thunder Ct
- 5400 LSVL 40272 5940 B4

Thunder Dr
- 11000 LSVL 40272 5940 B3

Thunder Rd
- 100 BltC 40165 6162 E7

Thunderbolt Rd
- - HdnC 40121 6374 C1

Thurman Ct
- 10 SVLY 40216 5723 A3

Thurman Dr
- 2200 SVLY 40216 5723 B3

Thurman Rd
- 4800 LSVL 40299 5839 C2

Thyme Ct
- 10 LSVL 40258 5831 C4

Tiara Ct
- 6200 LSVL 40219 5836 A5

Ticonderoga Dr
- 7300 LSVL 40214 5832 E3
- 7300 LSVL 40214 5833 A3

Tidbit Rd
- 2100 MLHT 40219 5834 B6

Tidewater Ct
- 6100 PROS 40059 5400 E4
- 6100 PROS 40059 5401 A5

Tidwell Rd
- 2300 LSVL 40272 5941 D3

Tidworth Ct
- 1400 LSVL 40245 5622 E2

Tierney Av
- 11600 LSVL 40272 5939 E4

Tiffany Ct
- 100 BltC 40047 6056 A1

Tiffany Ct NE
- 6500 HsnC 47122 5501 B3

Tiffany Ln
- 100 HdnC 42701 6593 B5
- 100 RDCF 42701 6593 B5
- 500 RLGF 40207 5508 D7
- 500 RLGF 40207 5617 D1

Tiffany Brooke Ct
- 8500 LSVL 40228 5836 B5

Tiger Rd
- - HdnC 40121 6374 C1

Tile Factory Ln
- 1200 LSVL 40213 5725 E5
- 1200 LYNV 40213 5725 E6
- 1300 LSVL 40218 5725 E5

Tillman Rd
- 8200 HTBN 40222 5619 A3

Tim Ct
- 100 RDCF 40160 6483 D5

Timber Ln
- 10 ELZT 42701 6702 C7
- 10 HdnC 42701 6702 C7
- 100 ELZT 42701 6811 C1

Timber Trc
- 1700 LSVL 40214 5832 E3

Timber Wy
- - LSVL 40214 5723 D7

Timberbend Dr
- 6600 LSVL 40229 5944 E2
- 6700 LSVL 40229 5945 A2

Timber Bluff Ct
- 6900 PROS 40059 5400 D6

Timberbrook Dr
- 9700 JFTN 40223 5619 B5

Timberbrook Pl
- 800 JFTN 40223 5619 D5

Timber Creek Ct
- 5500 PROS 40059 5400 D6

Timber Crest Dr
- 6900 PROS 40059 5400 D6

Timberhaven Trc
- 2000 LSVL 40214 5832 E3

Timber Hill Rd
- 2900 LSVL 40272 5832 B6

Timber Hills Rd
- 2700 LSVL 40214 5832 C6
- 2800 LSVL 40272 5832 C6

Timber Hollow Ct
- 8600 LSVL 40219 5834 E6

Timber Hollow Dr
- 3700 LSVL 40219 5834 E7
- 3700 LSVL 40219 5835 A7

Timberlake Tr
- 400 LSVL 40245 5621 B3

Timberline Dr
- 8600 LSVL 40291 5837 A3

Timber Oak Dr
- 1100 JFTN 40223 5620 A6

Timber Pine Dr
- 4700 FydC 47150 5396 C3

Timber Ridge Ct
- 4600 OdmC 40014 5404 C2
- 6900 PROS 40059 5400 D6

Timber Ridge Dr
- 5500 PROS 40059 5400 D5

Timber Ridge Pl
- 6000 PROS 40059 5400 D5

Timber Ridge Rd
- 4100 OdmC 40014 5404 C2
- 5900 PROS 40059 5400 D5
- 6000 LSVL 40059 5400 D5

Timber Springs Cir
- 6900 LSVL 40241 5509 B3

Timberview Wy
- 9700 JFTN 40223 5619 D6

Timber Wolf Ct
- 3000 FydC 47150 5397 C3

Timberwood Cir
- - HTBN 40222 5619 D5
- 6900 CTWD 40014 5403 C7
- 9900 JFTN 40223 5619 D6

Timberwood Dr
- 800 RDCF 40160 6483 A2

Timmy Ct
- 6200 LSVL 40219 5836 A5

Timmy Ln
- 8100 LSVL 40219 5836 A6

Timothy Ln
- 4100 SVLY 40216 5723 B4

Timothy Pl
- 9200 ODGH 40014 5402 E7
- 9200 OdmC 40014 5402 E7

Timothy Wy
- 4200 OdmC 40014 5404 D7

Timtam Ct
- 10 HdnC 42701 6703 E4

Tina Ct
- 1000 HdnC 40160 6592 C4
- 1600 OdmC 40031 5297 C4

Tina Dr
- 4500 OdmC 40014 5404 D7

Tindall Ln
- 1100 LSVL 40245 5621 D7

Tin-Dor Cir
- - LGNG 40031 5296 E2

Tindor Cir
- 10 LGNG 40031 5296 E1

Tin Dor Wy
- 500 LSVL 40118 5942 D2

Tingle Dr
- - NALB 47150 5395 E7
- 10 NALB 47150 5504 E1

Tin Pan Al
- 1400 LSVL 40208 5615 D6

Tiny Ln
- 2500 SVLY 40216 5723 E1

Tioga Rd
- 6300 LSVL 40214 5832 D1

Tipton Pl
- 4800 LSVL 40272 5940 D3

Tip Top Ln
- 7700 LSVL 40219 5836 A5

Tirol Ct
- 2800 JFTN 40220 5728 B2

Tisha Ct
- 800 ELZT 42701 6702 D6

Titan Dr
- 9400 LSVL 40229 5944 A1

Titanic Wy
- 6100 LSVL 40258 5831 B3

Titleist Rd
- 2500 LDNP 40242 5510 B5
- 2600 LSVL 40242 5510 B5

Titus Ct
- 4400 LSVL 40218 5726 C5

Tiverton Ct
- 9400 RLGH 40242 5510 D6

Tiverton Wy
- 100 ELZT 42701 6702 E3
- 9100 WWOD 40242 5510 C6
- 9200 RLGH 40242 5510 C6
- 9700 MWVL 40242 5510 C6
- 9800 MWVL 40223 5510 C6

Tivis Ct
- 4700 LSVL 40218 5726 C5
- 4700 PLRH 40218 5726 C6

Tivoli Dr
- 5400 LSVL 40272 5940 B3

Todd Av
- 1600 LSVL 40213 5725 D2

Todd Dr
- 100 MTWH 40047 6056 A2
- 100 SbyC 40067 5732 D3

Todds Point Rd
- 8000 OdmC 40014 5513 D3
- 8000 SbyC 40245 5513 E3

Todds Point Rd SR-1408
- 8000 OdmC 40014 5513 D3
- 8000 SbyC 40245 5513 E3

Todds Point Rd SR-1818
- - OdmC 40014 5513 D2

Toebbe Ln
- 5700 LSVL 40229 5944 E1
- 5900 LSVL 40229 5945 A1

Toledo Ct
- 4800 LSVL 40272 5831 C7
- 4800 LSVL 40272 5940 D1

Toledo Ln
- 9600 LSVL 40272 5940 C1

Toliver Ct
- 100 HLVW 40229 5944 B7

Tolkien Ct
- 5000 LSVL 40229 5944 D1

Toll House Ct
- 10400 LSVL 40241 5511 A2

Toll House Ln
- 4600 LSVL 40241 5511 A2

Toll Plaza Dr
- - LSVL 40209 5725 A5

Tolls Av
- 8000 LSVL 40214 5833 D5

Tolls Ln
- 7900 LSVL 40214 5833 D6

Tollview Dr
- 100 SHDV 40165 6162 A3

Tomahawk
- - FydC 47150 5613 C2

Tomahawk Ln
- 300 FydC 47150 5613 D2

Tomahawk Rd
- 5200 INDH 40207 5508 E7

Tom Evans Rd
- 7600 FydC 47124 5283 E6
- 7600 FydC 47124 5284 A2
- 9500 ClkC 47106 5284 A2

Tomjoe Ct
- 2500 LSVL 40242 5509 D5

Tomjoe Dr
- 7400 LSVL 40242 5509 D5

Tommie Ct
- 7600 LSVL 40258 5830 D4

Tommy Gray Ct
- - ELZT 42701 6811 C2

Tompkins Rd
- 10800 LSVL 40291 5837 E4

Tom Wallace Rd
- - LSVL 40118 5942 B5

Tony Ln
- 3300 HBNE 40165 6053 D3

Tonya Ct
- 8100 LSVL 40214 5833 C5

Tooten Hill Rd
- 3400 ClkC 47130 5399 A3

Topaz Ct
- 4300 LSVL 40216 5722 E4

Topfield Rd
- 100 BltC 40229 5944 D7
- 100 HLVW 40229 5944 D7

Top Hat Ct
- 6100 LSVL 40258 5831 B3

Top Hill Rd
- 300 ELZT 42701 6812 B2
- 1100 LSVL 40118 5941 E5
- 1500 LSVL 40118 5942 B6
- 2400 LSVL 40206 5617 A3

Top Walnut Lp
- 11300 LSVL 40229 5945 A3

Tornado Rd
- 2400 HdnC 40121 6265 C7
- 2400 HdnC 40121 6374 C1

Torquay Ct
- 9900 LSVL 40241 5510 E1

Torrey Pines Ct
- 8200 LSVL 40291 5837 C6

Torrington Ct
- 5300 LSVL 40272 5940 B3

Torrington Rd
- 10300 LSVL 40272 5940 C2

Totem Rd
- 10 INDH 40207 5508 E7

Tottenham Rd
- 6600 WDYH 40207 5618 C1

Tower Dr
- 500 STMW 40207 5618 B4

Tower Rd
- 4000 LSVL 40219 5835 A3

Tower St
- 1100 CHAN 47111 5181 D3

Town Country Trailer Park Rd
- - HdnC 42701 6593 C7

Towne Dr
- 100 ELZT 42701 6702 D4

Towne Center Dr
- 4100 LSVL 40241 5511 A3

Towne Center Lp
- - ELZT 42701 6702 D4

Towne Creek Ct
- 100 MDTN 40243 5620 E4

Towne Creek Rd
- - MDTN 40223 5620 E4
- 12600 MDTN 40243 5620 E5

Townepark Cir
- - MDTN 40243 5620 E4

Townepark Wy
- 12600 MDTN 40243 5620 E4

Towner Pl
- 800 ANCH 40223 5620 B2

Townsend Rd
- 600 ClkC 47172 5289 A7

Townsend Ter
- 3100 SPVL 40241 5509 E4

Toy Ct
- 100 HLVW 40229 5944 A5

Tracey Ct
- 100 RDCF 40160 6483 D6

Trackers Wy
- 4800 LSVL 40216 5831 D1

Tracy Wy
- 5400 LSVL 40214 5723 E6

Trade Port Dr
- - LSVL 40258 5831 A7
- - LSVL 40272 5830 E7
- - LSVL 40272 5831 A7
- 7000 LSVL 40258 5830 E7

Trades Mill Dr
- 6400 LSVL 40291 5836 E3

Tradition Cir
- 2400 LSVL 40245 5512 C7

Tradition Dr
- 14900 LSVL 40245 5512 D7

Trafalgar Sq
- 100 LSVL 40218 5726 C2

Trail Creek Pl
- 3600 LSVL 40241 5509 D3

Trail Crest Ct
- 7300 LSVL 40241 5509 E3

Trail Gate Trc
- 7900 LSVL 40291 5836 E4

Trail Ridge Ct
- 7200 LSVL 40241 5509 D3

Trail Ridge Rd
- 3200 LSVL 40241 5509 E3

Trails End Rd
- 10 LSVL 40216 5722 E2

Training Officer Ter
- - LSVL 40210 5615 A6

Trakia Ct
- 8300 LSVL 40219 5836 A6

Tralee Ln
- 5900 LSVL 40219 5835 E5
- 5900 LSVL 40219 5836 A5

Trane Wy
- 1800 JFTN 40299 5619 D7

Tranquil Dr
- 1200 JFVL 47130 5507 B2

Tranquil Valley Ln
- 8700 LSVL 40299 5728 A4

Transylvania Av
- 600 ELZT 42701 6811 D2
- 6700 LSVL 40059 5400 C5
- 6700 PROS 40059 5400 C5

Transylvania Bch
- 6000 LSVL 40059 5400 B5

Trappers Cross
- 13300 OdmC 44026 5292 B3

Trappers Ln
- - BltC 40165 6051 E5

Trappers Rd
- 100 BltC 40165 6051 E6

Trappers Tr
- 10 LSVL 40216 5723 A2

Trappers Ridge Cir
- 5900 LSVL 40216 5722 D7

Trappers Ridge Ct
- - HdnC 40162 6591 A4

Travis Ln
- 100 BltC 40047 6055 E2

Travis Rd
- 100 BltC 40165 6054 D3

Travois Rd
- 100 WDYH 40207 5509 A7
- 200 INHC 40207 5509 A6
- 200 LSVL 40207 5509 A6

Trealor Rd
- 11100 ClkC 47143 5180 B1

Treasure Ct
- 10300 LSVL 40229 5944 A3

Treasure Bay Ct
- 100 SHDV 40165 6161 C3

Tree Ln
- 2900 JFTN 40299 5728 D3

Treece Ter
- - LSVL 40205 5616 C7
- - LSVL 40205 5725 E1

Tree Crest Ct
- 14100 LSVL 40245 5621 C3

Treeline Ct
- 14000 LSVL 40245 5621 C2

Treesdale Ct
- 3100 FydC 47172 5287 E6

Treesdale Dr
- 4200 FydC 47172 5287 D6

Tree Tops Dr
- 7900 LSVL 40291 5837 D5

Treeview Ct
- 3000 LSVL 40214 5832 C3

Trefoil Ln
- 5400 LSVL 40258 5831 C5

Tregaron Av
- 2400 JFTN 40299 5728 D2

Trellis Ct
- 3400 JFTN 40299 5728 D4

Tremont Dr
- 2800 LSVL 40205 5726 B1

Trena Tr
- 6100 LSVL 40258 5831 B2

Trent Av
- 1700 LSVL 40216 5832 A1

Trenta Ln
- 9200 LSVL 40291 5728 B7

Trentham Ct
- 9100 WWOD 40242 5510 C6

Trentham Ln
- 9000 WWOD 40242 5510 C6
- 9200 RLGH 40242 5510 C6

Trepio Ct
- 8900 JFTN 40299 5728 B6

Trestle Rd
- - HdnC 40177 6156 C6
- - HdnC 40177 6265 C3
- - WPT 40177 6156 B6

Treva Ct
- 100 MTWH 40047 6056 B3

Trevilian Wy
- - SMRV 40205 5617 B7
- 1000 LSVL 40213 5725 E2
- 1400 LSVL 40205 5725 E2
- 1600 LSVL 40205 5726 A1
- 1800 LSVL 40205 5617 A7
- 2500 SGDN 40205 5617 C6

Trevillian Ct
- 1200 JFVL 47130 5507 C2

Trevino Wy
- 7800 LSVL 40258 5831 B4

Trevor Ct
- - BltC 40047 6055 A5
- - LSVL 40245 5622 D1

Trevor Dr
- - LSVL 40245 5622 C1

Trewlaney Ct
- 4300 LSVL 40229 5944 B2

Trey Ct
- 4500 LSVL 40220 5727 D3

Trey Dr
- 100 MTWH 40165 6054 D5

Trey Pl
- 4500 LSVL 40220 5727 D3

Treyborne Pl
- 18600 LSVL 40023 5622 E5
- 18600 LSVL 40245 5622 E5

Triangle Dr
- 300 SLRB 47172 5288 D4
- 1300 CLKV 47129 5506 C2
- 6700 LSVL 40214 5832 D1

Triangle Ln N
- 3400 HLVW 40229 5943 E6
- 3500 HLVW 40229 5944 A6

Triangle Ln S
- - HLVW 40229 5944 A7

Triangle Ln W
- 2200 HLVW 40229 5943 E6
- 2200 HLVW 40229 5944 A6

Tribal Rd
- 100 INDH 40207 5508 D7

Tricia Ln
- 400 ELZT 42701 6811 E4

Trigg St
- 1600 LSVL 40213 5725 D2

Trillium Dr
- 7700 LSVL 40258 5831 B4

Trimingham Rd
- 10 FydC 47150 5504 C4
- 10 NALB 47150 5504 C4

Trinity Cir
- 4300 LSVL 40213 5725 C4

Trinity Rd
- 3100 LSVL 40206 5617 D4
- 3300 LSVL 40207 5617 D4

Trinity Hills Ln
- 400 STMW 40207 5618 A1

Trinity Park Dr
- 1300 LSVL 40213 5725 C5

Trio Av
- 1200 LSVL 40219 5835 B6

Trio Ln
- 2000 FydC 47122 5503 A3

Triple Acres Rd
- - HdnC 42701 6593 C7

Triple Crown Ct
- 12100 MDTN 40243 5620 C6

Triplett Ct
- 2700 LSVL 40216 5831 C1

Triplett Dr
- 6300 LSVL 40216 5831 B1
- 6300 LSVL 40258 5831 B1

Tripolee Rd
- 11000 FydC 47124 5392 A5

Trista Dr
- 300 MDTN 40243 5620 D3

Tristan Rd
- 100 BLMD 40222 5619 B3

Triton Park Blvd
- 13500 LSVL 40223 5512 B6

Triton Spring Ct
- 11300 LSVL 40299 5729 B6

Troon Ct
- 100 LSVL 40245 5621 B5

Troon Dr
- 14200 LSVL 40245 5621 B5

Troon Meadow Pl
- 300 LSVL 40245 5621 B5

Troon Village Wy
- 200 LSVL 40245 5621 B6
- 200 MDTN 40245 5621 B6

Trooper Hill Rd
- 10 HdnC 40162 6702 B2

Trophy Pl
- 12400 LSVL 40299 5729 B4

Tropic Ct
- 6800 LSVL 40219 5835 C3

Trotters Pointe Dr
- 10300 LSVL 40241 5511 A1
- 10400 LSVL 40241 5402 A7

Trotwood Pl
- 500 LSVL 40245 5621 D6

Trough Spring Ln
- 1800 LSVL 40205 5726 A1

Trout Creek Ct
- 3300 LSVL 40218 5726 B5

Troutwood Ct
- 8000 LSVL 40291 5836 E3

Trowbridge Ter
- 4700 BWDV 40207 5618 C3

Troy Av
- 600 RDCF 40160 6483 D5

Troy St
- 1700 NALB 47150 5505 D5

Trubart Ln
- 2500 LSVL 40216 5722 E5

Truckers Blvd
- 1400 JFVL 47130 5397 E7
- 1400 JFVL 47130 5398 A7
- 1400 JFVL 47130 5506 E1

Trudy Rural Ct
- 4500 JFTN 40299 5728 A6

Truman Dr
- - MTWH 40047 6054 E6
- 100 BltC 40047 6054 E5

Truman Wy
- 10400 JFTN 40299 5728 E5

Trump Av
- 13000 LSVL 40299 5729 D6

Trumpet Wy
- 4500 LSVL 40216 5722 D4

Trumpetvine Rd
- 2700 LSVL 40220 5727 E2

Truro Ct
- 10 LSVL 40216 5722 E4

Tuba Dr
- 3400 LSVL 40216 5722 D4

Tuberose Av
- 4500 LSVL 40213 5725 C7

Tubman Ct
- 4900 LSVL 40218 5726 D6

Tuckaho Rd
- 2300 RBNW 40207 5509 A5
- 2400 LSVL 40207 5509 A5
- 2600 LSVL 40207 5508 E5

Tuckaway Ct
- 7900 LSVL 40291 5837 C5

Tuckaway Dr
- - LSVL 40291 5837 D6

Tucker Av
- 600 CLKV 47129 5506 D2
- 3800 SVLY 40216 5723 C2

Tucker Blvd
- - LSVL 40205 5617 E6

Tucker Rd
- 2700 JFTN 40299 5728 C2

N Tucker Rd
- 1400 FydC 47122 5502 C4
- 1400 GEOT 47122 5502 C4

S Tucker Rd
- 500 FydC 47136 5502 D6

Tucker Lake Dr
- 13200 LSVL 40299 5729 D4

Tuckers Mhp Rd
- - RDCF 40160 6483 B1

Tucker Station Rd
- 200 MDTN 40243 5620 C5
- 400 DGSH 40243 5620 D6
- 800 DGSH 40299 5620 D6
- 1000 MDTN 40299 5620 D6
- 1400 LSVL 40299 5620 D7
- 1400 LSVL 40299 5729 D1
- 1500 JFTN 40299 5729 D3

Tucker Wood Ln
- 3300 LSVL 40299 5729 E3

Tucker Wood Pl
- 13300 LSVL 40299 5729 E4

Tucson Ct
- 9800 LSVL 40223 5510 D7

Tudor Ct
- 7500 GYDL 40222 5509 E7

Tuesday Wy
- 3700 LSVL 40219 5835 A5

Tufton Ct
- 9700 JFTN 40299 5728 C5

Tug Rd
- - LSVL 40209 5724 E5

Tulane Av
- 3900 LSVL 40214 5724 C3

Tulip Av
- 100 PWEV 40056 5512 D2

Tulip Cir
- 4100 LSVL 40219 5835 B7

Tulip Ct
- - JFVL 47130 5507 D3
- 100 RDCF 40160 6483 D7

Tulip Grove Ct
- 4300 LSVL 40241 5510 E3

Tuliphurst Dr
- 100 PWEV 40056 5512 C3

Tulip Oak Cir
- 100 ELZT 42701 6702 E3

Tulip Poplar Ct
- 9900 LSVL 40291 5946 D1

Tulip Tree Dr
- 10100 LSVL 40241 5510 E2

Tumbleweed Dr
- 100 HLVW 40229 5944 C5
- 100 LSVL 40229 5944 C5

Tumbleweed Rd
- 11400 HLVW 40229 5944 C5
- 11400 LSVL 40229 5944 C5

Tumeric Ln
- 5000 LSVL 40258 5831 C4

Tunbridge Wells Ln
- - INHC 40207 5509 A7
- 700 WDYH 40207 5509 A7

Tunisian Wy
- 1600 LSVL 40214 5723 E7
- 1600 LSVL 40214 5832 E1

Tunnel Rd
- 100 FydC 47122 5503 B4

Tunnel Wy
- 9900 LSVL 40291 5946 C3

Tunnel Hill Rd
- 1800 ELZT 42701 6703 E5
- 1800 HdnC 42701 6703 E5

Tunnel Hill Rd N
- 10 HdnC 42701 6703 E3
- 1900 ELZT 42701 6703 E5

Tunnel Mill Rd
- 1400 CHAN 47111 5181 E4
- 1400 ClkC 47111 5181 E4
- 1500 ClkC 47111 5182 A3

Tupelo Ct
- 2300 CLKV 47129 5397 C6

Tupelo Dr
- 2200 CLKV 47129 5397 C6

Tupelo Pass
- 5300 LSVL 40213 5726 A7
- 5500 LSVL 40219 5726 A7

Tuppence Trc
- 10000 JFTN 40223 5619 D5

Turf Ct
- 10600 LSVL 40241 5511 A3

Turfland Wy
- 10800 LSVL 40241 5511 B2

Turkey Ridge Rd
- 10 MdeC 40175 6373 A6

Turnberry Dr
- 4700 FydC 47119 5503 D1
- 8000 LSVL 40291 5837 D6

Turnberry Wy
- 400 ELZT 42701 6702 D1

Turnbridge Pl
- 6500 PROS 40059 5400 D3

Turnbridge Wy
- 7500 PROS 40059 5400 D3

Turner Av
- - OdmC 40014 5403 C7

Turner Ct
- 13000 LSVL 40299 5729 D6

Turner Dr
- 100 RDCF 40160 6592 E1

Turner Ridge Rd
- 7400 OdmC 40014 5403 A7

Turnover Ct
- 3200 LSVL 40216 5722 C6

Turnpike View Dr
- 9600 LSVL 40229 5943 E2

Turnside Dr
- 8400 LSVL 40242 5510 A5
- 8400 PNTN 40242 5510 A5

Turnstile Ct
- 10300 JFTN 40223 5619 E5

Turnstile Trc
- 400 JFTN 40223 5619 E5

Turpin Dr
- 1800 CLKV 47129 5397 C6

Turquoise Dr
- 1500 LSVL 40214 5832 E2

Turtle Bay Ct
- 100 SHDV 40165 6161 C3

Turtle Creek Tr
- 17400 LSVL 40245 5622 D3

Tuscany Wy
- 4700 LSVL 40299 5728 D6

Tuscarora Wy
- 4100 LSVL 40215 5724 A5

Tuts Rd
- 100 BltC 40165 6160 D6

Tutts Rd
- - BltC 40165 6160 D6

Tuxford Wy
- 4100 LSVL 40241 5510 E3

Tween Rd
- 4600 BWDV 40207 5618 C2

Twelve Oaks Ct
- 3300 FydC 47172 5397 B1

Twelve Oaks Dr
- 100 MTWH 40047 6056 C3

Twilight Dr
- 10100 LSVL 40272 5939 E2

Twillingate Ln
- 4300 LSVL 40241 5510 C2

Twin Dr
- 1500 LSVL 40213 5725 C3
- 6800 LSVL 40258 5831 E2

Twin Acres Dr
- 100 BltC 40165 6052 A5

Twin Brook Dr
- 100 BltC 40165 6053 A4
- 100 FXCH 40165 6053 A4
- 1700 ClkC 47172 5288 C5
- 1700 SLRB 47172 5288 C5

Twinbrook Dr
- 1700 ClkC 47172 5288 B6
- 1700 CLKV 47172 5288 B6

Twinbrook Rd
- 400 WDYH 40207 5618 A1

Twin Cir Dr
- 3100 FydC 47119 5504 B1

Twin Elms Ct
- 4300 LSVL 40241 5509 B1

Twin Hill Rd
- 2100 LSVL 40207 5508 D5
- 2100 RVWD 40207 5508 D5

Twinkle Dr
- 5200 LSVL 40258 5831 C2

Twin Lakes Ct
- 8200 LSVL 40214 5832 B5

Twin Oak Ln
- 3200 LSVL 40219 5725 E7
- 3300 LSVL 40219 5726 A7

Twin Oaks Dr
- 10 HdnC 40160 6484 A7
- 100 BltC 40047 6055 A2
- 1700 NALB 47150 5505 C1

Twin Ridge Ct
- 8700 LYDN 40242 5510 B7
- 8700 LYDN 40242 5619 B1

Twin Ridge Rd
- 1400 LYDN 40242 5510 B7
- 1400 LYDN 40242 5619 B1

Twin Springs Ct
- 8500 CLKV 47172 5288 B6

Twin Springs Dr
- 6800 CLKV 47172 5288 A6
- 8500 ClkC 47172 5288 A6

Twin View Ct
- 3500 FydC 47119 5394 E7

Twin Willows Ln
- 1200 LSVL 40214 5833 A4

Twisted Pine Rd
- 8300 LSVL 40219 5835 E6

Two Mile Ln
- 2000 FydC 47150 5613 C3

Two Mules Dr
- 10 HdnC 42701 6593 E4

INDEX 49
Two Springs Ln
Louisville Metro Street Index
Velva Dr

STREET Block City ZIP Map# Grid
Two Springs Ln
6000 WDYH 40207 5509 B7
Two Springs Pl
1600 WDYH 40207 5509 C7
Tyanne Pl
3700 LSVL 40220 5727 B1
Tycoon Wy
1300 LSVL 40213 5725 E2
Tye Av
4000 FydC 47150 5396 C4
4000 NALB 47150 5396 C5
Tyler Av
- BltC 40047 6055 E1
400 MTWH 40047 6055 E1
2300 LSVL 40212 5506 A7
2700 LSVL 40212 5505 E7
Tyler Cir
10 ELZT 42701 6703 C6
Tyler Dr
400 NALB 47150 5505 A1
Tyler Ln
100 CLKV 47129 5396 E6
1800 LSVL 40205 5726 B1
2100 SMRG 40205 5726 C1
2200 SMRG 40205 5617 C7
2300 KGLY 40205 5617 C7
2300 LSVL 40205 5617 C7
Tyler Pkwy
100 SHDV 40165 6161 A6
1600 LSVL 40204 5616 D6
Tyler St
2100 ClkC 47172 5397 D1
Tyler Wy
- LSVL 40299 5729 E5
Tyler Park Dr
1300 LSVL 40204 5616 C6
Tyler Woods Ct
12400 LSVL 40299 5729 D5
Tyne Rd
200 BWDV 40207 5618 C3
Tynebrae Ct
3800 LSVL 40241 5510 D3
Tyrone Dr
2000 LSVL 40218 5726 C3
3500 WBHL 40218 5726 C3
Tyson Pl
2800 LSVL 40218 5727 B2

U

Ulery Av
- LSVL 40218 5726 E4
- WBHL 40218 5726 E4
Ulrich Av
900 LSVL 40219 5834 E2
Ulrich Rd
4800 JFTN 40299 5728 A6
Underhill Ct
5100 LSVL 40207 5508 E4
Underwood Tr
7300 LSVL 40299 5840 D6
Undine Dr
5500 LSVL 40216 5722 C5
Unger Rd
100 HdnC 40121 6373 E5
Unicorn Regiment Rd
- HdnC 40121 6374 C1
Union Av
1200 LSVL 40213 5725 B3
Union St
100 NALB 47150 5505 A4
3700 LSVL 40213 5725 C2
United Blvd
11200 HTCK 40229 5945 E4
Universal Coach Dr
7000 LSVL 40258 5830 E6
University Av
500 LSVL 40206 5617 A1
University Dr
- FydC 47150 5396 C3
- NALB 47150 5396 B3
200 RDCF 40160 6483 C4
500 ELZT 42701 6811 E3
University Rd
3000 LSVL 40206 5508 A7
3000 LSVL 40206 5617 A1
University Woods Dr
10 NALB 47150 5396 C7
Unruh Ct
1900 NALB 47150 5396 C7
Unruh Dr
8000 GEOT 47122 5502 C3
Unseld Blvd
4400 LSVL 40218 5726 C6
4600 PLRH 40218 5726 C6
4700 LSVL 40213 5726 C6
Upland Rd
500 LSVL 40206 5617 A3
Upper Hunters Trc
1800 LSVL 40216 5723 A7
2100 LSVL 40216 5722 E7
6000 LSVL 40216 5831 D1
6600 LSVL 40258 5831 D2
Upper River Rd
2000 LSVL 40206 5507 D7
3700 LSVL 40207 5508 B6
4700 ClkC 47130 5400 A4
4700 UTCA 47130 5400 A5
UPS Dr
1600 LYDN 40223 5510 E7
1600 LYDN 40223 5619 E1
Upshur Pl
11400 FCSL 40241 5511 C2
Upsliner Rd
700 LSVL 40213 5834 B1
Upton Rd
- HdnC 40121 6265 D7
- HdnC 40121 6374 D1
Uranus Dr
7000 LSVL 40258 5831 C3
Ursuline Rd
- LSVL 40205 5616 C7
Urton Ln
100 MDTN 40223 5621 A6
100 MDTN 40243 5621 A6
12500 MDTN 40243 5620 E6
12500 MDTN 40299 5620 E6
US-31
- ClkC 47129 5397 E4
- ClkC 47129 5506 E7
- ClkC 47130 5397 E4
- ClkC 47130 5398 A2
- ClkC 47172 5288 E7
- ClkC 47172 5397 E7
- ClkC 47172 5398 A2
- CLKV 47129 5397 E4
- CLKV 47129 5506 D4
- CLKV 47130 5506 E6
- CLKV 47172 5397 E7
- CLKV 47172 5398 A2
- JFVL 47129 5397 E4
- JFVL 47130 5397 E4
- JFVL 47130 5506 E7
- SLRB 47172 5288 E5
- SLRB 47172 5397 E1
US-31 S 2nd St
100 LSVL 40202 5615 E2
US-31 George R Clark Mem Br
- CLKV 47129 5506 E7
- CLKV 47129 5615 E1
- JFVL 47130 5506 E7
- JFVL 47130 5615 E1
- LSVL 40202 5615 E1
US-31 N Indiana Av
- ClkC 47172 5288 E2
100 SLRB 47172 5288 E2
US-31 S Indiana Av
100 SLRB 47172 5288 D4
US-31 Pearl St
- CLKV 47130 5506 E6
- JFVL 47130 5506 E6
US-31E
- BltC 40047 5947 B7
- BltC 40047 6056 C4
- LSVL 40291 5947 A6
- MTWH 40047 6056 C4
US-31E S 1st St
200 LSVL 40202 5615 E2
US-31E Bardstown Rd
- BltC 40047 5947 A6
- LSVL 40291 5946 E1
1000 LSVL 40204 5616 C5
1400 LSVL 40205 5616 D6
1900 LSVL 40205 5617 B7
2700 SMRM 40205 5617 B7
2700 SMRV 40205 5617 B7
2800 SMRG 40205 5726 C1
2900 WLTN 40205 5726 C1
3500 WBHL 40218 5726 D3
10800 LSVL 40291 5947 A5
US-31E E Liberty St
500 LSVL 40202 5616 B4
US-31E W Market St
100 LSVL 40202 5615 E3
US-31 Frontage Lp E
- BltC 40047 6056 D5
US-31 N Indiana Av
10900 ClkC 47143 5288 E1
US-31E Bardstown Rd
2700 SMRG 40205 5617 C7
2800 LSVL 40205 5726 C1
3300 LSVL 40218 5726 D2
4100 LSVL 40218 5727 A4
4600 LSVL 40291 5727 D6
5200 LSVL 40291 5728 A7
5300 LSVL 40291 5837 C5
US-31E Baxter Av
100 LSVL 40206 5616 B3
200 LSVL 40204 5616 D5
US-31E Buechel Byp
- LSVL 40218 5726 E4
- WBHL 40218 5726 E4
4100 LSVL 40218 5727 D6
US-31E E Chestnut St
- LSVL 40204 5616 B3
US-31E E Liberty St
100 LSVL 40202 5615 E3
700 LSVL 40204 5616 A3
US-31E Main St
- BltC 40047 5947 B7
US-31E E Main St
100 LSVL 40202 5615 E2
400 LSVL 40202 5616 B3
700 LSVL 40206 5616 A2
US-31E W Main St
100 LSVL 40202 5615 E2
US-31EX Main St
- BltC 40047 5947 A7
- MTWH 40047 5947 A7
100 BltC 40047 6056 C4
100 MTWH 40047 6056 C3
US-31W
- ELZT 42701 6593 C7
- ELZT 42701 6702 D3
- ELZT 42701 6812 D6
- HdnC 40121 6373 E4
- HdnC 40121 6374 A5
- HdnC 40160 6374 A6
- HdnC 40177 6155 D7
- HdnC 40177 6156 D2
- HdnC 40177 6264 D7
- HdnC 42701 6593 B4
- HdnC 42701 6702 D3
- LSVL 40272 6156 D2
- MdeC 40108 6264 D7
- MdeC 40121 6264 D7
- MRGH 40155 6264 C4
- RDCF 40160 6374 A7
- RDCF 40160 6483 B1
- RDCF 40160 6593 B3
- RDCF 42701 6593 B3
- RDCF 42701 6702 C1
- WPT 40177 6155 D7
- WPT 40177 6156 D1
US-31W S 22nd St
100 LSVL 40212 5615 A2
400 LSVL 40211 5615 A3
800 LSVL 40210 5615 A4
1300 LSVL 40210 5614 E7
US-31W Bernheim Ln
- LSVL 40210 5614 E7
US-31W S Dixie Av
- ELZT 42701 6812 C3
US-31W W Dixie Av
- ELZT 42701 6702 E6
- ELZT 42701 6703 A7
600 ELZT 42701 6812 A1
US-31W S Dixie Blvd
2100 RDCF 40160 6484 A7
2200 RDCF 40160 6593 A1
US-31W Dixie Hwy
- HdnC 40177 6156 D2
- LSVL 40272 6156 E1
1900 LSVL 40210 5614 E7
2100 LSVL 40216 5614 E7
2300 LSVL 40210 5723 E1
2300 LSVL 40216 5723 E1
2300 SVLY 40216 5723 E1
5100 LSVL 40216 5832 A1
5300 LSVL 40258 5832 A2
6400 LSVL 40258 5831 C7
9100 LSVL 40272 5831 C7
9700 LSVL 40272 5940 B1
11700 LSVL 40272 5939 E5
13000 LSVL 40272 6048 C4
US-31W N Dixie Hwy
1000 ELZT 42701 6702 E5
US-31W S Dixie Hwy
- HdnC 40160 6483 E4
- RDCF 40160 6483 E5
- RDCF 40160 6484 A7
- RDCF 40160 6593 C7
- RDCF 42701 6593 A2
US-31W Dr WJ Hodge St
200 LSVL 40203 5615 A4
200 LSVL 40212 5615 A3
400 LSVL 40211 5615 A4
600 LSVL 40210 5615 A4
US-31W Dumesnil St
2100 LSVL 40210 5615 A5
US-31W BYP Elizabethtown Byp
- ELZT 42701 6702 E6
- ELZT 42701 6811 E2
- ELZT 42701 6812 A3
US-31W Louisville Rd
- ELZT 42701 6702 D3
US-31W W Main St
200 LSVL 40202 5615 E2
1000 LSVL 40203 5615 B2
2000 LSVL 40212 5615 B2
US-31W W Market St
200 LSVL 40202 5615 E2
1000 LSVL 40203 5615 C2
2000 LSVL 40212 5615 C2
US-31WX
- HdnC 40177 6156 A4
- WPT 40177 6156 A4
US-42
- GSHN 44026 5292 D3
- HSDS 40222 5509 C3
- HSDS 40241 5509 C3
- LSVL 40059 5400 D7
- LSVL 40059 5401 A1
- LSVL 40059 5509 D1
- LSVL 40222 5509 C5
- LSVL 40241 5400 D7
- LSVL 40241 5509 D1
- NHFD 40222 5509 C5
- OdmC 40059 5292 C5
- OdmC 40059 5401 A1
- OdmC 44026 5292 E3
- PROS 40059 5400 E2
- RVBF 40059 5401 B1
US-42 Brownsboro Rd
- LSVL 40222 5509 B6
- NHFD 40222 5509 A7
- WDYH 40207 5508 E7
1700 LSVL 40206 5616 D2
2700 LSVL 40206 5617 A2
3200 LSVL 40207 5617 A2
3600 BWNV 40207 5617 D1
3700 DRDH 40207 5617 D1
3700 INDH 40207 5617 A2
4200 INDH 40207 5508 E7
4200 INHC 40207 5508 E7
4200 LSVL 40207 5508 E7
4400 INHC 40207 5509 A7
4500 LSVL 40207 5509 A7
4700 WNDF 40207 5509 B6
4800 WDYH 40207 5509 B6
US-42 E Main St
1000 LSVL 40206 5616 B2
US-42 Mellwood Av
1400 LSVL 40206 5616 C2
US-42 Story Av
1000 LSVL 40206 5616 B2
US-60
- HdnC 40177 6155 D7
- HdnC 40177 6156 D2
- HdnC 40177 6264 D7
- LSVL - 5723 D5
- LSVL 40023 5623 B6
- LSVL 40245 5623 B6
- LSVL 40272 6156 D2
- MdeC 40108 6264 D7
- MdeC 40121 6264 C7
- MdeC 40175 6264 D7
- MdeC 40175 6373 A1
- MRGH 40155 6264 C4
- SbyC 40067 5623 B6
- SVLY - 5723 C5
- WPT 40177 6155 D7
- WPT 40177 6156 D1
US-60 TRK S 1st St
200 LSVL 40202 5615 E2
US-60 ALT S 3rd St
2500 LSVL 40208 5724 A3
US-60 ALT 7th St Rd
3700 LSVL 40215 5723 D3
3700 LSVL 40216 5723 D3
3700 SVLY 40216 5723 D3
US-60 TRK S 12th St
700 LSVL 40203 5615 C3
700 LSVL 40210 5615 C4
US-60 TRK S 13th St
100 LSVL 40203 5615 B2
US-60 ALT Bardstown Rd
1300 LSVL 40204 5616 D5
1400 LSVL 40205 5616 D6
US-60 TRK Baxter Av
100 LSVL 40206 5616 B3
200 LSVL 40204 5616 B3
US-60 ALT Berry Blvd
1300 LSVL 40215 5724 A3
1500 LSVL 40215 5723 C4
1800 SVLY 40216 5723 C4
US-60 BUS W Broadway
1200 LSVL 40203 5615 A3
1300 LSVL 40210 5615 A3
US-60 ALT Cherokee Pkwy
2000 LSVL 40204 5616 D6
2300 JfnC 40204 5616 E5
US-60 TRK E Chestnut St
- LSVL 40204 5616 B3
US-60 Dixie Hwy
- HdnC 40177 6156 D2
- LSVL 40272 6156 E1
4400 SVLY 40216 5723 A7
4700 LSVL 40216 5723 B6
5100 LSVL 40216 5832 A1
5300 LSVL 40258 5832 A2
6400 LSVL 40258 5831 C7
9100 LSVL 40272 5831 C7
9700 LSVL 40272 5940 B1
11700 LSVL 40272 5939 E7
13000 LSVL 40272 6048 C4
US-60 ALT Dixie Hwy
4000 LSVL 40216 5723 D4
4000 SVLY 40216 5723 C4
US-60 BUS Dixie Hwy
700 LSVL 40203 5615 A3
700 LSVL 40210 5615 A3
1500 LSVL 40210 5614 E6
2100 LSVL 40216 5614 E7
2300 LSVL 40210 5723 E1
2300 LSVL 40216 5723 E1
2300 SVLY 40216 5723 E1
US-60 ALT Eastern Pkwy
300 LSVL 40208 5724 D1
400 LSVL 40217 5724 E1
700 LSVL 40217 5725 A1
900 LSVL 40217 5616 A7
1300 LSVL 40204 5616 C6
1300 LSVL 40213 5616 C6
1500 LSVL 40205 5616 C6
US-60 TRK Frankfort Av
1600 LSVL 40206 5616 D2
2500 LSVL 40206 5617 E3
3300 LSVL 40207 5617 B4
3400 STMW 40207 5617 D3
US-60 ALT Grinstead Dr
2500 JfnC 40204 5616 E4
2500 JfnC 40206 5616 E4
2500 LSVL 40204 5616 E4
2500 LSVL 40206 5616 E4
US-60 Henry Watterson Expwy
- LSVL - 5617 E7
- LSVL - 5618 A7
- LSVL - 5723 E5
- LSVL - 5724 C4
- LSVL - 5725 D4
- LSVL - 5726 A3
- STMW - 5618 A7
- WSNP - 5726 A3
US-60 TRK W Hill St
1200 LSVL 40210 5615 B6
US-60 ALT Lexington Rd
- JfnC 40206 5617 A4
- LSVL 40204 5617 A4
2400 JfnC 40206 5616 E4
2400 LSVL 40206 5616 E4
2500 LSVL 40206 5617 A4
3300 LSVL 40207 5617 D3
US-60 TRK E Liberty St
100 LSVL 40202 5615 E3
500 LSVL 40202 5616 A3
700 LSVL 40204 5616 A3
US-60 TRK E Main St
100 LSVL 40202 5615 E2
400 LSVL 40202 5616 A2
700 LSVL 40206 5616 A2
US-60 TRK W Main St
100 LSVL 40202 5615 E2
1000 LSVL 40203 5615 C2
US-60 TRK W Market St
100 LSVL 40202 5615 E2
1000 LSVL 40203 5615 C2
US-60 TRK Mellwood Av
1400 LSVL 40206 5616 C2
US-60 Shelbyville Rd
7500 STMW 40222 5618 E3
7600 LSVL 40222 5618 E3
7600 NRWD 40222 5618 E3
7800 LYDN 40222 5618 E3
7900 HTBN 40222 5619 A3
7900 LSVL 40222 5619 A3
7900 LYDN 40222 5619 A3
8400 BLMD 40222 5619 B3
8800 BLMD 40223 5619 B4
8900 LYDN 40223 5619 C4
9300 JFTN 40223 5619 D4
9400 WDWD 40223 5619 D4
9800 LSVL 40223 5619 D4
10000 BRMR 40223 5619 E4
10300 SCMR 40223 5619 E4
10400 BRMR 40223 5620 A4
10400 DGSH 40243 5620 A4
10400 SCMR 40223 5620 A4
10600 LSVL 40243 5620 A4
10700 LSVL 40223 5620 A4
11300 MDTN 40243 5620 A4
12700 MDTN 40223 5620 E4
12800 MDTN 40223 5621 A4
12800 MDTN 40243 5621 A4
13500 LSVL 40245 5621 B4
13500 MDTN 40245 5621 B4
15700 LSVL 40245 5622 A5
16800 LSVL 40023 5622 E5
18200 LSVL 40023 5623 E7
18200 LSVL 40245 5623 E7
18200 SbyC 40067 5623 E7
US-60 TRK Shelbyville Rd
- LSVL 40222 5618 D3
- NRWD 40222 5618 E3
- STMW 40222 5618 D3
3800 LSVL 40207 5617 E3
3800 STMW 40207 5617 E3
3900 LSVL 40207 5618 A3
3900 STMW 40207 5618 A3
4100 RHLN 40207 5618 A3
4200 FRMD 40207 5618 B3
4400 BWDV 40207 5618 B3
US-60 TRK Story Av
1000 LSVL 40206 5616 C2
US-60 ALT Taylor Blvd
2700 LSVL 40208 5724 C1
3000 LSVL 40215 5724 B2
US-60 ALT Winkler Av
300 LSVL 40208 5724 C1
US-62 Bardstown Rd
- ELZT 42701 6703 E7
US-62 Leitchfield Rd
1600 ELZT 42701 6812 A4
1700 ELZT 42701 6811 A6
2100 HdnC 42701 6811 A6
US-62 N Mulberry St
100 ELZT 42701 6812 D1
1800 ELZT 42701 6703 E7
US-150
- BltC 40047 5947 B7
- BltC 40047 6056 C4
- FydC - 5503 E2
- FydC - 5504 E4
- FydC 47119 5393 E3
- FydC 47119 5394 A4
- FydC 47119 5503 D1
- FydC 47122 5503 D2
- FydC 47124 5283 A6
- FydC 47124 5393 B1
- GNVL 47124 5283 B6
- GNVL 47124 5393 A1
- LSVL - 5505 D6
- LSVL - 5506 A7
- LSVL 40203 5615 A1
- LSVL 40212 5615 A1
- LSVL 40291 5947 A6
- MTWH 40047 6056 C4
- NALB - 5504 D3
- NALB - 5505 A5
US-150 N 21st St
100 LSVL 40203 5615 A2
100 LSVL 40212 5615 A2
US-150 N 22nd St
- LSVL 40203 5506 A7
- LSVL 40212 5506 A7
100 LSVL 40212 5615 A1
400 LSVL 40203 5615 A1
US-150 S 22nd St
100 LSVL 40212 5615 A2
400 LSVL 40211 5615 A2
US-150 Bardstown Rd
- BltC 40047 5947 A6
- LSVL 40291 5946 E1
1000 LSVL 40204 5616 C5
1400 LSVL 40205 5616 D6
1900 LSVL 40205 5617 B7
2700 SMRG 40205 5617 C7
2700 SMRM 40205 5617 B7
2700 SMRV 40205 5617 B7
2800 LSVL 40205 5726 C1
2800 SMRG 40205 5726 C1
2900 WLTN 40205 5726 C1
3200 LSVL 40218 5726 D2
3500 WBHL 40218 5726 D3
4100 LSVL 40218 5727 A4
4600 LSVL 40291 5727 D6
5200 LSVL 40291 5728 A7
5300 LSVL 40291 5837 C5
10800 LSVL 40291 5947 A5
US-150 Baxter Av
700 LSVL 40204 5616 D5
US-150 E Broadway
100 LSVL 40202 5615 E4
100 LSVL 40203 5615 E4
500 LSVL 40202 5616 B4
500 LSVL 40203 5616 B4
700 LSVL 40204 5616 A4
US-150 W Broadway
100 LSVL 40202 5615 D4
100 LSVL 40203 5615 C3
1300 LSVL 40210 5615 C3
2000 LSVL 40211 5615 C3
US-150 Buechel Byp
- LSVL 40218 5726 E4
- WBHL 40218 5726 E4
4100 LSVL 40218 5727 B5
US-150 Dr WJ Hodge St
100 LSVL 40203 5615 A3
100 LSVL 40212 5615 A3
400 LSVL 40211 5615 A2
600 LSVL 40210 5615 A3
US-150 Main St
- BltC 40047 5947 B7
US-150 Mary Anderson Mem Hwy
- FydC 47119 5503 D2
- FydC 47122 5503 D2
US-150 Sherman Minton Br
- LSVL - 5505 E6
- NALB - 5505 B6
Usar School Rd
- HdnC 40121 6374 C1
Utah Av
2800 LSVL 40208 5724 B2
3200 LSVL 40215 5724 A2
Utah Ct
100 ELZT 42701 6812 A2
E Utah St
10 HdnC 40121 6374 E2
W Utah St
- HdnC 40121 6374 D3
Ute St
- HdnC 40121 6374 E2
Utica Rd
6300 LSVL 40214 5832 D1
E Utica St
100 SLRB 47172 5288 E4
800 ClkC 47172 5288 E4
800 ClkC 47172 5289 A5
800 SLRB 47172 5289 A5
W Utica St
100 SLRB 47172 5288 D3
Utica Charlestown Rd
400 UTCA 47130 5400 A4
600 ClkC 47130 5399 E4
600 UTCA 47130 5399 E4
Utica Pike
300 JFVL 47130 5507 C6
2100 JFVL 47130 5508 C2
4700 JFVL 47130 5399 D7
5100 ClkC 47130 5399 D7
5600 UTCA 47130 5399 D7
Utica Sellersburg Rd
600 ClkC 47130 5399 A3
600 UTCA 47130 5399 E6
1400 JFVL 47130 5399 A3
3700 ClkC 47130 5398 E3
4100 ClkC 47172 5398 D2
6100 ClkC 47172 5289 A5
6100 SLRB 47172 5289 A5
Utopia Dr
- RDCF 40160 6483 A1
Utz Rd
9100 FydC 47122 5392 E7

V

Vagabond Ln
4700 LSVL 40219 5835 C5
Valdosta Av
3600 LSVL 40218 5727 D4
Vale Cir
3500 LSVL 40241 5509 E3
Vale Ct
1800 NALB 47150 5505 C1
Vale Dr
700 CLKV 47129 5506 D3
Vale Rd
100 MDTN 40223 5620 E4
Vale Hill Dr
3600 FydC 47119 5394 B7
Valeridge Ct
8700 LYDN 40242 5619 B1
Vale Wood Ct
3200 JFTN 40220 5728 A3
Valhalla Ct
2800 LDNP 40242 5510 B5
Valhalla Dr
- RDCF 40160 6483 B1
Valhalla View Dr
100 LSVL 40245 5621 D5
Valiant Dr
5100 LSVL 40216 5723 A7
5100 LSVL 40216 5832 A1
Valla Rd
100 LSVL 40219 5726 A7
4700 LSVL 40213 5726 B7
4700 PLRH 40213 5726 B7
Valletta Ln
- SGDN 40205 5617 C6
2300 LSVL 40205 5617 B6
Valletta Rd
2400 LSVL 40205 5617 C6
2400 SGDN 40205 5617 C6
2600 KGLY 40205 5617 C7
Valley Dr
100 MTWH 40047 6056 B2
400 CHAN 47111 5181 E4
1200 ANPK 40213 5725 C2
1200 LSVL 40213 5725 C2
2800 JFTN 40299 5728 E3
12000 OdmC 44026 5292 C3
12200 GSHN 44026 5292 C3
Valley Ln
100 BltC 40165 6162 D5
Valley Rd
10 LSVL 40204 5616 C6
10 LSVL 40213 5616 C6
100 HLVW 40229 5944 B6
600 ELZT 42701 6812 A1
Valley Brook Rd
1500 GYDL 40222 5510 A7
1500 GYDL 40222 5619 C3
1500 LYDN 40222 5619 A1
Valley College Dr
- LSVL 40272 5940 D2
500 LSVL 40272 5831 D7
Valley Creek Ln
10 ELZT 42701 6812 E4
10 HdnC 42701 6812 E4
Valley Creek Rd
200 ELZT 42701 6812 D6
800 HdnC 42701 6812 E5
Valley Creek Rd SR-567
800 ELZT 42701 6812 E5
800 HdnC 42701 6812 E5
Valley Dale
4200 FydC 47150 5396 A4
Valleydale Dr
300 FydC 47150 5396 A4
300 NALB 47150 5396 A4
Valley Fair Wy
9800 LSVL 40272 5830 D7
9800 LSVL 40272 5939 D1
Valley Forge Wy
1700 LSVL 40215 5723 E3
Valley Meadow Wy
12000 LSVL 40272 5940 C2
Valley Park Ct
12400 LSVL 40299 5729 C7
12400 LSVL 40299 5838 C1
Valley Park Dr
5400 LSVL 40299 5729 C7
5500 LSVL 40299 5838 C1
Valley Pine Dr
12500 LSVL 40299 5729 C7
Valleyside Ct
3100 LSVL 40214 5832 C2
Valley Spring Ct
7800 LSVL 40220 5618 E7
Valley Station Rd
3900 LSVL 40272 5940 C2
Valley Station Rd SR-907
4600 LSVL 40272 5940 C2
Valley Terrace Dr
4200 FydC 47150 5396 A4
Valley View Ct
10 NALB 47150 5504 E3
10 NALB 47150 5505 A2
Valley View Dr
- ELZT 42701 6702 E7
100 VNGV 40160 6483 B7
100 VNGV 40160 6592 B1
100 VNGV 40175 6483 A7
300 VNGV 40175 6482 E6
4000 SVLY 40216 5723 C4
E Valley View Dr
300 BltC 40047 6056 A7
6200 GNVL 47124 5284 B7
N Valley View Dr
8500 GNVL 47124 5284 B7
S Valleyview Dr
100 BltC 40165 6162 D4
Valley View Rd
1000 NALB 47150 5504 E3
11400 ANCH 40223 5511 C7
Valley View Ter
1300 LSVL 40229 5944 C1
Valley View Trc
700 NALB 47150 5504 E4
N Valley View Trc
800 NALB 47150 5504 E4
Valley Vista Rd
2200 LSVL 40205 5616 E7
2300 LSVL 40205 5725 E1
2400 LSVL 40205 5726 A1
Van Ct
6200 LSVL 40291 5836 E2
Vance Av
1700 NALB 47150 5505 B2
Vanderbilt Dr
600 ELZT 42701 6811 D2
Vandre Av
6500 LSVL 40219 5836 B5
6500 LSVL 40228 5836 B5
Vaneto Dr
4400 LSVL 40216 5722 D4
Vanguard Dr
3500 LSVL 40229 5943 E1
3500 LSVL 40229 5944 A1
Vanherr Dr
12000 LSVL 40299 5729 B4
Van Hoose Rd
4700 LSVL 40216 5722 E6
4700 SVLY 40216 5722 E6
Vannah Av
700 LSVL 40223 5619 E2
Vantage Pl
3900 JFTN 40299 5728 E5
Vantage Rd
10300 JFTN 40299 5728 E5
Vantage Pointe Cir
3700 JFTN 40299 5728 C5
Vantage Pointe Dr
3600 JFTN 40299 5728 C5
Vantage View Ct
11000 JFTN 40299 5728 E5
Van Winkle Dr
3300 LSVL 40216 5722 E2
3300 LSVL 40216 5723 A3
Varble Av
1500 JFVL 47130 5507 C5
4500 LSVL 40211 5614 A3
Vasa Wy
500 JFVL 47130 5507 D5
Vassar Av
5200 LSVL 40258 5831 D3
Vassar Ct
10 ELZT 42701 6811 D2
Vaughn Ln
100 ELZT 42701 6812 C4
Vaughn Mill Rd
7200 SPML 40228 5836 C4
7600 LSVL 40228 5836 C6
Vaxter St
1400 CLKV 47129 5397 D7
1400 CLKV 47129 5506 D1
Veech Rd
10 SpnC 40023 5949 E1
Veechdale Rd
- SbyC 40067 5732 E3
Veenia Av
2500 LSVL 40205 5617 B7
Vega Al
- ELZT 42701 6812 C2
Vega Ln
9900 LSVL 40272 5941 A1
Veirs Ln
- MdeC 40175 6482 A4
Velden Dr
2900 JFTN 40220 5728 B3
Velle Vista Dr
5300 LSVL 40272 5831 B7
5300 LSVL 40272 5940 B1
Velva Dr
100 HLVW 40229 5943 E5
100 HLVW 40229 5944 A5

INDEX 50
Ven Ct
Louisville Metro Street Index
Watson Sellersburg Rd

STREET Block City ZIP Map# Grid

Ven Ct
100 HLVW 40229 5944 B7
Venado Dr
10300 LSVL 40291 5837 E3
Venango Dr
6300 LSVL 40258 5831 B3
Venetian Ct
1900 LSVL 40214 5832 E2
Venetian Wy
100 NALB 47150 5396 A7
7000 LSVL 40214 5832 E3
Venhoff Av
4500 SVLY 40216 5723 C6
Venkata Wy
- LSVL 40059 5401 C7
Ventura Dr
4900 LSVL 40272 5940 C1
Venus Dr
5200 LSVL 40258 5831 D2
Vera Av
4500 LSVL 40213 5725 C7
Veranda Wy
11700 LSVL 40299 5729 C6
Verbena Av
4500 LSVL 40213 5834 C1
Verity Wy
1000 GSHN 44026 5292 C3
1000 OdmC 44026 5292 C4
Vermissa Ct
8200 LYDN 40222 5619 A2
Vermont Av
3100 LSVL 40211 5614 C2
Vermont Ct
500 ELZT 42701 6811 E2
Vermont St
500 ClkC 47172 5288 E2
Verna Rd
3200 SVLY 40216 5723 B2
Verne Ct
3100 LSVL 40205 5726 A2
Vernetta Wy
9600 LSVL 40291 5946 C5
Vernon Av
100 LSVL 40206 5616 D2
Vernon Ct
2100 LSVL 40206 5616 E2
Verona Wy
7200 LSVL 40218 5727 D3
Veronica Dr
2500 LSVL 40216 5722 E5
2500 LSVL 40216 5723 A5
Veronica Pl
700 JFVL 47130 5507 A6
Versailles Ln
3300 LSVL 40219 5834 E3
3400 LSVL 40219 5835 A3
Vertrees Ct
100 ELZT 42701 6812 C3
Vesper Ln
5400 LSVL 40272 5940 B2
Veterans Pkwy
- CLKV 47129 5397 C7
- JFVL 47129 5397 E6
- JFVL 47130 5397 E6
- JFVL 47130 5398 A6
Veterans Wy
- ELZT 42701 6702 C4
Veterans Memorial Pkwy
- CTWD 40014 5404 A6
- OdmC 40014 5404 A7
Veterans Mem Pkwy SR-329 BYP
- CTWD 40014 5404 A6
- OdmC 40014 5404 A7
Vetter Av
3300 LSVL 40215 5724 A3
Vevey Rd
9200 LSVL 40291 5728 C7
Vevia Ct
12200 LSVL 40272 5940 B6
Vevia Pl
5500 LSVL 40272 5940 B5
VFW Blvd
700 JFVL 47130 5506 E6
Viburnum Wy
1100 MDTN 40243 5620 C7
Vicki Ln
8400 LSVL 40258 5831 C6
Vickie Wy
100 BltC 40165 6053 B4
Vicky Ct
10 HdnC 42701 6593 C5
Victor Dr
2000 NALB 47150 5505 E1
Victor Pl
2700 LSVL 40206 5617 A2
Victoria Ct
700 NALB 47150 5396 B6
Victoria Dr
100 BltC 40165 6160 D6
200 ELZT 42701 6703 C7
2700 ClkC 47172 5288 A7
2700 CLKV 47172 5288 A7
2900 FydC 47172 5287 E7
7200 LSVL 40228 5836 B4
Victoria Pl
700 INHC 40207 5509 A7
700 WDYH 40207 5509 A7
Victoria Wy
6800 LSVL 40228 5836 B3
7000 LSVL 40219 5836 B3
Victorson St
10 HdnC 40162 6702 B1
Victory Ct
1600 OdmC 40059 5291 E2
2700 CLKV 47129 5506 B2
Victory Ln
- OdmC 40059 5291 E1
Victory Ridge Ct
400 LSVL 40245 5621 B5
Victory Ridge Dr
14100 LSVL 40245 5621 B5
14100 MDTN 40245 5621 B5

Vienna Rd
10 CHAN 47111 5181 D1
10 ClkC 47111 5181 C1
Viers Ct
10 MdeC 40175 6482 A3
Viers Ln
10 MdeC 40175 6482 A3
Vieux Carre Dr
- JFTN 40223 5619 D4
100 WDWD 40223 5619 D4
N View Dr
100 BltC 40165 6052 E7
View Pt
- NALB 47150 5504 D1
Viewcrest Dr
1100 HYVA 40118 5942 E3
1100 LSVL 40118 5942 E3
1100 LSVL 40118 5943 A3
Viewpointe Dr
3500 JFTN 40299 5728 E4
Viking Ct
1900 JFVL 47130 5507 D4
Viking Dr
1900 JFVL 47130 5507 D4
Viking Pl
400 JFVL 47130 5507 D5
Viking Wy
1900 JFVL 47130 5507 D5
Villa Ct
1400 CHAN 47111 5181 D2
1900 OdmC 40031 5295 C6
Villa Dr
300 SLRB 47172 5288 E5
10300 LSVL 40272 5940 B2
Villa Pl
5100 OdmC 40031 5295 C6
Villa Fair Ct
4800 JFTN 40291 5728 C6
Villa Fair Rd
4900 JFTN 40291 5728 C6
4900 LSVL 40291 5728 C7
Village Cir
400 NALB 47150 5395 E7
400 NALB 47150 5504 E1
Village Dr
200 BltC 40165 6161 B2
200 ELZT 42701 6812 B1
200 SHDV 40165 6161 B2
500 ELZT 42701 6703 B7
2300 LSVL 40205 5617 A6
Village Dr E
10 NALB 47150 5505 B2
Village Dr N
10 NALB 47150 5505 A2
Village Dr W
10 NALB 47150 5505 A2
Village Ln
100 MTWH 40047 6056 B2
300 BltC 40047 6056 B1
Village Vly
- SHDV 40165 6162 B2
Village Gate Ct
8000 LSVL 40291 5836 E4
Village Gate Trc
6900 LSVL 40291 5836 E4
Village Green Blvd
- LSVL 40245 5512 D4
- OdmC 40056 5512 D4
1900 JFVL 47130 5507 E2
Village Green Ct
9200 OdmC 40056 5512 D4
Village Green Dr
3800 LSVL 40299 5727 E4
3800 LSVL 40299 5728 A4
Village Lake Dr
400 LSVL 40245 5621 B3
Village Pine Dr
200 NALB 47150 5504 E1
Village Point Dr
7900 LSVL 40291 5836 E2
Village West Dr
600 LSVL 40203 5615 C3
Villanova Ct
8700 JFTN 40220 5728 A3
Villanova Dr
3200 JFTN 40220 5728 A3
Villa Park Dr
1300 LSVL 40219 5835 D6
Villa Ray Dr
10 HdnC 40160 6592 B2
10 HdnC 40175 6592 B2
Villa Rd Dr NE
3000 HsnC 47136 5611 A3
Villiage Green Blvd
6800 OdmC 40056 5512 D4
6900 LSVL 40245 5512 D4
Vim Dr
1200 LSVL 40213 5725 D7
Vincennes St
10 NALB 47150 5505 C3
Vincennes St SR-111
10 NALB 47150 5505 C3
Vincennes Tr
6000 FydC 47124 5393 A1
6000 GNVL 47124 5393 A1
Vincent Wy
7200 LSVL 40214 5832 B3
Vine Av
7700 LSVL 40245 5512 A2
7700 OdmC 40014 5512 A2
7700 OdmC 40245 5512 A2
Vine St
100 SHDV 40165 6161 D4
100 VNGV 40175 6591 D1
700 LSVL 40204 5616 B5
1300 NALB 47150 5505 A3
7700 OdmC 40014 5512 A2
E Vine St
100 RDCF 40160 6483 D5
E Vine St SR-144
100 RDCF 40160 6483 D5
W Vine St
100 RDCF 40160 6483 C5
1500 HdnC 40160 6483 B6

W Vine St
1600 VNGV 40160 6483 B6
1900 VNGV 40175 6483 A6
W Vine St SR-144
100 RDCF 40160 6483 C5
1500 HdnC 40160 6483 B6
1600 VNGV 40160 6483 B6
1900 VNGV 40175 6483 A6
Vinecliff Pl
4700 LSVL 40299 5728 E6
Vine Crest Av
7800 LYDN 40222 5618 E2
8000 LYDN 40222 5619 B2
Vinedale Av
2400 LSVL 40220 5618 D5
Vine Grove Rd
- HdnC 40121 6373 C7
- MdeC 40175 6373 C7
- RDCF 40160 6483 A2
- RDCF 40175 6483 A2
800 HdnC 40121 6374 A4
Vine Grove Connector Rd
- HdnC 40160 6592 E2
- RDCF 40160 6592 E2
- RDCF 40160 6593 A3
- RDCF 42701 6593 A3
- VNGV 40160 6483 A6
- VNGV 40160 6592 C1
- VNGV 40175 6483 A6
Vine Grove Connector Rd SR-313
- HdnC 40160 6592 E2
- RDCF 40160 6592 E2
- RDCF 40160 6593 A3
- RDCF 42701 6593 A3
- VNGV 40160 6483 A6
- VNGV 40160 6592 C1
- VNGV 40175 6483 A6
Vineleaf Dr
500 LYDN 40222 5618 E2
Vinewood Rd
1100 LSVL 40219 5834 E1
Vineyard Dr
3300 WSNP 40213 5725 E4
Vining Pl
10500 LSVL 40241 5511 A2
Vinita Wy
4600 LSVL 40272 5831 D6
Vintage Creek Ct
4700 LSVL 40299 5728 D6
Vintage Creek Dr
10500 JFTN 40299 5728 D6
10500 LSVL 40299 5728 D6
Viola Dr
4500 JFVL 47130 5398 B5
Virgil Ct
100 RDCF 40160 6593 A2
7100 ClkC 47172 5288 B6
7100 CLKV 47172 5288 B6
Virgil Dr
100 RDCF 40160 6593 A2
3600 ClkC 47130 5398 C4
Virgin Al
800 JFVL 47130 5507 B6
Virginia
800 JFVL 47130 5507 C5
Virginia Av
400 NALB 47150 5505 E3
400 NRWD 40222 5618 E3
400 STMW 40222 5618 D2
700 JFVL 47130 5508 A3
1000 ELZT 42701 6812 D1
2600 LSVL 40210 5614 E5
4100 LSVL 40211 5614 A4
7400 LSVL 40258 5831 D4
S Virginia Av
900 CLKV 47129 5506 D6
Virginia Ct
200 NALB 47150 5505 A3
1500 LGNG 40031 5297 A2
Virginia Dr
10 JFVL 47130 5508 A4
150 LGNG 40031 5297 A1
Virginia Hts
9100 ClkC 47172 5288 A5
Virginia Rd
8200 LSVL 40258 5831 C5
Virginia St
200 ClkC 47172 5288 E2
N Virginia St
- HdnC 40121 6374 E2
S Virginia St
- HdnC 40121 6374 E2
Vision Pl
8600 HTCK 40229 5945 E4
Vissing Dr
- JFVL 47130 5508 B2
Vista Dr
- ELZT 42701 6811 E3
500 ELZT 42701 6812 C5
Vista Greens Ct
3400 LSVL 40241 5511 C5
Vista Greens Dr
11100 LSVL 40241 5511 B5
Vista Hills Blvd
9800 LSVL 40291 5946 E3
Vista John Dr
5200 LSVL 40214 5832 D2
Vivian Ct
10 ELZT 42701 6703 C7
Vivian Ln
1500 LSVL 40205 5618 A6
Vivian Wy
100 BltC 40047 6055 B3
Vixen Ct
1400 FydC 47150 5396 E1
Voelker Dr NE
1000 HsnC 47112 5610 B7
Vogt Av
3400 LSVL 40211 5723 A2
3400 LSVL 40216 5723 A2
Vogue Av
- LSVL 40218 5727 B2
3000 LSVL 40220 5727 B2

Volar Ln
7200 LSVL 40258 5831 C3
Volney Ct
5000 LSVL 40291 5728 A7
Volpaire Dr
10500 LSVL 40223 5619 E2
Von Allman Rd
7200 FydC 47119 5287 A5
Vonda Ct
100 RDCF 40160 6592 E2
Vondine Dr
9000 SPVW 40219 5834 C7
Vonoa Dr
2500 RDCF 40160 6592 E1
Von Spiegel St
3700 LSVL 40211 5614 B6
Vorster Av
1800 LSVL 40210 5614 E6
Voyles Rd
7100 FydC 47124 5283 C5
7100 GNVL 47124 5283 C6
8000 FydC 47165 5283 C5
9500 ClkC 47106 5283 C5

W

Wabash Av
3300 FydC 47150 5396 D3
Wabash Ct
4100 OdmC 40031 5404 E2
Wabash Pl
4900 LSVL 40214 5724 D6
Wabash St
- HdnC 40121 6265 D7
- HdnC 40121 6374 D1
Wabasso St
300 LSVL 40209 5724 D6
300 LSVL 40214 5724 D6
Waco Ct
2400 LSVL 40216 5723 A5
Waddell Ln
100 BltC 40165 6054 A1
Wadell Wy
- JFTN 40299 5729 C1
Wadsworth Av
2200 LSVL 40205 5726 C1
2200 WLTN 40205 5726 C1
Wagner Av
1000 LSVL 40217 5616 B7
Wagner Dr
3500 FydC 47119 5395 A1
Wagon Rd
- BltC 40165 6162 E7
Wagon Tr
10 LSVL 40216 5722 E2
10 LSVL 40216 5723 A2
Wagon Wheel Tr
400 RDCF 40160 6593 A1
Wagram Wy
6000 GNVH 40222 5509 B4
Wahl St Blvd
4100 LSVL 40218 5727 B5
Wahoo Dr
2800 NALB 47150 5505 B1
Waino Cir
1100 OdmC 40014 5405 E1
Waino Ct
1100 OdmC 40014 5405 E1
Waino Dr
3700 OdmC 40014 5405 E1
Wainwright Av
500 LSVL 40208 5724 E1
500 LSVL 40217 5724 E1
Wainwright Dr
200 NALB 47150 5505 C2
Wainwright Pl
1100 ELZT 42701 6702 E7
Waitfield Pl
600 LSVL 40206 5617 D4
Wake Ct
10500 LSVL 40272 5940 D2
Wakefield Pl
14200 LSVL 40245 5621 C4
Wakefield Trc
200 LSVL 40245 5621 C4
Wakulla Ct
9200 JFTN 40299 5728 C4
Walbridge Ct
11000 LSVL 40299 5838 A1
Walbrook Dr
2500 LSVL 40222 5509 C5
2500 NHFD 40222 5509 C5
Walden Dr
4600 LSVL 40229 5944 C3
Waldner Ct
2000 OdmC 40014 5405 C5
Waldoah Beach Rd
2900 LSVL 40207 5508 A6
Waldwick Ct
7500 LSVL 40258 5831 A3
Wales Ct
9500 LSVL 40272 5941 C1
Wales Run Rd
- BltC 40047 6055 D3
- MTWH 40047 6055 D3
Wales Run Rd SR-2706
- BltC 40047 6055 D3
- MTWH 40047 6055 D3
E Walford Dr
1200 JFVL 47130 5507 E2
1200 JFVL 47130 5508 A2
N Walford Dr
2900 JFVL 47130 5507 E2
S Walford Dr
2900 JFVL 47130 5508 A3
W Walford Dr
1100 JFVL 47130 5507 E2
Walhampton Ct
9200 RLGH 40242 5510 C6
Walhampton Dr
9300 RLGH 40242 5510 D6
Walker Av
- CLKV 47129 5506 C2

Walker Ct
100 ELZT 42701 6812 B3
Walker Rd
100 MdeC 40108 6264 C3
100 MRGH 40155 6264 C3
8200 LSVL 40258 5831 C5
Wall St
- ELZT 42701 6812 B2
100 JFVL 47130 5507 A7
1000 JFVL 47130 5506 E6
Wallace Av
- STMW 40207 5618 A4
300 LSVL 40207 5617 E3
300 STMW 40207 5617 E3
2400 LSVL 40205 5617 B6
Wallace Ct
100 ELZT 42701 6812 B3
Wallace Ln
6500 LSVL 40258 5831 A4
Waller Ln
6800 LSVL 40258 5831 B3
Wallie Ann Ct
2100 LSVL 40210 5614 E7
2100 LSVL 40210 5615 A7
2100 LSVL 40210 5723 E1
2200 SVLY 40210 5723 E1
2200 SVLY 40216 5723 E1
Wallingford Ct
2900 LSVL 40218 5727 C3
Wallingford Ln
4100 LSVL 40218 5727 C4
4100 LSVL 40220 5727 C3
Walls Hllw N
100 BltC 40165 6051 D7
Walls Hollow Rd
100 BltC 40165 6051 D7
500 BltC 40165 6160 D1
Walmart Dr
10 ELZT 42701 6702 E4
Walnut Al
- LSVL 40245 5511 E2
E Walnut Al
- LGNG 40031 5296 E3
- LGNG 40031 5297 A2
W Walnut Al
- LGNG 40031 5296 E3
Walnut Av
100 BltC 40047 6056 A4
200 BltC 40047 6055 E4
Walnut Dr
- BltC 40109 5943 E5
100 BltC 40047 6056 D5
Walnut Ln
1400 ANCH 40223 5620 B1
Walnut Pl
2100 LSVL 40205 5617 A6
Walnut Rd
2100 OdmC 40031 5297 C5
Walnut St
- HdnC 40121 6265 B7
- MdeC 40108 6264 C4
- MRGH 40155 6264 C4
- UTCA 47130 5400 A5
100 JFVL 47130 5507 A6
100 VNGV 40175 6591 E1
200 CHAN 47111 5181 E5
400 ELZT 42701 6812 C2
1400 NALB 47150 5505 A3
9000 GEOT 47122 5501 E3
N Walnut St
100 LGNG 40031 5296 E2
100 SHDV 40165 6161 C4
S Walnut St
100 LGNG 40031 5296 E3
200 LGNG 40031 5297 A3
Walnut Wy
10 ELZT 42701 6702 D1
10 HdnC 42701 6702 D1
100 BltC 40047 6055 A6
1600 RDCF 40160 6483 A4
5500 LSVL 40229 5944 E4
Walnut Creek Ct
7000 LSVL 40229 5945 A4
Walnut Creek Rd
10 HdnC 42701 6702 A6
Walnut Grove Av
4700 LSVL 40216 5723 B7
4700 SVLY 40216 5723 B7
Walnut Grove Rd
100 CLKV 47129 5396 E6
Walnut Hill Rd
500 ELZT 42701 6812 A1
Walnut Hills Dr
4700 LSVL 40299 5727 E6
Walnut Ridge Tr
6200 LSVL 40059 5400 D3
6200 PROS 40059 5400 D3
Walnut Trace Cir
100 ELZT 42701 6812 A2
Walnut View Wy
11600 JFTN 40299 5729 A5
11600 LSVL 40299 5729 A5
Walnutwood Ct
- LGNG 40031 5297 A5
Walnutwood Wy
9500 JFTN 40299 5728 C4
Walpole Av
1800 JFVL 47130 5507 D4
Walpole Ct
- JFVL 47130 5507 D4
Walrich Dr
2200 LSVL 40211 5614 B7
Walser Rd
700 WLNP 40207 5618 C1
800 WDYH 40207 5618 C1
Walsh Dr
4500 LSVL 40272 5831 D7
Walsh St
4300 HdnC 40121 6374 A2
Walter Av
1300 LSVL 40215 5724 A6
1500 LSVL 40215 5723 E6
9000 LSVL 40219 5835 B4
9000 LSVL 40229 5835 B4

Walter Av
9000 LSVL 40229 5944 A1
Walter Rd
100 BltC 40047 6056 E3
Walter Boone Rd
- HdnC 40162 6592 D7
- HdnC 40162 6702 A3
- HdnC 42701 6702 B2
- RDCF 42701 6702 C2
Walter Dale Ter
2200 LSVL 40205 5617 A7
Walters Rd NE
3400 HsnC 47136 5610 E3
3400 HsnC 47136 5611 A3
Walterwood Ct
1500 LGNG 40031 5296 D1
1500 LGNG 40031 5297 A1
Waltlee Ct
5400 LSVL 40291 5728 C7
Waltlee Rd
8700 LSVL 40291 5728 B7
Walton Wy
- OdmC 40014 5403 D6
Walts Rd
1000 FydC 47122 5502 A5
1200 GEOT 47122 5502 A5
Walts Rd NE
10 FydC 47122 5502 A6
E Wampum Av
100 LSVL 40214 5724 D5
300 LSVL 40209 5724 D5
W Wampum Av
100 LSVL 40214 5724 C5
Wampum Rd
10 INDH 40207 5508 D7
Wanda Wy
8000 LSVL 40219 5836 A5
Wanlou Dr
9000 LSVL 40272 5831 D7
Wansee Dr
1200 LSVL 40219 5834 E2
1200 LSVL 40219 5835 A2
Warbler Wy
4900 LSVL 40213 5725 D6
4900 LYNV 40213 5725 D6
Ward Av
10600 LSVL 40223 5620 A2
10800 ANCH 40223 5620 A2
Wardshire Pl
600 LSVL 40223 5620 A2
Wareham Rd
2600 LDNP 40242 5510 C5
Warehouse St
10 HdnC 40121 6374 B4
Wareing Ct
11700 LSVL 40272 5940 B5
Warfield Rd
- LSVL 40228 5836 B6
E Warfield St
100 ELZT 42701 6812 C2
W Warfield St
300 ELZT 42701 6812 B2
Warhawk St
4300 HdnC 40121 6374 A2
Warm Spring Ct
4900 CDSM 40245 5511 C1
Warner Av
3400 LSVL 40207 5617 E4
3400 STMW 40207 5617 E4
3800 STMW 40207 5618 A4
Warner Dr
12300 GSHN 44026 5292 C4
12300 OdmC 44026 5292 C4
E Warnock St
200 LSVL 40208 5724 D1
400 LSVL 40217 5724 E1
Warren Av
3300 LSVL 40215 5724 B3
Warren Dr
400 HdnC 40160 6592 A5
Warren Ln
100 BltC 40165 6052 C5
Warren Rd
10 LSVL 40206 5616 D1
Warren St
- MdeC 40108 6264 B4
- MRGH 40155 6264 B4
4200 LSVL 40213 5725 D4
Warren St SR-1638
- MdeC 40108 6264 B4
- MRGH 40155 6264 B4
Warrenton Hill Ct
7400 LSVL 40291 5837 B4
Warrington Wy
1800 CSGT 40222 5509 C6
1900 NHFD 40222 5509 C6
Warrior Rd
10 INDH 40207 5508 D7
Warson Ct
3300 JFTN 40299 5728 B3
Warwick Av
- STMW 40222 5618 D2
8000 LYDN 40222 5618 E1
8100 LYDN 40222 5619 A1
Warwickshire Ct
3300 LSVL 40213 5725 E6
Warwickshire Dr
- LSVL 40219 5725 E7
5300 LSVL 40213 5725 E7
Washburn Av
400 LYDN 40222 5618 E2
400 NRWD 40222 5618 E3
600 STMW 40222 5618 D1
700 LSVL 40222 5618 D1
Washington Av
10 MTWH 40047 6056 A2
Washington Blvd
1600 LYDN 40242 5510 B7
1600 LYDN 40242 5619 C1
Washington Cir
100 LGNG 40031 5297 A2
Washington Dr
1800 ClkC 47172 5397 C1
8400 MTWH 40047 6056 A1

Washington Pl
200 NALB 47150 5505 B6
400 JFVL 47130 5507 A4
Washington Sq
3800 BLWD 40207 5617 D2
3800 STMW 40207 5617 D2
Washington St
400 ELZT 42701 6812 A2
E Washington St
100 LGNG 40031 5296 E4
100 LSVL 40202 5615 E2
200 LGNG 40031 5297 A3
600 LSVL 40202 5616 A2
1500 LSVL 40206 5616 C2
W Washington St
100 LGNG 40031 5296 E3
200 CLKV 47129 5506 C3
600 LSVL 40202 5615 D2
Washington Wy
900 JFVL 47130 5398 E7
900 JFVL 47130 5399 A7
Washington State Ct
7600 LSVL 40228 5836 D5
Wataga Dr
600 LSVL 40206 5617 A3
Watch Hill Ct
7400 HWCK 40228 5836 C2
Watch Hill Rd
6400 HWCK 40228 5836 D2
Water St
- ClkC 47111 5181 D5
100 MTWH 40047 6056 B3
800 CHAN 47111 5181 E4
800 LSVL 40206 5616 A2
1200 HdnC 40121 6374 B3
9100 GEOT 47122 5501 E4
E Water St
- LSVL 40202 5616 A2
- LSVL 40206 5616 A2
100 NALB 47150 5505 B6
W Water St
100 NALB 47150 5505 B6
Waterbury St
900 LSVL 40203 5615 E5
Watercrest Ct
4400 LSVL 40241 5510 B1
Waterdancer Ln
- LSVL 40229 5944 D1
Waterfall Ct
3600 HBNE 40165 6053 D3
Waterfern Wy
7900 LSVL 40291 5836 E3
Waterfield St
1100 RDCF 40160 6484 A5
Waterford Cir
4000 STMW 40207 5618 B4
Waterford Pl
- ELZT 42701 6702 D4
12200 LSVL 40291 5947 A6
Waterford Rd
700 WDYH 40207 5509 B7
11400 BltC 40047 5947 A6
11400 LSVL 40291 5947 A6
Waterford Rd SR-660
11400 BltC 40047 5947 A6
11400 LSVL 40291 5947 A6
Watergate Dr
100 BltC 40165 6162 D2
Waterglen Pl
3100 LSVL 40207 5508 D4
Watering Pl
7800 LSVL 40291 5837 A5
Waterleaf Ct
3500 LSVL 40207 5617 D2
Waterleaf Wy
200 LSVL 40207 5617 C2
Waterline Rd
- ClkC 47111 5290 D5
- ClkC 47130 5290 E6
- ClkC 47130 5291 A6
- ClkC 47130 5400 A1
Waterloo Wy
10600 LSVL 40223 5620 A3
Waterman Al
- LSVL 40203 5615 E4
Water Oaks Ct
10700 LSVL 40241 5511 A2
Waters Edge Dr
14000 LSVL 40245 5621 B3
Waters Edge Pkwy
2700 JFVL 47130 5399 A5
Waterside Ct
14100 LSVL 40245 5621 C6
Waterwood Ln
11200 HLVW 40229 5944 B5
11200 LSVL 40229 5944 B5
Waterworks Rd
100 BltC 40047 6056 B7
1500 LGNG 40031 5296 E1
1500 OdmC 40031 5296 E1
1600 LGNG 40031 5297 A1
1600 OdmC 40031 5297 A1
Watford Ct
6900 STMW 40222 5509 D7
6900 STMW 40222 5618 B2
Wathen Ln
1600 LSVL 40210 5723 E1
1600 LSVL 40215 5724 A1
1600 LSVL 40216 5723 E1
1600 SVLY 40210 5723 E1
1600 SVLY 40210 5724 A1
1600 SVLY 40216 5723 E1
1600 SVLY 40216 5724 A1
Wathen Farm Rd
2500 JFVL 47130 5507 E4
Watkins Prairie Ln
100 NALB 47150 5396 A6
Watson Ln
6800 LSVL 40272 6048 C1
Watson Ln SR-1230
6800 LSVL 40272 6048 C1
Watson Sellersburg Rd
4000 ClkC 47130 5398 D2
4000 ClkC 47172 5398 C1

INDEX 52
Wild Oak Ct
Louisville Metro Street Index
Woodcreek Ct

STREET
Block City ZIP Map# Grid

Wild Oak Ct
500 LYDN 40222 5619 A2
Wildon Pl
8700 JFTN 40220 5728 A2
Wild River Ct
5300 LSVL 40229 5944 D2
Wildwood Cir
7000 LSVL 40291 5727 C7
Wildwood Ct
9800 WDWD 40223 5619 D3
Wildwood Dr
- LSVL 40219 5834 D6
900 NALB 47150 5504 C3
2600 CLKV 47129 5506 B3
Wildwood Ln
100 JFTN 40223 5619 D4
100 LSVL 40223 5619 D3
100 WDWD 40223 5619 D3
9100 LSVL 40272 5832 C7
Wildwood Pl
300 LSVL 40206 5617 A3
Wildwood Rd
- NALB 47150 5504 D4
10 JFVL 47130 5508 A2
500 SLRB 47172 5288 D5
Wildwood Tr
100 BltC 40047 6057 B3
Wilhemina Av
- CHAN 47111 5181 D3
Wilke Farm Av
5500 LSVL 40216 5831 B1
Wilken Wy
13500 LSVL 40272 6048 D1
Wilkerson Av
2500 LSVL 40216 5722 D6
Wilkerson Dr
- BltC 40047 5946 C7
Wilkie Rd
3000 LSVL 40216 5722 C6
Will Wy
10000 LSVL 40291 5837 C4
Willabrook Dr
100 BltC 40109 6052 E1
100 HLVW 40109 6052 E1
Willard Av
2100 NALB 47150 5505 D2
Willenhall Ct
400 DGSH 40243 5620 A5
Willett Pl
6900 CTWD 40014 5403 C7
William St
100 LSVL 40206 5616 C2
William Beckett Dr
- LSVL 40211 5614 C6
William Clark Dr
6700 LSVL 40228 5836 B7
William Cummins Ct
8500 LSVL 40228 5836 C6
William E Summers III Av
1600 LSVL 40211 5614 B6
William E Summers III Ct
1800 LSVL 40211 5614 B5
William G Penny Ln
8000 LSVL 40219 5835 B5
William M Diesen Rd
- LSVL 40216 5831 D1
- LSVL 40258 5831 D1
William O Vance Ct
10 NALB 47150 5505 A4
William Penn Ct
8800 LSVL 40228 5836 B7
William Penn Wy
8700 LSVL 40228 5836 B7
Williams Dr
100 CLKV 47129 5506 D4
Williams Ln
1400 CHAN 47111 5181 C1
1400 ClkC 47111 5181 C1
N Williams Ln
100 BltC 40109 5943 E7
100 BltC 40109 6052 E1
100 HLVW 40109 6052 E1
Williams Rd
8500 BltC 40071 5949 C1
8500 LSVL 40299 5949 C1
E Williams Rd
100 BltC 40071 5948 B4
Williams St
100 JFVL 47130 5507 A4
E Williams St
100 ELZT 42701 6812 C2
W Williams St
100 ELZT 42701 6812 C2
Williamsborough Ln
9500 LSVL 40291 5837 C2
Williamsburg Ct
1000 STMW 40207 5618 A5
Williamsburg Dr
1200 ELZT 42701 6811 B5
1200 HdnC 42701 6811 B5
Williamsburg Plz
9400 HTBN 40222 5619 C4
9500 JFTN 40223 5619 D5
Williamsburg Sta
4600 FydC 47119 5503 C1
Williams-Landfill Rd
- BltC 40071 5949 C3
Williamson Ct
1800 LSVL 40223 5512 B7
Williams Ridge Rd
1200 MDTN 40243 5620 C6
Willian Ln
2300 NALB 47150 5504 C6
2500 FydC 47150 5504 C6
Willinger Ln
100 JFVL 47130 5506 E3
Willis Av
3300 LSVL 40206 5617 D4
3300 LSVL 40207 5617 D4
3300 STMW 40207 5617 D4
Willis Dr
100 LSVL 40118 5942 C3
100 RDCF 40160 6483 D6
E Willis Rd
1100 FydC 47150 5503 D4
W Willis Rd
4700 FydC 47122 5503 C3
Willismore Dr
6200 LSVL 40272 5940 A3
Willmar Av
3700 LSVL 40218 5726 E2
3700 LSVL 40218 5727 A3
Willoughby Ct
200 LSVL 40245 5621 E6
Willow Av
1100 LSVL 40204 5616 D5
1300 JfnC 40204 5616 D5
1400 LSVL 40205 5616 D5
2100 NALB 47150 5505 E4
3600 JFTN 40299 5728 D4
Willow Ct
- LSVL 40213 5834 D1
500 ELZT 42701 6812 A2
3600 JFTN 40299 5728 D4
Willow Dr
1300 LSVL 40213 5725 E5
1300 LSVL 40218 5725 E5
1500 JFVL 47130 5506 E2
1500 NALB 47150 5396 E7
8300 BltC 40071 5949 A3
Willow Ln
- BltC 40109 5943 E5
10 JFVL 47130 5508 B3
11400 ANCH 40223 5620 B2
Willow Run
- NALB 47150 5396 C6
Willow St
- HdnC 40121 6265 C7
Willow Wy
1500 RDCF 40160 6482 E4
1500 RDCF 40160 6483 A4
3300 LSVL 40218 5726 D2
3500 HBNE 40165 6053 C2
3500 PNRV 40165 6053 C2
Willow Bend Dr
7400 OdmC 40014 5405 A7
7400 OdmC 40014 5514 A1
Willowbrook Cir
9800 JFTN 40223 5619 D5
Willowbrook Ct
2400 OdmC 40059 5292 E5
Willowbrook Dr
300 WDHL 40243 5620 D4
Willow Brook Rd
500 WDHL 40243 5620 D5
600 MDTN 40243 5620 D5
Willow Creek Ct
900 SbyC 40245 5513 D5
Willow Creek Dr
400 ELZT 42701 6812 A3
Willowcreek Dr
8800 LSVL 40219 5834 E7
8900 LSVL 40219 5835 A7
Willow Creek Ln
900 SbyC 40245 5513 D5
Willowcreek Rd
12900 OdmC 40059 5401 B1
Willow Crest Cir
6800 LSVL 40241 5509 B3
Willow Forest Dr
12900 LSVL 40245 5511 E3
12900 LSVL 40245 5512 A3
Willow Forest Pl
4700 LSVL 40245 5512 A3
Willow Gate Ct
7300 PROS 40059 5401 B3
Willow Glen Rd
12600 LSVL 40299 5729 C6
Willow Green Wy
7900 LSVL 40291 5837 B5
Willow Grove Cir
14200 LSVL 40245 5621 C3
Willow Grove Ct
14100 LSVL 40245 5621 C3
Willow Grove Wy
14100 LSVL 40245 5621 B3
Willowhurst Pl
500 JFTN 40223 5619 D5
Willow Lake Ct
10800 ANCH 40223 5511 A7
10800 LSVL 40223 5511 A7
Willow Oak Ct
10 HdnC 42701 6702 B6
6000 LSVL 40059 5402 A6
Willow Oak Ln
1100 LGNG 40031 5296 E1
Willow Park Cir
1100 MDTN 40299 5620 E6
Willow Park Dr
12700 MDTN 40299 5620 E6
Willow Reed Dr
13700 LSVL 40299 5729 E5
Willow Reed Pl
4100 LSVL 40299 5729 D5
Willow Ridge Dr
- JFTN 40223 5619 D5
Willowrun Ct
8600 OdmC 40056 5512 E4
Willowrun Ln
6600 OdmC 40056 5512 E4
Willow Springs Dr
1000 LYDN 40242 5619 C2
9100 LYDN 40223 5619 C2
Willow Stone Ct
11300 LSVL 40223 5620 B3
Willow Stone Wy
- DGSH 40243 5620 B4
100 LSVL 40223 5620 B3
500 MDTN 40243 5620 B3
Willow Tree Ln
12800 MDTN 40299 5620 E6
Willow View Blvd
3800 JFTN 40299 5729 A5
3800 LSVL 40299 5729 A5
Willowwick Ct
11200 LSVL 40272 5940 C4
Willowwood Ct
3600 JFTN 40299 5728 C4
Willow Wood Dr
100 MTWH 40047 6056 D3
Willowwood Dr
- MTWH 40047 6056 D3
Willowwood Wy
9000 LSVL 40299 5728 B4
9200 JFTN 40299 5728 B4
Wills Ct
1400 LSVL 40211 5614 D5
Wilma Av
- BltC 40165 5944 D5
- HLVW 40229 5944 D5
- LSVL 40229 5944 D5
100 RDCF 40160 6483 C5
Wilmington Av
- LSVL 40206 5617 D3
3500 LSVL 40207 5617 D3
3500 STMW 40207 5617 E3
Wilmington Dr
100 MTWH 40047 6056 A2
Wilmoth Av
4000 LSVL 40216 5722 A4
Wilshire Av
4300 LSVL 40216 5722 A3
Wilshire Blvd
10 LSVL 40214 5833 D6
Wilshire Blvd E
10 LSVL 40214 5833 D6
Wilshire Blvd W
10 LSVL 40214 5833 C6
Wilson Av
- LSVL 40245 5511 E2
- LSVL 40245 5512 A2
400 ELZT 42701 6812 A2
1800 LSVL 40210 5615 A5
2100 LSVL 40210 5614 E5
2500 LSVL 40211 5614 E5
Wilson Av SR-1934
1800 LSVL 40210 5615 A5
2100 LSVL 40210 5614 E5
2500 LSVL 40211 5614 E5
Wilson Ct
1200 LGNG 40031 5297 A3
Wilson Ln
5600 LSVL 40229 5944 E4
7000 ClkC 47129 5397 D1
7000 ClkC 47172 5397 D1
7000 CLKV 47129 5397 D1
7100 CLKV 47172 5397 D1
Wilson Rd
- HdnC 40177 6156 B7
- RDCF 40160 6374 C7
3100 HdnC 40121 6374 D1
6200 HdnC 40121 6265 C4
9000 HdnC 40177 6265 C4
23100 WPT 40177 6156 B6
N Wilson Rd
- HdnC 40121 6374 C7
- RDCF 40160 6374 C7
100 RDCF 40160 6483 C3
1000 HdnC 40121 6483 C2
1100 RDCF 40121 6483 C1
S Wilson Rd
100 RDCF 40160 6483 D3
1300 RDCF 40160 6592 E1
1700 RDCF 40160 6593 A1
2200 HdnC 40160 6593 A2
5900 ELZT 42701 6702 D3
S Wilson Rd SR-1500
1000 RDCF 40160 6483 E6
Wilson St
10 NALB 47150 5505 A7
100 MRGH 40155 6264 C4
8900 LYDN 40242 5510 B7
Wilton Dr
9700 LSVL 40118 5942 C2
Wiltonwood Ct
11700 LSVL 40272 5940 B5
Wiltshire Av
100 LSVL 40207 5617 E3
100 RDCF 40175 6482 E2
100 STMW 40207 5617 E3
Wimbledon Ct
400 LSVL 40218 5726 C2
Wimbley Ct
9300 LSVL 40241 5510 D4
Wimborne Wy
8400 HTBN 40222 5619 B4
Wimpleton Pl
600 LSVL 40206 5617 D3
Wimpole Ct
2900 LSVL 40218 5727 B3
Wimpole Rd
4000 LSVL 40218 5727 C3
Wimsatt Wy
8800 LSVL 40291 5837 B1
Wimstock Av
7200 LSVL 40272 6048 C1
7400 LSVL 40272 5939 C7
Winbledon Ct
7200 FydC 47122 5393 D5
E Winbourne Av
100 CLKV 47129 5506 D6
W Winbourne Av
200 CLKV 47129 5506 D6
Winburn Dr
1900 JFVL 47130 5507 D4
Winchester Blvd
900 ELZT 42701 6703 D6
Winchester Ct
100 BltC 40165 6054 C2
Winchester Dr
- BltC 40047 6056 A3
100 MTWH 40047 6056 A3
2700 CLKV 47172 5288 A7
2700 FydC 47172 5288 A7
Winchester Pl
600 NBNE 40207 5618 A4
600 STMW 40207 5618 A4
Winchester Rd
- JFVL 47130 5508 A1
2900 JFVL 47130 5507 E2
3300 LSVL 40207 5617 E5
3500 BFLD 40207 5617 E5
3600 BFLD 40207 5618 A4
3700 NBNE 40207 5618 A4
4500 FRMD 40207 5618 B3
4500 STMW 40207 5618 B3
N Winchester Acres Rd
3000 LSVL 40245 5511 E5
S Winchester Acres Rd
2800 LSVL 40223 5511 D5
Winchester Woods Pl
12300 LSVL 40223 5511 D5
Wind Bent Ct
7400 FydC 47124 5283 C5
Windbrook Ct
4000 LSVL 40220 5727 E4
Wind Dance Dr
7300 FydC 47124 5283 C6
7300 GNVL 47124 5283 C6
Wind Dance Pkwy
7300 FydC 47124 5283 C5
Windemere Dr
7200 LSVL 40214 5832 D2
Windemere Rd
400 CLKV 47129 5506 C2
Windfall Trc
9900 JFTN 40223 5619 D4
Windham Pkwy
6800 PROS 40059 5400 D3
Wind Hill Dr
10000 GNVL 47124 5283 C6
Windhurst Ct
900 WDYH 40207 5618 C1
Windhurst Rd
6600 WDYH 40207 5618 C1
Winding Rd
5400 LSVL 40214 5833 C3
Winding Bluff Ct
6000 LSVL 40207 5509 B6
Winding Bluff Trc
2000 LSVL 40207 5509 B6
Winding Creek Ct
14000 LSVL 40245 5621 C2
Winding Creek Pl
1200 LSVL 40245 5621 C2
Winding Creek Rd
4200 OdmC 40014 5404 C2
Winding Oaks Tr
700 ANCH 40223 5620 C3
700 MDTN 40243 5620 C3
Winding Ridge Tr
16000 LSVL 40299 5839 D3
Winding River Wy
10100 LSVL 40229 5944 D1
Winding Spring Cir
4900 CDSM 40014 5511 D1
4900 CDSM 40245 5511 D1
4900 JfnC 40014 5511 E1
Winding Spring Ct
12100 CDSM 40245 5511 D1
Winding Spring Pl
5000 CDSM 40245 5511 D1
Winding Stream Dr
6200 LSVL 40272 5940 A5
Winding Stream Wy
11600 LSVL 40272 5940 A5
Winding View Tr
16700 LSVL 40023 5731 C2
Winding Woods Tr
10 MTWH 40047 6055 E6
Windmill Ln
- JFVL 47130 5398 E7
Windover Rd
500 FydC 47150 5504 D2
500 NALB 47150 5504 D2
Wind Ridge Ct
6800 LSVL 40241 5509 D3
Wind River Dr
- FydC 47124 5283 B5
10000 GNVL 47124 5283 C6
Windrow Ct
10200 JFTN 40223 5619 E5
Windrow Pl
6100 WDYH 40207 5618 B1
Windsong Ct
6000 WDYH 40207 5618 B1
7000 CTWD 40014 5403 D7
Windsong Pl
900 STMW 40207 5618 B1
900 WDYH 40207 5618 B1
Windsong Wy
1000 STMW 40207 5618 B1
1000 WDYH 40207 5618 B1
Windsor Cir
1000 JFVL 47130 5507 B6
Windsor Ct
1100 JFVL 47130 5507 B6
1400 ELZT 42701 6703 D6
Windsor Dr
1100 JFVL 47130 5507 B6
8900 ClkC 47172 5288 B5
Windsor Pl
1600 LSVL 40204 5616 C5
Windsor Forest
100 HdnC 40162 6593 A6
Windsor Forest Dr
2200 LSVL 40214 5832 C6
2200 LSVL 40272 5832 C6
Windsor Forest Trail Park Rd
- HdnC 40162 6593 A6
Windsor Keep Dr
600 LYDN 40222 5618 E2
Windsor Lakes Ct
8100 LSVL 40214 5832 B5
Windsor Lakes Pkwy
2900 LSVL 40214 5832 B5
Windsor Park Dr
9200 LSVL 40272 5832 C7
Windsor View Dr
8600 LSVL 40272 5832 C7
Wind Valley Ct
7100 GNVL 47124 5283 C6
Windview Pl
1000 ELZT 42701 6703 D6
Windward Ct
2600 OdmC 40059 5292 D6
Windward Pl
4300 STMW 40207 5618 B1
Windward Wy
100 HLVW 40165 6052 E1
100 HLVW 40165 6053 A2
3600 LSVL 40220 5727 A1
Windwood Ct
8400 LSVL 40219 5834 E6
Windy Wy
2500 WDYH 40207 5509 C7
Windy Creek Wy
1900 FydC 47150 5288 A7
Windy Elm Ct
5700 LSVL 40214 5723 D7
Windygo Ct
6300 WDYH 40207 5509 B7
Windy Hill Rd
100 PNRV 40165 5944 C7
100 PNRV 40229 5944 C7
3800 BltC 40165 5944 D7
3800 BltC 40165 6053 D1
Windy Hills Dr
7500 FydC 47119 5287 B7
7500 FydC 47119 5396 B1
Windy Oaks Rd
4200 LSVL 40241 5511 A2
Windy Ridge Rd
- BltC 40165 6163 C6
Windy Willow Ct
11500 LSVL 40241 5511 C1
Windy Willow Dr
5100 LSVL 40241 5511 C1
5100 LSVL 40245 5511 C1
5200 LSVL 40241 5402 C7
5500 OdmC 40241 5402 C7
Winesap Wy
7500 LSVL 40228 5836 D6
Winfield Dr
300 NALB 47150 5504 E1
E Wing Dr
- LSVL 40209 5725 A3
S Wing Dr
- LSVL 40209 5725 A3
Wingard Dr
1200 RDCF 40160 6483 C1
Wingate Dr
7800 LSVL 40291 5837 E5
Wingate Rd
4300 WLNP 40207 5618 C1
Winged Foot Ct
1800 JFVL 47130 5507 A1
9900 LSVL 40223 5619 D2
Winged Foot Dr
9800 LSVL 40223 5619 D2
Wingfield Av
- LSVL 40291 5837 C5
2000 LSVL 40210 5615 A7
2000 SVLY 40210 5615 A7
Wingfield Cir
2000 OdmC 40031 5296 D6
Wingfield Ct
200 ELZT 42701 6702 E4
2200 LSVL 40210 5614 E7
2200 LSVL 40216 5614 E7
Wingfield Dr
100 ELZT 42701 6702 E4
100 ELZT 42701 6703 A4
Wingfield Ln
2100 LSVL 40210 5614 D7
2100 LSVL 40216 5614 D7
Wingfield Rd
- LSVL 40291 5837 C5
Winifrede Ln
10 LSVL 40206 5616 E1
Winkler Av
700 LSVL 40208 5724 B1
Winkler Av US-60 ALT
300 LSVL 40208 5724 C1
Winn Av
- LSVL 40214 5724 C3
- LSVL 40215 5724 C3
Winners Cir
1100 LYDN 40242 5619 B1
3500 OdmC 40031 5297 C7
Winning Colors
- MTWH 40047 6056 D2
Winning Colors Dr
100 MTWH 40047 6056 D2
Winnland Dr
3400 LSVL 40219 5834 E5
3400 LSVL 40219 5835 B5
Winnrose Wy
4100 LSVL 40211 5614 A5
Winsford Pl
1800 CSGT 40222 5509 C7
Winslow Cir
5300 LSVL 40272 5940 B3
Winslow Dr
5300 LSVL 40272 5940 B3
Winstead Dr
7100 LSVL 40258 5830 D5
Winstewart Rd
8100 FydC 47122 5502 B2
8100 GEOT 47122 5502 B2
Winston Av
1900 LSVL 40205 5726 B1
2100 LSVL 40205 5617 B7
2100 SMRG 40205 5617 B7
2300 KGLY 40205 5617 C7
Winston Ct
12000 HLVW 40229 5944 B6
Winter Av
1300 LSVL 40204 5616 B5
Winter Wy
3000 LSVL 40272 5940 A7
Winterberry Cir
3500 LSVL 40207 5617 C1
Winterberry Dr
100 ELZT 42701 6812 D2
Winterbourne Pl
8300 LYDN 40222 5619 C2
Winter Branch Wy
1200 LSVL 40245 5621 D3
Winter Garden Ct
4300 LSVL 40218 5727 C5
Winter Garden Wy
- OdmC 40014 5403 E4
Wintergreen Ct
8600 BRWD 40242 5510 B6
Wintergreen Dr
100 RDCF 40160 6592 D1
Wintergreen Rd
5400 LSVL 40272 5831 B7
Winterhaven Ct
2300 OdmC 40059 5292 E5
Winterhaven Rd
2800 LSVL 40220 5727 E2
Winter Hill Ct
8300 LSVL 40299 5728 A5
Winter Lake Dr
4000 LSVL 40272 5940 A6
Winter Leaf Dr
- BltC 40165 6161 B2
Winterleaf Dr
3600 LSVL 40207 5617 D2
Winter Park Dr
4200 LSVL 40218 5727 C5
Winter Park Pl
10 HdnC 42701 6812 A7
Winter Smith Ct
100 ELZT 42701 6812 B3
Winter Springs Ct
1200 MDTN 40243 5620 C7
Winter View Dr
5900 LSVL 40272 5940 A6
Winthrop Av
100 CHAN 47111 5181 D4
Winthrop Ln
6400 LSVL 40222 5509 C4
Winton Av
200 LSVL 40206 5617 B1
Winton Ln
400 LSVL 40206 5617 B1
Winwood Ct
4200 FydC 47119 5394 D3
Winyan Ln
500 LSVL 40223 5619 D3
Wirth Av
- LGNG 40031 5296 E2
3000 LSVL 40213 5725 A2
3000 LSVL 40217 5725 A2
Wirth Dr
100 BltC 40165 6054 B1
Wisdom Ln
8700 HTCK 40229 5945 E4
Wise Ct
100 HLVW 40229 5944 A7
Wise Ln
- ELZT 42701 6702 C4
- HdnC 42701 6702 C4
10 HdnC 40162 6592 D6
Wiseland Wy
4400 HLVW 40229 5944 B7
4400 PNRV 40229 5944 B7
Wiselyn Dr
- RDCF 40160 6592 D2
Wiseman Ct
5300 LSVL 40272 5940 B5
Wise Owl Tr
17300 LSVL 40299 5840 A5
Wisertown Rd
8400 LSVL 40214 5832 E5
Wismann Rd NE
4200 HsnC 47112 5610 B1
Wissman Rd
1000 FydC 47122 5501 E4
1000 FydC 47122 5502 A5
1000 GEOT 47122 5501 E4
Wisteria Av
400 LYDN 40222 5619 A2
Witawanga Av
1200 LYDN 40222 5619 A1
1200 LYDN 40242 5619 A1
E Witherspoon St
100 LSVL 40202 5615 E2
400 LSVL 40202 5616 A2
800 LSVL 40206 5616 A2
Withorn Sq
5100 LSVL 40241 5510 E1
Witlow Av
- LSVL 40245 5511 E2
- LSVL 40245 5512 A2
Witten Ct
- CHAN 47111 5181 D2
Witten Dr
5200 LSVL 40258 5831 C6
8100 ClkC 47111 5181 B5
Wizard Av
3300 LSVL 40215 5724 B3
WMU Dr
- LSVL 40206 5617 B4
Woehille Rd
- JFVL 47130 5398 B6
Woerner Av
1200 CLKV 47129 5506 E7
Wolf Dr
1800 OdmC 40031 5405 D2
Wolf Creek Ct
7800 LSVL 40241 5510 A1
Wolfcreek Ct
- LSVL 40241 5510 A1
Wolf Creek Pkwy
4500 LSVL 40241 5510 A1
Wolf Den Ct
3000 FydC 47150 5397 C3
Wolf Dr Ct
1800 OdmC 40031 5405 D3
Wolfe Av
1200 LSVL 40213 5725 B3
Wolfe Trc
10 NALB 47150 5505 B2
Wolfe Cemetery Rd
6500 GEOT 47122 5501 C3
6500 HsnC 47122 5501 C3
Wolfe Run Rd
- HdnC 42701 6702 B4
Wolfe Trace Ct
10 NALB 47150 5505 B2
Wolf Lair Ct
3000 FydC 47150 5397 C4
Wolf Lake Blvd
3000 FydC 47150 5397 C3
Wolford Dr
4700 FydC 47119 5394 D4
Wolford Ridge Ct
700 LSVL 40245 5621 C6
Wolf Pen Ln
10 LSVL 40059 5401 B7
10 LSVL 40059 5510 B1
Wolf Pen Trc
5600 LSVL 40059 5401 A6
Wolf Pen Branch Rd
6200 LSVL 40059 5400 C7
6900 GNSP 40241 5509 D1
6900 LSVL 40059 5509 D1
6900 LSVL 40241 5509 D1
6900 PROS 40059 5509 D1
7100 GNSP 40241 5400 E7
7100 LSVL 40241 5400 E7
7100 PROS 40059 5400 E7
7200 LSVL 40059 5401 A7
Wolf Pen Branch Wy
4500 LSVL 40059 5400 B7
4500 LSVL 40059 5509 D1
4500 PROS 40059 5400 B7
Wolf Pen Glen Ct
7600 LSVL 40059 5400 E7
7600 LSVL 40059 5401 A7
Wolf Pen Ridge Ct
7600 LSVL 40059 5400 E6
7600 LSVL 40059 5401 A7
Wolf Pen Ridge Dr
7700 LSVL 40059 5401 A7
7700 LSVL 40059 5510 A1
Wolf Pen Woods Ct
7400 LSVL 40059 5400 E7
Wolf Pen Woods Dr
5000 LSVL 40059 5400 E7
5000 LSVL 40059 5401 A7
5200 LSVL 40059 5510 A1
5300 PROS 40059 5400 E7
Wolf Ridge Ct
3000 FydC 47150 5397 B3
Wolf Ridge Dr
3000 FydC 47150 5397 C3
Wolf Ridge Rd
5600 LSVL 40059 5400 E6
Wolf Run Rd
500 LSVL 40118 5942 B3
Wolf Spring Ct
7600 LSVL 40241 5510 A1
Wolf Spring Dr
4400 LSVL 40241 5510 A1
4500 GNSP 40241 5509 E1
4500 LSVL 40241 5509 E1
Wolf Spring Trc
7300 GNSP 40241 5509 E1
7300 LSVL 40241 5509 E1
Wood Av
800 JFVL 47130 5507 B6
2100 NALB 47150 5505 D2
Wood Rd
100 BLMD 40222 5619 B3
100 HTBN 40222 5619 B3
100 LYDN 40222 5619 A3
6300 LSVL 40258 5831 A3
Wood St
- CHAN 47111 5181 D5
- HdnC 40121 6374 D2
200 MRGH 40155 6264 C5
Woodale Av
500 ELZT 42701 6812 C4
Woodbark Ln
6600 LSVL 40291 5837 B3
Woodbine Av
400 LSVL 40208 5615 E6
Woodbine Ln
100 NALB 47150 5504 E3
Woodbine St
200 LSVL 40208 5615 D6
Woodbluff Trc
14600 LSVL 40245 5621 D3
Woodbourne Av
2000 LSVL 40205 5617 B6
Woodbourne Dr
800 NALB 47150 5396 C6
Wood Briar Cir
7200 LSVL 40241 5509 E4
Wood Briar Ct
2900 LSVL 40241 5509 D4
Wood Briar Pl
7100 LSVL 40241 5509 E4
Wood Briar Rd
7100 LSVL 40241 5509 D4
Woodbridge Hill Ln
7700 LSVL 40059 5400 E3
7700 LSVL 40059 5401 A2
Woodbridge Meadows Ct
8900 LSVL 40219 5835 B3
Wood Brook Ct
100 LSVL 40229 5943 D2
Woodbrook Ct
- LSVL 40223 5620 E1
Woodbury Dr
7900 LSVL 40219 5835 A5
Woodchat Wy
9100 LSVL 40272 5831 E6
Woodchester Wy
1300 LSVL 40219 5834 A6
Woodcleft Rd
200 BLMD 40222 5619 B3
Woodcock Cir
4900 LYNV 40213 5725 D6
Woodcreek Ct
1500 LGNG 40031 5296 D1

INDEX 53
Woodcreek Ct — Louisville Metro Street Index — 5th Av

STREET
Block City ZIP Map# Grid

Woodcreek Ct
1500 LGNG 40031 5297 A1
8000 LYDN 40222 5619 A2
Wood Creek Dr
400 RDCF 40160 6483 C3
Woodcreek Dr
1200 LGNG 40031 5296 E1
1200 LGNG 40031 5297 A1
Woodcreek Rd
2500 SGDN 40205 5617 C6
Wood Creek Wy
2500 ClkC 47130 5399 C4
Woodcrest Ct
2800 OdmC 40059 5292 A6
Woodcrest Dr
7900 LSVL 40219 5835 B5
Woodcroft Ct
1100 JFTN 40223 5620 A6
Woodcross Pl
5500 LSVL 40229 5944 E3
Wooddale Dr
8900 LSVL 40272 5831 D7
Wood Duck Cir
200 JFVL 47130 5507 E4
Wood Duck Pl
200 JFVL 47130 5507 E4
Wooded Wy
100 HLVW 40229 5944 A5
3000 JFVL 47130 5398 D7
3000 JFVL 47130 5507 D1
3900 LSVL 40219 5835 B1
Wooded Bend Wy
4300 LSVL 40245 5512 B3
Wooded Creek Dr
6000 LSVL 40291 5837 B1
Wooded Crown Rd
300 MDTN 40243 5620 E5
Wooded Falls Rd
100 MDTN 40243 5620 E4
Wooded Forest Rd
12900 MDTN 40243 5620 E5
Wooded Glen Ct
8500 JFTN 40220 5728 A2
Wooded Glen Rd
8600 JFTN 40220 5728 A2
Wooded Hobbs Tr
10300 LSVL 40118 5942 D3
Wooded Lake Ct
11000 LSVL 40299 5838 A1
Wooded Lake Dr
- SbyC 40067 5623 C7
1000 SbyC 40067 5732 B2
5500 LSVL 40299 5838 A1
Wooded Meadow Ct
3000 LSVL 40241 5509 D4
Wooded Meadow Rd
7000 LSVL 40241 5509 D4
Wooded Oak Cir
4600 LSVL 40245 5511 C1
Wooded Springs Ct
3700 LSVL 40245 5512 B4
Wooded Trail Ct
8700 JFTN 40220 5728 A1
Wooded Valley Dr
100 FydC 47150 5504 D1
100 NALB 47150 5504 D1
Wooded View Dr
3600 FydC 47122 5393 B6
Wooden Branch Ln
11300 LSVL 40291 5837 E3
Woodfern Wy
7900 LSVL 40291 5836 E3
Woodfield Dr
1000 NALB 47150 5396 C5
4300 FydC 47119 5394 E7
Woodfield Rd
1800 HBNA 40220 5619 B7
1900 HBNA 40220 5728 B1
Woodfill Wy
1800 LSVL 40205 5726 A1
Woodford Pl
2000 LSVL 40205 5617 A6
Wood Gate Dr
- MTWH 40047 6056 A4
Woodgate Ln
3900 LSVL 40220 5727 C2
Woodgreen Ct
3700 LSVL 40215 5723 D5
Woodgrove Pl
3700 LSVL 40245 5512 D5
Woodhaven Rd
6700 LSVL 40228 5727 B7
7000 LSVL 40291 5727 C7
Woodhaven Pl Cir
6000 LSVL 40228 5727 B7
Woodhaven Pl Dr
6800 LSVL 40228 5727 B7
Woodhaven Ridge Ct
5900 LSVL 40291 5836 C1
Woodhill Ct
5000 OdmC 40014 5405 D3
Woodhill Ln
4900 LSVL 40219 5835 D4
Woodhill Rd
10 INDH 40207 5508 D6
Woodhill Valley Rd
7400 LSVL 40241 5509 C1
Wood Hollow Rd
9300 LSVL 40229 5944 D2
Woodhurst Ct
9200 HTBN 40222 5619 C6
Woodington Pl
12600 LSVL 40223 5511 E5
Woodknoll Rd
10200 BRMR 40223 5619 E4
10200 LSVL 40223 5619 E3
E Woodlake Cir
- MTWH 40047 6055 E3
- MTWH 40047 6056 A4
W Woodlake Cir
- BltC 40047 6056 A4
- MTWH 40047 6055 E4
- MTWH 40047 6056 A4
Woodlake Ct
- MTWH 40047 6056 A4
Wood Lake Dr
500 LGNG 40031 5296 D4
Woodlake Dr
- MTWH 40047 6056 A4
500 LSVL 40245 5621 D4
Woodlake Trc
14600 LSVL 40245 5621 D3
Woodland Av
- LSVL 40245 5511 E2
- LSVL 40245 5512 A2
2000 LSVL 40210 5615 A5
2100 LSVL 40210 5614 E5
2500 LSVL 40211 5614 D5
Woodland Ct
200 ELZT 42701 6811 E1
200 ELZT 42701 6812 A1
2000 JFVL 47130 5507 C2
Woodland Dr
- LSVL 40219 5834 D6
100 BltC 40165 6161 B1
100 NALB 47150 5505 B3
100 RDCF 40160 6483 C4
200 VNGV 40175 6482 D7
400 ELZT 42701 6812 A1
700 ELZT 42701 6702 E5
3300 LSVL 40216 5722 A6
6100 FydC 47124 5284 A7
6100 GNVL 47124 5284 A7
6100 GNVL 47124 5393 A1
6500 ClkC 47111 5181 B3
Woodland Dr SR-1600
400 ELZT 42701 6812 A1
N Woodland Dr
100 RDCF 40160 6483 C3
S Woodland Dr
1800 RDCF 40160 6483 D7
3000 RDCF 40160 6592 D1
Woodland Rd
10 JFVL 47130 5508 A2
100 BltC 40047 6055 B7
1600 NALB 47150 5504 D4
2000 JFVL 47130 5507 D2
11800 ANCH 40223 5620 C2
Woodland Heights Dr
900 LSVL 40245 5621 C3
Woodland Hills Dr
10 SpnC 40071 6057 E4
Woodland Lake Dr
- SbyC 40067 5732 B2
Woodland Lakes Dr
- LGNG 40031 5297 A1
- OdmC 40031 5297 A1
Woodland Ridge Cir
- LGNG 40031 5297 A1
Woodland Ridge Ct
- LGNG 40031 5297 A1
1000 LSVL 40245 5621 C3
Woodland Ridge Dr
14200 LSVL 40245 5621 C3
Woodland Springs Rd
6800 LSVL 40299 5839 B5
Woodland Trailer Park
- ELZT 42701 6702 D6
Woodlawn Av
100 JFVL 47130 5507 A3
100 LGNG 40031 5296 D3
E Woodlawn Av
100 LSVL 40214 5724 D6
300 LSVL 40209 5724 E5
W Woodlawn Av
100 LSVL 40214 5724 C5
500 LSVL 40215 5724 B5
Woodlawn Dr
1600 NALB 47150 5505 D1
Woodlawn Ovps
- LSVL 40209 5724 E5
- LSVL 40214 5724 D5
Woodlea Ln
10 LSVL 40207 5508 B7
10 MKBV 40207 5508 B7
Woodlea Wy
10100 LSVL 40229 5944 C2
Woodlily Tr
9000 LSVL 40229 5945 E5
Woodluck Av
1500 LSVL 40205 5618 A6
Woodmere Av
2600 SVLY 40216 5723 D1
Woodmont Dr
900 NALB 47150 5504 D4
2300 LSVL 40220 5618 D5
2600 SRPK 40220 5618 D6
Woodmont Ln
3900 LSVL 40245 5512 C5
Woodmont Park Ln
3700 LSVL 40245 5512 D5
Woodmont Park Pl
14800 LSVL 40245 5512 D5
Woodmore Av
10 LSVL 40214 5833 B3
Woodpecker Ct
3000 LSVL 40216 5722 C7
Woodpointe Blvd
- LSVL 40219 5835 A7
- LSVL 40229 5835 A7
Woodpointe Ct
- MTWH 40047 6056 A4
Woodreed Ct
9200 ODGH 40014 5402 E7
Woodreed Pl
7400 ODGH 40014 5402 E7
Woodridge Dr
100 CHAN 47111 5181 C5
100 ClkC 47111 5181 D5
7600 PWEV 40056 5512 B3
11400 LSVL 40272 5940 B4
Woodridge Rd
- PWEV 40056 5512 B3
Woodridge Lake Blvd
- LSVL 40272 5940 B4
Woodridge Lake Wy
11200 LSVL 40272 5940 B4
Wood Rock Rd
7200 LSVL 40291 5836 D1
Woodrose Ct
8200 PROS 40059 5401 B4
Woodrow Av
600 NALB 47150 5505 E3
Woodrow Wy
6600 LSVL 40228 5836 B4
6900 LSVL 40219 5836 B3
Woodruff Av
3500 LSVL 40215 5724 A4
Woods Ln
100 BltC 40109 5943 A6
Woods Bend Dr
200 BltC 40109 6052 C3
Woodsbend Rd
10 HdnC 42701 6703 C3
Woodsboro Rd
1800 OdmC 40014 5405 D3
Woods Club Ct
7000 LSVL 40241 5509 B3
Woods Club Rd
2800 LSVL 40241 5509 D4
Woodsdale Av
2600 LSVL 40220 5618 C6
Woodsend Rd
4900 LSVL 40229 5944 D1
Woods Hollow Dr
900 RDCF 40160 6483 A3
Woodside Ct
100 MTWH 40047 6056 C3
1000 RDCF 40160 6483 A2
Woodside Dr
10 HdnC 40160 6484 A6
10 RDCF 40160 6484 A6
900 NALB 47150 5396 C6
12600 OdmC 40059 5292 A6
Woodside Pl
2800 OdmC 40059 5292 B6
3600 GNVW 40222 5508 E3
Woodside Rd
2300 LSVL 40207 5508 E4
2300 RVWD 40207 5508 E5
3100 GNVW 40222 5509 A3
3400 GNVW 40222 5508 E3
Woodside Hill Rd
5100 GNVW 40222 5508 E3
5100 GNVW 40222 5509 A3
Woodside Point Ct
5300 LSVL 40207 5509 A4
Woodsman Ct
8300 LSVL 40219 5834 E5
Woodsong Ct
11300 LSVL 40291 5837 E2
Wood Springs Rd
400 LGNG 40031 5296 D3
Woodstock Dr
900 CLKV 47129 5397 C7
Woodstock Rd
10200 BRMR 40223 5619 E4
Woodstone Dr
4000 FydC 47119 5503 E1
Woodstone Wy
700 ELZT 42701 6703 A3
4000 LSVL 40241 5509 C1
Woodstone Ridge Wy
3900 LSVL 40241 5509 C2
Woodstream Pl
14600 LSVL 40245 5621 D3
Woodsview Ct
6000 FydC 47119 5395 D1
Woods View Pl
4100 LSVL 40245 5512 B4
Woodthrush Dr
10 ClkC 47111 5181 C2
Wood Thrush Trc
1600 LSVL 40245 5621 D2
Wood Twist Ct
10800 LSVL 40291 5837 E6
Wood Vail Ct
6500 LSVL 40241 5509 C2
Woodvalley Ct
8400 BltC 40299 5948 C3
Woodvalley Ln
100 BltC 40299 5948 C4
8700 LSVL 40299 5948 C4
Woodview Cir
500 MDTN 40243 5620 D3
Woodward Dr
2800 SRPK 40220 5618 D6
Woodway Ln
1000 LSVL 40211 5614 B4
Woodwind Ct
100 MTWH 40047 6055 E6
9800 JFTN 40223 5619 B5
Wood Wynd Wy
1100 JFTN 40223 5620 A6
Woody Av
1400 LSVL 40215 5724 A6
Woody Ln
4000 LSVL 40258 5832 A3
Wooldridge Av
100 OdmC 40014 5512 C1
100 PWEV 40056 5512 C1
Wooldridge Ferry Rd
10 HdnC 42701 6703 D1
Woolrich Rd
7100 GYDL 40222 5509 D7
World Top Ct
100 BltC 40165 6052 B7
Worldview Cir
300 BltC 40165 6052 B7
Worth Av
1300 PNRV 40165 6053 B1
Worth Rd
2600 OdmC 40014 5405 B3
Worthing Ct
400 LSVL 40245 5621 C4
Worthington Ln
10200 LSVL 40059 5402 B5
10600 OdmC 40014 5402 B6
10900 OdmC 40059 5402 B5
Worthington Wy
5900 LSVL 40059 5402 A6
Worthington Glen Dr
- LSVL 40241 5402 A7
10200 LSVL 40241 5511 A1
Worthington Pl Dr
5400 LSVL 40241 5511 B1
Wren Ct
- RDCF 40175 6482 E3
Wren Rd
2000 NALB 47150 5505 C1
3200 ANPK 40213 5725 B3
6700 CTWD 40014 5512 E1
Wrocklage Av
1900 LSVL 40205 5617 B7
Wrought Iron Wy
6500 FydC 47122 5502 E6
Wunderly Ct
6800 LSVL 40291 5836 D3
Wurtele Av
1400 LSVL 40208 5724 A1
1500 SVLY 40216 5724 A1
2900 SVLY 40216 5723 D2
Wyandot Ct
10 SHDV 40165 6161 E2
500 RDCF 40160 6483 C3
Wyandotte Av
1600 LSVL 40210 5614 D6
Wyckford Wy
2500 LSVL 40218 5726 E3
Wyckoff Ct
6700 LSVL 40258 5831 A3
Wyckshire Ct
1900 CLKV 47129 5397 B7
Wycliffe Ct
7500 PROS 40059 5400 C3
Wycliffe Dr
7400 PROS 40059 5400 C3
Wyeth Ct
2500 LSVL 40220 5727 D2
Wynbrooke Cir
3100 LSVL 40241 5510 E4
Wynbrooke Pl
9900 LSVL 40241 5510 E4
Wyncliff Ct
9900 LSVL 40241 5510 E4
Wyndefair Ct
7200 PROS 40059 5400 E7
Wynde Manor Dr
6700 LSVL 40228 5836 B2
Wyndemere Ct
3500 FydC 47150 5397 B1
Wyndemere Dr
- LSVL 40245 5621 B5
Wyndham Ct
3600 JFTN 40299 5728 C5
Wyndham Wy
3700 JFTN 40299 5728 E4
Wyndingbrook Dr
100 BltC 40165 6053 A4
Wyndridge Creek Wy
8700 LYDN 40242 5619 B1
Wyndstar Pl
8500 LYDN 40242 5619 B1
Wyndswept Ct
3400 FydC 47150 5397 B1
Wynfield Mw
3000 LSVL 40206 5617 B1
Wynfield Close
- LSVL 40206 5617 B1
Wynmeade Pl
12400 LSVL 40223 5511 D5
Wynnewood Cir
2200 NHFD 40222 5509 C5
Wynn Gate Ct
10 NALB 47150 5396 D6
Wyola Ct
4300 LSVL 40218 5727 A4
Wythe Hill Cir
6900 PROS 40059 5400 E4
Wythe Hill Pl
7100 PROS 40059 5400 E3

Y

Yager Av
200 LGNG 40031 5296 E3
Yager Ct
10500 LSVL 40241 5511 A2
Yager Ln
4500 LSVL 40241 5511 A2
Yakima St
1100 LSVL 40214 5832 E3
Yale Dr
600 ELZT 42701 6811 D2
700 CLKV 47129 5506 D3
1700 LSVL 40205 5617 A7
Yancy Ln
600 MYHE 40207 5617 E1
Yandell Dr
11300 LSVL 40223 5511 C5
Yankee Ln
5400 LSVL 40219 5835 D3
Yardley Ct
3800 LSVL 40299 5728 A4
Yarmouth Ct
9600 LSVL 40272 5941 C1
Yarwood Mobile Home Park Dr
- RDCF 40160 6483 E5
- RDCF 40160 6484 A5
Yates Cir
500 ELZT 42701 6812 B1
Yates Dr
500 RDCF 40160 6483 A3
Yaupon Ln
5000 LSVL 40213 5726 C6
Yearling Dr
10 BltC 40109 6052 C3
Yellow Brick Rd
3700 LSVL 40023 5731 B5
Yellowpine Ct
9500 LSVL 40229 5945 A2
Yellowpine Dr
6100 LSVL 40229 5945 A2
Yellow Sands Dr
6000 LSVL 40219 5835 D2
6100 LSVL 40219 5836 A3
Yellowstone St
- HdnC 40121 6374 D1
Yellow Wood Ct
- LYDN 40242 5619 C1
Yellow Wood Pl
8900 LYDN 40242 5619 C1
Yenowine Ln
10 FydC 47122 5503 B6
600 FydC 47136 5503 B7
600 FydC 47150 5503 B7
Ye Old Post Rd
5400 LSVL 40219 5835 E3
Yew Ln
5000 LSVL 40213 5726 C6
Yocumshire Dr
4600 JFTN 40299 5728 B6
Yolanda Dr
4400 LSVL 40216 5723 C6
York St
200 LSVL 40202 5615 D4
200 LSVL 40203 5615 D4
Yorkcliff Dr
- LGNG 40031 5296 E1
York River Rd
7200 LSVL 40214 5833 D3
Yorkshire Blvd
2800 LSVL 40220 5618 C7
Yorkshire Dr
1500 ELZT 42701 6703 D6
Yorktown Ct
7300 LSVL 40214 5833 D4
Yorktown Rd
7100 LSVL 40214 5833 D5
Yorktown Ter
7100 LSVL 40214 5833 D4
Yorkwood Pl
700 JFTN 40223 5619 D5
Young Av
3200 LSVL 40211 5614 C6
Young St
700 NALB 47150 5504 E5
9000 HdnC 40121 6374 B7
Youngland Av
1700 SVLY 40216 5723 D1
Youngstown Ct
3100 LSVL 40272 5940 D3
Youngstown Dr
10800 LSVL 40272 5940 D3
Youngstown Park Dr
100 MTWH 40047 6056 A2
Youngwood Rd
3700 LSVL 40218 5726 E3
Yucca Ln
5500 LSVL 40258 5831 C3
Yuma Wy
6700 LSVL 40258 5830 E7
6700 LSVL 40272 5830 E7
Yvette Ct
7700 LSVL 40228 5836 B5
Yvonne Ct
6800 LSVL 40228 5836 B5

Z

Zabel Wy
8700 LSVL 40291 5728 B7
Zachary Wy
8700 LSVL 40214 5833 B4
Zakery Dr
- OdmC 40031 5297 C4
Zane St
500 LSVL 40203 5615 C5
1000 LSVL 40210 5615 B4
Zaring Rd
- OdmC 40014 5295 A7
- OdmC 40014 5403 D1
- OdmC 40031 5295 A7
Zaring Mill Cir
3800 LSVL 40241 5510 D4
Zayre Rd
- LSVL 40216 5832 A1
Zebra Pl
5700 BltC 40165 6054 B1
Zelma Pl
10 BltC 40165 6054 B1
Zelma Fields Av
8000 LSVL 40228 5836 E6
8300 LSVL 40228 5837 A6
Zenith Wy
7700 LSVL 40219 5836 A5
Zephyr Ct
7500 LSVL 40220 5727 D2
Zermatt Ct
- OdmC 40014 5402 C6
Zeta Ct
4500 LSVL 40213 5725 D5
Zeus Ct
6700 LSVL 40258 5831 C2
Zev Wy
5400 LSVL 40272 5831 B7
Zhale Smith Rd
1700 LGNG 40031 5297 D5
1700 OdmC 40031 5297 D5
Zib Ln
2600 LSVL 40219 5834 D5
Ziegler St
- LSVL 40217 5615 E7
700 LSVL 40217 5616 C7
Zilma Dr
4700 LSVL 40216 5722 C5
Zinnia Rd
100 BltC 40229 5944 D6
100 HLVW 40229 5944 D6
Zinnia Wy
100 BltC 40165 6054 B2
Zix Dr
10200 LYDN 40223 5510 E7
Zoeller Av
4100 LSVL 40216 5722 E2
Zollman Dr NE
7400 LNVL 47136 5610 E5
Zoneton Rd
- BltC 40165 5945 E7
- LSVL 40165 5945 E7
- LSVL 40229 5945 E7
100 BltC 40165 6053 D1
400 BltC 40165 6054 E1
Zoneton Rd SR-1116
100 BltC 40165 6053 D1
400 BltC 40165 6054 B1
Zorn Av
300 LSVL 40206 5617 B1
400 LSVL 40207 5617 A1
700 LSVL 40206 5508 A7
700 LSVL 40207 5508 A7
1000 LSVL 40206 5507 E6
1000 LSVL 40207 5507 E6
Zorra Ct
5600 LSVL 40291 5836 E1
Zorro Pl
100 BltC 40165 6054 B1
Zulauf Av
500 JFVL 47130 5507 C5
Zurich Ct
- OdmC 40014 5402 B6
Zurschmeide Dr
2400 NALB 47150 5505 A2

#

1st Av
- JFVL 47130 5507 A4
- SHDV 40165 6161 C5
N 1st Av
100 LGNG 40031 5296 E2
100 OdmC 40031 5296 E1
N 1st Av SR-53
100 LGNG 40031 5296 E2
100 OdmC 40031 5296 E1
NE 1st Av
- ELZT 42701 6702 D4
S 1st Av
- LGNG 40031 5296 E3
S 1st Av SR-53
- LGNG 40031 5296 E3
1st St
- RDCF 40160 6483 B5
- SHDV 40165 6161 C5
- WPT 40177 6156 D2
10 HdnC 42701 6593 C7
100 CHAN 47111 5181 D1
100 ClkC 47111 5181 D1
100 HLVW 40229 5944 D5
100 LSVL 40229 5944 D5
100 MTWH 40047 6056 A2
200 MdeC 40177 6264 C3
200 MRGH 40155 6264 C3
200 VNGV 40175 6591 D1
E 1st St
- GNVL 47124 5283 D7
N 1st St
100 LSVL 40202 5615 E2
S 1st St
- LSVL 40208 5615 D7
100 LGNG 40031 5297 A3
100 LSVL 40202 5615 D6
600 LSVL 40203 5615 E4
3900 LSVL 40214 5724 D3
S 1st St SR-53
100 LGNG 40031 5297 A3
S 1st St US-31E
200 LSVL 40202 5615 E2
S 1st St US-60 TRK
200 LSVL 40202 5615 E2
W 1st St
- GNVL 47124 5283 D7
10 NALB 47150 5505 B5
100 SHDV 40165 6161 C4
1st Cross St
5500 FydC 47119 5393 D3
2nd Av
- ClkC 47130 5290 B7
- JFVL 47130 5507 B4
100 SHDV 40165 6161 C5
1500 HdnC 40121 6374 B2
N 2nd Av
100 LGNG 40031 5296 E2
S 2nd Av
100 LGNG 40031 5296 E3
2nd St
- RDCF 40160 6483 B5
10 HLVW 40229 5944 D5
10 LSVL 40229 5944 D5
100 CHAN 47111 5181 D1
100 ClkC 47111 5181 D1
200 MdeC 40177 6264 C3
200 MRGH 40155 6264 C3
200 VNGV 40175 6591 C1
800 ELZT 42701 6702 D4
E 2nd St
100 SHDV 40165 6161 C4
6900 GNVL 47124 5283 D7
N 2nd St
100 LSVL 40202 5615 E2
100 UTCA 47130 5400 A5
100 WPT 40177 6156 C2
S 2nd St
- WPT 40177 6156 C3
100 LSVL 40202 5615 D4
100 UTCA 47130 5400 A5
700 LSVL 40203 5615 D4
1200 LSVL 40208 5615 D5
2800 LSVL 40208 5724 D2
2900 LSVL 40214 5724 C3
6400 LSVL 40214 5833 C1
S 2nd St SR-1020
200 LSVL 40202 5615 E2
700 LSVL 40203 5615 D4
1200 LSVL 40208 5615 D5
S 2nd St US-31
100 LSVL 40202 5615 D4
W 2nd St
- GNVL 47124 5283 D7
100 SHDV 40165 6161 C4
2nd Cavalry Regiment Rd
- HdnC 40121 6374 B1
2nd Dragoons Rd
6500 HdnC 40121 6374 D1
3rd Al
3400 LSVL 40212 5505 D6
3rd Av
- JFVL 47130 5507 B4
10 HdnC 40121 6374 B2
100 SHDV 40165 6161 C5
S 3rd Av
- LGNG 40031 5296 E3
3rd St
- ClkC 47130 5290 B6
- ClkC 47130 5399 A1
- RDCF 40160 6483 B5
- SHDV 40165 6161 C4
10 HdnC 42701 6593 D7
100 CHAN 47111 5181 D1
100 ClkC 47111 5181 D1
100 HLVW 40229 5944 D5
100 LSVL 40229 5944 D5
200 MdeC 40177 6264 C3
200 MRGH 40155 6264 C3
800 CLKV 47129 5506 E7
800 JFVL 47130 5506 E7
E 3rd St
- GNVL 47124 5283 D7
10 NALB 47150 5505 B5
N 3rd St
100 LGNG 40031 5296 E2
100 LSVL 40202 5615 D2
100 UTCA 47130 5400 A5
100 WPT 40177 6156 C2
NE 3rd St
- ELZT 42701 6702 D4
S 3rd St
- WPT 40177 6156 C3
100 LSVL 40202 5615 D4
100 UTCA 47130 5400 A5
700 LSVL 40203 5615 D4
1200 LSVL 40208 5615 D5
2000 LSVL 40208 5724 C1
3900 LSVL 40214 5724 C6
6100 LSVL 40214 5833 C1
S 3rd St SR-1020
200 LSVL 40202 5615 D4
700 LSVL 40203 5615 D4
1200 LSVL 40208 5615 D5
2000 LSVL 40208 5724 C1
3000 LSVL 40214 5724 C2
S 3rd St US-60 ALT
2500 LSVL 40208 5724 C1
W 3rd St
- GNVL 47124 5283 D6
10 NALB 47150 5505 B6
100 SHDV 40165 6161 C4
3rd Alley St
- LSVL 40212 5505 D6
3rd Armored Division Rd
4400 HdnC 40121 6373 E4
4400 HdnC 40121 6374 A4
3rd St Rd
7400 LSVL 40214 5833 A5
7700 LSVL 40214 5832 D7
8000 LSVL 40272 5832 E6
9300 LSVL 40272 5941 A1
9700 LSVL 40272 5940 E1
3rd St Rd SR-907
7400 LSVL 40214 5833 A5
7700 LSVL 40214 5832 D7
8000 LSVL 40272 5832 E6
9300 LSVL 40272 5941 A1
9700 LSVL 40272 5940 E2
4th Av
100 SHDV 40165 6161 D6
1100 JFVL 47130 5507 B4
1400 HdnC 40121 6374 B2
N 4th Av
- LGNG 40031 5296 E2
S 4th Av
400 LGNG 40031 5296 E3
4th St
- ClkC 47130 5290 C6
- ClkC 47130 5399 B1
- RDCF 40160 6483 B5
- UTCA 47130 5399 E6
100 CHAN 47111 5181 D1
100 ClkC 47111 5181 D1
200 MdeC 40177 6264 C3
200 MRGH 40155 6264 C3
E 4th St
10 NALB 47150 5505 C5
1000 SHDV 40165 6161 D4
E 4th St SR-44
1000 SHDV 40165 6161 D4
N 4th St
100 LSVL 40202 5615 D2
100 UTCA 47130 5400 A5
100 WPT 40177 6156 C2
S 4th St
100 LSVL 40202 5615 D2
100 UTCA 47130 5400 A5
100 WPT 40177 6156 C3
200 UTCA 47130 5399 E6
700 LSVL 40203 5615 D4
1200 LSVL 40208 5615 D7
2100 LSVL 40208 5724 C1
3100 LSVL 40215 5724 C2
4800 LSVL 40214 5724 C6
W 4th St
10 NALB 47150 5505 B6
4th Army Division Rd
- HdnC 40121 6265 B7
4th Dam Rd
3100 CLKV 47129 5396 E5
3100 FydC 47129 5396 E5
3100 FydC 47150 5396 E5
3100 NALB 47129 5396 E5
3100 NALB 47150 5396 E5
5th Av
100 SHDV 40165 6161 D6
1400 HdnC 40121 6374 C2

INDEX 54
N 5th Av
Louisville Metro Street Index
745th Tank Battalion Rd

STREET Block City ZIP Map# Grid

N 5th Av
100 LGNG 40031 5296 E2
5th St
- ClkC 47130 5290 C7
- ClkC 47130 5399 C1
- RDCF 40160 6483 C6
100 CHAN 47111 5181 D1
100 ClkC 47111 5181 D1
100 WPT 40177 6156 C2
400 JFVL 47130 5506 E7
E 5th St
- GNVL 47124 5283 D7
10 NALB 47150 5505 C5
N 5th St
100 UTCA 47130 5399 E5
100 UTCA 47130 5400 A4
100 WPT 40177 6156 C2
S 5th St
- LSVL 40214 5833 B1
100 LSVL 40202 5615 D4
100 UTCA 47130 5399 E5
100 WPT 40177 6156 C3
600 LSVL 40203 5615 D4
1500 LSVL 40208 5615 C6
2400 LSVL 40208 5724 C1
3800 LSVL 40214 5724 C4
3800 LSVL 40215 5724 C4
W 5th St
400 JFVL 47130 5506 E7
600 NALB 47150 5505 A5
5th Armor Division Rd
- HdnC 40121 6374 D4
6th Av
- HdnC 40121 6374 D2
100 SHDV 40165 6161 D6
N 6th Av
100 LGNG 40031 5296 D2
S 6th Av
- LGNG 40031 5296 E3
6th St
- ClkC 47130 5290 C7
- ClkC 47130 5399 C1
- RDCF 40160 6483 B6
E 6th St
- GNVL 47124 5283 E7
200 NALB 47150 5505 C5
N 6th St
100 LSVL 40202 5615 D2
100 UTCA 47130 5399 E5
100 WPT 40177 6156 C2
200 HdnC 40177 6156 C2
S 6th St
100 LSVL 40202 5615 D2
100 UTCA 47130 5399 E5
100 WPT 40177 6156 C3
400 LSVL 40203 5615 C5
1200 LSVL 40208 5615 C5
2300 LSVL 40208 5724 C1
4400 LSVL 40214 5724 C5
4400 LSVL 40215 5724 C5
W 6th St
- CLKV 47129 5506 E6
- CLKV 47130 5506 E6
600 NALB 47150 5505 A5
7th Av
- SHDV 40165 6161 D6
100 HdnC 40121 6374 C3
7th St
- RDCF 40160 6483 B6
E 7th St
100 JFVL 47130 5507 A6
200 NALB 47150 5505 C5
N 7th St
100 LSVL 40202 5615 D2
100 WPT 40177 6156 C2
S 7th St
100 LSVL 40202 5615 B7
100 WPT 40177 6156 C3
200 LSVL 40203 5615 B7
1200 LSVL 40208 5615 C5
1800 LSVL 40210 5615 B7
S 7th St SR-1931
700 LSVL 40202 5615 B7
700 LSVL 40203 5615 B7
1200 LSVL 40208 5615 C5
1800 LSVL 40210 5615 B7
W 7th St
10 JFVL 47130 5507 A5
300 NALB 47150 5505 A5
400 JFVL 47130 5506 E7
600 CLKV 47130 5506 E7
700 CLKV 47129 5506 E7
900 NALB 47150 5504 E5
7th Armored Division Rd
500 HdnC 40121 6374 E7
500 HdnC 40121 6483 E1
500 HdnC 40121 6484 A1
7th St Rd
2000 LSVL 40208 5615 B7
2000 LSVL 40210 5615 B7
2300 LSVL 40208 5724 A1
2300 LSVL 40210 5724 A1
2300 SVLY 40216 5724 A1
2500 LSVL 40215 5724 A1
2900 LSVL 40215 5723 D4
2900 SVLY 40216 5723 D4
3700 LSVL 40216 5723 D3
7th St Rd SR-1931
2000 LSVL 40208 5615 B7
2000 LSVL 40210 5615 B7
2300 LSVL 40208 5724 A1
2300 LSVL 40210 5724 A1
2300 SVLY 40216 5724 A1
2500 LSVL 40215 5724 A1
2900 LSVL 40215 5723 D4
2900 SVLY 40216 5723 D4
7th St Rd US-60 ALT
3700 LSVL 40215 5723 D3
3700 LSVL 40216 5723 D3
3700 SVLY 40216 5723 D3
8th Av
400 HdnC 40121 6374 B3
8th St
- ClkC 47111 5290 D7

8th St
- ClkC 47130 5290 D7
- ClkC 47130 5399 D1
- RDCF 40160 6483 B6
E 8th St
10 JFVL 47130 5507 A6
400 NALB 47150 5505 C3
N 8th St
100 LSVL 40202 5615 C2
100 WPT 40177 6156 C2
S 8th St
100 LSVL 40202 5615 C3
100 WPT 40177 6156 C3
200 LSVL 40203 5615 C4
1400 LSVL 40208 5615 C6
4400 LSVL 40215 5724 B4
W 8th St
10 NALB 47150 5505 A6
100 JFVL 47130 5507 A4
400 JFVL 47130 5506 E6
700 NALB 47150 5504 E5
S 8th Armored Division Dr
100 HdnC 40121 6373 D4
8th Armored Division Rd
- HdnC 40121 6373 E4
8th Cavalry Regimen Rd
- HdnC 40121 6374 C1
9th Av
1600 HdnC 40121 6374 D3
9th St
- RDCF 40160 6483 B6
100 HdnC 40121 6374 E2
E 9th St
- JFVL 47130 5506 E6
10 NALB 47150 5505 C5
300 JFVL 47130 5507 A6
N 9th St
100 LSVL 40202 5615 C2
100 WPT 40177 6156 C2
S 9th St
- LSVL 40215 5724 B2
- WPT 40177 6156 C3
700 LSVL 40203 5615 C4
1400 LSVL 40208 5615 C6
2900 LSVL 40208 5724 B2
W 9th St
10 JFVL 47130 5506 E6
400 CLKV 47130 5506 E6
600 NALB 47150 5505 A5
700 NALB 47150 5504 E5
E 10th St
10 NALB 47150 5505 C5
100 JFVL 47130 5506 E6
200 JFVL 47130 5507 A6
2800 JFVL 47130 5398 D7
N 10th St
100 LSVL 40202 5615 C2
300 WPT 40177 6156 C2
S 10th St
100 LSVL 40202 5615 C3
100 WPT 40177 6156 C3
200 LSVL 40203 5615 C3
1200 LSVL 40210 5615 C5
1400 LSVL 40208 5615 B6
W 10th St
10 JFVL 47130 5506 E6
10 NALB 47150 5505 A6
800 NALB 47150 5504 E5
10th Armored Cavalry Rd
- HdnC 40121 6265 B6
2600 HdnC 40121 6374 C1
10th Tank Battalion St
7400 HdnC 40121 6374 D4
11th Av
300 HdnC 40121 6374 B4
E 11th St
100 JFVL 47130 5506 E6
700 JFVL 47130 5507 A5
700 NALB 47150 5505 C4
N 11th St
100 LSVL 40202 5615 C2
100 LSVL 40203 5615 C2
100 WPT 40177 6156 C2
S 11th St
100 LSVL 40202 5615 C2
100 LSVL 40203 5615 C4
700 LSVL 40210 5615 C4
1700 LSVL 40208 5615 B7
E 12th St
10 NALB 47150 5505 C5
100 JFVL 47130 5506 E6
400 JFVL 47130 5507 A5
N 12th St
100 LSVL 40203 5615 C2
100 WPT 40177 6156 B3
S 12th St
100 LSVL 40203 5615 C3
100 WPT 40177 6156 C3
700 LSVL 40210 5615 B4
S 12th St US-60 TRK
700 LSVL 40203 5615 B4
700 LSVL 40210 5615 B4
12th Armored Division Av
4300 HdnC 40121 6374 A1
E 13th St
10 NALB 47150 5505 D5
N 13th St
100 LSVL 40203 5615 C2
100 WPT 40177 6156 B2
S 13th St
200 WPT 40177 6156 B3
600 LSVL 40203 5615 B4
700 LSVL 40210 5615 B4
S 13th St US-60 TRK
100 LSVL 40203 5615 B3
W 13th St
10 CLKV 47130 5506 E6
10 JFVL 47130 5506 E6
13th Cavalry Rd
1100 HdnC 40121 6374 B3
E 14th St
10 NALB 47150 5505 D5

E 14th St
100 JFVL 47130 5506 E5
N 14th St
100 WPT 40177 6156 B3
S 14th St
100 WPT 40177 6156 B3
W 14th St
10 JFVL 47130 5506 E5
500 CLKV 47129 5506 E5
500 CLKV 47130 5506 E5
14th Armor Cavalry Rd
- HdnC 40121 6265 C7
14th Armored Division Rd
- HdnC 40121 6265 C7
E 15th St
10 NALB 47150 5505 D5
100 JFVL 47130 5506 E5
N 15th St
100 LSVL 40203 5615 B2
100 WPT 40177 6156 B3
S 15th St
100 LSVL 40203 5615 B3
600 LSVL 40210 5615 B3
W 15th St
100 JFVL 47130 5506 E5
15th Cavalry Dr
10 HdnC 40121 6265 C7
E 16th St
300 NALB 47150 5505 D4
N 16th St
- LSVL 40203 5615 B1
300 WPT 40177 6156 B3
S 16th St
100 LSVL 40203 5615 B3
1200 LSVL 40210 5615 B5
2000 SVLY 40210 5615 A7
N 17th St
600 LSVL 40203 5615 B1
S 17th St
100 LSVL 40203 5615 B2
1200 LSVL 40210 5615 A5
E 18th St
300 NALB 47150 5505 D4
N 18th St
1800 LSVL 40203 5615 B1
S 18th St
100 LSVL 40203 5615 B3
600 LSVL 40210 5615 A3
N 19th St
100 LSVL 40203 5615 B2
S 19th St
100 LSVL 40203 5615 A3
600 LSVL 40210 5615 A3
20th St
- ClkC 47111 5290 D3
- ClkC 47111 5291 B4
- ClkC 47130 5290 E4
- ClkC 47130 5291 B4
N 20th St
100 LSVL 40203 5615 A1
S 20th St
100 LSVL 40203 5615 A2
700 LSVL 40210 5615 A3
1800 LSVL 40210 5614 E7
N 21st St
100 LSVL 40203 5615 A2
100 LSVL 40212 5615 A2
N 21st St US-150
100 LSVL 40203 5615 A2
100 LSVL 40212 5615 A2
N 22nd St
- LSVL 40203 5506 A7
- LSVL 40212 5506 A7
100 LSVL 40212 5615 A1
400 LSVL 40203 5615 A1
N 22nd St US-150
- LSVL 40203 5506 A7
- LSVL 40212 5506 A7
100 LSVL 40212 5615 A1
400 LSVL 40203 5615 A1
S 22nd St
- LSVL 40216 5614 E7
100 LSVL 40212 5615 A2
400 LSVL 40211 5615 A2
1200 LSVL 40210 5614 E5
1200 LSVL 40210 5615 A4
S 22nd St US-31W
100 LSVL 40212 5615 A2
400 LSVL 40211 5615 A2
1200 LSVL 40210 5614 E5
1200 LSVL 40210 5615 A4
S 22nd St US-150
100 LSVL 40212 5615 A2
400 LSVL 40211 5615 A2
N 23rd Al
- LSVL 40212 5615 A1
N 23rd St
200 LSVL 40212 5615 A1
600 LSVL 40212 5506 A7
S 23rd St
100 LSVL 40212 5615 A2
600 LSVL 40211 5615 A3
800 LSVL 40210 5614 E4
900 LSVL 40211 5614 E4
2200 LSVL 40216 5614 E7
2200 LSVL 40216 5723 E1
N 24th St
100 LSVL 40212 5615 A1
500 LSVL 40212 5506 A7
S 24th St
200 LSVL 40212 5615 A2
300 LSVL 40212 5614 E3
800 LSVL 40211 5614 E4
1700 LSVL 40210 5614 E6
N 25th St
100 LSVL 40212 5614 E1
300 LSVL 40212 5615 A1
600 LSVL 40212 5506 A7
S 25th St
100 LSVL 40212 5614 E2
800 LSVL 40210 5614 E4
800 LSVL 40211 5614 E4

N 26th St
- LSVL 40212 5506 A7
100 LSVL 40212 5614 E1
400 LSVL 40212 5505 E7
S 26th St
100 LSVL 40212 5614 E3
400 LSVL 40211 5614 E4
900 LSVL 40210 5614 E4
26th Cavalry Dr
5900 HdnC 40121 6265 D6
N 27th St
300 LSVL 40212 5614 E1
600 LSVL 40212 5505 E7
800 LSVL 40212 5506 A6
S 27th St
400 LSVL 40212 5614 E2
500 LSVL 40211 5614 E3
N 28th St
300 LSVL 40212 5614 E1
600 LSVL 40212 5505 E7
S 28th St
200 LSVL 40212 5614 E2
1300 LSVL 40211 5614 D5
1900 LSVL 40210 5614 D7
2000 LSVL 40216 5614 D7
N 29th St
100 LSVL 40212 5614 E1
600 LSVL 40212 5505 E7
S 29th St
400 LSVL 40212 5614 E2
900 LSVL 40211 5614 D4
N 30th St
100 LSVL 40212 5614 E1
600 LSVL 40212 5505 E7
S 30th St
100 LSVL 40212 5614 D1
1500 LSVL 40211 5614 D6
1900 LSVL 40210 5614 D7
N 31st St
600 LSVL 40212 5505 E7
S 31st St
600 LSVL 40211 5614 D2
N 32nd St
100 LSVL 40212 5614 D1
600 LSVL 40212 5505 E6
S 32nd St
200 LSVL 40212 5614 D2
900 LSVL 40211 5614 D6
N 33rd St
100 LSVL 40212 5614 D1
500 LSVL 40212 5505 D6
S 33rd St
100 LSVL 40212 5614 D1
700 LSVL 40211 5614 D3
N 34th St
100 LSVL 40212 5614 D1
700 LSVL 40212 5505 D6
S 34th St
100 LSVL 40212 5614 D2
400 LSVL 40211 5614 D2
N 35th St
100 LSVL 40212 5614 D1
500 LSVL 40212 5505 D7
S 35th St
100 LSVL 40212 5614 D1
500 LSVL 40211 5614 C2
N 36th St
100 LSVL 40212 5614 C1
600 LSVL 40212 5505 D6
S 36th St
- LSVL 40212 5614 C2
2300 LSVL 40211 5614 C7
N 37th St
100 LSVL 40212 5614 C1
500 LSVL 40212 5505 D7
N 37th St SR-3217
500 LSVL 40212 5505 D7
S 37th St
100 LSVL 40212 5614 C1
2300 LSVL 40211 5614 C7
N 38th St
100 LSVL 40212 5614 C1
300 LSVL 40212 5505 C7
N 38th St SR-3216
500 LSVL 40212 5505 C7
S 38th St
100 LSVL 40212 5614 C2
600 LSVL 40211 5614 C3
38th Armored Infantry Btln Cir
4900 HdnC 40121 6373 C4
N 39th St
100 LSVL 40212 5614 C1
300 LSVL 40212 5505 C7
S 39th St
200 LSVL 40212 5614 C2
1600 LSVL 40211 5614 B7
N 40th St
100 LSVL 40212 5614 C1
S 40th St
100 LSVL 40212 5614 C1
600 LSVL 40211 5614 B3
N 41st St
100 LSVL 40212 5614 C1
300 LSVL 40212 5505 C7
S 41st St
100 LSVL 40212 5614 C1
400 LSVL 40211 5614 B2
N 42nd St
100 LSVL 40212 5614 C1
500 LSVL 40212 5505 C7
S 42nd St
100 LSVL 40212 5614 B1
1000 LSVL 40211 5614 B4
N 43rd St
100 LSVL 40212 5614 C1
200 LSVL 40212 5505 C7
S 43rd St
- LSVL 40212 5614 B2
700 LSVL 40211 5614 B3
N 44th St
100 LSVL 40212 5614 B1
300 LSVL 40212 5505 C7

S 44th St
100 LSVL 40212 5614 B1
700 LSVL 40211 5614 B3
N 45th St
100 LSVL 40212 5614 B1
200 LSVL 40212 5505 B7
S 45th St
100 LSVL 40212 5614 B1
700 LSVL 40211 5614 A4
N 46th St
100 LSVL 40212 5614 B1
200 LSVL 40212 5505 B7
S 46th St
- LSVL 40212 5614 B1
S 47th St
- LSVL 40211 5614 A3
70th Tank Battalion Rd
7700 HdnC 40121 6374 C4
82nd Recon Dr
10 HdnC 40121 6265 D7
191st Tank Battalion Rd
- BltC 40121 6160 A6
- BltC 40165 6160 A6
484th Engineer Rd
- HdnC 40177 6264 E4
- HdnC 40177 6265 A4
745th Tank Battalion Rd
- HdnC 42701 6593 C2

Louisville Metro Points of Interest Index

Louisville Metro Points of Interest Index

Subdivisions & Neighborhoods

Louisville Metro Points of Interest Index

FEATURE NAME Address City ZIP Code	MAP#	GRID
Plainview, JFTN	5619	E6
Plymouth Village, PLYV	5618	A4
Portland, LSVL	5505	C7
Prairie Village, LSVL	5940	E2
Prestonia, LSVL	5725	B4
Riverfront, LSVL	5615	E2
Riverside Gardens, LSVL	5722	A4
Robinswood, RBNW	5508	E5
Rolling Fields, JFVL	5507	D3
Rollington, PWEV	5512	C1
Routt, LSVL	5840	A5
Salt River, SHDV	6161	D5
Seatonville, LSVL	5839	A6
Seminary Village, LSVL	5617	D2
Shawnee, LSVL	5614	C1
Shelby, WSNP	5726	A4
Silver Hills, NALB	5504	E7
Smyrna, LSVL	5836	B6
South Park, LSVL	5943	A1
Springlee, SPLE	5618	A4
Stonestreet, LSVL	5941	A2
Strathmoor Gardens, SMRG	5617	C7
Sylvania, LSVL	5831	B2
Thixton, LSVL	5946	E3
Treasure Island, LSVL	5944	A2
Valley Downs, LSVL	5940	A1
Valley Gardens, LSVL	5831	C7
Valley Village, LSVL	6048	D2
Waverly Hills, LSVL	5831	E5
Whipps Millgate, WPMG	5510	D7
Winding Falls, WNDF	5509	B6
Woodland Hills, NALB	5504	C3
Zoneton, BltC	6053	C2

Transportation

FEATURE NAME Address City ZIP Code	MAP#	GRID
Greyhound-Louisville, LSVL	5615	C3

Visitor Information

FEATURE NAME Address City ZIP Code	MAP#	GRID
Louisville Convention & Visitors Bureau 401 W Main St, LSVL, 40202	5615	D2

RAND M⊃NALLY

Thank you for purchasing this Rand McNally Street Guide!
We value your comments and suggestions.

Please help us serve you better by completing this postage-paid reply card.
This information is for internal use ONLY and will not be distributed or sold to any external third party.

Missing pages? Maybe not... Please refer to the "Using Your Street Guide" page for further explanation.

Street Guide Title: Louisville Metro   ISBN-13# 978-0-5288-5969-4   MKT: LOU

Today's Date: _____   Gender: ☐M ☐F   Age Group: ☐18-24 ☐25-31 ☐32-40 ☐41-50 ☐51-64 ☐65+

1. What type of industry do you work in?

   ☐Real Estate ☐Trucking ☐Delivery ☐Construction ☐Utilities ☐Government
   ☐Retail ☐Sales ☐Transportation ☐Landscape ☐Service & Repair
   ☐Courier ☐Automotive ☐Insurance ☐Medical ☐Police/Fire/First Response
   ☐Other, please specify: _____

2. What type of job do you have in this industry?_____

3. Where did you purchase this Street Guide? (store name & city) _____

4. Why did you purchase this Street Guide? _____

5. How often do you purchase an updated Street Guide? ☐Annually ☐2 yrs. ☐3-5 yrs. ☐Other:_____

6. Where do you use it? ☐Primarily in the car ☐Primarily in the office ☐Primarily at home ☐Other: _____

7. How do you use it? ☐Exclusively for business ☐Primarily for business but also for personal or leisure use
   ☐Both work and personal evenly ☐Primarily for personal use ☐Exclusively for personal use

8. What do you use your Street Guide for?
   ☐Find Addresses ☐In-route navigation ☐Planning routes ☐Other: _____
   Find points of interest: ☐Schools ☐Parks ☐Buildings ☐Shopping Centers ☐Other:_____

9. How often do you use it? ☐Daily ☐Weekly ☐Monthly ☐Other: _____

10. Do you use the internet for maps and/or directions? ☐Yes ☐No

11. How often do you use the internet for directions? ☐Daily ☐Weekly ☐Monthly ☐Other:_____

12. Do you use any of the following mapping products in addition to your Street Guide?
    ☐Folded paper maps ☐Folded laminated maps ☐Wall maps ☐GPS ☐PDA ☐In-car navigation ☐Phone maps

13. What features, if any, would you like to see added to your Street Guide? _____
    _____

14. What features or information do you find most useful in your Rand McNally Street Guide? (please specify)
    _____
    _____

15. Please provide any additional comments or suggestions you have. _____
    _____
    _____

We strive to provide you with the most current updated information available if you know of a map correction, please notify us here.

Where is the correction? Map Page #:_____ Grid #:_____ Index Page #:_____

Nature of the correction: ☐Street name missing ☐Street name misspelled ☐Street information incorrect
☐Incorrect location for point of interest ☐Index error ☐Other: _____

Detail: _____

I would like to receive information about updated editions and special offers from Rand McNally
   ☐via e-mail   E-mail address: _____
   ☐via postal mail
   Your Name: _____   Company (if used for work): _____
   Address: _____   City/State/ZIP: _____

Thank you for your time and help. We are working to serve you better.
This information is for internal use ONLY and will not be distributed or sold to any external third party.